SOCIAL PSYCHOLOGY

Key Readings in Social Psychology

General Editor: ARIE W. KRUGLANSKI, University of Maryland at College Park

The aim of this series is to make available to senior undergraduate and graduate students key articles in each area of social psychology in an attractive, user-friendly format. Many professors want to encourage their students to engage directly with research in their fields, yet this can often be daunting for students coming to detailed study of a topic for the first time. Moreover, declining library budgets mean that articles are not always readily available, and course packs can be expensive and time-consuming to produce. **Key Readings in Social Psychology** aims to address this need by providing comprehensive volumes, each one of which will be edited by a senior and active researcher in the field. Articles will be carefully chosen to illustrate the way the field has developed historically as well as current issues and research directions. Each volume will have a similar structure, which will include:

- An overview chapter, as well as introductions to sections and articles,
- Questions for class discussion,
- Annotated bibliographies,
- Full author and subject indexes.

Published Titles

Emotions in Social Psychology	W. Gerrod Parrott
Intergroup Relations	Michael Hogg and Dominic Abrams
Motivational Science	E. Tory Higgins and Arie W. Kruglanski
Social Psychology and Human Sexuality	Roy F. Baumeister
Stereotypes and Prejudice	Charles Stangor
The Self in Social Psychology	Roy F. Baumeister
The Social Psychology of Organizational Behavior	Leigh L. Thompson

Titles in Preparation

Attitudes and Persuasion	Richard E. Petty, Shelly Chaiken, and Russell Fazio
Close Relationships	Harry Reis and Caryl Rusbult
Group Processes	John Levine and Richard Moreland
Interfaces of Social and Clinical Psychology	Robin M. Kowalski and Mark R. Leary
Language and Communication	Gün R. Semin
Political Social Psychology	John Jost and Jim Sidanius
Social Cognition	David Hamilton
Social Comparison	Diederik Stapel and Hart Blanton
Social Neuroscience	John T. Cacioppo and Gary Berntson
The Social Psychology of Health	Peter Salovey and Alexander J. Rothman

For continually updated information about published and forthcoming titles, please visit www.keyreadings.com

SOCIAL PSYCHOLOGY
A GENERAL READER

Edited by

Arie W. Kruglanski

*University of Maryland
at College Park, MD*

E. Tory Higgins

*Columbia University
New York, NY*

Psychology Press

New York and Hove

Psychology Press
29 West 35th Street
New York, NY 10001
www.psypress.com

Published in Great Britain by
Psychology Press, LTD.
27 Church Road
Hove, East Sussex
BN3 2FA
www.psypress.co.uk

Psychology Press is an imprint of the Taylor & Francis Group.
Printed in the United States of America on acid-free paper.

Cover Illustration: "Parade Before a Red Background." 1953 Fernand Leger. Réunion des Musées Nationaux/
Art Resource NY.
Cover Design: Two of Cups Studio.

10 9 8 7 6 5 4 3 2 1

Cataloging-in-Publication Data is available form the Library of Congress.

ISBN 0-86377-694-9 (hbk.); 0-86377-695-7 (pbk.)

Contents

v

About the Editors

Arie W. Kruglanski is one of the most credited researchers in Social Psychology, whose interests have centered on how people form judgments, beliefs, impressions and attitudes, and what consequences this has for their interpersonal relations, their interaction in groups and their feelings about various "out groups." He has served as Editor, or on the Editorial Board, of most major national and international journals in the field—most recently he was Editor of the *Journal of Personality and Social Psychology*. He has received numerous Honors and Awards, including the Donald T. Campbell Award for Distinguished Scientific Contribution to Social Psychology and the Humboldt Foundation Life Achievement Award (Forschungspreis). His recent activities include being appointed to the National Academy of Science: Social and Behavioral Panel on Counter-terrorism.

He is Editor on the two Psychology Press series: *Key Readings in Social Psychology* and *Principles of Social Psychology*, and recently agreed to edit a new series of upper-level texts called *Frontiers of Social Psychology*.

E. Tory Higgins received his Ph.D. at Columbia, where is he now the Stanley Schachter Professor of Psychology. His research interests have centered on social cognition; self and affect; motivation and cognition; and principles of self-regulation. He received a MERIT Award from the National Institute of Mental Health (1989), the Donald T. Campbell Award in Social Psychology (1996), and the Thomas M. Ostrom Award in Social Cognition (1999). In 2000 he was the recipient of both the William James Fellow Award from the American Psychological Society and the American Psychological Association Award for Distinguished Scientific Contributions.

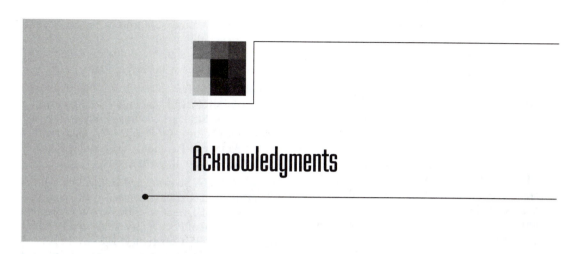

Acknowledgments

The Editors and Publishers are grateful to the following for permission to reproduce the articles in this book:

Reading 1: D. M. Buss, Mate Preferences in 37 Cultures. In W. J. Lonner and R. S. Malpass (Eds.), Psychology and Culture (pp. 197–202). Boston: Allyn and Bacon. Copyright © 1994 by Allyn & Bacon. Reprinted/adapted by permission.

Reading 2: J. T. Cacioppo, and G. G. Berntson, Social Psychology Contributions to the Decade of the Brain: Doctrine of Multilevel Analysis. American Psychologist, 47, 1019–1028. Copyright © 1992 by the American Psychological Association. Reprinted/adapted with permission.

Reading 3: S. E. Taylor, and J. D. Brown, Illusion and Well-Being: A Social Psychological Perspective on Mental Health. Psychological Bulletin, 103, 193–210. Copyright © 1998 by the American Psychological Association. Reprinted/adapted with permission.

Reading 4: H. H. Kelley, The Warm-Cold Variable in First Impressions of Persons. Journal of Personality, 18, 431-439. Copyright © 1950 by Blackwell Publishing. Reprinted with permission.

Reading 5: C. O. Word, M. P. Zanna, and J. Cooper, The Nonverbal Mediation of Self-Fulfilling Prophecies in Interracial Interaction. Journal of Experimental Social Psychology, 10, 109–120. Copyright © 1974 by Academic Press. Reprinted/adapted with permission.

Reading 6: M. Snyder and W. B. Swann, Jr., Hypothesis-Testing Processes in Social Interaction. Journal of Personality and Social Psychology, 57, 925–939. Copyright © 1978 by the American Psychological Association. Reprinted/adapted with permission.

Reading 7: E. T. Higgins, W. S. Rholes, and C. R. Jones, Category Accessibility and Impression Formation. Journal of Experimental Social Psychology, 13, 141–145. Copyright © 1977 by Academic Press. Reprinted by permission of the publisher.

Reading 8: J. A. Bargh, and P. Pietromonaco, Automatic Information Processing and Social Perception: The Influence of Trait Information Presented Outside of Conscious Awareness on Impression Formation. Journal of Personality and Social Psychology, 43(3), 437–449. Copyright © 1982 by the American Psychology Association. Reprinted/adapted with permission.

Reading 9: P. G. Devine, Stereotypes and Prejudice: Their Automatic and Controlled Components. Journal of Personality and Social Psychology, 56, 5–18. Copyright © 1989 by the American Psychological Association. Reprinted/adapted with permission.

Reading 10: D. L. Hamilton, D. M. Driscoll, and L. T. Worth, Cognitive Organization of Impressions: Effects of Incongruency in Complex Representations. Journal of Personality and Social Psychology, 57, 925–939. Copyright © 1989 by the American Psychological Association. Reprinted/adapted with permission.

Reading 11: H. H. Kelley, Attribution Theory in Social Psychology. In D. Levine (Ed.), Nebraska Symposium on Motivation (Vol. 15, pp. 192–238). Lincoln, NE: University of Nebraska Press. Reprinted from the 1967 Nebraska Symposium on Motivation by permission of the University of Nebraska Press. Copyright © 1967 by the University of Nebraska Press. Copyright © renewed 1995 by the University of Nebraska Press.

Reading 12: Y. Trope, and T. Alfieri, Effortfulness and Flexibility of Dispositional Judgment Processes. Journal of Personality and Social Psychology, 73(4), 662–674. Copyright © 1997 by the American Psychological Association. Reprinted/adapted with permission.

Reading 13: C. S. Carver and M. F. Scheier, Origin and Functions of Positive and Negative Affect: A Control-Process View. Psychological Review, 97, 19–35. Copyright © 1990 by the American Psychological Association. Reprinted/adapted with permission.

Reading 14: E. T. Higgins, R. N. Bond, R. Klein, and T. Strauman, Self-Discrepancies and Emotional Vulnerability: How Magnitude, Accessibility, and Type of Discrepancy Influence Affect. Journal of Personality and Social Psychology, 51(1), 5–15. Copyright © 1986 by the American Psychological Association. Reprinted/adapted with permission.

Reading 15: W. Mischel, Y. Schoda, and M. L. Rodriguez, Delay of Gratification in Children. Science, 244, 933–938. Reprinted with permission from Science. Copyright © 1989 American Association for the Advancement of Science.

Reading 16: E. S. Elliot, and C. S. Dweck, Goals: An Approach to Motivation and Achievement. Journal of Personality and Social Psychology, 54, 5–12. Copyright © 1998 by the American Psychological Association. Reprinted/adapted with permission.

Reading 17: P. M. Gollwitzer, H. Heckhausen, and B. Steller, Deliberative and Implemental Mind-Sets: Cognitive Tuning toward Congruous Thoughts and Information. Journal of Personality and Social Psychology, 59(6), 1119–1127. Copyright © 1990 by the American Psychological Association. Reprinted/adapted with permission.

Reading 18: R. H. Fazio, D. M. Sanbomatsu, M. C. Powell, and F. R. Kardes, On the Automatic Activation of Attitudes. Journal of Personality and Social Psychology, 50, 229–238. Copyright © 1986 by the American Psychological Association. Reprinted/adapted with permission.

Reading 19: A. Tesser, and D. Paulhus, The Definition of Self: Private and Public Self-Evaluation Management Strategies. Journal of Personality and Social Psychology, 44(4), 672–682. Copyright © by the American Psychological Association. Reprinted/adapted with permission.

Reading 20: N. Schwarz and G. L. Clore, Mood, Misattribution, and Judgments of Well-Being: Informative and Directive Functions of Affective States. Journal of Personality and Social Psychology, 45, 513–535. Copyright © 1983 by the American Psychological Association. Reprinted/adapted with permission.

Reading 21: D. M. Mackie, and L. T. Worth, Processing Deficits and the Mediation of Positive Affect in Persuasion. Journal of Personality and Social Psychology, 57, 27–40. Copyright © 1989 by the American Psychological Association. Reprinted/adapted with permission.

Reading 22: D. M. Wegner, and R. Erber, The Hyperaccessibility of Suppressed Thoughts. Journal of Personality and Social Psychology, 63, 903–912. Copyright © 1992 by the American Psychological Association. Reprinted/adapted with permission.

Reading 23: Z. Kunda, Motivated Inference: Self-Serving Generation and Evaluation of Causal Theories. Journal of Personality and Social Psychology, 53(4), 636–647. Copyright © 1987 by the American Psychological Association. Reprinted/adapted with permission.

Reading 24: A. Kruglanski, and T. Freund, The Freezing and Unfreezing of Lay Inferences: Effects on Impressional Primacy, Ethnic Stereotyping and Numerical Anchoring. Journal of Experimental Social Psychology, 19, 448–468. Copyright © 1983 by Academic Press. Reprinted/adapted with permission.

Reading 25: D. W. Griffin and K. Bartholomew, Models of Self and Other: Fundamental Dimensions Underlying Measures of Adult Attachment. Journal of Personality and Social Psychology, 67, 430–445. Copyright © 1994 by the American Psychological Association. Reprinted/adapted with permission.

Reading 26: C. Hazan, and P. R. Shaver, Love and Work: An Attachment-Theoretical Perspective. Journal of Personality and Social Psychology, 59, 270–280. Copyright © 1990 by the American Psychological Association. Reprinted/adapted with permission.

Reading 27: P. A. M. Van Lange, W. Otten, E. M. N. De Bruin, and J. A. Joireman, Development of Prosocial, Individualistic, and Competitive Orientations: Theory and Preliminary Evidence. Journal of Personality and Social Psychology, 73, 733–746. Copyright © 1997 by the American Psychological Association. Reprinted/adapted with permission.

Reading 28: W. Stroebe, M. S. Stroebe, G. Abakoumkin, and H. Schut, The Role of Loneliness and Social Support in Adjustment to Loss: A Test of Attachment versus Stress Theory. Journal of Personality and Social Psychology, 70, 1241–1249. Copyright © 1996 by the American Psychological Association. Reprinted/adapted with permission.

Reading 29: S. L. Murray, and J. G. Holmes, Seeing Virtues in Faults: Negativity and the Transformation of Interpersonal Narratives in Close Relationships. Journal of Personality and Social Psychology, 65(4), 707–722. Copyright © 1993 by the American Psychological Association. Reprinted/adapted with permission.

Reading 30: R. M. Krauss, P. S. Vivenkananthan, and S. Weinheimer, "Inner Speech" and "External Speech": Characteristics and Communication Effectiveness of Socially and Nonsocially Encoded Messages. Journal of Personality and Social Psychology, 9, 295–300. Copyright © 1968 by the American Psychological Association. Reprinted/adapted with permission.

Reading 31: E. T. Higgins, Achieving "Shared Reality" in the Communication Game: A Social Action That Creates Meaning. Journal of Language and Social Psychology, 11, 107–125. Copyright © 1992 by Sage Publications. Reprinted by Permission of Sage Publications.

Reading 32: G. R. Semin, and K. Fiedler, The Cognitive Functions of Linguistic Categories in Describing Persons: Social Cognition and Language. Journal of Personality and Social Psychology, 54, 558–568. Copyright © 1991 by the American Psychological Association. Reprinted/adapted with permission.

Reading 33: S. Chaiken, Heuristic versus Systematic Information Processing and the Use of Source versus Message Cues in Persuasion. Journal of Personality and Social Psychology, 39(5), 752–766. Copyright © 1980 the American Psychological Association. Reprinted/adapted with permission.

Reading 34: R. E. Petty, J. T. Cacioppo, and R. Goldman, Personal Involvement as a Predictor of Argument-Based Persuasion. Journal of Personality and Social Psychology, 41, 847–855. Copyright © 1981 by the American Psychological Association. Reprinted/adapted with permission.

Reading 35: A. W. Kruglanski and E. P. Thompson, Persuasion by a Single Route: A View from the Unimodel. Psychological Inquiry, 10, 83–110. Copyright © 1998 by LEA Publishers, Associates. Reprinted with permission.

Reading 36: C. J. Nemeth, Differential Contributions of Majority and Minority Influence. Psychological Review, 93, 23–32. Copyright © 1986 by the American Psychological Association. Reprinted/adapted with permission.

Reading 37: J. M. Levine, and R. L. Moreland, Group Socialization: Theory and Research. European Review of Social Psychology, 5, 305–336. Copyright © 1994 by John Wiley & Sons, Ltd. Reprinted by permission of John Wiley & Sons Limited.

Reading 38: D. Abrams, and M. A. Hogg, Comments on the Motivational Status of Self-Esteem in Social Identity and Intergroup Discrimination. European Journal of Social Psychology, 18, 317–334. Copyright © 1988 by John Wiley & Sons, Ltd. Reprinted by permission of John Wiley & Sons Limited.

Reading 39: A. Reid, and K. Deaux, Relationship Between Social and Personal Identities: Segregation or Integration? Journal of Personality and Social Psychology, 71, 1084–1091. Copyright © 1997 by the American Psychological Association. Reprinted/adapted with permission.

Reading 40: R. C. Jacobs, and D. T. Campbell, The Perpetuation of an Arbitrary Tradition Through Several Generations of a Laboratory Microculture. Journal of Personality and Social Psychology, 62, 649–658, 1961. Public Domain.

Preface

What makes us all social psychologists is a commitment to a domain of psychological phenomena where relations to other individuals play a critical role. What makes a phenomenon "social" is its concern with how people respond to, or take into account, other people. But the responses can be psychological, cognitive, affective, or behavioral; they can be individualistic or collective, controlled or spontaneous, and so on. Any approach, any level of analysis, any framework or perspective is in principle legitimate. Our approach to social psychology is nonreductionistic and characterized by a multiplicity of perspectives (see also Higgins & Kruglanski, 1996). Accordingly, our reader is ordered in terms of levels of analysis whereby social phenomena can be understood. We start with the biological level, and successively cover the cognitive, personal/motivational, interpersonal, and group and cultural levels. No one level of analysis is considered superior, more basic, or more adequate for explaining social phenomena than any other level, nor do these levels compete with each other. Rather, we believe that each level makes a vital contribution to the understanding of human social experience and that it does so in a unique way. Thus, the relations between the levels of analysis are complementary, and together they shed light on our social nature. The common thread running through this volume, at all its levels of analysis, is a concern with social psychology as a realm of phenomena.

Beyond the organization of the readings according to different levels of analysis, our choice of articles was guided by a commitment to the notion of *principles* of social behavior. We believe that a fundamental objective of scientific research is the discovery of lawful principles governing a realm of phenomena. From this viewpoint, empirical findings have to be understood as "evidence" in relation to possible principles rather than as "facts" about the social world. In other words, science, ultimately, is not about facts, nor even about theories if those represent particular investigators' perspectives. Rather, it is about discovering and understanding the true laws of nature as they manifest themselves through empirical observations. Now, we are not naively assuming that Truth as such is directly knowable or that we may ever be able to determine with finality whether or not we have attained it. Instead, we accept Popper's (1959) dictum that Truth should be the *regulating ideal* of scientific research, something to strive for relentlessly. This implies an "inter-theoretic" stance that eschews commitment to any one framework but insists on a continuous assessment of theories relative to each other to enable the next insight into the essential underpinnings of social psychological phenomena.

The articles we have selected not only include highly influential papers but also ones that seem to showcase important social psychological principles.

This was not an easy choice, to be sure. Of the thousands of articles in the social psychological literature, numerous papers on any given topic fit our selection criteria quite well. Thus, in order to balance our own subjective judgments of importance and impact, we sought the advice of esteemed colleagues, about the one or two most central and useful papers on a topic. All other things equal, we selected papers on basis of their readability, accessibility, and, yes, brevity, else this volume would have swollen to unmanageable proportions. In an attempt to correct the imbalance that any choice creates, each article in our anthology is accompanied by lists of suggested readings that round out the picture and provide additional background on the substantive issues, approaches, and methods in a given area of study. The discussion questions accompanying each selection are meant to be helpful to readers by focusing their attention on the gist of the contribution. We hope, therefore, that this reader conveys the vastness of domain, the versatility of approaches, and the tremendous vitality and excitement that characterize the empirically based study of social psychological principles.

REFERENCES

Higgins, E. T., & Kruglanski, A. W. (1996). *Social Psychology: A handbook of basic principles*. New York: Guilford.

Popper, K. R. (1959). *The logic of scientific discovery*. New York: Harper. (Originally published as *Logik der Forschung*. Viena, 1935)

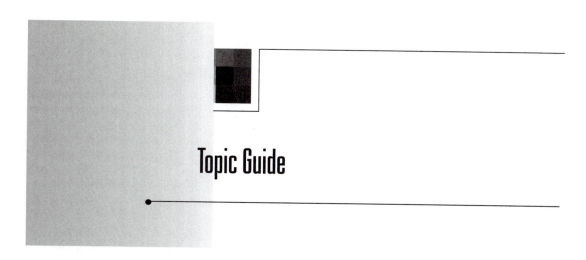

Topic Guide

This brief Topic Guide clearly shows which readings relate to the key topic areas in Social Psychology. Instructors and students will find this useful when mapping the contents of this reader with their course textbook. For a more detailed index, please see the Subject Index on page 643.

The Biological System

The mind-body problem, surely one of the greatest, most acute, and most profound philosophical issues of all times, is touched upon in the present section. It highlights the notion that our behavior, though in a certain sense free and self-directed, is nonetheless constrained by our biological makeup. In and of itself, this idea is not surprising. We are all aware that our bodily states, from fatigue, illness, or the influence of chemical substances, affect how we behave, perceive ourselves and others, and react emotionally to various situations. The scientific investigation of the crucial mind-body interface obviously went much beyond such everyday observations in exploring theoretical notions, experimental paradigms, and novel research technologies in order to delve into the intricate ways in which our biological and psychological aspects interact with one another.

The three selections in the present section illustrate some of the major approaches to the issue currently represented in social psychological research. The selection by Buss (1989) adopts an evolutionary approach, descendent from Darwin's influential theorizing, in order to study cross-culturally such fundamentally important social behavior as mate selection. Evolutionary theory, and the data Buss reports, suggest that such behavior has strong biological determinants and is not exclusively shaped by norms and practices forged by a given society at a given time and place. Taking a different approach, Cacioppo and Berntson (1992) examine the reciprocal relations between our biological makeup and our social behavior. They make a compelling case that, current preferences for specialization notwithstanding, a general psychological theory worthy of its name can only be constructed by considering multiple levels of analysis, including the physiological, cognitive, social, and cultural layers of behavioral organization. The third selection, by Taylor and Brown (1988), is less explicitly biological in its approach, but it also concerns functional adaptation. It describes how psychological mechanisms function to support adaptation to our social and physical environments and effective coping with traumatic events such as major illness. The provocative thesis put forth by Taylor and Brown is that adaptive functioning may often require that we bend reality a little to suit our needs by viewing life through rose-tinted glasses and engaging in positive illusions that promote well-being.

Mate Preferences in 37 Cultures

1989

David M. Buss • Professor of Psychology, University of Michigan

Editors' Notes

Are human mate preferences determined by cultural norms or practices or do they reflect biological mechanisms of universal (and hence transcultural) applicability? The present article examines several predictions derived from evolutionary theory regarding differential mate preferences of males and females. These predictions are examined across 37 cultures differing widely in their characteristics. Because these cultures are so divergent in their character, finding similarities across them would argue against the notion that mate preferences are the province solely of cultural forces. Indeed, impressive similarities are found, consistent with the evolutionary framework, in that across cultures males generally place greater emphasis than females on their mate's chastity and physical attractiveness (indicative of fertility or reproductive potential), whereas, compared to males, females generally prefer mates with greater potential for securing material resources. However, not all the evolutionary predictions were found to hold universally, and there was considerable variability among cultures in the degree to which the differences between males and females exhibited the predicted patterns.

Discussion Questions

1. How powerful is biology versus culture in determining mate preferences?
2. Can you think of culturally based alternative explanations for the differences reported by Buss?
3. How might the advent of new technologies and biotechnologies affect the future of mate preferences?

Suggested Readings

Buss, D. M., & Schmitt, D. P. (1993). Sexual strategies theory: An evolutionary perspective on human mating. *Psychological Review, 100,* 204–232.

Cosmides, L. (1989). The logic of social exchange: Has natural selection shaped how humans reason? *Cognition, 31,* 187–276.

Hamilton, W. D. (1964). The evolution of social behavior. *Journal of Theoretical Biology, 7,* 1–52.

Every person is alive because of a successful mating. People in the past who failed to mate are not our ancestors. But how do we choose our mates? What characteristics do we seek? And why?

Social scientists have long assumed that our mate preferences are highly culture-bound—that people in North America, for example, desire different characteristics than people in Asia or Africa. Even Charles Darwin, a pioneering scientist on the topic of mating, believed that mate preferences were largely arbitrary. But little scientific knowledge has been gathered about what we want in a mate. Until recently.

A startling new study shows that traditional scientific assumptions have been radically wrong. With 50 other scientists residing in 37 cultures around the world, I set out to discover what people want in a mate.

These findings, involving more than 10,000 *people in 37 cultures on six continents and five islands,* were extraordinarily difficult to obtain. In South Africa, the data collection was described as "a rather frightening experience" due to political turmoil and violence in shanty-towns. Government committees hindered data collection in some countries, and banned the study entirely in others. Revolutions and mail strikes prevented some collected data to be sent. It took us more than five years to gather all the information, and two years to perform the needed statistical analyses. But it was worth the wait.

We did find some striking differences across cultures, as scientists and common lore had long suspected. But we found apparently universal preferences as well—things that people worldwide expressed a desire for. And we found a few key differences between men and women in all cultures—universal differences that appear to be deeply rooted in the evolutionary history of our species. This chapter summarizes a few of the most important findings.

Universal Mate Preferences Shared by Men and Women

We asked people to tell us how desirable 32 characteristics were in a potential marriage partner. We used two instruments. The first was a rating instrument, where subjects indicated how important each of 18 characteristics was on a scale ranging from "0" (irrelevant or unimportant) to "3" (indispensable). The second instrument requested subjects to rank each of 13 characteristics from "1" (most desirable) to "13" (least desirable).

When we analyzed the data for each of the 37 cultures, we found that people in nearly every culture agreed about which were the top few most desirable characteristics. Not only was there agreement across cultures on the top few, men and women were statistically identical in nearly all of the 37 cultures on these most valued attributes. Everywhere, both men and women wanted a mate who was kind and understanding, intelligent, and was healthy (ranking instrument). Universally, as shown by the rating instrument, both men and women wanted a mate who possessed emotional stability and maturity, dependability, a pleasing disposition, and good health (see Table 1).

What about love? Many scientists believe that love is a Western notion, invented just a few hundred years ago. Our findings show those scientists to be wrong. People the world over value mutual attraction and love. Love is not merely something seen in Western Europe or even the Western world. Love is just as highly prized by the Chinese, Indonesians, Zambians, Nigerians, Iranians, and Palestinians. At least with respect to these character-

TABLE 1.1. Universally Desired Mate Characteristics

Universally Preferred Characteristics—Ranking Instrument

1. Kind and Understanding
2. Intelligent
3. Exciting Personality
4. Healthy

Universally Preferred Characteristics—Rating Instrument

1. Mutual Attraction—Love
2. Emotionally Stable and Mature
3. Dependable Character
4. Good Health
5. Pleasing Disposition

istics, people everywhere have roughly the same desires. Our scientific theories need revision. At least some mate preferences are not as culture-bound as we had thought.

Culturally Variable Mate Preferences

But it's not that simple. Not all characteristics showed uniformity across cultures. Indeed, for a few characteristics, what people desired in potential mates varied tremendously across cultures. Chastity—the lack of previous sexual intercourse—proved to be the characteristic most variable across culture (see Figure 1). This surprised our research team.

We expected that men worldwide would value chastity, and would value it more than women.

This is because of the differences between men and women in the certainty of their parenthood. Women are 100 percent certain that they are the mothers of their children. But men can never be entirely sure that they are the fathers. Over thousands of generations of human evolutionary history, this sex-linked adaptive problem should have imposed selection pressure on men to prefer mates for whom their paternity probability would be increased. Valuing chastity might have been one way that men could be more "confident" that they were the fathers. We found that not all men feel that way.

We were surprised that men and women from the Netherlands, for example, don't care about chastity at all. Neither is virginity valued much in the Scandinavian countries such as Sweden and Norway. Indeed, some people even wrote on the questionnaires that chastity was "undesirable" or "bad" in a prospective mate. In China, however, virginity is indispensable in a mate—marrying a non-virgin is virtually out of the question. People from India, Taiwan, and Iran also placed tremendous value on chastity. In between the Western European countries and the Asian countries were Nigeria, South Africa, Zambia, Japan, Estonia, Poland, and Columbia—they all saw chastity as only moderately desirable in a mate.

Cultures, however, do not seem to be infinitely variable in this regard. We could find no cultures where women valued virginity more than men. In fact, in two thirds of all of our cultures—an overwhelming majority—men desired chastity in marriage partners more than women. Culture does have

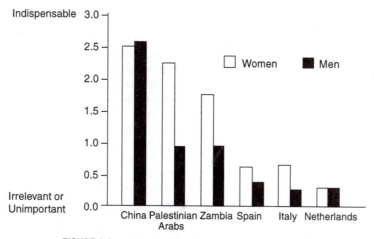

FIGURE 1.1 ■ Chastity: No previous sexual intercourse.

a large effect on how much chastity is valued. In the majority of cultures, though, so does whether one is a man or a woman.

Although the value men and women place on chastity in potential mates overwhelmingly showed the greatest cross-cultural variability, several other factors also showed large cultural differences. Examples include: *good housekeeper* (highly valued in Estonia and China, little valued in Western Europe and North America); *refinement/neatness* (highly valued in Nigeria and Iran, less valued in Great Britain, Ireland, and Australia); and *religious* (highly valued in Iran, moderately valued in India, little valued in Western Europe and North America). These large cultural differences, important as they undoubtedly are, probably mask a great deal of variability across individuals within cultures.

What Do Women Want?

From Aristotle to Freud to contemporary society, scholars have puzzled over the question: What do women want? Trivers's (1972, 1985) seminal theory of parental investment and sexual selection provided a powerful evolutionary basis for predicting some female preferences. Trivers argued that the sex that invested more in offspring should be selected to be relatively more choosy or discriminating than the sex that invested less. Poor mating decisions are more costly to the heavily investing sex. A woman who chooses poorly, for example, might end up abused or find herself raising her children alone—events that would have been reproductively damaging in ancestral (and likely modern) times. Because humans are like other mammals in that fertilization, gestation, and placentation are costs incurred by females rather than by males, it is clear that the *minimum* investment needed to produce a child is much greater in women than in men. But in other species, such as the Mormon cricket, the pipefish seahorse, and the poison arrow frog, males invest more heavily in offspring and in these species, males are more choosy than females about who they mate with. This highlights the fact that relative parental investment, not biological *sex per se*, is the driving force behind relative choosiness.

But in species where the less investing sex can accrue and defend resources, where they vary a lot in how many resources, they have to contribute, and where some show a willingness to devote resources, the more heavily investing sex is predicted to prefer mates who show an ability and willingness to invest resources. Folk wisdom has it that the concern with material resources is prevalent only in cultures with capitalist systems. Our international study of 37 cultures shows otherwise. In a striking confirmation of Trivers's theory, women value "good financial prospects" and "good earning capacity" more than men. From the Zulu tribe in South Africa to coastal dwelling Australians to city-dwelling Brazilians, women place a premium on good earning capacity, financial prospects, ambition, industriousness, and social status more than men—characteristics that all provide resources.

We were surprised to find these results even in socialist countries and communist countries where there is less income inequality. Women seem to value resources in mates more than men regardless of the political system. Women throughout human evolutionary history have needed material resources that can help their children survive and thrive.

Are women more choosy than men? Across nearly all cultures, women indeed were more discriminating and choosy than men. Women express more stringent standards across an array of characteristics—they want more of nearly everything. These findings support another key prediction from Trivers's evolutionary theory.

What Do Men Want in a Mate?

Men expressed more stringent standards than women on only two characteristics. The first is *youth*. Men worldwide prefer wives who are younger than they are (see Figure 2). But how much younger depends on the nature of the mating system. In cultures that permit men to acquire multiple wives, such as Zambia and Nigeria, men prefer brides who are much younger than they are—by as many as 7 or 8 years. In cultures that restrict men to one wife such as Spain, France, and Germany, men prefer brides who are only a few years younger. Interestingly, women in all cultures preferred husbands who were older—because men mature somewhat later than women and because older men often have access to more resources than younger men.

But youth is not the only thing that men want.

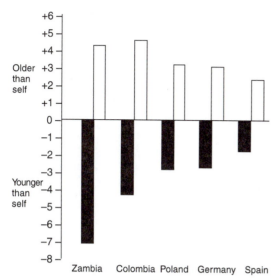

FIGURE 1.2 ■ Age difference preferred between self and spouse.

Men across the globe also value "physical attractiveness" in marriage partners more than women.

Traditional social science theories have assumed that what people find beautiful is culture-bound—that beauty is merely "in the eyes of the beholder" and that standards of beauty are rather arbitrary. We now know that these theories are partially wrong. The available evidence shows that people across cultures see clear and supple skin, absence of wrinkles, lustrous hair, full lips, clear eyes, good health, regular features, and other signs of youth and health as attractive. Although there are cultural preferences for slightly more plump or thin mates, men worldwide regard the same women as beautiful.

The importance men place on good looks is not limited to Western Europe or North America; nor is it limited to cultures saturated with visual media such as television, movies, and videos; nor is it limited to particular racial, ethnic, religious, or political groups. In *all* known cultures worldwide, from the inner-continental tribal societies of Africa and South America to the big cities of Madrid, London, and Paris, men place a premium on the physical appearance of a potential mate. And they do so for a very good reason.

According to a new scientific theory, these qualities provide the best signals to a man that the woman is fertile and has good reproductive ca-

pacity. This is not necessarily done at a conscious level. We like sweet foods without knowing the nutritional logic of caloric intake. Men prize physical appearance and youth without knowing that these qualities signal a woman's fertility and reproductive capacity.

Mate Preferences and Actual Marriage Decisions

People act on their preferences. Worldwide, men do marry women younger than they are, on average. And interestingly, men who possess a lot of resources can obtain younger and more physically attractive mates. Women who are physically attractive can obtain men with more resources and social status. In societies where men purchase their wives, young women command a higher "brideprice" than older women. Finally, among the most prevalent causes of marital dissolution worldwide are infertility, infidelity, and a man's failure to provide economically (Betzig, 1989). Mate preferences, in other words, are reflected in the actual mating decisions that people make.

Conclusions

Where does all this leave us? First, it is important to recognize that each person is at least somewhat unique, showing individual patterns of mate preferences. Second, culture clearly matters a lot. The tremendous cross-cultural variability on preferences for "chastity" demonstrate that even characteristics that are close to reproduction are not immutable, unchangeable, or intractable. Third, it is now apparent that men and women worldwide do differ consistently on a few key mate preferences—those where the sexes have faced different adaptive problems over human evolutionary history. Fourth, there are many preferences that men and women share the world over, with both sexes valuing them highly in a mate. In an important sense, as variable as we are across culture and across gender, we are all one species when it comes to mating.

REFERENCES

Betzig, L. (1989). Causes of conjugal dissolution. *Current Anthropology, 30,* 654–676.

Buss, D. M. (1989). Sex differences in human mate preferences: Evolutionary hypotheses tested in 37 cultures. *Behavioral and Brain Sciences, 12,* 1–49.

Buss, D. M. (in press). *Sexual strategies: The evolution of human mating.* New York: Basic Books.

Trivers, R. (1972). Parental investment and sexual selection. In B. Campbell (Ed.), *Sexual selection and the descent of man:* 1871–1971. Chicago: Aldine.

Trivers, R. (1985). *Social evolution.* Menlo Park, CA: The Benjamin/Cummings Publishing Company.

Social Psychological Contributions to the Decade of the Brain: Doctrine of Multilevel Analysis

John T. Cacioppo and Gary G. Berntson • Ohio State University

Editors' Notes

Is it the fate of psychology to disintegrate into a fragmented set of specific subdisciplines (neuroscience, cognitive science, social science) and lose the intellectual glue that has been binding it together thus far? Is it even relevant for students of social psychology to gain a basic understanding of the biological elements in behavior? And is it useful for neuroscience students to master a rudimentary understanding of social psychology? Cacioppo and Berntson put forth a doctrine of multiple levels of analysis whereby the construction of a general psychological theory requires examining its target phenomena on multiple levels of organization. Although useful science may be conducted on any single level of analysis as well, it is the integration across levels that affords a full-fledged understanding of psychological phenomena. Thus, contrary to the threat of fractionation, the present proposal makes a compelling plea for a unified, multilevel approach to psychology as a science.

Discussion Questions

1. Will neuroscience replace the study of social psychology? If so, why so? If not, why not?
2. What is the significance of the fact that the brain does not function in isolation from cognitive, social, and cultural phenomena?
3. What is to be gained, and what might be lost, by the increments in precision made possible by going down the hierarchy of levels of analysis?

Suggested Readings

Cohen, S., Tyrell, D. A. J., & Smith, A. P. (1991). Life events, perceived stress, negative affect and susceptibility to the common cold. *Journal of Personality and Social Psychology, 64*, 131–140.

Kiecolt-Glaser, J. K., Malarkey, W. B., Chee, M. A., Newton, T., et al. (1993). Negative behavior during marital conflict is associated with immunological down-regulation. *Psychosomatic Medicine, 55*, 395–409.

Authors' Abstract

The 1990s were declared by Congress to be the "decade of the brain." This declaration is important to all psychologists, not only neuroscientists, because with this declaration come expectations of the cognitive and behavioral sciences generally and because the brain does not exist in isolation but rather is a fundamental component of developing and aging individuals who themselves are mere actors in the larger theater of life. This article examines the importance of a multilevel, integrative approach to the study of mental and behavioral phenomena in the decade of the brain, reviews how this approach highlights the synergistic relationship between theoretical and clinically relevant research, and illustrates how this approach can foster the transition from microtheories to general psychological theories.

My concern is that the character of psychology is increasingly manifest in the rapid proliferation of narrowly focused and compulsively insular camps, a proliferation that seemingly knows no limits. (Bevan, 1991, p. 475)

Panoramic photographs of earth from space reveal agricultural runoffs that stretch hundreds of miles out to sea and vast clouds of fossil fuel emissions blanketing industrial areas. These disquieting images reflect the collective action of individuals, but the effect of these actions cannot be fully appreciated unless these phenomena are studied from a point of view that extends well beyond the level of individual actions. From this ionospheric perspective, one could easily visualize effects that could not be fully comprehended from a closer focal point. This simple example from space science illustrates a principle that seems so obvious in the physical sciences but that often appears incomprehensible in the psychological sciences and neurosciences. There are phenomena that may be explicable in terms of events at a microlevel of analysis but that are more easily studied and more fully comprehended by reference to broader and multiple levels of analysis.

Our aims in this article are to outline the importance of a multilevel, integrative approach to the study of mental and behavioral phenomena in the decade of the brain; to review how this approach highlights the synergistic relationship between theoretical and clinically relevant research; and to explore how this approach might foster the transition from microtheories to general psychological theories. We begin by examining the decade of the brain and its relevance to the social and psychological sciences. We then review several psychological principles underscoring the thesis that basic research cutting across levels, including the cultural, social, psychological, and biological, is an imperative rather than a luxury if the decade of the brain is to produce satisfactory answers to complex psychological phenomena and disorders.

Decade of the Brain

A fundamental assumption in the natural science of psychology is that neurophysiological processes underlie adaptive and maladaptive psychological phenomena. William James (1890/1950) was one of the first psychologists to articulate this assumption; to recognize that developmental, environmental, and sociocultural factors influence neurophysiological processes underlying psychological phenomena; and to acknowledge that these influences *could* be studied as neurophysiological transactions. James also asserted that unnecessary diseconomies and conundrums would result if neurophysiological events were the exclusive focus of psychological investigations (Cacioppo & Tassinary, 1990a).

William James drew these conclusions over a century ago. In decades past, studies of the neurophysiological structures and functions associated with psychological events were limited primarily to animal models, postmortem examinations, and observations of the occasional unfortunate individual (e.g., Phineas Gage, H.M.) who suffered trauma to or disorders of the brain. Developments in electrophysiological recording, brain imaging, and neurochemical techniques within the neurosciences have increasingly made it possible to investigate the role of neural structures and processes in normal and disordered thought in humans. The importance of these technical developments was underscored by Congress's declaration of the 1990s as the decade of the brain.

The congressional declaration of the decade of the brain is important to all psychological sciences for two reasons. First, this declaration may confer higher appropriations, but it clearly confers higher expectations for the unraveling of the mind's knots and nightmares. The credibility of the cognitive, behavioral, and social sciences, not just the neurosciences, is therefore at stake.

Second, the brain does not exist in isolation but rather is a fundamental but interacting component of a developing or aging individual who is a mere actor in the larger theater of life. This theater is undeniably social, beginning with prenatal care, mother-infant attachment, and early childhood experiences and ending with loneliness or social support and with familial or societal decisions about care for the elderly. In addition, mental disorders such as depression, schizophrenia, and phobia are both determined by and are determinants of social processes; and disorders such as substance abuse, juvenile delinquency, child and spousal abuse, prejudice and stigmatization, family discord, worker dissatisfaction and productivity, and the spread of acquired immunodeficiency syndrome (AIDS) are quintessentially social as well as neurophysiological phenomena. Social psychology, with its panoramic focus on the effects of human association and the impact of society on the individual, is therefore a fundamental although sometimes unacknowledged complement to the neurosciences. [1]

The importance of a social psychological perspective to the neurosciences is revealed in research demonstrating both that (a) neurochemical events influence social processes and (b) social processes influence neurochemical events. Studies of mating behavior in the ring-necked dove, for instance, indicate that social behaviors (e.g., male strutting and cooing) trigger hormonal changes (e.g., increased production of estrogen in the female) that predispose the female toward a new set of behaviors (e.g., courtship and copulation), which results in yet additional reciprocal influences between hormones and social behaviors until the newborns are reared (Erikson & Lehrman, 1964; Lehrman, 1964; Martinez-Vargas & Erikson, 1973). These reciprocal influences have also been found in primates. Testosterone levels in male primates, for example, have been found to promote sexual behavior, whereas the availability of sexually receptive females, in turn, has been found to influence testosterone levels in male primates (Bernstein, Gordon, & Rose, 1983; Bernstein, Rose, & Gordon, 1974; Rose, Gordon, & Bernstein, 1972; see, also, Davidson, Camargo, & Smith, 1979). Indeed, our understanding of the function of hormones would be far more rudimentary if not for analyses of their effects on social behavior and for the effects of social behavior on hormonal changes. Thus, comprehensive theoretical accounts of hormonal regulation (not just sexual behavior) necessitate consideration of social factors. There are, of course, physiological mechanisms underlying these phenomena, but the identification and understanding of these mechanisms are better served by systematic investigations within and across multiple (including social) levels of analysis rather than by a reductionistic focus alone.

The differences in social psychological and neuroscientific levels of analysis have occasion-

---

[1] We chose to focus here on social psychological contributions to the decade of the brain for two reasons. First, its complementarity to a neuroscience perspective is less understood than other psychological perspectives. Cognitive, behavioral, and developmental neuroscience, for instance, are all active areas of research, but social neuroscience strikes some as being an oxymoron (see Scott, 1991). It is not, as we hope to illustrate in this article. Second, the social and neuroscience perspectives represent two ends of a continuum of levels of organization studied in psychology. By illustrating the importance of considering both social and neuroscience perspectives and their intersections, we hope to illustrate the general importance of multilevel, integrative analyses of complex psychological phenomena.

ally obscured commonalities and isolated related research on and contributions to a psychological phenomenon. Before considering these commonalities and potential mutual contributions, we will review briefly ways in which the term *level of analysis* has been used in social psychology and in the neurosciences. We will then define how the term will be used here, review several basic principles in which the construct of levels is fundamental, and examine the implications of these principles for psychological theory and research.

Level of Analysis: Single Level Versus Multilevel Analysis

Single Level Analysis

The term *level of analysis* has been used in psychology to refer to the level of structural organization (e.g., Tolman, 1959; P. Weiss, 1941), the level of explanation (e.g., Shaw & Turvey, 1981), and the level of processing (e.g., Churchland & Sejnowski, 1988; Craik & Lockhart, 1972). In the present article, we will focus on the first usage of the term *levels*, which refers to the different scales into which the brain or behavior can be represented. What constitutes a level of organization, at least for lower mechanisms, is usually guided by knowledge of anatomy or physiology; but the ultimate criterion is the usefulness of the posited organization in shedding light on some designated biological, psychological, or behavioral phenomenon. Thus, the level of organization of psychological phenomena can vary from the molecular, to the cellular, to the tissue, to the organ, to the system, to the organism, to the physical environment, to the sociocultural context.

Levels of analysis in the neurosciences generally encompass the lower end of this spectrum, whereas in social psychology they capture the higher end—the individual and group within a sociocultural system. Thus, these fields differ in the level at which behavioral phenomena are unitized, although they need not differ in terms of the behavioral phenomenon under investigation. For instance, although both neuroscientists and social psychologists may study sexual behavior, aggression, or addiction, the elements into which the phenomena are partitioned and the dimensions of the measurements of these two levels of analysis are discordant. Consequently, the conceptual units

and dimensions of one level seldom map isomorphically into those of another. This lack of isomorphism is inherent across levels of analysis because (a) higher levels entail functional outcomes of interactive aggregates of lower processes and (b) a given outcome may arise from differing aggregates or states. Thus, social psychological analyses focus on social structures and processes that characterize *functional* aspects of neurophysiological mechanisms, but a particular function cannot be readily characterized in the terminology and concepts of neurophysiology. Moreover, a given function can be implemented by one or more neurophysiological mechanisms whose boundaries may not be obvious, at least initially, from anatomical considerations (Cacioppo & Tassinary, 1990b; Fodor, 1968).

Multilevel Integrative Analysis

Important advances have been made and will continue to be made using single levels of analysis. Indeed, one of the themes of this article is that such research is important and bears on issues relevant to investigators working on the same psychological phenomenon even when their particular level of analysis is quite different. We suggest there is an additional benefit to be gained, however, from a multilevel analysis of the phenomenon, wherein one considers not only the elements from two or more levels of analysis that bear on some phenomenon but also the relational features among these elements. Thus, by multilevel analysis we mean the study of a phenomenon from various structural scales or perspectives, ranging from the neuroscientific ("microscopic") to the social psychological ("macroscopic"). By integrative, we mean simply that analyses of a phenomenon at one level of organization can inform, refine, or constrain inferences based on observations at another level of analysis and, therefore, can foster comprehensive accounts and general theories of complex psychological phenomena. Given differences in the unitization of a phenomenon across levels of analysis, multilevel analyses require special considerations, which we will consider below.

There are at least three reasons to expect that multilevel analyses of complex social and behavioral problems will be integrative. First, complex systems as a rule cannot be understood as a simple extrapolation from the properties of their elementary components (Marr, 1982). Unless the properties of the system are the simple sum of those of its elementary components, a focus on elementary components contributes to an explanation only when considered in conjunction with events occurring at different levels of the system. Indeed, Fodor (1968; Fodor & Pylyshyn, 1988) observed that there are causal structures at each level of organization and that the causal structures at the macroscopic level in science cannot be predicted by the microscopic.[2] "No one expects the theory of protons to look very much like the theory of rocks and rivers, even though, to be sure, it is protons and the like that rocks and rivers are 'implemented in'" (Fodor & Pylyshyn, 1988, p. 63). Fodor and Pylyshyn further noted:

> Clearly it is pointless to ask whether one should or shouldn't do cognitive science by studying 'the interaction of lower levels' as opposed to studying processes at the cognitive level since we surely have to do *both*. Some scientists study geological principles, others study 'the interaction of lower level units' like molecules. But since the fact that there are genuine, autonomously-stable principles of geology is never in dispute, people who build molecular level models do not claim to have invented a 'new theory of geology' that will dispense with all that old fashioned 'folk geological' talk about rocks, rivers, and mountains! (p. 66)

For this reason, the study of the elements of a system (i.e., reductionism) may produce eloquent descriptions while falling short of a useful and comprehensive explanation.

We should emphasize that we are not suggesting that the study of the behavior of elementary components has disutility or is irrelevant to molar analyses but rather that reductionistic inquiries can precede (or co-occur or follow) and, in turn, stimulate (or be informed by) relatively molar research on the behavior of complex systems. The example from space science with which we began this article is a case in point. The study of the system as an aggregate may produce detailed descriptions of the molar behavior of the system while falling short of defining the underlying origins of this

behavior (i.e., individual and collective actions in the case of the pollution). Learned helplessness exemplifies a molar psychological phenomenon that was subsequently informed by, and in turn informed, lower levels of analysis. Early research demonstrated that inescapable shock led to a depressive syndrome characterized by inactivity, loss of escape/avoidance reactions, and a decrease in reactivity to pain (Seligman, 1975). This research led to a specific psychological explanation that ascribed this state of helplessness to the learning of a lack of contingency between responses and outcomes and to a pessimistic attributional style (Abramson, Seligman, & Teasdale, 1978; Peterson & Seligman, 1984). Research in the neurosciences, however, has further demonstrated that (a) brain catecholamine depletion can yield a similar syndrome, (b) inescapable shock can lead to a decrease in central catecholamines and an opiate-mediated analgesia, and (c) this syndrome can be effectively treated by antidepressants or other agents that enhance central catecholamines or block opiate receptors (Basbaum & Fields, 1984; Bodnar, 1990; Maier, 1984, 1986; Simson, Weiss, Hoffman, & Ambrose, 1986; J. M. Weiss, Goodman, Losito, Corrigan, & Bailey, 1981; J. M. Weiss et al., 1986). Thus, lower levels of analysis have illuminated physiological mechanisms that may underlie this helplessness syndrome and in turn may inform certain cases of human depression (Maier, 1984; J. M. Weiss et al., 1981). On the other hand, it has also become apparent that (a) there are both associative and nonassociative behavioral determinants of helplessness (Lysle & Fowler, 1988; Maier, Jackson, & Tomie, 1987; Minor, Dess, & Overmeir, 1991; Seligman, 1975), (b) the degree of stress-induced catecholamine depletion is related to the psychological factors of predictability and controllability (Maier, 1984; J. M. Weiss et al., 1981), and (c) physiological mechanisms for both opiate and nonopiate stress-induced analgesia are differentially invoked on the basis of the behavioral context (Bodnar, 1990; Maier, 1986, 1989). These reciprocal interactions between behavioral and physiological domains would seriously cloud studies limited to a single level of analysis. The point is that distinct levels of analysis might better be viewed as complementary rather than alternative approaches. The relationship between catecholamine depletion and depression in helplessness, for instance, did not originate in research on central catecholamine regulation but in

---

[2] Fodor's (1968) emphasis was on concepts and theories rather than elements (units, dimensions). Differences in the unitization of a phenomenon across levels of analysis and the consequent lack of isomorphism become even more notable when one progresses from elements to conceptual or theoretical schemata that must also specify relational features among dissimilar and nonisomorphic elements.

research on the effects of uncontrollable stressors on behavior and cognition.

A second reason multilevel analyses of complex social and behavioral problems tend to be integrative is that each level of organization constitutes a particular kind of representation with which to examine human mentation and behavior. Any particular representation makes certain information explicit at the expense of other information and, hence, renders some operations or insights easy and others quite difficult. Thus, no single level of behavioral organization is best for all psychological questions. An example can be found in the relative utility of specifying the sociocognitive versus the neurophysiological basis of patient delay following the onset of gynecologic cancer. Women can now survive most gynecologic cancers if the disease is diagnosed and treated early. Indeed, research on gynecologic cancer indicates that the prognosis for survival and for quality of life following medical treatment is directly related to the stage of the cancer at diagnosis (Andersen, 1986). Moreover, women with advanced rather than early-stage disease at diagnosis, even if they survive, are more likely to suffer depression, experience marital and family problems, and require extended and expensive medical treatment. Hence, patient delay in seeking a diagnosis is a serious problem that carries large and longterm personal, family, and societal costs. The form of the representation of patient delay offered by neuroscientific analyses of patient delay, although perhaps ultimately contributing to a more complete understanding of the phenomenon, is not optimal for identifying the determinants of patient delay or for developing effective interventions to minimize such delay. Huge savings in resources and human suffering are there to be reaped, not through a specification of the brain circuits underlying patient delay but by well-conceived public health campaigns that identify the early signs of cancer and minimize the material, emotional, and social costs of seeking diagnosis and treatment (Andersen, 1986; see also Rossi, 1991).

Third, Fodor and McLaughlin (1990) noted that precision is often gained when one moves from generalizations about operations on molar elements to generalizations about operations on microelements. However, this increased precision does not yield a truer depiction of the causal mechanism nor is the conceptual price paid for the precision necessarily worth the gain in preci-

sion. As Fodor and McLaughlin noted, if by moving to the more microscopic level of analysis one finds the macrolevel processes are not really causal, then it must mean the microlevel processes underlying these macrolevel processes are not causal either. Moreover:

> We get *still more* precision when we go down from unit-sensitive operations to molecule-sensitive operations to quark-sensitive operations. The moral is not, however, that the causal laws of psychology should be stated in terms of the behavior of quarks. Rather, the moral is that whether you have a level of causal explanation is a question, not just how much precision you are able to achieve, but also of *what generalizations you are able to express*. The price you pay for doing psychology at the level of units is that you lose causal generalizations that symbol-level theories are able to state. (Fodor & McLaughlin, 1990, p. 204)

Thus, if some designated set of neural events is a sufficient cause for a psychological phenomenon, the effects documented in experimentation in which the designated events are manipulated will be *replicable*. The illusion of generality may be achieved by the study of the behavior of simple systems rather than complex phenomena because of the replicability of an effect across laboratories worldwide. However, although lawfulness is established when a psychological phenomenon (e.g., aversive conditioning) is invariably affected by the manipulation of a specific neurophysiological system (e.g., lesions of the amygdaloid nucleus; see LeDoux, Iwata, Cicchetti, & Reis, 1988), generality is not established. Only if these neural events are also a necessary cause are the effects fully *generalizable*. If the designated events are sufficient but not necessary to produce the psychological phenomenon (e.g., the psychological phenomenon is multiply determined by independent sets of neural events), experimental manipulations of the designated events may reliably produce the psychological phenomenon only because other sufficient causes have been controlled in a particular experimental paradigm or assessment context.[3] In such

---

[3] It is rare for a single factor or determinant to assume a necessary and sufficient relationship with a complex psychological phenomenon (ψ), at least in a contextually generalized fashion. Rather, psychological phenomena are often subject to multiple determinants. This multiple determinism may assume one or both of two general forms. The first we term *parallel determinism*, in which any one of a number of factors is sufficient to evoke the psychological

cases, a "generalizing problem" is to be expected in natural (e.g., clinical) settings or populations. A well-known example can be found in the research on the physiological detection of lying. Although lying about a significant event typically produces an electrodermal response, efforts to detect lying on the basis of electrodermal responses are characterized by high false-alarm rates unless the myriad other sufficient causes of electrodermal responding have been controlled in the assessment procedure (Iacono & Patrick, 1988). From this point of view, the generalizing problem does not reflect a methodological quagmire but rather represents a theoretical challenge. That is, the observation that effects documented in carefully controlled experimentation lack generalizing power may not reflect any dubious feature of experimentation or particular level of analysis but may simply reflect the multiply determined nature of the phenomenon of interest.[4] Thus, boundary conditions for theories can be identified and new theoretical organizations can be discovered when generalizing problems arise. In this light, reductionistic studies demonstrating the sufficiency of a neurophysiological mechanism as a cause of some psychological phenomenon are immensely important, largely because they guide and constrain general theories of the psychological phenomenon.

Doctrine of Multilevel Analysis

We have suggested that multilevel analyses spanning neural and social perspectives can foster comprehensive accounts of psychological phenomena. The doctrine of multilevel analysis states that there

are psychological phenomena that derive from events at one level of analysis and that are only or more distinctly observable across levels of analysis. Consequently, order can uniquely emerge when psychological phenomena are examined from multiple levels of analysis.

The doctrine of multilevel analysis specifies that microanalyses of a psychological phenomenon can be particularly effective when pursued in addition to or in conjunction with molar analyses. It also holds a key argument for maintaining psychology as a coherent scientific discipline. Scott (1991) reflected on what he viewed to be the inevitable fractionation of psychology as a scientific discipline, with the growing abyss, for example, between the fields of social and biopsychology: "Most biopsychology students consider a core course in social psychology to be an impediment toward becoming a neuroscientist. . . . I assume that our students in social psychology reflect that sentiment about their core experience in biopsychology" (p. 975).

Methodological fractionation may be inevitable with the maturation of the subdisciplines in psychology. Furthermore, the expansion of basic empirical data and theory within these subdisciplines increases the difficulty of mastering the methods and theories of multiple levels of analysis. The doctrine of multilevel analysis makes it equally apparent, however, that the inevitable consequence of this fractionation is a devolution into fact lists and elaborated microtheories with limited generality. The demand for general theories of psychological phenomena may therefore be better served by at least a rudimentary training of graduate students in multiple subdisciplines within psychology and by forming multi-investigator research teams working together to bring differing levels of analysis to bear on a psychological problem.

The doctrine of multilevel analysis is composed of three principles and a corollary:

1. The principle of multiple determinism: A target event at one level of organization (e.g., neuroeffector response, evaluative response predisposition) may have multiple antecedents within or across levels of organization.
2. The corollary of proximity: The mapping between elements across levels of organization becomes more complex (e.g., many-to-many) as the number of intervening levels of organization increases.

---

phenomenon. Thus, if the manipulated factor or treatment (τ) is a sufficient but not a necessary cause of ψ, then evidence of the psychological phenomenon should be observed whenever τ has occurred and may be observed even when t has not occurred. In a second form of multiple determinism, termed *convergent determinism*, the convergence of a number of factors (or one or more factors in a specific context) is required to evoke the psychological phenomenon. Thus, if the manipulated factor or treatment is a necessary but not a sufficient cause of ψ, then evidence of ψ should not be observed if t has not occurred, and ψ may or may not be observed if τ has occurred (Cacioppo & Berntson, 1992).

[4] If a psychological phenomenon is multiply determined by synergistic variables that coexist in the laboratory but not typically in nonlaboratory settings, then a generalizing problem will again be encountered. The resolution of this generalizing problem will again rest on insight into the multiply determined nature of the psychological phenomenon.

3. The principle of nonadditive determinism: Properties of the collective whole are not always predictable from the properties of the parts until the properties of the whole have been clearly documented and studied across levels.
4. The principle of reciprocal determinism: There can be mutual influences between microscopic (e.g., biological) and macroscopic (e.g., social) factors in determining brain and behavioral processes.

An example of the principle of multiple determinism can be found in the extensive literature on drug abuse. It now seems clear that endogenous brain opioid receptor systems constitute ultimate bases for the physiological, cognitive, and affective actions of opiate drugs of abuse. Studies of these systems have illuminated, and will continue to clarify, the underlying dynamics and physiological consequences of drug self-administration. However, central opioid systems are common across individuals, only some of whom will succumb to drug abuse. Hence, central opiates merely constitute permissive substrates for substance abuse. The proximate and powerful determinants of drug abuse include the social factors of economics, opportunity, peer group influences, and family dynamics. These determinants will not be understood at an exclusively neuroscientific level in the near future. Rather, the interactions between social processes and the underlying neural substrates that support drug administration represent some of the most important issues currently facing our society. As is so often the case, it was the molar features of a phenomenon that prompted and guided inquiry into underlying mechanisms. Indeed, it was the profound psychological effects of the opiates and their abuse potential that stimulated research leading to the discovery of central opioid systems.

Considerable additional evidence has amassed over the past several decades demonstrating that elements in the physiological domain and elements in the psychological domain can be influenced by a multiplicity of factors within and across levels of organization (e.g., see Plomin, 1989). Consideration of these sets of factors can foster more comprehensive theoretical accounts than are achievable by limiting empirical and theoretical inquiries to the factor with the largest effect size or to a single level of analysis. This can be illustrated by returning to our example of drug (e.g.,

alcohol) abuse. An understanding of osmoreceptive mechanism and volume detectors, which monitor body water balance, can offer an eloquent account of facilitated ingestive reflexes, and the action of alcohol on central gamma-aminobutyric acid (GABA) receptors may constitute a partial explanation for its incentive value. These mechanisms, however, offer only a partial account of an animal bar-pressing for water, for which the principles of learning must be invoked. Nor do they tell us much about the drinking behavior of alcoholics in bars, which is heavily determined by social and contextual factors. Conversely, even extensive studies limited to operant performance or barroom behavior would be relatively uninformative about the fundamental mechanisms of thirst or alcoholism if conceptualized in isolation of the psychobiological underpinnings. Studies of the opiate system and addictive behavior, for example, have shown that drug administration results in opiate receptor changes, which in turn contribute to drug tolerance and addiction, which incline larger drug administrations, opiate changes, and so on. However, whether or not these developments result in a positive feedback loop and drug addiction depend also on the individual's social context. Clearly, research that specifies the conditions under which each of a set of factors or processes is operative, and that specifies the relationship between empirical observations at differing levels of analysis, sets the stage for integral theoretical advances.

A supplement to the principle of multiple determinism is the *corollary of proximity*, which states that the mapping between elements across levels of organization becomes more complex (e.g., many-to-many) as the number of intervening levels of organization increases. This is because an event at one level of organization (e.g., depressive or schizophrenic behavior) can have a multiplicity of determinants at an adjacent level of organization (e.g., cognitive), which in turn may have a multiplicity of implementations at the next level of organization (e.g., neurophysiological), and so forth. The implication is not to avoid venturing across the abyss separating the macroscopic and the microscopic levels of organization but to proceed incrementally across levels of analysis. These measured efforts can pay handsome dividends. As illustrated in research on learned helplessness (see above), understanding a behavioral problem at multiple levels of organization can result in a more general theory and can improve the selection and application of clinical interventions.

The principle of nonadditive determinism further highlights the order in behavioral data that can emerge when one uses a multilevel analysis to examine a phenomenon. According to this principle, properties of the collective whole are not always predictable from the properties of the parts until the properties of the whole have been clearly documented and studied across levels (Marr, 1982). Consider an illustrative study by Haber and Barchas (1983), who found that the administration of amphetamine appeared to have no reliable effect on primate behavior until the primate's position in the social hierarchy was considered. When this social factor was considered, amphetamine administration was found to increase dominance behaviors in primates high in the social hierarchy and to increase submissive behaviors in primates low in the social hierarchy. The importance of their study derives from its demonstration of how the effects of physiological changes on behavior can *appear* unreliable until the analysis is extended across multiple levels of organization. A physiological analysis, regardless of the sophistication of the measurement technology, may not have unraveled the orderly relationship that existed between the physiological manipulation and behavior. There are, of course, physiological mechanisms underlying these phenomena, but the identification and understanding of these mechanisms are often better served by systematic investigations within and across multiple (including social) levels of organization than by a reductionistic focus alone.

The evidence for the principle of reciprocal determinism further establishes the complementarity between social psychological and neuroscientific levels of analysis. Reciprocal determinism between biological and social factors is, of course, inherent in evolutionary analyses of social species. More interestingly, Plomin (1989) reviewed evidence in behavior genetics that suggests a wide variety of genetic influences are repressed unless or until certain environmental factors are introduced. Within social psychology, Zillmann (1984, 1989) has demonstrated that violent and erotic material influences the level of physiological arousal in males and that the level of physiological arousal has a reciprocal influence on the perceptions of and tendencies toward sex and aggression. As discussed earlier, testosterone in male primates pro-

motes sexual behavior, and the availability of sexually receptive females influences testosterone levels in male primates (Bernstein et al., 1983; Rose et al., 1972). Testosterone affects aggressive as well as sexual behavior, and increasing the level of testosterone in a castrated chimpanzee leads to behaviors by the primate that elevate his social rank (Clark & Birch, 1945; see, also, Bernstein, Rose, & Gordon, 1974). In addition, alterations of social rank influence testosterone levels. In an intriguing naturalistic investigation, for instance, Jeffcoate, Lincoln, Selby, and Herbert (1986) obtained repeated plasma samples from five men confined on a 38-foot boat during a 14-day sailing holiday around the north coast of Scotland. The men were physicians and were used to having blood samples taken. One of the five men surreptitiously recorded dominance/aggressive behaviors (e.g., bossiness, insistence on undertaking "important" tasks) to document the social hierarchy that emerged over the course of the holiday. Results revealed that the remaining four men had comparable testosterone levels before and after the holiday. Nevertheless, by the end of the second week on the boat, the individuals who had achieved the highest ranking in the social hierarchy also exhibited the highest testosterone levels, whereas the least dominant pair had the lowest levels of testerone (see also Keverne, Meller, & Eberhart, 1982). Of course, the reciprocal determinism between biological and social systems cannot be mapped if either level of organization is regarded as irrelevant, and achieving comprehensive accounts of the role of these systems in behavior is difficult in the absence of a mapping of their mutual influence.

It follows from each of the foregoing principles that an exclusive focus on a reductionistic (e.g., neurophysiological, molecular, genetic) level of analysis can mask contributions of other levels of organization to mental order and disorder and thereby constrain theoretical accounts of psychological phenomena. This supposition is apparent in research on the putative role of dopamine systems in schizophrenia. The hypothesis that excessive dopaminergic activity underlies schizophrenia was developed in part from correlative evidence linking the clinical efficacy of antipsychotic drugs with their ability to block dopamine receptors (Losonczy, Davidson, & Davis, 1987; Seeman, Lee, Chau-Wong, & Wong, 1976). Evidence that dopamine antagonists (neuroleptics) produce improvements in schizophrenic behavior has led to interpretations ranging from dopamine's being a "marker" of schizophrenia to the dopaminergic system's representing the mechanism responsible for the disorder. The fact that elevated dopamine levels produce autonomic and behavioral effects similar to those found in schizophrenics (e.g., Zahn, Rapoport, & Thompson, 1981) does not necessarily imply that the emergence or maintenance of schizophrenia is invariably (or even usually) initiated by excessive levels of dopamine, Indeed, dopamine abnormalities may not be present in all cases (Haracz, 1982; Losonczy et al., 1987; Meltzer, 1987). Thus, (a) the dopaminergic system may represent but one of many physiological mechanisms capable of producing schizophrenia; (b) dopamine may be one of a complex of biochemical variables in which subsets (coalitions) are capable of generating schizophrenia; or (c) an overabundance of dopamine is not an antecedent of schizophrenia but rather, like schizophrenia, a consequence of some other underlying process (Patterson, 1976; Spohn & Patterson, 1979; Zahn, 1986). However, the processes underlying schizophrenia may be best conceptualized and investigated across levels of analysis. For instance, there is no longer any doubt about the importance of genetic, social, and environmental events in triggering schizophrenia (e.g., Turpin, Tarrier, & Sturgeon, 1988). It is also clear that environmental stressors that can exacerbate schizophrenic symptoms exert powerful modulatory influences on central neurochemical systems (including dopamine). Clearly, the ultimate explication of the bases of schizophrenia will require attention to interactions between genetic and environmental factors and multiple central neurochemical systems.

In summary, the predictable yield from isolated research on discrete determinants of a multiply determined psychological outcome is a portfolio of fact lists and disparate microtheories. Each of these microtheories provides a limited account for the phenomenon of interest, however, and is at best a piece of a larger conceptual puzzle. Even determinants of a phenomenon that account for a modicum of variance are noteworthy if the goal is to achieve a comprehensive theory of the psychological phenomenon rather than a microtheory of the determinant. In addition, knowledge of the body and brain can usefully constrain and inspire concepts and theories of psychological function, inasmuch as there are any number of ways in which

a particular outcome might be achieved. Knowledge about the functional organization of ordered and disordered mental activities, however, can also usefully guide the study of the underlying brain processes, because the nature of the particular physiological mechanisms and events could be suggested by the observed mentation, behavior, or interaction. Although there are neurophysiological processes that are affected, for instance, by human association and that underlie the associated psychological and social phenomena, these phenomena shape physiological events in ways that may not be evident from studies of the physiology isolated from the social or environmental context in which they manifest. Hence, without attention to basic social psychological factors and processes, the decade of the brain may yield some spectacular images and experimental effects but rather limited answers to the problems of mental health.

Social Neuroscience?

We have thus far reviewed principles of behavior that underscore the theoretical utility of examining complex psychological phenomena and mental disorders from multiple levels of analysis. Although Bevan (1991) and Leshner (1991) have suggested that investigating the processes underlying mental health from multiple points of view may be the look of the future, it is not entirely new to social psychology. As Gordon Allport (1968) noted:

> An individual is a member of many publics, of many institutions, of many social systems. . . . It was Sapir who advised all social and psychological scientists to form the habit of looking at their data both from the concrete individual point of view and from the abstract social point of view. It enriches research and theory to do so. (p. 55)

Social psychological contributions to the neurosciences are particularly apparent in, and served as the impetus for, the explosive development of the field of psychoneuroimmunology. Classically, immune functions were considered to reflect specific and nonspecific physiological responses to pathogens or tissue damage (Roitt, Brostoff, & Male, 1985). It is now clear that immune responses are heavily influenced by central nervous processes that are shaped by psychological factors (see reviews by Ader, 1981; Kennedy, Glaser, & Kiecolt-Glaser, 1990). Indeed, effects of psychological context now appear to be among the most powerful determinants of the expression of immune reactions. It is clear that an understanding of immunocompetence will be inadequate in the absence of considerations of psychosocial factors. Research on these interactions was activated by research demonstrating the direct and moderating effects of psychosocial factors (e.g., conditioned stimuli, bereavement, social support, major life events) on immune competence (e.g., see Kennedy et al., 1990). Thus, major advances in the neurosciences can derive from increasing the scope of the analysis to consider the contributions of social factors and processes.

Our more general theme throughout this article, however, has been that reciprocal benefits and more general psychological theory can be achieved by considering or pursuing jointly macrolevel and microlevel analyses of psychological phenomena. Social psychological contributions to the understanding of complex, multiply determined mental processes and problems may be limited unnecessarily in scope to the extent that a parochial perspective is adopted by neuroscientists *or* by social psychologists. To illustrate, consider social psychological research on attitudes, which has produced a large corpus of data and theory, much of which can and has been applied to the study and resolution of mental problems (e.g., see Cooper & Aronson, 1992; Petty & Cacioppo, 1986). Theories of attitudes and attitude change, however, have only infrequently considered physiological factors and mechanisms or research on appetitive and defense motivational systems. Evaluative categorizations and response predispositions—criterial attributes of the construct of attitudes—are fundamental and ubiquitous in behavior. Mechanisms for differentiating hostile from nurturing environmental stimuli are imperative for the survival of species and for the formation and maintenance of social units. Indeed, all organisms have biological mechanisms for approaching, acquiring, or ingesting certain classes of stimuli and withdrawing from, avoiding, or rejecting others (Berntson, Boysen, & Cacioppo, in press; Cacioppo, 1991). Knowledge of the organization and operating characteristics of these underlying mechanisms may therefore lay down, at least in broad strokes, the rules by which biological and social factors alter evaluative categorizations and evaluative response dispositions. Protective flexor–withdrawal reflexes to pain stimuli are apparent, for example, even in the isolated spinal cord, and both decerebrate humans and rats display stereotyped orofacial ingestion/ejection reflexes to relevant gustatory stimuli (Grill & Berridge, 1985; Steiner, 1979). Although of constitutional origin and generally stereotyped in form, reflexive responses nevertheless demonstrate a sensitivity to motivational variables. Orofacial ingestion reflexes can be primed by metabolic deficits and can be modulated by conditioned taste aversions, even in the decerebrate organism (Berridge, 1991; Grill & Berridge, 1985). These inherent dispositions allow an organism, even at early stages of development and without previous experience, to adaptively respond to important classes of environmental stimuli.

There is an enormous additional adaptive advantage when an individual member of a species is also able to acquire new evaluative response dispositions (e.g., attitudes) toward the stimuli in its particular environment as a consequence of the contingencies in that environment. Thus, adaptive reflexes are functionally limited, but they represent only a single level in what appears to be a continuity of evaluative mechanisms (Berntson et al., in press; Cacioppo, Petty, & Berntson, 1991). Although decerebrate organisms display orofacial ingestion/ejection responses to gustatory stimuli, they do not evidence normal appetitive goal-seeking behavior (Berntson & Micco, 1976; Grill & Berridge, 1985). With the involvement of additional subcortical structures, such as the limbic system and striatum, the reactions of the decorticate animal to pain stimuli entail additional response components and evidence greater directedness, integration, serial coherence, and contextual adaptability (Berntson & Micco, 1976; Goldstein & Oakley, 1985). Furthermore, the ingestive behavior of the decorticate is more fully responsive to metabolic signals, and appetitive or goal-seeking components are apparent. These findings suggest that evaluative mechanisms are not localized to specific neuraxial levels but evidence a hierarchy or representation throughout the central nervous system. With progressively higher organizational levels in evaluative mechanisms, there appears to be a general expansion in the range and relational complexity of contextual controls and in the breadth and flexibility of adaptive response (Berntson et al., in press; Cacioppo et al., 1991). Although research on the interactions between evaluative mechanisms at differing levels of the neuraxis is still in its early stages, there appears to be considerable common ground for dialogue between social psychologists and neuroscientists.

In summary, reductionism has contributed to the solution of some of the most perplexing scientific problems in human history (e.g., see Boorstin, 1983) and has much to contribute to our understanding of social and psychological phenomena. However, it is counterproductive to presume that reductionism will convert the abstractions of the psychological sciences to "real" science in the coming millennium, just as it is counterproductive to presume that reductionism produces insights that are irrelevant to theories of social processes and phenomena. To do either ignores the distinction between levels of explanation, the scientific breakthroughs that can result from research at each of the levels of explanation and at or across levels of organization, the rich theoretical insights about the nature and timing of the relationships among variables that can be derived from descriptions of phenomena from multiple scales or perspectives, and the economy of thought to be reaped by capitalizing on the form of representation most appropriate for the task. In addition, it undermines multilevel, integrative analyses; alienates scientists working at "unchosen" levels of organization who might otherwise contribute relevant data and theory; and renders it acceptable to ignore relevant theory and data on a phenomenon of interest simply because they were not born from one's own level of analysis. Given there are phenomena that derive from events at one level of analysis that are only or distinctly observable at other or broader levels of analysis, then multilevel integrative analyses will play an important role in providing the empirical data and theoretical insight needed for a comprehensive understanding of basic behavioral processes, mental health, and mental disorders. Thus, the decade of the brain is more likely to be a gateway to a new millennium of the mind if we recognize that the brain is a single, pivotal component of an undeniably social species and if we recognize that the nature of the brain, behavior, and society is, in Bevan's (1991) words, orderly in its complexity rather than lawful in its simplicity.

ACKNOWLEDGMENTS

Lewis P. Lipsitt served as the action editor for this article.

Preparation of this article was supported by National Science Foundation Grants BNS-8940915 and DBS-9211483 to John T. Cacioppo and BNS-8820027 to Gary G. Berntson.

The determinism principles examined in this article were developed in recent conferences of the Behavioral Sciences Basic Research Branch of the National Institute of Mental Health (NIMH) and most notably by the NIMH Behavioral Sciences Assessment Panel. This panel met during 1987 and 1988 to develop a conceptual framework for the advancement of research in the behavioral sciences ("New Frontiers," 1989). The present article was developed from John T. Cacioppo's work on a subsequent panel.

We are grateful to the inaugural panel members, including Marilyn Brewer, Glen Elder, Walter Kintsch, Lewis Lipsitt, Martha McClintock, Anne Petersen (Chair), Robert Plomin, David Reiss, and Arnold Sameroff. We also thank Molly Oliveri, Diane Ruble, Phil Costanza, and an anonymous reviewer for comments on a draft of this article.

REFERENCES

Abramson, L. Y., Seligman, M. E., & Teasdale. J. D. (1978). Learned helplessness in humans: Critique and reformulation. *Journal of Abnormal Psychology, 87,* 49–74.

Ader, R. (1981). *Psychoneuroimmunology.* San Diego, CA: Academic Press.

Allport, G. H. (1968). The historical background of modern social psychology. In G. Lindzey & E. Aronson (Eds.), *The handbook of social psychology* (Vol. 1, pp. 1–80). Reading, MA: Addison-Wesley.

Andersen, B. L. (1986). *Women with cancer: Psychological perspectives.* New York: Springer-Verlag.

Basbaum, A. L., & Fields, H. L. (1984). Endogenous pain control systems: Brainstem spinal pathways and endorphin circuitry. *Annual Review of Neuroscience, 7,* 309–338.

Bernstein, I. S., Gordon, T. P., & Rose, R. M. (1983). The interaction of hormones, behavior, and social context in nonhuman primates. In B. B. Svare (Ed.), *Hormones and aggressive behavior* (pp. 535–561), New York: Plenum Press.

Bernstein, I. S., Rose, R. M., & Gordon, T. P. (1974). Behavioral and environmental events influencing primate testosterone levels. *Journal of Human Evolution, 3,* 517–525.

Berntson, G. G., Boysen, S. T., & Cacioppo, J. T. (in press). Neurobehavioral organization and the cardinal principle of evaluative bivalence. In F. M. Crinella & J. Yu (Eds.), *Brain mechanisms 1990: Papers in memory of Robert Thompson.* New York: New York Academy of Sciences.

Berntson, G. G., & Micco, D. J. (1976). Organization of brainstem behavioral systems. *Brain Research Bulletin, 1,* 471–483.

Berridge, K. C. (1991). Modulation of taste affect by hunger, caloric satiety, and sensory specific satiety in the rat. *Appetite, 16,* 103–120.

Bevan, W. (1991). A tour inside the onion. *American Psychologist, 46,* 475–483.

Bodnar, R. J. (1990). Effects of opioid peptides on peripheral stimulation and "stress" induced analgesia in animals. *Critical Reviews in Newbiology, 6,* 39–49.

Boorstin, D. J. (1983). *The discoverers: A history of man's search to know his world and himself.* London: J. M. Dent & Sons.

Cacioppo, J. T. (1991, May), *Attitudes.* Invited address at the annual meeting of the Midwestern Psychological Association, Chicago.

Cacioppo, J. T., & Berntson, G. G. (1992). The principles of multiple, nonadditive, and reciprocal determinism: Implications for social psychological research and levels of analysis. In D. Ruble, P. Costanzo, & M. Oliveri (Eds.), *Basic social psychological processes in mental health* (pp. 328–349). New York: Guilford Press.

Cacioppo, J. T., Petty, R. E., & Berntson, G. G. (1991). Persuasion. In R. Dulbecco (Ed.), *Encyclopedia of human biology* (Vol. 5, pp. 799–810). San Diego, CA: Academic Press.

Cacioppo, J. T., & Tassinary, L. G. (1990a). Centenary of William James' *Principles of Psychology*: From the chaos of mental life to the science of psychology. *Personality and Social Psychology Bulletin, 16*, 601–611.

Cacioppo, J. T., & Tassinary, L. G. (1990b). Inferring psychological significance from physiological signals. *American Psychologist, 45*, 16–28.

Churchland, P. S., & Sejnowski, T. J. (1988). Perspectives on cognitive neuroscience. *Science, 242*, 741–745.

Clark, G., & Birch, H. G. (1945). Hormonal modifications of social behavior. The effects of sex-hormone administration on the social status of male-castrate chimpanzee. *Psychosomatic Medicine, 7*, 321–329.

Cooper, J., & Aronson, J. M. (1992). Attitudes and consistency theories: Implications for mental health. In D. Ruble, P. Costanza, & M. Oliveri (Eds.), *Basic social psychological processes in mental health*. New York: Guilford Press.

Craik, F. I. M., & Lockhart, R. S. (1972). Levels of processing: A framework for memory research. *Journal of Verbal Learning and Verbal Behavior, 11*, 671–684.

Davidson, J. M., Camargo, C. A., & Smith, E. R. (1979). Effects of androgen on sexual behavior in hypogonadal men. *Journal of Clinical Endocrinology and Metabolism, 48*, 955–958.

Erikson, C., & Lehrman, D. (1964). Effects of castration of male ring doves upon ovarian activity of females. *Journal of Comparative and Physiological Psychology, 58*, 164–166.

Fodor, J. A. (1968). *Psychological explanation*. New York: Random House.

Fodor, J. A., & McLaughlin, B. P. (1990). Connectionism and the problem of systematicity: Why Smolensky's solution doesn't work. *Cognition, 35*, 183–204.

Fodor, J. A., & Pylyshyn, Z. W. (1988). Connectionism and cognitive architecture: A critical analysis. *Cognition, 28*, 3–71.

Goldstein, F. C., & Oakley, D. A. (1985). Expected and actual behavioral capacity after diffuse reduction in cerebral cortex: A review and suggestions for rehabilitative techniques with the mentally handicapped and head injured. *British Journal of Clinical Psychology, 24*, 13–24.

Grill, H. J., & Berridge, K. C. (1985). Taste reactivity as a measure of the neural control of palatability. In J. M. Sprague & A. N. Epstein (Eds.), *Progress in psychobiology and physiological psychology* (Vol. 11, pp. 1–61). San Diego, CA: Academic Press.

Haber, S. N., & Barchas, P. R. (1983). The regulatory effect of social rank on behavior after amphetamine administration. In P. R. Barchas (Ed.), *Social hierarchies: Essays toward a sociophysiological perspective* (pp. 119–132). Westport, CT: Greenwood Press.

Haracz, J. L. (1982). The dopamine hypothesis: An overview

of studies with schizophrenic patients. *Schizophrenia Bulletin, 8*, 438–469.

Iacono, W. G., & Patrick, C. J. (1988). What psychologists should know about lie detection. In A. K. Hess & I. B. Weiner (Eds.), *Handbook of forensic psychology* (pp. 205–233). New York: Wiley.

James, W. (1950). *Principles of psychology* (Vol. 1). New York: Dover. (Original work published 1890)

Jeffcoate, W. J., Lincoln, N. B., Selby, C., & Herbert, M. (1986). Correlation between anxiety and serum prolactin in humans. *Journal of Psychosomatic Research, 30*, 217–222.

Kennedy, S., Glaser, R., & Kiecolt-Glaser, J. (1990). Psychoneuroimmunology. In J. T. Cacioppo & L. G. Tassinary (Eds.), *Principles of psychophysiology: Physical, social, and inferential elements* (pp. 177–190). New York: Cambridge University Press.

Keverne, E. B., Meller, R. E., & Eberhart, A. (1982). Dominance and subordination: Concepts or physiological states? In A. B. Chiarelli & R. S. Curriccini (Eds.), *Advanced views in primate biology*. Berlin, Germany: Springer.

LeDoux, J. E., Iwata, J., Cicchetti, P., & Reis, D. J. (1988). Different projections of the central amygdaloid nucleus mediate autonomic and behavioral correlates of conditioned fear. *Journal of Neuroscience, 8*, 2517–2529.

Lehrman, D. (1964). The reproductive behavior of ring doves. *Scientific American, 211*, 48–54.

Leshner, A. I. (1991). Psychology research and NIMH: Opportunities and challenges. *American Psychologist, 46*, 977–979.

Losonczy, M. F., Davidson, M., & Davis, K. (1987). The dopamine hypothesis of schizophrenia. In H. Y. Meltzer (Ed.), *Psychopharmacology: A second generation of progress* (pp. 715–726). New York: Raven Press.

Lysle, D. T., & Fowler, H. (1988). Changes in pain reactivity induced by unconditioned and conditioned excitatory and inhibitory stimuli. *Journal of Experimental Psychology: Animal Behavior Processes, 14*, 376–389.

Maier, S. F. (1984). Learned helplessness and animal models of depressions. *Progress in Neuro-Psychopharmacology & Biological Psychiatry, 8*, 435–446.

Maier, S. F. (1986). Stressor controllability and stress-induced analgesia. *Annals of the New York Academy of Sciences, 467*, 55–72.

Maier, S. F. (1989). Determinants of the nature of environmentally induced hypoalgesia. *Behavioral Neuroscience, 103*, 131–145.

Maier, S. F., Jackson, R. L., & Tomie, A. (1987). Potentiation, overshadowing, and prior exposure to inescapable shock. *Journal of Experimental Psychology: Animal Behavior Processes, 13*, 260–270.

Marr, D. (1982). *Vision: A computational investigation into the human representation and processing of visual information*. New York: Freeman.

Martinez-Vargas, M. C., & Erikson, C. J. (1973). Some social and hormonal determinants of nest-building behaviour in the ring dove (*Streptopelia risoria*). *Behaviour, 45*, 12-37.

Meltzer, H. Y. (1987). Biological studies in schizophrenia. *Schizophrenia Bulletin, 13*, 77–111.

Minor, T. R., Dess, N. K., & Overmeir, J. B. (1991). Inverting the traditional view of "learned helplessness": A reinterpretation in terms of anxiety and modulator operations. In M. R. Denny (Ed.), *Aversive events and behavior* (pp. 87–133). Hillsdale, NJ: Erlbaum.

New frontiers in the behavioral sciences and mental health: An assessment. (1989). [Working paper.] Rockville, MD: National Institute of Mental Health, Behavioral Sciences Research Branch, Division of Basic Sciences.

Patterson, T. (1976). Skin conductance responding/nonresponding and pupillometrics in chronic schizophrenia: A confirmation of Gruzelier and Venables. *Journal of Nervous and Mental Disease, 163,* 200–209.

Peterson, C., & Seligman, M. E. (1984). Causal explanations as a risk factor for depression: Theory and evidence. *Psychological Review, 91,* 347–374.

Petty, R. E., & Cacioppo, J. T. (1986). *Communication and persuasion: Central and peripheral routes to attitude change.* New York: Springer-Verlag.

Plomin, R. (1989). Environment and genes: Determinants of behavior. *American Psychologist, 44,* 105–111.

Roitt, I., Brostoff, J., & Male, D. (1985). *Immunology.* St. Louis, MO: Mosby.

Rose, R. N., Gordon, T. P., & Bernstein, I. S. (1972). Plasma testosterone levels in the male rhesus: Influences of sexual and social stimuli. *Science, 178,* 643–645.

Rossi, J. S. (1991). Cancer risk and behavior change. *Science, 254,* 501.

Scott, T. R. (1991). A personal view of the future of psychology departments. *American Psychologist, 46,* 975–976.

Seeman, P., Lee, T., Chau-Wong, M., & Wong, K. (1976). Antipsychotic drug doses and neuroleptic/dopamine receptors. *Nature, 261,* 717–719.

Seligman, M. E. P. (1975). *Helplessness.* San Francisco: Freeman.

Shaw, R., & Turvey, M. T. (1981). Coalitions as models for ecosystems: A realist perspective on perceptual organization. In M. Kubovy & J. R. Pomerantz (Eds.), *Perceptual organization.* Hillsdale, NJ: Erlbaum.

Simson, P. G., Weiss, J. M., Hoffman, L. J., & Ambrose, M. J. (1986). Reversal of behavioral depression by infusion of alpha$_2$-adrenergic agonist into the locus coeruleus. *Neuropharmacology, 25,* 385–389.

Spohn, H. E., & Patterson, T. (1979). Recent studies of psychophysiology in schizophrenia. *Schizophrenia Bulletin, 5,* 581–611.

Steiner, J. E. (1979). Human facial expressions in response to taste and smell stimulation. *Advances in Child Development and Behavior, 13,* 237–295.

Tolman, E. C. (1959). Principles of purposive behavior. In S. Koch (Ed.), *Psychology: A study of a science* (pp. 92–157). New York: McGraw Hill.

Turpin, G., Tarrier, N., & Sturgeon, D. (1988). Social psychophysiology and the study of biopsychosocial models of schizophrenia. In H. L. Wagner (Ed.), *Social psychophysiology and emotion: Theory and clinical applications* (pp. 251–272). New York: Wiley.

Weiss, J. M., Goodman, P. A., Losito, B. G., Corrigan, S., & Bailey, W. H. (1981). Behavioral depression produced by uncontrollable stress: Relationship to norepinephrine, dopamine and serotonin levels in various regions of the rat brain. *Brain Research Reviews, 3,* 167–203.

Weiss, J. M., Simson, P. G., Hoffman, L. J., Ambrose, M. J., Cooper, S., & Webster, A. (1986). Infusion of adrenergic agonists and antagonists into the locus coeruleus and ventricular systems of the brain. *Neuropharmacology, 25,* 367–384.

Weiss, P. (1941). Self-differentiation of the basic patterns of coordination. *Comparative Psychology Monographs, 17*(4), 1–96.

Zahn, T. (1986). Psychophysiological approaches to psychopathology. In M. G. H. Coles, E. Donchin, & S. W. Porges (Eds.), *Psychophysiology: Systems, processes, and applications* (pp. 508–610). New York: Guilford Press.

Zahn, T., Rapoport, J. L., & Thompson, C. L. (1981). Autonomic effects of dextroamphetamine in normal men: Implications for hyperactivity and schizophrenia. *Psychiatry Research, 4,* 39–47.

Zillmann, D. (1984). *Connections between sex and aggression.* Hillsdale, NJ: Erlbaum.

Zillmann, D. (1989). Aggression and sex: Independent and joint operations. In H. Wagner & A. Manstead (Eds.), *Handbook of social psychophysiology* (pp. 229–260). New York: Wiley.

Illusion and Well-Being: A Social Psychological Perspective on Mental Health

Shelley E. Taylor • University of California, Los Angeles
Jonathon D. Brown • Southern Methodist University

Editors' Notes

In this selection Taylor and Brown deal with the fundamental "Truth or Consequences" question. The authors argue that, contrary to much received psychological wisdom, truth is not inevitably salutary in its consequences for such important matters as people's well-being, mental health, and ability to cope with adverse circumstances, such as a major illness. Quite to the contrary, it is often the ability to maintain an unrealistically rosy outlook in the face of clear and present adversity that characterizes normal (as opposed to pathological) human adaptation. This is not to say that all positive illusions are adaptive. Whether they are is both a matter of the degree to which one's private perceptions are at odds with socially shared realities (affecting one's ability to function interactively with others in one's group) and, a matter of the implications of veridical versus illusory judgments for specific decisions and actions. The relation of truth to psychological consequences, and the body of recent social-cognitive research relevant to this problem, are of the utmost importance for psychological theorists, researchers, and practitioners.

Discussion Questions

1. How is mental health served by positive illusions?
2. Are there domains, circumstances, or situations where veridicality is superior in its consequences to illusions? What might these be?

Suggested Readings

Kagan, J. (1992). Temperamental contributions to emotion and social behavior. In M. S. Clark (Ed.), *Emotion and social behavior* (pp. 99–118). Newbury Park, CA: Sage.

Kruglanski, A. W. (1989). The psychology of being "right": On the problem of accuracy in social perception and cognition. *Psychological Bulletin, 106,* 395–409.

Pennebaker, J. W. (1989). Confession, inhibition and disease. In L. Berkowitz (Ed.), *Advances in experimental social psychology* (Vol. 22, pp. 211–244). New York: Academic Press.

Wortman, C. B., & Silver, R. C. (1989). The myths of coping with loss. *Journal of Consulting and Clinical Psychology, 57,* 349–357.

Authors' Abstract

Many prominent theorists have argued that accurate perceptions of the self, the world, and the future are essential for mental health. Yet considerable research evidence suggests that overly positive self-evaluations, exaggerated perceptions of control or mastery, and unrealistic optimism are characteristic of normal human thought. Moreover, these illusions appear to promote other criteria of mental health, including the ability to care about others, the ability to be happy or contented, and the ability to engage in productive and creative work. These strategies may succeed, in large part, because both the social world and cognitive-processing mechanisms impose filters on incoming information that distort it in a positive direction; negative information may be isolated and represented in as unthreatening a manner as possible. These positive illusions may be especially useful when an individual receives negative feedback or is otherwise threatened and may be especially adaptive under these circumstances.

Decades of psychological wisdom have established contact with reality as a hallmark of mental health. In this view, the well-adjusted person is thought to engage in accurate reality testing, whereas the individual whose vision is clouded by illusion is regarded as vulnerable to, if not already a victim of, mental illness. Despite its plausibility, this viewpoint is increasingly difficult to maintain (cf. Lazarus, 1983). A substantial amount of research testifies to the prevalence of illusion in normal human cognition (see Fiske & Taylor, 1984; Greenwald, 1980; Nisbett & Ross, 1980; Sackeim, 1983; Taylor, 1983). Moreover, these illusions often involve central aspects of the self and the environment and, therefore, cannot be dismissed as inconsequential.

In this article, we review research suggesting that certain illusions may be adaptive for mental health and well-being. In particular, we examine evidence that a set of interrelated positive illusions—namely, unrealistically positive self-evaluations, exaggerated perceptions of control or mastery, and unrealistic optimism—can serve a wide variety of cognitive, affective, and social functions. We also attempt to resolve the following paradox: How can positive misperceptions of one's self and the environment be adaptive when accurate information processing seems to be essential for learning and successful functioning in the world? Our primary goal is to weave a theoretical context for thinking about mental health. A secondary goal is to create an integrative framework for a voluminous literature in social cognition concerning perceptions of the self and the environment.

Mental Health as Contact with Reality

Throughout psychological history, a variety of views of mental health have been proffered, some idiosyncratic and others widely shared. Within this theoretical diversity, a dominant position has maintained that the psychologically healthy person is one who maintains close contact with reality. For example, in her distillation of the dominant views of mental health at the time, Jahoda (1958) noted that the majority of theories considered contact with reality to be a critical component of mental health. This theme is prominent in the writings of Allport (1943), Erikson (1950), Menninger (1930), and Fromm (1955), among others.

Although it is not the only theoretical perspective on the mentally healthy person, the view that psychological health depends on accurate perceptions of reality has been widely promulgated and widely shared in the literature on mental health.

Social Congnition, Reality, and Illusion

Early theorists in social cognition adopted a view of the person's information-processing capabilities that is quite similar to the viewpoint just described. These theorists mantained that the social perceiver monitors and interacts with the world like a naive scientist (see Fischhoff, 1976; Fiske & Taylor, 1984; Nisbett & Ross, 1980, for discussions). According to this view, the person gathers data in an unbiased manner; combines it in some logical, identifiable fashion; and reaches generally good, accurate inferences and decisions. Theories of the causal attribution process (e.g., Kelley, 1967), prediction (see Kahneman & Tversky, 1973), judgments of covariation, and other tasks of social inference (see Fiske & Taylor, 1984; Nisbett & Ross, 1980) incorporated the assumptions of the naive scientist as normative guidelines with which actual behavior could be compared.

It rapidly became evident, however, that the social perceiver's actual inferential work and decision making looked little like these normative models. Rather, information processing is full of incomplete data gathering, shortcuts, errors, and biases (see Fiske & Taylor, 1984; Nisbett & Ross, 1980, for reviews). In particular, prior expectations and self-serving interpretations weigh heavily into the social judgment process.

At this point, we exchange the terms *error* and *bias* for a broader term, *illusion*. There are several reasons for this change in terminology. *Error and bias imply short-term mistakes and distortions, respectively, that might be caused by careless oversight or other temporary negligences* (cf. Funder, 1987). *Illusion, in contrast, implies a more general, enduring pattern of error, bias, or both that assumes a particular direction or shape.* As the evidence will show, the illusions to be considered (unrealistically positive self-evaluations, exaggerated perceptions of control, and unrealistic optimism) do indeed seem to be pervasive, enduring, and systematic. Illusion is defined as

> a perception that represents what is perceived in a way different from the way it is in reality. An illusion is a false mental image or conception which may be a misinterpretation of a real appearance or may be something imagined. It may be pleasing, harmless, or even useful. (Stein, 1982, p. 662)

Positive Illusions and Social Cognition

Any taxonomy of illusions is, to some extent, arbitrary. Many researchers have studied biases in the processing of self-relevant information and have given their similar phenomena different names. There is, however, considerable overlap in findings, and three that consistently emerge can be labeled *unrealistically positive views of the self, exaggerated perceptions of personal control,* and *unrealistic optimism.*

Unrealistically Positive Views of the Self

As indicated earlier, a traditional conception of mental health asserts that the well-adjusted individual possesses a view of the self that includes an awareness and acceptance of both the positive and negative aspects of self. In contrast to this portrayal, evidence indicates that most individuals possess a very positive view of the self (see Greenwald, 1980, for a review). When asked to indicate how accurately positive and negative personality adjectives describe the self, normal subjects judged positive traits to be overwhelmingly more characteristic of self than negative attributes (Alicke, 1985; Brown, 1986). Additionally, for most individuals, positive personality information is efficiently processed and easily recalled, whereas negative personality information is poorly processed and difficult to recall (Kuiper & Derry, 1982; Kuiper & MacDonald, 1982; Kuiper, Olinger, MacDonald, & Shaw, 1985). Most individuals also show poorer recall for information related to failure than to success (Silverman, 1964) and tend to recall their task performance as more positive than it actually was (Crary, 1966). Research on the self-serving bias in causal attribution documents that most individuals are more likely to attribute positive than negative outcomes to the self (see Bradley, 1978; Miller & Ross, 1975; Ross & Fletcher, 1985; Zuckerman, 1979, for reviews).[1]

Even when negative aspects of the self are acknowledged, they tend to be dismissed as inconsequential. One's poor abilities tend to be perceived as common, but one's favored abilities are seen as rare and distinctive (Campbell, 1986; G. Marks, 1984). Furthermore, the things that people are not proficient at are perceived as less important than the things that they are proficient at (e.g., Campbell, 1986, Harackiewicz, Sansone, & Manderlink, 1985; Lewicki, 1984; Rosenberg, 1979). And people perceive that they have improved on abilities that are important to them even when their performance has remained unchanged (Conway & Ross, 1984).

In sum, far from being balanced between the positive and the negative, the perception of self that most individuals hold is heavily weighted toward the positive end of the scale. Of course, this imbalance does not in and of itself provide evidence that such views are unrealistic or illusory. Evidence of this nature is, however, available.

First, there exists a pervasive tendency to see the self as better than others. Individuals judge positive personality attributes to be more descriptive of themselves than of the average person but see negative personality attributes as less descriptive of themselves than of the average person (Alicke, 1985; Brown, 1986). This effect has been documented for a wide range of traits (Brown, 1986) and abilities (Campbell, 1986; Larwood & Whittaker, 1977); individuals even believe that their driving ability is superior to others' (Svenson, 1981). Because it is logically impossible for most people to be better than the average person, these highly skewed, positive views of the self can be regarded as evidence for their unrealistic and illusory nature. People also tend to use their positive qualities when appraising others, thereby virtually assuring a favorable self-other comparison (Lewicki, 1983). And people give others less credit for success and more blame for failure than they ascribe to themselves (Forsyth & Schlenker, 1977; Green & Gross, 1979; Mirels, 1980; Schlenker & Miller, 1977; Taylor & Koivumaki, 1976).

A second source of evidence pertaining to the illusory quality of positive self-perceptions comes from investigations in which self-ratings have been compared with judgments made by observers.

Lewinsohn, Mischel, Chaplin, and Barton (1980) had observers watch college-student subjects complete a group-interaction task. Observers then rated each subject along a number of personality dimensions (e.g., friendly, warm, and assertive). Subjects also rated themselves on each attribute. The results showed that self-ratings were significantly more positive than the observers' ratings. In other words, individuals saw themselves in more flattering terms than they were seen in by others.

In sum, the perception of self that most individuals hold is not as well-balanced as traditional models of mental health suggest. Rather than being attentive to both the favorable and unfavorable aspects of self, normal individuals appear to be very cognizant of their strengths and assets and considerably less aware of their weaknesses and faults. Evidence that these flattering self-portrayals are illusory comes from studies in which researchers have found that (a) most individuals see themselves as better than the average person and (b) most individuals see themselves as better than others see them. For these reasons, overly positive views of the self appear to be illusory.[2]

Does there exist a group of individuals that is

---

[1]Despite a general pattern indicating that people accept more responsibility for positive outcomes than for negative outcomes, some evidence suggests that people may exaggerate their own causal role in the occurrence of highly negative events (e.g., Bulman & Wortman, 1977; Janoff-Bulman, 1979; Taylor, Lichtman, & Wood, 1984). These data might appear to be at odds with a general pattern of self-serving attributions, but they may not be. Self-attribution does not imply personal responsibility or self-blame (Shaver & Drown, 1986) and therefore may not produce any blow to self-esteem. Moreover, some have suggested that self-attribution may enable people to begin to achieve mastery over an adverse event, helping to maintain a sense of personal control (Bulman & Wortman, 1977; Taylor, 1983).

[2]One might argue that overly positive self-descriptions reflect public posturing rather than privately held beliefs. Several factors, however, argue against the plausibility of a strict self-presentational interpretation of this phenomenon. For example, Greenwald and Breckler (1985) reviewed evidence indicating that (a) self-evaluations are at least as favorable under private conditions as they are under public conditions; (b) favorable self-evaluations occur even when strong constraints to be honest are present; (c) favorable self-referent judgments are made very rapidly, suggesting that people are not engaging in deliberate (time-consuming) fabrication; and (d) self-enhancing judgments are acted on. For these as well as other reasons, a consensus is emerging at the theoretical level that individuals do not offer flattering self-evaluations merely as a means of managing a public impression of competency (see Schlenker, 1980; Tesser & Moore, 1986; Tetlock & Manstead, 1985).

accepting of both the good and the bad aspects of themselves as many views of mental health maintain the normal person is? Suggestive evidence indicates that individuals who are low in self-esteem, moderately depressed, or both are more balanced in self-perceptions (see Coyne & Gotlieb, 1983; Ruehlman, West, & Pasahow, 1985; Watson & Clark, 1984, for reviews). These individuals tend to (a) recall positive and negative self-relevant information with equal frequency (e.g., Kuiper & Derry, 1982; Kuiper & MacDonald, 1982), (b) show greater evenhandedness in their attributions of responsibility for valenced outcomes (e.g., Campbell & Fairey, 1985; Kuiper, 1978; Rizley, 1978), (c) display greater congruence between self-evaluations and evaluations of others (e.g., Brown, 1986), and (d) offer self-appraisals that coincide more closely with appraisals by objective observers (e.g., Lewinsohn et al., 1980). In short, it appears to be not the well-adjusted individual but the individual who experiences subjective distress who is more likely to process self-relevant information in a relatively unbiased and balanced fashion. These findings are inconsistent with the notion that realistic and evenhanded perceptions of self are characteristic of mental health.

Illusions of Control

In a series of studies adopting gambling formats, Langer and her associates (Langer, 1975; Langer & Roth, 1975) found that people often act as if they have control in situations that are actually determined by chance. When manipulations suggestive of skill, such as competition, choice, familiarity, and involvement, are introduced into chance situations, people behave as if the situations were determined by skill and, thus, were ones over which they could exert some control (see also Goffman, 1967). For example, people infer that they have greater control if they personally throw dice than if someone else does it for them (Fleming & Darley, 1986; Langer, 1975). Similarly, a large literature on covariation estimation indicates that people substantially overestimate their degree of control over heavily chance-determined events (see Crocker, 1982, for a review). When people expect to produce a certain outcome and the outcome then occurs, they often overestimate the degree to which they were instrumental in bringing it about (see Miller & Ross, 1975).

Is there any group in which this illusion of control appears to be absent? Mildly and severely depressed individuals appear to be less vulnerable to the illusion of control (Abramson & Alloy, 1981; Golin, Terrell, & Johnson, 1977; Golin, Terrell, Weitz, & Drost, 1979; M. S. Greenberg & Alloy, in press). When skill cues are introduced into a chance-related task or when outcomes occur as predicted, depressed individuals provide more accurate estimates of their degree of personal control than do nondepressed people. Similarly, relative to nondepressed people, those in whom a negative mood has been induced show more realistic perceptions of personal control (Alloy, Abramson, & Viscusi, 1981; see also Shrauger & Terbovic, 1976). This is not to suggest that depressed people or those in whom a negative mood has been induced are always more accurate than non-depressed subjects in their estimates of personal control (e.g., Abramson, Alloy, & Rosoff, 1981; Benassi & Mahler, 1985) but that the preponderance of evidence lies in this direction. Realistic perceptions of personal control thus appear to be more characteristic of individuals in a depressed affective state than individuals in a nondepressed affective state.

Unrealistic Optimism

Research suggests that most people are future oriented. In one survey (Gonzales & Zimbardo, 1985), the majority of respondents rated themselves as oriented toward the present and the future (57%) or primarily toward the future (33%) rather than toward the present only (9%) or toward the past (1%). Optimism pervades people's thinking about the future (Tiger, 1979). Research suggests that most people believe that the present is better than the past and that the future will be even better (Brickman, Coates, & Janoff-Bulman, 1978). Questionnaires that survey Americans about the future have found the majority to be hopeful and confident that things can only improve (Free & Cantril, 1968). When asked what they thought was possible for them in the future, college students reported more than four times as many positive as negative possibilities (Markus & Nurius, 1986).

Is there any evidence, however, that such optimism is actually unrealistic? Although the future may well hold more subjectively positive events than negative ones for most individuals, as with excessively positive views of the self, evidence for the illusory nature of optimism comes from studies comparing judgments of self with judgments of others. The evidence indicates that although the warm and generous vision of the future that individuals entertain extends to all people, it is decidedly more in evidence for the self. People estimate the likelihood that they will experience a wide variety of pleasant events, such as liking their first job, getting a good salary, or having a gifted child, as higher than those of their peers (Weinstein, 1980). Conversely, when asked their chances of experiencing a wide variety of negative events, including having an automobile accident (Robertson, 1977), being a crime victim (Perloff & Fetzer, 1986), having trouble finding a job (Weinstein, 1980), or becoming ill (Perloff & Fetzer, 1986) or depressed (Kuiper, MacDonald, & Derry, 1983), most people believe that they are less likely than their peers to experience such negative events. In effect, most people seem to be saying, "The future will be great, especially for me." Because not everyone's future can be rosier than their peers', the extreme optimism that individuals display appears to be illusory.

In contrast to the extremely positive view of the future displayed by normal individuals, mildly depressed people and those with low self-esteem appear to entertain more balanced assessments of their likely future circumstances (see Ruehlman et al., 1985, for a review). Relative to judgments concerning others, these individuals fail to exhibit the self-enhancing tendency to see positive events as more likely for self and negative events as less likely for self (Alloy & Ahrens, 1987; Brown, 1985; Pietromonaco & Markus, 1985; Pyszczynski, Holt, & Greenberg, 1987). Thus, although in some cases such tendencies may reflect pessimism on the part of depressed people, it appears to be individuals who are high, not low, in subjective well-being who evince more biased perceptions of the future.

Mental-Health-Promoting Aspects of Illusion

It is one thing to say that positive illusions about the self, personal control, and the future exist and are true for normal people. It is another to identify how these illusions contribute to mental health. To do so, one first needs to establish criteria of mental health and then determine whether the consequences of the preceding positive illusions fit those criteria. One dilemma that immediately arises is that, as noted earlier, many formal definitions of mental health incorporate accurate self-perceptions as one criterion (see Jahoda, 1958; Jourard & Landsman, 1980). In establishing criteria for mental health, then, we must subtract this particular one.

When we do so, what is left? The ability to be happy or, at least, relatively contented, has been one central criterion of mental health and well-being adopted by a variety of researchers and theorists (e.g., Menninger, 1930; see E. Diener, 1984; Jahoda, 1958 for reviews). In her landmark work, Jahoda (1958) identified five additional criteria of positive mental health: positive attitudes toward the self; the ability to grow, develop, and self-actualize; autonomy; environmental mastery in work and social relationships; and integration (i.e., the balance of psychic forces of the id, ego, and superego). Reviewing both older and more recent formulations, Jourard and Landsman (1980, p. 131) distilled very similar criteria: positive self-regard, the ability to care about others and for the natural world, openness to new ideas and to people, creativity, the ability to do productive work, the ability to love, and the ubiquitous realistic self-perceptions. Because positive self-regard has already been considered in our section on exaggeratedly positive self-perceptions, we will not review it here. Thus, the common elements in these criteria that we examine in the next section are happiness or contentment, the ability to care for and about others, and the capacity for productive and creative work.

Happiness or Contentment

Most people report being happy most of the time. In surveys of mood, 70% to 80% of respondents report that they are moderately to very happy. Whereas most respondents believe that others are average in happiness, 60% believe that they are happier than most people (Freedman, 1978). Positive illusions have been tied to reports of happiness. People who have high self-esteem and self-confidence, who report that they have a lot of control in their lives, and who believe that the future will bring them happiness are more likely than people who lack these perceptions to indicate that they are happy at the present (Freedman, 1978).

As alluded to earlier, when the perceptions of

happy people are compared with those of people who are relatively more distressed, happy people have higher opinions of themselves (e.g., Beck, 1967; Kuiper & Derry, 1982; Kuiper & MacDonald, 1982; Kuiper et al., 1985; Lewinsohn et al., 1980; see Shrauger & Terbovic, 1976), are more likely to evince self-serving causal attributions (Kuiper, 1978; Rizley, 1978), show exaggerated beliefs in their ability to control what goes on around them (Abramson & Alloy, 1981; Golin et al., 1977; Golin et al., 1979; M. S. Greenberg & Alloy, in press), and are more likely to be unrealistically optimistic (Alloy & Ahrens, 1987).

The association between illusions and positive mood appears to be a consistent one, but the evidence is largely correlational rather than causal. Some evidence that illusions directly influence mood has, however, been reported. For example, we noted earlier that individuals are more inclined to attribute success than failure to the self. MacFarland and Ross (1982) tested whether such a self-serving pattern promotes positive mood states. These investigators had subjects perform a laboratory task in which they manipulated success and failure. Some subjects were led to attribute success (failure) to the self, whereas other subjects were led to attribute success (failure) to the task. Mood measures were then gathered. In line with the hypothesis that the self-serving attributional bias causally influences positive mood states, subjects led to attribute success to the self and failure to the task reported more positive mood after success and less negative mood after failure.

Ability to Care for Others

The ability to care for Others has been considered an important criterion of mental health, and evidence suggests that positive illusions are associated with certain aspects of social bonding. For example, research with children indicates that high self-evaluations are linked to both perceived and actual popularity among peers (Bohrnstedt & Felson, 1983; Felson, 1981). Optimism may also improve social functioning. One study found that people with high self-esteem and an optimistic view of the future were better able to cope with loneliness at college than were individuals who displayed an absence of these tendencies (Cutrona, 1982).

Illusions may also affect the ability to care for and about others indirectly by means of their ca-

pacity to create positive mood. Research indicates that when a positive (as opposed to negative or neutral) mood has been induced, people are generally more likely to help others (e.g., Batson, Coke, Chard, Smith, & Taliaferro, 1979; Cialdini, Kenrick, & Baumann, 1982; Moore, Underwood, & Rosenhan, 1973), to initiate conversations with others (Batson et al., 1979; Isen, 1970), to express liking for others and positive evaluations of people in general (Gouaux, 1971; Griffith, 1970; Veitch & Griffitt, 1976), and to reduce the use of contentious strategies and increase joint benefit in bargaining situations (Carnevale & Isen, 1986). Summarizing the research evidence, Isen (1984) concluded, "Positive affect is associated with increased sociability and benevolence" (p. 189; see also E. Diener, 1984).

Overall, then, there is evidence associating positive illusions with certain aspects of social bonding. This relation may also be facilitated indirectly by means of positive mood.

Capacity for Creative, Productive Work

Positive illusions may promote the capacity for creative, productive work in two ways: First, these illusions may facilitate intellectually creative functioning itself; second, they enhance motivation, persistence, and performance.

Facilitation of intellectual functioning. The evidence for direct effects of positive illusions on intellective functioning is sparse. Whether unrealistic optimism or exaggerated beliefs in personal control affect intellectual functioning directly is unknown. There may, however, be intellectual benefits to self-enhancement. Memory tends to be organized egocentrically, such that people are able to recall self-relevant information well. Greenwald (1980) suggested that there are cognitive benefits to an egocentrically organized memory: The self as a well-known, highly complex, densely organized system allows for rapid retrieval of information and extensive links among elements in the system. As yet, it is unclear, however, whether self-enhancement biases directly facilitate egocentrically organized memory.

Motivation, persistence, and performance. Self-enhancing perceptions, a belief in personal control, and optimism appear to foster motivation, persistence at tasks, and ultimately, more effective performance.

Evidence for the impact of self-enhancing perceptions on motivation, persistence, and performance comes from several sources. Positive conceptions of the self are associated with working harder and longer on tasks (Felson, 1984); perseverance, in turn, produces more effective performance and a greater likelihood of goal attainment (Bandura, 1977; Baumeister, Hamilton, & Tice, 1985; see also Feather, 1966, 1968, 1969). People with high, as compared to low, self-esteem also evaluate their performance more positively (Vasta & Brockner, 1979), even when it is equivalent to that of low-self-esteem people (Shrauger & Terbovic, 1976). These perceptions then feed back into enhanced motivation. People with high self-esteem have higher estimations of their ability for future performance and higher predictions of future performance, even when prior performance on the task would counterindicate those positive estimations (McFarlin & Blascovich, 1981).

Evidence relating beliefs in personal control to motivation, persistence, and performance comes from a variety of sources. Research on motivation has demonstrated repeatedly that beliefs in personal efficacy (a concept akin to control) are associated with higher motivation and more efforts to succeed (Bandura, 1977; see also Brunstein & Olbrich, 1985; Dweck & Licht, 1980). In a series of studies, Burger (1985) found that individuals high in the desire for control responded more vigorously to a challenging task and persisted longer. They also had higher (and, in this case, more realistic) levels of aspiration and higher expectations for their performance than did individuals low in desire for control.

Individual-difference research on mastery also indicates the value of believing that one has control. C. I. Diener and Dweck (1978, 1980) found differences between mastery-oriented and helpless children in their interpretation of success and failure. Even when their performance was equivalent to that of helpless children, mastery oriented children (i.e., those with a sense of control over the task) remembered their success better, were more likely to see success as indicative of ability, expected successes in the future and were less daunted by failure. Following failure, mastery-oriented children chose to focus on ways to overcome the failure. In fact, they seemed not to recognize that they had failed (C. I. Diener & Dweck, 1978).

Several lines of research suggest that optimism is associated with enhanced motivation and performance. High expectations of success prompt people to work longer and harder on tasks than do low expectations of success (Atkinson, 1964; Mischel, 1973; Weiner, 1979). Gonzales and Zimbardo (1985) found that a self-reported orientation toward the future was associated with self-reports of higher income, higher motivation to work, more goal seeking, more pragmatic action, more daily planning, and less fatalism. Indirect evidence for the relation of optimism to effort, perseverance, and ultimately, goal attainment comes from studies of depression and studies of learned helplessness. Beck (1967) maintained that pessimism is one of the central attributes of depression,[3] and it is also prominent in learned helplessness (Seligman, 1975). One of the chief symptoms of depression is inactivity, and researchers in learned helplessness have also noted the centrality of generalized deficits of motivation in this syndrome (Seligman, 1975). Negative mood, then, depresses activity level, perhaps because it facilitates seeing the negative consequences attached to any action. This pessimism may then reduce motivation and consequent activity toward a goal.

Overall, then, research evidence indicates that self-enhancement, exaggerated beliefs in control, and unrealistic optimism can be associated with higher motivation, greater persistence, more effective performance, and ultimately, greater success. A chief value of these illusions may be that they can create self-fulfilling prophecies. They may help people try harder in situations with objectively poor probabilities of success; although some fail-

---

[3]Positive mood provides a potential secondary route whereby illusions may foster motivation and persistence. Manipulated positive mood enhances perceived probability of success and the tendency to attribute success to personal stable factors (Brown, 1984). By way of perpetuating the cycle of positive mood-perseverance-success, people in a naturally occurring or experimentally induced positive mood are also more likely to believe that they have succeeded and to reward themselves accordingly (Mischel, Coates, & Raskoff, 1968; Wright & Mischel, 1982). Their performance also increases more in response to increases in incentives than does that of people in a negative mood (Weinstein, 1982). Manipulated negative mood is associated with lower expectations for future success, with attributions of success to unstable factors (Brown,1984), and with less self-reward (Mischel et al., 1968; Wright & Mischel, 1982). Motivation and positive mood appear to influence each other reciprocally: Involvement in activity elevates mood, and elevated mood increases involvement in activity (E. Diener, 1984). Overall, the links between being happy and being active are so well-established that one of our earliest psychologists, Aristotle, maintained that happiness is a by-product of human activity (Freedman, 1978).

ure is inevitable, ultimately these illusions will pay off more often than will lack of persistence (cf. Greenwald, 1980). [4]

Accommodating Illusions to Reality

The previous analysis presents some theoretical and practical dilemmas. On the one hand, we have an established view of mental health coming largely from the fields of psychiatry and clinical psychology that stresses the importance of accurate perceptions of the self, one's circumstances, and the future. On the other hand, we have a sharply different portrait from cognitive and social psychology of the normal individual as one who evidences substantial biases in these perceptions. Moreover, these biases fall in a predictable direction, namely, a positive one. How are we to reconcile these viewpoints?

A second dilemma concerns the functional value of illusions. On the one hand, positive illusions appear to be common and, more important, appear to be associated with positive outcomes that promote good mental health. On the other hand, this evidence flies in the face of much clinical wisdom as well as commonsense notions that people must monitor reality accurately to survive. Thus, it is important to consider how positive illusions can be maintained and, more important, can be functional in the face of realistic and often contradictory evidence from the environment.

Reconciling Contradictory Views of Mental Health

In addressing the first dilemma, a useful point of departure in a reconciliation is to examine the potential flaws in the datagathering methods of the relevant clinical and social psychological literatures in deriving their respective portraits. Historically, clinical constructions of mental health have been dominated by therapy with and research on abnormal people. Many psychologists and psychiatrists who have written about mental health devote their research and clinical endeavors to individuals whose perceptions are disturbed in a variety of ways. How might an understanding of mental health be influenced when abnormality is an implicit yardstick? Contrasts between pathological and normal functioning are likely to loom large. Because an attribute of many psychologi-

cally disturbed people is an inability to monitor reality effectively, the healthy individual may be portrayed as one who maintains very close contact with reality. More subtle deviations in perceptions and cognitions from objectively accurate standards may well go unnoticed.

But just as a strict clinical view of mental health may result in an overemphasis on rationality, a view of mental health derived solely from social cognition research may be skewed to reveal an overemphasis on illusions. Much research in social cognition extricates individuals from the normal settings in which they interact for the purpose of providing them with experimentally manipulated information and feedback. Yet social and cognitive research on the prevalence and usefulness of schemata makes clear that people rely heavily on their prior expectations for processing incoming data (see Fiske & Taylor, 1984; Hastie, 1981; Taylor & Crocker, 1981, for reviews). To the extent that manipulated information and feedback are similar to the information and feedback that people normally encounter in their chosen environments, one might expect to see perceptions similar to those that people usually develop in their normal world. However, to the extent that the information and feedback that are provided experimentally deviate from the usual information and feedback that an individual might encounter in the real world, the implications of any errors and biases in perception and cognition are unclear. Within social cognition, these experimentally documented errors and biases are often interpreted as evidence for flaws in human information-processing strategies. Another interpretation, however, is at least as tenable. Individuals may merely assimilate unfamiliar or unexpected data to their prior

---

[4]We have assumed that the relation between illusions and persistence generally results in positive outcomes. Perseverance may sometimes be maladaptive, however, as when an individual persists endlessly at a task that is truly intractable (see Janoff-Bulman & Brickman, 1982). Although some evidence (e.g., McFarlin, Baumeister, & Blascovich, 1984) suggests that such nonproductive perseverance may be most prevalent among people with high self-esteem (i.e., those who are most apt to display self-enhancing illusions), other studies (e.g., Baumeister & Tice, 1985; McFarlin, 1985) suggest that people with high self-esteem may be most apt to desist from persisting endlessly at an unsolvable task when they are given the opportunity to do so. Thus, the nature of the relation between unproductive persistence and self-enhancing illusions is unclear and needs further empirical clarification.

beliefs with relatively little processing at all. If prior beliefs include generally positive views of the self, personal efficacy, and the future, then interpretation of any negative feedback may appear, falsely, to be error prone in a positive direction.

Taking these respective flaws of the social and clinical portraits into account, what kind of reconciliation can we develop? First, a certain degree of contact with reality seems to be essential to accomplish the tasks of everyday life. If the errors and biases identified by social cognition dominated all inferential tasks, it would be difficult to understand how the human organism could learn. On the other hand, it is also evident that when errors and biases do occur, they are not evenly distributed. They consistently stray in a positive direction, toward the aggrandizement of the self and the world in which one must function. The key to an integration of the two views of mental health may, then, lie in understanding those circumstances under which positive illusions about the self and the world may be most obvious and useful. The nature of these circumstances is suggested both by social cognition research itself and by research on victims of misfortune.

If one assumes either that people's prior beliefs about themselves, their efficacy, and their future are positive or that their information-processing strategies bias them to interpret information in this way, then it follows that errors and biases will be most obvious when feedback from the real world is negative. In fact, in experimental circumstances examining positive biases, research reveals that positive biases are more apparent as threats to the self increase (Greenwald, 1981). The importance of information may also alter the prevalence of positive biases. Greenwald (1981) found self-enhancing biases to be more in evidence as the importance of the situation increased. Thus, for example, the self-serving causal attribution bias is more likely to occur for behaviors that are important to an individual than for personally trivial events (e.g., Miller, 1976).

Consistent with both points, research with victims of misfortune, such as cancer patients, suggests that illusions about the self, one's efficacy, and the future are in evidence in dealing with these potentially tragic events (Taylor, 1983). For example, a study of patients with breast cancer found that the belief that one's coping abilities were extraordinary (Wood, Taylor, & Lichtman, 1985) and the belief that one could personally prevent the cancer from coming back, even in the face of a likely recurrence, were quite common (Taylor, Lichtman, & Wood, 1984). More to the point, they were associated with successful psychological adjustment to the cancer.

To summarize then, evidence from converging sources suggests that positive illusions about the self, one's control, and the future may be especially apparent and adaptive under circumstances of adversity, that is, circumstances that might be expected to produce depression or lack of motivation. Under these circumstances, the belief in one's self as a competent, efficacious actor behaving in a world with a generally positive future may be especially helpful in overcoming setbacks, potential blows to self-esteem, and potential erosions in one's view of the future.

Management of Negative Feedback

Social construction of social feedback. A variety of social norms and strategies of social interaction conspire to protect the individual from the harsher side of reality. Research indicates that, although people are generally unwilling to give feedback (Blumberg, 1972), when it is given, it is overwhelmingly likely to be positive (Blumberg, 1972; Parducci, 1968; Tesser & Rosen, 1975). Evaluators who must communicate negative feedback may mute it or put it in euphemistic terms (Goffman, 1955), thus rendering it ambiguous. In a similar vein, studies of opinion moderation (Cialdini, Levy, Herman, & Evenbeck, 1973; McGuire, 1985; M. Snyder & Swann, 1976; Tetlock, 1983) reveal that when people expect that others will disagree with them, they often moderate their opinions in advance to be less extreme and thereby more similar to what they perceive to be the attitudes of their audience. If a person holds negative beliefs about another, he or she is highly likely to discontinue interaction with the person, rather than communicate the negative feedback (Darley & Fazio, 1980). Implicitly, then, people collectively subscribe to norms, ensuring that they both give and receive predominantly positive feedback (see also Goffman, 1955).

The construction of social relationships with friends and intimates also facilitates positive self-impressions. People select friends and intimates who are relatively similar to themselves on physical resources, nearly equal on ability and achievement, similar in attitudes, and similar in background characteristics (Eckland, 1968; Hill, Rubin, & Peplau, 1976; Richardson, 1939; Spuhler, 1968; see Swann, 1984, for a review). This selection process reinforces one's beliefs that one's attitudes and attributes are correct. People form relationships with people who see them as they see themselves (Secord & Backman, 1965; Swann, 1983) and tend to be unhappy in relationships in which they are not seen as they want to be seen (Laing, Phillipson, & Lee, 1966). Tesser and his associates (Tesser, 1980; Tesser & Campbell, 1980; Tesser, Campbell, & Smith, 1984; Tesser & Paulhus, 1983) have suggested that people select friends whose abilities on tasks central to the self are somewhat inferior to their own but whose abilities on tasks less relevant to the self are the same or superior. In this way, individuals can achieve the best of both worlds: They can value their friends for exceptional qualities irrelevant to the self (thereby enhancing the self by means of association) without detracting from their own positive self-evaluations.

Some negative feedback, such as losing a job or being abandoned by a spouse, is difficult to rebut, and under such circumstances, one's friends and family may help in the esteem-restoring process by selectively focusing on one's positive qualities, on the positive aspects of the unpleasant situation, and on the negative aspects of the former situation. In analyses of the social support process, researchers have uniformly regarded the maintenance of self-esteem as a major benefit of social support (e.g., Cobb, 1976; House, 1981; Pinneau, 1975; Schaefer, Coyne, & Lazarus, 1981), and research indicates that social support buffers people from physical and emotional distress during periods of high stress (Cobb, 1976; Cohen & Hoberman, 1983; Cohen & McKay, 1983; Kaplan, Cassel, & Gore, 1977; LaRocco, House, & French, 1980). Experimental studies are consistent with this conclusion (e.g., Backman, Secord, & Peirce, 1963; Swann & Predmore, 1985) by showing that friends' agreement on one's personal attributes can act as a buffer against disconfirming feedback.

Biases in encoding, interpretation, and retrieval. Social interaction itself, then, is one filter that biases the information an individual receives in a positive direction. Another set of filters is engaged as the cognitive system encodes, interprets, or retrieves information. People generally select, interpret, and recall information to be consistent with their prior beliefs or theories (see Fiske & Taylor,

1984; Greenwald, 1980; Taylor & Crocker, 1981, for reviews). [5] Consequently, if a person's prior beliefs are positive, cognitive biases that favor conservatism generally will maintain positive illusions more specifically.

Some potentially contradictory information never gets into the cognitive system. Preexisting theories strongly guide the perception of information as relevant (Howard & Rothbart, 1980; Rothbart, Evans, & Fulero, 1979; see Fiske & Taylor, 1984; Nisbett & Ross, 1980). Ambiguous information tends to be interpreted as consistent with prior beliefs (see Taylor & Crocker, 1981, for a review); thus, a behavior that is neither clearly a success nor clearly a failure is likely to be seen as positive by most individuals. In particular, ambiguous feedback from others may be perceived as more favorable than it really is (Jacobs, Berscheid, & Walster, 1971).

If feedback is not positive, it may simply be ignored. In their review of approximately 50 studies, Shrauger and Schoeneman (1979) examined the evidence relating self-perceptions to evaluations by significant others in natural settings. They found little evidence that self-evaluations are consistently influenced by others' feedback, nor did they find evidence of congruence between self-perceptions and evaluations by others (see also Shrauger, 1982). They did, however, find substantial evidence that people's views of themselves and their perceptions of others' evaluations of them were correlated. People who thought well of themselves believed that they were well-thought-of, and people who thought poorly of themselves believed that others did as well (see also Schafer & Keith, 1985).

Interpretational biases also mute the impact of incoming information. Generally speaking, discrepant self-relevant feedback is more likely to be perceived as inaccurate or uninformative than is feedback that is consistent with the self (Markus, 1977; Swann & Read, 1981a, 1981b). It is scrutinized more closely than is confirmatory information in terms of the evaluator's motives and credibility, with the result that it is likely to be

---

[5]Hastie and Kumar (1979) and others (see Higgins & Bargh, 1987, for a review) have found that under certain circumstances, inconsistent information is better recalled than consistent information. This finding appears to occur primarily under impression-formation conditions, however, which are unlikely to characterize self-inference.

discounted (Halperin, Snyder, Shenkel, & Houston, 1976; Shavit & Shouval, 1980; Shrauger, 1982). One manifestation of this tendency is that, because self-perceptions are generally positive, negative feedback is seen as less credible than positive feedback (C. R. Snyder, Shenkel, & Lowery, 1977), especially by people with high self-esteem (Shrauger & Kelly, 1981; Shrauger & Rosenberg, 1970; see Shrauger, 1975, for a review). When all else fails, discrepant behaviors may be explained away by excuses that offer situational explanations for the behavior (C. R. Snyder, Higgins, & Stucky, 1983). In those cases in which personal responsibility for failure cannot be denied, one can maintain that the attributes on which one is successful are important, whereas the attributes on which one fails are not (e.g., Tesser & Paulhus, 1983).

Finally, information that is consistent with a prior theory is, generally speaking, more likely to be recalled (e.g., Anderson & Pichert, 1978; Owens, Bower, & Black, 1979; Zadny & Gerard, 1974). People are better able to remember information that fits their self-conceptions than information that contradicts their self-conceptions (see Shrauger, 1982; Silverman, 1964; Suinn, Osborne, & Page, 1962; Swann, 1984; Swann & Read, 1981a, 1981b, for reviews). When social feedback is mixed in its implications for the self, people preferentially recall what confirms their self-conceptions (Swann & Read, 1981a, 1981b). Typically, these self-conceptions are positive.

Cognitive drift. If negative or otherwise contradictory information succeeds in surmounting the social and cognitive filters just described, its effects may still be only temporary. Research demonstrates that beliefs may change radically in response to temporary conditions and then drift back again to their original state (e.g., Walster & Berscheid, 1968). This characteristic, cognitive drift, can act as another method of absorbing negative feedback, For example, a dramatic change in self-perception may occur following a negative experience, such as failing a test or being accused of insensitivity by a friend. But, with time, any single encounter with negative feedback may fade into the context of other so-called evidence bolstering positive self-conceptions (cf. Swann, 1983).

Some direct evidence for cognitive drift exists in the literature on self-serving attributions. In a series of experiments, Burger and Huntzinger (1985) found that initially modest attributions for successful and failed performance became more self-serving over time. Similarly, in research on attributions for joint performance, Burger and Rodman (1983, Experiment 2) found that people gave a partner more credit than the self for a joint task immediately following the task (an attribution that may have considerable social value) but later gave themselves more credit for the joint product, as the self-centered bias predicts. Markus and Nurius (1986) made a similar point in noting that the working self-concept is highly responsive to the social environment, whereas the stable self-concept is more robust and less reactive. Cognitive drift, then, is a conservative mechanism that can protect against change in the cognitive system. To the extent that beliefs about one's self and the environment are positive, cognitive drift also maintains positive self-conceptions.

Acknowledged pockets of incompetence. Certain kinds of negative feedback recur repeatedly and, therefore, elude the social and cognitive filters just described. Presumably, this negative information has validity and therefore must be dealt with in some way that acknowledges its existence without undermining generally positive conceptions of the self and the world. One such method is accepting a limitation in order to avoid situations that would require it. In essence, one creates an acknowledged pocket of incompetence. Each person may have a few areas of life (e.g., finances, tennis, artistic or musical ability, fashion sense, or ability to dance) in which he or she readily acknowledges a hopeless lack of talent. People may relegate such behaviors to others and avoid getting themselves into circumstances in which their talents would be tested.

Summary and Conclusions

Evidence from social cognition research suggests that, contrary to much traditional, psychological wisdom, the mentally healthy person may not be fully cognizant of the day-to-day flotsam and jetsam of life. Rather, the mentally healthy person appears to have the enviable capacity to distort reality in a direction that enhances self-esteem, maintains beliefs in personal efficacy, and promotes an optimistic view of the future. These three illusions, as we have called them, appear to foster traditional criteria of mental health, including the ability to care about the self and others, the ability to be happy or contented, and the ability to engage in productive and creative work.

Are positive illusions always adaptive? Might there not be long-term limitations to positive illusions? Indeed, each of the positive illusions described would seem to have inherent risks. For example, a falsely positive sense of accomplishment may lead people to pursue careers and interests for which they are ill-suited. Faith in one's capacity to master situations may lead people to persevere at tasks that may, in fact, be uncontrollable; knowing when to abandon a task may be as important as knowing when to pursue it (Janoff-Bulman & Brickman, 1982). Unrealistic optimism may lead people to ignore legitimate risks in their environments and to fail to take measures to offset those risks. False optimism may, for example, lead people to ignore important health habits (Weinstein, 1982) or to fail to prepare for a likely catastrophic event, such as a flood or an earthquake (Lehman & Taylor, in press). Faith in the inherent goodness of one's beliefs and actions may lead a person to trample on the rights and values of others; centuries of atrocities committed in the name of religious and political values bear witness to the liabilities of such faith. If positive illusions foster the use of shortcuts and heuristics for making judgments and decisions (Isen & Means, 1983), this may lead people to oversimplify complex intellectual tasks and to ignore important sources of information.

It is not clear that the preceding points are limits of positive illusions, only that they are possible candidates. It is important to remember that people's self-evaluations are only one aspect of judgments about any situation, and there may be non-ego-related information inherent in situations that offsets the effects of illusions and leads people to amend their behavior. For example, a man who does poorly at a job may fail to correctly interpret negative feedback as evidence that he is doing a poor job, but he may come to feel that he does not like the job, his boss, or his co-workers very much; consequently, he may leave. The certitude that one is right may lead to discrimination against or hatred of others who hold different beliefs. People may be dissuaded, however, from committing certain actions, such as murder or incarceration of others, in service of their beliefs because they believe the means are wrong or because they know they will be punished; this recognition may, nevertheless, leave their beliefs intact. Potential liabilities associated with one illusion may be canceled out by another. For example, false optimism may lead people to underestimate their vulnerability to cancer, but mastery needs may lead people to control their smoking, diet, or other risk factors. The preceding argument is not meant to suggest that positive illusions are without liabilities. Indeed, there may be many. One should not, however, leap to any obvious conclusions regarding potential liabilities of positive illusions without an appreciation of possible countervailing forces that may help offset those liabilities.

In conclusion, the overriding implication that we draw from our analysis of this literature is that certain biases in perception that have previously been thought of as amusing peccadillos at best and serious flaws in information processing at worst may actually be highly adaptive under many circumstances. The individual who responds to negative, ambiguous, or unsupportive feedback with a positive sense of self, a belief in personal efficacy, and an optimistic sense of the future will, we maintain, be happier, more caring, and more productive than the individual who perceives this same information accurately and integrates it into his or her view of the self, the world, and the future. In this sense, the capacity to develop and maintain positive illusions may be thought of as a valuable human resource to be nurtured and promoted, rather than an error-prone processing system to be corrected. In any case, these illusions help make each individual's world a warmer and more active and beneficent place in which to live.

ACKNOWLEDGMENTS

Preparation of this article was supported by National Science Foundation Grant BNS 83-08524, National Cancer Institute Grant CA 36409, and Research Scientist Development Award MH 00311 from the National Institute of Mental Health to Shelley E. Taylor. Jonathon D. Brown was supported by a University of California, Los Angeles, Chancellor's fellowship and by a Southern Methodist University new-faculty seed grant.

We owe a great deal to a number of individuals who commented on earlier drafts: Nancy Cantor, Edward Emery, Susan Fiske, Tony Greenwald, Connie Hammen, Darrin Lehman, Chuck McClintock, Dick Nisbett, Lee Ross, Bill Swann, Joanne Wood, and two anonymous reviewers.

REFERENCES

Abramson, L. Y., & Alloy, L. B. (1981). Depression, non-depression, and cognitive illusions: A reply to Schwartz. *Journal of Experimental Psychology, 110,* 436–447.

Abramson, L. Y., Alloy, L. B., & Rosoff, R. (1981). Depression and the generation of complex hypotheses in the judgment of contingency. *Behaviour Research and Therapy, 19,* 35–45.

Alicke, M. D. (1985). Global self-evaluation as determined by the desirability and controllability of trait adjectives. *Journal of Personality and Social Psychology, 49,* 1621–1630.

Alloy, L. B., Abramson, L. Y., & Viscusi, D. (1981). Induced mood and the illusion of control. *Journal of Personality and Social Psychology, 41,* 1129–1140.

Alloy, L. B., & Ahrens, A. H. (1987). Depression and pessimism for the future: Biased use of statistically relevant information in predictions for self versus others. *Journal of Personality and Social Psychology, 52,* 366–378.

Allport, G. W. (1943). *Becoming: Basic considerations for a psychology of personality.* New Haven, CT: Yale University Press.

Anderson, R. C., & Pichert, J. W. (1978). Recall of previously unrecallable information following a shift in perspective. *Journal of Verbal Learning and Verbal Behavior, 17,* 1–12.

Atkinson, J. W. (1964). *An introduction to motivation.* Princeton, NJ: Van Nostrand.

Backman, C. W., Secord, C. F., & Peirce, J. R. (1963). Resistance to change in the self-concept as a function of consensus among significant others. *Sociometry, 26,* 102–111.

Bandura, A. (1977). *Social learning theory.* Englewood Cliffs, NJ: Prentice–Hall.

Batson, C. D., Coke, J. S., Chard, F., Smith, D., & Taliaferro, A. (1979). Generality of the "glow of good will": Effects of mood on helping and information acquisition. *Social Psychology Quarterly, 42,* 176–179.

Baumeister, R. F., Hamilton, J. C., & Tice, D. M. (1985). Public versus private expectancy of success: Confidence booster or performance pressure? *Journal of Personality and Social Psychology, 48,* 1447–1457.

Baumeister, R. F., & Tice, D. M. (1985). Self-esteem and responses to success and failure: Subsequent performance and intrinsic motivation. *Journal of Personality, 53,* 450–467.

Beck, A. T. (1967). *Depression: Clinical, experimental and theoretical aspects.* New York: Harper & Row.

Becker, E. (1973). *The denial of death.* New York: Free Press.

Benassi, V. A., & Mahler, H. I. M. (1985). Contingency judgments by depressed college students: Sadder but not always wiser. *Journal of Personality and Social Psychology, 49,* 1323–1329.

Blumberg, H. H. (1972). Communication of interpersonal evaluations. *Journal of Personality and Social Psychology, 23,* 157–162.

Bohrnstedt, G. W., & Felson, R. B. (1983). Explaining the relations among children's actual and perceived performances and self-esteem: A comparison of several causal models. *Journal of Personality and Social Psychology, 45,* 43–56.

Bradley, G. W. (1978). Self-serving biases in the attribution process: A reexamination of the fact or fiction question. *Journal of Personality and Social Psychology, 36,* 56–71.

Brickman, P., Coates, D., & Janoff-Bulman, R. (1978). Lottery winners and accident victims: Is happiness relative? *Journal of Personality and Social Psychology, 35,* 917–927.

Brown, J. D. (1984). Effects of induced mood on causal attributions for success and failure. *Motivation and Emotion, 8,* 343–353.

Brown, J. D. (1985). [Self-esteem and unrealistic optimism about the future]. Unpublished data, University of California, Los Angeles.

Brown, J. D. (1986). Evaluations of self and others: Self-enhancement biases in social judgments. *Social Cognition, 4,* 353–376.

Brown, J. D. (1987). *Evaluating one's abilities: The self-assessment versus self-enhancement debate revisited.* Manuscript submitted for publication.

Brown, J. D., & Taylor, S. E. (1986). Affect and the processing of personal information: Evidence for mood-activated self-schemata. *Journal of Experimental Social Psychology, 22,* 436–452.

Brunstein, J. C., & Olbrich, E. (1985). Personal helplessness and action control: Analysis of achievement-related cognitions, self-assessments, and performance. *Journal of Personality and Social Psychology, 48,* 1540–1551.

Bulman, R. J., & Wortman, C. B. (1977). Attributions of blame and coping in the "real world": Severe accident victims react to their lot. *Journal of Personality and Social Psychology, 35,* 351–363.

Burger, J. M. (1985). Desire for control and achievement-related behaviors. *Journal of Personality and Social Psychology, 48,* 1520–1533.

Burger, J. M., & Huntzinger, R. M. (1985). Temporal effects on attributions for one's own behavior: The role of task outcome. *Journal of Experimental Social Psychology, 21,* 247–261.

Burger, J. M., & Rodman, J. L. (1983). Attributions of responsibility for group tasks: The egocentric bias and the actor-observer difference. *Journal of Personality and Social Psychology, 45,* 1232–1242.

Campbell, J. D. (1986). Similarity and uniqueness: The effects of attribute type, relevance, and individual differences in self-esteem and depression. *Journal of Personality and Social Psychology, 50,* 281–294.

Campbell, J. D., & Fairey, P. J. (1985). Effects of self-esteem, hypothetical explanations, and verbalization of expectancies on future performance. *Journal of Personality and Social Psychology, 48,* 1097–1111.

Cantril, H. (1938). The prediction of social events. *Journal of Abnormal and Social Psychology, 33,* 364–389.

Carnevale, P. J. D., & Isen, A. M. (1986). The influence of positive affect and visual access on the discovery of integrative solutions in bilateral negotiation. *Organizational Behavior and Human-Decision Processes, 37,* 1–13.

Cialdini, R. B., Kenrick, D. T., & Baumann, D. J. (1982). Effects of mood on prosocial behavior in children and adults. In N. Eisenberg (Ed.), *The development of prosocial behavior* (pp. 339–359). New York: Academic Press.

Cialdini, R. B., Levy, A., Herman, C. P., & Evenbeck, S. (1973). Attitudinal politics: The strategy of moderation. *Journal of Personality and Social Psychology, 25,* 100–108.

Cobb, S. (1976). Social support as a moderator of life stress. *Psychosomatic Medicine, 38,* 300–314.

Cohen, S., & Edwards, J. R. (in press). Personality characteristics as moderators of the relationship between stress and disorder. In R. W. J. Neufeld (Ed.), *Advances in the investigation of psychological stress*. New York: Wiley.

Cohen, S., & Hoberman, H. M. (1983). Positive events and social supports as buffers of life change stress. *Journal of Applied Social Psychology, 13,* 99–125.

Cohen, S., & McKay, G. (1983). Social support, stress, and the buffering hypothesis: A theoretical analysis. In A. Baum, S. E. Taylor, & J. Singer (Eds.), *Handbook of psychology and health* (Vol. 4, pp. 253–267). Hillsdale, NJ: Erlbaum.

Conway, M., & Ross, M. (1984). Getting what you want by revising what you had. *Journal of Personality and Social Psychology, 47,* 738–748.

Coyne, J. C., & Gotlieb, I. H. (1983). The role of cognition in depression: A critical appraisal. *Psychological Bulletin, 94,* 472–505.

Crandall, V. J., Solomon, D., & Kelleway, R. (1955). Expectancy statements and decision times as functions of objective probabilities and reinforcement values. *Journal of Personality, 24,* 192–203.

Crary, W. G. (1966). Reactions to incongruent self-experiences. *Journal of Consulting Psychology, 30,* 246–252.

Crocker, J. (1982). Biased questions in judgment of covariation studies. *Personality and Social Psychology Bulletin, 8,* 214–220.

Cutrona, C. E. (1982). Transition to college: Loneliness and the process of social adjustment. In L. A. Peplau & D. Perlman (Eds.), *Loneliness: A sourcebook of current theory, research and therapy* (pp. 291–309). New York: Wiley.

Darley, J. M., & Fazio, R. H. (1980). Expectancy confirmation processes arising in the social interaction-sequence. *American Psychologist, 35,* 867–881.

deCharms, R. (1968). *Personal causation: The internal affective determinants of behavior*. New York: Academic Press.

Diener, C. I., & Dweck, C. S. (1978). An analysis of learned helplessness: Continuous changes in performance, strategy, and achievement cognitions following failure. *Journal of Personality and Social Psychology, 36,* 451–462.

Diener, C. I., & Dweck, C. S. (1980). An analysis of learned helplessness: II. The processing of success. *Journal of Personality and Social Psychology, 39,* 940–952.

Diener, E. (1984). Subjective well-being. *Psychological Bulletin, 95,* 542–575.

Duval, S., & Wicklund, R. A. (1972). *A theory of objective self-awareness*. New York: Academic Press.

Dweck, C. S., & Licht, B. G. (1980). Learned helplessness and intellectual achievement. In M. E. P. Seligman & J. Garber (Eds.), *Human helplessness: Theory and applications* (pp. 197–222). New York: Academic Press.

Eckland, B. K. (1968). Theories of mate selection. *Eugenics Quarterly, 15,* 71–84.

Erikson, E. H. (1950). *Childhood and society* (2nd ed.). New York: Norton.

Feather, N. T. (1966). Effects of prior success and failure on expectations of success and subsequent performance. *Journal of Personality and Social Psychology, 3,* 287–298.

Feather, N. T. (1968). Change in confidence following success or failure as a predictor of subsequent performance. *Journal of Personality and Social Psychology, 9,* 38–46.

Feather, N. T. (1969). Attribution of responsibility and valence of success and failure in relation to initial confidence and task performance. *Journal of Personality and Social Psychology, 13,* 129–144.

Felson, R. B. (1981). Ambiguity and bias in the self-concept. *Social Psychology Quarterly, 44,* 64–69.

Felson, R. B. (1984). The effect of self-appraisals of ability on academic performance. *Journal of Personality and Social Psychology, 47,* 944–952.

Fenichel, O. (1945). *The psychoanalytic theory of neurosis*. New York: Norton.

Fenigstein, A., Scheier, M. F., & Buss, A. H. (1975). Public and private self-consciousness: Assessment and theory. *Journal of Consulting and Clinical Psychology, 43,* 522–528.

Fischhoff, B. (1976). Attribution theory and judgment under uncertainty. In J. H. Harvey, W. J. Ickes, & R. F. Kidd (Eds.), *New directions in attribution research* (Vol. 1, pp. 421–452). Hillsdale, NJ: Erlbaum.

Fiske, S. T., & Taylor, S. E. (1984). *Social cognition*. Reading, MA: Addison-Wesley.

Fleming, J., & Darley, J. M. (1986). *Perceiving intention in constrained behavior: The role of purposeful and constrained action cues in correspondence bias effects*. Unpublished manuscript, Princeton University, Princeton, NJ.

Forsyth, D. R., & Schlenker, B. R. (1977). Attributing the causes of group performance: Effects of performance quality, task importance, and future testing. *Journal of Personality, 45,* 220–236.

Frank, J. D. (1953). Some psychological determinants of the level of aspiration. *American Journal of Psychology, 47,* 285–293.

Frankel, A., & Snyder, M. L. (1978). Poor performance following unsolvable problems: Learned helplessness or egotism? *Journal of Personality and Social Psychology, 36,* 1415–1423.

Franzoi, S. L. (1983). Self-concept differences as a function of private self-consciousness and social anxiety. *Journal of Research in Personality, 17,* 272–287.

Free, L. A., & Cantril, H. (1968). *The political beliefs of Americans: A study of public opinion*. New York: Clarion.

Freedman, J. (1978). *Happy people: What happiness is, who has it, and why*. New York: Harcourt Brace Jovanovich.

Fromm, E. (1955). *The sane society*. New York: Rinchart.

Funder, D. C. (1987). Errors and mistakes: Evaluating the accuracy of social judgment. *Psychological Bulletin, 101,* 75–90.

Gibbons, F. X. (1986). Social comparison and depression: Company's effect on misery. *Journal of Personality and Social Psychology, 51,* 140–149.

Goffman, E. (1955). On face-work: An analysis of ritual elements in social interaction. *Psychiatry: Journal for the Study of Interpersonal Processes, 18,* 213–231.

Goffman, E. (1967). *Interaction ritual*. Newport Beach, CA: Westcliff.

Golin, S., Terrell, T., & Johnson, B. (1977). Depression and the illusion of control. *Journal of Abnormal Psychology, 86,* 440–442.

Golin, S., Terrell, T., Weitz, J., & Drost, P. L. (1979). The illusion of control among depressed patients. *Journal of Abnormal Psychology, 88,* 454–457.

Gonzales, A., & Zimbardo, P. G. (1985, March). Time in perspective. *Psychology Today*, pp. 21–26.

Gouaux, C. (1971). Induced affective states and interpersonal attraction. *Journal of Personality and Social Psychology, 20,* 37–43.

Green, S. K., & Gross, A. E. (1979). Self-serving biases in

implicit evaluations. *Personality and Social Psychology Bulletin, 5,* 214–217.

Greenberg, J., Pyszczynski, T., & Solomon, S. (1986). The causes and consequences of a need for self-esteem: A terror management theory. In R. R. Baumeister (Ed.), *Public self and private life* (pp. 189–212). New York: Springer-Verlag.

Greenberg, M. S., & Alloy, L. B. (in press). Depression versus anxiety: Differences in self and other schemata. In L. B. Alloy (Ed.), *Cognitive processes in depression.* New York: Guilford Press.

Greenwald, A. G. (1980). The totalitarian ego: Fabrication and revision of personal history. *American Psychologist, 35,* 603–618.

Greenwald, A. G. (1981). Self and memory. In G. H. Bower (Ed.), *The psychology of learning and motivation* (Vol. 15, pp. 201–236). New York: Academic Press.

Greenwald A. G., & Breckler, S. J. (1985). To whom is the self presented. In E. Schlenker (Ed.), *The self and social life* (pp. 126–145). New York: McGraw-Hill.

Griffith, W. B. (1970). Environmental effects on interpersonal affective behavior: Ambient temperature and attraction. *Journal of Personality and Social Psychology, 15,* 240–244.

Haan, N. (1977). *Coping and defending.* New York: Academic Press.

Hall, J., & Taylor, S. E. (1976). When love is blind. *Human Relations, 29,* 751–761.

Halperin, K., Snyder, C. R., Shenkel, R. J., & Houston, B. K. (1976). Effects of source status and message favorability on acceptance of personality feedback. *Journal of Applied Psychology, 61,* 85–88.

Harackiewicz, J. M., Manderlink, G., & Sansone, C. (1984). Rewarding pinball wizardry: Effects of evaluation and cue value on intrinsic interest. *Journal of Personality and Social Psychology, 47,* 287–300.

Harackiewicz, J. M., Sansone, C., & Manderlink, G. (1985). Competence, achievement orientation, and intrinsic motivation: A process analysis. *Journal of Personality and Social Psychology, 48,* 493–508.

Hastie, R. (1981). Schematic principles in human memory. In E. T. Higgins, C. P. Herman, & M. P. Zanna (Eds.), *Social cognition: The Ontario Symposium* (Vol. 1, pp. 39–88). Hillsdale, NJ: Erlbaum.

Hastie, R., & Kumar, P. (1979). Person memory: Personality traits as organizing principles in memory for behaviors. *Journal of Personality and Social Psychology, 37,* 25–38.

Heider, F. (1958). *The psychology of interpersonal relations.* New York: Wiley.

Hendrick, I. (1942). Instinct and the ego during infancy. *Psychoanalytic Quarterly, 11,* 33–58.

Higgins, E. T., & Bargh, J. A. (1987). Social cognition and social perception. *Annual Review of Psychology, 38,* 369–425.

Hilgard, E. R., & Bower, G. H. (1966). *Theories of learning.* New York: Appleton-Century-Crofts.

Hill, C. T., Rubin, Z., & Peplau, L. A. (1976). Breakups before marriage: The end of 103 affairs. *Journal of Social Issues, 32,* 147–168.

House, J. A. (1981). *Work stress and social support.* Reading, MA: Addison-Wesley.

Howard, J. W., & Rothbart, M. (1980). Social categorization and memory for ingroup and outgroup behavior. *Journal of Personality and Social Psychology, 38,* 301–310.

Ingram, R. E., & Smith, T. W. (1984). Depression and internal versus external focus of attention. *Cognitive Therapy and Research, 8,* 139–151.

Irwin, F. W. (1944). The realism of expectations. *Psychological Review, 51,* 120–126.

Irwin, F. W. (1953). Stated expectations as functions of probability and desirability of outcomes. *Journal of Personality, 21,* 329–335.

Isen, A. M. (1970). Success, failure, attention, and reactions to others: The warm glow of success. *Journal of Personality and Social Psychology, 36,* 1–12.

Isen, A. M. (1984). Toward understanding the role of affect in cognition. In R. Wyer & T. Srull (Eds.), *Handbook of social cognition* (pp. 174–236). Hillsdale, NJ: Erlbaum.

Isen, A. M., & Daubman, K. A. (1984). The influence of affect on categorization. *Journal of Personality and Social Psychology, 47,* 1206–1217.

Isen, A. M., Daubman, K. A., & Nowicki, G. P. (1987). Positive affect facilitates creative problem solving *Journal of Personality and Social Psychology, 52,* 1122–1131.

Isen, A. M., Johnson, M. M. S., Mertz, E., & Robinson, G. (1985). The influence of positive affect on the unusualness of word association. *Journal of Personality and Social Psychology, 48,* 1413–1426.

Isen, A. M., & Means, B. (1983). The influence of positive affect on decision-making strategy. *Social Cognition, 2,* 18–31.

Isen, A. M., Shalker, T., Clark, M., & Karp, L. (1978). Affect, accessibility of material in memory, and behavior: A cognitive loop? *Journal of Personality and Social Psychology, 36,* 1–12.

Jacobs, L., Berscheid, E., & Walster, E. (1971). Self-esteem and attraction. *Journal of Personality and Social Psychology, 17,* 84–91.

Jahoda, M. (1953). The meaning of psychological health. *Social Casework, 34,* 349.

Jahoda, M. (1958). *Current concepts of positive mental health.* New York: Basic Books.

Janoff-Bulman, R. (1979). Characterological versus behavioral self-blame: Inquiries into depression and rape. *Journal of Personality and Social Psychology, 37,* 1798–1809.

Janoff-Bulman, R., & Brickman, P. (1982). Expectations and what people learn from failure. In N. T. Feather (Ed.), *Expectations and action: Expectancy-value models in psychology* (pp. 207–272). Hillsdale, NJ: Erlbaum.

Jourard, S. M., & Landsman, T. (1980). *Healthy personality: An approach from the viewpoint of humanistic psychology* (4th ed.). New York: Macmillan.

Kahneman, D., & Tversky, A. (1973). On the psychology of prediction. *Psychological Review, 80,* 237–251.

Kaplan, B. H., Cassel, J. C., & Gore, S. (1977). Social support and health. *Medical Care, 15*(Suppl. 1), 47–58.

Kelley, H. H. (1967). Attribution theory in social psychology. In D. Levine (Ed.), *Nebraska Symposium on Motivation* (Vol. 15, pp. 192–240). Lincoln: University of Nebraska Press.

Kuiper, N. A. (1978). Depression and causal attributions for success and failure. *Journal of Personality and Social Psychology, 36,* 236–246.

Kuiper, N. A., & Derry, P. A. (1982). Depressed and nondepressed content self-reference in mild depression. *Journal of Personality, 50,* 67–79.

Kuiper, N. A., & MacDonald, M. R. (1982). Self and other

perception in mild depressives. *Social Cognition, 1,* 233–239.

Kuiper, N. A., MacDonald, M. R., & Derry, P. A. (1983). Parameters of a depressive self-schema. In J. Suls & A. G. Greenwald (Eds.), *Psychological perspectives on the self* (Vol. 2, pp. 191–217). Hillsdale, NJ: Erlbaum.

Kuiper, N. A., Olinger, L. J., MacDonald, M. R., & Shaw, B. F. (1985). Self-schema processing of depressed and nondepressed content: The effects of vulnerability on depression. *Social Cognition, 3,* 77–93.

Laing, R. D., Phillipson, H., & Lee, A. R. (1966). *Interpersonal perception: A theory and a method of research.* New York: Springer Publishing.

Langer, E. J., (1975). The illusion of control. *Journal of Personality and Social Psychology, 32,* 311–328.

Langer, E. J., & Benevento, A. (1978). Self-induced dependence. *Journal of Personality and Social Psychology, 36,* 886–893.

Langer, E. J., & Roth, J. (1975). Heads I win, tails it's chance: The illusion of control as a function of the sequence of outcomes in a purely chance task. *Journal of Personality and Social Psychology, 32,* 951–955.

LaRocco, J. M., House, J. S., & French, J. R. P., Jr. (1980). Social support, occupational stress, and health. *Journal of Health and Social Behavior, 21,* 202–218.

Larwood, L., & Whittaker, W. (1977). Managerial myopia: Self-serving biases in organizational planning. *Journal of Applied Psychology, 62,* 194–198.

Lazarus, R. S. (1983). The costs and benefits of denial. In S. Breznitz (Ed.), *Denial of stress* (pp. 1–30). New York: International Universities Press.

Lehman, D. R., & Taylor, S. E. (in press). Date with an earthquake: Coping with a probable, unpredictable disaster. *Personality and Social Psychology Bulletin.*

Lewicki, P. (1983). Self-image bias in person perception. *Journal of Personality and Social Psychology, 45,* 384–393.

Lewicki, P. (1984). Self-schema and social information processing. *Journal of Personality and Social Psychology, 47,* 1177–1190.

Lewicki, P. (1985). Nonconscious biasing effects of single instances on subsequent judgments. *Journal of Personality and Social Psychology, 48,* 563–574.

Lewinsohn, P. M., Mischel, W., Chaplin, W., & Barton, R. (1980). Social competence and depression: The role of illusory self-perceptions. *Journal of Abnormal Psychology, 89,* 203–212.

Lund, F. H. (1975). The psychology of belief: A study of its emotional and volitional determinants. *Journal of Abnormal and Social Psychology, 20,* 63–81.

MacFarland, C., & Ross, M. (1982). The impact of causal attributions on affective reactions to success and failure. *Journal of Personality and Social Psychology, 43,* 937–946.

Marks, G. (1984). Thinking one's abilities are unique and one's opinions are common. *Personality and Social Psychological Bulletin, 10,* 203–208.

Marks, R. W. (1951). The effect of probability, desirability, and "privilege" on the stated expectations of children. *Journal of Personality, 19,* 332–351.

Markus, H. (1977). Self-schemata and processing information about the self. *Journal of Personality and Social Psychology, 35,* 63–78.

Markus, H., & Nurius, P. (1986). Possible selves. *American Psychologist, 41,* 954–969.

Maslow, A. H. (1950). Self-actualizing people: A study of psychological health. *Personality.* Symposium No. 1, 11–34.

McFarlin, D. B. (1985). Persistence in the face of failure: The impact of self-esteem and contingency information. *Personality and Social Psychology Bulletin, 11,* 153–163.

McFarlin, D. B., Baumeister, R. F., & Blascovich, J. (1984). On knowing when to quit: Task failure, self-esteem, advice, and nonproductive assistance. *Journal of Personality, 52,* 138–155.

McFarlin, D. B., & Blascovich, J. (1981). Effects of self-esteem and performance feedback on future affective preferences and cognitive expectations. *Journal of Personality and Social Psychology, 40,* 521–531.

McGuire, W. (1960). A syllogistic analysis of cognitive relationships. In M. Rosenberg, C. Hovland, W. McGuire, R. Abelson, & J. Brehm (Eds.), *Attitude organization and change* (pp. 65–111). New Haven, CT: Yale University Press.

McGuire, W. J. (1985). Attitudes and attitude change. In G. Lindzey & E. Aronson (Eds.), *Handbook of social psychology* (3rd ed., Vol. 2, pp. 233–346). New York: Random House.

Menninger, K. A. (1930). What is a healthy mind? In N. A. Crawford & K. A. Menninger (Eds.), *The healthy-minded child.* New York: Coward-McCann.

Miller, D. T. (1976). Ego involvement and attributions for success and failure. *Journal of Personality and Social Psychology, 34,* 901–906.

Miller, D. T., & Ross, M. (1975). Self-serving biases in attribution of causality: Fact or fiction? *Psychological Bulletin, 82,* 213–225.

Mirels, H. L. (1980). The avowal of responsibility for good and bad outcomes: The effects of generalized self-serving biases. *Personality and Social Psychology Bulletin, 6,* 299–306.

Mischel, W. (1973). Toward a cognitive-social learning reconceptualization of personality. *Psychological Review, 80,* 252–283.

Mischel, W., Coates, B., & Raskoff, A. (1968). Effects of success and failure on self-gratification. *Journal of Personality and Social Psychology, 10,* 381–390.

Moore, B. S., Underwood, B., & Rosenhan, D. L. (1973). Affect and altruism, *Developmental Psychology, 8,* 99–104.

Nisbett, R. E., & Ross, L. (1980). *Human inference: Strategies and shortcomings of social judgement.* Englewood Cliffs, NJ: Prentice-Hall.

Owens, J., Bower, G. H., & Black, J. B. (1979). The "soap-opera" effect in story recall. *Memory and Cognition, 7,* 185–191.

Parducci, A. (1968). The relativism of absolute judgments. *Scientific American, 219,* 518–528.

Perloff, L. S., & Fetzer, B. K. (1986). Self-other judgments and perceived vulnerability of victimization. *Journal of Personality and Social Psychology, 50,* 502–510.

Pietromonaco, P. R., & Markus, H. (1985). The nature of negative thoughts in depression. *Journal of Personality and Social Psychology, 48,* 799–807.

Pinneau, S. R., Jr. (1975). *Effects of social support on psychological and physiological stress.* Unpublished doctoral dissertation, University of Michigan, Ann Arbor.

Pruitt, D. G., & Hoge, R. D. (1965). Strength of the relationship between the value of an event and its subjective probability as a function of method of measurement. *Journal of Experimental Psychology, 5,* 483–489.

Pyszczynski, T., Holt, K., & Greenberg, J. (1987). Depression, self-focused attention, and expectancies for positive and negative future life events for self and others. *Journal of Personality and Social Psychology, 52,* 994–1001.

Richardson, H. M. (1939). Studies of mental resemblance between husbands and wives and between friends. *Psychological Bulletin, 36,* 104–120.

Rizley, R. (1978). Depression and distortion in the attribution of causality. *Journal of Abnormal Psychology, 87,* 32–48.

Robertson, L. S. (1977). Car crashes: Perceived vulnerability and willingness to pay for crash protection. *Journal of Community Health, 3,* 136–141.

Rosenberg, M. (1979). *Conceiving the self.* New York: Basic Books.

Ross, M., & Fletcher, G. J. O. (1985). Attribution and social perception. In G. Lindzey & E. Aronson (Eds.), *The handbook of social psychology* (3rd ed., pp. 73–122). Reading. MA: Addison-Wesley.

Roth, D. L., & Ingram, R. E. (1985). Factors in the Self-Deception Questionnaire: Associations with depression. *Journal of Personality and Social Psychology, 48,* 243–251.

Rothbart, M., Evans, M., & Fulero, S. (1979). Recall for confirming events: Memory processes and the maintenance of social stereotyping. *Journal of Experimental Social Psychology, 15,* 343–355.

Rothbaum, F., Weisz, J. R., & Snyder, S. S. (1982). Changing the world and changing the self: A two-process model of perceived control. *Journal of Personality and Social Psychology, 42,* 5–37.

Ruehlman, L. S., West, S. G., & Pasahow, R. J. (1985). Depression and evaluative schemata. *Journal of Personality, 53,* 46–92.

Sackeim, H. A. (1983). Self-deception, self-esteem, and depression: The adaptive value of lying to oneself. In J. Masling (Ed.), *Empirical studies of psychoanalytical theories* (Vol. 1, pp. 101–157). Hillsdale, NJ: Analytic Press.

Sackeim, H. A., & Gur, R. C. (1979). Self-deception, other-deception, and self-reported psychopathology. *Journal of Consulting and Clinical Psychology, 47,* 213–215.

Schaefer, C., Coyne, J. C., & Lazarus, R. S. (1981). The health-related functions of social support. *Journal of Behavioral Medicine, 4,* 381–406.

Schafer, R. B., & Keith, P. M. (1985). A causal model approach to the symbolic interactionist view of the self-concept. *Journal of Personality and Social Psychology, 48,* 963–969.

Schlenker, B. R. (1980). *Impression management.* Monterey, CA: Brooks/Cole.

Schlenker, B. R., & Miller, R. S. (1977). Egocentrism in groups: Self-serving biases or logical information processing? *Journal of Personality and Social Psychology, 35,* 755–764.

Schneider, D. J., Hastorf, A. H., & Ellsworth, P. C. (1979). *Person perception.* Reading, MA: Addison-Wesley.

Schulz, D. (1977). *Growth psychology: Models of the healthy personality.* New York: Van Nostrand Reinhold.

Sears, D. O. (1983). The person-positivity bias. *Journal of Personality and Social Psychology, 44,* 233–250.

Secord, P. F., & Backman, C. W. (1965). An interpersonal approach to personality. In B. A. Maher (Ed.), *Progress in experimental personality research* (Vol. 2, pp. 91–125). New York: Academic Press.

Seligman, M. E. P. (1975). *Helplessness: On depression, development and death.* San Francisco: Freeman.

Shaver, K. G., & Drown, D. (1986). On causality, responsibility, and self-blame: A theoretical note. *Journal of Personality and Social Psychology, 4,* 697–702.

Shavit, H., & Shouval, R. (1980). Self-esteem and cognitive consistency effects on self-other evaluation. *Journal of Experimental Social Psychology, 16,* 417–425.

Sherman, S. J. (1980). On the self-erasing nature of errors of prediction. *Journal of Personality and Social Psychology, 39,* 211–221.

Shrauger, J. S. (1975). Responses to evaluation as a function of initial self-perception. *Psychological Bulletin, 82,* 581–596.

Shrauger, J. S. (1982). Selection and processing of self-evaluative information: Experimental evidence and clinical implications. In G. Weary & H. L. Mirels (Eds.), *Integrations of clinical and social psychology* (pp. 128–153). New York: Oxford University Press.

Shrauger, J. S., & Kelly, R. J. (1981). *Self-confidence and endorsement of external evaluations.* Unpublished manuscript.

Shrauger, J. S., & Rosenberg, J. E. (1970). Self-esteem and the effects of success and failure feedback on performance. *Journal of Personality, 38,* 404–417.

Shrauger, J. S., & Schoeneman, T. J. (1979). Symbolic interactionist view of self-concept: Through the looking glass darkly. *Psychological Bulletin, 86,* 549–573.

Shrauger, J. S., & Terbovic, M. L. (1976). Self-evaluation and assessments of performance by self and others. *Journal of Consulting and Clinical Psychology, 44,* 564–572.

Silverman, I. (1964). Self-esteem and differential responsiveness to success and failure. *Journal of Abnormal and Social Psychology, 69,* 115–119.

Smith, T. W., & Greenberg, J. (1981). Depression and self-focused attention. *Motivation and Emotion, 5,* 323–331.

Smith, T. W., Ingram, R. E., & Roth, D. L. (1985). Self-focused attention and depression: Self-evaluation, affect, and life stress. *Motivation and Emotion, 9,* 381–389.

Snyder, C. R., Higgins, R. L., & Stucky, R. J. (1983). *Excuses: Masquerades in search of grace.* New York: Wiley.

Snyder, C. R., Shenkel, R. J., & Lowery, C. R. (1977). Acceptance of personality interpretations: The "Barnum effect" and beyond. *Journal of Consulting and Clinical Psychology, 45,* 104–114.

Snyder, M., & Swann, W. B. (1976). When actions reflect attitudes: The politics of impression management. *Journal of Personality and Social Psychology, 34,* 1034–1042.

Spuhler, J. N. (1968). Assortative mating with respect to physical characteristics. *Eugenics Quarterly, 15,* 128–140.

Stein, J. (Ed.). (1982). *The Random House dictionary of the English language* (unabridged ed.). New York: Random House.

Suinn, R. M., Osborne, D., & Page, W. (1962). The self-concept and accuracy of recall of inconsistent self-related information. *Journal of Clinical Psychology, 18,* 473–474.

Svenson, O. (1981). Are we all less risky and more skillful than our fellow drivers? *Acta Psychologica, 47,* 143–148.

Swann, W. B., Jr. (1983). Self-verification: Bringing social reality into harmony with the self. In J. Suls & A. G.

Greenwald (Eds.), *Social psychology perspectives* (Vol. 2, pp. 33–66). Hillsdale, NJ: Erlbaum.

Swann, W. B., Jr. (1984). Quest for accuracy in person perception: A matter of pragmatics. *Psychological Review, 91,* 457–477.

Swann, W. B., Jr., & Hill, C. A. (1982). When our identities are mistaken: Reaffirming self-conceptions through social interaction. *Journal of Personality and Social Psychology, 43,* 59–66.

Swann, W. B., Jr., & Predmore, S. C. (1985). Intimates as agents of social support: Sources of consolation or despair? *Journal of Personality and Social Psychology, 49,* 1609–1617.

Swann, W. B., Jr., & Read, S. J. (1981a). Acquiring self-knowledge: The search for feedback that fits. *Journal of Personality and Social Psychology, 41,* 1119–1128.

Swann, W. B., Jr., & Read, S. J. (1981b). Self-verification processes: How we sustain our self-conceptions. *Journal of Experimental Social Psychology, 17,* 351–370.

Tajfel, H., & Turner, J. C. (1986). The social identity theory of intergroup behavior. In S. Worchel & W. Austin (Eds.), *Psychology of intergroup relations* (pp. 7–24). Chicago: Nelson-Hall.

Taylor, S. E. (1983). Adjustment to threatening events: A theory of cognitive adaptation. *American Psychologist, 38,* 1161–1173.

Taylor, S. E., & Crocker, J. (1981). Schematic bases of social information processing. In E. T. Higgins, C. P. Herman, & M. P. Zanna (Eds.), *Social cognition: The Ontario Symposium* (Vol. 1, pp. 89–134). Hillsdale, NJ: Erlbaum.

Taylor, S. E., & Koivumaki, J. H. (1976). The perception of self and others: Acquaintanceship, affect, and actor-observer differences. *Journal of Personality and Social Psychology, 33,* 403–408.

Taylor, S. E., Lichtman, R. R., & Wood, J. V. (1984). Attributions, beliefs about control, and adjustment to breast cancer. *Journal of Personality and Social Psychology, 46,* 489–502.

Tesser, A. (1980). Self-esteem maintenance in family dynamics. *Journal of Personality and Social Psychology, 39,* 77–91.

Tesser, A., & Campbell, J. (1980). Self-definition: The impact of the relative performance and similarity of others. *Social Psychology Quarterly, 43,* 341–347.

Tesser, A., Campbell, J., & Smith, M. (1984). Friendship, choice and performance: Self-evaluation maintenance in children. *Journal of Personality and Social Psychology, 46,* 561–574.

Tesser, A., & Moore, J. (1986). On the convergence of public and private aspects of self. In R. F. Baumeister (Ed.), *Public self and private life* (pp. 99–116). New York: Springer-Verlag.

Tesser, A., & Paulhus, D. (1983). The definition of self: Private and public self-evaluation management strategies. *Journal of Personality and Social Psychology, 44,* 672–682.

Tesser, A., & Rosen, S. (1975). The reluctance to transmit bad news. In L. Berkowitz (Ed.), *Advances in experimental psychology* (Vol. 8, pp. 193–232). New York: Academic Press.

Tetlock, P. E. (1983). Accountability and complexity of thought. *Journal of Personality and Social Psychology, 45,* 74–83.

Tetlock, P. E., & Manstead, A. S. R. (1985). Impression management versus intrapsychic explanations in social psychology: A useful dichotomy? *Psychological Review, 92,* 59–77.

Tiger, L. (1979). *Optimism: The biology of hope.* New York: Simon & Schuster.

Turner, R. G. (1978). Effects of differential request procedures and self-consciousness on trait attributions. *Journal of Research in Personality, 12,* 431–438.

Vaillant, G. (1977). *Adaptation to life.* Boston: Little, Brown.

Vasta, R., & Brockner, J. (1979). Self-esteem and self-evaluation covert statements. *Journal of Consulting and Clinical Psychology, 47,* 776–777.

Veitch, R., & Griffitt, W. (1976). Good news-bad news: Affective and interpersonal effects. *Journal of Applied Social Psychology, 6,* 69–75.

Walster, E., & Berscheid, E. (1968). The effects of time on cognitive consistency. In R. P. Abelson, E. Aronson, W. J. McGuire, T. M. Newcomb, M. J. Rosenberg, & P. H. Tannenbaum (Eds.), *Theories of cognitive consistency: A sourcebook* (pp. 599–608). Chicago: Rand McNally.

Watson, D., & Clark, L. A. (1984). Negative affectivity: The disposition to experience aversive emotional states. *Psychological Bulletin, 96,* 465–490.

Weiner, B. (1979). A theory of motivation for some classroom experiences, *Journal of Educational Psychology, 71,* 3–25.

Weinstein, N. D. (1980). Unrealistic optimism about future life events. *Journal of Personality and Social Psychology, 39,* 806–820.

Weinstein, N. D. (1982). Unrealistic optimism about susceptibility to health problems. *Journal of Behavioral Medicine, 5,* 441–460.

White, R. W. (1959). Motivation reconsidered: The concept of competence. *Psychological Review, 66,* 297–335.

Wood, J. V., Taylor, S. E., & Lichtman, R. R. (1985). Social comparison in adjustment to breast cancer. *Journal of Personality and Social Psychology, 49,* 1169–1183.

Wright, J., & Mischel, W. (1982). Influence of affect on cognitive social learning person variables. *Journal of Personality and Social Psychology, 43,* 901–914.

Wurf, E., & Markus, H. (1983, August). *Cognitive consequences of the negative self.* Paper presented at the annual convention of the American Psychological Association, Anaheim, CA.

Zadny, J., & Gerard, H. B. (1974). Attributed intentions and informational selectivity. *Journal of Experimental Social Psychology, 10,* 34–52.

Zuckerman, M. (1979). Attribution of success and failure revisited, or: The motivational bias is alive and well in attribution theory. *Journal of Personality, 47,* 245–287.

The Cognitive System

Social psychology has been cognitive from its very inception as a modern scientific discipline. Its intellectual forefathers, such as Kurt Lewin, Solomon Asch, and Fritz Heider, pervasively employed cognitive terminology, such as "cognitive structures," "naïve theories," and "expectancies." From the beginning they were willing to "peek" into what radical behaviorists considered a "black box" whose secrets can never be known and hence were not worth theorizing about. The cognitive leanings of social psychologists received an additional boost in the 1970s with the advent of the cognitive revolution in psychology at large. This general Zeitgeist inspired a new generation of social psychologists who proceeded to launch a minirevolution of their own, embodied in a movement known as "social cognition." Social cognition is more than a topical area within the larger domain of social psychology. Rather, it is a way of looking at almost all social-psychological phenomena, including those usually stated at the interpersonal, group, or even intergroup levels of analysis. It is an approach that attempts to explain manifold social psychological phenomena by pointing to their cognitive underpinnings. It takes as one of its missions the exploration of how much of such phenomena can be explained by cognitive factors. Far from being just passive consumers of the work of cognitive psychologists, social psychologists themselves developed theories about the cognitive structures and processes involved in categorization, causal inference, knowledge activation, automaticity, and mental representation. The following set of selections amply attest to the utility of the cognitive perspective in social psychology.

The papers by Kelley (1950) and Word, Zanna, and Cooper (1974) explore the effects of prior expectancies on how we interact with others. Snyder and Swann (1978) look at how our interpersonal impressions can be influenced by the hypothesis-testing process itself. The paper by Higgins, Rholes, and Jones (1977) addresses the role of construct accessibility in interpreting ambiguous information about persons. The Bargh and Pietromonaco (1982) paper employs the concept of automaticity and illustrates how information presented outside of awareness may impact the impressions we form of others. Devine's (1989) article suggests how automatic activation of ethnic stereotypes may lead people to act "against their will" in a discriminatory way (i.e., even if their conscious attitudes were liberal and nonbigoted). Hamilton, Driscoll, and Worth's (1989) paper delves into the "inside" of our memory to explore how our impressions of others are organized. Kelley (1967) systematically theorizes about how hypotheses about the causal role of others are tested, and Trope and Alfieri (1997) tie the problem of causal hypothesis testing to issues of automaticity and control discussed in the previous selections.

The Warm-Cold Variable in First Impressions of Persons

Harold H. Kelley • University of Michigan

Editors' Notes

How do expectations of a person we are about to meet influence our impressions of this person? Harold Kelley argues that, consistent with Solomon Asch's theorizing, some expectations are especially important and influential in this regard. He proposes that expectations about "central traits," more than expectations about other traits, exert "ripple effects" on other aspects of the impression being formed, causing a reorganization of the impression along the lines of the central traits. Impressions are important because they do not stay in the perceivers' heads but, rather, are likely to affect subsequent behavior as well. The data presented by Kelley provide strong and compelling support for this theorizing.

Discussion Questions

1. In what ways did the expectation that a stimulus person is "warm" or "cold" affect participants' impressions of this person?
2. In your opionion, why didn't the participants base their impressions on what they themselves saw, heard, and experienced during their interaction with the stimulus person?
3. Why are "warm" and "cold" considered "central" traits by Asch and by Kelley? What might centrality of traits depend on? Can you think of other traits that would be "central"? In what circumstances might they be so?

Suggested Readings

Asch, S. E. (1946). Forming impressions of personality. *Journal of Abnormal Social Psychology, 41,* 258–290.

Ross, M., & Olson, J. M. (1981). An expectancy-attribution model of the effects of placebos. *Psychological Review, 88,* 408–437.

Wishner, J. (1960). Reanalysis of "impressions of personality." *Psychological Review, 67,* 96–112.

This experiment is one of several studies of first impressions (3), the purpose of the series being to investigate the stability of early judgments, their determinants, and the relation of such judgments to the behavior of the person making them. In interpreting the data from several nonexperimental studies on the stability of first impressions, it proved to be necessary to postulate inner-observer variables which contribute to the impression and which remain relatively constant through time. Also some evidence was obtained which directly demonstrated the existence of these variables and their nature. The present experiment was designed to determine the effects of one kind of inner-observer variable, specifically, *expectations* about the stimulus person which the observer brings to the exposure situation.

That prior information or labels attached to a stimulus person make a difference in observers' first impressions is almost too obvious to require demonstration. The expectations resulting from such preinformation may restrict, modify, or accentuate the impressions he will have. The crucial question is: What changes in perception will accompany a given expectation? Studies of stereotyping, for example, that of Katz and Braly (2), indicate that from an ethnic label such as "German" or "Negro," a number of perceptions follow which are culturally determined. *The present study finds its main significance in relation to a study by Asch (1)* which demonstrates that certain crucial labels can transform the entire impression of the person, leading to attributions which are related to the label on a broad cultural basis or even, perhaps, on an autochthonous basis.

Asch read to his subjects a list of adjectives which purportedly described a particular person. He then asked them to characterize that person. He found that the inclusion in the list of what he called *central* qualities; such as "warm" as opposed to "cold," produced a widespread change in the entire impression. This effect was not adequately explained by the halo effect since it did not extend indiscriminately in a positive or negative direction to all characteristics. Rather, it differentially transformed the other qualities, for example, by changing their relative importance in the total impression. Peripheral qualities (such as "polite" versus "blunt") did not produce effects as strong as those produced by the central qualities.[1]

The present study tested the effects of such central qualities upon the early impressions of *real* persons, the same qualities, "warm" vs. "cold," being used. They were introduced as preinformation about the stimulus person before his actual appearance; so presumably they operated as expectations rather than as part of the stimulus pattern during the exposure period. In addition, information was obtained about the effects of the expectations upon the observers' behavior toward the stimulus person. An earlier study in this series has indicated that the more incompatible the observer initially perceived the stimulus person to be, the less the observer initiated interaction with him thereafter. The second purpose of the present experiment, then, was to provide a better controlled study of this relationship.

No previous studies reported in the literature have dealt with the importance of first impressions for behavior. The most relevant data are found in the sociometric literature, where there are scattered studies of the relation between choices among children having some prior acquaintance and their interaction behavior. For an example, see the study by Newstetter, Feldstein, and Newcomb (8).

---

[1] Since the present experiment was carried out, Mensh and Wishner (6) have repeated a number of Asch's experiments because of dissatisfaction with his sex and geographic distribution. Their data substantiate Asch's very closely. Also, Luchins (5) has criticized Asch's experiments for their artificial methodology, repeated some of them, and challenged some of the kinds of interpretations Asch made from his data. Luchins also briefly reports some tantalizing conclusions from a number of studies of first impressions of actual persons.

Procedure

The experiment was performed in three sections of a psychology course (Economics 70) at the Massachusetts Institute of Technology.[2] The three sections provided 23, 16, and 16 subjects respectively. All 55 subjects were men, most of them in their third college year. In each class the stimulus person (also a male) was completely unknown to the subjects before the experimental period. One person served as stimulus person in two sections, and a second person took this role in the third section. In each case the stimulus person was introduced by the experimenter, who posed as a representative of the course instructors and who gave the following statement:

Your regular instructor is out of town today, and since we of Economics 70 are interested in the general problem of how various classes react to different instructors, we're going to have an instructor today you've never had before, Mr.————. Then, at the end of the period, I want you to fill out some forms about him. In order to give you some idea of what he's like, we've had a person who knows him write up a little biographical note about him. I'll pass this out to you now and you can read it before he arrives. *Please read these to yourselves and don't talk about this among yourselves until the class is over so that he won't get wind of what's going on.*

Two kinds of these notes were distributed, the two being identical except that in one the stimulus person was described among other things as being "rather cold" whereas in the other form the phrase "very warm" was substituted. The content of the "rather cold" version is as follows:

Mr.———— is a graduate student in the Department of Economics and Social Science here at M.I.T. He has had three semesters of teaching experience in psychology at another college. This is his first semester teaching Ec. 70. He is 26 years old, a veteran, and married. People who know him consider him to be a rather cold person, industrious, critical, practical, and determined.

The two types of preinformation were distributed randomly within each of the three classes and in such a manner that the students were not aware that two kinds of information were being given

out. The stimulus person then appeared and led the class in a twenty-minute discussion. During this time the experimenter kept a record of how often each student participated in the discussion. Since the discussion was almost totally leader-centered, this participation record indicated the number of times each student initiated verbal interaction with the instructor. After the discussion period, the stimulus person left the room, and the experimenter gave the following instructions:

Now, I'd like to get your impression of Mr. ——. This is not a test of you and can in no way affect your grade in this course. This material will not be identified as belonging to particular persons and will be kept strictly confidential. It will be of most value to us if you are completely honest in your evaluation of Mr. ——. Also, please understand that what you put down will not be used against him or cause him to lose his job or anything like that. This is not a test of him but merely a study of how different classes react to different instructors.

The subjects then wrote free descriptions of the stimulus person and finally rated him on a set of 15 rating scales.

Results and Discussion

1. *Influence of warm-cold variable on first impressions.* The differences in the ratings produced by the warm-cold variable were consistent from one section to another even where different stimulus persons were used. Consequently, the data from the three sections were combined by equating means (the S.D.'s were approximately equal) and the results for the total group are presented in Table 1. Also in this table is presented that part of Asch's data which refers to the qualities included in our rating scales. From this table it is quite clear that those given the "warm" preinformation consistently rated the stimulus person more favorably than do those given the "cold" preinformation. Summarizing the statistically significant differences, the "warm" subjects rated the stimulus person as more considerate of others, more informal, more sociable, more popular, better natured, more humorous, and more humane. These findings are very similar to Asch's for the characteristics common to both studies. He found more frequent attribution to his hypothetical "warm" personalities of sociability, popularity, good naturedness, gen-

---

[2] Professor Mason Haire, now of the University of California, provided valuable advice and help in executing the experiment.

TABLE 4.1. Comparison of "Warm" and "Cold" Observers in Terms of Average Ratings Given Stimulus Persons

Item	Low End of Rating Scale	High End of Rating Scale	Average Rating		Level of Significance of Warm-Cold Difference	Asch's Data: Per Cent of Group Assigning Quality at Low End of Our Rating Scale*	
			Warm N = 27	Cold N = 28		Warm	Cold
1	Knows his stuff	Doesn't know his stuff	3.5	4.6			
2	Considerate of others	Self-centered	6.3	9.6	1%		
3†	Informal	Formal	6.3	9.6	1%		
4†	Modest	Proud	9.4	10.6			
5	Sociable	Unsociable	5.6	10.4	1%	91%	38%
6	Self-assured	Uncertain of himself	8.4	9.1			
7	High intelligence	Low intelligence	4.8	5.1			
8	Popular	Unpopular	4.0	7.4	1%	84%	28%
9†	Good natured	Irritable	9.4	12.0	5%	94%	17%
10	Generous	Ungenerous	8.2	9.6		91%	08%
11	Humorous	Humorless	8.3	11.7	1%	77%	13%
12	Important	Insignificant	6.5	8.6		88%	99%
13†	Humane	Ruthless	8.6	11.0	5%	86%	31%
14†	Submissive	Dominant	13.2	14.5			
15	Will go far	Will not get ahead	4.2	5.8			

*Given for all qualities common to Asch's list and this set of rating scales.
†These scales were reversed when presented to the subjects.

erosity, humorousness, and humaneness. So these data strongly support his finding that such a central quality as "warmth" can greatly influence the total impression of a personality. This effect is found to be operative in the perception of real persons.

This general favorableness in the perceptions of the "warm" observers as compared with the "cold" ones indicates that something like a halo effect may have been operating in these ratings. Although his data are not completely persuasive on this point, Asch was convinced that such a general effect was *not* operating in his study. Closer inspection of the present data makes it clear that the "warm-cold" effect cannot be explained altogether on the basis of simple halo effect. In Table 1 it is evident that the "warm-cold" variable produced differential effects from one rating scale to another. The size of this effect seems to depend upon the closeness of relation between the specific dimension of any given rating scale and the central quality of "warmth" or "coldness." Even though the rating of intelligence may be influenced by a halo effect, it is not influenced to the same degree to which considerateness is. It seems to make sense to view such strongly influenced items as considerateness, informality, good naturedness,

and humaneness as dynamically more closely related to warmth and hence more perceived in terms of this relation than in terms of a general positive or negative feeling toward the stimulus person. If first impressions are normally made in terms of such general dimensions as "warmth" and "coldness," the power they give the observer in making predictions and specific evaluations about such disparate behavior characteristics as formality and considerateness is considerable (even though these predictions may be incorrect or misleading).

The free report impression data were analyzed for only one of the sections. In general, there were few sizable differences between the "warm" and "cold" observers. The "warm" observers attributed more nervousness, more sincerity, and more industriousness to the stimulus person. Although the frequencies of comparable qualities are very low because of the great variety of descriptions produced by the observers, there is considerable agreement with the rating scale data.

Two important phenomena are illustrated in these free description protocols, the first of them having been noted by Asch. *Firstly* the characteristics of the stimulus person are interpreted in terms of the precognition of warmth or coldness. For example, a "warm" observer writes about a rather shy and retiring stimulus person as follows: "He makes friends slowly but they are lasting friendships when formed." In another instance, several "cold" observers describe him as being ". . . intolerant: would be angry if you disagree with his views . . ."; while several "warm" observers put the same thing this way: "Unyielding in principle, not easily influenced or swayed from his original attitude." *Secondly*, the preinformation about the stimulus person's warmth or coldness is evaluated and interpreted in the light of the direct behavioral data about him. For example, "He has a slight inferiority complex which leads to his coldness," and "His conscientiousness and industriousness might be mistaken for coldness." Examples of these two phenomena occurred rather infrequently, and there was no way to evaluate the relative strengths of these countertendencies. Certainly some such evaluation is necessary to determine the conditions under which behavior which is contrary to a stereotyped label resists distortion and leads to rejection of the label.

A comparison of the data from the two different stimulus persons is pertinent to the last point in so far as it indicates the interaction between the properties of the stimulus person and the label. The fact that the warm-cold variable generally produced differences in the same direction for the two stimulus persons, even though they are very different in personality, behavior, and mannerisms, indicates the strength of this variable. However, there were some exceptions to this tendency as well as marked differences in the *degree* to which the experimental variable was able to produce differences. For example, stimulus person A typically appears to be anything but lacking in self-esteem and on rating scale 4 he was generally at the "proud" end of the scale. Although the "warm" observers tended to rate him as they did the other stimulus person (i.e., more "modest"), the difference between the "warm" and "cold" means for stimulus person A is very small and not significant as it is for stimulus person B. Similarly, stimulus person B was seen as "unpopular" and "humorless," which agrees with his typical classroom behavior. Again the "warm" observers rated him more favorably on these items, but their ratings were not significantly different from those of the "cold" observers, as was true for the other stimulus person. Thus we see that the strength or compellingness of various qualities of the stimulus person must be reckoned with. The stimulus is

not passive to the forces arising from the label but actively resists distortion and may severely limit the degree of influence exerted by the pre-information. [3]

2. *Influence of warm-cold variable on interaction with the stimulus person.* In the analysis of the frequency with which the various students took part in the discussion led by the stimulus person, a larger proportion of those given the "warm" preinformation participated than of those given the "cold" preinformation. Fifty-six per cent of the "warm" subjects entered the discussion, whereas only 32 per cent of the "cold" subjects did so. Thus the expectation of warmth not only produced more favorable early perceptions of the stimulus person but led to greater initiation of interaction with him. This relation is a low one, significant at between the 5 per cent and 10 per cent level of confidence, but it is in line with the general principle that social perception serves to guide and steer the person's behavior in his social environment.

As would be expected from the foregoing findings, there was also a relation between the favorableness of the impression and whether or not the person participated in the discussion. Although any single item yielded only a small and insignificant relation to participation, when a number are combined the trend becomes clear cut. For example, when we combine the seven items which were influenced to a statistically significant degree by the warm-cold variable the total score bears considerable relation to participation, the relationship being significant as well beyond the 1 per cent level. A larger proportion of those having favorable total impressions participated than of those having unfavorable impressions, the biserial correlation between these variables being .34. Although this relation may be interpreted in several ways, it seems most likely that the unfavorable perception led to a curtailment of interaction. Support for this comes from one of the other studies in this series (3). There it was found that those persons having

---

[3] We must raise an important question here: Would there be a tendency for "warm" observers to distort the perception in the favorable direction regardless of how much the stimulus deviated from the expectation? Future research should test the following hypothesis, which is suggested by Gestalt perception theory (4, pp. 95-98) : If the stimulus differs but slightly from the expectation, the perception will tend to be *assimilated* to the expectation; however, if the difference between the stimulus and expectation is too great, the perception will occur by contrast to the expectation and will be distorted in the opposite direction.

unfavorable impressions of the instructor at the end of the first class meeting tended less often to initiate interactions with him in the succeeding four meetings than did those having favorable first impressions. There was also some tendency in the same study for those persons who interacted least with the instructor to change least in their judgments of him from the first to later impressions.

It will be noted that these relations lend some support to the autistic hostility hypothesis proposed by Newcomb (7). This hypothesis suggests that the possession of an initially hostile attitude toward a person leads to a restriction of communication and contact with him which in turn serves to preserve the hostile attitude by preventing the acquisition of data which could correct it. The present data indicate that a restriction of interaction is associated with unfavorable preinformation and an unfavorable perception. The data from the other study support this result and also indicate the correctness of the second part of the hypothesis, that restricted interaction reduces the likelihood of change in the attitude.

What makes these findings more significant is that they appear in the context of a discussion class where there are numerous *induced* and *own* forces to enter the discussion and to interact with the instructor. It seems likely that the effects predicted by Newcomb's hypothesis would be much more marked in a setting where such forces were not present.

Summary

The warm-cold variable had been found by Asch to produce large differences in the impressions of personality formed from a list of adjectives. In this study the same variable was introduced in the form of expectations about a real person and was found to produce similar differences in first impressions of him in a classroom setting. In addition, the differences in first impressions produced by the different expectations were shown to influence the observers' behavior toward the stimulus person. Those observers given the favorable expectation (who, consequently, had a favorable impression of the stimulus person) tended to interact more with him than did those given the unfavorable expectation.

ACKNOWLEDGMENT

The writer acknowledges the constructive advice of Professor Dorwin Cartwright, University of Michigan.

REFERENCES

1. ASCH, S. E. Forming impressions of personality. *J. abnorm. soc. Psychol.,* 1946, 41, 258–290.
2. KATZ, D., & BRALY, K. W. Verbal stereotypes and racial prejudice. In Newcomb, T. M. and Hartley, E. L. (eds.), *Readings in social psychology.* New York: Holt, 1947. Pp. 204–210.
3. KELLY, H. H. First impressions in interpersonal relations. Ph.D. thesis, Massachusetts Institute of Technology, Cambridge, Mass. Sept., 1948.
4. KRECH, D., & CRUTCHFIELD, R. S. *Theory and problems of social psychology.* New York: McGraw-Hill, 1948.
5. LUCHINS, A. S. Forming impressions of personality: a critique. *J. abnorm. soc. Psychol.,* 1948, 43, 318–325.
6. MENSH, I. N., & WISHNER, J. Asch on "Forming impressions of personality": further evidence. *J. Personal.,* 1947, 16, 188–191.
7. NEWCOMB, T. M. Autistic hostility and social reality. *Hum. Relations.,* 1947, 1, 69–86.
8. NEWSTETTER, W. I., FELDSTEIN, M. J., & NEWCOMB, T. M. *Group adjustment: a study in experimental sociology.* Cleveland: Western Reserve University, 1938.

The Nonverbal Mediation of Self-Fulfilling Prophecies in Interracial Interaction

Carl O. Word, Mark P. Zanna, and Joel Cooper • Princeton University

Editors' Notes

One of the most intriguing phenomena in social interaction is the self-fulfilling prophecy. Specifically, an expectancy that one person has of another may cause the former to behave toward the latter in ways that elicit from the latter just the behaviors that the former had expected. In this connection, the importance of the present reading selection is twofold. First, it provides a clear experimental demonstration of each phase of the self-fulfilling prophecy process. Second, it ties this phenomenon to the important issue of stereotyping and prejudice. When white American interviewers have negative expectancies about African-Americans, they can act in ways that communicate these negative attitudes nonverbally to African-American interviewees. This, in turn, can elicit less friendly reactions from these interviewees than from white interviewees. This paper shows that such destructive interaction patterns can be demonstrated even in the confines of an experimental laboratory. Given that these forces are much more powerful in the real world, this research has important implications for interracial relations in the workplace and elsewhere. Note the clever experimental ways in which this issue was tackled in the present selection; they illustrate a uniquely social-psychological approach to the study of major social concerns.

Discussion Questions

1. What is the significance of the fact that in experiment 1, the confederate applicants were naïve with respect to the hypotheses? What might have been the interpretative problem had they not been naïve?

2. In experiment 2, all participants were white. In what sense, then, are the authors justified in claiming that their results are relevant to white-black relations in the workplace?

3. What are the psychological mechanisms whereby expectancies produce self-fulfilling prophecies?

Suggested Readings

Downey, G., Freitas, A. L., Michaelis, B., & Khouri, H. (1998). The self-fulfilling prophecy in close relationships: Rejection sensitivity and rejection by romantic partners. *Journal of Personality and Social Psychology, 75,* 545–560.

Jussim, L. (1986). Self-fulfilling prophecies: A theoretical and integrative review. *Psychological Review, 93,* 429–445.

Lord, C. G., Ross, L., & Lepper, M. (1979). Biased assimilation and attitude polarization: The effects of prior theories on subsequently considered evidence. *Journal of Personality and Social Psychology, 37,* 2098–2109.

Snyder, M., Tanke, E. D., & Berscheid, E. (1977). Social perception and interpersonal behavior: On the self-fulfilling nature of social stereotypes. *Journal of Personality and Social Psychology, 35,* 656–666.

Authors' Abstract

Two experiments were designed to demonstrate the existence of a self-fulfilling prophecy mediated by nonverbal behavior in an interracial interaction. The results of Experiment I, which employed naive, white job interviewers and trained white and black job applicants, demonstrated that black applicants received (a) less immediacy, (b) higher rates of speech errors, and (c) shorter amounts of interview time. Experiment 2 employed naive, white applicants and trained white interviewers. In this experiment subject-applicants received behaviors that approximated those given either the black or white applicants in Experiment 1. The main results indicated that subjects treated like the blacks of Experiment 1 were judged to perform less adequately and to be more nervous in the interview situation than subjects treated like the whites. The former subjects also reciprocated with less proximate positions and rated the interviewers as being less adequate and friendly. The implications of these findings for black unemployment were discussed.

S ociologist Robert Merton (1957), by suggesting that an originally false definition of a situation can influence the believer to act in such a way as to bring about that situation, is generally credited with focusing attention on the phenomenon of the self-fulfilling prophecy. The present investigation is concerned with such a phenomenon in face-to-face, dyadic interactions. In this context it is hypothesized that one person's attitudes and expectations about the other person may influence the believer's actions, which in turn, may induce the other person to behave in a way that confirms the original false definition. Interpersonally, this phenomenon has been documented in schools, with teachers' expectations influencing students' performances, and in psychology laboratories, with experimenters' expectations influencing subjects' responses (cf. Rosenthal, 1971).

In the present study attention will be directed toward (1) possible nonverbal mediators of this effect, and (2) the reciprocal performances of the interactants. The focus, in addition, will be on the interaction of black and white Americans with a view toward examining the employment outcomes of black job applicants interviewed by whites.

Attitudes and Immediacy

Mehrabian (1968) has recently reported a series of studies linking attitudes toward a target person and the concomitant nonverbal behavior directed toward that person. The results of these studies have consistently found that closer interpersonal distances, more eye contact, more direct shoulder orientation, and more forward lean are a consequence of more positive attitudes toward an addressee. Mehrabian (1969) has considered such nonverbal behaviors in terms of "immediacy" and has defined immediacy "as the extent to which communication behaviors enhance closeness to and nonverbal interaction with another. Greater immediacy is due to increasing degrees of physical proximity and/or increasing perceptual availability of the communicator to the addressee" (p. 203).

A related series of studies has been conducted by Kleck and his associates (Kleck, 1968; Kleck, Buck, Goller, London, Pfeiffer, & Vukcevic, 1968; Kleck, Ono, & Hastorf, 1966) pursuing Goffman's (1963) observation that normals tend to avoid stigmatized persons. They have begun to document what might be called a nonverbal stigma effect. For example, normal interactants were found to terminate interviews sooner (Kleck et al., 1966) and to exhibit greater motoric inhibition (Kleck, 1968) with a handicapped person (i.e., leg amputee), and to employ greater interaction distances with an epileptic stranger (Kleck et al., 1968). This set of studies, then, also suggests that those persons who possess a personal characteristic which is descrediting in the eyes of others are treated with less immediate behaviors. In addition to such discrediting characteristics as a physical disability or a criminal record, Goffman (1963) includes blackness in a white society as a stigmatizing trait.

Thus, a body of data suggests that (1) attitudes toward an individual are linked with nonverbal behavior emitted toward that individual, and (2) positive attitudes lead to more immediate nonverbal behaviors. Two questions that now arise are concerned with whether such behaviors are (1) decoded or understood by the target and (2) reciprocated.

Decoding and Reciprocating Immediacy

Recent studies suggest that such evaluative, nonverbal behaviors are both decoded and reciprocated. Mehrabian (1967) found friendliness ratings of an interviewer varied as a function of the physical interaction distance, and the immediacy of head and body positions given subjects. Eye

contact has been extensively investigated. Both Kleck and Nuessle (1968) and Jones and Cooper (1971) found that a high degree of eye contact produced higher evaluations of the communicator and produced more positive evaluations on the part of the subjects than did low eye contact.

Since individuals apparently are able to decode affective components of communications from variations in immediacy behavior, it seems reasonable to expect they would reciprocate such variations. This proposition also has received support. Rosenfeld (1967), for example, found that subjects treated to more smiles and positive head nods did reciprocate with more of each.

Thus individuals apparently decode less immediacy as indicating less friendly behavior and reciprocate with less friendly (i.e., less immediate) behavior of their own. Since individuals seldom are able to monitor their own nonverbal behaviors, they are more likely to attribute the reciprocated immediacy, not to their own, original nonverbal behavior, but instead to some disposition inherent in their cointeractant (cf. Jones & Nisbett, 1971). With this nonverbal reciprocation, then, a self-fulfilling prophecy is born.

White–Black Interaction in a Job Interview Setting

So far we have been concerned with describing possible mechanisms of interpersonal, self-fulfilling prophecies. The discussion now turns to consider such a process in black–white, dyadic interactions. It has been demonstrated time and again that white Americans have generalized, negative evaluations (e.g., stereotypes) of black Americans. This has been shown most recently in our own subject population by Darley, Lewis, and Glucksberg (1972). Such negative evaluations, of course, represent the kind of attitudes that can initiate an interpersonal, self-fulfilling prophecy. The general hypothesis that the present study sought to investigate, therefore, was that whites interacting with blacks will emit nonverbal behaviors corresponding to negative evaluations and that blacks, in turn, will reciprocate with less immediate behaviors. If the context in which the interaction occurs involves a job interview, with the white interviewing the black, such reciprocated behavior may be interpreted as less adequate performance, thus confirming, in part, the interviewer's original attitude.

These general expectations are operationalized by two subhypotheses: First, black, as compared to white, job applicants will receive less immediate nonverbal communications from white job interviewers; second, recipients of less immediate nonverbal communications, whether black or white, will reciprocate these communications and be judged to perform less adequately in the job interview situation than recipients of more positive nonverbal communications. The first hypothesis was tested in Experiment 1, which employed naive, white job interviewers and trained white and black job applicants; the second in Experiment 2, which used naive, white job applicants and trained white job interviewers who were instructed to emit either immediate or nonimmediate cues.

Experiment 1

Method

OVERVIEW

In the context of a study on group decision-making white subjects, as representatives of a team in competition with other teams, interviewed both white and black job applicants. The applicants were trained to respond similarly in both the verbal and nonverbal channels. The interview situation itself was arranged to give the subject-interviewers the opportunity to treat their applicants differentially without the knowledge (1) that their own behavior was being monitored, or (2) that race of the applicants was the experimental variable.

SUBJECTS (INTERVIEWERS) AND CONFEDERATES (APPLICANTS AND TEAM MEMBERS)

Subject-interviewers were 15 white, Princeton males recruited to participate in a study of group decision-making conducted by Career Services and the Psychology Department. They were informed that the study would last approximately one hour and a half and that they would be paid $2.00 and possibly $5.00 more. One of the subjects was eliminated when he indicated that he was aware of the purpose of the study before the debriefing period. No other subject volunteered this sort of information after intensive probing, leaving an *n* of 14.

Confederate-applicants were two black and three white high school student volunteers referred by their high school counselor. Each was told that the study was concerned with cognitive functioning and that the experimenter was interested in finding out how subjects made up their minds when forced to choose between nearly identical job applicants. All confederates in both experiments were naive with respect to the hypotheses. Intensive probing following the experiment indicated that they did not become aware. The three confederates who served as the subject's "team members" and the experimenter were male Princeton volunteers.

PROCEDURE

Upon arrival the subjects entered a room containing two confederate team members, who introduced themselves and acted friendly. Another confederate entered and acted friendly, as well. Then the experimenter entered, handed out written instructions and answered any questions.

The instructions informed subjects that the four people in the room constituted a team; that they were to compete with four other teams in planning a marketing campaign; and that they needed to select another member from four high school applicants. In order to increase incentive and concern, an additional $5.00 was promised to the team which performed best in the competition. Using a supposedly random draw, the subject was chosen to interview the applicants. He was then handed a list of 15 questions which was to serve as the interview material, told he had 45 minutes to interview all four high school students and taken to the interview room where the first confederate-applicant was already seated.

In order to measure the physical distance that the interviewer placed himself from the applicant, the experimenter upon entering the interview room, feigned to discover that there was no chair for the interviewer. Subjects were then asked to wheel in a chair from an adjoining room.

Subjects were led to believe that there would be four interviews so that the race variable would be less apparent to them. In addition, to eliminate any special effect that might occur in the first and last interview, an a priori decision was made not to analyze the data from the first "warm-up" interview and not to have a fourth interview. The "warm-up" job candidate was always white. Half the subjects then interviewed a black followed by a white applicant; the other half interviewed a white then a black candidate. After completion of the third interview, subjects were told that the fourth applicant had called to cancel his appointment. After the third interview, subjects were paid and debriefed.

APPLICANT PERFORMANCE

Confederate-applicants were trained to act in a standard way to all interviewers. First, they devised answers to the 15 questions such that their answers, though not identical, would represent equally qualifying answers. Confederates then rehearsed these answers until two judges rated their performances to be equal. Confederates were also trained to seat themselves, shoulders parallel to the backs of their chairs (10° from vertical) and to make eye contact with the interviewer 50% of the time. A code was devised to signal confederates during their interviews if they deviated from the pose or began to reciprocate the gestures or head nods given them.

DEPENDENT MEASURES

Immediacy behaviors. Following Mehrabian (1968, 1969), four indices of psychological immediacy were assessed: (1) Physical Distance between interviewer and interviewee, measured in inches; (2) Forward Lean, scored in 10° units, with zero representing the vertical position and positives scores representing the torso leaning toward the confederate; (3) Eye Contact, defined as the proportion of time the subject looked directly at the confederate's eyes; and (4) Shoulder Orientation, scored in units of 10° with zero representing the subject's shoulders parallel to those of the confederate and positive scores indicating a shift in either direction. Two judges,[1] placed behind one-way mirrors, scored the immediacy behaviors.

More distance and shoulder angle represent less immediate behaviors while more foreward lean and more eye contact represent more immediate behaviors. An index of total immediacy was constructed by summing the four measures, standardized, and weighted according to the regression equation beta weights established by Mehrabian (1969). Final scores of this index represent (-.6) distance + (.3) forward lean + (.3) eye contact + (-.1) shoulder orientation. Positive scores represent more immediate performances.

Related Behaviors. Two related behaviors, which indicate differential evaluations of the applicants (cf. Mehrabian, 1969), were also assessed: (1) Interview length indicates the amount of time from the point the subject entered the interview room until he announced the interview was over, in minutes. This measure was taken by the experimenter. (2) Speech Error Rate, scored by two additional judges from audiotapes, represents the sum of (a) sentence changes, (b) repetitions, (c) stutters, (d) sentence incompletions, and (e) intruding, incoherent sounds divided by the length of the interview and averaged over the two judges. Higher scores represent more speech errors per minute.

Results

Reliabilities and Order Effects

Reliabilities, obtained by correlating the judges' ratings, ranged from .60 to .90 (see Table 1). Preliminary analyses also indicated that there were no effects for the order in which confederate-applicants appeared, so that the results are based on data collapsed across this variable.

Immediacy Behaviors

The results, presented in Table 1, indicate that, overall, black job candidates received less immediate behaviors than white applicants ($t = 2.79$; $df = 13$; $p < .02$). On the average, blacks received a negative total immediacy score; whites received a positive one. This overall difference is primarily due to the fact that the white interviewers physically placed themselves further from black than white applicants ($t = 2.36$; $df = 13$; $p < .05$). None of the other indices of immediacy showed reliable differences when considered separately.

Related Behaviors

The results for interview length and speech error rate are also presented in Table 1. Here it can be seen that blacks also received less immediate be-

---

[1]All judges employed in the present research were Princeton undergraduates. Each worked independently and was naive concerning the hypothesis under investigation. Intensive probing indicated that they did not become aware of the hypothesis.

TABLE 5.1. Mean Interviewer Behavior as a Function of Race of Job Applicant: Experiment 1

Behavior	Reliability	Blacks	Whites	t^b	p
Total immediacy[a]	—	−.11	.38	2.79	<.02
Distance	.90	62.29 inches	58.43 inches	2.36	<.05
Forward lean	.68	−8.76 degrees	−6.12 degrees	1.09	n.s.
Eye contact	.80	62.71%	61.46%	<1	n.s.
Shoulder orientation	.60	22.46 degrees	23.08 degrees	<1	n.s.
Related behaviors					
Interview length	—	9.42 min.	12.77 min.	3.22	<.01
Speech error rate	.88	3.54 errors/min.	2.37 errors/min.	2.43	<.05

[a]See text for weighting formula, from Mehrabian (1969).
[b]t test for correlated samples was employed.

haviors. White interviewers spent 25% less time ($t = 3.22$; $df = 13$; $p <.01$) and had higher rates of speech errors ($t = 2.43$; $df = 13$; $p <.05$) with black as compared to white job candidates.

The results of the first experiment provide support for the hypothesis that black, as compared to white, job applicants receive less immediate nonverbal communications from white job interviewers. Indirectly the results also provide support for the conceptualization of blackness as a stigmatizing trait. The differences in time (evidenced by 12 of 14 interviewers), in total immediacy (evidenced by 10 of 14 interviewers), and in speech error rate (evidenced by 11 of 14 interviewers) argues for an extension of the stigma effect obtained by Kleck and his associates to include black Americans.

Experiment 2

Method

OVERVIEW

A second experiment was conducted to ascertain what effect the differences black and white applicants received in Experiment 1 would have on an applicant's job interview performance. In the context of training job interviewers, subject-applicants were interviewed by confederate-interviewers under one of two conditions. In the Immediate condition, as compared to the Nonimmediate condition, interviewers (1) sat closer to the applicant, (2) made fewer speech errors per minute, and (3) actually took longer to give their interviews. The main dependent measures were concerned with the interview performance of the applicant, both in terms of its judged adequacy for obtaining the job and in terms of its reciprocation of immediacy behaviors.

SUBJECTS (JOB APPLICANTS) AND CONFEDERATES (INTERVIEWERS)

Thirty white male Princeton University students were recruited ostensibly to help Career Services train interviewers for an upcoming summer job operation. No subjects were eliminated from the study, leaving an n of 15 in each condition. The two confederate-interviewers were also white male Princeton students.

PROCEDURE

Upon arrival each subject was given an instruction sheet which informed him that Career Services had contracted with the Psychology Department to train Princeton juniors and seniors in the techniques of job interviewing and that one of the techniques chosen included videotaping interviewers with job applicants for feedback purposes. The subject was then asked to simulate a job applicant, to be honest, and to really compete for the job, so as to give the interviewer real, lifelike practice. To make the simulation more meaningful, subjects were also informed that the applicant chosen from five interviewed that evening would receive an additional $1.50.

Subjects were taken to the interview room and asked to be seated in a large swivel chair, while the Experimenter turned on the camera. The confederate-interviewer then entered, and assumed either an immediate or nonimmediate position which will be described in more detail below. Exactly five minutes into the interviewing in both conditions, a guise was developed whose result was that the experimenter had to reclaim the chair in which the subject was sitting. The subject was then asked to take a folding chair leaning against the wall and to continue the interview. The distance from the interviewer which the subject placed his new chair was one of the study's dependent measures designed to assess reciprocated immediacy.

When the interview ended, the experimenter took the subject to another room where a second investigator, blind as to the condition of the subject, administered self-report scales and answered any questions. Subject was then paid and debriefed.

IMMEDIACY MANIPULATION

As in the Kleck and Nuessle (1968) and the Jones and Cooper (1971) studies, systematic nonverbal variations were introduced by specifically training confederates. Two confederate-interviewers alternated in the two conditions. In the Immediate condition, confederates sat at a chair on the side of a table. In the Nonimmediate condition, confederates sat fully behind the table. The difference in distance from the subject's chair was about four inches, representing the mean difference in distance white interviewers gave black and white interviewers gave black and white applicants in Experiment 1.[2]

In addition, the confederate-interviewers in the Immediate condition were trained to behave as precisely as possible like the subject-interviewers in Experiment 1 had acted toward white applicants. In the Nonimmediate condition, interviewers were trained to act as subject-interviewers had acted toward blacks in Experiment 1. The factors used to simulate the immediacy behaviors found in the first experiment were speech error rate, length of interview and, as has been previously mentioned, physical distance. Eye contact, shoulder orientation and forward lean did not show significant differences in Experiment 1 and thus were held constant in Experiment 2 (with levels set at 50% eye contact, 0° shoulder orientation and 20° forward lean).

DEPENDENT MEASURES

Three classes of dependent variables were collected: (1) judges' ratings of interview performance; (2) judges' ratings of reciprocated immediacy behaviors; and (3) subjects' ratings of their post-interview mood state and attitudes toward the interviewer.

Applicant performance. Applicant interview performance and demeanor were rated by a panel of two judges from videotapes of the interviews.

The videotapes were recorded at such an angle that judges viewed only the applicant, not the confederate-interviewer. The judges were merely instructed about the type of job subjects were applying for, and were asked to rate (1) the overall adequacy of each subject's performance and (2) each subject's composure on five (0–4) point scales. High scores, averaged over the judges, represent more adequate and more calm, relaxed performances, respectively.

Reciprocated immediacy behaviors. Two additional judges, placed behind one-way mirrors as in Experiment 1, recorded subjects' forward lean, eye contact, and shoulder orientation in accordance with the procedures established by Mehrabian (1969). Distance was directly measured after each interview, and represents the distance, in inches, from the middle of the interviewer-confederate's chair to the middle of the subject's chair, after the interruption. Speech errors were scored by another panel of two judges from audiotapes of the interviews, also according to Mehrabian's (1969) procedures. High scores represent more speech errors per minute.

Applicant mood and attitude toward the interviewer. After the interview, subjects filled out a series of questionnaires designed to assess their mood state and their attitudes toward the interviewer. Following Jones and Cooper (1971), subjects' moods were expected to vary as a function of immediacy conditions. The mood scale adapted from that study was employed. It consisted of six polar adjectives (e.g., happy–sad) separated by seven-point scales. Subjects were asked to respond to each pair according to "the way you feel about yourself."

Two measures of subjects' attitudes toward the interviewer were collected. First, subjects were asked to rate the friendliness of the interviewer on an 11-point scale, with zero representing an "unfriendly" and 10 representing a "friendly" interviewer, respectively. Second, in order to asses subjects' attitudes concerning the adequacy of the interviewer as an individual, they were asked to check the six adjectives best describing their interviewer from a list of 16 drawn from Gough's Adjective Checklist. Final scores represent the

---

[2]By having the interviewer sit either behind or at the side of the table, the impact of the four inch difference in distance was intentionally maximized in terms of psychological immediacy.

TABLE 5.2. Mean Applicant Responses Under Two Conditions of Interviewer Immediacy: Experiment 2

Response	Reliability	Nonimmediate	Immediate	F	P
Applicant performance					
Rated performance	.66	1.44	2.22	7.96	<.01
Rated demeanor	.86	1.62	3.02	16.46	<.001
Immediacy behaviors					
Distance	—	72.73 inches	56.93 inches	9.19	<.01
Speech error rate	.74	5.01 errors/min.	3.33 errors/min.		
Self reported mood and attitudes					
Mood	—	3.77	5.97	1.34	n.s.
Interviewer friendliness	—	4.33	6.60	22.91	<.001
Interviewer adequacy	—	−1.07	1.53	8.64	<.01

number of positive adjectives chosen minus the number of negative adjectives checked.

Results

Reliabilities and Interviewer Effects

Reliabilities, obtained by correlating judges' ratings, ranged from .66 to .86 (see Table 2). Preliminary analyses also indicated that there were no effects for interviewers, so that the results presented are based on data collapsed across this variable.

Applicant Performance

It was predicted from an analysis of the communicative functions of nonimmediacy that applicants would be adversely affected by the receipt of nonimmediate communications. Those effects were expected to manifest themselves in less adequate job-interview performances.

Subjects in the two conditions were rated by two judges from videotapes. The main dependent measure, applicant adequacy for the job, showed striking differences as a function of immediacy conditions (see Table 2). Subjects in the Nonimmediate condition were judged significantly less adequate for the job ($F = 7.96; df = 1/28; p <.01$). Subjects in the Nonimmediate condition were also judged to be reliably less calm and composed ($F = 16.96; df = 1/28; p <.001$).

Reciprocated Immediacy Behaviors

Following Rosenfeld (1967) among others, it was expected that subjects encountering less immediate communications would reciprocate with less immediate behaviors of their own. This expectation was supported by both the measures of physical distance and speech error rate (see Table 2).

Subjects in the Immediate condition, on the average, placed their chairs eight inches closer to the interviewer after their initial chair was removed; subjects in the Nonimmediate conditions placed their chairs four inches further away from their interviewer. The mean difference between the two groups was highly significant ($F = 9.19; df = 1/28; p <.01$).

As in Experiment 1 mean comparisons for the forward lean, eye contact, and shoulder orientation measures of immediacy did not reach significance. The combination of these measures, using the weighting formula devised by Mehrabian (1969), however, was reliably different (means of −.29 and .29 in the Nonimmediate and Immediate conditions, respectively; $F = 5.44; df = 1/28; p < .05$).

The rate at which subjects made speech errors also tended to be reciprocated with subjects in the Nonimmediate condition exhibiting a higher rate than subjects in the Immediate condition ($F = 3.40; df = 1/28; p < .10$).

Applicant Mood and Attitude Toward the Interviewer

It was expected that subjects receiving less immediate (i.e., less positive) communication would (1) feel less positively after their interviews, and (2) hold less positive attitudes toward the interviewer himself. These expectations were only partially supported (see Table 2). Although subjects in the Nonimmediate condition reported less positive moods than subjects in the Immediate condition, this difference was not statistically reliable.

Subjects in the less immediate condition did, however, rate their interviewers to be less friendly ($F = 22.91$; $df = 1/28$; $p <.001$) and less adequate overall ($F = 8.64$; $df = 1/28$; $p <.01$) than subjects in the more immediate condition.

Discussion

Results from the two experiments provide clear support for the two subhypotheses, and offer inferential evidence for the general notion that self-fulfilling prophecies can and do occur in interracial interaction.

The results of Experiment 1 indicated that black applicants were, in fact treated to less immediacy than their white counterparts. Goffman's (1963) conception of blackness as a stigmatizing trait in Anglo-American society is, thus, given experimental support—insofar as that classification predicts avoidance behaviors in interactions with normals. These results may also be viewed as extending the stigma effect documented by Kleck and his associates with handicapped persons.

That the differential treatment black and white applicants received in Experiment 1 can influence the performance and attitudes of job candidates was clearly demonstrated in Experiment 2. In that experiment those applicants, treated similarly to the way blacks were treated in Experiment 1, performed less well, reciprocated less immediacy, and found their interviewers to be less adequate. Taken together the two experiments provide evidence for the assertion that nonverbal, immediacy cues mediate, in part, the performance of an applicant in a job-interview situation. Further, the experiments suggest that the model of a self-fulfilling prophecy, mediated by nonverbal cues, (1) is applicable to this setting, and (2) can account, in part, for the less adequate performances of black applicants (cf. Sattler, 1970).

Social scientists have often tended to focus their attention for such phenomena as unemployment in black communities on the dispositions of the disinherited. Such an approach has been termed "victim analysis" for its preoccupation with the wounds, defects and personalities of the victimized as an explanation for social problems (Ryan, 1971). The present results suggest that analyses of black-white interactions, particularly the area of job-seeking blacks in white society, might profit if it we assumed that the "problem" of black performance resides not entire within the black, but rather within the interaction setting itself.

ACKNOWLEDGMENTS

This research was supported by N.I.H. Biomedical Research Grants #5 S05 FR07057-04 and #5 S05 RR07057-07.

REFERENCES

Darley, J. M., Lewis, L. D., & Glucksberg, S. Stereotype persistence and change among college students: one more time. Unpublished Manuscript, Princeton University, 1972.

Goffman, E. *Stigma: notes on the management of spoiled identity.* Englewood Cliffs, New Jersey: Prentice–Hall, 1963.

Jones, R. E., & Cooper, J. Mediation of experimenter effects. *Journal of Personal and Social Psychology*, 1971, *20*, 70–74.

Jones, E. E., & Nisbett, R. E. The actor and the observer: divergent perceptions the causes of behavior. In E. E. Jones, D. E. Kanouse, H. H. Kelley, R. E. Nesbett, S. Valins and B. Weiner (Eds.), *Attribution: perceiving the causes behavior.* New York: General Learning Press, 1971.

Kleck, R. E. Physical stigma and nonverbal cues emitted in face-to-face interaction *Human Relations*, 1968, *21*, 19–28.

Kleck, R., Buck, P. L., Goller, W. L., London, R. S., Pfeiffer, J. R., & Vukcevic, D. P. Effects of stigmatizing conditions on the use of personal space. *Psychological Reports*, 1968, *23*, 111–118.

Kleck, R. E., & Nuessle, W. Congruence between indicative and communicative functions of eye contact in interpersonal relations. *British Journal of Social and Clinical Psychology*, 1968, *7*, 241–246.

Kleck, R. E., Ono, H., & Hastorf, A. H. The effects of physical deviance upon face-to-face interaction. *Human Relations*, 1966, *19*, 425–436.

Mehrabian, A. Orientation behaviors and nonverbal attitude communication. *Journal of Communication*, 1967, *17*, 324–332.

Mehrabian, A. Inference of attitudes from the posture, orientation, and distance of a communicator. *Journal of Consulting and Clinical Psychology*, 1968, *32*, 296–308.

Mehrabian, A. Some referents and measures of nonverbal behavior. *Behavior Research Methods and Instrumentation*, 1969, *1*, 203–207.

Merton, R. K. *Social theory and social structure.* New York: Free Press, 1957.

Rosenfeld, H. M. Nonverbal reciprocation of approval: an experimental analysis. *Journal of Experimental and Social Psychology*, 1967, *3*, 102–111.

Rosenthal, R. Teacher expectations. In G. S. Lesser (Ed.), *Psychology and the educational process.* Glenview, Illinois: Scott, Foresman, 1971.

Ryan, W. *Blaming the victim.* New York: Pantheon, 1971.

Sattler, J. Racial "experimenter effects" in experimentation, testing, interviewing and psychotherapy. *Psychological Bulletin*, 1970, *73*, 136–160.

Hypothesis-Testing Processes in Social Interaction

Mark Snyder and William B. Swann, Jr. • University of Minnesota

Editors' Notes

Whereas the previous selection addressed the case in which participants in an interaction were assumed to possess clear expectations about their interaction partners, the present selection addresses the case in which individuals form their expectancies from scratch by testing hypotheses about their partner's properties during the course of the interaction. Snyder and Swann propose that this hypothesis-testing process is not exactly objective and unbiased. Rather, once individuals have formulated a hypothesis, they tend to ask questions in ways that are likely to yield answers which confirm the hypothesis. The kinds of questions asked tend to prompt the individuals questioned to provide hypothesis-confirming answers. Thus, it is possible that the self-fulfilling phenomenon begins even before a strong expectancy is formulated. Instead, it may begin already with the hypothesis-testing process itself; that is, in circumstances where individuals feel that they are quite impartial and objective about their information seeking.

Discussion Questions

1. What are the stages of the hypothesis-testing process identified by Snyder and Swann?
2. Why might participants in the Snyder and Swann studies be reluctant to abandon their hypothesis-confirming strategy, even if they believed their hypothesis was incorrect or even when given a monetary incentive to be accurate?
3. What are the implications of a hypothesis-confirming process for social interaction in general and stereotyping in particular?
4. Do people always follow a hypothesis-confirming process? When might they follow a more objective process?

Suggested Readings

Klayman, J., & Ha, Y. W. (1987). Confirmation, disconfirmation, and information in hypothesis testing. *Psychological Review, 94,* 211–228.

Kruglanski, A. W., & Mayseless, O. (1988). Contextual effects in hypothesis testing: The role of competing hypotheses and epistemic motivations. *Social Cognition, 6,* 1–20.

Trope, Y., & Thompson, E. P. (1997). Looking for truth in all the wrong places? Asymmetric search of individuating information about stereotyped group members. *Journal of Personality and Social Psychology, 79,* 229–241.

Authors' Abstract

This research is concerned with the processes by which individuals use social interaction to actively test hypotheses about other people. In four separate empirical investigations, female participants were provided with hypotheses about the personal attributes of other individuals ("targets"). Participants then prepared to test these hypotheses (i.e., that their targets were extraverts or that their targets were introverts) by choosing a series of questions to ask their targets in a forthcoming interview. In each investigation, participants planned to test these hypotheses by preferentially searching for behavioral evidence that would confirm these hypotheses. Moreover, these search procedures channeled social interaction between participants and targets in ways that caused the targets to provide actual behavioral confirmation for the participants' hypotheses. A theoretical analysis of the psychological processes believed to underlie and generate both the preferential search for hypothesis-confirming behavioral evidence and the interpersonal consequences of hypothesis-testing activities is presented.

In the course of social relationships, individuals often attempt to make judgments about the personal attributes of other people. At times, this quest for knowledge may involve the testing of hypotheses about other people. When we form our early impressions of new acquaintances, we may wish to test hypotheses based upon our expectations about their personal dispositions (Is this new acquaintance as friendly as a mutual friend has led me to believe? Is that new acquaintance as boring as every other graduate of the same college?). When we question the accuracy of existing beliefs about friends, we may wish to test hypotheses based on alternate interpretations of their natures (Is this friend whom I have always liked really as mean-tempered as everyone now tells me? Is that friend's unexpected change in behavior a sign of a corresponding change in character?). In these and other circumstances in which we form hypotheses about other people, we may use our subsequent social interactions as opportunities to collect behavioral evidence with which to test these hypotheses.

Having formed a hypothesis about another person, how might an individual use social interaction to actually test that hypothesis? Consider the case of an individual who wishes to test the hypothesis that another person is friendly and sociable. In conversation, the individual might ask that person a series of questions designed to determine whether or not that person's actual behavior and life experiences match those of a characteristically sociable and outgoing person. In choosing these questions, the individual may adopt one of at least three hypothesis-testing strategies. In one strategy, the individual might preferentially search for behavioral evidence that would tend to confirm the hypothesis under scrutiny. Thus, the individual might devote most of the conversation to probing for instances of sociable and outgoing behavior. For example, the individual might ask about those times when the person went to parties, those times when the person sought out new friends, and so forth. In another strategy, the individual might preferentially search for evidence that would disconfirm the hypothesis. Thus, the individual might devote most of the conversation to probing for instances of shy and retiring behavior. For example, the individual might ask about those times when the person wanted to spend time alone or those times when the person avoided meeting new people. In a third strategy, the individual might search for hypothesis-confirming and hypothesis-disconfirming evidence with equal diligence. Thus, the individual might devote equal amounts of the conversation to probing for instances of friendly–sociable and shy retiring behaviors.

What strategies do individuals actually formulate to test hypotheses about other individuals with whom they interact? Do individuals systematically adopt "confirmatory" strategies and preferentially search for evidence that would confirm their beliefs? Or, do individuals systematically adopt "disconfirmatory" strategies and preferentially search for evidence that would disconfirm their beliefs? Or, do individuals adopt "equal opportunity" strategies and search for confirming and disconfirming behavioral evidence with equal diligence? We have sought answers to these questions in our empirical investigations of hypothesis-testing processes.

Investigation 1: Formulation of Strategies for Hypothesis Testing

The initial investigation examined strategies that individuals formulate to test hypotheses about others with whom they anticipate social interaction. Each participant received a hypothesis about another individual (the target) and then prepared to test the hypothesis by planning a series of questions to ask the target. Some participants attempted to assess how extraverted the target was; other participants attempted to assess how introverted the target was. Each participant also received information designed to influence estimates of the likelihood that the hypothesis would prove to be accurate or inaccurate. We included this factor because hypotheses vary in the likelihood that they will prove true; accordingly, we wanted to assess

the impact of this factor on hypothesis-testing strategies.

Method

Participants

Participants in these investigations were female undergraduates at the University of Minnesota who received extra credit in their introductory psychology course. The use of participants of one sex was essentially one of convenience; when this research was initiated, there was a substantially greater availability of female participants than male participants. Fifty-eight women participated individually in the first investigation.

Procedure

The experimenter informed participants that they were in an investigation of how people come to understand each other. The experimenter explained that one way to learn about other people is to ask them questions about their likes and dislikes, their favorite activities, their life experiences, and their feelings about themselves. Each participant would attempt to find out about another person (supposedly waiting in another room) by asking questions designed to determine whether that person was the type whose personality was outlined on a card provided by the experimenter. These personality profiles provided the participants with hypotheses about the other individual.

The hypotheses. Participants randomly assigned to the *extravert hypothesis* conditions were instructed to assess the extent to which the target's behavior and experiences matched those of a prototypic extravert. According to the personality profile:

> Extraverts are typically outgoing, sociable, energetic, confident, talkative, and enthusiastic. Generally confident and relaxed in social situations, this type of person rarely has trouble making conversation with others. This type of person makes friends quickly and easily and is usually able to make a favorable impression on others. This type of person is usually seen by others as characteristically warm and friendly.

Participants randomly assigned to the *introvert hypothesis* conditions were instructed to determine the extent to which the target's behavior and experiences matched those of a prototypic introvert. According to the personality profile:

> Introverts are typically shy, timid, reserved, quiet, distant, and retiring. Usually this type of person would prefer to be alone reading a book or have a long serious discussion with a close friend rather than to go to a loud party or other large social gathering. Often this type of person seems awkward and ill at ease in social situations, and consequently is not adept in making good first impressions. This type of person is usually seen by others as characteristically cool and aloof.

Certainty of the hypothesis. The experimenter also provided participants with information about the (supposed) origins of the profile. Participants assigned randomly to the *high certainty* conditions learned that "the personality profile is a summary of the results of a personality test the other person took last week. Thus, according to the test results, the person whom you will interview is an extravert/introvert." The intent here was to give the hypothesis some credibility by having it "emerge" from the target's own actions. Moreover, pretesting had indicated that undergraduates at the University of Minnesota have considerable faith in the validity of personality assessment procedures.

The intent in the *low certainty* conditions was to make clear that the hypothesis had no connection to any actions of the target. These participants learned that "the personality profile is a description of a type of person familiar to us all—the extravert/introvert. You are to find out how well this profile describes the person you interview." They were given no reasons to believe that the hypothesis was either true or false. Their task simply was to discover whether their target was the type of person described in the personality profile.

Formulating a hypothesis-testing strategy. The experimenter then explained that the profile (the hypothesis) dealt in abstract generalities and global characteristics. However, getting to know someone involves finding out concrete information and specific facts about what that person actually thinks, feels, and does. Accordingly, the participant would choose 12 questions that would help find out whether the target's specific beliefs, attitudes, and actions in life situations matched the general characteristics described in the profile.

The experimenter then provided participants with a list of 26 "Topic Areas Often Covered by Interviewers" from which to choose their 12 questions. The questions on the topic sheet inquired about a wide range of beliefs, feelings, and actions within the domains of personal experience and interpersonal relationships. Nine undergraduate rater-judges had previously classified these questions into three categories.

1. *Extraverted questions.* These 11 questions were ones that the majority of the rater-judges thought would typically be asked of people *already known* to be extraverts, for example, "What would you do if you wanted to liven things up at a party?" "What kind of situations do you seek out if you want to meet new people?" "In what situations are you most talkative? What is it about these situations that makes you like to talk?"
2. *Introverted questions.* According to the majority of the rater-judges, these 10 questions would characteristically be asked of individuals *already known* to be introverts, for example, "In what situations do you wish you could be more outgoing?" "What factors make it hard for you to really open up to people?" "What things do you dislike about loud parties?"
3. *Neutral questions.* The 5 questions for which there was no consensus that they were extraverted questions or introverted questions and those classified by the majority of the rater-judges as irrelevant to introversion and extraversion were classified as neutral questions, for example, "What kinds of charities do you like to contribute to?" "What are your career goals?" "What do you think the good and bad points of acting friendly and open are?"

Participants selected the 12 questions that they estimated would provide them with the information to best test the hypothesis about the target. The experimenter then informed each participant that the interview would not actually take place and thoroughly debriefed each participant.

Results

What strategies did participants formulate to test hypotheses about targets with whom they anticipated social interaction? Did they plan to preferentially search for evidence that would confirm the hypothesis? Did they plan to preferentially

TABLE 6.1. Formulating Strategies for Hypothesis Testing

Type of question	Investigation 1				Investigation 2		Investigations 1 & 2 comparison means		Investigation 3		Investigation 4	
	Extravert hypothesis		Introvert hypothesis		Extravert hypothesis (n = 20 dyads)	Introvert hypothesis (n = 20 dyads)	Extravert hypothesis	Introvert hypothesis	Many extraverts (n = 15)	Few extraverts (n = 15)	$25 extravert hypothesis (n = 15)	$25 extravert hypothesis (n = 15)
	High certainty (n = 14)	Low certainty (n = 15)	High certainty (n = 14)	Low certainty (n = 15)								
Extraverted[a]												
M	6.93	7.67	4.64	4.33	7.25	4.80	7.43	4.60	6.93	6.07	7.20	5.07
SD	2.05	1.72	1.69	1.95	2.24	1.73	2.01	1.81	1.33	1.28	2.14	1.67
Introverted[b]												
M	2.43	2.47	5.57	5.60	2.80	5.90	2.66	5.77	3.00	3.87	2.93	4.93
SD	2.17	1.99	1.87	2.16	2.31	1.62	2.15	1.85	1.77	1.30	2.25	1.87
Neutral[c]												
M	2.64	1.87	1.78	2.07	1.95	1.30	1.91	1.63	2.07	2.07	1.87	2.00
SD	.84	1.18	.80	1.03	.89	1.08	1.01	1.11	.80	1.03	.91	.92

[a] Range = 0–11. Higher means indicate greater numbers of extraverted questions (as identified by the rater-judges) chosen for purposes of hypothesis testing.
[b] Range = 0–10. Higher means indicate greater numbers of introverted questions (as identified by the rater-judges) chosen for purposes of hypothesis testing.
[c] Range = 0–5. Higher means indicate greater numbers of neutral questions (as identified by the rater-judges) chosen for purposes of hypothesis testing.

search for evidence that would disconfirm the hypothesis? Or were there no systematic preferences in the participants' strategies?

To answer these questions, we examined the numbers of extraverted, introverted, and neutral questions (for means, see Table 1) that participants planned to ask their targets. A 2 (extravert hypothesis–introvert hypothesis) × 2 (high certainty–low certainty) multivariate analysis of variance (Overall & Klett, 1972) yielded a highly reliable main effect of the manipulation of the participants' hypotheses, multivariate $F(3, 52) = 11.5, p < .00001$. However, choice of questions was not noticeably affected by the certainty of the hypothesis, multivariate $F(3, 52) < 1$, nor was there any interaction between the hypothesis and certainty factors, multivariate $F(3, 52) = 1.63$, *ns*.

To specify the nature of the main effect of the participants' hypotheses on their choices of questions, we examined the outcomes of univariate analyses of variance. Participants planned to ask extraverted questions more frequently when preparing to test the hypothesis that their targets were extraverted individuals than when preparing to test the hypothesis that their targets were introverted individuals, $F(1, 54) = 33.04, p < .001$. Similarly, participants chose to ask introverted questions more frequently when planning to test the hypothesis that their targets were introverts than when preparing to test the hypothesis that targets were extraverts, $F (1, 54) = 33.75, p < .001$. Finally, participants chose neutral questions with equal frequency whether they were testing the extravert or the introvert hypothesis, $F (1, 54) = 1.44$, *ns*.

Discussion

The initial investigation provided evidence that individuals will systematically formulate confirmatory strategies for testing hypotheses about other people. To test the hypothesis that their targets were extraverts, participants were particularly likely to choose to ask those questions that one typically asks of people already known to be extraverts. Similarly, to test the hypothesis that their targets were introverts, participants were particularly likely to choose to ask those questions that one typically asks of people already known to be introverts. Moreover, participants were as likely to plan to search preferentially for evidence that would confirm the hypothesis when they had no

reason to believe that the hypothesis was true as when they had some reason to anticipate that the hypothesis was true.

Investigation 2: Consequences of Confirmatory Hypothesis Testing

Of what consequence is the preferential search for confirming evidence? What would happen if we allowed participants to actually interview their targets and "collect the data" that their hypothesis-testing activities would provide them? Would these evidence-gathering procedures generate behaviors that would confirm the hypotheses? Would targets who are being "tested" for extraversion actually come to behave in relatively sociable and outgoing fashion and targets who are being "tested" for introversion actually come to behave in relatively shy and reserved fashion? After all, the more often one inquires about another's person's extraversion, the more opportunities that person will have to provide instances of extraverted behaviors. Similarly, the more often one inquires about another person's introversion, the more often that person will have opportunities to provide instances of introverted behaviors. That is, a confirmatory hypothesis-testing strategy may constrain interaction in ways that cause the target to provide actual *behavioral confirmation* for the hypothesis being tested. In the second experimental investigation, participants first formulated their hypothesis-testing strategies and then carried out these strategies by actually interviewing their targets.

Method

Participants

Participants ($N = 80$) were scheduled in pairs of previously unacquainted individuals who were instructed to arrive at separate experimental rooms located on different corridors. Each participant was assigned randomly to one of two "roles," interviewer or target.

Procedure

The procedure was identical to that of the initial investigation except that participants assigned to the interviewer role actually interviewed participants assigned to the target role. Half of the interviewer participants ($n = 20$) were instructed to assess the extent to which their target's behavior and experiences matched those of a prototypic extravert. The other half of the interviewer-participants ($n = 20$) were instructed to assess the extent to which their target's behavior and experiences matched those of a prototypic introvert. The instructions to interviewer-participants in the extravert hypothesis and introvert hypothesis conditions were identical to those of the initial investigation. As in the low certainty conditions of the initial investigation, interviewer-participants were given no reasons to anticipate that the hypothesis would prove accurate or inaccurate. Interviewer-participants were simply instructed to assess the extent to which their targets were like a familiar, but hypothetical, type of person.

While interviewer-participants were choosing their questions from the topic sheet, the experimenter informed participants assigned to the role of target that they would be interviewed by another student. Targets were simply instructed to answer all the questions in as informative, open, and candid a manner as possible.

Each dyad then participated in an interview in which the interviewer-participant asked 12 questions and the target-participant answered these 12 questions. Interviews were conducted by means of microphones and headphones connected through a Sony TC-570 stereophonic tape recorder. Each participant's voice was recorded on a separate channel of the tape. The experimenter then thoroughly debriefed the participants.

To assess the extent to which the answers of the target-participants provided behavioral confirmation for the attributes of the interviewer-participants' hypotheses, six male and six female judges listened to tape recordings of the interviews. These listener-judges were unaware of the purpose of this investigation and knew nothing of the hypotheses being tested by the interviewer-participants. They heard only the track of the tape containing the target-participants' voices. Specifically, they listened to two segments of each interview: the target-participant's answers to three questions from the beginning of the interview and the target-participant's answers to three questions from the end of the interview. Listener-judges then rated each target-participant on 10 6-point bipolar scales: talkative–quiet; unsociable–sociable; friendly–

unfriendly; poised–awkward; introverted–extraverted; enthusiastic–apathetic; shy–outgoing; energetic–relaxed; cold–warm; unconfident–confident. These 10 attributes were chosen from the profiles of the prototypic extravert and prototypic introvert that constituted the interviewer-participants' hypotheses. Accordingly, these dependent measures provide indexes of the extent to which specific attributes that define the interviewer-participants' hypotheses were actually reflected in the target-participants' behavior (as perceived by the listener-judges) in this interview context.

Results

We examined the effects of the manipulation of the interviewer-participants' hypotheses on (a) the hypothesis-testing strategies formulated by the interviewer-participants and (b) the target-participants' behavioral self-presentation during the interviews, as measured by the listener-judges' evaluations of the tape recordings.

INTERVIEWER-PARTICIPANTS' HYPOTHESIS-TESTING STRATEGIES

Interviewer-participants appear to have formulated confirmatory hypothesis-testing strategies. A multivariate analysis of variance revealed a reliable main effect of the manipulation of the participants' hypotheses, multivariate $F(3, 36) = 7.92, p < .0005$. Univariate analyses of variance on the individual dependent measures (for means, see Table 1) specified the nature of this outcome. Interviewer-participants chose to ask extraverted questions more frequently when planning to test the introvert hypothesis, $F(1, 38) = 14.91, p < .001$. Interviewer-participants chose to ask introverted questions more frequently when preparing to test the introvert hypothesis than when planning to test the extravert hypothesis, $F(1, 38) = 28.18, p < .001$. In addition, interviewer-participants in the extravert hypothesis condition chose neutral questions more frequently than did their counterparts in the introvert hypothesis condition, $F(1, 38)\ 4.32, p < .05$.

TARGET-PARTICIPANTS' BEHAVIORAL CONFIRMATION

Interviewer-participants tested hypotheses about their targets by preferentially searching for evidence that would confirm these hypotheses. Moreover, during the interview itself, target-participants came to behave in ways that appeared to confirm specific attributes of the hypotheses being tested by the interviewer-participants. A multivariate analysis of variance (with the 10 dimensions used by the listener-judges as multiple correlated dependent measures) revealed that the listener-judges did view the target-participants in the extravert hypothesis condition quite differently from target-participants in the introvert hypothesis condition, multivariate $F(10, 29) = 2.37$, $p = .034$.

The nature of the differences detected by the listener-judges may be inferred from group differences on the individual dependent measures. Univariate analyses of variance revealed group differences reliable at better than the .05 level for four of the attributes that had defined the interviewer-participants' hypotheses. Target-participants in the extravert hypothesis condition were regarded as more extraverted, $F(1, 38) = 4.70$, $p = .036$; confident, $F(1, 38) = 8.41$, $p = .006$; poised, $F(1, 38) = 12.78$, $p = .001$; and energetic, $F(1, 38) = 6.59$, $p = .014$, than target-participants in the introvert hypothesis condition. Two other attributes, when considered individually, yielded group differences reliable at better than the .10 level. Target-participants in the extravert hypothesis condition were seen as more outgoing, $F(1, 38) = 3.55$, $p = .067$, and more enthusiastic, $F(1, 38) = 3.12$, $p = .085$, than those in the introvert hypothesis condition. Group differences for the remaining four attributes are all in the same direction. Target-participants in the extravert hypothesis condition were rated as more (although not reliably more) sociable, warm, friendly, talkative, all Fs £ 2.36, ps ³ .13. And, if one simply sums the 10 dimensions to create an overall measure (with an internal consistency of .95, as assessed by coefficient alpha), a univariate analysis of variance reveals that target-participants in the extravert hypothesis condition presented themselves in more extraverted fashion during the interviews than did participants in the introvert hypothesis condition, $F(1, 38) = 4.56$, $p = .04$.

Evidently, answers of the target-participants to the interviewer-participants' questions did provide behavioral confirmation for the hypotheses being tested by the interviewer-participants. Moreover, it should be recalled that these behavioral differences were detectable to naive listener-judges who had access only to tape recordings of just the target-participants contributions to the interviews.

Discussion

In this investigation, we were able to witness these stages of the process of hypothesis testing in social interaction: the interviewer-participants' formulation of confirmatory strategies, the interviewer-participants' use of these search procedures in their interviews, and the target-participants' behavioral confirmation of the interviewer-participants' hypotheses. But, did the interviewer-participants regard the hypotheses as having been confirmed by the actions of the target-participants? Although this investigation does not answer this question directly, other reserch (e.g., Swann, 1978) has demonstrated that after interacting with other people for purposes of testing hypotheses, individuals do regard their hypotheses as having been confirmed.

It appears that the critical link in the chain of events of hypothesis testing in social interaction is the formulation of a confirmatory strategy. Once the individual chooses to search preferentially for hypothesis-confirming evidence, the actual behavior of the target then may be constrained in ways that actually provide hypothesis-confirming evidence. Accordingly, we next focused on defining the boundary conditions within which individuals formulate confirmatory hypothesis-testing strategies.

Investigations 3 and 4:
In Search of the Limits of Confirmatory Hypothesis Testing

In the initial investigation, it mattered not at all whether participants had any reason to suspect that the hypothesis would prove to be accurate. When participants had no reason to believe that the hypothesis would prove accurate, they were as likely to plan to search preferentially for confirming evidence as when they had some reason to suspect that the hypothesis might describe the target accurately. How pervasive is this hypothesis-testing strategy? In the third and fourth investigations, we attempted to identify circumstances in which individuals would avoid confirmatory strategies.

Method: Investigation 3

Will individuals avoid confirmatory hypothesis-testing strategies if they have compelling reasons to believe that the hypothesis may prove to be in-accurate? Participants in the third investigation (N = 30) chose 12 questions to test the hypothesis that their targets were extraverts. The procedure was identical to that of the initial investigation, except that participants received concrete infor-mation designed to graphically convey the likeli-hood that the hypothesis would prove accurate or inaccurate.

To make it seem unlikely that the targets were extraverts, we informed participants in the few extraverts condition (n = 15) that:

> She is a sophomore, a psychology major, and a member of a sorority. From a recent study we did, we know that very few of the 30 members of this particular sorority are extraverts. That is, of the 30 girls in the sorority, 7 of them are extraverts. Your task is to find out if she is one of the very few extraverts in her sorority.

To make it seem likely that the targets were ex-traverts, we informed participants in the many extraverts condition (n = 15) that:

> She is a sophomore, a psychology major, and a member of a sorority. From a recent study we did, we know that most of the 30 members of this par-ticular sorority are extraverts. That is, of the 30 girls in the sorority, 23 of them are extraverts. Your task is to find out if she is one of the many extra-verts in her sorority.

To assess understanding of the implications of the composition of the sorority, we had partici-pants answer, on a 6-point scale, the question, "In view of the number of extraverts in her sorority, how likely is it that the person you are about to interview is an extravert?" We included this ques-tion because we were aware that there are times when people fail to appreciate the implications of statistical information about other people (e.g., Nisbett & Borgida, 1975).

Results: Investigation 3

Did it matter to participants whether their targets were one of very many or very few extraverts in the sorority? They appear to have understood the implications of the information about the soror-ity. Participants in the many extraverts condition estimated that it was much more likely that their targets were extraverts (M = 5.0) than did partici-pants in the few extraverts condition (M = 3.8), $F(1, 28)$ = 12.39, $p < .001$. But, did this informa-tion affect the formulation of hypothesis-testing strategies?

As standards of comparison for assessing the extent to which participants in the many extraverts and the few extraverts conditions formulated con-firmatory strategies, we created extravert hypoth-esis and introvert hypothesis comparison condi-tions. The extravert hypothesis comparison condition (n = 35) was created by combining par-ticipants in the extravert hypothesis–low certainty condition of the first investigation and participants in the extravert hypothesis condition of the sec-ond investigation. The introvert hypothesis com-parison condition (n = 35) was created by com-bining the introvert hypothesis–low certainty condition of the first investigation and the intro-vert hypothesis condition of the second investiga-tion. These comparison conditions provide our best estimates of the mean numbers of extraverted, in-troverted, and neutral questions chosen to test hy-potheses when there are no reasons to expect that the hypotheses will prove accurate or inaccurate.[1]

How did the hypothesis-testing strategies for-mulated by participants in the many extraverts and few extraverts conditions compare with those of participants in the extravert hypothesis and intro-vert hypothesis comparison conditions? A one-way multivariate analysis of variance revealed reliable differences in the pattern of extraverted, intro-verted, and neutral questions chosen by the four groups, multivariate $F(9, 229)$ = 5.18, $p < .001$. Subsequent univariate analyses of variance re-vealed reliable between-group differences for

---

[1] Before combining results from the relevant conditions of the first and the second investigations, we first ascertained that our "hypothesis-testing" effect (that is, preferential choice of hypothesis-confirming questions) did not differ across the two investigations. Indeed, if we perform a 2 (introvert hypothesis–extravert hypothesis) × 2 (Investigation 1–Investigation 2) multivariate analysis of variance with numbers of extraverted, introverted, and neutral questions as dependent variables, there are neither main nor interaction effects involving the investigation factor, multivariate $Fs(3, 64)$ = ≤ 1.60, $ns;$ there is, of course, a reliable main effect of the hypothesis factor, multivariate $F(3, 64)$ = 13.71, $p < .001$.

mean numbers of extraverted questions and introverted questions chosen, Fs (3, 96) = 16.13 and 17.62, respectively, $ps < .001$, but no reliable between-groups differences in mean numbers of neutral questions chosen, $F(3, 96) = 1.03$, ns.

To infer the nature of these between-groups differences, we then examined the pattern of the group means for extraverted and introverted questions. It appears that participants planned to ask equally many *extraverted questions* (for means, see Table 1) whether they were in the many extraverts, few extraverts, or extraverts hypothesis comparison conditions; and participants in the many extraverts, few extraverts, and extravert hypothesis comparison conditions all planned to ask more extraverted questions than participants in the introvert hypothesis comparison condition, $F(1, 96) = 42.10$, $p < .001$.[2] Moreover, participants planned to ask equally few *introverted questions* whether they were in the many extraverts, few extraverts, or extravert hypothesis comparison conditions; and participants in the many extraverts, few extraverts, and extravert hypothesis comparison conditions all planned to ask fewer introverted questions than participants in the introvert hypothesis comparison conditions, $F(1, 96) = 48.54$, $p < .001$.[3]

Method: Investigation 4

Would participants formulate confirmatory hypothesis-testing strategies if offered substantial incentives to test hypotheses as accurately as possible? We made the following offer to participants in the fourth investigation ($N = 30$):

> To give you a little incentive, we are offering $25 to the person who develops the set of questions that will tell the most about the extraversion/introversion of the interviewee. You should therefore try to be as accurate as possible in finding out what the interviewee is like.

Participants in the $25 extravert hypothesis condition ($n = 15$) and those in the $25 introvert hypothesis condition ($n = 15$) then chose 12 questions to test the hypotheses that their targets were extraverts or introverts, respectively.[4]

Results: Investigation 4

Did participants avoid the preferential search for confirming evidence when offered a $25 incentive for accuracy? Or, more modestly, were these participants any less likely to formulate confirmatory strategies than individuals who had not been offered such large incentives for accuracy (i.e., the extravert hypothesis and introvert hypothesis comparison conditions)? Evidently not. When we entered choices of extraverted, introverted, and neutral questions into a 2 (extravert hypothesis–introvert hypothesis) × 2 ($25–comparison) multivariate analysis of variance, there emerged a reliable main effect of the hypothesis manipulation, multivariate $F(3, 94) = 16.36$, $p < .0001$, but neither a reliable main effect of the investigation factor nor a reliable interaction between the hypothesis and investigation factors, multivariate $Fs < 1$.

Moreover, separate univariate analyses (for means, see Table 1) indicated that participants in the $25 extravert hypothesis condition planned to ask more extraverted questions than participants in the $25 introvert hypothesis condition, $F(1, 28) = 9.25$, $p = .005$; and participants in the $25 introvert hypothesis condition planned to ask more introverted questions than participants in the $25 extravert hypothesis condition, $F(1, 28) = 7.01$, $p = .013$. Apparently, the offer of substantial monetary incentives was not sufficient even to diminish, let alone override, the propensity to search preferentially for confirming evidence.

---

[2]This F Value is the outcome of a single contrast with the following weights: many extraverts = +1; few extraverts = +1; extravert hypothesis = +1; introvert hypothesis = –3. Not only is this contrast highly significant but it accounts for 87.01% of the systematic between-conditions variance. Moreover, the many extraverts, few extraverts, and extravert hypothesis comparison means for extraverted questions do *not* differ from each other at the .05 level of confidence, using Scheffé's procedure for multiple comparisons.

[3]This F value is the outcome of a single contrast with the following weights: many extraverts = –1; few extraverts = –1; extraverts hypothesis = –1; introvert hypothesis = +3. Not only is this contrast highly reliable but it accounts for 91.84% of the systematic between-conditions variance. Moreover, the many extraverts, few extraverts, and extravert hypothesis comparison means for introverted questions do *not* differ from each other at the .05 level of confidence, using Scheffé's procedure for multiple comparisons.

[4]We did award $25 to one participant in the fourth investigation. Our criterion for identifying "accuracy" was somewhat arbitrary. We awarded $25 to one of the only two participants (she was identified by the flip of a coin) who planned to ask precisely equal numbers of extraverted and introverted questions of their targets.

Discussion: Investigations 3 and 4

In each investigation, we have observed the formulation of confirmatory hypothesis-testing strategies. It seemed not to matter to participants where their hypotheses orginated (Investigation 1), how likely it was that their hypotheses would prove accurate (Investigation 3), or whether substantial incentives for accurate hypothesis testing were offered (Investigation 4). In each case, participants planned to preferentially search for evidence that would tend to confirm their hypotheses. It is true that all participants in these investigations were females. However, we know of no reason why the outcomes ought not be generalizable to males. In fact, other research on hypothesis testing in social interaction has documented the preferential search for hypothesis-confirming evidence with male participants (Swann, 1978). Nonetheless, we recognize that we are in no position to claim that individuals always adopt confirmatory hypothesis-testing strategies. At the very least, we can assert that we have yet to identify any procedure that will induce individuals to eschew such strategies in favor of either disconfirmatory or equal opportunity strategies.

Hypothesis Testing: A Theoretical Analysis

Why did individuals who participated in these empirical investigations construct and enact confirmatory strategies for testing hypotheses about other people? We believe that the structure and process of human thought fosters and promotes the ready and willing adoption of confirmatory strategies for hypothesis testing. First of all, there is every reason to believe that it is easier for the individual to think of the target behaving in accord with his or her hypothesized nature than it is for the individual to think of the target violating the hypothesis. Considerable research on concept formation and concept utilization indicates that people prefer and use positive instances of concepts over negative ones (e.g., Hovland & Weiss, 1953). Moreover, confirming instances generally have more impact on inductive conclusions than do disconfirming instances (e.g., Gollob, Rossman, & Abelson, 1973), and covariation between positive instances leads to estimates of greater relationships than does covariation between negative

or mixed instances (e.g., Jenkins & Ward, 1965; Smedslund, 1963). Furthermore, in judgments of similarity, individuals preferentially look for common features rather than distinctive features (e.g., Tversky, 1977). Similarly, investigations of logical reasoning (e.g., Wason & Johnson-Laird, 1972) make clear that when attempting to decide whether general propositions (e.g., all Norwegian men are handsome) are true, individuals almost always look for instances that could verify the proposition (e.g., Norwegian men who are handsome) and almost never look for falsifying instances (e.g., nonhandsome men who are Norwegian). Even researchers in the behavioral sciences tend to design empirical investigations that seek to confirm, rather than disconfirm, their hypotheses (Greenwald, 1975). Accordingly, when anticipating what events are to appear as their interaction unfolds, the individual may find it easier to construct mental scenarios of the events of the forthcoming interaction in which the target acts in accord with the individual's hypothesis than to construct scenarios in which the target betrays the hypothesis.

If representations of the target behaviorally confirming the individual's hypothesis are more cognitively "available" than representations of the target violating the hypothesis, then there is every reason to believe that the individual will overestimate the likelihood that the target will, in fact, behave in ways that confirm the hypothesis. Considerable evidence suggests that individuals use "availability" as a heuristic for estimating frequency: Events that are easy to bring to mind are thought to occur with greater frequency than events that are difficult to bring to mind (e.g., Tversky & Kahneman, 1973). If so, by virtue of contemplating the forthcoming interaction with the target in the light of the hypothesis, the individual not only will find it easier to think of the target confirming the hypothesis but also will believe that these hypothesis-confirming actions will occur in great numbers and that these hypothesis-confirming behaviors will be representative of the target's true personal nature.

To the extent that the individual believes that hypothesis-confirming behaviors are typical of the target's activities, he or she may consider it not unreasonable to confine the conversation to those topics about which the target can provide the most informative and meaningful facts about his or her life. Accordingly, the individual may use their social interaction as an opportunity to collect preferentially evidence that confirms the hypothesis under scrutiny.

Such a preferential evidence-gathering procedure may generate a sample of evidence in which hypothesis-confirming evidence will be overrepresented and hypothesis-disconfirming evidence will be underrepresented. For there is every reason to believe that most people, as targets, will be "generous" in providing specific instances of hypothesis-confirming actions. There is sufficient situation-to-situation variability in human social behavior that most people about whom hypotheses are tested will have behaved, in some situations and at some times, consistently with the hypothesis under scrutiny (e.g., Mischel, 1968). However, these same people probably will have behaved, in other situations and at other times, in ways that would tend to disconfirm that same hypothesis. Accordingly, to the extent that the individual preferentially solicits hypothesis confirming instances of the target's behavior, such a search procedure will be particularly successful in generating a sample of data in which confirming evidence is overrepresented and in which disconfirming evidence is underrepresented. Of course, it will be this sample of data upon which the individual will base the decision to accept or reject the hypothesis in question. Accordingly, the individual may accept this hypothesis more readily than the "data" of actual events in the target's life truly warrant.

Whatever the ultimate fate of this admittedly speculative analysis of the processes that underlie and generate the preferential search for hypothesis-confirming evidence, the possible social and interpersonal consequences of confirmatory hypothesis-testing strategies cannot be ignored. To the extent that individuals chronically formulate and enact confirmatory strategies for assessing the accuracy of their hypotheses and beliefs about other people, they may create for themselves a world in which hypotheses become self-confirming hypotheses and beliefs become self-perpetuating beliefs (for other demonstrations of the self-perpetuating nature of beliefs, see Snyder & Swann, 1978; Snyder, Tanke, & Berscheid, 1977; Snyder & Uranowitz, 1978). From this perspective, it becomes easier to understand why so many popular beliefs about other people (in particular, clearly erroneous social and cultural stereotypes) are so stubbornly resistant to change. Even if one

were to develop sufficient doubt about the accuracy of these beliefs to proceed to test them actively, one nevertheless might be likely to "find" all the evidence one needs to confirm and retain these beliefs. And, in the end, one may be left with the secure (but totally unwarranted) feeling that these beliefs must be correct because they have survived (what may seem to the individual) perfectly appropriate and even rigorous procedures for assessing their accuracy.

ACKNOWLEDGMENTS

This research and the preparation of this manuscript were supported in part by National Science Foundation Grants SOC 75-13872, "Cognition and Behavior: When Belief Creates Reality," and BNS 77-11346, "From Belief to Reality: Cognitive, Behavioral, and Interpersonal Consequences of Social Perception," to Mark Snyder. We thank Steve Anderson, Bruce Campbell, Bill Gavin, Pat Hanafan, Steve Kramasz, John Lardy, and LaRaye Osborne, who assisted in the empirical phases of these investigations. We thank Berna Skrypnek, Seymour Uranowitz, and D. Kendzierski for their careful reading of this manuscript.

REFERENCES

Gollob, H. F., Rossman, B. B., & Abelson, R. P. Social inference as a function of the number of instances and consistency of information presented. *Journal of Personality and Social Psychology,* 1973, 27, 19–33.

Greenwald, A. G. Consequences of prejudice against the null hypothesis. *Psychological Bulletin,* 1975, 82, 1–20.

Hovland, C. I., & Weiss, W. Transmission of information concerning concepts through positive and negative instances. *Journal of Experimental Psychology,* 1953, 45, 175–182.

Jenkins, H. M., & Ward, W. C. Judgment of contingency between responses and outcomes. *Psychological Monographs,* 1965, 79(1, Whole No. 594).

Mischel, W. *Personality and assessment.* New York: Wiley, 1968.

Nisbett, R. E., & Borgida, E. Attribution and the psychology of prediction. *Journal of Personality and Social Psychology,* 1975, 32, 932–943.

Overall, J. E., & Klett, C. J. *Applied multivariate analysis.* New York: Mc Graw-Hill, 1972.

Smedslund, J. The concept of correlation in adults. *Scandinavian Journal of Psychology,* 1963, 4, 165–173.

Snyder, M., & Swann, W. B., Jr. Behavioral confirmation in social interaction: From social perception to social reality. *Journal of Experimental Social Psychology,* 1978, 14, 148–162.

Snyder, M., Tanke, E. D., & Berscheid, E. Social perception and interpersonal behavior: On the self-fulfilling nature of social stereotypes. *Journal of Personality and Social Psychology,* 1977, 35, 656–666.

Snyder, M., & Uranowitz, S. W. Reconstructing the past: Some cognitive consequences of person perception. *Journal of Personality and Social Psychology,* 1978, 36, 941–950.

Swann, W. B., Jr. *The interpersonal nature of self-conceptions.* Unpublished doctoral dissertation, University of Minnesota, 1978.

Tversky, A. Features of similarity. *Psychological Review,* 1977, 84, 327–352.

Tversky, A., & Kahneman, D. Availability: A heuristic for judging frequency and probability. *Cognitive Psychology,* 1973, 5, 207–232.

Wason, P. C., & Johnson-Laird, P. N. *Psychology of reasoning: Structure and content.* London: D. T. Batsford, 1972.

Category Accessibility and Impression Formation

E. Tory Higgins, William S. Rholes, and Carl R. Jones • Princeton University

Editors' Notes

When a stored contruct is activated in our memory by some contextual stimulus (priming), its accessibility is temporarily increased. This increased accessibility makes it more likely to be used subsequently in another situation to interpret ambiguous information. Thus, the way things appear to us at a given moment depends not only on their own features but also on which constructs have been recently primed in the preceding context. This means that there can be considerable variability in how different individuals evaluate the same behaviors of others; the interpretation depends upon the contexts in which the individuals happen to be prior to observing the behaviors. Such recent priming induces a certain type of bias in their reacting cognitively to subsequent experiences, a bias of which people are unaware but which nonetheless influences their evaluations of those experiences.

Discussion Questions

1. Why did Higgins, Rholes, and Jones (1977) choose ambiguous stimuli to demonstrate the effects of construct accessibility?
2. What was the significance of Higgins et al. (1977) manipulating the applicability of the activated constructs to the stimulus descriptions?
3. In what ways does the research of Higgins et al. (1977) go beyond previous findings (e.g., Kelley, 1950) that an exposure to prior verbal labeling (e.g., the terms *warm* or *cold*) affects the impressions we form of others?

Suggested Readings

Higgins, E. T., King, G. A., & Mavin, G. H. (1982). Individual construct accessibility and subjective impressions and recall. *Journal of Personality and Social Psychology, 43,* 35–47.

Sedikides, C., & Skowronski, J. J. (1991). The law of cognitive structure activation. *Psychological Inquiry, 2,* 169–184.

Srull, T. K., & Wyer, R. S. (1980). Category accessibility and social perception: Some implications for the study of person memory and interpersonal judgment. *Journal of Personality and Social Psychology, 38,* 841–856.

Taylor, S. E., & Fiske, S. T. (1978). Salience, attention, and attribution: Top of the head phenomena. In L. Berkowitz (Ed.), *Advances in experimental social psychology* (Vol. 11, pp. 249–288). New York: Academic Press.

Authors' Abstract

The present study examined the immediate and delayed effects of unobtrusive exposure to personality trait terms (e.g., "reckless," "persistent") on subjects' subsequent judgments and recollection of information about another person. Before reading a description of a stimulus person, subjects were unobtrusively exposed to either positive or negative trait terms that either could or could not be used to characterize this person. When the trait terms were applicable to the description of the stimulus person, subjects' characterizations and evaluations of the person reflected the denotative and evaluative aspects of the trait categories activated by the prior exposure to these terms. However, the absence of any effects for nonapplicable trait terms suggested that exposure to trait terms with positive or negative associations was not in itself sufficient to determine attributions and evaluations. Prior verbal exposure had little effect on reproduction of the descriptions. Moreover, no reliable difference in either evaluation or reproduction was found between subjects who overtly characterized the stimulus person and those who did not. Exposure to applicable trait terms had a greater delayed than immediate effect on subjects' evaluations of the stimulus person, suggesting that subjects may have discounted their categorizations of the stimulus person when making their immediate evaluations. The implications of individual and situational variation in the accessibility of different categories for judgments of self and others are considered.

The present study examined whether previous exposure to personality trait terms would affect subjects' subsequent characterizations and evaluations of a stimulus person. The results of a number of studies in the area of object and person perception suggest that an experimenter's verbal description of a stimulus prior to, or during, its presentation can affect how that stimulus is remembered and evaluated (e.g., Bach & Klein, 1957; Carmichael, Hogan, & Walter, 1932, Kelley, 1950; Thomas, DeCapito, Caronite, LaMonica, & Hoving, 1968). For example, Kelley (1950) found that students' ratings of a new instructor were more favorable when the instructor was described as a "warm" person by the experimenter prior to the instructor's arrival at class than when the instruc-

tor was described as a "cold" person. One interpretation of the results of these studies is that the experimenter's verbal description of the stimulus affects subjects' storage and retrieval of the stimulus information. However, the procedure of past studies, whereby the verbal description expresses the experimenter's personal judgment of the stimulus, suggests an alternative interpretation of the findings. In their public responses subjects may have simply conformed to the experimenter's judgment of the stimulus, without these responses necessarily reflecting the subjects' private judgment or recollection of the stimulus. One purpose of the present study is to distinguish between these alternative interpretations.

Bartlett (1932), Bruner (1957, 1958) and others have suggested that a fundamental process of person perception is to connect the input information with some stored category. The readiness with which a person classifies information in terms of a particular category is an indication of the *accessibility* of that category (cf. Bruner, 1957). Since prior activation of a trait *category* (i.e., stored conceptual information that distinguishes a particular quality of persons, such as particular behavior, appearance, intentions, etc.) increases its accessibility, exposure to the experimenter's trait *term* (i.e., the name of the trait category) should increase the likelihood that subjects will categorize the stimulus person in terms of the activated category.[1] The act of categorization may in turn affect how the stimulus information is processed.

The categorization that occurs upon presentation of information about a stimulus person can have both direct and indirect effects on later judgments of the person. The categorization can have the *indirect* (or mediating) effect of introducing bias and distortion into both the initial comprehension and storage of this information and its later retrieval and representation (cf. Bartlett, 1932; Neisser, 1967). Bruner (1958) gives an example of an average-sized Black sitting on a park bench during his lunch break who is categorized as "lazy" by an observer and is later remembered as a big, healthy, Black sprawling idly in the park doing nothing all day. With respect to the *direct* effects of categorization, the category activated by the categorization process is an integral part of the memory itself and, along with the stored details of the input information, forms a basis for judgments (Bartlett, 1932; Neisser, 1967). Information processing models suggest that a subject's judgment of a stimulus person will depend upon the sample of information about the person that the subject retrieves at the time his or her judgment is made (cf. Salancik, 1974; Wyer, 1973). The subject's previous categorization of a stimulus person could therefore affect his or her judgments of this person both indirectly, through its effect on the construction and reconstruction of the stimulus information, and directly, through the category's own denotative and evaluative implications.

One can thus interpret the effects of an experimenter's description of a stimulus on subjects' judgments and recollections of the stimulus as being mediated by the information processes described above. However, it is necessary to distinguish such effects from experimenter demand effects. To avoid the problem of experimenter demand effects in the present study, the relative accessibility of different trait categories was manipulated by exposing subjects to trait terms that were unobtrusively embedded in a previous "unrelated" task. Exposure to a trait term should activate its trait category meaning, and this meaning will then "prime," or further activate, closely associated trait categories. For example, exposure to the trait term "reckless" may activate the trait category 'reckless' which in turn may prime closely related coordinate categories, such as 'daredevil' or 'foolhardy,' as well as its superordinate category 'seeking adventure in a careless, thoughtless way.' Indirect evidence for this was obtained by Warren (1972). In this study, subjects were instructed to name as quickly as possible the color of ink in which a target word was written, while ignoring the word itself. Prior exposure to words closely related to the target word was expected to make it more difficult to ignore the target word itself (as priming would increase the target word's accessibility). As predicted, subjects' naming of a target word's ink color was slower when subjects had previously been exposed to words (e.g., "elm," "oak," "maple") related to the target word (e.g., "tree") rather than words unrelated to the target word. The major advantage of this procedure is that exposure to a trait term can be unobtrusive and yet be effective in activating a trait category. In fact, verbal exposure may affect subjects' responses to the stimulus even when subjects cannot recall any of the priming words. Tulving (1972) distinguishes semantic memory, which includes organized knowledge about words and their meanings and referents, from episodic memory, which includes information about temporally dated episodes or events. Thus prior exposure to "elm" could affect naming the ink color of "tree" because of the close association of the meanings of these words in semantic memory, even if the actual experience of perceiving "elm" is not itself available in episodic memory.

One would expect prior verbal exposure to have its greatest effect when the stimulus can be categorized in alternative ways with approximately equal likelihood and when the alternative catego-

---

[1]Throughout the paper double quotes (e.g., "warm") will be used for words and verbal expressions, and single quotes (e.g., 'warm') will be used for stored conceptual categories.

ries themselves lack clearly defined boundaries. Social stimuli and the categories pertaining to them often have these characteristics (Kanouse, 1971; Neisser, 1967). Our first hypothesis was that subjects would categorize an ambiguous stimulus person using whichever category or categories had been previously activated or primed. We expected the effects of these categorizations to be reflected both in subjects' later characterizations and evaluations of the stimulus person, and in their reproduction of the input information. The characterization of a stimulus involves assigning an appropriate trait name to whatever stimulus information is retrieved or available at the time the judgment is made, while its evaluation involves a judgment of the desirability of the kind of person to which the retrieved information makes reference (cf. Higgins & Rholes, 1976). We therefore predicted that subjects would evaluate the stimulus person more favorably when the trait terms to which they were exposed had favorable referents as opposed to unfavorable referents.

Three additional factors were considered in the present study, to clarify the interpretation of the anticipated results. First, the above hypothesis assumes that the effect of prior exposure to trait terms on subjects' subsequent evaluation of a stimulus person is mediated by categorization processes. However, exposure to trait terms with either positive or negative associations may simply evoke a positive or negative affective state in subjects that could have a direct effect on subjects' evaluation of the stimulus person, independent from this mediating categorization. To examine this issue, the effects of exposing subjects to trait terms that were applicable for characterizing the stimulus person were compared to the effects of exposing subjects to equally favorable or unfavorable trait terms that were not applicable for characterizing the stimulus person.

Second, the proposed formulation suggests that prior exposure to applicable trait terms should affect subjects' evaluation of the stimulus person whether or not subjects overtly characterize the stimulus person. However, the overt characterization of a stimulus person is a salient public behavior that may increase one's commitment to the evaluative implications of the characterization (cf. Janis, 1968). It is also an overt behavior that a person could use to infer his or her attitude toward the stimulus person (cf. Bem, 1972). These possibilities were explored.

Third, as we noted above, Bartlett (1932) and Neisser (1967) suggest that the categorization of input information tends to introduce bias into the reconstructive process through assimilation of the input information to the activated category. Bartlett (1932) also suggests that the delayed influence of the categorization on reproduction and judgment may be greater than the immediate influence, as the stored details of the input information are more rapidly forgotten than the categorization. In order to examine this issue for reproduction and evaluation, both immediate and delayed measures were obtained.

Method

Overview. As part of a "reading comprehension" study, 60 Princeton University undergraduates read a paragraph ambiguously describing a stimulus person. Prior to reading the paragraph, all subjects participated in an "unrelated" study on "perception" in which they were exposed to different personality trait terms. There were six different verbal exposure conditions that constituted the between-subject experimental conditions, with 10 subjects being randomly assigned to each condition. Forty subjects were exposed to trait terms that were applicable for characterizing the stimulus person. Half of these subjects were later asked to characterize the stimulus person (the Applicable–Overt condition) while the other half were not (the Applicable–No Overt condition). Twenty subjects were exposed to trait terms that were not applicable for characterizing the stimulus person, and all of these subjects were later asked to characterize the stimulus person (the Nonapplicable–Overt condition). In each of these three verbal exposure conditions, half of the subjects were exposed to trait terms with positive desirability and the other half were exposed to trait terms with negative desirability. As a within-subject variable, the dependent measures were given both immediately after subjects read the paragraph and again 10 to 14 days later. The dependent measures consisted of asking subjects to rate the overall desirability of the stimulus person, and to rewrite exactly, word for word, the paragraph about the stimulus person.

Construction of descriptive essay. Twenty bipolar adjective pairs were selected. The members of each pair referred to quite similar behavior but differed in desirability (e.g., neat/obsessive; assertive/aggressive; cautious/fearful; etc.). An ambiguous desription was constructed to exemplify both members of each adjective pair. (Some examples are given below.) Each of these descriptions was given to 30 pilot subjects to determine whether it did, in fact, elicit both adjective poles with approximately equal frequency. Subjects were asked to characterize with a single word the kind of person portrayed by each description. The four most ambiguous descriptions exemplified the following trait category pairs (the percentage of subjects using a trait term from one or the other pole of each pair is given in parentheses): adventurous (43%)/reckless (43%); self-confident (50%)/conceited (40%); independent (43%)/aloof (43%); persistent (53%)/stubborn (43%). These four descriptions were then combined into a single paragraph as follows (the trait category pair for each description is given in parentheses):

"Donald spent a great amount of his time in search of what he liked to call excitement. He had already climbed Mt. McKinley, shot the Colorado rapids in a kyack, driven in a demolition derby, and piloted a jet-powered boat—without knowing very much about boats. He had risked injury, and even death, a number of times. Now he was in search of new excitement. He was thinking, perhaps, he would do some skydiving or maybe cross the Atlantic in a sailboat (adventurous/reckless). By the way he acted one could readily guess that Donald was well aware of his ability to do many things well (self-confident/conceited). Other than business engagements, Donald's contacts with people were rather limited. He felt he didn't really need to rely on anyone (independent/aloof). Once Donald made up his mind to do something it was as good as done no matter how long it might take or how difficult the going might be. Only rarely did he change his mind even when it might well have been better if he had (persistent/stubborn)."

Procedure. Each subject was asked to participate in two studies. Subjects were told the purpose of the first study was to examine the effects of information processing on perception. Subjects were shown a series of 10 slides containing different words (e.g., "tree," "yellow," "sky") on different colored backgrounds and were told to name the color of the background as quickly as possible. Before each slide, subjects auditorily received a "memory" word that they had to repeat immedi-

ately after naming the background color. This meant that they had to retain each "memory" word for 8–10 seconds. The 10 memory words included six object-nouns (e.g., "furniture," "corner," etc.) and four personality trait terms. The four trait terms always occupied the 3rd, 5th, 7th, and 8th positions in the series. The experimental manipulation of category accessibility involved varying the set of four trait terms for the different conditions. The trait terms used in each condition were as follows:

(a) *Applicable, positive*: "adventurous," "self-confident," "independent," "persistent."
(b) *Applicable, negative*: "reckless," "conceited," "aloof," "stubborn."
(c) *Nonapplicable, positive*: "obedient," "neat," "satirical," "grateful."
(d) *Nonapplicable, negative*: "disrespectful," "listless," "clumsy," "sly."

The mean likability of the four sets of traits, based upon norms compiled by Anderson (1968), were 416, 149, 418, and 152, respectively, along a scale from 0 to 600. The selection of the Nonapplicable trait terms was made on an intuitive basis. However, the validity of the selection was indicated by the fact that none of the 30 pilot subjects used any of the Nonapplicable trait terms to characterize the descriptions.

Following the "perception" study, which took about five minutes, subjects were given the "reading comprehension" study. They were given the paragraph about "Donald" described above and were told to familiarize themselves with it because later they would have to answer questions about it. It took subjects about two minutes to read the paragraph.

After subjects read the paragraph, they were given a questionnaire. There were two kinds of questionnaires. On the first page of one questionnaire, subjects were asked to characterize each of the four descriptions of Donald (e.g., "Considering only Donald's attitude towards contacts with other people, how might one characterize, with a single word, this aspect of his personality?"). Half the subjects in the Applicable Positive and Applicable Negative conditions, and all the subjects in the Nonapplicable conditions, were given a questionnaire containing this front page. The presence or absence of this question constituted the manipulation of *Overt*, as opposed to *No Overt*, characterization. The remaining three pages of each questionnaire were the same for all subjects. The first of these contained eight factual questions about the paragraph (e.g., "In what manner was Donald thinking he might cross the Atlantic?"). This reading comprehension test was included to maintain the credibility of the task. The next page asked subjects to take into account all the information contained in the paragraph and then to rate how desirable they considered Donald to be on a 10-point scale ranging from extremely undesirable to extremely desirable, with no neutral point. (The scale is described in more detail below.) The final page of both questionnaires asked subjects to re-write exactly, word for word, the paragraph about Donald.

All subjects returned 10 to 14 days later to participate in "another reading comprehension study." Before beginning the "new" study, subjects were asked to fill out a questionnaire concerning the previous study which contained both the desirability and reproduction measures.

The desirability scales in the first and second sessions were identical 10-point scales except that different numbers were assigned to minimize any attempt to simply repeat one's previous response. One scale ranged from –50 (extremely undesirable) to +50 (extremely desirable), whereas the other scale ranged from +10 (extremely desirable) to –10 (extremely undesirable).[2] The order of these scales across the two sessions was counterbalanced, so that an equal number of subjects in each condition used each type of scale in each session. Prior to analysis, the scores on each scale were transformed to their equivalent scores on a standard 10-point scale ranging from +5 to –5.

Upon completion of the delayed questionnaire, subjects were questioned about the study. No subject guessed the true purpose of the study nor reported being suspicious. In order to check further on possible demand effects induced by the "perception" task, nine subjects in the Applicable–Overt condition were asked at the end of the first session to recall all the "memory" words. The mean percentage recall for the trait "memory" words (53%) was actually slightly less than that for the object-noun "memory" words (56%). These nine subjects were then told that we wished to know whether *anything* about the "perception" study interfered with or affected their behavior in the "reading comprehension" study, as it was still easy for us to change our procedure to avoid such problems. Only one subject even noticed that some of the "memory" words coincided with his characterization of Donald, and even this subject did not

suspect the reason for this relation. (This subject's data was excluded from the subsequent analysis and another subject was added to maintain 10 subjects in that condition.)[3] Thus the verbal exposure procedure did not make the trait words themselves particularly salient or raise any suspicions about the study.

Results

Effects of Verbal Exposure on Overt Attributions

Our first prediction was that if a stimulus person could be categorized by different traits with approximately equal likelihood, subjects would characterize this person with whichever of the categories had been previously activated. To test this hypothesis, we considered only those overt characterizations that were applicable. There was almost perfect agreement between two "blind" and independent judges as to whether or not a characterization was applicable. About 95% of subjects' characterizations were applicable, and the percentage of applicable characterizations was similar for the Applicable and Nonapplicable conditions (96 vs. 94%, respectively). Subjects were divided into the following types depending upon how they had applicably characterized the four descriptions of Donald: (1) with a majority of positive characterizations (positive); (2) with a majority of negative characterizations (negative); and (3) with an equal number of positive and negative characterizations (mixed).

The number of subjects who produced different types of characterization is shown in Table 1 as a function of their verbal exposure condition. As predicted, more subjects were positive than negative characterizers in the Applicable–Positive condition, whereas fewer subjects were positive than negative characterizers in the Applicable–Negative condition. This difference in the number of positive and negative characterizers within each

---

[2]As there was no zero point, this scale did not consist of equal intervals throughout. Thus it is important to point out that all comparisons which were significant by parametric analysis were also significant by nonparametric analysis (which does not involve an equal interval assumption).

[3]A comparison of subjects in the Applicable–Overt condition who did (8) or did not (12) participate in this recall task showed no effect on subjects' desirability and reproduction responses in the second session as a function of participation.

TABLE 7.1. Frequency of Subjects Producing Different Types of Overt Characterization as a Function of Verbal Exposure Condition

Types of overt characterization	Applicable		Nonapplicable	
	Positive	Negative	Positive	Negative
Positive	7	1	2	5
Negative	1	7	5	3
Mixed	2	2	3	2

condition was significant, Fisher Exact Test, $p <$ .02 two-tailed. In direct contrast, there was, if anything, a nonsignificant tendency in the opposite direction for subjects in the Nonapplicable condition. Thus, as predicted, the desirability of activated categories was not sufficient alone to affect subjects' characterizations of the stimulus person. In fact, the slight reversal in the Nonapplicable condition could be due to some of the activated categories being denotatively inconsistent with a particular description (e.g., 'listless' with respect to adventurous/reckless).

The above effect of applicable verbal exposure on characterizations was not simply a lexical choice phenomenon, as only 45% of the trait terms subjects used to characterize the stimulus person were those used in the manipulation. The remaining 55% of the trait terms subjects used were denotative and evaluative synonyms (e.g., "loner" instead of "aloof"; "self-centered" instead of "conceited"; "daring" instead of "adventurous").[4] Furthermore, a reanalysis of the characterization data excluding those trait terms used in the manipulation revealed essentially the same pattern shown in Table 1—a significant effect in the predicted direction in the Applicable condition ($p <$ .02, two-tailed), and a slight reversal in the Nonapplicable condition. Thus, as hypothesized, the verbal exposure manipulation activated trait categories and not just trait terms.

Effects of Verbal Exposure on Desirability Ratings

We predicted that if a stimulus person could be categorized by different traits with approximately equal likelihood, subjects would evaluate the person in a manner consistent with the desirability of whichever categories had been previously activated. Table 2 presents the mean desirability ratings of Donald for the immediate and delayed measures, and the change in ratings between these measures, for each condition. In the Applicable condition, an overall Valence (Positive vs. Negative verbal exposure) × Characterization (Overt vs. No Overt characterization) × Time (Immediate vs. Delayed measure) analysis of variance yielded a significant Valence × Time Interaction, $F(1, 36) =$ 4.04, $p <$ .05, but no other significant effects. The significant Valence × Time interaction reflects the fact that the desirability ratings became more negative over time in the Applicable–Negative condition (mean change of -1.1) than in the Applicable–Positive condition (mean change of $+0.2$).

A further analysis of the above Valence × Time interaction indicated that the difference in evaluation under positive and negative conditions was small and nonsignificant on the immediate measure ($M = .8$ and .3 under positive and negative conditions, respectively), $t(38) = 0.72, p > .25$ two-tailed; but was substantial and significant on the delayed measure ($M = 1.0$ and $-.8$ under positive and negative conditions, respectively), $t(38) = 2.06$, $p <$ .05 two-tailed.[5] This delayed difference in

[4] In contrast, in the memory check for the "memory" words described above, 100% of the words recalled were those used in the manipulation. This exemplifies the need to distinguish episodic from semantic memory (Tulving, 1972).

[5] There was also a nonsignificant tendency on the delayed measure for the desirability ratings to be more positive in the Applicable–No Overt condition than in the Applicable–Overt condition. The difference appears greater in Table 2 because the difference in the means (-0.6 vs. $+0.8$, respectively) is greater than the difference in the medians (0.0 vs. $+0.4$, respectively).

TABLE 7.2. Mean Immediate, Delayed, and Change Desirability Ratings for Each Verbal Exposure Condition

	Applicable				Nonapplicable	
	Overt characterization		No overt characterization		Overt characterization	
	Positive	Negative	Positive	Negative	Positive	Negative
Immediate	0.0	0.2	1.6	0.4	0.3	0.3
Delayed	0.3	−1.4	1.6	−0.1	0.2	-0.2
Change	0.3	−1.6	0.0	-0.5	−0.1	-0.5

Note. Scores could range from +5 (extremely desirable) to –5 (extremely undesirable).

evaluations was also evident in the numbers of subjects who rated Donald as desirable or undesirable under the positive and negative verbal exposure conditions. Donald was rated as desirable by more subjects in the Positive than in the Negative condition (13 vs. 6 subjects), and as undersirable by more subjects in the Negative than in the Positive condition (14 vs. 7 subjects), $\chi^2(40)$ = 3.61, p < .05 one-tailed. Thus on the delayed desirability measure, 27 out of 40 subjects in the Applicable condition evaluated the stimulus person in a manner consistent with the evaluative tone of the trait terms to which they were exposed. In the Nonapplicable condition there was, if anything, an opposite tendency on the delayed measure—only nine out of 20 subjects evaluated the stimulus person in a manner consistent with the evaluative tone of the trait terms to which they were exposed. This difference between the Applicable and Nonapplicable conditions suggests that for verbal exposure to affect the evaluation of a stimulus person, it is critical that the trait terms involved be applicable to the stimulus person.

Effects of Verbal Exposure on Reproduction

The paragraph that subjects had to reproduce contained four separate ambiguous descriptions of the target person. Each description could be either reproduced in its original ambiguous form, distorted toward the positive or negative evaluative member of its bipolar pair, or deleted entirely. Each reproduction was coded for the number of descriptions that remained ambiguous, became either positive or negative, or were deleted, with these four "scores" being mutually exclusive. Two independent and "blind" coders scored the reproductions of 15 randomly chosen subjects. Excluding deletions (for which there was 100% agreement), interrater agreement was over 85%. In cases of disagreement, a third judge chose between the alternatives. The reproductions were also coded for additional descriptions reflecting traits not included in the original paragraph; however, less than 3% of the reproductions included such information.

We predicted that if a stimulus person could be categorized by different traits with approximately equal likelihood, subjects would distort their reproduction of the stimulus information in a manner consistent with whichever of the categories had been previously activated. For each reproduction,

the number of negative distortions was subtracted from the number of positive distortions. Except for a weak tendency in the predicted direction for immediate reproductions in the Applicable condition (mean difference score of .8 for Applicable–Positive vs. .2 for Applicable–Negative), there was no support for the prediction in any condition on either immediate or delayed reproductions.

Separate 3(Applicable–Overt vs. Applicable–No Overt vs. Nonapplicable–Overt) × 2(Positive vs. Negative) × 2(Immediate vs. Delayed) analyses of variance were then performed for the ambiguous and deleted scores. Only the main effect of time was reliable. Specifically, more descriptions were deleted in the delayed than in the immediate reproductions (23 vs. 14%), $F(1,48)$ = 19.17, p < .001; and more descriptions remained ambiguous in the immediate than the delayed reproductions (47 compared to 31%), $F(1,48)$ = 23.88, p < .001. A measure of the polarization for each reproduction that was not confounded by the amount of deletion was obtained by summing the positive and negative descriptions reproduced and then dividing this sum by the total number of positive, negative, and ambiguous descriptions. This ratio was greater for delayed (.70) than immediate reproductions (.53), $F(1,54)$ = 13.68, p < .001. This result indicates that the descriptions were reproduced in a more polarized form over time.

Discussions and Conclusions

The results of the present study may be summarized as follows: (1) In characterizing the stimulus person, subjects used trait categories that had been previously activated or primed through unobtrusive exposure to trait terms, but only when the trait categories were applicable to the stimulus person. (2) Subjects' delayed evaluations of the stimulus person were consistent with the evaluative implications of those trait categories that had been previously activated or primed, but only when the trait categories were applicable to the stimulus person. (3) The effect of prior verbal exposure on subjects' evaluations did not significantly depend upon whether subjects had overtly characterized the stimulus person. (4) The delayed effect of prior verbal exposure on subjects' evaluations was greater than the immediate effect. (5) Prior verbal exposure had no significant effect on subjects' reproductions of the information about the stimulus person. (6) Subjects' reproductions of the information about the stimulus person became more polarized over time.

As discussed in the introduction, a person's previous categorization of a stimulus person can affect his or her later judgments of the stimulus person either indirectly, through its effect on the construction and reconstruction of the stimulus information, and/or directly, through the category's own denotative and evaluative implications. The absence of a significant reproduction effect in the present study suggests that the characterization and evaluation effects found were due mainly to a direct effect of categorization on judgment. However, in a recent study of audience opinion effects on communicators' message summaries of stimulus information about another person, we did find a significant relation among subjects' categorizations, evaluations, *and* reproductions of the stimulus information (Higgins & Rholes, Note 2). The major difference between the two studies was that subjects in the present study probably felt they should memorize the stimulus information because it was part of a "reading comprehension" test, whereas in the other study there was no reason for subjects to try to memorize the stimulus information. Spiro (1975) has found that reconstructive errors in reproduction do not occur when subjects are instructed to memorize the input information, but will occur otherwise. Reproductive errors consistent with the activated categories might have occurred in the present study if subjects had been given different instructions for the stimulus information (e.g., to summarize the information for another person).

There was no evidence in the present study that the stimulus information became increasingly distorted over time toward the trait categories activated by the prior verbal exposure. Therefore, the fact that prior verbal exposure had an increasing effect on evaluation over time cannot be explained in terms of such indirect effects of category activation. However, it can be explained in terms of changes in the direct effects of category activation. It may be that an awareness that one's categorizations are biased accounts of the stimulus information can function as a "discounting cue" (Hovland, Lumsdaine, & Sheffield, 1949) that attenuates the direct impact of the categorizations. In the Applicable condition, any bias in categorizing the stimulus information is most likely to be noticed when the categorizations occur immediately prior to evaluation and are overtly communicated. In addition, any bias is most likely to be compensated for in subjects' evaluations when the categorizations have a negative (i.e., prejudicial) bias. Both the results in Table 2 and some additional correlational evidence support this discounting interpretation. In the Applicable–Overt condition, a significant positive correlation was found between the positivity of subjects' overt characterizations (the number of positive characterizations minus the number of negative characterizations) and the positivity of their delayed evaluations of the stimulus person, $r = .46$, $p < .05$, two-tailed (Pearson Product Moment Correlation), but there was little correlation with their immediate evaluations of the stimulus person, $r = .13$, $p > .25$, two-tailed.

The delayed-action effect in the Applicable condition is particularly interesting given the general lack of evidence for "sleeper effects" in particular and delayed-action effects in general (cf. Gillig & Greenwald, 1974). In addition, the delayed-action effect in the Applicable–Overt condition indicates that subjects' evaluations of the stimulus person did not result simply from their desire to be consistent with their previous responses.

The effects of verbal exposure on subjects' characterizations found in the present study are consistent with previous findings that verbal exposure increases the accessibility of primed categories (cf. Posner & Warren, 1972; Forbach, Stanners, & Hochhaus, 1974). This increased accessibility can occur for several items simultaneously, and can last as long as ten minutes (cf. Forbach et al., 1974). The attribution results of the present study suggest that attributions are not determined solely by the behavioral, dispositional, and/or situational information about a stimulus person, or even one's attitude toward this person. At least in ambiguous situations, category accessibility can also determine how a stimulus person is characterized.

Given that category accessibility can affect how a person characterizes another person, it may also affect how a person characterizes his or her own behavior and internal processes. For example, Becker (1966) states that because of the ambiguity of certain marihuana-produced sensations, a new user must learn from more experienced users to define his drug experience as pleasurable. Exposure to generally positive labels may cause a new user to select positive rather than negative categories to characterize his or her own ambiguous sensations (e.g., 'warm' as opposed to 'hot'; 'exciting' as opposed to 'agitating'). Furthermore, category accessibility can be varied by nonverbal as well as by verbal means. Exposure to particular social behaviors (e.g., euphoric behavior of a stooge) or group compositions (e.g., the only male in an otherwise all female group) can affect subjects' self-descriptions and attitude responses by increasing the accessibility of certain categories (cf. Schachter & Singer, 1962; Ruble & Higgins, 1976). There may even be individual differences in the relative accessibility of different categories. Sapir (1927) and Nunnally (1965) have suggested that individual differences in word usage have a close relation to individual differences in personality characteristics and emotional state. This relation may be due in part to individual differences in the accessibility of different categories being related to individual differences in both word selection and the characterizations of self and others.

ACKNOWLEDGMENTS

This research was begun as a Senior Thesis by Carl R. Jones (Note I) under the direction of the first author. We are grateful to Joseph Danks and Mark Zanna for their helpful comments on an earlier draft of this paper. Address reprint requests to E. Tory Higgins, Psychology Department, Princeton University, Princeton, NJ 08540.

REFERENCES

Anderson, N. H. Likableness ratings of 555 personality-trait words. *Journal of Personality and Social Psychology*, 1968, *9*, 272–279.

Bach, S. & Klein, G. S. Conscious effects of prolonged subliminal exposure of words. *American Psychologist* 1957, *12*, 397.

Bartlett, F. C. *Remembering*. London: Cambridge University Press, 1932.

Becker, H. S. Becoming a marihuana user. In D. Solomon (Ed.), *The marihuana papers*. New York: Signet Books, 1966.

Bem, D. J. Self-perception theory. In L. Berkowitz (Ed.), *Advances in experimental social psychology*: Vol. 6. New York: Academic Press, 1972.

Bruner, J. S. On perceptual readiness. *Psychological Review*, 1957, *64*, 123–152.

Bruner, J. S. Social psychology and perception. In E. E. Maccoby, T. M. Newcomb, & E. L. Hartley (Eds.), *Readings in social psychology*. New York: Holt, Rinehart and Winston, 1958.

Carmichael, L., Hogan, H. P., & Walter, A. A. An experimental study of the effect of language on the reproduction of visually perceived form. *Journal of Experimental Psychology*, 1932, *15*, 72–86.

Forbach, G. B., Stanners, R. F., & Hochhaus, L. Repetition and practice effects in a lexical decision task. *Memory and Cognition*, 1974, *2*, 337–339.

Gillig, P. M., & Greenwald, A. G. Is it time to lay the sleeper effect to rest? *Journal of Personality and Social Psychology*, 1974, *29*, 132–139.

Higgins, E. T., & Rholes, W. S. Impression formation and role fulfillment: A "holistic reference" approach. *Journal of Experimental Social Psychology*, 1976, *12*, 422–435.

Hovland, C. I., Lumsdaine, A. A., & Sheffield, F. D. *Experiments on mass communication*. Princeton: Princeton University Press, 1949.

Janis, I. L. Attitude change via role playing. In R. P. Abelson, E. Aroson, W. J. McGuire, T. M. Newcomb, M. J. Rosenberg, & P. H. Tannenbaum (Eds.), *Theories of cognitive consistency: A sourcebook*. Chicago: Rand McNally and Company, 1968.

Kanouse, D. E. Language, labeling, and attribution. In E. E. Jones, D. E. Kanouse, H. H. Kelley, R. E. Nisbett, S. Valins, & B. Weiner (Eds.), *Attribution: Perceiving the causes of behavior*. Morristown: NJ: General Learning Press, 1971.

Kelley, H. H. The warm-cold variable in first impressions of persons. *Journal of Personality*, 1950, *18*, 431–439.

Neisser, U. *Cognitive Psychology*. New York: Appleton-Century-Crofts, 1967.

Nunnally, J. C. Individual differences in word usage. In S. Rosenberg (Ed.), *Directions in Psycholinguistics*. New York: MacMillan, 1965.

Posner, M. I., & Warren, R. E. Traces, concepts, and conscious constructions. In A. W. Melton & E. Martin (Eds.), *Coding processes in human memory*. Washington, DC: V. H. Winston & Sons, 1972.

Ruble, D. N., & Higgins, E. T. Effects of group sex composition on self-presentation and sex-typing. *Journal of Social Issues*, 1976, *32*, 125–132.

Salancik, G. R. Inference of one's attitude from behavior recalled under linguistically manipulated cognitive sets. *Journal of Experimental Social Psychology*, 1974, *10*, 415–427.

Sapir, E. Speech as a personality trait. *American Journal of Sociology*, 1927, *32*, 892–905.

Schachter, S., & Singer, J. E. Cognitive, social and physiological determinants of emotional state. *Psychological Review*, 1962, *69*, 379–399.

Spiro, R. J. Inferential reconstruction in memory for connected discourse. Technical Report No. 2, Laboratory for Cognitive Studies in Education, University of Illinois, October, 1975.

Thomas, D. R., DeCapito, Caronite, A., LaMonica, G. L., & Hoving, K. L. Mediated generalization via stimulus labeling: A replication and extension. *Journal of Experimental Psychology*, 1968, *78*, 531–533.

Tulving, E. Episodic and semantic memory. In E. Tulving & W. Donaldson (Eds.), *Organization of memory*. New York: Academic Press, 1972.

Warren, R. E. Stimulus encoding and memory. *Journal of Experimental Psychology*, 1972, 94, 90–100.

Wyer, R. S., Jr. Category ratings as "subjective expected values": Implications for attitude formation and change. *Psychological Review*, 1973, *80*, 446–467.

REFERENCE NOTES

1. Jones, Carl R. *An experiment on the effect of language on nonlinguistic behavior*. Senior Thesis, Princeton University, 1974.

2. Higgins, E. T., & Rholes, W. S. *Message production effects on impression formation*. Unpublished manuscript, Princeton University, 1976.

Automatic Information Processing and Social Perception: The Influence of Trait Information Presented Outside of Conscious Awareness on Impression Formation

John A. Bargh • New York University
Paula Pietromonaco • University of Michigan

Editors' Notes

The present selection further explores the notions of priming and construct accessibility as they may affect the impressions we form of others. The research shows that the degree to which cognitive categories are activated depends on the frequency with which an individual is exposed to these categories in a previous context. Most significant, the research shows that the exposure which primes the constructs can occur outside of conscious awareness. That is, people's impressions of a target person can be affected by recent priming of which they were not even aware. Even if people are conscious of priming in one context, it does not mean that they are aware of its influence on their judgments in a subsequent context (e.g., Higgins, Rholes, & Jones, 1977). But under some conditions awareness of recent priming could allow them to avoid, control, or counteract its biasing effects if these were deemed undesirable. The effects of unconscious priming demonstrated by Bargh and Pietromonaco show that in certain situations individuals couldn't possibly counteract the bias or avoid it, simply because they lacked the "basic piece of the puzzle," namely, awareness that the priming ever occurred.

Discussion Questions

1. What are some of the ways in which construct activation or priming has been accomplished in social cognition research?
2. What was the significance of the second study of the Bargh and Pietromonaco research? In what ways did it complement and strengthen the first study?
3. What are the implications of the finding that the proportion of hostile words presented affected the general negativity with which the target person was perceived? How can one account for this particular finding?

Suggested Readings

Bargh, J. A., Lombardi, W. J., & Higgins, E. T. (1988). Automaticity of chronically accessible constructs in person x situation effects on person perception: It's just a matter of time. *Journal of Personality and Social Psychology, 55,* 599–605.

Gilbert, D. T., Pelham, B. W., & Krull, D. S. (1988). On cognitive busyness: When person perceivers meet persons perceived. *Journal of Personality and Social Psychology, 54,* 733–740.

Wegner, D. M., & Erber, R. (1992). The hyperaccessibility of suppressed thoughts. *Journal of Personality and Social Psychology, 63,* 903–912.

Authors' Abstract

The accessibility of a category in memory has been shown to influence the selection and interpretation of social information. The present experiment examined the possibility that information relevant to a trait category (hostility) presented outside of conscious awareness can temporarily increse that category's accessibility. Subjects initially performed a vigilance task in which they were exposed unknowingly to single words. Either 0%, 20%, or 80% of these words were semantically related to hostility. In an ostensibly unrelated second task, subjects read a behavioral description of a stimulus person that was ambiguous regarding hostility, and then rated the stimulus person on several trait dimensions. The amount of processing subjects gave to the hostile information and the negativity of their ratings of the stimulus person both were reliably and positively related to the proportion of hostile words to which they were exposed. Several control conditions confirmed that the words were not consciously perceived. It was concluded that social stimuli of which people are not consciously aware can influence conscious judgments.

The social perceiver is continuously confronted with a formidable array of environmental information interpret. Bruner (1957, 1958) was one of the first to recognize that this information is manageable only by selectively attending to certain features of the stimulus field and by further reducing this limited range of information by assigning it to cognitive *categories*—abstract representations of conceptually related information. In this increasingly popular view (e.g., Cantor, 1981; Mischel, 1979; Neisser, 1976; Norman & Bobrow, 1976), perception consists of the interaction between the cognitive structure of the perceiver and the environmental context.

The relative accessibilities of these categories, therefore, partly determine the selection and interpretation of social information (Bruner, 1957; Higgins & King, 1981; Wyer & Srull, 1981). The more accessible a category, the more likely it is to be used to process relevant information. Category accessibilities are critical to the outcome of social perception because a considerable percentage of social information is at least somewhat ambiguous (Bruner, 1958), and an ambiguous stimulus will tend to be "captured" by the most accessible category for which it is relevant.

Categories can become more accessible through greater recency or frequency of activation. A category's *acute* or temporary accessibility is directly related to its recency of activation: The more recently a category has been used, the greater its acute accessibility (Hayes-Roth, 1977; Higgins & King, 1981; Srull & Wyer, 1979, 1980). In a study by Higgins, Rholes, and Jones (1977), subjects first performed a color-naming task in which they were presented with a word to hold in memory until the color had been named. These memory words included four personality trait terms, either positive or negative and either relevant or irrelevant to the stimulus material of the next task. In the second task, allegedly unrelated to the first, all subjects read the same behavioral description of a stimulus person. Subjects exposed to the relevant trait terms evaluated the stimulus person in line with the denotative character of those traits (i.e., either positively or negatively), whereas the positive and negative irrelevant trait terms had no effect on subjects' evaluations. Higgins et al. (1977) concluded that the earlier exposure to the trait terms had activated trait categories that influenced subsequent processing of trait-relevant but not trait-irrelevant information.

Srull and Wyer (1979, 1980) replicated and extended this finding. In an ostensibly unrelated first task, subjects were exposed to behavioral exemplars of a trait. In a second task, they read a behavior description relevant to that trait. Evaluations of the stimulus person on the relevant trait (e.g., "hostile"), and also on evaluatively similar traits (e.g., "conceited" and "narrow-minded"), were influenced by the earlier exposure to the trait-relevant information. Apparently, although an activated trait category only influences the processing of category-relevant information (Higgins et al., 1977), the effect of this processing can be to influence judgments along other trait dimensions as well (Srull & Wyer, 1979). It should also be noted that presenting the priming information after the behavioral description has no effect on trait ratings (Srull & Wyer, 1980), underscoring the importance of category accessibility during information acquisition in determining how that information will be interpreted.

A given category also can differ across individuals in its long-term, or *chronic*, acessibility. In general, the more frequently a category is activated the more accessible it becomes, requiring decreasing amounts of stimulus energy to detect congruent information (Bruner, 1957; Higgins & King, 1981; Shiffrin & Schneider, 1977).[1] Individuals will vary in the frequency with which different categories become active, due to variance in their past experiences, and their repertoires of chronically accessible categories will vary accordingly. A recent study by Higgins, King, and Mavin (1982) illustrated the influence of chronically accessible categories. Subjects read a behavioral description of a stimulus person. After an intervening task, they wrote down the behavioral description as accurately as they could, followed by their impression of the stimulus person. The contents of the story reproductions and impressions varied with the subjects' individual category accessibilities, which had been assessed previously via a card-sorting task. More accessible trait information was included in both the reproductions and impressions than was inaccessible trait information.

Higgins and King (1981) have argued that category priming effects can be passive, that is, not require a conscious expectancy or set on the part of subjects. They held that subjects in the Higgins et al. (1977) study were not aware of the connection between the two allegedly unrelated experiments they participated in, and that this, coupled with the subjects' relatively low level of recall for the adjectives used in the first task, demonstrated a lack of conscious awareness of the priming information during performance of the second task. The subjects had certainly been *momentarily* aware of the priming adjectives during the color-naming task, however, and were able to recall over half of these adjectives after evaluating the stimulus person, so that to an extent they still were conscious of the prior presence of the priming adjectives at the time they read the description of the stimulus person.

A more stringent and conclusive test of the existence of passive, automatic priming effects would require the priming information to be presented outside of subjects' conscious awareness. In an

[1]This point is a source of difference between the category accessibility models of Higgins and King (1981) and Wyer and Srull (1981). In the Wyer and Srull "storage bin" model, a category not frequently used can still have long-term effects as long as it was the *most recently* used (i.e., is on the top of

investigation of the influence of social constructs on selective attention, Bargh (1982) found that people for whom the trait category of independence was chronically accessible (i.e., a trait very frequently used in reference to the self) showed evidence of processing independence-related information of which they were not consciously aware. This suggests that chronically accessible categories are capable of becoming active outside of consciousness. Therefore, presentation of category-consistent stimuli below the threshold of conscious recognition should result in the activation of chronically accessible categories, with this automatic activation resulting in passive priming effects.

To test this prediction, a partial replication of the Srull and Wyer (1979) Experiment 1 was conduced.[2] In an initial vigilance task, subjects reacted as quickly as they could to "flashes" on a cathode-ray tube (CRT) screen by pressing a button. The flashes were actually words, some related to hostility, the remainder unrelated. The word flashes appeared on the screen very briefly (100 msec each) and were immediately masked. In addition, the time and location of their occurrence on the screen were made unpredictable, and they were presented outside of the subjects' foveal visual field. These steps were taken to ensure that no conscious awareness of the word content occurred. Depending on the condition to which the subject had been randomly assigned, either 0%, 20%, or

---

the bin). In the Higgins and King model, as here, frequent activation is a necessary condition for chronic accessibility.

[2]Srull and Wyer (1979) also used stimulus words related to kindness in a second experiment. Our original intention was to do the same, but subjects were able to consciously detect the presence of the "kind" words on the CRT screen. Subjects in the momentary awareness condition correctly guessed 9.2% of the kind words presented, whereas subjects trying to guess the hostile words were correct on only 6%. Moreover, subjects exposed to the 80% kind-word list recognized reliably more kind words on the memory test than did subjects in the 20% condition (58% vs. 47%, $p = .06$). This difference in sensitivity between kind and hostile words is most likely due to the much greater frequency of the former in the English language, with a mean frequency of 109 per million, compared to 13 per million for the hostile words (Carroll, Davies, & Richman. 1971). Subjects would thus have a lower recognition threshold for the kind words (Solomon & Postman, 1952); unfortunately, the physical specifications of the apparatus used in the experiment did not permit words to be flashed any faster than 100 msec. Hence we were unable to replicate Srull and Wyer's (1979) Experiment 2 with subliminal stimulus presentation. In addition, Srull and Wyer (1979) did not utilize a baseline 0% condition, as we did here.

80% of the experimental trials contained hostile words. Next, subjects read a behavioral description of a stimulus person that was somewhat ambiguous with regard to the trait of hostility. Finally, they rated the stimulus person on several trait scales, half of which were related to the trait of hostility and half of which were not.

This design allows the replication and extension of an earlier study that demonstrated automatic processing of trait information (Bargh, 1982). The presence of automatic processing of the words would be indicated by relatively fewer correct responses and longer reaction times to the flashes, as less of the subject's limited processing capacity (Kahneman, 1973; Miller, 1956; Norman & Bobrow, 1976) would be available for the vigilance task. In two control conditions, subjects did not rate the stimulus person but were tested either for recognition memory or for momentary awareness of each word flashed on the screen. These conditions were included to ensure that subjects had not been conscious of the hostile information.

Experiment 1

Method

OVERVIEW

Subjects were randomly assigned to either the rate, test, or guess condition. Those assigned to the rate condition were exposed to either 0%, 20%, or 80% hostile words (the remainder being neutral control words) while performing the initial vigilance task. This task required subjects to react as quickly as they could to flashes (actually words, but subjects were told nothing about the nature of the flashes) on a CRT screen. After completing the 100 trials of the vigilance task, rate-condition subjects read a brief description of a stimulus person and rated him on 12 trait dimensions, half of which were related to hostility and half unrelated. Subjects assigned to the test condition were exposed to either 20% or 80% hostile words in the vigilance task and then were given a recognition memory test on the hostile and control words to which they had been exposed. All subjects assigned to the guess condition were exposed to 80% hostile words during the initial phase of the experiment. Unlike all other subjects, however, guess-condition subjects did not perform the vigilance task. Instead, they were informed that the flashes they would see were actually words and that they should try to guess each word as it was presented.

SUBJECTS

The subjects were 108 male undergraduate students participating to partially fulfill a requirement for the introductory psychology course at the University of Michigan. Subjects were randomly assigned to one of the six cells of the design and participated in groups of one to four. Subjects were asked before the start of the experimental session if they had normal or corrected-to-normal vision and if English was their native language. One subject was excused from the experiment and replaced in the design because he could not see the CRT screen clearly.

APPARATUS AND MATERIALS

Experimental room. The main room was divided into six individual booths, three on either side of the room. These booths had doors that, when closed, allowed each subject to perform the tasks with a minimum of external distraction.

Each booth contained a chair and a table. On the table was a GBC model MV-12 CRT screen and two response panels, all directly connected to a Digital Equipment Corporation PDP-11/20 minicomputer located in a separate control room. Each response box contained a single button: one was located on the table to the subject's left and was labeled "LEFT," the other was located to the subject's right and was labeled "RIGHT."

The CRT display was under computer program control. The computer recorded each response and its latency (to the nearest msec) for each subject. The chair was located at a fixed and constant distance from the table. The location of the chair was such that the distance from the subject's eyes to the center of the CRT screen (where a fixation point was situated) was 56 cm when the subject sat straight in the chair, so that the stimuli would be presented outside of the subject's foveal visual field (see next section). It was considered necessary to establish the *maximum* possible eye-to-screen distance; if subjects leaned forward it could only restrict the span of the foveally processed region around the fixation point.

CRT screen display. At the center of the display were three Xs, constituting a fixation point on which subjects were told to focus their gaze at all times. The background state of the screen was total illumination; characters appeared as "black on white," that is, as patterns of no illumination. All screens were at the same background level of illumination of 4.3 tx.

Each stimulus word was presented for 100 msec, followed immediately by a 100-msec masking string of 16 Xs at one of four locations equidistant from the fixation point (two each to the left and right). The location order was randomized and was the same for all subjects. Of the total of 100 trials, 25 were presented at each location. Each word was centered within its location, so that the center of each word was 3.6 cm from the center of the fixation point.

No character of any word appeared closer than 2.7° of visual angle from the fixation point, or farther than 6° of visual angle. This placed the stimuli within the parafoveal visual field (from 2° to 6° of visual angle). Studies of text reading and picture viewing (Allport 1977; Nelson & Loftus, 1980; Rayner, 1978) have found the semantic content of stimulation in this area to be processed to a small degree outside of awareness (which is generally reserved for the foveal area).

Stimulus words. Three 100-word stimulus lists were composed, containing either 0, 20, or 80 hostile words, with the remainder being control words. Each of the 100 words was flashed at one of the four locations around the fixation point on the CRT display. Subjects in the rate and test conditions were instructed to react as quickly as possible to each flash by pressing the response button corresponding to the side of the fixation point where the flash had occurred; these subjects were not informed that the flashes were actually words. Subjects in the guess condition were told that the flashes were indeed words, and were instructed to try to guess each word as it was flashed.

The 15 hostile words were taken from among those used by Srull and Wyer (1979). They were *hostile, insult, unkind, inconsiderate, thoughtless, dislikable, hate, hurt, rude, curse, beat, whip, punch, stab, and unfriendly.* The 15 control words were selected from among the 200 most frequently appearing words in the English language (Carroll et al., 1971); the selection criterion was that they be of approximately the same length as the hostile words. The control words were *water, long, number, people, what, little, many, something, together, different, between, said, every, another, and always.* High-frequency words were used as control words in order to rule out an alternative explanation for a finding of relatively greater stimulus word processing by the 20% and 80% hostile word groups in terms of the subjects' greater familiarity with hostile words. Given the greater frequency of the control words, a familiarity effect would be exactly the opposite of that predicted for a category-activation effect. The 0% hostile-word group was exposed to 100% control words, whereas the 80% hostile-word group was exposed to only 20% control words.

Word presentation order was randomized. The positions of the minority items (hostile words in the 20% list and control words in the 80% list) were the same for the 20% and the 80% lists. Each of the 15 hostile and 15 control words appeared approximately the same number of times in each list as the other hostile and control words, respectively.

Ten additional low-frequency words (e.g., *colonder, fresco*) were used during the initial practice task.

The brief duration of each word, its immediate masking, its unpredictable location and time of occurrence, and its placement outside the foveal area were all intended to prevent subjects from becoming conscious of the word contents. As a manipulation check, the following recognition test was administered to subjects in the test condition.

Recognition memory test. The 60 items of this test were composed of equal numbers of hostile targets (actually presented), hostile distractors (not presented) control targets, and control distractors. The hostile distractors were taken from the hostile words to which subjects in the Srull and Wyer (1979) study were exposed but that were not presented in the vigilance task here (e.g., *malicious, unfair, kill*). Like the control targets, the control distractors were taken from among the 200 most frequent words in the English language (e.g., *down, house, about*). The presentation order of the items was randomized.

Behavioral description. Subjects in the rate condition did not take the recognition memory test but were given a 12-sentence paragraph to read (from Srull & Wyer, 1979). The paragraph described a stimulus person engaging in somewhat hostile behaviors. The degree to which these "hostile" acts were due to dispositional rather than situational reasons was ambiguous (e.g., "A salesman knocked at the door, but Donald refused to let him enter. He also told me that he was refusing to pay

his rent until the landlord repaints the apartment.")

Trait rating form. Immediately after reading the behavioral description, subjects in the rate condition were given a form consisting of 12 traits on which to rate the stimulus person. Subjects indicated their rating by circling a number from 0 (not at all) to 10 (extremely) for each trait. Six of the trait scales were descriptively similar to hostility. Three were negative in evaluative tone (*hostile, unfriendly, dislikable*) and three were positive (*kind, considerate, thoughtful*). The remaining six trait scales were evaluatively denotative but not related to hostility. Three were negative (*boring, conceited, narrow-minded*) and three were positive (*dependable, interesting, intelligent*). The presentation order of the 12 scales was randomized.

PROCEDURE

Rate and test conditions. After arriving at a waiting room each subject was seated in an individual booth within the experimental room. Subjects were told that the experiment would consist of two separate parts, and that instructions for the second part would be given following completion of the first part. Subjects were next informed as to the nature of the vigilance task. They were instructed to sit in an upright but comfortable position, to maintain their gaze on the fixation point on the screen in front of them throughout the task and, as quickly as they could after seeing a flash, to press the button corresponding to the side of the fixation point on which the flash had occurred. Maintaining both accuracy (pressing the correct button) and speed throughout the entire task was stressed. Subjects first performed a 10-flash practice version of the task in the experimenter's presence to ensure that they understood the task. Any questions were answered, the booth doors were closed and each subject responded to the 100 experimental trials of the vigilance task. An equal number of the 75 subjects in the rate condition were exposed to the 0%, 20%, and 80% hostile-word lists; half of the 24 subjects in the test condition were presented with the 20% list and half with the 80% list. The vigilance task took approximately 12 minutes to complete.

In the rate condition, the experimenter next announced that the second part the experiment would concern how people form impressions of other people. The subjects were given the behavioral description to read through one time. As soon as a subject had finished reading the paragraph, he was given the trait rating form to complete.

After subjects in the test condition had completed the vigilance task, the experimenter explained that the flashes on the screen actually had been words. The recognition memory test was distributed, and subjects were instructed to check those items they thought had been presented. They were informed that some of the items on the test had been flashed during the vigilance task and others had not been.

Guess condition. The nine subjects in the guess condition participated one at a time. After being seated in individual booths, they were informed that words would be flashed on the CRT screen very quickly at one of four specified locations around the central fixation point. Their task was to try to guess each of these words immediately after it was flashed. They were instructed to maintain their gaze on the fixation point, as this was the best strategy for seeing each word given its unpredictable location. All subjects in this condition were exposed to the 80% hostile-word list. Subjects were encouraged to make a guess for every word, and not to worry about whether or not they were correct. The experimenter sat behind and to the right of the subject, and recorded each guess alongside a number indicating to which flash it corresponded.

At the conclusion of the experiment, all subjects were debriefed fully as to the purpose and design of the experiment and thanked for their participation.

Results

AWARENESS MEASURES

Momentary awareness. The nine subjects in the guess condition were exposed to the 80% hostile word list and tried to guess each word. They had considerable trouble in even making a guess, as they made no response at all for 705 of the total of 900 trials. Of the 195 guesses made, only 16 were correct, as scored by a lenient criterion of correctness.[3] Of these 16 guesses, 12 were control words and 4 were hostile words. That is, only 6% of the hostile words were guessed correctly. The fact that three times as many control words as hostile words were correctly recognized is most likely due to the higher frequency of the control words in the language (see Footnote 2). When the incorrect

guesses were examined for their hostility relatedness, 11 were found to be related to kindness (e.g., *loving, friend, helping, smile*), and none were related to hostility.[4] The extremely low hit rate for hostile words and the nearly three times as many kindness-related incorrect guesses that were given argue that subjects were not momentarily aware of the contents of the hostile words. If subjects had been momentarily aware of anything it would have been kindness information and not hostility information, which would work against confirmation of the hypotheses.

The fact that the subjects were unable to make a guess on so many of the trials is problematic, however. Subjects may have been using a strict criterion of accuracy that inhibited responding when they lacked the necessary confidence in their guess. A lower response criterion, one that allowed a guess to be made on every trial, may have served to increase the number of hostile targets detected.

Recognition test. The hit rates and false alarm rates for both the hostile and control recognition test items were computed for each test-condition subject. A repeated-measures analysis of variance of hostile test item endorsement rates, with proportion (80% vs. 20% hostile word groups) as the between-subjects factor, and item type (target vs. distractor) as the within-subjects factor, found no reliable main effects or interactions. Accepting the null hypothesis of no differences between conditions when it is in fact false is the more critical statistical decision error here, however, because our intent is to demonstrate a lack of differences between the groups in recognition memory for the hostile items. Therefore a series of *t* tests was performed, comparing the endorsement rates of the 20% and 80% conditions on each item type. The hit rates of the two groups on both hostile and control items did not differ reliably, and all were at the .50 level expected by chance alone (see Table 1). The 80% group did make more hostile false alarms, however, $t(22) = 2.08$, $p < .05$. Thus, al-

---

[3]The addition or deletion of letters was acceptable, except to the word base, and as long as the alteration did not change the basic meaning of the word (e.g., as when the prefix "un" is omitted from "unfriendly").

[4]Two judges blind to the experiment scored the incorrect guesses on their relatedness to hostility. Neither found any hostile words. The judges scored the same 11 words to be related to kindness, with one judge scoring 2 additional words as related (*welcome and laughter*). The lower consensus total of 11 was considered the true number.

TABLE 8.1. Mean Hit and False Alarm Rates for the Recognition Test, Experiment 1

	Percentage hostility-related words	
Rate	20%	80%
Hostile		
Hit	.49	.51
False alarm	.45	.60
Control		
Hit	.48	.52
False alarm	.41	.27

though subjects could not detect hostile targets at better than a chance level, the amount of hostile words they were exposed to influenced their endorsement of hostile false alarms. The results of the recognition test, although clearly not demonstrating any memory for the items actually presented, are not conclusive as to whether subjects were aware of the *type* of item presented.

AMOUNT-OF-PROCESSING MEASURES

Assuming for the moment that subjects were not aware of the hostile stimuli, any differential perceptions of the stimulus person by the three proportion groups would strongly suggest that subjects had automatically processed the contents of the flashed hostile words. However, direct support for the proposed mediating process of automatic category activation would be provided by poorer performance on the vigilance task by the 80% hostile word group relative to the 20% group, and by the 20% group relative to the 0% group. As argued previously, to the degree to which the hostile trait category had been activated, the subject would have less of his limited processing capacity for the demands of the vigilance task, resulting in poorer performance. Together with subjects' lack of awareness of the hostile word contents, such differences in task performance would provide compelling evidence of automatic activation of the hostile trait category. The two measures of vigilance task performance were the number of correct responses and the average reaction time to the word flashes.

Number of correct responses. For each subject, the percentage of correct responses (pressing the correct left or right button within 3.5 seconds after a flash had occurred), incorrect responses (pressing the wrong button), response latencies, and misses (failing to press either button) were

tabulated for each 20-word trial block of the task. Calculating a separate score for each trial block allowed examination of the amount of processing given to the task over its time course.

An analysis of variance was conducted on the percentage of correct responses, with proportion of hostile trials (0%, 20%, or 80%) as the between-subjects factor and trial block as the within-subjects factor. There were reliable main effects for the proportion factor, $F(2, 92) = 4.47$, $p < .025$, and trial block factor, $F(4, 368) = 5.11$, $p < .001$. The Proportion × Trial Block interaction was marginally significant, $F(8, 368) = 1.87$, $p < .07$.

Figure 1 illustrates these effects. New-man-Keuls tests (Winer, 1971, pp. 518–532) revealed that the 80% condition made fewer correct responses than either the 20% or the 0% groups ($p < .05$). In addition, the trial block main effect was attributable solely to Block 5, which was significantly lower than every other block ($p < .01$). Given the marginally significant Proportion × Trial Block interaction, however, and the patterns of means shown in Figure 1, contrasts were performed between the three proportion conditions at each trial block. These contrasts indicated that the proportion factor had a reliable simple main effect both at Trial Block 1, $F(1, 92) = 4.35$, $p < .05$, and at Block 5, $F(1, 92) = 14.79$, $p < .001$. Finally, comparisons of individual means within Blocks 1 and 5 showed that the 80% group differed marginally from the other two at Block 1, $F(1, 92) = 3.78$, $p < .06$, and the 80% and 20% groups both differed reliably from the 0% group at Block 5: 80% group, $F(1, 92) = 15.06$, $p < .001$; 20% group, $F(1, 92) = 8.36$, $p < .01$.[5]

Incorrect responses and misses. An examination of the nature of the incorrect responses shows that most were incorrect button presses (left instead of right and vice versa), with the remainder being complete misses (no response made at all).

---

[5]Because the simple main effects of the between-subjects factor at single levels of the within-subjects factor were being tested, the denominator of the F statistic for the contrasts was formed by pooling the between-subjects and within-subjects mean square errors. The denominator degrees of freedom for the corresponding F distribution is given by Satterwaite's. The numerator for the test of the simple main effects is the mean square for the proportion factor at the given level of the trial block factor (Winer, 1971, pp. 518–532). Due to the unequal number of subjects at each level of the proportion factor, the numerator of the contrasts between the three proportion means within a trial block is $(2A–B–C)^2$ divided by the summed ratios of the squared weights and cell ns (Winer, 1971, p. 215).

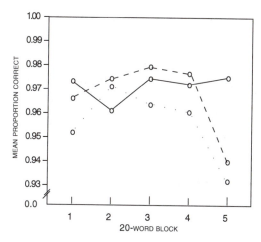

FIGURE 8.1 ■ Proportion correct responses over time. Experiment 1 (0 = 0% hostility-related words, 2 = 20%, 8 = 80%).

The pattern of the incorrect responses by proportion over trial blocks is nearly identical to the inverse of Figure 1. The analysis of variance reveals the proportion and trial block main effects and their interaction all to be reliable. In addition, comparisons of the individual proportion means at Block 1 show the 80% group to have made significantly more incorrect responses than the 20% or 0% groups, $F(1, 92) = 6.65, p < .02$.

The very low number of misses (1% of all trials) did not allow trial block to be included as a factor in the analysis of misses. Although the pattern of mean proportion misses was consistent with the previously given findings (80% group = .018; 20% group = .009; 0% group = .011), the proportion main effect was not reliable.

Reaction times. An analysis of variance of average reaction time,[6] again with proportion and trial block as factors, found a reliable effect of trial block, $F(4, 368) = 45.70, p < .001$. In general, response latencies increased over time, most likely due to fatigue. There was no reliable effect of the proportion factor.

It appears, therefore, that the differential processing of the hostile information had its effect on response accuracy instead of speed. Subjects had been instructed to be both accurate and fast, but when they were not able to perform both accu-

rately and quickly they traded accuracy for speed.

In summary, accuracy reliably decreased as the amount of hostile information presented increased, supporting the argument that the processing of the hostile information would take capacity away from the vigilance task.

IMPRESSION OF STIMULUS PERSON

An overall hostility rating was computed for each subject by taking the mean of the ratings on the six hostile traits, after reversing the scales for the three kindness traits. Similarly, an overall hostility-unrelated trait rating was computed for each subject by taking the means of the ratings on the six hostility-unrelated traits after scale reversal on the three positive traits. These average ratings were then subjected to a repeated-measures analysis of variance, with proportion as the between-subjects factor and relatedness (ratings on hostility-related vs. unrelated traits) as the within-subjects factor. This analysis is summarized in Table 2.

In general, the higher the proportion of hostile words to which a subject was exposed, the more negative his impression of the stimulus person (see Table 3). Subjects also rated the stimulus person in a more extremely negative direction on those traits related to hostility than on the hostility-unrelated traits. To determine the source of the significant interaction between proportion and relatedness, a series of planned comparisons was conducted. An examination of the simple main effect of proportion on hostility-related traits showed the 80% hostile-word group to have rated the stimulus person significantly more negatively than the other two groups, $F(1, 128) = 4.15, p < .05$ (see Footnote 5). For hostility-unrelated traits, however, both the 80% and 20% groups rated the stimulus person reliably more negatively than the 0% group, $F(1, 128) = 10.06, p < .01$. For both hostility-related and unrelated traits, therefore,

---

[6]This measure included reaction times to both correct and incorrect responses. A separate analysis of correct-response reaction times alone produced nearly identical results.

TABLE 8.2. Summary of the Analysis of Variance of Trait Ratings, Experiment 1

Source	df	MS	F	p <
Proportion (P)	2	6.84	3.67	.03
Error between	72	1.86	—	—
Relatedness (R)	1	87.16	98.98	.001
R X P	2	3.34	3.79	.03
Error within	72	.88	—	—
Total	149	—	—	—

TABLE 8.3. Mean Rating of Stimulus Person by Trait Type and Proportion Experiment 1

Trait type	Percentage hostile information		
	0%	20%	80%
Hostility related	6.99	6.78	7.47
Hostility unrelated	4.95	5.77	5.94

Note. 0 = extremely positive: 10 = extremely negative.

those subjects exposed to more hostile words during the vigilance task rated the stimulus person reliably more negatively, replicating the finding of Srull and Wyer (1979).

Discussion

The ambiguity of the results of the two awareness conditions does not permit an evaluation of the hypothesis of automatic processing of the hostile stimuli until it is demonstrated beyond any doubt that subjects were not aware of the hostile stimuli during the vigilance task. The greater hostile item false alarm rate for the 80% group may well be another manifestation of the automatic processing of the hostile stimuli that presumably produced the differences in impressions of the stimulus person—a bias toward hostile items caused by passive priming. But it could also be argued that the false alarm rate difference indicates a degree of awareness that hostile words had been presented. Certainly the other results provide substantial support for the hypothesis of automatic priming if subjects' lack of awareness is assumed. Increases in the proportion of hostile words presented decreased task performance, indicating a usurpation of limited processing capacity by the automatic processing of the stimuli, and also increased the negativity of subjects' impressions of the stimulus person.

The persuasiveness of these converging lines of evidence hinges upon a more convincing demonstration of the subjects' lack of conscious awareness of the contents of the flashed words. Accordingly, a second experiment was conducted that was designed to eliminate the problems in interpretation of the awareness conditions used in Experiment 1. The guess-condition procedure was altered so that subjects were told that they *must* guess on every trial, and were prompted to do so if at first they did not. This was intended to lower their guessing criterion and to provide a fairer test of

their momentary awareness of the stimuli. In the test condition, instead of taking the recognition test after all 100 trials had been completed, subjects selected the word they thought had been presented on each trial from three alternatives supplied to them on the CRT screen immediately after that trial. Better than chance performance on this test would indicate that subjects were aware of the stimulus words to some degree.

Experiment 2

Method

OVERVIEW

The experimental setting, apparatus, and stimulus word list used in the second experiment were the same as those used in the first experiment. The 80% hostile-word list was presented on the CRT screens to subjects at the same random locations and random time intervals. Each word was again presented for 100 msec and was followed immediately by a 100-msec masking string of Xs.

SUBJECTS

Twenty male undergraduates enrolled in the introductory psychology course at the University of Michigan volunteered to participate in the experiment and were paid $3 each for their time. They were randomly assigned to either the guess or the test condition.

PROCEDURE

The procedures for the guess and the test conditions were identical to those used in Experiment 1, except for certain modifications intended to eliminate the earlier deficiencies.

Guess condition. Subjects were told that they must make a guess for each word presented, even making a blind guess if necessary, in order to respond on every trial. If a subject did not guess on a trial, he was prompted by the experimenter to do so. Each subject was first presented with the 10 practice trials, and the experimenter made certain during this time that the subject understood the necessity of guessing on every trial. The experimenter wrote down all guesses for the 100 experimental trials as the subject made them. To give subjects more time to make guesses than they had in Experiment 1, the intertrial interval was increased to 6 seconds.

Test condition. The major change here was that a forced-choice recognition test was used, with subjects indicating which of three words they thought had been presented on each trial. One second after each word flash occurred, three alternatives appeared on the screen. Subjects were instructed to choose the target word from among these alternatives. The choices were presented for 3 seconds, followed by 3 additional seconds before the next trial began. During the latter interval, subjects indicated their choice on an answer sheet that listed the three alternatives for each trial. To help subjects keep track of the trial number, it was displayed for 2 seconds before the trial began.

Subjects first worked through the 10 practice trials and during this time the experimenter made certain that they understood the procedure. For the 100 experimental trials, the three alternatives consisted of two hostile words and one neutral word, all taken from the 80% hostile-word list. The three words were as equal in length as possible. For the 80 trials on which a hostile word was the target, this word was one of the three alternatives, along with a distractor hostile word and a distractor neutral word. For the 20 trials on which a neutral word was the target, the neutral word was an alternative along with two hostile distractors. The presentation order of the three alternatives was randomized for each trial, with the constraint that the targets and the neutral words appeared first, second, and third equally often.

Results and Discussion

GUESS CONDITION

The 10 subjects made a total of 995 guesses, failing to make a guess on only 5 of the 1,000 total trials. Thus the procedural change was successful in relaxing subjects' criterion for responding, allowing a true test of their degree of sensitivity to the hostile word contents.

The same lenient criterion of correctness was used in the scoring of the guesses as was used in Experiment 1. Subjects correctly guessed 10 hostile words out of the 800 presented—a hit rate of 1.3%. They were able to correctly guess 6 of the 200 neutral words presented, for a hit rate of 3%. As before, the neutral word hit rate was appreciably higher than that for the hostile words. The

doubling of the hostile hit rate from 6% in Experiment 1 is most likely a function of the increase in the proportion of trials on which guesses were made, from .217 in Experiment 1 to .995 in Experiment 2.

Incorrect guesses were once again examined for their relatedness to hostility or to kindness. Both of the judges were blind to the experimental hypotheses (these were not the same judges used in Experiment 1). More words were scored as related to kindness than as related to hostility (10 vs. 6 for Judge 1, 18 vs. 9 for Judge 2).

These results parallel those of the first experiment. There was again a very low hit rate on hostile words, and nearly twice as many kindness-related words as hostility-related words were given as incorrect guesses. Summing together all of the correct and incorrect guesses made that were related to kindness and summing all those related to hostility (in order to obtain an overall index of the amount of awareness of the two types of information) results in 28 kindness-related guesses compared to 25 hostility-related guesses. Again, subjects were at least as likely to be momentarily aware of kindness-related information that was not presented as they were of hostility-related stimuli that were presented. Momentary awareness of the hostile information does not appear to be a viable explanation of the impression-formation results of Experiment 1.

TEST CONDITION

By chance alone, one would expect subjects to guess correctly 33% of the target items, as three alternatives were presented after each trial. Overall, subjects were correct on 30.7% of the 100 words, clearly not better than chance detection of the presented stimulus words. On the 80 hostile-word trials, subjects were correct on 29% of the trials, again performing no better than chance. Among the incorrect responses on the hostile-word trials, subjects preferred the hostile over the neutral distractors 40.9% to 30.1%. This was a significant difference: Hotelling's one-sample $T^2(2,8) = 36.22$, $p < .01$ (see Harris, 1975, pp. 67–73). Finally, subjects correctly guessed the neutral items when they were flashed 37.5% of the time, but this was not reliably greater than the chance level of 33% $t(9) < 1$.

Thus, even when subjects had the flashed word in front of them in a lineup of three alternatives, they were not able to select it at a better than chance level. Furthermore, the significantly higher endorsement rate for the hostile distractor items indicates that although the subjects were not consciously aware of the word contents, their meaning was still influencing subjects' responses.

The outcome of these two additional control conditions allows us to state unequivocally that subjects were at no time during the experiment aware of the contents of the flashed words. Together with the finding of Experiment I that vigilance task performance declined with increases in the amount of hostile information presented, this confirms the prediction that the hostile information would be processed outside of conscious awareness.

General Discussion

The pattern of results strongly suggests that the impression subjects formed of the stimulus person was directly related to the amount of hostile information to which they had been exposed (of which they had not been consciously aware). The more hostile information to which rate-condition subjects were exposed in Experiment 1, the more negatively they perceived the stimulus person, on both hostility-related and hostility-unrelated traits.

These findings extend those of Higgins et al. (1977) and Srull and Wyer (1979) by showing that social categories can be primed passively by presenting the priming information outside of the subject's awareness. Subjects in the Higgins et al. (1977) study recalled over half of the trait adjectives that had influenced their interpretation of the behavioral description (Srull & Wyer, 1979, 1980, did not explicitly test subjects' memory for the priming information). Thus, the present experiment rules out the necessity of momentary awareness and substantial memory of the priming information for passive priming effects.

Which social category was primed by the hostile stimuli is not clear from the impression rating data. The greater the proportion of hostile words presented, the more negatively the stimulus person was perceived, both in terms of hostility-related and hostility-unrelated traits. The hostile stimuli produced a negative halo effect resulting in an overall negative reaction to the stimulus person. This could have occurred in two ways. First, the hostile stimuli could have activated the hostile

trait category, with this activation spreading along associative pathways in memory to other trait categories (cf. Collins & Loftus, 1975). The traits that are associated with hostility in one's implicit personality theory (Rosenberg & Sedlak, 1972) are likely to be negatively toned as well (e.g., unreliable, foolish, boring), and so their activation would result in a negative halo effect. Alternatively, perhaps a more general social category, such as "undesirable" or "unpleasant," was directly primed by the hostile stimuli. The activation of this more global concept would then influence all trait ratings in a negative direction, regardless of their relatedness to hostility.

A third alternative interpretation does not assume that any social category was primed by the hostile stimuli. Rather, subjects may have extracted the emotional tone of the information, and this affective processing may have produced both the vigilance task performance decrements (again because of concomitant reductions in the already limited processing capacity) and the differential trait ratings. Hostile words are certainly fraught with emotional content. A recent study by Nielsen and Sarason (1981) found that sexually related words were able to attract attention in a dichotic listening task even when subjects were trying to ignore the channel on which they were presented. Nielsen and Sarason (1981) argued that emotionally salient information can receive processing outside of conscious awareness.

The automatic processing of self-relevant trait words by subjects in the Bargh (1982) study (which also used the dichotic listening technique) can be seen as further support for this interpretation when one considers the emotional nature of information related to the self (e.g., Zajonc, 1980). Of course, the mental categories for sexual as well as for self-relevant stimuli should also be very accessible, given the high frequency of their occurrence in thought. Future studies should focus on the viability of both the category accessibility and the emotional salience accounts of selective attention and automatic processing effects.

The performance curves of the three proportion conditions over the five trial blocks of the vigilance task (see Figure 1) are very suggestive as to the time course of automatic category activation, and therefore to the issue of the conditions necessary for category activation by external stimuli. The 80% hostile-word group made more incorrect responses during the first 20-word block than the other two groups, suggesting that the amount of hostile information in the first block (16 of 20 words) was sufficient to arouse the hostile trait category. The continued presence of the category-congruent information, however, apparently caused the habituation of the category, resulting in markedly lower amounts of hostile-word processing. This is evidenced by the similarity in task performance by the three proportion groups over the middle three trial blocks. As a similar fatigue effect has been found with repeated suboptimal presentations of single letters (Pomerantz, Kaplan, & Kaplan, 1969), perhaps a category also can become fatigued through continuous subconscious activation.

On the final trial block, the performance of both the 80% and 20% groups dropped markedly. The hostile-trait category of the 80%-condition subjects apparently became fully activated again due to the continuing presence of the congruent information, whereas the hostile-trait category of the 20%-condition subjects became aroused for the first time. Given the lower proportion of hostile information for this group relative to the 80% condition, it might well have taken longer for the accumulation of an amount of relevant stimulation sufficient to activate the trait category. It is intriguing in this light that the number of hostile words that the 20% group had been exposed to just prior to the start of the fifth trial block (20% of 80 words = 16) was the same number to which the 80% group was exposed during the first trial block (80% of 20 words = 16) when their hostile-trait category was first activated. This implies that automatic processing may require a certain amount of external stimulation. It appears that this level can be reached both immediately and through the accumulation over time of congruent information. This implication merits further investigation, as does the apparent habituation of the automatically activated category with continued external stimulation.

The accessibility of categories is an important factor in determining the sources of environmental stimulation that will receive attention, how that information will be interpreted and encoded, and whether it will be remembered. Automatic category activation by congruent information increases the category's acute accessibility and thus its influence on the interpretation of subsequent information. One does not have to be aware of a source of environmental information for it to affect conscious judgments such as impressions of other people. The present research therefore extends the work of Nisbett and Wilson (1977) by showing that not only do people lack awareness of the ways in which they *process* information, they can also be unaware of the *presence* of influential information.

ACKNOWLEDGMENTS

This article is based on part of a doctoral dissertation in social psychology at the University of Michigan by John A. Bargh. He thanks Hazel Markus, Stephen Kaplan, William Kunst-Wilson, and Robert Zajonc for their constant support while serving as his committee. We are grateful to them and to Yaacov Schul, Richard Sorrentino, and Thomas Srull for their detailed comments on an earlier version of this article. We also thank Thomas Srull for supplying the stimulus materials used in the experiment.

REFERENCES

Allport, D. A. On knowing the meaning of words we are unable to report: The effects of visual masking. In S. Dornic (Ed.), *Attention and performance VI*. Hillsdale, NJ: Erlbaum. 1977.

Bargh, J. A. Attention and automaticity in the processing of self-relevant information. *Journal of Personality and Social Psychology*, 1982, *43*, 425–436.

Bruner, J. S. On perceptual readiness. *Psychological Review*, 1957, *64*, 123–152.

Bruner, J. S. Social psychology and perception. In E. E. Maccoby, T. M. Newcomb, & E. L. Hartley (Eds.), *Readings in social psychology* (3rd ed.). New York: Holt, Rinehart & Winston, 1958.

Cantor, N. A. cognitive-social approach to personality. In N. Cantor & J. F. Kihlstrom (Eds.), *Personality, cognition, and social interaction*. Hillsdale, NJ: Erlbaum, 1981.

Carroll, J. B., Davies, P., & Richman, B. *The American Heritage word frequency book*. New York: Houghton Miffin, 1971.

Collins, A. M., & Loftus, E. F. A spreading activation theory of semantic processing. *Psychological Review*, 1975, *82*, 407–428.

Harris, R. J. *A primer of multivariate statistics*. New York: Academic Press, 1975.

Hayes-Roth, B. Evolution of cognitive structures and processes. *Psychological Review*, 1977, *84*, 260–278.

Higgins, E. T., & King, G. Accessibility of social constructs: Information-processing consequences of individual and contextual variability. In N. Cantor & J. F. Kihlstrom (Eds.), *Personality, cognition, and social interaction*. Hillsdale, NJ: Erlbaum, 1981.

Higgins, E. T., King, G. A., & Mavin. G. H. Individual construct accessibility and subjective impressions and recall. *Journal of Personality and Social Psychology*, 1982, *43*, 35–47.

Higgins, E. T., Rholes, W. S., & Jones, C. R. Category accessibility and impression formation. *Journal of Experimental Social Psychology*, 1977, *13*, 141–154.

Kahneman, D. *Attention and effort*. Englewood Cliffs, NJ: Prentice-Hall, 1973.

Miller, G. A. The magical number seven, plus or minus two: Some limits on our capacity for processing information. *Psychological Review*, 1956, *63*, 81–97.

Mischel, W. On the interface of cognition and personality. Beyond the person-situation debate. *American Psychologist*, 1979, *34*, 740–754.

Neisser, U. *Cognition and reality*. San Francisco: Freeman, 1976.

Nelson, W. W., & Loftus, G. R. The functional visual field during picture viewing. *Journal of Experimental Psychology: Human Learning and Memory*, 1980, *6*, 391–399.

Nielsen, S. L., & Sarason, I. G. Emotion, personality, and selective attention. *Journal of Personality and Social Psychology*, 1981, *41*, 945–960.

Nisbett, R. E., & Wilson, T. D. Telling more than we can know: Verbal reports on mental processes *Psychological Review*, 1977, *84*, 231–259.

Norman, D. A., & Bobrow, D. G. On the role of active memory processes in perception and cognition. In C. N. Cofer (Ed.), *The structure of human memory*. San Francisco: Freeman, 1976.

Pomerantz, J. R., Kaplan, S., & Kaplan, R. Satiation effects in the perception of single letters. *Perception & Psychophysics*, 1969, *6*, 129–132.

Rayner, K. Foveal and parafoveal cues in reading. In J. Requin (Ed.), *Attention and performance VIII*. Hillsdale, NJ: Erlbaum. 1978.

Rosenberg, S. E., & Sedlak, A. Structural representations of implicit personality theory. In L. Berkowitz (Ed.), *Advances in experimental social psychology* (Vol. 6). New York: Academic Press, 1972.

Shiffrin, R. M., & Schneider, W. Controlled and automatic human information processing: II. Perceptual learning, automatic attending, and a general theory. *Psychological Review*, 1977, *84*, 127–190.

Solomon, R. L., & Postman, L. Usage as a determinant of visual duration thresholds of words. *Journal of Experimental Psychology*, 1952, *43*, 195–201.

Srull, T. K., & Wyer, R. S., Jr. The role of category accessibility in the interpretation of information about persons: Some determinants and implications. *Journal of Personality and Social Psychology*, 1979, *37*, 1660–1672.

Srull, T. K., & Wyer, R. S., Jr. Category accessibility and social perception: Some implications for the study of person memory and interpersonal judgments. *Journal of Personality and Social Psychology*, 1980, *38*, 841–856.

Winer, B. J. *Statistical principles in experimental design* (2nd ed.). New York: McGraw-Hill, 1971.

Wyer, R. S., Jr., & Srull, T. K. Category accessibility: Some theoretical and empirical issues concerning the processing of social stimulus information. In E. T. Higgins, C. P. Herman, & M. P. Zanna (Eds.), *Social cognition: The Ontario Symposium* (Vol. 1). Hillsdale, NJ: Erlbaum, 1981.

Zajonc, R. B. Cognition and social cognition: A historical perspective. In L. Festinger (Ed.), *Retrospections on social psychology*. New York: Oxford University Press, 1980.

READING 9

Stereotypes and Prejudice: Their Automatic and Controlled Components

Patricia G. Devine • University of Wisconsin–Madison

Editors' Notes

Stereotyping and prejudice are surely among the most often studied problems in contemporary social psychology. The reasons for this are twofold: (1) the societal significance of understanding intergroup beliefs and feelings that continue to underlie major conflicts within and between societies; and (2) the theoretical and methodological advances in social psychology occasioned by the cognitive and social-cognitive revolutions that offered new approaches to understanding and investigating the phenomena of stereotyping and prejudice, The disturbing message of the present selection is that at some level we all have the potential for prejudicial behavior. Specifically, Devine argues that exposure to members of a stereotyped group can automatically activate the group stereotype in all of us. Only those opposed to prejudice would attempt to prevent the stereotypic ideas from actually affecting their judgments and behavior. Because controlling stereotypic thoughts requires mental resources, when resources are depleted the activated stereotypes may affect the judgments, decisions, and actions of even those opposed to prejudice.

Discussion Questions

1. What logic led Devine to conclude that stereotypes are activated automatically upon an encounter with a member of the stereotyped group?
2. Do Devine's results directly support the notion that an encounter with a member of a stereo-typed group leads to automatic stereotype activation? How might you explain her results differently?

3. What are the implications of the Devine model for societal efforts to combat prejudice? Are we all prejudiced? How can stereotyping and prejudice be reduced?

Suggested Readings

Bodenhausen, G. V. (1990). Stereotypes as judgmental heuristics: Evidence of circadian varia-tion in discrimination. *Psychological Science, 1,* 319–322.

Hamilton, D. L., & Rose, T. L. (1980). Illusory correlation and the maintenance of stereotypic beliefs, *Journal of Personality and Social Psychology, 39,* 832–845.

Stangor, C., Lynch, L., Duan, C., & Glass, B. (1992). Categorization of individuals on the basis of multliple social features. *Journal of Personality and Social Psychology, 62,* 207–218.

Author's Abstract

Three studies tested basic assumptions derived from a theoretical model based on the dissociation of automatic and controlled processes involved in prejudice. Study 1 supported the model's assumption that high- and low-prejudice persons are equally knowledgeable of the cultural stereotype. The model suggests that the stereotype is automatically activated in the presence of a member (or some symbolic equivalent) of the stereotyped group and that low-prejudice responses require controlled inhibition of the automatically activated stereotype. Study 2, which examined the effects of automatic stereotype activation on the evaluation of ambiguous stereotype-relevant behaviors performed by a race-unspecified person, suggested that when subjects' ability to consciously monitor stereotype activation is precluded, both high- and low-prejudice subjects produce stereotype-congruent evaluations of ambiguous behaviors. Study 3 examined high- and low-prejudice subjects' responses in a consciously directed thought-listing task. Consistent with the model, only low-prejudice subjects inhibited the automatically activated stereotype-congruent thoughts and replaced them with thoughts reflecting equality and negations of the stereotype. The relation between stereotypes and prejudice and implications for prejudice reduction are discussed.

Social psychologists have long been interested in stereotypes and prejudice, concepts that are typically viewed as being very much interrelated. For example, those who subscribe to the tripartite model of attitudes hold that a stereotype is the cognitive component of prejudiced attitudes (Harding, Proshansky, Kutner, & Chein, 1969; Secord & Backman, 1974). Other theorists sug-gest that stereotypes are functional for the indi-vidual, allowing rationalization of his or her preju-dice against a group (Allport, 1954; LaViolette & Silvert, 1951; Saenger, 1953; Simpson & Yinger, 1965).

In fact, many classic and contemporary theo-rists have suggested that prejudice is an inevitable consequence of ordinary categorization (stereotyp-ing) processes (Allport, 1954; Billig, 1985; Ehrlich, 1973; Hamilton, 1981; Tajfel, 1981). The basic argument of the *inevitability of prejudice* perspective is that as long as stereotypes exist, prejudice will follow. This approach suggests that stereotypes are automatically (or heuristically) applied to members of the stereotyped group. In essence, knowledge of a stereotype is equated with prejudice toward the group. This perspective has serious implications because, as Ehrlich (1973) argued, ethnic attitudes and stereotypes are part of the social heritage of a society and no one can escape learning the prevailing attitudes and ste-reotypes assigned to the major ethnic groups.

The inevitability of prejudice approach, how-ever, overlooks an important distinction between knowledge of a cultural stereotype and acceptance or endorsement of the stereotype (Ashmore & Del

Boca, 1981; Billig, 1985). That is, although one may have *knowledge of a stereotype*, his or her *personal beliefs* may or may not be congruent with the stereotype. Moreover, there is no good evidence that knowledge of a stereotype of a group implies prejudice toward that group. For example, in an in-depth interview study of prejudice in war veterans, Bettleheim and Janowitz (1964) found no significant relation between stereotypes reported about Blacks and Jews and the degree of prejudice the veterans displayed toward these groups (see also Brigham, 1972; Devine, 1988; Karlins, Coffman, & Walters, 1969).

Although they may have some overlapping features, it is argued that stereotypes and personal beliefs are conceptually distinct cognitive structures. Each structure represents part of one's entire knowledge base of a particular group (see Pratkanis, in press, for a supporting argument in the attitude domain). Beliefs are propositions that are endorsed and accepted as being true. Beliefs can differ from one's knowledge about an object or group or one's affective reaction toward the object or group (Pratkanis, in press). To the extent that stereotypes and personal beliefs represent different and only potentially overlapping subsets of information about ethnic or racial groups, they may have different implications for evaluation of and behavior toward members of the ethnic and racial groups. Previous theorists have not adequately captured this distinction and explored its implications for responding to stereotyped group members. The primary goal of the three studies reported here was to examine how stereotypes and personal beliefs are involved in responses toward stereotyped groups.

This work challenges the inevitability of prejudice framework and offers a model of responses to members of stereotyped groups that is derived largely from work in information processing that distinguishes between automatic (mostly involuntary) and controlled (mostly voluntary) processess (e.g., Posner & Snyder, 1975; Schneider & Shiffrin, 1977; Shiffrin & Schneider, 1977). Automatic processes involve the unintentional or spontaneous activation of some well-learned set of associations or responses that have been developed through repeated activation in memory. They do not require conscious effort and appear to be initiated by the presence of stimulus cues in the environment (Shiffrin & Dumais, 1981). A cru-

cial component of automatic processes is their inescapability; they occur despite deliberate attempts to bypass or ignore them (Neely, 1977; Shiffrin & Dumais, 1981). In contrast, controlled processes are intentional and require the active attention of the individual. Controlled processes, although limited by capacity, are more flexible than automatic processes. Their intentionality and flexibility makes them particularly useful for decision making, problem solving, and the initiation of new behaviors.

Previous theoretical and empirical work on automatic and controlled processes suggests that they can operate independently of each other (Logan, 1980; Logan & Cowan, 1984; Neely, 1977; Posner & Snyder, 1975). For example, by using a semantic priming task, Neely demonstrated that when automatic processing would produce a response that conflicted with conscious expectancies (induced through experimenter instructions), subjects inhibited the automatic response and intentionally replaced it with one consistent with their conscious expectancy.

For example, Neely (1977) examined the influence of a single-word prime on the processing of a single-word target in a lexical decision task (i.e., whether the target was a word). The prime was either semantically related to the target (e.g., *body-arm*) or related to the target through experimenter instructions (e.g., subjects were told that *body* would be followed by a bird name such as sparrow). In this latter condition, subjects had a conscious expectancy for a bird name when they saw the *body* prime, but *body* should also have automatically primed its semantic category of body parts.

Neely (1977) found that with brief intervals between the prime and target (i.e., 250 ms), the prime facilitated decisions for semantically related targets regardless of experimenter instructions. Neely argued that this facilitation was a function of automatic processes. At longer delays (i.e., 2,000 ms), however, experimenter-induced expectancies produced both facilitation for expected targets and inhibition for unexpected targets regardless of their semantic relation to the prime. Before such inhibition of automatically activated responses can occur, there has to be enough *time* and *cognitive capacity* available for the conscious expectancy to develop and inhibit the automatic processes.

Automatic and Controlled Processes: Implications for Activation of Stereotypes and Personal Beliefs

The present model assumes that primarily because of common socialization experiences (Brigham, 1972; Ehrlich, 1973; P. Katz, 1976; Proshansky, 1966), high- and low-prejudice persons are equally knowledgeable of the cultural stereotype of Blacks. In addition, because the stereotype has been frequently activated in the past, it is a well-learned set of associations (Dovidio, Evans, & Tyler, 1986) that is *automatically* activated in the presence of a member (or symbolic equivalent) of the target group (Smith & Branscombe, 1985). The model holds that this unintentional activation of the stereotype is equally strong and equally inescapable for high- and low-prejudice persons.

A major assumption of the model is that high- and low-prejudice persons differ with respect to their personal beliefs about Blacks (Greeley & Sheatsley, 1971; Taylor, Sheatsley, & Greeley, 1978). Whereas high-prejudice persons are likely to have personal beliefs that overlap substantially with the cultural stereotype, low-prejudice persons have *decided* that the stereotype is an inappropriate basis for behavior or evaluation and experience a conflict between the automatically activated stereotype and their personal beliefs. The stereotype conflicts with their nonprejudiced, egalitarian values. The model assumes that the low-prejudice person must create a cognitive structure that represents his or her newer beliefs (e.g., belief in equality between the races, rejection of the stereotype, etc.). Because the stereotype has a longer history of activation (and thus greater frequency of activation) than the newly acquired personal beliefs, overt nonprejudiced responses require intentional inhibition of the automatically activated stereotype and activation of the newer personal belief structure. Such inhibition and initiation of new responses involves controlled processes.

This analysis suggests that whereas stereotypes are automatically activated, activation of personal beliefs require conscious attention. In addition, nonprejudiced responses require both the inhibition of the automatically activated stereotype and the intentional activation of nonprejudiced beliefs (see also Higgins & King, 1981). This should not be surprising because an individual must overcome a lifetime of socialization experiences. The present

model, which suggests that automatic and controlled processes involved in stereotypes and prejudice can be dissociated, posits that the inevitability of prejudice arguments follow from tasks that are likely to engage automatic processes on which those high and low in prejudice are presumed not to differ (i.e., activation of a negative stereotype in the absence of controlled stereotype-inhibiting processes). Interestingly, the model implies that if a stereotype is automatically activated in the presence of a member of the target group and those who reject the cultural stereotype do not (or perhaps cannot) monitor consciously this activation, information activated in the stereotype could influence subsequent information processing. A particular strength of the model, then, is that it suggests how knowledge of a stereotype can influence responses even for those who do not endorse the stereotype or have changed their beliefs about the stereotyped group.

The present studies were designed to test implications of the dissociation of automatic and controlled processes in prejudice. Study 1 examined the validity of the assumption that high- and low-prejudice subjects are equally knowledgeable of the cultural stereotype. Study 2 explored the implications of automatic racial stereotype priming on the evaluation of ambiguous stereotype-relevant behaviors. This task permitted examination of the effects of automatic stereotype activation independently of controlled processes relevant to the stereotype. Finally, Study 3 examined the likelihood that high- and low-prejudice subjects will engage in controlled processes to inhibit prejudiced responses in a consciously directed thought-listing task.

Study 1: Stereotype Content and Prejudice Level

Method

Subjects and procedure. Forty White introductory psychology students participated in groups of 4–6 for course credit. To ensure anonymity, subjects were isolated from each other and the experimenter left the room after giving general instructions. Written instructions told subjects that the questionnaire was designed to help researchers better understand social stereotypes and that interest centered on the cultural stereotype of Blacks. The experimenter informed them that she was not interested in their personal beliefs but in their knowledge of the content of the cultural stereotype. Subjects were provided with a page with several blank lines on which to list the components of the stereotype and were asked not to write any identifying marks on the booklet.

After listing the components of the stereotype, subjects completed the seven-item Modern Racism Scale (McConahay, Hardee, & Batts, 1981). The Modern Racism Scale is designed to measure subjects' anti-Black attitudes in a nonreactive fashion. The Modern Racism Scale has proven to be useful in predicting a variety of behaviors including voting patterns and reactions to busing (Kinder & Sears, 1981; Sears & Kinder, 1971; Sears & McConahay, 1973). Subjects indicated their agreement with each of the items on the 5-point rating scale that ranged from –2 (*disagree strongly*) to +2 (*agree strongly*). Subjects put the completed booklet into an unmarked envelope and dropped it into a large box containing several envelopes. Finally, subjects were debriefed and thanked for their participation. The Modern Racism Scale ranges from –14 (*low prejudice*) to +14 (*high prejudice*). The scale had good reliability (Cronbach's alpha=.83). Subjects were assigned to a high-prejudice ($N = 21$) or a low-prejudice ($N = 19$) group on the basis of a median split of scores on the scale.

Results and Discussion

The coding scheme, based primarily on the previous stereotype assessment literature, included traits such as lazy, poor, athletic, rhythmic, ostentatious, and so on. In addition, a category was included for themes related to hostility, violence, or aggressiveness. Although these terms have not been included in the traditional assessment literature, the assumption that Blacks are hostile or aggressive has guided much of the research on the effect of racial stereotypes on perception and behavior (Donnerstein & Donnerstein, 1972; Donnerstein, Donnerstein, Simon, & Ditrichs, 1972; Duncan, 1976; Sager & Schofield, 1980). Trait listings, however, do not completely capture the components of cultural stereotypes. For example, subjects also listed descriptive features (e.g., afro, brown eyes) and family characteristics (e.g., many children, single-parent homes). Coding categories for these components and a miscellaneous category

TABLE 9.1. Proportion of Thoughts Listed in Each of the Coding Categories as a Function of Prejudice Level

Category	High prejudice	Low prejudice
Poor	.80	.75
Aggressive/tough	.60	.60
Criminal	.65	.80
Low intelligence	.50	.65
Uneducated	.50	.50
Lazy	.55	.75
Sexually perverse	.50	.70
Athletic	.75	.50
Rhythmic	.50	.40
Ostentatious	.50	.40
Inferior	.20	.30
Food preferences	.25	.35
Family characteristic	.25	.30
Dirty/smelly	.20	.30
Descriptive terms	.55	.50

Note. None of these differences is significant.

for components listed that did not clearly fit into the existing categories were included. In all, there were 16 coding categories (see Table 1).

Two judges, blind to subjects' prejudice level, were provided with the coding instructions and the 40 protocols in different random orders. Each characteristic listed received one classification by each judge; the judges agreed on 88% of their classifications.

Table 1 shows coding categories and the proportion of high- and low-prejudice subjects who used the coding category in describing the stereotype. There are several noteworthy aspects of these data. First, the most striking aspect of these data is that the most common theme in subjects' protocols was that Blacks are aggressive, hostile, or criminal-like (see Table 1). All subjects listed either the aggressive or criminal categories and many listed both categories. This finding is important because, as was suggested earlier, much of the intergroup perception literature has been predicated on the assumption that Blacks are hostile and aggressive. Second, consistent with the stereotype assessment literature, the protocols were dominated by trait listings and were predominately negative. Third, there appeared to be few differences in the content reported by high- and low-prejudice subjects.

The prediction of no difference between the high- and low-prejudice subjects' knowledge of the cultural stereotype was tested in two different ways. First, none of the differences in Table 1 was statistically reliable. Second, two separate judges were given subjects' protocols and were instructed to read the content listed and to separate the protocols into high- and low-prejudice groups. The judges could not reliably predict the subjects' prejudice level from the content of their protocols. These data validate Ehrlich's (1973) assumption as well as the first assumption of the present model: High- and low-prejudice persons are indeed equally knowledgeable of the cultural stereotype.

Study 2: Automatic Priming, Prejudice Level, and Social Judgment

Study 1 showed that prejudice has little effect on direct reports of stereotype content. However, the free response task directly involved controlled processes. Subjects were explicitly instructed to be bias-free when making these reports. These data, then, are not necessarily informative regarding the implicit cognitive structures that are accessed during automatic processing. What is needed is a task in which the controlled processes do not provide an alternative explanation for the automatic processes. Thus, the goal of Study 2 was to examine automatic stereotype priming effects for both high- and low-prejudice subjects.

Nonconscious priming was of particular interest in this research because it is this type of processing that would allow the clearest dissociation of automatic and controlled processes involved in responses to members of a stereotyped group. Thus, the priming technique developed by Bargh and Pietromonaco (1982) was used in this study to automatically or passively prime the racial stereotype. Because the priming task activates the stereotype without conscious identification of the primes, the effects of stereotype activation can be studied independently of controlled stereotype-related processes. Specifically, interest centered on the effect of automatic racial stereotype activation on the interpretation of ambiguous stereotype-related behaviors performed by a race-unspecified target person.

In this study, evaluation of ambiguously hostile behaviors was examined because the assumption that Blacks are hostile is part of the racial stereotype (Brigham, 1971; Study 1) and because it has guided research in intergroup perception (Duncan, 1976; Sager & Schofield, 1980; Stephan, 1985). Because interest centered on the effects of activation of the stereotype on the ratings of a target person's hostility, no words directly related to hostility were used in the priming task. This study explicitly examined Duncan's (1976) hypothesis that the activation of the racial stereotype, which presumably activates a link between Blacks and hostility, explains why ambiguously aggressive behaviors were judged as being more aggressive when performed by a Black than a White actor.

Method

Subjects and selection criteria. Data were collected over two academic quarters. Introductory psychology students were pretested on the seven-item Modern Racism Scale embedded in a number of political, gender, and racial items. This was done to minimize the likelihood that subjects would identify the scale as a measure of prejudice. The experimenter told subjects that completion of the questionnaire was voluntary and that responses would be kept confidential. Subjects were also provided with a form concerning participation in subsequent experiments and provided their names and phone numbers if they were willing to be contacted for a second study for which they could earn extra credit.

Over the two quarters a total of 483 students filled out the Modern Racism Scale. Participants from the upper and lower third of the distribution of scores were identified as potential subjects ($N = 323$). When contacted by phone, potential subjects were asked about their vision, and only subjects with perfect vision or corrected perfect vision were considered eligible. High-prejudice subjects' scores on the Modern Racism Scale fell within the upper third of scores (between +2 and +14), and low-prejudice subjects' scores fell within the lower third of scores (between –9 and –14). The scale had good reliability (Cronbach's alpha = .81). From this sample of 323 subjects, 129 who agreed and had good vision participated in the experiment. After replacing 3 Black subjects, 1 subject who reported having dyslexia following the vigilance task, and 3 subjects who failed to follow instructions, the sample consisted of 78 White subjects in the judgment condition, 32 White subjects in the recognition condition, and 12 White subjects in the guess condition.

The experimenter remained blind to subjects' prejudice level, priming condition, and stimulus replication condition. Subjects were telephoned by one experimenter, who prepared the materials (with no treatment information) for the second experimenter, who conducted the experiment.

The method and procedure for this study were modeled after Bargh and Pietromonaco (1982). The only difference between their procedure and the one in this study was that in this study, stimuli were presented tachistoscopically rather than on a computer monitor. The experimental room contained a Scientific Prototype two-channel tachistoscope connected to an experimenter-controlled panel for presenting stimuli. Subjects placed their heads against the eyepiece such that the distance from subjects' eyes to the central fixation point was constant. The presentation of a stimulus activated a Hunter Model 120 Klockounter on which the interval between stimulus onset and the response was recorded to the nearest millisecond. Subjects indicated their responses by pushing one of two buttons (labeled *left* or *right*) on a response box. The experimenter recorded each response and its latency.

The stimuli were black and presented on a white background. Each stimulus was presented for 80 ms and was immediately followed by a mask (a jumbled series of letters). In addition, following Bargh and Pietromonaco (1982), the interstimulus interval was 2–7 s. The stimuli (words) were centered in each quadrant, with the center of each word being approximately 2.3 in. (0.06 m) from the central fixation point. The eye-to-dot distance was 31 in. (0.79 m) for the Scientific Prototype tachistoscope. As a result, to keep the stimulus within the parafoveal visual field (from 2° to 6° of visual angle), words could not be presented closer than 1.08 in. (0.03 m) or farther than 3.25 in. (0.08 m) from the fixation point. Twenty-five of the 100 trials within each replication were randomly assigned to each quadrant.

Stimulus materials. Words that are labels for the social category *Blacks* (e.g., Blacks, Negroes, niggers) or are stereotypic associates (e.g., poor, lazy, athletic) were the priming stimuli. Twenty-four primes were used to generate two stimulus replications. Efforts were made to produce roughly equivalent content in the two replications. Replication 1 primes included the following: nigger, poor, afro, jazz, slavery, musical, Harlem, busing, minority, oppressed, athletic, and prejudice. Replication 2 primes included the following: Negroes, lazy, Blacks, blues, rhythm, Africa, stereotype, ghetto, welfare, basketball, unemployed, and plan-

tation. Twelve neutral words (unrelated to the stereotype) were included in each replication. All neutral words were high-frequency words (Carrol, Davies, & Richman, 1971) and were matched in length to the stereotype-related words. Neutral words for Replication 1 included the following: number, considered, what, that, however, remember, example, called, said, animal, sentences, and important. Replication 2 neutral words included the following: water, then, would, about, things, completely, people, difference, television, experience, something, and thought. Ten additional neutral words were selected and used during practice trials.

Within each stimulus replication, the stereotype-related and neutral words were used to generate two separate 100-word lists. One list contained 80 stereotype-related words (the rest were neutral words) and the other contained 20 stereotype-related words (the rest were neutral words). The lists were organized into blocks of 20 words. In the 80% stereotype-priming condition, each block contained 16 stereotype-related words and 4 neutral words. Within each block, to make 16 stereotype-related words, 4 of the 12 stereotype-related words were randomly selected and presented twice.

For both stimulus replications, the words within each block were randomly ordered with the restriction that the first stereotype-related word was a label for the group (e.g., Negro or nigger). The positions of the minority items (stereotype-related words in the 20% priming list and neutral words in the 80% priming list) were the same for the 20% and 80% priming lists. Each of the 12 stereotype-related and the 12 control words appeared approximately the same number of times as the other stereotype-related and neutral words, respectively.

Judgment condition. The experimenter told subjects that they would participate in two separate tasks. First, they were seated at the tachistoscope and then provided with a description of the vigilance task. The experimenter told subjects that the vigilance task involved identifying the location of stimuli presented for brief intervals. Subjects also learned that stimuli could appear in one of the four quadrants around the dot in the center of the screen. They were to identify as quickly and as accurately as possible whether the stimulus was presented to the left or the right of the central dot. Subjects indicated their responses by pressing the button labeled *left* or *right* on the response panel. The experimenter informed subjects that the timing and the location of the stimuli were unpredictable. Because both speed and accuracy were emphasized, subjects were encouraged to concentrate on the dot, as this strategy would facilitate detection performance. All subjects first completed 10 practice trials and then 100 experimental trials. Overall, the vigilance task took 11–13 min to complete.

Following the vigilance task, the second task was introduced. Subjects were told that the experimenter was interested in how people form impressions of others. They were asked to read a paragraph describing the events in the day of the person about whom they were to form an impression. This paragraph is the now familiar "Donald" paragraph developed by Srull and Wyer (1979, 1980; see also Bargh & Pietromonaco, 1982, and Carver et al., 1983). This 12-sentence paragraph portrays Donald engaging in a series of empirically established ambiguously hostile behaviors. For example, Donald demands his money back from a store clerk immediately after a purchase and refuses to pay his rent until his apartment is repainted.

After reading the paragraph, subjects were asked to make a series of evaluative judgments about Donald. Subjects rated Donald on each of 12 randomly ordered trait scales that ranged from 0 (*not at all*) to 10 (*extremely*). Six of the scales were descriptively related to hostility; 3 of these scales were evaluatively negative (hostile, dislikeable, and unfriendly) and 3 were evaluatively positive (thoughtful, kind, and considerate). The remaining 6 scales were not related to hostility; 3 of these scales were evaluatively negative (boring, narrow-minded, and conceited) and 3 were evaluatively positive (intelligent, dependable, and interesting).

After completing the rating scales, the experimenter questioned subjects about whether they believed that the vigilance task and the impression-formation task were related. No subject reported thinking the tasks were related or indicated any knowledge of why the vigilance task would have affected impression ratings. The experimenter then explained the nature of priming effects to the subjects. During this debriefing, however, the fact that subjects had been selected for participation on the basis of their Modern Racism Scale scores was not revealed. Subjects were then thanked for their participation.

Recognition test condition. Up through completion of the vigilance task, recognition test subjects were treated exactly the same as the judgment subjects. Subjects in this condition were exposed to either the 80% or 20% priming lists of Replication 1 or Replication 2. Following the vigilance task, however, the experimenter explained that the stimuli were actually words and that subjects would be asked to try to recognize the words previously presented. The recognition test was distributed and subjects were instructed to check off the items that they believed had been presented. The experimenter told them that only half of the words on the list had been presented during the vigilance task.

The 48 items of this test consisted of the 24 words in Replication 1 (12 stereotype-related and 12 neutral words) and the 24 words in Replication 2 (12 stereotype-related and 12 neutral words). Words in Replication 2 served as distractors (words not presented) for Replication 1 targets (words actually presented), and Replication 1 words were used as distractors for Replication 2 targets during the recognition test. The recognition test items were randomly ordered.

Guess condition. The experimenter told subjects in this condition that the words would be presented quickly in one of four locations around the central fixation point. Their task was to guess each word immediately following its presentation. The experimenter instructed subjects to maintain their gaze on the fixation point, as this was the best strategy for guessing words given their unpredictable location and timing. Subjects saw either the 80% list of Replication 1 or the 80% list of Replication 2. Subjects were to make a guess for each word presented, even making blind guesses if necessary, and were prompted to guess if they failed to do so spontaneously. This requirement was introduced to lower subjects' guessing criterion so as to provide a fair test of their immediate awareness of the stimuli (Bargh & Pietromonaco, 1982).

Results

Several checks on subjects' awareness of the content of primes were included in this study. Attentionless processing should allow detection but not immediate or delayed recognition of the stimuli.

Guess condition: A check on immediate awareness. Six high- and 6 low-prejudice subjects were run in this condition. Half of each group were presented with the 80% list of Replication 1 and half with the 80% list of Replication 2. If word content were truly not available to consciousness under the viewing conditions of this study, then subjects should not have been able to guess the content of the stereotype-related or neutral words. Subjects reported that this was a difficult task and that they had no idea of the content of the stimuli. Overall, they made few accurate guesses.

Of the 1,200 guesses, subjects guessed 20 words accurately, a hit rate of 1.67%. Overall, subjects guessed 1.4% of the stereotype-related words and 3.33% of the neutral words. Replicating Bargh and Pietromonaco (1982), the neutral word hit rate was appreciably higher than that for stereotype-related words. The neutral words were high-frequency words and thus would presumably be more easily detectable under the viewing conditions in this study.

Incorrect guesses were examined for their relatedness to the racial stereotype. Only three of the incorrect guesses could be interpreted as being related to the stereotype. Twice *Black* appeared as a guess, once from a high-prejudice subject and once from a low-prejudice subject. These data suggest that neither high- nor low-prejudice subjects were able to identify the content of the priming words at the point of encoding, thus satisfying one criterion for attentionless processing.

Recognition condition: A check on memory for primes. Although subjects could not guess the content of the words at the point of stimulus presentation, it is possible that a recognition test would provide a more sensitive test of subjects' awareness of the content primes. On the basis of their performance on the recognition test, subjects were assigned a hit (correct recognition of presented items) and a false alarm (incorrect recognition of new items) score for both stereotype-related and neutral words.

The hits and false alarms were used to generate d' scores for both stereotype-related and neutral words, which corresponded to subjects' ability to correctly identify previously presented information. Green and Swets (1966) have tabled d' scores for all possible combinations of hits and false alarms. The primary analysis concerned whether subjects performed the recognition task better than would be expected by chance. Over all subjects, neither d' for stereotype-related words ($M = .01$) nor for neutral words ($M = .07$) differed significantly from zero ($ps > .42$). These same comparisons were also done separately for high- and low-

prejudice subjects. These analyses, like the overall analysis, suggest that subjects could not reliably recognize the primes. High-prejudice subjects' mean d' scores for stereotyped-related and neutral words were .02 and .12, respectively ($ps > .40$). Low-prejudice subjects' mean d' scores for stereotype-related and neutral words were .01 and .02, respectively ($ps > .84$).

In addition, the d' scores were submitted to a four-way mixed-model analysis of variance (ANOVA)—Prejudice Level × Priming × Replication × Word Type—with word type (stereotype-related vs. neutral) as a repeated measure.[1] Interest centered on whether (a) high- and low-prejudice subjects were differentially sensitive to stereotype-related and neutral words on the recognition test and (b) priming affected recognition performance. The analysis revealed that prejudice level did not affect subjects' overall performance, $F(1, 24) = 0.07, p = .78$, and that it did not interact with word type, $F(1, 24) = 0.04, p = .84$.

The second crucial test concerned whether increasing the number of primes interacted with recognition of the word type or subjects' prejudice level to affect performance on the recognition test. None of these tests was significant. Priming did not interact with word type, $F(1, 24) = 0.47, p = .50$, or affect the Prejudice × Word Type interaction, $F(1, 24) = 0.32, p < .56$. The analysis revealed no other significant main effects or interactions. Subjects were not able to reliably recognize either stereotype-related or neutral words, suggesting that subjects did not have conscious access to the content of the primes, thus establishing the second criterion for attentionless processing.

Automatic stereotype activation and hostility ratings. The major issue concerned the effect of automatic stereotype activation on the interpretation of ambiguous stereotype-congruent (i.e., hostile) behaviors performed by a race-unspecified target person. Following Srull and Wyer (1979) and Bargh and Pietromonaco (1982), two subscores were computed for each subject. A hos-

---

[1] The overall hit and false alarm rates for stereotype-related and neutral words were also examined as a function of prejudice level, priming, and replication. These data were submitted to a five-way mixed-model analysis of variance. Prejudice level, priming, and replication were between-subjects variables; word type (stereotype-related vs. neutral) and response type (hits vs. false alarms) were within-subject variables. This analysis, like the d' analysis, revealed no significant main effects or interactions.

tility-related subscore was computed by taking the mean of the six traits denotatively related to hostility (hostile, dislikeable, unfriendly, kind, thoughtful, and considerate). The positively valenced scales (thoughtful, considerate, and kind) were reverse scored so that higher mean ratings indicated higher levels of hostility. Similarly, an overall hostility-unrelated subscore was computed by taking the mean of the six hostility-unrelated scales. Again, the positive scales were reverse scored.

The mean ratings were submitted to a mixed-model ANOVA, with prejudice level (high vs. low), priming (20% vs. 80%), and replication (1 vs. 2) as between-subjects variables and scale (hostility related vs. hostility unrelated) as a within-subjects variable. The analysis revealed that the Priming × Scale interaction was significant, $F(1, 70) = 5.04$, $p < .03$. Ratings on the hostility-related scales were more extreme in the 80% ($M = 7.52$) than in the 20% ($M = 6.87$) priming condition.[2] The hostility-unrelated scales, however, were unaffected by priming ($Ms = 5.89$ and 6.00 for the 20% and 80% priming conditions, respectively). Moreover, the three-way Prejudice Level × Priming × Scale interaction was not significant, $F(1, 70) = 1.19$, $p = .27$. These results were consistent with the present model and suggest that the effects of automatic stereotype priming were equally strong for high- and low-prejudice subjects. Activating the stereotype did not, however, produce a global negative evaluation of the stimulus person, as only trait scales related to the behaviors in the ambiguous passage were affected by priming.

These analyses suggest that the automatic activation of the racial stereotype affects the encoding and interpretation of ambiguously hostile behaviors for both high- and low-prejudice subjects. To examine this more closely, separate tests on the hostility-related and hostility-unrelated scales were conducted. If high- and low-prejudice subjects are equally affected by the priming manipulation, then prejudice level should not interact with priming in either analysis. The analysis on hostility-related scales revealed only a significant priming main effect, $F(1, 70) = 7.59$, $p < .008$. The Prejudice Level × Priming interaction was nonsignificant, $F(1, 70) = 1.19$, $p = .28$. None of the other main effects or interactions was significant. In the analysis of the hostility-unrelated scales, neither the priming main effect, $F(1, 70) = 0.23$, $p = .63$, nor

the Prejudice Level × Priming interaction, $F(1, 70) = 0.02$, $p = .88$, reached significance.

Subjects' prejudice level did enter into several higher order interactions. The Prejudice Level × Priming × Replication interaction, $F(1, 70) = 4.69$, $p < .03$, indicated that the priming effect was slightly reversed for low-prejudice subjects exposed to Replication 1. A Prejudice Level × Scale Relatedness × Replication interaction, $F(1, 70) = 4.42$, $p < .04$, suggested that the difference between scores on hostility-related and hostility-unrelated scales was greater for low-prejudice subjects in Replication 1 and high-prejudice subjects in Replication 2.

Discussion

Study 2 examined the effects of prejudice and automatic stereotype priming on subjects' evaluations of ambiguous stereotype-related behaviors performed by a race-unspecified target person under conditions that precluded the possibility that controlled processes could explain the priming effect. The judgment data of this study suggest that when subjects' ability to consciously monitor stereotype activation is precluded, both high- and low-prejudice subjects produce stereotype-congruent or prejudice-like responses (i.e., stereotype-congruent evaluations of ambiguous behaviors).

In summary, the data from Studies 1 and 2 suggest that both those high and low in prejudice have cognitive structures (i.e., stereotypes) that can support prejudiced responses. These data, however, should not be interpreted as suggesting that all people are prejudiced. It could be argued that neither task allowed for the possibility of nonprejudiced responses. Study 1 encouraged subjects not to inhibit prejudiced responses. Study 2 suggested that when the racial category is activated and subjects' ability to consciously monitor this activation is bypassed, their responses reflect the activation of cognitive structures with a longer history (i.e., greater frequency) of activation. As previously indicated, it appears that these structures are the culturally defined stereotypes

---

[2] The primary analysis was repeated for high- and low-prejudiced subjects separately. The two-way Priming × Scale Related interaction was obtained for both high- and low-prejudice subjects (both $ps < .05$), thus supporting the primary analysis.

(Higgins & King, 1981), which are part of people's social heritage, rather than necessarily part of subjects' personal beliefs.

The present data suggest that when automatically accessed the stereotype may have effects that are inaccessible to the subject (Nisbett & Wilson, 1977). Thus, even for subjects who honestly report having no negative prejudices against Blacks, activation of stereotypes can have automatic effects that if not consciously monitored produce effects that resemble prejudiced responses. Study 3 examined the responses of high- and low-prejudiced subjects' personal beliefs about Blacks (in addition to the automatically activated stereotype).

Study 3: Controlled Processes and Prejudice Level

The present model suggests that one feature that differentiates low- from high-prejudice persons is the effort that they will put into stereotype-inhibition processes. When their nonprejudiced identity is threatened, low-prejudice persons are motivated to reaffirm their nonprejudiced self-concepts (Dutton, 1976; Dutton & Lake, 1973). Thus, when the conflict between their nonprejudiced personal beliefs and the stereotype of Blacks is made salient, low-prejudiced persons are likely to resolve the conflict by denouncing the stereotype and expressing their nonprejudiced beliefs. To express stereotype-congruent ideas would be inconsistent with and perhaps threaten their nonprejudiced identities.

Study 3 tested this hypothesis by asking high- and low-prejudice subjects to list their thoughts about the racial group *Blacks* under anonymous conditions. This type of task is likely to make the stereotype–personal belief conflict salient for low-prejudice subjects. The model suggests that under these conditions, high- and low-prejudice subjects will write different thoughts about Blacks. High-prejudice subjects, because their beliefs overlap with the stereotype, are expected to list stereotype-congruent thoughts. Low-prejudice subjects, it is argued, will take this opportunity to demonstrate that they do not endorse the cultural stereotype; they are likely to inhibit stereotype-congruent thoughts and intentionally replace them with thoughts consistent with their nonprejudiced personal beliefs. According to the model, resolution

of the conflict between personal beliefs and the cultural stereotype in the form of nonprejudiced responses requires controlled inhibition (Logan & Cowan, 1984; Neely, 1977) of the automatically activated stereotype.

Method

Subjects. Subjects were 67 White introductory psychology students who participated for course credit.[3] Subjects were run in groups of 3–6 and were seated at partitioned tables so that subjects were isolated from each other. These procedures were used to enhance anonymity so that subjects would not feel inhibited and would write whatever came to mind.

An additional precaution was taken to ensure anonymity. Before subjects were given instructions regarding the thought-listing task, their experimental participation cards were collected, signed, and left in a pile in the front of the room for subjects to pick up after the study. The experimenter asked subjects not to put any identifying information on their booklets. These procedures were followed so that it would be clear that subjects' names could not be associated with their booklets and that they would receive credit regardless of whether they completed the booklet. No subject refused to complete the measures.

Procedure. After subjects' cards were signed the experimenter asked them to turn over and read the general instructions on the first page of the booklet. Subjects' first task was to list as many alternate labels as they were aware of for the social group *Black Americans*. They were told that the experimenter was interested in how people think about and talk informally about social groups. As such, the experimenter told them that slang or other unconventional group labels were acceptable. Subjects were allowed 1 min to complete this task. The purpose of this task was to encourage activation of subjects' cognitive representation of Blacks. If, for example, high- and low-prejudice persons refer to the social group with different labels (i.e., pejorative vs. nonpejorative) and the labels have

---

[3]Four Black students signed up to participate. These students did not fill out the thought-listing or Modern Racism measure but were given credit for showing up to participate. The nature of the study was described to them, and they were told why interest centered on the responses of White subjects.

different associates, this could provide a basis for explaining any potential differences in content between high- and low-prejudice subjects.

Following the label-generation task, subjects read the thought-listing instructions that asked them to list all of their thoughts in response to the social group *Black Americans* and to the alternate labels they generated. The experimenter told them that any and all of their thoughts (e.g., beliefs, feelings, expectations), flattering or unflattering, were acceptable. Subjects were encouraged to be honest and forthright. The experimenter provided them with two pages of 10 thought-listing boxes in which to record their thoughts and asked them to put only one thought in each box. They were allowed 10 min to complete the task. Finally, subjects completed the seven-item Modern Racism Scale and read through a debriefing document that described the goals of the research and thanked them for their participation.

Results

Coding scheme. On the basis of a pilot study[4] a scheme for coding the types of thoughts generated was developed. Two judges, blind to subjects' prejudice level, were provided with the coding scheme instructions. A statement or set of statements listed in a box was considered one thought and was assigned one classification by each judge. Each judge rated the 67 protocols in different random orders. The judges agreed on 92% of their classifications. A third judge resolved discrepancies in scoring.

The major interest in this study was in whether the content of thoughts generated would differ as a function of prejudice level.[5] Before examining those data, however, the alternate labels subjects generated for Black Americans were examined. If high-prejudice subjects generate more negative labels (e.g., nigger, jigaboo, etc.) than low-prejudice subjects and pejorative labels are more strongly associated with stereotype-congruent information, this could explain possible differences between high- and low-prejudice subjects. Subjects were divided into high-prejudice ($N = 34$) and low-prejudice ($N = 33$) groups on the basis of a median split of scores on the Modern Racism Scale.

The proportion of pejorative and nonpejorative labels generated was calculated for each subject. Pejorative labels included terms such as the following: niggers, coons, spades, spear-chuckers, jungle bunnies, and jigs. Nonpejorative labels included the following: Blacks, Afro Americans, Brothers, and colored people. One high-prejudice subject was eliminated from this comparison because she failed to generate any alternate labels. The comparison indicated that the proportion of pejorative alternate labels did not differ between high-prejudice ($M = .53$) and low-prejudice ($M = .44$) subjects, $t(64) = .68, p > .10$. It appears, then, that high- and low-prejudice subjects were aware of the various pejorative labels.

---

[4]The coding scheme was developed and pretested in a pilot study, the goal of which was to demonstrate that subjects' cognitive representations of social groups are richer and more complex than simple traitbased structures. The coding scheme was developed on the basis of considerations of the stereotype assessment, prejudice, attitude, and cognitive organization literature. The stereotype literature, for example, led to an examination of the types of traits (i.e., positive or negative) listed in response to the category label. The prejudice and attitude measurement literature, however, led to examination of whether positive (e.g., statements of equality, recognition of Blacks' plight historically, etc.) or negative (resentment of affirmative action, avoid interactions with Blacks) belief thoughts would be elicited by the label.

The cognitive organization literature (Collins & Quillian, 1969; Rips, Shoben, & Smith, 1973) suggested that both criterial (e.g., physical descriptors) as well as noncriterial (e.g., associated terms) should be examined. On the basis of Rosch's (1978) categorization model, the coding scheme included a category for basic (e.g., athletes) and subordinate (e.g., Richard Pryor) level exemplars of the social category. Superordinate labels were not included because subjects had been asked to generate alternate labels prior to the thought-listing task. Strong support for the coding scheme was found in the pilot study. The pilot study did not examine the complexity of thought listings as a function of subjects' prejudice level. That was the goal of this study.

[5]As a prerequisite to examining the content of the protocols, an analysis on the number of thoughts and the number of alternate labels generated by high- and low-prejudice subjects was performed to examine whether prejudice level affected these tasks. Although it was expected that subjects would generate more thoughts than alternate labels, the key tests of interest were provided by the prejudice-level main effect (whether one group listed more items than the other) and the Prejudice Level × Task interaction (whether prejudice level differentially affected the tasks). These data were submitted to a Prejudice Level (high vs. low) × Task (label generation vs. thought generation) mixed-model analysis of variance. The analysis revealed that subjects generated a greater number of thoughts ($M = 12.67$) than labels ($M = 4.72$), $F(1, 65) = 156.83$, $p < .0001$. However, neither the prejudice main effect, $F(1, 65) = 0.66, p < .42$, nor the Prejudice Level × Task interaction, $F(1, 65) = 0.01, p < .94$, was significant.

Examination of the thought-listing protocols, however, revealed important differences between high- and low-prejudice subjects. The important differences appeared to be associated with the belief and trait categories.[6] Negative beliefs included thoughts such as "Blacks are free loaders"; "Blacks cause problems (e.g., mugging, fights)"; "Affirmative action sucks"; and so on. Positive-belief thoughts included "Blacks and Whites are equal"; "Affirmative action will restore historical inequities"; "My father says all Blacks are lazy, I think he is wrong" (e.g., negation of the cultural stereotype); "It's unfair to judge people by their color—they are individuals"; and so on. The positive and negative traits were typically listed as single words rather than being written in complete sentences. Negative traits included hostile, lazy, stupid, poor, dirty, and so on. The positive traits included musical, friendly, athletic, and so on.

The frequency of these positive-belief, negative-belief, and trait thoughts listed in subjects' protocols were submitted to a Prejudice Level (high vs. low) × Valence (positive vs. negative) × Thought Type (trait vs. belief) mixed-model ANOVA. Prejudice level was a between-subjects variable, and valence and thought type were within-subjects variables. The analysis revealed the expected Prejudice Level × Valence interaction, $F(1, 65) = 28.82$, $p < .0001$. High-prejudice subjects listed more negative ($M = 2.06$) than positive ($M = 1.48$) thoughts, and low-prejudice subjects listed more positive ($M = 2.28$) than negative ($M = 1.10$) thoughts. In addition, there was a Prejudice Level × Type interaction, $F(1, 65) = 18.04$, $p < .0001$. This interaction suggested that high-prejudice subjects were more likely to list trait ($M = 2.56$) than belief ($M = 1.52$) thoughts. In contrast, low-prejudice subjects were more likely to list belief ($M=2.86$) than trait ($M=1.12$) thoughts. These interactions are important because the Black stereotype traditionally has been largely negative and composed of traits (Brigham, 1971). Ascription of negative components of the streotype was verified in these data only for high-prejudice subjects.

These two-way interactions were qualified, however, by a significant Prejudice Level × Valence × Thought Type interaction, $F(1, 65) = 4.88$, $p < .03$. High-prejudice subjects most often listed negative traits ($M = 3.32$). A post hoc Duncan test ($p = .05$) revealed that for high-prejudice subjects, the frequency of negative trait thoughts differed significantly from each of the other three thoughts

types but that the frequency of positive-belief ($M = 1.17$), negative-belief ($M = 1.18$), and positive trait ($M = 1.79$) thoughts did not differ from each other. In contrast, low-prejudice subjects most frequently listed positive-belief thoughts ($M = 4.52$). This mean differed significantly (Duncan test, $p = .05$) from the negative-belief ($M = 1.21$), positive trait ($M = 1.24$), and negative trait ($M = 1.00$) means, but the latter three means did not differ from each other.

It was argued earlier that this type of task would encourage subjects to intentionally access and report thoughts consistent with their personal beliefs. Trait ascriptions are part of high-prejudice, but not low-prejudice, subjects' beliefs according to the present model. It appears that in this task, both high- and low-prejudice subjects' thoughts reflected their beliefs. High-prejudice subjects reported primarily traits and low-prejudice subjects reported beliefs that contradicted the cultural stereotype and emphasized equality between the races.

To follow up implications from the previous studies, subjects' protocols were examined to determine whether the themes of hostility, aggressiveness, or violence were present. Statements such as "They are hostile," "Blacks are violent," "Blacks are aggressive," and so on were considered to reflect this theme. Non-trait-based thoughts such as "They rape women" or "I'm scared of them" were less frequent but were also considered to reflect the general theme. Sixty percent of the high-prejudice subjects directly included such themes in their thought-listing protocols. In contrast, only 9% of the subjects scoring low in prejudice included hostility themes in their protocols. A z test on proportions indicated that this difference was reliable ($z = 4.41$, $p < .01$).

Discussion

Taken together, these sets of analyses indicate that high- and low-prejudice subjects were willing to

---

[6]A canonical discriminant function analysis in which subjects' prejudice level was predicted as a function of the best linear combination of the 10 coding categories revealed a single canonical variable (Wilks's lambda = 0.63), $F(10, 56) = 3.25$, $p < .002$. The canonical squared multiple correlation was 0.37. Positive-belief thoughts were located at one extreme of the canonical structure (–0.88) and negative trait thoughts at the other (0.78). None of the other categories discriminated significantly between high- and low-prejudice groups.

report different thoughts about Blacks. In addition, these analyses suggested that there were sufficient levels of variability in prejudice levels among the subjects to detect the effects of prejudice in the previous studies should those effects exist. The thought-listing task was one in which subjects were likely to think carefully about what their responses implied about their prejudice-relevant self-concepts. For those who valued a nonprejudiced identity, writing stereotype-congruent thoughts would have been inconsistent with and perhaps would have threatened their nonprejudiced identity.

Thus, even under anonymous conditions, low-prejudice subjects apparently censored and inhibited (Neely, 1977) the automatically activated negative stereotype-congruent information and consciously replaced it with thoughts that expressed their nonprejudiced values. Low-prejudice subjects wrote few pejorative thoughts. Their thoughts were more likely to have reflected the importance of equality or the negation of the cultural stereotype. Moreover, low-prejudice subjects appeared reluctant to ascribe traits to the group as a whole. In contrast, the protocols of high-prejudice subjects seemed much more consistent with the cultural stereotype of Blacks. Their thoughts were primarily negative, and they seemed willing to ascribe traits to the group (especially negative traits).

A most important comparison for the present three studies, and for the intergroup perception literature more generally, concerns the likelihood of subjects reporting thoughts reflecting the theme of hostility. Much of the intergroup perception literature has assumed that the hostility component of the stereotype influences perceptions of Blacks (Donnerstein et al., 1972; Duncan, 1976; Sager & Schofield, 1980), and Studies 1 and 2 suggested that hostility is strongly associated with Blacks for both high- and low-prejudice subjects. Study 2 in particular suggested that hostility is automatically activated when the category label and associates are presented. The present data, however, suggest that high- and low-prejudice subjects differ in their willingness to attribute this characteristic to the entire group. High-prejudice subjects included thoughts suggesting that Blacks are hostile and aggressive much more frequently than did low-prejudice subjects. The present framework suggests that this difference likely reflects low-prejudice subjects engaging in controlled, stereo-type-inhibiting processes. Low-prejudice subjects apparently censored negative, what they considered inappropriate, thoughts that came to mind.

General Discussion

The model examined in these studies makes a clear distinction between knowledge of the racial stereotype, which Study 1 suggested both high- and low-prejudice persons possess, and personal beliefs about the stereotyped group. Study 2 suggested that automatic stereotype activation is equally strong and equally inescapable for high- and low-prejudice subjects. In the absence of controlled stereotype-related processes, automatic stereotype activation leads to stereotype-congruent or prejudice-like responses for both those high and low in prejudice. Study 3, however, provided evidence that controlled processes can inhibit the effects of automatic processing when the implications of such processing compete with goals to establish or maintain a nonprejudiced identity.

In conclusion, it is argued that prejudice need not be the consequence of ordinary thought processes. Although stereotypes still exist and can influence the responses of both high- and low-prejudice subjects, particularly when those responses are not subject to close conscious scrutiny, there are individuals who actively reject the negative stereotype and make efforts to respond in nonprejudiced ways. At least in situations involving consciously controlled stereotype-related processes, those who score low in prejudice on an attitude scale are attempting to inhibit stereotypic responses (e.g., Study 3; Greeley & Sheatsley, 1971; Taylor et al., 1978; see also Higgins & King, 1981). The present framework, because of its emphasis on the possible dissociation of automatic and controlled processes, *allows for the possibility* that those who report being nonprejudiced are in reality low in prejudice.

This analysis is not meant to imply that prejudice has disappeared or to give people an excuse for their prejudices. In addition, it does not imply that only low-prejudice persons are capable of controlled stereotype inhibition. High-prejudice persons could also consciously censor their responses to present a non-prejudiced identity (probably for different reasons than low-prejudice persons, however). What this analysis requires is that theoreticians be more precise on the criteria established for labeling behavior as prejudiced or nonprejudiced. The present model and set of empirical studies certainly does not resolve this issue. However, the present framework highlights the potential for nonprejudiced behaviors when social desirability concerns are minimal (Study 3) and invites researchers to explore the variables that are likely to engage controlled stereotype-inhibiting processes in intergroup settings.

ACKNOWLEDGMENTS

This article is based on a dissertation submitted by Patricia G. Devine to the Ohio State University Graduate School in partial fulfillment of the requirement for the doctoral degree. This research was supported by a Presidential Fellowship and by a Graduate Student Alumni Research Award both awarded by the Ohio State University Graduate School.

Thanks are extended to Thomas M. Ostrom, chair of the dissertation committee, and to the other members of the committee, Anthony G. Greenwald and Gifford Weary.

REFERENCES

Allport, G. W. (1954). *The nature of prejudice*. Reading, MA: Addison-Wesley.

Ashmore, R. D., & Del Boca, F. K. (1981). Conceptual approaches to stereotypes and stereotyping. In D. L. Hamilton (Ed.), *Cognitive processes in stereotyping and intergroup behavior* (pp. 1–35). Hillsdale, NJ: Erlbaum.

Bargh, J. A. (1984). Automatic and conscious processing of social information. In R. S. Wyer Jr., & T. K. Srull (Eds.), *The handbook of social cognition* (Vol. 3, pp. 1–43). Hillsdale, NJ: Erlbaum.

Bargh, J. A., Bond, R. N., Lombardi, W. J., & Tota, M. E. (1986). The additive nature of chronic and temporary sources of construct accessibility. *Journal of Personality and Social Psychology, 50,* 869–878.

Bargh, J. A., & Pietromonaco, P. (1982). Automatic information processing and social perception: The influence of trait information presented outside of conscious awareness on impression formation. *Journal of Personality and Social Psychology, 43,* 437–449.

Baxter, G. W. (1973). Prejudiced liberals? Race and information effects in a two person game. *Journal of Conflict Resolution, 17,* 131–161.

Bettleheim, B., & Janowitz, M. (1964). *Social change and prejudice*. New York: Free Press of Glencoe.

Bolota, D. A. (1983). Automatic semantic activation and episodic memory encoding. *Journal of Verbal Learning and Verbal Behavior, 22,* 88–104.

Billig, M. (1985). Prejudice, categorization, and particularization: From a perceptual to a rhetorical approach. *European Journal of Social Psychology, 15,* 79–103.

Brigham, J. C. (1971). Ethnic stereotypes. *Psychological Bulletin, 76,* 15–33.

Brigham, J. C. (1972). Racial stereotypes: Measurement variables and the stereotype-attitude relationship. *Journal of Applied Social Psychology, 2,* 63–76.

Carrol, J. B., Davies, P., & Richman, B. (1971). *The American Heritage word frequency book*. New York: Houghton Mifflin.

Carver, C. S., Ganellin, R. J., Froming, W. J., & Chambers, W. (1983). Modeling: An analysis in terms of category accessibility. *Journal of Experimental Social Psychology, 19,* 403–421.

Collins, A. M., & Quillian, M. R. (1969). Retrieval time from semantic memory. *Journal of Verbal Learning and Verbal Behavior, 8,* 240–247.

Crosby, F., Bromley, S., & Saxe, L. (1980). Recent unobtrusive studies of black and white discrimination and prejudice: A literature review. *Psychological Bulletin, 87,* 546–563.

Devine, P. G. (1988). *Stereotype assessment: Theoretical and methodological issues*. Unpublished manuscript, University of Wisconsin—Madison.

Donnerstein, E., & Donnerstein, M. (1972). White rewarding behavior as a function of the potential for black retaliation. *Journal of Personality and Social Psychology, 24,* 327–333.

Donnerstein, E., Donnerstein, M., Simon, S., & Ditrichs, R. (1972). Variables in interracial aggression: Anonymity, expected retaliation, and a riot. *Journal of Personality and Social Psychology, 22,* 236–245.

Dovidio, J. F., Evans, N. E., & Tyler, R. B. (1986). Racial stereotypes: The contents of their cognitive representation. *Journal of Experimental Social Psychology, 22,* 22–37.

Duncan, B. L. (1976). Differential social perception and attribution of intergroup violence: Testing the lower limits of stereotyping of blacks. *Journal of Personality and Social Psychology, 34,* 590–598.

Dutton, D. G. (1976). Tokenism, reverse discrimination, and egalitarianism in interracial behavior. *Journal of Social Issues, 32,* 93–107.

Dutton, D. G., & Lake R. A. (1973). Threat of own prejudice and reverse discrimination in interracial situations. *Journal of Personality and Social Psychology, 28,* 94–100.

Ehrlich, H. J. (1973). *The social psychology of prejudice*. New York: Wiley.

Fowler, C. A., Wolford, G., Slade, R., & Tassinary, L. (1981). Lexical access with and without awareness. *Journal of Experimental Psychology: General, 110,* 341–362.

Gaertner, S. L. (1976). Nonreactive measures in racial attitude research: A focus on "liberals." In P. A. Katz (Ed.), *Towards the elimination of racism* (pp. 183–211). New York: Pergamon Press.

Gaertner, S. L., & Dovidio, J. F. (1977). The subtlety of white racism, arousal, and helping. *Journal of Personality and Social Psychology. 35,* 691–707.

Gaertner, S. L., & McLaughlin, J. P. (1983). Racial stereotypes: Associations and ascriptions of positive and negative characteristics. *Social Psychology Quarterly, 46,* 23–30.

Gilbert, G. M. (1951). Stereotype persistence and change among college students. *Journal of Abnormal and Social Psychology, 46,* 245–254.

Greeley, A., & Sheatsley, P. (1971). Attitudes toward racial integration. *Scientific American, 222,* 13–19.

Green, D. M., & Swets, J. A. (1966). *Signal detection theory and psychophysics*. New York: Wiley.

Greenwald, A. G., Klinger, M., & Liu, T. J. (in press). Unconscious processing of word meaning. *Memory & Cognition*.

Hamilton, D. L. (1981). Stereotyping and intergroup behavior: Some thoughts on the cognitive approach. In D. L.

Hamilton (Ed.), *Cognitive processes in stereotyping and intergroup behavior* (pp. 333–353). Hillsdale, NJ: Erlbaum.

Harding, J., Proshansky, H., Kutner, B., & Chein, I. (1969). Prejudice and ethnic relations. In G. Lindzey (Ed.), *Handbook of social psychology* (Vol. 5). Reading, MA: Addison-Wesley.

Higgins, E. T., & King, G. (1981). Accessibility of social constructs: Information-processing consequences of individual and contextual variability. In N. Cantor & J. F. Kihlstrom (Eds.), *Personality and social interaction* (pp. 69–121). Hillsdale, NJ: Erlbaum.

Holender, D. (1986). Semantic activation without conscious identification in dichotic listening, parafoveal vision, and visual masking: A survey and appraisal. *Behavioral and Brain Sciences, 9,* 1–66.

Karlins, M., Coffman, T. L., & Walters, G. (1969). On the fading of social stereotypes: Studies in three generations of college students. *Journal of Personality and Social Psychology, 13,* 1–16.

Katz, D., & Braly, K. (1933). Racial stereotypes in one hundred college students. *Journal of Abnormal and Social Psychology, 28,* 280–290.

Katz, P. A. (1976). The acquisition of racial attitudes in children. In P. A. Katz (Ed.), *Towards the elimination of racism* (pp. 125–154). New York: Pergamon Press.

Kinder, D. R., & Sears, D. O. (1981). Prejudice and politics: Symbolic racism versus racial threats to the good life. *Journal of Personality and Social Psychology, 40,* 414–431.

Klatzky, R. L. (1984). *Memory and awareness.* San Francisco: Freeman.

LaViolette, F., & Silvert, K. H. (1951). A theory of stereotypes. *Social Forces, 29,* 237–257.

Linn, L. S. (1965). Verbal attitudes and overt behavior: A study of racial discrimination. *Social Forces, 43,* 353–364.

Logan, G. D. (1980). Attention and automaticity in Stroop and priming tasks: Theory and data. *Cognitive Psychology, 12,* 523–553.

Logan, G. D., & Cowan, W. G. (1984). On the ability to inhibit thought and action: A theory of act control. *Psychological Review, 91,* 295–327.

Marcel, A. J. (1983a). Conscious and unconscious perception: Experiments on visual masking and word recognition. *Cognitive Psychology, 15,* 197–237.

Marcel, A. J. (1983b). Conscious and unconscious perception: An approach to the relations between phenomenal experience and perceptual processes. *Cognitive Psychology, 15,* 238–300.

McConahay, J. B., Hardee, B. B., & Batts, V. (1981). Has racism declined? It depends upon who's asking and what is asked. *Journal of Conflict Resolution, 25,* 563–579.

Neely, J. H. (1977). Semantic priming and retrieval from lexical memory: Roles of inhibitionless spreading activation and limited-capacity attention. *Journal of Experimental Psychology, 106,* 226–254.

Nisbett, R. E., & Wilson, T. D. (1977). Telling more than we can know: Verbal reports on mental processes. *Psychological Review, 84,* 231–259.

Pettigrew, T. (1987, May 12). "Useful" modes of thought contribute to prejudice. *New York Times,* pp. 17, 20.

Porter, J. D. R. (1971). *Black child, white child: The development of racial attitudes.* Cambridge, MA: Harvard University Press.

Posner, M. I., & Snyder, C. R. R. (1975). Attention and cognitive control. In R. L. Solso (Ed.), *Information processing and cognition: The Loyola Symposium.* Hillsdale, NJ: Erlbaum.

Pratkanis, A. R. (in press). The cognitive representation of attitudes. In A. R. Pratkanis, S. J. Breckler, & A. G. Greenwald (Eds.), *Attitude structure and function.* Hillsdale, NJ: Erlbaum.

Proshansky, H. M. (1966). The development of intergroup attitudes. In L. W. Hoffman & M. L. Hoffman (Eds.), *Review of child development research* (Vol. 2, pp. 311–371). New York: Russell Sage Foundation.

Rips, L. J., Shoben, E. J., & Smith, E. E. (1973). Semantic distance and the verification of semantic relations. *Journal of Verbal Learning and Verbal Behavior, 12,* 1–20.

Ronis, D. L., Yates, J. F., & Kirscht, J. P. (in press). Attitudes, decisions, and habits as determinants of repeated behavior. In A. R. Pratkanis, S. J. Breckler, & A. G. Greenwald (Eds.), *Attitude structure and function.* Hillsdale, NJ: Erlbaum.

Rosch, E. (1978). Principles of categorization. In E. Rosch and B. B. Lloyd (Eds.), *Cognition and categorization* (pp. 28–48). Hillsdale, NJ: Erlbaum.

Saenger, G. (1953). *The social psychology of prejudice.* New York: Harper.

Sager, H. A., & Schofield, J. W. (1980). Racial and behavioral cues in black and white children's perceptions of ambiguously aggressive acts. *Journal of Personality and Social Psychology, 39,* 590–598.

Schneider, W., & Shiffrin, R. M. (1977). Controlled and automatic human information processing: I. Detection, search, and attention. *Psychological Review, 84,* 1–66.

Sears, D. O., & Kinder, D. R. (1971). Racial tensions and voting in Los Angeles. In W. Z. Hirsch (Ed.), *Los Angeles: Viability and prospects for metropolitan leadership* (pp. 51–88). New York: Praeger.

Sears, D. O., & McConahay, J. B. (1973). *The politics of violence: The new urban blacks and the Watts riot.* Boston: Houghton Mifflin.

Secord, P. F., & Backman, C. W. (1974). *Social psychology.* New York: McGraw-Hill.

Shiffrin, R. M., & Dumais, S. T. (1981). The development of automatism. In J. R. Anderson (Ed.), *Cognitive skills and their acquisition* (pp. 111–140). Hillsdale, NJ: Erlbaum.

Shiffrin, R. M., & Schneider, W. (1977). Controlled and automatic human information processing: II. Perceptual learning, automatic attending, and a general theory. *Psychological Review, 84,* 127–190.

Simpson, G. E., & Yinger, J. M. (1965). *Racial and cultural minorities* (rev. ed.) New York: Harper & Row.

Smith, E. R. (1984). Model of social inference processes. *Psychological Review, 91,* 392–413.

Smith, E. R., & Branscombe, N. R. (1985). *Stereotype traits can be processed automatically.* Unpublished manuscript, Purdue University, West Lafayette, IN.

Srull, T. K., & Wyer, R. S., Jr. (1979). The role of category accessibility in the interpretation of information about persons: Some determinants and implications. *Journal of Personality and Social Psychology, 37,* 1660–1672.

Srull, T. K., & Wyer, R. S., Jr. (1980). Category accessibility and social perception: Some implications for the study of person memory and interpersonal judgments. *Journal of Personality and Social Psychology, 38,* 841–856.

Stephan, W. G. (1985). Intergroup relations. In G. Lindzey & E. Aronson (Eds.), *The handbook of social psychology* (3rd ed., Vol. 2, pp. 559–658). Hillsdale, NJ: Erlbaum.

Tajfel, H. (1981). *Human groups and social categories: Studies in social psychology*. Cambridge, England: Cambridge University Press.

Taylor, D. G., Sheatsley, P. B., & Greeley, A. M. (1978). Attitudes toward racial integration. *Scientific American, 238,* 42–49.

Weitz, S. (1972). Attitude, voice, and behavior: A repressed affect model of interracial interaction. *Journal of Personality and Social Psychology, 24,* 14–21.

Wyer, R. S., Jr., & Srull, T. K. (1981). Category accessibility: Some theoretical and empirical issues concerning the processing of social stimulus information. In E. T. Higgins, C. P. Herman, & M. P. Zanna (Eds.), *Social cognition: The Ontario Symposium* (Vol. 1, pp. 168–197). Hillsdale, NJ: Erlbaum.

READING 10

Cognitive Organization of Impressions: Effects of Incongruency in Complex Representations

David L. Hamilton and Denise M. Driscoll • University of California, Santa Barbara
Leila T. Worth • Pennsylvania State University

Editors' Notes

The present selection represents a central interest of social cognition researchers in how information about persons is stored and organized in memory. Whereas we do not have any psychological X rays to answer these questions directly, there are indirect behavioral measures that can be used, such as examining the relative probability of recalling various informational items about the person and the conditional probabilities of recalling some items given that others were recalled. The use of such innnovative techniques requires an understanding of how a hypothesized structure of person information in memory is likely to lead to specific differences in recall. The present paper illustrates the sophistication and rigor with which model construction and testing can be approached in social cognition research.

Discussion Questions

1. What specific person-memory models are presented by Hamilton et al. (1989), and how do the results of the reported experiments relate to these various models?
2. How do Hamilton et al. (1989) explain the fact that, contrary to numerous prior experiments, no differences were found in the present studies in memory for incongruent versus congruent information?

3. In what ways, according to Hamilton et al. (1989), are the processes invoked in simple impression formation contexts different from those invoked in more complex situations?

Suggested Readings

Hastie, R., & Kumar, P. (1979). Person memory: Personality traits as organizing principles in memory for behaviors. *Journal of Personality and Social Psychology, 37,* 25–38.

Rothbart, M., Fulero, S., Jensen, C., Howard, J., & Birrell, P. (1978). From individual to group impressions: Availability heuristics in stereotype formation. *Journal of Experimental Social Psychology, 14,* 235–255.

Smith, E. R., & DeCoster, J. (1998). Knowledge acquisition, accessibility, and use in person perception and stereotyping: Simulation with a recurrent connectionist network. *Journal of Personality and Social Psychology, 74(1),* 21–35.

Srull, T. K., Lichtenstein, M., & Rothbart, M. (1985). Associative storage and retrieval processes in person memory. *Journal of Experimental Psychology: Learning, Memory, and Cognition, 11,* 316–345.

Authors' Abstract

Two experiments investigated the organization in memory of expectancy-congruent and expectancy-incongruent information pertaining to multiple trait concepts in an impression-formation task. In Experiment 1, when multiple trait concepts were represented in the information describing the target person, both congruent and incongruent items reflecting the same trait concept were stored together and were directly associated in memory, and both types of items were recalled equally well. In Experiment 2, when only one trait concept was represented in the information, incongruent items were recalled with higher probability than congruent items, and the latter were not directly associated in memory. Results suggest that with increasing categorical complexity of stimulus information, processes are invoked that do not occur in simpler impression-formation contexts. Implications for theoretical models of person memory are discussed.

In recent years researchers interested in impression formation have adopted an information-processing orientation in order to understand how information available about a person is acquired, stored, and used in developing an impression of that person. Although this research has investigated a variety of topics, a central focus of this work has been on how information that is either congruent or incongruent with an initial impression or expectation about a target person is processed, represented in memory, and subsequently retrieved.

In an important article, Hastie and Kumar (1979) established a paradigm that has proven to be extremely useful for studying these issues, and their work has been the catalyst for numerous subsequent investigations. Their subjects, whose task was to form an impression of a target person, were first presented with a set of homogeneous trait adjectives describing the person. This description created a strong initial impression about the person on a single trait dimension. Subjects then read a series of sentences describing behaviors performed by the person. Some of the behaviors were congruent with the initial impression, some were incongruent with it, and some were irrelevant to the trait initially established in the impression. Subsequently, subjects were asked to recall as many of the behaviors as they could. Hastie and Kumar found that behaviors incongruent with the initial impression were recalled with higher probability than were impression-congruent behaviors, with irrelevant behaviors being the least likely to be recalled. Those basic findings have been replicated in numerous subsequent experiments (e.g., Bargh & Thein, 1985; Belmore & Hubbard, 1987; Crocker, Hannah, & Weber, 1983; Driscoll, Hamilton, & Sorrentino, 1989; Hastie, 1980, 1984; Hemsley & Marmurek, 1982; Srull, 1981; Srull, Lichtenstein, & Rothbart, 1985; Stern, Marrs, Millar, & Cole, 1984; Wyer & Gordon, 1982; Wyer & Martin, 1986).

This finding has been theoretically explained in terms of an associative network model, first proposed by Hastie (1980) and subsequently developed and extended by Srull (1981). In this model, shown in Figure 1, the subject's conception of the target person (including the initial expectancy) is represented by a "node" to which items of information about the person become attached as they are encoded, represented by the vertical lines connecting individual behaviors to the node. During encoding, if the subject thinks about, compares, or integrates one behavioral item with another, an associative pathway directly connecting those two items in memory can be formed, as indicated by the horizontal lines in the figure. Hastie (1980) and Srull (1981) have postulated that this associative activity is likely to occur during the encoding of impression-incongruent behaviors, but not during the encoding of impression-congruent behaviors. As a consequence, all of the direct interitem connections (horizontal pathways) involve incongruent behaviors, for it was during their encoding that these associations (with both congruent and other incongruent behaviors) were formed. However, there is never an instance of a direct interitem connection between two congruent items.[1]

The model also specifies a retrieval process that would, in conjunction with the assumed representation, produce the differences in recall probabilities for congruent and incongruent behaviors. Spe-

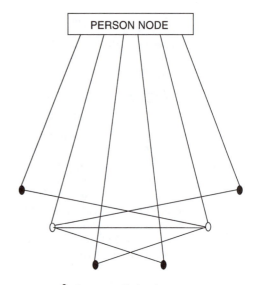

● Congruent behaviors
○ Incongruent behaviors

FIGURE 10.1 ■ Associative network representation of behaviors congruent and incongruent with a single trait.

cifically, when asked to recall the behavioral information, the subject accesses the memory network through the person node and traverses one of the vertical pathways to recall the first item. The model then assumes that, if possible, the retrieval process will move horizontally across a pathway directly connecting the recalled item to another behavior, which will then be recalled. If such a pathway is not available, however, the retrieval process will return to the person node and search for another vertical pathway to recall another behavioral item. This process continues until the subject can no longer recall additional items. Given the representation shown in Figure 1, the outcome of this process is a higher probability that incongruent, compared with congruent, behaviors will be recalled because there are more pathways leading to the incongruent than to the congruent items in the network. Thus, the model is highly effective in accounting for the recall results obtained in the studies cited earlier.

In addition, data obtained from two other kinds of analyses provide further support for the model. The first concerns an analysis of the sequential properties of subjects' recall performance. The model predicts that having recalled a congruent item, the next item recalled is likely to be an incongruent item, whereas when an incongruent item

---

[1]The nature of this associative activity is not specified in the model per se, but a likely candidate is the attribution process. That is, there is now fairly good evidence that expectancy-incongruent information triggers the attribution process (Clary & Tesser, 1983; Hamilton, 1988; Hastie, 1984; Weiner, 1985). The attempt to "explain" why a person engaged in a behavior that is incongruent with one's impression of that person may include reviewing, and thinking about the causal implications of, other information already acquired about the person, thereby producing the pattern of interitem associations posited by the Hastie–Srull model (Hamilton, 1988; Hamilton, Grubb, Acorn, Trolier, & Carpenter, 1989).

is recalled, the following item may be either congruent or incongruent. These predictions follow from the pattern of interitem associations represented in the model. To test those predictions, Srull (1981) calculated the conditional probabilities for recall of congruent and incongruent items, given that the previously recalled item was congruent or incongruent. The probabilities conformed nicely to the model's predictions.

The second analysis is based on measurement of the time interval between successively recalled items. The assumption is that the transition in recall from one item to the next should be shorter if those two items are directly connected than if moving from one to the other requires going through the person node. This assumption translates into the simple prediction that time intervals between successively recalled items should be shorter when at least one of those items is an incongruent behavior than when neither item is an incongruent behavior. Srull et al. (1985) measured these interrecall intervals and reported results consistent with this prediction.

In sum, results obtained from three different measures—probability of recall, sequential properties of recall, and interrecall intervals—provide strong support for the assumptions of the associative network model proposed by Hastie (1980) and Srull (1981). Information incongruent with an impression is more likely to be recalled than impression-congruent information. Moreover, as represented in memory, incongruent items are often directly connected with other (congruent and incongruent) items, whereas these associative pathways do not form between two impression-congruent items.

It is important to note, however, that in the paradigm used in almost all of those studies, subjects learned about, and hence based their impression representation on, information that pertained to only one personality trait dimension. That is, the initial impression conveyed by the trait ensemble, the congruent behaviors, and the incongruent behaviors all referred to the same attribute dimension. In this article we argue that this feature of the commonly used paradigm may impose serious constraints on the generality of the findings obtained from that research.

Other person memory researchers have investigated the organization of impressions in terms of multiple trait categories. Hamilton, Katz, and Leirer (1980; Hamilton, 1981) reported a series of experiments showing that subjects in an impression formation task organized behavior-descriptive information about a target person in terms of prominent trait categories represented in the descriptive information. Their evidence for this conclusion was based on analyses of clustering in subjects' free recall of the behavior-descriptive sentences. Specifically, subjects were presented with a series of statements describing a target person's behaviors. The behavior descriptions provided several instances of the person manifesting each of several different traits (sociable, intelligent, athletic, etc.). All behaviors were positive manifestations of one of the attributes (i.e., no inconsistencies were included in the stimulus list). The series of items was presented in random order and, following a brief filler task, subjects were asked to recall the stimulus behaviors. Although behaviors representing the same trait were dispersed in the stimulus presentation sequence, clustering analyses indicated that they tended to be grouped together in subjects' recall protocols. In other words, in forming their impressions, subjects had imposed an organization on the behavior-descriptive information they received on the basis of trait categories, an organization that was not present in the stimulus sequence.

Although Hamilton et al. (1980) did not discuss their results in an associative network framework, it is not difficult to consider their findings in terms of a model similar to that shown in Figure 1. Also, to integrate this work with the findings of Hastie (1980), Srull (1981), and others, it is important to consider how incongruent behaviors would be incorporated into these representations. In the following discussion we differentiate among three possible models that make somewhat different assumptions about processing.

Trait-Specific Hastie Model

One plausible strategy is to assume that the type of representation proposed by Hastie (1980) develops separately for each trait category included in the stimulus information. Consider a simple case in which each of two traits (e.g., friendliness, intelligence) is represented by four behavioral items, three congruent and one incongruent with the trait. If items are grouped in memory according to the traits they manifest, then there should be two groupings of behaviors under the person node, with

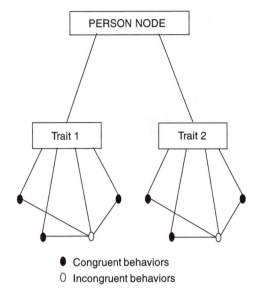

● Congruent behaviors
○ Incongruent behaviors

FIGURE 10.2 ■ Trait-specific Hastie model of congruent and incongruent behaviors for two traits.

one cluster corresponding to each trait. As shown in Figure 2, each behavioral item becomes attached to a trait subnode as it is encoded. Incongruent items would be stored in the appropriate trait clusters and would form associative pathways with other items (congruent and incongruent) within that cluster. In contrast, no direct connections between pairs of congruent behaviors are established. In recall, subjects would proceed from the person node through one of the trait subnodes to one of the behaviors. Having recalled that behavior, the retrieval process would either traverse a horizontal pathway or return to the trait subnode and then, if possible, to another behavior within the same grouping. If no other behavior within that grouping can be recalled, retrieval would return to the person node and proceed to the other trait subnode and to recall of behaviors in that grouping.

As shown in Figure 2, this approach simply assumes that in a multitrait context, the processes and representations discussed earlier for a single-trait context will occur for each trait concept. This model, then, would produce trait-based clustering in free recall and would preserve the assumption that associative pathways are not formed directly between congruent behaviors. Therefore, within a trait cluster, incongruent behaviors are more likely to be recalled than are congruent behaviors.

Complete Association Model

On the other hand, an intuitive consideration of the impression-formation task with multiple trait concepts implies that associations between congruent items would be formed. That is, an important aspect of processing the behavioral information and forming an impression seemingly would involve not only interpreting a new behavior in terms of an appropriate trait concept but also comparing that item with previously acquired behaviors of the same type to determine their degree of fit as manifestations of the same trait. This kind of integrative activity has been prevalent in many discussions of the impression-formation process (Asch, 1946; Hamilton et al., 1980; Srull, 1983).

This process of evaluating whether behaviors belong together in the emerging representation (impression) of the target person may be applied to both congruent and incongruent behaviors. If so, then this comparison or matching process would produce direct associations between behaviors as they are represented in memory. Such a representation is shown in Figure 3. This type of processing would seem particularly likely when trait concepts have not already been activated, as in the Hamilton et al. (1980) study. However, even when prior expectancies have been created, this

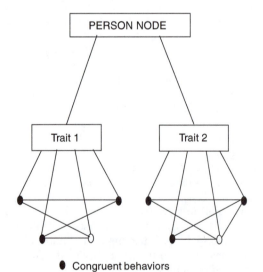

● Congruent behaviors
○ Incongruent behaviors

FIGURE 10.3 ■ Complete association model of congruent and incongruent behaviors for two traits.

process of comparing new items with previously acquired items that instantiated the same concept may be more likely to occur when the information pertains to multiple trait concepts rather than just one concept. Thus, in contrast to the assumptions of the trait-specific Hastie model, congruent items would be directly associated with each other as they are represented in memory.

The retrieval process would proceed in the same manner described for the previous model. The pattern of interitem connections would facilitate recall of items within the same grouping, thereby producing trait-based clustering in recall. Note, however, that because the comparison or matching process assumed to occur in this multitrait case has produced direct associations between congruent (as well as incongruent) items, there no longer are more pathways leading to the incongruent behaviors. Therefore, an important implication of this model is that in the case of multitrait information, there will be no difference in the probability of recall of congruent and incongruent behaviors.

Dual-Coding Model

A third model, initially proposed by Wyer and Gordon (1982, 1984) and recently formalized by Srull and Wyer (1989; see also Wyer, 1989; Wyer, Bodenhausen, & Srull, 1984), assumes that each incoming item of information receives a dual coding and hence becomes represented twice in the subject's memory. One of the codings is based on the subject's interpretation of the behavior in terms of a trait concept to which that item becomes attached. When several items are interpreted in terms of the same trait concept, they become grouped together in memory under a trait node, forming a trait-behavior cluster. Because behaviors that are denotatively incongruent with each other (e.g., friendly and unfriendly behaviors) instantiate different trait concepts, they would be stored in different, independent trait–behavior clusters in this representation. In addition, the subject forms a second, separate representation of the items solely on the basis of their evaluative properties. This representation is organized around a person node that reflects the subject's evaluative impression of the target person as likable or unlikable, and each behavioral item describing the person is attached to this node as well. The evaluative property of each behavior determines whether the item is con-

gruent or incongruent with the overall evaluative impression; the model makes the same assumptions about interitem associations as were made by Hastie (1980) and Srull (1981). That is, incongruent items are connected to other items, but pathways do not form directly between two congruent items. In this model, however, it is explicitly assumed that it is evaluative, not descriptive, incongruency that is the basis for the formation of these interitem associations (Srull & Wyer, 1989; Wyer & Gordon, 1982, 1984).

This dual-representation model has considerable flexibility in accounting for the empirical findings discussed earlier. That is, retrieval of information from the trait–behavior clusters would produce the trait-based organization of recall reported by Hamilton et al. (1980), whereas retrieval from the evaluative representation would produce the advantage in recall of incongruent, compared with congruent, items.

If this dual representation exists, it becomes important to know which representation a person will use in retrieving information under any given condition. As just illustrated, retrieval of information from one of the representations may produce a recall protocol that would differ in meaningful ways from that obtained from retrieval based on the other representation of the same information. Unfortunately, the conditions under which retrieval will occur from the trait clusters and when it will be based on the evaluative representation have not been fully specified. In the most recent statement of this model, Srull and Wyer (1989, p. 64) postulated that retrieval is more likely to be based on the representation that was used most recently. This principle may be useful for understanding retrieval at some later time, but it provides no guidelines regarding retrieval following the initial, simultaneous representation of information, as in the typical experiment.

Nevertheless, it was possible to evaluate some implications of this model in our research. For example, if retrieval is based on the evaluative representation, subjects should have better recall for incongruent than for congruent behaviors, but recall protocols should not be organized according to trait categories. Alternatively, if retrieval is based on trait clusters, no difference in recall of congruent and incongruent behaviors would be expected. In this case trait-based clustering would be predicted. However, in this model, positive (e.g., friendly) and negative (e.g., unfriendly) manifestations of the same trait are regarded as different trait concepts. Therefore, congruent and incongruent behaviors would be stored independently, under different trait nodes, and hence should not be associated in recall (Srull & Wyer, 1989, pp. 67 and 69).

Experiment 1

In the first experiment we investigated how behavioral information about a target person is organized and represented in memory when that information pertains to several trait categories and includes, for some of those traits, expectancy-incongruent items. All subjects were told that the experiment was a study of how people form first impressions of others. A general description was provided at the outset to create an initial impression of the target person prior to reading the behavioral information. Instead of describing a single trait domain, however, this description was designed to establish expectancies regarding three personality attributes. The stimulus sentences provided information about the target person's behaviors pertaining to the various attributes and, in some of the experimental conditions, included behaviors incongruent with the initial impression. The dependent measures were derived from subjects' recall of these behaviors. As already indicated, the three models described earlier make differing predictions about subjects' recall for congruent and incongruent behaviors. Additional differences are developed and discussed as the results of the experiment are reported.

Method

Overview. Subjects participated in an experiment on impression formation. They first read a paragraph presenting either a positive or a negative description of a person named Bob. This description was designed to create an initial impression about Bob on three dimensions; friendliness, intelligence, and adventurousness. Subjects then read a series of sentences describing behaviors that Bob performed. The behaviors were congruent or incongruent with the initial expectancies or were irrelevant to any of the three traits conveyed in the paragraph. Subjects were then asked to recall all of the behaviors that they could remember. Three measures were derived from subjects' recall pro-

tocols: the proportion of congruent and incongruent behaviors recalled, the sequence in which these items were recalled, and the time interval between successively recalled behaviors.

Subjects. Subjects in the experiment were 151 University of California, Santa Barbara, undergraduate students who participated in order to partially fulfill a psychology course requirement. Subjects were run in groups of 1–4 persons.

Pretesting of stimulus materials. Fifty undergraduate students not in the actual experiment rated a large number of behavioral sentences on four 11-point scales, with high numbers representing the positive pole of each dimension. The four scales on which each sentence was rated were adventurous-unadventurous, friendly–unfriendly, intelligent–unintelligent, and desirable–undesirable. On the basis of subjects' ratings, we selected five sentences to represent each pole of each of the first three dimensions. Also selected were 15 behaviors irrelevant to any of the dimensions. Mean desirability ratings ranged from 2.7 to 4.0 for behaviors representing the negative pole and from 7.6 to 8.4 for behaviors representing the positive pole of the dimensions.

The same pretest subjects then read a paragraph portraying either a positive or a negative impression of Bob and, on the basis of this description, rated Bob on 11-point scales measuring the following dimensions: adventurous–unadventurous, friendly–unfriendly, intelligent–unintelligent, and like–dislike. The overall mean ratings for the positive and negative paragraphs of Bob were 9.61 and 3.96, respectively. Table 1 shows the mean ratings of both the behavioral sentences and the impression paragraphs on each dimension.

Construction of stimulus sets. All subjects were given a booklet containing 30 pages, each of which presented one behavior-descriptive sentence about Bob. Each behavior description was congruent or incongruent with one of the three traits described in the impression paragraph or was irrelevant to any of the three traits.

Fourteen versions of this stimulus packet were constructed. Seven booklets presented predominantly desirable behaviors, whereas the other 7 consisted of predominantly negative behaviors. In all cases there were five behaviors from one pole (positive or negative) of all three trait dimensions (friendliness, intelligence, and adventurousness). These items were always congruent with the impression created by the initial paragraph. The 7

Table 10.1. Mean Ratings of Stimulus Behaviors and Initial Impression Paragraphs

Sentence/paragraph type	Rating scale			
	Friendly–unfriendly	Intelligent–unintelligent	Adventurous–unadventurous	Desirable–undesirable
Type of sentence				
Friendly	9.99	7.55	7.02	8.36
Unfriendly	2.34	4.14	5.26	2.95
Intelligent	6.92	9.80	6.82	7.61
Unintelligent	5.73	2.90	6.28	2.71
Adventurous	6.89	6.35	10.03	7.70
Unadventurous	5.46	5.58	2.31	4.03
Irrelevent	6.53	6.97	6.09	7.20
Initial impression paragraph				
Positive	9.60	9.40	9.84	9.36
Negative	2.96	4.24	4.68	4.60

booklets in each of the subsets differed in the nature of the remaining 15 sentences. Table 2 illustrates, for the positive-impression condition, each of the three major conditions of the study: the all congruent condition, the one incongruent category condition, and the two incongruent categories condition. In the all congruent condition, one stimulus set (in both the positive and negative versions) contained the five impression-congruent behaviors for each trait, along with 15 behaviors that were irrelevant to any of the three traits. No items incongruent with the initial impression were included in this condition. In the one incongruent category condition, three other packets (in both positive and negative versions) included, in addition to the 15 congruent behaviors, five behaviors that were incongruent with one of the three traits. The three packets in this condition differed in which of the three traits had the incongruent behaviors. To keep the total length of the stimulus list constant (at 30 items), only 10 irrelevant behaviors were included in these packets. In the two incongruent categories condition, the final three packets (in both positive and negative versions) included the 15 congruent behaviors along with 5 incongruent behaviors for each of two traits. The three packets in this condition differed in which pair of traits had incongruent behaviors. Again, total list length was held constant by reducing the number of irrelevant behaviors to five.

In all 14 versions of the stimulus packet, items were presented in a random order, with the constraint that two items representing the same trait dimension (positive or negative) never occurred in succession.

Procedure. On entering the laboratory subjects were told that "the experiment you will be participating in today involves forming an impression about a person named Bob. Please concentrate on forming this impression as it is important for the experiment." Subjects were then given a sheet of paper providing either a positive or a negative ini-

Table 10.2. Example of Distribution of Stimulus Items in Experimental Conditions

Condition	Type of stimulus behavior						
	Friendly		Intelligent		Adventurous		
	Positive	Negative	Positive	Negative	Positive	Negative	Irrelevant
Consistent items only in all categories	5	0	5	0	5	0	15
Inconsistent items in one category	5	5	5	0	5	0	10
Inconsistent items in two categories	5	5	5	5	5	0	5

Note. All possible combinations of incongruency across the three trait categories were included in the experiment.

tial description of Bob. Subjects in the positive-impression condition read the following:

In the packet of materials in front of you (turned face down) you will find a number of behaviors performed by an individual named Bob. Bob tends to be much more friendly and sociable than the average person. He enjoys making new friends, meeting with old ones, and generally tends to value social activities. Bob is also very intelligent. His sharp, quick mind has always helped him to excel at almost anything he does. Bob tends to be very adventuresome, as well. He enjoys new and exciting activities and actively seeks out adventures and experiences with uncertain outcomes. When I say begin, please turn the packet over and read each behavior carefully as you form your impression of Bob.

For subjects in the negative-impression condition, the first and last sentences were identical but the descriptive passage read as follows:

Bob tends to be a bit less friendly and sociable than the average person. He enjoys spending time alone, and generally doesn't value social activities. Bob is also of below average intelligence. His mind works slowly and has always prevented him from excelling at anything he does. Bob tends to be very timid as well. He is scared of doing new things and prefers sticking to a daily routine and activities he knows he can do.

When subjects finished reading the paragraph, they were asked to turn it face down on the table. They were then given one of the stimulus packets and instructed to read each behavior carefully, keeping in mind their impression of Bob. Each behavioral sentence was typed and centered on a sheet of paper. Subjects were paced through the booklet, reading one sentence every 6 s.

After being paced through the behavioral packets, a short (3-min) filler task was administered. Each subject was then escorted to a separate room and was given an instruction sheet that read as follows:

Earlier in this experiment you read a series of sentences, each of which described a behavior performed by a person named Bob. We would like you to recall as many of these behaviors as possible. We realize that it would be impossible for you to remember the behaviors word for word, but please try to recall as many as you can as precisely as possible. The order in which you recall these behaviors is not important. We will be tape recording your recall of Bob's behaviors, so please speak into the tape recorder.

The experimenter emphasized that the subjects' task was to recall the behaviors they had read earlier and not to provide their general impressions of Bob. Subjects were also informed that the experimenter would return in a few minutes to shut off the tape recorder and to let the tape keep running regardless of whether they were still remembering behaviors. Subjects were given 4 min to recall the behavioral sentences. When this task was completed they were thoroughly debriefed and thanked for their participation.

Dependent measures. Three dependent measures were scored and analyzed, all of which were derived from the subjects' tape-recorded recall protocols. The recall protocol for each subject was coded by assistants who were unaware of the purpose of the experiment. The coding procedure required listening to each subject's tape-recorded recall twice. The first time through the tape, the assistant wrote down the behavioral sentences recalled by the subject in the order in which they were recalled. Two dependent measures were derived from this record: amount of recall and conditional probabilities. First, the amount of recall for each subject was calculated. In addition to a total recall score, the subject's recall of various types of items (congruent and incongruent items for each trait category as well as irrelevant items) was determined. Second, from the sequence of recalled items we calculated conditional probabilities that various types of items were recalled in successive positions.

The second coding of each subject's recall tape was done to record the time intervals between successively recalled items. Using a computer program written to facilitate recording of these *interrecall times*, the assistant pressed a button on hearing the last word of one recalled sentence and then pressed another button on hearing the first word of the next recalled sentence. The computer recorded the time interval (in milliseconds) between the button presses. Sentences never presented during the study but recalled by the subjects were coded as intrusions and were ignored when coding interrecall times. The frequency of these intrusion was low and did not have an impact on the data. For the measurement of interresponse intervals, the interjudge reliability of two coders was calculated for a sample of 20 subjects. The codings of two assistants correlated .999, indicating high reliability. Therefore, only one assistant coded response intervals for the total sample, and her codings for all subjects were used in data analyses.

As noted, subjects were given 4 min to complete this recall task. Typically subjects would complete most of their recall within the first 2 min, and after some lengthy passage of time an additional item or two might come to mind. This latter feature created some abnormally long interrecall intervals that could have a substantial influence on cell means and variances. To avoid those effects, we decided to include subjects' recall performance up to the point of their first 50-s interval between successively recalled items and to exclude items recalled following that interval.[2] This criterion resulted in dropping an average of 1.09 items from subjects' recall scores. All three dependent measures were based on data from this reduced recall protocol.

Results and Discussion

Recall. Our first analysis was an examination of the overall recall performance of subjects in various conditions of the experiment. To this end, a 2 (positive and negative initial impression) × 3 (all congruent, one incongruent category, and two incongruent categories) analysis of variance (ANOVA) was conducted on subjects' total recall scores. This analysis yielded a nearly significant main effect for initial impression, $F(1, 145) = 3.73$, $p < .06$, with subjects who read the positive-impression paragraph recalling somewhat more items ($M = 10.86$) than subjects in the negative first-impression condition ($M = 9.73$). Neither the main effect for congruency conditions nor the interaction of the two factors were significant. Thus, subjects' overall recall did not differ as a function of whether the stimulus behavior did or did not include incongruent behaviors, or if they did, whether those incongruencies occurred in one- or two-true categories. Therefore, any effects obtained in subsequent analyses could not be attributed to differences among these conditions in overall recall performance.

The recall analysis of primary interest concerned the differential recall of congruent, incongruent,

and irrelevant behaviors. The three models outlined earlier make somewhat differing predictions about subjects relative recall of congruent and incongruent behaviors. As an extension of the single-trait case studied in past research, the trait-specific Hastie model predicts that subjects will recall a higher proportion of incongruent than congruent behaviors. The same prediction would be made by the dual-representation model, assuming that items are retrieved from the evaluation-based representation. In contrast, the complete association model posits that because all items within a trait category can be directly associated with each other, the proportion of congruent and incongruent behaviors recalled should not differ.

To test these predictions, we determined the proportion of each sentence type recalled by each subject and analyzed the data in a 2 (initial impression) × 2 (one incongruent category and two incongruent categories) × 3 (congruent, incongruent, and irrelevant item type) ANOVA with repeated measures on the last factor. Cell means from this analysis are shown in Table 3. The only significant result in this analysis was the main effect of item type, $F(2,218) = 7.45$, $p < .001$. Newman-Keuls tests indicated that subjects had significantly poorer ($p < .01$) recall for impression-irrelevant behaviors ($M = .278$) than for either of the other two types of items but that their recall of congruent ($M = .349$) and incongruent ($M = .353$) behaviors did not differ. These results are consistent with the complete association model but conflict with the predictions of the trait-specific Hastie model and the dual-representation model.

We performed additional analyses to test other predictions of the models. One implication of both the trait-specific Hastie model and the dual-representation model is that the presence of incongru-

---

[2]This criterion is somewhat arbitrary and reflects a compromise in the necessary trade off between (a) reducing the adverse effects of long and unrepresentative interrecall intervals and (b) reducing the length of the recall protocols on which the analyses are based.

TABLE 10.3. Proportion of Congruent, Incongruent, and Irrelevant Items Recalled: Experiment 1

Condition	Item type		
	Congruent	Incongruent	Irrelevant
Incongruent items in one category			
Positive impression	.372	.336	.290
Negative impression	.304	.384	.312
Incongruent items in two categories			
Positive impression	.395	.362	.239
Negative impression	.325	.339	.271

ent items in the stimulus list will actually facilitate recall of congruent items because of the associations that are formed during the encoding of incongruent behaviors. This result has been obtained in past research using one trait category (Srull, 1981). In all stimulus conditions in Experiment 1 subjects read 5 behaviors congruent with each of the three trait categories (a total of 15 congruent behaviors). To test the theoretical prediction just noted, we calculated the number of congruent items recalled by each subject and conducted a 2 (initial impression) × 3 (congruency conditions) ANOVA on the resulting scores. The main effect of initial impression was significant, $F(1,145) = 18.34$, $p < .001$, with positive-impression subjects recalling more congruent items ($M = 6.17$) than negative-impression subjects ($M = 4.73$). However, the prediction that recall of congruent behaviors would increase with increasing numbers of incongruent behaviors was not supported because the main effect of congruency conditions was not significant. If anything, there was a nonsignificant trend in the opposite direction, with subjects in the all congruent condition recalling slightly more of the items ($M = 6.03$) than did subjects exposed to incongruent behaviors in either one ($M = 5.16$) or two ($M = 5.37$) trait categories.

The preceding analysis collapsed across the three trait categories. Perhaps the predicted effects were masked by this collapsing, particularly if the results were stronger for some traits than for others. Therefore, we also conducted comparable analyses separately for each trait category to determine whether the effects of incongruency on recall of congruent items was specific to within-category descriptive inconsistency. For example, recall of congruent friendly items was compared for the all congruent condition, the one incongruent category condition in which incongruent friendly items were presented, and both of the two incongruent categories conditions that included unfriendly behaviors. Parallel analyses were conducted on recall of congruent intelligent and congruent adventurous behaviors. None of these analyses yielded any significant effect of congruency conditions, either as a main effect or in interaction with the initial impression manipulation. These results, then, do not support this prediction derived from the trait-specific Hastie model and the dual-representation model.

The most important finding in these analyses of subjects' recall scores was the lack of any ad-vantage in recall of incongruent, compared with congruent, behaviors. Given its apparent inconsistency with the results of several previous studies, this finding may seem puzzling. Additional analyses, focused on measures that are potentially more diagnostic of the way the behavioral information was encoded and represented in memory, provide a basis for understanding these results and their implications for theoretical accounts of how information is processed during impression formation.

Conditional probabilities. One strategy for examining the way information is organized and represented in memory is to analyze the sequential properties of subjects' recall protocols. Following Srull (1981), we determined the likelihood that certain kinds of item pairs were recalled in succession. Specifically, we calculated conditional probabilities of the following kind: Given that an item of Type X had just been recalled, what was the probability that the next item recalled would be of Type Y? We determined whether the conditional probabilities varied as a function of the congruency or incongruency of the items and whether the two items were from the same or different trait categories. These values are shown in Table 4. The three congruency conditions of the experiment define the major sections of the table, and within each one, all possible combinations of sequences of recalling congruent and incongruent behaviors are identified as rows of the table. For each combination, we calculated the conditional probabilities separately depending on whether both items were from the same or different trait categories; this distinction defines the columns of the table.

Several aspects of these data are informative regarding how the behavioral information was organized in memory. First, it is clear that the behaviors manifesting the same trait category were more likely to be recalled in succession than were behaviors representing different trait categories. That is, for every combination listed in Table 4, within-category sequences occurred with higher (in most cases, considerably higher) probability than its between-categories counterpart. Note that in many cases—specifically, those for which the second entry is a congruent item—by chance alone one would expect higher values in the between-categories than in the within-category column. Consider, for example, the first row for each condition in the table, where two items congruent with the initial impression are recalled in succession.

TABLE 10.4. Conditional Probabilities for Different Recall Sequences: Experiment 1

Condition	Conditional probabilities		
	Item sequence	Within category	Between categories
All congruent	C–C	.28	.15
Incongruent items in	C–C	.26	.13
one category	C–I	.23	.14
	I–C	.26	.13
	I–I	.25	Not possible
Incongruent items in	C–C	.31	.15
two categories	C–I	.23	.13
	I–C	.20	.14
	I–I	.25	.13

Note. C = congruent behavior and I = incongruent behavior.

Given that a congruent item has just been recalled, there are twice as many congruent behaviors reflecting a different trait than reflecting the same trait as the just-recalled item. The fact that within-category sequences in recall were more likely, even in these cases, is an indication of the extent to which the behavioral information was organized in terms of the trait categories they implied.

Second, the results for the second and third conditions—in which the stimulus sets included incongruent behaviors for one or two of the trait categories—indicate that this general tendency for trait-based organization was not meaningfully altered by the incongruent information. In particular, it is clear that incongruent items were more likely to be associated with other items, congruent and incongruent, reflecting the same trait than with items representing other trait categories. This result is problematic for the dual-representation model in two respects: (a) If items are being recalled from the evaluation-based representation, in which trait content is not specified, then within-category sequences should be no more (or less) likely than between-categories sequences. The differences between the two columns of Table 4 clearly contradict this prediction of the model. (b) Alternatively, it may be that items were being retrieved from the trait clusters. However, if in this model positive (friendly) and negative (unfriendly) manifestations of a trait constitute different concepts, and hence form distinct clusters, then congruent (C)–incongruent (I) and I–C sequences within a category should be much less likely than C–C and I–I within-category sequences. The data do not support this prediction either.

Third, it is theoretically important that two congruent items manifesting the same trait were just

as likely to be recalled in succession regardless of whether the stimulus set did or did not include incongruent behaviors. This result is problematic for the trait-specific Hastie model and for retrieval based on the evaluative representation of the dual-coding model. Specifically, the horizontal pathways involving incongruent items (see Figure 2) should result in recall of congruent items being followed by recall of incongruent items, thus reducing the likelihood of C–C sequences compared with the all congruent condition. There is no evidence in Table 4 for such a reduction.

The primary message conveyed by these conditional probabilities is that the behavioral items were organized in memory according to the trait categories that they implied. Behaviors that manifest the trait concepts, whether congruent or incongruent, are stored together in memory and separately from items manifesting other traits. From these results there appear to be no differences between congruent and incongruent items in the extent to which items are associated with each other in memory. Although these findings are problematic for the dual-representation and trait-specific Hastie models, they are entirely consistent with the complete association model.

Interrecall intervals. A final strategy for investigating the nature of subjects' memory representations of the stimulus behaviors was to analyze the amount of time between subjects' recall of successive items in their recall protocols. On the basis of the models discussed at the outset, interitem retrieval times are assumed to vary according to the retrieval route traversed in getting from one item to the next. Thus, successive recall of two items that are directly connected by an associative pathway should be relatively easy, with little time passing between recall of one item and the next. In contrast, when successive recall of two items would require, for example, leaving one trait grouping by going through the person node into another trait grouping, the time interval between the successive recall of the items should be considerably longer. Given those assumptions, short interrecall intervals would be interpreted as reflecting close association in memory and possibly direct association between the two items, whereas long interrecall times would be diagnostic of items stored in separate locations and not directly connected to each other.

Analysis of the interrecall times required creating what Srull et al. (1985) called "pseudosubjects." Because the recall protocols of many subjects did not include all possible combinations of interitem transitions, individual subjects often did not have complete interrecall time date. Therefore, we formed subgroups of subjects such that when their data were combined, each subgroup or pseudosubject possessed an interrecall time for every type of interitem transition (specifically, all of those shown in Table 4). Pseudosubjects were constructed separately for each of the six cells defined by the two initial impressions and the three congruency conditions of the experiment. The pseudosubjects were established by the following procedure: First, we identified the interrecall transition that occurred with the lowest frequency in any of the conditions; this determined the maximum number of pseudosubjects that could be created for that condition (in this case, 15). Subjects with interrecall times for that transition were identified and assigned to different pseudosubjects. In order to equate pseudosubject sample size for all conditions, 15 pseudosubjects were also estab-

lished in the other conditions. Second, we then identified the next least frequent transition type and, from the remaining subjects, identified those with entires for that recall sequence. These subjects were randomly assigned to the pseudosubjects defined by the first set of subjects. Third, this process continued until all pseudosubjects had an interrecall time entry for all types of interitem transition. Fourth, any remaining subjects were randomly assigned to the pseudosubjects. Finally, for each transition type except the least frequent (for which there was only one entry), the interrecall times for the members of each pseudosubject were averaged. Every pseudosubject, then, had an interrecall time for each transition type. Analyses of the interrecall time data were based on these samples.

Mean interrecall times for both within-category and between-categories instances of the various types of recall transitions are reported separately for each congruency condition in Table 5. Because of the nature of the design, we analyzed the data in a series of nonindependent analyses focusing on different theoretically relevant comparisons.

In the first analysis, for each congruency condition, the interrecall times between successively recalled congruent items (C–C transitions) were examined as a function of whether the two items were from the same or from different trait categories. A 2 (positive or negative initial impression) × 3 (congruency conditions) × 2 (within- vs. between-categories transition) ANOVA, with repeated measures on the last factor, was conducted on the interrecall times for C–C transitions. This analysis in effect compares the data in the first row of each of the major conditions shown in Table 5. This analysis yielded a highly significant main

TABLE 10.5. Mean Interrecall Intervals for Different Recall Sequences: Experiment 1

Condition	Interrecall times (in seconds)		
	Item sequence	Within category	Between categories
All congruent	C–C	3.3	9.7
Incongruent items in one category	C–C	4.8	11.9
	C–I	4.6	7.6
	I–C	5.8	9.5
	I–I	4.1	Not possible
Incongruent items in two categories	C–C	3.9	10.2
	C–I	8.5	9.8
	I–C	7.7	7.3
	I–I	5.1	5.4

Note. C = congruent behavior and I = incongruent behavior.

effect attributable to within- vs. between-categories transitions, $F(1,39) = 25.91$, $p < .001$, such that the time interval between successively recalled congruent items from the same trait category was considerably shorter ($M = 4.00$) than the interval between two impression-congruent items manifesting different traits ($M = 10.60$). No other main effects or interactions were significant.

This difference in interrecall intervals for within- and between-categories transitions was substantial and, as indicated by the nonsignificant interactions, was not moderated either by the predominant evaluation of the impression or by the presence or absence of incongruent information. The magnitude of this difference is consistent with the interpretation that behaviors reflecting the same trait are stored together in memory in clusters that are distinct from those representing other trait concepts (Hamilton et al., 1980).

In a second analysis we compared the within- and between-categories interrecall times for different types of transitions in the two conditions that included incongruent items. We performed a 2 (initial impression) × 2 (one vs. two incongruent categories) × 3 (C–C, C–I, and I–C transition type) × 2 (within- vs. between-categories) ANOVA, with repeated measures on the last two factors, on the interrecall times. (In the one incongruent category condition, it was impossible to have successive recalls of incongruent items from different categories, and this empty cell prevented including I–I transitions in this analysis.) Again, the only significant result was the main effect attributable to within- vs. between-categories transitions, $F(1, 26) = 18.41$, $p < .001$; within $M = 5.88$, between $M = 9.36$. Examination of Table 5 suggests that in both conditions the difference represented by this main effect was greater for C–C transitions than for transitions involving incongruent items, but the relevant interaction term did not approach significance, $F(2, 52) = 1.97$, $p = .15$.

We conducted an additional analysis on the two incongruent categories condition in order to include comparisons with the transitions between two incongruent items: a 2 (initial impression) × 4 (C–C, C–I, I–C, and I–I transition types) × 2 (within vs. between categories) ANOVA with repeated measures on the last two factors. Consistent with the preceding results, this analysis yielded only a significant main effect attributable to the within versus the between variable, $F(1, 13) = 4.70$, $p < .05$; within $M = 6.29$, between $M = 8.16$. Al-

though the means shown in Table 5 indicate that this difference was meaningful only for C–C transitions, the interaction of transition type with the within versus the between variable was not statistically significant, $F(3, 39) = 1.46$, $p > .20$. Simple effects analyses, conducted as if the interaction were significant and examining comparisons between means in each row, indicated that the within versus between difference was significant for the C–C transition, $F(1, 13) = 7.99$, $p < .01$, but was not significant for the other three cases. In contrast, comparisons among means in each column indicated that the time intervals for the four within-category transitions did not differ significantly and that those for between-categories transitions showed only a weak trend ($p < .11$) due to the I–I transition being somewhat faster than the other three cases. This general lack of significance probably reflects the reduced sample size for within-condition analyses as well as the considerable variation of values around each of the means.[3]

The results of Experiment 1 provide strong evidence that behavior-descriptive information about a target person was organized and stored in memory in terms of the trait categories manifested in the behavioral information. These findings further document that given the general processing goal of forming an impression of a target person, initial impressions are organized around the personality themes that are prominent in the available information (Hamilton et al., 1980). Of particular importance, both the conditional probability data and the interrecall times support the view that both congruent and incongruent items reflecting the same trait category are stored together and are directly associated with each other in the memory representation. These findings are consistent with the complete association model but are incompatible with both the trait-specific Hastie model and the dual-representation model.

Moreover, in this experiment subjects did *not* demonstrate better recall of incongruent compared with congruent behaviors. This finding raises the possibility that there may be differences in the processes involved in forming simple, unitrait

---

[3]We are dubious about the reliability of the mean values for the within-category congruent–incongruent (C–I) and I–C transitions. In a similar experiment (see Hamilton, 1989, for details) the mean interrecall times for these transitions were considerably shorter than the present values and were comparable to other within-category times.

impressions versus more complex, multitrait impressions. However, before any such conclusions can be drawn, additional evidence is required in order to rule out certain alternative accounts for our findings. It is possible that our failure to obtain results comparable to previously reported findings was not caused by including information about multiple trait domains in the stimulus materials but was a consequence of the specific materials and procedures used in our experiment. For example, we sought to establish initial expectancies through a paragraph-length description of the target person, whereas prior studies have typically done so by presenting a set of homogenous trait terms. Perhaps our procedure was a less effective expectancy-induction technique, with the consequence that incongruent items were not perceived as being incongruent to the same degree. Alternatively, it is possible that the behavior descriptions were not adequate instantiations of the trait concepts. For these reasons, we considered it important to test whether these materials, if presented for only one trait domain, would produce results comparable to those obtained in previous studies. We therefore conducted a second experiment to that end.

Experiment 2

Subjects in this experiment were instructed to form an impression of a target person described in the information presented to them. In contrast to Experiment 1, all of the descriptive information (other than irrelevant items) pertained to only one trait domain. Three versions of the stimulus materials (initial descriptions, congruent and incongruent behaviors) were developed, one version based on each of the three trait categories included in the first experiment. These replications were presented to different groups of subjects. We again assessed recall by having subjects speak into a tape recorder. Our hypothesis was that under these conditions, subjects would recall significantly more incongruent than congruent behaviors, as in previous studies in which only one trait dimension was represented in the descriptive information. In addition, we predicted that evidence for direct interitem connections between congruent items would not be obtained with these single-dimension materials.

Method

Subjects. Subjects in the experiment were 68 undergraduate students who participated in partial fulfillment of a course requirement. None of the subjects had participated in Experiment 1. Subjects were run in groups of 1–4 persons.

Stimulus materials. The stimulus materials were similar to those of Experiment 1 except that each subject received information pertinent to only one (rather than three) trait dimension. All stimulus booklets in Experiment 2 included both congruent and incongruent behaviors. In order to equate the total list length with that used in the first study, we doubled the number of behavior descriptions representing each pole of a dimension as well as the number of irrelevant behaviors, compared with the corresponding conditions of Experiment 1. Thus, each booklet consisted of 10 congruent and 10 incongruent behaviors, all of which pertained to the same trait dimension, and 10 irrelevant behaviors. One such booklet was prepared for each of the three trait domains used in Experiment 1. Which pole of the dimension was congruent or incongruent was determined by whether a positive or negative initial impression was created by the preliminary descriptive information provided to the subjects. This initial description also was limited to only one of the trait domains.

Procedure. The procedure was identical to that of Experiment 1. After receiving the instructions describing the impression-formation task, subjects were given a positive or negative initial description on one trait dimension. These were constructed by removing, from the paragraphs used in Experiment 1, those sentences pertaining to the other two dimensions. Thus, for example, subjects who received a positive friendly description of Bob read the following:

> In the packet of materials in front of you (turned face down) you will find a number of behaviors performed by an individual named Bob. Bob tends to be much more friendly and sociable than the average person. He enjoys making new friends, meeting old ones, and generally tends to value social activities. When I say begin, please turn the packet over and read each behavior carefully as you form your impression of Bob.

Similar paragraphs were presented for the intelligent and adventurousness stimulus sets.

Subjects were then paced through their stimulus booklet of 30 sentences, reading one sentence every 6 s. When completed, subjects again performed a 3-min filler task, were escorted to individual rooms, and were asked to recall the behavior sentences by speaking them into a tape recorder.

Dependent measures. As in Experiment 1, subjects' recall of congruent, incongruent, and irrelevant behaviors, their conditional probabilities for various recall sequences, and the time interval between successively recalled items were calculated from their tape-recorded recall protocols. Again, all measures were based on subjects' recall performance up to the first 50-s interval in their recall protocols (reducing subjects' recall scores, on average, by 0.85 items).

Results and Discussion

Recall. The number of congruent, incongruent, and irrelevant items recalled by each subject was determined and the resulting scores were analyzed in a 2 (positive and negative initial impression) × 3 (friendliness, intelligence, and adventurousness trait dimensions) × 3 (congruent, incongruent, and irrelevant item types) ANOVA with repeated measures on the last factor. The only significant result in this analysis was the main effect attributable to item type, $F(2, 124) = 27.50$, $p < .001$. Newman-Keuls tests confirmed that subjects recalled significantly ($p < .05$) more incongruent behaviors ($M = 3.99$) than congruent behaviors ($M = 3.54$) and that both of these were recalled significantly more often than irrelevant behaviors ($M = 2.44$, $p < .01$, in both cases). The lack of significant interactions indicates that this result was not qualified by either the desirability of the initial impression or the trait dimension described in the stimulus information.

Conditional probabilities. As in Experiment 1, conditional probabilities representing the likelihood that each type of item was recalled, given the nature of the preceding item in the recall sequence, were calculated for each subject's recall protocol. These individual conditional probabilities were then averaged across subjects, and the resulting means are shown in Table 6. It can be seen that recall of a congruent item was more likely to be followed by recall of an incongruent than another congruent item, whereas recall of an in-

TABLE 10.6. Conditional Probabilities for Different Recall Sequences: Experiment 2

Previous item	Subsequent item		
	Congruent	Incongruent	Irrelevant
Congruent	.28	.50	.22
Incongruent	.40	.37	.23
Irrelevant	.42	.25	.33

congruent item was equally likely to be followed by a congruent or an incongruent item. This pattern of results is exactly the same as that reported by Srull (1981) and is consistent with the network model for representation of single-trait information (Hastie, 1980; Srull, 1981).

Interrecall intervals. Time intervals between successively recalled items were measured as in the first experiment. Unfortunately, because trait domain was now a between-subjects factor and given the limited sample size, we were not able to create a sufficient number of pseudosubjects to perform a meaningful analysis of these data.

The findings from the recall measures and the conditional probabilities provide substantial evidence compatible with the Hastie–Srull model. Consistent with the findings of numerous other experiments using this paradigm with a single trait dimension, subjects recalled a higher proportion of incongruent than congruent behaviors. In addition, the conditional probability data were directly parallel to results of a comparable analysis reported by Srull (1981) and provide a more process-based measure that also fits the predictions of the Hastie–Srull model. Clearly, then, when the stimulus behaviors were limited to one trait domain, the findings were compatible with those typically obtained in studies using this paradigm.

General Discussion

Whereas the results of Experiment 2 replicate previous findings, they are also in strong contrast to the results of Experiment 1. In that experiment subjects did not have advantaged recall of incongruent items, and both conditional probability and interrecall interval data based on recall sequences indicated that congruent items were as closely associated with each other in memory as with incongruent items. The primary difference between the experiments was the dimensional complexity of the stimulus information. In Experiment 2 the impressions subjects formed were based primarily on information pertaining to a single trait dimension. In Experiment 1 the impressions were based on information reflecting multiple trait categories. The difference in the pattern of results suggests that somewhat different processes are operating in the two cases.

Equally important, the results of Experiment 1 conflict in several important respects with some central predictions derived from the Hastie–Srull model and applied in two of the more complex formulations introduced earlier. Specifically, in our experiment (a) items that were incongruent with initial expectancies were *not* recalled with higher probability than were expectancy-congruent items; (b) congruent items were *not* more likely to be followed by incongruent than by other congruent items in subjects' recall protocols; and (c) the time interval between successively recalled items was *not* longer for congruent–congruent transitions than for transitions involving incongruent items. These three findings are incompatible with the trait-specific Hastie model. They also conflict with retrieval based on the evaluative representation of the dual-coding model, which presumably would be centrally involved when the behavioral information includes evaluative incongruencies. These models, then, failed to receive support for some of their core hypotheses.

One of the strengths of the model originally proposed by Hastie (1980) is that it is specific regarding both how information becomes represented in memory and how it is retrieved. It is this specificity that has made it so useful in permitting a variety of empirical tests of its implications during the last decade. The trait-specific Hastie model and the complete association model retain this specificity regarding both representational and retrieval processes. The dual-coding model, although clearly postulating that each item is simultaneously represented in two independent structures pertaining to the target person, is ambiguous regarding the retrieval process. In particular, it is not clear when information will be retrieved from one representation as opposed to the other, even though properties of the recall protocol would differ in the two cases. This aspect of the model needs to be clarified if it is to make useful predictions.

Given the fact that numerous experiments have reported significantly better memory for incongruent than for congruent information, the absence of this difference in the results of Experiment 1 may seem problematic. However, other data provide the basis for understanding this outcome. Specifically, both the conditional probabilities and the interrecall times indicate that the primary basis for organization in memory was the trait domain to which the behaviors referred and that, within a trait domain, associative pathways were formed among those items, including pathways directly between pairs of congruent items. If congruent items are directly associated with each other in the memory network, as our data suggest, then the theoretical basis for explaining the greater recall of incongruent items would no longer hold. That is, there would no longer be more pathways leading to incongruent items than there are leading to congruent items. Consequently, under those conditions one would not expect any advantage in retrieving either type of item.

That behaviors were represented in memory according to trait domain may suggest that the results reflect retrieval from the trait-cluster aspect of the dual-representation model. According to that model, however, opposite poles of the same trait dimension (e.g., friendly, unfriendly) would be represented by different trait concepts. Therefore, behaviors manifesting those concepts would form independent trait clusters and hence should be recalled separately. In contrast to this hypothesis, both the conditional probability data and the interrecall interval results provided strong evidence that behaviors that were congruent and incongruent with the same trait were closely associated with each other as they were represented in memory.

The results of Experiment 1 also clarify findings obtained in a similar study by Hamilton and Worth (cited in Hamilton, 1989), who found better recall of incongruent than congruent behaviors in a multitrait context. As noted earlier, interpretation of this result was clouded by the unequal numbers of congruent and incongruent behaviors included in their stimulus sets. The lack of this recall effect in Experiment 1 suggests that the earlier result was a reflection of set-size effects. This interpretation is bolstered by the finding that the conditional probability and interrecall interval results for the two studies were highly comparable.

We have argued that Experiment 1's findings reflect, at least in part, processes that are invoked in more complex impression-formation situations, but that may not be influential in a simpler context, such as the single-trait paradigm often used in person memory research. This interpretation is bolstered by the results of Experiment 2, in which subjects received information pertaining to only one of the three trait domains presented in Experiment 1. In this case, analyses of the same dependent measures produced a predictably different pattern of results, a pattern that is now characteristic of studies using materials restricted to one trait domain. Thus, the differences in the results of our two experiments appear to reflect effects associated with the categorical complexity of the impression-relevant information that was presented.

In conclusion, our research has shown that the cognitive representations formed in complex, multitrait impression-formation tasks can involve different processes and produce different patterns of results than those that have been studied in previous person memory research. Our findings suggest that current theoretical models and experimental paradigms need to be extended to incorporate these more complex features of the impression-formation process.

ACKNOWLEDGMENTS

This research was supported by National Institute of Mental Health Grant MH 40058.

We are grateful to Diane M. Mackie for her contribution to the development of these studies and to Leslie Beckwith, Leslie Hoover, Hayley Jones, and Pilar Pablo for their assistance.

REFERENCES

Asch, S. (1946). Forming impressions of personality. *Journal of Abnormal and Social Psychology, 41,* 258–290.

Bargh, J. A., & Thein, R. D. (1985). Individual construct accessibility, person memory, and the recall-judgment link: The case of information overload. *Journal of Personality and Social Psychology, 49,* 1129–1146.

Belmore, S. M., & Hubbard, M. L. (1987). The role of advance expectancies in person memory. *Journal of Personality and Social Psychology, 53,* 61–70.

Clary, E. G., & Tesser, A. (1983). Reactions to unexpected events: The naive scientist and interpretive activity. *Personality and Social Psychology Bulletin, 9,* 609–620.

Crocker, J., Hannah, D. B., & Weber, R. (1983). Person memory and causal attributions. *Journal of Personality and Social Psychology, 44,* 55–66.

Driscoll, D. M., Hamilton, D. L., & Sorrentino, R. M. (1989). *Uncertainty orientation and recall of person-descriptive information.* Unpublished manuscript, University of California, Santa Barbara.

Gordon, S. E., & Wyer, R. S. Jr. (1987). Person memory: Cat-

egory-set-size effects on the recall of a person's behaviors. *Journal of Personality and Social Psychology, 53,* 648–662.

Hamilton, D. L. (1981). Cognitive representations of persons. In E. T. Higgins, C. P. Herman, & M. P. Zanna (Eds.), *Social cognition: The Ontario Symposium* (Vol. 1, pp. 135–159). Hillsdale, NJ: Erlbaum.

Hamilton, D. L. (1988). Causal attribution viewed from an information processing perspective. In D. Bar-Tal & A. W. Kruglanski (Eds.), *The social psychology of knowledge* (pp. 359–385). Cambridge, England: Cambridge University Press.

Hamilton, D. L. (1989). Understanding impression formation: What has memory research contributed? In P. R. Solomon, G. R. Goethals, C. M. Kelley, & B. R. Stephens (Eds.), *Memory: Interdisciplinary approaches* (pp. 221–242). New York: Springer-Verlag.

Hamilton, D. L., Grubb, P. D., Acorn, D. A., Trolier, T. K., & Carpenter, S. (1989). *Attribution difficulty and memory for attribution-relevant information.* Unpublished manuscript, University of California, Santa Barbara.

Hamilton, D. L., Katz, L. B., & Leirer, V. O. (1980). Organizational processes in impression formation. In R. Hastie, T. M. Ostrom, E. B. Ebbesen, R. S. Wyer, Jr., D. L. Hamilton, & D. E. Carlston (Eds.), *Person memory: The cognitive basis of social perception* (pp. 121–153). Hillsdale, NJ: Erlbaum.

Hastie, R. (1980). Memory for behavioral information that confirms or contradicts a personality impression. In R. Hastie, T. M. Ostrom, E. B. Ebbesen, R. S. Wyer, Jr., D. L. Hamilton, & D. E. Carlston (Eds.), *Person memory: The cognitive basis of social perception* (pp. 155–177). Hillsdale, NJ: Erlbaum.

Hastie, R. (1984). Causes and effects of causal attribution. *Journal of Personality and Social Psychology, 46,* 44–56.

Hastie, R., & Kumar, P. A. (1979). Person memory: Personality traits as organizing principles in memory for behavior. *Journal of Personality and Social Psychology, 37,* 25–38.

Hemsley, G. D., & Marmurek, H. H. C. (1982). Person memory: The processing of consistent and inconsistent person information. *Personality and Social Psychology Bulletin, 8,* 433–438.

Srull, T. K. (1981). Person memory: Some tests of associative storage and retrieval models. *Journal of Experimental Psychology: Human Learning and Memory, 7,* 440–462.

Srull, T. K. (1983). Organizational and retrieval processes in person memory: An examination of processing objectives, presentation format, and the possible role of self-generated retrieval cues. *Journal of Personality and Social Psychology, 44,* 1157–1170.

Srull, T. K., Lichtenstein, M., & Rothbart, M. (1985). Associative storage and retrieval processes in person memory. *Journal of Experimental Psychology: Learning, Memory, and Cognition, 11,* 316–345.

Srull, T. K., & Wyer, R. S., Jr. (1989). Person memory and judgment. *Psychological Review, 96,* 58–83.

Stern, L. D., Marrs, S., Millar, M. G., & Cole, E. (1984). Processing time and the recall of inconsistent and consistent behaviors of individuals and groups. *Journal of Personality and Social Psychology, 47,* 253–262.

Weiner, B. (1985). "Spontaneous" causal thinking. *Psychological Bulletin, 97,* 74–84.

Wyer, R. S., Jr. (1989). Social memory and social judgment. In P. R. Solomon, G. R. Goethals, C. M. Kelley, & B. R.

Stephens (Eds.), *Memory: Interdisciplinary approaches* (pp. 243–270). New York: Springer-Verlag.

Wyer, R. S., Jr., Bodenhausen, G. V., & Srull, T. K. (1984). The cognitive representation of persons and groups and its effect on recall and recognition memory. *Journal of Experimental Social Psychology, 20,* 445–469.

Wyer, R. S., Jr., & Gordon, S. E. (1982). The recall of information about persons and groups. *Journal of Experimental Social Psychology, 18,* 128–164.

Wyer, R. S., Jr., & Gordon, S. E. (1984). The cognitive representation of social information. In R. S. Wyer, Jr., & T. K. Srull (Eds.), *Handbook of social cognition* (Vol. 2, pp. 73–150). Hillsdale, NJ: Erlbaum.

Wyer, R. S., Jr., & Martin, L. L. (1986). Person memory: The role of traits, group stereotypes, and specific behaviors in the cognitive representation of persons. *Journal of Personality and Social Psychology, 50,* 661–675.

Attribution Theory in Social Psychology

Harold H. Kelley • University of California, Los Angeles

Editors' Notes

The simple question "Why?" is probably one of the most significant and frequently posed queries about the behavior of others. Why did she act that way? Why did he say that? Did they really mean it? Did they have a hidden agenda? What might that agenda be? Should I expect them to do the same thing in future situations? Would other people in their place do the same thing? Answering such questions is critically important in determining our attitudes toward others, our trust in their attitudes toward us, and the interpersonal decisions we make in regard to them. The present selection provides an important social-psychological perspective on the topic of causal attribution. In it Harold Kelley proposes a bold thesis that the causal reasoning of lay persons resembles in its essence the way trained scientists go about their causal inferences. The paper traces the implications of this analysis in several major domains of social-psychological research. Whereas Kelley's basic analysis is cognitive, he also considers the ways motivation may impact the process, and he discusses in attributional terms other major topics in the psychology of interpersonal relations.

Discussion Questions

1. In what way, according to Kelley, do lay persons' causal attributions resemble the statistical logic of an analysis of variance. What would be the numerator of the F-ratio in this analysis? What would the denominator be?
2. Why is it important to apportion causality as between the person and the environment?
3. In what way does attribution theory contribute to our understanding of persuasion?

Suggested Readings

Bem, D. J. (1965). An experimental analysis of self-persuasion. *Journal of Experimental So-cial Psychology, 1,* 199–218.

Jones, E. E., & Davis, K. E. (1965). From acts to dispositions: The attribution process in person perception. In L. Berkowitz (Ed.), *Advances in experimental social psychology* (Vol. 2, pp. 219–266). New York: Academic Press.

Ross, L. (1977). The intuitive psychologist and his shortcomings: Distortions in the attribution process. In L. Berkowitz (Ed.), *Advances in experimental social psychology* (Vol. 10, pp. 173–220). San Diego, CA: Academic Press.

Schachter, S., & Singer, J. E. (1962). Cognitive, social and physiological determinants of emotional state. *Psychological Review, 69,* 379–399.

The Attribution Process

Attribution refers to the process of inferring or perceiving the dispositional properties of entities in the environment. These are the stable features of distal objects such as color, size, shape, intention, desire, sentiment, and ability. Any given stable feature may manifest itself in many ways. A given rectangular surface produces many specific retinal images. A person's desire to benefit me is expressed by many different actions. In our perception, we tend to interpret, analyze, and order this "variable manifold of mediating events" in order to achieve an understanding of the "contents of the distal environment" (Heider, p. 296).

This understanding is gained by way of a causal analysis that is "in a way analogous to experimental methods" (Heider, p. 297) and that has the purpose of disentangling which effects are to be attributed to which of several factors present. In the basic case, where the person is concerned with the dispositional properties of his surrounding environment, the choice is between external attribution and internal (self) attribution. This can be illustrated by an example concerning the attribution of object desirability vs. personal desire. Am I to take my enjoyment of a movie as a basis for an attribution to the movie (that it is intrinsically enjoyable) or for an attribution to myself (that I have a specific kind of desire relevant to movies)? The inference as to where to locate the dispositional properties responsible for the effect is made by interpreting the raw data (the enjoyment) in the context of subsidiary information from experiment-like variations of conditions. A naive version of J. S. Mills' method of difference provides the basic analytic tool. The effect is attributed to

that condition which is present when the effect is present and which is absent when the effect is absent. This basic notion of covariation of cause and effect is used to examine variations in effects (responses, sensations) in relation to variations over (a) entities (movies), (b) persons (other viewers of the movie), (c) time (the same person on repeated exposures), and (d) modalities of interaction with the entity (different ways of viewing the movie). The attribution to the external thing rather than to the self requires that I respond *differentially* to the thing, that I respond *consistently*, over time and over modality, and that I respond *in agreement* with a consensus of other persons' responses to it. In other words, the movie is judged enjoyable if I enjoy only it (or at least, not all movies), if I enjoy it even the second time, if I enjoy it on TV as well as at the drive-in theater, and if others also enjoy it. If these conditions are not met, there is indicated an attribution to the self (I enjoy all movies, or I alone have a weakness for this particular type) or to some juxtaposition of circumstances (I was in an especially susceptible mood on the one occasion).

The logic of the analysis is obviously akin to that employed in analysis of variance and can be illustrated by the diagram in Figure 1. Along the vertical axis are listed *entities* which correspond to things in the environment (e.g., movies). Along one horizontal axis are various *persons* who interact with the entities and along the other, the various *modalities* of interaction and the *times* at which these interactions may occur. The X, Y, and Z's represent *effects* such as experiences, sensations, or responses. These effects are defined from a given person's point of view (the "self" in Figure 1) inasmuch as we are dealing with one person's as-

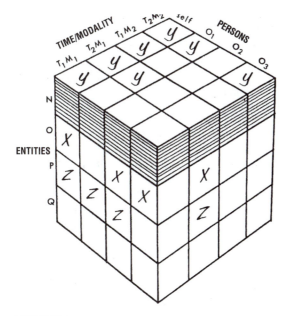

FIGURE 11.1 ■ Data pattern indicating attribution of effect Y to entity N.

sembly of information in order to make an attribution. This person makes the attribution of effect Y to entity N when, as in the figure, Y and Y alone occurs exclusively within the horizontal plane corresponding to N. This means that the effect Y varies only as between entities, is uniquely associated with N, and occurs consistently over time, modality, and persons when N is present. In general, we might say that the subjective criteria for the possession of valid knowledge about the external world are distinctiveness of response coupled with consistency and consensus.

Heider gives a number of similar examples which involve the assignment of an effect to a cause either in the environment or in the person. In addition to the problem of environmental vs. personal factors in enjoyment (in the illustration above), his examples include difficulty of task as an environmental factor vs. ability as a personal factor, objective requirements vs. personal wishes in relation to values and norms, and external vs. personal responsibility for a person's compliance to another's influence. In all these cases, the attribution is presumed to follow the rules outlined above: External attribution (problem difficulty; norms and values reflecting objective, invariant standards; external responsibility) is made when evidence exists as to the distinctiveness, con-

sistency, and consensus of the appropriate effects.

I have emphasized the allocation of causality between the environment and the self because when cast in these terms the theory bears on the central issue in psychological epistemology; namely, the basis of subjective validity. But the analysis is also applicable to other cause-effect problems. For example, an observer may witness my pleasure at attending the movie and may consider whether to conclude something about me or about the movie. Or, I may have the problem of assigning responsibility for some effect, good or bad, between two other persons. Or the problem may be the one in social perception that Jones and Davis analyze, involving my inferring a person's intentions from knowledge of the consequences of his actions. Before considering at greater length some of these problems of social perception, attention needs to be directed to the implications of the basic self-environment analysis for a central area of social psychology, namely, social influence.

Informational Influence

As noted above, in the analysis of external *vs.* internal ascription, attribution theory confronts the problem of the phenomenology of attribution validity. When a person has an impression that something is true of an entity, how does he ascertain that the impression reflects the inherent properties of the entity and not his own characteristics or some peculiar interaction with the entity? The four criteria for external validity are those mentioned above:

1. *Distinctiveness*: the impression is attributed to the thing if it uniquely occurs when the thing is present and does not occur in its absence.
2. *Consistency over time*: each time the thing is present, the individual's reaction must be the same or nearly so.
3. *Consistency over modality*: his reaction must be consistent even though his mode of interaction with the thing varies. (For example, he sees it to have an irregular outline and he feels it to be rough; or first he estimates the answer to the problem and then he calculates it.)
4. *Consensus*: attributes of external origin are experienced the same way by all observers.

To the degree a person's attributions fulfill these criteria, he feels confident that he has a true picture of his external world. He makes judgments quickly and with subjective confidence, and he takes action with speed and vigor. When his attributions do not satisfy the criteria, he is uncertain in his views and hesitant in action. It is not assumed that fulfillment of these criteria implies veridicality of the person's attributions. The specified evidence provides a basis for subjective validity (as manifested, for example, in confidence in the validity of one's attributions) but not necessarily a basis for their objective validity.

These concepts are useful in organizing a great deal of the social psychological literature on the conditions governing (a) susceptibility to persuasion, (b) immediate success of persuasion, and (c) the persistence of its effects.

Person A will be more susceptible to influence the more variable his prior attribution has been. Attribution instability (and, hence, susceptibility to influence) will be high for a person who has (a) little social support, (b) prior information that is poor or ambiguous, (c) problems difficult beyond his capabilities, (d) views that have been disconfirmed because of their inappropriateness or nonveridicality, and (e) other experiences engendering low self-confidence. (The reader need not be reminded of the vast amount of social psychological research that bears upon these various points.)

With regard to B's success in persuading A, we may first assert that A will be influenced by B if B's message enables A subsequently to achieve a higher level of distinctiveness and stability in his attributions than before. However, the factors relevant to this influence and the persistence of its effects will depend upon which of two methods of influence B uses. As B tries to create stability for A for a new attribution, he may operate on either the *consistency* aspects or the *consensus* aspects of A's attribution process. (Of course, he may do both, and persuaders usually do, but for simplicity I will consider only the two pure cases.)

In the first instance (usually called education or *instruction*), B attempts to provide A with the means of obtaining consistency, both over time and over modality, in the new attribution. For example, B may demonstrate a new way of looking at or interacting with the entity which enables A to find consistency in his subsequent confrontations with it. What B provides may consist of new analytic methods, problem-solving procedures, practice in the use of a given modality in order to increase its

consistency, new perspectives and frameworks for evaluating items, training in discrimination and judgment, the suggestion of crucial comparisons in order to sharpen discriminations and evaluations, a demonstration of the relevance of facts and information that A had not previously appreciated, or instruction in relevant verbal labels. These methods have in common the property that they may be used by A independently of B (once A has learned them) and they contribute directly to the fulfillment of the consistency criteria and, in that manner, enhance the subjective validity of whatever attribution they lead to. The content of this influence will be adopted and held by A because it affords him attributional stability, and not because of B's expertness or credibility. (However, the latter may be relevant to A's willingness to pay attention to B at the outset.)

The second influence method (usually referred to as *persuasion*) is more thoroughly dependent on A's evaluation of B. In this case, B conveys information about his own conclusions, attributions, evaluations, or about other persons' opinions. The information contributes wholly to fulfilling the consensus criteria and if accepted increases A's stability of attribution by that means. The question is whether A will accept B's information. On this point, A is confronted with a second type of problem of causal analysis, the one I mentioned earlier in which an observer makes an attribution of the action of another person. *Person B's message is itself an effect*, and A's problem is to attribute it, either to that part of their common environment under discussion (in which case it is considered valid), to B himself (his role, desires, etc.), or to the situation or target (A himself, the particular circumstances).

In this attribution process, although they are used for a different purpose than in an earlier example (other person-environment attribution here *vs.* self-environment attribution in the earlier case), the familiar four criteria are again relevant:

1. *Distinctiveness.* Does B report this attribution only for this particular entity? If not, the cause of his report by this entity is cast in doubt.
2. *Consistency over time.* Does B report the same evaluation to all target audiences and not to A only? Does he make the same attribution in all situations, regardless of his motivation or circumstances? If not, there is indicated an attribution of his report to "irrelevant" causal fac-

tors such as A himself or B's own need state.

3. *Consistency over modality.* Does B report the same attribution when he thinks about the matter in different ways or when he approaches it with different observational methods? Is there any evidence in his presentation of his uncertainty, vacillation, indecisiveness, or weakness of response? These would be cues as to inconsistency and would suggest interference from other causal factors.

4. *Consensus.* Do other people agree with him? Does he convey information that others agree with him? (If so, this message itself creates a *further* problem of attribution and validation.) Or, does B provide information which implies that the reactions of other sensible persons might be different from his own? The latter would violate the consensus criterion for A, raise questions about whether B's reactions are really caused by the object, and reduce A's acceptance of B's assertions. (This may be illustrated by the ineffectiveness of a two-sided communication with less educated persons, in the study by Hovland, Lumsdaine, and Sheffield, 1949.)

The analysis of the validity of B's assertions can be summarized as in Figure 2. Person A (the "self" in this analysis) focuses on the "slice" of the data table produced by B (indicated by O_1) and tests for B's differential response to N, the consistency of his report (where the time categories refer to different situations or different target audiences), and his agreement with other observers of the same entities. I have left blank A's own "slice" of the data table (that corresponding to self) in order to emphasize his dependence upon B and other social sources of information. It is not uncommon, however, for A to have some reactions of his own to the entity, in which case the consistency between these and B's is an important determiner of the effect of B's message.

The communicator factors usually considered relevant to A's acceptance of a persuasive communication are B's expertness and trustworthiness. These notions are readily reduced to attribution terms. *Expertness* can be defined as the communicator's contact with or mediation of the *relevant* external causal factors. An expert is one who, by virtue of his modes of interaction with the environment, is capable of attaining a high information level in his own attributions and (un-

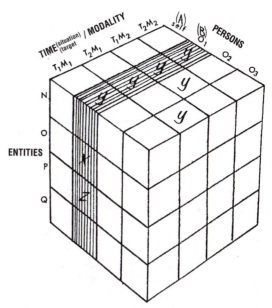

FIGURE 11.2 ■ Data pattern indicating attribution of B's message, Y, to entity N.

less other causal factors interfere) of making attributional statements presumed to have high validity. *Trustworthiness* implies the *absence of irrelevant* causal factors (personal motives, role demands) in the person's statements. In view of the basic attributional relevance of these two concepts, it is perhaps no accident of method or approach that they have repeatedly appeared as defining the primary and exhaustive categories for the classification of communicator variables in research on persuasive communication.

Social Perception

The analysis of social influence has led us indirectly to the problem of perceiving the causes of another person's behavior (*viz.*, the behavior of a communicator). Jones and Davis (1965) have directly attacked this central problem in social perception. They employ attributional principles adopted from Heider to analyze the process of inferring another person's intentions from his actions. The authors define the task of their observer as that of identifying the intentions of the actor insofar as they depart from the normal or typical person in the same situation. In other words, the task is that of inferring the actor's *personal* attributes—the ways in which he is unique as a causal agent. The basic principles of their analysis are simple. It is first assumed that the observer believes the actor "was aware his action would have the observed effects" (p. 220) and has the "ability to bring about the effects observed" (p. 221). In other words, the effects may not be considered accidental. Under certain further conditions, the observer will then make a *correspondent inference* from the effects to the actor's intentions. By correspondent inference the authors mean that the effects and the attributes or intentions of the actor may be described in similar terms; e.g., behavior having the effect of dominating another person will be taken as a basis for inferring the actor's intention to dominate. The central hypothesis is that a correspondent inference will be made to the degree (a) there are *some but few* effects of the action that are unique (noncommon) to it as compared with other alternative actions available to the actor, and (b) these effects are *low* in assumed social desirability. The first part means that information is revealed about the actor's intentions only from the ways in which his chosen action differs from other actions he might have taken and that this information is less ambiguous the fewer such differences there are. The second part of the hypothesis means that the action yields information about the actor's idiosyncratic intentions only insofar as the effects are not those that people in general would have produced under similar circumstances. In brief, the fewer distinctive reasons a person might have for an action (assuming he has some) and the less these reasons are widely shared in the culture, the more informative that action is concerning the characteristics of the person.

The matter of social desirability must be considered carefully. It is not implied that desirable effects are not relevant to the inference of intentions. Indeed, Jones and Davis note that we usually assume a person took an action out of regard for the good consequences it produced (assuming foresight and control, as we have) rather than with the intention of achieving its negative consequences. However, their purpose is to analyze the process of inferring *unique* intentions and "it is . . . clear that attribute-effect linkages based on universally desired effects are not informative concerning unique characteristics of the actor" (p. 227). In more general attributional terms, it might be said that effects widely produced by virtue of their desirability tell us more about the properties of external situations or states—their intrinsic desirability, demand characteristics, etc.—than about the properties of persons who act to produce them.

The reader will note some general parallels between the Jones and Davis analysis and my earlier one. (Indeed the reader may be puzzled that the correspondence is not more apparent, inasmuch as both analyses are alleged to stem from Heider. This is partly a reflection of the richness of Heider's ideas, but also an indication of the complexity of the problems at hand.) Let me try to explain the similarities and differences. To begin with a difference, the observer's focus in the two cases is essentially at opposite ends of the person-environment polarity. In my earlier analyses, dealing respectively with the self-environment and the other-environment problems, the person is concerned about the validity of an attribution regarding the environment. He applies the several criteria in an attempt to rule out person-based sources or "error" variance. In the problems specified by Jones and Davis, the observer has exactly the opposite orientation. He is seeking for person-caused variance (that caused by the particular actor under scrutiny) and in doing so, he must rule out environmental or situation-determined causes of variations in effects. He does this by looking for deviations from the general entity and situation trends, for example, as these are revealed in between-actor consistencies. This is the reason for the assumption that socially undesirable effects are more informative than socially desirable ones.

In terms of the data table I have been using in this paper, the pattern of data fulfilling the Jones and Davis criteria is the one shown in Figure 3. The entries in the table represent various persons' actions as they are experienced by the self (i.e., in terms of their "effects"). As in the case of the persuasive communicator's message, these actions are themselves effects which must be subjected to causal analysis. The time dimension of the table includes (as in the analysis of the persuasive communication) the various situations in which the actions occur and different targets of these actions (the self and various others).

The Jones and Davis criteria lead to an inference of *intention* when the particular observed effect, Y, produced by O_1 at T_1M_1, deviates from the data trends for:

1. *Situations and targets.* The effect is not what most persons (or even this particular actor) pro-

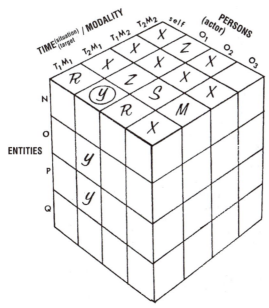

FIGURE 11.3 ■ Data pattern indicating attribution of effect Y to actor's intention.

duce in the same situation in relation to this particular target person, T_1. (Effects X and R are more common). This is essentially the criterion of low social desirability. The situation or person, or both, do not have "demand characteristics" such that most persons would produce the observed effect.

2. *The actor*, O_1. The effect is not to be accounted for by limitations in or peculiarities of the actor's available actions. Other actions that are known to be available to him have different effects (e.g., X and Z) even with the same target person and in the same situation (summarized by T_1). This deviation indicates that the observed effect is not to be attributed to the actor's "traits," habits, or response biases.

In brief, intention, as a reflection of a deliberate act of choice to produce the observed effect, is manifested in deviation of the observed effect from those attributable to situational demands and personal characteristics of the actor. From the present analysis, it might be added that the observed effect should also deviate from trends for:

3. *Entities.* The effect cannot be considered a reflection of the properties of some entity N that happens to be present.

4. *Modalities.* The effect is not a result of a particular way of the actor's interacting with, relating to, or viewing the self—a way that would induce any person to take an action with the same effect.

The second criterion above, deviations from the actor's "typical" effects, makes it clear why Jones and Davis assume that the observer believes the actor has foreknowledge and control. The actor's knowledge and ability enable him to choose among and employ his actions deliberately and with regard for their various effects. To the degree the effect of his selected action is different from those of other actions he might have taken, the observer has evidence of the actor's willful intervention as a causal agent, exercising choice to cause a special effect.

This second criterion forms part of Jones and Davis' criterion of noncommon effects, specifying as it does that an inference as to intention requires that the observed effect deviate from those resulting from other actions of the actor. However, they also propose that *number* of noncommon effects is important—that the observer's inference about the actor's intention will be more firmly based the *fewer* are the effects that differentiate the selected action from the available alternative actions. The logic of this assumption is not clear. It seems reasonable to suppose that with fewer noncommon effects, it will usually be easier for an observer to label or rate the intention, but there seems no reason in principle why all or most of the various unique effects of an action may not be taken as evidence of the intention (or set of intentions) guiding the choice of that action. (In the present analysis, letters such as X, Y, and Z are used to indicate effects without regard to the number of identifiable components, and the term "effect" is used in a broad sense to include any single effect or set of consequences produced by an action, perceptual response, etc.)

As noted above, situational consistencies are introduced indirectly by Jones and Davis, by way of the concept of social desirability. To show the importance of social desirability, Jones, Davis, and Gergen (1961) present evidence from a study of observers' judgments of job applicants being interviewed for a job. Some applicants act in line with the requirements of the desired occupation and other applicants behave inconsistently with the requirements. The observers made more extreme attributions of the latter applicants and made the attributions with greater confidence. The interpretation is that inasmuch as most applicants would have acted in conformity with the situational requirements, it is only deviation from this conforming behavior that affords a basis for causal attributions to the individual person.

Jones and Davis' use of the criterion of social desirability and this experimental example contain an important point for our analysis: the observer may not need actually to examine variations in behavior over a number of persons. From his knowledge of social pressures, shared values, and situational demands, he may be able to make confident estimates about the amount of consensus of response to be expected. If made with sufficient confidence, whether correct or not, these estimates can supplant observation of the actual consensus and afford a basis for the attribution process. *This assumes*, of course, *that the individual has already made a firm attribution about the situation*; namely, that it has inherent properties such that most or all people respond to it in a given manner. The important general point is that once certain attributions are made, they become the basis for making further ones and they permit the individual to bypass some of the processes we have been describing here.

One aspect of my earlier analysis is missing from that of Jones and Davis, the criterion of temporal consistency. Their reason for omitting this from their scheme seems to be that they are exclusively interested in the inference of momentary intentions and not in "dispositional structures." This criterion would certainly be important in inferring enduring personal dispositions (e.g., the traits and response biases ruled out by criterion 2 above) and Jones and Davis imply as much. Temporal consistency might also be relevant in cases where the observer could not assume foresight and control. He might find it desirable to test this assumption by considering stability *vs.* change in actions after the actor has had opportunities over successive trials to observe and learn the effects of his actions.

Self Perception

Earlier, the question of attribution to the self *vs.* the environment was considered. I now wish to review several other approaches to the phenomena of self perception. Although these other approaches are consistent with this analysis of attribution theory, they pose new problems for the theory and suggest further directions for its development.

Recently Daryl Bem (1965, 1967) arguing from a radical behaviorist position, has proposed that the processes of arriving at inferences about the self are identical with those used in drawing inferences about others. For example, an observer judges another's attitude on the basis of his behavior and the stimulus conditions under which it occurs. In the same way, a person judges his own attitude from observing his own behavior and taking account of the conditions under which it occurs. The latter assertion seems to contradict our everyday experience that we have direct and private access to our own attitudes. On the other hand, it is consistent with the present view that an attribution about the environment (an attitude would be a specific case) involves checking the consistency of one's responses, on successive occasions and over different modalities of interaction with the environment. In the sense that this checking process involves verbal responses, I would agree to the appropriateness of the comment from E. M. Forster, "How can I tell what I think till I see what I say."

The notion that the processes of self- and other-perception are similar is quite compatible with the present attribution analysis. Our examples have suggested that the same framework is used in making causal analyses whether the problem involves attribution to self *vs.* environment or to another person *vs.* his environment. This implies the same conclusion as Bem's, that given analogous information a person will draw the same conclusion whether in regard to himself or to another individual he is observing. However, this should not be taken to mean that the *same* information will always be available for the self as for another individual. To give a simple example, a person, being keenly aware of variations in the intensity of his own efforts, may observe correlated variations in his success on a series of tasks and attribute to himself a degree of control over this type of task. On the other hand, an observer to whom the variations in "trying" may not be apparent may interpret the various performance outcomes as mere random variations in task difficulty and, consequently, may attribute no skill to the person. Another example would involve a difference between the actor and the observer (in the Jones and Davis problem of intention inference) in the set of alternative actions seen to be available to the actor. If different instances of TM (in Figure 3) are salient for the two persons, they will differ in the sets of actions (or effects) with which they compare the observed action, Y, and may differ, accordingly, in the intention to which they attribute it.

The specific problem Bem deals with in the context of self-perception *vs.* other-perception is that of inferring a person's "true" attitude from his verbal report or similar actions. This is a familiar problem at least insofar as it concerns inferring *another* person's true attitude. Earlier it was reported that the attribution analysis elicited by a communication of mere opinion by another person focused upon the assessment of the degree to which his opinion varied with variations in the entities but was consistent over time (situation, need state, etc.) and modalities, and with other persons' opinions. It is reasonable to expect the same analysis to be applied in the determination of one's *own* true attitude.

Bem employs B. F. Skinner's distinction between *tact* and *mand* in his conceptual analysis of this problem, and it appears that these categories of behavior have direct correspondence to our attributional analysis. Consider two classes of behavior (verbal response, or whatever), the first consisting of behavior that covaries with entities (and is consistently and consensually enacted) and the second consisting of behavior that varies with time (situation, need, target of the verbal behavior) rather than with entities. The first class corresponds to "tacts" which are responses under the discriminative control of some portion of the environment. Tacts consist of those portions of the behavioral repertoire that have been shaped by social training (largely language training) to vary only with entities; that is, to be uniquely distinctive for different entities, but highly consistent (in all the respects we have considered) for a given entity. They are "comments about the world" and are epitomized by naming responses and descriptive statements. The second class of behavior, that behavior which varies not with entities but with situations, constitutes "mands." They are responses under the control of specific reinforcing contingencies such as might characterize a particular behavioral situation. Mands—which include commands, demands, and requests—are "comments" about the reinforcing properties of social situations as these have relevance to the needs of the actor.

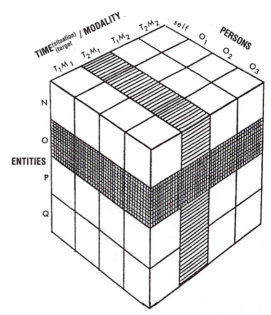

FIGURE 11.4 ■ Attribution interpretation of distinction between tacts and mands.

In our data table, the distinction between tacts and mands would appear as in Figure 4. Consistency within a horizontal slice of the table, corresponding to a given entity, would imply the response has tact properties. On the other hand, consistency of response within a vertical slice corresponding to a given situation would indicate the behavior has mand properties.

Bem assumes (as I would, on the basis of this analysis) that tacts are considered by observers to reflect the actor's attribution to the entity—his true attitude or evaluation. Mands are considered (again, as they would be according to this analysis) to convey no information about the person's attributions to entities. They constitute attributions to the reward/punishment contingencies inherent in the response situation, but they are not relevant to entity properties.

Bem's (implicit) rule for determining whether a response is under cue or reinforcement control involves a simple presence-absence test. If a strong reward or threat contingency is present, the behavior is considered likely to have mand properties. If not, if the response situation is neutral or bland in terms of reinforcement consequences, the behavior is regarded as having tact properties. At this point, the reasoning strongly resembles that of Jones and Davis. Implicit in the judgment of *strong* reinforcement contingencies, as in the judgement of social desirability, is the notion that most or all persons in the same situation would make a response having the same effect. This is a significant implication to which we must return later in discussing Bem's critique of certain experimental studies of cognitive dissonance theory.

Biases, Errors, and Illusions In Attribution

Like all other perceptual and cognitive systems, attribution processes are subject to error. Heider suggests that errors can be traced to instances in which, first, the relevant situation is ignored; second, egocentric assumptions are made; third, the relevant effects have affective significance for the observer; and fourth, the surrounding situation is misleading. I will discuss the first three very briefly and then consider the fourth in more detail. Finally, as a fifth point, I wish to consider briefly some means for the deliberate induction of attributional errors that have appeared in the recent experimental literature.

1. With regard to *ignoring the relevant situation*, Jones and Harris (1966) report evidence which they suggest may indicate a tendency to attach too much significance to the behavior and its effects, and too little to its situational context. In a situation in which a person was observed to express an unpopular and unexpected opinion, the judgment of his true opinion was very much influenced by his expressed opinion *even when the expression had been elicited by strong, legitimate external pressure*. Jones and Harris note that although there is some ambiguity in the interpretation of this effect, it may support Heider's point that "behavior in particular has such salient properties it tends to engulf the total field rather than be confined to its proper position as a local stimulus whose interpretation requires the additional data of a surrounding field . . ." (Heider, p. 54).

In some cases, as in complex causal environments, the relevant causal factors in the situation are not ignored but are simply not perceptible to the person. Under these circumstances, there may occur quite accidentally a covariation between actions and consequences which will create a strong impression of self-control over events that are really externally controlled. For example, if the reinforcing environment gradually becomes

increasingly beneficent (e.g., during an inflationary period when the profits of certain businesses increase almost without regard to what they do), an action a person happens to take early in the trend will be reinforced and increase in its frequency. By this effect, the rate of that particular response (or effort, amount of trying, etc.) may rise along with the rising rate of reward. The resulting covariation would provide compelling evidence for attributing the environmental changes to the self. (Experimental evidence for somewhat similar phenomena comes from studies of "superstitious" behavior. See Kimble, 1961, pp. 197–198). The reader will note that an attribution error of this type, in which a self-attribution is made for what is actually an externally caused change, is likely to be asymmetrical, occurring only in situations of increasing environmental benevolence. If the external causal system is declining in its rate of reward, the person is likely to make repeated adjustments in his behavior in an attempt to stem the decline. Since it is unlikely that he will experience any covariation, one way or the other, between his actions and his rewards, he will probably attribute the decline to external factors and not blame himself.

2. *Egocentric assumptions* are important when the evidence for the attribution is incomplete. For example, Heider suggests that attributions are often made on the basis of what he refers to as the "minimum data pattern" which is the simple presence-absence test: one instance of presence of both object and effect coupled with one instance in which both are absent. This simple experience leads to an attribution to the object which then often leads to assumptions that the other attribution criteria will also be fulfilled: What I now enjoy I will enjoy again and other persons will also enjoy. It is not clear to what degree assumptions of this sort are likely to be in error in such domains as those of desire and pleasure (where Heider makes this point), but at least they make it possible for there to be systematic differences in attributions between an individual and a person observing him. As Heider puts it, the individual may have only the minimum data pattern, but an observer of his reactions will also have (at the very least) the additional evidence of his *own* reactions. Under these circumstances, the individual's *external* attribution of his reaction will often be in contrast to the observer's *personal* one. Specifically, if the observer fails to share the individual's reac-

tion, he will attribute it to personal characteristics of the individual himself.

But the egocentricity extends also to the observer. When the reaction he observes the individual to make differs from his own, he is inclined not only to attribute the former to personal characteristics but also to attribute the latter to the object world. "The person tends to attribute his own reactions to the object world, and those of another, when they differ from his own, to personal characteristics in [the other]" (Heider, p. 157). This, in brief, is Heider's theoretical account for what he refers to as "a tendency for attribution in general to be leveled at the environment" (p. 156).

Yet this problem of egocentric assumptions has not been fully analyzed. Against examples given above, in which the individual erroneously assumes his reaction to be common, we can pose counter-examples in which the individual erroneously assumes his reaction to be unique. This seems to lie at the basis of the phenomenon of *pluralistic ignorance* where each person assumes that everyone except himself accepts and conforms to social norms. (The attributional implication is that everyone else is assumed to find the norms to have the properties of objective standards rather than arbitrary social rules, but each individual finds evidence in his own experience contrary to this external attribution.) The phenomenon of pluralistic ignorance exists when there is a strong consensus in the public labeling of the relevant behavior (as if it reflected external attributions) but careful concealment of the behavior itself. The consequences of these two circumstances is that people are led to draw an erroneous equation between what is socially desirable and what is common. Intuitively, it seems probable that the condition underlying this state of affairs is a social norm that is based on assumptions about attributes of external objects that are highly nonveridical, is too weak to prevent individuals from interacting directly with the objects, and is therefore repeatedly disconfirmed in the individuals' own experience.

3. *The magnitude of the affective consequences* involved in an attribution may also bias the interpretation made. Heider suggests that a negative self-attribution may be avoided because it would undermine the individual's self-esteem. Uniformly critical action toward a person by his associates will be attributed by an observer to the person inasmuch as he is the constant factor in the situation. But to protect his pride the individual may attribute the common treatment to a conspiracy against him, perhaps based on jealousy of his superior attributes. Ego-protective attribution of this sort is illustrated by results from an interesting study by Johnson, Feigenbaum, and Weiby (1964). Their experimental subject attempted to teach a student some arithmetic materials. The student did not actually exist, but he was represented convincingly to the subject by a prearranged set of completed work sheets. He "did poorly" on the first unit of material and the instructor taught him a second unit. After this second instruction, the student improved for some instructors but for others he continued to do badly. The subject-instructors for whom the student showed no improvement tended to attribute the performance to the student, whereas those for whom the student improved tended to take credit themselves for the improvement, even to the extent of making more favorable evaluations of their own second presentations. The former attribution, that made to the student, would seem to be ego-defensive in character.

Jones and Davis (1965) deal with affective consequences in terms of the *hedonic relevance* of the actions for the observer. They suggest that as the hedonic relevance increases, the observer is likely to assimilate various effects of the actor's behavior to a single theme suggested by the predominant hedonic value. The effect is, they suggest, to reduce the number of unique (noncommon) effects perceived to result from the behavior. This permits the observer to make a more confident inference as to the actor's intentions. We might also suspect that the important negative or positive consequences (and particularly the negative ones) of a person's action make the affected person keenly aware of the other actions that might have been taken with less extreme consequences. Thus, the set of alternative actions the interested observer considers in evaluating the chosen one is likely to be biased in a manner that makes the latter appear to be more unique than it would otherwise. There is, unfortunately, little evidence bearing upon either of these interpretations of hedonic relevance. In fact, the evidence that *any* bias results from hedonic relevance is less than adequate at present.

4. Let us now consider cases of attribution in which the *surrounding situation is misleading*. Here, the concern is with cases analogous to optical *illusions* where the field in which the figure is embedded exerts a distorting influence on the per-

ception of the figure. Some examples in the area of social causation can be provided by returning to Bem's critique of cognitive dissonance experiments.

Bem uses his version of attribution analysis to interpret certain "forced compliance" experiments conducted as tests of cognitive dissonance theory. The reader will recall that in the classical experiment on this problem, by Festinger and Carlsmith (1959), the subject was induced, with either a $20 or a $1 payment, to misrepresent to another subject his views about a dull and boring task. Consistent with the hypothesis of insufficient justification (derived from cognitive dissonance theory), the smaller the incentive provided the subject for this misrepresentation, the more he was found subsequently to hold favorable attitudes about the task.

Given Bem's theoretical viewpoint, in which the processes of self-perception are considered identical with those in social perception, it occurred to him to ask what attitude an observer would attribute to subjects in the Festinger and Carlsmith experiment, given knowledge of the conditions and their behavior. Accordingly, Bem conducted what he calls "interpersonal replications" of several congnitive dissonance experiments. In his interpersonal replication of Festinger and Carlsmith (Bem, 1967), his subjects listened to a tape recording which described the *circumstances* of a subject in one of the experimental conditions (the boring task, the request made of him to describe the task to another subject as being interesting, the payment given him for doing so) and his *actions* (the comments he made in complying with the request). Bem's (observer) subjects were then asked to estimate that subject's attitude toward the task. The results closely paralleled those from the original experiment. "Observers" of the person who complied with the request when given the $1 incentive, estimated his attitude to be more favorable than did those making similar judgments of a subject who complied in response to the $20 offer. Presumably, in the latter case, the large reward is taken to be the cause of the behavior (describing the task as interesting), but in its absence, the behavior is taken as having *tact* value. The same attribution interpretation is also made of the actual subjects in the Festinger and Carlsmith experiment. When they were asked about their opinions of the task at the end of the experiment, they reviewed their recent experience, their behavior in relation to the task, the conditions of its occur-

rence, and from this they inferred their attitude toward the task. When they recalled speaking highly of it in the presence of the large reward, they attributed this behavior to situational constraints and not to the task itself. The latter attribution was made when the incentive was small.

In brief, Bem interprets the post-experiment report as an attribution statement that reflects the individual's causal attribution of his earlier behavior—whether it was caused by irrelevant incentives (situation) or by the properties of the task (entity). In view of this interpretation, Bem concludes that such studies as that of Festinger and Carlsmith do not require the postulation of a post-decision dissonance reduction process.

I do not intend here to consider the appropriateness of Bem's critique as a general alternative to cognitive dissonance interpretations of experimental results. Rather, I wish to subject both Bem's analysis and the procedures of certain cognitive dissonance experiments to close scrutiny from an attribution theory point of view. The analysis has two problems even as applied to the forced compliance experiments, and both of these problems, when carefully analyzed, suggest the possible existence within experimental procedures characteristic of cognitive dissonance research of *attributional illusions*. I shall refer to these two problems as (a) the illusion of freedom, and (b) the effects of unanticipated consequences.

(a) *The illusion of freedom.* Although Bem does not make it explicit, the high- and low-incentive conditions would seem to imply different degrees of consensus in compliance with the experimenter's request. That is, the $20 incentive would induce all or most subjects to comply and this would be one indication of its role as a strong situational cause. The $1 incentive would induce compliance only from subjects whose private attitudes are more or less favorable toward the task. And it does not seem likely that all subjects would feel favorable, in view of the boring nature of the task. Thus, the observer's judgment that the attitude of a $1 complier is more favorable than that of a $20 complier is probably associated with assumptions (unchecked in Bem's work, as far as I know) that there is a distribution of opinion toward the task, and only the more favorable subjects complied in the $1 case and almost all, favorable or not, complied in the $20 case.

But at this point we encounter a problem. Any assumption of differential rates of compliance in the Festinger and Carlsmith experiment (and in similar, well-conducted experiments of the cognitive dissonance genre) would be quite unwarranted. Virtually all subjects in both incentive conditions complied with the request to describe the task as interesting and exciting. Thus, an observer to the *actual* Festinger and Carlsmith experiment, seeing all subjects comply in both conditions, would not have this basis for making different attributions regarding the cause of their behavior. Of course, this fact of uniform compliance in both conditions does not vitiate Bem's procedure because insofar as possible, he gives his "observer" the *same* information about the circumstances and the behavior as the corresponding subject has in the actual experiment.

If, then, we are to accept an attribution interpretation of the Festinger and Carlsmith experiment (or a Bemian one), we must deal with the problem that the attribution made in the low incentive condition is one that assumes less than total compliance to the situational demands existing there, when in fact the compliance is virtually complete. (I need hardly point out that it is the complete compliance which makes the result nonobvious and interesting to us, as observers of the experiment with total knowledge about the conditions and effects. If only some of the subjects complied under conditions of low incentive, the results would be quite trivial, readily interpretable in terms of subject self-selection.)

A resolution to this puzzle is achieved by assuming that *it is possible to induce a person to feel he has total freedom to express himself when in fact he has none.* That is, it is possible to induce a person to state a particular opinion under special misleading conditions such that he and all other persons will do so, but on looking back at it he will feel he was free to express his own opinion. If this line of argument is at all plausible, it leads us to examine typical procedures in forced compliance experiments for clues about how to create this particular attributional illusion, the illusion of freedom.

Certainly a key feature of the typical cognitive dissonance study is concealment of the fact that everyone conforms. In fact, there is often the implication that the individual is the *only* person of whom the request is being made. This would seem to divert his attention, at that moment and later, away from any consideration of whether other persons did (or would) comply.

A second common procedure is to label the decision a free choice: "It's up to you to decide what you want to do." There may even be contained in this kind of comment an encouragement for the person to think about the problem, to process the pros and cons, and even to have some feelings of wavering, indecision, and hesitancy such as are associated with the impression of voluntariness (cf. the earlier discussion of Brehm and Cohen).

The Jones and Davis analysis suggests that the "socially undesirable" action will be judged by the person as reflecting his own decision, and in a similar vein, Brehm and Cohen imply that compliance to illegitimate pressure is self-attributed. A number of the forced compliance experiments contain the direct suggestion or at least the strong implication that the subject's compliance will be an exception to the social rule. (Brehm & Cohen, 1962, p. 75: After indicating that other subjects had written anti-police essays, the experimenter says, "What we really need now are some essays favoring the police side." Davis & Jones, 1960, p. 404: "Surprisingly enough, most of my recent subjects have been choosing to read the flattering evaluation of the person, so . . . I'd like to ask you to read the negative evaluation. . . ." Davidson, 1964, p. 50: "Thus far we've run some 52 pairs of subjects and, well, quite understandably, we've had 46 cases where the subject has chosen to read the positive evaluation." The subject is then asked to read the negative evaluation.)

In some cases, the nature of the compliant behavior itself is fairly clearly socially undesirable, as for example, telling a lie directly and with seeming sincerity to some person who is innocently involved in the situation, as in the original Festinger and Carlsmith experiment and in one of the conditions of the Carlsmith, Collins, and Helmreich (1966) experiment.

Finally, the experimental procedures seem to include much pressure and constraint which is exerted so diffusely that the subject's attention is never called to its presence. The usual appeal is to the needs of the experimenter or experimental design, but these are mentioned in mild terms and always with a qualifier or offsetting statement. ("As far as I'm concerned you may read either . . . but I would like to ask you . . . Do you think that you'll be able to do this for me?" Davis & Jones, 1960, p. 404). There is often a complicated justification in terms of experimental design that probably serves to befuddle the subject, exerting pressure on him but leaving him unable to recapture the reasons or justification for his decision.

Unfortunately, much of the interchange between experimenter and subject that occurs in these experiments—the social process by which the pressure is exerted—is left ad lib—to the experimenter. The published experimental instructions often indicate where the experimenter paused for the subject's reaction, the implication being that the experimenter dealt with these reactions as he saw fit at the moment. As a consequence, many details of the process by which pressure may be exerted without being made salient are not available to us.

In view of these common elements in experiments on forced compliance, it seems not too far-fetched to believe that the successful experiment is one in which strong situational demands, entirely sufficient to produce total or near-total compliance, are successfully camouflaged by a network of cues as to self-determination. From an attribution point of view, the situation surrounding the behavior is misleading. The central attribution assumption in Bem's analysis, then, becomes tenable—that when the subject in the low-incentive condition reviews his recent behavior, it does not occur to him to attribute it to the situation and it is possible for him plausibly to make an entity attribution. Apparently having been free to speak his mind at that point, and having addressed himself to the entity, the subject views his response as having been entity-caused. In the high-incentive condition, the salient fact of the large payment suggests to him a situation-attribution for his behavior.

Conclusion

In this paper, I have explored the parallels that exist among the ideas of persons who, from various different theoretical backgrounds and for different purposes, have been dealing with what are essentially problems of causal attribution. I believe there is a genuine covergence of concepts in this area, despite the fact that some investigators begin with Heider, others with Skinner, and still others with Festinger.

As lengthy as this paper has become, I have not been able to deal with many of the significant aspects of attribution theory and its implications. I should at least *mention* a few more:

1. Attributions about the self and the basis of need for information about the self. Investigation of this topic might involve an analysis of social situations (e.g., *T* groups or sensitivity training situations) in which unique information regarding the self is presumed to be gained.

2. The assignment of credit and blame. The understanding of the effects of unanticipated consequences, briefly discussed in this paper, may be of great importance in dealing with matters of unwarranted guilt. The other side of the coin is the defensive dismissal of anticipated consequences with the result that feelings of personal responsibility are inappropriately absent.

3. The interplay between language and attribution. The importance of labeling for attribution stability would seem to require analysis.

4. Problems of establishing trust in interpersonal relationships. Attribution theory has important statements to make about the conditions and dilemmas here, as illustrated by Strickland's (1958) provocative study of the matter.

5. The development of attribution processes, with analysis of the stages of attribution as a function of maturation, socialization, and language training.

6. Personality differences in attribution processes. Significant work has been done by Seeman (1963), Rotter (1966), and others on self- *vs.* external-attributions of causality. A different line of investigation would be to examine individual differences in preferred modes of attribution, reliance on different criteria for stability, and egocentric biases in attribution.

7. The relation between the common man's attribution processes and the more systematic processes incorporated in scientific methods.

I hardly need to point out the potential importance of some of the problems considered within this framework. To take but one example from the present paper, the question of the illusion of freedom. This is a matter of high importance for a society that is dedicated to ideas of freedom but that seems to find it increasingly necessary to insist on conformity of behavior and expression. Understanding the conditions under which this illusion is created may enable us to avoid adopting the spurious solution it suggests to the problem of the tension between our ideals and the short-run advantages of uniformity.

ACKNOWLEDGMENTS

While I assume full responsibility for this paper, I gratefully acknowledge the many fruitful conversations on these topics with Melvin Seeman, John Thibaut, and the students in three graduate seminars. The preparation of the paper was facilitated by Grant GS-1121X from the National Science Foundation.

REFERENCES

Asch, S. E. *Social psychology*. New York: Prentice-Hall, 1952.

Bavelas, A., Hastorf, A. H., Gross, A., & Kite, W. R. Experiments on the alteration of group structure. *J. exp. soc. Psychol.*, 1965, *1*, 55–70.

Bem, D. J. An experimental analysis of self-persuasion. *J. exp. soc. Psychol.*, 1965, *1*, 199–218.

Bem, D. J. Self perception: An alternative interpretation of cognitive dissonance phenomena. *Psychol. Rev.*, 1967, *74*, 183–200.

Bramel, D. A. dissonance theory approach to defensive projection. *J. abnorm. soc. Psychol.*, 1962, *64*, 121–129.

Bramel, D. Selection of a target for defensive projection. *J. abnorm. soc. Psychol.*, 1963, *66*, 318–324.

Brehm, J. W. Increasing cognitive dissonance by a *fait-accompli. J. abnorm. soc. Psychol.*, 1959, *58*, 379–382.

Brehm, J. W., & Cohen, A. R. *Explorations in cognitive dissonance*. New York: Wiley, 1962.

Carlsmith, J. M., Collins, B. E., & Helmreich, R. L. Studies in forced compliance: I. The effect of pressure for compliance on attitude change produced by face-to-face role playing and anonymous essay writing. *J. Pers. soc. Psychol.*, 1966, *4*, 1–13.

Davidson, J. R. Cognitive familiarity and dissonance reduction. In L. Festinger (Ed.), *Conflict, decision, and dissonance*. Stanford: Stanford University Press, 1964. Pp. 54–59.

Davis, K. E., & Jones, E. E. Changes in interpersonal perception as a means of reducing cognitive dissonance. *J. abnorm. soc. Psychol.*, 1960, *61*, 402–410.

Festinger, L. Informal social communication. *Psychol. Rev.*, 1950, *57*, 271–282.

Festinger, L. A theory of social comparison processes. *Hum. Relat.*, 1954, *7*, 117–140.

Festinger, L., & Carlsmith, J. M. Cognitive consequences of forced compliance. *J. abnorm. soc. Psychol.*, 1959, *58*, 203–210.

Gerard, H. B., Deviation, conformity, and commitment. In I. D. Steiner & M. Fishbein (Eds.), *Current studies in social psychology*. New York: Holt, Rinehart & Winston, 1965. Pp. 263–277.

Gerard, H. B., & Rabbie, J. Fear and social comparison. *J. abnorm. soc. Psychol.*, 1961, *62*, 586–592.

Hastorf, A. H., Kite, W. R., Gross, A. E., & Wolfe, L. J. The perception and evaluation of behavior change. *Sociometry*, 1965, *28*, 400–410.

Heider, F. *The psychology of interpersonal relations*. New York: Wiley, 1958.

Hovland, C. I., Lumsdaine, A. A., & Sheffield, F. D. *Experiments on mass communication*. Princeton: Princeton University Press, 1949.

Jecker, J. D. The cognitive effects of conflict and dissonance. In L. Festinger (Ed.), *Conflict, decision and dissonance*. Stanford: Stanford University Press 1964. Pp. 21–30.

Johnson. T. J., Feigenbaum, R., & Weiby, M. Some determinants and consequences of the teacher's perception of causation. *J. educ. Psychol.*, 1964, *55*, 237–246.

Jones, E. E., & Davis, K. E. From acts to dispositions. In L. Berkowitz (Ed.), *Advances in experimental social psychology*. Vol. 2. New York: Academic Press, 1965, Pp. 219–266.

Jones, E. E., Davis, K. E., & Gergen, K. J. Role playing variations and their informational value for person perception. *J. abnorm. soc. Psychol.*, 1961, *63*, 302–310.

Jones, E. E., & Harris, V. A. The attribution of attitudes. Unpublished manuscript, Duke University, 1966.

Kelley, H. H., & Thibaut, J. W. Group problem solving. In G. Lindzey & E. Aronson (Eds.), *Handbook of social psychology*. (2d ed.) Reading, Mass.: Addison-Wesley, in press.

Kelman, H. C., & Hovland, C. I. "Reinstatement" of the communicator in delayed measurement of opinion change. *J. abnorm. soc. Psychol.*, 1953, *48*, 327–335.

Kimble, G. *Conditioning and learning*. New York: Appleton-Century-Crofts, 1961.

Ring, K. Some determinants of interpersonal attraction in hierarchical relationships: A motivational analysis. *J. Pers.*, 1964, *32*, 651–665.

Rotter, J. B. Generalized expectancies for internal versus external control of reinforcement. *Psychol. Monogr.*, 1966, *80*, No. 1 (Whole No. 609).

Schachter, S., & Singer, J. E. Cognitive, social and psychological determinants of emotional states. *Psychol. Rev.*, 1962, *69*, 379–399.

Seeman, M. Alienation and social learning in a reformatory. *Amer. J. Sociol.*, 1963, *69*, 270–284.

Strickland, L. H. Surveillance and trust. *J. Pers.*, 1958, *26*, 200–215.

Thibaut, J. W., & Kelley, H. H. *The social psychology of groups*. New York: Wiley, 1959.

Thibaut, J. W., & Riecken, H. W. Some determinants and consequences of the perception of social causality. *J. Pers.*, 1955, *24*, 113–133.

Valins, S. Cognitive effects of false heart-rate feedback. *J. Pers. soc. Psychol.*, 1966, *4*, 400–408.

Walster. Elaine. Assignment of responsibility for an accident. *J. Pers. soc. Psychol.*, 1966, *3*, 73–79.

Effortfulness and Flexibility of Dispositional Judgment Processes

Yaacov Trope and Thomas Alfieri • New York University

Editors' Notes

What is the role of situational constraints in determining our attributions? Generally, it has been thought that observed situational constraints diminish the perceived role of the person as causally responsible for an action. This is based on the logic that under strong situational pressures everyone would behave in the same way, hence the behavior is not informative in regards to the actor's unique personal attributes. Trope's and Alfieri's insightful analysis suggests, however, that things often aren't as simple as all that. This is because situational constraints may play a dual role in causal attribution. When a behavior is ambiguous, it is the situational constraints that can serve to disambiguate it. For example, an actor's mysterious facial expression may be interpreted as "sad" if the context is a funeral, and as "happy" if the context is a party. This means that the behavior is *assimilated to the context* and assumes the character implied by the context. However, in order to determine the causal role that the actor's unique personality played in producing the behavior, the context is now *subtracted* from the behavior. Thus, if the context was a funeral and the actor's expression was "sad," it is not concluded necessarily that this individual is a "sad person." After all, most people would wear a sad expression at a funeral. The dual role that the context plays in dispositional attributions (i.e., the assimilative and the subtractive roles) is further complicated by the fact that the former may occur (semi)automatically and without the individual's awareness, whereas the latter is often highly conscious and deliberative. These notions are tested in a pair of elegant experiments reported in the present selection.

Discussion Questions

1. What is the dual role of situational constraints in the dispositional attribution process?
2. Which of the two phases of the attributional process is more accessible to conscious awareness? What evidence do Trope and Alfieri adduce in this regard?
3. What are the implications of the automatic nature of the initial behavior identifications for how new information is dealt with when it is inconsistent with these identifications?

Suggested Readings

Chun, W.-Y., Spiegel, S., & Kruglanski, A. W. (2002). Assimilative behavior identification can also be resource dependent: A unimodal-based analysis of dispositional attribution phases. *Journal of Personality and Social Psychology.*

Gilbert, D. T., Pelham, B. W., & Krull, D. S. (1988). On cognitive busyness: When person perceivers meet persons perceived. *Journal of Personality and Social Psychology, 54,* 733–739.

Higgins, E. T., & Winter, L. (1993). The "acquisition principle": How beliefs about a behavior's prolonged circumstances influence correspondent inference. *Personality and Social Psychology Bulletin, 19,* 605–619.

Trope, Y. (1986). Identification and inferential processes in dispositional attribution. *Psychological Review, 93,* 239–257.

Authors' Abstract

Two experiments investigated how situational information is used to identify behavior (assimilative identification) and to adjust dispositional inferences from the identified behavior (inferential adjustment). Participants heard an ambiguous or unambiguous evaluation of a job candidate by an evaluator who was under situational pressure to present either a positive or negative evaluation. In Experiment 1 participants were under low or high cognitive load. In Experiment 2 the situational information was either validated or invalidated. Results showed that cognitive load and invalidation eliminated the use of situational information for inferential adjustment. Behavior ambiguity determined the use of situational information for assimilative identification. The results suggest that the use of situational information for assimilative identification is resource independent but inflexible, whereas inferential adjustment is flexible but resource dependent.

Situational information may affect dispositional inferences in two opposite ways. By means of *assimilative behavior identification*, situational information may produce an additive effect on dispositional inference, whereas by means of *inferential adjustment* it may produce a subtractive effect on dispositional inference. The effect on behavior identification presumably reflects an implicit and relatively uneffortful assimilation process (Bargh, 1989; Higgins & Stangor, 1988; Jacoby, Lindsay, & Toth, 1992; Schwarz & Bless, 1992; Sedikides & Skowronski, 1991). Information about the situation, like prior information about the target, may serve as context to which the immediate behavior is assimilated. It is important to note that these situationally derived identifications may be treated as reflecting the properties of the behavioral input and may, therefore, persevere even after situational information is invalidated. Assimilative identification effects should depend on such factors as the ambiguity of the behavior and the order in which situational and behavioral information is processed (see Trope et al., 1988; Trope, Cohen, & Alfieri, 1991) but should be independent of attentional resources and whether situational information is validated or invalidated (see Wilson & Brekke, 1994).

The use of situational information to adjust the implications of the identified behavior regarding the corresponding disposition is presumably a more effortful and deliberate process and, therefore, is likely to depend on perceivers' processing resources. In hypothesis-testing terms, inferential adjustment requires diagnostic inferences, namely, taking into account both the extent to which the disposition is sufficient and necessary to produce the behavior (see Trope & Liberman, 1993, 1996). Situational demands presumably make the disposition seem unnecessary (by making the behavior seem probable regardless of this disposition) and thus attenuate the diagnostic value of behavior. Under suboptimal processing conditions (e.g., high cognitive load or low motivation for accuracy), perceivers are likely to rely on a simpler inference rule, called the *pseudodiagnostic heuristic*, wherein behavior is attributed to the corresponding disposition to the extent that the disposition is seen as sufficient to produce the behavior. The necessity of the disposition is ignored, and inferences are therefore unadjusted for situational demands. Moreover, as a deliberate process, inferential adjustment should be performed flexibly, so that, unlike assimilative behavior identification, inferential adjustment should be annulled when situational information is invalidated (see Wilson & Brekke, 1994).

In this dual-process model, these two opposite effects of situational information determine the overall effect of situational information on dispositional judgment (see Figure 1). Situational information will produce an overall subtractive effect if this information is used for adjusting dispositional inferences from the behavior but not for identifying the behavior (see Quadrant B of Figure 1). When either one of these two requirements is violated, situational information will produce weak or null effects on dispositional judgment (Quadrants A and D). Thus, null effects may result from failure to adjust for situational demands (Quadrant A). However, null effects may also result from assimilative effects of situational information on behavior identification (Quadrant D). Here, situationally produced behavior identifications are used as independent evidence for the corresponding disposition, thus offsetting inferential adjustment. For example, knowing that an audience expects a pro-choice speech is unlikely to attenuate attribution of pro-choice attitudes to the speaker if this knowledge about the audience leads

perceivers to identify the speech as pro-choice when in fact it is not pro-choice. Finally, when both behavior identification and inferential adjustment requirements are violated, information about situational demands will produce additive (discounting reversal) effects on dispositional judgment; that is, situational demands to produce a behavior will increase rather than decrease attribution of the correspondent disposition (Quadrant C). In this case, perceivers use situational information to identify behavior but not to adjust the inferences regarding the correspondent disposition. For example, an additive effect will occur when information that an audience is pro-choice leads perceivers to misidentify a speech as pro-choice but not to adjust the diagnostic value of this identification regarding the speaker's true attitudes.

We designed two experiments to test the present distinction between assimilative identification and inferential adjustment as two processes that combine to determine the overall effect of situational information on dispositional judgment. Both experiments partitioned the overall effect of situational information into an indirect effect (reflecting assimilative identification) and a direct effect (reflecting inferential adjustment). The first experiment examined the dependency of the two processes on attentional resources. The main hypothesis tested in this experiment is that the use of situational information to adjust dispositional inferences from behavior depends on attentional resources, whereas the use of situational information to identify behavior depends on behavioral

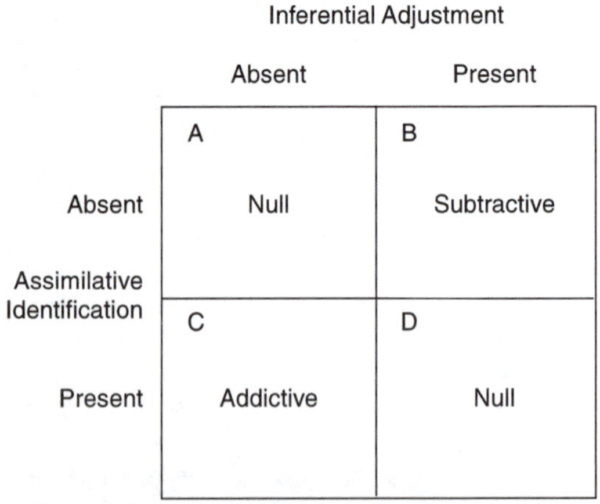

Inferential Adjustment

		Absent	Present
		A	B
	Absent	Null	Subtractive
Assimilative Identification		C	D
	Present	Addictive	Null

FIGURE 12.1 ■ Overall effects of situational information on dispositional judgment as a function of inferential adjustment and assimilative identification.

ambiguity and is independent of attentional resources. Past research has shown that cognitive
load attenuates the overall effect of situational information on dispositional judgment (e.g., Gilbert
et al., 1988). In our first experiment we extended
this research by testing the hypothesis that cognitive load interferes with inferential adjustment but
not with assimilative identification. This experiment thus tested the unique prediction that cognitive load may produce additive overall effects of
situational information on dispositional judgment.

In the second experiment we examined the flexibility of assimilative identification and inferential adjustment. The main hypothesis was that the
use of situational information to adjust dispositional inferences from behavior will be annulled
when situational information is invalidated,
whereas the use of situational information to identify behavior will depend on behavioral ambiguity and will persevere after situational information is invalidated.

Experiment 1

Participants heard a student working in a dean's
office describe to the dean a job candidate whom
the dean either liked or disliked. The dean's attitude toward the candidate created situational demands on the evaluator to present either a positive
or a negative evaluation of the candidate. The
evaluation that participants heard was either *unambiguously* positive or *ambiguous*. Furthermore,
the evaluation was presented either under cognitive load (participants kept in memory an 8-digit
number) or under no cognitive load. Participants
then judged the favorability of the evaluation (behavior identification) and the evaluator's true opinion of the candidate (dispositional judgment).

Method

PARTICIPANTS

A total of 165 undergraduate students (107 women
and 58 men) participated in this experiment as part
of a course requirement. Participants were randomly assigned to conditions that comprised a 2
(situational demands: positive or negative) × 2
(behavior ambiguity: unambiguous or ambiguous
evaluation) × 2 (cognitive load: present or absent)
factorial design.

PROCEDURE

Participants were tested individually. The experimenter read aloud background information as participants read this same information. The background information described a scenario with three
characters and began as follows:

> John is a sophomore at a small liberal arts college
> in New York. John wants to run for treasurer of
> the student council at his college. In order to be
> able to run for office, John has to hand in an ap-
> plication as well as be approved by the Dean of
> Student Affairs. Stephen is also a student at this
> college. He knows John from their psychology
> class. Stephen has been working part-time in the
> Dean's office for the past several months. Stephen
> hopes that the Dean will let him work there again
> next year.
>
> The Dean has received John's application to run
> for Treasurer and is reviewing John's academic
> record. One day when Stephen was working in
> the Dean's office, the Dean said the following:

Situational demands. What the dean said varied according to the situational demands conditions. In the positive demand condition the dean
said

> I know that mixed feelings exist concerning John:
> some people seem to like John but others do not
> like him. I think that John would be a good candi-
> date for Treasurer. I think that John is a persever-
> ing and economically minded individual, and,
> therefore, he is qualified for the position.

In the negative demand conditions the dean said

> I know that mixed feelings exist concerning John;
> some people seem to like John but others do not
> like him. I think that John would be a poor candi-
> date for Treasurer. I think that John is a stubborn
> and stingy person and, therefore, he is unquali-
> fied for the position.

Behavior ambiguity: Participants were told that
the dean approached Stephen and asked him what
he thought about John. At this point, Stephen's
answer was played to the participant on audiotape.
Half of the participants heard Stephen give the
following unambiguously positive evaluation:

> Well, I've known John for a year now. We met
> when he started to work for the student council.
> My experiences with John make me think that he
> is a person who keeps promises. Nothing seems
> to deter him from coming through on his word.
> He has been involved with the student council for
> the last year, and he has worked on a number of

student council functions. We are both psychology majors, and we took a class together last semester. I've worked with him on a few projects, both in the student council and in the class we took together. John has always finished the tasks he starts; when he has a job to do he sticks with it. I know that he earns extra money by working a few hours a week at a part-time job. He is good at saving money, and doesn't spend his money unwisely.

Half of the participants heard Stephen give the following ambiguous evaluation:

Well, I've known John for a year now. We met when he started to work for the student council. My experiences with John make me think that he doesn't change his mind very often. Once he has made a decision, it would be difficult to convince him to change it. He has been involved in the student council for the last year, and he has worked on a number of student council functions. We are both psychology majors and we took a class together last semester. I've worked with him on a few group projects, both in the student council and in the class we took together. When John works in a group, and this group arrives at what seems to be the best course of action, he resists making changes to this initial plan. I know that he earns extra money by working a few hours a week at a part-time job, though he doesn't spend much of it. He's very exact with his expenses and tightly holds onto his money. John can argue and argue his point of view; he likes people to agree with him. When push comes to shove, John refuses to take no as an answer.

We pretested these evaluations to ensure that they were either unambiguous or ambiguous. Thirty-six undergraduate students rated these evaluations without situational context. Pretest participants listened to the evaluations, presented in counterbalanced order, and were asked to rate them on 7-point scales. Half of the participants rated the evaluations in response to the following three questions: (1) To what extent does this description portray John as being a persevering person? (2) To what extent does this description portray John as being an economically minded person? (3) To what extent does this description portray John in a positive manner? The other half of the participants rated the evaluations in response to the following three questions: (1) To what extent does this description portray John as being a stubborn person? (2) To what extent does this description portray John as being a stingy person?

(3) To what extent does this description portray John in a negative manner? In all cases, the scales were anchored with the labels *not at all* (0) and *extremely* (6). As expected, the unambiguously positive evaluation was judged as portraying John as persevering ($M = 4.70$) but not stubborn ($M = 1.13$), $t(34) = 3.45$, $p < .01$; economically minded ($M = 5.25$) but not stingy ($M = 1.31$), $t(34) = 4.38$, $p < .01$; and positive ($M = 5.00$) but not negative ($M = 0.38$), $t(34) = 6.36$, $p < .01$. The ambiguous evaluation, however, was judged as portraying John as persevering ($M = 4.25$) and stubborn ($M = 4.81$), economically minded ($M = 5.35$) and stingy ($M = 3.75$), and as both moderately positive ($M = 3.10$) and moderately negative ($M = 2.69$, all *ts ns*). These ratings ensure that the unambiguously positive evaluation is perceived as describing John in only positive terms, whereas the ambiguous evaluation can be judged as describing John in either positive or negative terms.

Cognitive load. Half of the participants were placed under cognitive load while listening to the situational information and the evaluation, whereas the other half of the participants were under no cognitive load. Before the experimenter read the situational information to participants in the cognitive load conditions, the experimenter asked them to keep an 8-digit number in memory. The experiment then proceeded as above. After the participants heard the evaluation, the experimenter asked them to write down the number. Therefore, no participants were under cognitive load when providing responses to the dependent variables.

As a manipulation check, participants were asked, in addition to the dependent variables described below, to rate the dean's opinion of John, the applicant. These ratings were made on 11-point scales ranging from 0 (*very negative*) to 10 (*very positive*). We performed an analysis of variance (ANOVA) on these ratings using behavior ambiguity (ambiguous or unambiguous), situational demands (positive or negative), and cognitive load (present or absent) as between-subject variables. Results of this ANOVA revealed that participants in the positive situation conditions judged the dean's opinion to be significantly more positive ($M = 1.95$) than in the negative situation conditions ($M = 1.96$), $F(1, 157) = 710.26$, $p < .001$. Furthermore, cognitive load did not affect these ratings. In the positive situation conditions, the means for the load and no-load conditions were 8.09 and 7.79, respectively. In the negative situation conditions, the means for the load and no-load conditions were 1.82 and 2.10, respectively. The Situational Demand × Cognitive Load interaction was not significant. $F(1, 157) < 1$. These data indicate that participants remembered the situational demands in both the load and the no-load conditions.

DEPENDENT VARIABLES

After listening to either the unambiguous or the ambiguous evaluation, participants completed a short questionnaire. They rated the contents of the evaluation describing the applicant on an 11-point scale ranging from 0 (*very negative*) to 10 (*very positive*). We used responses to this item as a measure of behavior identification. Participants also rated what they believed to be Stephen's true attitude toward the applicant, again on an 11-point scale ranging from 0 (*very negative*) to 10 (*very positive*). We used responses to this item as a measure of dispositional judgments. Items were presented in counterbalanced order.

Results

BEHAVIOR IDENTIFICATION

We examined participants' ratings of the favorability of the evaluation to test the predictions that (a) information about situational demands will produce an assimilative effect on the identification of the ambiguous evaluation but not

on the identification of the *unambiguous* evaluation and (b) cognitive load would not interfere with the situation's assimilative effect. Figure 2 presents mean ratings of the favorability of the evaluations. We performed an ANOVA on these data using situational demands (positive or negative), behavior ambiguity (ambiguous or unambiguous), and cognitive load (present or absent) as between-subjects variables. As predicted, this ANOVA revealed a significant Situational Demands × Behavior Ambiguity interaction, $F(1, 157) = 14.23, p < .001$. This interaction indicated that situational demands produced an assimilative effect on the identification of the ambiguous evaluation but not on the identification of the unambiguous evaluation. The ambiguous evaluation was perceived as more favorable when the evaluator was said to be under pressure to make a positive evaluation ($M = 5.72$) than when he was said to be under pressure to make a negative evaluation ($M = 3.55$), $t(157) = 2.81, p < .01$. In contrast, perception of the unambiguous evaluation was completely unaffected by information about the positive or negative situations ($Ms = 8.54$ and 8.53, respectively).

As expected, the effect of situational demands on behavior identification was independent of cognitive loads ($Fs < 1$) for both the Situational Demands × Cognitive Load interaction and the Behavior Ambiguity × Situational Demands × Cognitive Load interaction. The means in Figure 2 indicate that the assimilative effect of situational information was the same for perceivers who were under cognitive load and for perceivers who were not.

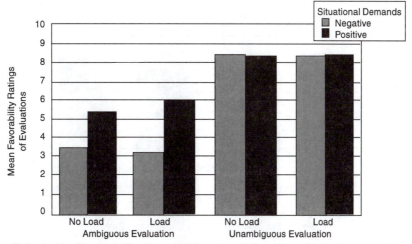

FIGURE 12.2 ■ Behavior identification in Experiment 1: Mean favorability ratings of evaluations as a function of situational demands, evaluation ambiguity, and cognitive load.

The ANOVA also revealed a significant main effect of behavior ambiguity, $F(1, 157) = 190.23$, $p < .001$, indicating that the unambiguously positive evaluation was perceived as more positive than the ambiguous evaluation ($Ms = 8.53$ and 4.68, respectively). The main effect of situational demands also was significant, with the positive situational demands leading to more positive ratings ($M = 7.01$) than the negative situations ($M = 5.91$), $F(1, 157) = 17.02, p < .001$. The interpretation of this effect, however, is completely qualified by the significant Behavior Ambiguity × Situational Demands interaction discussed above. As can be seen in Figure 2, only the identification of the ambiguous evaluation showed an assimilative effect of situational information. No other effects were significant.

These data support the hypothesis that the effect of situational information on behavior identification (a) depends on the ambiguity of the behavior and (b) is independent of attentional resources.

DISPOSITIONAL JUDGMENT

We proposed that the overall effect of situational information on dispositional judgment depends on behavior ambiguity and cognitive load because the former determines assimilative identification and the latter determines inferential adjustment. Theoretically, assimilative identification and inferential adjustment are independent determinants of overall situational effects. Hence, behavior ambiguity and cognitive load should independently influence situational effects on dispositional judgment.

Figure 3 presents mean ratings of the speaker's true attitude toward the applicant (dispositional judgment). We performed an ANOVA on these data using situational demands, behavior ambiguity, and cognitive load as between-subjects variables. As expected, the analysis showed that both ambiguity of the evaluation and cognitive load determined the effect of situational demands on attitude judgments. First, a significant Situational Demands × Behavior Ambiguity interaction, $F(1, 157) = 5.52, p < .05$, indicated that situational demands (positive vs. negative) were more likely to produce additive effects on attitude judgments when the evaluation was ambiguous ($Ms = 5.24$ and 3.86, respectively) than when it was unambiguous ($Ms = 7.62$ and 7.82, respectively). Second, a significant Situational Demands × Cognitive Load interaction, $F(1, 157) = 4.22, p < .05$, indicated a parallel effect of cognitive load. That is, situational demands (positive vs. negative) were more likely to produce additive effects on attitude judgments when perceivers were under cognitive load ($Ms = 6.65$ and 5.40, respectively) than when they were not ($Ms = 5.95$ and 6.08, respectively). The three-way interaction (Situational Demands × Behavior Ambiguity x Cognitive Load) was not significant, $F(1, 157) < 1$, thus supporting our hypothesis that ambiguity and cognitive load are

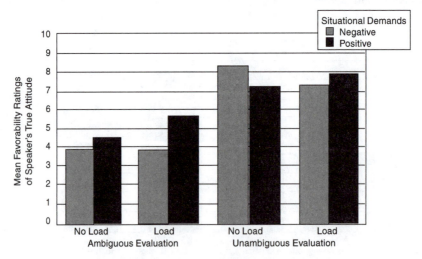

FIGURE 12.3 ■ Dispositional judgments in Experiment 1: Mean favorability ratings of the speaker's true attitude toward the candidate as a function of situational demands, evaluation ambiguity, and cognitive load.

independent determinants of the effect of situational demands on attitude judgment.

The ANOVA yielded two additional effects: One was a main effect of behavior ambiguity, $F(1, 157) = 99.25$, $p < .001$, indicating that the unambiguously positive evaluation was attributed to a more positive attitude ($M = 7.71$) than was the ambiguous evaluation ($M = 4.58$). The other was a main effect of situational demands, $F(1, 157) = 4.04$, $p < .05$. As discussed before, the interpretation of this effect is qualified by ambiguity and cognitive load.

PATH MODELS

We performed regression analyses to partition the total effect of situational demands on dispositional judgments into the direct effect of situational demands on dispositional judgment (reflecting inferential adjustment) and the indirect effect of situational demands on dispositional judgment by means of assimilative behavior identification. We expected that these direct and indirect effects would vary across the four Behavior Ambiguity × Cognitive Load conditions (i.e., ambiguous behavior, no load; ambiguous behavior, load; unambiguous behavior, no load; unambiguous behavior, load). Specifically, we predicted that the indirect effect of situational demands on dispositional judgment depends on behavior ambiguity and the direct effect of situational demands on dispositional judgment depends on cognitive load. Beta weights

(i.e., standardized regression coefficients) representing the direct and indirect effects in the four Behavior Ambiguity × Cognitive Load conditions are presented as path models in Figure 4.[1]

The results of these analyses support our hypotheses. First, the assimilative effect of situational demands depended on behavior ambiguity and not on cognitive load. Consistent with the ANOVA on behavior identification ratings, the path coefficients from situational demands to behavior identification were significantly higher for ambiguous behavior ($bs = .45$ and $.31$) than for unambiguous behavior ($bs = .04$ and $.09$), as indicated by the significant Situational Demands × Behavior Ambiguity interaction, $t(157) = 2.13$, $p < .05$.

As a consequence of this significant interaction, the indirect effects of situational demands on dispositional judgment (i.e., the effects of situational demands on dispositional judgment by means of behavior identification) were significantly greater than zero in the ambiguous behavior conditions but not in the unambiguous behavior conditions.[2] The indirect effect in the ambiguous-behavior-and-no-load condition was $\beta = .25$, $z = 2.49$, $p < .01$, and the indirect effect in the ambiguous-behavior-and-load condition was $\beta = .38$, $z = 3.23$, $p < .01$. The corresponding indirect effects were not significantly greater than zero in the unambiguous behavior conditions ($\beta s = .03$ and $.07$, $zs < 1$). As expected, the indirect effects of situational demands on dispositional judgments did not vary as a function of cognitive load.

---

[1] The regression analyses performed to obtain the beta weights presented in Figure 4 are presented here. The first regression analysis was designed to produce beta weights for the unique (i.e., simultaneous) relationships between (a) situational demands and dispositional judgment and (b) behavior identification and dispositional judgment in the four Behavior Ambiguity × Cognitive Load conditions. In this analysis, dispositional judgment was regressed onto behavior identification, situation demands (coded 1 = positive, 0 = negative), behavior ambiguity (dummy coded, 1 = unambiguous, 0 = ambiguous), cognitive load (dummy coded, 1 = present, 0 = absent), five 2-way interactions (Behavior Ambiguity × Cognitive Load, Behavior Ambiguity × Situational Demands, Behavior Ambiguity × Behavior Identification, Cognitive Load × Situational Demands, and Cognitive Load × Behavior Identification), and two 3-way interactions (Behavior Ambiguity × Cognitive Load × Situational Demands, and Behavior Ambiguity × Cognitive Load × Behavior Identification). The second regression analysis was designed to estimate beta weights of the relationship between situational demands and behavior identification in each of the four Behavior Ambiguity × Cognitive Load conditions. Behavior identification was

regressed onto situational demands (coded 1 = positive, 0 = negative), behavior ambiguity (dummy coded, 1 = unambiguous, 0 = ambiguous), cognitive load (dummy coded, 1 = present, 0 = absent), the three 2-way interactions (i.e., Situational Demands × Behavior Ambiguity, Situational Demands × Cognitive Load, and Behavior Ambiguity × Cognitive Load), and the three-way interaction. Following well-established procedures (see, e.g., Cohen & Cohen, 1983), we converted the standardized regression weights obtained from these analyses into the beta weights presented in Figure 4. The beta weights presented in Figure 7 (Experiment 2) were calculated in the manner outlined here, substituting the variable "validation condition" for "cognitive load."

[2] We calculated indirect effects of situational demands on dispositional judgments by multiplying the beta weights of the paths associated with the effect, that is, the beta weight of the path linking situational demands to behavior identification multiplied by the beta weight of the path linking behavior identification to dispositional judgments. The standard error of the indirect effect was calculated with LISREL VII (Jöreskog & Sörbom, 1989), thus allowing us to construct a z score to test the hypothesis that these effects were significantly greater than zero.

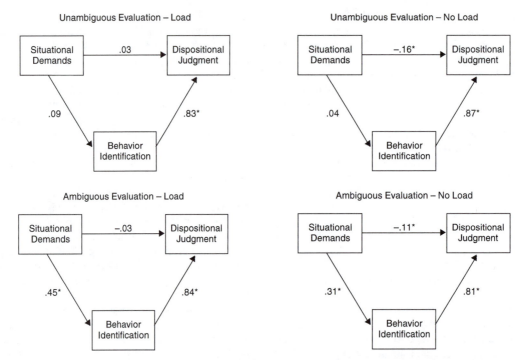

FIGURE 12.4 ■ Direct and indirect effects of situational demands on dispositional judgment in Experiment 1 as a function of evaluation ambiguity and cognitive load. Situational demands are coded as 0 = negative, 1 = positive. *$\beta \neq 0$, $p < .05$.

Second, the direct effect of situational demands on dispositional judgment, representing the use of situational demands for inferential adjustment, depended on cognitive load but not on behavior ambiguity. The direct paths from situational demands to dispositional judgment, that is, the effects of situational demands on dispositional judgment when controlling for behavior identification, were significantly stronger in the no-cognitive-load conditions (βs = −.11 and −.16) than in the cognitive load conditions (βs = -.03 and .03), as indicated by the significant Situational Demands × Cognitive Load interaction, $t(155) = 2.02$, $p < .05$. As expected, these paths were independent of behavior ambiguity, as indicated by the nonsignificant Situational Demands × Behavior Ambiguity interaction, $t(155) = 0.33$, and the Situational Demands × Behavior Ambiguity × Cognitive Load interaction, $t(155) = 0.29$.

Together, the results of Experiment 1 suggest that the use of situational information to identify behavior depends on its ambiguity, whereas the use of situational information to adjust inferences

from the identified behavior depends on cognitive load. These results are consistent with the present dual-process model wherein the use of situational information for behavior identification is a resource-independent process, whereas the use of situational information for inferential adjustment is a resource-dependent process.

Experiment 2

This experiment was designed to determine whether the effects of situational demands persevere after these demands are invalidated. Suppose perceivers are initially led to believe that an audience expects the speaker to take a certain stance but later, after hearing the speech, perceivers learn that the speaker was actually unaware of this demand. The question is whether perceivers' beliefs about situational demands will continue to influence judgment after these beliefs are invalidated. A considerable amount of research suggests that it is often difficult to reverse the initial effect of evidence on judgment when this evidence is subsequently disproved (see L. Ross, Lepper, & Hubbard, 1975; Schul & Burnstein, 1985; Wilson & Brekke, 1994). From the present dual-process perspective, assimilative identification and inferential adjustment should differ in this respect. Theoretically, inferential adjustment is a deliberate process of diagnostic reasoning (Trope & Liberman, 1993, 1996). Perceivers should therefore be able to perform it flexibly. That is, they should be able to reverse or refrain from inferential adjustment for situational demands when these demands are invalidated. Assimilative identification is presumably an implicit process leading perceivers to treat their behavior identifications as perceptual data rather than as situationally derived inferences (Banaji, Hardin, & Rothman, 1993; Bruner, 1957; Higgins, 1989; Jacoby et al., 1992; Martin, Seta, & Crelia, 1990; Moskowitz & Roman, 1992; Stapel, Koomen, & van der Pligt, 1997). Assimilative behavior identification should therefore be relatively inflexible in that it should be unaffected by invalidation of situational information.

According to the present analysis, then, when situational demands are invalidated, their assimilative effect on behavior identification will persevere, but their use for inferential adjustment will be annulled. Thus, invalidation of situational demands can diminish the effect of situational demands on dispositional judgment by means of inferential adjustment but not their effect by means of behavior identification. When behavior is ambiguous, situational demands will produce assimilative identification independent of situational invalidation. By diminishing inferential adjustment, invalidation will therefore act to increase overall additive effects of situational demands on dispositional attributions of ambiguous behavior. When behavior is unambiguous, situational demands cannot affect identification, and invalidation of situational demands can act only to diminish their overall subtractive effect on dispositional judgment.

Method

In this experiment we used the same basic attitude judgment paradigm as in Experiment 1. Participants heard a student (speaker) describe to the dean a job candidate whom the dean either liked or disliked. The description strongly implied, but did not actually state, that the speaker knew the dean's opinion about the candidate and thus was under demand to present a positive or negative evaluation. Participants then heard either an unambiguously positive evaluation or an ambiguous evaluation. After hearing the evaluation, participants in the validation condition were told that the speaker did indeed know the dean's opinion of the target when he gave his evaluations. Participants in the invalidation condition were told that the evaluator was actually unaware of the dean's opinions about the target. All participants then judged the favorability of the evaluation (behavior identification) and the evaluator's true feelings toward the target (dispositional inference).

PARTICIPANTS

Eighty-three undergraduate students (60 women and 23 men) participated in this experiment as part of a course requirement. Participants were approximately equally divided into the 2 (situational demands: positive or negative) × 2 (behavior ambiguity: unambiguous or ambiguous) × 2 (validation: situational demands validated or invalidated) experimental design.

PROCEDURE

The procedure and manipulations of the dean's attitude toward the candidate (situational demand) and the speaker's evaluation (behavior ambiguity) were the same as in the no-load condition in Experiment 1. After hearing the speaker's evaluation, and before completing the dependent variables, participants received additional information designed to validate or invalidate situational demands. In the validation condition, participants read the following information (depending on whether they were in the positive or negative situational demand condition):

> The Dean often speaks his positive (negative) opinion of John in the office; therefore, Stephen knew that the Dean had a positive (negative) opinion of John. When Stephen said the things that he did, Stephen knew that the Dean liked (did not like) John. Stephen knew that the Dean's opinion of John was that John was a persevering and economically minded (stubborn and stingy) person.

In the invalidation condition participants read:

Although the Dean often speaks his positive (negative) opinion of John in the office, Stephen did not know how the Dean actually felt about John. When Stephen said the things that he did, Stephen did not know if the Dean liked or disliked John. Stephen did not know the Dean's opinion of John.

The dependent measures were similar to those used in Experiment 1. Participants rated on 9-point scales ranging from –4 (*very negative*) to 4 (*very positive*) the favorability of the dean's opinion about the candidate, the favorability of the evaluation presented by the speaker, and the favorability of the speaker's true opinion about the candidate. The order of these items was counterbalanced across participants.

Participants' ratings of the favorability of the dean's opinion about the applicant served as a check on the manipulation of situational demands. We performed an ANOVA on these data with situational demands (positive or negative), behavior ambiguity (ambiguous or unambiguous), and validation condition (situational demands validated or invalidated) as between-subjects variables. As expected, the analysis yielded a significant main effect of situational demands, $F(1, 57) = 184.0, p < .001$, indicating that participants rated the opinion of the positive dean as more favorable toward the candidate ($M = 2.22$) than the opinion of the negative dean ($M = -2.51$). No other effects were significant in this analysis. Thus, participants were able to remember correctly the dean's opinion whether it was validated or invalidated.

Results

BEHAVIOR IDENTIFICATION

Mean ratings of the favorability of the evaluation are presented in Figure 5. A Situational Demands × Behavior Ambiguity × Validation Condition ANOVA of these ratings yielded the predicted Situational Demands × Behavior Ambiguity interaction, $F(1, 75) = 14.59, p < .001$. This interaction indicates that situational demands to present a positive rather than a negative evaluation produced an assimilative effect on the identification of the content of the ambiguous evaluation ($Ms = -0.38$ and -2.22, respectively) but not on the content of the unambiguous evaluation ($Ms = 2.35$ and 2.72, respectively). The main effect of behavior ambiguity was significant, $F(1, 75) = 184.46, p < .001$, indicating that the positive evaluation was perceived as more favorable than was the ambiguous evaluation ($Ms = 2.59$ and -1.23, respectively). A significant main effect of situational demands, $F(1, 75) = 5.40, p < .05$, indicated that the evaluations were perceived as more favorable when the situation demanded a positive evaluation rather than a negative evaluation ($Ms = 0.95$ and 0.64, respectively). However, the interpretation of these effects is qualified by the interaction discussed above.

It is important to note that the assimilative effect of situational demands was independent of whether they were validated or invalidated ($Fs < 1$) for effects involving validation condition. As can be seen in Figure 5, invalidation of situational

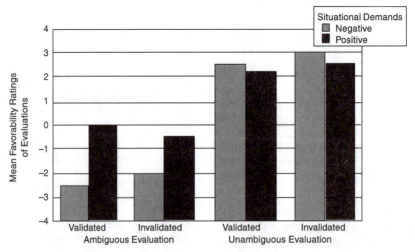

FIGURE 12.5 ■ Behavior identification in Experiment 2: Mean favorability ratings of evaluations as a function of situational demands, evaluation ambiguity, and situational validation.

demands did not eliminate their effect on behavior identification. On the contrary, their effect on behavior identification was as strong as that of validated situational demands. These results are consistent with our hypothesis that assimilative identification depends on the ambiguity of the behavior and is independent of whether situational demands are validated or invalidated.

DISPOSITIONAL JUDGMENT

Ratings of the speaker's true opinion about the candidate served as a measure of dispositional judgment. Mean ratings are presented in Figure 6. An ANOVA performed on these ratings yielded the predicted Situational Demands × Validation Condition interaction, $F(1, 75) = 9.24$, $p < .01$. This interaction indicates that situational demands (positive vs. negative) produced a subtractive effect on dispositional judgment (reflecting inferential adjustment) when they were validated (Ms = -0.29 and 1.22, respectively) but not when they were invalidated (Ms = 1.05 and 0.50, respectively). In addition, consistent with the results of Experiment 1, situational demands (positive vs. negative) produced this subtractive effect when the evaluation was unambiguous (Ms = 1.00 and 1.71, respectively) but not when the evaluation was ambiguous (Ms = -0.24 and -0.39, respectively). However, the Situational Demands × Behavior Type interaction was not significant, $F(1, 75) = 1.16$, $p = .29$.

Note in Figure 6 that validated situational demands produced a subtractive effect on dispositional judgment even when behavior was ambiguous (Ms = -0.90 and 0.11 for positive vs. negative demands). Apparently, validation of the situational demands enhanced inferential adjustment to an extent that was sufficient to offset the assimilative identification of ambiguous behavior. Finally, the main effect for behavior ambiguity was significant, $F(1, 75) = 17.30$, $p < .001$, indicating that the unambiguously positive evaluation was attributed to a more positive attitude ($M = 1.39$) than was the ambiguous evaluation ($M = -0.31$). There were no other significant effects.

PATH MODELS

As in Experiment 1, we performed regression analyses to assess the direct effect of situational demands on dispositional judgment (reflecting inferential adjustment), to assess the indirect effect of situational demands on dispositional judgment by means of assimilative behavior identification, and to compare these effects in the four Behavior Ambiguity × Validation conditions (see footnote 1). We predicted that the indirect effect of situational demands on dispositional judgment depends on behavior ambiguity and that the direct effect of situational demands on dispositional judgment depends on validation condition. The resulting path models are presented in Figure 7.

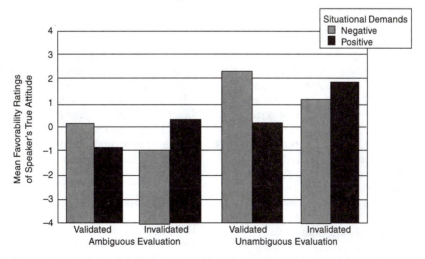

FIGURE 12.6 ■ Dispositional judgments in Experiment 2: Mean favorability ratings of the speaker's true attitude toward the candidate as a function of situational demands, evaluation ambiguity, and situational validation.

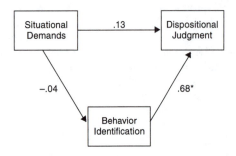

Unambiguous Evaluation – Situation Invalidated

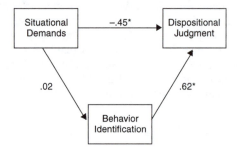

Unambiguous Evaluation – Situation Validated

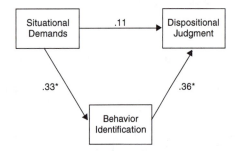

Ambiguous Evaluation – Situation Invalidated

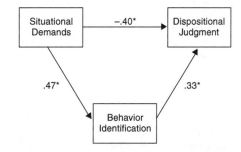

Ambiguous Evaluation – Situation Validated

FIGURE 12.7 ■ Direct and indirect effects of situational demands on dispositional judgment in Experiment 2 as a function of evaluation ambiguity and situational validation. Situational demands are coded as 0 = negative, 1 = positive. *$\beta \neq 0$, p < .05.

The results support our predictions. First, consistent with the ANOVA results, the path coefficients from situational demands to behavior identification were significantly higher for ambiguous behavior (bs = .47 and .33) than for unambiguous behavior (bs = .02 and −.04), as indicated by the significant Situational Demands × Behavior Ambiguity interaction, $t(75) = 3.03$, $p < .05$. Indirect effects of situational demands on dispositional judgment were significantly greater than zero for the ambiguous-behavior–situation-validated condition $b = .16$, $z = 1.72$, $p < .05$, one-tailed, and the ambiguous-behavior–situation-invalidated condition, $b = .12$, $z = 1.67$, $p < .05$, one-tailed. The indirect effects of the situation in the unambiguous behavior conditions were negligible (bs = .01 and −.03, zs < 1). As expected, indirect effects did not vary as a function of whether situational demands were validated or invalidated.

Second, the direct paths from situational demands to dispositional judgment, reflecting the effects of situational demands on dispositional judgment when behavior identification is partialed out, were significantly more negative after situ-

ational validation (bs = −.40 and −.45) than after situational invalidation (bs = .11 and .13), $t(71) = 1.99$, $p < .05$, for the Situational Demands × Validation Condition interaction. It is important to note that these paths were independent of behavior ambiguity (ts < 1) for all effects involving behavior ambiguity.

Overall, these results are consistent with our proposal that (a) behavior ambiguity determines the indirect effect of situational demands by means of assimilative identification, (b) validation or invalidation of situational demands determines their direct (inferential adjustment) effect on dispositional judgment, and (c) these two effects add to determine the overall effect of situational demands on dispositional judgment.

General Discussion

The present experiments investigated how situational information is used to (a) identify behavior (assimilative identification) and (b) adjust dispositional inferences from the identified behavior (inferential adjustment). In Experiment 1 we varied behavior ambiguity and cognitive load and assessed their effect on assimilative identification and inferential adjustment. The results were straightforward: Behavior ambiguity determined assimilative identification, whereas cognitive load determined inferential adjustment. More specifically, information about situational demands affected the interpretation of behavior to the extent that the behavior was ambiguous. For example, information indicating that a listener expected a positive evaluation rather than a negative evaluation of a job candidate led participants to interpret an ambiguous evaluation as positive rather than negative. Cognitive load did not interfere with the use of situational information for identifying the behavior. If anything, situational information produced a slightly stronger effect on behavior identification when participants were under cognitive load than when they were under no load.

Although cognitive load did not affect the use of situational information for behavior identification, it did affect the use of this information for adjusting dispositional inferences from the identified behavior. Under no cognitive load, participants adjusted dispositional inferences from the identified behavior for the influence of situational demands. For example, information indicating that a listener expected a positive evaluation rather than a negative evaluation attenuated attribution of the positive evaluation to a positive attitude. In contrast, under cognitive load, participants attributed the identified behavior to the corresponding disposition without adjusting these attributions for situational demands. The ambiguity of behavior, which determined the use of situational information for identifying behavior, had no effect on the use of situational information for drawing inferences from the identified behavior.

In Experiment 2 we investigated how behavior ambiguity and validation versus invalidation of situational information affect assimilative behavior identification and inferential adjustment. The results are again easy to summarize: Assimilative identification depended on behavior ambiguity, whereas inferential adjustment depended on the validation or invalidation of situational information. More specifically, consistent with the results of Experiment 1, situational information produced an assimilative effect on identification of ambiguous behavior but not on the identification of unambiguous behavior. Moreover, the assimilative

effect of situational information on behavior identification was independent of the validity of the situational information. Information about situational demands on the speaker continued to bias participants' interpretation of the content of the speaker's evaluation even when this situational information was invalidated.

Unlike the use of situational information for behavior identification, the use of situational information for inferential adjustment depended on its validity, not on the ambiguity of behavior. Participants adjusted their inferences for situational demands when these demands were validated. It is interesting that the situational validation condition enhanced inferential adjustment not only in comparison to the invalidation condition but also in comparison to the no-load conditions of Experiment 1, in which situational information was neither validated nor invalidated. Apparently, the increased salience of validated situational information enhanced its use for inferential adjustment.

When situational information was invalidated, however, inferential adjustment was eliminated. Dispositional judgments under these circumstances fully corresponded to behavior identifications, indicating that inferential adjustment was completely annulled. It seems, then, that the validity of situational information was taken into account in inferential adjustment but not in assimilative identification. This finding is consistent with research on belief perseverance showing that people are better able to correct their judgment for the direct effect of some information than for the indirect effect of this information by means of its influence on the construal of other pieces of information (see Anderson, Lepper, & Ross, 1980; Golding, Fowler, Long, & Latta, 1990; L. Ross, Lepper, Strack, & Steinmetz, 1977; Schul & Burnstein, 1985; Wilson & Brekke, 1994).

Overall, the results of the present experiments support the distinction between the use of situational information for identifying behavior and for drawing dispositional inferences from the identified behavior. The two processes presumably differ in the attentional capacity they require and their flexibility. The first, assimilative identification, is inflexible and independent of attentional resources. It occurs when behavior is ambiguous and preceded by situational information (see Trope, 1986; Trope et al., 1991, 1988). Whether the perceiver is under cognitive load and whether situational information is validated or invalidated does not eliminate or even diminish the use of the situation for identifying behavior. Theoretically, when one of the alternative interpretations of the ambiguous behavior matches situational expectations, the meaning of behavior is disambiguated with little conscious awareness (see Banaji et al., 1993; Bruner, 1957; Higgins, 1989; Jacoby et al., 1992; Martin et al., 1990; Moskowitz & Roman, 1992; Stapel et al., 1997). Perceivers presumably think their identifications reflect the properties of the behavioral input and, therefore, treat them as independent evidence for inductive inferences about the target's general dispositions, without realizing that these identifications are context derived.

The use of situational information for adjusting dispositional inferences from behavior is an effortful process that is hard to perform when processing capacity is reduced by cognitive load. It requires diagnostic reasoning, namely, taking into account not only whether the disposition is sufficient to produce the behavior but also whether the disposition is necessary to produce the behavior (see Trope & Liberman, 1993, 1996). Moreover, our findings suggest that inferential adjustment is conditional on the validity of situational information. When information about situational demands is invalidated, adjustment for these demands is annulled (suppressed or reversed). Thus, inferential adjustment appears to be an effortful but flexible process.

By varying simultaneously determinants of assimilative identification (behavior ambiguity) and inferential adjustment (cognitive load and validation of situational information), we were able to test the assumption that the two processes independently affect dispositional judgment. That is, if assimilative identification and inferential adjustment represent independent mediators of the situational effect on dispositional judgment, then this effect should be an additive function of assimilative identification and inferential adjustment determinants. The results fully support this prediction. Neither cognitive load nor situational validation interacted with behavior ambiguity in determining the effect of situational information on dispositional judgment. Behavior ambiguity, on the one hand, and cognitive load and situational validation, on the other hand, acted independently to diminish or reverse negative situational effects on dispositional judgment.

ACKNOWLEDGMENT

We thank Ben Gervey for his assistance in preparing this work.

REFERENCES

Anderson, C. A., Lepper, M. R., & Ross, L. (1980). Perseverance of social theories: The role of explanation in the persistence of discredited information. *Journal of Personality and Social Psychology, 39,* 1037–1049.

Banaji, M. R., Hardin, C., & Rothman, A. J. (1993). Implicit stereotyping in person judgment. *Journal of Personality and Social Psychology, 65,* 272–281.

Bargh, J. A. (1989). Conditional automaticity: Varieties of automatic influence in social perception and cognition. In J. S. Uleman & J. A. Bargh (Eds.), *Unintended thought* (pp. 3–51). New York: Guilford Press.

Bassili, J. N. (1989). Traits as action categories vs. traits as person attributes in social cognition. In J. N. Bassili (Ed.), *On-line cognition in person perception* (pp. 61–89). Hillsdale, NJ: Erlbaum.

Bruner, J. (1957). On perceptual readiness. *Psychological Review, 64,* 123–152.

Cohen, J., & Cohen, P. (1983). *Applied multiple regression/correlation analysis for the behavior sciences.* Hillsdale, NJ: Erlbaum.

Devine, P. G., Hirt, E. R., & Gehrke, E. M. (1990). Diagnostic and confirmatory strategies in trait hypothesis-testing. *Journal of Personality and Social Psychology, 58,* 952–963.

Dweck, C. S., Hong, Y., & Chiu, C. (1993). Implicit theories: Individual differences in the likelihood and meaning of dispositional inference. *Personality and Social Psychology Bulletin, 19,* 633–643.

Dweck, C. S., & Leggett, E. L. (1988). The social–cognitive approach to motivation and personality. *Psychological Review, 95,* 256–273.

Gidron, D., Koehler, D. J., & Tversky, A. (1993). Implicit quantification of personality traits. *Personality and Social Psychology Bulletin, 19,* 594–604.

Gilbert, D. T. (in press). Folk personology. In D. T. Gilbert, S. T. Fiske, & G. Lindzey (Eds.), *The handbook of social psychology* (4th ed.). New York: McGraw-Hill.

Gilbert, D. T., & Krull, D. S. (1988). Seeing less and knowing more: The benefits of perceptual ignorance. *Journal of Personality and Social Psychology, 54,* 93–102.

Gilbert, D. T., & Malone, P. S. (1995). Correspondence bias. *Psychological Bulletin, 117,* 21–38.

Gilbert, D. T., & Osborne, R. E. (1989). Thinking backward: The curable and incurable consequences of cognitive busyness. *Journal of Personality and Social Psychology, 57,* 940–949.

Gilbert, D. T., Pelham, B. W., & Krull, D. S. (1988). On cognitive busyness: When person perceivers meet persons perceived. *Journal of Personality and Social Psychology, 54,* 733–740.

Golding, J. M., Fowler, S. B., Long, D. L., & Latta, H. (1990). Instructions to disregard potentially useful information: The effects of pragmatics on evaluative judgments and recall. *Journal of Memory and Language, 29,* 212–227.

Heider, F. (1958). *The psychology of interpersonal relations.* New York: Wiley.

Higgins, E. T. (1989). Knowledge accessibility and activation: Subjectivity and suffering from unconscious sources. In J. S. Uleman & J. A. Bargh (Eds.), *Unintended thought* (pp. 75–152). New York: Guilford Press.

Higgins, E. T., & Stangor, C. (1988). Context-driven social judgment and memory: "When behavior engulfs the field" in reconstructive memory. In D. Bar-Tal & A. W. Kruglanski (Eds.), *The social psychology of knowledge* (pp. 262–298). New York: Cambridge University Press.

Hilton, J. L., Fein, S., & Miller, D. T. (1993). Suspicion and dispositional inference. *Personality and Social Psychology Bulletin, 19,* 501–512.

Jacoby, L. L., Lindsay, D. S., & Toth, J. P. (1992). Unconscious influences revealed: Attention, awareness, and control. *American Psychologist, 47,* 802–809.

Jones, E. E. (1979). The rocky road from acts to dispositions. *American Psychologist, 34,* 107–117.

Jones, E. E., & Nisbett, R. E. (1972). *The actor and the observer: Divergent perception of the causes of behavior.* Morristown, NJ: General Learning Press.

Jöreskog, K., & Sörbom, D. (1989). *LISREL VII: Analysis of linear structural relationships by maximum likelihood, instrumental variables, and least squares methods.* Mooresville, IN: Scientific Software.

Krull, D. S. (1993). Does the grist change the mill? The effect of the perceiver's inferential goal on the process of social inference. *Personality and Social Psychology Bulletin, 19,* 340–348.

Lupfer, M. B., Clark, L. F., & Hutcherson, H. W. (1990). Impact of context of spontaneous trait and situational attributions. *Journal of Personality and Social Psychology, 58,* 239–249.

Martin, L. L., Seta, J. J., & Crelia, R. A. (1990). Assimilation and contrast as a function of people's willingness and ability to expend effort in forming an impression. *Journal of Personality and Social Psychology, 59,* 27–37.

Moskowitz, G., & Roman, R. J. (1992). Spontaneous trait inferences as self-generated primes: Implications for conscious social judgment. *Journal of Personality and Social Psychology, 62,* 728–738.

Newman, L. S., & Uleman, J. S. (1993). When are you what you did? Behavior identification and dispositional inference in person memory, attribution and social judgment. *Personality and Social Psychology Bulletin, 19,* 513–525.

Reeder, G. D. (1993). Trait–behavior relations and dispositional inference. *Personality and Social Psychology Bulletin, 19,* 586–593.

Reeder, G. D., & Brewer, M. B. (1979). A schematic model of dispositional attribution in interpersonal perception. *Psychological Review, 86,* 61–79.

Ross, L. (1977). The intuitive psychologist and his shortcomings. In L. Berkowitz (Ed.), *Advances in experimental social psychology* (Vol. 10, pp. 173–220). New York: Academic Press.

Ross, L., Lepper, M. R., & Hubbard, M. (1975). Persever-

ance in self-perception and social perception: Biased attributional processes in the debriefing paradigm. *Journal of Personality and Social Psychology, 32,* 880–892.

Ross, L., Lepper, M. R., Strack, F., & Steinmetz, J. (1977). Social explanation and social expectation: Effects of real and hypothetical explanations on subjective likelihood. *Journal of Personality and Social Psychology, 35,* 817–829.

Schul, Y., & Burnstein, E. (1985). When discounting fails: Conditions under which individuals use discredited information in making a judgment. *Journal of Personality and Social Psychology, 49,* 894–903.

Schwarz, N., & Bless, H. (1992). Constructing reality and its alternatives: An inclusion/exclusion model of assimilation and contrast effects in social judgment. In L. L. Martin & A. Tesser (Eds.), *The construction of social judgments* (pp. 217–245). Hillsdale, NJ: Erlbaum.

Sedikides, C., & Skowronski, J. J. (1991). The law of cognitive structure activation. *Psychological Inquiry, 2,* 169–184.

Stapel, D. A., Koomen, W., & van der Pligt, J. (1997). Categories of category accessibility: The impact of trait concepts versus exemplar priming on person judgment. *Journal of Experimental Social Psychology, 47*–76.

Taylor, S. E., & Fiske, S. T. (1978). Salience attention and attribution: Top of the head phenomena. In L. Berkowitz (Ed.), *Advances in experimental social psychology* (Vol. 11, pp. 249–288). New York: Academic Press.

Trope, Y. (1986). Identification and inferential processes in dispositional attribution. *Psychological Review, 93,* 239–257.

Trope, Y. (1997). Dispositional bias in person perception: A hypothesis-testing perspective. In J. Cooper & J. M. Darley (Eds.), *Attribution processes, person perception, and social interaction: The legacy of Ned Jones* (pp. 26–48). Washington, DC: American Psychological Association.

Trope, Y., Cohen, O., & Alfieri, T. (1991). Behavior identification as a mediator of dispositional inference. *Journal of Personality and Social Psychology, 61,* 873–883.

Trope, Y., Cohen, O., & Maoz, I. (1988). The perceptual and inferential effects of situational inducements. *Journal of Personality and Social Psychology, 55,* 165–177.

Trope, Y., & Higgins, E. T. (1993). The what, how, and when of dispositional inference: New questions and answers. *Personality and Social Psychology Bulletin, 19,* 493–500.

Trope, Y., & Liberman, A. (1993). Trait conceptions in identification of behavior and inferences about persons. *Personality and Social Psychology Bulletin, 19,* 553–562.

Trope, Y., & Liberman, A. (1996). Social hypothesis-testing: Cognitive and motivational mechanisms. In E. T. Higgins & A. W. Kruglanski (Eds.), *Social psychology: Handbook of basic principles* (pp. 239–270). New York: Guilford Press.

Wilson, T. D., & Brekke, N. (1994). Mental contamination and mental correction: Unwanted influences on judgments and evaluations. *Psychological Bulletin, 116,* 117–142.

Personal and Motivational Systems

The previous set of readings dealt with cognitive phenomena of social-psychological significance. The research interests of social and personality psychologists, however, extends well beyond cognitive phenomena occurring in individuals' heads. It includes interests in the remaining major facets of human psychology, including motivation, feelings, and actions. Indeed, a major emphasis in the following set of readings is given to the interrelations among these fundamental aspects of the human experience, such as the relation of motivation to action, and of both to feeling. What are the mechanisms and processes whereby self-regulation toward important objectives is accomplished? Why is it that some individuals persist with their chosen pursuit no matter what the obstacles or the temptations, whereas others cannot resist alluring distractions and are easily distracted from their carefully considered intentions and resolutions? Why is it that some individuals are devastated by failure, whereas others are relatively unperturbed by it, and what implications does this have for achievement behavior ? How can one ever ensure that her or his intentions are carried out? How do we evaluate objects and events, including our own happiness and general life satisfaction? What effects do our moods have on our ability to think, and how do our motivations affect our thought processes? These questions and others are addressed in the present section.

A general outline of the way our self-regulatory processes are structured is offered in the paper by Carver and Scheier (1990). The affect generated in the course of unsuccessful regulation is looked at by Higgins, Bond, Klein, and Strauman (1986). Mischel, Shoda, and Rodriguez (1989) examine delay-of-gratification mechanisms and their impact on children's subsequent success in their social and academic pursuits. Elliott and Dweck (1988) theorize about and investigate the differences between children whose concern is with performance versus those more interested in learning and mastery. Gollwitzer, Heckhausen, and Steller (1990) look at what it takes to translate one's formulation of a goal into the undertaking of successful goal pursuit via appropriate action. Fazio, Sanbonmatsu, Powell, and Kardes (1986) deal with the automaticity of our evaluations, and Tesser and Paulhus (1983) discuss the management of our own self-evaluations. The papers by Schwarz and Clore (1983) and by Mackie and Worth (1989) address different ways in which mood affects cognition. Wegner and Erber (1992) discuss how mental control may be exercised. Finally, Kunda (1987) and Kruglanski and Freund (1983) discuss different ways in which our motivations may impact our judgmental processes.

Origins and Functions of Positive and Negative Affect: A Control-Process View

Charles S. Carver • University of Miami
Michael F. Scheier • Carnegie Mellon University

Editors' Notes

This paper has dual significance. First, it outlines a sophisticated control theory of behavior in which cognition, meta-cognition, and action are coherently interrelated. Second, it ties these notions to the concept of affect that has typically been thought of in very different terms, and often separately from the individual's self-regulatory concerns. The control-theory framework is a general cognitive alternative to behavioristic construals of action. Rather than assuming a mechanistic model wherein reinforcement enhances the probability of behavior and internal mediators retain the status of a "black box," control theoretic notions describe the processes that underlie behavior. This includes people's sensitivity to feedback, both in terms of generating action patterns and in engendering emotion. The model postulates that the quality and magnitude of emotions vary as a function of people's goal-related expectancies, the degree to which these are met or frustrated by the consequences of their actions, and the rate of progress in goal attainment.

Discussion Questions

1. What is the relation of emotion to disengagement processes?
2. According to Carver and Scheier (1990), what is the function of the meta-loop in self-regulation?
3. What is the relation between pace of progress toward the goal and emotional phenomena?

Suggested Readings

Cantor, N. (1990). From thought to behavior: "Having" and "doing" in the study of personality and cognition. *American Psychologist, 45,* 735–750.

Higgins, E. T. (1997). Beyond pleasure and pain. *American Psychologist, 52,* 1280–1300.

Mischel, W., & Shoda, Y. (1995). A cognitive-affective system theory of personality: Reconceptualizing situations, dispositions, dynamics, and invariance in personality structure. *Psychological Review, 102,* 246–268.

Authors' Abstract

The question of how affect arises and what affect indicates is examined from a feedback-based viewpoint on self-regulation. Using the analogy of action control as the attempt to diminish distance to a goal, a second feedback system is postulated that senses and regulates the rate at which the action-guiding system is functioning. This second system is seen as responsible for affect. Implications of these assertions and issues that arise from them are addressed in the remainder of the article. Several issues relate to the emotion model itself; others concern the relation between negative emotion and disengagement from goals. Relations to 3 other emotion theories are also addressed. The authors conclude that this view on affect is a useful supplement to other theories and that the concept of emotion is easily assimilated to feedback models of self-regulation.

Self-Regulation of Behavior

Control Processes and Self-Regulation

We construe intentional behavior as reflecting a process of feedback control (see, e.g., Carver, 1979; Carver & Scheier, 1981, 1982a, 1986a, in press; MacKay, 1963, 1966; Norman, 1981; Powers, 1973). When people move (physically or psychologically) toward goals, they manifest the functions of a negative (discrepancy reducing) feedback loop (see Figure 1). That is, people periodically note the qualities they are expressing in their behavior (an input function). They compare these perceptions with salient reference values—whatever goals are temporarily being used to guide behavior (a comparison process inherent in all feedback systems).[1] If the comparisons indicate discrepancies between reference value and present state (i.e., between intended and actual qualities of behavior), people adjust behavior (the output function) so that it more closely approximates the reference value.

Taken as an organized system, these component functions act to "control" the quality that is sensed as input to the system. That is, when a feedback loop is functioning properly, it induces the sensed

quality closer to the reference value. In terms of human behavior, the exercise of feedback control means that the person acts to minimize any discernable discrepancy between current actions and the behavioral reference value. To put it more simply, when people pay attention to what they are doing, they usually do what they intend to do, relatively accurately and thoroughly.

This brief description obviously omits a great deal that is important, and space limitations preclude treatment of all of the issues relevant to conceptualizing behavior. Two more sets of theoretical principles are needed, however, for us to address emotion and its role in self-regulation.

---

[1]A brief comment on our use of terms such as *reference value, standard,* and *goal:* We use these terms interchangeably here, despite the fact that they have slightly different connotations to many people. Reference values are qualities that are taken as guides, qualities to be approximated in one's actions. Although the word *standard* is often taken as implying social definitions of appropriateness, that is not meant here (see Carver & Scheier, 1985, for detail). The term *goal* often evokes an image of a "final state," but we do not mean to imply a static, statelike quality. People have many goals of continuous action—for example, the goal of being engaged in sailing or skiing or the goal of having a successful career. Indeed, most goals underlying behavior would seem to be of this sort. This emphasis on dynamic goals in self-regulation will become more obvious later in the article.

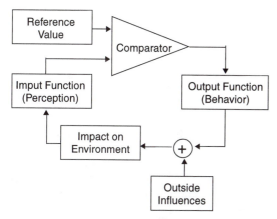

FIGURE 13.1 ■ Schematic depiction of a feedback loop, the basic unit of cybernetic control. (In such a loop a sensed value is compared to a reference value or standard, and adjustments are made, if necessary, to shift the sensed value in the direction of the standard.)

Hierarchical Organization of Behavior

One of these principles is the notion that behavior is organized hierarchically (e.g., Broadbent, 1977; Dawkins, 1976; Gallistel, 1980; Martin & Tesser, in press; Ortony, Clore, & Collins, 1988; Powers, 1973; Vallacher & Wegner, 1985, 1987). In con-

trol-process terms, the output of a superordinate feedback system (the system directing behavior at the level of present current concern—cf. Klinger, 1975; Shallice, 1978) is the resetting of reference values at the next lower level of abstraction (Figure 2). Powers (1973) argued that an identity between output at one level and resetting of standards at the next lower level is maintained from the level that is presently superordinate, down to the level of setting reference values for muscle tensions. Thus, the hierarchy creates the physical execution of whatever action is taking place.

We have adopted Powers' position as a conceptual heuristic, focusing on its implications at high levels of abstraction, the levels of our own interest (see Marken, 1986, and Rosenbaum, 1987, regarding the usefulness of similar notions at lower levels). The hierarchical organization in Figure 2 shows three high levels of control. At the highest level shown (labeled *system concepts*) are such values as the global sense of idealized self. Although self is not the only reference value at this level, it provides what may be the most intuitive illustration of the type of quality that occurs here, and it may be the most frequently used value at this level. Other possibilities include the idealized sense of a relationship or of a society.

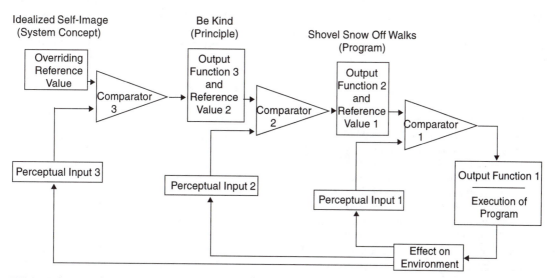

FIGURE 13.2 ■ Three-level hierarchy of feedback loops showing the top three levels of control in the model proposed by Powers (1973) and illustrating the kinds of content that reference values at these three levels can assume. (This diagram portrays the behavior of someone who is presently attempting to conform to his ideal self-image, by using the principle of kindness to guide his actions, a principle that presently is being manifest through the program of shoveling snow from a neighbor's sidewalk.)

Reference values at this level are abstract and difficult to define. How do people minimize discrepancies between their behavior and such abstract qualities? What behavioral outputs are involved? The answer suggested by Powers (1973) is that the behavioral output of this high-order system consists of providing reference values at the next lower level, which he termed the level of *principle* control. Thus, people act to "be" who they think they want (or ought) to be by adopting any of the guiding principles that are implied by the idealized self to which they aspire. (The constituents of the idealized self to which the person aspires—and what principles are thereby implied—obviously will differ from person to person.)

Principles begin to provide some form for behavior. Principles are probably the most abstract aspects of behavior that have names in everyday language—for example, honesty, responsibility, and expedience. Principles are not specifications of acts but of qualities that can be manifest in many acts. People do not just go out and "do" honesty, or responsibility, or thrift. Rather, people manifest any one (or more) of these qualities while doing more concrete activities.

The concrete activities are termed *programs* (cf. Schank & Abelson's 1977, discussion of scripts). Principles influence the program level by influencing what programs occur as potential reference values and by influencing choices made within programs. Programs of action are the sorts of activities that most people recognize more clearly as "behavior," although even programs are still relatively abstract. Going to the store, cooking dinner, writing a report—all these are programs.

Programs, in turn, are made up of movement *sequences*. One difference between programs and sequences is that programs involve choice points at which decisions must be made (ranging from trivial to important), whereas the constituents of a sequence are executed all-at-a-piece. When an action becomes sufficiently well learned that its enactment (once begun) is automatic rather than effortful (e.g., Shiffrin & Schneider, 1977), it can be thought of as having become a sequence rather than a program.

An important implication of the notion of hierarchical organization is that the higher one goes into this organization, the more fundamental to the overriding sense of self are the qualities encountered. A second, related implication is that the importance of a reference value at a low level is at least partly a product of the degree to which its attainment contributes to success in the attempt to reduce discrepancies at higher levels.

A last point concerning the hierarchical model is that self-regulation does not inevitably require engaging the full hierarchy from the top downward. We tentatively assume that whatever level of the hierarchy is temporarily focal is functionally superordinate at that moment, with self-regulation at any level higher suspended until attention is redirected toward reference values at the higher level. In practice, much of human behavior is probably self-regulated at the program level, with little or no consideration of values higher than that.

Difficulty, Disengagement, and Withdrawal

A final set of theoretical principles concerns the fact that people are not always successful in attaining their goals. Sometimes the physical setting precludes intended acts. Sometimes personal inadequacies prevent people from accomplishing what they set out to do. Regardless of the source of the impediment, and regardless of the level of abstraction at which it occurs (e.g., principle, program), there must be a way to construe the fact that people sometimes put aside their goals, aspirations, and intentions.

Assessing expectancies. We believe that behavior proceeds smoothly until and unless people encounter impediments (Figure 3). When people encounter enough difficulty to disrupt their efforts, we assume that they step outside the behavioral stream momentarily and assess the likelihood that the desired outcome will occur, given further effort. Potential impediments to action that come to mind before action begins presumably act the same in this respect as do those confronted during the action.

This sequence of interruption and expectancy assessment can be initiated in several ways. The simplest initiator is frustration—existence of an obstacle to goal attainment, either external (impediments or constraints) or internal (deficits of skill, knowledge, or effort). Another major class of interruptors is anxiety, which is aroused in circumstances in which a contemplated or ongoing action is in some way threatening. Although other interruptors are certainly possible, most represent

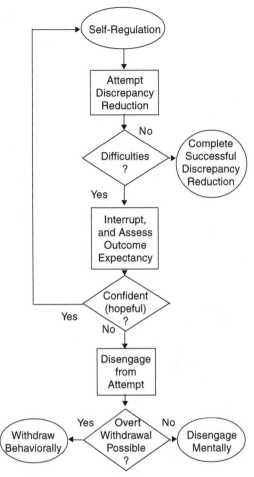

FIGURE 13.3 ■ Flow diagram of the various consequences that can follow when a person attempts to match his or her behavior to a standard of comparison. (Although self-regulation often proceeds unimpeded, discrepancy reduction efforts may be interrupted if difficulties or impediments are encountered, or anticipated. What follows this interruption is determined by the person's expectations about whether continued efforts will promote a good outcome.)

conditions that hamper or interfere with goal attainment.

The process of assessing outcome expectancy (whatever the interruptor) may make use of a wide variety of information pertaining to the situation and to internal qualities such as skill, anticipated effort, and available response options (cf. Lazarus, 1966). In many cases, however, expectancy assessment relies quite heavily on memories of prior experiences. Thus, a preexisting sense of confidence or doubt with respect to some activity can be a particularly important determinant of situational expectancies. If the expectancies that emerge from this assessment process are sufficiently favorable, the person renews his or her efforts. If the expectancies are sufficiently unfavorable, however, the person begins to disengage from the attempt at goal attainment.

Our research on this rough dichotomy among responses to adversity occurred in the context of our explorations of the effects of self-directed attention (Carver, Blaney, & Scheier, 1979a, 1979b; Carver, Peterson, Follansbee, & Scheier, 1983; Carver & Scheier, 1981; Scheier & Carver, 1982). This line of thought has also been extended to certain problems in self-management, including both test anxiety and social anxiety (Carver et al.,1983; Carver & Scheier, 1984, 1986a, 1986b; Carver, Scheier, & Klahr, 1987; see also Burgio, Merluzzi, & Pryor, 1986; Galassi, Frierson, & Sharer, 1981; Rich & Woolever, 1988; Schlenker & Leary, 1982). These discussions all emphasize the idea that expectancies about one's eventual outcome are an important determinant of whether the person responds to adversity by continuing to exert effort at goal attainment or, instead, by disengaging from the attempt. This analysis has a good deal in common with other expectancy models of behavior (e.g., Abramson, Seligman, & Teasdale, 1978; Bandura, 1977, 1986; Kanfer & Hagerman, 1981, 1985; Rotter, 1954; Wortman & Brehm, 1975), although there are also differences among theories (for more detail, see Scheier & Carver, 1988).

Expectancies and affect. We have assumed for some time that the behavioral consequences of divergent outcome expectancies are paralleled by differences in affective experience (Carver, 1979), and research evidence tends to support this position (Carver & Scheier, 1982b; Andersen & Lyon, 1987; see also Weiner, 1982). When expectancies are favorable, people tend to have positive feelings, which are variously experienced as enthusiasm, hope, excitement, joy, or elation (cf. Stotland, 1969). When expectancies are unfavorable, people have negative feelings—anxiety, dysphoria, or despair. The specific tone of these feelings varies (in part) with the basis for the expectancies (Scheier & Carver, 1988). The latter is a theme that has been developed in much greater detail by Weiner (1982).

A More Elaborated View: Meta-Monitoring and Emotion

We have characterized people's conscious self-regulation as a process of monitoring their present actions and comparing the qualities that they perceive therein with the reference values that presently are salient, making adjustments as necessary to render discrepancies minimal. In what follows, we will use the term *monitoring* to refer to this feedback process. As indicated earlier, we see this monitoring loop as fundamental to the control of intentional behavior.

We suggest, however, that there is also a second feedback process that (in a sense) builds on this one, in a fashion that is orthogonal to the hierarchical organization discussed earlier. This second function operates simultaneously with the monitoring function and in parallel to it, whenever monitoring is going on. The second feedback system serves what we will term a *meta-monitoring* function.

Discrepancy Reduction and Rate of Reduction

The most intuitive way to begin in describing this meta-monitoring function is to say that the meta loop is checking on how well the action loop is doing at reducing the behavioral discrepancies that the action loop is monitoring. More concretely, we propose that the perceptual input for the meta-monitoring loop is a representation of the *rate of discrepancy reduction in the behavioral (monitoring) system over time*. What is important to the meta loop is not merely whether discrepancies are being reduced at the level of the action loop, but how rapidly they are being reduced. If they are being reduced rapidly, the action loop's progress toward its goal (as perceived by the meta loop) is high. If they are being reduced slowly, the action loop's progress is lower. If they are not being reduced at all, the action loop's progress is zero. Any time discrepancies are enlarging at the level of action monitoring, of course, the action loop's progress is inverse. [2]

Although it may be somewhat less intuitive than the foregoing, we find an analogy useful in de-

scribing the functioning of these two systems, an analogy that may also have more literal implications. Because action implies change between states, consider behavior to be analogous to distance (construed as a vector, because perception of one's action incorporates both the difference between successive states and also the direction of the difference). If the monitoring loop deals with distance and if (as we just asserted) the meta loop assesses the rate of progress of the monitoring loop, then the meta loop is dealing with the psychological equivalent of velocity (also directional). In mathematical terms, velocity is the first derivative of distance over time. To the extent that this physical analogy is meaningful, the perceptual input to the meta loop we are postulating presumably is the first derivative over time of the input information used by the action loop.

We propose that the meta-monitoring process functions as a feedback loop. It thus involves more than the mere sensing of the rate of discrepancy reduction in the action loop. This sensing constitutes an input function, but no more. As in any feedback system, this input is compared against a reference value (cf. Frijda, 1986, 1988). In this case, the reference value is an acceptable or desired rate of behavioral discrepancy reduction.

As in other feedback systems, the comparison determines whether there is a discrepancy or deviation from the standard. If there is, an output function is engaged to reduce the discrepancy.

We suggest that the outcome of the comparison process that lies at the heart of this loop is manifest phenomenologically in two forms. The first is a hazy and nonverbal sense of outcome expectancy. The second is affect, a feeling quality, a sense of positiveness or negativeness.

When sensed progress in the action loop conforms to the desired rate of progress, the meta-monitoring system accordingly registers no discrepancy (see Table 1, Example 1). Given an absence of discrepancy at the meta level, affect is neutral. When the action loop is making continuous, steady progress toward reducing its own discrepancy, but its rate of discrepancy reduction is slower than the meta-monitoring system's reference value, a discrepancy exists for the meta loop (Table 1, Example 2). The result in this case should be a degree of doubt and negative affect, proportional to the size of this meta-level discrepancy. When the rate of discrepancy reduction in the action loop is higher than the meta loop's reference

---

[2]For convenience, we will treat as equivalent phrases such as *progress of the action loop* and *rate of discrepancy reduction in the action loop.*

TABLE 13.1. Three Conditions of Behavior Over Time, How They Would Be Construed at the Level of the Action Loop, How They Would Be Construed at the Level of the Meta-Monitoring Loop, and the Affect That Theoretically Would Be Experienced

Depiction of behavior	Action-loop construal	Meta-loop construal	Affect
1. Progress toward goal, at a rate equal to the standard	Discrepancy reduction	No discrepancy	None
2. Progress toward goal, at a rate lower than the standard	Discrepancy reduction	Discrepancy	Negative
3. Progress toward goal, at a rate higher than the standard	Discrepancy reduction	Positive discrepancy	Positive

value (Table 1, Example 3), there is a positive discrepancy at the meta loop, an overshoot of the reference value that is reflected in confidence and in positive feelings.

It is clear that the two systems under discussion (monitoring and meta-monitoring) are related to each other, but we argue that only one of them has implications for affect. In all three cases shown in Table 1, the action loop is successfully reducing discrepancies. The fact that it is doing so does not, however, determine affect. Affect may be neutral, it may be positive, or it may even be negative (Examples 1, 2, and 3, respectively), depending on the adequacy of the *rate* of discrepancy reduction. Assessing the adequacy of the rate of operation of one system implies the use of a second system.

It is also important to note that the size of the discrepancy confronted by the action loop at any given point does not play an important role in the perceptual input to the meta loop. A large discrepancy—even a *very* large discrepancy—perceived at the level of the action loop can be associated with perceptions of either abundant or insufficient progress. This same discrepancy thus can be associated with either favorable or unfavorable expectancies and with either positive or negative affect. What matters with respect to the meta-monitoring system is solely whether the perceived *rate of progress* in the action system is adequate.

The same point can also be made of cases in which the behavioral discrepancy is relatively small. If the meta-monitoring system senses that there is an abundant rate of change toward discrepancy elimination, there should be positive affect and confidence. If it senses an inadequate rate of change, there should be negative affect and doubt.

Thus, ironically, it should be possible for a person who has a large discrepancy at the action loop to feel more positively than a person who has a small discrepancy at the action loop, if the first

person is perceiving a more acceptable rate of progress than the second person. In terms of the physical analogy, the first person is more distant from the goal, but is moving toward it with a higher velocity.

It is important to recognize that we are not suggesting that affect is the controlled quality in this loop, but rate. Positive feelings reflect a positive discrepancy, which is good. To a system whose goal is controlling sensed rate, however, a discrepancy is a discrepancy and any sensed discrepancy should be reduced.

The existence of a natural tendency that has the effect of causing positive affect to be short-lived seems, at first glance, highly improbable, A plausible basis for such a tendency can be seen, however, in the idea that human behavior is hierarchically organized and involves multiple current concerns. That is, people typically are working toward several goals more or less simultaneously, and many lower level efforts contribute to minimizing discrepancies at high levels. To the extent that movement toward goal attainment is more rapid than expected in one domain, it permits the person to shift attention and effort toward goal strivings in another domain, at no cost. To continue the unneccessarily rapid pace in the first domain might increase positive affect with respect to that activity, but by diverting efforts from other goals, that action may create the potential for negative affect in other domains.

Changes in Rate and the Abruptness of Change

Although we have limited ourselves thus far to addressing various rates of progress toward action goals, it should be obvious that the rate of discrepancy reduction at the action loop can change. Changes in rate at the action loop are subjectively manifest, not as affect but as *change* of affect. Increases in rate are reflected in shifts toward more positive feelings, with the actual experience depending on the initial and final rates. When the change is from a rate far below the meta standard to a rate closer to the standard but still below it, affect should change from more negative to less negative. If the change is instead to a value that exceeds the meta standard, affect should change from negative to positive.

In the same manner, downward changes in sensed rate at the action loop are also reflected in affective shifts, with the quality of the experience again depending on the initial and final rates. When the change is from a rate that exceeds the meta standard to a rate below the standard, the affective change should be from positive to negative. When the change is from just below the standard to far below the standard, the affective change should be from mildly negative to very negative.

Shifts in rate of progress at the action loop can be gradual, or they can be more abrupt. The more abrupt an increase in the action loop's progress, the more the subjective experience incorporates a rush of exhilaration, reflecting the contrast between the more negative feelings and the more positive feelings (cf. the description of "sentimentality" by Frijda, 1988, p. 350). The more abrupt a slowing of the action loop's progress, the more the subjective experience should incorporate the well-known sinking feeling (de-exhilaration?) that reflects the contrast when feelings suddenly shift in a negative direction. Indeed, it seems reasonable to suggest that a discernible shift toward more negative feelings is often precisely the experience that causes people to interrupt ongoing action and consciously evaluate the probability of their eventual success.

We suggested earlier that the quality the meta loop senses as its input is analogous to the physical quality of velocity. Let us carry this analogy one step further. What we are addressing now is not velocity but change in velocity—acceleration. Acceleration is the second derivative of distance over time. Given that people apparently are equipped to sense these experiences, the analogy seems to suggest that some neural processor is computing a second derivative over time of the information input to the action loop. Does this imply the need to postulate a third layer of feedback control (complete with reference value and comparator)? Not necessarily. It is possible to sense a quality that is not involved in a feedback

loop. In part because it is difficult for us to know what might be the implications of such a third layer of control, we are hesitant at this stage to assume its existence.

With respect to a final point, however, we are more confident. In the same way that distance and velocity are independent of each other, both are independent of acceleration. (An object moving 20 ft per second can be accelerating, decelerating, or its velocity can be constant; the same is true of an object moving 80 ft per second.) We suggest that the same independence exists on the other side of the analogy. We argued earlier that affect experienced is independent of the degree of discrepancy at the action level (Table 1). In the same fashion, we argue that the rush associated with acceleration is independent of the size of the discrepancy at the action level and also independent of the rate of discrepancy reduction at the action level.

As an example, a person with a large discrepancy at the action level will have positive affect if the rate of discrepancy reduction is greater than needed. This positive affect will be free of exhilaration if the rate of discrepancy reduction is constant. If the rate has suddenly shifted upward (to the same ending value), the positive feelings will be accompanied by a sense of exhilaration.

Reference Values Used in Meta-Monitoring

One important question is what reference value is being used by the meta-monitoring system. We assume that this system is capable of using widely varying definitions of adequate progress for the action loop. Sometimes the reference value is imposed from outside (as in tenure review decisions), sometimes it is self-imposed (as in someone who has a personal timetable for career development), and sometimes it derives from social comparison (as when people are in competition with each other). Sometimes the reference value is very demanding, sometimes it is less so.

As an example in which the meta standard is both stringent and externally imposed, consider the requirements of degree programs in medical or law school. In such cases, even continuous progress in an absolute sense (i.e., successful mastery of required material) is adequate only if it occurs at or above the rate required by the degree program. Thus, as the person attempts to attain the action goal of becoming a physician or a lawyer, the reference value for meta-monitoring will be a relatively stringent one.

How stringent a standard is used at the meta level has straightforward implications for the person's emotional life. If the pace of progress used as a reference point is too high, it will rarely be matched, even if (objectively) the person's rate of progress is extraordinarily high. In such a case, the person will experience negative affect often and positive affect rarely. If the pace of progress used as a reference point is low, the person's rate of behavioral discrepancy reduction will more frequently exceed it. In this case, the person will experience positive affect more often and negative affect more rarely.

What variables influence the stringency of the meta level standard being used? One important determinant is the extent to which there is time pressure on the activity being regulated, which varies greatly from one activity to another. Some actions are clearly time dependent ("Have that report on my desk by 5 o'clock"), others are more vaguely so (it's about the time of year to fertilize the lawn), and the time dependency is even hazier for others (I want to go to China some day; I'd like to have a boat before I get too old to enjoy it). When an activity has demanding time constraints, the meta-level reference value used necessarily is stringent. When there is a relative lack of time pressure, a relatively lax standard is more likely to be used.

Although time dependence is clearest in situations that require a rapid pace, there also appears to be a second sort of time dependence. This occurs for behavioral activities that people wish to have completed but have no desire to do (a common view of chores). Such goals are highly time dependent, in the sense that people wish their attainment to be instantaneous. Given this, the meta-level reference value must necessarily be at a very high level. Because the rate of progress therefore cannot meet the standard, positive affect is nearly impossible and aversiveness is almost inevitable when the activity is being engaged in. (On the other hand, the intensity of this affect is proportional to the importance of the activity, which is often relatively low.) This set of relations would seem to define the experience of drudgery.

Changing Meta-Level Standards

As noted in the preceding section, reference values for the meta loop differ across people and across categories of behavior. Reference values at the meta level can also shift as a result of time and experience (see also Lord & Hanges, 1987). To put it differently, as people accumulate more experience in a given domain, adjustments can occur in the pacing that they expect and demand of their efforts.

Sometimes the adjustment is downward. For example, a researcher experiencing difficulty in his attempt to be as productive as his colleagues may gradually adopt less stringent standards of pacing. One consequence of this is a more favorable balance of positive to negative affect across time (cf. Linsenmeier & Brickman, 1980). In other cases, the adjustment is up-ward. A person who gains work-related skills may undertake greater challenges, requiring quicker handling of each action unit. Upward adjustment has the side effect of decreasing the potential for positive affect and increasing the potential for negative affect.

This adjusting of meta-level reference values over the course of experience looks suspiciously like a self-corrective feedback process in its own right, as the person reacts to insufficient challenge by taking on a more demanding pace, and reacts to too much challenge by scaling back the criterion.[3] If a feedback process is responsible for changing standards at the meta level (or contributes to such changes), it is much slower acting than are those that are the focus of this article. Shifting the reference value downward is not the immediate response when the person has trouble keeping up with a demanding pace. First the person tries harder to keep up. Only more gradually, if the person cannot keep up, does the meta standard shift to accommodate. Similarly, an upward shift is not the immediate response when the person's rate of discrepancy reduction exceeds the standard. The more typical response is to coast for a while. Only when the overshoot is frequent does the standard shift to accommodate.

_____

[3]A possibility that may be worth considering is that this shift of meta standard reflects the long-term consequences of the *opponent process* discussed by Solomon (1980). Solomon proposed the existence of a system that acts to dampen emotional reactions, in two senses: In the short term the opponent process causes the affect evoked by a given event to return to neutral. In the longer term (after repeated experiences of similar events), the event comes to elicit less of the emotional response than it did at first. This latter effect seems comparable in some ways to the idea that there has been a shift in meta standard.

The idea that these changes are produced by a slow-acting feedback system may help to account for why it can be so difficult to shift meta standards voluntarily. That is, one can make a verbal change easily ("Stop being so demanding of yourself, and be more satisfied with what you are accomplishing"), but this sort of self-verbalization rarely takes effect immediately. If a true shift in standard relies on a slow-acting feedback loop, that would account for why subjective experience tends to lag behind the self-instruction.

It is of some interest that these patterns of shift in reference value (and the concomitant effects on affect) imply a mechanism within the organism that functions in such a way as to prevent the too-frequent occurrence of positive feeling, as well as the too-frequent occurrence of negative feeling. That is, the (bidirectional) shifting of the rate criterion over time would tend to control pacing of behavior in such a way that affect continues to vary in both directions around neutral. We earlier suggested that the meta system does not function to maximize positive affect. In the same manner, an arrangement for changing meta-level reference values such as we are suggesting here would not work toward maximization of pleasure and minimization of pain. Rather, the affective consequence would be that the person experiences more or less the same range of variation in his or her affective experience over extended periods of time.

Time Frames for Input to Meta-Monitoring

Another question to be raised about the model concerns the span of time over which the action loop's progress at discrepancy reduction is processed to form a perceptual input (a sensed rate) for the meta system. The time period across which information is merged may by brief or it may be quite long.[4] There seems to be nothing inherent in the meta-monitoring process per se that dictates whether it focuses on a short or a long time period. Whether input information is merged over a short or a long time period, however, can have important implications for the subjective experiences that result.

Consider the case of a person whose actions create gradual but erratic progress toward some goal (see Figure 4). If the input function to this person's meta-monitoring loop assesses rate of discrepancy reduction over a very short time frame,

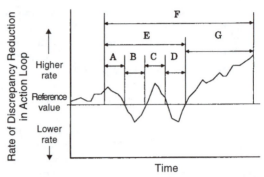

FIGURE 13.4 ■ Assessing rate of discrepancy reduction across different lengths of time can produce different patterns of emotional experience. (If assessment bears on brief time spans [periods A, B, C, and D], the experience is alternately positive feelings [A and C] versus negative feelings [B and D]. If assessed rate of discrepancy reduction is merged across a longer interval [E], experienced mood does not fluctuate. Assessing across too long a period, however [F], can be misleading because it can obscure meaningful changes that occur over a shorter term [G, compared with E].)

the person will be intermittently happy (periods A and C) and dysphoric (periods B and D). That is, the rate of progress exceeds the standard during periods A and C (thus yielding positive affect) but falls short of the standard during period B and most of period D (thus yielding negative affect). If the person takes a longer view on the same set of events (i.e., merges across all of period E), the frequent deviations upward and downward from the standard will be blurred (in effect, averaged) in the derivation of perceptual input for the meta system. In the general case, this will produce affect (and a concomitant sense of expectancy) that is

---

[4]We should distinguish between the matter under discussion here and other issues embedded in a growing literature on goal setting. One issue in goal setting concerns whether goals are close or distant in time (see Kirschenbaum, 1985, for a discussion of this and other variables). How distant a goal is in time, although important in its own right, is conceptually distinct from what we are discussing here, In general, assessment of progress toward any goal—whether close or distant—may still be made with respect to either a long or a short span of time and effort. Of course, with goals that are very close in time, one's freedom to assess over long time spans diminishes. Nor are we discussing the frequency with which a person "samples" perceptual input. That can also vary, from sampling often to sampling rarely. What is presently under discussion is the breadth of time (or the number of discrete bits of information) over which progress is merged to *form* a perceptual input.

both more stable and more moderated. In the specific case of period E, the affect experienced will be near neutral, because the upward and downward deviation cancel each other out.

This reasoning might seem to argue that it is desirable to take the broader view of events. There is, however, a potential disadvantage of deriving input through the broader view. Merging data over a very long period can result in insensitivity to what are actually meaningful changes in the rate of discrepancy reduction at the action loop. Period G reflects considerably faster progress than took place across period E, but awareness of that shift in rate will be blunted if the input is merged across period F. Thus, taking too long a view in creating input for the meta system can be as bad as taking too short a view.

This general line of reasoning suggests a possible process basis for the fact that people seem naturally to differ in how variable their moods are (e.g., Diener, Larsen, Levine, & Emmons, 1985; Larsen, 1987; Wessman & Ricks, 1966). Perhaps these differences in emotional variability reflect default differences in the time spans merged for input by people's meta-monitoring systems.

Multiple Affects from a Single Event, and the Independence of Positive and Negative Affect

Our theoretical discussion was focused on the existence of one feeling at a time. Affect associated with goal-directed effort need not be purely positive or purely negative, however. A single event may produce both of these feelings, depending on how it is viewed in meta-monitoring.

Sometimes there is more than one view on an event, even with respect to a single goal (cf. Ortony et al., 1988, pp. 51–52). For example, it may happen that the experience of a failure yields the realization of how to attain future success. The failure is displeasing, but the insight is elating. Feelings from the event thus are mixed. Focusing more on the present failure to attain the goal (inadequate progress) will yield a greater sense of negative affect. Focusing more on the insight (progress toward future success) will yield a greater sense of positive affect. Both feelings, however, are produced by different aspects of the same outcome, and both can be felt at once (or as alternating time-shared experiences).

It is perhaps more common that an action or an outcome has implications for two distinct goals. The goals making up the hierarchy of a person's self-definition are not always perfectly compatible with each other, and occasionally two conflicting goals become salient at the same time (see also Emmons, 1986; Van Hook & Higgins, 1988). For example, the goal of career advancement and the goal of spending a lot of time with one's young children may both be desirable, but the 24-hr day imposes limitations on the time available for trying to attain them. Sometimes the actions that permit progress toward one goal (working extra hours at the office) simultaneously interfere with progress toward the other goal (spending time with one's children). To the extent that both goals remain salient, the result is mixed feelings. In this case, however, the two feeling qualities stem from meta-monitoring with respect to each of two distinct goals.

This line of discussion also suggests a perspective on the assertion, made frequently in recent years, that positive and negative affective experiences are not at opposite poles of a continuum but rather are independent (e.g., Diener & Emmons, 1984; Diener & Iran-Nejad, 1986; Warr, Barter, & Brownbridge, 1983; Watson & Tellegen, 1985; Zevon & Tellegen, 1982). This argument usually focuses on the experience of moods, not on the nature of affect.[5] As a statement about mood, the argument means in part that people's moods can incorporate mixed feelings. A mood can be partly good and partly bad, though only rarely are both of these feelings intense at the same time (Diener & Iran-Nejad, 1986).

This argument also means that knowing a person is not depressed does not make it reasonable to infer that the person is happy. Knowing a person is not happy does not make it reasonable to infer that the person feels bad. Sometimes people

---

[5]Careful examination of Watson and Tellegen's (1985) position on the structure of mood reveals, however, the involvement of another issue that is beyond the scope of this discussion. Specifically, their dimension of negative affect has heavy overtones of anxiety, rather than depression. Higgins (1987) has recently argued for the importance of a distinction between these two emotion qualities, and his argument seems to require distinctions beyond those we are making here (as does the Watson & Tellegen position). This distinction does not, however, detract in any way from the points we are making here. We address the Higgins (1987) model in more detail in a later section of the article.

are affectively neutral. The relative independence of these qualities thus has important methodological implications. To know about both qualities in people's overall feelings, one must assess both (cf. Wortman & Silver, 1989).

Although these two qualities of mood have been observed to vary relatively independently, there has been very little discussion of why this is so. Diener and Iran-Nejad (1986) noted that their subjects sometimes reported moderate amounts of both positive and negative affect but did not speculate why. Watson and Tellegen (1985) noted the possibility that different parts of the brain might be involved in the two affect qualities, but did not address the question of why people might ever experience mixed feelings.

The preceding discussion suggests a very simple explanation for these findings. People often have many goals at once. A person who is making rapid progress on some current concerns and poor progress on others should experience positive feelings with respect to the former and negative feelings with respect to the latter. This experience must be common, even in the course of a single day. The diversity of these "progress reports" from the meta-monitoring system should disrupt any inverse correlation between reports of having experienced positive affect and reports of having experienced negative affect in a given time span, particularly if that span is relatively long. As the time span narrows to a given "emotional" event, one would expect the independence of the two affects to diminish, because the person is more likely to be dealing with only one goal (and only one perspective on it) than would otherwise be the case, This is precisely what seems to happen (Diener & Iran-Nejad, 1986).

Effects of Existing Emotion on Subsequent Experience

Our main theoretical interest is on the processes by which we think affect is created in the behaving person. We should note, however, that once an affect exists, it also influences later processing. It is now widely believed, for example, that emotional state influences the ease with which affectively toned material is brought from memory (e.g., Blaney, 1986; Bower & Cohen, 1982; Clark, Milberg, & Ross, 1983; Clark & Waddell, 1983). Positive affect makes positively valenced material

more accessible, negative affect makes negatively valenced material more accessible.

It seems a reasonable inference from this that a current affective state may influence the outcomes of subsequent meta-monitoring. This is not a restatement of the point made earlier that people's consciously derived expectancies are subject to influences beyond current sensed progress. The point we are making now is that even sensed progress per se may be affected by current affect. That is, perceptions relevant to meta-monitoring (as well as monitoring) are determined partly by information drawn from the situation as it exists, and partly by information from memory (Figure 5). Any bias in the use of either of these sources of information will cause bias in the output of the meta process.

A current affective state may exert a bias by rendering external information consistent with current affective tone more salient for input processing, which may reflect easier access to memories consistent with that affective tone (cf. Masters & Furman, 1976; Pyszczynski, Holt, & Greenberg,

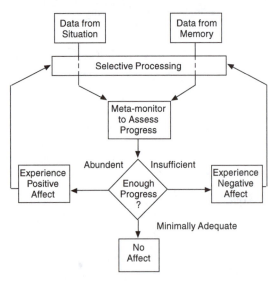

FIGURE 13.5 ■ Current affect is both a consequence of, and an influence on, one's perceptions of how well one is doing at moving toward one's behavioral goals. (If meta-monitoring yields affect, that affect can cause the person to preferentially code affect-consistent information inherent in the situation itself and to preferentially extract affect-consistent information from memory. Both of these influences can bias subsequent assessments at the meta level, perpetuating the tone of the current mood.)

1987). More simply, being in a good mood may cause a current situation to be viewed more positively (Forgas & Moylan, 1987), because of selective encoding of favorable aspects of the situation (cf. Antes & Matthews, 1988), which may be facilitated by enhanced access to memories of prior successes. Being in a bad mood may cause a current situation to be viewed more negatively through selective coding of unfavorable elements of the situation, facilitated by enhanced access to memories of prior bad outcomes.

The effect of such a processing bias would be to perpetuate the original emotional tone. Being in a bad mood causes people to see things in a way that tends to keep them in a bad mood. What causes emotions ever to fade, then? An answer is provided by Solomon's (1980) argument that every emotion evokes a second, slower acting process that acts in opposition to the initial emotion. The relevant aspect of Solomon's theory in this context is that (in normal self-regulation, at least) the opponent process dampens affective tone. The opponent process itself implies the existence of a feedback system beyond the ones on which we are focusing, in that whichever the direction of the initial emotional response (positive or negative), the opponent process acts to return the person to a neutral state.

Breadth of Intended Application

A final question to be raised about the model concerns its intended scope. Although most examples in this article come from domains of achievement and instrumental activity, this is not a theory of achievement-related affect. This analysis is intended to apply to all goal-directed behavior, including attempts to attain goals that are amorphous and poorly specified, and goals for which the idea of assessing the rate of progress toward discrepancy reduction might at first glance seem odd.

Human goals such as developing and maintaining a sound relationship, being a good mother or father, dealing honorably and pleasantly with acquaintances, seeing someone you care for be happy and fulfilled, having a full and rich life, and even becoming immersed in the fictional lives portrayed in a novel or film are fully amenable to analysis in these terms. These are all qualities of human experience toward which people attempt to move, goals that evolve or recur across time, as do most

goals underlying human action. To the extent that progress toward goals such as these is taken by the person as important, to the extent that people are invested in experiencing these qualities in their lives sooner rather than later, the meta loop produces positive and negative feelings as progress is faster or slower than the standard being used. Sometimes pacing toward such goals matters little, but sometimes it matters a lot. In the latter circumstances, we suggest, these events are capable of producing affect.

Issues Relating Emotion to Disengagement

Hierarchical Organization Sometimes Creates an Inability to Disengage

One issue stems from the idea that behavior is hierarchically organized and that goals are increasingly important as one moves upward through the hierarchy. Presumably, in most cases disengagement from values low in the hierarchy of control is easy. Indeed, the nature of programs is such that disengagement from efforts at subgoals is quite common, even while the person continues to pursue the overall goal of the program (e.g., if you go to buy something and the store is closed for inventory, you are likely to head for another store rather than give up altogether).

Sometimes, however, lower order goals are more closely linked to values at a higher level. To disengage from lower level goals in this case enlarges discrepancies at higher levels. These higher order qualities are values that are important, even central, to one's life. One cannot disengage from them, or disregard them, or tolerate large discrepancies between those values and currently sensed reality, without substantially reorganizing one's value system (Carver & Scheier, 1986c; Kelly, 1955; Millar, Tesser, & Millar, 1988). In such a case, disengagement from concrete behavioral goals is quite difficult.

Now recall the affective consequences of being in this situation. The desire to disengage was prompted in the first place by unfavorable expectancies for discrepancy reduction. These expectancies are paralleled by negative affect. In this situation, then, the person is experiencing negative feelings (because of an inability to progress toward behavioral discrepancy reduction) and is unable to do anything about the feelings (because of an inability to give up the behavioral reference value). The person simply stews in the feelings that arise from irreconcilable discrepancies (see also Martin & Tesser, in press). In our view, this bind—being unable to let go of something that is unattainable—lies at the heart of exogenous depression (cf. Hyland, 1987; Klinger, 1975; Pyszczynski & Greenberg, 1987). It seems important to us to recognize that this bind often stems from the hierarchical nature of people's goal structures.

Disengagement Requires That There Be an Override Mechanism

The idea that people's efforts give way to disengagement from the goal as expectancies become more negative also raises a second issue. We believe that this characterization is reasonable as part of a model of motivated action. But there is a conceptual discontinuity between this idea and the feedback theories we have espoused regarding behavioral self-regulation and—now—affective experience.

Where in the model of affect is the mechanism to produce disengagement? We portrayed metamonitoring as a feedback system in which discrepancies (inadequate progress) produce doubt and negative affect. Why should this system (and the corresponding behavioral monitoring system) not continue endlessly to attempt to reduce discrepancies, however ineffectively? Why should the negative affect not simply persist or intensify? What permits the person ever to disengage?

The answer has to be that in normal self-regulation there is an override that is capable of taking precedence over this feedback system and causing disengagement from the reference value currently being used to guide action. In the jargon of the computer field, there must be something akin to a *break* function, which permits ongoing action to be suspended or abandoned altogether. When disengagement is adaptive, it is so because it frees the system to take up other reference values and enables the person to turn to the pursuit of substitute or alternative goals. Such an override function has a critically important role in human self-regulation, inasmuch as there are any number of goals from which people simply must disengage,

either temporarily or permanently (see Klinger, 1975, for a broader discussion of commitment to and disengagement from incentives).

Failure to override. Although it seems necessary to assume an override function in adaptive self-regulation, it should also be reemphasized that disengagement does not always occur, even when the desire to disengage is there. As we noted just earlier, when the goal toward which the person is unable to make progress is central to that person's implicit definition of self, the person for that reason often cannot disengage from it. Disengagement from such a goal means disengagement from oneself. Such an inability to disengage, we said, yields depression.

Consistent with this general line of thought is a variety of evidence that the inability (or unwillingness) to disengage correlates with depression. Depression has been linked to behavioral indicators of failing to disengage mentally from experimentally created failures (Kuhl, 1984, 1985; Pyszczynski & Greenberg, 1985, 1987), to concurrent self-reports of a tendency to perseverate mentally on failure (Carver, La Voie, Kuhl, & Ganellen, 1988), and to ruminative thoughts during forced suspension of personally valued activities (Millar et al., 1988). Mental perseveration among depressed people is not limited to major life goals, but can occur even for transient and relatively trivial intentions (Kuhl & Helle, 1986). Thus, there is evidence that depression is bound up with a general failure to override and disengage. It is not clear why this should be so, but in some sense this failure seems to be at the core of the dynamics of depression (see also Klinger, 1975).

Discussion of this issue also raises a broader question. People clearly vary in how easily they put previously valued goals behind them and move on to new ones. This is true whether the goal has been removed permanently by some external event, for example, the death of a loved one (cf. Wortman & Silver, 1989), or whether the person has simply decided that the previously sought-after goal should no longer be pursued, as happens when people break off close relationships or give up previously desired careers. Some people disengage quickly and move on, experiencing relatively little distress; others take longer to disengage, and consequently (in our view) experience more negative affect. An important question would seem to be what makes people differ from each other in this way.

Conclusion

In the preceding pages, we have tried to indicate some of the ways in which a control-process model of the self-regulation of behavior can incorporate assumptions about the nature and functions of certain qualities of emotion. We have attempted to specify how we think these affective qualities are created, and we have pointed to a link between them and another element that is important to self-regulation of action: expectancies. We have also tried to give a sense of how the model as a whole can provide a vehicle for conceptualizing some of the emotional difficulties that people periodically experience.

We obviously have not presented a comprehensive model of the nature of all emotional experiences (cf. Frijda, 1986; Leventhal, 1984). Nor have we catalogued the varieties of emotional experience (cf. Izard, 1977; Ortony et al., 1988; Plutchik, 1980; Tomkins, 1984). Doing so was not our intent. Our goal was less ambitious and more focused: To indicate how the nature of some emotions, as they are presently understood, seems compatible with the logic of control theory.

Our intent throughout this discussion was twofold. First, we wanted to contribute to an emerging line of argument that holds that the domain of human experience reflected in concepts such as *feeling* and *affect* is in no way inimical to information-processing or feedback models of thought and action. We believe that we have been able to address feeling states here in terms that do little or no violence either to feedback concepts or to intuitions and knowledge concerning the subjective experience of feeling states. To the extent we have done this successfully, our discussion contributes to this line of argument.

We have not, however, been entirely blind to broader concerns. To the contrary, we believe that our attempt to create a control-process account of affect has led us to conclusions that complement and supplement in useful ways other accounts of emotion. For example, we agree with Frijda (1988) that emotions arise in response to meaning structures of situations. In some sense, what we have tried to do here is to specify in generic terms what kinds of meaning structures—as inputs—may give rise to emotions. In brief, we assert that emotions intrinsically are related to goal values, and that they reflect differences between expected and experienced rates of movement toward (or away from) those goals. They represent an organismic monitoring of "how things are going" with respect to those values.

Clearly, others have been intuitively aware of this quality of affect (see Frijda, 1988), but the importance of this aspect of the picture has rarely been emphasized. What we have done is simply to approach the subject from a somewhat different angle, which has served to make this aspect more salient. Independent of the origins of our effort (i.e., the desire to fit affect to control theory), we hope that others will find merit in the ideas developed here.

ACKNOWLEDGMENTS

Preparation of this article was facilitated by support from the National Science Foundation (BNS 87-06271 and BNS 87-17783).

We would like to thank Paul Blaney, Donald Broadbent, Deniz Ergener, Michael Hyland, William Powers, and Roxane Silver for their comments on earlier versions of this article.

REFERENCES

Abramson, L. Y., Seligman, M. E. P., & Teasdale, J. D. (1978). Learned helplessness in humans: Critique and reformulation. *Journal of Abnormal Psychology, 87,* 49–74.

Andersen, S. M., & Lyon, J. E. (1987). Anticipating desired outcomes: The role of outcome certainty in the onset of depressive affect. *Journal of Experimental Social Psychology, 23,* 428–443.

Antes, J. R., & Matthews, G. R. (1988, November). *Attention and depression: Do the depressed focus on sad themes?* Paper presented at the meeting of the Psychonomic Society, Chicago.

Averill, J. A. (1983). Studies on anger and aggression. *American Psychologist, 38,* 1145–1160.

Bandura, A. (1977). *Social learning theory.* Englewood Cliffs, NJ: Prentice-Hall.

Bandura, A. (1986). *Social foundations of thought and action: A social cognitive theory.* Englewood Cliffs, NJ: Prentice-Hall.

Beck, A. T. (1972). *Depression: Causes and treatment.* Philadelphia: University of Pennsylvania Press.

Berscheid, E. (1983). Emotion. In H. H. Kelley, E. Berscheid, A. Christiansen, J. H. Harvey, T. L. Huston, G. Levinger, E. McClintock, L. A. Peplau, & D. R. Peterson (Eds.), *Close relationships* (pp. 110–168), San Francisco: Freeman.

Blaney, P. H. (1986). Affect and memory: A review, *Psychological Bulletin, 99,* 229–246.

Bower, G. H., & Cohen, P. R. (1982). Emotional influences in memory and thinking: Data and theory. In M. S. Clark & S. T. Fiske (Eds.), *Affect and cognition: The 17th Annual Carnegie Symposium on Cognition* (pp. 291–331), Hillsdale, NJ: Erlbaum.

Broadbent, D. E. (1977). Levels, hierarchies, and the locus of control. *Quarterly Journal of Experimental Psychology, 29,* 181–201.

Burgio, K. L., Merluzzi, T. V., & Pryor, J. B. (1986). The effects of performance expectancy and self-focused attention on social interaction. *Journal of Personality and Social Psychology, 50,* 1216–1221.

Carver, C. S. (1979). A cybernetic model of self-attention processes. *Journal of Personality and Social Psychology, 37,* 1251–1281.

Carver, C. S., Blaney, P. H., & Scheier, M. F. (1979a). Focus of attention, chronic expectancy, and responses to a feared stimulus. *Journal of Personality and Social Psychology, 37,* 1186–1195.

Carver, C. S., Blaney, P. H., & Scheier, M. F. (1979b). Reassertion and giving up: The interactive role of self-directed attention and outcome expectancy. *Journal of Personality and Social Psychology, 37,* 1859–1870.

Carver, C. S., La Voie, L., Kuhl, J., & Ganellen, R. J. (1988). Cognitive concomitants of depression: A further examination of the roles of generalization, high standards, and self-criticism. *Journal of Social and Clinical Psychology, 7,* 350–365.

Carver, C. S., Peterson, L. M., Follansbee, D. J., & Scheier, M. F. (1983). Effects of self-directed attention on performance and persistence among persons high and low in test anxiety. *Cognitive Therapy and Research, 7,* 333–354.

Carver, C. S., & Scheier, M. F. (1981). *Attention and self-regulation: A control-theory approach to human behavior.* New York: Springer-Verlag.

Carver, C. S., & Scheier, M. F. (1982a). Control theory: A useful conceptual framework for personality–social, clinical, and health psychology. *Psychological Bulletin, 92,* 111–135.

Carver, C. S., & Scheier, M. F. (1982b). Outcome expectancy, locus of attribution for expectancy, and self-directed attention as determinants of evaluations and performance. *Journal of Experimental Social Psychology, 18,* 184–200.

Carver, C. S., & Scheier, M. F. (1984). Self-focused attention in test anxiety: A general theory applied to a specific phenomenon. In H. M. van der Ploeg, R. Schwarzer, & C. D. Spielberger (Eds.), *Advances in test anxiety research* (Vol. 3, pp. 3–20). Hillsdale, NJ: Erlbaum.

Carver, C. S., & Scheier, M. F. (1985). Aspects of self, and the control of behavior. In B. R. Schlenker (Ed.), *The self and social life* (pp. 146–174). New York: McGraw-Hill.

Carver, C. S., & Scheier, M. F. (1986a). Functional and dysfunctional responses to anxiety: The interaction between expectancies and self-focused attention. In R. Schwarzer (Ed.), *Self-related cognitions in anxiety and motivation* (pp. 111–141). Hillsdale, NJ: Erlbaum.

Carver, C. S., & Scheier, M. F. (1986b). Analyzing shyness: A specific application of broader self-regulatory principles. In W. H. Jones, J. M. Cheek, & S. R. Briggs (Eds.), *Shyness: Perspectives on research and treatment* (pp. 173–185), New York: Plenum Press.

Carver, C. S., & Scheier, M. F. (1986c). Self and the control of behavior. In L. M. Hartman & K. R. Blankstein (Eds.), *Perception of self in emotional disorder and psychotherapy* (pp. 5–35). New York: Plenum Press.

Carver, C. S., & Scheier, M. F. (in press). Principles of self-regulation: Action and emotion. In R. Sorrentino & E. T. Higgins (Eds.), *Handbook of motivation and cognition* (Vol. 2). New York: Guilford.

Carver, C. S., Scheier, M. F., & Klahr, D. (1987). Further explorations of a control-process model of test anxiety. In R. Schwarzer, H. M. van der Ploeg, & C. D. Spielberger (Eds.), *Advances in test anxiety research* (Vol. 5, pp. 15–22). Lisse: Swets & Zeitlinger.

Clark, M. S., Milberg, S., & Ross, J. (1983). Arousal cues arousal-related material in memory: Implications for understanding effects of mood on memory. *Journal of Verbal Learning and Verbal Behavior, 22,* 633–649.

Clark, M. S., & Waddell, B. A. (1983). Effects of moods on thoughts about helping, attraction, and information acquisition. *Social Psychology Quarterly, 46,* 31–35.

Dawkins, R. (1976). Hierarchical organisation: A candidate principle for ethology. In P. P. G. Bateson & R. A. Hinde (Eds.), *Growing points in ethology* (pp. 7–54). Cambridge, England: Cambridge University Press.

DeAngelis, D. L., Post, W. M., & Travis, C. C. (1986). *Positive feedback in natural systems* (Biomathematics, Vol. 15). New York: Springer-Verlag.

Diener, E., & Emmons, R. A. (1984). The independence of positive and negative affect. *Journal of Personality and Social Psychology, 47,* 1105–1117.

Diener, E., & Iran-Nejad, A. (1986). The relationship in experience between various types of affect. *Journal of Personality and Social Psychology, 50,* 1031–1038.

Diener, E., Larsen, R. J., Levine, S., & Emmons, R. A. (1985). Intensity and frequency: Dimensions underlying positive and negative affect. *Journal of Personality and Social Psychology, 48,* 1253–1265.

Dweck, C. S., & Elliott, E. S. (1983). Achievement motivation. In P. H. Mussen (Ed.), *Handbook of child psychology* (4th ed., pp. 643–691). New York: Wiley.

Dweck, C. S., & Leggett, E. L. (1988). A social–cognitive approach to motivation and personality. *Psychological Review, 95,* 256–273.

Elliott, E. S., & Dweck, C. S. (1988). Goals: An approach to motivation and achievement. *Journal of Personality and Social Psychology, 54,* 5–12.

Emmons, R. A. (1986). Personal strivings: An approach to personality and subjective well being. *Journal of Personality and Social Psychology, 51,* 1058–1068.

Finlay-Jones, R., & Brown, G. W. (1981). Types of stressful life event and the onset of anxiety and depressive disorders. *Psychological Medicine, 11,* 803–815.

Forgas, J. P., & Moylan, S. (1987). After the movies: Transient mood and social judgments. *Personality and Social Psychology Bulletin, 13,* 467–477.

Frijda, N. H. (1986). *The emotions.* Cambridge, England: Cambridge University Press.

Frijda, N. H. (1988). The laws of emotion. *American Psychologist, 43,* 349–358.

Galassi, J. P., Frierson, H. T., Jr., & Sharer, R. (1981). Behavior of high, moderate, and low test anxious students during an actual test situation. *Journal of Consulting and Clinical Psychology, 49,* 51–62.

Gallistel, C. R. (1980). *The organization of action: A new synthesis.* Hillsdale, NJ: Erlbaum.

Gray, J. A. (1981). A critique of Eysenck's theory of personality. In H. J. Eysenck (Ed.), *A model for personality* (pp. 246–276). Berlin: Springer-Verlag.

Gray, J. A. (1982). *The neuropsychology of anxiety: An enquiry into the functions of the septo-hippocampal system.* New York: Oxford University Press.

Hamilton, V. (1983). *The cognitive structures and processes of human motivation and personality*. Chichester, England: Wiley.

Higgins, E. T. (1987). Self-discrepancy: A theory relating self and affect. *Psychological Review, 94,* 319–340.

Hyland, M. (1987). Control theory interpretation of psychological mechanisms of depression: Comparison and integration of several theories. *Psychological Bulletin, 102,* 109–121.

Izard, C. E. (1977). *Human emotions*. New York: Plenum Press.

Kanfer, F. H., & Hagerman, S. (1981). The role of self-regulation. In L. P. Rehm (Ed.), *Behavior therapy for depression: Present status and future directions* (pp. 143–179). New York: Academic Press.

Kanfer, F. H., & Hagerman, S. (1985). Behavior therapy and the information processing paradigm. In S. Reiss & R. R. Bootsin (Eds.), *Theoretical issues in behavior therapy* (pp. 3–33). New York: Academic Press.

Kelly, G. A. (1955). *The psychology of personal constructs*. New York: Norton.

Kirschenbaum, D. S. (1985). Proximity and specificity of planning: A position paper. *Cognitive Therapy and Research, 9,* 489–506.

Klinger, E. (1975). Consequences of commitment to and disengagement from incentives. *Psychological Review, 82,* 1–25.

Kuhl, J. (1984). Volitional aspects of achievement motivation and learned helplessness: Toward a comprehensive theory of action control. In B. A. Maher (Ed.), *Progress in experimental personality research* (Vol. 13, pp. 99–170). New York: Academic Press.

Kuhl, J. (1985). Volitional mediators of cognition–behavior consistency: Self-regulatory processes and action versus state orientation. In J. Kuhl & J. Beckmann (Eds.), *Action control: From cognition to behavior* (pp. 101–128). New York: Springer-Verlag.

Kuhl, J., & Helle, P. (1986). Motivational and volitional determinants of depression: The degenerated-intention hypothesis. *Journal of Abnormal Psychology, 95,* 247–251.

Kukla, A. (1972). Foundations of an attributional theory of performance. *Psychological Review, 79,* 454–470.

Larsen, R. J. (1987). The stability of mood variability: A spectral analytic approach to daily mood assessments. *Journal of Personality and Social Psychology, 52,* 1195–1204.

Lazarus, R. S. (1966). *Psychological stress and the coping process*. New York: McGraw-Hill.

Leventhal, H. (1984). A perceptual–motor theory of emotion. In L. Berkowitz (Ed.), *Advances in experimental social psychology* (Vol. 17, pp. 117–182). New York: Academic Press.

Linsenmeier, J. A. W., & Brickman, P. (1980). *Expectations, performance, and satisfaction*. Unpublished manuscript.

Lord, R. G., & Hanges, P. J. (1987). A control system model of organizational motivation: Theoretical development and applied implications. *Behavioral Science, 32,* 161–178.

MacKay, D. M. (1963). Mindlike behavior in artefacts. In K. M. Sayre & F. J. Crosson (Eds.), *The modeling of mind: Computers and intelligence* (pp. 225–241). Notre Dame, IN: University of Notre Dame Press.

MacKay, D. M. (1966). Cerebral organization and the conscious control of action. In J. C. Eccles (Ed.), *Brain and conscious experience* (pp. 422–445). Berlin: Springer-Verlag.

Mandler, G. (1984). *Mind and body: Psychology of emotion and stress*. New York: Norton.

Mandler, G. & Watson, D. L. (1966). Anxiety and the interruption of behavior. In C. D. Speilberger (Ed.), *Anxiety and behavior* (pp. 263–288). New York: Academic Press.

Marken, R. S. (1986). Perceptual organization of behavior: A hierarchical control model of coordinated action. *Journal of Experimental Psychology: Human Perception and Performance, 12,* 267–276.

Markus, H., & Nurius, P. (1986). Possible selves. *American Psychologist, 41,* 954–969.

Martin, L., & Tesser, A. (in press). Toward a model of ruminative thought. In J. S. Uleman & J. A. Bargh (Eds.), *Unintended thought: The limits of awareness, intention, and control*. New York: Guilford.

Masters, J. C., & Furman, W. (1976). Effects of affective states on noncontingent outcome expectancies and beliefs in internal or external control. *Developmental Psychology, 12,* 481–482.

Mayer, J. D., & Gaschke, Y. N. (1988). The experience and meta-experience of mood. *Journal of Personality and Social Psychology, 55,* 102–111.

Millar, K. U., Tesser, A., & Millar, M. G. (1988). The effects of a threatening life event on behavior sequences and intrusive thought: A self-disruption explanation. *Cognitive Therapy and Research, 12,* 441–458.

Norman, D. A. (1981). Categorization of action slips. *Psychological Review, 88,* 1–15.

Ogilvie, D. M. (1987). The undesired self: A neglected variable in personality research. *Journal of Personality and Social Psychology, 52,* 379–385.

Ortony, A., Clore, G. L., & Collins, A. (1988). *The cognitive structure of emotions*. Cambridge, England: Cambridge University Press.

Plutchik, R. (1980). *Emotion: A psychoevolutionary synthesis*. New York: Harper & Row.

Powers, W. T. (1973). *Behavior: The control of perception*. Chicago: Aldine.

Pyszczynski. T., & Greenberg, J. (1985). Depression and preference for self-focusing stimuli after success and failure. *Journal of Personality and Social Psychology, 49,* 1066–1075.

Pyszczynski, T., & Greenberg, J. (1987). Self-regulatory perseveration and the depressive self-focusing style: A self-awareness theory of reactive depression. *Psychological Bulletin, 102,* 122–138.

Pyszczynski, T., Holt, K., & Greenberg, J. (1987). Depression, self-focused attention, and expectancies for positive and negative future life events for self and others. *Journal of Personality and Social Psychology, 52,* 994–1001.

Rich, A. R., & Woolever, D. K. (1988). Expectancy and self-focused attention: Experimental support for the self-regulation model of test anxiety. *Journal of Social and Clinical Psychology, 7,* 246–259.

Rogers, C. R. (1980). *A way of being*. Boston: Houghton Mifflin.

Rosenbaum, D. A. (1987). Hierarchical organization of motor programs. In S. P. Wise (Ed.), *Higher brain functions: Recent explorations of the brain's emergant properties* (pp. 45–66). New York: Wiley.

Rotter, J. B. (1954). *Social learning and clinical psychology*. New York: Prentice-Hall.

Schachter, S., & Singer, J. E. (1962). Cognitive, social, and physiological determinants of emotional state. *Psychological Review, 69,* 379–399.

Schank, R. C., & Abelson, R. P. (1977). *Scripts, plans, goals, and understanding.* Hillsdale, NJ: Erlbaum.

Scheier, M. F., & Carver, C. S. (1982). Cognition, affect, and self-regulation. In M. S. Clark & S. T. Fiske (Eds.), *Affect and cognition: The 17th Annual Carnegie Symposium on Cognition* (pp. 157–183). Hillsdale, NJ: Erlbaum.

Scheier, M. F., & Carver, C. S. (1987). Dispositional optimism and physical well-being: The influence of generalized outcome expectancies on health. *Journal of Personality, 55,* 169–210.

Scheier, M. F., & Carver, C. S. (1988). A model of behavioral self-regulation: Translating intention into action. In L. Berkowitz (Ed.), *Advances in experimental social psychology* (Vol. 21, pp. 303–346), New York: Academic Press.

Schlenker, B. R., & Leary, M. R. (1982). Social anxiety and self-presentation: A conceptualization and model. *Psychological Bulletin, 92,* 641–669.

Schönpflug, W. (1983). Coping efficiency and situational demands. In G. R. Hockey (Ed.), *Stress and fatigue in human performance* (pp. 299–333). Chichester, England: Wiley.

Schönpflug, W. (1985). Goal directed behavior as a source of stress: Psychological origins and consequences of inefficiency. In M. Frese & J. Sabine (Eds.), *Goal-directed behavior: The concept of action in psychology* (pp. 172–188). Hillsdale, NJ: Erlbaum.

Shallice, T. (1978). The dominant action system: An information-processing approach to consciousness. In K. S. Pope & J. L. Singer (Eds.), *The stream of consciousness: Scientific investigations into the flow of human experience* (pp. 117–157). New York: Wiley.

Shiffrin, R. M., & Schneider, W. (1977). Controlled and automatic human information processing: II. Perceptual learning, automatic attending, and a general theory. *Psychological Review, 84,* 127–190.

Simon, H. A. (1967). Motivational and emotional controls of cognition. *Psychological Review, 74,* 29–39.

Soloman, A. (1987). Motives, mechanisms, and emotions. *Cognition and Emotion, 1,* 217–233.

Solomon, R. L. (1980). The opponent–process theory of acquired motivation: The costs of pleasure and the benefits of pain. *American Psychologist, 35,* 691–712.

Srull, T. K., & Wyer, R. S., Jr. (1986). The role of chronic and temporary goals in social information processing. In R. M. Sorrentino & E. T. Higgins (Eds.), *Handbook of motiva-*

tion and cognition: Foundations of social behavior (pp. 503–549). New York: Guilford.

Stotland, E. (1969). *The psychology of hope.* San Francisco: Jossey-Bass.

Tomkins, S. S. (1984). Affect theory. In K. R. Scherer & P. Ekman (Eds.), *Approaches to emotion.* Hillsdale, NJ: Erlbaum.

Vallacher, R. R., & Wegner, D. M. (1985). *A theory of action identification.* Hillsdale, NJ: Erlbaum.

Vallacher, R. R., & Wegner, D. M. (1987). What do people think they're doing? Action identification and human behavior. *Psychological Review, 94,* 3–15.

Van Hook, E., & Higgins, E. T. (1988). Self-related problems beyond the self-concept: Motivational consequences of discrepant self-guides. *Journal of Personality and Social Psychology, 55,* 625–633.

Warr, P., Barter, J., & Brownbridge, G. (1983). On the independence of positive and negative affect. *Journal of Personality and Social Psychology, 44,* 644–651.

Watson, D., & Tellegen, A. (1985). Toward a consensual structure of mood. *Psychological Bulletin, 98,* 219–235.

Weiner, B. (1982). The emotional consequences of casual ascriptions. In M. S. Clark & S. T. Fiske (Eds.), *Affect and cognition: The 17th Annual Carnegie Symposium on Cognition* (pp. 185–209). Hillsdale, NJ: Erlbaum.

Wessman, A. E., & Ricks, D. F. (1966). *Mood and personality.* New York: Holt, Rinehart & Winston.

Wills, T. A. (1981). Downward comparison principles in social psychology. *Psychological Bulletin, 90,* 245–271.

Wood, J. V., Taylor, S. E., & Lichtman, R. R. (1985). Social comparison in adjustment to breast cancer. *Journal of Personality and Social Psychology, 49,* 1169–1183.

Wortman, C. B., & Brehm, J. W. (1975). Responses to uncontrollable outcomes: An integration of reactance theory and the learned helplessness model. In L. Berkowitz (Ed.), *Advances in experimental social psychology* (Vol. 8, pp. 277–336). New York: Academic Press.

Wortman, C. B., & Silver, R. C. (1989). The myths of coping with loss. *Journal of Consulting and Clinical Psychology, 57,* 349–357.

Zajonc, R. B. (1980). Feeling and thinking: Preferences need no inferences. *American Psychologist, 35,* 151–175.

Zevon, M. A., & Tellegen, A. (1982). The structure of mood change: An idiographic/nomothetic analysis. *Journal of Personality and Social Psychology, 43,* 111–122.

Self-Discrepancies and Emotional Vulnerability: How Magnitude, Accessibility, and Type of Discrepancy Influence Affect

E. Tory Higgins, Ronald N. Bond, Ruth Klein, and Timothy Strauman
• New York University

Editors' Notes

Whereas motivation, cognition, and emotion have often been considered in separate terms and have been accorded separate theoretical treatments, the present selection (like the previous one) clarifies how motivation, cognition, and affect are intricately intertwined, and it illustrates how we can hardly have the one without the other. Self-discrepancies, on the one hand, are motivational constructs in that they denote a distance from attaining a desired end-state, which can represent an aspiration or hope (an "ideal") or a duty or obligation (i.e., an "ought"). Yet, at the same time, self-discrepancies are cognitively represented and are capable of being rendered chronically or situationally accessible. Moreover, self-discrepancies generate affective states whose distinctive quality is determined by the nature of the specific goal from which one is discrepant (dejection feelings like sadness from an "ideal" discrepancy or agitation feelings like tension from an "ought" discrepancy). Thus, affective experiences depend on the type of discrepancy, its magnitude, and its mental accessibility.

Discussion Questions

1. How did Higgins et al. (1986) measure self-discrepancies? How did they measure affect?
2. What is the reason why a discrepancy from an ought guide results in agitation-type emotions whereas a discrepancy from an ideal guide results in dejection-type emotions?

3. How did Higgins et al. (1986) operationally define chronic accessibility of a self-discrepancy? How did these authors operationally define momentary accessibility?

Suggested Readings

Higgins, E. T. (1987). Self-discrepancy: A theory relating self and affect. *Psychological Review, 94,* 319–340.

Strauman, T. J. (1989). Self-discrepancies in clinical depression and social phobia: Cognitive structures that underlie emotional disorders? *Journal of Abnormal Psychology, 98,* 14–22.

Houston, D. A. (1990). Empathy and the self: Cognitive and emotional influences on the evaluation of negative affect in others. *Journal of Personality and Social Psychology, 59,* 859–868.

Authors' Abstract

Two studies examined whether the type of emotional change experienced by individuals is influenced by the magnitude and accessibility of the different types of self-discrepancies they possess. In both studies, subjects filled out a measure of self-discrepancy a few weeks prior to the experimental session. Subjects were asked to list up to 10 attributes each for different self-states—their actual self, their ideal self (their own or others' hopes and goals for them), and their ought self (their own or others' beliefs about their duty and obligations). Magnitude of self-discrepancy was calculated by comparing the attributes in the actual self to the attributes in either the ideal self or the ought self, with the total number of attribute pairs that matched being subtracted from the total number of attribute pairs that mismatched. In Study 1, subjects were asked to imagine either a positive event or a negative event and were then given a mood measure and a writing-speed task. Subjects with a predominant actual:ideal discrepancy felt more dejected (e.g., sad) and wrote more slowly in the negative event condition than in the positive event condition, whereas subjects with a predominant actual:ought discrepancy, if anything, felt more agitated (e.g., afraid) and wrote more quickly in the negative event condition. In Study 2, subjects were selected who were either high in both kinds of discrepancies or low in both. Half of the subjects in each group were asked to discuss their own and their parents' hopes and goals for them (ideal priming), and the other half were asked to discuss their own and their parents' beliefs concerning their duty and obligations (ought priming). For high-discrepancy subjects, but not low-discrepancy subjects, ideal priming increased their dejection whereas ought priming increased their agitation. The implications of these findings for identifying cognitive-motivational factors that may serve as vulnerability markers for emotional problems is discussed.

When people expect that something terrible is going to happen they feel apprehensive or afraid, but when they believe that they will never obtain some desired goal they feel sad or disappointed. More generally, there are two basic kinds of negative psychological situations that are associated with different kinds of emotional states (see Higgins, 1984; Jacobs, 1971; Lazarus, 1968; Mowrer, 1960; Roseman, 1979): the presence (actual or expected) of negative outcomes, which is associated with agitation-related emotions (e.g.,

fear, apprehension, edginess), and the absence (actual or expected) of positive outcomes, which is associated with dejection-related emotions (e.g., dissatisfaction, disappointment, sadness). These psychological situations, as for social-psychological experiences generally (e.g., Asch, 1952; Lewin, 1951; Merton, 1957), are a function of both the nature of external events and individuals' interpretations of those events. It is well known that there are individual differences in how external events are interpreted (e.g., Coyne & Lazarus, 1980;

Kelly, 1955; Klein, 1970; Murray, 1938). To the extent that there are individual differences in the likelihood of experiencing one or the other kind of negative psychological situation, there should be individual differences in vulnerability to the kinds of emotional problems associated with each psychological situation. Recently, we have begun to examine one possible source of such differences—differences in the magnitude and accessibility of different types of self-discrepancies that individuals possess (Higgins, Klein, & Strauman, 1985; Higgins, Strauman, & Klein, 1986).

There is a long history in psychology of distinguishing among different facets of the self or self-images. Even a brief review of the literature yields descriptions of a normative, socially prescribed self that involved individuals' beliefs about what others believe they ought to be like (e.g, Freud, 1923/1961; James, 1890/1948; Schafer, 1967); a hopeful, aspiring self that involves individuals' personal goals and wishes (e.g., Allport, 1955; Colby, 1968; Rogers, 1959, 1961); a dutiful, conscientious self that involves individuals' own sense of moral duty and obligations (e.g., Ausubel, 1955; Colby, 1968; Freud, 1923/1961); and a social ideal self that involves individuals' beliefs about others' hopes, goals, and aspirations for them (e.g, Cooley, 1902/1964; James, 1890/1948; Piers & Singer, 1971). In addition to these potential selves (see James, 1890/1948; Cantor, Markus, Niedenthal, & Nurius, 1986), one finds descriptions of two kinds of actual selves: what kind of person an individual believes he or she actually is and what kind of person an individual believes that others think he or she actually is (e.g., Erikson, 1950/1963; Lecky, 1961; Mead, 1934).

Although theorists have distinguished between various subsets of these different aspects of the self (see Greenwald & Pratkanis, 1984), there has been no systematic framework for revealing the interrelations of the aspects. In an attempt to do so, Higgins (1984) proposed that two cognitive dimensions underlie these disparate self-state representations: domains of the self and standpoints on the self.

1. *Domains of the self.* There are three basic domains of the self: the *actual* self, which is a person's representation of the attributes that someone (self or other) believes the person actually possesses; the *ideal* self, which is a person's representation of the attributes that someone (self or other) would like the person, ideally, to possess (i.e., someone's hopes, goals, or wishes for the person); and the *ought* self, which is a person's representation of the attributes that someone (self or other) believes the person should or ought to possess (i.e., someone's sense of the person's duty, obligations, or responsibilities).

2. *Standpoints on the self.* A standpoint on the self is a point of view or position that reflects a set of attitudes or values and from which a person can be judged (see Turner, 1956). There are two basic standpoints on the self: a person's *own* personal standpoint and the standpoint of some significant *other* (e.g., mother, father, sibling, closest friend). A person can have self-state representations for each of a number of significant others.

Combining each of the domains of the self with the standpoints on the self yields six basic kinds of self-state representations: actual/own, actual/other, ideal/own, ideal/other, ought/own, and ought/other. The first two self-state representations, particularly actual/own, constitute what is typically meant by a person's "self-concept" (see Wylie, 1979). The four remaining self-state representations are self-directive standards or acquired guides for being (see Higgins et al., 1986). Self-discrepancy theory (Higgins, 1984) proposes that people are motivated to reach a condition where their actual state matches their ideal and ought states; that is, where their self-concept matches their self-guides. The theory also proposes that there are individual differences in which self-guide a person is especially motivated to meet. Indeed, not everyone is expected to possess all of the self-guides—some people may possess only ought self-guides whereas others may possess only ideal self-guides; some may possess only own-standpoint self-guides whereas others may possess only other-standpoint self-guides.

To the extent that an individual's actual/own self-concept does not match one of the individual's self-guides, self-discrepancy theory predicts that the individual will experience discomfort. Just as the motivational or emotional response to a performance is determined by an individual's beliefs about the consequences or significance of the performance and not by the properties of the performance per se, the motivational or emotional effects of an individual's actual-self attributes are determined not by the nature of the attributes per se but by the individual's beliefs about the consequences or significance of possessing such attributes, which in turn reflect their *relation* to his or her self-guides. And relations between individuals' actual-self states and different types of self-guides represent different negative psychological situations that have different motivational or emotional significance, as follows:

1. Actual/own versus ideal/own and actual/own versus ideal/other: These discrepancies involve conditions in which the current state of an individual's actual attributes, from the individual's own standpoint, does not match the ideal state that he or she personally wishes to attain or that he or she believes some significant other person wishes him or her to attain. The discrepancy represents the general psychological situation of the absence of positive outcomes (i.e., the nonobtainment of goals and desires); thus the individual is predicted to be vulnerable to dejection-related emotions.

2. Actual/own versus ought/own and actual/own versus ought/other: These discrepancies involve conditions in which the current state of an individual's actual attributes, from the individual's own standpoint, does not match the state that the individual himself or herself believes it is his or her duty to attain or that he or she believes some significant other person believes it is his or her duty or obligation to fulfill. Because violation of prescribed duties and obligations is associated with sanctions (e.g., punishment), this discrepancy represents the general psychological situation of the presence of negative outcomes; thus the individual is predicted to be vulnerable to agitation-related emotions.

There is some indirect evidence consistent with these proposed associations in the psychological literature on the self and emotions (see Higgins, 1984). For example, Duval and Wicklund (1972) reported that individuals become increasingly dissatisfied or disappointed with themselves as they focus on their real-self/ideal-self discrepancy (see also Scheier & Carver, 1977), and others have observed that actual:ideal discrepancies are associated with disappointment, shame, and dissatisfaction (e.g., Cooley, 1902/1964; James, 1890/1948; Rogers, 1961). And many psychologists have reported that when individuals transgress their own or society's moral standards, which would involve an actual:ought discrepancy, they feel guilty, fearful, and anxious (e.g., Freud, 1923/1961; Hoffman, 1975; James, 1890/1948; Perry & Gawel, 1953).

There is also some direct supporting evidence for these hypothesized relations from our own recent studies (Higgins, Klein, & Strauman, 1985, in press). Using a variety of standard measures of depression and anxiety (e.g., Beck Depression Inventory; Hopkins Symptom Checklist), Higgins, Klein, and Strauman (1985) measured both undergraduates' self-concept discrepancies (see Method section for a description of the procedure) and their emotional problems. As predicted, partial correlational analyses revealed that discrepancies between individuals' self-concepts and their ideal self-guides (e.g., actual/own:ideal/own and actual/own:ideal/other discrepancies) were more closely associated with dejection-related emotions (e.g., dissatisfied, shame, feeling blue) than with agitation-related emotions (e.g., guilt, panic, fear), whereas the reverse was true for discrepancies between individuals' self-concepts and their ought self-guides (i.e., actual/own:ought/own and actual/own:ought/other discrepancies). In another study (Higgins et al., in press), we found that the magnitude of undergraduates' actual: ideal discrepancies predicted whether they would suffer from depressive symptoms approximately 2 months later better than the magnitude of their actual:ought discrepancies did. The magnitude of their actual:ought discrepancies, on the other hand, predicted whether they would suffer from anxious and paranoid emotional symptoms better than the magnitude of their actual:ideal discrepancies did.

Self-discrepancy theory proposes the following general hypothesis: The greater the magnitude and accessibility of a particular type of self-discrepancy possessed by an individual, the more the individual will experience the type of discomfort associated with that self-discrepancy. The results of our previous studies are consistent with this hypothesis, but they are limited in a couple of respects. First, they do not provide evidence for the causal direction predicted by the model. Although the studies found the predicted pattern of associations between different types of self-concept discrepancies and different types of emotions, they were not designed to demonstrate that activation of a discrepancy induces discomfort. Second, these studies tested only the role of magnitude and type of self-discrepancy in relation to emotional discomfort—not the role of the accessibility of the self-discrepancy.

As reflected in the general hypothesis, self-discrepancy theory proposes that individuals' emotional discomfort is influenced by two factors. First, emotional discomfort is influenced by the magnitude of an individual's available types of self-discrepancies, where the greater the magnitude of a particular type of discrepancy the more intensely the individual will experience the type of discomfort associated with that discrepancy. Thus, everything else being equal, an individual will experience most intensely the type of discomfort that is associated with the self-discrepancy that has the greatest magnitude. Second, emotional discomfort is influenced by the accessibility of an individual's available types of self-discrepancies, where the greater the accessibility of a particular type of discrepancy the more likely the individual will experience the type of discomfort associated with that discrepancy. Thus, everything else being equal, an individual will experience most intensely the type of discomfort that is associated with the self-discrepancy that has the greatest accessibility. The impact of the relative accessibility of stored constructs on people's interpretation of social events has been demonstrated in a number of studies (see Higgins & King, 1981; Wyer & Srull, 1981). Higgins, King, and Mavin (1982), for example, demonstrated that individuals who had the same person constructs available to them in conceptual memory formed different impressions of a stimulus person because of individual differences in which available constructs were chronically accessible (see also Bargh & Thein, 1985).

The purpose of the present studies was to test the causal direction predicted by self-discrepancy theory with respect to the impact of both the magnitude and accessibility of individuals' self-discrepancies on the nature of emotional change. The purpose of Study 1 was to examine whether focusing on an event that is likely to be experienced as a negative psychological situation (e.g., receiving a grade of D in a course, which could be experienced as either the absence of a positive outcome or the presence of a negative outcome) would produce different types of discomfort depending on the relative magnitude of an individual's different types of self-concept discrepancies. We predicted that exposure to such an event would cause predominant actual:ideal discrepancy individuals to

feel more dejected but would cause predominant actual:ought discrepancy individuals to feel more agitated. We also expected that such differences, as a function of an individual's predominant type of discrepancy, would be less evident when individuals focused on an event that was unlikely to be experienced as a negative psychological situation (e.g., receiving a grade of A in a course).

The purpose of Study 2 was to examine whether increasing the accessibility of a self-concept discrepancy would produce different types of emotions depending on the magnitude and type of discrepancy involved. The accessibility of individuals' cognitive structures can be momentarily modified by contextual factors that temporarily increase their retrievability (see Higgins, Bargh, & Lombardi, 1985; Higgins & King, 1981; Higgins, Rholes, & Jones, 1977; Posner, 1978; Shiffrin & Schneider, 1977; Wyer & Srull, 1981). Study 2 used a priming technique (e.g., activating a construct through recent exposure to an instance of or label for the construct) to increase the accessibility of individuals' self-concept discrepancies. We predicted that when individuals' actual:ideal and actual:ought self-concept discrepancies were both high in magnitude, that the individuals would feel more dejected when their actual:ideal discrepancies were primed and would feel more agitated when their actual:ought discrepancies were primed. Because little, if any, discomfort is expected when the magnitude of individuals' self-concept discrepancies is low, we predicted that differential priming would have relatively little effect when individuals' discrepancies were low in magnitude.

Study 1

The major purpose of our first study was to examine whether the type of discomfort that occurred from focusing on a negative event would vary depending on the type of self-concept discrepancy that was predominant for an individual. Subjects were asked to imagine either a positive event in which performance matched a common standard (e.g., receiving a grade of A in a course) or a negative event in which performance failed to match a common standard (e.g., receiving a grade of D in a course that was necessary for obtaining an important job). For the negative event condition, we expected that subjects would experience the event in terms of the negative psychological situation associated with their predominant self-concept discrepancy, such that individuals whose predominant discrepancy was an actual: ideal discrepancy would have an increase in dejection-related emotions, whereas individuals whose predominant discrepancy was an actual:ought discrepancy would have an increase in agitation-related emotions. For the positive event condition, we expected that subjects' predominant self-concept discrepancies would have less impact on their emotions because the negative psychological situations associated with the discrepancies would be less applicable to positive events, and because actively focusing on such nondiscrepant events might temporarily even block the chronic effects of such discrepancies (see Higgins & King, 1981).

Two other variables were included in the study: (a) protagonist (self or other) and (b) type of attribute (achievement or interpersonal). These two variables were included for reasons not directly germane to the issues of concern in the present paper.[1] The type of attribute variable, however, does provide a test of whether self-discrepancy theory can be generalized across different kinds of attributes, and the protagonist variable permits a preliminary test of whether activation of individuals' self-discrepancies is greater for a self-referent event than for an other-referent event. With regard to this latter issue, one might expect that the more self-referent an event is, the more likely it is to activate an individual's discrepancies. Chronically accessible constructs, however, are easily activated by other-referent stimuli to which they apply (e.g., Higgins et al., 1982), and people typically imagine the psychological state of others by considering their own psychological state under the same circumstances (see Higgins, 1981; Tagiuri, 1969). Thus, no clear prediction of the effect of the protagonist variable on individuals' mood could be made.

Method

Subjects

One hundred seventeen undergraduates were recruited from the introductory psychology subject pool at New York University. Seven students were excluded from the data analyses owing to their self-reported failure to follow the event-focus instruc-

tions. Of the remaining 110 subjects, 93 had filled out all sections of the self-concept discrepancy measure in the battery of tests given a few weeks earlier. Only the results for these 93 subjects are reported. All subjects received course credit for their participation.

Materials

Three measures were used to assess subjects' mood state:

1. *Semantic differential*. Subjects rated themselves on six 7-point bi-polar scales (e.g., sad–happy, alert–tired, slow–fast). Half of the items were keyed in the positive direction and half were keyed in the negative direction in order to control for response biases. A composite general mood score was calculated by summing the item scores such that higher scores were indicative of a negative mood state. The composite score, which has been found to be sensitive to differences in mood (Natale & Hantas, 1982), was used as a general assessment of subjects' mood prior to the manipulation of the activating of individuals' self-concept discrepancies. Subjects' general mood prior to the manipulation was obtained to use as a covariate in our subsequent analyses so as to control for the influence of prior feelings on subjects' subsequent emotional responses.

2. *Multiple Affect Adjective Checklist (MAACL; Zuckerman & Lubin,* 1965). Subjects were given a list of positive and negative emotional adjectives from which they were asked to select those that best described their current feelings. The MAACL has been found to be sensitive to transient changes in mood (Gatchel, Paulus, & Maples, 1975; Metalsky, Abramson, Seligman, Semmel, & Peterson, 1982; Miller & Seligman, 1975).

For our purposes, the positive emotions were scored 1 if not checked, and the negative emotions were scored 1 if checked. Therefore, higher scores reflected greater discomfort. Of the emotions

---

[1]Study 1 was part of a larger study conducted by the second author for his dissertation to partially fulfill the requirements for the degree of Doctor of Philosophy at New York University. These two variables were relevant to other theoretical issues addressed in that study. These other issues also led to the inclusion of additional dependent measures (e.g., attributional style) that will not be discussed. The results of the study presented in this article were independent of the results on these other measures.

listed, 20 were clearly dejection-related or agita-tion-related—9 positive and negative dejection-related items (e.g., happy, satisfied, blue, discour-aged, low) and 11 positive and negative agitation-related items (e.g., calm, quiet, afraid, agitated, desperate). Consistent with clinical us-age, items were considered dejection-related or agitation-related if they (or, in the case of positive items, their negation) described a sad, unmotivated, dissatisfied state or a frightened, threatened, ner-vous state, respectively. In selecting dejection-re-lated items and agitation-related items, we did not simply use the depression subscale of the MAACL for the dejection items and the anxiety subscale of the MAACL for the agitation items because many of the items in these subscales either do not dis-criminate between dejection and agitation clearly enough (e.g., anxiety subscale—pleasant, loving, upset; depression subscale—healthy, suffering, terrible), or they confuse the distinction (e.g., anxi-ety subscale—cheerful; depression subscale—safe). Two independent coders were given the 20 items we selected and were asked to classify them as either dejection-related or agitation-related. Both coders were in 100% agreement with our classification of the items.

This measure of subjects' dejection-related and agitation-related emotions was given to subjects after exposure to the positive or negative event in order to test for the hypothesized emotional changes. For each subject, the average score of the dejection-related items was calculated (as de-scribed earlier) to yield an overall dejection score, and the average score of the agitation-related items was calculated to yield an overall agitation score. Each score could vary from 0 to 1.

3. *Writing-speed task.* Before and after the manipulation of activating their self-concept dis-crepancies, subjects were asked to perform a simple writing-speed task. The writing task re-quired subjects to write a list of numbers by ones, in decreasing order, starting from 100. The writ-ing-speed score was the number of digits recorded in a 1-min period. This task has been found to be sensitive to differences in momentary mood, with subjects' writing speed decreasing following a sad mood induction and increasing following a happy mood induction (Natale & Hantas, 1982). This measure was included in order to have a behav-ioral index of emotional change. We expected that activating actual:ideal discrepancies (e.g., making

subjects more dejected) would cause a decrease in writing speed. It was less clear what we should predict would happen to writing speeds when ac-tual/ought discrepancies were activated. Increased agitation can reduce performance if it includes fear of failure. But in this case the task was simple and the subjects were given no indication that their performance would be judged. Moreover, agita-tion involves arousal, and arousal can enhance performance on simple tasks (see Zajonc, 1966). Thus, one might even predict an increase in writ-ing speed when actual:ought discrepancies were activated.

In addition to these three measures of mood state, subjects' self-concept discrepancies were measured a few weeks prior to the experimental session (as part of a general battery of measures given to Introductory Psychology students). The measure used was the Selves questionnaire used in Higgins, Klein, & Strauman (1985). This mea-sure asks subjects to list up to 10 traits or attributes associated with different self-states. By having subjects spontaneously list the attributes associ-ated with each of their self-states (as opposed to a constrained, checklist procedure), we increased the likelihood that the attributes would be important to each subject. In the present study, only subjects' responses to self-states that involved their own standpoint were used. Subjects were given these instructions:

> In the following questionnaire, you will be asked to list the attributes of the type of person you think you actually, ideally, and ought to be:
>
> Actual self: Your beliefs concerning the attributes you think you *actually* possess.
>
> Ideal self: Your beliefs concerning the attributes you would like *ideally* to possess; your ultimate goals for yourself.
>
> Ought self: Your beliefs concerning the attributes you believe you *should* or *ought to* possess; your normative rules or prescriptions for yourself.

A two-stage process was used to quantify the discrepancy between the actual/own self-concept and each of the two self-guides (i.e., ideal/own and ought/own). First, the attributes in the actual/own self-concept were compared to the attributes in the self-guide to determine which attributes matched (i.e., the self-concept and the self-guide have the same attributes, including synonyms) and which attributes mismatched (i.e., an attribute in the self-concept was the opposite or antonym of an attribute in the self-guide). Synonyms and antonyms were operationally defined in terms of *Roget's Thesaurus*. Second, the self-concept discrepancy score was calculated by subtracting the total number of matches from the total number of mismatches. For the entire sample of subjects, the correlation between subjects' actual/own:ideal/own discrepancy and actual/own:ought/own discrepancy was $r(91)=.23$, $p <.05$.

Procedure

When the subjects arrived at the experimental session they were told that the purpose of the study was to see how people perceive various life events. The subjects completed the semantic differential questionnaire and then performed the first of the writing-speed tasks. They then received a guided imagery task, modeled after a procedure used by Wright and Mischel (1982), to manipulate the activation of their self-concept discrepancies.

The entire procedure for the imagery task was prerecorded to ensure that it was standardized for the subjects in each condition. The subjects were given 4 min to imagine an event as vividly as possible, with one reminder of the event being given after 2 min. The subjects were randomly assigned to eight experimental conditions that were produced by factorially combining two levels each of event focus (positive event, negative event), protagonist in the event (self, other), and type of attribute in the event (achievement, interpersonal). In the positive event condition, subjects were asked to imagine that they (or another person) either received a grade of A in a course (the achievement theme) or just spent the evening with someone they (or the other person) had admired for some time (the interpersonal theme). In the negative event condition, subjects were asked to imagine that they (or another person) either received a grade of D in a course necessary for obtaining an important job (the achievement theme) or that their (or another person's) lover had just left them (the interpersonal theme). During the guided imagery task, the subjects were given a detailed description of the event in order to make the event as vivid and realistic as possible (e.g., describing the time of day, the time of year, the weather, the surroundings, etc.). No reference, however, was made to the feelings that the protagonist might experience in order not to

influence the subjects' spontaneous emotional reactions.

Following the guided imagery task, subjects were given the writing speed test for the second time. Upon completion of this test, subjects filled out the MAACL questionnaire to measure their current feelings. At the end of the session, the subjects were debriefed, thanked for their participation, and asked not to discuss the study with other subjects. As part of the debriefing, the subjects were given the opportunity to discuss their experiences in the study and express any concerns they might have. The discussion with each subject continued until it was clear that the effects of the guided imagery task had dissipated.

Results and Discussion

Mood

The major purpose of the study was to examine whether focusing on a negative event would induce different types of discomfort depending on an individual's predominant discrepancy. To test this, we first divided the 93 subjects into high and low actual:ideal discrepant groups on the basis of a median split of their actual/own:ideal/own discrepancy scores, and into high and low actual:ought discrepancy groups on the basis of a median split of their actual/own:ought/own discrepancy scores. These divisions were then used to create two distinct sets of subjects varying on which kind of discrepancy was predominant—a high actual:ideal discrepancy/low actual:ought discrepancy group ($N=16$) and a high actual:ought discrepancy/low actual:ideal discrepancy group ($N=23$). Because there were empty cells when the complete five-way analysis of variance (ANOVA) was performed, 2 four-way ANOVAS were performed. First, a Type of Self-Concept Discrepancy (predominant actual:ideal discrepancy; predominant actual:ought discrepancy) × Event Focus (positive event; negative event) × Type of Attribute (achievement; interpersonal) × Type of Mood (Dejection-related; Agitation-related) ANOVA was performed on the postmanipulation mood scores, using subjects' premanipulation mood (as measured by the semantic differential) as a covariate. As shown in Table 1, there was a significant Type of Self-Concept Discrepancy × Event Focus × Type of Mood interaction, $F(1,31) = 6.39$, $p <.02$, which reflected the fact that, as predicted, the predominant actual:ideal discrepancy subjects were more dejected following the negative event-focus than following the positive event-focus, whereas the predominant actual:ought discrepancy subjects were, if anything, slightly more agitated following the negative event-focus than following the positive event-focus. Morever, planned comparisons (using t rations; Kirk, 1968) indicated that in the negative event condition, as expected, predominant actual:ideal discrepancy subjects felt significantly ($p <.001$) more dejected than predominant actual:ought discrepancy subjects, whereas predominant actual:ought discrepancy subjects tended to feel more agitated than predominant actual:ideal discrepancy subjects ($p <.08$). In addition predominant actual:ideal discrepancy subjects felt significantly ($p <.001$) more dejected in the negative event condition than in the positive event condition.

Thus, focusing on a negative event had different effects on subjects' emotions depending on their predominant self-concept discrepancy, whereas subjects' emotions were less influenced by the relative magnitude of their discrepancies when they were exposed to a positive event. An additional partial correlational analysis provides further support for this conclusion. In both the positive event and negative event conditions separately, the unique relations between each type of discrepancy and dejection and agitation were calculated, with the contributions to the relations both from the other type of discrepancy and premanipulation mood (as measured by the semantic differential) being partialed out. All 93 subjects for whom all the requisite scores were available were included in this analysis. In the negative event condition, magnitude of actual:ideal discrepancy was positively correlated with amount of

dejection, $pr(41) = .39$, $p <.01$, whereas actual:ought discrepancy was uncorrelated with dejection, $pr(41) = -.04$(ns); and magnitude of actual:ideal discrepancy was negatively correlated with amount of agitation, $pr(41) = -.33$, $p <.05$, whereas magnitude of actual:ought discrepancy was positively correlated with amount of agitation, $pr(41) = .46$, $p <.003$. These differences in the negative event condition between actual:ideal discrepancy and actual:ought discrepancy in their relation to dejection and agitation were both significant—dejection, $t(40) = 2.32$, $p <.05$; agitation, $t(40) = 4.98$, $p <.01$. In contrast, in the positive event condition there were no significant relations for either type of discrepancy between magnitude of discrepancy and amount of discomfort (all $ps >$ .20 except for a positive correlation between actual:ought discrepancy and agitation, $pr(44) =$ .26, $p =.09$).

The first ANOVA analysis also revealed a significant Type of Self-Concept Discrepancy × Type of Attribute × Type of Mood interaction, $F(1,31)$ $= 5.03$, $p <.05$, which reflected the fact that predominant actual:ideal discrepancy subjects felt especially dejected when they focused on an achievement attribute ($M = .20$; for all other conditions, M was less than .10). A Type of Self-Concept Discrepancy × Event Focus × Protagonist (self; other) × Type of Mood ANOVA was also performed. No significant effects of protagonist were found.

To further test our hypothesis using a behavioral index of emotional consequences, a Type of Self-Concept Discrepancy × Event Focus × Type of Attribute ANOVA was first performed on the percentage increase in subjects' writing speed (specifically, the arcsine transformation of the proportion—postspeed minus prespeed divided by prespeed), again using subjects' premanipulation

TABLE 14.1. Mean Dejection-Related and Agitation-Related Mood Scores as a Function of Type of Self-Concept Discrepancy and Event Focus

Self-concept discrepancy	Positive event		Negative event	
	Dejection	Agitation	Dejection	Agitation
High actual:ideal discrepancy	.03	.03	.24	.00
High actual:ought discrepancy	.06	.09	.04	.11

Note. Scores could range from 0 to 1. All means are adjusted for premanipulation mood.

mood as a covariate.[2] There was a significant Type of Self-Concept Discrepancy × Event Focus interaction, $F(1,29) = 7.08$, $p < .05$, which reflected the fact that, as predicted, the predominant actual:ideal discrepancy subjects were slower following the negative event focus (mean percentage increase in writing speed, adjusted for premanipulation mood, $M = -5.1\%$) but were faster following the positive event focus ($M = 4.3\%$), whereas predominant actual:ought discrepancy subjects were faster following the negative event focus ($M = 3.9\%$) and showed little change following the positive event focus ($M = 0.5\%$). Moreover, planned comparisons indicated that in the negative event condition, as expected, predominant actual:ideal discrepancy subjects had a significantly ($p < .05$) greater decrease in writing speed than predominant actual: ought discrepancy subjects. Predominant actual:ideal discrepancy subjects also had a significantly ($p < .05$) greater decrease in writing speed in the negative event condition than in the positive event condition.

Thus, the event-focus manipulation had different effects on subjects' mood-related behavior depending on a subject's predominant self-concept discrepancy. An additional, partial correlational analysis provides further support for this general conclusion. In both the positive event and negative event conditions separately, the unique relations between each type of discrepancy and the percentage increase in subjects' writing speed were calculated, with the contribution to the relations both from the other type of discrepancy and premanipulation mood (as measured by the semantic differential) being partialed out. All 92 subjects for whom all the requisite scores were available were included in the analysis. In the negative event condition, there was a negative correlation between actual:ideal discrepancy and percentage increase in writing speed, $pr(41) = -.30$, $p < .06$, reflecting the fact that the greater the magnitude of subjects' actual:ideal discrepancy as measured weeks before, the greater was the decrease in their writing speed following exposure to a negative event. In contrast, the nonsignificant relation between actual:ought discrepancy and percentage increase in writing speed was, if anything, in the opposite direction, $pr(41) = .17$ (*ns*). This differ-

ence in the negative event condition, between actual:ideal discrepancy and actual:ought discrepancy in their relation to increase in writing speed, was significant, $t(40) = t(40) = 2.47$, $p < .02$. In the positive event condition, neither type of discrepancy was related to percentage increase in writing speed ($p > .15$). It is interesting, however, that the direction of the correlations was reversed (actual:ideal, $pr(43) = .19$; actual: ought, $pr(43) = -.13$), perhaps caused by relief from the type of discomfort normally associated with each type of discrepancy.

The first ANOVA also revealed a significant Event Focus × Type of Attribute interaction, $F(1,29) = 5.39$, $p < .05$, reflecting the fact that in the negative event condition there was a greater decrease in writing speed when subjects focused on an achievement attribute ($M = -5.9\%$) than when they focused on an interpersonal attribute ($M = 4.8\%$), whereas there was no difference in the positive event condition (achievement, $M = 2.1\%$; interpersonal, $M = 2.2\%$).

A Type of Self-Concept Discrepancy × Event Focus × Protagonist ANOVA was also performed, and it revealed a significant three-way interaction, $F(1,29) = 8.52$, $p < .01$, which reflected the fact that predominant actual:ideal discrepancy subjects had the greatest decrease in their writing speed in the negative event/self protagonist condition ($M = -9.6\%$), whereas predominant actual:ought discrepancy subjects had the greatest increase in their writing speed in this condition ($M = +6.5\%$). On this behavioral measure, then, there was support for the notion that individuals' unique emotional vulnerability would have its greatest impact when the self was directly focused upon (see Scheier & Carver, 1977).

The results of this study support the hypothesis of self-discrepancy theory that focusing on an event that is likely to be experienced as a negative psychological situation will induce different emotions and emotionally related behaviors depending on an individual's predominant type of self-concept discrepancy. In particular, individuals with predominant actual:ideal discrepancy became more dejected, whereas individuals with predominant actual:ought discrepancy, if anything, tended to become slightly more agitated.

It might be argued that subjects' predominant type of discrepancy was predictive of the quality of discomfort induced by focusing on a negative

---

[2]One subject was dropped from this analysis because of failure to complete the postwriting-speed measure.

event, but that the magnitude of their self-concept discrepancy did not influence the intensity of their discomfort. Instead, the magnitude of discrepancy inherent in the negative event itself was the source of the intensity of subjects' experience. As described earlier, however, the magnitude of subjects' actual:ideal and actual:ought discrepancies as measured weeks before the experimental session predicted the intensity of their dejected and agitated response to the same negative event.

The results of this study also suggest that *whether* a mood induction procedure such as the guided imagery task is effective, and *what* mood is induced when it is effective, depends on the relation between the particular procedure used and the subjects' particular self-concept discrepancies. In fact, it may be that most mood induction procedures, like the guided imagery task used in our study, are more relevant to actual:ideal discrepancies that actual:ought discrepancies (i.e., subjects are not asked to imagine the event in terms of duty or obligations), which could explain why such procedures are typically described as manipulating dejection (i.e., happy vs. sad). However, if a different kind of procedure were used, one that was more relevant to actual:ought discrepancies (i.e., framed in terms of subjects' sense of duty and moral obligation), then it could be used more effectively to manipulate agitation (i.e., calm vs. agitated). In any case, it would be useful for researchers using mood-induction paradigms to be sensitive to this issue.

The weaker results for actual:ought discrepancy than for actual:ideal discrepancy in this study, then, could be because the negative events we used were more closely related to an actual:ideal psychological situation than an actual:ought psychological situation. At least with respect to the achievement situation, which was associated with the strongest dejection effects, an examination of subjects' matching and mismatching attributes revealed that the attribute *smart* or *intelligent* did appear somewhat more often among predominant actual:ideal discrepancy subjects' ideal attributes (25.0%) than among predominant actual:ought discrepancy subjects' ought attributes (4.3%). This difference by itself, however, would not be sufficient to account for the generally stronger results for actual:ideal discrepancy, although it may contribute somewhat to the difference for the achievement situation.

More generally, it should be noted that there was considerable overlap between predominant actual:ideal discrepancy subjects and predominant actual:ought discrepancy subjects for *most* of the attributes they listed (e.g., friendly, hardworking, outgoing, understanding, caring, patient, sensitive). Predominant actual:ideal discrepancy subjects did list *good-looking* and *sense of humor* more often than did predominant actual:ought discrepancy subjects, who in turn listed *responsible* and *honest* more often than did predominant actual:ideal discrepancy subjects. But these attributes were not listed frequently enough to draw any clear conclusions at this point.

It is also possible that the results for the actual:ought discrepancy would have been stronger if actual/own:ought/other rather than actual/own:ought/own had been used as the actual:ought discrepancy because we have found that the former discrepancy has a stronger relation to agitation-related emotions than the latter (e.g., Higgins, Klein, & Strauman, 1985). Indeed, the magnitude of predominant actual:ought discrepancy subjects' actual/own:ought/own discrepancy was significantly smaller than the magnitude of predominant actual:ideal discrepancy subjects' actual/own:ideal/own discrepancy, $t(37) = 3.43$, $p < .01$, which could account for the weaker results of the former discrepancy.

Study 2

The results of Study 1 indicated that emotional change from focusing on an event that is likely to be experienced as a negative psychological situation varied as a function of the kind of self-concept discrepancy that was predominant for an individual. Thus, the hypothesized relation between the relative magnitude of individuals' different types of discrepancies and differences in emotional change was demonstrated by comparing individuals who had a high magnitude of discrepancy for only one type of self-concept discrepancy. The purpose of Study 2 was to demonstrate our second hypothesized relation, between the relative accessibility of individuals' different types of discrepancies and differences in emotional change. Thus, individuals were compared who had high magnitudes of both kinds of self-concept discrepancies but had a different discrepancy primed by the momentary context.

Method

Subjects

Thirty-six undergraduates were recruited from the introductory psychology subject pool at New York University; all had filled out the self-concept discrepancy measure in the battery of tests given a few weeks earlier. All subjects received course credit for their participation.

Procedure

Four to 6 weeks prior to the experimental session, the students were given the Selves questionnaire (Higgins, Klein, & Strauman, 1985). In this study, the students' discrepancies from *other* self-guides were calculated as well as their discrepancies from *own* self-guides. The students' ideal/other and ought/other self-guides were obtained by asking them to select their most relevant significant other for each of these domains (e.g., for ideal/other, "Whose hopes, goals, or wishes for you are most relevant or meaningful to you?"). This method of selecting *other* standpoints assures that the standpoint associated with each self-state is relevant to each student. We attempted to control for standpoint relevance as much as possible because self-discrepancy theory purposes that it influences the magnitude of felt disparity (see Higgins, 1984). The students were asked to list the attributes of the type of person this *other* individual (e.g., mother) would like them *ideally* to be (ideal/other) or believes they *should* or *ought to* be (ought/other). After the students' Selves questionnaires were collected, their actual:ideal discrepancies (i.e., actual/own:ideal/own discrepancy and actual/own:ideal/other discrepancy combined) and actual:ought discrepancies (i.e., actual/own: ought/own discrepancy and actual/own:ought/other discrepancy combined) were calculated. The students' scores on these two types of (combined) discrepancies were later used to select subjects (as described below).

The questionnaire measuring self-concept discrepancy was modified for this study in order to distinguish more clearly between matches and mismatches and between degrees of mismatches. For each of the self-states (i.e., actual/own, ideal/own, ideal/other, ought/own, and ought/other), after the students listed the attributes, they were asked to rate the extent to which they or their most relevant other believed they actually possessed, ideally possessed, or ought to possess each attribute they listed. The 4-point rating scale ranged from 1 (*slightly*) to 4 (*extremely*). The addition of this rating scale to the Selves questionnaire permitted a new distinction to be made in calculating discrepancies—true matches, where synonymous attributes in two self-states had a rating that varied by no more than one scale point, versus synonymous mismatches, where synonymous attributes in two self-rates had ratings that varied by two or more scale points (e.g., actual/own: slightly attractive vs. ideal/own: extremely attractive). In order to reflect degree of mismatch, synonymous mismatches were given a weight of 1 whereas antonymous mismatches (e.g., actual/own: unattractive vs. ideal/own: extremely attractive) were given a weight of 2. Synonymous matches were given the same weight as synonymous mismatches (i.e., 1). The interrater reliability of this measure was tested in a previous study where two rates independently scored 80 actual/own:ideal/own discrepancies. The interrater correlation was .89. With our previous self-discrepancy measure an individual who had two antonymous mismatches and two matches would have received the same discrepancy score as an individual who had no mismatches or matches (i.e., zero for both). With our new measure, the former individual would receive a higher discrepancy score (i.e., 2 or 6 depending on whether the two matches were true matches or were synonymous mismatches) than the latter individual (i.e., zero).

From among 200 undergraduates in the subject pool who had filled out the Selves questionnaire completely, 60 students were randomly selected with the constraint that their scores should reflect the full range of actual:ideal and actual:ought discrepancy scores in the pool. A median split was performed on the actual:ideal discrepancy scores to identify students who had either relatively high or relatively low actual:ideal discrepancies, and a median split was performed on the actual:ought discrepancy scores to identify students who had either relatively high or relatively low actual:ought discrepancies. Two sets of subjects were then recruited for the experimental study—subjects who were relatively high on both discrepancies (the high actual:ideal and actual:ought discrepancy group) and subjects who were relatively low on both discrepancies (the low actual:ideal and actual:ought discrepancy group).

The ostensible purpose of the experimental study was to obtain the self-reflections of an undergraduate, youth sample in order to compare them to the self-reflections of preadolescent, middle-aged, and retired samples of males and females as part of a large life-span developmental study on self-perception. The subjects were told that their mood during the study would be checked because previous research indicated that mood can sometimes influence people's self-reflections, and there might possibly be life-span developmental differences in general mood. This cover story provided the rationale for obtaining mood measures both before and after the experimental manipulation.

Half of the subjects in each discrepancy group were randomly assigned to an ideal priming condition and half were assigned to an ought priming condition. In the ideal priming condition, subjects were asked, in a series of questions, to describe the kind of person that they and their parents would ideally like them to be, to list the attributes that they and their parents hoped they would have, and to discuss whether there had been any change over the years in these hopes and goals for them. We expected that priming subjects' ideal standards would increase the accessibility of their actual:ideal discrepancies (see Higgins & King, 1981). In the ought priming condition, subjects were asked to describe the kind of person that they and their parents believed they ought to be, to list the attributes that they and their parents believed it was their duty or obligation to have, and to discuss whether there had been any change over the years in these beliefs concerning their duty and obligations. Again, we expected that priming subjects' ought standards would increase the accessibility of their actual:ought discrepancies. Both before and after this experimental manipulation, subjects were given a mood questionnaire that contained dejection-related emotions (e.g., sad, disappointed, enthusiastic [reversed for scoring]) and agitation-related emotions (e.g., tense, nervous, calm [reversed for scoring]). The subjects were asked to rate the extent to which they *now* were feeling each emotion on a 6-point scale that ranged from 0 (*not at all*) to 5 (*a great deal*). The scores for the eight dejection-related emotions were combined to create a dejection measure, and the scores for the eight agitation-related emotions were combined to create an agitation measure. At the end of the study, all subjects were given the Velten (1968) elation mood induction to ensure

that they left the study in a positive mood. They were then fully debriefed.

Results and Discussion

For the subjects who had high actual:ideal and actual:ought discrepancies, we predicted that the priming manipulation would increase whichever kind of discomfort was associated with the self-concept discrepancy, the accessibility of which was increased by the priming—an increase in dejection-related emotions in the ideal priming condition versus an increase in agitation-related emotions in the ought priming condition. In contrast, for the subjects who had low actual:ideal and actual:ought discrepancies, we predicted that the priming manipulation would, if anything, slightly decrease whichever kind of discomfort was associated with the primed discrepancy (i.e., make subjects feel better by reminding them of goals or obligations they have met)—a slight decrease in dejection-related emotions in the ideal priming condition versus a slight decrease in agitation-related emotions in the ought priming condition. To test these predictions, a Level of Discrepancy (high actual:ideal and actual:ought discrepancy; low actual:ideal and actual:ought discrepancy) × Type of Priming (ideal priming; ought priming) × Type of Discomfort (dejection-related; agitation-related) ANOVA was performed on subjects' mood change scores (i.e., for the dejection measure and the agitation measure separately, the postpriming score minus the prepriming score).

As shown in Table 2, a significant Level of Discrepancy × Type of Priming × Type of Discomfort interaction was found, $F(1,32) = 7.43$, $p < .01$, which reflected the fact that, as predicted, the major impact of ideal priming was to increase high-discrepancy subjects' dejection and slightly decrease low-discrepancy subjects' dejection, whereas the major impact of ought priming was to increase high-discrepancy subjects' agitation and slightly decrease low-discrepancy subjects' agitation. Planned comparisons indicated that ought priming for high-discrepancy subjects caused a significantly greater increase in agitation ($p < .05$) than either ought priming for low-discrepancy subjects or ideal priming for high-discrepancy subjects.

The fact that the priming manipulations increased high-discrepancy subjects' discomfort (either increasing dejection or increasing agitation

TABLE 14.2. Mean Change in Dejection-Related Emotions and Agitation-Related Emotions as a Function of Level of Self-Concept Discrepancies and Type of Priming

Self-concept discrepancies	Ideal priming		Ought priming	
	Dejection	Agitation	Dejection	Agitation
High actual:ideal and actual:ought discrepancies	3.2	−0.8	0.9	5.1
Low actual:ideal and actual:ought discrepancies	−1.2	0.9	0.3	−2.6

Note. Each emotion was measured on a 6-point scale from *not at all* to *a great deal*, and there were eight dejection emotions and eight agitation emotions. The more positive the number, the greater the increase in discomfort.

depending on the type of priming) but did not increase low-discrepancy subjects' discomfort indicates that the priming manipulations did not by themselves induce discomfort by temporarily creating self-discrepancies. If they had, low-discrepancy subjects would also have experienced an increase in discomfort as a result of these manipulations. In fact, the priming manipulations had, if anything, and opposite effect on the low-discrepancy subjects' mood.

Thus, this study demonstrates that changing the accessibility of different types of self-concept discrepancies causes changes in different types of discomfort. Moreover, it shows that this is true even when individuals possess both types of discrepancies. The fact that individuals with both high actual:ideal discrepancy and high actual:ought discrepancy could experience either an increase in dejection or an increase in agitation depending on which type of discrepancy was temporarily more accessible accounts for why some individuals suffer from both dejection and agitation in their lives.

General Discussion and Conclusions

Self-discrepancy theory (Higgins, 1984) proposes that people's emotions are influenced by the magnitude, accessibility, and type of discrepancy they have between their self-concept and their self-guides. The results of the present studies support this proposal. With respect to magnitude of discrepancy, Study 1 found that subjects exposed to an event that was likely to be experienced as a negative psychological situation felt different types

of discomfort depending on which of their self-concept discrepancies was greater in magnitude, and Studies 1 and 2 found that both the intensity and direction (i.e., increase or decrease) of subjects' change in discomfort were related to the magnitude of their self-concept discrepancy (as measured weeks before). With regard to accessibility, Study 2 found that increasing the accessibility of a particular type of self-concept discrepancy induced a change in whichever type of discomfort was associated with that type of discrepancy. And with respect to type of discrepancy, both Study 1 and Study 2 found that activating actual:ideal discrepancies induced changes in dejection-related emotions, whereas activating actual:ought discrepancies induced changes in agitation-related emotions.

It should be noted that actual:ideal discrepancy is the type of self-concept discrepancy that most closely represents how *low self-esteem* has been conceptualized in the self-concept literature (see Wylie, 1979). Our results indicate, then, that low self-esteem needs to be distinguished from other kinds of self-discrepancies, such as actual:ought discrepancy, if its relation to emotional problems is to be specified. In addition, our results indicate that it is not sufficient to measure only the negativity of individuals' self-concept, which has also been used to define low self-esteem, because the relation between a negative self-concept and emotional problems depends on the self-guide from which the negative self-concept is discrepant (i.e., ideal vs. ought). In Study 2, for example, subjects with both high actual: ideal discrepancy and high actual:ought discrepancy experienced different types of discomfort depending on which type of self-guide was primed, even though their self-concept (i.e., the actual self) was not manipulated.

Even if one defined negativity in terms of whether it did or did not match a self-guide, thus defining actual-self negativity idiographically, it would still not account for our findings. Negative actual selves associated with actual: ideal discrepancies and negative actual selves associated with actual:ought discrepancies would not be qualitatively distinct because regardless of how they came to be judged as negative they would be equivalent in their negativity. In our model, discomfort is not induced by individuals' possession of negative actual selves per se. Mismatching actual selves are not assumed to be negative outcomes in themselves, nor are they assumed to be negative in absolute terms (e.g., positive actual self attributes involved in synonymous mismatches). Rather, discomfort is considered to be induced by the negative psychological situation that the self-concept discrepancy as a whole represents.

In recent years there has been an increasing interest in identifying cognitive factors that may serve as vulnerability markers for emotional problems (e.g., Beck, Rush, Shaw, & Emery, 1979; Kuiper, Olinger, MacDonald, & Shaw, 1985). The results of the present studies suggest that one such cognitive factor may be individuals' self-discrepancies. A self-discrepancy is a cognitive structure that represents a psychological situation, with different self-discrepancies representing different psychological situations. For example, actual:ideal discrepancies represent the absence of a positive outcome, whereas actual:ought discrepancies represent the presence of a negative outcome. Like any cognitive construct, when a self-discrepancy reaches a threshold level of activation it is ready to be used to interpret stimulus events (see Higgins, Bargh, & Lombardi, 1985). The psychological situation represented by a self-discrepancy can become sufficiently accessible to be used in interpreting past, present, or future life events either by frequent activation that leads to a chronic accessibility (see Higgins et al., 1982) or by contextual priming that temporarily increases its accessibility. In the latter case, the self-discrepancy would be an endogenous vulnerability factor, and the contextual priming would be an exogenous factor. Together, they would produce the emotional symptoms associated with the psychological situation represented by the self-discrepancy—dejec-tion-related symptoms in the case of an actual:ideal discrepancy and agitation-related symptoms in the case of an actual:ought discrepancy.

Another emotional vulnerability factor would be the chronic accessibility of a self-discrepancy. Frequent activation of a self-discrepancy, as might occur when a child's parents are constantly bemoaning their lost hopes and desires for the child or when threatening punishment for the child's bad behaviors, could lead to a chronically accessible self-discrepancy that is easily activated by even an ambiguous life event. Higgins and King (1981) suggested that depressed individuals may have more chronically accessible negative constructs than nondepressed individuals, and there is evidence that supports this hypothesis (e.g., Bargh & Tota, 1985; Gotlib & McCann, 1984). This cognitive feature of depressed individuals, however, may reflect an episode marker rather than a vulnerability factor. We propose that it is the chronic accessibility of self-discrepancies, rather than negative self-constructs per se, that is the vulnerability factor.

The present studies were restricted to examining the emotional impact of actual:ideal and actual:ought discrepancies. Self-discrepancy theory, however, distinguishes within these particular types of self-discrepancies and among other types of self-discrepancies. Within actual:ideal discrepancies, for example, it predicts that actual:ideal/own discrepancy will be more associated with dejection from perceived loss of mastery or self-fulfillment, whereas actual:ideal/other discrepancy will be more associated with dejection from perceived or anticipated loss of social affection or esteem. There is evidence consistent with these predictions (Higgins, 1984). In addition, there are other types of self-discrepancies that do not involve discrepancy from the actual self. For example, there are ideal:ought discrepancies that represent a conflict between competing types of self-guides, such as between an individual's personal desires (ideal/own) and his or her own sense of duty (ought/own) or between the hopes and wishes of one parent for an individual (ideal/other$_1$) and the prescibed rules of the other parent for the individual (ought/other$_2$). By distinguishing among these different types of self-discrepancies and the psychological situations they represent, we hope to discover a set of cognitive-motivational factors that underlie different types of emotional vulnerabilities.

ACKNOWLEDGMENTS

A brief version of this paper was presented at the Symposium on Affect and Cognition, American Psychological Association meetings, Toronto, 1984, at the International Conference on the Self and Identity, Cardiff, Wales, July 1984, and as an invited address at the Eastern Psychological Association meetings, Boston, 1985. The research was supported in part by Grant MH39429 from the National Institute of Mental Health to the first author. The authors would like to express their thanks to John Bargh, Marty Hoffman, Diane Ruble, and Robin Wells for their helpful comments and suggestions on earlier versions of the ideas expressed in this paper.

REFERENCES

Allport, G. W. (1955). *Becoming*. New Haven, CT: Yale University Press.

Asch, S. E. (1952). *Social psychology* Englewood Cliffs, NJ: Prentice-Hall.

Ausubel, D. P. (1955). Relationships between shame and guilt in the socializing process. *Psychological Review, 62*, 378–390.

Bargh, J. A., & Thein, R. D. (1985). Individual construct accessibility, person memory, and the recall-judgment link: The case of information overload. *Journal of Personality and Social Psychology, 49*, 1129–1146.

Bargh, J. A., & Tota, M. E. (1985). *Automatic processing in depression: Sensitivity to negative input with regard to self but not others*. Unpublished manuscript, New York University.

Beck, A. T., Rush, A. J., Shaw, B. F., & Emery, G. (1979). *Cognitive therapy of depression*. New York: Guilford Press.

Cantor, N., Markus, H., Niedenthal, P., & Nurius, P. (1986). On motivation and the self-concept. In R. M. Sorrentino & E. T. Higgins (Eds.), *Handbook of motivation and cognition: Foundations of social behavior* (pp. 96–121). New York: Guilford Press.

Colby, K. M. (1968). A programmable theory of cognition and affect in individual personal belief systems. In R. P. Abelson, E. Aronson, W. J. McGuire, T. M. Newcomb, M. J. Rosenberg & P. H. Tannenbaum (Eds.), *Theories of cognitive consistency: A source book* (pp. 520–525). Chicago: Rand McNally.

Cooley, C. H. (1964). *Human nature and the social order*. New York: Schocken Books. (Original work published 1902)

Coyne, J. C., & Lazarus, R. S. (1980). Cognitive style, stress perception, and coping. In I. L. Kutash & L. B. Schlesinger (Eds.), *Handbook on stress and anxiety* (pp. 144–158). San Francisco: Jossey-Bass.

Duval, S., & Wicklund, R. A. (1972). *A theory of objective self-awarness*. New York: Academic Press.

Erikson, E. H. (1963). *Childhood and society* (2nd ed). New York: Norton. (Original work published 1950)

Freud, S. (1961). The ego and the id. In J. Strachey (Ed. and Trans.), *The standard edition of the complete psychological works of Sigmund Freud* (Vol. 19, pp. 3–66). London: Hogarth Press. (Original work published 1923)

Gatchel, R. J., Paulus, P. B., & Maples, C. W. (1975). Learned helplessness and self-reported affect. *Journal of Abnormal Psychology, 84*, 732–734.

Gotlib, I. H., & McCann, C. D. (1984). Construct accessibil-ity and depression: An examination of cognitive and affective factors. *Journal of Personality and Social Psychology, 47*, 427–439.

Greenwald, A. G., & Pratkanis, A. R. (1984). The self. In R. S. Wyer & T.K. Srull (Eds.), *Handbook of social cognition* (pp. 129–178). Hillsdale, NJ: Erlbaum.

Higgins, E. T. (1981). Role taking and social judgment: Alternative developmental perspectives and processes. In J. H. Flavell & L. Ross (Eds.), *Social cognitive development: Frontiers and possible futures* (pp. 119–153). New York: Cambridge University Press.

Higgins, E. T. (1984). *Self-discrepancy: A theory relating self and affect*, Unpublished manuscript, New York University.

Higgins, E. T., Bargh, J. A., & Lombardi, W. (1985). The nature of priming effects on categorization. *Journal of Experimental Psychology: Learning, Memory, and Cognition, 11*, 59–69.

Higgins, E. T., & King, G. (1981). Accessibility of social constructs: Information processing consequences of individual and contextual variability. In N. Cantor & J. Kihlstrom (Eds.), *Personality, cognition, and social interaction* (pp. 69–121). Hillsdale, NJ: Erlbaum.

Higgins, E. T., King, G. A., & Mavin, G. H. (1982). Individual construct accessibility and subjective impressions and recall. *Journal of Personality and Social Psychology, 43*, 35–47.

Higgins, E. T., Klein, R., & Strauman, T. (1985). Self-concept discrepancy theory: A psychological model for distinguishing among different aspects of depression and anxiety. *Social Cognition, 3*, 51–76.

Higgins, E. T., Klein, R., & Strauman, T. (in press). Self-discrepancies: Distinguishing among self-states, self-state conflicts, and emotional vulnerabilities. In K. M. Yardley & T. M. Honess (Eds.), *Self and identity: Psychosocial perspectives*. New York: Wiley.

Higgins, E. T., Rholes, W. S., & Jones, C. R. (1977). Category accessibility and impression formation. *Journal of Experimental Social Psychology, 13*, 141–154.

Higgins, E. T., Strauman, T., & Klein, R. (1986). Standards and the process of self-evaluation: Multiple affects from multiple stages. In R. M. Sorrentino & E. T. Higgins (Eds.), *Handbook of motivation and cognition: Foundations of social behavior* (pp. 23–63). New York: Guilford Press.

Hoffman, M. L. (1975). Sex differences in moral internalization. *Journal of Personality and Social Psychology, 32*, 720–729.

Jacobs, D. (1971). Moods-emotion-affect: The nature of and manipulation of affective states with particular reference to positive affective states and emotional illness. In A. Jacobs & L. B. Sachs (Eds.), *The psychology of private events* (pp. 121–156). New York: Academic Press.

James, W. (1948). *Psychology*. New York: World. (Original work published 1890)

Kelly, G. A. (1995). *The psychology of personal constructs*. New York: Norton.

Kirk, R. E. (1968). *Experimental design: Procedures for the behavioral sciences*. Belmont, CA: Brooks/Cole.

Klein, G. S. (1970). *Perception, motives and personality*. New York: Knopf.

Kuiper, N. A., Olinger, L. J., MacDonald, M. R., & Shaw, B. F. (1985). Self-schema processing of depressed and nondepressed content: The effects of vulnerability to depression. *Social Cognition, 3*, 77–93.

Lazarus, A. A. (1968). Learning theory and the treatment of depression. *Behavior Research and Therapy, 6*, 83–89.

Lecky, P. (1961). *Self-consistency: A theory of personality.* New York: Shoe String Press.

Lewin, K. (1951). *Field theory in social science.* New York: Harper.

Mead, G. H. (1934). *Mind, self, and society.* Chicago: University of Chicago Press.

Merton, R. K. (1957). *Social theory and social structure.* Glencoe, IL: Free Press.

Metalsky, G. I., Abramson, L. Y., Seligman, M. E. P., Semmel, A., & Peterson, C. (1982). Attributional styles and life events in the classroom: Vulnerability and invulnerability to depressive mood reactions. *Journal of Personality and Social Psychology, 43*, 612–617.

Miller, W. R., & Seligman, M. E. P. (1975). Depression and learned helplessness in man. *Journal of Abnormal Psychology, 84*, 228–238.

Mowrer, O. H. (1960). *Learning theory and behavior.* New York: Wiley.

Murray, H. A. (1938). *Exploration in personality.* New York: Oxford University Press.

Natale, M., & Hantas, M. (1982). Effect of temporary mood states on selective memory about the self. *Journal of Personality and Social Psychology, 42*, 927–934.

Perry, H. S., & Gawel, M. L. (Eds.). (1953). *The collected works of Harvey Stack Sullivan* (Vol. 1). New York: Norton.

Piers, G., & Singer, M. B. (1971). *Shame and guilt.* New York: Norton.

Posner, M. I. (1978). *Chronometric explorations of the mind.* Hillsdale, NJ: Erlbaum.

Rogers, C. R. (1959). A theory of therapy, personality, and interpersonal relationships, as developed in the client-centered framework. In S. Koch (Ed.), *Psychology: A study of a science: Volume 3, Formulations of the person and the social context* (pp. 184–256). New York: McGraw-Hill.

Rogers, C. R. (1961). *On becoming a person.* Boston: Houghton Mifflin.

Roseman, I. (1979). *Cognitive aspects of emotion and emotional behavior.* Paper presented at the 87th Annual Convention of the American Psychological Association, New York City.

Schafer, R. (1967). Ideals, the ego ideal, and the ideal self. In R. R. Holt (Ed.), Motives and thought: Psychoanalytic essays in honor of David Rapaport [Special issue]. *Psychological Issues, 5*(2–3), 131–174.

Scheier, M. F., & Carver, C. S. (1977). Self-focused attention and the experience of emotion: Attraction, repulsion, elation, and depression. *Journal of Personality and Social Psychology, 35*, 625–636.

Shiffrin, R. M., & Schneider, W. (1977). Controlled and automatic human information processing: II. Perceptual learning, automatic attending, and a general theory. *Psychological Review, 84*, 127–190.

Tagiuri, R. (1969). Person perception. In G. Lindzey & E. Aronson (Eds.), *The handbook of social psychology* (Vol. 3, 2nd ed., pp. 395–449). Reading, MA: Addison-Wesley.

Turner, R. H. (1956). Role-taking, role standpoint, and reference-group behavior. *American Journal of Sociology, 61*, 316–328.

Velten, E. (1968). A laboratory task for induction of mood states. *Behavior Research and Therapy, 6*, 473–482.

Wright, J., & Mischel, W. (1982). Influence of affect on cognitive social learning person variables. *Journal of Personality and Social Psychology, 43*, 901–914.

Wyer, R. S., & Srull, T. K. (1981). Category accessibility: Some theoretical and empirical issues concerning the processing of social stimulus information. In E. T. Higgins, C. P. Herman, & M. P. Zanna (Eds.), *Social cognition: The Ontario Symposium* (pp. 161–197). Hillsdale, NJ: Erlbaum.

Wylie, R. C. (1979). *The self-concept.* Lincoln: University of Nebraska Press.

Zajonc, R. B. (1966). *Social psychology: An experimental approach.* Belmont, CA: Brooks/Cole.

Zuckerman, M., & Lubin, B. (1965). *Manual for the Multiple Affect Adjective Check List.* San Diego, CA: Educational and Industrial Testing Service.

READING 15

Delay of Gratification in Children

Walter Mischel, Yuichi Shoda, and Monica L. Rodriguez

Editors' Notes

The issue of self-control, a fundamental problem in self-regulation, is addressed in this selection. The quintessential issue of self-control arises when a short-term temptation threatens the undermining of a more important long-term goal. Common experience tells us that some individuals are better at overcoming temptations than others. The results reported in the present article support that intuition. Children's early ability to delay gratification has a number of important concurrent associations such as intelligence, achievement strivings, and social responsibility. Follow-up studies conducted years later indicate that high delayers of gratification are likely to grow up to be more academically and socially successful than their low-delaying counterparts. These results indicate the importance of the ability to delay gratification in guiding the social development of children. But it is also important to ask how do the high delayers manage to forego immediate rewards for the sake of subsequent, more important ones. The paper provides evidence for a number of successful strategies of delay, including shifting one's attention away from the immediate temptations, self-distraction, and focusing on symbolic or abstract representations of the delayed rewards.

Discussion Questions

1. How do cognitive processes mediate children's ability to delay gratification?
2. What is the psychological process whereby delay of gratification mediates academic and social success?
3. How do children acquire effective delay strategies? What are the implications for improving the lot of disadvantaged children?

Suggested Readings

Baumeister, R. F., & Heatherton, T. F. (1996). Self-regulation failure: An Overview. *Psychological Inquiry, 7,* 1–15.

Klinger, E. (1975). Consequences of commitment to and disengagement from incentives. *Psychological Review, 82,* 1–25.

Mischel, W., Shoda, Y., & Peake, P. K. (1988). The nature of adolescent competencies predicted by preschool delay of gratification. *Journal of Personality and Social Psychology, 54,* 687–699.

Authors' Abstract

To function effectively, individuals must voluntarily postpone immediate gratification and persist in goal-directed behavior for the sake of later outcomes. The present research program analyzed the nature of this type of future-oriented self-control and the psychological processes that underlie it. Enduring individual differences in self-control were found as early as the preschool years. Those 4-year-old children who delayed gratification longer in certain laboratory situations developed into more cognitively and socially competent adolescents, achieving higher scholastic performance and coping better with frustration and stress. Experiments in the same research program also identified specific cognitive and attentional processes that allow effective self-regulation early in the course of development. The experimental results, in turn, specified the particular types of preschool delay situations diagnostic for predicting aspects of congnitive and social competence later in life.

For almost a century, the infant has been characterized as impulse-driven, pressing for tension reduction, unable to delay gratification, oblivious to reason and reality, and ruled entirely by a pleasure principle that demands immediate satisfaction (*1*). The challenge has been to clarify how individuals, while remaining capable of great impulsivity, also become able to control actions for the sake of temporally distant consequences and goals, managing at least sometimes to forgo more-immediate gratifications to take account of anticipated outcomes. The nature of this future-oriented self-control, which develops over time and then coexists with more impetuous behaviors, has intrigued students of development, who have made it central in theories of socialization and in the very definition of the "self" (*2*). Such goal-directed self-imposed delay of gratification is widely presumed to be important in the prevention of serious developmental and mental health problems, including those directly associated with lack of resilience, conduct disorders, low social responsibility, and a variety of addictive and antisocial behaviors (*3–9*).

To explain how people manage to exercise self-control, concepts like "willpower" or "ego strength" are readily invoked, although these terms provide little more than labels for the phenomena to which they point. Some people adhere to difficult diets, or give up cigarettes after years of smoking them addictively, or continue to work and wait for distant goals even when tempted sorely to quit, whereas others fail in such attempts to better regulate themselves in spite of affirming the same initial intentions. Yet the same person who exhibits self-control in one situation may fail to do so in another, even when it appears to be highly similar (*6*). The research program reviewed here addresses the nature of these individual differences, the psychological processes that underlie them, and the conditions in which they may be predictable.

Overview

We review findings on an essential feature of self-regulation: postponing immediately available gratification in order to attain delayed but more valued outcomes. Studies in which 4-year-old children attempt this type of future-oriented self-control reveal that in some laboratory situations individual differences in delay behavior significantly predict patterns of competence and coping assessed more than a decade later (10). Experiments in the same laboratory situations have identified specific cognitive and attentional processes that allow the young child to sustain goal-directed delay of gratification even under difficult, frustrating conditions (11).

We begin with a summary of major individual differences associated with this type of self-regulation early in life, and the long-term developmental outcomes that they predict. Then we examine the specific processes that seem to underlie effective self-imposed delay of gratification in young children, as revealed by the experimental studies. These results, in turn, pointed to the types of preschool delay situations diagnostic for predicting aspects of cognitive and social competence in adolescence. Finally, we consider the development of the child's understanding of self-control and the concurrent links found among components of self-regulation in children with behavioral problems.

Measuring Self-Control: From Choice to Execution

Two complementary methods were used to investigate delay of gratification in the research program reviewed here. Initially preferences for delayed, more valuable versus immediate but less valuable outcomes were studied as choice decisions. In this approach individuals choose under realistic conditions among outcomes that vary in value and in the expected duration of time before they become available. Sets of such choices were given to people from a wide range of sociocultural backgrounds, family structure, and economic circumstances (5, 12). As expected these choices are affected predictably by the anticipated delay time and the subjective value of the alternatives. For example, preferences for delayed rewards decrease when the required time for their attainment increases and increases with the expectation that the delayed outcomes will occur (13, 14). The choice to delay (i) increases with the values of the delayed rewards relative to the immediate ones; (ii) increases with the subject's age; and (iii) is susceptible to a variety of social influences, including the choice behavior and attitudes that other people display (3, 5, 11, 13). Choices to delay were

related significantly to a number of personal characteristics assessed at about the same time. For example, children who tend to prefer delayed rewards also tend to be more intelligent (13), more likely to resist temptation (15), to have greater social responsibility (9, 16), and higher achievement strivings (17). The obtained concurrent associations are extensive, indicating that such preferences reflect a meaningful dimension of individual differences, and point to some of the many determinants and correlates of decisions to delay (18).

As efforts at self-reform so often attest, however, decisions to forgo immediate gratification for the sake of later consequences (for example, by dieting) are readily forgotten or strategically revised when one experiences the frustration of actually having to execute them. Because intentions to practice self-control frequently dissolve in the face of more immediate temptations, it is also necessary to go beyond the study of initial decisions to delay gratification and to examine how young children become able to sustain delay of gratification as they actually try to wait for the outcomes they want. For this purpose, a second method was devised and used to test preschool children in the Stanford University community (19, 20).

In this method, the experimenter begins by showing the child some toys, explaining they will play with them later (so that ending the delay leads to uniform positive consequences). Next, the experimenter teaches a game in which he or she has to leave the room and comes back immediately when the child summons by ringing a bell. Each child then is shown a pair of treats (such as snacks, small toys, or tokens) which differ in value, established through pretesting to be desirable and of age-appropriate interest (for example, one marshmallow versus two; two small cookies versus five pretzels). The children are told that to attain the one they prefer they have to wait until the experimenter returns but that they are free until the waiting period whenever they signal; if they do, however they will get the less preferred object and forgo the other one. The items in the pair are selected to be sufficiently close in value to create a conflict situation for young children between the temptation to stop the delay and the desire to persist for the preferred outcome when the latter requires delay. After children understand the contingency, they are left on their own during the delay period while their behavior is observed unobtrusively, and the duration of their delay is recorded until they terminate or the experimenter returns (typically after 15 minutes). With this method, "self-imposed delay of gratification" was investigated both as a psychological process in experiments that varied relevant features in the delay situation and as a personal characteristic in studies that examined the relation between children's delay behavior and their social and cognitive competencies.

A recent follow-up study of a sample of these children found that those who had waited longer in this situation at 4 years of age were described more than 10 years later by their parents as adolescents who were more academically and socially competent than their peers and more able to cope with frustration and resist temptation. At satistically significant levels, parents saw these children as more verbally fluent and able to express ideas; they used and responded to reason, were attentive and able to concentrate, to plan, and to think ahead, and were competent and skillful. Likewise they were perceived as able to cope and deal with stress more maturely and seemed more self-assured (21, 22). In some variations of this laboratory situation, seconds of delay time in preschool also were significantly related to their Scholastic Aptitude Test (SAT) scores when they applied to college (23). The demonstration of these enduring individual differences in the course of development, as well as the significance attributed to purposeful self-imposed delay of gratification theoretically, underline the need to understand and specify the psychological processes that allow the young child to execute this type of self-regulation in the pursuit of desired outcomes.

Effects of Attention to the Rewards

Theoretical analyses of the delay process have assumed for almost a century that the individual's attention during the delay period is especially important in the development of the ability to delay gratification (1, 24). William James, noting a relation between attention and self-control as early as 1890, contended that attention is the crux of self-control, Beginning with Freud, it has been proposed that attention to the delayed grantifications in thought, mental representation, or anticipation provides the mechanism that allows the young child to bridge the temporal delay required for their

attainment. When children become able to represent the anticipated gratifications mentally, it was reasoned, they become able to delay for them by focusing on these thoughts or fantasies, thereby inhibiting impulsive actions. Some learning theorists also have speculated that the cognitive representation of rewards allows some sort of anticipatory or symbolic covert reinforcement that helps sustain effort and goal-directed behavior while external reinforcement is delayed (11).

In spite of the fact that rewards were given paramount importance in psychological attempts to explain the determinants of behavior, their role in the delay process had remained mostly speculative because of the difficulty of objectively studying thoughts about rewards, particularly in young children. To study how their thinking about the rewards affects self-imposed delay, preschool children in the Stanford University community were assessed in several variations of the self-imposed delay situation described earlier. If thinking about the rewards facilitates delay, then children who are exposed to the rewards or encouraged to think about them should wait longer. The first study varied systematically whether or not the rewards were available for attention while the children were waiting (19). For example, in one condition they waited with both the immediate (less preferred) and the delayed (more preferred) rewards facing them, exposed. In a second condition, both rewards were also present but obscured from sight (covered), and in two other conditions either the delayed reward only or the immediately available reward was exposed during the delay period. The results were the opposite of those the investigators predicted: attention to the rewards consistently and substantially decreased delay time instead of increasing it. Preschool children waited an average of more than 11 minutes when no rewards were exposed, but they waited less than 6 minutes on average when any of the rewards were exposed during delay.

To test the effects of thinking about the rewards more directly, in a second study different types of thoughts were suggested to orient the children's attention with regard to the rewards (20). The results showed that when preschoolers were cued to think about the rewards when waiting, delay time was short, regardless of whether the objects were exposed or covered (Fig. 1). When distracting ("fun") thoughts were suggested, children waited for more than 10 minutes, whether or not the rewards were exposed. On the other hand, when no thoughts were suggested, delay time was greatly reduced by reward exposure, confirming the earlier findings. Distracting thoughts counteracted the strong effects of exposure to the actual rewards, allowing children to wait about as long as they did when the rewards were covered and no thoughts were suggested. In contrast, when the rewards were covered and the children were cued to think about them, the delay time was as short as when the rewards were exposed and no distractions were suggested (25, 26). Thus the original prediction that attention and thought directed to the reward objects would enhance voluntary delay was consistently undermined.

Observation of children's spontaneous behavior during the delay process also suggested that those who were most effective in sustaining delay seemed to avoid looking at the rewards deliberately, for example, covering their eyes with their hands and resting their heads on their arms. Many children generated their own diversions: they talked quietly to themselves, sang, created games with their hands and feet, and even tried to go to sleep during the waiting time. Their attempts to delay gratification seemed to be facilitated by external conditions or by self-directed efforts to reduce their frustration during the delay period by selectively directing their attention and thoughts away from the rewards (11). However, it also seemed unlikely that sheer suppression or distraction from the frustration caused by the situation is the only determinant of this type of self-control. Indeed, when certain types of thoughts are focused

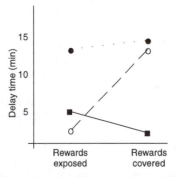

FIGURE 15.1 ■ Average delay time shown by 52 Stanford preschoolers when different types of thoughts were suggested (●, fun thoughts; ■, thoughts about the rewards; O, no thoughts suggested) and the rewards were exposed or covered [based on figure 4 in (20)].

on the rewards they can facilitate self-control substantially, even more than distraction does, as the next set of experiments found.

From Distraction to Abstraction

The results so far show that exposure to the actual rewards or cues to think about them undermine delay, but the studies did not consider directly the possible effects of images or symbolic representations of rewards. Yet it may be these latter types of representation—the images of the outcomes, rather than the rewards themselves—that mediate the young child's ability to sustain delay of gratification (1, 27). To explore this possibility, the effects of exposure to realistic images of the rewards were examined by replicating the experiments on the effects of reward exposure with slide-presented images of the rewards. It was found that although exposure to the agrual rewards during the delay period makes waiting difficult for young children, exposure to images of the rewards had the opposite effect, making it easier. Children who saw images of the rewards they were waiting for (shown life-size on slides) delayed twice as long as those who viewed slides of comparable control objects that were not the rewards for which they were waiting, or who saw blank slides (27). Thus, different modes of presenting rewards (that is, real versus symbolic) may either hinder or enhance self-control.

To test more directly the effects of the cognitive representations of rewards on delay behavior, preschool children were taught to transform "in their heads" the stimuli present during delay (real rewards or pictures of them) by turning real rewards into pictures and pictures into real rewards in their imagination (28). How the children represented the rewards cognitively was a much more potent determinant of their delay behavior than the actual reward stimulus that they were facing. For example, children facing pictures of the rewards delayed almost 18 minutes, but they waited less than 6 minutes when they pretended that the real rewards, rather than the pictures, were in front of them. Likewise, even when facing the real rewards they waited almost 18 minutes when they imagined the rewards as if they were pictures.

This pattern of results may reflect two different aspects of reinforcing (rewarding) stimuli that, in turn, may have completely different effects on self-control behavior. Consistent with earlier work (29), we hypothesized that stimuli can be represented both in an arousing (consummatory) and in an abstract (nonconsummatory) informative manner. In an arousing representation, the focus is on the motivating, "hot" qualities of the stimulus that tend to elicit completion of the action sequence associated with it, such as eating a food or playing with a toy. In an abstract representation the focus is on the more informative, "cool," symbolic aspects of the stimulus, for example, as in a cue or reminder of the contingency or reason for delaying the action sequence associated with it (30).

Specifically, it was suggested to one group of children that they could focus their thoughts on the arousing qualities of the rewards (such as the pretzel's crunchy, salty taste), and to another group of children that they could focus on the reward's abstract qualities and association (by thinking about pretzel sticks, for example, as long, thin brown logs). Two other groups were given the same type of suggestions as to how they could think while waiting, but directed at comparable control objects that were not the rewards (Fig. 2). When encouraged to focus on the abstract qualities of the rewards children waited an average of more than 13 minutes but they waited less than 5 minutes when the same type of thoughts were directed at the comparable objects that were not the rewards, suggesting that the abstract representation of the actual reward objects provides more than just distraction.

The longest mean delay time (almost 17 minutes) occurred when the suggested thoughts were also about control objects but with regard to their arousing qualities (for example, children waiting for marshmallows who had been cued to think about the salty, crunchy taste of pretzels). Thus, while hot ideation about the rewards made delay difficult, such ideation directed at comparable objects that are not the reward on which one is waiting may provide very good distraction. The results support the view that attention to the rewards may have either a facilitating or an interfering effect on the duration of delay, depending on whether the focus is arousing or abstract.

The experimental results, taken collectively, help specify how young children can become able to sustain self-imposed delay gratification for substantial periods. Delay is difficult for the preschooler when the rewards are exposed, unless distractions are provided or self-generated. Suggestions to think about the rewards or attention to them, can facilitate or interfere with delay, depending on whether the rewards are represented in ways that lead to a focus on their arousing or abstract features. An abstract focus on the rewards can help self-imposed delay even more than comparable distractions; an arousing focus makes delay exceedingly difficult. How the child represents the rewards congnitively in this regard, rather than whether they are exposed physically or as images, crucially influences the duration of delay.

Preschool Delay Conditions for Predicting Long-Term Developmental Outcomes

On the basis of the experimental research reviewed so far, it also becomes possible to specify the types of preschool delay conditions in which the child's behavior will be more likely to predict relevant long-term developmental outcomes. The significant links noted earlier between delay of gratification at age 4 years and adolescent competence did not take account of the particular delay conditions. When the rewards are exposed, delay becomes highly frustrative for preschoolers, so that to sustain their goal-directed waiting they must use effective strategies, for example, by distracting themselves or by representing the rewards cognitively in an abstract, "cool" way. When preschoolers are not given strategies for sustain-

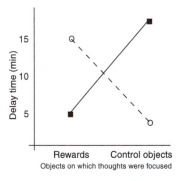

FIGURE 15.2 ■ Delay time as a function of objects on which thoughts were focused (rewards versus comparable control objects) and type of cognitive representation in thoughts [arousing (■) versus abstract (O)]. All 48 Stanford preschool children were facing the exposed rewards [data are from table 1 in (30)].

ing delay but the rewards are exposed, they must generate and execute such strategies on their own to delay, and therefore their behavior should reveal most clearly individual differences in this type of competence. To the degree that this ability is stable and has enduring consequences for adaptation, we expected that preschool delay time when the rewards are exposed and no strategies are suggested would be diagnostic for predicting relevant developmental outcomes. In contrast, when the rewards are obscured, delay behavior was not expected to reflect children's ability to generate effective self-control strategies because that situation does not require the use of such strategies.

These expectations were supported in another follow-up study of the Stanford preschool children, in which we increased the sample of respondents so that the role of conditions could be analyzed in relation to long-term outcomes (23). To obtain a more objective measure of cognitive academic competences and school-related achievements in adolescence, we also included Scholastic Aptitude Test (SAT) scores. In conditions in which the rewards were exposed and no strategies were supplied, those children who delayed longer as preschoolers were rated in adolescence by their parents as significantly more attentive and able to concentrate, competent, planful, and intelligent. They also were seen as more able to pursue goals and to delay gratification, better in self-control, more able to resist temptation, to tolerate frustration, and to cope maturely with stress. Beyond parental ratings, in the same conditions SAT scores were available for 35 children, and both their verbal and quantitative SAT scores were significantly higher related to seconds of preschool delay time. The linear regression slope predicting SAT verbal scores from seconds of preschool delay time was 0.10 with a standard error of 0.04; for predicting SAT quantitative scores, the slope was 0.13 with a standard error of 0.03. The correlations were 0.42 for SAT verbal scores and 0.57 for SAT quantitative scores. In contrast, individual differences in delay behavior when the rewards were obscured did not reliably predict either parental ratings or SAT performance.

The significant correlations between preschool delay time and adolescent outcomes, spanning more than a decade, were relatively large compared to the typically low or negligible associations found when single measures of social behavior are used to predict other behaviors, especially over a long developmental period (6). On the other hand, although the obtained significant associations are at a level that rivals many found between performances on intelligence tests repeated over this age span (31, 32), most of the variance still remains unexplained. The small size of the SAT sample dictates special caution in these comparisons and underlines the need for replications, especially with other populations and at different ages.

As previously noted, preschool delay time in the diagnostic condition was significantly related not only to academic abilities of the sort assessed by the SAT but also to other indices of competence. Even after statistically controlling for SAT scores, preschoolers who had delayed longer were later rated by parents as more able to cope with a number of social and personal problems, suggesting that the relation between preschool delay time and later parental judgments is not completely attributable to school-related competencies as measured by the SAT.

The causal links and mediating mechanisms underlying these long-term associations necessarily remain speculative, allowing many different interpretations. For example, an early family environment in which self-imposed delay is encouraged and modeled also may nurture other types of behavior that facilitate the acquisition of social and cognitive skills, study habits, or attitudes which may be associated with obtaining higher scores on the SAT and more positive ratings by parents. It also seems reasonable, however, that children will have a distinct advantage beginning early in life if they use effective self-regulatory strategies to reduce frustration in situations in which self-imposed delay is required to attain desired goals. By using these strategies to make self-control less frustrating, these children can more easily persist in their efforts, becoming increasingly competent as they develop.

Of course, the self-regulatory strategies that have been described are not the only ones useful for sustaining goal-directed delay and effort. The particular strategies required depend on the type of delay situation, for example, self-imposed versus externally imposed delay (26). During the delay process children may use a variety of strategies, including self-instructions, rehearsal of the specific contingencies for goal attainment while avoiding an arousing focus on the rewards themselves, and self-monitoring of progress (11). Related research in variations of the delay of gratification situation with young children showed the value for self-control of specific, carefully rehearsed and elaborated plans for inhibiting temptations to terminate goal-directed efforts (33). Such plans are used spontaneously, in varying degree, even by preschool children. Similar self-regulatory strategies have been identified in research on the acquisition of cognitive skills for mastery of other tasks requiring self-control, like reading (34) and impulse inhibition (35). It is also plausible that the specific competencies necessary for effective self-regulation are a component of a larger ability or set of abilities involving both cognitive and social knowledge and skill. Whereas self-regulatory competencies in the pursuit of goals are not even considered as a factor in traditional conceptions and tests of intelligence (36), they are directly relevant to more recent attempts to devise a theory of social intelligence that integrates findings from cognitive, social, and developmental psychology to thoroughly reconstruct the analysis of intelligent behavior (37).

The Development of Knowledge about Effective Self-Regulatory Strategies

In the course of development, children show increasing understanding and awareness of the strategies that facilitate various kinds of self-control. In a sample of middle-class children in the Stanford community, from preschool through grade six, the children's knowledge of the strategies that might help during the delay process were assessed (38). The overall results indicate that 4-year-olds often prefer the least effective strategies for self-imposed delay, thereby inadvertently making self-control exceedingly difficult for themselves. For example, they significantly prefer to expose the rewards during the delay period and to think about them (for example, "because it makes me feel good"), thus defeating their own effort to wait. Within a year, most children understand and choose more effective strategies. They soon prefer to obscure the temptations and consistently reject arousing thoughts about them as a strategy for self-control. At that age many begin to recognize the problem of increased temptation produced by thinking about the arousing attributes of the rewards and try to self-distract ("just sing a song"). They also start to see the value of self-instructions, focusing on the contingency and reiterating it ("I'll wait, so

I can get the two marshmallows instead of one" or "I'll say, 'do not ring the bell.' . . . If you ring the bell and the teacher comes in, I'll just get that once." The self-control rule that does not seem to become available until some time between the third and sixth grades requires recognition of the value of abstract rather than arousing thoughts, suggesting possible links between the development of this type of understanding and the child's achieving operational thought in the Piagetian sense (39).

Extensions to Older Children at Risk

The research described so far specified some of the strategies that facilitate delay experimentally and summarized the development of children's growing knowledge and understanding of those strategies. However, the links between children's knowledge of effective strategies, their spontaneous use of such strategies when attempting to control themselves in the pursuit of delayed goals, and their success in sustaining delay remained unexamined. The delay process in older children with behavior problems, such as aggressiveness, conduct disorders, or hyperactivity, has been surprisingly unstudied, although these are the very individuals for whom effective attention deployment and sustained delay of gratification are assumed to be especially difficult (40). So far, research on delay of gratification has concentrated on preschool children without known developmental risks. Therefore, a recent study extended the delay paradigm to a population of older children, described as having a variety of social adjustment difficulties, such as aggressiveness and withdrawal (41).

In this sample, ages 6 to 12 years, assessed in a summer residential treatment facility, children's knowledge of self-control processes was significantly correlated with duration of their self-imposed delay. For example, those who knew that an abstract rather than an arousing representation would make waiting easier also delayed longer. Similarly, the children's spontaneous attention deployment during the delay period was significantly related to their actual delay time: as the delay increased, those who were able to sustain self-control spent a higher proportion of the time distracting themselves from the frustrative situation than did those who terminated earlier. Even when controlling statistically for the effects of verbal intelligence, the relations among knowledge of self-control, spontaneous use of effective delay strategies, and duration of delay remained significant. In addition, those individuals who scored higher on these indices of self-control in the delay situation, especially when the rewards were exposed, also were rated as significantly less aggressive throughout the summer (42). The overall findings obtained with older children at risk indicate that the cognitive attentional strategies that allow effective delay of gratification, as identified in the earlier experiments, also seem to be used spontaneously by individuals who delay longer.

Summary

Taken collectively, the results from the research programs we reviewed specify some of the cognitive processes that underlie this type of delay of gratification early in life. Whether or not attention to the rewards, or distraction from them, is the better strategy for sustaining self-control depends on how the rewards are represented cognitively. A focus on their arousing features makes self-control exceedingly difficult; a focus on their more abstract, informative features has the opposite effects. Moreover, the type of cognitive representation generated can overcome, and reverse, the effects of exposure to the rewards themselves.

Significant links were found between self-control behavior as measured in this paradigm and relevant social and cognitive outcomes years later. The experimental research allowed identification of the conditions in which these long-term relations were most clearly visible. The child's spontaneous understanding of effective self-regulatory strategies also was found to develop in a clear age related sequence. Finally, delay of gratification in the same paradigm with older children at risk showed the expected concurrent relations to knowledge of effective self-control strategies and spontaneous attention deployment while trying to exercise self-control. An unanswered question now is whether or not teaching delay of gratification skills and strategies of the sort identified to those who lack them, early in life, would in fact reduce later developmental risks such as school failure. Postponing gratification sometimes may be an unwise choice, but unless individuals have the competencies necessary to sustain delay when they want to do so, the choice itself is lost.

REFERENCES AND NOTES

1. S. Freud, *Collected Papers* (Basic Books, New York, 1959), vol. 4, pp. 13–2.1.
2. S. Harcer, in *Handbook of Child Psychology*, P. H. Mussen, Ed. (Wiley, New York, 1983), vol. 4, pp. 275–385.
3. A. Bandura and W. Mischel, *J. Pers, Soc. Psychol* 2, 698 (1965).
4. A. Bandura, *Social Foundations of Thought and Action: A Social-Cognitive Theory* (Prentice-Hall, Englewood Cliffs, NJ, 1986).
5. W. Mischel, *Progess in Experimental and Personality Research, B, Maher, Ed.* (Academic Press, San Diego, CA 1966); vol. 3, pp. 85–132.
6. W. Mischel, *Personality and Assessment* (Wiley, New York, 1968).
7. ———, *Introduction to Personality: A New Look* (Holt, Rinehart & Winston, New York, ed. 4, 1986).
8. M. Rutter, *Am. J. Orthopsychiatry* 57, 316 (1987).
9. J. S. Strumphauzer, *J. Pers. Soc. Psychol* 21, 10 (1972).
10. W. Mischel, Y. Shoda, P. K. Peake, *ibid* 54, 687 (1988).
11. W. Mischel, in *Advances in Experimental Social Psychology*, L. Berkowitz, Ed. (Academic Press, New York, 1974), vol. 7, pp. 249–292.
12. S. L. Klincberg, *J. Soc. Pers. Psychol.* 8, 253 (1968); L. Mclilcian. *J. Soc. Psychol* 50, 81 (1959); T. Graves, *Southerest. J. Anthsopol.* 23, 337 (1967).
13. W. Mischel and R. Metzner, *J. Abnorm. Soc. Psychol.* 64, 425 (1962).
14. W. Mischel and E. Staub, *J. Pers. Soc. Psychol*, 2, 625 (1965).
15. W. Mischel and C. Gilligan, *J. Abnorm. Soc. Psychol.* 69, 411 (1964).
16. W. Mischel, *ibid* 62, 1 (1961).
17. ———, *ibid*, p. 543.
18. Researchers in other areas, beyond the scope of the present article, have pursued somewhat parallel problems in self-control. In one direction, a large operant conditioning literature has investigated self-control in lower organisms by using analogous situations to those in the present article. Typically, a pigeon in a Skinner box has to choose among alternatives varying in the amount and delay of the reinforcer. This research indicates that organisms sharply discount future rewards as a function of the temporal distance from the time of choice [G. W. Ainslie, *Psychol. Bull.* 82, 463 (1975); A. W. Logue, *Brain Behav. Sci.* 4, 665 (1988); A. W. Logue, M. L. Rodriguez, T. E. Pena-Correal, K. Mauro, *J. Exper. Anim. Behav.* 41, 53 (1984); H. Rachlin and L. Green, *ibid* 17, 15 (1972); H. Rachlin, A. W. Logue, I. Gibbon, M. Frankel, *Psychol Rev.* 93, 33 (1986); M. L. Rodriguez and A. W. Logue, *J. Exp. Psychol. Anim. Behav. Proc.* 14, 105 (1988)]. Preference for a small, immediate reward, over a larger, more delayed one, reverts as the time between choice and delay of rewards increases (Rachlin and Green, above, Logue, Rodriguez, Pena-Correal, Manro, above). Moreover, by using analog to the self-imposed delay of gratification situation described in this article, parallel results also were reported with pigeons [J. Grosch and A. Neuringer. *J. Exp. Anim. Behav.* 35, 3 (1981)]. In a second direction, economists have studied how delayed outcomes affect economic decisions and savings behavior of humans, again with interesting par-

allels to the research reported here [I. Fisher, The Theory of Interest (Macmillan, London, 1930); H. M. Shefrin and R. H. Thaler, *Ecom.* Inq. 26, 609 (1988)].

19. W. Mischel and E. B. Ebbesen, *J. Pers. Soc. Psychol.* 16, 329. (1970).

20. —A. R. Zeiss, *ibid.* 21, 204 (1972).

21. W. Mischel, Y. Shoda, P. K. Peake, *ibid* 54, 687 (1988).

22. Studies following children's development over many years, using other measures of self-control requiring different types of delay of gratification, also found evidence of enduring psychological qualities [D. C. Funder, J. H. Block, J. Block, *J. Pers. Soc. Psychol.* 44, 1198 (1983)]. The particular qualities, however, depend on the specific type of delay behaviors sampled [see Table 5 in (21) for comparisons of long-term correlates obtained].

23. Y. Shoda, W. Mischel, P. K. Peake, in preparation.

24. W. James, *Principles of Psychology* (Holt, New York, 1890).

25. When the rewards were exposed, children cued to think about fun did not differ significantly from those who faced the covered rewards with no thoughts suggested or who were cued to think about fun. Delay time also was not significantly different for children waiting with the rewards exposed when no thoughts were suggested and those cued to think about the rewards.

26. When children waited in a similar self-imposed delay situation they also estimated the delay to be longer when the reward was present physically, supporting the interpretation that exposure to the rewards in this situation increases frustration (D. T. Miller and R. Karniel, *J. Pers Soc. Psychol* 34, 310 (1976)].

27. W. Mischel and B. Moore, *ibid* 28, 172 (1973).

28. B. Moore, W. Mischel, A. Zeise, *ibid*, 34, 419 (1976).

29. D. Berlyne, *Conflict, Arousal and Curiosity* (McGraw-Hill, New York, 1960).

30. W. Mischel and N. Baker. *J. Pers. Soc. Psychol.* 31, 254 (1975).

31. B. S. Bloom, *Stability and Change in Human Characteristics* (Wiley, New York, 1964).

32. M. P. Honzik, J. W. Macfarlane, L. Allen, *J. Exp. Educ.* 17, 309 (1948).

33. W. Mischel and C. J. Patterson in *Minnesota Symposium on Child Psychology*, W. A. Collins, Ed. (Erlbaum, Hillsdale, NJ, 1978). vol. 11, pp. 199–230.

34. A. L. Brown and J. S. DeLoache, in *Children's Thinking: What Develops?* R. S. Sieglet, Ed. (Erlbaum, Hillsdale, NJ, 1978). pp. 3–25; A. L. Brown, J. D. Bransford, R. A. Ferrara, J. C. Campione, in *Handbook of Child Psychology*, P. H. Mussen, Ed. (Wiley, New York, 1983), vol. 3, pp. 77–166.

35. D. H. Meichenbaum and J. Goodman, *J. Ab. Psychol.* 77, 115 (1971).

36. R. J. Sternberg and D. K. Detterman, Eds., *What Is Intelligence? Contemporary Viewpoints* (Ablet, Norwood, NJ, 1986).

37. N. Cantor and J. F. Kihlstrom, *Personality and Social Intelligence* (Prencice-Hall, Englewood Cliffs, NJ, 1987).

38. H. N. Mischel and W. Mischel, *Child Dev.* 54, 603 (1983).

39. J. Piaget and B. Inhelder, *L'image Mentale Chez l'Enfant* (Presses Universitaires de France, Paris, 1966).

40. D. M. Ross and S. A. Ross, *Hyperactivity: Current Issues, Research and Theory* (Wiley, New York, 1982).

41. M. L. Rodriguez, W. Mischel, Y. Shoda, *J. Pers, Soc. Psychol.*, in press.

42. M. L. Rodriguez, Y. Shoda, W. Mischel, J. Wright, "Delay of gratification and children's social behavior in natural settings," paper presented at the Eastern Psychological Association, Boston, March 1989.

43. Although more reviewers than can be thanked here provided constructive criticism on earlier drafts, we are especially grateful to J. Hochberg and H. Zukier who were exceptionally generous with their time and commentary.

READING 16

Goals: An Approach to Motivation and Achievement

Elaine S. Elliott and Carol S. Dweck • Harvard University

Editors' Notes

Whereas some persons are more successful than others, probably all people fail sometimes in their lives at some activity. A person who is good at academic pursuits is not necessarily a successful athlete and vice versa. A person who does very well at business pursuits is not necessarily invariably successful in her or his interpersonal relations. Thus, failure is a seemingly inseparable feature of the human predicament, and the ability to cope with failure is invaluable. The present selection examines the cognitive and motivational attributes of persons who cope well versus those who do poorly with the experience of failure. As the results indicate, much of it has to do with the goals persons adopt. If the goal is to shine in one's performance, failure can be devastating. On the other hand, if the goal is to improve one's ability at a task, failure is perceived as a challenge that can encourage further mobilization of efforts and the judicious choice of strategies. Compared to a performance goal, a learning goal induces minimal negative affect from failure. These findings suggest that failure in and of itself does not produce unique psychological effects. Rather, its effects depend on what the task goals were to begin with.

Discussion Questions

1. Discuss the relation between adopting a performance goal and exhibiting the learned helplessness syndrome.
2. How did the experimenter induce the learning and performance goals in participants?
3. To what do children with performance goals attribute their failure? What are the attributes of children with learning goals?

4. How can one instill in children performance or learning goals? There are clear advantages of learning goals. Can you think of any advantages of adopting performance goals?

Suggested Readings

Dweck, C. S., Chiu, C., & Hong, Y. (1995). Implicit theories and their role in judgments and reactions: A world from two perspectives. *Psychological Inquiry, 6,* 267–285.

Gollwitzer, P. M., & Wicklund, R. A. (1985a). Self-symbolizing and the neglect of others' perspectives. *Journal of Personality and Social Psychology, 48,* 702–715.

Rhodewalt, F. (1994). Conceptions of ability, achievement goals, and individual differences in self-handicapping behavior: On the application of implicit theories. *Journal of Personality, 62,* 67–85.

Authors' Abstract

This study tested a framework in which goals are proposed to be central determinants of achievement patterns. Learning goals, in which individuals seek to increase their competence, were predicted to promote challenge-seeking and a mastery-oriented response to failure regardless of perceived ability. Performance goals, in which individuals seek to gain favorable judgments of their competence or avoid negative judgments, were predicted to produce challenge-avoidance and learned helplessness when perceived ability was low and to promote certain forms of risk-avoidance even when perceived ability was high. Manipulations of relative goal value (learning vs. performance) and perceived ability (high vs. low) resulted in the predicted differences on measures of task choice, performance during difficulty, and spontaneous verbalizations during difficulty. Particularly striking was the way in which the performance goal-low perceived ability condition produced the same pattern of strategy deterioration, failure attribution, and negative affect found in naturally occurring learned helplessness. Implications for theories of motivation and achievement are discussed.

Past research (Diener & Dweck, 1978, 1980) documented and described two strikingly different reactions to failure. Despite previous success on a task, children displaying the "helpless" response quickly began to attribute their failures to low ability, to display negative affect, and to show marked deterioration in performance. In contrast, those with the mastery-oriented response did not focus on failure attributions; instead, they exhibited solution-oriented self-instructions, as well as sustained or increased positive affect and sustained or improved performance.

Although the research has clearly demonstrated these different patterns, the question that remains unanswered is why two groups of children who are completely equal in ability would react to failure in such discrepant ways—that is, why do helpless children react as though they have received

an indictment of their ability, but mastery-oriented children react as though they have been given useful feedback about learning and mastery. These findings suggested that helpless and mastery-oriented children are pursuing different goals in achievement situations, with helpless children seeking to document their ability (but failing to do so) and mastery-oriented children seeking to increase their ability (and receiving information on how to do so).

The purpose of our study was to experimentally test the hypothesis that different goals set up the observed helpless and mastery-oriented patterns.

Specifically, we propose that there are two major goals that individuals pursue in achievement situations: (a) performance goals, in which individuals seek to maintain positive judgments of their ability and avoid negative judgments by seeking to prove, validate, or document their ability and not discredit it; and (b) learning goals, in which individuals seek to increase their ability or master new tasks (Nicholls & Dweck, 1979). It is hypothesized that performance goals, which focus individuals on the adequacy of their ability, will render them vulnerable to the helpless response in the face of failure, setting up low ability attributions, negative affect, and impaired performance. In contrast, it is hypothesized that learning goals, which focus individuals on increasing their ability over time, will promote the mastery-oriented response to obstacles, strategy formulation, positive affect, and sustained performance.

To elaborate, one may view each goal as generating its own set of concerns and as creating its own framework for processing incoming information. Individuals who pursue performance goals are concerned with the measurement of their ability and can be seen as posing the question, Is my ability adequate? Subsequent events, such as failure outcomes, may be seen as providing information that is relevant to this question, leading some individuals (particularly those who may already doubt their ability) to low ability attributions and their sequelae.

In contrast, individuals who pursue learning goals are concerned with developing their ability over time and can be seen as posing the question, How can I best acquire this skill or master this task? Subsequent events, such as failure outcomes, may then provide information that is relevant to this question, leading individuals to alter their strategies or escalate their efforts. Here, even individuals with poor opinions of their current ability should display the mastery-oriented pattern, because (a) they are not focused on judgments of their current ability, (b) errors are not as indicative of goal failure within a learning goal, and (c) low current ability in a valued area may make skill acquisition even more desirable.

The specific hypotheses of our study are depicted in Table 1. It is predicted that when goals (performance or learning) and perceptions of current ability level (low or high) are induced experimentally, the following patterns will result: (a) Performance goals and high perceived ability will allow a mastery-oriented response (but will lead subjects to sacrifice learning opportunities that involve the risk of errors), (b) performance goals and low perceived ability will create the helpless response, and (c) learning goals and either high or low perceived ability will result in the mastery-oriented response to failure.

How, more specifically, might the performance goal-low perceived ability condition act to create debilitation? What are the particular mechanisms through which impairment occurs? Although these factors are not tested separately here, we suggest that this condition can in itself generate many of the different congitive and affective factors that have been found to be associated with performance disruption during difficulty: (a) low ability attributions that lead to a loss of belief in the utlity of effort (e.g., Ames, 1984; Diener & Dweck, 1978; Dweck, 1975); (b) defensive withdrawal of effort, given that continued effort may further document low ability (e.g., Frankl & Snyder, 1978; Leggett,

TABLE 16.1. Summary of Goals and Predicted Achievement Patterns

Goal value	Confidence (perceived level of ability*)	Predicted achievement pattern	
		Task choice	Response to difficulty
Performance goal is highlighted	High	Sacrifice learning and choose moderate or moderately difficult task to display competance	Mastery-orientation of effective problem solving
	Low	Sacrifice learning and choose moderately easy task to avoid display of incompetence	Learned-helpless response of deterioration in problem solving and negative affect
Learning goal is highlighted	High or low	Choose learning at risk of displaying mistakes to increase competence	Mastery-orientation of effective problem solving

*A distinction is made between perceived current ability (perceived level of current skill) and potential ability (perceived capacity to acquire new skills). Perceived current ability was manipulated to be high or low. Perceived potential ability was manipulated to be high and constant across all conditions.

1986; Nicholls, 1976, 1984; (c) worry about goal failure that can divert attention from the task (e.g., Spielberger, Morris, & Liebert, 1968; Wine, 1971, 1982); (d) negative affect, such as anxiety or shame, that can motivate escape attempts (e.g., Weiner, 1972, 1982); and (e) blockage of intrinsic rewards from task involvement, solution-oriented effort, or even progress, due to threatened negative judgment (Deci & Ryan, 1980; Lepper, 1980; Lepper & Greene, 1978). Thus, *goal* may be a construct that organizes these previously distinct congnitive and affective factors and helps us to understand the conditions under which they arise.

The focus of individuals who pursue learning goals (whether they believe their ability to be high or low) is on improving ability over time, not on proving current ability. As noted, obstacles will not as readily be seen to imply goal failure and will, therefore, not require defensive maneuvers, not as readily generate anxiety, and not detract from the intrinsic rewards shown to derive from involvement and progress on a valued task.

Method

Overview

There were four experimental contrasts: feedback that the child's current skill level on the experimental task was either low or high was crossed with task instructions that highlighted the value of either a performance (look competent) or a learning (increase competence) goal.

Children's beliefs about their current level of skill on the experimental task were manipulated via feedback on a pattern recognition task. Half the children were told that this task revealed that they currently had high ability and half were told that they currently had low ability for the experimental task. All were told that they had the capacity to acquire new knowledge or skills from the task.

In the second part of the study, another experimenter, who was unaware of the child's ability feedback, gave instructions that highlighted (relatively) either a learning or a performance goal (i.e., high value for learning and moderate value for performance vs. high value for performance and moderate value for learning). Half the children were assigned to each of the goal value conditions.

There were three dependent variables: choice

of tasks, performance during difficulty, and spontaneous verbalizations during difficulty. All children were given a choice of tasks, each embodying one goal: (a) one described as a learning task (i.e., continued risks of mistakes and confusion during the acquisition process, but the task would promote skill development); and (b) another described as a performance task (i.e., nothing new would be learned, but the task would allow one to display or avoid display of one's skills by choice of three difficulty levels). In fact, all were given the same discrimination task, which was designed to allow comparison of groups on effectiveness of problem-solving strategies and on spontaneous verbalizations (e.g. attributions, expression of positive or negative affect, etc.).

Predictions for each of the experimental groups are summarized in Table 1.

Participants

The participants were 101 fifth-grade children (57 girls and 44 boys) from semirural schools. Roughly equal numbers of subjects had been randomly assigned to conditions, but due to time limits imposed by the school's schedules, several sessions could not be completed, resulting in unequal cell sizes: 15 girls and 12 boys in the learning goal-low ability condition, 14 girls and 10 boys in the learning goal-high ability condition, 13 girls and 10 boys in the performance goal-low ability condition, and 15 girls and 12 boys in the performance goal-high ability condition.

An additional 9 girls and 8 boys and 15 girls and 14 boys participated in the first and second pilot study, respectively.

Tasks and Procedures

Tasks and procedures for manipulating ability perceptions. A pattern recognition task adapted from Glanzer, Huttenlocher, and Clark (1963) was used to manipulate perceptions of ability. Each stimulus consisted of some combination of five geometric forms drawn in yellow or blue on a card. The subject was shown a card for 2 s and was then asked to recognize the pattern from among three alternative cards. Each subject was administered 10 cards. This task was sufficiently complex so that subjects were unsure of the correctness of their responses. This allowed the tester to give predetermined feedback on performance.

The experimenter instructed the children that their performance would indicate how good they presently were at this type of work and explained the details of the task. To ensure that children who would be receiving high ability feedback did not attribute their performances to good luck, children were told that even the kinds of guesses they made would indicate how they would do on the later work. Children were randomly assigned to the low and high ability feedback conditions.

All children were told that they had the capacity to acquire knowledge from the tasks to be presented by the experimenter. This was done in order to ensure that all children had high confidence in their ability to learn. Hence, if children sacrificed learning, it would be known that sacrifice of learning did not come from low confidence in learning. It could also be shown that learned helplessness occurs with the presence of a performance goal despite high confidence in ability to learn. In other words, a strong case is made if the learning option has a high expectancy and moderately high value (i.e., if there is a good alternative and it is not taken and not kept in mind for mastery purposes).

Tasks and procedures for highlighting goal value. After the children were given the instructions described above, the first experimenter introduced the second experimenter to the children and left the room with her materials. The next experimenter was blind to the children's ability condition. She presented all children with two boxes, one described as containing the learning task and the other described as containing the performance task with its three levels of difficulty; moderately easy, moderate, and moderately difficult. The identical discrimination task had been placed in both boxes.

The presentation of the boxes was counterbalanced. (Differences between goal value manipulations are described below.) All children were given the following description of the tasks in the two boxes.

Performance task. In this box we have problems of different levels. Some are hard, some are easier. If you pick this box, although you won't learn new things, it will really show me what kids can do.

Learning task. If you pick the task in this box, you'll probably learn a lot of new things. But you'll probably make a bunch of mistakes, get a little confused, maybe feel a little dumb at times—but eventually you'll learn some useful things.

Under conditions that highlighted the value of the performance goal, children were told that their performance was being filmed and would be normatively evaluated by experts. It was assumed that the filming instructions would make the value of displaying competence high and that the general description of the learning task would make the value of increasing competence moderate.

Under conditions that highlighted the value of the learning goal, no film was mentioned. In addition to the general description of the learning task, children were told that the learning task might be a big help in school, because it "sharpens the mind" and learning to do it well could help their studies. It was assumed that this added information about the learning task would make the value of increasing competence high and that the mere presence of the experimenter would make the value of displaying competence moderate.

As can be seen, we made both goals available in each condition rather than presenting one goal per condition. This was done to mimic realworld choices in which the two goals are valued and available, and in which individuals must sacrifice one goal as a result of high value on the other. That is, the learning goal leads individuals to risk performance failure and the performance goal makes individuals sacrifice learning opportunities.

Procedures for measuring dependent variables. There were three dependent variables; task choice, problem-solving effectiveness during the discrimination task, and spontaneous verbalizations during the discrimination task.

Children's task choice preferences were taken after the manipulation of the goal. To ensure that children felt no demand from the experimenter to choose a particular task, children were told that different children like to choose different tasks and that she was only interested in what tasks children choose.

After children indicated preferences, all worked on the same discrimination task, which was found in both the learning and the performance boxes. For those who chose the learning box, instructions for the discrimination task were given immediately. For those who chose the performance task, the three levels were reviewed and the children were asked to indicate their two preferences. All children who chose the performance task were then given the "moderate" task, which could be presented as consonant with their choice in that it was either one of their two choices or could be described as the average of their two choices. This allowed comparison of the experimental groups when subjects believed that they were performing a task that allowed inferences about ability.

The discrimination task, used to measure problem-solving effectiveness and spontaneous verbalizations, was adopted from Diener and Dweck (1978). Each child was presented with four training problems and three test problems. A problem consisted of a deck of cards with each card displaying two figures that varied on three dimensions; color (e.g., red or blue), form (e.g., square or triangle), and symbol in the center of the form (e.g., dot or star, see Figure 1). At the beginning of each new deck of cards the experimenter named each of the six stimulus values and told the child only one was correct for the entire deck. Children pointed to the left or right figure and the experimenter said "correct" if the figure contained the stimulus value that was chosen for the deck.

To monitor hypothesis testing on Training Problems 3 and 4 and all test problems, the children received feedback about the correctness of their responses on every fourth card (Levine, 1966). A hypothesis was defined as the consistent selection of a particular stimulus property, such as the color red, over four trials prior to feedback. The cards were varied in a systematic fashion so that the child's hypothesis about the correct solution could be inferred unambiguously from his or her pattern of choices of the left or right side. For example, a child who is testing the hypothesis, "triangle," would choose cards in the sequence of left, left, right, left, as can be seen in Figure 1.

On the fourth training problem, the children were asked to begin "thinking out loud" (see Diener & Dweck, 1978) when they worked on the problems. They were told that we were interested in what kinds of things children think about while they do tasks of this nature. To dispel inhibitions about making task irrelevant statements, it was stressed that children think about many different kinds of things.

Because one goal of the study was to examine the effects of failure feedback on problem-solving strategies during the testing, rather than to test children's hypothesis use per se, each child was given extensive training prior to the test problems. The experimenter repeated a training problem until the child reached a criterion of six successive correct responses. A hint was provided each time the training deck was repeated (e.g., "The correct

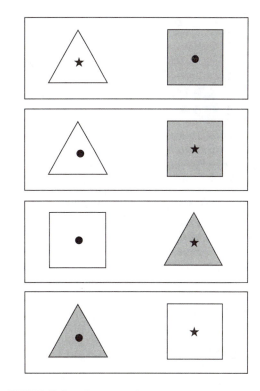

FIGURE 16.1 ■ Example of four consecutive stimulus cards that allowed the tracking of a hypothesis over the no-feedback trials.

answer is one of the two shapes, either the square or triangle.")

On the three test problems, the child received feedback after every fourth response and was asked to verbalize his or her thoughts. Each of the three test decks was gone through only once. This allowed the children to search for the solution but ensured that, given their strategy level, they would not have tested all possible solutions. The feedback always consisted of "wrong," thus permitting the monitoring of strategy change following continued failure feedback.

Children were very carefully debriefed to make sure that all left feeling proud of their performance. The second experimenter told them that they certainly did very well on her tasks. She also said that sometimes children who do poorly on the first task really do show a lot of talent, that it does not always indicate how well children will do. She added that because they had done such good work, she had even put in some problems that were intended for older children.

TABLE 16.2. Ability and Goal Value Manipulations

Pilot question	Manipulation	M	df	t
Right now, how good do you think you are on these tasks?	High present ability feedback Low present ability feedback	5.33 4.37	15	2.04**
How good do you think you'll be at learning new things, developing new skills from these tasks?	High present ability feedback Low present ability feedback	5.00 5.12	15	.23
How important is it to you that I (experimenter)/experts think your work is good?	High evaluation Moderate evaluation	5.40 4.54	27	1.83**
How important is it to you that you learn new things and develop new abilities from these tasks?	High skill utility instruction Moderate skill utility instruction	6.23 5.40	27	1.54*

*$p<.10$. **$p<.05$.

Two pilot studies were run to ensure the effectiveness of the ability manipulation and goal value manipulation. The pilot questions and results are presented in Table 2.

Results

Pilot Studies

Pilot Studies 1 and 2 revealed that the ability and the goal value manipulations were effective (Table 2).

Choice of Tasks

The number of children in each of the four conditions who chose the learning and the performance box was analyzed by means of a chi-square test. As expected, no significant effect was found for ability feedback. The data were collapsed across ability and a chi-square test was performed on the number of children who chose either the learning or the performance box in performance and learning conditions. As predicted, children more often chose the learning box (82.4%) when the utility of the knowledge was high and the performance box (66%) when the importance of evaluation was high, $\chi^2(1, N = 101) = 22.35, p < .001$.

The number of children in the high and low ability feedback conditions who chose each of the three difficulty levels was analyzed. The results supported our predictions. About 33% of the children who were given low feedback chose the moderately easy level and none of the children chose the moderately hard level. On the other hand, only 9% of the children who were given high feedback chose the moderately easy level and 14% chose the moderately difficult level, $\chi^2(2, N = 42)=5.91, p = .05$.

Performance Measures

Classification of strategies. To assess the effectiveness of each group's problem-solving efforts, their hypotheses were classified as useful strategies (dimension checking and hypothesis checking, in descending order of sophistication) or as ineffectual strategies (stimulus preference, position alternation, and position preference, also in descending order of sophistication). Useful strategies are sequences of hypotheses that, when followed perfectly, will lead to problem solution. Ineffectual strategies are sequences of hypotheses that can never lead to problem solution (see Diener & Dweck, 1978, for a fuller description of strategies).

Training measures: Performance prior to failure. To determine the comparability of groups prior to the test trials, several case-of-training measures were analyzed: number of hints, number of ineffectual hypotheses, and number of times children used dimension checking versus hypothesis checking during training. These training trial measures were not significant except for a single effect on Trial 2 and on Trial 3, and all differences were eliminated by the training trial immediately preceding the failure test trials.

An Ability × Goal interaction was found on Trial 2 for the number of hints $F(1,97) = 8.51, p < .005$, (mean number of hints was 0.1 for the performance goal-low perceived ability group, 0.7 for the performance goal-high perceived ability group, 0.5 for the learning goal-low perceived ability group, and 0.3 for the learning goal-high perceived ability group). A main effect on Trial 3 was also found for the stimulus preference hypothesis, with groups under the performance conditions ($M = 51$) using this ineffectual hypothesis more often than groups under the learning conditions ($M = .24$), $F(1,94) = 4.08, p < .05$.

Strategy use on Trials 3 and 4 was also analyzed. A chi-square analysis was performed on the number of children in each condition using hypothesis checking versus dimension checking. No significant effects were found for Trials 3 or 4.

Test measures: Strategy change after failure. Analyses were performed to test for the predicted changes in strategy use from Test 1 to Test 3. To ensure that there were no baseline differences between groups on Test 1, a chi-square analysis was performed on the number of children in each conditon using ineffectual hypotheses, hypothesis checking, or dimension checking. No significant differences were found between the low and high ability groups in the learning condition, $\chi^2(2, N = 51) = 1.72, p = .42$, nor in the performance condition, $\chi^2(2, N = 50) = 3.02, p = .22$.

Given no significant baseline differences in Test 1, children's strategies (ineffectual strategy use, hypothesis checking, or dimension checking) were classified as improving, remaining the same, or deteriorating on Test 1 versus Test 3 (Table 3).

As predicted, there were differences between low and high ability groups under performance but not under learning conditions, although this difference fell just short of significance. Under the performance condition, 43.5% of the low ability group deteriorated and only 8.7% improved from Test 1 to Test 3. In contrast, only 29.6% of the high ability children deteriorated, whereas 37.0% of them actually improved, $\chi^2(2, N = 50) = 5.47, p =.06$.

In addition to the chi-square, a McNemar test (Siegel, 1956) for the significance of change was used to test the significance of the observed changes for each of the four experimental groups. There were no significant changes from Test 1 to Test 3 for any group except the performance goal-low perceived ability group. These children showed a significant tendency to deteriorate in use

TABLE 16.3. Percentage of Low and High Ability Feedback Children in Each Condition Whose Hypothesis-Testing Strategy Improved, Remained the Same, or Deteriorated over the Three Failure Trails

| | Condition | | | |
| | Learning goal | | Performance goal | |
Strategy status	Low	High	Low	High
Improved	22.2	20.8	8.7	37.0
No change	44.4	45.8	47.8	33.3
Deteriorated	33.3	33.3	43.5	29.6

of problem-solving strategies from Test 1 to Test 3, $\chi^2(1, N = 23) = 4.08, p < .05$. These results replicated the Diener and Dweck (1978, 1980) findings for children with learned helplessness.

Verbalizations

Raters. Two independent raters, blind to the condition of each subject, categorized verbalizations according to the classification used by Diener and Dweck (1978). The mean interrater reliability for these categories was computed by using the conservative method of evaluating percentage agreements for each category separately. Only categories with mean interrater reliabilities greater than 80% were used in the study. These categories included statements of useful task strategy, statements of ineffectual task strategy, attributions, statements of negative affect, and solution-irrelevant statements. Only verbalizations on which there was agreement were used in the analyses.

Training. Verbalizations were recorded on the last training trial prior to failure trials. Analyses showed that as in the Diener and Dweck (1978) study, there were no verbalization differences among groups during training.

Testing. Contingency tables for verbalizations were analyzed with a chi-square or a Fisher's exact test. Several significant differences were found among the verbalizations of the different groups (Table 4). The attributional category includes statements that attribute performance on the task to lack or loss of ability, lack of effort, task difficulty, experimenter's unfairness, or lack of luck. An analysis of the number of children in each group who made attributional statements during the failure trials supported the original predictions. Under the learning condition there was no difference

TABLE 16.4. Percentage of Low and High Ability Children in Each Condition Who Make Verbalizations During the Failure Problems

	Condition			
	Learning goal		Performance goal	
Verbalizations	Low	High	Low	High
Statements of attribution	3.7	8.3	26.1	3.7
Statements of negative affect	3.7	0.0	30.4	3.7

between low and high ability groups. Neither high nor low ability groups were likely to make attributions for failure. However, under the performance conditions there was a significant difference between low and high ability groups. Under the performance condition, children given low ability feedback more frequently made attributions for failure, whereas only 4% of the high ability feedback group made such an attribution (Fisher's exact test, $p = .03$).

Particularly noteworthy is that all of the children in the performance goal-low perceived ability group attributed failure to an uncontrollable cause. None attributed failure to lack of effort, a controllable and modifiable factor. Of the low ability group who made attributional statements, half attributed their failures to themselves. These statements reflected a perceived lack or loss of ability such as "I'm not very good at this" or "I'm confused." The remaining children in this group made statements that fit into various attributional categories including luck ("I accidentally picked the wrong one"), task difficulty ("This is hard and still getting harder"), and experimenter unfairness ("Seems like you're switching on me").

Analysis of verbalizations of negative affect also supported predictions. Under the learning conditions, neither low nor high ability groups were likely to express negative affect during the failure trials. Under the performance condition, however there was a significant difference between ability groups (Fisher's exact test, $p = .01$) as 30% of the low ability group expressed negative affect during the failure test trials. These included statements like "After this (problem), then I get to go?" "This is boring," "My stomach hurts," and "I'm going to hate this part" (stated prior to a "wrong" feedback). Only one child in the high ability group expressed negative affect during the failure test trials.

There were no differences among groups in the remaining verbalization categories: solution-irrelevant statements and statements of effective and ineffectual task strategy.

Similar to the learned helpless children in the Diener and Dweck (1978) study, verbalizations of the performance goal-low perceived ability group were characterized by attributions for their failure to uncontrollable factors and by statements of negative affect. In contrast, similar to the mastery-oriented children of the Diener and Dweck study, verbalizations of the performance goal-high perceived ability condition and verbalization of both high and low ability-learning goal conditions were marked by an absence of both attributions and negative affect during the failure trials.

Discussion

This study addressed the question of children's behavioral, cognitive, and affective patterns in achievement situations. When will children undertake challenging achievement tasks and exhibit the mastery-oriented response to difficulty? What underlies children's avoidance of challenging tasks and the more interfering, learned helpless response to failure? Why do these children allow little latitude for learning and focus prematurely on negative outcomes as a reflection of a personal deficit (i.e., low ability)?

The results of this study suggest that children's achievement goals are critical determinants of these patterns. When these achievement goals were fostered experimentally, the constellation of mastery-oriented and helpless achievement responses were created in their entirety. Specifically, when the value of the performance goal was highlighted and children believed they had low ability, they responded to feedback about mistakes in the characteristic learned helpless manner; making the attribution that mistakes reflected a lack of ability, responding to them with negative affect, and giving up attempts to find effective ways of overcoming those mistakes despite "ability to learn."

When the value of a performance goal was highlighted and children believed their current skills were high, they responded in a mastery-oriented manner in the face of obstacles. These children persisted in attempts to find solutions and did not make attributions for failure or express negative affect. Yet, like the performance-goal children who believed their current skills were low, performance-goal children with high perceived ability also passed up the opportunity to increase their skills on a task that entailed public mistakes.

In contrast to the condition in which the value of the performance goal was highlighted, when the learning goal value was salient, children's beliefs about their current skills were irrelevant in determining their achievement behavior. Regardless of whether they perceived their skills to be high or low, they sought to increase competence. That is, they opted for challenging tasks and did not forego opportunities to learn new skills, even with public errors. These children, regardless of their beliefs about their current skills, responded to failure in a mastery-oriented manner—their problem-solving strategies became more sophisticated.

Future studies are necessary to tease apart the aspects of the manipulations that affected the observed results. For example, our attempts to increase the salience of evaluation could have heightened concern about evaluation by adult experts or could have increased feelings of competition with peers. Regardless, we assume this would impact on the value of the performance goal. Dweck and Elliott (1983) considered other factors (e.g., intrinsic motivation and expectancies) that may influence goal values and confidence.

More generally, the results of our study suggest that learning and performance goals may be a very useful approach to understand achievement patterns (see also Dweck & Elliott, 1983; and Nicholls, 1984, for further discussion of this approach). Our research suggests that each of the achievement goals runs off a different "program" with different commands, decision rules, and inference rules, and hence, with different congnitive, affective, and behavioral consequences. Each goal, in a sense, creates and organizes its own world— each evoking different thoughts and emotions and calling forth different behaviors.

We believe this learning and performance goals framework has the potential to build and expand on past approaches to achievement behavior. Past studies may be classified into two categories: (a) approaches that focus on specific mediators of achievement, which include the attributional approach (Weiner, 1972, 1982; Weiner, Frieze, Kukla, Reed, Rest, & Rosenbaum, 1971), the evaluation anxiety approach (Mandler & Sarason, 1952; Sarason, Davidson, Lighthall, Waite, & Ruebush, 1960; Sarason & Mandler, 1952; Wine,

1971, 1982), and the social learning approach (Battle, 1965, 1966; V. C. Crandall, 1967, 1969; V. J. Crandall, 1963; V. J. Crandall, Katkovsky, & Preston, 1960); and (b) approaches that focus on general energizers of achievement behavior, which include the work within the need for achievement tradition (Atkinson, 1957, 1964; Atkinson & Feather, 1966; Heckhausen, 1967; McClelland, Atkinson, Clark, & Lowell, 1953).

Similar to researchers in the first category, we attempted to precisely delineate specific mediators and link these to specific achievement behaviors in testable ways. Our approach, however, puts specific motivational measures within a broader context of a more general theory of achievement goals and attempts to show how mediators such as attributions and anxiety follow from a focus on particular goals and how they represent part of a coherent pattern of mediators.

As to the second category of researchers who have attempted to measure the underlying motives by using global measures (such as the Thematic Apperception Test [Murray, 1938]) and then to use these to predict achievement behavior, we suggest these global motive measures may be viewed as the "grand sum" of the cognitive and affective measures that are found by researchers focusing on specific mediators. It may be that this property makes their approach useful for predictions (e.g., task choice) but less useful for understanding the specific motivational mediators and for precisely elucidating the pattern of individual and situational influences. Our approach, instead, suggests the ways in which goal orientation interacts with confidence to set in motion a sequence of specific processes that influence, in turn, task choice, performance, and persistence.

In conclusion, our experiment provides support for an approach to achievement behavior that emphasizes learning and performance achievement goals as the critical determinants of achievement patterns. It is suggested that this framework can provide a general, yet precise, context for systematically understanding the specific mediators of individual differences in and situational influences on motivational patterns. To the extent that performance and learning goals can be adopted with respect to any personal attribute and not just ability (to judge/validate the attribute vs. to develop the attribute), our framework may provide a useful tool for the general study of motivation.

ACKNOWLEDGMENTS

This research was conducted in partial fulfillment of the requirement for the doctoral degree at the University of Illinois by Elaine S. Elliott.

We wish to thank the people who have contributed in various ways to this study. In particular, we would like to acknowledge Susan Harner for serving as experimenter and Mary Bandura for her input on drafts of this article.

REFERENCES

Ames, C. (1984). Achievement attributions and self-instructions under competitive and individualistic goal structures. *Journal of Educational Psychology, 76,* 478–487.

Atkinson, J. W. (1957). Motivational determinants of risk-taking behavior. *Psychological Review, 64,* 359–372.

Atkinson, J. W. (1964). *An introduction to motivation.* Princeton, NJ: Van Nostrand.

Atkinson. J. W., & Feather, N. T. (Eds.). (1966). *A theory of achievement motivation.* New York: Wiley.

Battle, E. S. (1965). Motivational determinants of academic task persistence. *Journal of Personality and Social Psychology, 2,* 209–218.

Battle, E. S. (1966). Motivational determinants of academic competence. *Journal of Personality and Social Psychology, 4,* 634–642.

Crandall, V. C. (1967). Achievement behavior in the young child. In W. W. Hartup (Ed.), *The young child; Review of research* (pp. 165–185). Washington, DC: National Association for the Education of Young Children.

Crandall, V. C. (1969). Sex differences in expectancy of intellectual and academic reinforcement. In C. P. Smith (Ed.), *Achievement-related motives in children* (pp. 11–45). New York: Russell Sage Foundation.

Crandall, V. J. (1963). Achievement. In H. Stevenson (Ed.), *Child psychology: Sixty-second yearbook of the National Society for the Study of Education* (pp. 416–459). Chicago: University of Chicago Press.

Crandall, V. J. Katkovsky, W., & Preston, A. (1960). A conceptual formulation for some research on children's achievement development. *Child Development, 31,* 787–797.

Deci, E. L., & Ryan, R. M. (1980). The empirical exploration of intrinsic motivational process. In L. Berkowitz (Ed.), *Advances in experimental social psychology* (Vol. 13, pp. 39–80). New York: Academic Press.

Diener, C. L., & Dweck, C. S. (1978). An analysis of learned helplessness: Continuous changes in performance, strategy and achievement cognitions following failure. *Journal of Personality and Social Psychology, 36,* 451–462.

Diener, C. I., & Dweck, C. S. (1980). An analysis of learned helplessness: II. The processing of success. *Journal of Personality and Social Psychology, 39,* 940–952.

Dweck, C. S. (1975). The role of expectations and attributions in the alleviation of learned helplessness. *Journal of Personality and Social Psychology, 31,* 674–685.

Dweck, C. S., & Elliott, E. S. (1983). Achievement motivation. In E. M. Hetherington (Ed.), *Socialization, personality, and social development* (pp. 643–691). New York: Wiley.

Frankl, A., & Snyder, M. L. (1978). Poor performance following unsolvable problems: Learned helplessness or ego-tism? *Journal of Personality and Social Psychology, 36,* 1415–1423.

Glanzer, M., Huttenlocher, J., & Clark, W. H. (1963). Systematic operations involving concept problems. *Psychological Monographs, 77,* 1–14.

Heckhausen, H. (1967). *The anatomy of achievement motivation.* New York: Academic Press.

Legget, E. (1986, April). *Individual differences in effort-ability inference rules: Implications for causal judgments.* Paper presented at the meeting of the Eastern Psychological Association, New York, NY.

Lepper, M. R. (1980). Intrinsic and extrinsic motivation in children: Detrimental effects of superfluous social controls. In W. A. Collins (Ed.), *Minnesota symposium on child psychology* (Vol. 14, pp. 155–214). Hillsdale, NJ: Erlbaum.

Lepper, M. R., & Greene, D. (Eds.). (1978). *The hidden costs of reward: New perspectives on the psychology of human motivation.* Hillsdale, NJ: Erlbaum.

Levine, M. (1966). Hypothesis behavior by humans during discrimination learning. *Journal of Experimental Psychology, 71,* 331–338.

Mandler, G., & Sarason, S. B. (1952). A study of anxiety and learning. *Jornal of Abnormal and Social Psychology, 47,* 166–173.

McClelland, D. C., Atkinson, J. W., Clark, R. A., & Lowell, E. L. (1953). *The achievement motive.* New York: Appleton-Century-Crofts.

Murray, H. A. (1938). *Explorations in personality.* New York: Oxford University Press.

Nicholls, J. G. (1976). Effort is virtuous but it's better to have ability: Evaluative responses to perceptions of effort and ability. *Journal of Research in Personality, 10,* 306–315.

Nicholls, J. G. (1984). Achievement motivation: Conceptions of ability, subjective experience, task choice, and performance. *Psychological Review, 91,* 328–346.

Nicholls, J. G., & Dweck, C. S. (1979). *A definition of achievement motivation.* Unpublished manuscript. University of Illinois at Champaign-Urbana.

Sarason, S. B., Davidson, K., Lighthall, F., Waite, F., & Ruebush, B. (1960). *Anxiety in elementary school children.* New York: Wiley.

Sarason, S. B., & Mandler, G. (1952). Some correlates of test anxiety. *Journal of Abnormal and Social Psychology, 47,* 561–565.

Siegel, S. (1956). *Nonparametric statistics for the behavioral sciences.* New York: McGraw-Hill.

Spielberger, M., Morris, L., & Liebert, R. (1968). Cognitive and emotional components of test anxiety. Temporal factors. *Psychological Reports, 20,* 451–456.

Weiner, B. (1972). *Theories of motivation: From mechanism to cognition.* Chicago: Markham.

Weiner, B. (1982). An attribution theory of motivation and emotion. In H. Krohne & L. Laux (Eds.), *Achievement, stress, and anxiety* (pp. 223–245). Washington, DC: Hemisphere.

Weiner, B., Frieze, I. H., Kukla, A., Reed, L., Rest, S., & Rosenbaum, R. M. (1971). *Perceiving the causes of success and failure.* Morristown, NJ: General Learning Press.

Wine, J. D. (1971). Test anxiety and direction of attention. *Psychological Bulletin, 76,* 92–104.

Wine, J. D. (1982). Evaluation anxiety: A cognitive-attentional construct. In H. W. Krohne & L. Laux (Eds.), *Achievement, stress, and anxiety* (pp. 207–219). Washington, DC: Hemisphere.

READING 17

Deliberative and Implemental Mind-Sets: Cognitive Tuning Toward Congruous Thoughts and Information

Peter M. Gollwitzer, Heinz Heckhausen, and Birgit Steller
• Max-Planck-Institut für psychologische Forschung, Munich, Federal Republic of Germany

Editors' Notes

What is the psychological process whereby our wishes and desires are translated into actions? The German psychological tradition of the Würzburg School approached this problem by subdividing the road from wishes to actions into phases. This particular perspective is represented in the present selection. Each of the phases is characterized by a different task and a different mind-set. That is, each phase has a specific problem that the would-be actor attempts to resolve. The predecisional phase is characterized by a deliberative mind-set wherein the individual attempts to select a goal to which he or she is willing to commit. Once such commitment takes place, the individual moves to a postdecisional phase in which the means of implementing the goal intention are determined. The present selection presents studies testing the cognitive implications of different mind-sets accompanying the different phases. During the deliberative predecisional phase, individuals' thoughts are preoccupied with issues related to goal-choice, whereas during the implementational postdecisional phase, they are occupied with issues of execution and means identification. Of particular interest, the thoughts populating people's minds may generalize to other tasks. For instance, people in a deliberative set would approach a neutral problem with goal-deliberation in mind (or why questions), whereas their counterparts in an implementational set would approach the same task with thoughts about ways of carrying it out (or how questions). Furthermore, individuals in different mind-sets are likely to remember different portions of task information corresponding to their mind-set. In short, the road from wishes to actions leads through shifting mental sets that affect what we think about, attend to, and remember.

Discussion Questions

1. What are the issues a person in a deliberative mind-set versus an implemental mind-set is likely to think about?
2. What do the findings of Gollwitzer et al. (1990) imply about the relation between motivation and cognition? How do they relate to the distinction sometimes drawn between "hot" and "cold" cognition? Are there motivational processes to be found that are not cognitive? Are there cognitions that do not have a motivational background?
3. How do Gollwitzer et al. (1990) deal with the possibility that the implementational and deliberative information might vary in evaluative tone, which in turn might influence information processing?

Suggested Readings

Ajzen, I. (1991). The theory of planned behavior. *Organizational Behavior and Human Decision Processes, 50,* 179–211.

Gollwitzer, P. M. (1996). The volitional benefits of planning. In P. M. Gollwitzer & J. A. Bargh (Eds.), *The psychology of action: Linking cognition and motivation to behavior* (pp. 287–312). New York: Guilford.

Authors' Abstract

Study 1 established either deliberative mind-set by having Ss (Subjects) contemplate personal change decision or implemental mind-set by having Ss plan execution of intended personal project. Ss were subsequently requested to continue beginnings of 3 fairy tales, each describing a main character with a decisional conflict. Analysis revealed that deliberative mind-set Ss ascribed more deliberative and less implementational efforts to main characters than implemental mind-set Ss. In Study 2, Ss were asked to choose between different test materials. Either before or after making their decision, Ss were given information on deliberative and implementational thoughts unrelated to their task at hand. When asked to recall these thoughts, predecisional Ss recalled more deliberative and less implementational thoughts, whereas for postdecisional Ss the reverse was true. These findings suggest that deliberative and implemental mind-sets tune thought production and information processing.

A course of action may be conceived rather narrowly as extending from its initiation (starting point) to its termination (end point). Alternatively, one may adopt a broader perspective that embraces the motivational origins of an action as the actual starting point and the individual's evaluative thoughts about the achieved action outcome as the final end point. In the present article, we take this broader perspective and segment the course of action into four distinct, sequential phases (Heckhausen, 1986).

The first segment is the *predecisional* phase, where potential action goals entailed by a person's many wants and wishes are deliberated. When a decision to pursue one of these goals is made, a transition to the *postdecisional* (preactional) phase takes place, where the individual becomes concerned with implementing the chosen goal. However, this phase ends and the *actional* phase starts when actions geared toward achieving the chosen goal are initiated. Once these actions have resulted in a particular outcome, the *postactional* phase is entered and the individual proceeds to evaluate the achieved outcome.

We postulate that each of these phases is accompanied by a distinct mind-set (Gollwitzer, 1990). Following the lead of the Würzburg School (Kulpe, 1904; Marbe, 1901; Watt, 1905; for reviews, see Boring, 1950, pp. 401-406; Gibson, 1941; and Humphrey, 1951, pp. 30-131), we assume that the characteristics of each of these mind-sets are determined by the unique qualities of the different tasks to be solved within each phase. That is, the different mind-sets tailor a person's cognitive apparatus to meet phase-typical task demands, thus creating a special preparedness for solving these tasks. This preparedness should extend to a person's thought production, to the encoding and retrieval of information, and to the inferences drawn on the basis of this information. In this article, we explore the issue of mind-set congruous thought production as well as the encoding and retrieval of congruous information. As was done in a previous analysis of mind-set effects on a person's inferences (see Gollwitzer & Kinney, 1989, on illusion of control), we limit the analysis of cognitive tuning toward mind-set congruous thoughts and information to the *deliberative* mind-set of the predecisional phase and the *implemental* mind-set of the post-decisional, but preactional, phase.

What are the issues to which deliberative as compared with implemental mind-sets are attuned? To answer this question, one must consider the specific tasks that need to be tackled in the respective action phases. In the predecisional phase, people's task is to choose between action goals suggested by their wants and wishes. The likelihood of a "good" choice should be enhanced when the individual thoroughly ponders the attractiveness of the expected consequences (i.e., expected value) of these goals. Clearly, failing to think about the attractiveness of proximal and distant consequences will lead to problematic decisions associated with unexpected negative consequences. Accordingly, the deliberative mind-set should gear

a person's thinking toward the expected values of potential action goals.

In the postdecisional (preactional) phase, however, people are confronted with quite a different task: The chosen goal awaits successful implementation. Postdecisional individuals should therefore benefit from an implemental mind-set that guides their thoughts toward the questions of *when, where,* and *how* to implement the chosen action goal. In this phase, thoughts about the goal's expected value should be distractive rather than useful, because they are not immediately related to implementational issues.

The classic definition of mind-set ("Einstellung") as advanced by the Würzburg School suggests that mind-set effects are based on cognitive processes that promote solving the task that stimulated the rise of the mind-set. With respect to deliberative and implemental mind-sets, these may be conceived of as cognitive procedures relating to how one chooses between various goal alternatives or to the planning of actions one must take in order to attain a chosen goal, respectively. A deliberative mind-set should, for instance, entail procedures of weighing pros and cons, whereas an implemental mind-set should entail procedures of timing and sequencing of goal-oriented actions.

As Smith and Branscombe (1987) pointed out in their procedural model of social inferences, cognitive procedures may transfer from a training (priming) task to a subsequent (test) task. If these procedures are sufficiently strengthened through intensive practice in the training task, and if there is overlap in the applicability of procedures, transfer is very likely. This model suggests the following test of the postulated effects of deliberative and implemental mind-sets. If we succeed in creating strong deliberative and implemental mind-sets by either having subjects intensively contemplate potential goals or plan the execution of a chosen project (training task), we should find the postulated mind-set effects in an unrelated subsequent task (test task). A prerequisite would be that the subsequent task allows for those cognitive procedures that were strengthened in the training task, that is, the cognitive procedures characteristic of a deliberative or implemental mind-set.

Experiment 1, testing the postulate of mind-set congruous thought production, was designed along this premise. Subjects' first task (training task) was to either thoroughly contemplate an unresolved decisional problem of their own (deliberative mind-set) or to make a detailed plan of how to pursue a pressing personal project (implemental mind-set). Then they were confronted with a second, allegedly unrelated task (test task) that requested the spontaneous production of ideas. Because these ideas could be deliberative or implementational in nature, we expected both deliberative and implemental mind-sets to guide thought production in a mind-set congruous direction.

This transfer assumption allowed us to go beyond a recent experiment reported by Heckhausen and Gollwitzer (1987), where the thoughts of deliberative and implemental mind-set subjects were sampled during the training task. In this study, the classification of the reported thoughts clearly evidenced cognitive tuning toward mind-set congruous thoughts. This study, however, lacks an unrelated rest task, and therefore the results might be based on experimenter demands.

Experiment 1: Ascribing Deliberative and Implementational Efforts to Others

Asking subjects to deliberate unresolved personal problems that are pending a change decision should create strong deliberative mind-sets. Alternatively, asking subjects to plan the execution of chosen projects should evoke strong implemental mind-sets. Other experiments have indicated that deliberative and implemental mind-sets can reliably be produced through such a procedure (Gollwitzer, Heckhausen, & Ratajczak, 1990: Gollwitzer & Kinney, 1989). Accordingly, in the present experiment one third of the subjects were first asked to name an unresolved personal problem (e.g., Should I move from home? or Should I terminate my college education?) and then asked to contemplate whether or not to make a respective change decision. Another third of the subjects were to indicate a personal goal or project they planned to execute in the near future (e.g., moving from home or terminating one's college education) and then were to plan when, where, and how they wanted to accomplish it. The final third, a control group, were asked to passively view nature slides.

We tested whether deliberative and implemental mind-sets tune people's thought production in a mind-set congruous direction by asking subjects to fabricate ideas on an unrelated second task. To this end, we presented subjects with the beginings

of three fairy tales in which the main character of each story faced a different decisional conflict (e.g., a king had to go to war, but had nobody to whom he could entrust his young daughter). Subjects were asked to spontaneously compose the next three sentences for each of these fairy tales.

The mind-set congruency hypothesis implies that deliberative efforts (i.e., contemplating possible goals) are most frequently ascribed to the main characters of the stories in the deliberative mind-set condition, less frequently in the control condition, and even less so in the implemental mind-set condition. In contrast, implementational efforts (i.e., executing a chosen solution to the conflict) should be most frequently ascribed in the implemental mind-set condition, less frequently in the control condition, and least frequently in the deliberative mind-set condition.

Method

SUBJECTS

The 97 participants were male students at the Ruhr-Universität Bochum. Up to 4 subjects were invited to each experimental session and randomly assigned to one of three conditions. Subjects were recruited on the premise that they were willing to participate in two different studies, one on people's personal problems and projects, the other a test of their creativity. Subjects were separated by partitions, such that they could easily view the experimenter but none of the other participants. They were paid DM 10 (approximately $5.50) for participating.

DESIGN

Subjects in either a deliberative or implemental mind-set were asked to continue three different, incomplete fairy tales. Subjects' stories were analyzed with respect to whether deliberative or inplemand efforts were ascribed to the main characters of the fairy tales. Subjects in the control condition passively viewed photographs of various outdoor scenes before receiving the fairy tales.

PROCEDURE

Cover story. The female experimenter explained that subjects would take part in two different experiments. In the first experiment, subjects would be requested to reflect on personal issues or on nature photographs. Subjects were told that this study was designed to answer the question of whether intense reflection on personal issues would help people act more effectively in everyday life. In the second experiment their creativity would be tested. For this purpose, three different creativity tasks would be used, all of which would request the spontaneous creation of ideas.

In order to ensure that subjects perceived the two experiments as unrelated, the format of the written materials was different in each study (e.g. typeface, color of paper, and writing style). In addition, the materials of each alleged experiment were distributed and collected separately.

Deliberative and implemental mind-set manipulation. Deliberative mind-set subjects were asked to weigh the pros and cons of making or not making a personal change decision. First, they had to indicate an unresolved personal problem (e.g., Should I switch my major?). Then they were to list both potential positive and negative, short-term and long-term consequences (i.e., to elaborate on the expected value). In contrast, implemental mind-set subjects were asked to plan the implementation of chosen personal projects. They were instructed to first name a personal project they intended to accomplish within the following 3 months (e.g., to move from home). Then they had to list the five most crucial implementational steps and commit themselves to when, where, and how to execute these steps.

As a manipulation check, both groups of subjects were then asked to fill out a final questionnaire consisting of the following items:

1. "On the line below, please indicate the point that best represents your distance from the act of change decision." (For this purpose, a horizontal line of 13 cm was provided. The starting point was labeled "far from having made a change decision," the 6.5-cm mark "act of change decision," and the end point "past having made a change decision.")
2. "How determined do you feel at this moment?"
3. "Do you feel that you have committed yourself to a certain implementational course of action?"
4. "Do you feel that you have committed yourself to make use of a certain occasion or opportunity to act?"

Items 2–4 were accompanied by unipolar 9-point answer scales ranging from *not at all* to *very.*

Control subjects. Subjects in the control condition received a booklet containing numerous black-and-white photographs depicting various nature scenes. Subjects were instructed to passively view the pictures for about 30 min (i.e., the amount of time deliberative and implemental subjects needed to complete their tasks). Thereafter, the alleged second experiment was started.

Dependent variable. The experimenter began the alleged second study by distributing three different fairy tales, the order of which was counterbalanced across conditions. Subjects received the following instructions:

> All of these fairy tales end at a certain point in the plot. You are to fill in the next three sentences of each fairy tale. You should *not* write a "novel," and the fairy tales need not have an ending. When continuing the stories, give free rein to your fantasy and don't hesitate to write down your own creative thoughts, however unusual they may be. After you have finished the three sentences, please go on to the next fairy tale.

The first fairy tale read as follows:

> Once upon a time there was a king who loved the queen dearly. When the queen died, he was left with his only daughter. The widowed king adored the little princess who grew up to be the most beautiful maiden that anyone had ever seen. When the princess turned 15, war broke out and her father had to go to battle. The king, however, did not know of anyone with whom he could entrust his daughter while he was away at war. The king . . .

The second fairy tale was a king who had a huge forest by his castle. One day he had sent out a hunter into the forest who did not return. The two hunters he sent to look for the lost hunter also failed to return. The third fairy tale described a rather hedonistic tailor who had attended a christening party out of town. Late at night and after a few drinks too many, he was on his way home and got lost in a dark forest. He suddenly found himself standing in front of a huge rock wall with a passage just large enough to permit a person to pass.

Thought production scoring. Subjects' stories were scored by two independent blind raters. The raters proceeded as follows: First, they underlined verbs relating to the main characters of the three fairy tales. Then, they classified the episodes denoted by these verbs with respect to whether the main character tackled the predecisional task of choosing between action goals or the post-decisional task of implementing a chosen action goal. For this purpose, a coding scheme was developed (two mutually exclusive categories are depicted in the Appendix). Each category could be check-marked as often as necessary, depending on how many relevant episodes the subjects' stories contained. Eighty-one percent of the episodes could be placed into the categories provided by the coding scheme; the rest formed the category "unassignable episodes" (19%). Agreement between raters was determined by counting the number of "hits," defined as classifications on which the two raters agreed. Interater reliability was high with 91% of the ratings being hits.

Debriefing. When the subjects had finished working on the third fairy tale the experiment was terminated and the subjects were debriefed. During the debriefing session, we probed whether subjects perceived the two experiments as related or not. As it turned out subjects were only concerned with how well they had performed on the creativity task. None of the subjects raised the issue of the two experiments being potentially related or reported suspicions after being probed.

Results

EQUIVALENCE OF GROUPS

Deliberative and implemental mind-set subjects did not differ in the domains covered by their problems and projects, respectively. Unresolved personal problems (deliberative mind-set subjects) and personal projects (implemental mind-set subjects) were classified according to three different domains: career-related (42%), lifestyle-related (31%), and interpersonal (27%), the percentages being basically identical for both unresolved personal problems and personal projects.

The three groups of subjects also did not differ significantly in the number of words they wrote when continuing the three fairy tales: $M = 110.2$ for the deliberative mind-set group, $M = 112.5$ for the implemental mind-set group, and $M = 119.7$ for the control group, $F(2, 84) = .52$, ns.

MANIPULATION CHECKS

Subjects had indicated their proximity (in time) to the act of making a change decision on a hori-zontal line. Nearly all (24 of 26) deliberative mind-set subjects indicated that they had not yet made the decision. The reverse was found for implemental mind-set subjects; 25 of 26 subjects indicated that they had already made the decision. In addition, deliberative mind-set subjects ($M=4.6$) felt less determined than implemental mind-set subjects ($M=8.2$), $F(1, 50) = 50.8$, $p < .001$. Implemental mind-set subjects ($M= 7.6$) felt more committed to executing a certain implementational course of action than deliberative mind-set subjects ($M = 5.0$), $F(1, 50) = 26.67$, $p < .001$; the same pattern held true for feelings of commitment with respect to making use of a certain occasion or opportunity to act ($M = 6.7$ vs. $M = 5.1$), $F(1, 50) = 4.6$, $p < .04$.

DEPENDENT VARIABLES

To analyze subjects' stories, episodes ascribing deliberative efforts to the main characters (i.e., deliberating action goals and turning to others for advice) were added together to create a deliberative efforts index; actual acting on a chosen goal and thinking about the implementation of the chosen goal were added together to form an implementational efforts index (see Appendix). Scores on these indices were submitted to further analyses.

To test the hypothesis that ascribing deliberative and implementational efforts varies in a mind-set congruous direction, two one-way analyses of variance (ANOVAs) with linear contrast weights (see Rosenthal & Rosnow, 1985) were conducted. For ascribing deliberative efforts, these weights tested the hypothesis that the highest frequencies would be obtained among deliberative mind-set subjects, followed by control subjects and then deliberative subjects. These analyses revealed that ascribing deliberative and implementational efforts significantly varies in a mind-set congruous direction, $F(1,84) = 4.06$, $p < .025$ (one-tailed), and $F(1,84) = 8.48$, $p < .005$ (one-tailed), respectively. Pearson coefficients obtained by correlating ascribing deliberative and implementational efforts with the respective linear contrast coding of mind-set conditions underlined these results (see Table 1).

When the frequencies of ascribing deliberative and implementational efforts were submitted to an ANOVA with ascribed effort (deliberative vs. implementational) as a within-subjects variable and condition (deliberative, implemental, and con-

TABLE 17.1. Mean Deliberative and Implementational Efforts Ascribed to the Main Characters of the Three Fairy Tales

Type of ascribed efforts	F	r	Mind-set conditions		
			Deliberative ($n = 26$)	Control ($n = 35$)	Implemental ($n = 26$)
Deliberative	4.06*	.21*	1.00	0.71	0.38
Implementational	8.48**	.29**	5.81	6.94	7.85

Note. Means reflect the number of episodes in which subjects ascribed either deliberative or implementational efforts.
*$p \leq .05$. **$p \leq .01$

trol group) as a between-subjects variable, a significant main effect of ascribed effort emerged, $F(1,84) = 322.5$, $p < .001$, which is qualified by the predicted interaction effect, $F(2,84) = 4.65$, $p = .015$. We checked whether the pattern of data is different for each of the three fairy tales by computing a $3 \times 2 \times 3$ (Fairy Tale × Ascribed Effort × Condition) ANOVA. The significant Ascribed Effort × Condition interaction effect was *not* qualified by an interaction and did not reach significance ($F < 1.0$). In addition, the order in which the fairy tales were presented also failed to affect the critical interaction ($F < 1.0$). Finally, we explored how the episodes that could not be classified by our coding scheme were distributed across conditions. There were no significant differences among the conditions ($F < .25$).

DISCUSSION

Subjects requested to ponder a personal problem in order to determine whether or not they should make a change decision fabricated fewer implementational and more deliberative ideas when writing a creative fairy tale than subjects who had been asked to plan the execution of a chosen personal goal. Deliberating and planning created distinct mind-sets that persisted even after subjects had turned to the subsequent task of writing creative fairy tales. The ideas that spontaneously entered the subjects' minds when inventing their fairy tales corresponded to their deliberative or implemental mind-sets.

All groups of subjects imputed more implementational than deliberative efforts to the main characters of the fairy tales. Apparently, the task of writing creative endings to unfinished fairy tales predominantly relies on cognitive procedures characteristic of the implemental mind-set. As Rabkin (1979) and Rumelhart (1975, 1977) pointed out,

fairy tales seem to follow a certain grammar. A "good" fairy tale is not complete until the problem faced by the main character is solved. Because such solutions commonly require the main character to take action, ascribing implementational efforts is more in the style of a good fairy tale. Still, despite few deliberative efforts ascribed overall, we observed the predicted mind-set congruency effect. However, the scarcity of ascribing deliberative efforts in the present study serves as a reminder that testing the postulated mind-set congruency effects through a subsequent (test) task has its limits. If working on a subsequent task does not allow for the cognitive procedures entailed by a deliberative or implemental mind-set (e.g, solving an arithmetic task), mind-set congruency effects cannot be observed.

Studies conducted on category accessibility effects on social judgments seem relevant to the paradigm used here (Higgins, Rholes, & Jones, 1977; Srull & Wyer, 1979). Assuming that social constructs (e.g, kindness) are stored in memory, these constructs were first primed by confronting subjects either with trait words closely related to the target construct (Higgins et al.) or descriptions of relevant behaviors (Srull & Wyer). Then, in a presumedly unrelated second experiment, subjects read descriptions of a target character who shows either ambivalent (Higgins et al.) or vague (Srull & Wyer) indications of possessing the critical personal attribute. Finally, when subjects were asked to rate the target character, distortions in the direction of the primed category were observed. Both groups of researchers suggested that priming changes some property of the critical construct's representation in memory (i.e, activation or location in a storage bin, respectively) that makes it comparatively more accessible and more likely to be used in interpreting the behavior of the target person.

As in these priming experiments, subjects in Experiment 1 were also exposed to ambiguous information about a target character (i.e., the main character of the open-ended fairy tales) in an alleged second experiment. However, the ambiguity is about the main character's course of action and not about a potential personality attribute. We believe that subjects' ascribing of deliberative or implementational efforts was affected by cognitive procedures (or productions; Anderson, 1983) that have been strengthened through prior deliberation and planning processes. The activation of declarative knowledge (specific episodic and general semantic) through the contents touched by subjects' deliberation and planning should have played a minor role. This assumption is supported by the fact that the observed mind-set effects were rather long-lived (one quarter to half an hour), whereas conceptual priming effects were generally extremely short-lived (a matter of seconds or a few minutes). As Smith and Branscombe (1987) demonstrated, studies on category accessibility effects only manage to produce long-lasting effects (several hours) when procedural strengthening is involved.

Experiment 2: Recalling Deliberative Versus Implementational Thoughts of Others

Experiment 1 demonstrated that deliberative and implemental mind-sets favor the production of congruous thoughts. This should facilitate the task of choosing between goal options and the task of implementing a chosen goal, respectively. However, both of these tasks should also be facilitated by effective processing of task-relevant information. Therefore, one would expect that people in a deliberative mind-set show superior processing of information that speaks to the expected value of goal options, whereas people in an implemental mind-set should show superior processing of information that speaks to the issue of when, where, and how to execute goal-oriented behavior.

Our test of the superior processing of mind-set congruous information was also based on the transfer assumption of Smith and Branscombe's (1987) model of procedural strengthening and transfer. Instead of offering deliberative and implemental mind-set subjects information relevant to their decisional and implementational problem at hand, we offered information on other people's decisional and implementational problems. As this information could easily be identified as either expected value-related or implementation-related, we expected mind-set congruency effects with respect to subjects' recall of this information.

This information was depicted on eight pairs of slides. The first slide of each pair showed a person said to be experiencing a personal conflict of the following kind: Should I do x or not (e.g, sell my apartment)? The second slide presented four thoughts entertained by the person depicted on the first slide. Two of these thoughts were deliberative in nature, as they referred to the expected value of making a change decision. The other two thoughts were of an implementational nature, both addressing the issue of when (timing) and how (sequencing) to execute goal-oriented actions. When constructing these sentences, we used pilot subjects to establish that both types of information (expected value vs. implementation) were recalled about equally well.

A deliberative mind-set was established by asking subjects to contemplate the choice between one of two available creativity tests. An implemental mind-set was assumed for subjects who had just chosen between tests and were waiting to start working. A control group received and recalled the information without expecting to make a decision or to implement one already made.

Deliberative mind-set subjects should show superior recall of the expected value-related information, despite its being unrelated to the decision subjects were contemplating. Implemental mind-set subjects should show superior recall of the implementation-related information, despite its being unrelated to working on the chosen creativity test. Control subjects were expected to recall both expected value-related information and implementation-related information about equally well.

Method

SUBJECTS AND EQUIPMENT

The participants were 69 male students from the University of Munich. Two subjects were invited to each experimental session. They received DM 15 (approximately $8.00) for participation. A female experimenter ushered subjects into separate experimental cubicles where they received tape-recorded instructions through an intercom system.

Each cubicle was equipped with a projection screen.

DESIGN

Subjects were randomly assigned to one of three conditions. In the deliberative mind-set condition, information on both expected values and implementational issues was received and recalled prior to making a choice between two available creativity tests. In the implemental mind-set condition, subjects received and recalled this information while waiting to begin working on their chosen creativity test. Finally, control subjects received and recalled this information without either expecting to make a choice or having made one.

PROCEDURE

Cover story. Subjects were told that two different personality traits, that is, social sensitivity and artistic creativity, would be assessed during the course of the experiment. The experimenter further explained that for measuring each of these traits two alternative test materials had been prepared. It was stated that subjects would be allowed to choose between test materials, because only if subjects chose the test material more appropriate for them personally would test scores reflect their "true" social or creative potential. The experimenter then distributed a short questionnaire consisting of the following items: (a) "How creative do you think you are?" (b) "How confident are you that you are capable of creative achievements?" and (c) "How important is it for you to be a creative person?" Parallel questions were asked with respect to social sensitivity. (All items were accompanied by 9-point answer scales ranging from *not at all* to *very.*)

The first trait measured was *social sensitivity.* The experimenter presented subjects with short descriptions of two different interpersonal conflicts. Subjects were first asked to select the problem they personally found most engaging and then to suggest an appropriate solution to the conflict by writing a short essay. Subjects were told that they would later receive feedback concerning the usefulness of their suggested solutions.

Then the experimenter turned to the presumed second part of the experiment, that is, assessing subjects' *artistic creativity.* She explained that sub-jects would create collages from material cut out of different newspapers. It was the subjects' task to select various elements (e.g., people, animals and objects) needed to depict a certain theme provided by the experimenter. Finally, subjects should place the selected elements on a white sheet of paper and arrange them so that a creative picture emerged. When they had discovered the most appealing arrangement, they should glue the collage segments onto the white sheet of paper and then hand it to the experimenter.

Most important, however, two different sets of collage materials (black-and-white vs. color elements) would be available for this task. Subjects would be given a choice because they could reach their full creative potential only if they chose that set of elements they found personally most appealing. To help subjects choose properly, she would present four black-and-white as well as four color slides. She explained that these slides originated from a previous study on artistic creativity in which subjects had to invent the thoughts of people depicted on the slides. Subjects should view all of the slides carefully to determine which set of slides (color or black and white) would bring out their full creative potential.

However, subjects were instructed to refrain from making a choice of test material while viewing the slides. Impulsive choices, as well as choices based on initial preferences only, were said to have proven problematic. Therefore, subjects should take their time, lean back, and ponder the best choice. In addition, shortly before viewing the sample pictures subjects were given false feedback with respect to the quality of their performance on the social sensitivity test. All subjects were told that if they had chosen the alternative test material, their score would have been higher than the rather modest score achieved. This feedback, as well as the instructions to refrain from impulse choices, was given for the sole purpose of stimulating intense deliberation.

Information materials. The sample pictures were grouped into eight pairs of slides. Each pair consisted of a first slide that pictured a person said to be pondering a decisional problem (e.g., an elderly lady). On the subsequent slide, subjects read that she was reflecting on the following decisional problem: Should I invite my grandchildren to stay at my house during the summer—or shouldn't I?

The slide also contained her thoughts on the expected value of a change decision. The first thought centered on possible positive consequences (i.e., *It would be good, because* they could help me keep up my garden); the second thought focused on possible negative consequences (*i.e., It would be be bad, because* they might break my good china).

In addition, the slide depicted two thoughts related to the implementation of a potential change decision: One focused on the timing of a necessary implementational step (i.e., *If I decide yes, then* I won't talk to the kids *before* my daughter has agreed); the other thought mapped out the sequence of two further implementational steps (i.e., *If I decide yes, then I'll first* write my daughter *and then* give her a call).

Altogether, eight different persons, each facing a specific decisional conflict, were presented (e.g, a young man who pondered the question of becoming a sculptor, a young lady who reflected on whether to quit her waitressing job, and a middle-aged man who deliberated whether or not to sell his condominium). Four slides depicting persons were in color, and four were in black and white. The verbal information was always presented in the same format. The underlined parts of each sentence (see the example of the elderly lady above) remained analogous for each person and were written in black. The rest of the sentences were written in red.

Deliberative mind-set condition. Once subjects had viewed the eight pairs of slides, the experimenter told them that she would look for a second set of slides that might make it easier for subjects to make up their minds. While she was purportedly trying to set up this second set, subjects were to fill their time by working on a couple of tasks. Then the experimenter gave the instructions for a 5-min distractor (subjects counted the planes of several different geometrical figures drawn on a sheet of paper) and a subsequent recall test (as described below). When subjects were finished, the experimenter explained that she had failed to set up the additional set of slides. Therefore, subjects should make their decision based solely on viewing the original set of slides.

Implemental mind-set condition. Subjects were introduced to the choice option between two sets of collage materials and were instructed to deliberate on the question of which set of collage elements they found most appealing. After subjects had indicated their decision, the experimenter explained that it would take several minutes for her

to bring the chosen collage elements to the subject's cubicle. In the meantime, the subjects would view slides and solve a number of different tasks. The eight pairs of slides were then presented; the origin of these slides was described to the subjects in the same words as in the deliberative mind-set condition. Following the distractor, subjects worked on the recall test.

Control condition. Control subjects were not made to either expect a decision between collage elements or work on a set of collage elements. They were shown the slides after being told solely about their origin. Finally, subjects' recall performance was assessed following the completion of the distractor task.

Recall procedure. Following the 5-min distractor task, subjects were again shown the eight slides depicting the persons said to be experiencing a decisional conflict. In addition, they were given a booklet consisting of eight pages, each one entitled with the deliberation problem of one of the eight characters pictured on the slides. Subjects found those parts of the sentences printed in black on the slides that presented the depicted persons' thoughts and were instructed to complete them (i.e., fill in the parts of the sentences printed in red on the original slides). For this recall procedure, the slides depicting the characters were shown in the order in which they were originally presented.

Postexperimental questionnaire and debriefing. Deliberative and implemental mind-set subjects were asked to complete a final questionnaire that contained the following items accompanied by 9-point answer scales ranging from *not at all* to *very:* (a) "How important is it for you to show a creative performance on the collage creativity test?" (b) "How difficult was the choice between the two sets of collage elements?" (c) "How important is it for you to work with the appropriate collage elements?" (d) "How certain are you that you picked the appropriate collage elements?" (e) "I generally prefer black-and-white pictures over color ones" (*don't agree-agree*), and (f) "*I generally prefer color pictures over black-and-white ones!*" (*don't agree-agree*). After the subjects had completed this questionnaire, the experimenter debriefed them and paid them for their participation.

The debriefing was started by probing for suspicions. None of the subjects guessed our hypothesis. One subject (implemental mind-set) guessed that we were testing whether the information as sociated with the chosen type of material (black and white vs. color) is recalled better. The rest of the subjects took the incidental recall test as a check of whether they were good subjects who collaborated in an attentive and concentrated manner. As in other studies using this paradigm (Heckhausen & Gollwitzer, 1986, 1987), subjects were primarily concerned with the upcoming creativity test, on which they wanted to give their best.

Results

EQUIVALENCE OF MIND-SET GROUPS

Subjects' answers on the postexperimental questionnaire did not differ between groups: There were no differences with respect to the belief in one's creativity (Ms = 5.65 vs. 5.66), the confidence in one's capability for creative achievements (Ms = 5.76 vs. 5.72), and the importance assigned to being a creative person (Ms = 6.94 vs. 6.67), all Fs < 1.0. The relatively high means (unipolar 9-point scales) indicate that the subjects valued being creative and were quite certain of their possessing this desirable trait.

Subjects' answers on the postexperimental questionnaire also did not indicate any differences. The importance (Ms = 4.89 vs. 5.17), and difficulty (Ms = 6.35 vs. 6.67), of succeeding in the collage creativity test were perceived as similar in both conditions, as was also the case for the perceived importance of making the correct choice (Ms = 5.53 vs. 5.17), all Fs < 1.0. These data suggest that deliberative and implemental subjects took the collage test as a valid means to demonstrate being creative, and that they felt making the correct choice would influence their performance on this test.

Although black-and-white elements were chosen more than twice as often as color collage elements (25 vs. 10), this ratio did not differ across conditions, $\chi^2(1,N = 35)$ = .01, p = .91; nor did their general preference for black-and-white or for color collage elements (both Fs < 1.0)

DEPENDENT VARIABLES

Recall performance scores for expected value-related thoughts and implementation-related thoughts were determined by counting the respective thoughts that were recalled correctly. Deliberative mind-set subjects showed the predicted superior recall for expected value-related thoughts

(M = 7.29) as compared with implementation-related thoughts (M = 4.88), $t(16)$ = 2.25, $p < .02$ (one-tailed). Implemental mind-set subjects also evidenced mind-set congruous recall, recalling implementation-related thoughts (M =8.17) significantly better than expected value-related thoughts (M = 6.11), $t(17)$ = 2.02, p = <.03 (one-tailed). As expected, control subjects recalled expected value-related thoughts (M = 6.88) and implementation-related thougths (M = 6.63) about equally well, $t(15)$ = .24, ns (see Table 2).

To test the hypothesis that the recall performance for expected value-related and implementation-related information varies in a mind-set congruous direction, we conducted two separate one-way ANOVAs with linear contrast weights. With respect to the implementation-related information, the weights were set to test the hypothesis that its recall is highest for implemental mind-set subjects, followed by control subjects and then deliberative mind-set subjects. This analysis revealed a significant $F(1,48)$ = 4.03, p = .025 (one-tailed); the respective correlation coefficient is $r(51)$ = .28, p < .025. For expected value-related information, the weights were set to test the hypothesis that this information is recalled best by deliberative mind-set subjects, followed by control subjects and then implemental mind-set subjects, $F(1,48)$ = 1.02, $ns;$ $r(51)$ = .15, p = .15.

Although these findings indicate that for expected value-related information there is comparatively less mind-set congruous recall than for implementation-related information, recall of expected value-related information and implementation-related information combined to produce strong mind-set congruous recall (as can be seen from the difference scores reported in Table 2). When this difference index is submitted to a one-way ANOVA with linear contrast weights, a highly significant $F(1,48)$ = 9.15, $p < .003$ (one-tailed) emerges; the respective correlation coefficient is

TABLE 17.2. Mean Recall of Information on Expected Value and Implementation

Mind-set condition	Type of information		
	Thoughts about expected value	Thoughts about implementation	Difference
Deliberative	7.29	4.88	2.41
Control	6.87	6.63	0.24
Implemental	6.11	8.17	−2.06

Note. Higher numbers indicate better recall performance.

$r(51) = .41, p < .002$. This indicates that the superior recall for expected value-related information in the deliberative mind-set group was strongly reduced in the control group and reversed in the implemental mind-set group.

DISCUSSION

Deliberative mind-set subjects recalled expectecd value-related information better than implementation-related information, whereas implemental mind-set subjects showed better recall of implementation-related information than of expected value-related information. This pattern of data supports our hypothesis of superior recall of mind-set congruous information.

POSSIBLE CONFOUNDINGS

This conslusion rests on the assumption that the expected value-related information as well as the implementation-related information did not differ in other features (e.g., affective tone or complexity) that might be responsible for the recall performance of deliberative and implemental mind-set subjects. It might be argued, however, that implementation-related information was more positive in tone and that implemental mind-set subjects, because they were in a comparatively more positive mood, had an easier time recalling this information than deliberative mind-set subjects. Two reasons speak against this argument. First, it is unlikely that the implementation-related information was more positive in affective valence than the expected value-related information, because both types of information entailed positive and negative aspects (i.e., pleasant and unpleasant actions vs. positive and negative consequences, respectively). Second, the implemental mind-set cannot generally be assumed to produce a better mood than the deliberative mind-set. Planning may be as difficult and painful as deliberating; it all depends on the issue at hand.

Also, one might argue that the implementation-related information was worded such that it was more difficult to encode and retrieve than the expected value-related information. The recall performance of control subjects speaks against this argument; they recalled both types of information about equally well. Moreover, there are no convincing reasons why implemental mind-set subjects would be more effective in processing complex information as compared with deliberative mind-set subjects.

VARIOUS KINDS OF CONGRUOUS INFORMATION

Future studies should try to explore recall of other kinds of mind-set congruous information other than that used in the present experiment. With respect to implementation-related information, for instance, one might offer information on *where* to act, thus overcoming the present study's limitation to *when* (timing) and *how* (sequencing). With respect to deliberation-related information, one might want to extend the present study's limitation to *expected values*. Choosing between potential goals demands reflection about one's chances to implement these goals; otherwise, one would choose goals that are attractive but cannot be reached. Information on the feasibility of potential goals is thus congruous to a deliberative mind-set and should therefore also be processed more effectively in a deliberative as compared with an implemental mind-set.

ENCODING VERSUS RETRIEVAL

The present study is mute to the question of whether the observed mind-set congruous recall was achieved more by encoding or retrieval. This question, however, can be answered by testing both mind-set congruous recognition and recall in deliberative and implemental subjects. Recognition would capture the availability of the critical information (i.e., whether it was encoded or not), whereas recall would speak to the accessibility of stored information (i.e., whether it was easily retrieved or not; see Bargh & Thein, 1985; Srull, 1981, 1984).

An alternative approach may be taken by solely employing a recall procedure in a four-group design. In addition to the two groups tested in the present study, a third group would encode the critical information in a deliberative mind-set and recall it in an implemental mind-set. Finally, the fourth group would encode the information in an implemental mind-set and recall it in a deliberative mind-set. Comparisons among these four groups would allow one to determine the relative contribution of encoding and retrieval for mind-set congruous recall of expected value-related and implementation-related information.

In general, one would expect mind-sets to affect people's encoding of information in a mind-set congruous direction. This should be particularly pronounced when subjects are confronted with informational competition, that is, when more information than they can process impinges on them. Then, subjects must allocate attention to only some of the information available. Subjects' mind-sets should guide selective attention and thus favor the processing of congruous information.

But retrieval processes may also contribute to mind-set congruous recall. Assuming that subjects' retrieval attempts necessitate constructing descriptions of what they are trying to retrieve (Bobrow & Norman; 1975; Norman & Bobrow, 1976, 1979), it seems plausible that mind-sets provide perspectives (Bobrow & Winograd, 1977) that allow for the easy construction of specific descriptions. The deliberative mind-set, for instance, should favor descriptions phrased as pros and cons, benefits and costs, or hopes and fears. As Norman and Bobrow (1979) pointed out, quick construction of specific descriptions at the time of retrieval furthers successful retrieval. It seems possible, then, that deliberative and implemental mind-sets favor congruous recall by means of the prompt construction of appropriate descriptions (e.g., pros and cons vs. when and how).

General Discussion

The tasks people face in the various action phases create distinct mind-sets that tune people towards congruous thoughts and information. This finding is important for any theorizing on the course of action; in particular, it speaks to the question of whether the course of action should be conceptualized as homogeneous or heterogeneous, that is, compartmentalized into a number of distinct, qualitatively different phases. Lewin (Lewin, Dembo, Festinger, & Sears, 1944) suggested that the realm of goal-oriented behavior entails at least two distinct phenomena—goal setting and goal striving. He believed that goal setting may be accounted for by expectancy × value theories, whereas different theories should be developed to account for goal striving. However, researchers interested in goal-oriented behavior did not develop distinct theories to account for goal striving; rather, they stretched expectancy × value notions, making them account for both goal setting and goal striving (e.g.,

Atkinson, 1957). This has been criticized on the grounds that the extended expectancy × value theories have only been very modestly successful in predicting vital aspects of goal performance (see Klinger, 1977, pp. 22–24; 329–330).

The present experiments support Lewin's contention that goal setting and goal striving differ in nature. Individuals deliberating action goals were tuned toward thoughts and information that were different from those of individuals planning the implementation of a chosen goal. In recent experiments, further differences were observed between deliberating and planning individuals with respect to the inferences they made on the basis of available information (Gollwitzer & Kinney, 1989) and with respect to the absolute amount of available information they processed (Heckhausen & Gollwitzer, 1987, Study 2). These findings attest to differences in the natures of goal setting and goal striving; in addition, they bring to mind Lewin's claim that goal setting and goal striving deserve distinct theorizing.

ACKNOWLEDGMENTS

The help of Eva-Maria Detterbeck, Andrea Ennerest, Roswitha Flüge and Angelika Lengfelder in collecting and analyzing the data reported is greatly appreciated. We thank Christine Liu, Gabriele Oetingen, Fritz Strack, Robert Wicklund, and four anonymous reviewers, all of whom made valuable comments on an earlier version of this article.

REFERENCES

Anderson, J. R. (1983). *The architecture of cognition*. Cambridge, MA: Harvard University Press.

Atkinson, J. W. (1957). Motivational determinants of risk-taking behavior. *Psychological Review, 64,* 359–372.

Bargh, J. A., & Thein, R. D. (1985). Individual construct accessibility, person memory, and the recall-judgment link: The case of information overload. *Journal of Personality and Social Psychology, 49,* 1129–1146.

Bobrow, D. G., & Norman, D. A. (1975). Some principles of memory schemata. In D. G. Bobrow & A. Collins (Eds.), *Representation and understanding* (pp. 131–149). New York: Academic Press.

Bobrow D. G., & Winograd, T. (1977). An *overview of KRL*, a knowledge representation language. *Cognitive Science, 1,* 3–46.

Boring, E. G. (1950). *A history of experimental psychology*. New York: Appleton-Century-Crofts.

Gibson, J. J. (1941). A critical review of the concept of set in contemporary experimental psychology. *Psychological Bulletin, 38,* 781–817.

Gollwitzer, P. M. (1990). Action phases and mind sets. In E. T. Higgins & R. M. Sorrentino (Eds.), *Handbook of motivation and cognition: Foundations of social behavior* (Vol. 2, pp. 53–92). New York: Guilford Press.

Gollwitzer, P. M., Heckhausen, H., & Ratajczak, H. (1990). From weighing to willing. Approaching a change decision through pre- or postdecisional mentation. *Organizational Behavior and Human Decision Processes, 45,* 41–65.

Gollwitzer, P. M., & Kinney, R. F. (1989). Effects of deliberative and implemental mind-sets on illusion of control. *Journal of Personality and Social Psychology, 56,* 531–542.

Heckhausen, H. (1986). Why some time out might benefit achievement motivation research. In J. H. L. van den Bercken, T. C. M. Bergen, & E. E. J. De Bruyn (Eds.), *Achievement and task motivation* (pp. 7–39). Lisse, The Netherlands: Swets & Zeitliner.

Heckhausen, H., & Gollwitzer, P. M. (1986). Information processing before and after the formation of an intent. In F. Klin & H. Hagendorf (Eds.), *In memorian Hermann Ebbinghaus: Symposium on the structure and function of human memory* (pp. 1071–1082). Amsterdam: Elsevier/North Holland.

Heckhausen, H., & Gollwitzer, P. M. (1987). Thought contents and cognitive functioning in motivational vs. volitional states of mind. *Motivation and Emotion, 11,* 101–120.

Higgins, E. T., Rholes, W. S., & Jones, C. R. (1977). Category accessibility and impression formation. *Journal of Experimental Social Psychology, 13,* 141–154.

Humphrey, G. (1951). *Thinking.* London: Methuen.

Klinger, E. (1977). *Meaning and void.* Minneapolis: University of Minnesota Press.

Kulpe, O. (1904). Versuche uber Abstraktion [Experiments on abstraction]. *Bericht uberden l. Kongreb fur Experimentelle Psychologie, 1,* 56–68.

Lewin, K., Dembo, T., Festinger, L. A., & Sears, P. S. (1944). Level of aspiration. In J. McV. Hunt (Ed.), *Personality and the behavior disorders* (Vol. I, pp. 333–378). New York: Ronald.

Marbe, K. (1901). *Experimentell-psychologische Untersuchungen über das Urtell* [Experimental studies on judgement]. Leipzig: W. Engelmann.

Norman, D. A., & Bobrow, D. G. (1976). On the role of active memory processes in perception and cognition. In C. N. Cofer (Ed.), *The structure of human memory* (pp. 114–132). San Francisco: Freeman and Company.

Norman, D. A., & Bobrow, D. G. (1979). Descriptions: An intermediate stage in memory retrieval. *Cognitive Psychology, 11,* 107–123.

Rabkin, E. S. (1979). *Fantastic worlds: Myths, tales and stories.* Oxford, England: Oxford University Press.

Rosenthal, R., & Rosnow, R. L. (1985). *Contrast analysis: Focused comparisons in the analysis of variance.* New York: Cambridge University Press.

Rumelhart, D. E. (1975). Notes on a schema for stories. In D. G. Bobrow & A. M. Collins (Eds.), *Representation and understanding* (pp. 211–236). New York: Academic Press.

Rumelhart, D. E. (1977). Understanding and summarizing brief stories. In D. LaBerge & J. Samuels (Eds.), *Basic processes in reading and comprehension* (pp. 265–303). Hillsdale, NJ: Erlbaum.

Smith, E. R., & Branscombe, N. R. (1987). Procedurally mediated social inferences: The case of category accessibility effects. *Journal of Experimental Social Psychology, 23,* 361–382.

Srull, T. K. (1981). Person memory: Some tests of associative storage and retrieval models, *Journal of Experimental Psychology: Human Learning and Memory, 7,* 440–463.

Srull, T. K. (1984). Methodological techniques for the study of person memory and social cognition. In R. S. Wyer & T. K. Srull (Eds.), *Handbook of social cognition* (Vol. 2, pp. 1–72). Hillsdale, NJ: Erlbaum.

Srull, T. K., & Wyer, R. S. (1979). The role of category accessibility in the interpretation of information about persons: Some determinants and implications. *Journal of Personality and Social Psychology, 37,* 1660–1672.

Watt, H. J. (1905). Experimentelle Beitrage zu einer Theorie des Denkens (Experiments on a theory of thinking). *Archiv für die gesamie Psychologie, 4,* 289–436.

Appendix
Coding Scheme for Subjects' Stories

Ascribing Deliberative Efforts to Main Character

Deliberation aimed at making a goal decision: "The king racked his brains, wondering what to do . . ."; "The king was thinking things over for many days and nights, weighing whether to stay at home."

Turning to others for advice and listening to their suggestions. "The king asked a monk to give him advice . . ."; "The king listened to a fortune teller . . ."

Ascribing Implementational Efforts to Main Character

Actual acting on a chosen goal: "The tailor forced himself through the rock passage . . ."; "The king sent out more men to search the forest . . ."; "The king ordered a trusted officer to stay at the castle and protect his daughter . . ."

Thinking about the implementation of the chosen goal: "The king asked himself how could he find a trusted person who would stay home and protect his daughter . . ."; "The tailor wondered how to climb up the steep wall . . ."

On the Automatic Activation of Attitudes

Russell H. Fazio, David M. Sanbonmatsu, Martha C. Powell, and Frank R. Kardes
• Indiana University

Editors' Notes

The concept of attitude is widely used both in popular parlance and by social scientists. But what precisely is an attitude? This selection adopts a cognitive approach to attitudes. From its perspective, an attitude constitutes an association between two things—an evaluation and an object. This deceptively simple conception is quite powerful because, methodologically, it suggests that cognitive methods can be used to study attitudes, and, conceptually, it suggests a continuum of attitude strength. After all, at one end of the continuum one might not possess strong attitudes in regard to some objects in the world (e.g., badminton, Polish sausage, or the viola da gamba), while at the other end of the continuum one might have definite positive or negative attitudes (e.g., love, death, cockroaches, and butterflies). In cognitive terms, the former objects do not have a strong association with an evaluation, whereas the latter do. An innovative aspect of the research reported in this selection is the measurement of these associations through reaction-time procedures. Positive or negative objects to which one has an "accessible" attitude prompt quick evaluations. Objects to which one's attitudes are "inaccessible" or nonexistent yield slower evaluations. A major focus of the paper is on the automaticity of attitude evocation. If an attitude is automatically evoked upon presentation of its associated object, then this evaluation can facilitate or inhibit the evaluation of a subsequent object depending on whether these two objects have the same or opposite valence. These effects are also measured with the response-time technique. Thus, cognitive theorizing and research methods make a significant contribution to an understanding of the popular, and important, concept of attitudes.

Discussion Questions

1. Do all objects evoke an automatic attitude activation? If so, why so? If not, why not?
2. When should prior presentation of an attitude object facilitate the evaluation of a subsequent object and when should it inhibit the evaluation?
3. How does the notion of attitude accessibility relate to the "attitude-nonattitude" continuum?
4. How can the strength of an attitude be externally manipulated?

Suggested Readings

Bargh, J. A., Chaiken, S., Govender, R., & Pratto, F. (1992). The generality of the automatic attitude activation effect. *Journal of Personality and Social Psychology, 62,* 893–912.

Fazio, R. H., & Zanna, M. P. (1981). Direct experience and attitude-behavior consistency. *Advanced Experimental Social Psychology, 14,* 161–202.

Martin, L. K., Harlow, T. F., & Strack, S. (1992). The role of one's own bodily sensations in the evaluation of social events. *Personality and Social Psychology Bulletin, 18,* 412–419.

Zajonc, R. B. (1968). Attitudinal effects of mere exposure. *Journal of Personality and Social Psychology Monograph, 9,* 1–28.

Authors' Abstract

We hypothesized that attitudes characterized by a strong association between the attitude object and an evaluation of that object are capable of being activated from memory automatically upon mere presentation of the attitude object. We used a priming procedure to examine the extent to which the mere presentation of an attitude object would facilitate the latency with which subjects could indicate whether a subsequently presented target adjective had a positive or a negative connotation. Across three experiments, facilitation was observed on trials involving evaluatively congruent primes (attitude objects) and targets, provided that the attitude object possessed a strong evaluative association. In Experiments 1 and 2, preexperimentally strong and weak associations were identified via a measurement procedure. In Experiment 3, the strength of the object-evaluation association was manipulated. The results indicated that attitudes can be automatically activated and that the strength of the object-evaluation association determines the likelihood of such automatic activation. The implications of these findings for a variety of issues regarding attitudes—including their functional value, stability, effects on later behavior, and measurement—are discussed.

Our focus in this article is on the activation of attitudes from memory. The essential question to be addressed is whether attitudes are capable of being activated automatically upon the individual's encountering the attitude object. Consider such an encounter. One possibility is that the individual's attitude will be activated spontaneously and without any conscious effort on his or her part upon observation of the attitude object. On the other hand, it might be that activation of the attitude requires that the individual engage in a far more reflective process in which he or she actively considers his or her attitude toward the object. Our concern is with the extent to which the former possibility occurs and the degree to which the likelihood of its occurrence depends upon characteristics of the attitude in question.

The two possibilities regarding attitude activation outlined above correspond to the distinction offered by cognitive psychologists between automatic and controlled processes (e.g., Schneider & Shiffrin, 1977; Shiffrin & Schneider, 1977). Shiffrin and Dumais (1981) characterized as automatic any process that leads to the activation of some concept or response "whenever a given set of external initiating stimuli are presented, regardless of a subject's attempt to ignore or bypass the distraction" (p. 117). The key feature of such automatic activation, then, is its inescapability. The implication for attitudes is that, upon presentation of an attitude object, an individual's attitude would be activated despite the lack of any reflection whatsoever on his or her part. In contrast, a controlled process requires the active attention of the individual. Upon becoming aware of a situational cue implying the importance of considering one's attitude toward an object, the individual might attempt to retrieve a previously stored evaluation of the attitude object or might actively construct such an attitude on the spot. In either case, the process is reflective and active in nature.

The occurrence of an automatic process requires the existence of a previously well-learned set of associations or responses. For example, Shiffrin and Schneider (1977) observed that a target stimulus developed the ability to attract attention automatically only following extensive training. The experimenters first trained subjects to respond to a set of characters (letters). On the critical trials of a subsequent task, these characters served as distractor items. That is, one such character might appear on a display in a location that was irrelevant to the subject's task. Despite this irrelevance, these characters to which the subject had earlier been trained to attend did attract attention, as indicated by relatively poorer performance on the primary task. Shiffrin (in press) reviewed a number of such investigations concerning the development of automatism.

Given that automatic processes require such well-learned responses, it appears doubtful that automatic activation is likely for all of the attitudes that an individual might hold. Only for well-learned ones is the expectation of automatic activation even a possibility. Social psychologists have long recognized that attitudes vary in their "strength." Indeed, a variety of attempts have been made to quantify and assess the centrality or importance of an attitude issue for a given individual. The notion of ego-involvement in the context of social judgment theory serves as an illustration of such an approach (Hovland, Harvey, & Sherif, 1957; M. Sherif & Cantril, 1947). More recently, various indices of the "strength" of an attitude have been identified as moderators of the relation between attitudes and behavior. As examples, the

confidence with which an attitude is held (Sample & Warland, 1973; Fazio & Zanna, 1978a, 1978b); how clearly defined the attitude is, as measured by the width of the latitude of rejection (C. Sherif, Kelly, Rodgers, Sarup, & Tittler, 1973; Fazio & Zanna, 1978a); and the consistency between affective and cognitive components of the attitude (Norman, 1975) have each been found to relate to attitude-behavior consistency.

Relevant to this idea of attitudes varying in strength is the so-called *attitude/nonattitude* distinction. A number of years ago, both Hovland (1959) and Converse (1970) attempted to reconcile differences that had been observed between survey and laboratory research on attitude change. In so doing, they each—but Converse in particular—focused on a distinction between attitudes and nonattitudes. The distinction centered on the observation that a person may respond to an item on an attitude survey even though that particular attitude does not really exist in any a priori fashion for the individual. The attitude object may be one that the individual has not even considered prior to administration of the attitude survey. For Converse (1970), the attitude/nonattitude distinction centered on measurement error. An individual's nonattitude was characterized by unreliable measurement (in fact, virtually random responding) across the waves of a panel survey.

The attitude/nonattitude dichotomy might be more fruitfully conceived as a continuum. At one end of the continuum is the nonattitude. No a priori evaluation of the attitude object exists. As we move along the continuum, an evaluation does exist and its accessibility from memory grows increasingly strong. At the other extreme of the continuum, then, is a well-learned attitude that is highly accessible from memory.

A particular conception of attitudes underlies this view of the attitude/nonattitude continuum. In a recent series of experiments concerning attitude accessibility, Fazio and his colleagues (Fazio, Chen, McDonel, & Sherman, 1982; Fazio, Powell, & Herr, 1983; Powell & Fazio, 1984) proposed that attitudes be viewed as simple associations between a given object and a given evaluation. The term *object* is used in a broad sense. Individuals may have evaluations of a wide variety of potential attitude objects, including social issues, categories of situations, categories of people, and specific individuals, as well as physical objects. Likewise, the term *evaluation* is used in a broad sense. It may range in nature from a very "hot" affect (the attitude object being associated with a strong emotional response) to a "colder" more cognitively-based judgment of one's affect (feelings of favorability or unfavorability) toward the object (see Abelson, Kinder, Peters, & Fiske, 1982; Zanna & Rempel, 1984).

More relevant to the present purposes is the notion of association between the attitude object and the evaluation, regardless of the precise nature of this evaluation. The definition of an attitude implies that the strength of an attitude, like any other construct based on associative learning, can vary. That is, the strength of the association between the object and the evaluation can vary. This associative strength may determine the accessibility of the attitude from memory and the likelihood that the attitude will be activated automatically upon the individual's encountering the attitude object. Only if it is strongly associated with the attitude object is it likely that the evaluation will be spontaneously activated upon mere presentation of the attitude object. In general, what is being suggested is that the activation of one's affect toward an object (be it a hot or a cold linkage) depends on the strength of the association.

In testing this view of attitudes as object-evaluation associations, Fazio and his associates (Fazio et al., 1982; Powell & Fazio, 1984) employed latency of response to an attitudinal inquiry a measure of the associative strength. Subjects were asked indicate as quickly as possible whether they felt positively negatively toward a given attitude object. Subjects who had been induced to express their attitudes repeatedly—which should have the consequence of strengthening the object-evaluation association —were able to respond relatively quickly to these direct inquiries about their attitudes. For example, Powell and Fazio (1984) manipulated the number of times that an attitude was expressed in a within-subjects design by varying the number of semantic differential scale items that appeared relevant to a given attitude issue. In this way, subjects expressed their attitudes either one, three, or six times toward a given object. [1] In a subsequent task, subjects were presented with each attitude object and were instructed to make a good or bad judgment about each attitude object as quickly as possible. Latency of response (from stimulus onset to response) was found to relate to the number of previous attitudinal expressions. The

greater the number of expressions, the faster the latency of response to the attitudinal inquiry.

These findings imply that attitudes characterized by object-evaluation associations may be more accessible from memory. However, it is important to recognize that these finding are not at all informative with respect to the issue of whether the attitude activation stems from an automatic or a control process. Responding quickly to a direct attitudinal inquiry does not necessarily mean that the stored evaluation was activated automatically. Instead, the evaluation simply may have been retrieved efficiently via an effortful, controlled process.

In order to examine the automatic activation of attitudes from memory, the present research employed a priming technique. The procedure is a variant of a now well-tested method often employed to investigate automatic processing. It involves consideration of the extent to which the presentation of a prime automatically activates concepts that facilitate responding to the target word. For example, Neely (1977) found that use of a category label as a prime (e.g., bird) facilitated the speed with which subjects could identify a subsequently presented target word as a word, provided that the target was semantically related to the category (e.g., robin). The technique has been used to study activation from memory in a variety of contexts, including text processing (e.g., McKoon & Ratcliff, 1980; Ratcliff & McKoon, 1978) and spatial representations (e.g., McNam, Ratcliff, & McKoon, 1984), as well as semantic relations (e.g., Neely, 1976, 1977; deGroot, 1983).

In the present context, the subjects' primary task was to indicate as quickly as possible whether a target adjective (e.g., pleasant) had a positive or negative connotation. Latency of response served as the dependent measure. Our concern was with the extent to which such a judgment would be facilitated by the presentation of an attitude object as the prime. We reasoned that presentation of an attitude object would automatically activate any strong association to that object. Such activation is assumed to spread along the paths of the memory network, including any evaluative associations.

---

[1] This manipulation had no effect on the extremity of the final attitudinal expression. Thus, the results appear to be due to the strength of the object-evaluation association as a consequence of repeated attitudinal expression.

Consequently, the activation levels of associated evaluations are temporarily increased. If a target word that corresponds in valence to one of these previously activated evaluations is subsequently presented for judgment, then less additional activation is required for the activation level of the target word to reach threshold and, consequently, for a judgment to be made. Responding to a target word that has received some activation as a result of presentation of the prime is thus facilitated. That is, the individual should be able to respond relatively quickly.

As an example, let's assume that the attitude object *vodka* is evaluated positively by an individual. Presentation of vodka as the prime may automatically activate a positive evaluation. If the target adjective that is presented is also positive, then the individual may be able to indicate relatively quickly that the target has a positive connotation. That is, facilitation should occur. In a similar manner, facilitation is expected in the case of a negatively valued object serving as the prime when it is followed by a negative target adjective, as in *cockroach/disgusting*. What is meant by facilitation is simply that the latency is faster in such cases than in a trial involving the same target word preceded by a letter string (e.g., BBB). Such trials provide a no-prime baseline. Thus, the technique relies on the presence of facilitation as an indication that the evaluation associated with the primed attitude object has been activated upon its mere observation.

Of course, we would not expect such facilitation to occur for all attitude objects. Relating the methodology to the previous discussion of the attitude/nonattitude continuum, we would expect facilitation to occur only if the object-evaluation association is quite strong. In Experiments 1 and 2, the strength of the object-evaluation association was assessed with regard to a large number of potential attitude objects and strong versus weak primes were selected on an individual basis for each and every subject. In Experiment 3, the strength of the object-evaluation association was manipulated.

Experiment 1

The first experiment involved selecting attitude objects toward which a given individual possessed

a strong versus a weak evaluative association and then testing whether those objects produced facilition when presented as primes in the major experimental task. In order to assess the strength of object-evaluation associations, we employed the operationalization that had been used successfully in the studies of attitude accessibility mentioned earlier (Fazio et al., 1982; Powell & Fazio, 1984). Recall that the findings from this previous research indicated that latency of response to an attitudinal inquiry appears to index the strength of an object-evaluation association satisfactorily.

In the present experiment, attitude objects toward which a given subject displayed very fast or very slow latencies of response to an attitudinal inquiry were identified. If the latency was fast, we consider the object-evaluation association strong and, hence, facilitation should occur in the procedure described earlier. That is, positive target adjectives should be identified as having a positive connotation relatively more quickly when preceded by a positively valued object. Likewise, negative target adjectives should be identified as having a negative connotation relatively more quickly when preceded by a negatively valued object. Such facilitation is far less likely in the case of a weak object-evaluation association, as indicated by a slow latency of response to the direct inquiry. Thus, the hypothesis leads to a prediction of a three-way interaction (Strength of Association × Valence of Prime × Valence of Target). Greater facilitation is expected on trials involving congruent valences than on trials involving incongruent valences (i.e., a simple interaction of Prime Valence × Target Valence) for primes involving a strong evaluative association but not for primes involving a weak association.

Method

Subjects. Twenty-two Indiana University undergraduates participated in the experiment in partial fulfillment of an introductory psychology course requirement.

Procedure. Subjects were told that the experiment concerned word recognition and meaning and that a number of different tasks relevant to word judgment would be performed during the course of the experiment. They were also told that these tasks would grow increasingly complex as we progressed through the procedure.

The experimental procedure consisted of two major phases, the first devoted to prime selection and the second involving the actual priming task. A list of 70 attitude objects (including the names of some individuals, animals, foods, social groups, nations, activities, and physical objects) formed the pool of potential primes. Subjects were told that the first and simplest word-judgment task that they would be performing involved the presentation of a single word on the computer screen on any given trial. Their task was to press a key labeled *good* or a key labeled *bad* as quickly as possible to indicate their judgment of the object. Subjects were instructed to maximize both the speed and accuracy of their responses. The presentation was controlled by an Apple II+ computer. The order in which the words were presented was randomized for each subject. A given word remained visible on the screen until the subject responded. A 3-s interval separated each trial. The subject's response was recorded, along with the latency of response (from word onset to response) to the nearest millisecond. Subjects' performance of this task was preceded by a block of practice trials involving different words than those used as the potential primes, so as to familiarize subjects with the procedure.

After performing the task, subjects were excused from the laboratory for a short break. During this time, 16 words were selected on the basis of the subject's data as the primes. Four words were selected in each of four categories: strong good, strong bad, weak good, and weak bad. The 4 words toward which the subject had responded *good* and the 4 toward which the subject had responded *bad* most quickly served as the strong primes. The 4 good and the 4 bad words involving the slowest latencies served as the weak primes.[2] These 16 words, along with four different strings of three identical letters (e.g., BBB), which were intended to provide nonprime baselines, were employed as the primes in the next task.

A list of 10 evaluative adjectives that were clearly positive in connotation (e.g., "appealing," "delightful") and a list of 10 adjectives that were clearly negative (e.g., "repulsive," "awful") were prepared. These words served as the target words in the next phase of the experiment. Subjects were told that this task was a more complex one involving their again making a judgment of a word, but that this time they would have to remember another word while making the judgment. They were informed that a memory word would be presented followed by an adjective. They were to press the good or bad key as quickly as possible to indicate whether the adjective had a positive or negative connotation and to then recite the memory word aloud. Subjects were told to recite the memory word, that is the prime, solely to ensure that they attended to the prime. (In the case of a letter string such as BBB, subjects were instructed to recite "Triple B.") A cassette recorder was positioned adjacent to the computer to bolster the presumption that the experimenter was concerned about the subjects' recitation of the memory word.

On any given trial, a prime was presented for 200 ms, followed by a 100-ms interval before onset of the target word. Thus, the interval between prime onset and target onset, commonly referred to as the stimulus onset asynchrony (SOA), was 300 ms. The target word disappeared upon the subject's pressing a key. A 4-s interval passed before presentation of the next prime.

A total of five blocks of trials were presented. Each block consisted of 20 trials, in which each of the 20 primes (including the four letter strings) and each of the 20 target adjectives were presented once. Within each of the five prime categories (strong good, strong bad, weak good, weak bad, and letter string), 2 of the primes were followed by positive adjectives and 2 by negative adjectives. Across blocks, each target adjective was paired once with a prime from each of the five prime categories (strong good, strong bad, weak good, weak bad, and letter string). Thus, a target adjective appeared equally often in each of the five prime conditions. As with the prime selection task, subjects underwent a series of practice trials before performing the actual task so as to familiarize them with the procedure.

---

[2]Which attitude objects from the pool of 70 potential primes were selected for use as primes was quite idiosyncratic across subjects. Nevertheless, the following tabulation is intended to provide the reader with some sense of the nature of the attitude objects that served as priming stimuli. The most frequently selected objects in each of the four prime categories and the number of subjects for whom each object was selected are listed: strong good—gift (7), music (7), party (6), and cake (5); strong bad—death (11), hell (7), guns (6), and crime (5); weak good—crosswords (8), Republicans (7), Democrats (7), and rum (6); and weak bad—mazes (9), radiation (7), Democrats (7), and recession (6). Some of the other objects that also were selected for use as primes relatively frequently, but in varying categories, included vodka (8), snow (8), spider (8), television (7), dentist (6), sports (6), storms (6), Reagan (5), coffee (5), and Iran (4).

Results and Discussion

Subjects committed very few errors in making judgments of the connotation of the target adjectives. The average error rate across subjects was 1.95%. In these few cases, the latency was excluded from the analysis. For each subject, the mean response latency in each of the 10 cells of the design (Five Prime Categories × Positive vs. Negative Targets) was computed. Facilitation scores were then computed. Each mean in a positive target condition was subtracted from the nonprime baseline provided by trials in which positive targets were preceded by a letter string. The same was done with respect to the negative target conditions. [3] The resulting facilitation scores are depicted in Figure 1.

A 2 (strength of association) × 2 (prime valence) × 2 (target valence) analysis of variance was performed on the facilitation scores. The analysis revealed that the expected three-way interaction was statistically significant, $F(1, 21) = 6.86$, $p < .02$. In the case of primes involving a strong evaluative association, the predicted interaction between prime valence and target valence was very apparent, $F(1, 21) = 15.30$, $p < .001$. Just as we predicted, facilitation occurred in the cases of congruency between the valence of the primed object and the valence of the target adjective, but not in the cases of incongruency. That is, facilitation is apparent for positively valued attitude objects when followed by a positive target and for negatively valued objects when followed by a negative target. Inhibition is apparent for positively valued attitude objects when followed by a negative target and for negatively valued objects when followed by a positive target.

As indicated by the significant three-way interaction, the data pattern is quite different for those objects involving a weak evaluative association. Most important, there is no interaction between prime valence and target valence, $F < 1$, and no evidence of facilitation in the case of the weak primes. The only effect is a main effect of the valence of the primed object, $F(1, 21)$ 14.58, $p < .001$. Negative objects produced inhibition regardless of the valence of the target adjective. Apparently, the negative objects involving a weak association somehow distracted subjects from the

---

[3]For the benefit of any reader interested in considering raw latencies, the positive target and negative target baselines were 1,065 ms and 1,090 ms, respectively.

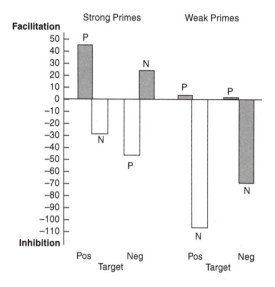

FIGURE 18.1 ■ Mean facilitation scores in Experiment 1 as a function of the strength of the object-evaluation association, the valence of the prime (P = positive; N = negative), and the valence of the target adjective (Pos = positive; Neg = negative). (Conditions involving congruent valences are darkened; incongruent ones are not.)

central task. However, this effect should be interpreted cautiously because, unlike the effect observed for strong primes it does not replicate in the later experiments to be reported.

On the basis of these findings, it appears that at least some attitudes may be activated from memory automatically upon mere presentation of the attitude object. What is critical is that the present evidence for subjects' attitudes having been activated is found in a situation in which the subject was merely exposed to the attitude object. The subjects were never asked during the second phase of the experiment to consider their attitudes. Nor was it to the subjects' advantage to do so, for the subjects' task was simply to respond to the target word and then to recite the memory word. Nevertheless, despite this irrelevance of attitudes to the immediate task concerns, exposure to objects for which subjects presumably possessed strong affective associations appears to have prompted activation of the associated evaluation.

Thus, the very nature of the task leads to the suggestion that the facilitation observed in the case of the strong primes was a result of automatic, rather than controlled, processing. Nevertheless, it might be argued that subjects did for some reason actively consider their evaluations of the prime and, hence, were "prepared" for a target word of congruent valence. To explain the findings, such an interpretation would have to maintain that the SOA that was employed allowed sufficient time for subjects to actively retrieve their evaluation in the case of strong primes, but was insufficient for such active retrieval in the case of weak primes. In order to examine this possibility, a second experiment involving manipulation of the SOA was conducted.

Experiment 2

If the facilitation observed in Experiment 1 were due to a controlled process, then allowing the subjects more time should, if anything, enhance the extent of facilitation. Most important, facilitation might be observed even in the case of weak primes. On the other hand, if the task is such, as we have argued, that the findings in Experiment 1 reflect automatic processing, then no such facilitation is to be expected for weak primes even at a longer SOA. Assuming that the interpretation in terms of automatism is valid, then whether facilitation in the case of strong primes is observed at a longer SOA will depend on the level of activation of the associated evaluation at the time the target word is presented. If the level of activation has dissipated (possibly due to its irrelevance to the immediate task concerns) then no facilitation is to be expected at the longer SOA. If the level of activation has not yet returned to baseline, then some facilitation might be expected.

Method

Subjects. Twenty-three individuals who had responded to a newspaper advertisement participated in the experiment in return for a payment of $6.

Procedure. The experimental procedure followed that employed in Experiment 1. The only major difference was that, following prime selection, subjects underwent the actual priming task twice. They did so once with an SOA of 300 ms and once with an SOA of 1000 ms. The order in which they did so was counterbalanced across subjects.

The only other procedural changes made were minor ones aimed at enhancing the power of the experiment. The pool of potential primes employed in the prime selection phase of the experiment was expanded to 92 attitude objects.[4] In addition, a few target adjectives that had produced relatively short or long latencies when preceded by letter strings were replaced by other words.

Results and Discussion

As in Experiment 1, errors were minimal (mean error rate = 1.39%) and when they did occur, the respective latency was omitted from the analysis. Facilitation scores[5] are depicted in Figure 2. Because the order of the blocks of trials involving SOAs of 300 versus 1,000 ms did not qualify any of the effects to be reported, the facilitation scores are presented collapsed across the order variable. As is clear from Figure 2, left column, the findings with an SOA of 300 ms replicate those observed in Experiment 1 when one considers attitude objects involving a strong evaluative association. Most important, there was a significant interaction of prime and target valence for strong primes at this SOA, $F(1, 22) = 4.87$, $p < .05$. Facilitation was greater in the case of congruent valences than in the case of incongruent valences. Furthermore, the extent of facilitation in the congruent cases ($M = 37$ ms) differed significantly from zero, $t(22) = 2.17$, $p < .05$. No significant facilitation was apparent in any of the other cells of the design—strong primes presented at the longer SOA or weak primes at either SOA. This pattern of data led to the observation of a significant SOA × Strength of Association × Prime Valence × Target Valence interaction, $F(1, 22) = 4.35$, $p < .05$. Only in the case of strong primes and the shorter SOA was facilitation found on trials involving congruent evaluations.

---

[4]The attitude objects most frequently selected for use as primes in each of the four categories (and the number of subjects for whom the object was selected) were as follows: strong good—music (7), friend (7), dancing (5), and cake (5); strong bad—war (8), death (8), cancer (6), and rats (6); weak good—Monday (9), dormitory (5), landlords (5), and Reagan (4); and weak bad—anchovies (8), landlords (6), exams (6), and recession (6). Some of the other objects that also were selected for use as primes relatively frequently, but in varying categories, included priest (8), fraternity (7), dentist (6), liver (6), mosquito (6), worms (6), guns (5), spider (5), taxes (5), and disco (4).

[5]The positive and negative target baselines were 830 ms and 880 ms, respectively, at the SOA of 300, and 770 ms and 790 ms, respectively, at the SOA of 1,000.

Thus, even when subjects were provided with additional time, no evidence of facilitation was observed for weak primes. It does not appear that the evaluative association was activated upon presentation of the attitude object when the association was weak in nature. This null finding tends to undermine the plausibility of the controlled processing alternative outlined earlier. If subjects had been actively retrieving their attitudes, then greater facilitation was to be expected at the longer SOA.

Apparently, facilitation in the present task is the result of automatic activation of the evaluation upon presentation of the attitude object. However, such automatic activation requires the existence of a strong association between the attitude object and the evaluation. The findings regarding SOA imply that the level of activation in such cases dissipated quickly (or, conceivably, was actively suppressed). Such quick dissipation may have been a consequence of the irrelevance of the subject's attitudes to the major task that was occupying the subject's attention, that is, identifying the connotation of the target adjective. In effect, presentation of the target adjective 1,000 ms after presentation of the attitude object appears to have been too late for the prime to facilitate responding to adjectives of the same valence. At the 300-ms interval, on the other hand, the level of activation of the associated evaluation was apparently sufficient to facilitate responding to evaluatively congruent adjectives. This finding is reminiscent of one from Neely's (1977) investigation. Subjects had been instructed that the prime *bird* implied that a target

word corresponding to a body part would be presented. Despite this instruction, responses to a specific bird exemplar (e.g., robin) as the target were facilitated at a short SOA. However, no such facilitation was observed at a longer SOA. In a fashion parallel to the present case, the level of activation of whatever exemplars had been activated by the presentation of the category prime apparently dissipated quickly.

Experiment 3

In each of the two experiments reported thus far, evidence supportive of the possibility of automatic activation of one's attitude upon mere exposure to the attitude object was found. Such automatic activation was restricted, however, to attitudes involving a strong object-evaluation association. Associative strength was measured via latency of response to an attitudinal inquiry. Attitudes that individuals could report relatively quickly were considered to involve strong object-evaluation associations. Such attitudes were compared to ones that required more time for subjects to report. These two classes of attitudes were found to differ with regard to the likelihood of presentation of the attitude object automatically activating the attitude from memory. We have argued that the strength of the object-evaluation association was the critical difference responsible for this differential likelihood. Nevertheless, as is the case any time a conceptual variable is measured rather than

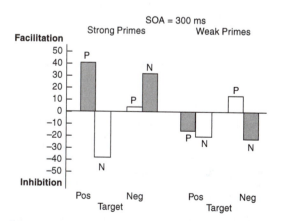
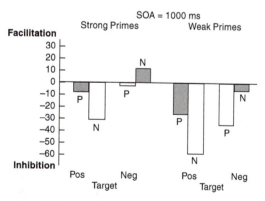

FIGURE 18.2 ■ Mean facilitation scores in Experiment 2 as a function of SOA (stimulus onset asynchrony), the strength of the object-evaluation association, the valence of the prime (P = positive; N = negative), and the valence of the target adjective (Pos = positive; Neg = negative). (Conditions involving congruent valences are darkened; incongruent ones are not.)

manipulated, other differences might exist between the two classes of attitudes that were identified via our measurement technique.

Experiment 3 was aimed at demonstrating more conclusively the critical importance of the strength of the object-evaluation association by manipulating rather than measuring it. Subjects were induced to express their attitudes toward a number of attitude objects repeatedly, as in the study described earlier by Powell and Fazio (1984). Another set of attitude objects was presented equally often but subjects were asked to make a non-evaluative judgment regarding each of these objects. In this way, the object-evaluation association was strengthened for some attitudes and not for others. These objects then served as primes in the subsequent task. The experimental design was the same as that of Experiment 2. The only difference was that strong versus weak primes were created experimentally rather than being selected on the basis of measured preexperimental strength. A four-way interaction similar to that found in Experiment 2 is to be expected. That is, facilitation should be greater in the cases of congruency between the evaluation of the prime and the evaluation of the target than in the cases of incongruency only for strong primes presented 300 ms before the target words.

Method

Subjects. Eighteen Indiana University undergraduates participated in the experiment in partial fulfillment of an introductory psychology course requirement.

Procedure. As before, subjects were led to believe that the experiment concerned word recognition and that the experimenter was interested in the "speed and accuracy with which people could perform various word recognition tasks." In the initial task, a word and a question appeared simultaneously on the computer screen. In some instances, the question asked "One syllable word?" and the subject was to respond by pressing a yes or no key as quickly as possible. In other instances, the question was "Good or bad?" and subjects responded by pressing the appropriate key as quickly as possible. The words and accompanying question were presented in a random order for each subject. Three seconds separated each trial. Subjects underwent a series of practice trials before

performing the actual task so as to ensure their understanding of the task.

A total of 16 attitude objects served as the stimuli that were subject to manipulation. The words were selected from the pool of 92 potential primes employed in Experiment 2 on the basis of the response and response latency data from the prime selection phase of Experiment 2. Two relevant criteria were employed to guide this process. First, objects that were endorsed as positive or negative with near unanimity across the subjects were selected. Second, of these objects that produced nearly uniform responses, the ones with the longest average response latencies across subjects were chosen. In this way, 8 positively valued ("aquarium," "baby," "cake," "chocolate," "eagle," "Friday," "parade," and "silk") and 8 negatively valued ("divorce," "hangover," "litter," "radiation," "recession," "toothache," "virus," and "weeds") attitude objects were selected.[6] These words were then randomly divided into two lists each consisting of 4 positive and 4 negative objects. For any given subject, one list was associated with the attitude expression question and one with the syllable identification question. Which specific list was used for which purpose was counterbalanced across subjects.

The actual task consisted of five blocks of 30 trials each. In any given block, the 16 words of interest appeared once. Thus, across blocks, subjects expressed their attitudes toward 8 of the objects 5 times[7] and answered the syllable question with respect to each of the 8 words from the other list 5 times. In this way, the number of presentations of the critical words was held constant. Filler words were included to bring the number of trials in each block to 30. Sixteen filler words were presented once throughout the series of blocks and another 18 filler words were presented a total of 3 times across all blocks. Half of the filler words

---

[6]An additional 6 subjects who participated in the experiment were not included in the analysis because their evaluative judgments of the objects chosen as experimental stimuli were not in accordance with these expectations. Four of these subjects disagreed concerning one of the attitude objects (e.g., judging negatively what had been selected as a positively valued object) and 2 did not concur with respect to two attitude objects.

[7]As is to be expected, subjects were significantly faster at indicating their evaluations the fifth time that they did so ($M = 910$ ms) than the first time ($M = 1,330$ ms), $F(1, 17) = 73.95$, $p < .001$.

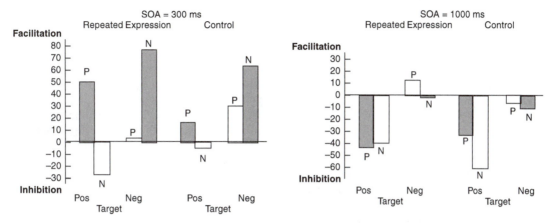

FIGURE 18.3 ■ Mean facilitation scores in Experiment 3 as a function of SOA (stimulus onset asynchrony), repeated expression, valence of the prime (P = positive; N = negative), and valence of the target adjective (Pos = positive; Neg = negative). (Conditions involving congruent valences are darkened; incongruent ones are not.)

were paired with the evaluation question and half with the syllable question.

The 4 positive and the 4 negative objects toward which evaluations had been expressed repeatedly in the above task are referred to as the *repeated expression* primes. The 4 positive and 4 negative objects that had been paired with the syllable question served as the control primes. The actual priming task proceeded as in Experiment 2. Following the priming task, subjects completed a questionnaire that asked them to evaluate each of the 50 attitude objects that had been presented in the first phase of the experiment (i.e., both the experimental and the filler words). These evaluations were made on a 7-point scale with endpoints labeled *very good* and *very bad*.

Results

As in the previous experiments, the number of errors that subjects made in judging the connotation of the target adjectives was minimal (mean error rate = 1.94%). Any latencies associated with a response error were omitted from the analysis.

The facilitation scores[8] are presented in Figure 3. An analysis of variance on these data revealed the predicted four-way interaction of SOA × Repeated Expression × Prime Valence × Target Valence, $F(1, 17) = 9.22$, $p < .01$. Similar to what had been observed for preexperimentally strong primes in Experiment 2, the critical simple interaction of prime and target valence was found for

the experimentally created strong primes (repeated expression condition) when the shorter SOA was involved, $F(1, 17) = 8.86$, $p < .01$. In this case, greater facilitation was observed when positively valued primes were followed by positive targets and when negatively valued primes were followed by negative targets than when the prime-target pairs were incongruent in valence. Furthermore, the extent of facilitation observed on these congruent trials ($M = 73.61$ ms) was once again statistically reliable, $t(17) = 4.37$, $p < .001$. Statistically reliable facilitation ($M = 43.19$ ms) was also apparent on congruent trials with control primes when the trials involved the 300-ms SOA, $t(17) = 3.30$, $p < .005$[9]. However, in a manner that is consistent with the hypothesis, the extent of such facilitation was significantly greater in the repeated expression condition than in the control condition, $t(17) = 2.61$, $p < .02$. No facilitation on congruent trials was apparent with either the repeatedly expressed or the control primes when the trials involved the longer SOA.

Note that the present data regarding the consequences of repeated attitudinal expression are not confounded by attitude extremity. That is, repeated

---

[8]The positive and negative target baselines were 780 ms and 840 ms, respectively, at the SOA of 300 ms, 710 ms, and 760 ms, respectively, at the SOA of 1,000.

[9]Due to the selection requirement concerning unanimity, the control attitude objects in Experiment 3 involved stronger evaluative associations than did the weak primes in Experiments 1 and 2.

expression did not enhance the extremity of subjects' self-reported attitudes at the end of the experiment. Attitudes toward each of the 16 experimental objects were examined by comparing the attitude scores of those subjects who had repeatedly expressed their attitudes toward the given object to the attitude scores of those who had not. Only 1 of these 16 comparisons, well within what is to be expected by chance alone, revealed a more extreme attitude among the repeated expression subjects. Such a null effect of repeated expression on attitude extremity is consistent with past research that has employed the repeated attitudinal expression manipulation. Powell and Fazio (1984) did not detect any reliable differences in attitude extremity as a function of repeated expression across 12 attitude issues. Thus, the present findings regarding attitude activation following repeated expression can be attributed to the resulting strength of the object-evaluation association and not to the extremity of the associated evaluation.

General Discussion

Together, the three present experiments suggest that some sorts of attitudes indeed can be activated from memory automatically upon one's mere observation of the attitude object. Such activation appears to be both spontaneous and inescapable. Even though attitude activation was irrelevant to the task that subjects were required to perform, we found evidence that evaluations were activated upon exposure to appropriate attitude objects. However, the likelihood of such automatic activation of an attitude appears to depend upon the strength of the association between the attitude object and the evaluation. Regardless of whether this associative strength was measured or manipulated experimentally, evidence of automatic activation of the attitude was far stronger when the association could be characterized as strong.

The findings also lend support to the utility of the proposed view of attitudes as evaluative associations with objects. These associations can vary in strength, ranging from *not existing at all* (the case of a nonattitude) to a *weak association* that is unlikely to be capable of automatic activation to a *strong association* that can be activated automatically. This continuum provides an interesting way of conceptualizing the strength of an attitude. The

attitudes of two individuals with identical scores from some attitude measurement instrument may still differ markedly with regard to their strength, that is, with regard to their likelihood of activation upon the individual's mere exposure to the object. When they encounter the attitude object in a given situation, the attitude of one individual may be activated whereas the attitude of the other may not. As a result, the two individuals may construe any information that is available concerning the object quite differently; that is, selective processing is more likely in the case of the individual whose attitude has been activated. A difference of this sort is apt to have a number of important implications.

First of all, the degree to which the attitude is likely to be evoked automatically is apt to affect the resistance of the attitude to counterinfluence. An attitude involving a strong association is apt to be activated upon the presentation of information concerning the attitude object and, as a result, color one's judgments of the information. Consistent with this notion, Wood (1982) found that attitude change in response to a persuasive communication is moderated by the degree to which individuals can rapidly retrieve from memory beliefs about the attitude object and past behaviors that they had performed relevant to the attitude object. The implication is that the stronger the object-evaluation association, the more resistant the attitude is to change and the greater the stability of the attitude over time.

A second implication concerns attitude-behavior consistency. If an attitude is activated automatically upon the individual's encountering the attitude object, it is far more likely to guide the individual's behavior toward that object than if it is not. Without activation of the attitude, behavior toward the object may proceed without the object having been considered in evaluative terms or on the basis of judgments of whatever features of the object happen to be salient in the immediate situation. In either case, the behavior may not be congruent with the individual's attitude.

Fazio (in press) has proposed a model of the process by which attitudes guide behavior that views activation of the attitude as critical in precisely this manner. The model assumes that behavior in any given situation is largely a function of the individual's definition of the event that is occurring. The critical question concerns the extent to which the attitude will influence one's construction of the event. In some situations, a cue implying the relevance of attitudinal considerations may prompt individuals to access their attitudes from memory. However, in cue-free situations, it is the chronic accessibility of the attitude, that is, the strength of the object-evaluation association, that is important. If the attitude is activated upon one's observation of the attitude object, it is likely to lead to some selective processing of the information available in the immediate situation. Thus, the individual's definition of the event is more likely to be congruent with his or her attitude toward the object in cases involving strong object-evaluation associations than in cases involving weak ones. Consequently, behavior is more likely to follow from a definition of the event that is attitudinally based in the former cases than in the latter.

Thus, there appear to be important implications of automatic attitudinal activation for both persuasion and attitude-behavior consistency. More generally, the present conceptualization and findings are relevant to the very functionality of attitudes. Attitude theorists have long considered one of the major functions served by attitudes to be that of organizing and structuring a rather chaotic universe of objects (Katz, 1960; Smith, Bruner, & White, 1956). An attitude is presumed to provide "a ready aid in 'sizing up' objects and events in the environment" (Smith et al., 1956, p. 41). The degree to which a given attitude actually fulfills this object appraisal function would appear to depend on the likelihood that the attitude is activated automatically when the individual observes the attitude object and, hence, on the strength of the object-evaluation association. Attitudes involving a strong association are highly functional. They free the individual from the processing required for reflective thought about his or her evaluation of the object and, through the process outlined earlier, can guide the individual's behavior in a fairly automatic manner. Thus, the individual is behaving in a fairly automatic manner. Thus, the individual is freed from much of the effort of having to engage in deliberate reasoning processes before behaving toward the object in question.

ACKNOWLEDGMENTS

The present research was supported by Grant MH 38832 from the National Institute of Mental Health.

The authors thank Paget Gross, Margaret Intons-Peterson, Steven Sherman, and Richard Shiffrin for their helpful comments on an earlier draft of the article.

REFERENCES

Abelson, R. P., Kinder, D. R., Peters, M. D., & Fiske, S. T. (1982). Affective and semantic components in political person perception. *Journal of Personality and Social Psychology, 42,* 619–630.

Anderson, J. R., & Pirolli, P. L. (1984). Spread of activation. *Journal of Experimental Psychology: Learning, Memory, and Cognition, 10,* 791–798.

Converse, P. E. (1970). Attitudes and non-attitudes: Continuation of a dialogue. In E. R. Tufte (Ed.), *The quantitative analysis of social problems* (pp. 168–189). Reading, MA: Addison-Wesley.

deGroot, A. (1983). The range of automatic spreading activation in word priming. *Journal of Verbal Learning and Verbal Behavior, 22,* 417–436.

deGroot, A., Thomassen, A., & Hudson, P. (1982). Associative facilitation of word recognition as measured from a neutral prime. *Memory and Cognition, 10,* 358–370.

Fazio, R. H. (in press). How do attitudes guide behavior? In R. M. Sorrentino & E. T. Higgins (Eds.), *The handbook of motivation and cognition: Foundations of social behavior.* New York: Guilford Press.

Fazio, R. H., Chen, J., McDonel, E. C., & Sherman, S. J. (1982). Attitude accessibility, attitude-behavior consistency, and the strength of the object-evaluation association. *Journal of Experimental Social Psychology, 18,* 339–357.

Fazio, R. H., Powell, M. C., & Herr, P. M. (1983). Toward a process model of the attitude-behavior relation: Accessing one's attitude upon mere observation of the attitude object. *Journal of Personality and Social Psychology, 44,* 723–735.

Fazio, R. H., & Williams, C. (1985). *Attitude accessibility as a moderator of the attitude-perception and attitude-behavior relations: An investigation of the 1984 presidential election.* Unpublished manuscript, Indiana University.

Fazio, R. H., & Zanna, M. P. (1978a). Attitudinal qualities relating to the strength of the attitude-behavior relationship. *Journal of Experimental Social Psychology, 14,* 398–408.

Fazio, R. H., & Zanna, M. P. (1978b). On the predictive validity of attitudes: The roles of direct experience and confidence. *Journal of Personality, 46,* 228–243.

Fiske, S. T. (1982). Schema-triggered affect: Applications to social perception. In M. S. Clark & S. T. Fiske (Eds.), *Affect and cognition: The 17th Annual Carnegie Symposium on Cognition* (pp. 55–78). Hillsdale, NJ: Erlbaum.

Fiske, S. T., & Pavelchak, M. A. (in press). Category-based versus piece-meal-based affective responses: Developments in schema-triggered affect. In R. M. Sorrentino & E. T. Higgins (Eds.), *The handbook of motivation and cognition: Foundations of social behavior.* New York: Guilford Press.

Hovland, C. I. (1959). Reconciling conflicting results derived from experimental and survey studies of attitude change. *American Psychologist, 14,* 8–17.

Hovland, C. I., Harvey, O. J., & Sherif, M. (1957). Assimilation and contrast effects in reactions to communication and attitude change. *Journal of Abnormal and Social Psychology, 55,* 244–252.

Jones, E. E., & Sigall, H. (1971). The bogus pipeline: A new paradigm for measuring affect and attitude. *Psychological Bulletin, 76,* 349–364.

Jonides, J., & Mack, R. (1984). On the cost and benefit of cost and benefit. *Psychological Bulletin, 96,* 29–44.

Katz, D. (1960). The functional approach to the study of attitudes. *Public Opinion Quarterly, 24,* 163–204.

McKoon, G., & Ratcliff, R. (1980). Priming in item recognition: The organization of propositions in memory for text. *Journal of Verbal Learning and Verbal Behavior, 19,* 369–386.

McNamara, T. P., Ratcliff, R., & McKoon, G. (1984). The mental representation of knowledge acquired from maps. *Journal of Experimental Psychology: Learning, Memory, and Cognition, 10,* 723–732.

Neely, J. H. (1976). Semantic priming and retrieval from lexical memory: Evidence for facilitatory and inhibitory processes. *Memory and Cognition, 4,* 648–654.

Neely, J. H. (1977). Semantic priming and retrieval from lexical memory: Roles of inhibitionless spreading activation and limited-capacity attention. *Journal of Experimental Psychology: General, 106,* 225–254.

Norman, R. (1975). Affective-cognitive consistency, attitudes, conformity, and behavior. *Journal of Personality and Social Psychology, 32,* 83–91.

Powell, M. C., & Fazio, R. H. (1984). Attitude accessibility as a function of repeated attitudinal expression. *Personality and Social Psychology Bulletin, 10,* 139–148.

Ratcliff, R., & McKoon, G. (1978). Priming in item recognition: Evidence for the propositional structure of sentences. *Journal of Verbal Learning and Verbal Behavior, 17,* 403–417.

Ratcliff, R., & McKoon, G. (1981). Does activation really spread? *Psychological Review, 88,* 454–462.

Sample, J., & Warland, R. (1973). Attitude and prediction of behavior. *Social Forces, 51,* 292–304.

Schneider, W., & Shiffrin, R. M. (1977). Controlled and automatic human information processing: I. Detection, search, and attention. *Psychological Review, 84,* 1–66.

Sherif, C. W., Kelly, M., Rodgers, H. L., Sarup, G., & Tittler, B. I. (1973). Personal involvement, social judgment, and action. *Journal of Personality and Social Psychology, 27,* 311–328.

Sherif, M., & Cantril, H. (1947). *The psychology of ego involvements.* New York: Wiley.

Shiffrin, R. M. (in press). Attention. In R. C. Atkinson, R. J. Herrnstein, G. Lindzey, & R. D. Luce (Eds.), *Stevens' handbook of experimental psychology* (2nd ed.). New York: Wiley.

Shiffrin, R. M., & Dumais, S. T. (1981). The development of automatism. In J. R. Anderson (Ed.), *Cognitive skills and their acquisition* (pp. 111–140). Hillsdale, NJ: Erlbaum.

Shiffrin, R. M., & Schneider, W. (1977). Controlled and automatic human information processing: II. Perceptual learning, automatic attending, and a general theory. *Psychological Review, 84,* 127–190.

Smith, M. B., Bruner, J. S., & White, R. W. (1956). *Opinions and personality.* New York: Wiley.

Wood, W. (1982). Retrieval of attitude-relevant information from memory: Effects on susceptibility to persuasion and on intrinsic motivation. *Journal of Personality and Social Psychology, 42,* 798–810.

Zanna, M. P., & Rempel, J. K. (1984). *Attitudes: A new look at an old concept.* Paper presented at the Conference on Social Psychology of Knowledge, Tel Aviv.

The Definition of Self: Private and Public Self-Evaluation Management Strategies

Abraham Tesser • University of Georgia
Del Paulhus • University of British Columbia, Vancouver, British Columbia, Canada

Editors' Notes

Whereas the previous selection dealt with the evaluation of objects, the present one deals with self-evaluation and with the self-concept more generally. One might think that grown-ups have plenty of self-knowledge and know exactly what they are and what they are not. A very different perspective on self-definition is implied by Tesser's Self-Esteem Maintenance model (SEM). That model predicts a fluctuation of our self-concepts depending on the outcomes of our social comparisons with others. Social comparison, in turn, is carried out with others who are similar to rather than dissimilar from oneself. Therefore, comparison with them carries greater weight in our self-definitions. To what extent, for example, do you think that academic success constitutes a central (versus a peripheral) part of your self-concept? How about athletics, music, interpersonal relations? As research in the present selection demonstrates, each of the above dimensions (and many others) will assume greater or lesser importance in your self-perception depending on how well you think you are doing on that particular dimension and with whom you are comparing yourself.

Discussion Questions

1. Tesser and Paulhus wonder whether their results may be due to an authentic change in self-evaluation versus an attempt to manage the impressions of others. What implications do the present findings have for this particular issue?
2. In what way does the present research extend the findings of Tesser & Campbell (1980)?

3. One might propose that if one does well on a given competition one tends to view it as important in order to enhance one's self-esteem ? How does this notion differ from the proposal of Tesser and Paulhus? Do they have evidence to distinguish these proposals?

Suggested Readings

Festinger, L. (1954). A theory of social comparison processes. *Human Relations, 1,* 117–140.

Taylor, S. E., Buunk, B. P., & Aspinwall, L. G. (1990). Social comparison, stress, and coping. *Personality and Social Psychology Bulletin, 16,* 74–89.

Tesser, A. (1988). Toward a self-evaluation maintenance model of social behavior. In L. Berkowitz (Ed.), *Advances in experimental social psychology* (Vol. 21, pp. 181–227). New York: Academic Press.

Authors' Abstract

Evaluation of subjects' own performances and beliefs about an audience's evaluation of subjects' own performances were manipulated to examine their effects on self-definition. Pairs of subjects worked independently on tasks said to be valid indicators of a fictitious trait called *cognitive perceptual integration* (CPI). Relevance of CPI to a subject's self-definition was indexed by (a) an oral measure taken by an interviewer, (b) a self-description measure, and (c) an unobtrusive behavioral measure. Subjects who believed they actually outperformed another subject indicated on all three indexes that CPI was more relevant than did subjects who were outperformed by the other subject. This difference was more pronounced when the other subject was described as similar than when described as dissimilar. Subjects confronted by an audience who believed that they (the subjects) outperformed the other subject (independent of the subjects' actual performances) indicated that CPI was more relevant than did subjects confronted by an audience who believed they were outperformed by the other. Similarity of the other subject did not moderate this effect. The results were interpreted as evidence for both private and public self-evaluation management strategies.

A classic problem for social psychology concerns the way in which people come to define themselves. Although some theorists believe that by late adolescence the core of one's self is relatively fixed (e.g., Block, 1981; Costa, McCrae, & Arenberg, 1980; Freud, 1940/1949), there is some research to show that one's self-identity is, at least to some extent, malleable (cf. Shrauger & Schoeneman, 1979). Below we sketch a model that argues that changes in self-conception do occur and that they occur in the service of maintaining a positive self-evaluation.

The Self-Evaluation Maintenance (SEM) Model

Recently, a self-evaluation maintenance model of social behavior has been proposed (Tesser, Note 1). One of the central postulates of the model suggests that the relevance of a particular attribute or dimension to one's self-definition is determined by one's social milieu and serves to protect or enhance one's self-evaluation. Self-evaluation is a hypothetical construct representing the relative worth individuals attach to themselves or that they believe others attach to them.

Suppose, for example, an individual is confronted by another person who performs better than he or she on some dimension. If that dimension were relevant or important to the individual's self-definition, his or her self-evaluation would be threatened, that is, he or she would suffer by comparison to the other. The psychological closeness of the other person also plays a role. This construct is similar to Heider's (1958) unit relation: Closeness increases with things like similarity in origin, age, background, looks, physical proximity, and so on. To the extent that the other is close, comparisons should be easier and the attendent threat to self-evaluation greater.

Now, suppose that the dimension on which the other person excelled was not relevant to one's own self-definition. Here we would not expect the individual to suffer by comparison. Indeed, to the extent that the other person is psychologically close, the individual's self-evaluation might be enhanced through a reflection process, that is, the individual can "bask in the reflected glory" of the close other's good performance (Cialdini et al., 1976).

The SEM model predicts that people will change their self-definition to protect or to enhance their self-evaluation. Thus, the relevance of a particular dimension to one's self-definition depends on the performance and closeness of others. To the extent that another's performance is better on some dimension, the relevance of that dimension to one's self-definition should decrease, particularly if the other is psychologically close (a more extended discussion of the model and its implications for self-definition can be found in Tesser & Campbell, in press).

The SEM model can be applied to the relative performance of siblings. To avoid unflattering comparisons with siblings, individuals should reduce relevance or define themselves as different from those siblings on performancelike attributes such as abilities, especially if the siblings are close (in age). For male respondents, as predicted by the model, Tesser (1980) found that when a respondent's sib was acknowledged to be a better all-around performer than the respondent, the respondent identified less with that sib if the sib was close (less than a 3-year difference in age) than if the sib was distant (more than a 3-year difference in age). If the respondent's sib was reported to be a poorer performer, there was more identification if the sib was close than if the sib was distant.

Perhaps the most relevant experimental study of changes in self-definition to date was conducted by Tesser and Campbell (1980). Female subjects were given an opportunity to perform on a "social sensitivity" task and on an "esthetic judgment" task with another "subject" (who was actually an experimental confederate). Some of the subjects were led to believe that the confederate was very similar to them (close), and the remaining subjects were led to believe that the other was dissimilar (distant). Half of the subjects found that they performed at the same level as the confederate on social sensitivity, and, although their absolute performance was a little better on the esthetic judgment than the social sensitivity task, the confederate was clearly better on this dimension. The remaining subjects did about the same as the confederate on esthetic judgment, but not as well as the confederate on social sensitivity. The model predicts that subjects will decrease the relevance of the task on which the confederate outperformed them and that this effect will be more pronounced when the other is close than when the other is distant. This expectation was realized on subjects' free choice of tasks to perform, on changes in their own self-descriptions, but not on an interview measure.

Private and Public Self-Evaluation Maintenance

The outcomes of the Tesser and Campbell (1980) study provide support for the model but raise an interpretational question that is important not only for the model but also, more generally, for research on the self. The question concerns whether the subjects behaved the way they did in order to protect their own private self-evaluation or to evoke a positive evaluation from the experimenter. This question has come to be important in a number of areas for at least two reasons. First, the management of impressions in interpersonal behavior is pervasive, and the use of impression management constructs for explaining social behaviors appears to be undergoing a renaissance (e.g., Baumeister & Jones, 1978; Frey, 1978; Schlenker, 1980; Snyder, 1977). Second, behavior originally thought to be the result of "intrapsychic" mechanisms can often be interpreted in impression management terms. For example, "consistent" behavior presumed to result from the reduction of cognitive dissonance can be plausibly interpreted as a self-presentation strategy (Alexander & Knight, 1971; Paulhus, 1982; Tedeschi, Schlenker, & Bonoma, 1971).

Tesser and Campbell (1980) raised the possibility of a public image management interpretation of their results. Instead of trying to protect their own private self-evaluation, subjects may have been trying to create a positive impression in the experimenter and/or avoid potential embarrassment. The fact that the interview measures (taken by the interviewer, who was not present during the performance manipulation) did not show the predicted effect, but the choice measure (taken by the experimenter, who was present during the manipulations) did show the effect is consistent with this interpretation (p. 346).

Thus, our major goal in the present study was to assess independently the extent to which changes in self-definition (relevance of a particular dimension) can be attributed to public self-evaluation management and private (personal) self-evaluation maintenance.

The Present Study

The general prediction from the SEM model is that the performance and closeness of another will interact in determining the relevance of the performance dimension to a person's self-definition. Suppose that performance is manipulated in two distinct and orthogonal ways. *Public* performance is a person's belief of what some audience thinks is his or her relative performance vis-à-vis another individual's. *Private* performance is what a person believes to be his or her actual relative performance and that of another person. (Note that the term *private* refers only to the subject's own belief about actual performance. It is not intended to imply that no one besides the subject is aware of the subject's actual performance.) If people simply want to maximize public self-evaluation, then the predicted effects should hold only for the public-performance manipulation. Moreover, these effects are more likely on measures of relevance that are monitored by an audience, for example, an experimenter, than on measures that are not monitored by the audience. On the other hand, if people simply aim to maximize private self-evaluation, then only the private-performance manipulation should produce the predicted effect, and that effect should manifest itself on all measures of relevance regardless of whether they are monitored by the audience. It is also possible that people seek to maintain both aspects of self-evaluation. If this is the case, measures of relevance should be affected by both public and private performance.

Method

SUBJECTS

Subjects were 96 males who volunteered for the study in partial fulfillment of a course requirement for introductory psychology.

PRETEST

In group sessions 2 to 3 weeks before the experiment, subjects completed a questionnaire consisting of a number of self-ratings on several fictitious traits, including one labeled *cognitive perceptual integration (CPI)*, described as the ability to match patterns and to track objects on a map. The three ratings on CPI (5-point scales) read as follows: (a) How important is it for you to be high in this ability? (b) Do you think of yourself in terms of things associated with this ability? (c) When others think of you, do they think of things associated with this ability? The three items were summed to form the pretest index.

The same subjects were later telephoned to be scheduled in pairs for the experimental session. They were led to believe they were to be paired on the basis of their pretest questionnaire responses; in fact, they were paired arbitrarily.

EXPERIMENTAL SESSION

Overview. Pairs of subjects were led to believe that they were very similar (or very dissimilar) to one another. The two subjects worked independently on tests said to measure CPI ability. It was arranged that one of the subjects would score higher on the CPI tests (this outcome is termed *private performance*). Subsequently, each subject met privately with an interviewer who communicated clearly that he or she believed the subject had scored relatively high or low on CPI independent of the subject's true private performance (the interviewer's stated belief regarding the subject's performance is termed the subject's *public performance*). It was possible to make public and private performances independent by staging a mix-up in the performance scores passed from the experimenter to the interviewer. Thus, public and private performances were manipulated independently. Finally, behavioral, oral self-report, and pencil-and-paper measures were taken of the subject's self-definition and his attitudes toward the study.

Procedure. An undergraduate experimenter greeted each subject and, after both subjects had arrived, explained that

this study concerns individual differences in a certain ability called cognitive perceptual integration, or CPI for short. This is the ability to do things like match patterns and track movements on a map. Psychologists studying this ability have found great differences in this ability among college students. It turns out that this kind of ability is characteristic of football quarterbacks, good pilots, skilled craftsmen and even some business managers. However, people who are low in CPI are just as successful in school and careers—they just tend to specialize in different areas.

Similarity manipulation. The experimenter explained that subjects were run in pairs to save time in completing the study. Subjects were led to believe they were paired on the basis of pretest responses.

> There should be no problem running you two together because you've been matched to be very similar (dissimilar). You have the same (different) ages and majors. And you've taken roughly the same (different) courses, and even your personality profiles seem very similar (different). In short, you're very (not at all) comparable to one another.

Private-performance manipulation. Subjects worked in separate rooms on two tasks said to be accurate indicators of CPI ability (the sequence of tasks was counterbalanced within each cell of the experimental design). One task was a computerized game called *aerial interception* programmed on a CBM 2001 microcomputer. The object was to avoid interception of the game player's aircraft by pursuing aircraft (all displayed on a grid map). The subject's score, which appeared on the computer screen, was said to be based on the logic of his moves, the speed of his reactions, and the length of time he could avoid interception. Several practice games were allowed, then the subject was scored over 6 minutes of successive games. Subjects assigned to the high-private-performance condition were given a score of 140; subjects in the low condition were given a score of 110. The second task was described as a figure-matching task and consisted of all three sections of the Embedded Figures Task (Witkin, 1950). Subjects were given 6 minutes to work on all three sections—only two subjects finished in that time. Scores were computed immediately and were said to be based on total items completed as well as the difficulty of items completed. Subjects assigned to the high-private-performance condition were given a score of 300; subjects in the low condition received a 220.

Public-performance manipulation: The mix-up. After subjects had completed the tasks, they were both led back to the microcomputer room. Each subject was asked to read his two scores aloud so

the experimenter could enter them into a computer program said to combine the subject's two scores into an overall index of CPI ability. They were told that the interviewer (said to be the experimenter's supervisor) would later meet with them individually and check their CPI index on the computer to see how high they were in CPI. As the subjects started to report their scores aloud, the experimenter expressed some confusion as to which subject's scores would be entered first. He spent a minute searching for the relevant instruction sheet, finally giving up. "Well, read me your scores anyway. I just hope I'm entering them in the correct order." After entering both subject's scores, the experimenter expressed dismay at this plight,

> I may be in trouble because I messed this up before and I'm getting paid for this—I hope I don't lose my job. You see, my supervisor's going to come in to check your overall scores on the computer. But I might actually have reversed your scores. No matter what shows up. I hope you won't tell him I screwed up—you won't say anything, will you?

After both subjects agreed not to disclose any mix-up in the scores, the experimenter announced that his duties were complete and so he was going home. The subjects were left in separate rooms to await the interviewer.

Dependent Measures

Behavioral measure of relevance: The observation period. The interviewer was older and less casually dressed than the experimenter, implying a higher status. The interviewer entered the room of the subject assigned to be interviewed second. The subject was told he would have to wait a few minutes for his interview and was asked to complete a short questionnaire labeled *Self-Report Inventory*. Before the subject started working on the questionnaire, the interviewer placed two loose-leaf binders, one red and one black, on a nearby desk while saying. "Please complete the questionnaire first. Then if there's extra time you might want to look at these biographies of famous people who have been tested on CPI." Lifting the red binder, the interviewer said, "These famous people are high in CPI." Lifting the black binder, the interviewer continued, "And these famous people are low in CPI. In any case, I'll try to get back to you as soon as I can." The interviewer then left the room. The books of biographies were clearly labeled *High CPI Biographies* and *Low CPI Biographies*, so that the subject would be clear about which one he was reading.

The subject was observed during this period through a two-way mirror that was covered with paper except for a strip along the bottom. After he had completed the self-report inventory, the subject's behavior was coded by 10-sec intervals into one of three categories: (a) subject looking at red book, (b) subject looking at black book, and (c) other. This coding period continued for 4 minutes starting at the instant the subject completed the self-report inventory.

The interview. The interviewer, carrying a clipboard, entered the room of the subject assigned to be interviewed first and introduced himself or herself as Dr.—. He or she began by asking a few general biographical questions. Next the interviewer checked the microcomputer, saying, "Let me see how you made out on the CPI tests." The computer indicated a percentile score of 75 for subjects assigned to the high-public-performance condition and a 55 for subjects assigned to the low condition. The interviewer continued, "Your score is a percentile rating compared with other college students taking our tests. I see you scored a lot higher (lower) than the other subject. That's all right—some people are just better at CPI than others." After a few more biographical questions, the subject was asked to rate his response aloud to the following question on a 7-point scale: How important is it for you to be high in CPI?

Postexperimental questionnaire. Finally, the subject was left alone to complete a questionnaire containing a number of 7-point rating scales. Four items were summed to serve as a self-description measure of the relevance of CPI: (a) How important is it for you to be high in CPI? (b) When you think of yourself, do you think of yourself in terms of the kinds of things associated with CPI? (c) When other people think about you, are they likely to think about things associated with CPI? and (d) To what extent do you think of yourself as a person with high CPI ability? The questionnaire also had several items concerning feelings about and perceptions of the experiment and experimenter.

When the subject finished the questionnaire, he was switched to the observation room, and the other subject was interviewed, Thus, half of the subjects in the study were observed reading the biographies before they were interviewed (includ-

ing the public-performance manipulation); the other half had received both the public- and private-performance manipulation before they were observed. This variable, interview order, was crossed with the other factors.

At this point the interviewer told the subjects that the "mix-up" was staged and that he was aware of their true performance. He explained that before he could elaborate, he wanted the subject to fill out a form "while events are still fresh in your mind." This partial debriefing was required so that subjects would be free to reveal their perception of the private-performance manipulation. To conclude the study, subjects were given a form containing manipulation-check items and then were given a final debriefing to determine degree of suspicion. Finally, subjects were given credit, thanked, and dismissed.

Results

MANIPULATION CHECKS

Three independent variables were manipulated in this study: similarity, private performance, and public performance. To test the effectiveness of these manipulations, subjects were asked to indicate (a) the extent to which they had seen themselves as similar to the other subjects (on a 7-point scale), (b) whether the subject or his partner had actually done better on the two CPI tasks, (c) whom the interviewer believed had done better on the tasks—the subject or the partner, and (d) how satisfied they were with their performance (on a 7-point scale).

The similarity manipulation was effective. Subjects saw themselves as more similar to the other subject in the similar condition ($M = 4.10$) than in the dissimilar condition ($M = 3.56$), $t(40) = 1.85$, $p < .04$, one-tailed. The private-performance manipulation was also effective. Subjects in the high-private-performance condition were more likely to say that they outperformed the other subject (89%) than subjects in the low-private-performance condition (11%), $\chi^2(1) = 52.2$, $p < .001$, and rated themselves as more satisfied with their performance ($M = 4.69$ vs. 3.69), $F(1, 40) = 13.92$, $p < .001$. Private performance did not interact with similarity on this measure, $F(1, 40) < 1$, *ns*. Finally, the public-performance manipulation was also successful. There was a difference between the high- and low-public-performance subjects in the likelihood with which they reported that the interviewer believed that the subject did better than his partner (63% vs. 36%), $\chi^2(1) = 5.02$,[1] $p < .03$. And high-public-performance subjects rated themselves as more satisfied with their performance ($M = 4.53$) than low-public-performance subjects ($M = 3.79$), $F(1, 40) = 6.31$, $p < .02$. Again, there was no interaction with similarity, $F(1, 40) < 1$, *ns*. Finally, preliminary analyses of the dependent variables revealed no experimenter or interviewer effects, so the data were collapsed over these variables for all subsequent analyses.

Data Analysis: Experimental Manipulations

There were two sources of dependency that were accounted for in the analysis: (a) Subjects were run in pairs, and (b) there were three measures on each subject. Therefore, a $2^4 \times 3$ hierarchically nested design (with a covariate) was used to divide the variance into effects that were between

pairs, effects that were within pairs, and effects that were within subjects. There were two between-pair variables: (a) the similarity manipulation with two levels and (b) interview order with two levels, that is, which participant was interviewed first. There were two within-pair variables: (a) public performance[2] with two levels and (b) private performance with two levels. There was one within-subject variable: measure of the relevance of CPI with three levels—(a) the behavioral measure (amount of biography examination time spent looking at the high-CPI biographies), (b) the interview[3] measure (the extent to which the subject described CPI as self-defining to the interviewer), and (c) the self-description measure (the extent to which the subject described CPI as self-defining on the final questionnaire). The distribution on each dependent variable was standardized prior to analysis. Because the pretest index contained items similar to those used in the self-description index, the pretest index was used as a covariate. Although the covariate was highly significant, $F(1, 40) =$

---

[1]This difference probably underestimates the effectiveness of the public-performance manipulation. It had been necessary to check the manipulations after a partial debriefing in which the interviewer told the subject that he or she knew about the "mix-up" in scores. Thus, some subjects may have answered the question in terms of what they just learned the interviewer actually knew rather than what they thought the interviewer knew during the experiment.

[2]The computation of the error term for the public-performance manipulation is rather complicated. Recall that by design, both public and private performance were manipulated relatively (not absolutely). It is not that one subject performed well or poorly regardless of the other's performance; each subject simply did better or worse than the other. Thus, although levels of public and private performance were manipulated within pairs, there were only two pair types: (a) One subject did better and the other did worse in both the public and private conditions; and (b) one subject did better than the other in the private condition, and the other subject did better than the first in the public condition. Therefore, level of private performance (a within-pair variable) and pair type (a between-pair variable) completely specify level of public performance: High public performance is associated with high private performance in the Type 1 pairs and with low private performance in the Type 2 pairs; low public performance is associated with low private performance in Type 1 pairs and high private performance in the Type 2 pairs. Thus, if one were to compute a public-performance effect within levels of private performance, the comparison would be between pairs: high-public/high-private (Type 1 pairs) versus low-public/high-private (Type 2 pairs) and high-public/low-private (Type 2 pairs) versus low-public/low-private (Type 1, pairs). But note also that across levels of private performance the public-performance effect is a within-

pair comparison. All pairs (Type 1 pairs and Type 2 pairs) have one member with high public performance and one member with low public performance. Because the public-performance effect viewed this way is partially within and partially between pairs, the data were analyzed as follows: Private performance was treated as a within-pair factor, and a dummy variable—type of pair—was treated as a between-pair factor. Public performance was not explicitly included in the analysis. (Recall that public performance is completely specified by private performance and pair type.) This analysis scheme permits a clean partitioning of between- and within-pair variance and thereby allows the computation of appropriate error terms. However, it leads to some confusion regarding the labeling of the public-performance effects. Using this analysis, what would ordinarily be the public-performance main effect is indexed by the Private Performance × Pair-Type interaction (a within-pair effect), and what would ordinarily be the Public × Private Performance interaction is indexed by the pair-type main effect (between pairs). In order to avoid this confusion in the text, we have used the appropriate error terms as described here but used the more usual labels to describe the results. For example, in the text, we do not mention the dummy variable—pair type—and we discuss the analysis as if the public performance were actually used as a factor in the analysis.

[3]As noted earlier, this index was composed of four items, three of which referred to how self-definitional CPI was to the subject and a fourth that asked subjects to indicate the extent to which other people thought CPI was relevant to the subject's self-definition. Previous research (Tesser & Campbell, 1980) had found that the latter item was not as sensitive as the former items. Preliminary analyses in this experiment revealed that all the items were similarly affected by the manipulations.

13.04 $p < .001$, the results were similar with and without the covariate.

THE EFFECTS OF PRIVATE PERFORMANCE ON RELEVANCE

The SEM model leads us to expect that persons will decrease the relevance of a particular attribute such as CPI to the extent that another outperforms them on CPI. Further, this effect should be more pronounced when the other is psychologically close (i.e., similar) than when the other is distant. This set of expectancies can be summarized in a planned comparison (cf. Tesser & Campbell, 1980), which assumes that the four means will be ordered (starting with CPI least relevant to CPI most relevant) as follows: low-performance/similar, low-performance/dissimilar, high-performance/dissimilar, high-performance/similar.

As can be seen in Figure 1, the means are ordered exactly as predicted. The planned comparison is highly significant, $t(40) = 4.75$, $p < .001$ (all a priori hypotheses are evaluated using one-tailed t tests). Further, when the variance associated with the planned comparison is removed, the remaining variation among the four means is negligible ($F < 1$). It is also possible to test both of the components of the planned comparison separately. As is obvious in the figure, CPI is more relevant

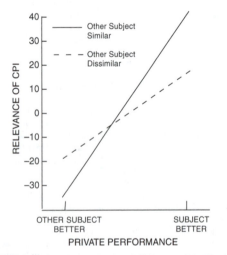

FIGURE 19.1 ■ Relevance of CPI to subject's self-definition as a function of private performance and similarity of other subject. (Means are collapsed over the standardized self-description, interview, and behavioral measures of relevance of CPI. CPI = cognitive perceptual integration.)

to subjects when they do better than the confederate than when the confederate does better than they, $t(40) = 4.40$, $p < .0001$. And, this private-performance effect is stronger when the confederate is similar to the subject than when the confederate is dissimilar, $t(40) = 1.84$, $p < .05$.

One might ask whether the overall effects shown in Figure 1 hold equally well on the self-report, interview, and behavioral measures of relevance. Because these were treated as a repeated measures factor in the analysis, differences in the effect would show up as interactions with private performance. Neither the Private Performance × Measure interaction nor the Similarity × Private Performance × Measure interaction was significant ($F < 1$ for both). There was, however, a significant Interview Order × Similarity × Private Performance × Measure interaction, $F(2, 80) = 3.90$, $p < .05$. This complex interaction indicates that the simple, simple Similarity × Performance interaction is stronger on the behavioral measure than the self-report or interview measure when the subject was interviewed first and weaker when the subject was interviewed second. In sum, except for the qualification associated with the four-factor interaction, the SEM predictions with respect to private performance seem to be supported across all three measures of the relevance of CPI to self-definition.

THE EFFECTS OF PUBLIC PERFORMANCE

The above results suggest that self-evaluation maintenance processes serve to maintain an individual's private self-evaluation. Self-evaluation processes may also serve a public or "self-presentation" function. Thus, we expect that public performance (what the interviewer believes about the subject) should affect measures of relevance in a way that is analogous to that of private performance.

Again, it is possible to apply the overall planned comparison, this time using public performance rather than private performance. The means[4] implicated in this analysis are shown in Figure 2.

---

[4]These means are based on the self-description measure and the oral measure for all subjects and the behavioral measures from subjects who were interviewed first but not subjects interviewed second. Recall that subjects interviewed second responded to the biographies, that is, the behavioral measure, prior to being interviewed. Because public performance was manipulated in the interview, the behavior of subjects who responded to the behavioral measure prior to the interview could not have been affected by the public manipulation.

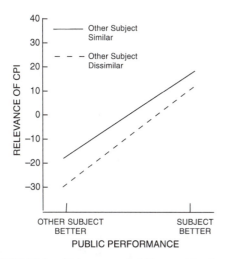

FIGURE 19.2 ■ Relevance of CPI to subject's self-definition as a function of public performance and similarity of other subject. (Means are collapsed over the standardized self-description, interview, and behavioral measures of relevance of CPI for subjects who were interviewed first and over the self-description and interview measures of relevance of CPI for subjects who were interviewed second. CPI = cognitive perceptual integration.)

Although the overall planned comparison is significant, $t(40) = 2.51, p < .01$, it is clear from Figure 2 that the means are not completely ordered as predicted. As expected, subjects indicated that CPI was more relevant to their self-definition when the interviewer expressed the belief that the subject outperformed the confederate than when the interviewer expressed the belief that the confederate outperformed the subject, $t(40) = 2.76, p < .01$. However, this public-performance effect was not more pronounced when the confederate was similar than when the confederate was dissimilar $(t < 1)$.

Again we may ask if the effects of public performance are the same on each of the measures. We might expect, for example, that if the public-performance effect is merely image management, then it would show itself most strongly on "public" measures of relevance. The interview measure (the oral rating of CPI in the interview) is the most directly public measure, the self-description is slightly less public (it was left unclear as to whether the interviewer would see it), and the behavioral measure is least public because it was taken when the subject believed he was not being observed.

However, type of measure did not interact with public performance, by itself, $(F < 1)$, or with public performance in combination with any other variable. This indicates that each of the dependent variables was similarly affected by the public-performance manipulation. In sum, what the interviewer professed to believe about the subject's performance, independent of what the subject knew to be his actual performance, affected the subject's self-definition on both public and private measures.

OTHER EFFECTS

The overall analysis yielded two additional effects. Interview order interacted with measure, $F(2, 80) = 4.52, p = .01$. CPI was more relevant to subject's self-definition on the self-description and interview measures than on the behavioral measure for subjects interviewed first, whereas the reverse was true for subjects interviewed second. More interesting is the interaction between public and private performance, $F(1, 40) = 4.65, p < .05$. As can be seen in Table 1, the effects of private performance are more pronounced when the interviewer expresses the belief that the subject performed better than the confederate, $F(1, 40) = 15.06, p < .001$, than when the interviewer expresses the beliefs that the subject performed poorer than the confederate $(F < 1)$; the effects of public performance are more pronounced when the subject believes he actually outperformed the confederate, $F(1, 80) = 8.63, p < .01$, than when he believes the confederate outperformed him $(F < 1)$.

Discussion

The results of this study provided some support for the specific hypotheses, raised some new questions, and supported some general conclusions. First, we will discuss the effects of private perfor-

TABLE 19.1. Relevance of Cognitive Perceptual Integration to Subject's Self-Definition as a Function of Public and Private Performance

Private performance	Public performance	
	Other better	Subject better
Other better	−.288	−.266
Subject better	−.154	.536

Note. See Footnote 4.

mance, then public performance, and finally some of the implications.

PRIVATE PERFORMANCE

The data provide some support for the notion that people change their views of themselves as a joint function of their own relative performance and the similarity of those around them. This is manifested in the way subjects describe themselves to others in a face-to-face interview, the way they describe themselves on a questionnaire, and even in their private behavior (i.e., their choice of reading material). These effects all indicate that an attribute is made less relevant to the extent that an individual is outperformed by another on that attribute, particularly if that other person is similar.

Further, the data nicely complement the findings of Tesser and Campbell (1980). The results of the two studies with respect to (private) performance and closeness/similarity are virtually identical. This was obtained in spite of the fact that the performance dimensions are different, the sex of subjects is different, the experimenters are different, the specific operations are different, and the specific dependent measures are different. Comparable results were also obtained in the correlational study on sibling identification (Tesser, 1980) that was described in the introduction. It appears that the effect is robust.

It might be argued that the effects that we are attributing to private self-evaluation are actually impression management strategies. After all, the experimenter (not the interviewer) and the other subject knew the subjects' "actual" performance. This does not seem plausible to us for several reasons. First, the experimenter and the other subject were not present when any of the dependent measures were collected, nor did the subject expect the experimenter to see them. Second, the predicted effects emerged even in the face of a high-status interviewer whose beliefs about the subject's performance were independent of the subject's actual performance. Finally, the effect was evident on a measure of relevance that the subjects believed was not witnessed by anyone, namely, the amount of time he spent looking at high-CPI biographies.

The work of Mischel, Ebbesen, and Zeiss (1973) may suggest a "warm glow" explanation of these results. That is, subjects who scored high on CPI tasks may have experienced a generalized positive affect toward anything associated with CPI.

Accordingly, they spend more time looking at high-CPI biographies. However, the warm glow hypothesis cannot explain the interaction of performance with similarity of partner unless one assumes that the glow is warmer when one outperforms a similar partner. Thus, unless the warm glow hypothesis is bolstered by ad hoc assumptions, it cannot account for all the present data.

A self-attribution explanation might also be proposed for the present results. Subjects may have inferred from a successful performance that they were good at CPI and that it was therefore relevant to their self-definition. This inference would be weaker when their partner was dissimilar to them, because the differences in age, major, courses taken, and so forth provide reasons for discounting differential performance as an indicator of the trait (Goethals & Darley, 1977; Kelley, 1971). Such a hypothesis might account for the present data, but the interpretation must be viewed in the context of other findings bearing on the self-evaluation maintenance model. For example, Tesser and Campbell's (1980) subjects were given the opportunity to define themselves relative to (a) absolute standards (percentiles of college students) or (b) the performance of a confederate. Because absolute standards are a more clear-cut source of information, they should be used in self-perception. The SEM model predicts that the confederate's relative performance is more important to self-definition. The latter outcome was obtained, thus favoring the SEM model.

Further, the SEM model is systemic: Each parameter is both an effect and a cause of the other parameters. Here we have seen how closeness and performance affected relevance of the performance dimension to one's self-definition. In previous research we have found that relevance, in interaction with closeness, affects people's willingness to facilitate or to hinder the performance of another (Tesser & Campbell, 1982, Tesser & Smith, 1980) and that relevance, in interaction with relative performance, affects people's attempts to alter their closeness to another (Pleban & Tesser, 1981; Tesser, 1980). It is difficult to see how a self-attribution account can handle all these findings as easily as the SEM model.

PUBLIC PERFORMANCE

We manipulated subjects' beliefs regarding what the interviewer believed about their performance to explore the role of changes in self-definition as self-presentation strategy. The data suggest that there is indeed a case to be made for a self-presentation function. What an audience believed about the subject's performance, irrespective of what the subject himself believed about his performance, affected subjects' reports of the relevance of that performance dimension.[5]

Although the results of public performance clearly show an effect of an audience's belief about one's performance relative to another on one's self-definition, the psychological closeness (similarity) of that other does not appear to moderate this relationship as it does in the case of private performance. This may mean that the determinants of self-presentation are less subtle than the determinants of private self-evaluation maintenance. On the other hand, perhaps it is because the interviewer simply did not specifically indicate that he or she knew whether the subjects were similar or dissimilar to one another. (However, it should be borne in mind that it was not necessary to emphasize the similarity variable in this way for it to affect private performance.)

The behavioral measure of the relevance of CPI was unobtrusive and therefore should not involve self-presentation, so we expected to find a reduced impact of public performance on this measure. However, the effect of the interviewer's belief showed itself on this measure no less strongly than on the other measures. Why should a subject's private behavior be influenced by the beliefs of an experimenter who was clearly unaware of their actual performance? Apparently, subjects' private self-definitions are determined in part by how they believe others see them (Mead, 1934; cf. Shrauger & Schoeneman, 1979). Subjects may come to believe the arbitrary evaluation assigned to them by the audience. Private effects of public evaluation have been reported in the literature (cf. Schlenker, 1980). For instance, Frey (1978) found that a public revelation of subjects' performance on an IQ test had a strong impact on their private evaluations of the test. In Frey's study, however, the audience knew the true performance; in the present study, subjects knew that the audience's belief was arbitrary. If such an effect were shown to be reliable in future research, it would suggest a greater, more arbitrary kind of plasticity of the self-concept than has heretofore been suspected.

The effects of public and private performance were not independent of one another. The effect of public performance was more pronounced when private performance was high, and the effect of private performance was more pronounced when public performance was high. This interaction was unanticipated, and we can only speculate about it. Subjects may be uncomfortable about acting on their own beliefs (private performance) when there is a discrepancy between those beliefs and the audience's beliefs. Perhaps an audience's belief in the subject's good performance acts as a "releaser" for allowing the subject's private beliefs to be consequential in his self-definition. On the other hand, the subjects may have been motivated to act on the audience's belief but reluctant to do so if they believed that they actually performed poorly. Perhaps, subjects' "confidence" in their own performance set the stage for allowing the audience's beliefs to impact their self-definition.

GENERAL IMPLICATIONS

We started off by asking the question of whether self-definitional behavior was a private self-evaluation maintenance strategy, a public self-presentation strategy, or both. We now have some data to address the question, and the answer that emerges is that one's self-definition serves both functions and appears to do so in relatively similar ways. This conclusion suggests that the original question is often phrased in a nonproductive way in terms of incompatability of these processes: If a behavior is in the service of image management, it can't be in the service of private self-evaluation maintenance, and vice versa. Our own data suggest that these processes can and do operate concurrently.

ACKNOWLEDGMENTS

This research was supported in part by National Science Foundation Grant BNS-8003711. This study was run while the second author was a postdoctoral fellow with the Institute for Behavioral Research at the University of Georgia.

The authors wish to thank Jeff Bald and Steve Miller for serving as experimenters; Sandy Bernstein for serving as one of the interviewers; and Jennifer Campbell, Bill Graziano, and David Shaffer for comments on a previous draft of this article.

---

[5] We also correlated the interview and behavioral measures with scores on the Crowne-Marlowe (1964) need for approval scale. The correlation was significant for the most public measure, the interview, $r(78) = .24$, $p < .05$, but not significant for the most private measure, the behavioral measure, $r(78) = .06$. These results are also consistent with the self-presentation interpretation.

REFERENCE NOTE

1. Tesser, A. A self-evaluation maintenance model of social behavior. Unpublished manuscript, University of Georgia, 1980.

REFERENCES

Alexander, C. N., & Knight, G. W. Situated identities and social psychological experimentation. *Sociometry*, 1971, 34, 65–82.

Baumeister, R. F., & Jones, E. E. When self-presentation is constrained by the target's knowledge: Consistency and compensation. *Journal of Personality and Social Psychology*, 1978, 36, 608–618.

Block, J. Some enduring and consequential structures of personality. In A. I. Rabin (Ed.), *Further explorations in personality*. New York: Wiley-Interscience, 1981.

Cialdini, R. B., et al. Basking in reflected glory: Three (football) field studies. *Journal of Personality and Social Psychology*. 1976, 34, 366–375.

Costa, P. T., McCrae, R. R., & Arenberg, D. Enduring dispositions in adult males. *Journal of Personality and Social Psychology*, 1980, 38, 793–800.

Crowne, D. P., & Marlowe, D. *The approval motive: Studies in evaluative dependence*. New York: Wiley, 1964.

Freud, S. *An outline of psychoanalysis*. New York: Norton, 1949. (Originally published 1940.)

Frey, D. Reactions to success and failure in public and private conditions. *Journal of Experimental Social Psychology*, 1978, 14, 172–179.

Goethals, G. R., & Darley, J. M. Social comparison theory: An attributional approach. In J. Suls & R. L. Miller (Eds.), *Social comparison processes*. New York: Wiley, 1977.

Heider, F. *The psychology of interpersonal relations*. New York: Wiley, 1958.

Kelley, H. H. *Causal schemata and the attribution process*. Morristown, N.J.: General Learning Press, 1971.

Mead, G. H. *Mind, self and society*. Chicago: University of Chicago, 1934.

Mischel, W., Ebbesen, E. B., & Zeiss, A. R. Selective attention to the self: Situational and dispositional determinants. *Journal of Personality and Social Psychology*, 1973, 27, 129–142.

Paulhus, D. L. Individual differences, self-presentation, and cognitive dissonance: Their concurrent operation in forced compliance. *Journal of Personality and Social Psychology*, 1982, 43, 838–852.

Pleban, R., & Tesser, A. The effects of relevance and quality of another's performance of interpersonal closeness. *Social Psychology Quarterly*, 1981, 44, 278–285.

Schlenker, B. R. *Impression management*. Monterey, Calif.: Brooks/Cole, 1980.

Shrauger, J. S., & Schoeneman, T. J. Symbolic interactionist view of self-concept: Through the looking-glass darkly. *Psychological Bulletin*, 1979, 86, 549–573.

Snyder, M. Impression management. In L. Wrightsman (Ed.), *Social psychology* (2nd ed.). Belmont, Calif.: Wadsworth, 1977.

Tedeschi, J. T., Schlenker, B. R., & Bonoma, T. V. Cognitive dissonance: Private ratiocination or public spectacle? *American Psychologist*, 1971, 26, 685–695.

Tesser, A. Self-esteem maintenance in family dynamics. *Journal of Personality and Social Psychology*. 1980, 39, 77–91.

Tesser A., & Campbell, J. Self definition: The impact of the relative performance and similarity of others. *Social Psychology Quarterly*, 1980, 43, 341–347.

Tesser, A., & Campbell, J. Self-evaluation maintenance and the perception of friends and strangers. *Journal of Personality*, 1982, 50, 261–279.

Tesser, A., & Campbell, J. Self-definition and self-evaluation maintenance. In J. Suls & A. Greenwald (Eds.), *Social psychological perspectives on the self* (Vol. 2). Hillsdale, N.J.: Erlbaum, in press.

Tesser, A., & Smith, J. Some effects of task relevance and friendship on helping: You don't always help the one you like. *Journal of Experimental Social Psychology*, 1980, 16, 582–590.

Witkin, H. A. Individual differences in case of perception of embedded figures. *Journal of Personality*, 1950, 19, 1–15.

READING 20

Mood, Misattribution, and Judgments of Well-Being: Informative and Directive Functions of Affective States

1983

Norbert Schwarz • University of Heidelberg, Federal Republic of Germany
Gerald L. Clore • University of Illinois at Urbana-Champaign

Editors' Notes

Like the previous selection, this selection demonstrates the malleability of our self-knowledge. The Tesser and Paulhus article demonstrated that the centrality of a dimension to our self-concept can vary according to the outcomes of our momentary social comparisons. The present selection demonstrates a similar fluidity with regard to our general life satisfaction. One might think that one's general life satisfaction would be the sum total of all of one's major successes and failures and would be relatively insensitive to transient fluctuations in mood. The present selection tellingly demonstrates that this is not the case. It shows that our momentary moods, induced by remembering just one happy or unhappy event or even by learning about the current weather outdoors, can significantly color our general assessment of our lives. Importantly, Schwarz and Clore also provide evidence about the process whereby transient moods affect our life satisfaction. It turns out that mood can serve as information from which general satisfaction is cognitively inferred. However, when the validity of the mood as evidence for satisfaction is called into question, the relation between mood and perceived life satisfaction is eliminated.

Discussion Questions

1. What is the significance of the attribution manipulation in the Schwarz and Clore experiments? What does it intend to accomplish?

263

2. How do Schwarz and Clore manipulate mood in their two experiments? Can you think of an alternative mood manipulation?

3. What do the authors mean by the directive-effects hypothesis? How does this hypothesis relate to wishful thinking?

Suggested Readings

Schwarz, N., Bless, H., Strack, F., Klumpp, G., Rittenauer-Schatka, H., & Simons, A. (1991). Ease of retrieval as information: Another look at the availability heuristic. *Journal of Personality and Social Psychology, 61,* 195–202.

Strack, F. (1992). The different routes to social judgments: Experiential versus informational strategies. In L. L. Martin & A. Tesser (Eds.), *The construction of social judgments* (pp. 249–275). Hillsdale, NJ: Erlbaum.

Zillmann, D., Johnson, R. C., & Day, K. D. (1974). Attribution of apparent arousal and proficiency of recovery from sympathetic activation affecting excitation transfer to aggressive behavior. *Journal of Experimental Social Psychology, 10,* 503–515.

Authors' Abstract

Two experiments investigated whether judgments of happiness and satisfaction with one's life are influenced by mood at the time of judgment. In Experiment 1, moods were induced by asking for vivid descriptions of a recent happy or sad event in respondents' lives; in Experiment 2, moods were induced by interviewing participants on sunny or rainy days. In both experiments, subjects reported more happiness and satisfaction with their life as a whole when in a good mood than when in a bad mood. However, the negative impact of bad moods was eliminated when subjects were induced to attribute their present feelings to transient external sources, irrelevant to the evaluation of their lives. Subjects who were in a good mood, on the other hand, were not affected by misattribution manipulations. The data suggest (a) that people use their momentary affective states as information in making judgments of how happy and satisfied they are with their lives in general and (b) that people in unpleasant affective states are more likely to search for and use information to explain their state than are people in pleasant affective states. Thus the data demonstrate informative and directive functions of affective states.

The present studies investigate the role of mood-related factors in judgments of general well-being, that is, judgments of happiness and satisfaction with one's life. Pilot work suggested that thinking about a single happy or sad event in one's life affects the evaluation of that life as a whole. Why is this the case? Thinking about a happy or sad event not only may change a person's mood but also may increase the availability of this and similarly valenced events in memory (Tversky & Kahneman, 1973). Either of these factors could influence the person's judgments of general well-being.

In Experiment 1, we attempted to separate these processes. To do this, we used a procedure con-ceptually similar to that developed by Zanna and Cooper (1976) to isolate the role of arousal in cognitive-dissonance phenomena. Specifically, we held constant the activity of thinking about positive and negative life events while varying the apparent relevance of any feelings resulting from this activity to judgments about one's life. This was accomplished by offering some subjects the suggestion that their feelings might be due to a situational factor that was irrelevant to the evaluation of their lives. If respondents attribute their feelings to such factors, they should be less likely to use them as an informational basis for evaluating their lives. To the extent that such misattributions of mood or feelings reduce the relationship between thinking about happy or sad events and judgments of general well-being, one can conclude that respondents used these momentary feelings as a basis for judgment. An alternative hypothesis is that writing about a happy or a sad event increases the availability of other similarly valenced life events from memory, leading subjects to overestimate the frequency of such events in their life. If the availability of these mood-congruent memories rather than present feelings is the basis of subjects' happiness and satisfaction judgments, then they should be influenced in all conditions regardless of the attribution manipulation, because the impact of these memories should not depend on the explanation of an individual's present mood.

Experiment 2 was a field study rather than a laboratory study in which mood was governed by whether subjects were interviewed on sunny or rainy spring days. The same set of hypotheses were tested, but in some respects this study is the reverse of the first. In Experiment 1, we induced subjects to attend to a situational factor that did not actually produce their mood, but in Experiment 2, they were induced to attend to a situational factor that did produce their mood. In both studies, attributions to situational factors were expected to reduce the likelihood that subjects would attribute their moods to more personally relevant aspects of their lives.

Experiment 1

In the first experiment, we asked subjects to give vivid descriptions of either a happy or a sad event in their recent past. On the one hand, this task should increase the cognitive availability of positive or negative events, and on the other hand, it should change subjects' mood. To isolate the effect of mood, we ran the experiment in an unusual soundproof room and suggested to some subjects that the room might make them feel good and to others that it might make them feel bad (adapted from Fazio, Zanna, & Cooper, 1977). A third group of subjects was not given any expectations concerning the effects of the room.

We expected that subjects who described negative life events would report being less happy and less satisfied than control subjects, who did not describe any past life events, whereas subjects who described positive life events would report being

more happy and more satisfied than control subjects. However, if persons use their affective state as a basis for evaluating the quality of their life, both discounting and augmentation effects (Kelley, 1971) should result from the room manipulation.

Specifically, subjects who described negative life events should discount the bad feelings resulting from thinking about negative life events when the bad feelings can be misattributed to the room, that is, to a transient source, irrelevant to the evaluation of thier lives. These subjects should report less unhappiness and dissatisfaction than those with no room expectations. On the other hand, when they expect the room to make them feel elated, they should report more unhappiness and dissatisfaction than the no-expectation group. That is, we expect augmentation effects when subjects realize they feel badly in spite of conditions presumably fostering good feelings.

Similarly, subjects who described positive life events should report lower well-being when they attribute their positive feelings to the room (discounting) and higher well-being when they expect the room to make them feel bad (augmentation) compared to those who have no room expectations.

Method

Participants. Sixty-one introductory psychology students who were randomly assigned to experimental conditions received course credit for their participation. They were run in groups of three or four persons each.

Overview. To set up the misattribution possibilities, the experiment was conducted in an odd-looking soundproof room. Participants were first told that the room might make them feel either tense or elated, or they were given no expectation concerning the room's effect. They then heard a series of three-note piano progressions on tape as part of a bogus "sound-memory task" (intended to legitimize the soundproof room). Next they wrote about a life event that had made them feel good or bad. The dependent variables were then assessed using questions about life satisfaction and happiness, present mood, and some causal-attribution scales. The design was therefore a 2 × 3 factorial involving two types of life-event descriptions (positive or negative) and three types of expectations about room effects (tense, elated, or no effect). In addition, a control condition was run in which subjects reported their life satisfaction without having previously described a life event and without having been in the soundproof room.

Expectation. Participants were given one of the three expectations about the soundproof room. Those given a *bad-mood expectation* were told that participants in an earlier study had complained about feeling "tense" and "depressed" in the room. Those given a *good-mood expectation* were told that earlier participants felt "elated" and "kind of high" in the room, perhaps because of its sound-proof quality. Subjects in these conditions were then told the Department of Psychology wanted to find out what caused these feelings. They were given a one-page questionnaire on which to rate the room for comfort, lighting, ventilation, and so on. Participants with *no mood expectation* sat in the same room but were not told about the reactions of earlier participants and were not given a questionnaire.

All subjects received the questionnaire at the beginning of the experiment, but it was desirable to suggest that the room might have its effects later (during the period when life events were described). To accomplish this, the cover page of the questionnaire for the expectation groups contained an instruction to the experimenter from the Department of Psychology to hand the questionnaire to some subjects at the beginning, to some subjects during, and to some subjects at the end of the experiment. It explained that the impact of the room might depend on the amount of time spent in it. In addition, subjects were asked to indicate at which of these times they received the questionnaire. This instruction was intended to convey the impression that subjects' moods might change over the course of the experiment.

Mood. Following the ratings of the experimental room, subjects were exposed to a series of three-note tonal progressions as part of the bogus sound-memory task and were then asked to collaborate on a 25-minute filler task prior to the sound-recognition test. The sound-memory task simply provided an excuse for running the experiment in a soundproof room. The filler task actually constituted the main part of the study. Specifically, subjects were asked to collaborate on the development of a "life-event inventory," purportedly a test instrument to assess events in people's lives. Printed instructions asked them to describe "as vividly and in as much detail as possible" a recent event that made them feel "really good" or one that made them feel "really bad." They were told that these

descriptions would provide the basis for the generation of items for the life-event inventory. Subjects were given 20 minutes to complete the task. To ensure that they attended to the emotional aspects of the event, they were asked to indicate how the experience made them feel, what aspects made them feel that way, what the experiences made them think about, and so on. Positive and negative mood conditions were run in each experimental session, and the experimenter was blind to the condition.

Half of the essays from each experimental condition were randomly selected and rated for the pleasantness of the described event. No differences, according to room expectations, emerged either for the positive ($F < 1$) or the negative descriptions, $F(2, 12) = 1.32$, ns, which indicated that the descriptions were equally positive or negative across the three expectation conditions.

Measures. Following these descriptions, participants were asked to answer some general questions, purportedly to help in the selection of appropriate response scales for the life-event inventory being developed. The questions, which were answered along either 7- or 11-point rating scales, included two measures of general well-being. One of these pertained to general happiness (How happy do you feel about your life as a whole?) and the other to life satisfaction (How satisfied are you with your life as a whole these days?). Both of these questions had previously been used in other surveys of well-being (cf. Andrews & McKennel, 1980). Following these measures, subjects' present affective states were assessed by the questions "How happy (unhappy) do you feel right now, at this moment?" and "How good (bad) do you feel at this moment?"

Finally, to assess causal attributions for their momentary moods, participants were asked two questions, one about how much their present feelings were due to what they thought about (an internal attribution) and one about how much their feelings were due to the room (an external attribution).

Participants in a nonfactorial control group, run concurrently with the experimental conditions, responded to the same dependent measures without first describing events from their lives.

Results

Temporary mood. The task of describing pleasant and unpleasant life even influenced mood, as expected. Compared to participants who described positive life events, those who described negative life events reported feeling significantly less happy at this moment ($Ms = 3.7$ vs. 5.5 on a 7-point scale) and less good ($Ms = 5.8$ vs. 8.4 on an 11-point scale), $Fs(2, 54) = 22.7$ and 20.7, respectively, $ps < .001$. Moreover, compared to control group subjects ($Ms = 5.1$ and 7.9), subjects who described negative events felt only less happy and less good at this moment, $ts(54) = 2.97$ and 3.06, $ps < .004$, whereas subjects who described positive events felt only somewhat happier and better, $ts(54) = 1.32$ and 1.30, respectively, $ps < .20$. That is, compared to the control group, the instruction to think about negative events had a more pronounced effect on subjects' mood than did the instruction to think about positive events. This finding, however, seems to be due primarily to the preexisting positive mood of the control group.

As expected, the manipulation of subjects' expectations for how the room would make them feel did not affect their reported mood ($Fs \leq 1$). In other words, opportunities to explain the source of the mood did not change the level of the mood itself.

General well-being. Table 1 shows the effects of event descriptions and room expectancies on ratings of both general happiness and life satisfaction. The pattern of results was similar in each case and consistent with the hypotheses. That is, subjects who had described positive life events reported being happy and satisfied with their lives regardless of their expectations about the effects of the room they were in. However, when subjects had described negative experiences, their ratings depended on the extent to which the room could potentially account for their negative feelings. That is, they reported less happiness and less life satisfaction when the room was described as likely to

make them elated and reported more happiness and satisfaction when it was described as likely to make them sad than when no expectations about the room's effects were given. These conclusions are confirmed statistically for both happiness and life satisfaction by main effects for the type of event described, $Fs(2, 54) = 59.2$ and 32.8, respectively, $ps < .001$, and by an Event Description × Room Expectations interaction, $Fs(2, 54) = 10.6$ and 5.6, respectively, $ps < .01$.

Thus the data are consistent with both informative and directive effects hypotheses. That is, subjects who were in a bad mood tried to explain their feelings in terms of transitory situational factors and therefore discounted them as reasonable sources of information about their life situation when they could attribute their feelings to the room they were in. Indeed, the discounting was sufficiently complete that the bad-mood-expectation condition no longer differed from the good-mood condition. On the other hand, participants who felt bad but who expected the room to make them feel "elated" or "kind of high" reported nonsignificantly less happiness than did those who expected no side effects and much less happiness than did participants with the same expectations who were in the good-mood condition.

In contrast, subjects who were in a good mood were not influenced by possible situational explanations of their mood. This fact may indicate that subjects were not motivated to search for factors that could account for positive affective states.

Attributions. In general, we expected attributions for mood states to be consistent with the information provided. For example, compared to subjects without expectations about the room, those expecting the room to make them feel tense should attribute bad moods externally to the room and good

TABLE 20.1. General Happiness and Life-Satisfaction Ratings: Experiment 1

Description of event	Expectation about room				
	Tense	No mood	Elated	Total	Control
General happiness (7-point scale)					
Positive	6.5$_{a,b}$	6.4$_{a,b}$	6.7$_a$	6.5	
Negative	6.1$_{a,b}$	4.1$_c$	3.6$_c$	4.5	5.5$_b$
Life satisfaction (11-point scale)					
Positive	9.6$_a$	8.6$_a$	9.7$_a$	9.3	
Negative	8.6$_a$	5.7$_b$	4.4$_b$	6.2	8.9$_a$

Note. Means that do not share a common subscript differ at $p < .05$ (Newman–Keuls test).

moods internally to their thoughts. Data relevant to this hypothesis are summarized in Table 2. Because within-cell variability in responses to these attribution scales was high, the expected effects were not significant. However, three of the four comparisons between means for subjects expecting elation versus tension were in the predicted direction (although the mean for the no-expectation group was often misplaced). The pattern of the data supports the misattribution reasoning, the only deviation being that participants in the bad-mood condition who expected the room to make them feel "elated" still attributed their bad mood more to the room and less to their thoughts than did the no-expectation group. This pattern of attribution may account for the weakness of the augmentation effect found in this condition.

Correlational analyses. Additional support for the hypothesis that subjects based their assessment of general well-being on their affective state at the time of judgment is provided by correlational analyses. Specifically, subjects' reports of momentary mood were generally correlated significantly with their reports of both general happiness and satisfaction with their lives; this was true for control subjects ($rs = .74$ and $.79$, respectively, $p < .002$). It was also true for subjects in the no-misattribution conditions after describing positive events ($r = .57$, $p < .07$ and $r = .67$, $p < .04$) and after describing negative events ($r = .81$, $p < .01$ and $r = .58$, $p < .07$). None of the correlations in the misattribution conditions, on the other hand, reached significance at the .10 level. Contrary to expectations, the correlation of mood with happiness was not significantly higher in any of the conditions than was its correlation with satisfaction.

TABLE 20.2. Causal Attributions of Subjects' Present Affective State

Description of event	Expectation about room			
	Tense	Neutral	Elated	Control
	Attribution to thoughts			
Positive	9.8$_b$	7.9$_{a,b}$	7.3$_a$	
Negative	8.9$_{a,b}$	9.3$_b$	8.0$_{a,b}$	5.4$_a$
	Attribution to the room			
Positive	2.8$_{a,b}$	1.5$_a$	3.5$_{a,b}$	
Negative	5.6$_b$	2.4$_{a,b}$	3.5$_{a,b}$	2.4$_{a,b}$

Note. Scales range from 1 to 11. Within each variable, means that do not share a common subscript differ at $p < .05$ (Newman–Keuls test).

Discussion

Writing vivid and detailed descriptions of pleasant and unpleasant life experiences appears to influence not only subjects' momentary mood states but also their judgments of how happy and satisfying their lives are in general. Considered in isolation, this could occur for two reasons. First, writing about a happy or a sad life event may increase the availability of similarly valenced events in memory. This, in turn, could lead subjects to overestimate the prevalence of such events in their lives (Tversky & Kahneman, 1973) and bias their judgments. Second, people may use their mood at the time of judgment as information in evaluating the quality of their lives. The results favor the second interpretation. That is, when subjects were given a chance to attribute their *bad* mood to a transient source, irrelevant to the quality of their lives, the description task no longer influenced their judgment of general well-being. In the terminology of attribution research, this is referred to as a "discounting effect" (Kelley, 1971), because subjects discounted aspects of their own lives as a cause of their bad moods when another external cause (the soundproof room) was made salient. Thus, these data demonstrate informational functions of affective states.

Discounting occurs when alternative plausible causes for an effect are made salient. Augmentation effects have also been reported (e.g., Schwarz, Servay, & Kumpf, 1981) when aspects of a situation are made salient that could reasonably produce a state opposite to that of the subject. Augmentation effects were anticipated primarily in the condition in which subjects were in a bad mood but had expected to be made giddy and elated. The results showed only a trend toward augmentation effects. Judging from the pattern of attribution results, subjects may have found it less credible that the soundproof room could produce elation than that it would produce tension, making augmentation effects in the bad-mood condition unlikely.

On the other hand, subjects who thought about positive events and reported being in a good mood were not influenced by the misattribution manipulations and reported high well-being regardless of experimental condition. This result is in line with the hypothesis that affect has a directive influence and that persons are more likely to seek explanations for negative than for positive feelings. It should be noted, however, that the momentary mood of subjects who described positive events was only insignificantly better than was the mood of control subjects, whereas the mood of subjects who described negative life events was significantly worse. That is, the mood of subjects who described negative events deviated more from what might be considered "normal" than did the mood of subjects who described positive events, a finding that seems to reflect the well-known tendency of people to report positive resting moods (see Matlin & Stang, 1978, for a review).

Experiment 2

The results of Experiment 1 support the hypothesis that people use their momentary mood state as information in evaluating the quality of their lives. The evidence came, however, from a relatively complex laboratory experiment involving some extraordinary stage managing. We decided, therefore, to test the hypothesis again in a more naturalistic way.

In this second study, well-being was assessed as part of a telephone interview conducted either on warm and sunny days or on rainy spring days. Cunningham (1979) had previously shown that weather had a reliable effect on mood. If people use their affective states as information to evaluate their lives, they should report greater well-being and life satisfaction on sunny days than on rainy days. This effect should be attenuated, however, when respondents are led to attribute their mood to the weather, that is, to a transitory source irrelevant to the evaluation of their lives. In this case, their mood should be discredited as reliable information concerning their general well-being. In addition, if only negative affective states lead respondents to seek explanations, then this attenuation of the effect of weather on well-being should occur only when the weather is bad and not when the weather is good.

Method

In a 2 × 3 factorial design, subjects were called either on sunny or on rainy spring days and were asked to answer questions on life satisfaction as part of a telephone survey. The salience of the weather as a plausible explanation for mood was varied. Weather either was not mentioned at all, was mentioned in passing as small talk, or was mentioned as a primary focus of the experiment.

Respondents. Ninety-three telephone numbers randomly selected from the student directory of the University of Illinois at Urbana-Champaign were called, and the persons answering the phone served as respondents. They were called by a female interviewer on either sunny or rainy weekdays during April and May. Nine respondents refused to participate in the interview, five on rainy days and four on sunny days, which left 84 subjects in the analysis.

Procedure. The interviewer always opened the conversation with "Hello, I'm ——, we're doing research for the psychology department at Circle Campus in Chicago." This university was selected as the interviewer's alleged affiliation under the pretense that the interviewer was calling from out of town.

In *indirect-priming* conditions the interviewer continued with an irrelevant aside: "By the way, how's the weather down there?" After the subject's response the interviewer continued, "Well, let's get back to our research. What we are interested in is people's moods. We randomly dial numbers to get a representative sample. Could you just answer four brief questions?"

In *direct-priming* conditions the interviewer continued after saying hello and indicating that she was calling from Chicago Circle with the words, "We are interested in how the weather affects persons' mood. We randomly dial numbers. . . . "

In no-priming conditions the interview continued after the standard opening as in the indirect-priming condition without the aside about the weather.

Following one of these introductions, the interview continued with the assessment of the respondent's perceived quality of life and present feeling state:

1. First, on a scale of 1 to 10, with 10 being the happiest, how happy do you feel about your life as a whole?
2. Thinking of how your life is going now, how much would you like to change your life from what it is now? This is also on a scale of 1 to 10. Ten means "change a very great deal" and one means "not at all."
3. All things considered, how satisfied or dissatisfied are you with your life as a whole these days? (with number 10 being the most satisfied).

4. And, how happy do you feel at this moment? Again, 10 is the happiest. That's all the questions I have. Thank you for your time and cooperation.

On any given rainy or sunny day the same number of calls were made in each priming condition. Thus a confounding of weather and priming was avoided. Finally, it should be noted that the interviewer was blind to the experimental hypothesis and did not expect an interaction effect of weather and priming but did expect a main effect of weather.

Results

Mood. An analysis of "momentary happiness" ratings showed that subjects called on sunny days felt happier ($M = 7.5$) than did subjects called on rainy days ($M = 5.4$), $F(1, 78) = 39.90$, $p < .001$, and that this mood measure was not affected by the priming manipulation, $F(2, 78) = 1.58$, *ns.*

Well-being. The effects of weather and priming manipulations on each dependent variable are shown in Table 3. In each case, the pattern of results is similar and consistent with predictions. That is, respondents on sunny days reported themselves to be generally happy and satisfied with their lives, and they had little desire to change. This tendency was similar under all conditions and planned comparisons of the no-priming condition with both priming conditions revealing no significant differences, $ts(78) = .20, .75,$ and $.80$, respectively. In contrast, respondents on rainy days reported themselves to be generally less happy, $t(78) = 3.68$, $p < .001$, and less satisfied, $t(78) = 3.56$, $p < .001$, and desiring more change, $t(78) = 1.96$, $p < .06$, in the no-priming condition than in either the direct- or the indirect-priming condition. In other words, the influence of the weather on these life judgments was appreciable only under no-priming conditions. Moreover, as shown in Table 3, respondents' appraisals of their lives on rainy days under no-priming conditions generally differed from their responses in the other five conditions, which did not differ from each other. However, the results for the "desire to change" measure were not as strong as for the happiness and the satisfaction measures.

In summary, the data of this study replicated both the informational and the directive effects of subjects' affective states found in Experiment 1.

Correlational analyses. As in Experiment 1,

TABLE 20.3. Mean Ratings of General Happiness, Desire to Change, and Life Satisfaction: Experiment 2

Dependent variable	Priming		
	None	Indirect	Direct
General happiness			
Sunny	7.43$_a$	7.29$_a$	7.79$_a$
Rainy	5.00$_b$	7.00$_a$	6.93$_a$
Desire to change			
Sunny	3.93$_a$	3.43$_a$	3.57$_a$
Rainy	5.79$_b$	4.57$_{a,b}$	4.93$_{a,b}$
Life satisfaction			
Sunny	6.57$_a$	6.79$_a$	7.21$_a$
Rainy	4.86$_b$	6.71$_a$	7.07$_a$

Note. $n = 14$ per cell. Means that do not share a common subscript differ at $p < .05$ (Newman–Keuls test).

there was a tendency for the correlation of subjects' reported present affective state with their reported happiness to be higher under no-priming conditions ($r = .79$) than under both priming conditions ($r = .63$, $z = 1.36$, *ns*). The correlation with satisfaction, on the other hand, was the same in the no-priming ($r = .49$) and the priming conditions ($r = .48$) and was lower than the correlation with happiness in both the no-priming ($z = 1.89$, $p < .06$) and the priming conditions ($z = 1.11$, *ns*).

General Discussion

Informative Functions of Affective States

The two experiments reported here, one in the laboratory and one involving telephone interviews, both provide evidence that respondents use their momentary moods to make judgments about their general happiness and life satisfaction. Both thinking about good versus bad experiences and being in sunny versus rainy weather influenced subjects' reports of general well-being. However, this influence was not direct. Instead, it appeared to occur only insofar as these factors affected subjects' moods, and these moods were considered to provide reliable information about well-being. Subjects appear to seek personally irrelevant explanations for an unpleasant mood state when such explanations are available. As a consequence, they then do not use their mood as information about their well-being. When in a good mood, however, subjects do use their mood as a basis for judging the quality of their life regardless of the availability of alternative explanations for the mood.

The impact of (mis)attribution manipulations on subjects' judgments, under bad-mood conditions make the results difficult to interpret in terms of the effect of mood on the availability of mood-consistent ideas (Bower, 1981; Isen et al., 1978). According to this reasoning, mood-congruent events should be more available in memory, leading subjects to overestimate the prevalence of positive or negative events in their lives. To the extent that subjects base their evaluations on this recalled evidence, they should report higher well-being under positive than under negative mood. Note, however, that the implications of the recalled events should not be altered by the attribution manipulations. That is, the mood-congruent-availability notion should predict a main effect of mood but not an interaction of mood and attribution. On the other hand, the attribution manipulation should affect the diagnostic value of subjects' present affective state, resulting in the interaction effect found in both studies. Therefore, the data provide evidence that moods themselves have an informational function.

Directive Effects of Affective States

Although opportunities for attribution and misattribution had strong effects on the reported well-being of participants in negative moods, those in positive moods reported high well-being regardless of experimental conditions, as predicted by the directive-effects hypothesis. This evidence is consistent with the results reported by Williams, Ryckman, Gold, and Lenny (1982), who used misattribution procedures to study the role of affect in the attitude-similarity-attraction paradigm. As in the present study, they found that subjects took the opportunity to attribute away negative but not positive affect. Also, Arkin et al. (1976) reported that subjects who received positive feedback about their performance (presumably putting them in a good mood) were insensitive to situational factors that could account for this feedback.

In this regard, we have favored the hypothesis that people are more motivated to seek explanations for negative than for positive moods, and we suggested that this might be primarily due to the fact that most people experience negative moods as deviating from their usually positive feelings. By the same logic, depressed persons for whom bad moods are usual, and persons in social situations in which bad moods are expected (e.g., fu-

nerals), should show attempts to explain any good feelings they might experience. Similarly, persons in unusually positive mood states might attempt to find out the causes of their feelings. Unfortunately, the present studies do not allow an evaluation of these issues because the positive mood induced through thinking about positive life events was not significantly better than was the mood of control group subjects. Also, rainy and sunny weather, used as a mood manipulation in the second study, does not lend itself easily to the creation of a "neutral" control group. Thus it seems reasonable to assume that extreme positive moods might produce effects similar to the ones we found for negative moods. We would like to suggest, however, that for most people most of the time unpleasant states are more likely to trigger explanations than pleasant states are.

Motivational Bias

By itself, the tendency to attribute bad moods but not good moods to external sources may indicate the operation of a motivational self-serving bias. Two pieces of data from Experiment 1, however, lead us to suggest that some factors, in addition to motivational bias, are at work. Both pieces of data are instances in which subjects did not take opportunities to increase the perceived quality of their lives. They suggest a two-stage branching system in which subjects must first seek explanations before available explanations are adopted. At the first stage, bad moods but not good moods are problematic and tend to activate explanation-searching activity. This stage, in which subjects do or do not seek explanations, could be motivated by a desire to maintain or reinstate feelings of well-being. Results at the next stage, however, are not always consistent with such a motivation. Thus, for example, subjects who felt good subsequent to describing positive life-events but who expected the room to make them feel bad could have augmented their feelings of well-being, but like other good-mood subjects, did not take the explanation-seeking branch. As a result, the opportunity to augment their good mood through attributional enhancement was foreclosed. There was no evidence of such augmentation effects in the good-mood condition. Conversely, bad-mood subjects, who generally did take the explanation-search branch, sometimes opened themselves to explanations that worsened their already negative level of well-being. Thus, for example, subjects who felt bad as a result of describing negative life events but who expected the room to make them feel elated, further decreased their sense of well-being. Though this effect was not significant, the pattern of means was nevertheless inconsistent with an unembellished motivational interpretation. Thus, although the present data are certainly not strong enough to allow a straightforward rejection of a self-serving bias explanation, they nevertheless seem to favor an informational interpretation: It appears that once subjects are in an explanation-search mode, processing of the information available is not motivationally biased even if the original decision to search might have involved such factors.

ACKNOWLEDGMENTS

The research reported in this article was conducted during the first author's postdoctoral year at the University of Illinois and was partially supported by a fellowship from the Deutsche Forschugsgemeinschaft to Norbert Schwarz and National Science Foundation Grant BNS 76-24001 to Robert S. Wyer, Jr.

The authors wish to thank Bob Wyer and Fritz Strack for their helpful comments at various stages of this research and Peggy Clark for her provocative critique of an earlier draft of this article. Experiment 1 was presented at the 1981 meeting of the Midwestern Psychological Association, Michigan, May 1981.

REFERENCE NOTE

1. Kerber, K. W., & Clore, G. L. *Causal relationships in the affect-cognition cycle: Interpersonal implications, intentionality and liking.* Unpublished manuscript, College of the Holy Cross, 1982.

REFERENCES

Andrews, F. M., & McKennel, A. C. Measures of self-reported well-being: Their affective, cognitive, and other components. *Social Indicators Research*, 1980, *8*, 127–155.

Arkin, R. M., Gleason, J. M., & Johnston, S. Effect of perceived choice, expected outcome, and observed outcome of an action on the causal attributions of actors. *Journal of Experimental Social Psychology*, 1976, *12*, 151–158.

Bower, G. H. Mood and memory. *American Psychologist*, 1981, *36*, 129–148.

Bradburn, N. M. *The structure of psychological well-being.* Chicago: Aldine, 1969.

Calvert-Boyanowsky, J., & Leventhal, H. The role of information in attenuating behavioral responses to stress: A reinterpretation of the misattribution phenomenon. *Journal of Personality and Social Psychology*, 1975, *32*, 214–221.

Cunningham, M. R. Weather, mood, and helping behavior: Quasi experiments with the sunshine samaritan. *Journal of Personality and Social Psychology*, 1979, *37*, 1947–1956.

Fazio, R. H., Zanna, M. P., & Cooper, J. Dissonance and self-perception: An integrative view of each theory's proper domain of application. *Journal of Experimental Social Psychology*, 1977, *13*, 464–479.

Goldings, M. J. On the avowal and projection of happiness. *Journal of Personality*, 1954, *23*, 30–47.

Isen, A. M., Shalker, T. E., Clark, M., & Karp. L. Affect, accessibility of material in memory, and behavior: A cognitive loop? *Journal of Personality and Social Psychology*, 1978, *36*, 1–12.

Kelley, H. H. Causal schemas and the attribution process. In E. E. Jones et al. (Eds.), *Attribution: Perceiving the causes of behavior*. Morristown, NJ: General Learning Press, 1971.

Matlin, M. W., & Stang, D. J. The *Pollyanna principle: Selectivity in language, memory, and thought.* Cambridge, MA: Schenkman, 1978.

Schwarz, N., Servay, W., & Kumpf, M. *Attribution of arousal as a mediator of the effectiveness of fear-arousing communications.* Paper presented at the meeting of the Eastern Psychological Association, New York, April 1981. (ERIC Document Reproduction Service No. ED 205 867)

Staub, E., & Kellett, D. S. Increasing pain tolerance by information about aversive stimuli. *Journal of Personality and Social Psychology*, 1972, *21*, 198-203.

Tversky, A., & Kahneman, D. Availability: A heuristic for judging frequency and probability. *Cognitive Psychology*, 1973, *5*, 207–232.

Wessman, A. E., & Ricks, D. F. *Mood and personality.* New York: Holt, Rinehart & Winston, 1966.

Williams, S., Ryckman, R. M., Gold, J. A., & Lenny, E. The effects of sensation seeking and misattribution of arousal on attraction. *Journal of Research on Personality*, 1982, *16*, 217–226.

Wyer, R. S., & Carlston, D. *Social cognition, inference, and attribution.* Hillsdale, NJ: Erlbaum, 1979.

Zanna, M. P., & Cooper, J. Dissonance and the attribution process. In J. Harvey et al. (Eds.), *New directions in attribution research* (Vol. 1). Hillsdale, NJ: Erlbaum, 1976.

READING 21

Processing Deficits and the Mediation of Positive Affect in Persuasion

Diane M. Mackie • University of California, Santa Barbara
Leila T. Worth • Pennsylvania State University

Editors' Notes

Whereas momentary mood can serve as evidence for making inferences (e.g., inferences about one's general life satisfaction), it can have other effects as well on our judgmental processes. This selection shows that mood can limit our cognitive capacity and thereby reduce our ability to engage in thorough information processing, such as that needed to distinguish between good and specious arguments. This selection also demonstrates how careful experimental design allows investigators to separate competing explanations of previous findings. People in a positive mood may be cognitively lazy and refrain from extensive processing simply because such processing could spoil their positive mood (e.g., the information encountered might be unpleasant, or the processing task itself could be difficult). Alternatively, the presence of positive mood could activate a lot of positive material from memory whose processing consumes cognitive capacity, thus reducing the ability to engage in the task at hand. Note how the investigators attempt to replicate their findings by using different ways of manipulating mood and different attitude issues.

Discussion Questions

1. What are the implications of a cognitive capacity versus a motivational explanation of reduced systematic processing under positive mood? Would participants be able, if they wanted, to engage in systematic processing under positive mood?

2. What are the specific reasons for carrying out experiment 2 after having obtained significant results in experiment 1? Which alternative interpretations of the findings is the second experiment controlling for?

3. What is the reason for measuring the recall of arguments?

4. Under what conditions would positive mood enhance task performance and under what conditions would it worsen it?

Suggested Readings

Bower, G. H. (1981). Mood and memory. *American Psychologist, 36,* 129–148.

Forgas, J. P. (1992). Affect in social judgments and decisions: A multi-process model. In M. P. Zanna (Ed.), *Advances in experimental social psychology* (Vol. 25, pp. 227–275). New York: Academic Press.

Isen, A., & Levin, P. F. (1972). Effect of feeling good on helping: Cookies and kindness. *Journal of Personality and Social Psychology, 21,* 384–388.

Authors' Abstract

Motivational and cognitive mediators of the reduced processing of persuasive messages shown by recipients in a positive mood were tested. Ss (Subjects) in positive or neutral moods read strong or weak counterattitudinal advocacies for either a limited time or for as long as they wanted. Under limited exposure conditions, neutral mood Ss showed attitude change indicative of systematic processing, whereas positive mood Ss showed no differentiation of strong and weak versions of the message. When message exposure was unlimited, positive mood Ss viewed the message longer than did neutral mood Ss and systematically processed it rather than relying on persuasion heuristics. These findings replicated with 2 manipulations of mood and 2 different attitude issues. We interpret the results as providing evidence that reduced cognitive capacity to process the message contributes to the decrements shown by positive mood Ss.

A recent resurgence of interest in the possible interaction of affective states and cognitive processes (Bower, 1981; Bower & Cohen, 1982; Clark & Fiske, 1982; Clark & Isen, 1982; Simon, 1967, 1982; Zajonc, 1980) has offered a new perspective from which to view the impact of positive mood states on persuasion. This interactional perspective focuses attention on processes other than the direct transfer of affect (see Zanna, Kiesler, & Pilkonis, 1970, for a representative example of associationistic approaches) that could mediate the impact of moods on acceptance of persuasive messages (see, for example, Gardner & Raj, 1983; Lutz, 1985; Mitchell & Olson, 1981; Srull, 1983).

Worth and Mackie (1987) provided evidence for the interactional approach by demonstrating that the way in which persuasive messages were cognitively processed mediated the impact of positive mood on acceptance of the advocated position. Subjects in whom a positive mood had been induced and subjects in a neutral mood were both exposed for a limited amount of time to a message concerned with controlling the impact of acid rain. Messages were delivered by either an expert or a nonexpert and comprised either strong and valid or weak and specious arguments for the advocated position. Subjects in a positive mood appeared to engage in little systematic processing of the message, as indicated by their failure to differentiate strong from weak arguments in their postexposure attitudes (Petty & Cacioppo, 1981; Petty, Wells, & Brock, 1976) and by their reduced elaboration and retrieval of message-relevant material in recall protocols (Chaiken, 1980; Cook & Flay, 1978; Craik & Lockhart, 1972). In addition, the postexposure attitudes of subjects experiencing positive mood showed greater relative impact of a heuristic cue (expertise of the source) in the persuasion context. In contrast, both the postexposure attitudes and the cognitive response listings of subjects in a neutral mood indicated the persuasive impact of strong (but not of weak) arguments and the relative lack of impact of the heuristic cue. The relative failure of recipients experiencing positive mood to engage in systematic or central route processing of messages presented for a limited time has also been demonstrated by Bless, Bohner, Schwarz, and Strack (in press).

The results of these studies in the persuasion domain parallel findings regarding the impact of affective states on problem solving and judgmental tasks (see Isen, 1984, for a general review). People in a positive mood exhibit little systematic processing of complex information and an increased reliance on rapid, less effortful judgment heuristics. Whether these strategies result in efficient or effective processing depends on the nature of the task. Although the factors that determine when positive mood results in superior task performance have not yet been isolated, it is clear that people in a positive mood use different and often truncated processing strategies in dealing with information as compared with people in a neutral mood (Forgas, Burnham, & Trimboli, 1988; Isen, Means, Patrick, & Nowicki, 1982).

One possible explanation of these findings is motivational in nature and is concerned with the subjective experience of being in a positive mood. Subjects act to maintain subjective feelings of well-being, preferring to expose themselves to positively rather than negatively toned material (Isen & Simmonds, 1978; Mischel, Ebbesen, & Zeiss, 1973) and to engage in behaviors that maintain rather than destroy positive mood (Isen & Levin, 1972). If extensive thinking about an issue is difficult (Janis & Mann, 1977), or if processing a message may result in exposure to aversive information, message recipients in a positive mood might be motivated to avoid such processing in order to maintain their good mood (Isen et al., 1982). In the motivational view, therefore, people in a positive mood suffer motivational deficits: They can systematically process incoming material, but they just do not want to.

A second explanation of the findings assumes that increased use of judgmental heuristics is in-

duced by cognitive changes brought about by the positive mood state itself. A positive mood state appears to activate positive material stored in memory, which in turn activates other material to which it is linked (Bower, 1981; Isen, Shalker, Clark, & Karp, 1978). More material, and more diverse material, comes to mind (Boucher & Osgood, 1969; Bousfield, 1944, 1950; Isen, 1984; Isen, Daubman, & Gorgoglione, 1987). The easy accessibility of this material, or its presence in working memory, could reduce cognitive capacity for several possible reasons. The presence of such material might merely reduce space in a capacity-limited system (Isen et al., 1982; Shiffrin & Schneider, 1977), or the easy and simultaneous accessibility of material might defocus attention (Isen, Daubman, & Nowicki, 1987). A conscious decision may be made to deal with the material in some way (Sherman, 1987), or the presence of positively toned material in working memory might automatically draw available attention to itself (Nielson & Sarason, 1981; Zajonc, 1980). Mood might therefore function as a distraction, interfering with the ability to engage in careful elaborative processing (Petty & Brock, 1981). Regardless of the mechanism by which positive mood might have its effect, the ultimate consequence of the induction of a positive mood would be to reduce the overall capacity available for other processing tasks (see Ellis & Ashbrook, 1988, for a similar argument about negative mood). From this perspective, then, people in a positive mood may wish to process incoming information systematically, but because their capacity and attention are being used elsewhere, they cannot.

Worth and Mackie's (1987) results indicated that subjects experiencing a positive mood engaged in less systematic processing of the presented message, but did not distinguish between possible motivational and cognitive mediators of the effect. In the present experiments, we attempted to provide further evidence for the possible contribution of cognitive influences, and for deficits in capacity in particular, to the decreased systematic processing shown by subjects in positive moods.

Experiment 1

In this experiment, we exposed subjects in a positive mood and subjects in a neutral mood to a persuasive message for a limited amount of time. This procedure provided a replication of our earlier findings, as well as a comparison baseline of the extent of systematic processing of the message under limited exposure conditions. In another set of conditions, other subjects in positive or neutral moods were exposed to an identical message but were told that they could look at the message for as long as they chose. Subjects in this study were therefore given the opportunity to process the message to whatever extent they needed. The cognitive explanation of processing decrements would be supported if subjects experiencing positive mood freely chose to expose themselves to the message longer than did subjects in a neutral mood, and engaged in systematic processing while doing so.

We hypothesized that the limited exposure conditions would replicate our earlier findings. Thus, subjects in a positive mood should engage in less systematic processing of the message than subjects in a neutral mood. As the occurrence of systematic processing is reflected in the impact of argument quality on persuasion, we expected that subjects in a neutral mood would differentiate between messages comprising strong or weak arguments, but that subjects in a positive mood would fail to do so when exposed to the message for only a limited period of time. On the basis of the cognitive position detailed in the preceding paragraph, we further hypothesized that any processing decrements shown by subjects in a positive mood would result from cognitive capacity deficits, for which subjects would compensate if given the opportunity. We therefore predicted that when message exposure was unlimited, subjects in a positive mood as compared with those in a neutral mood would spend more time looking at the message in order to compensate for their cognitive deficit (see Chaiken & Eagly, 1976, for a similar argument as regards the advantage of written over auditorily presented information). As a result of this extended exposure, we expected positive mood subjects in the unlimited exposure conditions to engage in systematic processing and to show as much differentiation of strong and weak arguments as neutral mood subjects. We therefore expected to find the differentiation of strong and weak messages characteristic of systematic processing in all conditions except the one in which subjects in a positive mood saw the persuasive communication for only a limited amount of time.

Method

OVERVIEW

Subjects in whom either a positive mood or no mood had been induced read a persuasive communication about acid rain. Subjects were always exposed to a counterattitudinal message, which comprised either strong or weak arguments. Half of the subjects in each of these conditions were given a limited amount of time to read the message. The other half were allowed to take as much time as they wanted to look at the message. The amount of time subjects chose to expose themselves to the message, the extent of attitude change toward the advocated position, the latency of responses to answer questions about the message, and the recall of and cognitive responses to the message were all measured.

SUBJECTS AND DESIGN

Subjects were 215 University of California, Santa Barbara, students recruited from an introductory psychology course who received partial course credit for their participation (men and women were represented in approximately equal numbers).[1]

Subjects were randomly assigned to the cells of a 2 (positive or neutral mood) × 2 (limited or unlimited exposure) × 2 (strong or weak arguments) factorial design. Subjects were run in groups of 3–7.

PROCEDURE

Subjects were placed in separate rooms, each of which contained an IBM PC-XT. They began the experimental session by filling out a 20-item opinion survey in which the key attitude issue was embedded. This item read "Governmental controls should be imposed to minimize the effects of acid rain on the northeastern U.S." We measured pretest attitude scores by asking subjects to check an anchored 11-cm line later transposed into a scale ranging from 1 to 9 (1 = *strong disagreement*, 9 = *strong agreement*). A 10-min filler task was used

---

[1]We eliminated data from 7 subjects whose exposure times were very extreme (longer or shorter than 2 standard deviations from the condition mean) from all analyses. Elimination of these data did not alter the significance of any other reported analysis.

to separate the pretesting of the attitude issue from the main experimental session. The experimenter then informed the subjects that all subsequent instructions would appear on the computer screen. The presentation of instructions (including practice using the response scales), manipulations, persuasive message, and response scales was controlled by the computer.

Manipulation of mood. Subjects were told that the experiment was concerned with the effects of winning money in lotteries on future risk taking. Subjects in whom a positive mood was to be induced were told that some subjects would be randomly selected by the computer to win $2; subjects were asked to check an envelope next to their terminal to determine whether they had won $2. All subjects in the positive mood condition were selected to win and kept the $2 found in their envelope, a procedure shown in previous research to reliably induce a mildly positive mood (Worth & Mackie, 1987). Subjects in the neutral mood condition were simply asked if they had ever participated in a lottery. All subjects were then told that a risk questionnaire would be constructed for them on the basis of whether they won money (positive mood condition) or whether they had ever participated in a lottery (neutral mood condition). While this was being accomplished, they were asked to complete another task.

Presentation of message and manipulation of argument quality. Subjects read that this second task concerned people's perceptions of how delegates represent the views of their constituents at conferences. Subjects were asked to read a speech delivered by a delegate at a student-run environmental conference and to answer some questions about the delegate's performance. After presentation of instructions and manipulations, subjects pressed a computer key to initiate presentation of a persuasive message on the issue of governmental controls and acid rain. All subjects read a speech in which the delegate advocated a position that was counterattitudinal. Thus, subjects initially opposing the issue (i.e., those checking below 5.5 cm on the 11-cm line) read a speech in which the delegate was in favor of imposing controls, and subjects initially supporting the issue (i.e., those checking above 5.5 cm on the 11-cm line) read a speech in which the delegate was opposed to their position.[2] Half of the subjects read a message comprising eight points that pretesting had demonstrated to be strong and valid ($M = 6.23$, where 9

= very strong). The rest of the subjects saw a message containing eight points pretested as weak ($M = 3.82$), $F(1, 40) = 18.36, p < .0001$. During pretesting, subjects were asked to judge the strength or weakness of the arguments independently of their agreement with the position advocated in the argument. The four versions of the message were approximately equal in length, comprising 24 lines of text.

Manipulation of exposure time. For half of the subjects, the persuasive message was presented on the screen for a limited period of 65 s (limited exposure). Pretesting had determined that 65 s was the average time that a sample of pilot subjects took to read the message through once without pausing. Subjects in the limited exposure condition were told to read the speech while it was on the screen. They were informed that the speech would remain on the screen for a time that was just long enough for them to read the message through once and that the dependent measures would then appear automatically. The subjects were therefore aware that they were under time constraints to read the speech. The other half of the subjects (unlimited exposure) were also told to read the speech when it appeared on the screen. In addition, they were told that they could press the space bar to proceed to the dependent measures whenever they were ready. Thus, these subjects were aware that they could look at the speech for as long as they wanted. We designed the instructions to ensure that subjects in both conditions were equally motivated to process and believed their processing task to be equally important. All subjects controlled the onset of the message.

DEPENDENT MEASURES

Subjects responded to dependent measures accompanied by 9-point scales. The first dependent measure presented was a second assessment of subjects' attitudes on the acid rain issue. Five other items designed to assess subjects' perceptions of the content and source of the message followed. Both responses and reaction times to these measures were recorded. Subjects were then given a sheet of paper and asked to

---

[2]An initial analysis indicated that the side of the issue advocated in the message had no significant effects; we eliminated this variable from all further analyses.

list any and all thoughts [they] had while reading the speech; these can include anything related to what the speaker said in his/her speech, the speaker him/herself and his/her personality, the topic of the speech, the context in which the speaker spoke, or anything else [they] might have been thinking, including totally unrelated things.

Following this, subjects were given a free-recall test of message content with no forewarning.

Results

EFFECTIVENESS OF MANIPULATION OF ARGUMENT QUALITY

We analyzed subjects' ratings of the strength of the arguments in the message (1 = very weak, 9 = very strong) in a 2 × 2 × 2 (Mood × Exposure × Argument Quality) analysis of variance (ANOVA). Subjects perceived the strong messages to contain stronger arguments ($M = 5.88$) than the weak messages ($M = 3.99$), $F(1, 200) = 50.85$, $p < .0001$, confirming the validity of this manipulation.

ATTITUDE CHANGE

After ascertaining that there were no differences in premessage attitudes between conditions, we calculated an individual index of attitude change toward the position advocated in the persuasive message from a comparison of each subject's premessage and postmessage positions on the issue. Positive scores indicated movement toward the advocated position.[3]

The primary analysis of these attitude change data consisted of a planned contrast that tested the specific pattern of means predicted by our hypothesis. That is, we expected all subjects to process the message systematically and consequently to differentiate between strong and weak arguments, except for those subjects in the positive mood–limited exposure condition. We expected these subjects to show no differential attitudinal impact of strong and weak messages. The planned contrast thus compared differential attitude change to the strong and weak versions of the message in the positive mood–limited exposure condition (given a contrast weight of 3) with that in the other three conditions (each given contrast weights of –1). This contrast proved to be significant, $F(1, 200) = 6.35$, $p < .02$, and confirmed our predictions; the three-way interaction approached significance,

TABLE 21.1. Attitude Change Toward the Position Advocated in the Message as a Function of Induced Mood, Exposure, and Argument Quality

Mood and exposure	Argument quality		Difference
	Strong	Weak	
Positive			
Limited	1.33	1.59	−0.26
Unlimited	1.59	0.39	1.20
Neutral			
Limited	1.81	0.71	1.10
Unlimited	1.52	0.43	1.09

Note. The higher the score (out of a possible 8), the more movement toward the advocated position.

$F(1, 200) = 2.45$, $p < .12$. As can be seen in Table 1, subjects in the positive mood–limited exposure condition showed equal amounts of attitude change to messages comprising strong or weak arguments. In contrast, all other subjects evidenced more attitude change following exposure to strong arguments than following exposure to weak arguments. To explore the specific nature of these differences, we performed further contrasts with pooled variance estimates separately on the attitude change data from subjects in a neutral mood and from subjects in a positive mood.

The results of the analysis for subjects in a neutral mood revealed that systematic processing of the message had occurred. A main effect for argument quality indicated that subjects showed more attitude change in response to strong arguments than to weak ones, $F(1, 200) = 9.68$, $p < .005$. This effect was equally strong when these subjects were exposed to the message for a limited amount of time as when they controlled their own exposure time, $F(1, 200) < 1$ for the Quality × Exposure interaction.

Analysis of the attitude change shown by subjects in a positive mood revealed a quite different pattern, as expected. If positive mood subjects were experiencing cognitive deficits, the manipulation of exposure time would have a significant impact on their processing of the message. Specifically, we expected that these subjects, when exposed to the message for a limited period of time, would be unable to process systematically. We expected that removal of the processing time constraints would

[3]Analyses with premessage and postmessage attitudes entered as a repeated measure yielded results parallel to those using the index of attitude change.

result in systematic processing of the message, as subjects could compensate for the cognitive deficits. The existence of this pattern in the data was confirmed by a significant interaction between exposure and argument quality, $F(1, 200) = 5.19$, $p < .025$. As can be seen in Table 1, subjects in the unlimited exposure condition displayed the usual indications of systematic processing, showing more change in response to strong than weak messages, $F(1, 200) = 6.84$, $p < .01$. In contrast, subjects in the limited exposure condition appeared not to differentiate between strong and weak messages, $F(1, 200) < 1$.

EXPOSURE TIMES

We expected that subjects experiencing positive mood would compensate for their processing difficulty by increasing the length of their exposure to the message when given the opportunity to do so. We therefore entered the amount of time subjects kept the message on the screen in the unlimited exposure conditions in a 2 × 2 (Mood x Argument Quality) between-subjects ANOVA. This analysis revealed the expected main effect of mood, $F(1, 95) = 5.32$, $p < .025$, indicating that positive mood subjects chose significantly longer exposure times ($M = 78.37$) than did neutral mood subjects ($M = 69.49$). As expected, the mean exposure time for positive mood subjects was also significantly greater than the time allotted for processing in the limited exposure condition, $t(54) = 4.32$, $p < .01$. The mean exposure time for neutral mood subjects did not, however, significantly differ from the limited exposure time, $t(43) = 1.90$, ns.

The presence of a significant interaction between mood and argument quality, $F(1, 95) = 4.92$, $p < .03$ (see Table 2 for means), indicated that the increase in exposure time for positive mood subjects as compared with neutral mood subjects occurred primarily for subjects exposed to a message containing strong arguments, $F(1, 95) = 9.11$, $p < .005$. This increase was not significant for subjects exposed to weak messages, $F(1, 95) < 1$. This result is discussed in more detail later.

RECALL OF MESSAGE ARGUMENTS

Accurately recalled arguments provided an index of how extensively message content was processed (Cook & Flay, 1978; Craik & Lockhart, 1972; Eagly & Chaiken, 1984). The primary analysis of

TABLE 21.2. Exposure Times for Subjects in the Unlimited Exposure Condition as a Function of Mood and Argument Quality

Mood	Argument quality		M
	Strong	Weak	
Positive	85.91	71.09	78.37
Neutral	68.12	70.74	69.49

Note. Exposure times are in seconds.

the recall data consisted of a planned contrast testing our hypothesis. Specifically, we predicted that subjects in the positive mood–limited exposure condition would recall fewer of the arguments, reflecting lack of extensive processing, as compared with subjects in any other condition. This contrast (means are presented in Table 3) was highly significant, $F(1, 196) = 7.94$, $p < .01$. As expected, recall in the positive mood–limited exposure condition ($M = 1.86$) was significantly lower than the mean of the other three conditions ($M = 2.58$). Separate analyses indicated a significant impact of exposure time on recall for positive mood subjects, $F(1, 196) = 8.76$, $p < .005$, but not for neutral mood subjects, $F(1, 196) < 1$.

In addition, an overall 2 × 2 × 2 (Mood × Exposure × Argument Quality) ANOVA revealed a main effect of exposure, $F(1, 196) = 6.74$, $p < .02$, indicating that subjects in the unlimited exposure condition recalled more arguments ($M = 2.68$) than did subjects in the limited exposure condition ($M = 2.08$). As indicated by the result of the planned contrast (see previous paragraph), this effect is disproportionately due to the reduced recall in the positive mood–limited exposure condition.

COGNITIVE RESPONSES

Subjects' cognitive responses were coded by two independent judges. Interjudge reliability was 95%, and all disagreements were resolved by discussion. Reactions and responses to the message were classified as favorable or unfavorable mes-

TABLE 21.3. Accurate Free Recall (Out of a Possible Eight) as a Function of Mood and Exposure

Mood	Exposure	
	Limited	Unlimited
Positive	1.86	2.74
Neutral	2.35	2.61

TABLE 21.4. Index of Overall Favorability Toward the Issue and Message Content by Mood, Exposure, and Argument Quality

	Mood			
	Positive		Neutral	
Argument quality	Limited exposure	Unlimited exposure	Limited exposure	Unlimited exposure
Weak	−1.48	−2.71	−2.71	−3.13
Strong	−0.07	−0.52	−0.16	−1.05
Differentiation	1.41	2.19	2.55	2.08

sage or issue-related elaborations, as favorable or unfavorable comments of a more general kind,[4] or as totally unrelated comments.

Elaborations of issue and message content. We calculated a single index of overall favorability toward the message by subtracting each subject's unfavorable elaborations about the message or issue from his or her favorable ones. These scores were entered in a $2 \times 2 \times 2$ (Mood × Exposure × Argument Quality) ANOVA. The means from this analysis, all of which indicate a relatively negative response to the message on the part of the subjects, are presented in Table 4. The analysis revealed a main effect for argument quality, $F(1, 200) = 21.61$, $p < .0001$, which indicated that subjects had on the whole responded less negatively to the strong version of the message and more negatively to the weak version. As can be seen in Table 4, subjects in the positive mood–limited exposure condition showed less differentiation between strong and weak versions of the message than did subjects in any other condition, as expected. However, a planned comparison contrasting differentiation in the positive mood–limited exposure condition with differentiation in the other three cells did not reach significance. To further test our hypotheses, we performed separate contrasts of the same form on reactions to the strong and weak versions of the message. Although the analysis of elaborations of the strong message did not reach significance, subjects in the positive mood–limited exposure condition reacted less negatively to the weak message ($M = -1.48$) than did subjects in the other conditions combined ($M = -2.84$), $F(1, 200) = 3.27$, $p < .065$.

Unrelated thoughts. We also coded and analyzed responses that were completely unrelated to the message, issue, or persuasion context. The only significant result was an interaction between the exposure and argument quality variables, $F(1, 200) = 4.00$, $p < .05$. Subjects produced equal numbers of unrelated thoughts when exposed to strong and weak messages for a limited amount of time, but produced more of these thoughts for the strong message when viewing the message for an unlimited amount of time. There were no main effects or interactions associated with the mood variable.

Prediction of Attitude Change from Cognitive Responses

We performed separate multiple regression analyses for subjects in a positive mood and subjects in a neutral mood at each level of the exposure variable. Extent of attitude change toward the position advocated in the message was used as the criterion variable, and the index of favorability toward issue and message content, unrelated thoughts, and number of freely recalled arguments were used as the predictor variables. Results of these analyses appear in Table 5. Systematic processing of the messages is indicated when the content favorability index reliably predicts attitude change. As can be seen, this was the case in every condition except the positive mood–limited exposure condition. The message-relevant cognitive responses of neutral mood subjects, regardless of exposure time, and those of subjects in the positive mood-unlimited exposure condition, reliably predicted their postexposure acceptance of the advocated position. These relations provide further evidence that systematic processing of the message occurred. In contrast, the number and kind of message-relevant cognitive responses produced by subjects in the positive mood–limited exposure condition bore no relation to the attitude change shown in this condition. Instead, the unrelated thoughts noted by these subjects appear to be significantly associated with their expressed attitude change.

---

[4]Analyses of the general comments (such as "What is acid rain anyway?") revealed no significant results.

TABLE 21.5. Multiple Regression Analyses Predicting Attitude Change from Issue and Message-Related Favorability, Unrelated Thoughts, and Number of Arguments Recalled as a Function of Mood and Exposure

	Mood			
	Positive		Neutral	
Predictor variables	Limited exposure	Unlimited exposure	Limited exposure	Unlimited exposure
Content	.10	.36**	.34*	.41**
Unrelated thoughts	.30*	.12	−.10	−.07
Arguments recalled	.05	.06	.11	−.05

Note. Numbers are beta weights.
*$p < .03$. ** $p < .01$.

Discussion

When exposed to a persuasive message for a limited amount of time, subjects experiencing a positive mood showed reduced processing as compared with subjects in a neutral mood. Under these conditions, subjects in a good mood exhibited no differentiation of strong and weak versions of the message in their attitude change. Their elaborations of issue and message content showed little differentiation of strong and weak arguments, and these responses failed to predict attitude change toward the message. In contrast, subjects in a neutral mood in the limited exposure condition exhibited the differentiation of strong and weak messages and the reliable relation between cognitive responses and attitude change indicative of systematic processing. These results replicate earlier findings (Bless et al., in press; Worth & Mackie, 1987) that subjects in a positive mood, unlike those in a neutral mood, engage in little, if any, systematic processing.

Our strategy in this experiment was to identify and test cognitive and motivational explanations of this processing decrement. The cognitive explanation tested was the notion of mood-induced limitations of active processing capacity. The motivational position assessed was the idea that a good mood is a rewarding state and that extensive processing that might eliminate positive mood will be avoided.

This motivational position fared rather badly in this experiment. The methodology we used—giving subjects control over their exposure time—allowed a clear test of whether good mood motivated people to avoid or reduce extensive processing. If subjects in a positive mood wanted to avoid processing, giving them control of exposure time meant that they need look at the message only long enough to gain the information necessary to make some reasonable response. In this experiment, however, they looked at the message longer than did neutral mood subjects, and when presented with strong arguments, did so for considerably longer. This finding is clearly incompatible with the motivational hypothesis. That these subjects chose to look at the message for fairly lengthy periods of time is especially compelling given the counterattitudinal nature of the message and the mildly negative connotations of the acid rain issue itself—both of which seemingly are counter to a motivation to maintain positive mood.

In contrast, the cognitive interpretation of the deficits was strengthened by these findings. When recipients in a positive mood were allowed to control their message exposure, they viewed the message for significantly longer than did neutral mood subjects, and having done so, exhibited all the usual indications of systematic processing. Their postexposure attitudes reflected the differentially persuasive impact of strong as compared with weak messages and their performance on recall and cognitive response measures matched that of the neutral mood subjects. Whereas very little systematic processing had occurred when exposure to the message was limited, unlimited exposure to the message dramatically increased the amount of extensive processing given to the material by subjects in a good mood. These results support the idea that these subjects wanted, needed, and used increased exposure time to compensate for reduced capacity.

Although Experiment 1's results are much more consistent with the operation of the cognitive than the motivational position tested, interpretation of the results would be strengthened by the elimination of possible methodological ambiguities and an important discrepancy in our data.

First, it is possible that, rather than being produced because the mood itself consumed cognitive capacity, our results were produced because our manipulation of positive mood was more unexpected, thought-provoking, and therefore distracting than our manipulation of neutral mood. Recall that to induce positive mood we had arranged for subjects to win $2 in a lottery "randomly." In comparison, subjects in the neutral mood condition were asked merely to answer questions about their participation in a lottery. It may be that the unexpected event of winning $2 caused subjects to engage in attributional processing (Wong & Weiner, 1981; including to wonder what an experimenter who gave away $2 was about to either request of them or do to them). Therefore, rather than dealing with the cognitive consequences of mood, subjects in the positive mood condition may merely have been distracted by thoughts about the particular manipulation we used.

In addition to this problem, the data were not uniformly consistent with the cognitive explanation. The most serious discrepancy was in the condition in which subjects in a good mood were given unlimited time to consider a message composed of weak arguments. Whereas subjects in a positive mood had found the weak messages persuasive in the limited exposure condition, they were clearly unimpressed by them in the unlimited exposure condition. This result is in line with our hypothesis that the unlimited exposure allowed subjects to compensate for cognitive deficits and engage in systematic processing (hence, they recognized the weak arguments as invalid). Although subjects in this condition appeared to be processing systematically, they did not, however, require any extra time to do so. It is quite possible that weak arguments require less capacity to process fully than strong arguments and can thus be comprehended in less time. If so, however, subjects in the limited exposure condition should have been able to deal more judiciously with the weak arguments than with the strong ones, and they did not. Because of the importance of these conditions for our hypotheses, we attempted in a second experiment to learn more about how and why positive mood has its effects under limited and unlimited exposure conditions.

Experiment 2

In this experiment, we attempted to replicate the central effects found in Experiment 1 and to eliminate alternative explanations of these findings on the basis of the peculiarities of the mood induc-

tion used or the attitude issue considered. We induced positive and neutral moods by having subjects view visual material designed to be equally interesting but also to induce positive or neutral affect differentially. Subjects in positive and neutral moods were then exposed to either a strong or weak counterattitudinal message delivered by either an expert or nonexpert source. The heuristic cue was provided to help distinguish between the motivational and cognitive consequences of mood. Some subjects were exposed to the message for a fixed amount of time, whereas other subjects controlled the length of time they were exposed to the message. Following Worth and Mackie (1987) and the results of Experiment 1, we expected that subjects experiencing positive mood and able to look at the message for only a fixed amount of time would show reduced systematic processing and increased reliance on persuasion cues as compared with subjects in a neutral mood. Furthermore, we expected that when subjects in a positive mood controlled their own exposure to the message, they would choose to process the message longer and as a consequence would show systematic processing of its content comparable to that shown by subjects in a neutral mood.

Method

OVERVIEW

Subjects in whom either a positive mood or no mood had been induced read a persuasive communication about handgun control. Subjects were always exposed to a counterattitudinal message, which comprised either strong or weak arguments and was delivered by either an expert source or a nonexpert source. Half of the subjects in each condition were given a limited amount of time to read the message. The other half were allowed to take as much time as they chose to look at the message. The amount of time subjects spent reading the message, the extent of attitude change toward the advocated position, the latency of responses to answer questions about the message, and recall of and cognitive responses to the message were all measured.

SUBJECTS AND DESIGN

Subjects were 260 University of California, Santa Barbara, students recruited from an introductory psychology course who received partial course credit for participation (men and women were represented in approximately equal numbers).[5]

Subjects were randomly assigned to the cells of a 2 (positive or neutral mood) × 2 (limited or unlimited exposure) × 2 (strong or weak arguments) × 2 (expert or nonexpert source) factorial design. Subjects were run in groups of 1–6.

PROCEDURE

As in Experiment 1, subjects began the experimental session by filling out a 20-item opinion survey in which a key attitude issue was embedded. This item read "Only those affiliated with law enforcement agencies should be allowed to possess handguns." We measured pretest attitude scores by asking subjects to check an anchored 11-cm line later transposed into a scale ranging from 1 to 9, in which 1 indicated strong disagreement with the item and 9 indicated strong agreement.

Manipulation of mood. The experimenter then told subjects that she was pretesting some video clips for an undergraduate project. Subjects were asked to watch one clip and answer some questions about it. Subjects in whom a positive mood was to be induced watched a 5-min comedy segment taken from the TV program "Saturday Night Live." Subjects in the neutral mood condition watched a 5-min segment on wine. After viewing the video clip, subjects were asked to rate their feelings "at the present moment" on two 9-point scales. These scales were anchored at the endpoints by *very sad* and *very happy* and by *not at all pleased* and *very pleased,* respectively. Subjects then indicated on anchored 9-point bipolar scales how entertaining, interesting, and suitable for presentation to students the clip was. This completed the first segment of the experiment.

Presentation of message and manipulation of source expertise. A second experimenter, blind to the subjects' mood condition, reseated subjects at individual, visually isolated IBM PC/XT computers that controlled presentation of stimulus materials and dependent measures. Subjects were given the same instructions and cover story as in Experiment 1. Half of the subjects were told that the delegate delivering the speech was an eminent legal scholar from the University of Virginia (expert source). The other half of the subjects were told that the delegate was a freshman at the University of Virginia (nonexpert source). All subjects

were then presented with a persuasive message on the issue of handgun control in which the delegate advocated a position that was counterattitudinal to the subject's initial position (subjects checking below 5.5 cm on the 11-cm line received a message supporting gun control; those checking above 5.5 cm received a message opposing gun control).

Manipulation of argument quality. Half of the subjects in each condition read a message comprising eight points that pretesting with 15 uninvolved but similar students had demonstrated to be strong and valid ($M = 6.24$, where 9 = very strong). The rest of the subjects saw a message containing eight points pretested as weak ($M = 3.93$), $F(1,14) = 67.41$, $p < .0001$. The difference between strong ($M = 6.62$) and weak ($M = 3.49$) arguments opposing gun control was greater than the difference between strong ($M = 5.89$) and weak ($M = 4.39$) arguments for gun control, $F(1, 14) = 6.25$, $p < .03$, but both differences were significant at $p < .01$. The four versions of the message were approximately equal in length, comprising 25 lines of text.

Manipulation of exposure time. Exposure time to the message was manipulated as in Experiment 1. For half of the subjects, the persuasive message was presented on the screen for a limited period of 70 s (limited exposure). Pretesting had determined that 70 s was the average time that a sample of pilot subjects took to read the message through once without pausing. Again, subjects were forewarned that they would have only enough time to read the message through once. The other half of the subjects controlled their own exposure time to the message (unlimited exposure). All subjects controlled onset of message presentation.

DEPENDENT MEASURES

The dependent measures used and their administration to subjects were the same as in Experiment 1.

Results

EFFECTIVENESS OF MOOD MANIPULATION

Subjects' responses to the questions about how happy and how pleased they felt immediately after viewing the video segments (Cronbach's $\alpha =$

---

[5]Three subjects were eliminated from all analyses because they failed to complete the mood manipulation check questions.

.82) were averaged to form a single index of subjective mood. Analysis of this index in a 2 (neutral or positive mood) × 2 (limited or unlimited exposure) × 2 (strong or weak arguments) × 2 (expert or nonexpert source) × 2 (side of issue presented) between-subjects ANOVA revealed the intended significant main effect of the mood manipulation, $F(1, 225) = 32.62$, $p < .0001$. Subjects who had watched the video intended to induce positive mood reported feeling happier and more pleased ($M = 6.70$, where 9 = very happy or pleased) than did subjects who had watched the neutral video ($M = 5.74$). No other main effects or interactions were significant. Subjects did *not* perceive the positive video ($M = 6.61$) to be significantly more interesting than the neutral video ($M = 6.32$), $F(1, 225) = 1.86$, *ns*. [6]

EFFECTIVENESS OF ARGUMENT STRENGTH AND EXPERTISE MANIPULATIONS

Subjects exposed to strong arguments rated the message they had seen as more strong and valid ($M = 6.33$, where 9 = very strong) than did subjects exposed to weak arguments ($M = 4.48$), $F(1, 225) = 37.48$, $p < .0001$, confirming the validity of this manipulation.[7] Also as intended, subjects who were told that the source was an expert in the field rated him as having more expertise ($M = 5.45$) than did subjects told that he was a nonexpert ($M = 4.37$), $F(1, 225) = 20.03$, $p < .0001$. Not surprisingly, subjects exposed to strong messages believed the source of those messages to be more expert ($M = 5.69$) than did subjects exposed to weak arguments ($M = 4.08$), $F(1, 225) = 48.12$, $p < .0001$.

ATTITUDE CHANGE

All subjects were exposed to a counterattitudinal message. After ascertaining that there were no differences in premessage attitudes between conditions, we calculated an individual index of attitude change toward the position advocated in the persuasive message from a comparison of each subject's premessage and postmessage positions on the issue. Positive scores indicated movement toward the advocated position.[8]

The primary analysis of these attitude change data consisted of the planned contrast that tested for systematic processing of the message (and consequent differentiation of strong and weak arguments) by all subjects except for those in the posi-

TABLE 21.6. Attitude Change Toward the Position Advocated in the Message as a Function of Induced Mood, Exposure, and Argument Quality: Experiment 2

Mood and exposure	Argument quality		
	Strong	Weak	Difference
Positive			
Limited	1.68	1.59	0.09
Unlimited	2.64	1.28	1.36
Neutral			
Limited	2.16	1.39	0.77
Unlimited	2.62	0.93	1.69

Note. The higher the score (out of a possible 8), the more movement toward the advocated position.

tive mood–limited exposure condition. These subjects were expected to show no differential attitudinal impact of strong and weak messages. The planned contrast thus compared differential attitude change to the strong and weak versions of the message in the positive mood–limited exposure condition (given a contrast weight of 3) with that in the other three conditions (each given a contrast weight of –1). This contrast proved to be significant, $F(1, 225) = 5.12$, $p < .025$, confirming our predictions; the three-way interaction was not significant, $F(1, 225) < 1$. As can be seen in Table 6, subjects in a positive mood given limited exposure to the message were equally influenced by strong and weak versions of the message. In contrast, all other subjects were more persuaded by strong arguments than by weak arguments.

Our second prediction concerned the use of the persuasion cue. We predicted that subjects in the positive mood–limited exposure condition would show greater reliance on available validity cues and thus be more persuaded by an expert source

---

[6]Subjects later assigned to conditions in which weak messages were seen found both videos to be more interesting ($M = 6.78$) than did subjects in the strong argument condition ($M = 6.13$), $F(1, 225) = 7.34$, $p < .007$.

[7]Ratings of argument strength also produced a four-way interaction, $F(1, 225) = 3.80$, $p < .052$, that suggested that all subjects in a positive mood saw pro-gun-control arguments as being stronger than anti-gun-control arguments, except those given limited exposure to a nonexpert's message, whereas all subjects in a neutral mood saw the anti-gun-control arguments as being stronger than the pro-gun-control arguments, except those given limited exposure to a nonexpert's message.

[8]Analyses with premessage and postmessage attitudes entered as a repeated measure yielded results parallel to those with the index of attitude change.

TABLE 21.7. Attitude Change Toward the Position Advocated in the Message as a Function of Induced Mood, Exposure, and Source Expertise: Experiment 2

Mood and exposure	Source expertise		
	Expert	Nonexpert	Difference
Positive			
Limited	2.25	1.09	1.16
Unlimited	1.90	1.97	−0.07
Neutral			
Limited	1.84	1.69	0.15
Unlimited	2.03	1.44	0.59

Note. The higher the score (out of a possible 8), the more movement toward the advocated position.

and less impressed with a nonexpert source than would subjects in any other condition. Our second planned contrast thus compared differential attitude change to the expert and nonexpert versions of the message in the positive mood–limited exposure condition (given a contrast weight of 3) with that in the other three conditions (each given contrast weights of −1). This contrast was marginally significant, $F(1, 225) = 3.25$, $p < .07$; the associated three-way interaction also approached significance, $F(1, 225) = 3.22$, $p < .07$. (Means appear in Table 7.) Subjects in the positive mood–limited exposure condition were much more impressed with the arguments of the expert source and were little influenced by the nonexpert source. Attitude change in the other conditions was independent of the presence or absence of the persuasion cue.

To explore the specific nature of both these differences, we performed further contrasts using pooled variance estimates separately on the attitude change data from neutral mood and positive mood subjects. The results for subjects in a neutral mood were quite straightforward. The main effect of argument quality was highly significant, $F(1, 225) = 9.58$, $p < .005$, and unqualified by any interaction between quality and exposure, $F(1, 225) = 1.60$, $p > .2$. Thus, neutral mood subjects systematically processed the message in both the limited and unlimited exposure conditions. These subjects were not significantly influenced by source expertise, $F(1, 225) = 2.01$, ns, and this was equally true in both the limited and unlimited exposure conditions, $F(1, 225) < 1$.

Analysis of the attitude change shown by subjects in a positive mood revealed the two significant predicted interactions. First, a significant in-

teraction between exposure and argument quality, $F(1, 225) = 4.79$, $p < .04$, indicated that subjects in the unlimited exposure condition showed more change in response to strong than weak messages, $F(1, 225) = 10.12$, $p < .002$, whereas subjects in the limited exposure condition failed to differentiate between strong and weak messages, $F(1, 225) < 1$. As expected, subjects with unlimited exposure to the message dealt with it systematically, whereas those with limited exposure showed no signs of systematic processing. In addition, the significant interaction between exposure and source expertise, $F(1, 225) = 3.99$, $p < .05$, reflected the fact that subjects with limited exposure differentiated the messages of the expert and the nonexpert sources, $F(1, 225) = 5.75$, $p < .025$, whereas those with unlimited access did not do so, $F(1, 225) < 1$.[9]

EXPOSURE TIMES

As in Experiment 1, we expected that subjects experiencing a positive mood would compensate for any difficulty processing the message by increasing their exposure to the message when given the opportunity to do so. We therefore entered the amount of time subjects kept the message on the screen in the unlimited exposure conditions into a $2 \times 2 \times 2 \times 2$ (Mood x Argument Quality x Source Expertise x Side of Issue Presented) between-subjects ANOVA. This analysis revealed the expected main effect of mood, $F(1, 116) = 6.49$, $p < .01$, indicating that positive mood subjects spent significantly longer looking at the message ($M = 84.15$) than did neutral mood subjects ($M = 74.87$; see Table 8 for means). Note that this difference

---

[9]The overall analysis of the index of attitude change also revealed a number of additional effects. Overall, there were main effects of quality, $F(1, 225) = 13.77$, $p < .0003$, and expertise, $F(1, 225) = 4.32$, $p < .04$. There was also an interaction between exposure and quality, $F(1, 225) = 5.88$, $p < .02$, indicating that, overall, subjects differentiated more between strong and weak arguments when they controlled their own exposure to the message (strong argument $M = 2.63$, weak argument $M = 1.12$) than when the exposure time was fixed (strong argument $M = 1.92$, weak argument $M = 1.48$). In addition, an interaction between quality and side of issue, $F(1, 225) = 4.03$, $p < .05$, indicated that although subjects were equally persuaded by the pro-gun-control ($M = 2.32$) and anti-gun-control ($M = 2.22$) messages when they contained strong arguments, they were more persuaded by the weak message that argued against gun control ($M = 1.80$) than by the weak message arguing in favor of gun control ($M = 0.96$).

TABLE 21.8. Exposure Times for Subjects in the Unlimited Exposure Condition as a Function of Mood and Argument Quality: Experiment 2

Mood	Argument quality		M
	Strong	Weak	
Positive	84.96	83.37	84.15
Neutral	73.61	75.97	74.87

Note. Exposure times are in seconds.

was true for subjects receiving both strong and weak arguments—the problematic finding of Experiment 1 was not replicated. As expected, the mean exposure time for subjects in a positive mood also proved to be significantly greater than the time allotted for processing in the limited exposure condition (70 s), $t(70) = 6.09$, $p < .001$. The mean exposure time chosen by subjects in a neutral mood was also significantly different from the limited exposure time, $t(62) = 2.04$, $p < .05$. The only other significant effect was a main effect of the side of the issue, $F(1, 116) = 11.16$, $p < .001$, indicating that subjects exposed to anti-gun-control arguments spent significantly longer looking at the message ($M = 87.01$) than did subjects exposed to the pro-gun-control message ($M = 74.94$).

RECALL OF MESSAGE ARGUMENTS

More arguments were recalled ($M = 3.51$) when subjects had unlimited exposure to the message than when exposure was limited ($M = 3.16$), $F(1, 225) = 5.39$, $p < .02$.

COGNITIVE RESPONSES

Subjects' cognitive responses were coded by two independent judges. Interjudge reliability was 91%, and all disagreements were resolved by discussion. The responses of most interest here were those classified as favorable or unfavorable message or issue-related elaborations and those classified as favorable or unfavorable comments about the source.[10]

Elaborations of issue and message content. We calculated a single index of overall favorability toward the message by subtracting each subject's unfavorable elaborations about the message or issue from his or her favorable ones. We entered these scores (which were again largely negative) into a 2 × 2 × 2 × 2 × 2 (Mood × Exposure × Argument Quality × Source Expertise x Side of Issue Presented) ANOVA. The analysis revealed a main effect for argument quality, $F(1, 225) = 17.93$, $p < .0001$, which indicated that subjects had on the whole responded positively to the strong version of the message ($M = .29$) and negatively ($M = -1.11$) to the weak version. As seen in Table 9, subjects in the positive mood–limited exposure condition showed less differentiation between strong and weak versions of the message than did subjects in other conditions, as expected. However, a planned comparison contrasting differentiation in the positive mood–limited exposure condition

---

[10]Analysis of responses that were generally favorable or unfavorable revealed only that more negative ($M = 1.01$) than positive ($M = 0.38$) responses were produced, $F(1, 225) = 60.32$, $p < .0001$, and that this was less true when people in a good mood received a weak message from a nonexpert than in any other condition, $F(1, 225) = 4.58$, $p < .03$. We also coded and analyzed those responses completely unrelated to the message, issue, or persuasion context (some of which included references to thoughts about the mood manipulation tapes). The only significant result was a four-way interaction between the mood, exposure, argument quality, and side of issue variables, $F(1, 225) = 5.19$, $p < .02$. Subjects in a good mood produced more unrelated thoughts when exposed to anti-gun-control than pro-gun-control messages in some conditions and the reverse in others, whereas subjects in a neutral mood always produced slightly more unrelated thoughts while thinking about the pro-gun-control messages as compared with the anti-gun-control messages.

TABLE 21.9. Index of Overall Favorability Toward the Issue and Message Content by Mood, Exposure, and Argument Quality

	Mood			
	Positive		Neutral	
Argument quality	Limited exposure	Unlimited exposure	Limited exposure	Unlimited exposure
Weak	−0.76	−1.27	−1.09	−1.27
Strong	0.03	0.32	0.72	0.04
Differentiation	0.79	1.59	1.81	1.31

TABLE 21.10. Index of Overall Favorability Toward the Source by Mood, Exposure, and Argument Quality

	Mood			
	Positive		Neutral	
Argument quality	Limited exposure	Unlimited exposure	Limited exposure	Unlimited exposure
Weak	−0.97	−0.47	−0.42	−1.00
Strong	1.00	0.35	0.78	0.66
Differentiation	1.97	0.82	1.20	1.66

with differentiation in the other three cells only approached significance, $F(1, 225) = 2.27, p < .09$.

Responses about the source. We subtracted subjects' negative comments about the source from their positive comments to form an overall index of favorability toward the source of the message. Analysis of these scores in a 2 × 2 × 2 × 2 × 2 (Mood × Exposure × Argument Quality × Source Expertise × Side of Issue Presented) ANOVA revealed a main effect for argument quality, $F(1, 225) = 39.95, p < .0001$, and a main effect for source expertise, $F(1, 225) = 6.54, p < .01$. Both of these effects were qualified by a significant interaction between the mood, exposure, and argument quality variables, $F(1, 225) = 3.83, p < .051$. As can be seen in Table 10, subjects in the positive mood–limited exposure condition made more positive than negative comments about the source as compared with subjects in any other condition, $F(1, 225) = 4.35, p < .03$, but there was no tendency for these subjects to distinguish between the expert and nonexpert source more than did other subjects.

PREDICTION OF ATTITUDE CHANGE FROM COGNITIVE RESPONSES

We performed separate multiple regression analyses for subjects in a positive mood and subjects in a neutral mood at each level of the exposure variable, as we did in Experiment 1. Extent of attitude change toward the position advocated in the message was used as the criterion variable, and the index of overall favorability toward issue and message content, the index of favorability toward the source, and the number of freely recalled arguments were used as the predictor variables. Results of these analyses appear in Table 11. Systematic processing (implicated when the content favorability index reliably predicts attitude change) appears to have occurred when subjects were in a neutral mood, regardless of exposure time, and when subjects in a positive mood were given unlimited access to the message. In contrast, the relative favorability of content-related responses produced by subjects in the positive mood-limited exposure condition bore no relation to the attitude change shown in this condition. Instead, the relative number of favorable reactions to the source was significantly associated with attitude change. This result is consistent with the use of a source heuristic and thus corroborates the attitude change data.

Discussion

Experiment 2's results are important in advancing our understanding of the processing decrement shown by positive mood subjects for several reasons. First, they replicate Experiment 1's results with a new manipulation of mood and a different

TABLE 21.11. Multiple Regression Analyses Predicting Attitude Change from Issue and Message-Related Favorability, Source Favorability, and Number of Arguments Recalled as a Function of Mood and Exposure

	Mood			
	Positive		Neutral	
Predictor variables	Limited exposure	Unlimited exposure	Limited exposure	Unlimited exposure
Content favorability	.04	.44***	.31**	.39***
Source favorability	.28*	.16	.15	.09
Arguments recalled	.16	.16	.13	−.00

Note. Numbers are beta weights.
*$p < .03$. ** $p < .01$. *** $p < .0003$.

(and more involving) attitude issue. Once again, subjects experiencing positive mood showed reduced processing as compared with subjects in a neutral mood when they were exposed to a persuasive message for a limited amount of time. Subjects in a good mood given unlimited access to the message showed increased exposure times and, under these conditions, showed as much systematic processing as did subjects in a neutral mood. Replication of these effects in Experiment 2 successfully eliminated the surprising nature of the lottery manipulation and the possible peculiarities of the acid rain issue as explanations of our results.

Second, the ability of subjects in a positive mood to process systematically again appeared to depend on increased exposure to the message, as indicated by the significantly longer time subjects in a good mood looked at the message. These subjects spent just as long looking at weak as at strong messages. This consistent increase in exposure to the message strengthens the argument that such an increase is a prerequisite for positive mood subjects' complete processing of the message.

Third, the experiment's results further questioned the viability of an explanation based on the motivation to avoid processing by revealing more about the processing strategies of subjects in a good mood. Those with inadequate time to process the message fully made greater use of an available persuasion heuristic (replicating Worth & Mackie, 1987). Even more important, subjects in a good mood given unlimited access to the message showed no greater reliance on this heuristic than did subjects in a neutral mood. This argues against the idea that subjects in a good mood were simply unmotivated to process.[11]

General Discussion

The important advance to be made in this area of research is an understanding of whether and how motivational and cognitive factors underlie the processing decrement effect shown by subjects in a good mood. In these experiments, we compared a motivational explanation of the effect with a cognitive explanation. Although it may be extremely difficult to fully disentangle motivational from cognitive processes, especially when it is likely that both are involved (Tetlock & Levi, 1982), it is nevertheless possible to conduct experiments that

make it highly unlikely that certain kinds of processes can effectively account for the results. In establishing, at least in our experimental conditions, that the exposure manipulation affects the processing performance of positive mood subjects, our results have proven incompatible with the motivational argument that those in a good mood wish to avoid extensive processing.

First, we were able to create an experimental situation that assessed the impact of positive mood states under conditions of high incentive. Several pieces of evidence indicate that subjects in both the limited and unlimited exposure conditions were motivated to complete the experimental task and to complete it well. For example, the fact that neutral mood subjects (and performance in the limited exposure condition was particularly important) showed extensive systematic processing of the message in both Experiments 1 and 2 indicates that our experimental situation was motivationally akin to the high involvement and high motivation conditions of dozens of previous studies (see Petty & Cacioppo, 1986, for a review). The situation was identical for positive mood subjects, with the added influence of their positive mood. Moreover, the results of the unlimited condition show that these positive mood subjects were motivated to process the message and that they did so. These aspects of our data suggest that all our subjects had ample incentive to process.

Second, as compared with neutral mood subjects, subjects in a good mood showed no indication of systematic processing when exposure was limited, but were influenced instead by the presence or absence of a persuasion cue. Third, when given control of exposure to the message, subjects feeling good spent more time looking at the message than did neutral mood subjects. Fourth, this

---

[11] Another aspect of our results helps to undermine the viability of another motivational explanation of these findings. Positive mood might well increase confidence and optimism (Johnson & Tversky, 1983; Kavenaugh & Bower, 1985), so that message recipients in a good mood believe they can judge the validity of the message accurately and successfully without extensive processing. Although increased confidence has been found to contribute to the quicker decision times found in other studies, it did not appear to be a factor in either of our studies. Not only did subjects in a positive mood take longer to process the message when given the opportunity, but they also took longer to make judgments about the message and the source and longer to report their own position regardless of exposure condition; $F(1, 200) = 8.24$, $p < .005$, in Experiment 1, and $F(1, 225) = 2.43$, $p < .12$, in Experiment 2).

extended exposure time resulted in systematic processing of the message by positive mood subjects, as indicated by multiple measures. Finally, subjects in the positive mood–unlimited exposure condition were uninfluenced by the presence or absence of a persuasion cue that effectively indicated message validity.

Although the idea that people in a positive mood are motivated to avoid processing could neither generate nor explain this pattern of findings, our results do not rule out every possible motivational explanation. One alternative possibility is that rather than avoiding processing altogether (the motivational position tested) and rather than finding positive mood inevitably distracting (the cognitive view investigated), subjects might choose momentarily to continue to savor a good mood before turning to the experimental task. Recall that in our experiments, subjects controlled message presentation, and so subjects in a good mood could have "basked" for as long as they chose before they turned to the message. Recall also that these subjects would have had to make the decision to continue basking in their mood despite being forewarned that the message would be available for only a limited period of time. The "savor-then-process" view nevertheless suggests that positive mood subjects might initiate message presentation, then savor their mood, delaying careful processing of the arguments. When subjects do turn to the task, however, they are quite capable of systematically processing the material. What evidence is there for this more specific "savor the moment, then buckle down" hypothesis?

In the unlimited exposure condition such a strategy would produce just the results we found: Positive mood subjects spent longer processing the message than did neutral mood subjects, and did systematically process it. However, what results would the savor-then-process hypothesis predict for the limited exposure condition? First, because processing was delayed, subjects would have been able to systematically process only some portion of the message before it disappeared. If this were so, subjects in this condition should have had better recall of arguments in the first (systematically processed) part of the message than in the second. They did not. Analyses of the arguments recalled showed that the argument presented last in the message was recalled by as many subjects in the positive mood condition ($N = 8$ of 58) as in the neutral mood conditions ($N = 6$ of 48), $\chi^2 = .0085$,

ns. Second, if subjects in this condition were indeed processing the content of the message, then attitude change should not have been affected by the presence of a heuristic cue. The results of Experiment 2 showed that such a cue had a significant impact in this condition. Third, if subjects were systematically processing even a third of the arguments, there should have been some signs, albeit weak ones, of an effect for argument quality. Such an effect was found in neither study: In Experiment 1, weak arguments were slightly more persuasive than strong arguments. In sum, although this alternative motivational hypothesis may be viable under some conditions and is worthy of further investigation, the total pattern of our results provided no evidence consistent with it.

A second motivational alternative suggests that the unlimited exposure conditions provided motivational compensation. For example, even though our subjects were operating under high incentive, positive mood might have been enough to reduce motivation to process the message, producing the results found in the limited exposure condition. Telling these subjects that they could process the message for as long as they liked, however, might have provided a motivational boost (because it made the task seem more important to them or because they now had no excuse—the limited processing time—not to process). If this possibility were correct, this motivational compensation should have allowed subjects in a good mood to go ahead and systematically process the message, performing no differently from neutral mood subjects. What do the results show? Given unlimited exposure, subjects in a good mood did systematically process the message, of course, but their performance differed from that of neutral mood subjects in a very significant way: They took much longer to do equivalently careful processing. The total pattern of findings is thus not adequately explained by appealing to the idea of motivational compensation either.

In contrast, the data are substantially compatible with an explanation emphasizing limitations in processing capacity induced by positive mood. This view is most strongly supported by the finding that giving positive mood recipients unlimited time to process eliminated the decrements found with limited exposure. Nevertheless, further research is needed to specify more precisely the cognitive implications of positive mood for processing. First, it is not clear whether (either experimental or naturally occurring) mood inductions result in substantial amounts of diverse material actually entering working memory or in such material becoming differentially accessible. Either eventuality would decrease attention and capacity and could influence performance on simultaneous processing tasks. Both the extent to which attention is redirected and the nature of the material to which it was redirected could influence what was processed in a persuasive message, as well as how much it was processed (Sherman, 1987). Second, the issue of how to distinguish control of the *consequences* of mood states from control of mood states themselves is of central importance. Reduction of processing capacity and diffusion of attention might require conscious clearing of the workspace or conscious focusing of attention away from mood-relevant material so that systematic processing might occur. Although in this sense the mood state itself can be said to be under motivational control, the assertion of such control is not only likely to be necessitated by capacity limitations, but, to the extent that the implementation of such strategies requires capacity, will also further reduce the kind of capacity necessary for systematic processing.[12] Empirical testing of these ideas would be helpful in advancing understanding of the impact of mood on processing tasks in general.

In arguing that the capacity reduction hypothesis provides the strongest and most parsimonious explanation of our findings in these experiments, we are not implying that motivational deficits never influence such processing. If processing the material was extremely difficult, if its content was extremely aversive, if people were highly motivated to maintain their positive moods, or if subjects had more pressing goals and interests (all conditions that have much higher probability outside than inside the laboratory), it is likely that they might choose not to deal extensively with a persuasive message. Our results suggest, however, that given adequate motivation to process, cognitive consequences of positive mood

and the need to deal with those consequences make it more difficult for people in a good mood to do so. The data presented in this article suggest that even if message recipients in a good mood are motivated to process incoming information, they do not do so as well in the same amount of time as do recipients in a neutral mood.

Arguing that the cognitive consequences of positive mood interfere with the execution of systematic processing does not imply that positive mood necessarily results in poorer performance on every type of task. Instead, the consequences of positive mood for speed, accuracy, and efficiency on a processing task depend on the nature of the task itself. Positive mood would not reduce performance speed on a heuristically processed task and, in cases in which utilized heuristics were valid paths to an accurate answer, would not impair accuracy either (Isen & Means, 1983). In fact, the nature of material occupying working memory as a result of positive mood might improve performance on tasks for which its presence is an advantage, for example, listing positive words (Isen, Johnson, Mertz, & Robinson, 1985) or finding creative "disassociative" solutions (Isen et al. 1987). Thus, the Isen et al. (1987) findings that subjects in a good mood are able to solve creativity problems more rapidly than are those in a neutral mood should not be taken as evidence that good mood produces no capacity deficits or as evidence that it routinely produces clearer thinking. Instead, the findings that mood states can have very different effects on different tasks and on different processing operations within the same task point to the need for more careful delineation of the interaction between the motivational and cognitive consequences of mood states and the cognitive and motivational demands of simultaneous processing tasks.

ACKNOWLEDGMENTS

The support of National Institute of Mental Health Grant MH44146 to Diane Mackie is gratefully acknowledged. Results from Experiment 2 were first presented at the 24th International Congress of Psychology, Sydney, Australia, August 1988.

We are particularly grateful to David L. Hamilton and Steven J. Sherman for their critical contribution to this and earlier versions of this article. Thanks are also due to several anonymous reviewers whose comments improved both our thinking and the manuscript; to Stephanie T. Nader, Laurie L. Kaufer, Linda M. Meneses, and Lorraine S. Hebb for help in collecting the data; and to Holly A. Schroth, Catherine L. Barber, and Marta S. Van Loon for coding the cognitive response data.

---

[12]Mood was in fact assessed again after subjects had listed cognitive responses to the message, but by this stage no differences remained between subjects originally exposed to the humorous video ($M = 5.02$) and those who saw the neutral video ($M = 5.16$), $F(1, 225) < 1$. These findings suggest that either the decision to process necessitated eliminating positive mood or that processing itself may have eliminated positive mood. Resolution of these issues awaits administration of multiple assessments of mood throughout the processing task.

REFERENCES

Bless, H., Bohner, G., Schwarz, N., & Strack, F. (in press). Happy and mindless? Moods and the processing of persuasive communications. *Personality and Social Psychology Bulletin*.

Boucher, J., & Osgood, C. E. (1969). The Pollyanna hypothesis. *Journal of Verbal Learning and Verbal Behavior, 8*, 1–8.

Bousfield, W. A. (1944). An empirical study of the production of affectively toned items. *Journal of General Psychology, 30*, 205–215.

Bousfield, W. A. (1950). The relationship between mood and the production of affectively toned associates. *Journal of General Psychology, 42*, 67–85.

Bower, G. H. (1981). Mood and memory. *American Psychologist, 36*, 129–148.

Bower, G. H., & Cohen, P. (1982). Emotional influences on learning and cognition. In M. S. Clark & S. T. Fiske (Eds.), *Affect and cognition* (pp. 291–331). Hillsdale, NJ: Erlbaum.

Chaiken, S. (1980). Heuristic versus systematic information processing and the use of source versus message cues in persuasion. *Journal of Personality and Social Psychology, 39*, 752–766.

Chaiken, S., & Eagly, A. H. (1976). Communication modality as a determinant of message persuasiveness and message comprehensibility. *Journal of Personality and Social Psychology, 34*, 605–614.

Clark, M. S., & Fiske, S. T. (1982). *Affect and cognition*. Hillsdale, NJ: Erlbaum.

Clark, M. S., & Isen, A. M. (1982). Toward understanding the relationship between feeling states and social behavior. In A. Hastorf & A. M. Isen (Eds.), *Cognitive social psychology* (pp. 73–108). New York: Elsevier.

Cook, T. D., & Flay, B. R. (1978). The temporal persistence of experimentally induced attitude change: An evaluative review. In L. Berkowitz (Ed.), *Advances in experimental social psychology* (Vol. 11, pp. 2–59). New York: Academic Press.

Craik, F. M., & Lockhart, R. S. (1972). Levels of processing: A framework for memory research. *Journal of Verbal Learning and Verbal Behavior, 11*, 671–684.

Eagly, A. H., & Chaiken, S. (1984). Cognitive theories in persuasion. In L. Berkowitz (Ed.), *Advances in experimental social psychology* (Vol. 17, pp. 268–361). New York: Academic Press.

Ellis, H. C., & Ashbrook. P. W. (1988). Resource allocation model of the effects of depressed mood states on memory. In K. Fiedler & J. Forgas (Eds.), *Affect, cognition and social behavior* (pp. 25–43). Toronto: Hogrefe.

Forgas, J. P., Burnham, D., & Trimboli, C. (1988). Mood, memory and social judgments in children. *Journal of Personality and Social Psychology, 54*, 697–703.

Gardner, M. P., & Raj, S. P. (1983). Responses to commercials in laboratory versus natural settings: A conceptual framework. In R. P. Bagozzi & A. M. Tybout (Eds.), *Advances in consumer research* (Vol. 10, pp. 142–146). Ann Arbor, MI: Association for Consumer Research.

Isen, A. M. (1984). Toward understanding the role of affect in cognition. In R. S. Wyer & T. K. Srull (Eds.), *Handbook of social cognition* (pp. 179–236). Hillsdale, NJ: Erlbaum.

Isen, A. M., Daubman, K. A., & Gorgoglione, J. M. (1987). The influence of positive affect on cognitive organization. In R. Snow & M. Farr (Eds.), *Aptitude, learning and instruction III: Conative and affective process analysis* (pp. 143–164). Hillsdale, NJ: Erlbaum.

Isen, A. M., Daubman, K. A., & Nowicki, G. P. (1987). Positive affect facilitates creative problem solving. *Journal of Personality and Social Psychology, 52*, 1122–1131.

Isen, A. M., Johnson, M. M. S., Mertz, E., & Robinson, G. F. (1985). The influence of positive affect on the unusualness of word associations. *Journal of Personality and Social Psychology, 48*, 1413–1426.

Isen, A. M., & Levin, P. F. (1972). The effect of feeling good on helping: Cookies and kindness. *Journal of Personality and Social Psychology, 21*, 384–388.

Isen, A. M., & Means, B. (1983). The influence of positive affect on decision making strategy. *Social Cognition, 2*, 18–31.

Isen, A. M., Means, B., Patrick, R., & Nowicki, G. (1982). Some factors influencing decision-making strategy and risk taking. In M. S. Clark & S. T. Fiske (Eds.), *Affect and cognition* (pp. 243–261). Hillsdale, NJ: Erlbaum.

Isen, A. M., Shalker, T. E., Clark, M., & Karp, L. (1978). Affect, accessibility of material in memory, and behavior: A cognitive loop? *Journal of Personality and Social Psychology, 36*, 1–12.

Isen, A. M., & Simmonds, S. (1978). The effect of feeling good on a task that is incompatible with good mood. *Social Psychology Quarterly, 41*, 346–349.

Janis, I. L., & Mann, L. (1977). *Decision making*. New York: Free Press.

Johnson, E. J., & Tversky, A. (1983). Affect, generalization, and the perception of risk. *Journal of Personality and Social Psychology, 45*, 20–31.

Kavenaugh, D. J., & Bower, G. H. (1985). Mood and self-efficacy: Impact of joy and sadness on perceived capabilities. *Cognitive Therapy and Research, 9*, 507–525.

Lutz, R. J. (1985). Affective and cognitive antecedents of attitude toward the ad: A conceptual framework. In L. F. Alwitt & A. A. Mitchell (Eds.), *Psychological processes and advertising effects: Theory, research, and applications* (pp. 45–64). Hillsdale, NJ: Erlbaum.

Mischel, W., Ebbesen, E., & Zeiss, A. (1973). Selective attention to the self: Situational and dispositional determinants. *Journal of Personality and Social Psychology, 27*, 129–142.

Mitchell, A. A., & Olson, J. C. (1981). Are product attribute beliefs the only mediator of advertising effects on brand attitude? *Journal of Marketing Research, 18*, 318–332.

Nielson, S. L., & Sarason, I. G. (1981). Emotion, personality, and selective attention. *Journal of Personality and Social Psychology, 41*, 945–960.

Petty, R. E., & Brock, T. C. (1981). Thought disruption and persuasion: Assessing the validity of attitude change experiments. In R. E. Petty, T. M. Ostrom, & T. C. Brock (Eds.), *Cognitive responses in persuasion* (pp. 55–80). Hillsdale, NJ: Erlbaum.

Petty, R. E., & Cacioppo, J. T. (1981). *Attitudes and persuasion: Classic and contemporary approaches*. Dubuque, IA: Wm. C. Brown.

Petty, R. E., & Cacioppo, J. T. (1986). The elaboration likelihood model of persuasion. In L. Berkowitz (Ed.), *Advances in experimental social psychology* (Vol. 19, pp. 124–205). New York: Academic Press.

Petty, R. E., Wells, G. L., & Brock, T. C. (1976). Distraction can enhance or reduce yielding to propaganda: Thought disruption versus effort justification. *Journal of Personality and Social Psychology, 34*, 874–884.

Sherman, S. J. (1987). Cognitive processes in the formation, change, and expression of attitudes. In M. P. Zanna, J. M. Olson, & C. P. Herman (Eds.), *Social influence: The Ontario Symposium* (Vol. 5, pp. 75–106). Hillsdale, NJ: Erlbaum.

Shiffrin, R. M., & Schneider, W. (1977). Controlled and automatic human information processing: II. Perceptual learning, automatic attending, and a general theory. *Psychological Review, 84,* 127–190.

Simon, H. A. (1967). Motivational and emotional controls of cognition. *Psychological Review, 74,* 29–39.

Simon, H. A. (1982). Comments. In M. S. Clark & S. T. Fiske (Eds.), *Affect and cognition* (pp. 333–342). Hillsdale, NJ: Erlbaum.

Srull, T. K. (1983). Affect and memory: The impact of affective reactions in advertising on the representation of product information and memory. In R. P. Bagozzi & A. M. Tybout (Eds.), *Advances in consumer research* (Vol. 10, pp. 520–525). Ann Arbor, MI: Association for Consumer Research.

Tetlock, P. E., & Levi, A. (1982). Attributional bias: On the inconclusiveness of the cognition-motivation debate. *Journal of Experimental Social Psychology, 18,* 68–88.

Wong, P. T. P., & Weiner, B. (1981). When people ask "why" questions, and the heuristics of attributional search. *Journal of Personality and Social Psychology, 40,* 650–663.

Worth, L. T., & Mackie, D. M. (1987). Cognitive mediation of positive affect in persuasion. *Social Cognition, 5,* 76–94.

Zajonc, R. B. (1980). Feeling and thinking: Preferences need no inferences. *American Psychologist, 35,* 151–175.

Zanna, M. P., Kiesler, C. A., & Pilkonis, P. A. (1970). Positive and negative attitudinal affect established by classical conditioning. *Journal of Personality and Social Psychology, 14,* 321–328.

The Hyperaccessibility of Suppressed Thoughts

Daniel M. Wegner • University of Virginia
Ralph Erber • DePaul University

Editors' Notes

The distinction between automatic and controlled processes in social cognition was articulated in readings 6, 12, and 18. It surfaces again in the present selection, this time in connection with the processes of thought suppression. Wegner and Erber postulate that thought suppression is carried out by two separate mechanisms. The sheer act of suppression and the search for distracters is assumed to be carried out deliberately and effortfully. The search for the targets to be suppressed, on the other hand, is considered to be automatic and effortless. Look in particular at how the investigators experimentally test the hypothesis that the automaticity of the monitoring process would render the suppressed targets more accessible than a nonsuppressed target. Using two separate methods, the investigators demonstrate that the to-be-suppressed words do indeed become highly accessible: they are responded to more quickly, and cause greater interference, with color naming. The authors end their paper by considering the implications of their findings for issues of broad psychological relevance, such as the problem of depression and Freudian slips.

Discussion Questions

1. What is the relation between time pressure and the phenomenon of thought suppression? What other operational variables apart from time pressure should, theoretically, yield the same results?
2. How did the researchers operationally define hyperaccessibility in experiment 1? How did they do so in experiment 2?

3. How does the theory featured in the present selection account for the high occurrence of unwanted thoughts in several psychological disorders such as obsessive-compulsion and depression?

Suggested Readings

Macrae, C. N., Bodenhausen, G. V., Milne, A. B., & Jetten, J. (1994). Out of mind but back in sight: Stereotypes on the rebound. *Journal of Personality and Social Psychology, 67,* 808–817.

Martin, L. L., & Tesser, A. (1989). Toward a motivational and structural theory of ruminative thought. In J. S. Uleman & J. A. Bargh (Eds.), *Unintended thought* (pp. 306–326). New York: Guilford.

Wegner, D. M., Schneider, D. J., Carter, S., & White, T. (1987). Paradoxical effects of thought suppression. *Journal of Personality and Social Psychology, 53,* 5–13.

Authors' Abstract

The accessibility of suppressed thoughts was compared with the accessibility of thoughts on which Ss were consciously trying to concentrate. In Experiment 1, Ss made associations to word prompts as they tried to suppress thinking about a target word (e.g., *house*) or tried to concentrate on that word. Under the cognitive load imposed by time pressure, they gave the target word in response to target-related prompts (e.g., *home*) more often during suppression than during concentration. In Experiment 2, reaction times for naming colors of words were found to be greater under conditions of cognitive load when Ss were asked to suppress thinking of the word than under conditions of no cognitive load or when Ss were asked to concentrate on the word. The results support the idea that an automatic search for the suppression target increases the accessibility of the target during suppression.

It is difficult to suppress an unwanted thought. We may try to attend to something else and even succeed for a while; but then we are somehow inevitably reminded, and the thought is with us again. During thought suppression, the thought we try to eliminate from attention remains remarkably near the surface and ready to return to consciousness with minimal prompting. This state of suppression-induced *hyperaccessibility* was the focus of our research.

Cognitive Processes in Suppression

We believe that the intention to suppress a thought initiates the operation of two cognitive processes, one controlled and the other automatic. First, there is a controlled process that attempts to avoid the unwanted thought by seeking out distracters. This *controlled distracter search* expends cognitive resources toward the goal of keeping a distracter in consciousness, and it is this process that operates when the person implements the plan to think of something else. Second, there is an automatic process that is initiated in the attempt to suppress as well—a process that operates outside of awareness and without conscious guidance even though it is instigated by the intention to suppress. From the inception of suppression, an *automatic target search* looks for the unwanted thought all the while. If this automatic search finds the target, the controlled distracter search can be launched to carry out the job of eliminating the thought. The ironic property of this automatic target search, however, is that it makes the person continually sensitive to the very thought that is unwanted.

The two processes that operate in suppression can be understood as components of a feedback mechanism aimed at the control of thought (cf. Uleman, 1989). Normally, control systems that operate through feedback are comprised of an operating process and a test process that detects the need for the operating process (Carver & Scheier, 1981; Miller, Galanter, & Pribram, 1960). The controlled search for distracters is the mental operating process that carries out the suppression, and this is the part of suppressing that seems effortful and requires conscious attentional guidance. The automatic target search can be understood as a relatively less effortful mechanism enlisted to test whether the operation of the controlled distracter search is needed at any particular moment. Like the "test" and "operate" components of a test-operate-test-exit or *TOTE* unit (Miller et al., 1960), then, these two processes in combination create a purposive system that functions to suppress a thought.

In normal suppression, the cyclic operation of the two processes is responsible for the phenomena of suppression that have been observed. Beginning with the intention to suppress, both processes are initialized. The automatic target search immediately indicates that the target is in consciousness and thus initiates the controlled distracter search. The controlled distracter search brings a series of distracters to mind until one is selected that absorbs attention. At this point, attention is drawn from the controlled distracter search to the absorbing distracter itself, and in this sense the controlled distracter search is no longer functioning. There occurs here a plateau of indeterminate length that may be called *successful* suppression. In the background, however, the automatic target search is still looking continually for signs of the target in consciousness. When an avenue of association to the thought is encountered, however vague or distant, the automatic target search is tuned to register this discovery, and so to return the unwanted thought to consciousness. This reintroduces the cycle from the start, and the controlled distracter search begins again.

This reasoning leads to the conclusion that during suppression, the unwanted thought is likely to be highly accessible to consciousness. The automatic target search introduced by suppression works to make the person unusually sensitive to any topics that might reintroduce the target thought to mind. If the controlled distracter search could be interrupted, it should be possible to observe the automatic target search operating relatively unimpeded to make the unwanted thought accessible in this way. Indeed, this automatic process could render the thought hyperaccessible, that is, even more accessible than it is during intentional concentration on the thought under similar conditions. This prediction was examined here in two experiments using divergent paradigms for the assessment of cognitive accessibility.

Experiment 1: Thought Suppression Under Time Pressure

This study examined the hyperaccessibility prediction in a setting that has been used often to examine the differential operation of automatic and controlled cognitive processes—the time-pressure paradigm (see, e.g., Bargh & Thein, 1985; Strack, Erber, & Wicklund, 1982). Under the assumption that time pressure disturbs the operation of controlled, resource-dependent processes while interfering only little with the operation of automatic processes, the research examined the nature of word associations made by subjects whose controlled processes were either undermined by time pressure or allowed free reign. The subjects were instructed either to think or not to think about a target word, and over several trials their tendency to respond with the target word to closely associated word prompts was observed. We expected that subjects suppressing under time pressure would show hyperaccessibility by responding frequently with the target word when prompted by an associated word.

Method

Overview and design. Subjects were instructed either to think about or not to think about a target word (e.g., *house*). During this concentration or suppression task, they heard prompts that were either related (e.g., *home*) or unrelated (e.g., *young*) to the concentration or suppression target and gave word associates for each prompt. Subjects responded to half of the prompts under high time pressure and half of the prompts under low time pressure.

Subjects. Undergraduates (46 women and 10 men) in introductory psychology classes at Trinity University in San Antonio participated in the study in return for extra class credit. Each was randomly assigned to a suppression condition or a concentration condition.

Procedure. Subjects participated individually in

a room equipped with two tape decks and a microphone. The experimenter said the study was to test "how various mental tasks affect the way people form associations between words" and told subjects they would perform several tasks during the experiment. He or she then gave the instructions for the first task. In the *concentration* condition subjects were asked to think of a target for 5 min: *house, child, mountain,* or *car*. In the *suppression* condition subjects were asked not to think about the target for this period. The experimenter then left the room.

On returning after 5 min, the experimenter asked subjects to continue to think or not to think about the target assigned to them and added that subjects were now to do another task concurrently. This task involved giving associates to words. Subjects were to listen to a list of words on a tape and for each word to generate one associate and verbalize it into the microphone for recording on the second tape deck. In some cases (*low time pressure*), subjects had 10 s to respond with an associate. So, after the prompt word was given, there would be a taped countdown from 10 to 1, before the end of which the response was to be delivered. In other cases (*high time pressure*), the response was to be given before 3 s was up and was signaled by a countdown from 3 to 1. The subject did three practice trials in the presence of the experimenter, and the experimenter then left the room and the subject began the task.

Stimulus materials. Subjects listened to a tape that presented them with 16 different prompts for their word-association task. Four of the prompt words were closely related to the word they were trying to concentrate on or suppress. These *target prompts* had been selected from the 6 most frequent associates of the target word according to the norms of Palermo and Jenkins (1964). Four of the prompt words were unrelated to the target; these *nontarget prompts* were selected as comparable associates of a different word. The remaining prompts were fillers unrelated to any of the targets.

The design included four between-subjects replications varying target and nontarget words. Subjects in the first two replications were given the target word *child* or *house*. The target prompts for *house* (*home, door, brick,* and *roof*) constituted the nontarget prompts for *child* and the target prompts for *child* (*mother, little, adult,* and *young*) were the nontarget prompts for *house*. For subjects in the other two replications, the target word was either *mountain* or *car*. The target prompts for *mountain* (*hill, high, top,* and *climb*) were the nontarget prompts for *car* and the target prompts for *car* (*wheel, bus, truck,* and *drive*) were the nontarget prompts for *mountain*. Within each replication subjects had to respond to half the words within 10 s (low time pressure) and half within 3 s (high time pressure). The manipulation of time pressure was counterbalanced between subjects such that the high time pressure words were switched with the low time pressure words half the time.

Results and Discussion

Prompted responses. The primary dependent measure was the number of prompted responses per trial. For *target-prompted* trials, this was the occurrence of the word the subject was trying to suppress or to concentrate on. For *nontarget-prompted* trials, this was the occurrence of the comparison word for which the subject had received no special instruction. So, for example, the measure for target-prompted trials was the number of times per trial subjects responded with *house* to prompts of *home, door, brick,* or *roof* while suppressing or concentrating on *house*. For nontarget-prompted trials, the measure was how often subjects responded with *child* to prompts of *mother, little, adult,* or *young* while suppressing or concentrating on *house*. This latter set of trials provided a baseline frequency for prompted responses in the absence of any instructions to concentrate on or to suppress a target word related to the prompt.

We submitted the number of prompted responses per trial to a three-way analysis of variance (ANOVA) with instruction (concentration vs. suppression) as a between-subjects variable and prompted word (target vs. nontarget) and time pressure (low vs. high) as within-subject variables. (Initial analyses indicated no significant main or interactive effects of the replication variable or time pressure counterbalancing.) The key result of this analysis was an interaction among all three factors, $F(1, 54) = 6.91, p < .02$, and significant lower-order interactions embedded in this one were not analyzed further. Analysis of simple effects indicated that the simple interaction of instruction and time pressure was significant for target-prompted trials, $F(1,54) = 16.94, p < .0001$, whereas this interaction was not significant for nontarget-prompted trials, $F(1, 54) < 1$. Means for the significant simple interaction are shown in Figure 1.

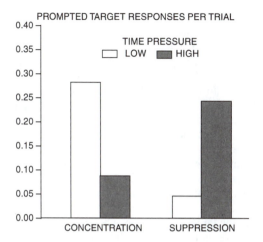

FIGURE 22.1 ■ Mean number of prompt-relevant associations per trial: Experiment 1. (Subjects who were suppressing or concentrating on a target thought gave associates to prompts for the target under low or high time pressure.)

The means for the significant simple interaction were compared as simple simple main effects among the conditions in which subjects were prompted with words related to the target. The hyperaccessibility prediction was clearly supported by these comparisons. Specifically, under high time pressure, subjects who were suppressing the target responded to target prompts with the target word more often ($M = 0.23$) than did subjects who were concentrating on the target ($M = 0.09$), $F(1, 54) = 4.09, p < .05$. Under low time pressure, in turn, this difference was significantly reversed. Subjects suppressing the target responded to target prompts with the target word less often ($M = 0.05$) than did those who were concentrating on the target ($M = 0.29$), $F(1, 54) = 9.29, p < .005$.

These four conditions can also be viewed in terms of differences between high and low time pressure within each instruction. Compared in this way, we found that subjects who were suppressing responded to the target prompts with the target more often when time pressure was high ($M = 0.23$) than when time pressure was low ($M = 0.05$), $F(1, 54) = 9.29, p < .005$. There was a significant reversal of this for subjects who were concentrating, as they responded to target prompts with the target more often when time pressure was low ($M = 0.29$) than when time pressure was high ($M = 0.09$), $F(1, 54) = 7.68, p < .01$.

One other set of comparisons was made to ex-

amine whether the means for target prompts departed significantly from the corresponding means for nontarget prompts. Recall that the nonsignificant simple interaction of instruction and time pressure within the nontarget prompt trials revealed a relatively flat pattern of response to nontarget prompts. The mean response to nontarget prompts per trial was .14 for suppressing subjects with high time pressure and .11 for each of the other conditions: suppression with low time pressure, concentration with high time pressure, and concentration with low time pressure. Simple simple main effects computed between target prompts and nontarget prompts indicated that target prompts yielded only marginally more target responses than nontarget responses that were yielded with nontarget prompts under suppression of the target with high time pressure ($M = 0.23$ vs. 0.14), $F(1, 54) = 1.66, p < .21$. Concentration with low time pressure produced more target responses to target prompts than nontarget responses to nontarget prompts ($M = 0.29$ vs. 0.11), $F(1, 54) = 7.68, p < .01$. No other comparisons in this set reached significance.

In sum, people suppressing a target who were prompted under time pressure to give the target as an associate were more prone to do this than people who were concentrating on the target. They were also more prone to do this than people who were suppressing but giving their response under low time pressure. Although the instruction and time pressure variables had no reliable impact on nontarget responses to nontarget prompts, people suppressing the target under time pressure were only marginally more inclined to give the target as their associate to a target prompt than to give the nontarget as an associate to a nontarget prompt.

Response time check. Response times were clocked by two judges for all trials. Their effective reliability across subjects averaged .98 over the within-subject conditions of the experiment, with a minimum of .96. The mean of the two judges was used as a measure of response time in the ANOVA (conducted on square-root-transformed response times to reduce the heterogeneity of within-cell variance). This analysis revealed a significant main effect for time pressure, $F(1, 54) = 31.30, p < .0001$. Subjects responding under high time pressure took significantly less time to respond ($M = 2.37$ s) than did subjects responding under low time pressure ($M = 3.80$ s). This result indicates that the manipulation of time pressure did in fact influence the speed of subjects' responses in the expected direction.

The analysis also indicated a significant interaction of instruction and time pressure, $F(1, 54) = 6.23$, $p < .02$. Subjects concentrating under low time pressure ($M = 4.64$ s) responded more slowly to target and nontarget prompts than did those concentrating under high time pressure ($M = 2.52$ s), those suppressing under low time pressure ($M = 2.95$ s), or those suppressing under high time pressure ($M = 2.20$ s). This effect suggests that concentration without time pressure may have imposed less of a sense of urgency on subjects than other tasks, but it does not qualify any of the primary results.

Finally, it is worth noting that correlations were computed separately between time to respond and response with the target word for each response trial within each condition of the Instruction x Time Pressure x Prompt design. None of these correlations was statistically significant, suggesting that differential response time within condition did not contribute to the observed variation in target responses.

Summary. The instruction to suppress a thought appears to render that thought hyperaccessible to consciousness. The evidence for this consists of word associations that subjects offered during a period of instructed suppression. When subjects were prompted by a word that was a close associate of the target they were suppressing and when they were under pressure to respond quickly, they often found themselves suffering the irony of blurting out exactly the suppressed thought as their word association. This was not as likely to happen when they were concentrating on the thought.

Experiment 2: Thought Suppression and Stroop Interference

Although the time pressure results offer important evidence in favor of the hyperaccessibility hypothesis, they are somewhat incomplete. The data are not entirely conclusive, for example, regarding the greater accessibility of suppressed thoughts in response to target prompts as opposed to the accessibility of nontarget thoughts in response to nontarget prompts. It can be argued more broadly that the time pressure paradigm may not capture response times as brief as those normally understood as indicative of automaticity (Logan,

1988). In Experiment 1, for instance, we observed that subjects with suppression instructions who were responding to target prompts under time pressure were more likely to respond with the target than those who were responding to target prompts without time pressure. This could be explained by the leisurely pace of the low-time-pressure interval, during which subjects who were suppressing thoughts may have made strategic replacements of their initial response. Such an explanation does not involve automatic accessibility at all, but turns instead on the activities individuals perform when they have plenty of response time.

The finding that suppression subjects responded with the target to target prompts under high time pressure more often than did concentration subjects is inconsistent with this weak conclusion, of course, as it contrasts suppression and concentration during the brief intervals for response under high time pressure. With very little time to respond, suppression still yields more frequent target response than does concentration. Nonetheless, it is important to gauge the degree to which suppression can augment accessibility during intervals so brief as to preclude any hint of strategic response replacement on the part of subjects. For this purpose, we chose to examine the influence of thought suppression on responding in a version of the Stroop (1935) color-word interference paradigm.

Method

Overview and design. Subjects were instructed either to think or not to think about one of the four targets used in the first study. During this task, they performed a two-color Stroop reaction time (RT) task. They pressed keys to indicate whether each of a series of words appearing on a computer monitor was printed in red or blue. The words included the target word, nontarget words, and target-related words. Half the subjects performed this task while simultaneously rehearsing a 9-digit number (high-cognitive-load condition), and the remainder did it while rehearsing a 1-digit number (low-cognitive-load condition).

Subjects. Undergraduates (27 men and 19 women) in introductory psychology classes at the University of Virginia participated in the experiment for course credit. Before their participation, subjects were screened for colorblindness and difficulty in reading words on a computer screen. Other subjects who were tested but whose data were not used in the analyses included 4 with high error rates (over 5%) and 5 with high mean RTs (over 750 ms). Subjects were randomly assigned to conditions, and the excluded subjects were evenly distributed among conditions.

Procedure. On arrival at the laboratory, each subject was seated at a computer and told that the experiment was concerned with how various mental tasks affect the way people name colors. The following instructions were shown on the computer screen:

> You will shortly see a series of words on the screen that are printed either in red or blue. If the word is in red, press the key labeled (R) at the righthand pad of the keyboard with your middle finger. If the word is in blue, press the key labeled (B) with your index finger. Your task is to indicate the color of each word as quickly and as accurately as you can. Try not to make mistakes, but try to be fast. Your reactions will be timed. An asterisk (*) will appear on the screen before each word appears to show you where to look.

Subjects then did 12 practice trials and completed another 12 trials if they made any mistakes. On completion of the practice the experimenter asked subjects to sit back from the computer and instructed them either to think or not to think about a house, a car, a mountain, or a child. The experimenter left the room and returned 5 min later to say the following:

> In addition to studying people's ability to name colors, we are also interested in finding out how they do when they perform another task at the same time. Your job will be to respond with the word colors and at the same time remember the following number. I will ask you to recall the number later on. You will have 25 seconds to commit the number to memory. I will ask you for the number at the end of the experiment. It is very important that you give me the number back exactly as it is on this paper. If you fail to remember the number, you will have to be disqualified from this study.

The experimenter then showed the subject a card containing either a 9-digit number or a 1-digit number and gave the subject 25 s to begin rehearsing the number (cf. Gilbert & Osborne, 1989).

Following this manipulation of cognitive load, the experimenter reminded subjects to continue to think or not to think about the object assigned to them, to continue to rehearse the number, and to begin the color-word task on the computer as during the practice trials. The experimenter then started the Stroop task program and left the room. When the task was completed, the experimenter returned and asked the subject to report the rehearsed number. All subjects recalled the number correctly.

Stimuli. The words were presented in the standard 24- × 80-character screen font on a 14" IBM-compatible EGA color monitor. Timing programs by Creeger, Miller, & Paredes (1990) were used to calibrate an IBM-AT-compatible computer for RT measurement in Microsoft Quickbasic 4.5. The program provided for each trial on a white screen to start with a 3-s pause followed by the 2-s presentation of a centered black asterisk. Then, the word appeared in red or blue at the asterisk focus and remained on-screen until a response was recorded.

The set of 64 stimulus words was the same for all subjects, although half the subjects were presented the words in reverse order. The word set contained a random ordering of 8 presentations of each of the 4 possible target words (*house, child, mountain*, and *car*) and 2 presentations of each of the 4 target-related words for each of the 4 possible targets (i.e., the 16 words selected as close associates of the targets in Experiment 1). Color was balanced such that half the presentations for each word were in each color. This set of stimuli allowed for the investigation of color-naming RTs for target words (e.g., *house* when the target is *house*), for target-unrelated words (e.g., *house* when the target is *child*), and for target-related words (e.g., *home* when the target is *house*) within each of the 4 target-word replications.

Results and Discussion

Mean RTs for correct responses to target-unrelated, target-related, and target words are shown in Figure 2. These were examined in an ANOVA with cognitive load (low vs. high), instruction (concentration vs. suppression), specific target word (*house, child, mountain*, and *car*), and stimulus word order (two orders) as between-subjects variables and word type (target, target-related, or target-unrelated word) as a repeated measure. A significant main effect was observed for cognitive load, $F(1, 20) = 6.28$, $p < .03$, indicating that subjects responded with the colors of all words more slowly under conditions of high load ($M = 549$ ms) than low load ($M = 485$ ms). A significant

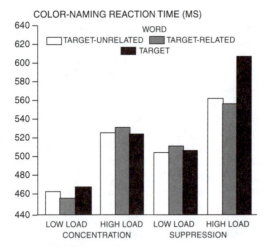

FIGURE 22.2 ■ Mean color-naming reaction times: Experiment 2. (Subjects who were suppressing or concentrating on a target thought made key press responses to name the colors of target-unrelated, target-related, and target words under low or high cognitive load.)

main effect was also found for instruction, $F(1, 20) = 5.53$, $p < .03$, in that subjects were slower to indicate colors of all words when they were suppressing a target ($M = 541$ ms) than when they were concentrating on it ($M = 493$ ms).

The interaction of load, instruction, and word type was marginally reliable, $F(2, 40) = 2.84$, $p < .07$, and its form was as predicted. As can be seen in Figure 2, target-unrelated and target-related words showed very similar patterns across the load and instruction conditions, corresponding generally to the main effects mentioned above. Reaction times for the target word itself, however, departed from this pattern with a noteworthy increment in the high-load-suppression condition. Analyses of the simple simple main effects of load on RT for the target word within the suppression condition showed that the high-load, color-naming RT for target words ($M = 600$ ms) was significantly greater than the low-load mean ($M = 508$ ms), $F(1, 20) = 5.02$, $p < .04$. The simple simple main effect of instruction on RT for target words within the high-load condition showed a marginally significant effect, $F(1, 20) = 3.36$, $p < .09$, as the color-naming RT for suppression ($M = 600$ ms) tended to exceed that for concentration ($M = 521$ ms). No other simple simple main effects were significant.

Another way to view the overall interaction is in terms of comparisons between RTs for target

words and target-unrelated words. Contrasts between target words and target-unrelated words within each of the Load × Instruction conditions revealed only one reliable difference. For subjects suppressing the target under high load, RT was significantly greater for target words ($M = 600$ ms) than for target-unrelated words ($M = 561$ ms), $F(1, 20) = 9.00$, $p < .01$. The only clear Stroop interference effect observed in this experiment, then, occurred for subjects who were suppressing a target under cognitive load and who were asked to name the color of the target.

The absence of inflated latencies for target words in the other conditions may have occurred for several reasons. Perhaps our implementation of the Stroop paradigm is capable of detecting only strong manipulations of accessibility. The two-color version of the Stroop situation used here may reduce interference in general because there are fewer response options, for example, or the two-finger keypress response (as compared with the more common voice-response method) may introduce sufficient response variance as to obscure interference effects. Given these obstacles, it may have been only under conditions promoting hyperaccessibility—the instruction to suppress under cognitive load—that this paradigm afforded the observation of interference effects. Alternatively, it may be that the absence of interference findings in the concentration conditions echoes research in which target primes that were presented for subjects' conscious perusal reduced rather than increased target accessibility (e.g., Lombardi, Higgins, & Bargh, 1987; Martin, 1986).

This study showed, in sum, that suppression increases the accessibility of an unwanted thought in that color-naming responses for that thought were slowed during an imposed cognitive load. When the target appeared as the colored stimulus, the instruction to suppress the target delayed color-naming responses during high cognitive load relative to low cognitive load. This slowing during high load and suppression was greater for presentations of the target word than for presentations of target-unrelated words. Color-naming of targets also tended to slow during suppression under high load as compared with concentration on the target under high load. This latter finding promotes the inference that suppression creates a state of hyperaccessibility of the target, a state in which the target is even more accessible than it is during the intentional attempt to think about it.

General Discussion

The intention to suppress a thought creates the opposite of what is wanted. This is particularly true when cognitive resources are assigned elsewhere even while the attempted suppression is ongoing. The results of these experiments indicate that a suppressed thought becomes more rather than less accessible to consciousness when time pressures or cognitive loads are imposed during suppression. The effect of this is that people may say the very word they are trying not to think (Experiment 1) or may attend to the very aspect of a stimulus they are trying not to think about (Experiment 2). We believe these hyperaccessibility effects occur as a result of the operation of an automatic search for the suppressed thought that is initiated when a thought is suppressed.

Automatic Target Search

If thought suppression triggers an automatic search for the suppression target, several consequences would be expected. In general, of course, there should be a tendency for the target to regain access to consciousness. Presumably, however, the automatic target search is normally balanced by the effortful activity of a controlled search for distracters, and as a result the unhampered enterprise of suppression can often yield apparent suppression success. This was shown in our studies when suppression was prompted with little or no cognitive load. Under these conditions, subjects in Experiment 1 managed to keep from giving the suppressed word as their associative response and subjects in Experiment 2 showed no greater latency for naming the color of a suppressed word.

The more pointed prediction offered by our formulation is that during suppression, the access of the suppressed thought to consciousness should be enhanced by the imposition of cognitive load. Such a load undermines the continued operation of the controlled distracter search and so unleashes the automatic target search. This prediction was substantiated in both studies, as higher relative levels of accessibility were observed for suppression with load than without load in both cases. Such findings provide substantial support for our conceptualization of the suppression process in terms of controlled distracter search and automatic target search.

The levels of accessibility produced by suppression with load at times even surpassed the accessibility of thoughts on which individuals were consciously trying to concentrate their attention. In Experiment 1, suppression under high time pressure led to more target associations than did concentration under high time pressure; in Experiment 2, suppression under high memory load led to a tendency for greater color-naming latency for the target word than did concentration with high load. It is in this sense that suppression can be most clearly identified as the source of hyperaccessibility. Normally, a thought that is accessible is defined as one that can come readily to mind, and that can thus participate more than other thoughts in judgments, reports, categorizations, or other mental processes (e.g., Bruner, 1957; Higgins & King, 1981). To the degree that intentional concentration marshals as much accessibility as can be engineered by conscious means, the finding that suppression under cognitive load yields yet greater levels of accessibility constitutes evidence for a higher degree of access—hyperaccess.

Suppression and Intrusive Thoughts

There are a variety of clinical and everyday problems in which people exhibit serious difficulties with intrusive thoughts. In depression, obsessive-compulsive disorder, phobia, posttraumatic stress disorder, and during dieting or treatment for addiction, for example, unwanted thoughts appear to recur and dominate the sufferer's mental landscape (cf. Wegner, 1989, 1992). Research on several of these problems has suggested that automaticity of particular classes of thought may be involved in the disorder. Depressive people exhibit automaticity in depressive thinking (Bargh & Tota, 1988; Gotlib & McCann, 1984), for example, and phobics show evidence of this in their phobic thinking (Watts, McKenna, Sharrock, & Trezise, 1986).

To date, automaticity of this kind has been understood by researchers primarily to be a consequence of learning. After all, automaticity is usually seen as a format that cognitive processes assume when they have been practiced repeatedly. Increments in automaticity accrue when a particular kind of social judgment is performed again and again (Smith & Lerner, 1986), for instance, and the automatic accessibility of attitudes follows when people repeat the attitude over and over

(Houston & Fazio, 1989). Attributing the development of automaticity to learning suggests that the people who exhibit automaticity in depressive, phobic, or other forms of pathological thinking have reached this pass by virtue of some sort of repetitive or habitual process. They have somehow been pressed to think these things too often, and so now have reached chronic levels of automatic activation of the thoughts (Higgins & King, 1981). This line of reasoning indicates that there must be considerable practice of unwanted thoughts occurring prior to the development of their automatic activation.

The hyperaccessibility of suppressed thoughts suggests that such repetition may not be so necessary. Instead, chronic levels of automatic activation may arise as a result of individuals' attempts to control their thinking through suppression. "Instant" automatic processes might develop without practice at all. The depressed person who is trying hard to suppress negative thoughts, for example, could unwittingly initiate and then suffer from an automatic target search that makes negative thoughts hyperaccessible to consciousness. Perhaps the cognitive stress that accrues from depression itself could exacerbate this process by serving as a continuous load (cf. Sullivan & Conway, 1989). More generally, the stresses that introduce cognitive load at many points in life may have the result of turning our struggle against unwanted, seemingly automatic mental states into an invitation for these states to overwhelm us.

The hyperaccessibility observed here could emerge whenever any psychological equivalent of our load manipulations impinges on the person who is actively suppressing a thought. Stress, distraction, arousal, busyness, and even the time pressures of normal living could introduce intrusions and perhaps even obsession or preoccupation with thoughts that were once suppressed. This reasoning suggests why we often find that the very thing we do not want to say or think comes forward when we are distracted or distressed. The phenomenon of Freudian slips that are precisely the least appropriate thing to say in a given situation might be explained in this way (Baars, 1985). Cognitive busyness or time pressure could interfere with processes of self-presentation, deception, or self-control that depend on thought suppression for their success, and so promote social blunders, unintentional disclosures of deceit, or self-control lapses that are not entirely random. Rather, because the

most unwelcome thoughts are typically chosen as targets for suppression, these very thoughts are the ones that are exposed when the controlled processes of suppression are disrupted. Hyperaccessibility of these unwanted thoughts can then come forward to produce chaos.

This suggestion is also consistent with the observation that stress exacerbates problems such as anxiety and phobia (Jacobs & Nadel, 1985). The individual who uses thought suppression as a strategy for the control of anxiety, for example, may effectively put upsetting thoughts out of mind as long as he or she has sufficient cognitive capacity to carry on the controlled search for distracters. This person might become absorbed in a variety of pursuits that aid in the enterprise of suppression and so lead a fairly peaceful life. The occurrence of some major stressor—loss of a job, or of a loved one, for instance—could interrupt this controlled distracter search with some disastrous psychological results. Beyond the negative emotions unleashed by the stressor, the person would now be subject to the hyperaccessibility of the suppressed anxiety-producing thought. A double dividend of negative emotion could be the consequence, because the originally suppressed thought could instigate its own emotional reaction.

Conclusions

The hyperaccessibility of suppressed thoughts has some useful implications, both theoretical and applied. For theory, these results suggest a useful way of understanding the potentially counter-intentional automatic processes that may be entailed by the intentional control of thinking. The observation of hyperaccessibility fulfills a key prediction made by our model of automatic and controlled processes in suppression, and it suggests that there may be some value to further research on how automatic processes may undermine the controlled ones that entail them. As for application, the results indicate in a preliminary way how people suffer from the choice to suppress thoughts. Although people may be quite able to distract themselves from unwanted thoughts under normal conditions, they can suffer from hyperaccessibility and the intrusive return of those thoughts when something happens to distract them from their distractions. The thoughts people are most desperate to suppress can come to mind at precisely the point of highest stress and produce the very thought and behavior that the suppression was enlisted to avoid.

ACKNOWLEDGMENTS

This research was supported by National Science Foundation Grants BNS 88-18611 and BNS 90-96263. We thank Todd Bennington, Stephen Blumberg, Miles Cortez, Rob Dillard, Vickie Fendley, Sonny Marks, and Jenn Taylor for assisting in the conduct of the research and John Bargh, Shelley Chaiken, Daniel Gilbert, Traci Giuliano, Stan Klein, Gordon Logan, Toni Wegner, Richard Wenzlaff, and Sophia Zanakos for their helpful comments on an earlier draft.

REFERENCES

Baars, B. J. (1985). Can involuntary slips reveal one's state of mind? With an addendum on the problem of conscious control of action. In T. M. Shlechter & M. P. Toglia (Eds.), *New directions in cognitive science* (pp. 242–261). Norwood, NJ: Ablex.

Bargh, J. A. (1984). Automatic and conscious processing of social information. In R. S. Wyer, Jr., & T. K. Srull (Eds.), *Handbook of social cognition* (Vol. 3, pp. 1–43). Hillsdale, NJ: Erlbaum.

Bargh, J. A. (1989). Conditional automaticity: Varieties of automatic influence in social perception and cognition. In J. S. Uleman & J. A. Bargh (Eds.), *Unintended thought* (pp. 3–51). New York: Guilford Press.

Bargh, J. A. (1990). Auto-motives: Preconscious determinants of social interaction. In E. T. Higgins & R. M. Sorrentino (Eds.), *Handbook of motivation and cognition* (Vol. 2, pp. 93–130). New York: Guilford Press.

Bargh, J. A., & Thein, R. D. (1985). Individual construct accessibility, person memory, and the recall–judgment link: The case of information overload. *Journal of Personality and Social Psychology, 49,* 1129–1146.

Bargh, J. A., & Tota, M. E. (1988). Context-dependent automatic processing in depression: Accessibility of automatic constructs with regard to self but not others. *Journal of Personality and Social Psychology, 54,* 925–939.

Bruner, J. S. (1957). On perceptual readiness. *Psychological Review, 64,* 123–152.

Carver, C. S., & Scheier, M. F. (1981). *Attention and self-regulation: A control-theory approach to human behavior.* New York: Springer-Verlag.

Creeger, C. P., Miller, K. F., & Paredes, D. R. (1990). Micromanaging time: Measuring and controlling timing errors in computer-controlled experiments. *Behavior Research Methods, Instruments, and Computers, 22,* 34–79.

Devine, P. G. (1989). Stereotypes and prejudice: Their automatic and controlled components. *Journal of Personality and Social Psychology, 56,* 5–18.

Fiske, S. T. (1989). Examining the role of intent, toward understanding its role in stereotyping and prejudice. In J. S. Uleman & J. A. Bargh (Eds.), *Unintended thought* (pp. 253–283). New York: Guilford Press.

Gilbert, D. T., Krull, D. S., & Malone, P. S. (1990). Unbelieving the unbelievable: Some problems in the rejection of false information. *Journal of Personality and Social Psychology, 59,* 601–613.

Gilbert, D. T., Krull, D. S., & Pelham, B. W. (1988). Of thoughts unspoken: Social inference and the self-regulation of behavior. *Journal of Personality and Social Psychology, 55,* 685–694.

Gilbert, D. T., & Osborne, R. E. (1989). Thinking backward: Some curable and incurable consequences of cognitive busyness. *Journal of Personality and Social Psychology, 57,* 940–949.

Gotlib, I. H., & McCann, C. D. (1984). Construct accessibility and depression: An examination of cognitive and affective factors. *Journal of Personality and Social Psychology, 47,* 427–439.

Hasher, L., & Zacks, R. T. (1979). Automatic and effortful processes in memory. *Journal of Experimental Psychology: General, 108,* 356–388.

Higgins, E. T., & King, G. (1981). Accessibility of social constructs: Information-processing consequences of individual and contextual variability. In N. Cantor & J. F. Kihlstrom (Eds.), *Personality, cognition, and social interaction* (pp. 69–121). Hillsdale, NJ: Erlbaum.

Houston, D. A., & Fazio, R. H. (1989). Biased processing as a function of attitude accessibility: Making objective judgments subjectively. *Social Cognition, 7,* 51–66.

Jacobs, W. J., & Nadel, L. (1985). Stress-induced recovery of fears and phobias. *Psychological Review, 92,* 512–531.

Jonides, J., Naveh-Benjamin, M., & Palmer, J. (1985). Assessing automaticity. *Acta Psychologica, 60,* 157–171.

Logan, G. D. (1983). On the ability to inhibit simple thoughts and actions: I. Stop-signal studies of decision and memory. *Journal of Experimental Psychology: Learning, Memory, and Cognition, 9,* 585–606.

Logan, G. D. (1988). Toward an instance theory of automatization. *Psychological Review, 95,* 492–527.

Lombardi, W. J., Higgins, E. T., & Bargh, J. A. (1987). The role of consciousness in priming effects on categorization: Assimilation versus contrast as a function of awareness of the priming task. *Personality and Social Psychology Bulletin, 13,* 411–429.

Martin, L. L. (1986). Set/reset: Use and disuse of concepts in impression formation. *Journal of Personality and Social Psychology, 51,* 493–504.

Miller, G. A., Galanter, E., & Pribram, K. H. (1960). *Plans and the structure of behavior.* New York: Holt.

Palermo, D. S., & Jenkins, J. J. (1964). *Word association norms.* Minneapolis: University of Minnesota Press.

Pennebaker, J. W. (1990). *Opening up.* New York: Morrow.

Posner, M. I., & Snyder, C. R. R. (1975). Attention and cognitive control. In R. L. Solso (Ed.), *Information processing and cognition: The Loyola Symposium* (pp. 55–88). Hillsdale, NJ: Erlbaum.

Shallice, T. (1972). Dual functions of consciousness. *Psychological Review, 79,* 383–393.

Smith, E. R., & Lerner, M. (1986). Development of automatism of social judgments. *Journal of Personality and Social Psychology, 50,* 246–259.

Strack, F., Erber, R., & Wicklund, R. A. (1982). Effects of salience and time pressure on ratings of social causality. *Journal of Experimental Social Psychology, 18,* 581–594.

Stroop, J. R. (1935). Studies of interference in serial verbal reactions. *Journal of Experimental Psychology, 18,* 643–662.

Sullivan, M. J. L., & Conway, M. (1989). Negative affect leads to low-effort cognition: Attributional processing for observed social behavior. *Social Cognition, 7,* 315–337.

Uleman, J. S. (1989). A framework for thinking intentionally about unintended thoughts. In J. S. Uleman & J. A. Bargh (Eds.), *Unintended thought* (pp. 425–449). New York: Guilford Press.

Watts, F. N., McKenna, F. P., Sharrock, R., & Trezise, L. (1986). Colour-naming of phobia-related words. *British Journal of Psychology, 77,* 97–108.

Wegner, D. M. (1989). *White bears and other unwanted thoughts.* New York: Viking/Penguin.

Wegner, D. M. (1992). You can't always think what you want: Problems in the suppression of unwanted thoughts. In M. Zanna (Ed.), *Advances in experimental social psychology* (Vol. 25, pp. 193–255). San Diego, CA: Academic Press.

Wegner, D. M., & Erber, R. (1993). Social foundations of mental control. In D. M. Wegner & J. W. Pennebaker (Eds.), *Handbook of mental control* (pp. 34–56). Englewood Cliffs, NJ: Prentice-Hall.

Wegner, D. M., & Schneider, D. J. (1989). Mental control: The war of the ghosts in the machine. In J. Uleman & J. Bargh (Eds.), *Unintended thought* (pp. 287–305). New York: Guilford Press.

Wegner, D. M., Schneider, D. J., Carter, S., III, & White, L. (1987). Paradoxical effects of thought suppression. *Journal of Personality and Social Psychology, 53,* 5–13.

Wegner, D. M., Shortt, J. W., Blake, A. W., & Page, M. S. (1990). The suppression of exciting thoughts. *Journal of Personality and Social Psychology, 58,* 409–418.

Wenzlaff, R., Wegner, D. M., & Roper, D. (1988). Depression and mental control: The resurgence of unwanted negative thoughts. *Journal of Personality and Social Psychology, 55,* 882–892.

Zillman, D. (1988). Mood management: Using entertainment to full advantage. In L. Donohew, H. E. Sypher, & E. T. Higgins (Eds.), *Communication, social cognition, and affect* (pp. 147–171). Hillsdale, NJ: Erlbaum.

READING 23

Motivated Inference: Self-Serving Generation and Evaluation of Causal Theories

Ziva Kunda • Princeton University

Editors' Notes

The present selection addresses the fundamental issue known in common parlance as wishful thinking; that is, believing or concluding what is convenient, pleasant, and desirable to believe. On a more general level, the issue being addressed here is the relation between motivation and cognition. The present research evaluates this problem by looking at the theories people tend to generate. The author proposes that these theories are often those that put the wishful thinkers in a particularly positive light. The research also examines how people evaluate evidence. The hypothesis is that when the evidence is threatening to the self, individuals tend to discredit it more than when the evidence is innocuous. Note how the investigator operationalizes the variables and guards against alternative interpretations of the findings. Insofar as this research intends to demonstrate a motivational effect on cognition, it needs to rule out the possibility that the results could be accounted for in purely cognitive terms.

Discussion Questions

1. Do the data of the first two studies completely rule out a cognitive interpretation? If so, why so? If not, why not?
2. How do the data of study 3 deal with a possible cognitive reinterpretation? In what way does study 3 deal more effectively with such a reinterpretation than the data of the former two experiments?
3. Does the theory featured in this selection claim that motivation represents an alternative route to judgment that competes with the cognitive route? What do the authors have to say on this issue?

Suggested Readings

Kruglanski, A. W. (1996). Motivated social cognition: Principles of the interface. In E. T. Higgins & A. W. Kruglanski (Eds.), *Social psychology: A handbook of basic principles*. New York: Guilford.

Miller, D. T., & Ross, M. (1975). Self-serving biases in the attribution of causality: Fact or fiction? *Psychological Bulletin, 82,* 213–225.

Author's Abstract

The results of four studies suggest that people tend to generate and evaluate causal theories in a self-serving manner. They generate theories that view their own attributes as more predictive of desirable outcomes, and they are reluctant to believe in theories relating their own attributes to undesirable events. As a consequence, people tend to hold theories that are consistent with the optimistic belief that good things will happen to them and bad things will not. I argue that these self-serving biases are best explained as resulting from cognitive processes guided by motivation because they do not occur in the absence of motivational pressures.

Most people tend to approach life with an optimistic stance. In general, we expect more desirable outcomes to be more likely (Irwin, 1953; Marks, 1951; Parducci, 1968; Pruitt & Hoge, 1965). We also think that we are more likely than our peers to experience positive outcomes and less likely than they to experience negative outcomes. Such optimism has been shown for a wide range of life domains, including beliefs about financial, professional, interpersonal, health-related, and crime-related outcomes (Weinstein, 1980, 1983, 1984; for a review see Perloff, 1983). Because logically we cannot all be better off than our peers, our belief that we are is bound to be unrealistic.

Where, then, does this unrealistic optimism come from? The present approach assumes that people do not merely proclaim that good things will happen and bad things will not. Rather, they support and maintain their optimistic beliefs through a network of interrelated theories about the causal determinants of positive and negative outcomes. They construct elaborate theories to explain how different attributes are related to various outcomes, but these theories are biased in a self-serving manner. People believe that their own attributes are more likely than other attributes to facilitate desired outcomes and to hinder feared outcomes. Such biased theories allow people to believe that they are more likely than others to experience the desired outcomes and to avoid the feared ones. In this article, I explore two potential sources for such biased theories: self-serving generation and self-serving evaluation of causal theories.

The first process assumes that people use their stored world knowledge to generate theories about the causes of positive and negative outcomes in a self-serving manner, favoring those theories that could help maintain optimism about their own likelihood of incurring such outcomes. For example, upon hearing that the divorce rate in this country is 50%, people might attempt to convince themselves that they will not fall victim to this misfortune. They could do this by searching through their knowledge about themselves and the world for factors that predispose them toward a happy marriage. Some people may remember, for example, that they have had several serious romantic relationships. They may then theorize that the understanding of others and of themselves gained through these relationships will make it easier for them to establish a stable relationship with their spouse.

The problem with such theorizing is that people possessing the opposite traits can just as easily generate theories about how their own traits predict happy marriage. Someone with no early romantic relationships might take comfort in the belief that entering marriage without any baggage of prior assumptions or hostility left over from earlier relationships is conducive to happy marriage. Thus no matter what people's attributes are, they may come to believe that their attributes will help them achieve desired outcomes and avoid feared outcomes.

Such self-serving theory generation is possible because people have great facility in generating causal theories linking any attribute to just about any outcome (Anderson & Sechler, 1986; Fischhoff, 1975; Kunda, 1985), and they have no way of determining the correctness of their theories. Indeed, they come to believe in the validity of any theory that they have been induced to generate (Anderson, Lepper, & Ross, 1980; Anderson & Sechler, 1986). Consequently, if people set out to generate a theory linking their own attributes to a desired or a feared outcome, they should be able to do so easily, no matter what their attributes are or what the outcome is. Once they generate such theories, these theories are likely to persist because people have enhanced memory for theories that they generate themselves (for review see Greenwald, 1981), because the arguments generated to support the theories remain available (Anderson, New, & Speer, 1985), and because people are not likely to generate alternative, contradictory theories spontaneously (Koriat, Lichtenstein, & Fischhoff, 1980).

The second form of self-serving processing examined here assumes that when confronted with evidence that has implications for optimistic beliefs, people evaluate it in a self-serving manner, applying more stringent criteria to evidence with less favorable implications to the self. For example, evidence implying that one is likely to incur health problems might be subjected to extensive scrutiny and criticism, whereas evidence implying good health might be accepted, at face value.

Such self-serving evidence evaluation is possible because people are capable of applying different inferential rules on different occasions (Kunda & Nisbett, 1986; Nisbett, Krantz, Jepson, & Kunda, 1983). Also, people are sadly lacking in the clear criteria needed to determine the appropriateness of a given rule to a given problem (Nisbett & Ross, 1980). When evaluating evidence, they may therefore apply to it only those inferential rules likely to produce a self-serving evaluation.

Through the repeated exercise of self-serving generation and self-serving evaluation of causal theories, people may come to possess a biased set of theories according to which their own attributes can cause desirable outcomes and deter undesirable ones. Such theories may help sustain unrealistic optimism.

There is now considerable evidence indicating that people use self-serving beliefs and processes in a variety of domains, including perception (Erdelyi, 1974), memory (Greenwald, 1980; Greenwald & Pratkanis, 1984), attribution of responsibility for one's own behaviors (Miller & Ross, 1975; Tetlock & Levi, 1982; Zuckerman, 1979) and for other people's behaviors (Lerner, 1980), value assessment (Tesser & Campbell, 1983), and social comparison (Pyszczynski, Greenberg & LaPrelle, 1985; Taylor, 1983). But there is little evidence concerning self-serving biases in inferential processes involving generation and evaluation of causal theories, although it is here that self-serving biases could have some of their most pervasive and consequential implications because of the dramatic and accumulating effects of such biases on beliefs. As a result of such biases, initially mildly optimistic beliefs could become increasingly polarized as one selectively generates and evaluates evidence (cf. Lord, Ross, & Lepper, 1979).

If self-serving biases in the generation and evaluation of evidence are found, it would also be interesting to determine whether these biases result from cold cognition processes or from hot cognition processes. Many of the biases initially introduced as resulting from hot, motivational processes have been reinterpreted in terms of entirely cold, cognitive processes. It has been argued that people may display such biases through no particular intention or effort of their own. Rather, the environment provides them with predominantly positive information, and their general inferential shortcomings lead them to act on this information so as to reason in an apparently self-serving manner (Miller & Ross, 1975; Nisbett & Ross, 1980).

Because most relevant self-serving biases can be interpreted in both cognitive and motivational terms, some theorists have argued that the hot-versus-cold cognition controversy cannot be resolved empirically (Ross & Fletcher, 1985; Tetlock & Levi, 1982). But others have argued that it is essential to assume motivational processing because many self-serving biases have been shown to occur only in the presence of arousal (e.g., Zanna & Cooper, 1976).

The present approach takes into account both motivational and inferential factors. In this view, the cognitive apparatus is harnessed in the service of motivational ends. People use cognitive inferential mechanisms and processes to arrive at their desired conclusions, but motivational forces determine which processes will be used in a given instance and which evidence will be considered. The conclusions therefore appear to be rationally supported by evidence, but in fact the evidence itself is tainted by motivation: its production and evaluation are guided by motivation (cf. Darley & Gross, 1983).

This position assumes that in order to generate causal theories about the relations between attributes and outcomes, one needs to search one's memory for beliefs about the attributes, the outcomes, and the world in general that could be woven together into a coherent theory. Also, in order to evaluate the validity and generalizability of evidence, one needs to search through memory for appropriate inferential rules. It has been shown that on different occasions people may access different facts and rules: They may make different social judgments (Higgins & King, 1981; Higgins, King, & Mavin, 1982), endorse different attitudes (Salancik & Conway, 1975; Snyder, 1982), assume different self-conceptions (Fazio, Effrein, & Falender, 1981; Markus & Kunda, 1986), and apply different inferential rules (Kunda & Nisbett, 1986; Nisbett et al., 1983). It seems possible that motivation may help determine which rules and facts people access when generating and evaluating causal theories and thus influence the content of these theories.

Several theorists have proposed similar processes to account for self-serving biases in other domains, but the implications of these ideas to the domain of theory generation and evaluation have not been elaborated, and there is little direct evidence for motivationally guided accessing of long-term memory in any domain (although considerable evidence suggests that motives may affect encoding, organization, and use of information coming from external sources; for a review see Srull & Wyer, 1986). The notion that motivational forces may drive inferential processes follows from dissonance theory (Festinger, 1957), but very little of the dissonance research was concerned directly with theory generation and evaluation. Most dissonance research examined the effects of motivational pressures resulting from choosing between equally attractive alternatives and from performing behaviors that would normally be avoided (for a review see Wicklund & Brehm, 1976). With few exceptions (e.g., Kassarjian & Cohen, 1965), the dissonance paradigm provided little direct support for the hypothesis that people rely on motivation-

ally directed inferential processes to sustain optimistic beliefs.

More recently, similar formulations, in which motivation is assumed to guide cognitive processes, have been proposed to account for self-serving attributions for one's own behavior (Anderson & Slusher, 1986; Pyszczynski & Greenberg, in press) and for phenomena such as stereotyping, anchoring, and primacy effects (Kruglanski & Freund, 1983). The aim of the present research is to extend the notion of motivated inference to a broader range of phenomena and to make a start at spelling out the cognitive mechanisms underlying such processes.

In this article, I examine whether people generate and evaluate causal theories in a self-serving manner and whether such biases are due to motivational factors. I argue that the motivational interpretation of such biases would be strengthened if they occurred only in the presence of motivational forces resulting from personal involvement with the outcomes in question.

Self-Serving Theory Generation

Study 1: Generating Self-Serving Theories About the Causes of Divorce

Study 1 examines whether people tend to generate theories in a self-serving manner so as to support the optimistic view that their own attributes predict good life outcomes but not bad ones. Do people believe that their own attributes are more predictive of desired outcomes than are other attributes? Do people possessing a given attribute view it as a better predictor of desired outcomes than do people who do not possess it?

It is important to study these processes in the context of highly desirable and undesirable outcomes about which people have little concrete information that would allow objective assessment of their odds. Young people's beliefs about the future outcomes of their marriages seem to fit these criteria. Almost everybody wants to be happily married and never to have to face the prospect of divorce. Yet few people, if any, have any way of assessing the actual likelihood that they will get divorced.

Nevertheless, most young people are quite convinced that they will remain married to their first spouse until death does them part (Lehman &

Nisbett, 1985). This is so despite their awareness of the well-publicized base rate. About half the marriages in the United States end in divorce. Such unrealistic optimism could be sustained by self-serving theorizing about the causal relation between one's attributes and the outcome of marriage.

To examine whether people engage in such self-serving theorizing, subjects read a description of a target person, consisting of one of two opposite sets of attributes, and were asked to assess the extent to which each of these attributes might have contributed to the outcome of the target's marriage. At the end, subjects were asked for their own standing on each of these attributes.

People were expected to judge their own attributes as better for marriage than the opposite attributes. Thus people who shared a given attribute with the target person were expected to judge that attribute as better for marriage than were people who possessed the opposite attribute. Within subjects, each person was expected to judge the subset of attributes that he or she shared with the target as better for marriage than the remaining attributes.

Subjects were also asked about the likelihood that they would get divorced, so as to verify that they were unrealistically optimistic in this regard.

Method. Subjects were 103 University of Michigan undergraduates of both sexes enrolled in introductory psychology. They participated in groups of 4 to 6 subjects.

The study was presented as concerned with people's memory, options, and beliefs. Subjects read a cover sheet that began with a reminder that the divorce rate in the United States was 50% and continued with a description of a research project designed to detect personality and background factors related to marriage outcomes. The researchers were said to have gathered information about the background factors of individuals who had attended the University of Michigan in the 1960s (almost half of whom were already divorced) and to have found some of the factors to be related to marriage outcomes. Because the researchers were also interested in people's beliefs about these issues, the study was to examine whether people knew which factors were likely to facilitate divorce and which were likely to hinder divorce.

Subjects then read a description of a person said to be one of the actual participants in the original study. The description consisted of one of two opposite sets of six attributes. Half the subjects read that (a) the person's mother was never employed outside the home; (b) as a college student the person was introverted and (c) independent; (d) the person was nonreligious; (e) the person identified with liberal political views; and (f) the person had at least one serious relationship with a member of the opposite sex before entering college. The other half of the subjects read that the person had the opposite set of attributes (employed mother, extravert, dependent, religious, conservative, no early romantic involvement). Half the subjects read that the person was male and half that the person was female. This variable had no effect on the dependent measures and will not be discussed further. A third of the subjects read that the target person was divorced, a third that the person was happily married, and a third were given no information about the outcome of the target person's marriage.

Subjects were next asked to indicate how each of the target person's attributes might have contributed to the eventual outcome of the target, person's marriage on a 9-point scale ranging from 1 (*made divorce much more likely*) through 5 (*had no influence*) to 9 (*made stable marriage much more likely*).

After responding to a series of unrelated questionnaires, subjects were asked about the probability that they would incur a number of positive and negative events, including divorce. At the end, subjects were asked to indicate their own standing on each of the background attributes (i.e., whether their own mother had been employed outside the home, etc.).[1]

Results and discussion. For each attribute, people who matched the target person on that attribute (i.e., possessed that attribute themselves) were expected to view it as better for the target person's marriage than were people who did not match the target person (i.e., possessed the opposite attribute). Table 1 shows that this pattern was found for 9 of the 12 possible comparisons. For example, subjects whose own mothers had been

---

[1] Subjects' self-reported attitudes were not affected by the target's outcome. For each outcome condition, the percentage of subjects who indicated that they matched the target on each attribute was calculated, and these percentages were averaged across attributes. On average, the percentage of subjects indicating that they matched the target in the happily married, divorced, and no-information conditions was 53, 55, and 53, respectively.

TABLE 23.1. Mean Rating of the Effect of Each Attribute on the Target Person's Marriage Given by Subjects Who Did and Who Did Not Match the Target Person on These Attributes

Target's attribute	Match	N	No match	N	Coef[a]	t
Employed mother	5.53	17	4.40	35		
Nonemployed mother	4.96	28	4.48	23	.40	2.75**
Introvert	3.65	17	4.37	30		
Extravert	5.70	37	5.30	10	−.09	.40
Independent	4.50	46	2.25	4		
Dependent	4.92	12	5.03	36	.36	1.14
Nonreligious	4.30	20	4.12	32		
Religious	6.81	27	6.33	24	.29	1.98**
Liberal	4.81	32	4.74	19		
Conservative	4.89	18	5.73	30	−.22	1.53
Early relationship	6.47	40	5.75	12		
No early relationship	4.43	23	3.57	28	.40	2.29**

Note. Ratings were made on a scale ranging from 1 (*made divorce much more likely*) to 9 (*made stable marriage much more likely*).
[a] These are multiple regression coefficients obtained in the prediction of subjects' responses from whether or not they matched the target person. *$p < .05$ ** $p < .01$.

employed outside the home viewed having had an employed mother as better for marriage and having had a nonemployed mother as worse for marriage than did subjects whose mothers had not worked outside the home.

A multiple regression was performed for each of the six items. In each case, subjects' responses were predicted from the target person's attribute (e.g., employed or nonemployed mother), the subject's attribute, and whether the subject matched the target person on this attribute. The key question was how the match/no-match variable (which was a dummy variable coded as 1 for *match* and as −1 for *no match*) contributed to the prediction of subject's responses. As seen in Table 1, four of the six regression coefficients were positive, indicating that subjects who matched the target person on a given attribute viewed that attribute as better for marriage than did subjects who did not match the target person. Three of these positive coefficients were significant at the .05 level or lower. Neither of the two negative coefficients was significant. This analysis is a between-subjects analysis comparing the responses of subjects possessing opposite positions on each dimension.

Subjects were also expected to view attributes that they possessed as better for marriage than attributes that they did not possess. Thus each subject was expected to rate the subset of attributes on which he or she matched the target person as better for the target person's marriage than the remaining attributes on which he or she did not match

the target person. To examine this, the mean rating of the items on which he or she matched the target person and the mean of the items on which he or she did not match the target person were calculated for each subject.[2] As seen in Figure 1, subjects judged items on which they matched the target person as better for marriage than items on which they did not match the target person. This was significant for each of the opposite attribute sets, pair-wise $t(50) = 2.73$, $p < .01$, and $t(48) = 2.04$, $p < .05$, as well as for both sets combined, $t(99) = 3.40$, $p < .01$.

Because of the combination of unequal cell sizes and unequal means for individual items, the effect may be somewhat exaggerated. To control for this, all items were standardized and the same analyses were carried out on the standardized scores. This procedure actually underestimates the magnitude of the effect. Nevertheless, these comparisons were all significant at $p < .05$.

Information about the outcome of the target's marriage did not interact with whether subjects matched the target ($p > .20$), but it did have a significant main effect on responses. Attributes were judged as best for marriage when the target was said to be happily married (5.82), as worst when the target was said to be divorced (4.38), and as intermediate when no information was given

---

[2]Only subjects with at least one match response and at least one no-match response were included in the within-subjects analyses in this and the following study.

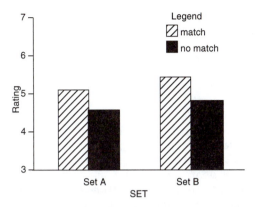

FIGURE 23.1 ■ For each attribute set, mean ratings given by subjects for the effects on the target person's marriage of attributes on which they did and did not match the target person.

(4.62), $F(2, 97) = 27.78$, $p < .001$. This suggests that subjects' theories about the causal determinants of divorce were not merely retrieved from memory. Rather, subjects appear to have generated the theories on the spot to meet the demands of the particular situation.

This main effect could be due to demand characteristics because subjects may have concluded that at least some of the attributes had to be related to the target's outcome. Also, their theories about these relations may have remained specific to the target person rather than becoming more general theories about the causes of divorce. However, in a follow-up study (Kunda, 1986), there was a similar main effect in the absence of such constraints. After explaining why a specific target was happily married or divorced, subjects indicated, in a setting made to appear unrelated so as to counteract demand, that they had generated general theories about the relations between target attributes and divorce.

These findings corroborate other research indicating that people are capable of generating theories linking any attribute to just about any outcome (Anderson & Sechler, 1986; Fischhoff, 1975). They are willing to do this even on the basis of a single instance (cf. Anderson, 1983), suggesting that people are constantly revising and updating their causal theories as they encounter individuals who have experienced various outcomes. The causal theories that are generated following exposure to such individuals appear to be shaped not only by these individuals' attributes and outcomes

and by general world knowledge but also by personal motivations and goals.

It seems that when generating theories about the influence of different attributes on marriage, people enhance the positive influence of their own attributes at the expense of other people's attributes. This process could enable people to maintain unrealistic optimism about the eventual outcomes of their own marriages. Indeed, even though subjects were reminded at the beginning of the study that the probability of divorce was 50%, subjects believed, on average, that the probability that they would get divorced was only 20%. These data suggest that this unrealistic optimism may be sustained at least in part through the selective generation of theories concerning the precursors of divorce when optimistic beliefs are questioned. If one believes that one's attributes are positively related to stable marriage, it follows that one is unlikely to get divorced. Motives, therefore, may exert their influence on reasoning by directing the memory search through relevant world knowledge and leading to greater activation and use of those knowledge structures that can support self-serving theories and beliefs.

Study 2: Generating Self-Serving Theories About Success in Professional School

Study 1 suggests that the mere possession of a given attribute leads one to view this attribute as more positively related to desired outcomes and less predictive of feared events. Thus people appear to generate causal theories in a self-serving manner. However, it is not clear that these findings necessarily imply motivationally directed theory generation. It is also possible, for example, that people with different attributes have different histories of unintentional exposure to information about these attributes and that this selective exposure highlights the positive aspects of these attributes in general and in relation to particular outcomes. If this were true, the effect could be due to purely cognitive factors (cf. Nisbett & Ross, 1980).

This alternative explanation implies that people's tendency to enhance the positivity of the relation between their own attributes and particular outcomes should be independent of the extent to which they are personally concerned about these outcomes. If it could be shown that people with different attributes have different beliefs about the relations between these attributes and outcomes only if they care about these outcomes, this alternative interpretation would be rendered less plausible, and the view that such differential beliefs result from motivationally directed theory generation would be strengthened.

Study 2 replicated Study 1, but this time the outcome concerned success or failure in a professional school such as for law or medicine. In this domain, it was possible to identify people who had no motivational involvement with the outcomes, namely those students who did not plan to go on to professional school. Unlike motivationally driven subjects, these disinterested subjects were not expected to consider their own attributes to be more predictive of success than other attributes.

Method. Subjects were 138 University of Michigan undergraduates of both sexes enrolled in introductory psychology. They participated in groups of 4 to 6 subjects.

Subjects read a cover sheet explaining that the study was part of a research project concerning the actual and believed causes of success and failure in professional schools such as for law, medicine, and business. They next read that the researchers had collected information about the background factors of many University of Michigan graduates who had gone on to professional schools and that some of these were found to be related to how well the students had done in professional school, even when grade point averages and Scholastic Aptitude Test (SAT) scores were held constant. The study was supposed to examine whether people knew which factors were likely to facilitate success in professional school and which were likely to hinder it.

Subjects then read a description of a person said to be one of the actual participants in the original study. The description consisted of one of two opposite sets of attributes. Half the subjects read that the person (a) was Catholic, (b) was the youngest child in his or her family, (c) had a mother who was never employed outside the home, (d) had a distant relationship with his or her father, (e) had at least one serious relationship with a member of the opposite sex before entering college, and (f) was insecure. The other half of the subjects read that the person had an opposite set of attributes (Protestant, oldest child, employed mother, close relationship with father, no early romantic relationship, secure). The person was said to be either male or female. This variable had no effect on the dependent measures and will not be discussed further. A third of the subjects read that the person had done very well in professional school, a third read that the person had done very poorly, and a third were given no information about how well the person did.

Subjects were next asked to indicate how each of the target person's attributes might have contributed to the person's performance in professional school, on a 9-point scale ranging from 1 (*made poor performance much more likely*) through 5 (*had no effect*) to 9 (*made excellent performance much more likely*). After responding to a series of unrelated questionnaires, subjects were asked to indicate their own standing on each of the background attributes.[3] Finally, subjects were asked to indicate, by checking *yes, no*, or *maybe*, whether they planned to attend a professional school after they graduated.

Results and discussion. Table 2 shows that the pattern of responses given to individual items replicates Study 1: In 10 of the 12 possible comparisons, subjects who matched the target person on a given attribute rated that attribute as better for the target person's success in professional school than did subjects who did not match the target person on that attribute.[4]

The results of the multiple regression analyses performed on each item also replicated Study 1. Subjects' responses to each item were predicted from the target's attribute, the subject's attribute, and whether the subject matched the target on this attribute. As seen in Table 2, five of the six regression coefficients obtained for the match variable were positive, indicating that subjects who matched the target person on a given attribute viewed that attribute as better for success than did subjects who did not match the target person. Two of these positive coefficients were significant at the .05 level or lower. The only negative coefficient was not significant.

As expected, the within-subjects analysis replicated Study 1 only for subjects who planned to

---

[3]Subjects' self-reported attitudes were not affected by the target's outcome. On average, the percentage of subjects indicating that they matched the target in the good-performance, poor-performance, and no-information conditions was 48, 46, and 47, respectively.

[4]Self-ratings for the last two items were obtained on 9-point scales. Subjects who placed themselves at the scale midpoints were excluded from the analyses for these items.

TABLE 23.2. Mean Rating of the Effect of Each Attribute on the Target Person's Success in Professional School Given by Subjects Who Did and Who Did Not Match the Target Person on These Attributes

Target's attribute	Match	N	No match	N	Coef[a]	t
Catholic	5.67	21	5.21	48		
Protestant	5.20	15	5.52	54	−.01	.02
Youngest child	5.58	31	4.84	38		
Oldest child	6.51	33	6.36	36	.36	2.09*
Nonemployed mother	5.74	34	4.76	33		
Employed mother	5.58	31	5.84	38	.17	1.13
Early relationship	5.51	47	5.50	22		
No early relationship	5.19	31	4.92	38	.07	.60
Insecure	4.38	13	3.89	44		
Secure	7.47	57	6.75	8	.29	1.10
Distant father	5.50	16	3.78	45		
Close father	6.62	42	6.00	14	.59	3.75**

Note. Ratings were made on a scale ranging from 1 (*made poor performance much more likely*) to 9 (*made excellent performance much more likely*).
[a] These are multiple regression coefficients obtained in the prediction of subjects' responses from whether or not they matched the target person. * $p < .05$ ** $p < .001$.

attend professional school or who were considering the possibility, as seen in Figure 2. These subjects rated items on which they matched the target person as better for success in professional school than items on which they did not match the target person. Planned comparisons yielded $t(126) = 2.77$, $p < .01$, and $t(126) = 2.93$, $p < .01$, respectively, for subjects who answered the question about whether they planned to attend professional school with *yes* and *maybe*. No such difference was found for subjects who did not plan to attend professional school, $t(126) = .27$. A 2 (match) × 2 (plans) repeated measures analysis of variance (ANOVA) in which responses of subjects replying *yes* and *maybe* were combined yielded a significant interaction, $F(1, 127) = 3.89$, $p < .05$, in addition to a significant main effect for the match variable, $F(1, 127) = 5.12$, $p < .05$. Analysis of standardized scores yielded similar results.

As in Study 1, information about the target's performance in professional school did not interact with whether subjects matched the target ($p > .20$) but did have a significant main effect on responses ($p < .001$). Attributes were judged as most conducive to success when the target was said to have done well (6.38), as least conducive to success when the target was said to have done poorly (4.71), and as intermediate when no information was given (5.51). This suggests once again that subjects were generating the theories on the spot.

These data suggest that people's tendency to view their own attributes as better than other attributes is probably due to motivational processes.

It appears that people generate theories favoring their own attributes to reassure themselves that they will obtain desired goals or avoid feared outcomes by virtue of the goodness of their attributes. Thus the motivation to obtain success may lead people to search memory for world knowledge that could support theories in which their own attributes are viewed as conducive to success. People with different attributes will access different world knowledge and generate different theories about the causes and determinants of success. This differential generation of theories seems closely tied in with concern about one's own likelihood of obtaining motivationally loaded outcomes because

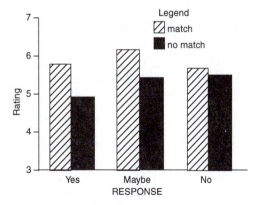

FIGURE 23.2 ■ Mean ratings given by subjects who thought that they would definitely, would probably, and would not attend professional school of attributes on which they did and did not match the target person.

when people do not care about the outcome in question, they do not bother to generate theories favoring their own attributes.

The data do not, however, completely rule out the possibility that these biases are due to entirely cognitive processes. It is possible, for example, that in comparison with people who are not concerned with a given outcome, people who are concerned with this outcome possess far more elaborate cognitive structures relevant to this outcome and that information contained in these structures is biased toward a favorable view of the causal consequences of their own attributes. Of course, one wonders whether the differential formation of such structures would not itself require motivationally guided inferential processes. Nevertheless, more conclusive arguments for the role of motivation in theory generation await research in which different theories are generated under different motivational conditions by the same subjects or by subjects randomly assigned to conditions and therefore assumed to possess similar knowledge structures.

Self-Serving Evidence Evaluation

So far, it has been suggested that optimistic beliefs may be maintained through self-serving theory generation. The following section focuses on whether optimistic beliefs may also be maintained through self-serving biases in the evaluation of evidence coming from an external source. Do people judge, evaluate, and believe scientific theories differentially, depending on the theories' implications for the self? And if they do, are these processes driven by motivational forces?

Study 3: Caffeine Consumption and the Evaluation of Evidence About Negative Effects of Caffeine

Study 3 examines whether people evaluate scientific evidence in a self-serving manner. Are people less likely to believe evidence linking an attribute to a negative outcome if they possess this dangerous attribute? Although other researchers have addressed similar questions (e.g., Kassarjian & Cohen, 1965; Pyszczynski & Greenberg, in press), there has been little attempt to examine biased evidence evaluation while attempting to rule out the possibility that the biases are produced entirely by prior beliefs (cf. Nisbett & Ross, 1980).

Subjects read an article about the negative effects of caffeine consumption on health. Heavy caffeine drinkers were expected to be less willing to believe the article than were people who did not consume much caffeine, because only the former would be personally threatened if the article were true. However, such results could be due to different prior beliefs about caffeine and its effects held by people who did and did not consume caffeine rather than to motivationally directed differential processing of evidence. In order to rule out this possibility, the negative effects were said to be specific to women. This allowed male subjects to serve as controls. Presumably, male and female heavy caffeine drinkers hold the same prior beliefs about caffeine, but only women should be motivated to disbelieve the evidence presented in this study because only they are personally threatened by it. Consequently, if the reduced willingness of caffeine drinkers to believe the article's contents is specific to women, it is probably due to motivational processes and not to prior beliefs.

Method. Subjects were 112 female and 104 male University of Michigan undergraduates enrolled in introductory psychology. Subjects who indicated that they had heard about the disease discussed in the study were eliminated from the analyses, leaving a total of 75 women and 86 men (the pattern of results remained identical when the other subjects were included in the analyses).

The study was presented as concerned with people's memory, opinions, and beliefs. Subjects read an article said to be adapted from the science section of *The New York Times* (in fact, the bulk of the article was adapted from a medical journal article, though the results were later disputed by other researchers). The article said that a recent review of research about the negative effects of caffeine consumption suggested that women were endangered by caffeine and were strongly advised to avoid caffeine in any form. The major risk for women was said to be fibrocystic disease, reportedly associated with often painful lumps in the breast that could go unnoticed in the early stages but that grew progressively worse with age. The disease was said to be serious because it was associated in its advanced stages with breast cancer. Women who regularly drank three or more cups of caffeine a day for a period of one year or longer were said to be at serious risk of contracting the disease. The article stated that caffeine induced the disease by increasing the concentration of a substance called cAMP in the breast, and thus concentration was higher than normal in women with fibrocystic disease and still higher in women with breast cancer.

The article then said that the damage caused by caffeine was either reversible (by eliminating caffeine from the diet) or irreversible. This variable had no significant effects on the dependent measures and will not be discussed further.

When subjects finished reading the article, they handed it back to the experimenter and were given a questionnaire concerning their recall of different portions of the article. These questions served to ascertain that subjects understood the connection between caffeine consumption and fibrocystic disease. The key dependent measures were embedded among these questions. Subjects were asked to assess the probability that within the next 15 years they would develop fibrocystic disease. After they were asked about the nature of these connections, they were asked to indicate how convinced they were of the connection between caffeine and fibrocystic disease and of the connection between caffeine and the dangerous substance cAMP on a 6-point scale ranging from 1 (*not at all convinced*) to 6 (*extremely convinced*).

Finally, subjects were asked whether they had heard before about fibrocystic disease. Subjects who indicated that they had were eliminated from the analysis. At the very end, subjects were asked to indicate their own level of caffeine consumption by checking *heavy, moderate, low*, or *no consumption*.

Following the study, subjects were fully debriefed, and the controversial nature of the study was explained to them.

Results and discussion. Responses of subjects indicating that they consumed heavy or moderate amounts of caffeine were grouped together, as were responses of subjects who indicated that they consumed low or no amounts of caffeine. These two groups will be referred to as heavy and low caffeine consumers, respectively.

As seen in Table 3, female heavy caffeine consumers thought that they were more likely to develop the caffeine-related disease than did female low consumers, suggesting that they were responsive to the threatening evidence. The comparable effect for men, who were not threatened by the evidence, was considerably smaller. The Sex × Caffeine Consumption interaction was highly significant, $F(1, 157) = 18.21, p < .0001$.

TABLE 23.3. Mean Estimates Given by Male and Female Heavy and Low Caffeine Consumers for the Likelihood That They Would Develop Fibrocystic Disease

Sex	Caffeine consumption	
	Heavy	Low
Female		
M	39%	11%
n	43	32
Male		
M	7%	2%
n	32	54

Despite this responsiveness of female heavy consumers to the evidence, Figure 3 shows that these women were not as convinced by the evidence as were female low consumers. Planned

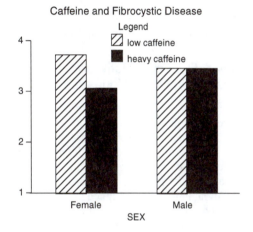

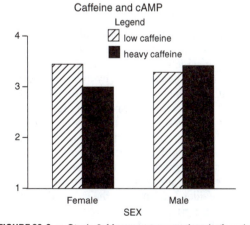

FIGURE 23.3 ■ Study 3: Mean responses given by female and male heavy and low caffeine consumers to questions about the extent to which they were convinced by information about the negative effects of caffeine.

comparisons yielded $t(155) = 2.31$, $p < .05$, and $t(153) = 1.92$, $p < .05$, respectively, for the connection between caffeine and fibrocystic disease and the connection between caffeine and the dangerous substance cAMP. As expected, no such effects were found for men, most of whom realized that they were not personally threatened by the research even if they were heavy caffeine consumers (both $ps > .50$). The Sex × Caffeine Consumption interactions were marginal for both variables, $F(1, 155) = 3.62$, $p < .10$, and $F(1, 153) = 2.40$, $p = .12$.

Thus it appears that those subjects who stood to suffer personal implications if the evidence were true were more likely to doubt its truth. Perhaps the motivation to maintain an optimistic view of their future health led these subjects to access those inferential rules and background beliefs that would allow them to reduce the credibility of the threatening research. However, the data do not allow for direct examination of these mediating processes.

Study 4: Reducing Motivational Pressures to Doubt Undesired Evidence

Study 3 showed that people who are personally threatened by negative evidence do not totally ignore this evidence, but they are not as convinced by it as are disinterested people. The reluctance of female heavy caffeine consumers to be convinced by the threatening evidence is probably due to motivational processes designed to preserve optimism about their future health rather than to different prior beliefs about the effects of caffeine. This is because male heavy caffeine consumers, who presumably hold the same prior beliefs about caffeine held by female heavy caffeine consumers but for whom no motivational pressure to disbelieve the evidence existed, did not show the same reluctance to be convinced by the evidence.

Still, a staunch critic of motivational processes might argue, female heavy caffeine consumers might hold different prior beliefs about caffeine than do male heavy caffeine consumers, and the results may be due to these differences in prior beliefs. If this were true, there should be similar differences in subjects' readiness to be convinced by the evidence even when the motivational pressures were greatly reduced. On the other hand, if the differences found are due to motivation, reducing the motivational pressures should reduce or eliminate the effect (cf. Miller, 1976). Study 4 addresses this issue.

Motivational pressures to disbelieve the article were reduced by making the negative implications of caffeine consumption seem much milder. The article stated that the disease said to be facilitated by caffeine was extremely common, so much so that doctors felt that it shouldn't even be considered a disease; more than 65% of women were said to suffer from it. The design was identical in all other respects to that used in Study 3.

Results and discussion. As seen in Table 4, subjects' beliefs about their likelihood of developing the caffeine-related disease replicated Study 3. Female heavy caffeine consumers thought that they were considerably more likely to develop the disease than did female low caffeine consumers, whereas the comparable effect for men was considerably smaller. The Sex × Caffeine Consumption interaction was highly significant, $F(1, 59) = 7.42$, $p < .01$.

Unlike in Study 3, female heavy consumers were no less convinced by the evidence than were female low consumers. As seen in Figure 4, the slight differences between the groups were actually in the opposite direction, but these differences did not approach significance on either measure (both $ps > .50$). Sex × Caffeine Consumption ANOVAs yielded no significant effects for either variable.

Thus when motivational pressures to disbelieve evidence are reduced, subjects who are personally threatened are less likely to disbelieve it. These data suggest that the reluctance of threatened subjects to believe the evidence presented in Study 3, where the motivational pressures were greater, was due to these motivational pressures. If it were due to different prior beliefs, it should have been found in Study 4 also because the relevant prior beliefs here should not differ in any significant way from those in Study 3.

Taken together, these studies suggest that people

TABLE 23.4. Mean Estimates Given by Male and Female Heavy and Low Caffeine Consumers for the Likelihood That They Would Develop Fibrocystic Disease

Sex	Caffeine consumption	
	Heavy	Low
Female		
M	46%	15%
n	16	16
Male		
M	6%	1%
n	18	13

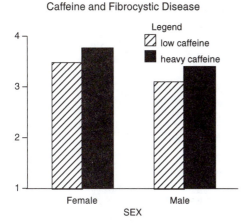

Caffeine and Fibrocystic Disease

Legend
▨ low caffeine
■ heavy caffeine

SEX

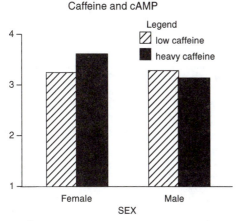

Caffeine and cAMP

Legend
▨ low caffeine
■ heavy caffeine

SEX

FIGURE 23.4 ■ Study 4: Mean responses given by female and male heavy and low caffeine consumers to questions about the extent to which they were convinced by information about the negative effects of caffeine.

do engage in motivationally directed inferential processes, but only when the levels of motivation are high. Even when motivation is high, they do not completely ignore negative evidence, they are responsive to it, but not as responsive as they might have been in the absence of motivational involvement.

General Discussion

These studies suggest that people tend to generate and evaluate causal theories in a self-serving manner; they spontaneously generate theories that view their own attributes as more predictive of desirable outcomes and are reluctant to believe in theories that imply that their own attributes might be related to undesirable events. As a consequence, people tend to hold theories that are consistent with the optimistic belief that good things will happen to them and bad things will not. These self-serving tendencies seem to be explained best as resulting from cognitive processes guided by motivational ends.

It is clear that motivational forces do not completely blind people to undesirable evidence or information. When generating causal theories to explain other people's life outcomes, people often do acknowledge that their own attributes might be related to undesirable outcomes. For example, subjects who had no early romantic relationships seemed to believe that this attribute was likely to be causally related to divorce (but they didn't believe the link to be as strong as did subjects who had early romantic relationships). Similarly, heavy caffeine consumers who read that caffeine consumption could lead to a disease thought they were more likely to suffer this disease than did low caffeine consumers. Thus, motivational forces could lead people to play down negative information but not to ignore it.

It is also clear, however, that it is difficult to account for people's optimistic beliefs without assuming some motivational biases. People's tendency to generate self-serving theories linking their attributes to desirable outcomes does not seem to be due to purely cognitive mechanisms, because this tendency was found only for people who cared about the outcomes. Only those subjects who considered attending professional school believed that their attributes were more likely than other attributes to be related to success in professional school. These findings do not, however, completely rule out an entirely cognitive interpretation, because they could also be explained in terms of preconceptions if one assumes that people who are concerned with an outcome also possess elaborate and biased cognitive structures related to this outcome.

The data supporting self-serving biases in the evaluation of evidence provide stronger support for the notion of motivationally driven processes and do not appear to lend themselves easily to alternative cognitive explanations based on prior beliefs. The results showed that people threatened by undesirable evidence were reluctant to believe this evidence, but only when its implications were perceived as serious. Thus female heavy caffeine consumers were less likely than female low consumers to be convinced by evidence indicating that caffeine consumption leads to disease in women, but only when the disease appeared serious. This effect was not due to differential prior beliefs held by heavy and low caffeine consumers because the effect was not found for male heavy caffeine consumers, who presumably possess the same prior beliefs about caffeine as do female heavy caffeine consumers but who were not personally threatened by the evidence in question. Furthermore, the effect was not found for female caffeine consumers when the implications of caffeine consumption were made to appear less serious, even though these women clearly held the same prior conceptions about caffeine as did their counterparts who believed the implications to be more serious.

Taken together, these two sets of studies suggest that people generate and evaluate causal theories in a self-serving manner only when they are motivated to do so. Such self-serving biases in inference may result from the influence of motivational forces on the choice of inferential procedures used in the generation and evaluation of evidence. People do rely on evidence when formulating their beliefs and do so in a seemingly rational way, but the evidence itself and the inferential rules used to evaluate it are tainted by self-protective motivational forces. Thus, the motivation to view oneself as likely to obtain desirable outcomes and avoid feared outcomes can trigger a memory search that is likely to activate information capable of supporting theories that view one's own attributes as conductive to obtaining the desirable outcome as well as inferential rules that could refute threatening evidence and validate reassuring evidence.

This view of motivation as guiding inference by influencing the search through memory for knowledge structures suggests a new way of investigating motivational biases. Rather than concentrating on the outcomes of such biases, that is, the biased conclusions people arrive at, it might be more fruitful to concentrate on investigating the underlying mechanisms responsible for these biases, that is, the biased activation and use of memories and rules (cf. Tetlock & Levi, 1982). Once these mechanisms are better understood, it should be possible to accumulate a body of literature capable of withstanding the cognitive critique that has shed doubt on the role of motivation in

producing the self-serving biases documented to date.

ACKNOWLEDGMENTS

This article is based on a doctoral dissertation submitted to the Department of Psychology of the University of Michigan. I am especially grateful to the chairs of my doctoral committee, Hazel Markus and Richard Nisbett, for their advice, and to John Jemmott and Edward Jones for comments on an earlier version of the article.

REFERENCES

Anderson, C. A. (1983). Abstract and concrete data in the perseverance of social theories: When weak data lead to unshakable beliefs. *Journal of Experimental Social Psychology 19*, 93–108.

Anderson, C. A., Lepper, M. R., & Ross, L. (1980). Perseverance of social theories: The role of explanation in the persistence of discredited information. *Journal of Personality and Social Psychology, 39*, 1037–1049.

Anderson, C. A., New B. L., & Speer, J. R. (1985). Argument availability as a mediator of social theory perseverance. *Social Cognition, 3*, 235–249.

Anderson, C. A., & Sechler, E. S. (1986). Effects of explanation and counterexplanation on the development and use of statistical theories. *Journal of Personality and Social Psychology, 50*, 24–34.

Anderson, C. A., & Slusher, M. P. (1986). Relocating motivational effects: A synthesis of cognitive and motivational effects. *Social Cognition, 4*, 270–292.

Darley, J. M., & Gross, P. H. (1983). A hypothesis-confirming bias in labeling effects. *Journal of Personality and Social Psychology, 44*, 20–33.

Erdelyi, M. H. (1974). A new look at the new look: Perceptual defense and vigilance. *Psychological Review, 81*, 1–25.

Fazio, R. H., Effrein, E. A., & Falender, V. F. (1981). Self-perceptions following social interaction. *Journal of Personality and Social Psychology, 41*, 232–242.

Festinger, L. (1957). *A theory of cognitive dissonance* Stanford, CA: Stanford University Press.

Fischhoff, B. (1975). Hindsight does not equal foresight: The effects of outcome knowledge on judgment under uncertainty. *Journal of Experimental Psychology: Human Perception and Performance, 1*, 288–299.

Greenwald, A. G. (1980). The totalitarian ego: Fabrication and revision of personal history. *American Psychologist, 35*, 603–618.

Greenwald, A. G. (1981). Self and memory. In G. H. Bower (Ed.), *The psychology of learning and motivation* (pp. 201–236). New York: Academic Press.

Greenwald, A. G., & Pratkanis, A. R. (1984). The self. In R. S. Wyer & T. K. Srull (Eds.), *Handbook of social cognition* (pp. 129–178). Hillsdale, NJ: Erlbaum.

Higgins, E. T., & King G. A. (1981). Accessibility of social constructs: Information-processing consequences of individual and contextual variability. In N. Cantor & J. F. Kihlstrom (Eds.), *Personality, cognition, and social interaction* (pp. 69–121). Hillsdale, NJ: Erlbaum.

Higgins, E. T., King, G. A., & Mavin, G. H. (1982). Individual construct accessibility and subjective impressions in recall. *Journal of Personality and Social Psychology, 73*, 35–47.

Irwin, F. W. (1953). Stated expectations as functions of probability and desirability of outcomes. *Journal of Personality, 21*, 329–335.

Kassarjian, H. H., & Cohen, J. B. (1965). Cognitive dissonance and consumer behavior. *California Management Review, 8*, 55–64.

Koriat, A., Lichtenstein, S., & Fischhoff, B. (1980). Reasons for confidence. *Journal of Experimental Psychology: Human Learning and Memory, 6*, 107–118.

Kruglanski, A. W., & Freund, T. (1983). The freezing and unfreezing of lay inference: Effects on impressional primacy, ethnic stereotyping, and numerical anchoring. *Journal of Experimental Social Psychology, 19*, 448–468.

Kunda, Z. (1985). *Motivation and inference: Self-serving generation and evaluation of causal theories.* Unpublished doctoral dissertation, University of Michigan, Ann Arbor.

Kunda, Z. (1986). *Generating theories from single instances.* Unpublished manuscript, Princeton University, Princeton, NJ.

Kunda, Z., & Nisbett, R. E. (1986). The psychometrics of everyday life. *Cognitive Psychology, 18*, 195–224.

Lehman, D., & Nisbett, R. E. (1985). *Effects of higher education on inductive reasoning.* Unpublished manuscript, University of Michigan, Ann Arbor.

Lerner, M. J. (1980). *The belief in a just world: A fundamental delusion.* New York: Plenum Press.

Lord, C. G., Ross, L., & Lepper, M. R. (1979). Biased assimilation and attitude polarization: The effects of prior theories on subsequently considered evidence. *Journal of Personality and Social Psychology, 37*, 2098–2109.

Marks, R. W. (1951). The effects of probability, desirability, and "privilege" on the stated expectations of children. *Journal of Personality, 19*, 332–351.

Markus, H., & Kunda, Z. (1986). Stability and malleability of the self-concept. *Journal of Personality and Social Psychology, 51*, 858–866.

Miller, D. T. (1976). Ego involvement and attributions for success and failure. *Journal of Personality and Social Psychology, 34*, 901–906.

Miller, D. T., & Ross, M. (1975). Self-serving biases in attribution of causality: Fact or fiction? *Psychological Bulletin, 82*, 213–225.

Nisbett, R. E., Krantz, D. H., Jepson, C., & Kunda, Z. (1983). The use of statistical heuristics in everyday inductive reasoning. *Psychological Review, 90*, 339–363.

Nisbett, R. E., & Ross, L. (1980). *Human inference: Strategies and shortcomings of social judgement.* Englewood Cliffs, NJ: Prentice-Hall.

Parducci, A. (1968). The relativism of absolute judgment. *Scientific American, 219*, 890.

Perloff, L. S. (1983). Perceptions of vulnerability to victimization. *Journal of Social Issues, 39*, 41–61.

Pruitt, D. G., & Hoge, R. D. (1965). Strength of the relationship between the value of an event and its subjective probability as a function of method of measurement. *Journal of Experimental Psychology, 69*, 483–489.

Pyszczynski, T., & Greenberg, J. (in press). A biased hypothesis testing approach to motivated attribution distortion. In L. Berkowitz (Ed.), *Advances in experimental social psychology.* New York: Academic Press.

Pyszczynski, T., Greenberg, J., & LaPrelle, J. (1985). Social comparison after success & failure: Biased search for information consistent with a self-serving conclusion. *Journal of Experimental Social Psychology, 21*, 195–211.

Ross, M., & Fletcher, G. J. O. (1985). Attribution and social perception. In G. Lindzey & E. Aronson (Eds.), *Handbook of social psychology* (pp. 73–122). New York: Random House.

Salancik, G. R., & Conway, M. (1975). Attitude inference from salient and relevant cognitive content about behavior. *Journal of Personality and Social Psychology, 32*, 829–840.

Snyder, M. (1982). When believing means doing: Creating links between attitudes and behavior. In M. P. Zanna, E. T. Higgins, & C. P. Herman (Eds.), *Consistency in social behavior: The Ontario Symposium* (Vol. 2, pp. 105–130). Hillsdale, NJ: Erlbaum.

Srull, T. K., & Wyer, R. S. (1986). The role of chronic and temporary goals in social information processing. In R. M. Sorrentino & E. T. Higgins (Eds.), *Handbook of motivation and cognition* (pp. 503–549). New York: Guilford Press.

Taylor, S. E. (1983). Adjustment to threatening events: A theory of cognitive adaptation. *American Psychologist, 38*, 1161–1173.

Tesser, A., & Campbell, J. (1983). Self-definition and self-evaluation maintenance. In J. Suls & A. Greenwald (Eds.), *Social psychological perspectives on the self* (Vol. 2, pp. 1–31). Hillsdale, NJ: Erlbaum.

Tetlock, P. E., & Levi, A. (1982). Attribution bias: On the inconclusiveness of the cognition–motivation debate. *Journal of Experimental Social Psychology, 18*, 68–88.

Weinstein, N. D. (1980). Unrealistic optimism about future life events. *Journal of Personality and Social Psychology, 39*, 806–820.

Weinstein, N. D. (1983). Reducing unrealistic optimism about illness susceptibility. *Health Psychology, 2*, 11–20.

Weinstein, N. D. (1984). Why it won't happen to me: Perceptions of risk factors and susceptibility. *Health Psychology, 3*, 431–457.

Wicklund, R. A., & Brehm, J. W. (1976). *Perspectives on cognitive dissonance.* Hillsdale, NJ: Erlbaum.

Zanna, M. P., & Cooper, J. (1976). Dissonance and the attribution process. In J. H. Harvey, W. J. Ickes, & R. F. Kidd (Eds.), *New directions in attribution research* (Vol. 1, pp. 199–217). Hillsdale, NJ: Erlbaum.

Zuckerman, M. (1979). Attribution of success and failure revisited, or: The motivational bias is alive and well in attribution theory. *Journal of Personality, 47*, 245–287.

The Freezing and Unfreezing of Lay-Inferences: Effects on Impressional Primacy, Ethnic Stereotyping, and Numerical Anchoring

Arie W. Kruglanski and Tallie Freund • Tel-Aviv University

Editors' Notes

The previous selection discussed cognitive biases introduced by a "directional" motivation; that is, a conclusional need to form specific, personally desirable judgments. But aside from such specific directional biases, motivation may impact judgments even if the individual isn't partial to particular (wished-for) conclusions. The present selection deals with two such motivations, referred to as the need for cognitive structure and the fear of invalidity. The need for structure is hypothesized to effect an early freezing on whatever information comes to mind that is relevant to one's judgmental task. The fear of invalidity, quite to the contrary, retards the freezing process and hence reduces the tendency to base one's judgment on early-appearing information. The power of this selection is that it applies the same motivational analysis to diverse judgmental phenomena, including primacy effects in impression formation, the use of ethnic stereotypes to judge persons, and the tendency to base one's judgments under uncertainty on arbitrary anchor points. Whereas these topics were treated previously as separate, the present analysis suggests that they are but special cases of a general process of judgment formation to which the same epistemic principles apply.

Discussion Questions

1. What does the theory of lay epistemology assert? What are its major postulates?

2. What is meant by the notions of "freezing" and "unfreezing"?

3. In what way does time pressure operationally define the need for structure, and evaluation apprehension operationally define the fear of invalidity? Can you think of alternative operational definitions of these constructs?

4. Can you think of other phenomena beyond those discussed by the authors to which the same analysis should apply? How would you test your ideas about those additional phenomena?

Suggested Readings

Kruglanski, A. W., & Webster, D. M. (1996). Motivated closing of the mind: "Seizing" and "freezing." *Psychological Review, 103,* 263–283.

Webster, D. M., & Kruglanski, A. W. (1994). Individual differences in need for cognitive closure. *Journal of Personality and Social Psychology, 67,* 1049–1062.

Authors' Abstract

Three experiments were conducted to test the hypothesis that primacy effects, ethnic stereotyping, and numerical anchoring all represent "epistemic freezing" in which the lay-knower becomes less aware of plausible alternative hypotheses and or inconsistent bits of evidence competing with a given judgment. It was hypothesized that epistemic freezing would increase with an increase in time pressure on the lay-knower to make a judgment and decrease with the lay-knower's fear that his/her judgment will be evaluated and possibly be in error. Accordingly, it was predicted that primacy effects, ethnic stereotyping, and anchoring phenomena would increase in magnitude with an increase in time pressure and decrease in magnitude with an increase in evaluation apprehension. Finally, the time-pressure variations were expected to have greater impact upon "freezing" when the evaluation apprehension is high as opposed to low. All hypotheses were supported in each of the presently executed studies.

An important issue in the domain of social cognition concerns people's readiness to modify their judgments in the light of new evidence. The present work examines this issue from a standpoint of a theory of lay epistemology developed recently by Kruglanski and his associates (cf. Kruglanski, 1980; Kruglanski & Jaffe, in press; Kruglanski & Ajzen, 1983). In previous papers on lay epistemology attempts were made to demonstrate how the lay-epistemic framework provides a basis for (1) integrating the various models of causal attribution (see in particular Kruglanski, 1980); (2) further synthesizing them with the cognitive-consistency theories (cf. Kruglanski & Klar, Note 1); and (3) reconceptualizing judgmental biases and errors in lay-epistemic terms (cf. Kruglanski & Ajzen, 1983). By contrast to these mainly theoretical attempts the present work explores some empirical implications of the lay-epistemic framework in particular concerning conditions under which judgments may be sensitive or insensitive to new evidence. But before specifically addressing those conditions let us outline the lay-epistemic theory in some detail.

The Theory of Lay Epistemology

The theory of lay epistemology concerns the process whereby people arrive at all their knowledge. Knowledge is considered in terms of its two aspects, its *content* and the *confidence* with which it is held. This suggests the two functions that the epistemic process has to fulfill. The contents of knowledge must be produced somehow. Thus we need to have a phase of *hypothesis generation*. Then a given degree of confidence needs to be bestowed on the knowledge in question. Thus we need to have a phase of hypothesis *evaluation or validation*.

The generation of hypotheses has to do with one's stream of associations and with the way ideas form in a person's mind. The validation of hypotheses is conducted in accordance with the principle of logical consistency: The individual deduces from a hypothesis under test some of its implications and tests them against the appropriate evidence. Should the evidence be logically consistent with the implications the individual's confidence in the hypothesis would be strengthened. And if no alternative hypotheses equally consistent with the evidence were apparent the individual might accept the hypothesis as true and come to regard it as firm knowledge. But the acceptance of any hypothesis is potentially revokable. For an individual could always become aware of a plausible alternative hypothesis or of an item of evidence inconsistent with the original hypothesis. A logical inconsistency can only be resolved *via* denying or conferring falseness on one of the contradictory propositions. Such attempts at denial are likely to be directed at the less firmly believed of those propositions. For instance, when a "hypothesis" clashes with a "fact" we usually abandon the "hypothesis." According to the present interpretation this is because a "hypothesis" represents a less firmly believed in proposition than a "fact."

If in principle an individual could generate cognitions inconsistent with any given hypothesis, a protracted belief in a hypothesis represents the "freezing" of the cognition-generation process: An individual accepts a given hypothesis as true because (s)he fails to generate a plausible enough alternative hypothesis or to become aware of a plausible enough bit of evidence inconsistent with the original hypothesis. The theory of lay epistemology specifies two categories of conditions affecting the tendency of the hypothesis-generation process to "freeze" at some point or, conversely, be "unfrozen." These categories are (1) the individual's *capacity* to produce various alternative hypotheses on a given topic, and (2) his/her motivation to do so. A person's capacity to engender hypotheses on a given topic may have to do with his/her store of past knowledge and with situational factors affecting the momentary saliency or availability of various ideas. The individual's motivation to generate alternative hypotheses is assumed to be affected by needs in three separate classes: (1) the need for structure, (2) the fear of invalidity, and (3) the need for specific conclusions (the need for conclusions contents).

The need for structure is the need to have some knowledge on a given topic, any knowledge as opposed to confusion and ambiguity. A need for structure once aroused is assumed to have an inhibiting or freezing influence on the hypothesis-generation process because the generation of alternative hypotheses endangers the existing hypothesis or structure. A need for structure may be heightened every time a person is under a pressure to form a clear opinion or reach a definite conclusion. A special case of this is when a person is under the pressure to act, for action often requires orienting knowledge for its execution. Indeed, research evidence indicates that time pressure and the need to quickly reach a decision intensify the tendency to seek cognitive closure and to refrain from critical probing of a given seemingly adequate solution to a problem (cf. Frenkel-Brunswick, 1949; Smock, 1955; Tolman, 1948).

The fear of invalidity stems from the perceived costs of committing a judgmental error. Opposite to the need of structure, the fear of invalidity is assumed to have a facilitating influence upon the hypothesis-generation process because of the expected dangers of committing oneself to a given, possibly mistaken hypothesis. For instance, the greater the ridicule expected from other people the stronger might be the individual's disposition to consider multiple alternative solutions to a given problem before accepting any one as valid. The foregoing analysis implies that where considerable costs hinge upon commission of an error, thus arousing the fear of invalidity, the individual will be more sensitive to evidence and ideas inconsistent with current beliefs and affording the generation of alternative or competing hypotheses.

The need for specific conclusions can sometimes

facilitate and sometimes inhibit the generation of alternative hypotheses: When the hypothesis is desirable from the standpoint of some need or wish the individual will feel more disposed to accept it and to refrain from generating rival alternative hypotheses. To the contrary, when the hypothesis is undesirable the individual will be more inclined to replace it by a plausible alternative. The foregoing implies that a person whose current beliefs are desirable or need-congruent will be less sensitive to evidence or ideas inconsistent with those beliefs than a person whose current beliefs are undesirable or need-incongruent. These ideas concerning conclusional biases are hardly novel. The thesis that people often engage in "wishful thinking" has long been a theme in psychological theorizing from psychoanalysis to the experimental study of perception (e.g., the "new look" approach of the 1950's).

Our epistemic analysis of "freezing" and "unfreezing" suggests that these processes pertain to judgments of all possible contents. Indeed, several heretofore disparate phenomena known to social–cognitive psychologists can be understood as instances of freezing manifest with different contents of judgment. In the present investigation we attempted to study from the epistemic perspective three such classical phenomena: Primacy effects in impression formation (cf. Luchins, 1957; Asch, 1946), ethnic stereotyping (cf. Hamilton, 1979), and anchoring phenomena (cf. Tversky & Kahneman, 1974). If all the above phenomena represent epistemic freezing they should be similarly affected by the hypothesized determinants of freezing such as the need of structure and the fear of invalidity mentioned earlier. One way to operationalize the need for structure would be *via* degrees of time pressure to reach a judgment. Thus we hypothesized that primacy effects, stereotypic judgments, and numerical anchoring would all be increased under a high-versus-low degree of time pressure. Furthermore, one way to operationalize the fear of invalidity would be *via* "evaluation apprehension" that is via anticipated costs to one's self-esteem of committing a judgmental error. Thus we hypothesized that primacy effects, stereotyping, or anchoring would all be *decreased* under high-versus-low degrees of evaluation apprehension. Finally, in situations where some judgment is ultimately required an interactive effect of time pressure and evaluation apprehension should be expected: The request to come up with a judgment

introduces an inherent demand for structure. When the evaluation apprehension is low such a demand might represent the only situational goal: due to a ceiling effect this might render any further time-pressure manipulations of little additional impact. By contrast, when evaluation apprehension is high the situational demand for structure is countered by an opposed goal and its effects on the epistemic process may be below the "ceiling" level. Thus, when evaluation apprehension is high and there is ample time to make a considered judgment epistemic freezing may be avoided. However, when time pressure is introduced it may counteract the effects of evaluation apprehension and allow freezing to take place. In other words, experimental manipulations of time pressure may exert a greater effect on primacy effects, stereotypic judgments, and anchoring phenomena under high as compared with low degree of evaluation apprehension. The foregoing possibilities were examined in three experimental studies described below.

Experiment 1: Primacy Effects

Primacy effects in judgmental behavior are generally said to exist when in judging an object or a person the individual bases his/her inferences predominantly on early information and appears to be affected less by late information (cf. Luchins, 1957). According to the present analysis, primacy effects can be interpreted as instances of epistemic freezing. On this view, an individual may attain closure early in the informational sequence and be relatively impervious to later information. For example, an individual might form a positive impression of another person if early information about this person was positive. Similarly, a person might form a negative impression of another if the early information was negative. All this, in relative disregard of later information which could often be inconsistent with the initial evidence.

In the present experiment we examined how primacy effects may be affected by the factors of time pressure and evaluation apprehension. Our epistemic analysis outlined earlier suggests that primacy effects should be *increased* under a high (versus low) degree of time pressure and should be *decreased* under a high (versus low) degree of evaluation apprehension. Finally, we predicted that the time-pressure variations would have greater impact upon primacy effects when the fear of invalidity is high rather than low.

Method

SUBJECTS AND EXPERIMENTAL DESIGN

Eighty high school students in Ashkelon, Israel, participated as subjects. They were tested in groups of four to six members. Subjects within groups were randomly assigned to experimental conditions in a $2 \times 2 \times 2$ factorial design with the independent variables: (1) time pressure (high versus low); (2) evaluation apprehension (high versus low); and (3) informational sequence depicting a target person's behaviors in a work-related context. In one condition positive information about the target person was presented first followed by negative information (positive-negative sequence). In the second condition, negative information was presented first followed by positive information (negative–positive sequence). The subjects' task was to judge the target person's likelihood of succeeding at a new job.

PROCEDURE

Each subject received typewritten text including a description of the experimental task and manipulations of the independent variables. An introductory paragraph emphasized the importance of developing new personel-selection methods in various organizations. The experimental task was portrayed as representing a particular selection method based on predicting a candidate's success at a job from this person's behaviors in a previous work situation. Specifically, the subjects had to predict a given person's future success as a president of a company from listening to a tape-recorded sequence of this person's on-the-job behaviors as a department head. The subjects then rated the candidate's likelihood of succeeding at the job on a scale ranging from 0 (not at all likely to succeed) to 10 (very likely to succeed).

Manipulating evaluation apprehension. In the high-evaluation-apprehension condition subjects were informed that the present research examines the ability to successfully predict another person's success at work. It was noted that such a predictive ability is of considerable importance so it is useful to know the extent to which one possesses this particular ability. The subjects were informed

that following task completion they would have to explain their predictions to other members of their group, and that their judgments would be compared with the target person's actual degree of job success as indexed by various objective criteria.

In the *low-evaluation-apprehension* condition subjects were informed that the selection method being investigated is at a pilot stage, and its validity is not yet well known. Subjects were also informed that "because of professional ethics" they would not be able to find out how well the target person actually did do at the new job, nor could they expect to find out how he was judged by other members of their group.

In the *high-time-pressure* condition subjects were informed that after listening to the tape-recorded sequence they would be given 3 min within which to complete their predictions. It was explained that a time constraint constitutes an essential element of the selection method under study. The passage of time was made vivid by means of a stopwatch visibly held by the experimenter during the experimental session. Indeed at the end of 3 min the experimenter proceeded to collect the response sheets from the subjects.

In the *low-time-pressure* condition the subjects were informed that after listening to the recorded sequence they would have an unlimited time within which to complete the predictive task. There was no indication of time measurement and the experimenter collected the subjects' response sheets at the end of 1 hr.

The recorded sequence. As noted earlier, the recorded sequence to which the subjects listened consisted of two parts. In one part the target person was portrayed in a positive light and in the second part in a negative light. Specifically, the positive part included behavioral events suggesting the target person's interest in the employees' performance and their welfare, courtesy to their clients and sensitivity to client needs, orderliness, and efficiency, as well as persuasiveness and leadership at a business conference. The negative part contained behavioral events suggesting the target person's inattentiveness to employee problems and a rejecting attitude toward their requests, wastefulness and inefficiency at troubleshooting, personal disorganization, and a lack of persuasiveness at a business conference. As mentioned earlier half of the subjects listened to the positive sequence first followed by the negative sequence and the other half listened to the negative sequence first followed by the positive sequence.

After the subjects made the requisite success ratings they were thoroughly debriefed and the experimental deceptions were disclosed to them. This concluded the experiment.

Results

Judgments in the *positive-negative* sequence were generally more positive than those in the *negative–positive* sequence ($F(1, 72) = 100.53$; $p < .01$).[1] This suggests that a general *primacy effect* was obtained. To analyze the primacy effects across the informational sequences a scale reversal was performed on scores in the *negative–positive* sequence. Insofar as informational sequence did not significantly interact with time pressure or evaluation apprehension we collapsed the data across the two informational sequences. These combined data are displayed in Table 1.

An analysis of variance performed on these results yielded two main effects and an interaction. Specifically, primacy effects were significantly more pronounced when time pressure was high rather than low ($F(1, 76) = 16.36$; $p < .01$) and when the evaluation apprehension was low rather than high ($F(1, 76) = 32.06$; $p < .01$). Finally, the difference between the time-pressure levels was greater when evaluation apprehension was high versus low ($F(1, 76) = 8.48$; $p < .01$).

Thus, the present data are consistent with the idea that primacy effects in impression formation reflect epistemic freezing and are appropriately influenced by the determinants of freezing such as the epistemic motivations for structure and the avoidance of invalidity, at least as these are represented by the degrees of time pressure and evaluation apprehension, respectively.

Experiment 2: Ethnic Stereotyping

In our second experiment we attempted to see whether an epistemic analysis of the freezing phenomenon may not apply also to ethnic stereotyping. An ethnic stereotype exists when a person perceives a given member of an ethnic group in terms of a generalized notion of the group as a category rather than in terms of specific information concerning the individual member (for an extensive treatment of stereotyping see Hamilton,

TABLE 24.1. Mean[a] Primacy Effects[b]

Degree of time pressure	Evaluation apprehension	
	High	Low
High	7.05	7.9
Low	4.9	7.5

[a] Data collapsed across the two informational sequences after the ratings in the negative–positive sequence were subjected to the appropriate scale reversals to allow for the combined testing for primacy effects.
[b] The higher the numbers the stronger the primacy effects.

1979). Ethnic stereotyping could be interpreted as an instance of epistemic freezing: An individual's conception of a given group could be decided on the basis of early information, and, be impervious to subsequent evidence inconsistent with this particular conception. If ethnic stereotyping reflects epistemic freezing it should be affected appropriately by the degrees of time pressure and evaluation apprehension. Just as with primacy effects, ethnic stereotyping should be more pronounced when time pressure is high versus low and when evaluation apprehension is low versus high. Furthermore, where the rendition of a judgment is ultimately required the time-pressure and evaluation-apprehension variables may be expected to interact: Variation of time pressure should have greater impact on ethnic stereotypes when evaluation apprehension is high as opposed to low.

Method

SUBJECTS AND EXPERIMENTAL DESIGN

The subjects were 144 female students at a Teachers' seminary in the Tel-Aviv area. All were in their final year of studies and within 1 month of graduation and receipt of their teaching diploma. Of the students 105 were of an Ashkenazi (Occidental) origin: their families had come to Israel from Europe or America. The remaining 39 students were of a Sepharadi (Oriental) origin; their families had come to Israel from Asia or Africa. The present experimental paradigm was adopted from Guttman and Bar-Tal (1982). In this particular paradigm, subjects assign grades to a composition written by a person of a given ethnic identity. Insofar as there were no significant differences in grade assign-

---

[1]All *p* values reported are two-tailed.

ments made by Ashkenazi-versus-Sepharadi subjects their data were combined and analyzed collectively.[2]

The subjects were tested in groups of five to seven persons. Subjects within groups were randomly assigned to cells of a 2 × 2 × 3 factorial design in which the independent variables were (1) degree of time pressure (high versus low); (2) degree of evaluation apprehension (high versus low); and (3) the target person's ethnic identity (Ashkenazi, Sepharadi, and ethnically unidentified). Each of the 12 cells in the above design contained 12 subjects.

PROCEDURE

Each subject received a set of typewritten sheets introducing the experimental task and manipulating the independent variables. The introduction, common to all subjects, stated that "evaluation of students' achievements is an essential part of a teacher's job" and that the experimental task consists of evaluating a Hebrew composition written by an 8th grader (the composition's topic being "an interesting event that happened to me"). The sheets given to subjects also included the written composition, some background information about the writer, and a rating scale on which the composition was to be graded for literary excellence. The scale ranged from 40 points (indicating failure) to 100 points (indicating excellent performance).

Manipulating evaluation apprehension. In the *high-evaluation-apprehension* condition the subjects' text stated that the research is intended to assess the teachers' evaluative ability prior to their graduation. The subjects were led to believe that each will have to explain her grade assignment to other members of the group. In addition, the subjects were informed that at the end they would be

---

[2]The absence of judgmental differences between Ashkenazi and Sepharadi subjects might seem contrary to our "conclusional-need" hypothesis, which could be interpreted to suggest that the Sepharadi subjects should rate the Sepharadi writer's product as more positive than the Ashkenazi subjects, with the reverse being the case for the Ashkenazi writer's product. But it is difficult to know precisely what may have been the Sepharadi subjects' needs in the present conditions. For instance, at least some subjects may have identified with the high status group and others might have "bent over backwards" to appear objective. To the extent that such needs were present they could well account for the lack of judgmental differences between Ashkenazi and Sepharadi subjects.

able to ascertain their evaluative ability *via* comparing their grade assignment with that made by a team of experienced teachers evaluating the same composition.

In the *low-evaluation-apprehension* condition the subjects' text indicated that evaluating achievements in humanistic domains is inherently difficult in the absence of clear-cut criteria for what constitutes quality in such domains. It was explained that when it comes to humanistic subjects there are no right or wrong evaluations and that the purpose of the research is not to assess correctness but rather to identify possible individual differences in evaluative style.

Manipulating time pressure. In the *high-pressure* condition the subjects were informed that because of scheduling problems the experiment had to be completed within 10 min. Indeed, at the end of 10 min the experimenter collected the subjects' response sheets and left the room. In the *low-pressure* condition the subjects were informed that they had a full hour at their disposal. In this condition, the experimenter collected the subjects' response sheets at the end of 1 hr from the beginning of the experiment.

The writer's ethnic identity. In one experimental condition (the Ashkenazi condition) the background information about the writer stated that his name was Isaac Blumenthal and that his father's birthplace was Poland. In a second experimental condition (the Sepharadi condition) the writer's name was alleged to be Isaac Abutbull (a typical Moroccan name) and his father's birthplace was Morocco. In a third experimental condition (the ethnically unidentified condition) the writer was only identified by his first name (Isaac) without any information being given about the father's birthplace, etc. To add realism, in all experimental conditions the writer was identified as an 8th grader, a resident of Tel-Aviv, born in 1969, and attending the "Maginim" public school. In fact, the composition was prepared by an 8th-grade Hebrew teacher as an example of what a reasonable composition by an 8th grader might look like.

After the subjects completed the task they were fully debriefed and the experimental manipulations and deceptions were explained to them.

Results

The subjects' grade assignments are summarized in Table 2. Grades assigned to the Sepharadi and

TABLE 24.2. Mean Grade Assignments as Function of Time Pressure, Evaluation Apprehension, and Writer's Ethnic Identity

	Epistemic motivation			
	High evaluation apprehension		Low evaluation apprehension	
Ethnic identity	High time pressure	Low time pressure	High time pressure	Low time pressure
Ashkenazi	−9.58	65.00	81.25	80.00
Sepharadi or unidentified	63.74	63.95	64.37	63.33

*The grades were recorded on a scale ranging from 40 points, representing failure, to 100 points, representing excellent performance.

unidentified writers were remarkably close in all the experimental conditions; they were, therefore, combined and displayed collectively.

As can be seen, the Ashkenazi writer is assigned systematically higher grades than the Sepharadi or the unidentified writers. The main effect for the writer's identity is highly significant ($F(1, 136) = 165.53$; $p < .01$) replicating the strong stereotyping effects reported by Guttman and Bar-Tal (1982).

More interesting from the present vantage are the effects on stereotyping of time pressure and evaluation apprehension indicated by the appropriate two- and three-way interactions. Specifically, the two-way interaction between the time-pressure variable and the writer's identity is statistically significant ($F(1, 136) = 14.78$; $p < .01$). A breakdown of this interaction given in Table 3 indicates that the Ashkenazi writer is assigned a higher grade when the time pressure is high as opposed to low whereas the time-pressure levels seem to have no effects on grades assigned the Sepharadi or unidentified writer. Earlier we noted that stereotypic judgments expressed themselves primarily in higher grade assignments to the Ashkenazi writer. Thus, the high (versus low) time pressure appears to significantly enhance the tendency toward stereotyping judgments just as suggested by the present epistemic analysis.

Furthermore, the two-way interaction between evaluation apprehension and the writer's ethnic identity is statistically significant ($F(1, 136) = 18.25$; $p < .01$). A breakdown of this interaction

given in Table 4 indicates that the grade assigned to the Ashkenazi writer is lower in the high-apprehension condition as compared with the low-apprehension condition, whereas the evaluation-apprehension levels seem to make little difference to grades assigned the Sepharadi or unidentified writer. Thus, the high (versus low) evaluation appears to significantly reduce the stereotyping effect, as predicted by the present epistemic analysis.

Finally, the three-way interaction between time pressure, evaluation-apprehension, and the writer's ethnic identity is statistically significant ($F(1, 136) = 13.97$; $p < .01$). A breakdown of this interaction given in Table 2 indicates that when evaluation apprehension is high, a high-versus-low degree of time pressure results in higher grade assignments to the Ashkenazi writer. Furthermore, the time-pressure levels have no apparent effects on grade assignments to the Sepharadi or the unidentified writer. Indeed, the two-way interaction between time pressure and the writer's identity at the *high evaluation-apprehension level* is statistically significant ($F(4, 132) = 7.03$; $p < .01$). However, at the *low evaluation-apprehension level* the time-pressure levels do not make any appreciable difference to grade assignments regardless of the writer's identity. The appropriate two-way interaction between time pressure and the writer's identity at the low evaluation-apprehension level is far from significant ($F = .005$). Thus, as predicted by the present epistemic analysis time pressure and evaluation apprehension exert an interactive effect

TABLE 24.3. Mean Grade Assignments as Function of Time-Pressure Levels and Writer's Ethnic Identity

	Time pressure	
Ethnic identity	High	Low
Ashkenazi	80.41	72.50
Sepharadi or unidentified	64.06	63.65

TABLE 24.4. Mean Grade Assignments as Function of Evaluation-Apprehension Levels and Writer's Ethnic Identity

	Condition	
	Fear invalidity	
Ethnic identity	High	Low
Ashkenazi	72.29	80.62
Sepharadi or unidentified	63.85	63.85

upon stereotypic judgments; the time-pressure variations have greater effect when the evaluation apprehension is high versus low.

So far, our epistemic analysis of freezing and unfreezing received support in experimental paradigms concerning disparate contents of social judgments: Judgments concerning first impressions of another person and of those concerning the stereotypic evaluation of another person's product. But the present epistemic analysis should generalize to judgments whose contents are not necessarily social. The next experiment in our series was explicitly designed to address this possibility.

Experiment 3: Numerical Anchoring

Tversky and Kahneman (1974) identified the tendency of numerical estimates to be anchored at initial values without being sufficiently adjusted in the light of subsequent calculations. For example such a tendency could lead to the overestimation of the probabilities of conjunctive events and to the underestimation of the probabilities of disjunctive events. A conjunctive event is defined as an intersection of several simple events with given probabilities. For example, consider the drawing (with replacement) of n marbles from an urn containing the proportion q of red marbles. A conjunctive event (x) would be, for example, coming up with a red marble on every single draw. The probability $p(x)$ of such an event can be calculated from the formula $p(x) = q^n$. Insofar as q is a fraction of some size, multiplying it by itself n times yields values which decrease with increase in n. Thus, the subjects are likely to overestimate $p(x)$ to the extent that their judgments are anchored at initial values suggested by the size of q.

While for a conjunctive event to occur the constituent simple events must all take place, for a disjunctive event to occur suffice it if at least one in a series of simple events took place. Returning to our example of n draws from an urn containing the proportion q of red marbles, an exemplary disjunctive event (y) would be coming up at least once out of n draws with a red marble. The probability of such an event is $p(y) = 1-(1-q)^n$. This quantity increases as a function of n. Thus subjects are likely to underestimate $p(y)$ to the extent that they are anchored at initial values suggested by q.

To demonstrate empirically the phenomenon of anchoring Bar-Hillel (1973) asked subjects to choose within pairs of events the one which is more likely to occur. Some pairs contrasted conjunctive events with simple events while other pairs contrasted simple events with disjunctive events. The q's of the constituent conjunctive events were in all cases larger than those of the yoked simple events; however, the final conjunctive probabilities were invariably smaller then those of the yoked simple events. The initial probabilities of the disjunctive events were in all cases smaller than those of the yoked simple events, yet the final disjunctive probabilities were in all cases larger. Under these circumstances Bar-Hillel (1973) was able to obtain impressive support for the anchoring phenomenon. As predicted, the subjects tended to significantly overestimate the probabilities of conjunctive events and to underestimate those of disjunctive events.

According to the present analysis, the anchoring phenomenon can be viewed as an instance of epistemic freezing in which the subjects' epistemic activities are frozen after an initial estimate is generated and slightly adjusted. Beyond this point subjects may refrain from *attending* to further relevant evidence and from revising their judgments in light of such evidence. If our analysis is correct the anchoring phenomenon should be more pronounced under a high-versus-low time pressure and under a low-versus-high evaluation apprehension. Furthermore, according to the logic explicated earlier the time-pressure variations should have greater impact upon anchoring when the evaluation apprehension is high rather than low.

Method

SUBJECTS AND EXPERIMENTAL DESIGN

One hundred and twenty high school students (male and female) from the Tel-Aviv area participated as subjects. They were all in their final year of high school (the 12th grade) and had had a degree of exposure to elementary probability theory. Sixty subjects participated in each of two separate subexperiments. In one subexperiment the subjects chose between simple and conjunctive events and in the second subexperiment, between simple and disjunctive events. The specific event pairs included each of the two subexperiments that were adopted from Bar-Hillel (1973) and are given in Table 5.

In each of the subexperiments all subjects re-

TABLE 24.5. Pairs[a] of Compound (Conjunctive or Disjunctive) and Simple Events in Two Subexperiments

	Subexperiment			
	1		2	
Event pair	Conjunctive event	Simple event	Disjunctive event	Simple event
1	$.7^2 = .490$	.50	$.1_7 = .522$	.50
2	$.9^9 = .387$	.40	$.2_6 = .738$	.70
3	$.6^2 = .360$	.40	$.3_4 = .832$	.80
4	$.8^7 = .210$	.25	$.4_5 = .922$	.90
5	$.5^4 = .062$	.10	$.1_9 = .613$	.60
6	$.9^2 = .478$	.50	$.2_8 = .832$	.80
7	$.5^2 = .250$	.30	$.3_2 = .918$	.90
8	$.75^6 = .178$	.20	$.5_4 = .938$	.90

[a] Adopted from Bar-Hillel (1973).

sponded to all event pairs. Also, in each of the experiments the subjects were tested in groups of six to nine persons. Subjects within groups were assigned randomly to the cells of a 2 × 2 factorial design with the independent variables of (1) time pressure (high versus low) and (2) evaluation apprehension (high versus low). All instructions and manipulations were accomplished *via* typewritten text provided to subjects. In all cases the experiment was described as testing a new educational game concerned with betting behavior. Each subject addressed eight pairs of bets and chose in each case the more likely bet in the pair.

Manipulating evaluation apprehension. Subjects in the *high-evaluation-apprehension* condition were informed that all pairs of bets were taken from an exam in advanced statistics. The subjects were told that after they make their choices the experimenter will write the right answers on the blackboard and each subject will be asked to state how many correct choices he/she made. It was explained to subjects that in this way they would be able to evaluate their personal level in statistics relative to the other members of the group. In the *low-evaluation-apprehension* condition the subjects were informed that because of a time shortage the researchers will not be able to check on the correctness of each subject's answers. It was further stated that the researchers are interested in group averages rather than in individual achievements.

Manipulating time pressure. In the *high-time-pressure* condition it was explained to subjects that in the betting game under study, the time element is of the essence. Correspondingly, the subjects were informed that they had at their disposal 3 min to complete their choices. In the *low-time-*

pressure condition the subjects were told that they have unlimited time to complete their task.

Following these manipulations each subject responded to eight pairs of bets in an order individually randomized for each respondent. After having done so the subjects were debriefed and the various deceptions used were fully revealed.

Results

Subjects' choices in the various experimental conditions are summarized in Tables 6 and 7.

As can be seen in Table 6 the proportions of the choosing conjunctive over simple events, indicative of the anchoring effect, are higher in the *high-* versus-*low* time-pressure condition. The corresponding main effect is significant statistically ($F(1, 56) = 8.15$); $p < .01$. Furthermore the proportions of conjunctive (versus simple) choices are *lower* in the *high-*versus-*low* evaluation apprehension conditions (main effect of fear invalidity, $F(1, 56) = 16.57$; $p < .01$). Finally, the time-pressure variations exert a greater effect on choosing conjunctive-versus-simple events under high-versus-low evaluation-apprehension (interaction of time pressure and evaluation apprehension, $F(1, 56) = 7.84$; $p < .01$). Highly similar effects appear in Table 7 where anchoring effects are indexed by

TABLE 24.6. Proportions of Choosing Conjunctive over Simple Events in Subexperiment 1

	Evaluation apprehension	
Time pressure	High	Low
High	.525	.575
Low	.325	.566

TABLE 24.7. Proportions of Choosing Simple over Disjunctive Events in Subexperiment 2

Time pressure	Evaluation apprehension	
	High	Low
High	.516	.541
Low	.316	.508

the proportions of choosing simple over disjunctive events. Those proportions are higher under high-versus-low *time pressure* (main effect of time pressure, $F(1, 56) = 8.86$; $p < .01$) and are lower under high-versus-low evaluation–apprehension (main effect of evaluation apprehension, $F(1, 56) = 7.56$; $p < .01$). Furthermore, the time-pressure variations have greater effect on choosing simple over disjunctive events when the evaluation apprehension is high versus low (interaction of time pressure × evaluation apprehension, $F(1, 56) = 4.47$; $p < .05$).

General Discussion

As predicted by our epistemic analysis, primacy effects in impression formation, stereotypic evaluations, and numerical anchorages were all more pronounced when the degree of evaluation apprehension was high versus low. Furthermore, the time-pressure and evaluation-apprehension variables interacted as expected in all of our experiments such that time pressure had greater impact on all of the presently studied phenomena when the evaluation apprehension was high versus low.

The above results are consistent with the idea that primacy effects, stereotypic judgments, and numerical anchorages all represent "epistemic freezing;" in particular, each of these phenomena seemed to be affected in the same way by factors theoretically relevant to "freezing," notably by the need for structure presently manipulated *via* degrees of time pressure and by the fear of invalidity presently manipulated *via* evaluation apprehension.

Process Similarities

The present data suggest that several phenomena that might seem as quite disparate and unrelated share important underlying commonalities. Take, for example, numerical anchoring investigated in

our third experiment. At first glance, this phenomenon may seem quite remote from primacy effects and stereotyping investigated in our first and second experiments. Furthermore, the observed effects of time pressure and evaluation apprehension on anchoring might seem quite different in kind from the effect on primacy and stereotyping phenomena: It seems intuitively plausible that under time pressure and/or when being right is not very important subjects would be unable and/or unmotivated to perform the calculations required for getting the right answer. This explanation readily accounts for the effects of our variables on anchoring, but can it also apply to primacy and stereotyping effects?

According to the epistemic analysis in all our studies the experimental tasks required the performance of various deductive operations on externally provided information. Time pressure was expected to inhibit, and evaluation apprehension to enhance, the process of attending to the information and/or deducing from it various implications relevant to the requisite judgments. What differed between our experiments were the *contents* of the specific deductions to be performed. In the impression-formation task of study 1 the relevant deductions had to do with the subjects' concept of "job-success" deducible as it may be from various items of information about the target person. In the product-evaluation task of study 2, subjects deduced the excellence of literary performance from various aspects of the target person's composition and, in the numerical-estimate task of study 3, subjects deduced (or calculated) a given quantity from numerical information relevant to that particular quantity. Now undoubtedly there exist many differences separating the numerical deductions of study 3 from the social ("success") or aesthetic ("literary excellence") deductions of studies 1 and 2. For instance, numerical deductions seem more objective or at least consensual (*any* educated person knows that $4 \times 4 = 16$, etc.) than social or aesthetic deductions, the latter being typically determined by reference to more subjective criteria. But from the present standpoint such differences have to do with the *contents* of judgments (numerical-versus-social or aesthetic) rather than with the judgmental process which as our data suggest, may be invariant across judgmental contents.

While quite encouraging, the present results may not be considered as conclusive evidence for the hypothesized effects on epistemic freezing of the needs for structure and the avoidance of invalidity. A major difficulty is that in all our three studies the specific manipulations of the relevant epistemic variables were highly similar. In particular, the need for structure was invariably manipulated *via* time pressure and the fear of invalidity, *via* evaluation apprehension aroused by the implied loss of face in case of a judgmental mistake. Further research is thus needed to demonstrate that alternative operationalizations of the same epistemic motivations would produce the same effects. For example, need for structure could be heightened by means of instructions stressing the value of clear-cut, unambiguous judgments. Similarly, need for structure could be lowered by means of instructions stressing the value of complexity and differentiation and/or disparaging oversimplification or overgeneralization. Furthermore, while in the present studies the fear of invalidity was manipulated *via* engaging the subjects' need for self-esteem, the same fear could be aroused by linking judgmental mistakes with threats to alternative needs, say economic needs, physical safety needs, etc.

Mediating Mechanisms of Motivational Effects

1. THE DISCOUNTING PHENOMENON

The present experimental findings are open to a number of interpretations that, on first glance at least, might appear to differ from our epistemic analysis. Specifically, Anderson and Jacobson (1965) showed that sometimes primacy effects may occur because of the tendency to discount later information inconsistent with an early information. It is thus possible that under a high degree of time pressure the tendency to discount later information is augmented resulting in the pronounced freezing observed in the high (versus low) time-pressure conditions of the present research. In order to see more precisely how the above interpretation relates to the epistemic analysis let us consider more closely Anderson's and Jacobson's notion of discounting.

First, as already noted, discounting is assumed to occur when different items of information are inconsistent with one another. Furthermore, Anderson and Jacobson hypothesized and found that in informational triads in which two items were con-

sistent with each other and were both inconsistent with a third item, it was the latter item which tended to be discounted. Finally, Anderson and Jacobson found that the discounting effect was augmented when subjects were led to believe that some of the informational items were implied to be (1) of a dubious validity or (2) inapplicable to the judgment being rendered.

It is noteworthy that all the above features of "discounting" are highly compatible with our epistemic theory, and in particular with its assumptions that (1) inconsistency is resolved *via* denying (or discounting) one of the inconsistent cognitions and that (2) denial is likely to be directed at the apparently less credible of the contradictory cognitions. For instance if two informational items are mutually consistent they cross-validate each other rendering the third inconsistent item less apparently credible and, hence, more likely to be discounted or denied. This tendency may well be augmented when some of the items are a priori known to be less valid than others. Furthermore, our lay epistemic analysis assumes that only information perceived as relevant or applicable would be considered when making a judgment. Implying (as did Anderson & Jacobson, 1965) that a given item of information is not relevant or applicable understandably reduces the tendency to take the item into account.

Finally, the lay-epistemic theory suggests that a heightened need for structure would enhance the tendency to resolve an inconsistency (preventing the attainment of structure). Thus, a heightened need for structure could well enhance the tendency to deny (discount) the inconsistent items of information in particular if they are considered as less valid than their opposing counterparts.

In short, the epistemic analysis is fully compatible with previous theory and findings concerning the discounting phenomenon (cf. Anderson & Jacobson, 1965). It also suggests that "discounting" may be particularly likely to occur under a heightened need for structure manipulated, for example, *via* a high degree of time pressure but also *via* other possible means.

2. ATTENTIONAL INCREMENTS

Anderson (1976) theorized that primacy effects may occur because of attentional decrements to successive items of information. In line with this analysis Anderson (1976) reported that primacy effects were eliminated in conditions where subjects were instructed to attend to all the informational items including those presented late in the series. Similar attentional increments could well be present in the high-apprehension conditions of our research and, underlying, the unfreezing effects observed in these conditions. In this sense, an "attentional increment" explanation is not incompatible with our "fear of invalidity" explanation. Rather, attentional increments could *mediate* fear-invalidity effects upon judgments. It is also well to note that according to the present analysis attentional increments *as such* are insufficient for a judgmental unfreezing to occur: Unfreezing is assumed to occur *providing* the attentional increments are aimed at improving the validity of one's judgments. Without such a guiding concern, attention might well be directed at irrelevant aspects of the information. Alternatively, new information could be attended to in an isolated fashion without it being brought to bear on previously formulated judgments. The above discussion suggests the need to refine the lay epistemic theory and to more specifically characterize the mediating mechanisms whereby the various epistemic motivations may exert their effects upon judgments.

Unfreezing Versus Rectifying

A simple interpretation of the present findings may depart from the assumption that the freezing of inferences represents a source of error; therefore factors like a lack of time pressure or a perceived importance of judgmental accuracy may be exerting a *rectifying* influence, and reduce the tendency to err. Such an interpretation is strongly at variance with our epistemic analysis of freezing and unfreezing. More specifically, we do not posit a systematic relation between the freezing or unfreezing of judgments on the one hand and judgmental accuracy on the other hand. According to our analysis, one's initial impressions could occasionally be "correct" in some sense, whereas further information that one might encounter could be of dubious "validity." In such circumstances, of course, stubbornly freezing on an initial judgment might result in a more correct inference than unfreezing and modifying the judgment in the light of incoming information. In short, allowing one ample time to complete a judgmental task and/or imploring one to be accurate need not improve the validity of inferences and might occasionally detract from inferential validity (for the details of this argument see Kruglanski & Ajzen, 1983).

Epistemic Analysis of Belief Perseverance

The foregoing discussion addresses some of the difficulties and alternative interpretations encountered by the present epistemic analysis of freezing and unfreezing. Without belittling the need for further research probing the validity of those competing alternatives it is well to point out that the epistemic analysis seems capable of ordering several previous findings on the phenomenon of "belief perseverance," viewed here as another instance of epistemic freezing. An individual is said to persevere with a belief when (s)he continues to subscribe to it despite discrediting evidence concerning the belief in question. For example, in research by Ross, Lepper, Strack, and Steinmetz (1977), the subjects' tendency to persevere with their beliefs about certain fictitious events was strengthened by instructions to provide causal explanations for those events. This could reflect a need for structure heightened by a requirement to *explain* the events, that is, imbed them in specific causal structures. Fleming and Arrowood (1979) also found an increase in perseverance under instructions to causally explain a given event: they further found a decrease in perseverance where subjects were distracted from thinking about the event, a condition which may well have reduced their need for structure concerning the event.

In an experiment by Lord, Ross, and Lepper (1977) subjects regarded as more reliable studies supporting their own position as compared to opposing studies. This could reflect the working of a conclusional need having to do with the subject's self-esteem. To the extent that the subject's self-esteem in the experimental situation hinged on being right they might find it pleasing to have their opinions confirmed and displeasing to have them disconfirmed. This could dispose the subjects to generate alternatives to the disconfirmatory conclusions and refrain from generating alternatives to the confirmatory conclusions. Finally, in the study by Ross, Lepper, and Hubbard (1975) belief perseverance was completely eliminated in a "process-debriefing" condition in which the subjects were specifically forewarned about perseverance and alerted to its possible dangers. This condition might well have heightened the subjects' fear of invalidity thus having sharpened their sensitivity to the debriefing information inconsistent with the original beliefs.

The present epistemic analysis ramifies to numerous additional topics in social cognition. In these closing paragraphs we should like to briefly mention a few. Consider, for example, Snyder's recent research on the confirmatory bias in hypothesis testing (cf. Snyder & Swann, 1978; Snyder & Gangestad, in press). In the experimental situations created by Snyder and his colleagues subjects were generally more sensitive to confirmatory evidence for a given hypothesis than to disconfirmatory evidence. But it seems appropriate to ask about the conditions under which confirmatory-versus-disconfirmatory evidence would be preferred as opposed to conditions under which the reverse might occur. For example, the present epistemic analysis suggests that subjects might be particularly sensitive to disconfirmatory evidence when their fear of invalidity is aroused or when the hypothesis being tested is highly incongruous with their wishes and desires. By contrast, subjects might be particularly insensitive to disconfirmatory evidence when their need for structure is high or when the hypothesis being tested is highly pleasing.

Alternatively, consider the topic of group problem solving (cf. Davis, 1969). It seems plausible to speculate that in the early phase of group problem solving validity concerns might be particularly salient for the group members. Under those circumstances, group members might welcome divergent ideas inconsistent with the group consensus. But in a late phase of group problem solving, as the time to reach a decision draws near, structure needs may become more dominant. Under these conditions the group may be less tolerant of divergent proposals controverting the emergent consensus.

Finally, consider the situation of the policy maker, say in government or business, as opposed to the outside consultant or advisor. To the extent that a great deal of decision making and action hinges on the established policies, the policy maker is likely to experience a high need for guiding structure. This might dispose the policy maker toward conservatism and close-mindedness to information inconsistent with the policy assumptions. By comparison, the outside advisor might have a relatively greater concern for the issue of validity and be more disposed to modify existing policies

in the light of new information. Such divergent perspectives could promote ample conflict and misunderstanding between policy makers and consultants. Taking into account the differences in epistemic motivation could furnish one avenue of dealing with these differences and possibly contribute to a bridging of the gaps involved.

Suggestions in the last few paragraphs are admittedly speculative and in need of extensive empirical probing for their validation. They do, however, illustrate the heuristic potential of the epistemic analysis and the range of social psychological problems to which it may apply.

ACKNOWLEDGMENTS

This paper was written while the first author was on a sabbatical leave from Tel-Aviv University and Fellow of the Social Science and Humanities Research Council of Canada at the University of Waterloo, Ontario. The work reported herein constituted research toward a master's degree conducted by the second author under the guidance of the first author.

REFERENCES

Anderson, N. H. Integration theory, functional measurement and the psychophysical law. In H. G. Geissler & Y. M. Zabrodin (Eds.), *Advances in psychophysics*, Berlin VEB Deutscher der Wissenschaften, 1976.

Anderson, N. H., & Jacobson, A. Effects of stimulus inconsistency and discounting instructions in personality impression formation. *Journal of Personality and Social Psychology*, 1965, *2*, 531–539.

Asch, S. E. Forming impressions of personality. *Journal of Abnormal and Social Psychology*, 1946, *41*, 258–290.

Bar-Hillel, M. On the subjective probability of compound events. *Organizational Behavior and Human Performance*, 1973, *9*, 396–406.

Davis, J. H. *Group performance*. Reading, Mass.: Addison-Wesley, 1969.

Fleming, J., & Arrowood, A. J. Information processing and the perseverence of discredited self-perceptions. *Personality and Social Psychology Bulletin*, 1979, *5*, 201–205.

Frenkel-Brunswick, E. Intolerance of ambiguity as emotional and perceptual personality variable. *Journal of Personality*, 1949, *18*, 108–143.

Guttman, J., & Bar-Tal, D. Stereotypic perceptions of teachers. *American Educational Research Journal*. 1982, *19*, 519–528.

Hamilton, D. L. A cognitive attribution analysis of stereotyping. In L. Berkowitz (Ed.), *Advances in experimental social psychology* (Vol. 12). New York: Academic Press, 1979.

Kruglanski, A. W. Lay epistemologic process and contents: Another look at attribution theory. *Psychological Review*, 1980, *87*, 70–87.

Kruglanski, A. W. The epistemic approach in cognitive therapy. *The International Journal of Psychology*, 1981, *16*, 275–297.

Kruglanski, A. W., & Ajzen, I. Bias and error in human judgment. *European Journal of Social Psychology*, 1983, *13*, 1–44.

Kruglanski, A. W., & Jaffe, Y. Lay epistemology: A theory for cognitive therapy. In L. Abramson (Ed.), *Social-personality inference in clinical psychology*. New York: Guilford Press, in press.

Lord, Ch. G., Ross, L., & Lepper, M. R. Biased assimilation and attitude polarization. The effects of prior theories on subsequently considered evidence. *Journal of Personality and Social Psychology*, 1977 *35*, 817–829.

Luchins, A. S. Experimental attempts to minimize the impact of first impressions. In C. E. Hovland (Ed.), *The order of presentation in persuasion*. New Haven, CT: Yale Univ. Press, 1957.

Ross, L., Lepper, M. R., & Hubbard, M. Perseverance in self-perception and social perception: Biased attributional process in the debriefing paradigm. *Journal of Personality and Social Psychology*, 1975, *32*, 880–892.

Ross, L., Lepper, M. R., Strack, F., & Steinmetz, J. Social explanation and social expectation. Effects of real and hypothetical explanations on subjective likelihood. *Journal of Personality and Social Psychology*, 1977, *35*, 817–829.

Smock, C. D. The influence of psychological stress on the "intolerance of ambiguity." *Journal of Abnormal and Social Psychology*, 1955, *50*, 177–182.

Snyder, M., & Gangestad, S. Hypothesis-testing processes. In J. H. Harvey, W. J. Ickes, & R. F. Kidd (Eds.), *New directions in attribution research* (Vol. 3). Hillsdale, NJ: Erlbaum, 1981.

Snyder, M., & Swann, W. B., Jr. Hypothesis-testing processes in social interaction. *Journal of Personality and Social Psychology*, 1978, *36*, 1202–1212.

Taylor, S. E., & Fiske, S. T. Salience, attention and attribution: Top of the head phenomena. In L. Berkowitz (Ed.), *Advances in experimental social psychology* (Vol. 11). New York: Academic Press, 1978.

Tolman. E. C. Cognitive maps in rats and man. *Psychological Review*, 1948, *55*, 189–208.

Tversky, A., & Kahneman, D. Judgment under uncertainty. Heuristics and biases. *Science*, 1974, *185*, 1124–1131.

Zuckerman, M. Attribution of success and failure revisited, or: The motivational bias is alive and well in attribution theory. *Journal of Personality*, 1979, *47*, 245–287.

REFERENCE NOTE

1. Kruglanski, A. W., & Klar, I. *A view from a bridge: Synthesizing the consistence and attribution paradigms from a lay epistemic perspective*. Unpublished manuscript, Tel-Aviv University, 1982.

The Interpersonal System

The selections thus far have addressed the intrapersonal level of social-psychological analysis. They depict how individuals think, act, and feel as they strive to understand the social world and self-regulate toward their various goals. But the central characteristic of our social nature is that we interact with others. Hence, the interpersonal level of analysis is crucial to our understanding of social psychology. The following set of selections represents, therefore, some major lines of work on ways in which people interact with one another. Such interaction begins very early and is related to the relations that develop between children and their adult caretakers. Our first two interpersonal selections address such relations from the point of view of attachment theory. Thus, the article by Griffin and Bartholomew (1994) reports work on the dimensions of adult attachment as they have evolved from early child-caretaker interactions, and Hazan and Shaver (1990) analyze how one's typical attachment style may imbue one's attitudes toward work. The way human outcomes are interdependent, and the impact this has on our social conduct, have been a major topic of interest to students of interpersonal phenomena. In the present volume it is represented in the selection by Van Lange, De Bruin, Otten, and Joireman (1997), which deals with different individual orientations to interdependence. The importance of social support is discussed in the article by Stroebe, Stroebe, Abakoumkin, and Schut (1996). The opposite issue, namely, that of interpersonal conflict, is addressed in the selection by Murray and Holmes (1993). Interpersonal communication is treated from very different perspectives in the articles by Krauss and Vivekananthan and Weinheimer (1968), Higgins (1992), and Semin and Fiedler (1988). The topic of persuasion, a major interpersonal concern, is addressed in selections by Chaiken (1980), Petty, Cacioppo, and Goldman (1981), and Kruglanski and Thompson (1999). Taken as a body, these selections provide a broad outline of the kind of issues that theory and research on the interpersonal system of social-psychological phenomena has addressed.

Models of the Self and Other: Fundamental Dimensions Underlying Measures of Adult Attachment

Dale Griffin • University of Waterloo, Canada
Kim Bartholomew • Simon Fraser University, Canada

Editors' Notes

The next two selections concern a major aspect of social development—a person's attachment to significant others. Griffin and Bartholomew conceptualize attachment in terms of two dimensions having to do with how positively (or negatively) one feels about one's own self and how positively (or negatively) one feels about generalized others. Based on a model that incorporates these two dimensions, the investigators proceed to test it psychometrically and in terms of its predicted outcome variables. Many of the previous selections in this book dealt with situationally induced, hence relatively transient, phenomena. In contrast, the present selection addresses broad personality styles having profound implications for how we feel about others and how we tend to interact with them. Note also that the methods employed in the present research are rather different than those we have seen in the previous selections. Specifically, this research utilizes questionnaire data and such psychometric techniques as confirmatory factor analysis and linear equation modeling. Despite these methodological differences, the gist of the methodological intent is the same as in the previous selections. It has the objective of validating one's concepts as against potential alternative interpretations of one's data. It is for that reason that several measurement variables are constructed to measure each latent variable, and a multitrait, multimethod strategy is employed by the investigators. In these ways, the present selection is valuable and instructive on both substantive and methodological levels.

Discussion Questions

1. What are the four attachment patterns identified by Bartholomew?
2. What is the contribution of this particular paper over and above Bartholomew's prior work?
3. What are the methodological advantages and contributions of the present research beyond previous work on adult attachment?

Suggested Readings

Andersen, S. M., Reznik, I., & Manzella, L. M. (1996). Eliciting facial affect, motivation, and expectancies in transference: Significant-other representations in social relations. *Journal of Personality and Social Psychology, 71,* 1108–1129.

Baldwin, M. W., & Holmes, J. G. (1987). Salient private audiences and awareness of the self. *Journal of Personality and Social Psychology, 52,* 1087–1098.

Moretti, M. M., & Higgins, E. T. (1999). Internal representations of others in self-regulation: A new look at a classic issue. *Social Cognition, 17,* 186–208.

Authors' Abstract

Three studies assessed the construct validity of the self- and other-model dimensions underlying the 4-category model of adult attachment (Bartholomew, 1990). Five methods were used to assess the hypothesized dimensions: self-reports, friend-reports, romantic partner reports, trained judges' ratings of peer attachment, and trained judges' ratings of family attachment. In each study, the convergent and discriminant validity of the dimensions were assessed by multitrait-multimethod matrices and by confirmatory factor analysis. Study 2 related the latent attachment dimensions to theoretically relevant outcome latent variables. As predicted, individuals' self models converged with direct measures of the positivity of their self-concepts, and individuals' other models converged with direct measures of the positivity of their interpersonal orientations. Study 3 related the latent attachment dimensions to 3 alternate self-report measures of adult attachment and showed that the 2 dimensions serve as an organizing framework for the different measurement approaches.

Attachment theory, as developed by John Bowlby (1973, 1980, 1982), conceptualizes the universal human need to form close affectional bonds. It serves both as a normative theory of how the in-born "attachment system" functions in all humans and as an individual-difference theory of the attachment strategies that are adopted in response to different life experiences (Hazan & Shaver, 1994). Since Hazan and Shaver (1987) introduced their three-category measure of adult attachment as an adult analog to Mary Ainsworth's classification of infants (Ainsworth, Blehar, Waters, & Wall, 1978), research on adult attachment has been focused almost exclusively on the correlates of individual differences in attachment (for an exception, see Hazan & Hutt, 1991). This has been a fruitful endeavor, as different attachment strategies have been related to (among other things) jealousy, parental drinking, well-being, relationship satisfaction, support seeking, self-disclosure, and religiosity (see Shaver & Hazan, 1993, for a comprehensive review).

Despite this impressive evidence for the predictive validity of attachment strategies in general, there has been little attention paid to basic measurement issues. Attachment patterns or strategies have variously been assessed by three-category and four-category interview procedures (e.g., Bartholomew & Horowitz, 1991; Main, Kaplan, & Cassidy, 1985), three-category and four-category self-report measures (Bartholomew & Horowitz, 1991; Hazan & Shaver, 1987), and multi-item scales that form either two (Simpson, Rholes, & Nelligan, 1992) or three (Collins &

Read, 1990) empirically derived factors. However, adult attachment research has lacked an integrated approach to measurement.

In this article, we take a theory-based or top-down look at the measurement of adult attachment. First, we briefly review one measurement model (Bartholomew, 1990; Bartholomew & Horowitz, 1991) that is derived directly from Bowlby's theoretical propositions. This two-dimensional model of adult attachment provides a promising framework for organizing the work of a variety of investigators. In the first two empirical sections, we assess the construct validity of this two-dimensional model. In the third and final section, we relate this model to three alternate measures of adult attachment and show that it serves to integrate much of the empirical work currently carried on in this area.

A Two-Dimensional Model of Adult Attachment

Bowlby proposed that the quality of childhood relationships with caregivers results in internal representations or "working models" of the self and others that provide the prototypes for later social relations (Bowlby, 1973, 1980, 1982). Building on the initial work applying an attachment perspective to adults (e.g., Hazan & Shaver, 1987; Main et al., 1985), Bartholomew has systematized Bowlby's definition of internal working models in a four-category classification of adult attachment (Bartholomew, 1990). Four prototypic attachment patterns are defined in terms of the intersection of two underlying dimensions—the positivity of a person's model of the self and the positivity of a person's model of hypothetical others. The positivity of the self model indicates the degree to which individuals have internalized a sense of their own self-worth and therefore expect others to respond to them positively; thus, the self model is associated with the degree of anxiety and dependency experienced in close relationships. The positivity of the other model indicates the degree to which others are generally expected to be available and supportive; thus, the other model is associated with the tendency to seek out or avoid closeness in relationships.

The self and other models represent general expectations about the worthiness of the self and the availability of others; in contrast, the four at-

tachment patterns are conceptualized as prototypic strategies for regulating felt security in close relationships. This conceptualization departs from earlier work by differentiating two patterns marked by a hesitancy to become intimate with others: a fearful pattern defined by a negative self and other model (high anxiety and high avoidance) and a dismissing pattern defined by a positive self model and negative other model (low anxiety and high avoidance). In contrast, the secure pattern is defined by positive self and other models (low anxiety and low avoidance) and the preoccupied pattern by negative self and positive other models (high anxiety and low avoidance). The four patterns and their relation to the underlying dimensions are illustrated in Figure 1. Each of these patterns is characterized by a distinct pattern of emotional regulation and interpersonal behavior. Fearful individuals are highly dependent on others for the validation of their self-worth; however, because of their negative expectations of others, they shun intimacy to avoid the pain of potential loss or rejection. Dismissing individuals also avoid closeness with others because of negative expectations; however, they maintain their high sense of self-worth by defensively denying the value of close relationships and stressing the importance of independence. Preoccupied individuals, like fearful individuals, have a deep-seated sense of unworthiness. However, their positive other model motivates them to validate their precarious self-worth through excessive closeness in personal relationships, leaving them vulnerable to extreme distress when their intimacy needs are not met. Finally, secure individuals are characterized both by an internalized sense of self-worth and comfort with intimacy in close relationships. See

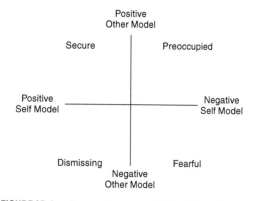

FIGURE 25.1 ■ Four-category model of adult attachment.

Bartholomew (1990) for discussion of the hypothesized developmental antecedents of the four patterns.

Previous work has demonstrated the utility of the four attachment categories in organizing and understanding individual differences in self-concept and interpersonal functioning (Bartholomew & Horowitz, 1991). However, the construct validity of the two dimensions hypothesized to underlie the four attachment patterns has not been examined explicitly. Can the two general models associated with the attachment patterns be reliably measured? Do the models of self and other derived from attachment measures correspond to more direct measures of an individual's self-evaluation and motivation to seek out others? Finally, how do these dimensions relate to other approaches to assessing adult attachment?

There is a growing body of evidence that two dimensions underlie adult attachment patterns and that these two dimensions are consistent with the dimensions proposed by the four-category model (for a review, see Shaver & Hazan, 1993). Some researchers have obtained attachment dimensions that appear to correspond directly to the self and other dimensions (e.g., Simpson et al.'s, 1992, avoidance and anxiety dimensions and Collins & Read's, 1990, comfort with closeness and anxiety dimensions). Other researchers have obtained dimensions that appear to correspond to the diagonals of the four-category model, that is, a 45° rotation from the self and other model dimensions (e.g., Brennan, Shaver, & Tobey's, 1991, secure vs. avoidant and high vs. low anxious-ambivalent dimensions, and Kobak's secure vs. insecure and dismissing vs. preoccupied dimensions; Kobak, Cole, Ferenz-Gillies, Fleming, & Gamble, 1991).

The purpose of this article is to validate the two dimensions underlying the four-category model and thereby to provide an underlying theoretical framework for the field of adult attachment. In contrast to exploratory work in this area that has been based on the descriptive use of correlational and factor-analytic methods, we take a confirmatory approach to construct validation. In particular, we use confirmatory factor analysis (CFA) and structural equation modeling to establish that the hypothesized underlying dimensions can be measured reliably and that they do validly represent the constructs of self and other models. Previous studies have either relied on a single method of assessing adult attachment (e.g., Hazan & Shaver, 1987; Kobak & Hazan, 1991), or, where multiple measures of adult attachment have been included (e.g., Bartholomew & Horowitz, 1991; Brennan et al., 1991), there has been no attempt to model underlying latent variables. In the present studies, we use a latent variable modeling approach that relies on multiple measures of each construct, including self-reports, friend reports, romantic partner reports, and trained judges' ratings.

Overview of the Studies

In each of three studies, the two dimensions hypothesized to underlie adult attachment were assessed by three different methods. In each study, we constructed a multitrait-multimethod matrix to examine the convergent and discriminant validity of the self-model dimension and other-model dimension. Each study also included a CFA to formally test the fit of the attachment measurement model. To assess the construct validity of the self- and other-model dimensions, Study 2 related the latent dimensions to theoretically relevant outcome latent variables (positivity of self-concept and interpersonal orientation). Study 3 related the latent attachment dimensions to three alternate self-report measures of adult attachment.

Study 1

This study presents a reanalysis of data originally presented in Study 2 of Bartholomew and Horowitz (1991). The attachment patterns of university students were assessed by three methods: self-reports, interviews on peer relationships, and interviews on family relationships. For each of the methods, two dimensions were derived from ratings of the four attachment patterns. A multitrait-multimethod matrix was constructed to examine the convergent and discriminant validity of the two dimensions. We hypothesized that correlations between different methods of measuring the same dimension would correlate more highly (convergent validity) than correlations between the same method of measuring different dimensions (discriminant validity). A CFA was performed to demonstrate that a two-dimensional structure was an appropriate representation of the observed correlations.

Method

PROCEDURE

Subjects were 69 undergraduate students (mean age 19.5 years) who participated for course credit. In a first session, subjects participated in two half-hour interviews (the Family Attachment Interview and the Peer Attachment Interview), both of which were audiotaped. One to two weeks later, subjects rated their own attachment patterns using the Relationship Questionnaire (RQ).

Family Attachment Interview (Bartholomew & Horowitz, 1991). The Family Attachment Interview is a semistructured interview exploring subjects' memories and evaluations of their experiences growing up in their families of origin. Participants are asked to describe their relationships with each parent, in particular their experiences of acceptance or rejection, to recount their experiences of separation and loss in childhood, to interpret their parents' behaviors and intentions, and to explain how their family experiences have shaped their adult personality. Two independent raters coded each interview for the individual's fit with each of the four attachment prototypes, and the final attachment ratings consisted of the mean of the two ratings for each of the four patterns (alphas ranged from .75 to .86).

Peer Attachment Interview (Bartholomew & Horowitz, 1991). The Peer Attachment Interview is a semistructured interview exploring subjects' past and present close friendships and romantic relationships. Participants are asked to describe the quality of their relationships, in particular their experiences of acceptance and rejection, their experiences of gaining and giving support, their responses to conflict and the threat of separation, and their expectations for the future. Two independent raters coded each interview in a manner parallel to that of the Family Interview (alphas ranged from .74 to .88).

Relationship Questionnaire. The RQ (Bartholomew & Horowitz, 1991) is made up of four short paragraphs, each describing a prototypical attachment pattern as it applies to close relationships in general. Participants are asked to rate their degree of correspondence to each prototype on a 7-point scale. For example, the dismissing prototype reads as follows "I am comfortable without close relationships. It is very important to me to feel independent and self-sufficient, and I pre-fer not to depend on others or have others depend on me."

For each of the three methods of measurement, two attachment dimensions were derived from the four pattern ratings. The self-model dimension was obtained by summing the ratings of the two attachment patterns with positive self models (secure and dismissing) and subtracting the ratings of the two patterns with negative self models (preoccupied and fearful). The other-model dimension rating was obtained by summing the ratings of the two attachment patterns with positive other models (secure and preoccupied) and subtracting the ratings of the two patterns with negative other models (dismissing and fearful).[1]

DATA ANALYSIS

Pearson product-moment correlations were computed among the six derived dimension variables (self-report, peer interview, and family interview ratings for self-model and other-model dimensions) and submitted to a CFA using the EzPATH program (Steiger, 1989). In addition to the standard maximum likelihood estimation procedures and statistical tests available on other structural equation modeling programs (e.g., LISREL, Jöreskog & Sörbom, 1986), EzPATH provides additional goodness of fit indices as well as confidence intervals for these statistics. Such confidence intervals are useful for assessing the fit of a hypothesized model when sample sizes are relatively small.

In cases of small sizes, the chi-square goodness of fit test has limited power to detect a poorly fitting model. Therefore, it is important to examine additional sample indices that are either independent of sample size or take the sample size into consideration. One commonly used index is the Jöreskog-Sörbom Adjusted Goodness of Fit Index (AGFI). Two additional indices recommended by Steiger (1989) are the Steiger-Lind Adjusted Root Mean Square Index (R*) and the Adjusted Population Gamma Index (T2). Values of the Steiger-

---

[1]To control for differential variances of the four ratings, we also computed dimension scores based on standardized attachment ratings (cf. Simpson, 1990). In addition, to control for individual differences in scale use, we computed dimension scores based on ipsatized attachment ratings (Cronbach, 1949). Because none of these "correction factors" had an appreciable effect on the results, we have chosen to present the results using the simpler unit-weighting procedure.

Lind Adjusted Root Mean Square Index less than .10 indicate a good fit and values less than .05 indicate an excellent fit. The Adjusted Population Gamma Index is a coefficient of model determination, adjusted for model complexity. Values of the Adjusted Population Gamma Index above .90 indicate a good fit, and values above .95 indicate an excellent fit. Confidence intervals around these indices provide an estimate of the power of the analysis to test the hypothesized model. Narrow confidence intervals indicate high precision of the goodness of fit estimates.

Results and Discussion

Table 1 presents a multitrait-multimethod matrix (Campbell & Fiske, 1959) for the six derived attachment variables. Inspection of the matrix reveals clear evidence of both convergent and discriminant validity. Convergent validity is demonstrated by the moderately high correlations within each attachment dimension across methods (the correlations within triangles). Discriminant validity is indicated by the relatively small correlations between attachment dimensions within methods (the circled correlations). The average within-dimension correlation was .43, whereas the average within-method correlation was −.09. (Note, here and elsewhere in the article, averages were computed on Fisher z-transformed correlations, and these averages were then transformed back to the raw correlation scale.)

A CFA of the six attachment variables verified the hypothesized two-dimensional structure underlying adult attachment patterns. As illustrated in Figure 2, the measurement model consisted of two factors (represented by the large circles corresponding to the two hypothesized dimensions), each measured by three methods (represented by the three rectangles asociated with each circle in the figure). We estimated the correlation between the factors (the double-headed arrow between the two circles), even though we expected them to be relatively independent. We first fit a preliminary model that inserted correlated errors between the three pairs of measures of shared method variance (e.g., the self-report measures of self-model and other-model). None of the correlated errors approached statistical significance, and so we proceeded to fit a model with no correlated errors of measurement. Figure 2 plays this model and the obtained parameter estimates. As expected, the

TABLE 25.1. Multitrait-Multimethod Matrix for Adult Attachment Dimensions: Study 1

Variable	1	2	3	4	5	6
Attachment self model						
1 Self-report	—					
2 Family Interview	.34	—				
3 Peer Interview	.39	.50	—			
Attachment other model						
4 Self-report	.03	.18	−.10	—		
5 Family Interview	.18	.09	.15	.39	—	
6 Peer Interview	.10	−.26	.21	.50	.45	—

Note. Correlations in triangles are within-dimension correlations (convergent validity), and circled correlations (on the diagonal) are within-method correlations (discriminant validity).

three measures of each dimension loaded moderately to highly on the appropriate dimensions. This indicates that both latent constructs were reliably measured by served variables. In addition, there was a modest (non-significant) negative correlation between the two latent variables.

Overall, the model fit the data well, $\chi^2(8, N = 69) = 10.29; p < .25$. The AGFI value of .88 indicated a good fit between and data. The Steiger-Lind index was .06, with a 90% confidence interval of .00 to .16. The Adjusted Population Gamma Index = .98, with a 90% confidence interval of .84 to 1.00. Both values Steiger-Lind Index and Adjusted Population Gamma values use indicate a good fit, and the relatively narrow confidence intervals around these values confirm that the fit of the model to the data is not simply a result of inadequate power.

These statistics indicate that a two-dimensional structure which each indicator is associated with only one of the underlying attachment dimensions is sufficient to explain the overall correlations. However, it is also important to demonstrate both dimensions are necessary to explain the observed pattern of data. Thus, we compared the two-dimensional model a simpler model in which all six indicators loaded on with underlying factor or dimension. This model showed a poor fit with the data, $\chi^2(9, N = 69) = 36.23, p < .001$, and the test of the difference in fit between the two competing models indicates that the hypothesized two-dimensional structure gave a significantly better fit, $\chi^2(1, N = 69) = 26.13, p < .001$.

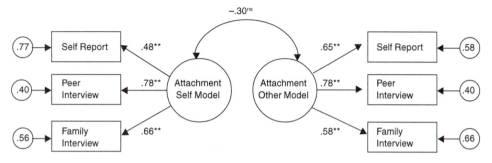

FIGURE 25.2 ■ Measurement model of adult attachment dimensions: Study 1. (*$p < .05$, ** $p < .01$.)

Study 2

Study 1 demonstrated the convergent and discriminant validity of the two hypothesized attachment dimensions. The first step in testing the construct validity of the two-dimensional model. In the current study, the measurement model of our first study was replicated on a new sample using a different set of methods for assessing adult attachment patterns (self-report ratings, interview ratings of peer relationships, and friend-ratings). Once again, CFA was used to test the appropriateness of the measurement model. Study 2 presents a reanalysis of data originally presented in Study 1 of Bartholomew and Horowitz (1991).

In addition to confirming the convergent and discriminant validity of the two-dimensional model, we assessed its construct validity by relating each latent attachment dimension to a theoretically dictated outcome variable. Recall that measures of the self-and other-model dimensions are derived by combining ratings of the four attachment prototypes, thus yielding indirect measures of the two dimensions. Furthermore, recall that the prototypes themselves are assessed in the context of individuals' close relationships. In the current study, we relate these indirect measures of the two general models to variables hypothesized to be direct measures of the same general models. Direct measures of the self-model dimension, which represents an individual's sense of self-worth ("positive self-concept"), were provided by self-report measures of self-esteem, subjective distress, and self-acceptance. Direct measures of the other-model dimension, which represents an individual's desire to seek or avoid closeness ("positive interpersonal orientation") were pro-

vided by self- and friend-reports of sociability and the warmth versus coldness dimension of the Interpersonal Circle. CFA was used to demonstrate the convergent and discriminant validity of these outcome variables. A full structural equation model then related the two attachment latent variables to the two latent variables representing the direct measures of the self and other models. We hypothesized that the attachment self model would largely correspond to the self-concept latent variable and be unrelated to interpersonal orientation; conversely, we hypothesized that the attachment other model would correspond to interpersonal orientation and be unrelated to self-concept. Finally, separate structural models were analyzed for each method of measuring attachment dimensions (i.e., self-report, friend-report, and interview) to determine whether the same pattern would be found at the level of individual measures.

Method

PROCEDURE

Target subjects were 77 undergraduate students (mean age 19.6 years) who participated for course credit. Each target subject was accompanied by a same-sex friend who was paid for his or her participation. In a first session, target subjects and their friends completed a series of questionnaires assessing, among other things, self-reports of the target subjects' attachment patterns, self-concepts, and interpersonal styles, and friend-reports of the target subjects' attachment patterns and interpersonal styles. One to two weeks later, target subjects were administered the Peer Attachment Interview.

MEASURES

Attachment measures. We assessed attachment patterns using an hour-long version of the Peer Attachment Interview, rated by three independent coders (alphas ranged from .87 to .95), and self-reports and friend-reports on the RQ. The friend-report version of the RQ was directly parallel to the self-report version with appropriate changes in wording. For example, the friend version of the dismissing prototype was "*F* is comfortable without close relationships. It is very important to *F* to feel independent and self-sufficient, and *F* prefers not to depend on others or have others depend on him or her." For each of the three methods of measurement, the two attachment dimensions of self and other models were derived as in Study 1.

Self-concept measures. Three self-report measures of self-concept were included. Self-esteem was assessed by the 10-item Rosenberg Self-Esteem Inventory (Rosenberg, 1965). A typical item is "I feel that I have a number of good qualities." (α = .85; note that this value and all subsequent alphas were calculated on the current data set). Self-acceptance was assessed by the 20-item Fey Self Acceptance Scale (Fey, 1955; α = .86). A typical item is "I'm pretty satisfied with the way I am." Subjective distress was assessed by a three-item scale measuring subjects' experienced depression, anxiety, and unhappiness (α = .68).

Interpersonal orientation measures. Two self-report and two friend-report measures of interpersonal orientation were included. Both self-reports and friend-reports of sociability were assessed by appropriately worded versions of the five-item Sociability Scale (Cheek & Buss, 1981; self-report α = .74; friend-report α = .78). A typical item is "I like to be with people." Self-reports and friend-reports of interpersonal warmth were assessed by appropriately worded versions of the Inventory of Interpersonal Problems (IIP; Horowitz, Rosenberg, Baer, Ureno, & Villasenor, 1988). Eight-item subscales of the IIP were created to correspond with the eight octants of the Interpersonal Circle (Alden, Wiggins, & Pincus, 1990; subscale alphas ranged from .66 to .89) and were combined to calculate a mean rating of interpersonal warmth according to the procedure described by Wiggins, Phillips, and Trapnell (1989). This score represents the degree to which reported interpersonal problems correspond to the warmth dimension of the Interpersonal Circle, a

model that conceptualizes interpersonal behavior in terms of two fundamental dimensions: Warmth versus Coldness and Dominance versus Submissiveness. Example items from the Overly Nurturant subscale include "*F* tries to please other people too much" (friend-report version) and "I put other people's needs before my own too much" (self-report version).

Result and Discussion

MEASUREMENT MODEL OF ATTACHMENT VARIABLES

Table 2 presents a multitrait-multimethod matrix for the six derived attachment variables. Once again, the matrix reveals evidence of both convergent validity (i.e., correlations within the triangles are moderately high) and discriminant validity (i.e., correlations within circles are relatively small). The average within-dimension correlation was .38, whereas the average within-method correlation was .90. These summary values are very similar to those obtained in Study 1. However, in this study, the correlation between two of the self-model measures, self- and friend-reports, was relatively small (r = .21). This discrepancy will be analyzed further below.

As illustrated in Figure 3, a CFA verified the hypothesized two-dimensional structure underlying the six attachment measures. As in Study 1, we first examined a model that included three correlated errors among the measured variables shar-

TABLE 25.2. Multitrait-Multimethod Matrix for Adult Attachment Dimensions: Study 2

Variable	1	2	3	4	5	6
Attachment self model						
1 Self-report						
2 Family Interview	.41					
3 Peer Interview	.34	.21				
Attachment other model						
4 Self-report	.12	.05	.19			
5 Family Interview	.12	.05	.17	.48		
6 Peer Interview	.05	−.21	.20	.42	.37	

Note. Correlations in triangles are within-dimension correlations (convergent validity), and circled correlations (on the diagonal) are within-method correlations (discriminant validity).

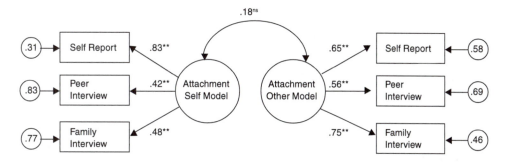

FIGURE 25.3 ■ Measurement model of adult attachment dimensions: Study 2. (*p < .05. **p < .01.)

ing a common method of measurement. None of the correlated errors approached significance, so we fit the simpler model presented in Figure 3. Once again, the three measures of each dimension loaded moderately to highly on the hypothesized dimensions, indicating that both latent constructs were reliably measured. In this study, there was a nonsignificant, positive correlation between the two latent variables.[2]

As in Study 1, the model fit the data well, $\chi^2(8, N = 77) = 10.76, p > .20$, with an AGFI value of .89. The Steiger-Lind Index was .07, with a 90% confidence interval of .00 to .16, and the Adjusted Population Gamma Index was .97 with a 90% confidence interval of .84 to 1.00. Again, the Steiger-Lind Index and Adjusted Population Gamma Index indicate good to excellent fit, and their confidence intervals confirm that the analysis had adequate power to reject an ill-fitting model. Again, the simpler unidimensional model was resoundingly rejected, $\chi^2(9, N = 77) = 29.21, p < .001$, and the hypothesized two-dimensional structure gave a significantly better fit, $\chi^2(1, N = 77) = 18.45, p < .001$.

MEASUREMENT MODEL OF OUTCOME VARIABLES

Correlations among the seven outcome variables are presented in Appendix A. Inspection of the correlation matrix reveals that the three self-concept measures intercorrelated highly, and the four interpersonal orientation measures intercorrelated at a moderate level. Between-construct correlations were generally low except for self-reported self-esteem and self-reported sociability ($r = .34, p <$

.01). Given that the content of these two measures does not overlap, we assumed that this correlation represented a common response bias, and therefore our CFA on the outcome variables included a correlated error term between self-esteem and self-reported sociability.[3]

Figure 4 presents the results of this analysis on the seven outcome measures. As expected, the three self-concept measures loaded highly on the latent variable of positive self-concept, and the four interpersonal measures loaded highly on the latent variable of positive interpersonal orientation. There was no correlation between the two latent variables. The correlated error between self-esteem and self-reported sociability was large and significant, indicating that the two variables shared a substantial amount of method variance. The two-construct

---

[2]This small positive correlation between the two latent dimensions contrasts with the moderate negative correlation found in Study 1. In fact, the two correlations differ significantly at the .05 level. We have no explanation for this discrepancy, except that peer reports replaced the Family Attachment Interview in Study 2. However, given that the two parallel correlations obtained in Study 3 are both small and positive, we assume that the negative correlation found in Study 1 is due to random fluctuation.

[3]According to standard measurement theory, the variance in an observed measure comes from three sources: common variance shared with other measures of the same construct, systematic error that may represent a response bias shared with other measures of the same type, and random error that is unrelated to any other measure. In this case, a significant correlated error means that some of the unique variance in self-reported sociability (that is, that part of this measure that is unrelated to any other interpersonal orientation measures) is related to some unique variance in self-reported self-esteem (that is, that part of this measure that is unrelated to any other self-concept measures).

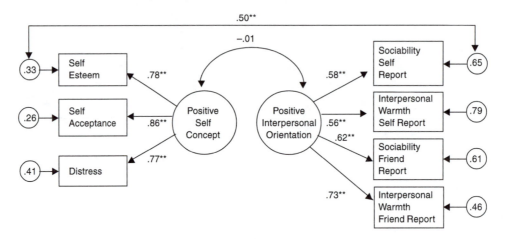

FIGURE 25.4 ■ Measurement model of outcome dimensions: Study 2. (*$p < .05$ **$p < .01$.)

model fit this data well: $\chi^2(12, N = 77) = 14.82, p > .25$, AGFI = .89, R* = .05, with a 90% confidence interval from 0 to .13; and G2 = .98, with a 90% confidence interval from .87 to 1.0. Again, a simpler unidimensional model failed to fit the data, $\chi^2(13, N = 77) = 63.27, p < .001$.

STRUCTURAL MODEL

Figure 5 displays the full structural model relating the attachment latent variables to the outcome latent variables. The causal model being tested implies that the attachment dimensions lead to the outcome variables. (Note that equivalent goodness of fit estimates would be obtained by reversing the direction of the so-called *causal paths*. See MacCallum, Wegener, Uchino, & Fabrigar, 1993). To enable the program to converge on a stable solution, it was necessary to specify two correlated errors between measures of the attachment other model and the interpersonal orientation measures. One correlated error was added between the self-reported attachment other model and self-reported interpersonal warmth. The other was added between the friend-reported attachment other model and friend-reported interpersonal warmth. These two correlated errors, like that between self-reported self-esteem and self-reported sociability identified above, represent common method variance and thus are theoretically plausible. Because the analysis of the attachment measurement model found a small, nonsignificant correlation between

the latent factors, this correlation was set to zero in the structural equation.

The standardized parameter estimates given in Figure 5 support the construct validity of the two-dimensional model. That is, the structural coefficient between each attachment dimension and its hypothesized outcome was very high (.96 and .93), whereas the coefficient between each attachment dimension and the noncorresponding outcome latent variable was virtually zero (.00 and .01). In fact, neither of the structural coefficients between the attachment latent variables and the corresponding outcome latent variables was significantly different from 1.0, indicating that the latent outcome variables (i.e., the "direct" measures of self-concept and interpersonal functioning) were not statistically distinguishable from the parallel latent attachment variables (i.e., the "indirect" measures of the self- and other-model dimensions). The implications of this remarkable finding are considered in the General Discussion. Goodness of fit statistics are presented in Figure 5.

All factor loadings were at least moderately high, except that for the friend-reported attachment self model, indicating that friend report is not a highly reliable measure of the self model.[4] To fur-

---

[4]The factor loadings change from the CFA of the measurement model (Figure 3) to the complete structural model (Figure 5) because the program finds the set of parameters that leads to the best fit of the entire correlation (or covariance) matrix. Thus, whereas the factor loadings of the attachment variables in Figure 3 reflect only the interrelations among the attachment

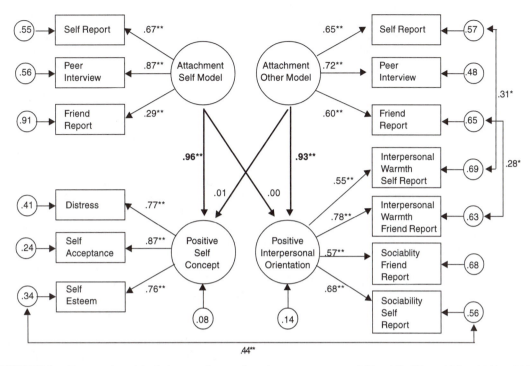

FIGURE 25.5 ■ Structural model relating attachment dimesions to outcome variables. ($N = 77$, $p > .13.$ $^*p < .05.$ $^{**}p < .01.$)

ther explore potential differences between methods of measuring the attachment dimensions, we then examined a separate structural equation model for each of the methods. For example, for self-report, the structural model consists of self-reported self model and self-reported other model, each predicting a corresponding outcome latent variable and a noncorresponding outcome latent variable. The parameter estimates for each of the three simplified structural models can be found in Table 3. Although goodness of fit values indicated that these simplified models fit the data adequately, the results are presented for descriptive purposes, and so the associated significance tests are not reported.

Inspection of Table 3 reveals two notable results. First, as suggested by the overall structural

indicator variables, the factor loadings of the attachment variables in Figure 5 reflect both the interrelations among the attachment indicator variables and the relations between the attachment indicator variables and the outcome indicator variables.

equation model, self-reports and interview ratings conform to the hypothesized model more closely than do friend-reports. In particular, friend-reports of the self-model dimension showed only modest predictive validity, whereas friend-reports of the

TABLE 25.3. Structural Relations (Standardized Coefficients) Between Individual Measures of Attachment Dimensions and Outcome Latent Variables: Study 2

	Outcome latent variables	
Method of measuring attachment dimensions	Positive self-concept	Positive interpersonal orientation
Self-report		
Self model	.64	.06
Other model	.06	.69
Friend-report		
Self model	.27	.02
Other model	.21	.67
Peer Interview		
Self model	.65	−.06
Other model	.09	.67

other-model dimension were highly predictive of the target subjects' interpersonal orientations. This finding may reflect the fact that observers are generally more accurate in judging observable characteristics such as extroversion or sociability than in judging less observable characteristics such as neuroticism or self-esteem (Kenrick & Funder, 1988). Second, the predictive validity of the interview ratings was comparable with that of the self-report ratings for both attachment dimensions and with the friend-reports for the other-model dimension. This finding is impressive because the latter two measurement methods shared common method variance with the outcome measures, whereas the interview ratings did not.

SUMMARY OF RESULTS

Study 2 replicated the measurement model tested in Study 1 with a different set of measurement methods. It showed that the two-dimensional model was both reliable, as demonstrated by CFA of the measurement model, and valid, as demonstrated by the structural equation relating the attachment latent variables to the outcome latent variables. As hypothesized, the self-model attachment dimension was strongly related to the latent self-concept variable and was unrelated to the latent interpersonal orientation variable. In contrast, the other-model dimension was strongly related to the latent interpersonal orientation variable and was unrelated to the latent self-concept variable. In separate analyses, this overall structure was also found for self-report and interview ratings of attachment. However, friends' reports of attachment showed greater construct validity for the other-model dimension than for the self-model dimension.

Study 3

In Study 3, the structure of the two-dimensional model was again tested with a different set of methods of assessing attachment (self-reports, romantic partner reports, and interview ratings) on a different population (committed couples). Unlike the previous two studies, the structure was tested separately for women and men. We hypothesized that the two-dimensional model would be appropriate for both women and men. In addition, three established self-report methods for assessing adult attachment that are not explicitly based on the two-dimensional model were related to the self-model and other-model dimensions. These methods are a multiple-item measure of Hazan's three attachment patterns (e.g., Mikulincer, Florian, & Tolmacz, 1990; Mikulincer & Nachshon, 1991; Simpson, 1990), Simpson's two attachment subscales (Simpson et al., 1992; see also Feeney, Noller, & Callan, 1994, for very similar scales), and Collins' three attachment subscales (Collins & Read, 1990).

The predictions for Simpson's and Collins' measures are relatively straightforward because both measures were originally conceptualized in dimensional terms. Simpson's two subscales of anxiety and avoidance were expected to correspond to the self- and other-model dimensions. Collins and Read (1990) identified three attachment subscales; anxiety, comfort with closeness, and comfort with depending on others. The first two are very similar to Simpson's two subscales and therefore were also expected to be predicted by the self-model and other-model dimensions, respectively. The dependence subscale appears to contain elements of both underlying attachment dimensions, although because of its correlation with the comfort with closeness subscale, it was expected to be most highly related to the other model dimension.

Our predictions for the measure of Hazan's three attachment patterns are less certain because the three categories are not explicitly defined in terms of attachment dimensions. Because Hazan's secure pattern is defined in terms of a lack of anxiety in close relationships and comfort with intimacy, we expected the secure subscale to be positively predicted by both the self-and other-model latent variables. Similarly, because Hazan's anxious-ambivalent pattern is defined in terms of a high degree of anxiety coupled with a desire for intimacy, we expected the ambivalent subscale to be negatively associated with the self-model dimension and positively associated with the other-model dimension. An examination of the items composing the avoidant subscale led us to expect that this subscale would be predicted primarily by the other model dimension. However, Brennan et al.'s (1991) comparison of self-report measures of the three- and four-category models of attachment suggested that Hazan's avoidant pattern may also contain a component of anxiety that might be negatively related to the self-model dimension.

Method

SUBJECTS

The sample consisted of 78 heterosexual couples who were part of a longitudinal study. Four women and six men were deleted from the analysis because of missing data on at least one variable. The criteria for inclusion in the study were minimum relationship length of 2 years, at least one partner aged 35 years or less, and both partners without children. The subjects' average age was 24.5 years; 28% were married, 44% were unmarried but cohabiting, and 28% were living separately. Subjects were recruited from a variety of university classes and from advertisements in the campus newspaper and elsewhere. Approximately 75% of the subjects were students. Each subject received $10 for participation as well as a chance to win a portion of $450 in lottery prizes.

PROCEDURE

In a first session, couples arrived together and separately completed a packet of questionnaires including measures of their own and their partner's attachment patterns. All subjects filled out self-reports and partner-reports on the RQ and then filled out self-reports on the Relationship Scales Questionnaire (RSQ; Griffin & Bartholomew, 1994). In a second session conducted within 2 weeks of the first, partners were individually administered the Peer Attachment Interview.

MEASURES

Attachment patterns were assessed by the Peer Attachment Interview and self-reports and partner-reports on the RQ. For each of the three methods of measurement, the two attachment dimensions were derived as in the previous two studies.

The RSQ is a 30-item self-report measure designed to yield a variety of attachment subscales. Included are items corresponding to the phrases in Hazan and Shaver's (1987) three-category attachment measure, Bartholomew and Horowitz's (1991) four-category attachment measure, as well as additional items used by Collins and Read (1990). In cases where items from different sources essentially overlapped, only one of the (conceptually identical) items was included in the RSQ. Each item is scored on a 5-point scale ranging from *not at all like me* to *very much like me*.

Measures of each of the three attachment styles identified by Hazan and Shaver (1987) were created by summing items derived from the corresponding prototypic description (see, e.g., Mikulincer et al., 1990; Mikulincer & Nachshon, 1991; and Simpson, 1990). The secure scale was composed of 5 items (e.g., "I find it relatively easy to get close to others"; $\alpha = .50$ for both women and men), the avoidance scale was composed of 4 items (e.g., "I am nervous when anyone gets too close to me"; $\alpha = .72$ for women and .74 for men), and the ambivalence scale was composed of 4 items (e.g., "I find that others are reluctant to get as close as I would like"; $\alpha = .77$ for women and .69 for men). The intercorrelations of the three scales were consistent with those reported by previous researchers: secure and avoidance scores correlated $-.59$ for women and $-.60$ for men, secure and ambivalence scores correlated $-.06$ for women and $-.23$ for men, and avoidance and ambivalence scores correlated .23 for women and .25 for men.

The three attachment subscales of closeness, anxiety, and dependence were created following the procedure of Collins and Read (1990). Each scale was composed of six items and all showed acceptable internal consistency (alphas ranged from .73 to .78). The intercorrelations among the three subscales were consistent with those reported by Collins and Read (1990): Closeness and anxiety were correlated .11 for women and $-.03$ for men, closeness and dependence were correlated .62 for women and .52 for men, and anxiety and dependence were correlated $-.27$ for women and $-.21$ for men. Finally, the two attachment subscales of anxiety and avoidance were created following the procedure of Simpson et al. (1992). The avoidance and anxiety scales were composed of eight and five items, respectively, and both showed acceptable internal consistency (alphas ranged from .75 to .82). The intercorrelations between the two scales were consistent with those reported by Simpson et al. (1992): $-.05$ for women and $-.20$ for men.

Results and Discussion

MEASUREMENT MODEL OF ATTACHMENT DIMENSIONS

Tables 4 and 5 contain two multitrait-multimethod matrices for the six derived attachment variables, one each for women and men. Inspection of the correlations for women reveals strong evidence of both convergent and discriminant validity. The within-dimension correlation was .44, and the average within-method correlation was .10. These values are comparable with those found with mixed-sex samples in the previous two studies. The correlation matrix for men, however, indicates that only the other-model dimension was reliably assessed by the three measures. Although the mean within-dimension correlation for the other-model dimension was a respectable .35, the mean within-dimension correlation for the self-model dimension was only .13, falling below the mean within-method correlation of .15.

Separate CFAs were conducted for women and men and are presented in Figures 6 and 7. For women, the results conformed closely to the hypothesized structure: The three measures of each dimension loaded moderately to highly on the appropriate attachment dimensions. Again, the two-dimensional model fit the data well (see Figure 6 for the goodness of fit statistics). For men, because partner-reports were uncorrelated with self-reports for the self-model dimensions, partner-reports of the self-model dimensions could not be included in the analysis. With only two variables available to define the self-model dimension, it was necessary to constrain both loadings to be equal to identify the model. As shown in Figure 7, this five-variable measurement model did fit the data for the men.

Table 25.4. Multitrait-Multimethod Matrix for Adult Attachment Dimensions: Study 3 Women

Variable	1	2	3	4	5	6
Attachment self model						
1 Self-report	—					
2 Peer Interview	.50	—				
3 Partner-report	.49	.40	—			
Attachment other model						
4 Self-report	.14	.06	.05	—		
5 Peer Interview	.25	.08	.09	.47	—	
6 Partner-report	.00	−.12	.07	.37	.39	—

Note. Correlations in triangles are within-dimension correlations (convergent validity), and circled correlations (on the diagonal) are within-method correlations (discriminant validity).

TABLE 25.5. Multitrait-Multimethod Matrix for Adult Attachment Dimensions: Study 3 Men

Variable	1	2	3	4	5	6
Attachment self model						
1 Self-report	—					
2 Peer Interview	.24	—				
3 Partner-report	−.03	.19	—			
Attachment other model						
4 Self-report	.20	.02	−.08	—		
5 Peer Interview	.02	.17	.01	.34	—	
6 Partner-report	−.02	−.03	.08	.32	.37	—

Note. Correlations in triangles are within-dimension correlations (convergent validity), and circled correlations (on the diagonal) are within-method correlations (discriminant validity).

Using mixed-sex samples in the two previous studies may have obscured any existing sex differences in the fit of the measurement model. To examine this possibility, we computed separate multitrait-multimethod matrices for men and women for each study. A comparison of these matrices revealed that although the average within-self-model dimension correlations for men were consistently (although nonsignificantly) lower than those for women (.34 vs. .48 in Study 1 and .27 vs. .36 in Study 2), both sexes showed adequate convergent validity. Correlations among measures of the other-model dimension showed no consistent ordering between sexes (.50 for men and .38 for women in Study 1, and .30 for men and .53 for women in Study 2). Thus, it appears that the difficulty in assessing the men's self-model dimension was restricted to Study 3.

To further explore this issue, we related each measure of the self-model dimension to the one relevant outcome measure that was available in this data set, a measure of self-esteem that was collected at a follow-up session conducted 8 months after the attachment measures were completed (the Rosenberg Self-Esteem Inventory, Rosenberg, 1965). For men, both the interview and self-report measures of the self-model dimension significantly predicted self-esteem 8 months later, $r(68) = .38, p < .001$, and $r(68) = −.31, p < .01$, whereas partner-report was unrelated, $r(68) = −.05$, ns. These results hardly changed when partial correlations were computed representing the unique

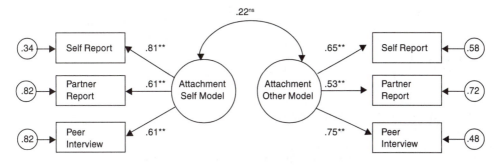

FIGURE 25.6 ■ Measurement model of adult attachment measures: Study 3 women. (N = 74, $p > .40$. $^*p < .05$. $^{**}p < .01$.)

relations between each separate attachment measure and self-esteem, interview $r(66) = .36$, $p < .01$; self-report $r(66) = .25$, $p < .05$; partner-report $r(66) = -.11$, ns. There are two notable aspects of these results. First, the interview ratings predicted later self-esteem at least as strongly as did self-report ratings of attachment, despite the interview ratings sharing no method variance with the self-esteem inventory. Second, the interview ratings and the self-reports of attachment independently predicted later self-esteem. Thus, although there was limited convergent validity among measures of the self-model dimension for men, both the interview and the self-report measures showed predictive validity.

For women, in contrast, all three self-model measures significantly predicted later self-esteem, interview $r(68) = .36$, $p < .01$; self-report $r(68) = .32$, $p < .01$; partner-report $r(68) = .30$, $p < .05$. When partial correlations were computed, only the interview rating showed any unique relationship with self-esteem, $r(66) = .23$, $p = .06$. (Other partial $rs < .15$, ns.) The small unique relationships compared with the moderate zero-order correlations are consistent with the high convergent validity of the different self model measures for women.

Overall, the results for women conformed closely to expectations. For men, there were two unexpected findings. First, partner-reports on the self-model dimension lacked both convergent and predictive validity. Note that partner-reports are fundamentally different from the peer-reports used in Study 2: In this study, reports came from opposite-sex, romantic partners, whereas in the prior study, reports came from same-sex, platonic friends. Romantic partners differ from same-sex peers on a number of dimensions such as time spent together, the contexts in which they observe their partner or friend, as well as the depth of emotional investment in the relationship and the concomitant motivation to idealize (or derogate) their partner or friend. Second, the interview and self-report measures of the self-model dimension were

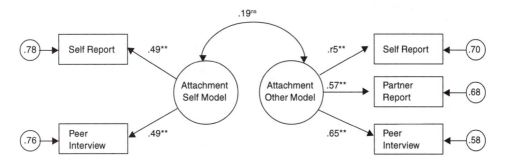

FIGURE 25.7 ■ Measurement model of adult attachment measures: Study 3 men. ($N = 72$, $p > .25$. $^*p < .05$. $^{**}p < .01$.)

only modestly correlated for men, and both independently predicted later self-esteem. It is not clear why this pattern was found only in Study 3, although there are a number of differences between this sample and those used in the previous studies. All subjects in this study were involved in long-term romantic relationships; they were about 6 years older, on average, than those sampled previously; and they participated in the context of a couples' study. Replications of these findings are necessary before substantive conclusions can be drawn.

RELATIONS WITH OTHER ATTACHMENT DIMENSIONS

We next related the latent attachment dimensions to each of the three self-report measures of attachment defined above. Separate analyses were conducted for men and women, with all analyses for men omitting the partner reports for the self-model dimension. Tables 6 and 7 present the results of the structural models predicting the three subscales derived from Hazan and Shaver's three-category model (1987). The results for men and women were remarkably consistent. For both samples, the Secure subscale was strongly predicted by the other-model dimension and only modestly related to the self-model dimension. The Avoidant subscale was strongly and inversely predicted by the other-model dimension and was also modestly negatively related to the self-model dimension. Finally, the Ambivalence subscale was primarily predicted by the self-model dimension (negatively), but there was a small negative relation between the Ambivalence scale and the other-model dimension for women only. To summarize, the other-model dimension seemed to underlie both the Secure and Avoidant subscales, whereas the self-model dimension seemed to underlie the Ambivalence subscale. Thus, although we hypothesized that the Secure and Ambivalence subscales would be associated with both attachment dimensions, our results indicate a simpler structure, that is, that the subscales roughly correspond to the dimensions rather than spanning them at a 45° angle.

Next, we examined how Collins and Read's three attachment subscales of Closeness, Anxiety, and Comfort With Dependence related to the self-model and other-model dimensions. As shown in

TABLE 25.6. Structural Relations (Standardized Coefficients) Between Latent Attachment Dimensions and Adult Attachment Subscales: Study 3 Women

Continuous attachment measures	Attachment latent variables	
	Positive self model	Positive other model
Hazan & Shaver (1987)		
Secure	.25*	.63**
Avoidant	−.27**	−.67**
Ambivalent	−.80**	−.18
Collins & Read (1990)		
Closeness	.09	.79**
Anxiety	−.77**	−.27*
Comfort with Dependence	.47**	.63**
Simpson et al. (1992)		
Avoidance	−.15	−.69**
Anxiety	−.80**	−.20

$* p < .05.$ $** p < .01.$

Tables 6 and 7, the results were generally consistent with our hypotheses and were comparable for men and women. The Anxiety subscale was strongly (and inversely) predicted by the self-model dimension, and the Comfort With Closeness subscale was strongly predicted by the other-model dimension. For men, there was a significant nonhypothesized path from the self model to the Closeness subscale, and for women there was a significant nonhypothesized path from the other model to the Anxiety subscale. However, these apparent sex differences were nonsignificant when

TABLE 25.7. Structural Relations (Standardized Coefficients) Between Latent Attachment Dimensions and Adult Attachment Subscales: Study 3 Men

Continuous attachment measures	Attachment latent variables	
	Positive self model	Positive other model
Hazan & Shaver (1987)		
Secure	.31**	.67**
Avoidant	−.38**	−.63**
Ambivalent	−.79**	−.10
Collins & Read (1990)		
Closeness	.29**	.86**
Anxiety	−.67**	−.20
Comfort with Dependence	.35**	.46**
Simpson et al. (1992)		
Avoidance	−.29**	−.86**
Anxiety	−.78**	−.10

$*p < .05.$ $**p < .01.$

the relevant paths for men and women were directly compared. In both samples, the Comfort With Dependence subscale was moderately related to both of the attachment latent variables.

The structural models relating the two subscales of Avoidance and Anxiety (Simpson et al., 1992) to the self-model and other model latent variables are also presented in Tables 6 and 7. The results were again consistent across samples. As hypothesized, the Anxiety subscale corresponded closely (and inversely) to the self-model dimension, whereas the Avoidance subscale corresponded closely to the other-model dimension. In addition, for men there was one significant—though modest—path from the self-model dimension to the Avoidance subscale (again, this path was not significantly larger than the corresponding path for women). Not surprisingly, the results for the two attachment subscales (Anxiety and Avoidance) were very similar to those for the corresponding subscales of Collins and Read (Anxiety and Closeness). The items making up these measures are largely overlapping. Thus, the two anxiety scales were correlated .86 for women and .82 for men, and the avoidance and closeness scales were correlated .98 for women and .96 for men.

In sum, Collins' and Simpson's dimensional measures were strongly predicted by the self- and other-model latent variables as expected. However, contrary to expectations, the dimensions underlying the multi-item measure of Hazan's three patterns also corresponded roughly to the self- and other-model latent variables. Researchers using these subscales may want to consider the implications of these findings when interpreting their own results. We should note, however, that the results obtained with these multi-item subscales may not hold with the single-item categorical measures originally developed by Hazan and Shaver (1987).

General Discussion

In three studies, using five different methods of assessment (self-reports, friend reports, romantic partner reports, trained judges' ratings of peer attachment, and trained judges' ratings of family attachment), we found strong support for the construct validity of the self- and other-model attachment dimensions. Across studies, the two attachment dimensions showed both discriminant

validity—that is, measures of different constructs were essentially independent—and convergent validity—that is, different measures of a given construct were highly related. In addition, Study 2 demonstrated the predictive validity of the two hypothesized dimensions: At the level of latent variables, the positivity of an individual's attachment self-model was highly (in fact, almost perfectly) related to the positivity of her or his self-concept, and the positivity of an individual's attachment other model was highly (again, almost perfectly) related to the positivity of her or his interpersonal orientation.

Study 2 also examined the predictive validity of the different methods of measuring the attachment dimensions. Results indicated that both self-report and interview measures were highly predictive of the corresponding latent outcome variables. However, for friend reports only, the self-model dimension showed rather poor predictive validity. Given that every one of the outcome measures was either a self-report or a friend-report, it was particularly striking that the interview-based attachment ratings predicted the outcome latent variables at least as well as self-reported and friend-reported attachment. Such high correlations across methods of measurement give an assurance that the results are not an artifact of the assessment procedures (Bank, Dishion, Skinner, & Patterson, 1990).

Study 2 provided the most dramatic example of the advantages of using multiple indicators in assessing constructs such as attachment. The standard strategy in the field of adult attachment has been to look at the associations between single indicators of attachment and outcome variables. Often both sets of measures also share a common method (typically, self-reports). Thus, the resulting associations are confounded with common method variance and with random measurement error: Depending on the situation, shared method variance may exaggerate or attenuate the apparent relation between two variables, and unreliability of either indicator may substantially attenuate the observed correlations (Green, Goldman, & Salovey, 1993). The present approach avoids both of these problems. For example, the simple correlation between self-report of the self-model dimension and self-reported self-esteem was approximately .5, and the correlation between self-reports of the self-model dimension and sociability was approximately .2. However, according to the structural equation model, the true correlation between the latent self-model dimension and the latent self-concept variable was .96 and the true correlation between the self-model dimension and the latent interpersonal orientation variable was zero.

In our final study, three continuous measures of adult attachment were examined, and all were shown to be measuring constructs similar to the self- and other-model latent dimensions underlying Bartholomew's four-category model. Study 3 also revealed the one anomalous finding in the measurement models presented here: Although men were able to reliably assess both their partners' self and other models, women seemed to be unreliable reporters of their partners' self models. At this point, we have no explanation for this finding and are hesitant to draw any conclusions until it has been replicated. It may represent random fluctuation, a systematic bias in women's perceptions of their romantic partners, or the failure of male partners to disclose their own self-evaluations. It offers an intriguing avenue for further investigation.

An important conclusion of these studies is that the two underlying attachment dimensions can be reliably assessed by self-report measures. For both theoretical and empirical reasons, we are considerably less confident that the individual attachment patterns can be reliably assessed by this method. Theoretically, these patterns are not necessarily conscious or open to introspection. Furthermore, multitrait-multimethod matrices and CFAs of attachment pattern ratings consistently fail to show convergent and discriminant validity (Griffin & Bartholomew, 1991). In some cases, ratings of theoretically "opposite" patterns such as secure and fearful correlated more highly (although negatively) than did ratings of the same patterns obtained by different methods. Therefore, we believe that results based on self-report ratings of attachment patterns should be validated by interview ratings whenever possible and that the development of a valid self-report measure of attachment patterns—preferably an implicit measure that does not directly ask for self-classification but instead offers socially desirable alternative characteristics of each pattern—should be a priority for future research.

ACKNOWLEDGMENTS

Preparation of this article was supported by Social Science and Humanities Research Council of Canada research grants to Dale Griffin and Kim Bartholomew and a sabbatical leave granted by the University of Waterloo to Dale Griffin.

We are grateful to Elaine Scharfe for her help in the collection and analysis of the data in Study 3, and to the Department of Psychology, University of British Columbia, for the use of their facilities during Dale Griffin's sabbatical leave.

REFERENCES

Ainsworth, M. D. S., Blehar, M. C., Waters, E., & Wall, S. (1978). *Patterns of attachment: A psychological study of the Strange Situation.* Hillsdale, NJ: Erlbaum.

Alden, L. E., Wiggins, J. S., & Pincus, A. L. (1990). Construction of circumplex scales for the Inventory of Interpersonal Problems. *Journal of Personality Assessment, 55.* 521–536.

Bank, L., Dishion, T., Skinner, M., & Patterson, G. R. (1990). Method variance in structural equation modeling: Living with "glop." In G. R. Patterson (Ed.), *Depression and aggression in family interaction* (pp. 247–279). Hillsdale, NJ: Erlbaum.

Bartholomew, K. (1990). Avoidance of intimacy: An attachment perspective. *Journal of Social and Personal Relationships, 7,* 147–178.

Bartholomew, K., & Horowitz, L. M. (1991). Attachment styles among young adults: A test of a four-category model. *Journal of Personality and Social Psychology, 61,* 226–244.

Bowlby, J. (1973). *Attachment and loss: Vol. 2. Separation: Anxiety and anger.* New York: Basic Books.

Bowlby, J. (1980). *Attachment and loss: Vol. 3. Loss: Sadness and depression.* New York: Basic Books.

Bowlby, J. (1982). *Attachment and loss: Vol. 1. Attachment* (2nd ed.). New York: Basic Books. (Original work published 1969).

Brennan, K. A., Shaver, P. R., & Tobey, A. E. (1991). Attachment styles, gender, and parental problem drinking. *Journal of Social and Personal Relationships, 8,* 451–466.

Campbell, D. T., & Fiske, D. W. (1959). Convergent and discriminant validation by the multitrait-multimethod matrix. *Psychological Bulletin, 56,* 81–105.

Cheek, J. M., & Buss, A. H. (1981). Shyness and sociability. *Journal of Personality and Social Psychology, 41,* 330–339.

Cliff, N. (1983). Some cautions concerning the application of causal modeling methods. *Multivariate Behavioral Research, 18,* 115–126.

Collins, N. L., & Read, S. J. (1990). Adult attachment, working models, and relationship quality in dating couples. *Journal of Personality and Social Psychology, 58,* 644–663.

Connell, J. P. (1987). Structural equation modeling and the study of child development: A question of goodness of fit. *Child Development, 58,* 167–175.

Connell, J. P., & Tanaka, J. S. (1987). Introduction to the special section on structural equation modeling. *Child Development, 58,* 2–3.

Cronbach, L. J. (1949). Statistical methods applied to Rorschach scores: A review. *Psychological Bulletin, 46*, 393–429.

Digman, J. M. (1990). Personality structure: Emergence of the five-factor model. *Annual Review of Psychology, 41*, 417–440.

Feeney, J. A., Noller, P., & Callan, V. J. (1994). Attachment style, communication and satisfaction in the early years of marriage. In K. Bartholomew & D. Perlman (Eds.), *Advances in personal relationships: Vol. 5. Attachment processes in adulthood* (pp. 269–308). London: Jessica Kingsley.

Fey, W. F. (1955). Acceptance by others and its relation to acceptance of self and others: A revaluation. *Journal of Abnormal and Social Psychology, 50*, 274–276.

Freedman, D. A. (1987). As others see us: A case study in path analysis. *Journal of Educational Statistics, 12*, 101–128.

Gifford, R., & O'Connor, B. (1987). The interpersonal circumplex as a behavior map. *Journal of Personality and Social Psychology, 52*, 1019–1026.

Green, D. P., Goldman, S. L., & Salovey, P. (1993). Measurement error masks bipolarity in affect ratings. *Journal of Personality and Social Psychology, 64*, 1029–1041.

Griffin, D., & Bartholomew, K. (1991, August). *A structural equation analysis of adult attachment styles.* Paper presented at the 99th Convention of the American Psychological Association, San Francisco.

Griffin, D. W., & Bartholomew, K. (1994). The metaphysics of measurement: The case of adult attachment. In K. Bartholomew & D. Perlman (Eds.), *Advances in personal relationships: Vol. 5. Attachment processes in adulthood* (pp. 17–52). London: Jessica Kingsley.

Hazan, C., & Hutt, M. J. (1991). *From parents to peers: Transitions in attachment.* Unpublished manuscript, Department of Human Development, Cornell University.

Hazan, C., & Shaver, P. (1987). Conceptualizing romantic love as an attachment process. *Journal of Personality and Social Psychology, 52*, 511–524.

Hazan, C., & Shaver, P. R. (1994). Attachment as an organizational framework for research on close relationships. *Psychological Inquiry, 5*, 1–22.

Horowitz, L. M., Rosenberg, S. E., Baer, B. A., Ureno, G., & Villasenor, V. S. (1988). Inventory of Interpersonal Problems: Psychometric properties and clinical applications. *Journal of Consulting and Clinical Psychology, 56*, 885–892.

Jöreskog, K. G., & Sörbom, D. (1986). *LISREL VI: Analysis of linear structural relationships by maximum likelihood, instrumental variables, and least squares methods* (4th ed.). Mooresville, IN: Scientific Software.

Kenrick, D. T., & Funder, D. C. (1988). Lessons from the person-situation debate. *American Psychologist, 43*, 23–34.

Kobak, R. R., Cole, H. E., Ferenz-Gillies, R., Fleming, W., & Gamble, W. (1991). *A dimensional analysis of adolescent attachment strategies.* Unpublished manuscript, Department of Psychology, University of Delaware, Newark.

Kobak, R. R., & Hazan, C. (1991). Attachment in marriage: The effects of security and accuracy of working models. *Journal of Personality and Social Psychology, 60*, 861–869.

MacCallum, R. C., Wegener, D. T., Uchino, B. N., & Fabrigar, L. R. (1993). The problem of equivalent models in applications of covariance structural analysis. *Psychological Bulletin, 114*, 185–199.

McCrae, R. R., & Costa, P. T., Jr. (1987). Validation of the five-factor model of personality across instruments and observers. *Journal of Personality and Social Psychology, 52*, 81–90.

McCrae, R. R., & Costa, P. T. (1989). The structure of interpersonal traits: Wiggins's circumplex and the five-factor model. *Journal of Personality and Social Psychology, 56*, 586–595.

Main, M., Kaplan, N., & Cassidy, J. (1985). Security in infancy, childhood, and adulthood: A move to the level of representation. In I. Bretherton & E. Waters (Eds.), *Growing points in attachment theory and research [Monograph]. Monographs of the Society for Research in Child Development, 50*, 66–106.

Mikulincer, M., Florian, V., & Tolmacz, R. (1990). Attachment styles and fear of personal death: A case study of affect regulation. *Journal of Personality and Social Psychology, 58*, 273–280.

Mikulincer, M., & Nachshon, O. (1991). Attachment styles and patterns of self-disclosure. *Journal of Personality and Social Psychology, 61*, 321–331.

Rosenberg, M. (1965). *Society and the adolescent self-image.* Princeton, NJ: Princeton University Press.

Scharfe, E., & Bartholomew, K. (1994). Reliability and stability of adult attachment patterns. *Personal Relationships, 1*, 23–43.

Shaver, P. R., & Brennan, K. A. (1992). Attachment styles and the "Big Five" personality traits: Their connections with each other and with romantic relationship outcomes. *Personality and Social Psychology Bulletin, 18*, 536–545.

Shaver, P. R., & Hazan, C. (1993). Adult romantic attachment: Theory and evidence. In D. Perlman & W. Jones (Eds.), *Advances in personal relationships* (Vol. 4, pp. 29–70). London: Jessica Kingsley.

Simpson, J. A. (1990). The influence of attachment styles on romantic relationships. *Journal of Personality and Social Psychology, 59*, 971–980.

Simpson, J. A., Rholes, W. S., & Nelligan, J. S. (1992). Support seeking and support giving within couples in an anxiety-provoking situation. *Journal of Personality and Social Psychology, 62*, 434–446.

Steiger, J. H. (1989). *EzPath: A supplementary module for SYSTAT and SYGRAPH.* Evanston, IL: SYSTAT.

Trapnell, P. D., & Wiggins, J. S. (1990). Extension of the Interpersonal Adjective Scales to include the Big Five dimensions of personality. *Journal of Personality and Social Psychology, 59*, 781–790.

Wiggins, J. S., Phillips, N., & Trapnell, P. (1989). Circular reasoning about interpersonal behavior: Evidence concerning some untested assumptions underlying diagnostic classifications. *Journal of Personality and Social Psychology, 56*, 296–305.

Appendix A

Multitrait-Multimethod Matrix for Outcome Variables: Study 2

Variable	1	2	3	4	5	6	7
Positive self-concept							
1 Distress							
2 Self-esteem	−.63	—					
3 Self-acceptance	.66	−.72	—				
Positive interpersonal orientation							
4 Sociability self-report	−.16	.34	−.13				
5 Sociability friend report	−.05	−.02	.10	.37	—		
6 Warmth self-report	.15	−.02	.10	.38	.20	—	
7 Warmth friend report	−.10	−.00	.05	.39	.49	.34	—

Note. Correlations in triangles are within-dimension correlations (convergent validity).

Love and Work:
An Attachment-Theoretical Perspective

Cindy Hazan • Cornell University

Phillip R. Shaver • State University of New York at Buffalo

Editors' Notes

A major contribution of attachment theory (by Bowlby, Ainsworth, and others) has been to explain patterns of significant adult behavior in terms of attachment modes developed in early childhood between an infant and her or his parents, in particular the mother. Influenced by Harlow's classic animal research, attachment theorists postulate a link between the availability to the infant of a supportive and protective parent and the tendency to confidently explore the environment. However, attachment theorists go beyond the period of infancy and hypothesize that attachment styles developed in early childhood extend into adulthood and affect such major domains of adult life as love and work that are analogous to childhood exploration. The results offer support for the notion that love and work are related and that patterns of attachment determine one's attitudes toward one's job as well as one's overall life satisfaction. Above all, this article (like the previous selection) supports the notion that early experiences determine lifelong attitudes, manner of functioning, and affective experience.

Discussion Questions

1. According to Bowlby, how are attachment and exploration related to each other?
2. What specific hypotheses do the authors put forward relating different attachment styles to work attitudes and experiences?
3. What three distinct patterns regarding work do the investigators identify, and how are these functionally similar to the three patterns of exploration in infancy and early childhood?

4. Hazan and Shaver mention a criticism of their prior work in terms of their constituting part of the same semantic network. How does the present research begin to counter this particular crititque?

Suggested Readings

Baumeister, R. F., & Leary, M. R. (1995). The need to belong: Desire for interpersonal attachment as a fundamental human motivation. *Psychological Bulletin, 117,* 497–529.

Clark, M. S., & Mills, J. (1979). Interpersonal attraction in exchange and communal relationships. *Journal of Personality and Social Psychology, 37,* 12–24.

Reis, H. T. (1990). The role of intimacy in interpersonal relations. *Journal of Social and Clinical Psychology, 9,* 15–30.

Authors' Abstract

The possibility that love and work in adulthood are functionally similar to attachment and exploration in infancy and early childhood was investigated. Key components of attachment theory–developed by Bowlby, Ainsworth, and others to explain the role of attachment in exploratory behavior–were translated into terms appropriate to adult love and work. The translation centered on the 3 major types of infant attachment and exploration identified by Ainsworth; secure, anxious/ambivalent, and avoidant. Two questionnaire studies indicated that relations between adult attachment type and work orientation are similar to attachment/ exploration dynamics in infancy and early childhood, suggesting that the dynamics may be similar across the life span. Implications for research on the link between love and work are discussed, as are measurement problems and other issues related to future tests of an attachment-theoretical approach to the study of adults.

Tolstoy, in a letter to Valerya Aresenyev, November 9, 1856, said, "One can live magnificently in this world if one knows how to work and how to love . . ." (Troyat, 1967, p. 158). Freud is purported to have said that the goal of psychotherapy is to allow the patient to love and to work (Erikson, 1963). The themes of love and work are central to some of the most influential theories of psychological well-being (e.g., Erikson, 1963; Maslow, 1954; Rogers, 1961); their importance for healthy functioning has been empirically documented (e.g., Baruch, Barnett, & Rivers, 1983; Gurin, Veroff, & Feld, 1960; Lee & Kanungo, 1984; Vaillant, 1977). Study after study has shown that satisfaction in one domain is associated with satisfaction in the other. But how are love and work related? What is the nature of the connection?

In the present article, we suggest that attachment theory can accommodate both love and work in a natural way. We argue that work is functionally similar to what Bowlby calls "exploration," that adult attachment supports work activity just as infant attachment supports exploration, and that the balance between attachment and exploration associated with healthy functioning early in life is, in important respects, similar to the love/work balance that marks healthy functioning in adulthood. By extending our research on adult attachment to include exploration, we hope to elucidate the role of love in adult life, to explain some of the links between love and work, and to further demonstrate the explanatory and integrative power of attachment theory.

Attachment and Exploration

According to Bowlby, attachment and exploration are linked as follows: To learn about and become competent at interacting with the physical and social environment, one must explore. But exploration can be tiring and even dangerous, so it is desirable to have a protector nearby, a haven of safety to which one can retreat. According to attachment theory, the tendency to form an attachment to a protector and the tendency to explore the environment are innate tendencies regulated by interlocking behavioral systems. The exploration system can function optimally only when the attachment system is relatively quiescent, namely, when an attachment figure feels sufficiently available and responsive (a state that Ainsworth, Blehar, Waters, & Wall, 1978, refer to as having a "secure base" and that Sroufe & Waters, 1977, call "felt security"). In other words, attachment needs are primary; they must be met before exploration can proceed normally.

The theorized link between attachment and exploration was initially tested by Ainsworth et al. (1978), who identified three patterns of infant attachment: secure, avoidant, and anxious/ambivalent. Secure infants match Bowlby's conception of nature's prototype in terms of both secure attachment to a caregiver and ability to use the caregiver as a secure base for exploration. Secure infants in Ainsworth et al.'s studies had mothers who were consistently sensitive and responsive to their signals and so could confidently explore their environment. (See Main, 1983, for further details concerning the secure toddler's exploratory behavior.)

Hypotheses

Just as attachments can be more or less healthy or secure, so can forms of work. In the same way that Ainsworth et al.'s (1978) avoidant infants appeared to explore to avoid seeking contact with their mothers, adults can approach their work compulsively or use it as a distraction from relational deficiencies. For someone with anxious/ambivalent proclivities, work can be viewed as an opportunity to satisfy attachment needs, a sideline that may interfere with job performance. On the basis of the documented attachment/exploration links in infancy and early childhood and of attachment theory's predictions concerning the dynamics of these two behavioral systems, a number of hypotheses can be derived, concerning the likely relations between attachment and exploration in adulthood.

Hypothesis 1

Securely attached subjects will report a secure orientation to work. This orientation will include high

(relative to those of insecurely attached subjects) ratings of work success and satisfaction, fewer work-related fears and worries concerning performance and evaluation by co-workers, and work habits that do not jeopardize health or relationships. Secure explorers, at any age, should be able to reap the most rewards from exploratory activity because they are not distracted by concerns over unmet attachment needs and do not explore primarily for the sake of pleasing or avoiding others.

Hypothesis 2

Anxious/ambivalently attached youngsters are typically too concerned with maintaining proximity to their caregivers to explore effectively. As these children develop, they may learn to use exploration as a means for achievement designed to attract the caregiver's attention and approval. Exploration then becomes a means of satisfying unmet attachment needs. Moreover, exploring merely as a means to win others' praise leaves a person vulnerable to feeling underappreciated.

We predict, therefore, that anxious/ambivalent attachment will be associated with an orientation to work that includes a preference for working with others rather than alone, a tendency to become overobligated as a way of pleasing others combined with feeling that one's own contribution is underappreciated, daydreaming about success and praise, and fearing failure and loss of esteem. Beyond affecting these social aspects of work, preoccupation with attachment concerns should be distracting and associated with inability to finish work projects, difficulty meeting deadlines, and poorer work performance.

Hypothesis 3

Like the avoidant infant, the avoidant adult will use exploration primarily as a means of keeping busy, avoiding uncomfortable interactions with others, and avoiding anxiety associated with unmet attachment needs. Because avoidant exploration is believed to reduce anxiety, avoidant people should be reluctant to stop working, to finish projects, or to take vacations (all nonsocial manifestations of avoidance). Avoidant attachment should be associated with exploratory behavior characterized by a preference for working alone, using work as an excuse to avoid socializing, and a compulsive approach to tasks that includes working during vacations, feeling nervous when not working, and working at the expense of health and relationships.

In addition to our interest in possible links between attachment and work, we want to investigate the effect of attachment on well-being more generally. We expect secure attachment, in relation to insecure attachment, to be associated with higher levels of physical and psychological health.

These hypotheses were tested in two related studies with overlapping subject samples. The first study examined the relation between attachment type and work orientation, assessed with measures taken from the research literature on work. This study was conducted to relate our hypotheses to an already existing body of work-related measures and findings. The second study was conducted in order to test our theory-based hypotheses more precisely.

Study 1

Study 1 involved publication of a love and work questionnaire in the Sunday magazine supplement of one of Colorado's largest circulation newspapers, the Denver *Post*. The overarching goal was to see if attachment type was related to exploration, here conceptualized as work orientation, in ways predicted by attachment theory.

Method

Subjects. Analyses reported here are based on the first 670 of over 1,000 replies received within 1 week following publication of the questionnaire. (The major findings were stable after the first few hundred, so additional replies were not keypunched.) Of the 670 replies, 143 were from men, 522 were from women, and 5 were from respondents who did not report their sex. The subjects ranged in age from 18 to 79, with a median age of 38 and a mean of 39 years. Average household income was $30,000 to $40,000; average education level was "graduated college." Ninety-six percent were heterosexual, 3% homosexual, and 1% bisexual. Forty-nine percent were married at the time of the survey (including those who were remarried); 27% were single; 25% were divorced or separated; 10% were "living with a lover"; and 3% were widowed. (Some respondents checked more than one category.)

Measures and procedure. The survey questionnaire, mentioned on the front page of the magazine, was titled "Loving/Working: Are they related? Tell psychologists your insights."

The measure of attachment type, described more fully by Hazan and Shaver (1987), offered respondents three answer alternatives, of which they were to choose the one that best described their feelings: (a) "I am somewhat uncomfortable being close to others; I find it difficult to trust them completely, difficult to allow myself to depend on them. I am nervous when anyone gets too close, and often, love partners want me to be more intimate than I feel comfortable being" (the avoidant type). (b) "I find that others are reluctant to get as close as I would like. I often worry that my partner doesn't really love me or won't want to stay with me. I want to get very close to my partner, and this sometimes scares people away" (the anxious/ambivalent type). (c) "I find it relatively easy to get close to others and am comfortable depending on them. I don't often worry about being abandoned or about someone getting too close to me" (the secure type). The attachment-type measure appeared after a measure of "most important love experiences" described by Hazan and Shaver (1987). This placement was designed to make love experiences salient before assessing attachment type.

Next came 21 items adapted from the existing literature on job satisfaction (e.g., Baruch et al., 1983; Crosby, 1984; Levinson, 1969; Parker, 1983; Smith, Kendall, & Hulin, 1969), covering such issues as job security, satisfaction with salary and co-workers, and opportunities for challenge. Subjects were asked to indicate, by circling 1, 2, 3, or 4 (indicating a range of responses from *not at all* to *extremely*) the extent to which they felt satisfied (or dissatisfied, in the case of 10 of the items) with each. This part of the questionnaire was followed by 8 individual questions concerning overall job satisfaction (response alternatives ranged from *extremely satisfied* to *extremely dissatisfied*); subject's perception of own work performance (*excellent* to *not very good*); judgment of co-workers' perception of subject's work performance (*excellent* to *not very good*); experience of romantic "crushes" on co-workers (*no, never* to *yes, it happens often*); experience of romantic affair(s) with co-workers (*no, never* to *yes, it happens often*); the degree to which relationship concerns interfere with work performance (*not at all* to *extremely*); the degree to which work concerns interfere with relationships (*not at all* to *extremely*); and the degree to which subject and partner have work-related arguments or disagreements (*not at all* to *extremely*).

For the next six items, subjects were asked to circle either "my relationship" or "my work" in relation to the following: which is more important, which usually brings the most pleasure, which usually brings the most pain, which has the greatest effect on overall life satisfaction, which (if forced to) would the subject choose, and which is considered to be primary. Next was a 14-item checklist measure of leisure activities, which was included in case such activities provided major avenues of exploration for some people. For the first half, subjects were asked to indicate, by circling items on an activity list (e.g., socializing, exercising, resting), how they spend their free time. For the second half, they were asked to say what they get from leisure activities, again by circling one or more items from a list of seven (e.g., renewed ties with others, improved health, relief from stress). This was followed by a 22-item symptom checklist used by Rubenstein and Shaver (1982) in a national study of loneliness.

The final section of the questionnaire focused entirely on demographic issues, such as age, marital status, educational background, income, religious affiliation, and occupation. The survey ended with a request for additional comments (the majority of respondents attached notes or letters) and an invitation to participate in a follow-up study, to which 58% responded by providing their name and telephone number. Subjects were asked to mail their replies to the Denver *Post* within 1 week.

Results and Discussion

Attachment type. Half (50%) of the subjects classified themselves as secure, 19% as anxious/ambivalent, and 30% as avoidant. These proportions were similar to those obtained in three previous studies (Hazan & Shaver, 1987, Studies 1 and 2; Shaver & Hazan, 1987) in which the frequency of self-classification as secure ranged from 51% to 56%, that of anxious/ambivalent ranged from 19% to 21%; and that of avoidant ranged from 23% to 28%.

Sex differences. There were few sex differences. Men more often than women reported having romantic crushes (*once or twice* vs. *never*) on co-workers, $t(657) = 2.15, p < .05$; men reported hav-

ing more frequent work-related arguments (*often* vs. *sometimes*) with their partners, $t(655) = 2.35, p < .05$; and on average, women were less well educated (*some college* vs. *graduated college*, $t(663) = 2.96, p < .01$) and had lower income ($10,000 to $20,000 vs. $20,000 to $30,000, $t(652) = 6.95, p < .001$).

Feelings about work. Hypotheses 1, 2, and 3 concerned the link between attachment type and work-related feelings and experiences. We predicted that each attachment type would be associated with a particular orientation to work which, in turn, would resemble the three patterns of exploration identified by Ainsworth et al. (1978). As an initial test of this hypothesized link, subjects were asked to indicate their degree of satisfaction and dissatisfaction on a number of items adapted from the research literature on work. Table 1 contains the mean item scores (each with a possible range of 1 to 4) for each attachment type, along with the F ratio from a one-way analysis of variance (ANOVA) on scores for each item. (An overall F that was based on all the items in the table was computed, using a multivariate analysis of variance procedure, or MANOVA, and proved to be highly significant: $F(42, 1218) = 2.05, p < .001$. We report ordinary ANOVAS in the table, rather than univariate Fs that were based on the MANOVA, so as not to reduce the Ns because of missing data.)

In line with Hypothesis 1, securely attached respondents reported relatively high levels of work satisfaction in terms of job security, co-workers, income, and opportunities for challenge and advancement. In line with Hypothesis 2, anxious/ambivalent attachment was associated with feelings of job insecurity, lack of appreciation and recognition by co-workers, and not getting desirable and deserved promotions. Compatible with Hypothesis 3, avoidantly attached respondents reported dissatisfaction with co-workers but were similar to secure respondents in their satisfaction with job security and opportunities for learning.

The differences among the attachment types in work-related feelings were generally small but in line with predictions. There is little in the descriptions of the attachment types that necessitates any particular pattern of responses on the work items, so the results are unlikely to be due to a mere semantic expansion of the independent variable. In addition, these work items, unlike the ones to be discussed later in connection with Study 2, were

TABLE 26.1. Mean Scores for Items Concerning Satisfaction/Disatisfaction with Work

Item	Attachment type			$F(2,658)$
	Avoidant	Anxious/ ambivalent	Secure	
Happy with				
Job security	2.76$_{ab}$	2.56$_a$	2.91$_b$	6.79***
Recognition	2.49$_a$	2.41$_a$	2.65$_b$	3.58*
Co-workers	2.78$_a$	2.88$_{ab}$	3.08$_b$	9.34***
Helping others	2.94$_a$	3.01$_{ab}$	3.19$_b$	6.47***
Competence	3.11$_a$	3.14$_a$	3.28$_b$	2.93
Variety	3.07$_a$	2.87$_b$	3.10$_a$	3.02*
Learning	2.93$_a$	2.62$_b$	3.00$_a$	6.43***
Working on own	3.36	3.39	3.45	0.88
Income	2.59	2.42	2.53	1.00
Advancement	2.10$_{ab}$	2.01$_a$	2.27$_b$	3.67*
Challenge	2.85$_{ab}$	2.67$_a$	2.95$_b$	3.42*
Unhappy with				
Too much work	2.01	1.86	1.84	2.35
No challenge	1.97	1.97	1.81	1.99
Job security	1.83$_a$	2.13$_b$	1.64$_a$	12.30***
Job conflicts	1.82	1.97	1.75	2.54
Advancement	2.20$_a$	2.32$_a$	1.92$_b$	8.61***
Recognition	2.18$_{ab}$	2.36$_a$	1.99$_b$	6.42***
Variety	1.80	1.89	1.67	2.58
Income	2.07	2.32	2.07	2.91
Advancement	2.22$_a$	2.34$_a$	2.08$_b$	3.08*
Co-workers	1.77$_a$	1.64$_{ab}$	1.53$_b$	6.03**

Note. Multivariate analysis of variance results for items in this table are reported in the text. Within each row, means with different subscripts differ significantly at $p = .05$.
*$p < .05$. **$p < .01$. ***$p < .001$.

not derived from attachment theory but were taken directly from studies of work. The pattern of differences, therefore, supports the claim that attachment types is related to feelings about work.

We predicted that the different attachment types would differ in overall job satisfaction and the balance between love and work. Table 2 contains the mean item scores for each attachment type and the results of a one-way ANOVA on scores for each item. (A MANOVA including all items in the table yielded a highly significant overall effect of attachment type: $F(28, 1,130) = 3.84$, $p < .001$.) Secure respondents reported higher overall work satisfaction, felt that they were good workers, and were confident that co-workers evaluated them highly. In contrast, anxious/ambivalent respondents expected co-workers to undervalue them, and avoidant respondents gave themselves lower ratings on job performance and expected similarly low ratings from co-workers.

In terms of the balance between love and work, secure attachment was associated with placing a higher value on, and deriving more pleasure from,

relationships than work. Secure subjects were also most likely to say that if forced, they would choose relationship success over work success. This fits with the notion that security is related to valuing and enjoying relationships. Anxious/ambivalent respondents were most likely to claim that love concerns interfere with work, perhaps referring to the kind of preoccupation with attachment needs that inhibits exploration. Attachment theory makes no predictions about the possible effects of exploration on attachment, and interestingly, the three attachment types did not differ in rate of reporting that concerns about work interfere with romantic relationships. Nor did the groups differ in their propensity to argue with love partners about work. Anxious/ambivalent subjects were also slightly, although not significantly, more likely to report romantic interest in co-workers. In addition, this group reported experiencing more pain in relation to love than to work. Avoidant respondents were most likely to emphasize the importance of work over love. For example, they were more likely to say they would choose work success over relation-

TABLE 26.2. Mean Scores and F Ratios for Items Concerning Work-Related Feelings and Experiences

| | Attachment type | | | |
Items	Avoidant	Anxious/ ambivalent	Secure	$F(2,658)$
Overall work satisfaction (6–pt.)	4.19$_a$	4.15$_a$	4.53$_b$	9.02***
How good are you at work? (5–pt.)	4.26	4.40	4.40	3.91*
How good would co-workers say you are? (5–pt.)	4.28$_a$	4.26$_a$	4.42$_b$	4.88**
Had crush on co-worker? (4–pt.)	1.67	1.79	1.62	2.70
Had affair with co-worker? (4–pt.)	1.48	1.59	1.45	1.67
How much does love interfere with work? (4–pt.)	1.77$_a$	1.86$_a$	1.63$_b$	7.19***
How much does work interfere with love? (4–pt.)	1.98	1.94	1.92	0.50
Argue with partner about work? (4–pt.)	1.51	1.55	1.50	0.22
Which is most important, work or relationship? (2–pt.)	1.62$_a$	1.67$_a$	1.81$_b$	12.34***
Which gives most pleasure, work or relationship? (2–pt.)	1.64$_a$	1.71$_a$	1.82$_b$	11.25***
Which causes most pain, work or relationship? (2–pt.)	1.47$_a$	1.67$_b$	1.37$_a$	17.58***
Which has greatest effect on overall happiness? (2–pt.)	1.59$_a$	1.70$_{ab}$	1.77$_b$	9.36***
Which would you choose? (2–pt.)	1.75$_a$	1.79$_{ab}$	1.87$_b$	6.59***
Which is more true, work supports love or love supports work? (2–pt.)	1.29$_a$	1.19$_{ab}$	1.16$_b$	6.00**

Note. Multivariate analysis of variance results for items in this table are reported in the text. Within each row, means with different subscripts differ significantly at $p = .05$. A high score on the 2-point scales indicates the love relationship alternative, except for the last scale, in which a high score indicates agreement with "work supports love."
*$p < .05$. **$p < .01$. ***$p < .001$.

ship success, that work has a greater overall effect on their happiness than do relationships, and that work success supports relationship success. Similar to avoidant infant explorers, avoidant adult workers tend to focus on work activity instead of relationships. In general, these findings lend additional support to the hypotheses.

Leisure activities. As stated earlier, not all jobs are well suited to provide the kind of challenge and stimulation typically associated with the term *exploration,* so subjects were also asked about activities outside of work (resting, socializing, exercising, shopping, traveling, and hobbies) and about what benefits they derive from leisure (improved health, relief from stress, renewed social ties, excitement, new knowledge, and sense of mastery). A MANOVA on the entire set of items proved significant: $F(28, 1290) = 2.54$, $p < .001$. Although scores on the majority of the items were not related to attachment type, the few that were are worth mentioning. Avoidant subjects were least likely to say they spent their free time socializing (42% vs. 58% and 59% for the anxious/ambiva-

lent and secure subjects, respectively) and least likely to say that leisure provided renewed social ties (34% vs. 54% and 57%). Anxious/ambivalent subjects were most likely to report that their leisure activities provide excitement (47% vs. 32% and 39% for the avoidant and secure types, respectively) and to report spending free time shopping (42% vs. 33% and 29%). (Shopping may be a form of immediate self-gratification; Rubenstein & Shaver, 1982, found that lonely people shop as one means of coping with negative feelings.) Avoidant subjects were least likely to report gaining new knowledge during free time (46% vs. 62% and 59% for anxious/ambivalent and secure subjects, respectively).

Well-being. The well-being measure used here was a symptom checklist previously used by Rubenstein and Shaver (1982) in a national study of loneliness. A principal-components analysis followed by equamax rotation was performed on the 22-item measure. Five factors had eigenvalues greater than 1.0. Items loading above .40 on one of the factors were analyzed for reliability, and the resulting coefficient alphas ranged from .52 for the Physical Illness factor to .89 for the Loneliness and Depression factor. Table 3 contains the results of a one-way ANOVA on the scale means for the three attachment types. Secure subjects were significantly less likely than insecure subjects were to report all five categories of symptoms. The results of Study 1 will be discussed more fully in the General Discussion section.

Study 2

The purpose of Study 2 was to pursue the effects of attachment type on work orientation, using items that were based on attachment theory and designed especially for this purpose.

Method

Subjects. Fifty-eight percent, or 387, of the 670 replies keypunched for Study 1 included a name and a telephone number. A supplementary questionnaire, to be described in the next paragraph, was mailed to the 290 respondents who, in addition, supplied a return address. They did not differ significantly from the larger sample in the prevalence of the three attachment types or in terms of sex, age, education, or average income.

Measures and procedure. A two-page love and work questionnaire was distributed by mail. It included one page of items concerning sexuality and caregiving (designed to pilot test measures for another research project) in addition to 35 work-related items derived from attachment theory and research. (These items are described in detail in a later section.) Responses to the 35 items were indicated by circling SD, D, A, or SA on a *strongly disagree* to *strongly agree* continuum. Subjects were asked to complete the questionnaire and return it within a week. A stamped, preaddressed envelope was included. Of the 290 questionnaires distributed, 260 were returned within a week, another 3 were returned by the post office for having an insufficient address, and 11 more arrived within a month, for a total return rate between 90% and 94%. Only the first 260 were keypunched.

It should be noted that these 260 subjects were not retested with the single-item attachment-type measure. Thus, the prediction of work items from attachment type extended over a period of more than 2 months.

Results and Discussion

The supplementary questionnaire items were designed to further test the predicted relationship between attachment and work (conceptualized as exploration). A principal-components analysis followed by equamax rotation was performed on the 35-item measure. Nine factors had eigenvalues greater than 1.0 and appeared to the left of the elbow in a scree test. Of these nine factors, seven scales consisting of the items that loaded above .40 on one of the factors were analyzed for reliability; and items that reduced coefficient alpha were deleted from the scales. Table 4 contains the names of the seven factor-based scales and sample

TABLE 26.3. Information and Mean Scores on 4-Point Symptom Scales

| Scale | No. items | Attachment type | | | $F(2,658)$ |
		Avoidant	Anxious/ ambivalent	Secure	
Loneliness and Depression (Crying easily, feeling hopeless)	8	2.02_a	2.05_a	1.49_b	60.73*
Anxiety (Feeling nervous, worrying)	6	2.23_a	2.16_a	1.77_b	42.87*
Hostility (Outbursts of temper, feeling irritable)	4	2.01_a	1.94_a	1.72_b	16.64*
Psychosomatic Illness (Muscle tension, intestinal problems)	5	1.63_a	1.57_a	1.39_b	19.50*
Physical Illness (Cold, flu)	4	1.85_a	1.83_a	1.65_b	10.40*

Note. Within each row, means with different subscripts differ significantly at $p = .05$.
*$p < .001$.

items, the number of items retained, coefficient alpha for each, and the results of one-way ANOVAs on the mean scale scores for the different attachment types. Some of the shorter scales had relatively low coefficient alphas but proved sufficiently reliable to reveal an association with attachment type. A MANOVA on the entire set of scales proved significant, $F(14,456) = 4.32$, $p < .001$.

The secure orientation to work. The securely attached respondents reported a relatively positive approach to work. In line with Hypothesis 1, they are least likely to put off work, least likely to have difficulty completing tasks, and least likely to fear failure and rejection from co-workers. They report enjoying their vacations and not allowing work to jeopardize their relationships or health.

The anxious/ambivalent orientation to work. Anxious/ambivalent respondents exhibited a different pattern of responses on the work items. As predicted, they preferred to work with others, reported feeling misunderstood and underappreciated, were motivated by approval, and worried that others would not be impressed with their work

performance or would reject them. As predicted, anxious/ambivalently attached subjects reported that interpersonal concerns interfered with productivity.

Not shown in Table 4 is a significant mean difference on the item "I don't like it when others try to become involved in my work." This item, which was not on any of the scales because it produced its own factor, was included to see whether anxious/ambivalent subjects, despite preferring to work with others, might resent others' intrusions into their work. (Ainsworth et al., 1978, characterized the mothers of anxious/ambivalent infants as intrusive.) The means on the feelings-about-intrusiveness item were 2.67 for secure subjects, 3.05 for avoidant subjects, and 3.20 for anxious/ambivalent subjects, $F(2, 233) = 6.20$, $p < .01$.

The avoidant orientation to work. In line with Hypothesis 3, avoidant respondents were more likely to indicate that they feel nervous when not working and that work interferes with their relationships and health. (Although the difference between avoidant and anxious/ambivalent subjects

TABLE 26.4. Mean Scores and Information on 5-Point Work Scales Derived from Attachment Theory ($N = 260$)

Scale	Alpha	No. items	Avoidant	Anxious/ ambivalent	Secure	$F(2, 233)$
			Attachment type			
Fears Failure/Disapproval Worries won't impress Fears rejection for poor work	.79	4	2.83$_a$	2.88$_a$	2.29$_b$	10.98***
Prefers Working with Others Hates working alone Works better with others	.77	4	2.53$_{ab}$	2.73$_a$	2.41$_b$	5.68**
Work Harms Health/ Relationships Overwork harms self/others Work interferes with relationships	74	4	2.50$_a$	2.25$_a$	1.93$_b$	12.31***
Distracted/Preoccupied Puts off work Difficulty finishing projects	.69	6	2.15$_{ab}$	2.36$_a$	2.04$_b$	5.43***
Feels unappreciated Work efforts misunderstood Work efforts unappreciated	.79	3	2.84$_{ab}$	3.20$_a$	2.51$_b$	8.54***
Needs/Desires to Keep Busy Vacations are pleasureless Nervous when not working	.48	3	2.55$_a$	2.37$_{ab}$	2.13$_b$	5.79**
Motivated by Approval Imagines praise Admiration is best reward	.45	3	3.11$_{ab}$	3.25$_a$	2.91$_b$	3.55*

Note. Within each row, means with different subscripts differ significantly at p = .05.
*p < .05. ** p < .01. *** p < .001.

on the Work Harms Health/Relationships Scale was not quite significant, it was significant for two of the scale's individual items: "Work interferes with relationships" and "work leaves no time for friends.") On the single item "I prefer to work alone," which did not fit with any of the scales, avoidant subjects obtained the highest score: 3.37, versus 3.09 for anxious/ambivalent subjects and 2.80 for secure subjects, $F(2, 233) = 4.36$, $p < .05$. Thus, according to avoidant subjects, work leaves little time for close relationships, and vacations are generally pleasureless.

Discriminant analyses. A question remains as to whether the differences are simply unidimensional, namely, simply a matter of security versus insecurity, rather than reflections of two distinct insecure patterns. Of 16 individual work items yielding significant differences among the three attachment groups, only 2 ("work leaves no time for friends" and "difficulty finishing projects") significantly distinguish the avoidant group from the anxious/ambivalent group. None of the multi-item scales in Table 3 distinguish significantly between the two insecure groups, although the two differ significantly from the secure group in distinctive ways. To address this issue and summarize differences among the three groups, two hierarchical discriminant-function analyses were performed to assess predictability of membership in the three attachment categories from work variables. Subjects with no missing data on any of the variables involved ($N = 224$) were included in the analyses. In the first analysis, both discriminant functions (two being the maximum possible number, given three target groups) were statistically significant, with a combined $\chi^2(24, N = 224) = 78.35$, $p < .001$. After removal of the first function, $\chi^2(11, N = 224) = 32.38$, $p < .001$, for the second function. The first function accounted for 59.5% of the between-groups variability; the second accounted for a sizable 40.5%, indicating that the differences between groups are not reducible to a single security–insecurity dimension. As shown in Figure 1, the first discriminant function separated secure subjects from insecure subjects. The second function separated avoidant subjects from anxious/ambivalent subjects. As can be seen in Table 5, 54.7% of the avoidant subjects were classified correctly, as were 55.8% of the anxious/ambivalent subjects and 64.0% of the secure subjects, for an overall correct classification percentage of 59.6% (in a three-category system, chance

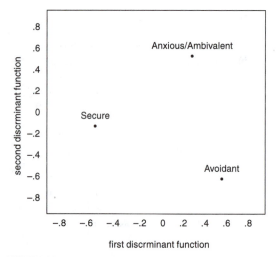

FIGURE 26.1 ■ Plot of three group centroids on two discriminant functions derived from work items ($N = 260$).

accuracy is 33.3%).

Correlations of the 19 predictor variables with the two discriminant functions are shown in Table 6. Only correlations of .20 or above are shown. The items that best discriminated between secure and insecure subjects included (a) work leaves no time for friends, (b) work interferes with relationships, (c) fears work failure, (d) work efforts are misunderstood, (e) rejects others' involvement, (f) nervous when not working, (g) prefers to work alone, and (h) work is useful for avoiding social events.

Because the same items were used for both the discrimination between secure and insecure types, on the one hand, and the discrimination between the two insecure types, on the other hand, we conducted a second analysis to investigate more clearly the best discriminators between avoidant subjects and anxious/ambivalent subjects. The discriminant function was significant, $\chi^2(35, N = 113) = 26.56$, $p < .001$, and correctly classified 76.6% of the

TABLE 26.5. Classification Results for the Discriminant Analysis

Actual group	Predicted group membership		
	Avoidant	Anxious/ ambivalent	Secure
Avoidant	54.7%	17.2%	28.1%
Anxious/ambivalent	23.1%	55.8%	21.2%
Secure	18.4%	17.5%	64.0%

TABLE 26.6. Correlations Between Work Items and Discriminant Functions for the Entire Study 2 Sample (N = 260)

Item	Function 1	Function 2
Work leaves no time for friends	.54	−.34
Work interferes with relationships	.53	−.20
Fears work failure	.52	
Work efforts misunderstood	.44	.43
Rejects others' involvement	.43	.22
Nervous when not working	.42	
Prefers to work alone	.42	
Work useful for avoiding social events	.40	
Overwork damages self/ significant others	.35	
Work efforts unappreciated	.35	.34
Worries about work performance	.34	
Vacations are pleasureless	.34	−.22
Worries others won't be impressed	.32	
Rejects advice for improving work	.24	
Fears rejection for poor work	.24	
Difficulty finishing projects		.58
Slacks off after praise		.25
Gets overinvolved in tasks	.21	.25
Overobligates self at work		.21

avoidant subjects and 63.5% of the anxious/ambivalents. Correlations of the 13 predictor variables (those with correlations of .20 or above) with the discriminant function are shown in Table 7. The items that best discriminated between the avoidant and anxious/ambivalent types, with positively correlated variables being those named more frequently by anxious/ambivalent subjects, included (a) difficulty finishing work projects, (b) work leaves no time for friends, (c) work efforts are misunderstood, (d) vacations are pleasureless, (e) work efforts are unappreciated, (f) work interferes with relationships, (g) works better with others, (h) slacks off after praise, (i) uses work to avoid social events, (j) gets overinvolved in tasks, (k) hates working alone, (l) prefers to work alone, and (m) day-dreams about success. All of these findings were in line with theory-based predictions.

Summary and comments. The results can be summarized by saying that secure subjects generally do not worry about work failure or feel unappreciated. In addition, they generally do not allow work to interfere with friendships or health and do take enjoyable vacations from work. Anxious/ambivalent subjects, in contrast, worry about their work performance, prefer to work with others but feel underappreciated and fear rejection for poor performance. They are also easily distracted, have trouble completing projects, and tend to slack off after receiving praise. Avoidant subjects prefer to work alone, use work to avoid having friends or a social life, and do not take enjoyable vacations from work.

Overall, the results of Study 2 support an attachment-theoretical approach to the study of love and work. There are three distinct patterns of feelings regarding work, and they are functionally similar to the three patterns of exploration seen in infancy and early childhood. Anxious/ambivalent attachment entails a preoccupation with attachment issues and an accompanying inability to focus on tasks, except when performance is perceived as an opportunity to work closely with others or to gain love and respect. Such distraction and preoccupation may be costly: Anxious/ambivalent subjects reported the lowest average income of the three groups—$20,000 to $30,000 compared with $30,000 to $40,000 for both the secure and avoidant subjects, $F(2,644) = 24.83, p < .001$. The income difference is independent of the sex difference in income reported earlier, and is not due simply to education. Attachment type was related to educational level; the secure group reported a significantly higher level of education than did the two insecure groups ("graduated college" vs. "some college"), $F(2,661) = 5.20, p < .01$. However, a three-way (Sex × Education × Attachment Type) ANOVA predicting income revealed no significant interaction between sex and attachment

TABLE 26.7. Correlations Between Work Items and Discriminant Functions for Avoidant and Anxious/Ambivalent Subjects (N = 113)

Item	Function 1
Difficulty finishing projects	.55
Work leaves no time for friends	−.43
Work efforts misunderstood	.34
Vacations are pleasureless	−.29
Work efforts unappreciated	.29
Work interferes with relationships	−.28
Works better with others	.27
Slacks off after praise	.25
Work useful for avoiding social events	−.24
Gets overinvolved in tasks	.24
Hates working alone	.21
Prefers to work alone	−.20
Daydreams about success	.20

type, $F(2,608) = 1.04$, *ns*, or between education and attachment type, $F(12,608) = 1.39$, *ns*.

The relatively low income reported by anxious/ambivalent respondents may be interpreted in a number of ways. One possibility is that anxious/ambivalent people are more likely to hold low-status jobs. However, only 2 of the 12 occupational categories were significantly related to attachment type: Teachers were more likely to endorse the secure attachment type, and technicians–skilled workers were more likely to describe themselves as anxious/ambivalent. Attachment type was not related to occupational categories such as artist, housewife, manager, or professional. Another possibility is that insufficient income causes relationship dissatisfaction, which is reflected in the endorsement of an insecure attachment type. However, this interpretation does not explain why avoidant respondents had an average income equal to that of the secure group. A third interpretation is that anxious/ambivalent attachment actually interferes with job performance and productivity, as predicted by attachment theory.

Avoidant attachment is associated with a compulsive approach to activity that serves as a way of avoiding other people. This approach to work is costly in terms of overall well-being, if not in terms of income. In contrast, secure attachment seems to support the healthiest and most satisfying approach to work: one that results in success but without the personal and social costs of the other two types.

General Discussion

Three hypotheses concerning the relation between attachment–love and exploration–work in adulthood were derived from attachment theory and research. We assessed adult attachment type by using a single-item measure that asked subjects to choose the one description among three that best summarized their feelings and behavior in romantic love relationships. The descriptions were designed by translating into adult terms the three patterns of attachment observed by Ainsworth et al. (1978).

In line with Hypothesis 1, secure respondents approach their work with the confidence associated with secure attachment. They enjoy work activity and are relatively unburdened by fears of failure. And, although they value work, they tend to value relationships more and generally do not allow work to interfere with those relationships. Securely attached people typically do not use work to satisfy unmet needs for love, nor do they use work to avoid social interaction.

In support of Hypothesis 2, anxious/ambivalent respondents reported that love concerns often interfere with work performance and that they frequently fear rejection for poor performance. They also reported a tendency to slack off following praise, which may indicate that their main motivation at work is to gain respect and admiration from others. Anxious/ambivalent respondents have the lowest average income of the three groups, even when differences in education are controlled.

Consistent with Hypothesis 3, avoidant respondents use work activity to avoid social interaction. They said that work interferes with having friends and a social life. Although they reported an average income equal to that of the secure group, they are less satisfied with their jobs. Nevertheless, they are least likely to take enjoyable vacations.

Secure attachment was also associated with greater overall well-being. In relation to insecure respondents, secure respondents are less likely to report suffering from loneliness and depression, anxiety, or irritability or are less likely to report having had colds or flu.

One possible criticism of our previous work on adult attachment (e.g., Hazan & Shaver, 1987) is that the measures of attachment type, on the one hand, and of relationship experiences (e.g., trust, jealousy, desire for reciprocation), on the other hand, were part of a shared semantic network. The supposed dependent variables may have been logical extensions or elaborations of the independent variable (as happens so often in personality research). We think the present studies begin to counter that criticism. Little in the descriptions of the three attachment types necessitates any particular pattern of responses on many of the work items. For instance, items such as feeling distrustful of others and being reluctant to take vacations from work (both endorsed more frequently by avoidant respondents) are semantically dissimilar but closely connected through the theory. Other items—such as an inability to finish tasks, slacking off after praise, or daydreaming about success—also go beyond a mere semantic expansion of the anxious/ambivalent attachment-type description. Note also that the same three attachment groups have been derived from subjects' descriptions of childhood relationships with parents, features of adult love experiences (Hazan & Shaver, 1987), and now from orientation to work. This is an indication of the broad integrative power of the theory and the validity of the three types. No other social-psychological theory of love offers this kind of integrative breadth (Shaver & Hazan, 1988).

ACKNOWLEDGMENTS

The research reported here was part of Cindy Hazan's doctoral dissertation at the University of Denver, for which Phillip R. Shaver served as adviser.

Preparation of this article was supported by National Science Foundation Grant BSN-8808736 to Cindy Hazan and Phillip R. Shaver. We are grateful to Richard Canfield, Harry Gollob, Susan Harter, Howard Markman, Judith Schwartz, Robert Sternberg, and three anonymous reviewers for many useful suggestions.

REFERENCES

Ainsworth, M. D. S., Blehar, M. C., Waters, E., & Wall, S. (1978). *Patterns of attachment: A psychological study of the strange situation*. Hillsdale, NJ: Erlbaum.

Baruch, G., Barnett, R., & Rivers, C. (1983). *Lifeprints: New patterns of love and work for today's women*. New York: McGraw-Hill.

Bowlby, J. (1969). *Attachment and loss: Vol. 1. Attachment*. New York: Basic Books.

Bowlby, J. (1973). *Attachment and loss: Vol. 2. Separation*. New York: Basic Books.

Bowlby, J. (1980). *Attachment and loss: Vol. 3. Loss*. New York: Basic Books.

Bowlby, J. (1988). *A secure base: Parent–child attachment and healthy human development*. New York: Basic Books.

Brennan, K. A., Hazan, C., & Shaver, P. R. (1989, April). *Multi-item assessment of adult attachment type*. Paper presented at the 60th annual convention of the Eastern Psychological Association, Boston, MA.

Campos, J. J., Barrett, K., Lamb, M. E., Goldsmith, H. H., & Stenberg, C. (1983). Socioemotional development. In M. M. Haith & J. J. Campos (Eds.), *Handbook of child psychology: Vol. 2. Infancy and psychobiology* (pp. 783–915). New York: Wiley.

Collins, N. L., & Read, S. J. (1990). Adult attachment, working models, and relationship quality in dating couples. *Journal of Personality and Social Psychology, 58*, 644–663.

Crosby, F. (1984). Job satisfaction and domestic life. In M. D. Lee & R. N. Kanungo (Eds.), *Management of work and personal life: Problems and opportunities* (pp. 41–60). New York: Praeger.

Egeland, B., & Farber, E. A. (1984). Infant–mother attachment: Factors related to its development and changes over time. *Child Development, 55*, 753–762.

Erikson, E. H. (1963). *Childhood and society* (2nd ed.). New York: Norton.

Feeney, J. A., & Noller, P. (1990). Attachment style as a predictor of adult romantic relationships. *Journal of Personality and Social Psychology, 58*, 281–291.

Fiedler, F. E. (1967). *A theory of leadership effectiveness*. New York: McGraw-Hill.

Gurin, G., Veroff, J., & Feld, J. (1960). *Americans view their mental health*. New York: Basic Books.

Hazan, C., & Hutt, M. J. (1989, October). Continuity and change in inner working models of attachment. In Keith Davis (Chair), *Adult Attachment, Mental Models, and Relationship Formation*. Symposium conducted at the annual meeting of the Society for Experimental Social Psychology, Santa Monica, CA.

Hazan, C., & Shaver, P. (1987). Romantic love conceptualized as an attachment process. *Journal of Personality and Social Psychology, 52*, 511–524.

Kanter, R. M. (1977). *Work and family in the United States: A critical review and agenda for research and policy*. New York: Sage.

Kohn, M. L., & Schooler, C. (1973). Occupational experience and psychological functioning: An assessment of reciprocal effects. *American Sociological Review, 38*, 97–118.

Lee, M. D., & Kanungo, R. N. (Eds.). (1984). *Management of work and personal life: Problems and opportunities*. New York: Praeger.

Levinson, H. (1969). Emotional toxicity of the work environment. *Archives of Environmental Health, 19*, 239–243.

Levy, M. B., & Davis, K. E. (1988). Lovestyles and attachment styles compared: Their relations to each other and to various relationship characteristics. *Journal of Social and Personal Relationships, 5*, 439–471.

Main, M. (1983). Exploration, play, and cognitive functioning related to infant–mother attachment. *Infant Behavior and Development, 6*, 167–174.

Maslow, A. (1954). *Motivation and personality*. New York: Harper & Row.

Mikulincer M., Florian, V., & Tolmacz, R. (1990). Attachment styles and fear of personal death: A case study of affect regulation. *Journal of Personality and Social Psychology, 58*, 273–280.

Parker, S. (1983). *Leisure and work*. London: George Allen & Unwin.

Piotrkowski, C. S. (1978). *Work and the family system: A naturalistic study of working-class and lower-middle-class families*. New York: Free Press.

Robinson, J. P. (1984). Work, free time, and the quality of life. In M. D. Lee & R. N. Kanungo (Eds.), *Management of work and personal life* (pp. 67–91). New York: Praeger.

Rogers, C. R. (1961). *On becoming a person*. Boston: Houghton Mifflin.

Rubenstein. C., & Shaver, P. (1982). *In search of intimacy*. New York: Delacorte.

Shaver, P., & Hazan, C. (1987). Being lonely, falling in love: Perspectives from attachment theory. In M. Hojat & R. Crandall (Eds.), Loneliness: Theory, research, and applications. [Special issue]. *Journal of Social Behavior and Personality, 2*, 105–124.

Shaver, P. R., & Hazan, C. (1988). A biased overview of the study of love. *Journal of Social and Personal Relationships, 5*, 473–501.

Shaver, P., Hazan, C., & Bradshaw, D. (1988). Love as attachment: The integration of three behavioral systems. In R. Sternberg & M. Barnes (Eds.). *The psychology of love* (pp. 69–99). New Haven, CT: Yale University Press.

Smith, P., Kendall, L. M., & Hulin, C. L. (1969). *The measurement of satisfaction in work and retirement: A strategy for the study of attitudes*. Chicago: Rand McNally.

Sroufe, L. A., & Waters, E. (1977). Attachment as an organizational construct. *Child Development, 48*, 1184–1199.

Troyat, H. (Ed.). (1967). *Tolstoy* New York: Doubleday.

Vaillant, G. E. (1977). *Adaptation to life: How the best and the brightest came of age*. Boston: Little, Brown.

Development of Prosocial, Individualistic, and Competitive Orientations: Theory and Preliminary Evidence

Paul A. M. Van Lange • Free University
Ellen M. N. De Bruin • Free University
Wilma Otten • University of Amsterdam
Jeffrey A. Joireman • Seattle Pacific University

Editors' Notes

The present selection is unique in that it brings together two separate lines of theorizing in social psychology. One line is already familiar from the last two readings, and it has to do with attachment styles. The second is novel to this selection and it derives from the theory of interdependence. The theory of interdependence relates the structure of the interpersonal situation to the individuals' outcome orientation. Of special interest are intermediate situations whose structure allows several possible response patterns. The present selection focuses on such a situation. An intermediate situation allows the following response patterns or social value orientations: a "prosocial" orientation (a desire to maximize outcomes for both oneself and the other party), an "individualist" orientation (caring only about one's own outcomes), and a "competitive" orientation (the desire to outdo one's partner at all costs). The previous selection has shown that attachment styles that are shaped in one's childhood can affect one's attitudes toward one's work and leisure activities. This selection demonstrates that attachment styles are also relevant to our typical style of interacting with others (i.e., our "social value orientations"). Also noteworthy about this selection is its extension to life-span issues, specifically regarding shifts in a person's social value orientations over his or her life span. Thus, we see here a remarkable tracing of a significant psychological mechanism (social value orientation) originating in childhood experiences and evolving over the course of one's lifetime.

371

Discussion Questions

1. How might different attachment styles relate to different social value orientations?
2. In what ways does study 2 go beyond and strengthen the argument made by Study 1?
3. According to the authors, why does the percentage of prosocial individuals increase over the course of one's lifetime?

Suggested Readings

Insko, C. A., Shopler, J., Hoyle, R. H., Dardis, G. J., & Graetz, K. A. (1990). Individual-group discontinuity as a function of fear and greed. *Journal of Personality and Social Psychology, 58,* 68–79.

Kelley, H. H., & Stahelski, A. J. (1970). Social interaction basis of cooperators' and competitors' beliefs about others. *Journal of Personality and Social Psychology, 16,* 66–91.

Rusbult, C. E. (1983). A longitudinal test of the investment model: The development (and deterioration) of satisfaction and committment in heterosexual involvements. *Journal of Personality and Social Psychology, 45,* 101–117.

Authors' Abstract

The authors adopt an interdependence analysis of social value orientation, proposing that prosocial, individualistic, and competitive orientations are (a) partially rooted in different patterns of social interaction as experienced during the periods spanning early childhood to young adulthood and (b) further shaped by different patterns of social interaction as experienced during early adulthood, middle adulthood, and old age. Congruent with this analysis, results revealed that relative to individualists and competitors, prosocial individuals exhibited greater levels of secure attachment (Studies 1 and 2) and reported having more siblings, especially sisters (Study 3). Finally, the prevalence of prosocials increased—and the prevalence of individualists and competitors decreased—from early adulthood to middle adulthood and old age (Study 4).

Although a variety of different social value orientations can be distinguished from a theoretical point of view (e.g., Knight & Dubro, 1984), in this article we address a three-category typology of social value orientation, examining differences between prosocial, individualistic, and competitive orientations. *Prosocials* tend to maximize outcomes for both themselves and others (i.e., cooperation) and to minimize differences between outcomes for themselves and others (i.e., equality); *individualists* tend to maximize their own outcomes with little or no regard for others' outcomes; and *competitors* tend to maximize their own outcomes relative to others' outcomes, seeking relative advantage over others. The three social value orientations are predictive of behavior in a variety of social dilemma tasks, with prosocials exhibiting clear tendencies toward cooperation (unless others fail to reciprocate), and individualists and competitors exhibiting tendencies toward maximizing their own and relative gain, even when interdependent others evidence high levels of cooperation (e.g., Kuhlman & Marshello, 1975; Liebrand & Van Run, 1985; McClintock & Liebrand, 1988; Sattler & Kerr, 1991; Van Lange & Kuhlman, 1994). Moreover, social value orientations are predictive of helping behavior, judgments of everyday life incidents of cooperation and competition, decisions and judgments regarding commuting choices, and willingness to sacrifice in close relationships (Beggan, Messick, & Allison, 1988; McClintock & Allison, 1989; Van

Lange, Agnew, Harinck, & Steemers, in press; Van Vugt, Meertens, & Van Lange, 1995).

Interdependence Analysis of Social Value Orientation

The concept of social value orientation reflects distinct ways in which outcomes for self and others are evaluated, some of which represent broader considerations that extend and complement the pursuit of immediate self-interest (e.g., prosocial and competitive motivation). Interdependence theory has conceptualized such broader considerations in terms of transformation of motivation, assuming that given interdependence situations (i.e., the given matrix) are transformed into subjective interdependence situations (i.e., the effective matrix) that ultimately guide interdependent behavior (Kelly & Thibaut, 1978). Such stable transformational tendencies, at least in part, are assumed to be shaped by *social interaction experiences*, which are a function of the interdependence features of a situation and the behavior of the two or more persons involved (cf. Kelley, 1997). For example, the experience of cooperative interaction is a function of the features of interdependence underlying a situation (i.e., whether such features permit cooperative and noncooperative choices, such as in the prisoner's dilemma) and the cooperative behavior exhibited by both persons.

One important interdependence feature of situations that guides social interaction is the correspondence of outcomes, or the degree to which preferences correspond versus conflict. A situation characterized by high correspondence does not permit cooperative and noncooperative choices, in that a choice serving one's own interests also tends to serve the other's interests (i.e., such situations challenge individuals' ability to coordinate). A situation characterized by intermediate correspondence generally does permit cooperative and noncooperative choices, in that the pursuit of the other's well-being and joint well-being can only occur at some cost to one's own well being. Situations characterized by perfect noncorrespondence represent a perfect conflict of interest, such that there is no basis for pursuing joint well-being. Prior research has revealed that experience with such situations may shape transformational tendencies. For example, individuals tend to develop norms and agreements to protect their own and others' well-being, particularly when joint well-being is increasingly challenged by a stronger conflict of interest (e.g., Thibaut, 1968; Thibaut & Faucheux, 1965).

Transformational tendencies may also be shaped by patterns of social interaction that are largely conditioned by another person's behavior. For example, repeated experience with others who tend to pursue self-interest or relative advantage over others may lead people to develop an individualistic or competitive orientation rather than a prosocial orientation. Alternatively, repeated experience with others who engage in prosocial transformations may lead people to develop a prosocial orientation. Consistent with this argument, prior research has revealed that prosocials expect others to be more cooperative than do individualists and competitors (e.g., Kuhlman & Wimberley, 1976). In a related manner, individuals' own tendencies to exhibit cooperation or noncooperation affect patterns of social interaction, which in turn are likely to shape (and confirm) one's own transformational tendencies. Indeed, initial beliefs regarding others' cooperative and noncooperative behavior are likely to be confirmed through individuals' own behavior (especially among those who approach others noncooperatively; cf. Kelley & Stahelski, 1970). Thus, on the basis of interdependence theory, we assumed that social interaction experiences, which are a function of the situation and the two (or more) persons involved, are the basis for the development of relatively stable social value orientations.

It is clear that different individuals experience different histories of social interaction. For example, young children who have repeatedly experienced interactions in which parents are very attentive to their elementary needs are likely to develop trust and security, which may promote prosocial orientation. Conversely, children who have repeatedly experienced interactions in which parents are not very attentive to their needs are likely to develop distrust and insecurity, which may enhance self-centered orientations. As another example, relative to individuals raised in small families, individuals raised in large families may have acquired greater experience with situations entailing some conflict of interest (e.g., scarcity of material or immaterial resources, such as the sharing of toys or attention from parents), which produces patterns of social interaction that may in turn shape individuals' social value orientations. Thus, as a consequence of such interaction experiences, individuals acquire interpersonal dispositions, reflected in the probability of approaching certain classes of interdependent situations in a prosocial, individualistic, or competitive manner.[1]

Although social value orientations are relatively stable over time, such transformational tendencies may be further shaped by patterns of social interaction as one experiences throughout a lifetime, from early adulthood to old age (cf. Erikson, 1980). It is plausible that throughout a lifetime, individuals acquire greater experience with a more varied set of social interactions (e.g., greater experience with others depending on you, greater experience with partners who differ in their approach to interdependence situations). Such extended experience may shape the further development of social value orientation.

Study 1

The purpose of Study 1 was to examine the relationship between social value orientation and attachment styles, a social disposition that is very explicitly assumed to be a product of past interaction experiences. Following traditional conceptualizations of attachment theory (Bowlby, 1969, 1973, 1980; see also Ainsworth, Blehar, Waters, & Wall, 1978), the field of personality and social psychology has recently emphasized the contribution of adult attachment styles in understanding patterns of interaction in ongoing relationships (e.g., Collins & Read, 1990; Hazan & Shaver, 1987; Simpson, 1990). It is important to note that attachment theory assumes that early childhood experiences with the primary caregiver (usually the mother) form the basis of the development of a particular attachment style. Traditionally, three attachment styles have been delineated, often called *secure, anxious–ambivalent*, and *avoidant* attachment (cf. Ainsworth et al., 1978). Secure individuals tend to find it easy to get close to others and do not tend to worry about being abandoned or about someone getting too close to them. Anxious–ambivalent individuals tend to seek closeness but feel that others are reluctant to become as close as they would like. Finally, avoidant individuals feel somewhat uncomfortable being close to others and tend to be somewhat distrustful of others.

Should the three differing social value orientations be associated with these three attachment styles? Recall that Bowlby (1969, 1973, 1980) reasoned that the dimension of security versus insecurity is most important in accounting for different behaviors and responses of young children (e.g., probability of crying when left alone), a claim supported by subsequent research by Ainsworth et al. (1978). How can the dimension of security versus insecurity be understood in terms of an interdependence analysis? We suggest that the early development of secure versus insecure attachment is at least partially a result of early patterns of social interaction, which presumably are importantly influenced by the primary caregiver. In particular, given that a young child is highly dependent on the primary caregiver, secure individuals have acquired greater experience than insecure individuals with interactions in which elementary needs and preferences are fulfilled by the primary caregiver.

Accordingly, secure individuals may have learned to perceive interdependent situations and partners as safe and secure, readily behaving in a trusting manner, thereby increasing the possibility of developing cooperative patterns of interactions with interdependent others. Such experiences are likely to enhance prosocial orientation. In contrast, insecure individuals may have learned to perceive interdependent situations and partners as dangerous and risky, behaving in a rather distrusting manner, thereby running the risk of developing noncooperative patterns of interaction with interdependent others. Such experiences are likely to enhance individualistic—and perhaps competi-

[1]Interaction experiences need not always be direct, but may also be vicarious (i.e., provided by social models; cf. Bandura, 1969) and complemented by explicit teaching of rules and norms relevant to interdependent behavior. Thus, we did not assume that social interaction experiences are limited to one's own, direct experience. Moreover, we did not assume that social interaction experiences are always carefully evaluated, nor that the development of social value orientation occurs in a calculated, systematic manner. We believe that, over extended experience with different social interactions, individuals develop habitual tendencies to react to specific patterns of interdependence situations in specific ways, such that the transformation process occurs quite rapidly, with little or no conscious thought. (Of course, this is not to argue that one never reevaluates habitual tendencies, even if one was to experience similar interdependent situations and partners; indeed, one is likely to do so when experiencing poor outcomes, when being reprimanded, or when interdependent others tend to react in unforeseen ways.)

tive—orientation. Thus, we advanced the general hypothesis that prosocials will exhibit greater levels of secure attachment than individualists and competitors. We refer to this prediction as the *prosocial-security hypothesis*.[2]

For more exploratory purposes, we were interested in examining the link between social value orientations and levels of anxious–ambivalent attachment and level of avoidant attachment. Given that higher levels of these attachment styles indicate a fair amount of insecurity, one could advance the prediction that, relative to individualists and competitors, prosocials will evidence lower levels of anxious–ambivalent attachment and lower levels of avoidant attachment. However, levels of anxious–ambivalent and avoidant attachment represent not only relatively low levels of security, but also differential preferences for seeking versus avoiding intimacy or interdependence (for further discussion, see Bartholomew & Horowitz, 1991; Shaver et al. 1996). Given that individualists and competitors are more likely than prosocials to avoid or withdraw from patterns of interdependence (e.g., Orbell & Dawes, 1993), another (albeit indirect) variation of the prosocial-security hypothesis would be that prosocials exhibit lower levels of avoidant attachment relative to individualsts and competitors. Given that prosocials might be more secure, as well as more appreciative of interdependent relationships than individualists and competitors, we advanced no formal hypothesis regarding social value orientation differences for levels of anxious–ambivalent attachment. Finally, past research has revealed no strong evidence indicating that men and women differ in terms of adult attachment styles (e.g., Shaver et al., 1996). In a highly exploratory vein, we examined whether the hypothesized relationship between social value orientation and level of secure attachment would be influenced by gender.

Method

Participants and design. A total of 573 individuals (338 women, 228 men, 7 unidentified) participated in this research (mean age: 22.3 years). They were recruited at several locations at the campus of the Free University, Amsterdam, including the university library and cafeteria. The design was a 3 (social value orientation: prosocials vs. individualists vs. competitors) × 2 (gender: women vs. men) factorial with measures of secure, avoidant,

and anxious–ambivalent attachment as the three dependent variables.

Procedure. Differences in social value orientation were assessed by using a series of decomposed games (Messick & McClintock, 1968), which involve making choices among combinations of outcomes for oneself and for another person. In the current study, we used a nine-item decomposed game measure of social value orientation, an efficient and easy-to-administer instrument that was adopted from prior research (e.g., Van Lange & Kuhlman, 1994; Van Lange et al., in press). The Appendix presents this decomposed game measure. As can be seen in this Appendix, the other was said to be someone whom participants did not know and whom they would never knowingly meet in the future. This allowed us to examine participants' general tendencies toward others. Also, the instructions noted that the other would also make choices; this allowed us to frame the choice situations as ones involving some interdependence between the participants and the other. Finally, outcomes were presented in terms of points, and participants were asked to imagine that the points had value to themselves as well as to the other person. Similar instructions have been used in past research (see Kuhlman & Marshello, 1975; McClintock & Allison, 1989; for other decomposed game measures, see Knight & Dubro, 1984; Liebrand, Jansen, Rijken, & Suhre, 1986). These measures of social value orientation have generally revealed good internal consistency and test–retest reliability over a period ranging from 2 months to 6 months (e.g., Kuhlman, Camac, & Cunha, 1986; Van Lange & Semin-Goossens, 1997).

---

[2]The prosocial-security hypothesis may also be based on comparisons of taxonomies of attachment styles and models of social value orientation. Recent taxonomies of attachment styles have conceptualized security in terms of the degree to which an individual has developed a positive model of both self and others; avoidance has been assumed to represent a positive model of self but a negative model of others; and anxious–ambivalent attachment has been assumed to represent a negative model of self but a positive model of others (e.g., Bartholomew & Horowitz, 1991). Similarly, the concept of social value orientation has been conceptualized in terms of self–other models, with prosocials assigning positive weights to the well-being of self and others, individualists assigning positive weights to primarily the well-being of self, and competitors assigning positive weight to the well-being of self and negative weight to the well-being of others (e.g., McClintock & Liebrand, 1988).

As can been seen in the Appendix, an example of a decomposed game is the choice among three options: Option A, 480 points for self and 80 points for other; Option B, 540 points for self and 280 points for other; and Option C, 480 points for self and 480 points for other. In this example, Option A represents the competitive choice, because it provides a larger difference between one's own and the other's outcomes (480 – 80 = 400) than does either Option B (540 – 280 = 260) or Option C (480 – 480 = 0). Option B represents the individualistic choice, because one's own outcomes are larger (540) than are those in Option A (480) or Option C (480). Finally, Option C represents the prosocial choice, because it provides a larger joint outcome (480 + 480 = 960) than does either Option A (480 + 80 = 560) or Option B (540 + 280 = 820); also, Option C represents a smaller discrepancy between one's own and other's outcomes (480 – 480 = 0) than does either Option A (480 – 80 = 400) or Option B (540 – 280 = 260).

Participants were classified as either prosocial, individualistic, or competitive if at least six choices were consistent with one of these social value orientations. Following these criteria, we identified 248 participants as prosocial, 164 as individualistic, and 46 as competitive; 115 participants (20%) could not be classified. Social value orientation exhibited a marginal relationship with gender, $c^2(2, N = 453) = 5.27, p < .10$, with prosocials being somewhat more prevalent among women (58.5%) than among men (47.7%) and individualists being somewhat less prevalent among women (32.2%) than among men (41.0%); the percentages of competitors were about equal among women (9.3%) and men (11.3%).

Measurement of adult attachment styles. Measurement of levels of secure, avoidant, and anxious–ambivalent attachment was based on a 13-item measure adapted from Hazan and Shaver (1987) and validated by Carnelley and Janoff-Bulman (1992). However, given that the purpose of Study 1 was to assess general attachment styles (i.e., attachment relevant to one's interpersonal dealings with others in general, not with one's close relationship partner per se), we excluded items that involved attachment to the current partner (e.g., "I worry that a love partner might not really love me"). Therefore, five items were used to assess level of secure attachment (e.g., "I find it easy to trust others," "I find it easy to get close to others," and "I feel comfortable having other people de-

pend on me"); level of avoidant attachment was measured by using three items (e.g., "I am nervous when anyone gets too close"); finally, level of anxious–ambivalent attachment was assessed by using three items (e.g., "I find that other people don't want to get as close as I would like"). The internal consistency of the latter two scales was acceptable (level of avoidant attachment, 3 items, $\alpha = .66$; level of anxious–ambivalent attachment, 3 items, $\alpha = .67$).

The internal consistency of the five items measuring level of secure attachment was judged to be unacceptable ($\alpha = .46$); however, after discarding two items the resultant internal consistency was judged to be acceptable ($\alpha = .57$). Therefore, in our analyses we examined the average scores of the three-item scales measuring level of secure, avoidant, and anxious–ambivalent attachment. The current scales parallel levels of internal consistency observed in the United States ($\alpha = .62, .59,$ and .68, respectively, for secure, avoidant, and anxious–ambivalent attachment; Carnelley & Janoff-Bulman, 1992). The data of three participants were discarded because of missing values.

Results and Discussion

We conducted a 3 (social value orientation: prosocials vs. individualists vs. competitors) × 2 (gender: women vs. men) multivariate analysis of variance (MANOVA) with the three-item measures of secure, anxious–ambivalent, and avoidant attachment styles as dependent measures. This analysis revealed a multivariate main effect for social value orientation, $F(6, 886) = 3.05, p < .01$. At the univariate level, the main effect for social value orientation was significant for level of secure attachment, $F(2, 444) = 7.07, p < .001$, and marginal for both level of avoidant attachment, $F(2, 444) = 2.47, p < .10$, and level of anxious–ambivalent attachment, $F(2, 444) = 2.76, p < .10$. The two-factor MANOVA did not reveal any effects involving gender, indicating that the association of social value orientation and secure attachment is independent of participant's gender.

Consistent with the prosocial-security hypothesis, prosocials ($M = 6.24, SD = 1.38$) exhibited greater levels of secure attachment than did individualists ($M = 5.92, SD = 1.35$) or competitors ($M = 5.51, SD = 1.59$). Subsequent planned comparisons revealed a significant contrast between prosocials versus individualists and competitors,

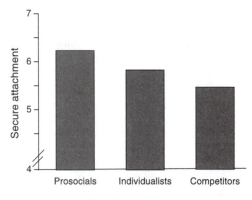

FIGURE 27.1 ■ Mean levels of attachment security among prosocials, individualists, and competitors (Study 1).

$F(1, 444) = 11.09, p < .001$, and a marginal difference between individualists and competitors, $F(1, 444) = 3.04, p < .10$. These findings are presented in Figure 1.

Second, congruent with the prosocial-security hypothesis, contrasts relevant to the marginal relationship between social value orientation and avoidant attachment revealed that prosocials ($M = 3.56, SD = 1.61$) exhibited lower levels of avoidant attachment than did individualists ($M = 3.92, SD = 1.48$) and competitors ($M = 3.86, SD = 1.48$), respectively, $F(1, 444) = 4.88, p < .05$. The contrast between individualists and competitors was not significant. Finally, relevant to the marginal relationship between social value orientation and levels of anxious–ambivalent attachment, subsequent comparisons revealed a significant contrast of prosocials ($M = 4.93, SD = 1.60$) versus individualists ($M = 4.63, SD = 1.71$) and competitors ($M = 4.55, SD = 1.80$), respectively, $F(1, 444) = 4.63, p < .05$. The contrast between individualists and competitors was not significant.

Study 2

Study 1 provided good support for the prosocial-security hypothesis, in that prosocials described their feelings and experiences relevant to others in general to be more secure (and somewhat less avoidant) than did individualists and competitors. Study 2 was designed to examine the association between social value orientation and partner-specific forms of secure attachment, focusing on feelings and experiences of secure attachment relevant to the current partner with whom participants were intimately involved.

Method

Participants and design. A total of 136 Dutch individuals (63 women, 73 men) participated in this research (mean age: 23.8 years). They were recruited at several locations at the campus of the Free University, Amsterdam, including the university library and cafeteria. All individuals were involved in a relationship of at least 3 months in duration (mean relationship duration: 31 months). The design was a 3 (social value orientation) × 2 (gender) factorial, with measures of secure, avoidant, and anxious–ambivalent attachment as the three dependent variables.

Procedure. The survey included an instrument measuring individuals' social value orientation and an instrument measuring levels of secure, avoidant, and anxious–ambivalent attachment. Social value orientations were measured as in Study 1 (see Appendix). Following the same criteria as in Study 1 (i.e., making at least six consistent choices), we identified 66 prosocials, 35 individualists, and 19 competitors (16 participants made fewer than six consistent choices and therefore could not be classified in one of the above groups). Unlike Study 1, there was no evidence of an association between social value orientation and gender, $\chi^2(2, N = 120) = 2.14, n.s.$

In measuring levels of secure, avoidant, and anxious–ambivalent attachment, we used descriptions adapted from Hazan and Shaver's (1987) three-prototype descriptions of how people typically feel in relationships. In light of the present purposes, there were three notable differences between Hazan and Shaver's measure and the present measure. First, whereas the descriptions used by Hazan and Shaver focus on feelings and experiences relevant to others in general, the current descriptions were reworded so as to measure feelings and experiences relevant to the participant's current partner. Second, rather than using phrases such as "getting close" or "being close," we used phrases such as "sharing intimate feelings and experiences." The reasons for this were that (a) the term "closeness" does not translate perfectly into Dutch and (b) we wanted to focus on fairly concrete experiences and feelings. Finally, whereas Hazan and Shaver asked participants to endorse the description that best described their feelings and experiences, we asked participants to rate each of these descriptions in terms of how well they described themselves (1 = *describes me not at all*, 4 = *describes me somewhat*, 7 = *describes me very well*; for similar procedures, see Shaver & Brennan, 1992).

Translated from Dutch, the respective descriptions measuring levels of secure, avoidant, and anxious–ambivalent attachment read as follows:

> I find it relatively easy to share intimate feelings and experiences with my partner and am comfortable to be dependent on one another. I don't often worry that my partner abandons me, or that my partner wants to share too intimate feelings and experiences. (*secure attachment*)
>
> I am somewhat uncomfortable when my partner and I share very intimate feelings and experiences. I find it difficult to trust my partner completely, difficult to allow myself to depend on him/her. I am nervous when we share very intimate feelings and experiences, and often my partner wants me to be more intimate than I feel comfortable being. (*avoidant attachment*)
>
> I wish that my partner would share more intimate feelings and experiences with me. I often worry that my partner doesn't really love me or won't want to stay with me. I want to merge completely with my partner, and this desire sometimes scares my partner. (*anxious–ambivalent attachment*)

Finally, given that individuals may be inclined to present themselves (or indirectly, their romantic partner or relationship) in a desirable manner, we included an instrument measuring tendencies toward social desirability (12 true–false items adapted from Crowne & Marlowe, 1964). As in some other research (e.g., Van Lange et al., 1997), the internal consistency ($\alpha = .49$) was clearly lower than ideal, yet we judged it to be acceptable in light of the fact that this scale focuses on several different tendencies and behaviors in a variety of situations (e.g., tendencies to gossip, tendencies to carefully read political programs prior to voting) and because this instrument has been widely used in prior research.

It appeared that only one of the constructs assessed in the present research was significantly linked to social desirability. There was a significant link between level of anxious–ambivalent attachment and social desirability, $r(115) = .26, p < .01$, suggesting that the expression of the desire for closeness, yet worrying that others do not wish

to become equally close, is to some degree desirable. Such links with levels of secure attachment, $r(115) = -.17$, and levels of avoidant attachment, $r(115) = .07$, were not significant. Moreover, social value orientation was not significantly linked to social desirability, $F(2, 115) = 2.53$, suggesting that the measurement of prosocial, individualistic, and competitive orientations by means of decomposed games is relatively free of tendencies toward presenting oneself in a socially desirable manner. In the analyses reported below, the data of two participants were discarded because of missing values.

Results and Discussion

We conducted a 3 (social value orientation) × 2 (gender) MANOVA, with the measures of secure, anxious–ambivalent, and avoidant attachment styles as dependent measures. This analysis revealed a significant multivariate main effect for social value orientation, $F(6, 222) = 3.27, p < .005$. At the univariate level, the main effect for social value orientation was found to be significant for level of secure attachment, $F(2, 112) = 5.53, p < .005$, and nonsignificant for both level of avoidant attachment, $F(2, 112) = 2.54$, and level of anxious–ambivalent attachment, $F(2, 112) = .12$. The two-factor MANOVA did not reveal any effects involving gender, indicating that the association of social value orientation and secure attachment is independent of participant's gender.

As can be seen in Figure 2, prosocials ($M = 5.25$,

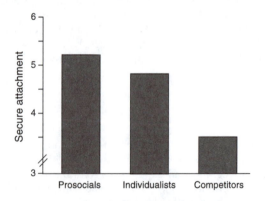

FIGURE 27.2 ■ Mean levels of attachment security among prosocials, individualists, and competitors (Study 2).

$SD = 1.90$) exhibited greater levels of secure attachment than did individualists ($M = 4.91$, $SD = 1.76$) or competitors ($M = 3.68$, $SD = 2.14$). Consistent with the prosocial-security hypothesis, planned comparisons revealed significant contrasts between prosocials versus individualists and competitors, $F(1, 112) = 4.94$, $p < .05$, and between individualists and competitors, $F(1, 112) = 6.11$, $p < .05$.

Study 3

Studies 1 and 2 were designed to provide evidence in support of the link between social value orientation and levels of secure attachment, which was explicitly assumed to be developed by early childhood experiences with the primary caregiver. Of course, demonstrating a simple link between social value orientation and level of secure attachment provides very indirect evidence in support of the more general claim that differences in social value orientation are at least partially rooted in childhood experiences of social interaction. Two limitations, in particular, are worth discussing. First, differences in level of secure attachment are assumed to be a function of interactions between caregiver and child. However, development of social value orientations may also be rooted in patterns of interaction with peers during young childhood and early adolescence. Second, demonstrating a link between secure attachment and social value orientation fails to provide direct insight into more "objective" features that may underlie differences in social interaction as experienced during childhood and early adolescence.

Study 3 addressed these limitations by examining the association between social value orientation and number of siblings. How might different transformational tendencies develop in the context of few versus many other siblings? We propose that the number of siblings has a substantial influence on interaction experiences, particularly during childhood. Number of siblings should be linked to the frequency—and possibly the intensity—with which one is confronted with situations characterized by intermediate or low correspondence of outcomes. The greater the number of siblings, the more likely is it that individuals will face situations in which particular resources have to be shared, resources that provide the basis for outcomes, material outcomes (e.g., toys, space) as well

as psychological outcomes (e.g., attention from parents; cf. Hoffman, 1991). How might such interdependence features affect social interactions? How might number of siblings shape social value orientation?

Given repeated experience with situations of intermediate or low correspondence, individuals may adapt in such a manner as to approach these situations in a cooperative and coordinating manner, thereby gradually learning the functional value of acting in a collectively beneficial manner. This reasoning suggests that individuals that are part of larger families are more likely to develop prosocial orientation. Indeed, the well-established finding that children raised in cultures characterized by high levels of collectivism and interdependence tend to exhibit greater cooperation than children raised in cultures characterized by relatively low levels of collectivism and interdependence is consistent with this argument, in that the former children typically have been raised in larger families than the latter children (e.g., children raised in rural parts of Mexico vs. children raised in the United States; Madsen & Shapira, 1977). Thus, this reasoning leads one to expect that prosocials will have a greater number of siblings than will individualists and competitors (i.e., *sibling-prosocial hypothesis*).

An alternative line of reasoning suggests that repeated experience with situations of intermediate or low correspondence, especially in the context of larger groups, gives rise to noncooperative interaction experiences. For example, prior research on social dilemmas has demonstrated that cooperative interactions decline as groups are somewhat larger in size (e.g., in comparisons of groups of 2, 3, and up to 7 persons; Bonacich, Shure, Kahan, & Meeker, 1976; Hamburger, Guyer, & Fox, 1975). If this is true, such noncooperative interaction experiences should give rise to somewhat lower levels of trust and increased pessimism regarding individuals' willingness and ability to act in a collectively beneficial manner, thereby instigating the development of proself (i.e., individualistic and competitive) orientation. Thus, this reasoning leads one to expect that prosocials will have a smaller number of siblings than will individualists and competitors (i.e., *sibling-proself hypothesis*).

Relevant to the two hypotheses noted above, we examined the relationship between social value orientation and birth order. Later borns obviously grow up with a sizable number of siblings, whereas early borns will only later experience the influence of more siblings. From this perspective, we can advance two specific predictions. According to the sibling-prosocial hypothesis, prosocials should have a greater number of older siblings than individualists and competitors. Conversely, according to the sibling-proself hypothesis, prosocials should have a smaller number of older siblings than individualists and competitors.

Finally, in a highly exploratory vein, we examined the relationship between social value orientation and the sex ratio of siblings. Prior research has revealed a link (albeit weak) between social value orientation and gender, such that among women prosocials tend to be a bit more prevalent than among men. Indeed, Study 1 revealed a marginal link between these variables. Hence, it is possible that the development of prosocial orientation increases with the presence of female siblings rather than male siblings. However, given the speculative nature of such reasoning and the fact that more complex lines of reasoning are possible (e.g., arguments suggesting specific patterns of interactions between one's own gender and the sex-ratio of siblings), we advanced no formal prediction for the link between social value orientation and the sex-ratio of siblings.

Method

Participants and design. A total of 631 Dutch individuals (335 women, 295 men, 1 unidentified; mean age: 24.0 years) participated in several survey and laboratory studies that included questions relevant to number of siblings, birth order, and sex ratio of siblings. In some studies, participants were recruited at specific locations at the Free University, Amsterdam (e.g., library, cafeteria), whereas in other studies participants were recruited by means of an advertisement in the university paper.

Procedure. In all studies, social value orientation was assessed as in Studies 1 and 2. Following the same criteria as in Studies 1 and 2 (i.e., making at least six consistent choices), we identified 311 prosocials (57%), 160 individualists (30%), and 73 competitors (13%), a distribution similar to those found in prior research (87 participants made fewer than six consistent choices and therefore could not be classified in one of the above groups). Unlike Study 1, there was no evidence of a significant association between social value ori-

entation and gender, $\chi^2(2, N = 544) = .84$, *n.s.* The questionnaire asked participants to list the total number of siblings older than themselves, the total number of siblings younger than themselves, as well as the total number of brothers and the total number of sisters. The data of three participants were discarded because of missing values.

Results and Discussion

The association between social value orientation and number of siblings was analyzed by using a 3 (social value orientation: prosocials vs. individualists vs. competitors) × 2 (gender: women vs. men) analysis of variance (ANOVA). Of course, this analysis did not assume that social value orientation causes variations in the so-called dependent measures—indeed, the reverse order of causation is more plausible. We used the ANOVA framework because the dependent measure complied with a ratio level of measurement (i.e., the same holds for the other dependent measures, including number of siblings older than the participant, the number of siblings younger than the participant, the number of brothers, and the number of sisters). This analysis revealed a significant main effect for social value orientation, $F(2, 535) = 4.82$, $p < .01$. Consistent with the sibling-prosocial hypothesis, Panel A of Figure 3 reveals that the number of siblings is greater for prosocials ($M = 2.03$, $SD = 1.56$) than for individualists ($M = 1.63$, $SD = 1.00$) and competitors ($M = 1.71$, $SD = 1.35$). Subsequent planned comparisons revealed a significant contrast between prosocials versus individualists and competitors, $F(1, 535) = 9.14$, $p < .005$. Differences between individualists and competitors were not significant. The 3 × 2 ANOVA did not reveal any other significant effects (i.e., main or interaction effects involving gender).

Next, we conducted a 3 (social value orientation) × 2 (gender) MANOVA on the number of older siblings, the number of younger siblings, the number of brothers, and the number of sisters.[3] This analysis revealed a multivariate main effect for social value orientation, $F(8, 1066) = 1.99$, $p < .05$. At the univariate level, we found a significant main effect for social value orientation for number of older siblings, $F(2, 535) = 3.64$, $p < .05$,

---

[3] We did not conduct a MANOVA for all five dependent measures because, logically, number of siblings is statistically related to the other four measures of siblings.

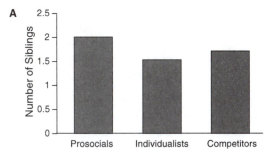

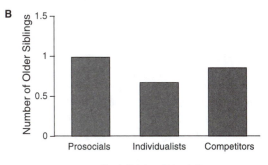

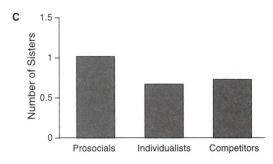

FIGURE 27.3 ■ Mean number of siblings (Panel A), older siblings (Panel B), and sisters (Panel C) among prosocials, individualists, and competitors.

and number of sisters, $F(2, 535) = 6.16, p < .005$. First, Panel B of Figure 3 reveals that the number of older siblings was greater for prosocials ($M = 0.96, SD = 1.25$) than for individualists ($M = 0.67, SD = 0.79$). Subsequent comparisons revealed a significant contrast between prosocials versus individualists and competitors, $F(1, 535) = 4.94, p < .05$. Differences between individualists and competitors ($M = 0.90, SD = 1.02$) were not significant. Second, Panel C of Figure 3 reveals that the number of sisters was greater for prosocials ($M =$

1.05, $SD = 1.14$) than for individualists ($M = 0.74, SD = 0.75$) or competitors ($M = 0.76, SD = 0.88$). Subsequent comparisons revealed a significant contrast between prosocials versus individualists and competitors, $F(1, 535) = 12.27, p < .001$. Differences between individualists and competitors were not significant. The 3×2 ANOVAs did not reveal any other significant effects (i.e., main or interaction effects involving gender). Although several specific explanations may account for these findings, they are congruent with the more general assumption that differences in social value orientation are partially rooted in different patterns of social interaction as experienced, at least in part, during the periods spanning early childhood to young adulthood.

Study 4

Study 4 was designed to provide evidence relevant to the claim that social value orientations are further shaped by different patterns of social interaction as experienced during early adulthood, middle adulthood, and old age. Our primary purpose was to examine the possible relationship between the distribution of three types of social value orientations (i.e., prosocials, individualists, and competitors) and age differences among a sample of adults in the Netherlands. There are several lines of reasoning why a relationship between these variables is plausible, advancing either (a) the hypothesis that the percentage of prosocials increases with age, whereas the percentage of individualists and competitors decreases with age (i.e., *prosocial-growth hypothesis*) or (b) the hypothesis that the percentage of prosocials decreases with age, whereas the percentage of individualists and competitors increases with age (i.e., *proself-growth hypothesis*).

What logic would underlie the prosocial-growth hypothesis? We suggest three complementary lines of reasoning. First, one may assume that all three social value orientations have functional value, depending on certain features of interdependence and behavior of interaction partners. At the same time, there is good reason to believe that across differing interdependent situations and interaction partners a prosocial orientation is more functional than an individualistic or competitive orientation. Individuals with a prosocial orientation tend to behave in a tit-for-tat manner, approaching others cooperatively and turning to noncooperation if others fail to cooperate. Such strategies tend to enhance both long-term personal well-being and collective well-being and have been asserted to be functional from an evolutionary perspective (cf. Axelrod, 1984; Trivers, 1971).[4] It is possible that over a lifetime, individuals increasingly detect the functional aspects of a prosocial orientation, thus becoming more prosocial and less individualistic or competitive over time.

Second, one might assume that the nature of interdependence situations changes over the course of a lifetime (cf. Levinson, 1986). For example, young adults may especially confront situations with rather low levels of correspondence, in that they typically have to compete for scarce resources (e.g., competing for jobs, partners). Later, when facing middle adulthood, individuals tend to establish themselves (e.g., in terms of careers and family) and increasingly face interaction situations in which others depend on their help and service (e.g., children, junior colleagues). Then, when facing old age, individuals tend to become somewhat more dependent on others for the provision of good outcomes (e.g., need for help because of some restraints following from old age). Because the interdependence features that are characteristic of later life phases call for tendencies toward helping others (and to some degree, being helped); it is likely that prosocial orientation increases as a function of age. Moreover, this second account complements the first explanation, in that a more varied set of interaction experiences may further help individuals to detect the functional aspects of prosocial orientation.

Third, over the course of this century, many societies, including the Netherlands, have become less collectivistic, yielding lower levels of interpersonal closeness and interdependence (i.e., a movement from rural, interpersonally close cultures to urbanized, interpersonally distant environments). Accordingly, the probability of being raised in collectivistic subcultures decreases with age. Given the association between levels of collectivism and prosocial orientation, one might speculate that, if the primary orientations are developed during early childhood, prosocial orientation should increase with age.

What logic would underlie the proself-growth hypothesis? One might assume that individuals assign greater weight and attention to patterns of interaction that are harmful to their own well-being than to patterns that are helpful to their own well-being (cf. Fiske, 1980; Skowronski & Carlston, 1989). Given that the cumulative experience with incidents of harm in settings of interdependence increases with age, one might argue that levels of trust in the prosocial motivation of others tend to gradually decline with age. Such decline in trust may be associated with a decline in prosocial orientation and an increase in individualistic or competitive orientations (cf. Kuhlman et al., 1986; Pruitt & Kimmel, 1977).

Of lesser relevance, Study 4 enabled us to examine two additional questions. First, the present research used a large sample of participants that was representative of the Dutch adult population. This allowed us to compare the distribution of social value orientations obtained in this study with distributions observed in prior research that has used samples of primarily college students (these samples are sometimes referred to as *convenience samples*). Indeed, it is fair to conclude that researchers' knowledge about social value orientation, issues of cooperation and competition, and related topics is primarily based on data from college students, thus providing a somewhat restricted database for researchers' knowledge and theoretical development (cf. Sears, 1986). Therefore, we explored whether (and if so, how) the prevalence of prosocials, individualists, and competitors in these convenience samples is different from that of the adult population in the real world.

Second, Study 4 examined the relationship between social value orientation and gender. Prior research has revealed some evidence that women are more likely than men to exhibit cooperative choice behavior, although such findings have been inconsistently observed (for a review, see Komorita & Parks, 1994; Van Lange, Liebrand, Messick, & Wilke, 1992). Moreover, several studies have examined a link between social value orientation and gender, finding weak evidence that women are more likely to be classified as prosocial and less likely to be classified as individualistic or competitive (e.g., McClintock & Liebrand, 1988; Van Lange, 1992). However, the (relatively small) samples in these studies consisted of primarily college students. By using a large sample that was

---

[4]Although few would doubt the functionality of tit for tat, it is not necessarily true that tit for tat would logically outperform all other possible interaction strategies (e.g. Selten & Hammerstein, 1984).

representative of the adult population, the present research examined whether the prevalence of prosocials is greater (and that of individualists and competitors smaller) among women than among men. Also, in an exploratory vein, we examined the association between social value orientation and level of education.

Method

Participants and design. A total of 1,728 individuals participated in this research. This sample comprised individuals who had agreed to participate once every week in surveys and research conducted by Telepanel, an organization linked to the University of Amsterdam. In exchange, each participant received a personal computer that was also used for surveys and research. This personal computer was connected with the main computer at Telepanel where the data were stored automatically. The Telepanel organization has made every attempt possible to recruit a sample of participants that is representative of the Dutch adult population. In the present sample, there were 940 (54.4%) men and 788 (45.6%) women; mean age was 45.7 years (age ranged from 15 years through 89 years). Slightly less than half of the participants had a (paid) job (48%), some were homemakers (20.1%), some were retired (14.3%), some were students (7.2%), a few were not able to work (3%), a few were unemployed (2.8%), and the remainder were involved in volunteer work or reported to be doing "something else" (4.6%). By using this sample, we examined the association between social value orientation (prosocials vs. individualists vs. competitors), age (15–29 years vs. 30–44 years vs. 45–59 years vs. 60 years and older), education (university or higher education vs. intermediate education vs. lower education), and gender (men vs. women).

Procedure. This study was part of a large survey that contained some questionnaires and a set of biographical questions to assess age, gender, and level of education. We included a series of six decomposed games (decomposed games 1 through 6; see Appendix) to assess participants' social value orientations. Paralleling the criteria used in prior research (i.e., at least 6 of 9 choices should be consistent with one of three social value orientations), participants were classified if they made at least five of six choices consistent with one of the three social value orientations. It appeared that 135 par-

ticipants (7.8%) made fewer than five consistent choices and thus were not classified. From the remaining 1,593 participants, 1,134 (71.2%) were classified as prosocial, 340 (21.3%) were classified as individualistic, and 119 (7.5%) were classified as competitive.

Results and Discussion

Association between social value orientation, age, education, and gender. The theoretical basis for classifying individuals into distinct age categories was the work of Erikson and colleagues (Erikson, 1980; Erikson, Erikson, & Kivnick, 1986), which distinguished among early adulthood (i.e., 20–35 years old), middle adulthood (35–65 years old), and old age (i.e., at least 65 years old). However, we also wanted groups that (a) were not extremely unequal in size and (b) represented equal intervals. We therefore differentiated among four groups varying in age, individuals who were (a) older than 15 years but younger than 30 years ($n = 270$); (b) at least 30 and younger than 45 years ($n = 523$); (c) at least 45 and younger than 60 years ($n = 529$); and (d) 60 years or older ($n = 271$).

Levels of education were varied in three groups as follows: those who had completed or were currently pursuing university or higher education ($n = 336$), those who had completed or were currently enrolled in intermediate levels of education ($n = 382$), and those who had completed lower levels of education or who had not completed any form of education ($n = 875$). The sample consisted of 868 men and 725 women.

The association of age, level of education, and gender with social value orientation was analyzed in a 3 (social value orientation) × 4 (age) × 3 (education) × 2 (gender) log-linear analysis. We used a so-called hiloglinear analysis because our analysis included four variables (allowing for 3 × 4 × 3 × 2 = 72 cells) and because the variables were skewed in their distribution (cf. Knoke & Burke, 1980; Reynolds, 1977). This analysis revealed significant main effects for social value orientation, partial $\chi^2(2, N = 1593) = 1061.72$; age, partial $\chi^2(3, N = 1593) = 166.88$; education, partial $\chi^2(2, N = 1593) = 314.90$; and gender, partial $\chi^2(1, N = 1593) = 12.85$, (all $ps < .001$), indicating that none of these distributions were equal.

More important, and relevant to the primary hypotheses (i.e., the prosocial-growth hypothesis and the proself-growth hypothesis), the analysis

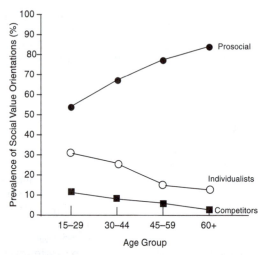

FIGURE 27.4 ■ The prevalence of social value orientations (in percentages) among groups differing in age.

revealed a Social Value Orientation × Age interaction, partial χ^2 (6, N = 1593) = 62.25, p < .001. As can be seen in Figure 4, the percentages of prosocials systematically elevated with increasing age (varying from 55.9% to 67.3%, 77.5%, and 81.5%), whereas the percentages of individualists (varying from 30.7% to 24.9%, 16.3%, and 15.1%) and competitors (varying from 13.3% to 7.8%, 6.2%, and 3.3%) decreased with increasing age. These findings are consistent with the prosocial-growth hypothesis and inconsistent with the proself-growth hypothesis.

Second, the analysis revealed a Social Value Orientation × Gender interaction, partial χ^2(2, N = 1593) = 15.61, p < .001. As predicted, the percentage of prosocials was higher among women (75.6%) than among men (67.5%), whereas the percentage of individualists was lower among women (18.1%) than among men (24.1%). The groups did not differ in terms of the percentage of competitors (6.3% and 8.4% for women and men, respectively). Third, we did not find a relationship between level of education and social value orientation; the Social Value Orientation × Education interaction was not significant, partial χ^2(4, N = 1593) = 7.46.[5]

Comparison of distributions of social value orientations across studies. Another purpose of this study was to compare the distribution of social value orientations observed in a sample that was fairly representative of the Dutch adult population

with the social value orientations observed in student populations, a common sample in research on social value orientations. We used data from two prior studies that have used identical instructions, except that these two data sets were based on nine decomposed games rather than six decomposed games as in the current work. The two prior studies involved sizable samples of primarily students living either in the United States or the Netherlands (Van Lange & Kuhlman, 1994, N = 394; Van Lange et al., in press, N = 336). However, because the distributions of social value orientations were almost identical in the two countries we do not further discuss the role of nation.

Table 1 presents the distributions observed in Van Lange and Kuhlman (1994), Van Lange et al. (in press), and the present study, broken down for different groups of individuals on the basis of age. As can be seen in Table 1, the distributions obtained in Van Lange and Kuhlman (1994) and Van Lange et al. (in press) were quite similar yet substantially different from the total, present distribution. In the present distribution, there was a greater percentage of prosocials and a lower percentage of individualists and competitors, χ^2(4, N = 2278) = 28.88, p < .001. Next, we compared the distributions of the two prior studies with the present one, focusing on the group of individuals who were older than 15 yet younger than 30—a group that is comparable in age to the participants in the two prior studies. The distributions were not significantly different, χ^2(4, N = 955) = 2.97, *n.s.* indicating that the percentages of prosocials, individualists, and competitors were indeed very similar in the three groups. We then compared the distributions of prior work with those of the present participants who were between 30 and 45 years of age, 45 and 60 years of age, and 60 years and older. Each comparison revealed significantly different distributions, χ^2(4, N = 1208) = 10.51, p < .05; χ^2(4, N = 1214) = 39.77, p < .001; and χ^2(4, N = 956) = 41.43, p < .001, respectively. Thus, these findings indicate that the distributions of social

[5]We observed three interaction effects that did not include social value orientation. First, an Age × Education interaction, partial χ^2(6, N = 1593) = 64.73, p < .001, revealed that individuals with higher education were more prominent in the more mature groups. Second, an Education × Gender interaction, partial χ^2(2, N = 1593) = 21.63, p < .001, revealed that men were relatively more prominent among individuals who had completed high levels of education. Third, an Age × Gender interaction, partial χ^2(3, N = 1593) = 9.54, p < .05, revealed lower percentages of women with increasing age.

TABLE 27.1. Percentages of Prosocials, Individualists, and Competitors for Differing Age Groups (Study 4) and Differing Studies (Van Lange & Kuhlman, 1994; Van Lange et al., in press)

Social value orientation	Groups differing in age (Study 4)				Van Lange & Kuhlman (1994)	Van Lange et al. (in press)
	15–29	30–44	45–60	60+		
Prosocials	55.9	67.3	77.5	81.5	60.8	60.5
Individualists	30.7	24.9	16.3	15.1	27.2	25.2
Competitors	13.3	7.8	6.2	3.3	12.0	14.3

value orientations were very similar to that obtained for a sample representative of the Dutch adult population insofar as this sample consists of individuals of similar ages (i.e., between 15 and 30 years old).

General Discussion

The present research provides preliminary evidence in support of the claim that differences in social value orientation are (a) partially rooted in different patterns of social interaction as experienced during the period from early childhood to young adulthood and (b) further shaped by different patterns of social interaction as experienced during early adulthood, middle adulthood, and old age. Consistent with the prosocial-security hypothesis, Studies 1 and 2 revealed that prosocials exhibit greater levels of secure attachment than do individualists and competitors. This finding is congruent with the contention that social value orientation is partially rooted in experiences of interaction between the individual and the primary caregiver. Indeed, we are not aware of any personality construct that is linked so directly (theoretically and empirically) to personal histories of social interaction (cf. Ainsworth et al., 1978; Bowlby, 1969, 1973, 1980; Hazan & Shaver, 1987).

It is interesting that past research has revealed that high levels of attachment security are associated with experiences of favorable life outcomes (i.e., healthy relationships with intimate partners, parents, coworkers) as well as with the relative absence of psychosomatic symptoms (for a review, see Shaver & Hazan, 1993). Demonstrating a link between level of secure attachment and social value orientation is also important because it may help researchers understand why the level of secure attachment is related to the favorable life outcomes noted above. Granted, it is plausible that interper-

sonal attitudes and feelings of security (i.e., mental models; Hazan & Shaver, 1987) are an important ingredient toward maintaining healthy relationships. However, it is unlikely that such mental models operate in a vacuum, independent of an individual's own behavior in interdependent relationships. The present evidence in support of the prosocial-security hypothesis suggests that the link between level of secure attachment and favorable life outcomes is to some extent mediated by one's own behavior in interdependent relationships. That is, favorable life outcomes may also be promoted by the inclination to approach interdependent others in a prosocial manner, behaving in ways that serve both one's own well-being and the others' well-being. Of course, this line of reasoning is speculative and remains to be tested in future research.

A second major finding was that prosocials reported having more siblings than did individualists and competitors. This finding, which supports the sibling-prosocial hypothesis, is congruent with the notion that patterns of social interaction—as determined by number of siblings—shape the development of social value orientation. This observation is also consistent with the well-established finding that prosocial patterns of behavior are more prevalent among individuals raised in cultures characterized by high (rather than low) levels of collectivism, interpersonal closeness, interdependence, and large (rather than small) family size. The present research suggests that, in fact, family size alone may partially account for this finding.[6]

---

[6]We are aware of one study that has examined whether cultural differences in cooperativeness and competitiveness are partially accounted for by family size differences (Knight & Kagan, 1982). This study compared Anglo American and Mexican American children and revealed greater levels of cooperation among Mexican American children (children who were raised in larger families). However, they did not find a link between degree of cooperativeness–competitiveness and

It is interesting that prosocials reported having more sisters than did individualists and competitors. Why is the number of sisters (rather than brothers) related to social value orientation? Studies 1 and 4 revealed that the prevalence of prosocials was somewhat greater—and that of individualists somewhat smaller—among women than among men. [7] One explanation would thus be that because sisters are more likely to be prosocial than brothers, individuals are more likely to adopt a prosocial orientation as the number of sisters increases (e.g., through patterns of reciprocity or modeling). A second—and somewhat more stereotypical—explanation would be that sisters more than brothers adopt a *mother role*, a repertoire of behaviors that involves nurturing, helping, and caring, thereby promoting prosocial orientation in the receiver (or the observer). Although these lines of reasoning are highly speculative, it is interesting to note that the current findings are in agreement with a recent finding indicating that, relative to fathers with no or a few sisters, fathers with many sisters devote greater time to raising their children (Duindam & Spruijt, 1996).

A third finding was that the prevalence of prosocials increased—and the prevalence of individualists and competitors decreased—with age, suggesting that differences in social value orientation are further shaped by different interaction experiences that are characteristic of early adulthood, middle adulthood, and old age. Why did we find support for the prosocial-growth hypothesis (and why did we not find support for the proself-growth hypothesis)? Earlier, we outlined three complementary lines of reasoning. The first explanation contends that over time and extended experience with interdependent situations and interaction partners, individuals may increasingly detect the functional aspects of prosocial motivation, an account that is congruent with the well-established finding that prosocial behavior among children and young adults increases with age. The second explanation assumes that the nature of interdependence situations and social interaction changes and evolves during a lifetime, suggesting that situations over a lifetime tend to increasingly call for tendencies toward helping others (and to some degree, being helped by others). Such features may also enhance prosocial orientation because they contribute to a more varied set of interaction experiences, which may further help individuals detect the functional aspects of prosocial orientation. The third explanation centers on the cultural-historical determinants of prosocial orientation, arguing that many societies, including the Netherlands, have become less rural, less collectivistic and more urban, more individualistic over the past decades. It should be clear that our findings do not enable us to draw any firm conclusions regarding the relative validity of these interrelated explanations.

It is important to note that our findings do not support the proself-growth hypothesis, a prediction that was based on the notion that levels of trust may decrease with increasing age. In retrospect, it might be questionable (a) whether individuals continue to assign greater weight to potentially harmful behavior, (b) if they do, whether individuals draw firm conclusions about humankind on the basis of such experiences, and (c) whether lower levels of trust necessarily translate in a movement away from prosocial orientation (cf. Parks, 1994). It could be that with increasing age, individuals become more prosocial, even though they (increasingly) believe that most people are not prosocial.

ACKNOWLEDGMENTS

Paul A. M. Van Lange and Ellen M. N. De Bruin, Department of Social Psychology, Free University, Amsterdam, the Netherlands; Wilma Otten, Department of Social Psychology, University of Amsterdam, Amsterdam, the Netherlands; Jeffrey A. Joireman, Department of Psychology, Seattle Pacific University.

This research was supported by Grant R-57-178 from the Netherlands Organization for Scientific Research. We are grateful to Hal Kelley, Caryl Rusbult, and Ben Slugoski for their valuable comments on a draft of this article.

---

number of siblings (or birth order). Thus, in this study, number of siblings and birth order did not account for the differences observed between Anglo American and Mexican American children.

[7]Social stereotypes suggest that women are considerably more prosocial and less competitive than are men. The current findings suggest that in actuality such differences tend to be rather small. Also, the current evidence in support of small differences between women and men is consistent with research on prosocial behavior among children, which also reveals modest differences between the genders (for a review, see Durkin, 1995).

REFERENCES

Ainsworth, M. D. S., Blehar, M. C., Waters, E., & Wall, S. (1978). *Patterns of attachment: A psychological study of the strange situation.* Hillsdale, NJ: Erlbaum.

Axelrod, R. (1984). *The evolution of cooperation*. New York: Basic Books.

Bandura, A. (1969). Social-learning theory of identificatory processes. In D. A. Goslin (Ed.), *Handbook of socialization theory and research* (pp. 213–262). Chicago: Rand McNally.

Bartholomew, K., & Horowitz, L. M. (1991). Attachment styles among young adults: A test of a four-category model. *Journal of Personality and Social Psychology, 61*, 226–244.

Beggan, J. K., Messick, D. M., & Allison, S. T. (1988). Social values and egocentric bias: Two tests of the "might over morality" hypothesis. *Journal of Personality and Social Psychology, 55*, 606–611.

Bonacich, P., Shure, G. H., Kahan, J. P., & Meeker, R. J. (1976). Cooperation and group size in the *N*-person prisoner's dilemma. *Journal of Conflict Resolution, 20*, 687–705.

Bowlby, J. (1969). *Attachment and loss: Attachment* (Vol. 1). London: Hogarth.

Bowlby, J. (1973). *Attachment and loss: Separation* (Vol. 2). London: Hogarth.

Bowlby, J. (1980). *Attachment and loss: Loss, sadness, and depression* (Vol. 3). Harmondsworth, England: Penguin.

Carnelley, K. B., & Janoff-Bulman, R. (1992). Optimism about love relationships: General vs. specific lessons from one's personal experiences. *Journal of Personal and Social Relationships, 9*, 5–20.

Collins, N. L., & Read, S. J. (1990). Adult attachment, working models, and relationship quality in dating couples. *Journal of Personality and Social Psychology, 58*, 644–663.

Crowne, D., & Marlowe, D. (1964). *The approval motive*. New York: Wiley.

Duindam, V., & Spruijt, E. (1996). *Caring fathers in the Netherlands*. Unpublished manuscript. University of Utrecht, the Netherlands.

Durkin, K. (1995). *Developmental social psychology: From infancy to old age*. Oxford, England: Blackwell.

Eisenberg, N., & Fabes, R. A. (1991). Prosocial behavior and empathy: A multimethod developmental perspective. In M. S. Clark (Ed.), *Prosocial behavior* (pp. 34–61). Newbury Park, CA: Sage.

Erikson, E. H. (1980). *Identity and the life cycle*. New York: Norton.

Erikson, E. H., Erikson, J. M., & Kivnick, H. Q. (1986). *Involvement in old age*. New York: Norton.

Fiske, S. T. (1980). Attention and weight in person perception: The impact of negative and extreme behavior. *Journal of Personality and Social Psychology, 38*, 889–906.

Hamburger, H., Guyer, M., & Fox, J. (1975). Group size and cooperation. *Journal of Conflict Resolution, 19*, 503–531.

Hazan, C., & Shaver, P. (1987). Romantic love conceptualized as an attachment process. *Journal of Personality and Social Psychology, 52*, 511–524.

Hoffman, L. W. (1991). The influence of the family environment on personality: Accounting for sibling differences. *Psychological Bulletin, 110*, 187–203.

Kelley, H. H. (1997). The "stimulus field" for interpersonal phenomena: The source of language and thought about interpersonal events. *Personality and Social Psychology Review, 1*, 140–169.

Kelley, H. H., & Stahelski, A. J. (1970). Social interaction basis of cooperators' and competitors' beliefs about others. *Journal of Personality and Social Psychology, 16*, 66–91.

Kelley, H. H., & Thibaut, J. W. (1978). *Interpersonal relations: A theory of interdependence*. New York: Wiley.

Knight, G. P., & Dubro, A. F. (1984). An individualized regression and clustering assessment of the social values of adults and children. *Journal of Research in Personality, 18*, 372–382.

Knight, G. P., & Kagan, S. (1982). Siblings, birth order, and cooperative–competitive social behavior: A comparison of Anglo-American and Mexican-American children. *Journal of Cross-Cultural Psychology, 13*, 239–249.

Knight, G. P., Kagan, S., & Buriel, R. (1981). Confounding effects of individualism in children's cooperation–competition social motive measure. *Motivation and Emotion, 5*, 167–178.

Knight, G. P., Kagan, S., Nelson, W., & Gumbiner, J. (1978). Acculturation of second- and third-generation Mexican American children: Field independence, locus of control, self-esteem, and school achievement. *Journal of Cross-Cultural Psychology, 9*, 87–97.

Knoke, D., & Burke, P. J. (1980). *Log-linear models*. Beverly Hills, CA: Sage.

Komorita, S. S., & Parks, C. D. (1994). *Social dilemmas*. Dubuque, IA: Brown & Benchmark.

Kuhlman, D. M., Camac, C., & Cunha, D. A. (1986). Individual differences in social orientation. In H. Wilke, D. Messick, & C. Rutte (Eds.), *Experimental social dilemmas* (pp. 151–176). New York: Verlag Peter Lang.

Kuhlman, D. M., & Marshello, A. (1975). Individual differences in game motivation as moderators of preprogrammed strategic effects in prisoner's dilemma. *Journal of Personality and Social Psychology, 32*, 922–931.

Kuhlman, D. M., & Wimberley, D. C. (1976). Expectations of choice behavior held by cooperators, competitors, and individualists across four classes of experimental games. *Journal of Personality and Social Psychology, 34*, 69–81.

Levinson, D. J. (1986). A conception of adult development. *American Psychologist, 41*, 3–13.

Liebrand, W. B. G., Jansen, R. W. T. L., Rijken, V. M., & Suhre, C. J. M. (1986). Might over morality: Social values and the perception of other players in experimental games. *Journal of Experimental Social Psychology, 22*, 203–215.

Liebrand, W. B. G., & Van Run, G. J. (1985). The effects of social motives across two cultures on behavior in social dilemmas. *Journal of Experimental Social Psychology, 21*, 86–102.

Luce, R. D., & Raiffa, H. (1957). *Games and decisions: Introduction and critical survey*, London: Wiley.

Madsen, M. C., & Lancy, D. F. (1981). Cooperative and competitive behavior: Experiments related to ethnic identity and urbanization in Papua New Guinea. *Journal of Cross-Cultural Psychology, 12*, 389–408.

Madsen, M. C., & Shapira, A. (1977). Cooperation and challenge in four cultures. *Journal of Social Psychology, 102*, 189–195.

McClintock, C. G. (1974). Development of social motives in Anglo-American and Mexican-American children. *Journal of Personality and Social Psychology, 29*, 348–354.

McClintock, C. G. (1978). Social values: Their definition, measurement, and development. *Journal of Research and Development in Education, 12*, 121–137.

McClintock, C. G., & Allison, S. (1989). Social value orientation and helping behavior. *Journal of Applied Social Psychology, 19*, 353–362.

McClintock, C. G., & Liebrand, W. B. G. (1988). The role of interdependence structure, individual value orientation, and other's strategy in social decision making: A transformational analysis. *Journal of Personality and Social Psychology, 55,* 396–409.

Messick, D. M., & McClintock, C. G. (1968). Motivational basis of choice in experimental games. *Journal of Experimental Social Psychology, 4,* 1–25.

Olweus, D. (1979). Stability of aggressive reaction patterns in males: A review. *Psychological Bulletin, 86,* 852–875.

Orbell, J. M., & Dawes, R. M. (1993). Social welfare, cooperators' advantage, and the option not to play. *American Sociological Review, 58,* 515–529.

Parks, C. D. (1994). The predictive ability of social values in resource dilemmas and public goods games. *Personality and Social Psychology Bulletin, 20,* 431–438.

Pruitt, D. G., & Kimmel, M. J. (1977). Twenty years of experimental gaming: Critique, synthesis, and suggestions for the future. *Annual Review of Psychology, 28,* 363–392.

Reynolds, H. T. (1977). *Analysis of nominal data.* Beverly Hills, CA: Sage.

Roth, A. E. (1988). Laboratory experimentation in economics: A methodological overview. *The Economic Journal, 98,* 974–1031.

Rusbult, C. E., & Van Lange, P. A. M. (1996). Interdependence processes. In E. T. Higgins & A. W. Kruglanski (Eds.), *Social psychology: Handbook of basic principles* (pp. 564–596). New York: Guilford Press.

Rushton, J. P. (1975). Generosity in children: Immediate and long-term effects of modeling, preaching, and moral judgment. *Journal of Personality and Social Psychology, 31,* 459–466.

Rushton, J. P., Fulker, D. W., Neale, M. C., Nias, D. K. B., & Eysenck, H. J. (1986). Altruism and aggression: The heritability of individual differences. *Journal of Personality and Social Psychology, 50,* 1192–1198.

Sattler, D. N., & Kerr, N. L. (1991). Might versus morality explored: Motivational and cognitive bases for social motives. *Journal of Personality and Social Psychology, 60,* 756–765.

Sears, D. O. (1986). College sophomores in the laboratory: Influences of a narrow data base on social psychology's view of human nature. *Journal of Personality and Social Psychology, 51,* 515–530.

Selten, R., & Hammerstein, P. (1984). Gaps in Harley's argument on evolutionary stable learning rules and in the logic of "tit for tat." *Behavioral and Brain Sciences, 7,* 115–116.

Shaver, P. R., & Brennan, K. A. (1992). Attachment styles and the "Big Five" personality traits: Their connections with each other and with romantic relationship outcomes. *Personality and Social Psychology Bulletin, 18,* 536–545.

Shaver, P. R., & Hazan, C. (1993). Adult romantic attachment: Theory and evidence. In D. Perlman & W. H. Jones (Eds.),

Advances in personal relationships (Vol. 4, pp. 29–70). London: Jessica Kingsley.

Shaver, P. R., Papalia, D., Clark, C. L., Koski, L. R., Tidwell, M. C., & Nalbone, D. (1996). Androgyny and attachment security: Two related models of optimal personality, *Personality and Social Psychology Bulletin, 22,* 582–597.

Simpson, J. A. (1990). The influence of attachment styles on romantic relationships. *Journal of Personality and Social Psychology, 59,* 273–280.

Skowronski, J. J., & Carlston, D. E. (1989). Negativity and extremity biases in impression formation: A review of explanations. *Psychological Bulletin, 105,* 131–142.

Thibaut, J. W. (1968). The development of contractual norms in bargaining: Replication and variation. *Journal of Conflict Resolution, 12,* 102–112.

Thibaut, J. W., & Faucheux, C. (1965). The development of contractual norms in a bargaining situation under two types of stress. *Journal of Experimental Social Psychology, 1,* 89–102.

Trivers, R. (1971). The evolution of reciprocal altruism. *Quarterly Review of Biology, 46,* 35–57.

Van Lange, P. A. M. (1992). Confidence in expectations: A test of the triangle hypothesis. *European Journal of Personality, 6,* 371–379.

Van Lange, P. A. M., Agnew, C. R., Harinck, F., & Steemers, G. (in press). From game theory to real-life: How social value orientation affects willingness to sacrifice in ongoing close relationships. *Journal of Personality and Social Psychology.*

Van Lange, P. A. M., & Kuhlman, D. M. (1994). Social value orientations and impressions of partner's honesty and intelligence: A test of the might versus morality effect. *Journal of Personality and Social Psychology, 67,* 126–141.

Van Lange, P. A. M., Liebrand, W. B. G., Messick, D. M., & Wilke, H. A. M. (1992). Social dilemmas: The state of the art. In W. B. G. Liebrand, D. M. Messick, & H. A. M. Wilke (Eds.), *Social dilemmas: Theoretical issues and research findings* (pp. 3–28). London: Pergamon Press.

Van Lange, P. A. M., Rusbult, C. E., Drigotas, S. M., Arriaga, X. B., Witcher, B. S., & Cox, C. L. (1997). Willingness to sacrifice in close relationships. *Journal of Personality and Social Psychology, 72,* 1373–1395.

Van Lange, P. A. M., & Semin-Goossens, A. (1997). *The boundaries of reciprocity.* Unpublished manuscript, Free University of Amsterdam.

Van Vugt, M., Meertens, R., & Van Lange, P. A. M. (1995). Car versus public transportation? The role of social value orientations in a real-life social dilemma. *Journal of Applied Social Psychology, 25,* 258–278.

Von Neuman, J., & Morgenstern, O. (1947). *Theory of games and economic behavior.* Princeton, NJ: Princeton University Press.

Appendix

An Instrument to Measure Social Value Orientation

In this task we ask you to imagine that you have been randomly paired with another person, whom we will refer to simply as the "Other." This other person is someone you do not know and that you will not knowingly meet in the future. Both you and the "Other" person will be making choices by circling either the letter A, B, or C. Your own choices will produce points for both yourself and the "Other" person. Likewise, the other's choice will produce points for him/her and for you. Every point has value: The more points you receive, the better for you, and the more points the "Other" receives, the better for him/her.

Here's an example of how this task works:

	A	B	C
You get	500	500	550
Other gets	100	500	300

In this example, if you chose A you would receive 500 points and the other would receive 100 points; if you chose B, you would receive 500 points and the other 500; and if you chose C, you would receive 550 points and the other 300. So, you see that your choice influences both the number of points you receive and the number of points the other receives.

Before you begin making choices, please keep in mind that there are no right or wrong answers—choose the option that you, for whatever reason, prefer most. Also, remember that the points have value: The more of them you accumulate, the better for you. Likewise, from the "other's" point of view, the more points s/he accumulates, the better for him/her.

For each of the nine choice situations, circle A, B, or C, depending on which column you prefer most:

	A	B	C
(1) You get	480	540	480
Other gets	80	280	480
(2) You get	560	500	500
Other gets	300	500	100
(3) You get	520	520	580
Other gets	520	120	320
(4) You get	500	560	490
Other gets	100	300	490
(5) You get	560	500	490
Other gets	300	500	90
(6) You get	500	500	570
Other gets	500	100	300
(7) You get	510	560	510
Other gets	510	300	110
(8) You get	550	500	500
Other gets	300	100	500
(9) You get	480	490	540
Other gets	100	490	300

Note. Participants are classified when they make 6 or more consistent choices. Prosocial choices are 1c, 2b, 3a, 4c, 5b, 6a, 7a, 8c, 9b; individualistic choices are 1b, 2a, 3c, 4b, 5a, 6c, 7b, 8a, 9c; and competitive choices are 1a, 2c, 3b, 4a, 5c, 6b, 7c, 8b, 9a.

READING 28

The Role of Loneliness and Social Support in Adjustment to Loss: A Test of Attachment versus Stress Theory

Wolfgang Stroebe and Margaret Stroebe • Utrecht University
Georgios Abakoumkin • University of Patras
Henk Schut • Utrecht University

Editors' Notes

Kurt Lewin, considered by many the father of contemporary social psychology, made the famous statement, "Nothing is as practical as a good theory." The present selection illustrates this idea by testing two clearly articulated theories in a real-world context of recently widowed women and men. The question posed by this research relates to the "prosocial" orientation discussed in the preceding selection. In the present case, the issue is the widowed individual's embeddedness in a network of family and friends who may extend needed support at time of stress, such as occasioned by the death of one's spouse. The research issue posed in this article is *not* whether social support enhances one's ability to cope with the bereavement situation. Both competing theories, stress theory and attachment theory, predict that it will. The question is whether social support will do so differentially; specifically, does social support enhance one's well-being only in moments of stress or generally? This selection argues that it does so generally, as predicted by attachment theory. Note the connection between this selection and Reading 20, which also investigated well-being. Whereas the previous selection viewed well-being as an inference from mood, this selection views it as a function of the social support one receives. Are the processes mediating subjective well-being entirely different in the two selections or do they contain similarities as well?

Discussion Questions

1. What is the theoretical rationale for the buffer hypothesis derived from stress theory?
2. What is the rationale for the competing attachment theory prediction?
3. What are the important design features of the Tübingen longitudinal study? Why are these features important?
4. How should the buffering effect be manifest in the data, if it did exist?

Suggested Readings

Hobfoll, S. E., Nadler, A., & Leiberman, J. (1986). Satisfaction with social support during crisis: Intimacy and self-esteem as critical determinants. *Journal of Personality and Social Psychology, 51,* 296–304.

Lakey, B., & Cassady, P. B. (1990). Cognitive processes in perceived social support. *Journal of Personality and Social Psychology, 59,* 337–343.

Vinokur, A., Schul, Y., & Caplan, R. D. (1987). Determinants of perceived social support: Interpersonal transactions, personal outlook, and transient affective states. *Journal of Personality and Social Psychology, 53,* 1137–1145.

Authors' Abstract

A longitudinal study of a matched sample of 60 recently widowed and 60 married men and women tested predictions from stress and attachment theory regarding the role of social support in adjustment to bereavement. Stress theory predicts a buffering effect, attributing the impact of bereavement on well-being to stressful deficits caused by the loss and assuming that these deficits can be compensated through social support. In contrast, attachment theory denies that supportive friends can compensate the loss of an attachment figure and predicts main effects of marital status and social support. Attachment theory further suggests that marital status and social support influence well-being by different pathways, with the impact of marital status mediated by emotional loneliness and the impact of social support mediated by social loneliness. Results clearly supported attachment theory.

One of the most widely shared truisms in bereavement research and practice is that support from family and friends is one of the most important moderators of bereavement outcome (e.g., Lopata, 1973; Sanders, 1993; W. Stroebe & M. Stroebe, 1987; Stylianos & Vachon, 1993). Yet, closer inspection of the bereavement literature suggests that the belief that social support can protect individuals against the deleterious effects of the death of a loved one is theoretically controversial and empirically not well supported. To clarify the role of social support in adjustment to bereavement, we first discuss predictions from the two major theoretical approaches relevant to bereavement: cognitive stress theory (e.g., Lazarus & Folkman, 1984; W. Stroebe & M. Stroebe, 1987) and attachment theory (Bowlby, 1979; Weiss, 1975, 1982). We then review previous research on the role of social support in adjustment to loss. Finally, we present data from our own longitudinal study that assess predictions from stress and attachment theory.

The Role of Social Support in Adjustment to Loss: A Theoretical Analysis

According to cognitive stress theories, critical life events such as bereavement are stressful because they require major readjustment. The intensity of stress created by a life event depends on the extent to which the perceived demands of the situation tax or exceed an individual's coping resources, given that failure to cope leads to important negative consequences (Lazarus & Folkman, 1984). Stress theory provides the theoretical underpinning for the "buffering model," which suggests that high levels of social support protect the individual against the deleterious impact of stress on health. According to Cohen and Wills (1985), there are two ways in which social support can buffer the individual against the negative impact of the stress experience. First, support can intervene between the stressful event and a stress reaction by attenuating or preventing a stress appraisal response. Second, adequate support may intervene between the experience of stress and the onset of the pathological response by eliminating the stress reaction or by directly influencing physiological processes. Whereas these two pathways reduce the individual's vulnerability to the impact of the stressful event, we propose a third way in which social support may affect individual stress response, namely, by aiding recovery. Thus, social support may also help individuals to recover more readily from the impact of the stressful life event.

The Deficit Model of Partner Loss was developed as an application of cognitive stress theory to bereavement (W. Stroebe & M. Stroebe, 1987; W. Stroebe, M. Stroebe, K. Gergen, & M. Gergen, 1980, 1982). On the basis of the interactional definition of stress, the deficit model offers an analysis of the situational demands characteristic of widowhood and of the coping resources needed to deal with these demands. Marital bereavement marks the end of a close mutual relationship, and the loss of a partner is likely to result in a number of deficits in areas in which the spouse had previously been able to rely on the partner. The Deficit Model suggests that the loss of a partner leads to deficits in areas that can broadly be characterized as loss of instrumental support, loss of validational support, loss of emotional support, and loss of social contact support. The Deficit Model postulates that social support alleviates the stress of bereavement, but only to the extent to which it helps to replace the deficits created by the loss of a partner.[1]

It follows from the Deficit Model that bereaved individuals are in greater need of social support than married individuals. The model therefore predicts an interaction of social support and marital status on the level of psychological symptoms (i.e., buffering effect). However, because it is unlikely that family and friends are able to alleviate completely the deficits caused by the loss of the partner, one would also expect a main effect of marital status on symptomatology.

In contrast, attachment theory rejects the notion that supportive friends can compensate for the loss of an attachment figure (Bowlby, 1969; Weiss, 1975). Bowlby (1969) proposed that the attachment figure, unlike other people in the social environment, was uniquely able to foster general feelings of security and that other people could not simply take over this function. He thus goes beyond optimal matching (e.g., Cutrona & Russell, 1990), by not only requiring a match between the characteristic of stressful events confronting the individual and the form of social support that is beneficial in this context, but by stating categorically that this type of social support can only be provided by one specific type of person.

Weiss (1975) elaborated these ideas in his relational theory of loneliness, in which he drew a fundamental distinction between emotional and social loneliness and argued that the two types of loneliness cannot compensate for each other. The loneliness of *emotional isolation* appears in the absence of a close emotional attachment and can only be remedied by the integration of another emotional attachment or the reintegration of the one that had been lost. Those experiencing this form of loneliness are apt to experience a sense of utter aloneness, whether or not the companionship of others is in fact accessible (Weiss, 1975). Thus, according to attachment theory, social support from relatives and friends cannot compensate for the major deficit caused by bereavement, namely, the loss of an attachment figure. However, social support should help with a second type of loneliness, namely, the loneliness of *social isolation*.

---

[1]These ideas form the basis of the analysis that the optimal matching theory of Cutrona and Russell (1990, p. 330) offers for the role of social support in ameliorating the impact of bereavement. Although matching theories of social support are still rooted in the cognitive stress framework, they stress the importance of matching the characteristics of stressful events confronting an individual and the specific form of social support that is most beneficial in this context. Buffering effects are thus restricted to situations where the social support available is matched to the specific support needs elicited by the stressful event.

Social loneliness is associated with the absence of an engaging social network, and this absence can only be remedied by access to such a network. The dominant feeling of this type of loneliness is boredom, together with feelings of marginality (Weiss, 1975).

Attachment theory thus suggests that marital status and social support influence well-being by distinctly different pathways, with the impact of marital status being mediated by emotional loneliness and the impact of social support by social loneliness (Figure 1). According to this Dual-Path Model, one would predict main effects of marital status and social support on measures of symptomatology, but no interaction. Because each of these main effects is assumed to be mediated by a different type of loneliness, one would further expect marital status to affect emotional but not social loneliness and social support to affect social but not emotional loneliness. Finally, one would expect that control for emotional loneliness should reduce or eliminate the impact of marital status on symptomatology, whereas control for social loneliness should reduce or eliminate the effect of social support on symptom levels.

The two major theories of bereavement outcome thus make different and partly contradictory predictions about the role of social support in adjustment to loss. Consistent with popular beliefs about the helpfulness of social support to the bereaved, cognitive stress theory predicts a Social Support/ Marital Status interaction on symptomatology (i.e., buffering effect) in addition to a main effect of marital status. In contrast, attachment theory predicts main effects of both marital status and social support on levels of symptoms, but no interaction. It further suggests that these two main effects on symptomatology are mediated by different types of loneliness. These predictions have not yet been addressed by empirical research.

The Role of Social Support in Adjustment to Loss: A Review of the Evidence

Guided by stress theory, research on the role of social support in adjustment to loss has focused exclusively on testing the buffering against the main effect model. As Cohen and Wills (1985) argued in their influential review of the literature on social support, such tests require a factorial design that includes at least two levels of stress and two levels of social support. Thus, to test whether social support buffers individuals against the negative impact of the loss of a marital partner, one has to compare the impact of social support in bereaved and married samples. Buffering effects would be reflected by a statistical interaction of social support with marital status on health.

In our earlier review of the literature on social support and bereavement up to 1986 (W. Stroebe & M. Stroebe, 1987), we found no studies that satisfied these criteria. In the meantime, a few studies using adequate designs, comparing the impact of levels of social support in bereaved samples to that of married controls, have been published. The results are not unanimous in favor of buffering. Although some do indeed report evidence of buffering (Krause, 1986; Norris & Murrell, 1990; Schwarzer, 1992), albeit using measures of social integration or received social support, others do not (Greene & Feld, 1989; Murphy, 1988).

Krause (1986) studied the impact of life stresses and social support on depressive symptoms in a random sample of 351 individuals older than 65 living in Galveston, Texas. Social support was assessed with a modified version of the Inventory of Socially Supportive Behaviors (ISSB; Barrera, Sandler, & Ramsay, 1981). Depressive symptomatology was assessed with the Center for Epidemiology Studies Depression Scale (CES-D; Radloff,

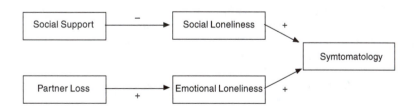

FIGURE 28.1 ■ Attachment theory: The dual-path model.

1977). Whereas no buffering effects occurred for the overall indicator of stressful life events, buffering was found for the numerically undefined subgroup of individuals who had been bereaved within the previous year. These buffering effects modified weak bereavement main effects.

As part of a larger study of individuals aged 55 and older, Norris and Murrell (1990) obtained interviews of three samples of older adults: 45 persons who had recently lost a spouse, 40 who had lost a parent or child, and 45 who were not bereaved. Depression was assessed with the CES-D. Social support was measured with the Louisville Social Support Scale (Norris & Murrell, 1987), which consists of two subscales reflecting social integration, or embeddedness in a social network, and "expected help." Expected help "taps the respondent's more specific expectations of help in an emergency from family, friends, and community" (p. 431) and thus appears to reflect aspects of perceived social support. Whereas expected help had no impact on depression, an ameliorative effect of social embeddedness on depression was reported. The more individuals were embedded in their social networks, the less they were depressed 9 months after their loss. This association between social embeddedness and depression was stronger for the widowed sample than for a combined control group consisting of individuals who were either nonbereaved or had lost a parent or child.

Schwarzer (1992) studied a sample of 248 individuals above the age of 60, of which 152 had lost a family member or a friend within the previous year. Social support was defined in terms of visits by children and family members. The criterion measure in this study was anxiety, assessed with a German version of the State-Trait Personality Inventory (Schwarzer & Schwarzer, 1983): When the sample was dichotomized into those who were visited at least every other week and those who received fewer visits, a clear buffering effect was observed, with loss having no impact on anxiety for individuals who received many visits but a strong impact on those who received few visits.

One puzzling feature of these studies is that buffering effects were observed for measures of social support that typically do not yield buffering effects. According to Cohen and Wills (1985), buffering effects ought only to be found with measures of perceived social support but not with network measures or scales assessing received social support. In contrast, the above studies report buffering effects with measures of social network (Krause, 1986) or received social support (Norris & Murrell, 1990; Schwarzer, 1992). The one study that assessed both social embeddedness and perceived social support did not find any effects for perceived social support (Norris & Murrell, 1990). It is plausible that this discrepancy has something to do with the fact that that study included only elderly individuals, a subgroup for whom the needs and provision (and consequently perhaps, perceptions) of social support are very different from those of younger groups.

Two studies, both using samples of more long-term bereaved, did not find buffering effects. In a follow-up assessment of 49 family members and close friends of 51 adult disaster victims of the Mount Saint Helens volcano eruption conducted 3 years after the disaster, in which their mental distress (measured with the Symptoms Checklist-90-R, SCL-90-R; Derogatis, 1977) was compared with that of a nonbereaved control group, there was no evidence of main or buffering effects (Murphy, 1988). Social support was measured with an index developed by Coppel (1980) that assesses social embeddedness as well as perceived social support.

Greene and Feld (1989) examined the relationship between social support and well-being in groups of 151 married women and 60 widowed women who had lost their partner within the previous five years. Respondents were drawn from a national sample of women aged 50 and older. Social support was assessed in terms of the number of social support functions for which respondents mentioned one or more social supporters. Well-being was measured with the Bradburn Affect Balance Scale (Bradburn, 1969). The buffering effect of social support on well-being was estimated by testing the differences in the relevant regression coefficients for widows versus married women. Although only marginally significant, there appeared to be a reverse buffering effect, with widows who had more social support reporting more negative affect.

In summary, the pattern that emerges from our review of research that used adequate designs to study buffering effects of social support in bereavement is not very conclusive. Although there is some evidence of buffering effects, it is limited to elderly samples and to the use of measures typically not associated with buffering in the general social support literature (Cohen & Wills, 1985). Furthermore, some studies also failed to find buffering effects, although this could be due to the fact that these studies used samples of longer-term bereaved individuals.

The Tubingen Longitudinal Study of Bereavement

To test predictions of stress theory against attachment theory, an in-depth, longitudinal study of a matched sample of recently bereaved and married men and women was conducted. Perceived social support was measured at the first time wave with a newly constructed questionnaire measure, the Perceived Social Support Inventory (PSSI). This was a German-language scale similar in many ways to the Interpersonal Support Evaluation List (ISEL; Cohen, Mermelstein, Kamarck, & Hoberman, 1985). Social support was related to depressive and somatic symptomatology assessed at three points in time. Social and emotional loneliness were also measured at the first time point.

The design of our study has thus three important features that distinguish it positively from the majority of earlier studies of the buffering effect; First, instead of using a cumulative index of reported life events as a measure of stress, a specific life event is used that is verifiable, datable, and listed as the most stressful event on the Social Readjustment Rating Scale (Holmes & Rahe, 1967). Second, the use of a longitudinal design with three points of measurement allows the assessment of the impact of social support on both stress vulnerability and recovery from the stressful event. Third, the assessment of two types of loneliness as potential mediators of the impact of bereavement on symptomatology allows for a test of stress versus attachment theory that is independent of the occurrence of a buffering effect.

Method

SAMPLE

Widowed and married individuals under the age of retirement, drawn from several towns in southern Germany, participated in the study. Names and addresses of all persons in this age category who had been maritally bereaved 4–7 months previously were supplied by the local registrars' offices.

Bereaved individuals were sent a letter describing the nature of the study and asking for their cooperation. No pressure was put on persons to participate if they were reluctant to do so. Those who did not decline participation by mail or phone were then contacted a few days afterward to arrange an interview. This procedure was continued until 30 widows and 30 widowers (mean age 53.05 years) had agreed to participate.

A comparison group of 30 married women and 30 married men (mean age 53.75 years) were individually matched to the widowed persons by sex, age, socioeconomic status, number of children, and town of residence. The comparison group was recruited from addresses of a larger number of matched individuals supplied by the registration offices of these towns. Letters were sent to these married persons, explaining that the study focused on the relationship between marital status and quality of life. Otherwise, the same procedure was followed as with the widowed group.

To achieve a sample size of 60 widowed persons for the interviews, 217 persons were approached. Of those who refused to participate in an interview, 24 were willing to fill out a mailed questionnaire containing some of the health measures. This allowed us to estimate the impact of selection on adjustment to loss (for a report, see M. Stroebe & W. Stroebe, 1989). Although the general level of acceptance was rather low, these rates are typical for research in this area (M. Stroebe & W. Stroebe, 1989). Of the individuals who agreed to be interviewed, 82% of the widowed and 90% of the married persons participated in all three interviews. There was no significant health difference between those who participated in all three sessions and those who dropped out.

TIMES OF MEASUREMENT

The participants were interviewed three times. The first interview was conducted 4–7 months after the loss and the second approximately 14 months after the loss. The third and final interview took place approximately 1 year after the second interview, that is, just over two years after the loss.

PROCEDURE

Data collection was based on structured interviews as well as self-report scales. The first two interviews were extensive and held at the homes of the interviewed. The third interview was shorter and conducted over the phone. At the end of each interview, participants were given (after face-to-face interviews at Times 1 and 2) or sent (following a telephone interview at Time 3) a questionnaire containing the health measures. They were asked to fill out this questionnaire within the following few days and to return it by mail. At Time 1, the questionnaire also contained the measure of perceived social support and of the two types of loneliness. All participants returned the questionnaire, but a few failed to respond to all the items. If more than 20% of the items of a given scale had not been completed, the scale was eliminated from analysis.

MEASURES

Perceived social support was assessed at Time 1 with the PSSI. The PSSI consists of 20 items that reflect four different functions of social support (instrumental, appraisal, emotional, social contact). Participants have to indicate in a true-false (T–F) format whether they have a person who, if the need arose, would provide them with one of the four kinds of support (e.g., "If I could not go shopping, I would have somebody who would do the shopping for me" [instrumental]. "If I would need advice on financial matters, I would have somebody whom I could rely on" [appraisal]. "I have nobody with whom I could talk about my feelings and problems" [emotional, negatively keyed]. "I have hardly any friends who share my interests" [contact, negatively keyed]). Since the four subscales assessing the different support functions are highly correlated with each other, only the overall score was used. The PSSI has high internal consistency ($\alpha = 0.90$).

Loneliness was assessed at Time 1, with two short scales constructed to assess the two types distinguished by Weiss (1982) using a T–F format. The measure of emotional loneliness consisted of the following two items ("I feel lonely even when I am with other people"; "I often feel lonely"). On the basis of the total sample, $\alpha = 0.78$ at Time 1. Social loneliness was also assessed with two items ("I have a really nice set of friends"; "I have friends and acquaintances with whom I like to be together"). At Time 1, $\alpha = 0.79$. The correlation between the two scales was .26.

Psychological symptoms were assessed at all three points in time with two measures: a measure of depression and one of somatic complaints. Depressive symptomatology was assessed with the German version of the Beck Depression Inventory (BDI; Beck, 1967; Kammer, 1983). The BDI consists of 21 items that assess the major symptoms of depression (e.g., sleep and appetite problems, self-reproach, loss of interest in everyday activities) with a multiple-choice format. Since pretests had shown that recently bereaved people resented having to respond to the "lack of sexual interest" item contained in the BDI, it was eliminated from the scale. Somatic complaints were assessed by a symptoms checklist (Beschwerdenliste, BL; von Zerssen, 1976), which is widely used in Germany and has high reliability. The BL lists 24 somatic complaints (e.g., dizziness, difficulty in swallowing, indigestion, excessive sweating, restlessness, neck and shoulder pain). Respondents indicate the extent to which they suffer from each symptom on a 4-point scale (0 = not at all; 3 = very much). The total score is the sum of these points.

Results

IMPACT OF MARITAL STATUS AND SOCIAL SUPPORT ON SYMPTOMATOLOGY

Table 1 presents the means and standard deviations of the BDI and BL scores of married and widowed individuals who participated in all three interviews and are below or above the median in their scores on the PSSI measured at Time 1.[2,3] A 2 (Social Support) × 2 (Marital Status) × 2 (Gender) × 3 (Time) ANOVA (with time as a within factor) conducted on the BDI scores yielded main effects of social support, $F(1,93) = 4.33, p < .05$; marital status, $F(1,93) = 4.95, p < .05$; gender, $F(1, 93) = 7.45, p < .01$; and time, $F(2, 186) = 5.10$,

[2]Cohen and Wills (1985) strongly recommend analyzing social support data with hierarchical linear regression procedures with the cross-product term (Marital Status × Support) forced into the equation after the main effect terms for marital status and support (e.g., Cohen & Wills, 1985) rather than using ANOVA or MANOVA. Regression avoids the loss of information that results from the need to divide the continuous social support variable into categorical data (e.g., median split) in order to use it as an independent variable in the MANOVA. However, our study differs in a number of respects from those reviewed by Cohen and Wills (1985), which makes the use of MANOVA preferable for our data: (a) Roughly 90% of the studies reviewed by Cohen and Wills (1985) assessed stress using cumulative life event measures. By having also to

TABLE 28.1. Means and Standard Deviations of the BDI and BL by Marital Status, Social Support, and Time for Individuals Who Participated in All Three Interviews

Variable and time	Married		Widowed	
	Low support	High support	Low support	High support
BDI[a]				
Time 1				
M	5.27	4.32	10.58	9.41
SD	5.87	4.62	9.06	5.53
Time 2				
M	7.09	3.87	8.54	8.14
SD	6.38	4.90	8.58	7.25
Time 3				
M	6.14	3.97	7.31	6.73
SD	6.27	4.26	8.33	6.06
N	22	31	26	22
BL[a]				
Time 1				
M	17.05	15.13	25.48	20.55
SD	9.20	11.33	17.40	13.83
Time 2				
M	18.73	14.26	20.78	18.09
SD	10.14	11.35	15.70	13.66
Time 3				
M	17.96	15.16	19.48	15.96
SD	11.76	12.58	16.45	10.31
N	22	31	27	22

Note. BDI = Beck Depression Inventory; BL = Beschwerdenliste.
[a] Higher means indicate higher levels of symptomatology.

$p < .01$. Individuals with high social support had lower BDI scores than those with low social support, married persons had lower scores than the widowed persons, and men had lower scores than women. The time main effect, a decrease in depression over time, was modified by the expected Time × Marital Status interaction, $F(2, 186) = 7.43$, $p < .001$. Whereas symptom levels of the bereaved persons decreased over time, those of the married persons showed little change. There was also a marginally significant Gender × Time interaction, $F(2, 186) = 2.95$, $p < .10$, with men improving

dichotomize (or trichotomize) the stress measure for the ANOVA in addition to the measure of social support, further loss of information occurred. Our study uses a stress measure that is already dichotomous (i.e., marital status). (b) Most of the studies reviewed by Cohen and Wills (1985) were cross-sectional. The few longitudinal studies reported used only two times of measurement. Thus, buffering in the cross-sectional studies could be tested in the course of one hierarchical regression analysis. (In the case of two time points, buffering was usually tested at Time 2, using symptomatology at Time 1 as the control variable). Our study has three points of measurement. Thus, using a repeated measures design, the MANOVA allowed us to analyze the impact of social support on adjustment measured at three points in time within the same design, whereas regression procedures would have required separate analyses for each point in time. We therefore argue that the added power of the repeated measures design more than compensates for the loss incurred in converting the continuous social support variable into categorical data. Furthermore, if the six regression analyses necessary to test for buffering for the two dependent measures at the three points

in time are calculated, there is no evidence of a Social Support × Marital Status interaction on either measure at any time point. We present the relevant outcomes of the analyses conducted at the first point of measurement as an example, because soon after the loss one would most likely expect a buffering effect: When the interaction of marital status and social support is forced into the equation in a second step (after the main effects of gender, marital status, and social support have already been entered), the interaction is associated with $F < 1$ for both the BDI and the BL. The R^2 change due to the interaction is .0024 for the BDI and .0004 for the BL. Thus, the buffering effect accounts for less than 0.2% of the variance of the BDI, and less than 0.04% of variance of the BL.

[3]The median was at 18. Scores on the PSSI of 18 and below fell below the median. The mean values of the PSSI for the widowed ($M = 15.29$, $SD = 5.26$) were significantly lower than for the married ($M = 18.00$, $SD = 2.87$), $t(1, 100) = -3.27$, $p < .001$. The lower level of social support experienced by the bereaved reflects the support deficit due to the loss of the partner.

more over time than women. There was no indication of a buffering effect: Neither the Social Support × Marital Status interaction ($F < 1$) nor the Social Support × Marital Status × Time interaction ($F < 1$) approached an acceptable level of significance.

The same analysis conducted on the BL resulted in a similar pattern. There were again main effects of social support, $F(1, 94) = 4.28, p < .05$; gender, $F(1.94) = 6.76, p < .05$; and time, $F(2, 188) = 4.59$, $p < .05$, with high social support individuals and men having lower BL scores than low social support individuals and women, and with somatic symptoms decreasing over time. As before, the time main effect was moderated by a Marital Status × Time interaction, $F(2, 188) = 7.62, p < .001$, reflecting the fact that there was more change over time for the bereaved than the married persons. There was also the unexpected Gender × Time interaction, $F(2, 188) = 3.25, p < .05$, with men improving faster over time than women. There was no indication of a buffering effect: Neither the Social Support/Marital Status interaction ($F < 1$) nor the Social Support × Marital Status × Time interaction ($F < 2$) approached an acceptable level of significance.

LONELINESS AS A MEDIATOR OF THE IMPACT OF MARITAL STATUS AND SOCIAL SUPPORT ON SYMPTOMATOLOGY

Table 2 presents the scores on the two measures of loneliness taken at Time 1 of married and widowed individuals who are above or below the median in their scores on the PSSI measured at Time 1. A 2 (Social Support) × 2 (Marital Status) × 2

(Gender) ANOVA on emotional loneliness revealed a highly significant main effect of marital status, $F(1, 109) = 81.65, p < .001$, but no significant main effect of social support. The same ANOVA on social loneliness resulted in the complementary pattern, with the main effect of social support becoming highly significant, $F(1, 112) = 10.36, p < .01$, but not the main effect of marital status ($F < 2$). Thus, consistent with attachment theory, marital status affected emotional loneliness but not social loneliness, whereas social support affected social loneliness but not emotional loneliness.

The analysis of the role of social and emotional loneliness as mediators of the impact of social support and bereavement on symptomatology suggests the reason our study failed to find a buffering effect of social support. According to Baron and Kenny (1986), a variable functions as a mediator when it meets the following three conditions: (a) Variations in the levels of the independent variable significantly account for variations in the presumed mediator, (b) variations in the mediator significantly account for variations in the dependent variable and finally (c) if the mediator is statistically controlled for, the effect of the independent on the dependent variable is substantially reduced or even eliminated.

To test for mediation, the following three regression models were estimated: First, the assumed mediator was regressed on the independent variable; second, the dependent variable was regressed on the independent variable; and third, the dependent variable was regressed on the independent variable, controlling for the assumed mediator by entering the mediator first in a hierarchical regres-

TABLE 28.2. Means and Standard Deviations of Emotional and Social Loneliness by Marital Status and Social Support

Type of loneliness[a]	Married		Widowed	
	Low support	High support	Low support	High support
Emotional				
M	0.21	0.03	1.27	1.17
SD	0.51	0.17	0.83	0.87
N	24	35	34	24
Social				
M	0.54	0.17	0.77	0.24
SD	0.83	0.51	0.88	0.60
N	24	36	35	25

[a] Higher scores indicate greater loneliness.

sion analysis. Because the assumed mediator was assessed at Time 1, whereas the two dependent variables were measured at Times 1, 2, and 3, only the last two regression models could be estimated for all three points in time (Tables 3 and 4).

Results were fully consistent with predictions from the Dual-Path Model. First, marital status had a highly significant effect on emotional loneliness (Table 3). Second, replicating the results of the earlier MANOVAs, the impact of marital status on depressive and somatic symptomatology was highly significant at Time 1, but weakened over time and did not reach significance at Time 3, suggesting that recovery had progressed. Third, when we controlled for the effect of emotional loneliness by entering it first into the regression, the impact of marital status on symptomatology was reduced to zero.

Obviously, the reduction was most impressive at Time 1, when the impact of marital status on symptomatology was substantial, accounting for 19% (BDI) and 8% (BL) of the variance. But even at Time 2, where marital status had a highly sig-

TABLE 28.3. Impact of Marital Status on Mediator and Symptomatology

Variable and time	β	R^2	F	df
Emotional loneliness				
Time 1	-.66	.44	89.26***	1,115
Depressive symptomatology (BDI)				
Time 1	-.44	.19	28.30***	1,117
Time 2	-.30	.09	10.70**	1,110
Time 3	-.17	.03	3.00	1,99
Somatic complaints (BL)				
Time 1	-.29	.08	10.33**	1,116
Time 2	-.18	.03	3.63	1,110
Time 3	-.07	.01	0.53	1,101
Controlling for emotional loneliness				
Depressive symptomatology (BDI)				
Time 1	-.15	.01[a]	2.07[b]	2,113
Time 2	-.02	.00[a]	0.86[b]	2,106
Time 3	.16	.01[a]	1.64[b]	2,96
Somatic complaints (BL)				
Time 1	.06	.00[a]	0.31[b]	2,113
Time 2	.16	.01[a]	1.71[b]	2,106
Time 3	.25	.03[a]	3.70[b]	2,97

Note. BDI = Beck Depression Inventory: BL = Beschwerdenliste.
**$p < .01$. ***$p < .001$.
[a] R^2 change.
[b] F change.

TABLE 28.4. Impact of Social Support on Mediator and Symptomatology

Variable and time	β	R^2	F	df
Social loneliness				
Time 1	-.50	.25	39.03***	1,118
Depressive symptomatology (BDI)				
Time 1	-.32	.10	13.30***	1,117
Time 2	-.18	.04	4.07[a]	1,110
Time 3	-.20	.04	4.30[a]	1,99
Somatic complaints (BL)				
Time 1	-.31	.09	12.08**	1,116
Time 2	-.17	.03	3.32	1,110
Time 3	-.20	.04	4.39*	1,101
Controlling for social loneliness				
Depressive symptomatology (BDI)				
Time 1	-.20	.03[a]	3.96[*ab]	2,116
Time 2	-.07	.00[a]	0.53[b]	2,109
Time 3	-.05	.00[a]	0.19[b]	2,98
Somatic complaints (BL)				
Time 1	-.25	.05[a]	6.16[*b]	2,115
Time 2	-.06	.00[a]	0.35[b]	2,109
Time 3	-.09	.01[a]	0.74[b]	2,100

Note. BDI = Beck Depression Inventory; BL = Beschwerdenliste.
* $p < .05$. ** $p < .01$. *** $p < .001$.
[a] R^2 change.
[b] F change.

nificant impact on the BDI and a marginally significant impact on the BL ($p = .06$), a total reduction in variance due to marital status was achieved by the introduction of emotional loneliness into the regression. According to Baron and Kenny (1986), perfect mediation is indicated by the fact that the impact of marital status on symptomatology is totally eliminated when controlling for the mediator. At Time 3 marital status no longer has a significant impact on symptomatology, thus preventing tests of the mediator role of emotional loneliness at this time point.

Analyses on the mediator role of social loneliness were also consistent with theoretical predictions. Social support had a highly significant effect on social loneliness (Table 4). Furthermore, the impact of social support on depressive and somatic symptomatology, although strongest at Time 1, still reaches significance at Time 3. Finally, the introduction of social loneliness into the regression substantially reduced the effect of social support on symptomatology. The fact that at least at Time 1 the social support effect remained significant even when we controlled for social loneliness suggests a case of less than perfect mediation.

Discussion

The pattern of findings observed in this study is consistent with predictions derived from attachment rather than stress theory. The analyses of the impact of social support and marital status on symptomatology revealed main effects for perceived social support and marital status on both the BDI and BL, but no indication of any buffering effects. Individuals who perceived the social support available to them as high reported less depressive and somatic symptomatology than individuals who perceived the availability of social support as low. Similarly, the bereaved persons had higher symptom levels than the married persons.

The design of our study allowed two ways for a buffering effect to emerge, namely, either as a Social Support × Marital Status interaction or as a Social Support × Marital Status × Time interaction. The Social Support × Marital Status interaction should have resulted if social support protected bereaved persons against the deleterious impact of the loss experience (i.e., the vulnerability factor). Then, highly supported bereaved persons should be less affected by the loss experience than unsupported persons, whereas these differences in social support should have little impact on married persons. If, rather than protecting bereaved persons, social support helped them to adjust more readily to their loss experience (i.e., the recovery factor), the immediate impact of social support should be similar for high and low support groups, but over time, highly supported bereaved persons should recover more readily from the loss experience than the less highly supported (Social Support × Marital Status × Time interaction). Contrary to these expectations, the presence or absence of social support had no greater impact on symptom levels of the bereaved than of the married persons at any time. In none of these analyses was there any indication of a buffering effect. There is even some suggestion of a reverse buffering effect in the pattern of means for the BDI at Times 2 and 3.

Because the discussion of buffering versus main effects in social support has been surrounded by a great deal of controversy regarding the use of re-gression versus analysis of variance procedures, our choice of MANOVA is justified in Footnote 2 as the most appropriate procedure given our longitudinal design and the use of a dichotomous stress measure rather than a life event scale. We would also like to point out that the sample we employed was of sufficient size to detect a buffering effect, should it have occurred in our study. Cohen and Wills (1985) reported numerous studies using functional measures that found buffering effects with samples that were smaller than or equal to ours, varying from 64 to 120 subjects (e.g., Cohen & Hoberman, 1983; Fleming, Baum, Gisriel, & Gatchel, 1982; Gore, 1978; Monroe, 1983; Paykel, Emms, Fletcher, & Rassaby, 1980; Surtees, 1980). Of the three bereavement studies that observed a buffering effect, described earlier, Norris and Murrell (1987) had a sample that was similar to ours. Furthermore, in a recent study of the role of social support in buffering the impact of unemployment, Schwarzer, Hahn, and Jerusalem (1994), who also employed a longitudinal design similar to ours, demonstrated highly significant buffering effects of social support (i.e., Employment Status/Social Support interaction) on symptomatology using a MANOVA with repeated measures. Finally, our chance of finding a buffering effect should have been increased by the fact that the stressor used in our study is reputed to be the most stressful life event (Holmes & Rahe, 1967).

Why, then, did we fail to find a buffering effect? For a buffering effect to occur, social support from friends and relatives must to some extent compensate for the support previously received from the lost person. The absence of a buffering effect is thus consistent with predictions from attachment theory, which does not allow for this type of compensation. Furthermore, attachment theory also makes assumptions about the processes that mediate the main effect. As noted above, according to attachment theory, marital status and social support influence well-being by distinctly different pathways, with the impact of marital status being mediated by emotional loneliness and the impact of social support by social loneliness (Figure 1). These hypotheses can be tested independently of whether buffering occurs. To our knowledge, our study provides the first indication that the impact of marital bereavement on health and well-being is mediated by emotional loneliness. Because the impact of bereavement on depressive and somatic symptomatology seems to be totally mediated by emotional loneliness, and because social support from friends and relatives does not seem to alleviate emotional loneliness, no buffering effect could have emerged in our study. Thus, our analysis of the mediating processes provides an additional test of the buffering hypothesis.

Overall, the pattern of findings observed in this study provides persuasive support for the predictions derived from attachment theory that losing a partner means losing a major attachment figure, and that social support from family and friends cannot compensate for this effect. The hypothesis from attachment theory that social support affects symptom levels through a different path, by social loneliness, was also clearly supported. Social support did not reduce emotional loneliness, and control for social loneliness substantially reduced the effect of social support. This pattern is quite consistent with the sentiment expressed by many of the bereaved persons interviewed in our study, who typically explained that, although their friends were a great help, they obviously could not replace the loved one.

ACKNOWLEDGMENTS

Wolfgang Stroebe, Margaret Stroebe, and Henk Schut, Research School of Psychology and Health, Utrecht University, Utrecht. The Netherlands; Georgios Abakoumkin, Department of Education, Psychology Section, University of Patras, Patras, Greece.

This research was financially supported through grants from the Deutsche Forschungsgemeinschaft.

REFERENCES

Baron, R. M., & Kenny, D. A. (1986). The moderator-mediator distinction in social psychological research: Conceptual, strategic, and statistical considerations. *Journal of Personality and Social Psychology, 51,* 1173–1182.

Barrera, M., Jr., Sandler, I. N., & Ramsay, T. B. (1981). Preliminary development of a scale of social support: Studies on college students. *American Journal of Community Psychology, 9,* 435–447.

Beck, A. T. (1967). *Depression: Clinical, experimental and theoretical aspects.* New York: Hoeber.

Bowlby, J. (1969). *Attachment and loss. Vol. 1: Attachment.* London: Hogarth Press; and New York: Basic Books.

Bowlby, J. (1979). *The making and breaking of affectional bonds.* London: Tavistock.

Bradburn, N. (1969). *The structure of psychological well-being.* Chicago: Aldine.

Cohen, S., & Hoberman, H. (1983). Positive events and social supports as buffers of life change stress. *Journal of Applied Social Psychology, 13,* 99–125.

Cohen, S., Mermelstein. R., Kamarck, T., & Hoberman, H.

M. (1985). Measuring the functional components of social support. In I. G. Sarason & B. R. Sarason (Eds.), *Social support: Theory, research and applications* (pp. 73–92). Dordrecht, The Netherlands: Martinus Nijhoff.

Cohen, S., & Wills, T. A. (1985). Stress, social support and buffering. *Psychological Bulletin, 98,* 310–357.

Coppel, D. (1980). *The relationship of perceived social support and self-efficacy to major and minor stresses.* Unpublished dissertation, University of Washington.

Cutrona, C. E., & Russell, D. W. (1990). Type of social support and specific stress: Toward a theory of optimal matching. In B. R. Sarason, I. G. Sarason, & G. R. Pierce (Eds.), *Social support: An interactional view* (pp. 319–366). New York: Wiley.

Derogatis, L. R. (1977). *SCL-90-R: Administration, scoring, and procedures manual—1.* Baltimore: Clinical Psychometric Research.

Fleming, R., Baum, A., Gisriel, M. M., & Gatchel, R. J. (1982). Mediating influences of social support on stress at Three Mile Island. *Journal of Human Stress, 8,* 14–22.

Gore, S. (1978). The effect of social support in moderating the health consequences of unemployment. *Journal of Health and Social Behavior, 19,* 157–165.

Greene, R. W., & Feld, S. (1989). Social support coverage and the well-being of elderly widows and married women. *Journal of Family Issues, 10,* 33–51.

Holmes, T. H., & Rahe, R. H. (1967). The social readjustment rating scale. *Journal of Psychosomatic Research, 11,* 121–218.

Kammer, D. (1983). Eine Untersuchung der psychometrischen Eigenschaften des deutschen Beck-Depressionsinventars (BDI). *Diagnostica, 28,* 48–60.

Krause, N. (1986). Social support, stress, and well-being among older adults. *Journal of Gerontology, 41,* 512–519.

Lazarus, R. S., & Folkman, S. (1984). *Stress, appraisal and the coping process.* New York: Springer.

Lopata, H. (1973). *Widowhood in an American city.* Cambridge, MA: Schenkman.

Monroe, S. M. (1983). Social support and disorder: Toward an untangling of cause and effect. *American Journal of Community Psychology, 11,* 81–96.

Murphy, S. (1988). Mental distress and recovery in a high-risk bereavement sample three years after untimely death. *Nursing Research, 37,* 30–35.

Norris, F., & Murrell, S. (1987). Transitory impact of life-event stress on psychological symptoms in older adults. *Journal of Health and Social Behavior, 28,* 197–211.

Norris, F. H., & Murrell, S. A. (1990). Social support, life events, and stress as modifiers of adjustment to bereavement by older adults. *Psychology and Aging, 5,* 429–436.

Paykel, E. S., Emms, E. M., Fletcher, J., & Rassaby, E. S. (1980). Life events and social support in puerperal depression. *British Journal of Psychology, 136,* 339–346.

Radloff, L. (1975). Sex differences in depression: The effects of occupation and marital status. *Sex Roles, 1,* 249–265.

Radloff, L. (1977). The CES-D Scale: A self-report depression scale for research in the general population. *Applied Psychological Measurement, 1,* 385–401.

Sanders, C. M. (1993). Risk factors in bereavement outcome. In M. Stroebe, W. Stroebe, & R. O. Hansson (Eds.), *Handbook of bereavement: Theory, research and intervention* (pp. 255–267). New York: Cambridge University Press.

Schwarzer, C. (1992). Bereavement, received social support, and anxiety in the elderly: A longitudinal analysis. *Anxiety Research, 4,* 287–298.

Schwarzer, R., Hahn, A., & Jerusalem, M. (1994). *Unemployment, social support and health complaints: A longitudinal study of stress in Eastern German refugees* (Technical Rep. No. 7). Berlin: Department of Educational Psychology, Humboidt University.

Schwarzer, R., & Schwarzer, C. (1983). The validation of the German form of the State-Trait Personality Inventory: A pilot study. In H. M. van der Ploeg, R. Schwarzer, & C. D. Spielberger (Eds.), *Advances in test anxiety research. Vol. 2* (pp. 215–221). Lisse, The Netherlands: Swets & Zeithinger; and Hillsdale, NJ: Erlbaum.

Stroebe, M., & Stroebe. W. (1989). Who participates in bereavement research? A review and empirical study. *Omega, 20,* 1–29.

Stroebe, W., & Stroebe, M. (1987). *Bereavement and health: The psychological and physical consequences of partner loss.* New York: Cambridge University Press.

Stroebe, W., Stroebe, M., Gergen, K., & Gergen, M. (1980). Der Kummer Effekt: psychologische Aspekte der Sterblichkeit von Verwitweten. *Psychologische Beiträge, 22,* 1–26.

Stroebe, W., Stroebe, M. S., Gergen, K., & Gergen, M. (1982). The effects of bereavement on mortality: A social psychological analysis. In J. R. Eiser (Ed.), *Social psychology and behavioral medicine* (pp. 527–560). Chichester, England: Wiley.

Stylianos, S. K., & Vachon, M. L. S. (1993). The role of social support in bereavement. In M. Stroebe, W. Stroebe, & R. O. Hansson (Eds.), *Handbook of bereavement: Theory, research and intervention* (pp. 397–410). New York: Cambridge University Press.

Surtees, P. G. (1980). Social support, residual adversity and depressive outcome. *Social Psychiatry, 15,* 71–80.

von Zerssen, D. (1976). *Die Beschwerdenliste (BL).* Weinhein, Germany: Beltz.

Weiss, R. S. (1975). *Loneliness: The experience of emotional and social isolation.* Cambridge, MA: MIT Press.

Weiss, R. S. (1982). Issues in the study of loneliness. In L. A. Peplau & D. Periman (Eds.), *Loneliness: A sourcebook of current theory research and therapy* (pp. 71–80). New York: Wiley.

Seeing Virtues in Faults: Negativity and the Transformation of Interpersonal Narratives in Close Relationships

Sandra L. Murray and John G. Holmes • University of Waterloo, Ontario, Canada

Editors' Notes

For the most part, studies included in the previous selection used highly structured ways of measuring the dependent variables, namely rating scales, reaction times, or choices in a gaming situation to mention a few. Of course, real life behaviors rarely involve responses to structured instruments. Instead, they unfold in a more spontaneous way like a personal narrative. In this selection, Murray and Holmes undertake the difficult task of tapping important interpersonal behavior in a relatively unconstrained way by having individuals convey their reactions via a free-wheeling narrative. The use of the narrative methodology has an additional advantage of special significance for the present research. It allows the participants considerable flexibility in their portrayal, more than would be revealed with structured questionnaires. Indeed, Murray and Holmes's main finding is that narratives are constructed flexibly and in a way that protects one's positive view of one's dating relationship (compare with Reading 23 on motivated reasoning). The use of the narrative methodology also allows a closer look at ways in which people restructure their narratives to fit their interests. Are such construals functional (compare with Reading 3) or detrimental because they distort the reality of the relationship? The authors' discussion here is notable for depicting the complex relation between truth and functionality in our close relations.

Discussion Questions

1. What was the paradox revealed by the participants' narratives in the Murray and Holmes studies?
2. How did the investigators support their prediction that participants were actively restructuring their narratives to suit the experimentally depicted value of conflict to improving intimacy?
3. In what ways did the design of study 2 complement that of study 1?
4. Were the investigators successful in affecting participants' beliefs in the relation between conflict and intimacy? How did they prove that they were indeed successful?

Suggested Readings

Braiker, H. H., & Kelley, H. H. (1979). Conflict in the development of close relationships. In R. L. Burgess & T. L. Huston (Eds.), *Social exchange in developing relationships* (pp. 135–168). New York: Academic Press.

Christensen, A., & Heavey, C. L. (1993). Gender differences in marital conflict: The demand/withdraw interaction pattern. In S. Oskamp & M. Costanzo (Eds.), *Gender issues in contemporary psychology*. Newbury Park, CA: Sage.

Holmes, J. G., & Boon, S. D. (1990). Developments in the field of close relationships: Creating foundations for intervention strategies. *Personality and Social Psychology Bulletin, 16*, 23–41.

Holtzworth-Munroe, A., & Jacobson, N. S. (1985). Causal attribution of marital couples: When do they search for causes? What do they conclude when they do? *Journal of Personality and Social Psychology, 48*, 1398–1412.

Authors' Abstract

It is proposed that individuals develop story-like representations of their romantic partners that quell feelings of doubt engendered by their partners' faults. In Study I, dating individuals were induced to depict their partners as rarely initiating disagreements over joint interests. Such conflict avoidance was then turned into a fault. In scaled questionnaires and open-ended narratives, low-conflict individuals then constructed images of conflict-engaging partners. These results suggest that storytelling depends on considerable flexibility in construal as low-conflict Ss possessed little evidence of conflict in their relationships. Study 2 further examined the construal processes underlying people's ability to transform the meaning of negativity in their stories (e.g., seeing virtues in faults), Paradoxically, positive representations of a partner may exist—not in spite of a partner's faults—but because of these imperfections.

Coming to terms with the reality of a less-than-perfect partner is perhaps the greatest challenge in the more serious stages of a relationship's development. Faults in an intimate may engender doubts about whether the partner really is the "right" person as well as underline the considerable risks posed by interdependence. Yet, in the face of such threats to their convictions, partners may continue to experience strong feelings of hope for their relationship's ultimate success. This juxta-position of hope and uncertainty enhances individuals' desire to "quell the babble of competing inner voices" underlying feelings of doubt (Jones & Gerard, 1967, p. 181).

We believe that individuals construct stories about their partners to diminish feelings of doubt, thereby affirming and protecting their positive convictions. Such convictions are prospective in nature, reflecting an individual's confidence that his or her partner really is the right person and can be counted on to be caring and responsive across time and situations (Holmes & Rempel, 1989). We propose that individuals protect these convictions by weaving cogent stories that depict potential faults or imperfections in their partners in the best possible light. As we explore, the potential for considerable flexibility in the construal of apparent negativity may be an integral feature of this defensive storytelling process (e.g., Gergen, Hepburn, & Fisher, 1986). For instance an individual might reconcile the threat posed by a partner's stubbornness during conflicts by interpreting it as a sign of integrity, rather than egocentrism. Such storytelling preserves the integrity of individuals' narratives, thereby promoting a sense of felt security in the face of the considerable risks posed by interdependence.

The structure of relationship-affirming narratives may change subtly over time as partners' positive and negative qualities become more or less salient. Early on in romantic relationships, individuals typically experience strong positive feelings as they attend almost exclusively to their partners' positive qualities (Holmes & Boon, 1990; Weiss, 1980). Self-presentation, interaction across restricted, positive domains, and intimates' desire not to perceive negative qualities (e.g., Brehm, 1988) likely all combine to create somewhat simple-minded, idealized narratives (Holmes & Rempel, 1989). As a result, individuals' initial sense of security in their relationships rests largely on the pull of positivity (cf. Brickman, 1987).

Yet, as interdependence increases, individuals begin interacting across broader, more conflictual domains, and the potential for partners to exhibit negative behaviors increases (Levinger, 1983). As the first, most directly affirming response to apparent negativity, individuals may simply deny that their partners' seemingly negative behavior reflects any underlying disposition or attribute. For example, individuals may avoid attributing negative traits to their partners by tagging behaviors suggestive of such traits to specific, unstable features of the situation (e.g., Bradbury & Fincham, 1990; Holtzworth-Munroe & Jacobson, 1985). However, as instances of negative behavior across disparate situations accumulate, dispositional attributions become increasingly difficult to avoid. Somewhat paradoxically though, individuals may become increasingly motivated not to see such faults, precisely because heightened negativity occurs coincident with increasing commitment and closeness

(e.g., Johnson & Rusbult, 1989). We argue that individuals restructure their stories about their partners in a way that transforms seemingly negative attributes, thus reducing their potential to threaten positive convictions.

Experiment 1

As we developed our paradigm, the nature of our theory forced us to confront some important and intriguing methodological considerations. First, if story construction masks negativity, examining individuals' preexisting, positive stories will shed very little light on precisely how negativity has been absorbed. Therefore, we decided to create a negative attribute in the laboratory. To do this, we essentially led individuals to reinterpret an apparent virtue in their partners as a significant fault. We believe that this procedure captures intimates' experiences in developing relationships. Early on, dating partners' impressions of one another are quite pristine; the realization of one another's faults then mars this positivity. Finally, our interest in narrative restructuring required that we develop ways of eliciting and analyzing narratives as a dependent measure (e.g., Baumeister, Stillwell, & Wotman, 1990; Gergen & Gergen, 1988; Harvey, Agostinelli, & Weber, 1989).

To explore the process of narrative transformation, we introduced a mild threat to individuals' convictions by suggesting that their partners possessed a significant fault. We first induced participants to depict their partners as rarely initiating disagreements over joint interests. We then turned such conflict avoidance into a fault by exposing experimental subjects to a bogus *Psychology Today* article that argued for the intimacy-promoting aspects of conflict engagement. In depicting low conflict negatively, we expected to counter our participants' a-priori theories that low conflict was diagnostic of intimacy and thus threaten experimental subjects' positive convictions about the level of intimacy in their relationships.

We modeled our methodology on a dissonance paradigm in the tradition of Aronson (1969) and Steele (1988). Within this tradition, dissonance arises from individuals' desire to reduce only those inconsistencies that pose a threat to the integrity of the self. In the present study, we expected threatened individuals to restructure their stories in ways that reduced the inconsistency between their initial accounts that their partners rarely initiated disagreements over joint interests and their awareness that conflict promoted intimacy. Participants' responses to two main dependent measures provided indices of such defensive restructuring. They first described their partners' willingness to initiate conflicts across a variety of domains exclusive of joint interests on a scaled measure of perceived conflict and then completed open-ended narratives depicting the development of intimacy in their relationships.

We expected threatened individuals to defuse the threat posed by the specter of a conflict-avoidant partner by constructing relationship–affirming narratives that both embellished their partners' virtues around conflict and refuted any faults. In other words, we expected threatened individuals to "see what they wanted to see"—conflict-engaging partners—despite their initial, public commitment to depictions of low-conflict partners. If threatened individuals were not completely successful in restoring the integrity of their narratives by enhancing their partners' conflict-related virtues, they were expected to construct narrative-bolstering refutations or rationalizations for any remaining weaknesses.

Earlier, we hypothesized that individuals restructure their narratives to protect their positive convictions from the threats posed by their partners' negative qualities. If this motivational hypothesis is correct, greater efforts to reconstruct narratives should be observed under conditions of greater threat. In the present study, the magnitude of the threat should depend on the degree to which individuals perceive their partners as falling short of the ideal standard of a conflict-engaging partner. Experimental participants who scored relatively low on a pretest index of disagreement over joint interests should be more threatened by the article than those who scored relatively high. Therefore, if threats to felt security drive story construction, then, paradoxically, low conflict experimental subjects should be the most motivated to construct stories describing high conflict partners.

From a somewhat more cognitive perspective, however, the availability of compelling data should moderate individuals' ability to construct desired narratives. For example, Kunda (1990) argued that individuals will come to believe what they want to believe only to the extent that reason permits. Thus, the availability of cogent data may constrain individuals' ability to construct desired stories. In the present study, individuals who scored relatively high on the pretest index of their partners' tendency to initiate disagreements over joint interests, but still labeled their partners as rarely initiating such conflicts, presumably possessed the most evidence of disagreement in their relationships. Therefore, it might be easiest for these high-conflict individuals to construct positive stories about conflict-engaging partners, whereas the paucity of convincing evidence of conflict could possibly curtail extensive narrative revision among low-conflict individuals.

Our strong expectation was that low-conflict individuals' desire to defuse the threat to their convictions would prove more important in determining the structure of their stories than the social reality of their partners' actual attributes or past behavior. Given our premise that individuals use considerable interpretive licence in their storytelling, we expected that even low-conflict subjects would experience little difficulty going beyond the available data in weaving their desired stories. Consequently, despite the apparent lack of supporting evidence, we expected that low-conflict, threatened subjects would be most likely to construct stories depicting conflict-engaging partners.

Method

SUBJECTS

University of Waterloo undergraduates (37 women; 14 men) who were currently involved in dating relationships between 3 and 24 months in length participated in the study. The mean age of these subjects was 20.2 years. The average relationship length was 11.56 months (SD = 6.19). Subjects received either course credit or $6.00 for their participation in the 75-min study.

PROCEDURE

On their arrival at the laboratory, participants were informed that the study had two primary foci. The first was the development of self-report strategies to assess individuals' perceptions of their partners and relationships. The second was an examination of how dating individuals evaluate research on dating relationships in the popular media.

Participants in the study were run either individually or in pairs. Subjects sat individually at one of two small tables separated by a screen. They were randomly assigned to either the experimental or control condition. Experimental and control subjects first completed a pretest battery assessing demographic characteristics and a variety of relationship quality variables, such as trust, love, and satisfaction.

Depicting a low-conflict partner. All participants then completed two short exercises designed to anchor their perceptions that their partners rarely initiated disagreements over the choice of joint interests and activities. In the first exercise, participants responded on 9-point scales to three statements about their partners' willingness to initiate disagreements over the choice of shared activities and interests (e.g., When I suggest an activity I enjoy but my partner does not enjoy, he or she is never reluctant to express his or her objection to this activity). In the second exercise, the respondents were given 2 min to list instances of their partners' initiating disagreements over joint activities or interests in the past month.

Participants were then provided with a written feedback sheet designed to consolidate the belief that their partners rarely initiated disagreements over joint interests. Finally, participants selected one of two descriptions as most characteristic of their partners' tendency to initiate disagreements over joint interests. The descriptions were (a) My partner tends to promote a sense of harmony in our interactions: My partner rarely initiates disagreements over the activities we may share, and (b) My partner is not particularly concerned with preserving harmony in our interactions: My partner quite frequently initiates disagreements over the activities we may share. The goal of the anchoring procedure was to induce subjects to choose the first description. The choice of this clear, salient label was designed to commit participants to the perception of a "conflict-avoidant" partner.[1]

Manipulation of the threat. Next, the experimenter reminded the participants that the study also examined people's evaluations of popular media articles on dating relationships. Experimental subjects then read the bogus *Psychology Today* article, "The Road to Intimacy." This article described how mature intimacy depended on partners' negotiation of accommodation periods. It contended that relationship intimacy depended on partners' willingness to engage issues by initiating disagreements over important sources of conflict. As an example, the article depicted partners who willingly engaged in disagreements over joint inter-

ests and activities as likely to be progressing toward a truly intimate relationship. Finally, the article concluded by noting that each couple might negotiate periods of accommodation in their own unique ways—ways that may not always include much open conflict. By linking the absence of disagreements to a less mature form of intimacy, we expected the article to threaten experimental participants' positive convictions about the level of intimacy in their relationships.

DEPENDENT MEASURES

Experimental subjects completed the four primary dependent measures after they read the article. They completed these measures in the order in which they appear below. Participants were informed that their evaluation of the article was of primary interest to the investigators and that the other exercises would help the investigators understand this evaluation. Control subjects completed the primary dependent measures before they read the *Psychology Today* article.

We took considerable care to reduce experimental demands in our procedures. First, the experimenter emphasized that the investigators were interested in participants' understanding of what made their relationships unique, thus providing threatened individuals with the opportunity to claim that the article's contentions did not apply to their own relationships. The participants were also given permission to reject the arguments because the experimenter emphasized that the study's focus was on their critical evaluation of the article.

Perceived conflict. This 7-item questionnaire assessed subjects' perceptions of their partners' tendency to risk disagreement and conflict in a variety of different domains exclusive of joint interests. Therefore, it provided an opportunity for threatened individuals to depict conflict-engaging partners. Examples of such items included (a) My partner clearly expresses his or her needs even when he or she knows that these needs conflict with my needs, and (b) My partner is certainly willing to risk an argument by expressing attitudes or thoughts that I oppose. Subjects responded to these items (and all following items) on 9-point scales (1 = not at all true, 9 = completely true).

---

[1] Only five participants indicated that their partners frequently initiated disagreements over joint interests. We included these participants in all analyses we report. Excluding them did not change the pattern of results.

Confidence in intimacy. Five items assessing participants' confidence in the degree of intimacy in their relationships were intermixed with the items assessing perceived conflict in order to provide a sensitive index of any dampening of feelings of confidence induced by the experimental manipulation (e.g., My partner makes me feel completely secure in our relationship).

Intimacy narratives. Participants were next given 10 min to write narratives describing the development of intimacy in their relationships. The instructions for experimental and control conditions were designed to be as similar as possible so as to give control subjects an optimal opportunity to include the role of conflict as part of their narratives. The instructions for the control subjects contained a preamble stating that the *Psychology Today* article examined whether expressing disagreements had any implications for relationship intimacy. The instructions for both experimental and control subjects concluded as follows:

> We are interested in your own account of the ways in which you feel your partner impedes or facilitates the development of intimacy in your relationship. Every relationship is different and partners may adjust to each other in ways that are quite different from those implied in the article. Please convey your honest feelings about the manner in which intimacy grows in your relationship.

Intimacy–conflict theories. Participants then completed a two-item measure designed to assess their theories regarding the relation between intimacy and conflict (e.g. In general, disagreement and conflict is good for my relationship).

Evaluation of the article. Finally, participants evaluated the contentions of the article on five dimensions (e.g., intuitiveness, reasonableness, and believability).

Upon completion of the dependent measures, the subjects were probed for suspicion, fully debriefed, and thanked for their participation.

INTIMACY NARRATIVES CODING DIMENSIONS

Three undergraduate raters (blind to condition and pretest conflict score) coded the intimacy narratives. One third of the narratives were randomly assigned to each rater. The narratives were parsed first into individual thought units. Then, the raters independently categorized each thought by its focus on conflict (presence of conflict, absence of conflict, or no mention of conflict), expansion of

meaning (embellishment, rationalization, or no enhancement), and valence (positive, neutral, or negative). To maintain a clear focus for the reader, we elaborate only on the subset of these categories that were central to our theoretical interests. Examples of these categories are included in the Results section.

Conflict engagement. Such statements focused on the partner's (or participant's) initiation of conflicts or attitude toward engaging conflicts. Such statements were further coded as referring to either the intimacy-promoting or intimacy-impeding aspects of conflict engagement.

Embellishment of conflict engagement. Statements embellishing the meaning of conflict mushroomed a simple reference to the intimacy-promoting nature of conflict by explicitly linking conflict engagement to enhanced feelings of closeness, security, and warmth.

Conflict avoidance. Such statements focused on the partner's (or participant's) tendency to avoid conflicts or attitude toward conflict avoidance. Such statements were further coded as referring to either the intimacy-promoting or intimacy-impeding aspects of conflict avoidance.

Rationalizations for conflict avoidance. Such rationalizations included both refutational statements and relationship-enhancing attributions for the intimacy-impeding aspects of conflict avoidance. *Refutational statements* (cf. Chaiken & Yates, 1985) acknowledged the partner's conflict avoidance but in some way refuted or downplayed its importance in the relationships. *Relationship-enhancing attributions* (e.g., Holtzworth-Munroe & Jacobson, 1985) speculated on the cause underlying conflict avoidance. Such attributions minimized the partner's responsibility for this fault by attributing it to the partner's good intentions or to unstable, specific factors.

Reliabilities. For each subject, we first calculated the number of occurrences of each category (e.g., conflict engagement statement, refutation for conflict avoidance). We then computed Cohen's Kappa for the narratives of 15 subjects. The interrater reliabilities were quite high, ranging from .85 to .95.

Results

We hypothesized that low-conflict experimental subjects would be most likely to depict conflict-engaging partners if threats to felt security moderate narrative restructuring. However, if data availability moderates narrative revision, high-conflict experimental subjects should be most likely to construct stories embellishing conflict. To examine these competing hypotheses, we conducted hierarchical regression analyses in which we first entered the main effects for condition (experimental vs. control) and the continuous pretest conflict index. We created this pretest index by averaging participants' responses to the three items assessing their partners' willingness to initiate disagreements over the choice of joint interests (a = .76). In the next step, we entered the condition by pretest conflict interaction term. In describing our results, we turn first to the analyses of the scaled measures and then discuss the content and structure of individuals' open-ended narratives. (No gender differences emerged in any of the analyses.)

Table 1 presents the regression statistics for each of the effects we describe below. For the purposes of interpretive clarity, we have also included the condition means for low and high pretest conflict groups (determined on the basis of a median split).

INTIMACY–CONFLICT THEORIES

Did the article change experimental subjects' theories concerning the relationship benefits of conflict? To examine this question, we first averaged participants' responses to the two theory items to create a single index of their theories of the relationship benefits of conflict ($\alpha = .77$). The regression analysis on this measure revealed a main ef-

fect for pretest conflict, a main effect for condition, and a significant interaction. As Table 1 illustrates, low-conflict experimental subjects were the most likely to revise their original theories that conflict was somewhat harmful (as evidenced in the baseline provided by low-conflict controls) to emphasize the importance of conflict in promoting intimacy. This interaction suggests that the manipulation posed the greatest threat to the integrity of low-conflict individuals' positive convictions: Their partners did not initiate certain types of conflicts and they now believed that conflict was diagnostic of intimacy.

CONFIDENCE IN INTIMACY

By depicting conflict avoidance as a fault, we expected to threaten experimental participants' positive convictions about the level of intimacy in their relationships. Consistent with this expectation the regression analysis conducted on participants' responses to the confidence items ($\alpha = .61$) yielded a marginal effect for condition ($p < .06$). The article appeared to dampen experimental subjects' confidence in the degree of intimacy in their relationships as these participants felt somewhat less secure and close to their partners than control subjects. This finding provides some tentative support for the success of the manipulation in instilling feelings of doubt in both low- and high-conflict subjects. We suspect this result would have been more pronounced (particularly for low-conflict subjects) if experimental subjects had not been

TABLE 29.1. Restructuring Indices for Study 1

| | Low conflict | | | | High conflict | | | | | | | | | |
| | Experimental | | Control | | Experimental | | Control | | Conflict pretest | | Condition | | Interaction | |
Dependent variable	M	SD	M	SD	M	SD	M	SD	F	dfs	F	dfs	F	dfs
Intimacy-conflict theories[a]	6.08	1.16	4.23	1.77	6.21	1.25	6.19	0.97	5.52**	1.49	5.23**	1.49	6.40**	1.48
Confidence in intimacy[b]	6.52	0.90	7.21	0.90	6.58	1.38	7.00	1.09	0.00	1.48	3.60*	1.48	1.28	1.47
Perceived conflict[c]	5.86	1.17	4.47	1.23	6.29	1.26	5.91	0.63	15.18****	1.49	7.78***	1.49	4.02**	1.48
Conflict engagement[c]	3.00	1.84	0.50	0.76	1.75	1.60	1.23	1.48	0.02	1.47	11.90***	1.47	4.73**	1.46
Embellishment of conflict engagement[c]	0.64	0.50	0.07	0.27	0.33	0.65	0.31	0.48	0.45	1.47	4.07**	1.47	2.16	1.46
Conflict avoidance[c]	1.27	1.49	0.14	0.36	0.17	0.58	0.08	0.28	2.72	1.47	6.49***	1.47	3.92**	1.46
Rationalizations for conflict avoidance[d]	2.36	2.25	0.33	0.50	0.00	0.00	0.00	0.00	2.55	1.34	6.45**	1.34	1.50	1.33
Proportion of refutations for conflict avoidance[e]	0.81	0.38	0.25	0.42	0.00	0.00	0.00	0.00	6.66**	1.18	3.77*	1.18	5.08**	1.17

[a] $N = 52$. [b] $N = 51$. [c] $N = 50$. [d] $N = 37$. [e] $N = 21$.
* $p < .10$. ** $p < .05$. *** $p < .01$. **** $p < .001$.

simultaneously fending off such feelings by describing their partners' willingness to initiate conflicts.

PERCEIVED CONFLICT

As the first route to alleviating any feelings of
concern, threatened individuals, particularly those
low in conflict, could construct images of partners who readily engaged conflicts in a variety of
domains exclusive of joint interests. We averaged
subjects' responses to the perceived conflict items
to create a single index of perceived conflict ($\alpha =$
.75). With regard to the construct validity of this
composite, we found a strong correlation between
control participants' scores on the pretest conflict
and perceived conflict indices, $r(26) = .70$, p <
.01. This correlation suggests that the pretest index of disagreement over joint interests did indeed
provide a reliable estimate of the general level of
conflict in these relationships.

The regression analysis on this measure yielded
significant main effects for pretest conflict and
condition and a significant interaction. Consistent
with the idea that threats to felt security moderate
narrative restructuring, low-conflict threatened
individuals constructed impressions of conflict-
engaging partners. They depicted their relationships as involving substantially greater conflict
than low-conflict controls. In fact, low- and high-
conflict experimental subjects did not even differ
on this measure of perceived conflict, even though
the self-reports of controls suggested that their
conflict histories differed dramatically. Apparently,
low-conflict threatened participants compensated
for their partners weaknesses around disagreeing
over joint interests by embellishing their tendency
to initiate conflicts across a variety of other, more
significant relationship domains.

INTIMACY NARRATIVES

If low-conflict subjects were actively restructuring their perceptions of conflict in their relationships in order to integrate the negative attribute
into stories about responsive and caring partners,
we would expect their intimacy narratives to contain the greatest emphasis on conflict. (One experimental and one control subject were eliminated
from the following analyses because they did not
provide narratives that could be coded on the dimensions we used.)

Conflict engagement. As a primary mechanism
of defense, low-conflict threatened individuals
should be quite motivated to embellish their partners' virtues around engaging conflicts. The regression analysis on the mean number of statements related to the intimacy-promoting aspects
of conflict engagement revealed a marginal main
effect for conflict pretest, a main effect for condition, and the expected interaction. As Table 1 illustrates, low-conflict threatened individuals' narratives contained the greatest focus on how their
partners' active engagement of conflicts in a variety of relationship domains facilitated intimacy
(e.g., "I feel he is facilitating our growth by increasingly being able to tell me when he disagrees
with my opinions in all areas"). (The regression
analysis applied to the mean number of statements
related to the intimacy-impeding aspects of conflict engagement revealed no significant effects.)

Embellishment of conflict engagement. Threatened individuals, particularly those low in conflict,
were also most likely to emphasize how their partners' willingness to initiate conflicts enhanced their
positive feelings about the degree of intimacy in
their relationships. They tended to mushroom
simple references to conflict engagement by explicitly linking it to enhanced feelings of closeness, security, and warmth (e.g. "We've had only
three disagreements . . . we were able to get to the
root of the problem, talk it out, and we managed
to emerge from it closer than before").

Conflict avoidance. If low-conflict threatened
individuals were indeed grappling with their partners' possible weaknesses around conflict, their
narratives should also contain the greatest reference to their partners' conflict avoidance impeding intimacy in their relationships. As expected,
the regression analysis on the mean number of such
statements revealed a marginal main effect for
conflict pretest, a main effect for condition, and
the expected conflict pretest by condition interaction. Low-conflict threatened subjects devoted the
most attention to how their partners' periodic unwillingness to initiate disagreements in particular
domains sometimes impeded the development of
intimacy in their relationships, although such references to conflict avoidance were far less frequent
than references to conflict engagement. One example of such an admission of fault is, "On many
occasions, I could tell that a problem existed, but
she refused to talk about it, almost afraid of an
argument." (Statements related to the intimacy-

promoting aspects of conflict avoidance were quite infrequent.)

Rationalizations for conflict avoidance. Low-conflict individuals' acknowledgment of their partners' weaknesses around initiating conflicts suggests that they were not completely successful in restoring the integrity of their narratives by embellishing their partners' conflict-related virtues. Therefore, we expected these individuals to construct relationship-bolstering rationalizations or refutations for their partners' isolated weakness in initiating conflicts. Such rationalizations function to defuse or take the sting away from these imperfections.

To examine this hypothesis, we combined instances of participants' refutations and relationship-enhancing attributions for conflict avoidance to form an index of rationalizations. We conducted the regression analysis only for those individuals who mentioned the intimacy-impeding nature of conflict avoidance. This analysis yielded a marginal main effect for conflict pretest and a significant main effect for condition. (An examination of the proportion of refutations related to conflict avoidance yielded the anticipated significant interaction.) As Table 1 illustrates, the narratives of the low-conflict threatened group contained almost the only rationalizations for their partners' conflict avoidance. Examples of such integrative, defensive story-telling included:

> On many occasions, I could tell that a problem existed, but she refused to talk about it, almost afraid of an argument . . . *on the other hand, she is very receptive to my needs, and willing to adapt if necessary. This is beneficial to our relationship.*

> My partner never really starts an argument *but knows that if something bothers me enough, I will bring it up. However, my partner has come to realize in the past few months that the development of intimacy is important to me and he seems to be more willing to negotiate problems that occur.*

Experiment 2

We designed our second experiment to explore the particular aspects of the construal process underlying individuals' ability to weave seemingly negative, contradictory elements into relationship-affirming narratives. First, such interpretive licence in storytelling may directly depend on intimates' interpretation of the meaning of apparent negativity (e.g., seeing virtues in faults). Also, to the extent that individuals are free to construct their past in line with their desired conclusions, differential retrieval of virtues and faults may facilitate storytelling (M. Ross, 1989). Finally, intimates may possess considerable licence in deciding which of their partners' virtues and faults are even relevant to the success of their relationships.

In developing a paradigm to examine these construal processes, we kept two specific goals in mind. First, in order to more directly examine how a desired story guides individuals' construal of negative or contradictory evidence, participants provided and then interpreted their own data. Study 1 may have provided the optimal context for poetic licence to assert itself because low-conflict individuals had little vivid, compelling evidence of low conflict staring them in the face, so to speak. Instead, they were able to introspect and selectively pick and choose among fragmented memories and impressions in order to construct images of conflict-engaging partners. Therefore, in Study 2, we attempted to push the boundaries of poetic licence by examining whether it extends to individuals' interpretation of self-generated, contradictory, vivid evidence.

Second, Study 1 could not provide strong evidence that self-reported data availability does not affect the type of story threatened individuals tell. After all, the salience of conflicts, once they were primed, likely buffered high conflict individuals from perceiving a motivating threat to their sense of security. Thus, a broader or more diffuse threat—the importance of recognizing differences—was used in Study 2. Given the sometimes covert nature of differences, we felt that even those individuals who claimed relatively high awareness of differences would have difficulty feeling that they were sufficiently aware of all their differences. By threatening even high-differences individuals, we hoped to examine whether claimed awareness of differences influenced the types of construal processes individuals used in weaving their desired stories.

In this study, we attempted to threaten individuals' positive convictions by linking their apparent inattention to differences to a less mature form of intimacy. In depicting little awareness of differences as negative, we expected to counter our dating participants' a-priori theories that perceiving only similarities was diagnostic of intimacy. We first induced participants to provide a pool of examples of similarities and differences, one that primarily consisted of similarities. Threatened individuals then read a bogus *Psychology Today* article that argued for the intimacy-promoting aspects of being aware of differences and warned against the dangers of assumed similarity. To directly explore the role of construal processes in shaping the meaning of specific pieces of evidence, we then gave participants the opportunity to provide any additional details they wished to their original pool of examples and to provide new examples of similarities and differences.

Despite having generated tangible evidence of their many similarities, we expected both low- and high-differences threatened individuals to reinterpret available evidence within stories that emphasized their awareness of differences. For instance, we expected threatened individuals to see virtues in faults by reconstruing the meaning of their similarities as evidence of their differences. They might also try to bolster their stories by mushrooming or exaggerating their original differences or by selectively remembering new differences and suppressing similarities. The latter construal processes may be particularly evident in high-differences individuals' constructions as the supporting evidence for such claims should be most readily available to them. Finally, if storytelling entails constructing idiosyncratic, relationship-enhancing theories about the importance of virtues and faults, threatened individuals might try to compensate for any potential weaknesses around recognizing differences by embellishing the significance of their similarities (Brickman, 1987). Alternatively, they might simply embellish the importance of their many virtues around recognizing differences.

Method

SUBJECTS

University of Waterloo undergraduates (50 women and 15 men) who were currently involved in dating relationships between 3 and 24 months in length participated in the study. Their mean age was 19.5 years. The average relationship length was 11.45 months (SD = 6.23). Subjects received course credit for their participation in the 90-min study.

PROCEDURE

On their arrival at the laboratory, subjects were greeted by a female experimenter and were given

a brief oral introduction to the study similar to that used in Study 1. Participants were run through the experimental procedures individually. They were randomly assigned to either the experimental or control condition.

Pretest measures. As in Study 1, participants first completed a pretest battery assessing demographic characteristics and a variety of relationship quality variables. An index of participants' awareness of differences between themselves and their partners was also included. This 7-item index consisted of items directly assessing participants' awareness of differences (e.g., My partner's needs and expectations for our relationship differ from my own in many ways) and items assessing perceived similarity. Perceived similarity and differences items were strongly negatively correlated, $r(63) = -.59$. Participants made their responses to these items (and all following items) on 9-point scales (1 = not at all true, 9 = completely true).

Claiming little awareness of differences. All participants then completed short exercises designed to anchor their perceptions that they were aware of few significant differences between themselves and their partners. In the first exercise, participants were given 3 min to list the similarities or differences they shared with their partners that they felt were most important for making their relationships work. All subjects were then provided with a feedback sheet designed to consolidate the belief that they were aware of few important differences. Then in an anchoring procedure, participants selected one of three alternatives as most representative of the respective ease with which they thought of differences and similarities. The goal was to induce subjects to endorse a description indicating that they had difficulty thinking of important differences.[2]

Manipulation of the threat. The experimenter then reminded the participants that the study also examined individuals' evaluations of popular media articles on dating relationships. Following this general introduction, the experimental subjects read the bogus *Psychology Today* article, "The Road to Intimacy." To control for elapsed time, control subjects read a filler article on subliminal perception.

---

[2]Fourteen participants indicated that they had little difficulty thinking of differences. We included these participants in all analyses we report. Excluding them did not change the pattern of results.

"The Road to Intimacy" described how the successful negotiation of accommodation periods depended on both partners' willingness to recognize and acknowledge their important, subtle differences. Recognition of differences was linked to partners' increased understanding and responsiveness to one another's needs. The article also suggested that blindly idealizing a partner impeded intimacy because rigidly held assumptions of similarity were inevitably violated and resulted in feelings of dissatisfaction. In summary, the article posed a threat to individuals' positive convictions by linking their inability to think of significant differences to a less mature form of intimacy.

DEPENDENT MEASURES

The measures are described in detail below, and participants completed them in the order in which they appear.

Providing additional details to the original examples. In an effort to support revised claims that they were aware of important differences, threatened subjects might subtly shift or reconstrue the nature of their reported similarities and differences. To examine this possibility, we asked participants to review their original examples and to provide any additional details they felt might help the investigators better understand the meaning of these examples. The experimenter also emphasized that subjects need not provide further details if they felt that their examples were already sufficiently detailed.

Provision of new examples. To bolster their perceptions that they were indeed aware of their differences, individuals might also selectively recall new differences and suppress evidence of similarities. Therefore, we gave participants the opportunity to provide any additional examples of similarities or differences that came to mind. Again, the experimenter emphasized that subjects might not be able to think of any new important similarities or differences.

Perceived differences questionnaire. This 16-item questionnaire assessed participants' perceptions of the degree to which they differed from their partners in a variety of domains. We included both perceived differences and similarity items in this index (e.g., I am aware of a variety of ways in which my partner's preferred ways of dealing with conflict differ greatly from my own, and My partner and I are just like two peas in a pod, we are

similar in so many ways). Similarity items were reverse scored in computing the index.

Confidence in intimacy. The five confidence items used in Study 1 were mixed with the perceived differences and similarities items to provide an index of any dampened feelings of confidence induced by the experimental manipulation.

Intimacy narratives. Participants were then given 10 min to write accounts describing the development of intimacy in their relationships. The instructions for experimental and control subjects were again designed to be as similar as possible to give control subjects an optimal opportunity to include differences in their narratives. Therefore, control instructions contained a preamble stating that the article examined whether partners' awareness of their differences had any implications for relationship intimacy. Otherwise, the instructions for writing the narratives for both experimental and control subjects mirrored those described in Study 1.

Intimacy-differences theories. This 6-item measure assessed participants' own theories concerning the relationship benefits of recognizing differences (e.g., In general, partners' recognizing their differences is very important for relationship intimacy).

Upon completion of the dependent measures, the subjects were probed for suspicion, fully debriefed, and thanked for their participation.[3]

CODING DIMENSIONS

Two raters (blind to condition and pretest differences score) independently coded the additional details, new examples, and intimacy narratives. One half of the subjects were randomly assigned to each rater. The original examples first were identified as either similarities or differences.

Additional details. The additional details that participants provided to their original examples were coded as belonging to one of the following

---

[3]We took considerable care in our debriefing procedures to ensure that all participants left the studies feeling positively about their relationships. In Study 1, we explained that conflict is an inevitable part of close relationships and that how couples handle conflict (whether through engagement or avoidance) is critical for feelings of satisfaction. In Study 2, we emphasized that similarities are indeed an integral part of good relationships while also noting that intimates are often unaware of their differences on dimensions critical for satisfaction. Further details regarding the debriefing procedures are available from the authors.

five mutually exclusive categories. *Defensive reconstrual* referred to the provision of details suggesting some degree of difference between partners to an example that was originally framed as a similarity. The category *offensive reconstrual* was applied when a participant provided details suggesting some degree of similarity between partners to an example that was originally framed as a difference. *Polarization* of similarities or differences referred to the provision of details suggesting that the similarity or differences was greater of more significant than the original example had indicated. *Meaning consistent elaboration* referred to a participant's provision of details that simply provided greater information about the similarity or difference without changing the meaning of the original example. *Examples left unchanged* were also categorized. Relevant examples of each category are included in the Results section.

Each example could then also be assigned either of the following codes. An *embellished meaning* code was applied if the participant provided details linking the similarity or difference to the presence of intimacy in the relationship, such as feelings of closeness and security. A *deemphasized meaning* code was applied if a participant provided details that refuted or lessened any potential bearing (usually negative) the similarity or difference might have on the quality of the relationship.

New examples. Each example was assigned to one of two categories. A *definitive difference* code was applied if a participant described a difference without providing any details suggesting any degree of underlying similarity. A *definitive similarity* code was applied if a participant described a similarity without providing any details suggesting any degree of underlying difference.

Intimacy narratives. The narratives were parsed first into individual thought units. Then, the raters independently coded each thought in terms of its focus on differences (presence, absence, or no mention) or similarities (presence, absence, or no mention), expansion of meaning (embellishment or not), and valence (positive, neutral, or negative).

Statements coded as *differences as facilitators* (or *impediments*) identified a participant's awareness of differences as promoting (or impeding) intimacy in his or her relationship. Differences statements were also identified as an example of an *articulated difference* (e.g., "He is more stubborn") or a simple *global declaration* that differences existed (e.g., "My partner and I are aware of

our differences"). Finally, *embellishment of differences* was identified using the criteria for assessing embellishment of conflict employed in Study 1. Relevant examples of each category are included in the Results section.

Reliabilities. For each subject, we first calculated the number of occurrences of each category (e.g., defensive reconstrual, differences as facilitators). We then computed Cohen's Kappa for each of the dependent indices for 20 subjects. The interrater reliabilities were quite high, ranging from 0.90 to 1.00.

Results

We expected both low- and high-differences individuals to dampen the threat to their convictions by weaving available evidence, memories, and introspections into depictions embellishing their awareness of differences. We also wished to explore whether self-proclaimed availability of data influenced how low-differences versus high-differences individuals restructured their narratives. As in Study 1, we conducted hierarchical regression analyses in which we first entered the main effects for condition (experimental vs. control) and the continuous pretest differences index. We created this pretest index by averaging participants' responses to the eight items assessing perceived similarities (reverse scored) and differences (a = .88). In the next step, we entered the condition by pretest differences interaction term. In describing our results, we turn first to the analyses of the scaled measures and then discuss the open-ended construal indices and narratives. (No gender differences emerged in any of the analyses.)

Table 2 presents the regression statistics for each of the effects we describe below. For interpretive clarity, we have also included the condition means.

INTIMACY-DIFFERENCES THEORIES

Were we successful in inducing a broader threat that challenged the theories of both low- and high-differences subjects? To answer this question, we averaged participants' responses to the six theory items assessing their perceptions of the relation between intimacy and recognizing differences (α = .71). The regression analysis on this index revealed only the expected main effect for condition. Threatened individuals revised their original theories that attending to differences was some-

TABLE 29.2. Restructuring Indices for Study 2

Dependent measure	Experimental		Control		Differences pretest		Condition		Interaction	
	M	SD	M	SD	F	dfs	F	dfs	F	dfs
Intimacy-differences theories[a]	5.66	1.33	4.81	1.13	1.92	1.62	5.10**	1.62	1.85	1.61
Confidence in intimacy[b]	6.42	1.38	7.03	1.08	39.69****	1.61	3.21*	1.61	0.03	1.60
Perceived differences[a]	5.10	1.28	4.25	1.00	72.51****	1.62	10.13***	1.62	0.00	1.61
Additional details										
Defensive reconstrual[a]	1.00	0.92	0.45	0.77	0.33	1.62	5.25**	1.62	2.64	1.61
Unequivocal defensive reconstrual[a]	1.00	0.92	0.23	0.56	1.26	1.62	12.49****	1.62	1.41	1.61
Polarization of differences[c]	0.64	0.91	0.09	0.29	6.63**	1.48	5.25**	1.48	1.63	1.47
Embellishment of differences[a]	0.32	0.59	0.06	0.25	0.01	1.62	4.52**	1.62	0.59	1.61
Deemphasis of differences[a]	0.12	0.41	0.48	0.85	0.35	1.62	3.81*	1.62	1.65	1.61
Embellishment of similarities[a]	0.74	1.21	0.16	0.45	0.06	1.62	5.84**	1.62	0.15	1.61
Intimacy narratives										
Differences as facilitators[a]	2.03	1.99	0.61	1.23	0.05	1.62	10.06***	1.62	0.01	1.61
Global declarations of differences[a]	1.79	1.84	0.23	0.67	0.05	1.62	17.62****	1.62	0.21	1.61
Embellishment of differences[a]	0.79	1.07	0.03	0.18	1.59	1.62	11.61***	1.62	1.31	1.61

[a] $N = 65$. [b] $N = 64$. [c] $N = 51$
*$p < .10$. **$p < .05$. ***$p < .01$. ****$p < .001$.

what harmful (as evidenced in the baseline provided by controls) to emphasize the importance of recognizing differences in promoting intimacy.

CONFIDENCE IN INTIMACY

By depicting little awareness of differences as an impediment to intimacy, we expected to threaten experimental participants' positive convictions in the level of intimacy in their relationships. The regression analysis on the confidence index ($\alpha = .69$) revealed a marginal effect for condition. As expected, the article appeared to dampen threatened subjects' confidence in the degree of intimacy in their relationships; they tended to feel less secure and close to their partners than control subjects.[4]

PERCEIVED DIFFERENCES QUESTIONNAIRE

We expected threatened individuals to claim awareness of a wide range of subtle differences in their efforts to lessen the inconsistency posed by their revised theories. We averaged participants' responses to the perceived differences and similarities items to create a single index of claimed awareness of differences ($\alpha = .83$). The regression analysis on this measure yielded significant main effects for pretest differences and condition. First, supporting the validity of the perceived differences pretest, high-differences individuals claimed greater awareness of differences than low

differences individuals. More importantly, threatened individuals, in comparison to controls, perceived more differences and fewer similarities across a variety of domains.

As the preceding analyses suggest, focusing on the importance of recognizing differences appeared to induce a more diffuse, less dismissable threat to the integrity of even high-differences individuals' narratives than was achieved in Study 1. We turn next to an examination of the open-ended process measures—the additional details, new examples, and intimacy narratives. We hoped that examining these measures would shed light on the construal processes underlying individuals' construction of relationship-affirming narratives centered around their awareness of differences.

PROVIDING ADDITIONAL DETAILS TO THE ORIGINAL EXAMPLES

The salient emphasis on similarities in threatened individuals' original examples likely presented a provoking contradiction to their desired narratives. We expected these individuals to redress this inconsistency by engaging considerable poetic licence to weave this data into evidence supporting their awareness of differences.

---

[4]We did not find very strong evidence of dampened feelings of confidence in either study. We are not particularly troubled by these findings because threatened subjects had already begun to tell their desired, confidence-boistering stories when they completed this measure.

Defensive reconstrual. In an effort to support a revised claim that they were indeed aware of important differences, experimental participants could depict certain similarities as encapsulating subtle differences. As expected, threatened individuals were more likely than controls to reconstrue their similarities as reflecting some degree of underlying difference. A closer examination of the nature of defensive reconstrual among experimental and control participants also revealed an intriguing qualitative disparity. Threatened individuals were more likely to encapsulate subtle, often important, differences within similarities and then to describe these differences quite unequivocally. In contrast, control participants tended to downplay the significance of such differences. Examples of threatened subjects' unequivocal depiction of differences included:

> We are of similar intellectual ability [original] . . . however, *when it comes to using this ability I like to spend more time on my schoolwork than she does or than she would have me do* [detailed].

> We both feel insecure about starting a relationship because of past experiences [original] . . . both my partner and I feel compelled to make our relationship work because of negative past experiences: *although we differ in that her fear is loneliness while mine is rejection* [detailed].

Polarization. To rid themselves of any nagging feelings of doubt instilled by the manipulation, experimental participants might also amplify or mushroom existing differences by suggesting that certain differences were more profound than they originally described. Threatened individuals did indeed polarize their differences to a greater extent than control subjects. As we expected, high-differences threatened individuals were far more likely to mushroom their existing differences ($M = 1.00$) than either low-differences threatened individuals ($M = 0.09$) or controls ($M = 0.09$; 0.09). Although the regression analysis was not sensitive to this interaction pattern, because of extremely low variance in three cells, a 2×2 analysis of variance (ANOVA) yielded the anticipated interaction, $F(1.47) = 6.29$, $p < .05$. Instances of such mushrooming of differences among high differences threatened subjects included:

> Differences between attitudes toward drinking alcohol [original] . . . *this reveals that she is a little more wanting to let loose whereas I feel I am a more conservative person* [detailed].

Personalities as to mood swings are not similar, or social habits [original] . . . *"I have a view that if I'm happy everything is fine. My partner feels that at times anger is necessary to fuel the relationship and make it work. I do not enjoy arguing whereas his mood swings and social habits (depressive drinker) are not to my liking. Thus, the dissimilarities in our attitudes or personalities are extreme* [detailed].

Embellishment of differences. We suggested earlier that poetic licence might also extend to intimates' impressions of which of their partners' faults and virtues are even relevant to the well-being and maintenance of their relationships. Threatened individuals, in comparison to controls, were the most likely to emphasize how attending to certain differences enhanced their positive feelings about the degree of intimacy in their relationships. Such linking of differences to the well-being of the relationship was reflected in this example.

> His views on important issues are the same as mine but he seems more firm in his beliefs [original] . . . I can see that he is very consistent with his feelings and attitudes and *therefore this makes it much easier for me to understand him and the reasons for his feelings and attitudes: it also makes me assess and understand myself* [detailed].

Deemphasis of differences. In contrast to experimental participants' emphasis on the central role differences played in promoting intimacy in their relationships, control participants tended to cast their differences in a relatively tangential role, although this effect was only marginally significant, $p < .06$. Comments such as "I like talking a lot about us . . . he is quiet a lot [original] . . . Actually *in general I talk a lot about anything so that is probably why he is more quiet*" [detailed] reflected control subjects' penchant for downplaying the significance of their differences.

Embellishment of similarities. The plethora of similarities in threatened individuals' original examples presented a potential impediment to their desired stories because the salience of similarities highlighted the threatening possibility that they were impeding intimacy by idealizing their partners. We expected individuals to compensate for this potential threat by embellishing the significance of their similarities in promoting intimacy (Brickman, 1987). The analysis of positive embellishment of similarities showed that experimental participants did indeed link their similarities to feelings of closeness, security, and warmth. Such evidence of compensation is reflected in this example.

> Similar in views of our families [original] . . . we both feel they are important in shaping our lives and yet both of us have great conflict with members of our families and *this leads to more bonding between us* [detailed].

NEW EXAMPLES

We expected threatened individuals to differentially recall new differences and suppress similarities to provide further support for their claims. Contrary to our hypothesis, they were not more likely to selectively retrieve more differences or fewer similarities in order to bolster their stories about the prevalence of differences in their relationships.

INTIMACY NARRATIVES

To this point, we have hypothesized that threatened individuals' desire to construct stories centered around differences guided their construal of particular instances of similarities and differences. Our examination of their intimacy narratives should shed light on whether such stories emerged from this process of reconstrual and redefinition.

Threatened individuals dramatically restructured their stories of the development of intimacy to emphasize the central role played by their awareness of differences. Their narratives contained the greatest focus on how their knowledge of their differences facilitated intimacy, especially as indexed by their simple, global declarations of such awareness (e.g., "We believe in many of the same things; however, we are very different people. I feel we are both aware of these differences"). (An examination of the number of statements depicting differences as impediments yielded no significant effects). In their depiction of the role of differences in their relationships, threatened subjects also mushroomed simple references to the intimacy-promoting nature of their attention to differences by explicitly linking such awareness to enhanced feelings of closeness and security (e.g., "Because we have recognized and negotiated the differences, this is why our relationship is so strong, and the closeness keeps growing").[5]

General Discussion

DEFUSING OUR APPARENT FAULTS

To this point, we have argued that our manipulations introduced threatening negative elements into individuals' positive stories. We then interpreted the subsequent story restructuring as a reflection of individuals' desire to defuse the threat. Is it possible, though, that the narrative restructuring we observed reflected something quite different from individuals' response to a threat to their convictions?

For instance, perhaps introducing the articles unintentionally confounded cognitive salience with threat. In other words, reviewing articles on conflict and differences may have simply made these dimensions quite salient for experimental subjects. They may then have produced a more differentiated, cognitively transformed story, not because they were threatened, but simply because information about these topics was so readily available. However, we made every attempt to make the topics of conflict and differences just as salient for control subjects.

First, they spent several minutes completing the perceived conflict and differences questionnaires immediately before they wrote their narratives. These measures tapped their perceptions in these domains in considerable depth and therefore made the local dimensions quite salient. In the preamble to control subjects' intimacy narratives, we also described the topic of the article, thereby ensuring that control subjects were focused on conflict or differences. In light of these precautions, differential salience seems a much less compelling explanation for the story restructuring. Further-

---

[5]Experimental participants exhibited greater variances than control subjects on many of the categorical indices for additional details, new examples, and intimacy narratives; this heterogeneity often resulted from very low condition means. However, nonparametric analyses of the condition main effects (Mann-Whitney U or Wilcoxon Rank Sum W Test) also revealed consistent, significant results, suggesting that this heterogeneity was not responsible for the findings. No significant condition effects or pretest differences by condition interactions were found for offensive reconstrual, polarization of similarities, meaning consistent elaboration of similarities and differences, negative embellishment of similarities and differences, or deemphasis of similarities. In the intimacy narratives, no significant effects were found for statements related to the absence of differences, statements related to the presence or absence of similarities, or embellishment of similarities.

more, we observed transformations in a direction opposite to subjects' original theories and perceptions, suggesting that salience alone did not produce our results. After all, we found a marked emphasis on conflict in low-conflict individuals' stories, an effect exactly opposite to what a more extensive sampling of their conflict experiences would produce.

Perhaps, low conflict and few differences are actually measures of relationship quality. If this is the case, low-conflict individuals might have restructured their narratives, not because their partners fell furthest from the conflict-engaging ideal, but simply because they were in better, happier relationships than high-conflict individuals. In other words, low-conflict individuals may simply have cared more about preserving a positive image of their partners. In Study 1, however, satisfaction was independent of perceived conflict scores, $r(50) = .16$, suggesting that low-conflict individuals were not any happier than high-conflict individuals (cf. Braiker & Kelley, 1979). In Study 2, awareness of differences did tap relationship quality, as high-differences individuals generally reported less satisfaction, $r(63) = -.69$. Yet, even these individuals restructured their stories in ways that preserved their generally positive representations. We certainly believe that the happiest, most committed individuals will be the most motivated to dispel threats. However, satisfaction did not statistically moderate the results in either study when it was entered as a covariate, suggesting that our participants all cared enough to need to defuse the threat.

In posing a threat to individuals' convictions, we changed their a-priori theories about the qualities that are desirable in an intimate partner. Therefore, it is possible that the story restructuring we observed simply reflected threatened individuals' desire to portray their relationships in a socially desirable light. In considering this threat to our interpretation of the results, it is critical to consider the intended audience for threatened individuals' revised narratives. If participants were striving to present a desirable account to themselves, this of course mirrors our contention that individuals need to believe the best of their partners.

On the other hand, if subjects were simply striving to "keep up appearances" and present a socially desirable account to the experimenter, this would certainly present a rival explanation for our findings. However, threatened individuals had numerous ways to do this apart from simply shaping their reports in the manner suggested by the articles. In their stories, they could have emphasized the many other ways in which their partners facilitated intimacy. Also, if presenting a desirable public image was their sole motivation, they would have wanted to avoid appearing inconsistent from the pretest to posttest, and most critically, they would not have described themselves as being less confident about the level of intimacy in their relationships.

Furthermore, if social desirability concerns were driving the effects in Study 1, high-conflict individuals could have easily emphasized conflict in their narratives. After all, they did depict their partners as rarely initiating disagreements over joint interests. Therefore, they should have been quite motivated to portray their relationships in a more desirable fashion if the audience was not a private, but a public one. However, high-conflict threatened individuals did not restructure their stories even though they could have easily impressed the experimenter by embellishing the amount of conflict in their relationships.

Finally, we also took a number of precautions to minimize any potential experimental demands. We emphasized throughout the experiment that we were interested in subjects' critical evaluation of the articles, thereby giving them explicit permission to reject them. We also stressed that we were interested in what made participants' relationships unique. We even concluded the articles with the caveat that partners may adjust to one another in ways quite different from those implied by the articles. To further minimize any need to impress the experimenter, we also emphasized that subjects' responses were anonymous and would be examined only in the context of the group's responses. In light of the preceding arguments and these many precautions, social desirability seems to be a less than parsimonious explanation for the overall pattern of results.

In the spirit of this article, we feel that these potential faults should be viewed within the context of the greater virtues of our paradigm. Eliciting individuals' open-ended accounts allowed us to examine how individuals spontaneously restructured their stories in response to negativity. Relying only on our scaled measures, however, might have been more revealing of the story we wanted threatened individuals to tell. Finding such strong, consistent results across both scaled and open-ended measures should therefore attest to the strength and validity of our findings.

Maintaining Convictions: The Role of Defensive Strategies

We suggest that intimates' storytelling efforts culminate in complex, integrative narratives that sustain their positive convictions. A sense of conviction or confidence is usually conceptualized as reflecting an attitude that has an unequivocal affective core (cf. Fazio, 1986). This affective core conclusion, as embodied in feelings of love or satisfaction, has been the focus of most research on close relationships. However, little research has examined the cognitive structure (e.g., mental representation of a partner) supporting this affective core. As our focus on narrative structure would attest, we doubt this affective conclusion can exist in isolation. In fact, McGuire and Papageorgis (1961) argued that such evaluative truisms may be quite vulnerable to threat if there is no supporting cognitive structure underlying the affect.

We believe that intimates' narratives provide this supportive cognitive structure. In confidence-instilling narratives, negative attributes must either be transformed or refuted, not left dangling as loose ends within the story. The potential for considerable poetic licence in storytelling may underlie such positive transformations of apparent negativity. In both studies, individuals were able to weave even the most seemingly compelling evidence of negativity into stories supporting their desired, positive conclusions. We suspect that individuals' continued confidence in their partners—their sense of felt security—depends on their continued struggle to weave stories that depict potential faults in their partners in the best possible light.

Seeing virtues in apparent faults appears to be a primary mechanism for weaving confidence-instilling stories in the face of negativity. For instance, threatened individuals constructed stories depicting conflict-engaging partners despite interpersonal histories suggestive of conflict avoidance. Similarly, in Study 2, threatened individuals constructed evidence of differences in data attesting to similarities. Intriguingly then, negativity need not be fully, consciously acknowledged as intimates weave their desired stories. Instead, the desired conclusion may function as an interpretive filter that colors, preconsciously, the meaning of negative attributes or behaviors. This hypothesized process bears a strong similarity to the perceptual defense phenomenon (e.g., Erdelyi, 1974). The glimmer of a potentially negative attribute may pose a threat preconsciously. However, defensive construal processes may largely preempt intimates' full, conscious recognition of negativity. Rather, constructed virtues appear figural rather than potential faults.

Although our data cannot definitively address how individuals turned apparent faults into virtues, a number of possibilities exist. First, there are often few clear, unequivocal behavioral exemplars for abstract personal qualities, such as trustworthiness or assertiveness. So, for instance, individuals may sustain positive impressions of their partners' willingness to engage conflicts by constructing idiosyncratic definitions that depict their partners' behaviors as evidence of this desired quality (e.g., Dunning. Meyerowitz, & Holzberg, 1989). Coupled with the ambiguity inherent in trait definitions, the meaning of behavior itself is often ambiguous. As a result, two individuals trying to sustain opposing conclusions about their partners' attributes may interpret apparently similar behaviors as evidence of these different, desired attributes (e.g., Gergen et al., 1986; Griffin & Ross, 1991). Thus, challenged individuals in Study 2 were able to reinterpret apparent similarities as evidence of their differences. Finally, revising the past may also enable individuals to see virtues where they once saw evidence of imperfections (Holmberg & Holmes, in press; McFarland & Ross, 1987); for example, individuals who are high versus low on conflict engagement may not always act in attribute-consistent ways from situation to situation (cf. L. Ross & Nisbett, 1991). Therefore, low-conflict individuals may construct images of conflict-engaging partners by remembering evidence of the virtue while suppressing evidence of the fault.

As a second general strategy for weaving faults into positive stories, individuals may also construct idiosyncratic theories about the relative importance of their partners' virtues and faults. By embellishing the significance of virtues and refuting the importance of faults, such personal theories maintain a consistent, positive theme in intimates' stories. For instance, threatened individuals maintained desired narratives by embellishing the significance of differences, whereas controls preserved positive narratives by dismissing the significance of these differences.

In their storytelling, individuals may relegate their partners' fault to the relatively tangential role dictated by their theories. In Study 1, low-conflict threatened individuals preserved the integrity of their narratives by constructing refutations and relationship-enhancing attributions that minimized the significance of their partners' conflict avoidance. By constructing such refutations intimates constrained the possible implications of this fault, thereby minimizing any potential links between their partners' conflict avoidance and their capacity to be good partners.

Individuals might also obscure imperfections simply by construing their partners' virtues in an even more positive light (cf. Brickman, 1987). For instance, threatened individuals in Study 2 were significantly more likely to embellish the value of their similarities for strengthening intimacy, as a counterpoint to the threat that they were not sufficiently aware of their differences. Similarly, research on compensation and self-interpretation suggests that individuals do indeed try to embellish their personal virtues to make up for perceived faults (Baumeister & Jones, 1978; Greenberg & Pyszczynski, 1985). Essentially, intimates may come to understand specific faults in the light of greater, more significant virtues that take the sting away from these imperfections (e.g., Holmes & Rempel, 1989).

Such defensive transformations of the meaning and significance of apparent faults may foster intimates' construction of idealized stories of "positive illusions" about one another. Individuals may discover new previously unrecognized virtues as they struggle to deal with one another's imperfections. For instance, low-conflict individuals discovered their partners' many important virtues around conflict engagement precisely because of their concerns about their partners' conflict avoidance. Similarly, as a counterpoint to the threat that they were simply idealizing their partners, threatened individuals in Study 2 discovered significant new virtues in recognizing difference. Individuals' struggle to deal with their own imperfections may also lead them to see even greater virtues in their partners. For example individuals seem to defuse doubts posed by their own attraction to desirable others by disparaging the attractiveness of these potential mates (Johnson & Rusbult, 1989). Individuals' own partners may then appear especially attractive and desirable in light of such unattractive alternatives. Paradoxically then, positive representations of a partner may prosper—not in spite of a partner's negative qualities—but precisely because of these imperfections (e.g., Brickman, 1987).

Construal and Catastrophe: A Latent Vulnerability?

To be resilient, individuals' stories must be capable of adapting to the challenges of their relationships' development. If positive affect is to be maintained over time, cogent narratives must evolve that realistically integrate the positive and negative aspects of intimates' experience.

As a primary response to the specter of negativity, committed dating partners may construct compelling stories that depict their intimates in the best possible light. Intimates' conviction in such stories may guide construal such that information processing serves a maintenance function. Individuals are potentially buffered from swings in emotion as a benign interpretation of negativity is largely predetermined. Defusing or minimizing faults in this way may also bolster feelings of efficacy by preventing intimates from construing faults as insurmountable. Thus, rather than inhibiting action, these narratives may provide intimates with sufficient hope and security to work negativity through interpersonally.

However, the reconstrual of negatives within narratives may also create the potential for catastrophe, leaving intimates vulnerable to a resurfacing of negative elements. As our theory would anticipate, individuals typically ignore apparent negativity and make decisions to marry largely on the basis of their positive feeling about their partners. In fact, apparent negativity, such as premarital conflict, is relatively orthogonal to feelings of love and satisfaction prior to and at the point of marriage (Braiker & Kelley 1979; Kelly, Huston, & Care 1985; Markman 1979). However, masking negativity in this way is not without its potential costs if individuals then fail to deal directly with troublesome issues. For instance, conflict and negativity before marriage, although initially divorced from reports of satisfaction, predict later declines in satisfaction (Kelly et al., 1985; Markman, 1981).

Whether integrative storytelling effectively defuses negativity over the longer term may depend on the fragility of the constructions. If a story appears to belie social reality constraints, the narrative woven around the negative attribute may unravel as evidence inconsistent with the individual's construction intrudes again and again. For example, if a fault in a partner is blatantly denied and transformed into a virtue, an individual may be quite vulnerable to the challenge posed by recurring evidence of this negative attribute. The construction of refutations that acknowledge but compartmentalize faults may prove more resilient to the resurfacing of negativity. Obviously, the utility of these defensive strategies—whether they ultimately bolster positivity or provide the basis for the relationship's eventual disintegration—remains a question for future research.

Our focus on the critical importance of efforts to accommodate to negativity mirrors recent attention given to the role of negativity in predicting relationship success (e.g., Huston & Vangelisti, 1991; Rusbult, Verette, Whitney, Slovik, & Lipkus, 1991). Rusbult et al. argued that avoiding destructive responses to negativity may ultimately be far more important for relationship satisfaction than attempting to maximize positive behaviors. Similarly, Huston and Vangelisti found that initial negativity in socioemotional behavior was the strongest predictor of declines in satisfaction among newly married couples two years into marriage.

Dealing with negativity may prove to be one of the greatest challenges in sustaining romantic relationships. As the above research (Huston & Vangelisti, 1991; Rusbult et al., 1991) attests, intimates' positive convictions may begin to waver if negativity is recurrent and exceeds their capacity to assimilate it into positive stories. Once this equilibrium is disturbed and intimates' confidence starts to erode, they may begin to test whether the partner really is someone they can count on to be responsive and caring. Rather than maintaining convictions, construal processes may then begin to serve a self-protective function. In effect, intimates may become risk averse in their interpretations in order to protect themselves from the further dashing of their hopes. Such a hypothesis-testing strategy may well support the feared conclusion as intimates become much more sensitized to the possible implications of negativity and less confident in the implications of positivity (Holmes & Boon, 1990).

Intriguingly, the very fragility of relationships may rest on the flexibility inherent in the construal process itself. Brickman (1987), for example, couched his description of romantic love in terms of catastrophe theory (Flay, 1978). He argued that passionate love is created out of intense ambivalence through intimates' commitment to idealized depictions of their partners. However, as ambivalence is only masked, recurring negativity may trigger a dramatic decrease in love. We suggest that interpretive license is the basis for such polar swings in emotion.

Although our research has focused on how the ambiguity inherent in the construal process sustains positive convictions, interpretive license may also support more negative conclusions. For instance, if an intimate is motivated to believe the best of her or his partner, occasional stubbornness could be interpreted as a sign of fortitude and integrity. However, an intimate less motivated to be generous might construe the same behavior as diagnostic of inconsiderateness and unresponsiveness. Thus, if feelings of doubt begin to erode positive convictions, intimates may find evidence of negativity in the same data that once supported positive stories. Such jaded interpretations may further escalate negative emotions. From a social-constructionist perspective, meaning may only be as lasting as the positive conclusion guiding the construal. If construals can be done, they can be undone with equal facility.

ACKNOWLEDGMENTS

We would like to thank Dale Griffin, Mike Ross, and Mark Zanna for their insightful comments on earlier versions of this article. We also benefited tremendously from the critiques and comments provided by Roy Baumeister and three anonymous reviewers. We are also indebted to Alisa Lennox, Julie Perks, Stephen Taylor, and Lee Westmaus for their assistance in conducting the research. This article was prepared with the support of a Social Sciences and Humanities Research Council of Canada (SSHRC) Doctoral Fellowship to Sandra L. Murray and a SSHRC research grant to John G. Holmes.

Portions of this article were presented at the Canadian Psychological Association annual convention in Calgary, Alberta, in June 1991; at the Society for Experimental Social Psychology annual meeting in Columbus, Ohio, in October 1991; and at the International Society for the Study of Personal Relationships convention in Orono, Maine, in July 1992.

REFERENCES

Allport, G. W. (1954). *The nature of prejudice*. Reading, MA: Addison-Wesley.

Aronson, E. (1969). The theory of cognitive dissonance: A current perspective. In L. Berkowitz (Ed.), *Advances in experimental social psychology* (Vol. 4, pp. 1–34). San Diego, CA: Academic Press.

Asch, S. E. (1946). Forming impressions of personality *Journal of Abnormal and Social Psychology, 41,* 258–290.

Asch, S. E., & Zukier, H. (1984). Thinking about persons. *Journal of Personality and Social Psychology, 46,* 1230–1240.

Bartholomew, K. (1990). Avoidance of intimacy: An attachment perspective. *Journal of Social and Personal Relationships, 7,* 147–178.

Baumeister, R. F., & Jones, E. E. (1978). When self-presentation is constrained by the target's knowledge: Consistency and compensation. *Journal of Personality and Social Psychology, 36,* 608–618.

Baumeister, R. F., Stillwell, A., & Wotman, S. R.(1990). Victim and perpetrator accounts of interpersonal conflict: Autobiographical narratives about anger. *Journal of Personality and Social Psychology, 59,* 994–1005.

Bowlby, J. (1977). The making and breaking of affectional bonds. *British Journal of Psychiatry, 130,* 201–210.

Bradbury, T. N., & Fincham, F. D. (1990). Attributions in marriage: Review and critique. *Psychological Bulletin, 107,* 3–33.

Braiker, H. B., & Kelley, H. H. (1979). Conflict in the development of close relationships. In R. L. Burgess & T. L. Huston (Eds.), *Social exchange in developing relationships* (pp. 135–168). San Diego, CA: Academic Press.

Brehm, S. S. (1988). Passionate love. In R. J. Sternberg & M. L. Barnes (Eds.), *The psychology of love* (pp. 232–263). New Haven, CT: Yale University Press.

Brickman, P. (1987). *Commitment, conflict, and caring.* Englewood Cliffs, NJ: Prentice-Hall.

Chaiken, S., & Yates, S. (1985). Affective-cognitive consistency and thought-induced polarization. *Journal of Personality and Social Psychology, 49,* 1470–1481.

Collins, N. L., & Read, S. J. (1990). Adult attachment, working models, and relationship quality in dating couples. *Journal of Personality and Social Psychology, 58,* 644–663.

Dunning, D., Meyerowitz, J. A., & Holzberg, A. D. (1989). Ambiguity and self-evaluation: The role of idiosyncratic trait definitions in self-serving assessments of ability. *Journal of Personality and Social Psychology, 57,* 1082–1090.

Erdelyi, M. H. (1974). A new look at the New Look: Perceptual defense and vigilance. *Psychological Review, 81,* 1–25.

Fazio, R. (1986). How do attitudes guide behavior? In R. M. Sorrentino & E. T. Higgins (Eds.), *The handbook of motivation and cognition: Foundations of social behavior* (pp. 204–243). New York: Guilford Press.

Flay, B. R. (1978). Catastrophe theory in social psychology: Some applications to attitudes and social behavior. *Behavioral Science, 23,* 335–350.

Gergen, K. J., & Gergen, M. M. (1988). Narrative and the self as relationship. In L. Berkowitz (Ed.), *Advances in experimental social psychology* (Vol. 21, pp. 17–56). San Diego, CA: Academic Press.

Gergen, K. J., Hepburn, A., & Fisher, D. C. (1986). Hermeneutics of personality description. *Journal of Personality and Social Psychology, 50,* 1261–1270.

Greenberg, J., & Pyszczynski, T. (1985). Compensatory self-inflation: A response to the threat to self-regard of public failure. *Journal of Personality and Social Psychology, 49,* 273–280.

Griffin, D. W., & Ross, L. (1991). Subjective construal, social inference and human misunderstanding. In M. P. Zanna (Ed.), *Advances in experimental social psychology* (Vol. 24, pp. 319–359). San Diego, CA: Academic Press.

Harvey, J. H., Agostineili, G., & Weber, A. L. (1989). Account-making and the formation of expectations about close relationships. In C. Hendrick (Ed.), *Review of personality and social psychology: Close relationships* (Vol. 10, pp. 39–62). Newbury Park, CA: Sage.

Hazan, C., & Shaver, P. (1987). Romantic love conceptualized as an attachment process. *Journal of Personality and Social Psychology, 52,* 511–524.

Holmberg, D., & Holmes, J. G. (in press). Reconstruction of relationship memories: A mental models approach. In N. Schwarz & S. Sudman (Eds.), *Autobiographical memory and the validity of retrospective reports.* New York: Springer-Verlag.

Holmes, J. G., & Boon, S. D. (1990). Developments in the field of close relationships: Creating foundations for intervention strategies. *Personality and Social Psychology Bulletin, 16,* 23–41.

Holmes, J. G., & Rempel, J. K. (1989). Trust in close relationships. In C. Hendrick (Ed.), *Review of personality and social psychology: Close relationships* (Vol. 10, pp. 187–219). Newbury Park, CA: Sage.

Holtzworth-Munroe, A., & Jacobson, N. S. (1985). Causal attributions of married couples: When do they search for causes? What do they conclude when they do? *Journal of Personality and Social Psychology, 48,* 1398–1412.

Huston, T. L., & Vangelisti, A. L. (1991). Socio-emotional behavior and satisfaction in marital relationships: A longitudinal study. *Journal of Personality and Social Psychology, 61,* 721–733.

Johnson, D. J., & Rusbult, C. E. (1989). Resisting temptation: Devaluation of alternative partners as a means of maintaining commitment in close relationships. *Journal of Personality and Social Psychology, 57,* 967–980.

Jones, E. E., & Gerard, H. B. (1967). *Foundations of social psychology.* New York: Wiley.

Kelly, C., Huston, T. L., & Care, R. M. (1985). Premarital relationship correlates of the erosion of satisfaction in marriage. *Journal of Social and Personal Relationships, 2,* 167–178.

Kunda, Z. (1990). The case for motivated reasoning. *Psychological Bulletin, 108,* 480–498.

Kunda, Z., & Sanitioso, R. (1989). Motivated changes in the self-concept. *Journal of Experimental Social Psychology, 25,* 272–285.

Levinger, G. (1983). Development and change. In H. H. Kelley, E. Berscheid, A. Christensen, J. H. Harvey, T. L. Huston, G. Levinger, E. McClintock, L. A. Peplau, & D. R. Peterson (Eds.), *Close relationships* (pp. 315–359). New York: Freeman.

Markman, H. J. (1979). Application of a behavioral model of marriage in predicting relationship satisfaction of couples planning marriage. *Journal of Consulting and Clinical Psychology, 47,* 743–749.

Markman, H. J. (1981). Prediction of marital distress. A five-year follow-up. *Journal of Consulting and Clinical Psychology, 49,* 760–762.

McFarland, C., & Ross, M. (1987). The relation between current impressions and memories of self and dating partners. *Personality and Social Psychology Bulletin, 13,* 228–238.

McGuire, W. J., & Papageorgis, D. (1961). The relative efficacy of various types of prior belief-defense in producing immunity against persuasion. *Journal of Abnormal and Social Psychology, 62,* 327–337.

Ross, L., & Nisben, R. E. (1991). *The person and the situation: Perspectives of social psychology.* New York: McGraw Hill.

Ross, M., (1989). Relation of implicit theories to the construction of personal histories. *Psychological Review, 96,* 341–357.

Ross, M., McFarland, C., & Fletcher, G. J. O. (1981). The effect of attitude on recall of past histories. *Journal of Personality and Social Psychology, 10,* 627–634.

Rusbult, C. E., Verette, J., Whitney, G. A., Slovik, L. F., & Lipkus, I. (1991). Accommodation processes in close relationships. Theory and preliminary research evidence. *Journal of Personality and Social Psychology, 60,* 53–78.

Sanitioso, R., Kunda, Z., & Fong, G. T. (1990). Motivated recruitment of autobiographical memories. *Journal of Personality and Social Psychology, 59,* 229–241.

Sroule, L. A. (1983). Infant–caregiver attachment and patterns of adaptation in preschool: The roots of maladaptation and competence. In M. Perlmutter (Ed.), *Minnesota symposium on child psychology* (Vol. 16, pp. 41–83). Hillsdale, NJ: Erlbaum.

Steele, C. M. (1988). The psychology of self-affirmation: Sustaining the integrity of the self. In L. Berkowitz (Ed.), *Advances in experimental social psychology* (Vol. 21, pp. 261–302). San Diego, CA: Academic Press.

Taylor, S. E. (1991). Asymmetrical effects of positive and negative events: The mobilization–minimization hypothesis. *Psychological Bulletin, 110,* 67–85.

Weiss, R. L. (1980). Strategic behavioral marital therapy: Toward a model for assessment and intervention. In J. P. Vincent (Ed.), *Advances in family intervention, assessment and theory* (Vol. 1, pp. 229–271). Greenwich, CT: JAI Press.

"Inner Speech" and "External Speech": Characteristics and Communication Effectiveness of Socially and Nonsocially Encoded Messages

Robert M. Krauss • Harvard University

P. S. Vivekananthan • Bell Telephone Laboratories, Murray Hill, New Jersey

Sidney Weinheimer • New York University

Editors' Notes

How do people communicate to others who do not share their perspective? Do persons make adjustments in fashioning such communications? If they do, how do they do so? And do the adjustments made improve communication effectiveness? A separate issue is, How does one go about studying such phenomena? These issues are addressed in the present selection. A major distinction is drawn between encoding information for one's own use or "internal speech" and encoding it for others, that is, "external speech." These two types of encoding differ in a number of important respects that relate to the ease of encoding and decoding the messages. The specific communication task selected was a referential task. It involved the naming of colored chips and the subsequent identification of which chip went with which name. The use of such a relatively simple task allows for a precise examination of differences in encoding information for one's own use versus other people's use and its consequences for decoding. Specifically, the research examined whether a message originally intended for others (or "external speech") is indeed better understood by others than a message originally intended for one's own use ("internal speech").

Discussion Questions

1. What were the defects the authors identify in prior studies of "internal" and "external" speech?

2. What was the authors' measure of communication effectiveness?

3. What were the lexical features that distinguished between "internal" and "external" speech? What were the functional reasons for these differences?

Suggested Readings

Clark, H. H., & Wilkes-Gibbs, D. (1986). Referring as a collaborative process. *Cognition, 22,* 1–39.

Fussell, S. R., & Krauss, R. M. (1992). Coordination of knowledge in communication: Effects of speakers' assumptions about others' knowledge. *Journal of Personality and Social Psychology, 62,* 378–391.

Authors' Abstract

1/2 of the *S*s supplied color chips with names that would later be used by *S*s themselves to identify the colors (nonsocial encoding condition), while the other 1/2 were told that the names were to be used by some other person (social encoding condition). Approximately 2 wks, later all *S*s were asked to match each of 72 names to the color which had elicited it. 24 of these names had been given previously by *S*s themselves (self-decoding condition), 24 had been given by a randomly selected *S* under social encoding instructions (other-social decoding condition), and the remaining 24 had been given by another *S* under nonsocial instructions (other-nonsocial decoding condition). Accuracy in identifying colors was greatest for names which *S*s themselves had supplied, intermediate for names given by others under social encoding instructions, and least for names given by others under nonsocial instructions. *S*s used their own color names with equal accuracy, regardless of whether the names had been given under social or nonsocial instructions. The nonsocial encoding condition produced more low-frequency (unusual) words than the social encoding condition; however, the number of words used by *S*s in the 2 conditions did not differ significantly. Data on the relationship between lexical characteristics of messages and decoding accuracy are also presented.

It frequently seems the case that the way a person encodes information for himself differs from the way he encodes it for some other person. One way of conceptualizing this difference is in the distinction between social or "external" speech and nonsocial or "inner" speech (see Vygotsky, 1962; Werner & Kaplan, 1963).

The difference between these two forms of verbal behavior is most clearly seen in the speech of young children. As Piaget (1926) has noted, the speech of young children is largely composed of verbalization which lacks a communicative function or is, to use Piaget's term, "egocentric." In more recent research, Glucksberg, Krauss, and Weisberg (1966) found that the messages uttered by 4-year-old speakers in a dyadic communication task communicated inadequately to others, although the same messages could be employed effectively in communication with the speaker himself.

Two relevant studies of inner and external speech using adult subjects (Kaplan, 1952; Slepian, 1959) have been reported in the literature (see Werner & Kaplan, 1963). In both, the inner speech of normal subjects was found to contain fewer words and fewer "communal referents," compared to the external speech of the same subjects. However, both studies have serious defects. In the first place, in both, the inner speech condition always preceded the external speech condition, thereby confounding treatments and sequence effects. Second, in both, the external speech condition was presented immediately after the subject had received negative feedback, that is, he had been told that the information provided in his message was insufficient to enable a listener to select the correct referent. Maclay and Newman (1960) have found that such feedback increases the number of words used by speakers to encode referents, and Krauss and Weinheimer (1966) have shown that this effect is especially strong where there is no direct interaction between speaker and listener, as was the case in the Kaplan (1952) and Slepian (1959) studies. So the effect of the negative feedback taken together with the sequence by treatment confounding, can explain the results of these two studies insofar as the number of words used is concerned. In addition, neither of these studies attempted to assess the communicative adequacy of inner or external speech by having listeners actually attempt to select a referent from among a set of referents on the basis of the two types of messages.

The present experiment attempts to examine differences in both the communication effectiveness and the lexical characteristics of inner and external speech. In addition, the data will enable some conclusions to be drawn concerning the relations between communication effectiveness and lexical characteristics. Following Werner and Kaplan's (1963) usage, messages which are socially encoded (i.e., encoded for others) will be defined as external speech and messages which are nonsocially encoded (i.e., encoded for oneself), as inner speech. The present measure of communication effectiveness is the same as that used by Lantz and Steffire (1964), namely, the accuracy with which a message enables a listener to select an object from a set of objects.

Method

Overview of the Experiment

Fifty-two female subjects named each of 24 color chips. Half of the subjects were told that the names would later be used by the subjects themselves to identify the colors (nonsocial encoding condition);

the remainder were told that the names would be used by some other person (social encoding condition). Approximately 2 weeks later all 52 subjects were called back, seated before the original 24-color stimulus array, and asked to match each of 72 names with the appropriate color. Twenty-four of these were names the subjects themselves had given in the first session (self-decoding condition), 24 were names given by another subject under social instructions (other-social decoding condition), and the remaining 24 had been given by another subject under nonsocial instructions (other-nonsocial decoding condition).

Subjects

Fifty-two female undergraduates, naive to the purposes of the experiment, served as subjects. All were randomly assigned to their treatment conditions. They were paid $1.50 for participating in the two sessions, which together ran about 35 minutes. In view of the low frequency of defective color vision among females (about .4% according to Judd, 1952), subjects were not screened for color blindness.

Stimulus Materials

Twenty-four 1/2 × 1/5-inch Munsell color chips comprised the stimulus array. The color array used here was originally employed by Brown and Lenneberg (1954), and the reader is referred to their paper for the Munsell renotation values of the 24 colors. Each chip was mounted on a white 3 × 5-inch card.

In the encoding sessions the chips were presented individually. The white card containing the color chip was placed in the center of a neutral gray field laid out on a table. Illumination was provided by two high-intensity lamps mounted 9 inches above and to either side of the stimulus display, 3 1/2 inches apart, providing an illumination level of 170 foot-candles. The subject, seated in front of the display, viewed it from above at an incident angle of about 75 degrees.

In the decoding sessions, the cards containing the 24 chips were displayed on a 25 × 20-inch sheet of white illustration board. They were systematically ordered on the hue dimension in four rows of six chips each. The illustration board was mounted up-right, and the subject viewed it at eye level from a distance of about 3 feet.

Procedure

In the first phase of the experiment, the encoding session, subjects were run individually. They were first shown the 24-color array and asked to examine the colors for about 1 minute. This procedure was followed to acquaint the subjects with the range of differences among the stimuli.

They were then told that they were participating in the first part of a two-part experiment and that they would be shown several color chips and asked to name them. Subjects were told that in the second part of the experiment they themselves (for nonsocial encoders) or some other girl (for social encoders) would be asked to identify the colors from these names. In part, the instructions read:

> . . . by the name of a color what I mean is any verbal label which will help [this other girl/you] to pick out that color in the second part of the experiment. That is, you don't have to restrict yourself to conventional color names if you don't want to.

The experimenter then exposed the 24 colors sequentially, using a different random order for each subject. The subject named each color aloud, and the experimenter transcribed each name verbatim.

In the second part of the experiment (the decoding sessions) all 52 subjects received a deck of 72 punch cards, each containing a single color name. Twenty-four of these names were the subject's own, 24 were those of a subject in the social encoding condition, and 24 were those of a subject in the nonsocial condition, randomly ordered. Random sampling without replacement was used, so that the names given by each subject were decoded by exactly two other subjects, one of whom had initially participated in the social encoding condition and the other in the nonsocial condition.[1] Subjects were run in groups numbering from two to four and worked in separate booths. They were instructed to go through the deck of punch cards, read the name at the top of the card, search the 24-color array in front of them and locate the color referred to, and write the identifying number of the color on the punch card. Subjects were told to go through the cards in the order given and not to skip any or go back. The instructions stressed that they were to assign a

number to every name and, if necessary, to guess when they were uncertain.

Results

Communication Effectiveness

The communication effectiveness of socially and nonsocially encoded messages was assessed by determining the frequency with which the names given in the encoding sessions enabled subjects in the decoding sessions to identify the colors which had elicited them. It is clear from an examination of the Brown and Lenneberg (1954) series that hue-adjacent colors are not equidistant. Initially, it had been the intention to multidimensionally scale the decoding data and establish intercolor distances so that values representing the degree of inaccurate identification could be assigned. Unfortunately, the decoding confusion matrices were unsuitable for multidimensional scaling. Hence, subjects' responses were assigned a binary score, 1 when the identification was correct and 0 when it was incorrect, regardless of how discrepant from the originally designated color it was. It should be noted that analyses based upon more refined scoring schemes produced the same configuration of results.

The configuration of treatments forms a 2 (encoding conditions) × 3 (decoding conditions) × 24 (colors) factorial experiment. Encoding condition is a between-subjects variable, and decoding condition and color are within-subjects variables. A mixed analysis of variance was performed on the data for accuracy of identification, and the results of this analysis appear in Table 1. The means, summed across colors, are shown in Table 2.

As these analyses indicate, there are clear differences in communication accuracy in the three decoding conditions ($F = 93.94$, $df = Z/100$, $p < .001$). Subjects were most accurate in identifying colors from their own encodings, they were next most accurate in identifying colors named by another person in the social encoding condition, and they were least accurate in identifying colors named by another person in the nonsocial encoding condition. As the Encoding–Decoding condition interaction indicates, a subject is equally good at identifying colors from his own (or others') names, irrespective of his original encoding condition. Indeed, the self-decoding means are iden-

[1]The authors gratefully acknowledge the efforts of Lee E. McMahon who wrote the computer program which produced the subjects' response cards.

TABLE 30.1. Analysis of Variance of Identification Data

Source	df	MS	F	Error term
Between Ss	S1			
Encoding condition (A)	1	0.0974	<1	Error (b)
Error (b)	50	0.2500		
Within Ss	3692			
Decoding condition (B)	2	11.0758	93.94*	E_1
Color (C)	23	3.1693	14.33*	E_2
A × B	2	0.1505	1.28	E_1
A × C	23	0.0726	<1	E_3
B × C	46	0.5135	4.54*	E_2
A × B × C	46	0.0854	<1	E_2
Error (w)	3550			
E_1 (B × Ss within groups)	100	0.1179		
E_2 (C × Ss within groups)	1150	0.2211		
E_3 (BC × Ss within groups)	2300	0.1130		
Total	3743			

*$p < .001$.

tical for subjects who encoded under social and nonsocial instructions, and this is the only contrast in which one would expect to find differences.

As the significant main effect for Color ($F = 14.33$, $df = 23/1150$, $p < .001$) indicates, colors vary in the accuracy with which they can be identified on the basis of a name. However, it is clear from the significant Decoding condition × Color interaction that this is not true to the same degree across colors; the same colors are differentially identifiable in the three decoding conditions. Upon further analysis these differences seem attributable to the fact that the 24 colors differ as to the ease with which they can be named—a property which Brown and Lenneberg (1954) termed "codability." Correlations, computed across colors within each of the three encoding conditions between the Brown and Lenneberg codability score (see Brown & Lenneberg, 1954, Table 1) and the decoding accuracy score show marked differences. For the self and other-social conditions, the correlation coefficients are not significantly different from zero (r's = .27, .31, respectively). For the other-nonsocial condition, $r = .58$ ($p < .01$). That is, de-

coding accuracy was more strongly associated with a color's codability in the other-nonsocial decoding condition than in the two other decoding conditions. It may be the case that nonsocial encoders tend to give idiosyncratic names to colors for which socially accepted names are not readily available. Because these names are idiosyncratic, they are difficult for another person to use in the identification task, although they present no great problem for the encoder himself.

Lexical Features

Name length. The length of each name (in number of words) was calculated for the two encoding conditions. In cases where it was not clear whether a pair of words should be counted as two separate words, a single word, or a hyphenated word the preferred usage as given by *Webster's New Collegiate Dictionary* (1949) was used as the criterion. For hyphenated words, hyphens were removed and the number of separate words counted. An analysis of variance performed on this measure indicated no significant difference in name length between the social and nonsocial encoding conditions ($F = 2.69$, $df = 1/50$, $p > .10$) contrary to the findings of Kaplan (1952) and Slepian (1959). This failure to confirm their results suggests that the confounding discussed above may indeed have been responsible for the greater length of external speech messages in Kaplan's and Slepian's experiments.

Type-token ratio. One commonly used measure

TABLE 30.2. Mean Proportion of Correct Identifications in the Six Decoding Conditions

Original encoding condition	Decoding of messages encoded by		
	Self	Other-Social	Other-Nonsocial
Social instructions	.744	.615	.577
Nonsocial instructions	.744	.620	.542

of vocabulary diversity is the ratio of the number of different words a speaker uses (types) to the total number of words he uses (tokens). A type-token ratio (TTR) was computed for each subject in each of the two encoding conditions, and a t test was performed on the TTR transformed to its radian. A significant difference in the TTRs for the two conditions was obtained ($t = 4.07$, $df = 50$, $p < .01$). Subjects in the nonsocial encoding condition employed more diverse vocabularies (i.e., larger TTRs) than their counterparts in the social encoding condition.

Word-frequency analysis. One may also characterize a vocabulary in terms of the portion of rank-frequency distribution from which it tends to be sampled. Persons using relatively esoteric vocabularies would tend, on the average, to use a great many low-frequency (high-rank) words. The authors compiled a lexicon of all the words used by subjects in both encoding conditions, ordered in terms of frequency of occurrence. Each word was assigned a rank corresponding to the ordinal position of its frequency. Each subject was then given a score based on the mean rank of the vocabulary she employed in encoding the 24 colors. A t test performed on the difference between mean rank of the vocabularies of subjects in the two encoding conditions revealed a significantly greater use of high-rank (i.e., relatively unusual) words for subjects in the nonsocial encoding condition ($t = 2.06$, $df = 50$, $p < .05$).

Another way of assessing differences in the word frequencies of the color names given in the two encoding conditions is in terms of the frequency of unique words (i.e., words used by only one subject). Subjects in the nonsocial encoding condition tended to use nearly twice as many unique words as subjects in the social condition (5.2 versus 2.8 words, respectively), but this difference does not quite achieve the conventionally accepted level for statistical significance ($t = 1.63$, $df = 50/.10 > p > .05$).

Lexical features and decoding. The authors have indicated above some aspects of the lexical differences between socially and non-socially encoded color names. Another area of interest concerns the relationship between the lexical features of color names and the extent to which they give rise to accurate identification. One may ask whether the use of unusual words tends to lead to accurate identification by (*a*) the subject who used them, and (*b*) other subjects. For socially encoded color names there is a significant negative correlation between mean rank and accurate identification in the self-decoding condition ($r = -.54$, $p < .05$), while for nonsocially encoded names the relationship is significant in a positive direction ($r = .12$, $p < .05$). In neither condition is mean rank related to decoding accuracy by others. The same pattern of relationships is found for the correlation of frequency of unique responses with accuracy. Apparently, then, the use of unusual words in the two encoding conditions reflects rather different processes.

Discussion

It seems clear that subjects instructed to produce color names either for their own use or for the use of others produce quite different sorts of names. Under nonsocial encoding instructions, subjects employ vocabularies which are more diverse and contain more unusual and unique words. However, their color names contain approximately the same number of words as the names given by subjects encoding under social instructions. Further, these lexical differences seem to be related to the accuracy with which names can be matched to the colors which elicited them. Socially encoded names elicit more accurate identification than do nonsocial names. However, in the self-decoding condition, social encoders and nonsocial encoders were equally accurate. This result is somewhat surprising, for intuitively it seems that the language one uses to encode messages for oneself is, in some sense, a more efficient code than the language one uses to communicate with others. Two factors may have mitigated this effect in the present experiment. First, subjects were not under time pressure for encoding or for decoding. It may be the case that inner speech is more efficient (if, in fact, it is more efficient) because one has readier access to it; that is, it permits production of names with shorter latencies. The second factor relates to the domain of stimulus objects. English provides a rich variety of conventional names for colors (see Chapanis, 1965), and it may well be the case that females are especially conversant with these names. Under such circumstances it may not be too surprising that self-decoding for socially or nonsocially encoded names is equally accurate. But it is clearly not the case that all subjects map color names onto the color array in precisely the same way. A subject using her own socially encoded names to identify colors performed more accurately than did other subjects using the same names. Undoubtedly there is some degree of idiosyncracy in the way individuals use certain conventional, but relatively rare, color names.[2] Perhaps with stimuli for which conventional names are less applicable (e.g., random shapes) or for which idiosyncratic associations might provide better mnemonics (e.g., faces), a difference in self-decoding would be found for socially and nonsocially encoded names.

The fact that accuracy in the self-decoding condition relates differently to the use of low-frequency words in the social and non-social encoding conditions (negatively in the former case and positively in the latter) suggests that rather different processes are represented in the two encoding conditions. One critical aspect of communication skill involves the speaker's ability to infer from a set of assumptions he makes about his listener the appropriateness of alternative ways of encoding a given informative content. As Brown (1965) put it, "Effective coding requires that the point of view of the auditor be realistically imagined [p. 132]." In the social encoding condition this would require that the subject assess the likelihood of another person being familiar with a given unusual color name or with objects whose color can be incorporated into a color name (as in "the color of the yolk of a hard-boiled egg"). The fact that a given social encoder finds it necessary to employ a great many unusual words might be taken to suggest a certain ineptness on his part, since good social names are by definition names which have a high degree of communality. And as these data indicate, this ineptness is reflected in the inability of such subjects to identify colors accurately on the basis of their own names. In contrast, the use of unusual words by a nonsocial encoder suggests the opposite, an ability to take advantage of his special knowledge of the characteristics of the message's recipient (i.e., himself) by using a spe-

cial vocabulary. This enhances the subject's ability to identify colors, as is indicated by the positive correlation between frequency of unusual words and self-decoding. What is surprising in all of this, and weakens the foregoing argument considerably, is the fact that in neither case is a relationship found between frequency of unusual words and decoding accuracy of others. Since, for social encoders, the frequency of unusual words and accuracy of self-decoding are negatively related, and, at the same time, self-decoding and other decoding are positively related, the authors are led both by speculation and by the configuration of relationships to expect a negative relationship between frequency of unusual words and decoding accuracy by others. The data simply do not support such an expectation.

REFERENCES

Brown, R. *Social psychology*. New York: Free Press of Glencoe, 1965.

Brown, R., & Lenneberg, E. H. A study in language and cognition. *Journal of Abnormal and Social Psychology*, 1954, 49, 454–462.

Chapanis, A. Color names for color space. *American Scientist*, 1965, 53, 327–346.

Glucksberg, S., Krauss, R. M., & Weisberg, R. Referential communication in nursery school children: Method and some preliminary findings. *Journal of Experimental Child Psychology*, 1966, 3, 333–342.

Judd, D. B. *Color in business, science and industry*, New York: Wiley, 1952.

Kaplan, E. An experimental study on inner speech as contrasted with external speech. Unpublished master's thesis, Clark University, 1952.

Krauss, R. M., & Weinheimer, S. Concurrent feedback, confirmation, and the encoding of referents in verbal communication. *Journal of Personality and Social Psychology*, 1966, 4, 343–346.

Lantz, D., & Stefflre, V. Language and cognition revisited. *Journal of Abnormal and Social Psychology*, 1964, 69, 472–481.

Maclay, H. S., & Newman, S. Two variable affecting the message in communication. In D. K. Wilner (Ed.), *Decisions, values, and groups*. New York: Pergamon Press, 1960.

Piaget, J. *The language and thought of the child* New York: Harcourt, Brace, 1926.

Pickford, R. W. *Individual differences in colour perception*. London: Routledge & Kegan Paul, 1951.

Slepian, H. A developmental study of inner vs. external speech in normals and schizophrenics. Unpublished doctoral dissertation, Clark University, 1959.

Vygotsky, L. S. *Thought and language*. New York: Wiley, 1962.

Webster's New Collegiate Dictionary. Springfield, Mass.: Merriam, 1949.

Werner, H., & Kaplan, B. *Symbol formation*. New York: Wiley, 1963.

---

[2]The authors abserved this in an early pilot study in which a non-color-defective male subject applied the name "chartreuse" to a pinkish-red color chip and insisted that the name was appropriate. It is the authors' impression that females tend to use such relatively rare color terms as "fuchsia," "cerise," etc., both more frequently and more accurately than do men. However, the operative factor here would seem to be familiarity (with color, names, or both) rather than perceptual acuity, given subjects whose color vision is normal (Pickford, 1951).

Achieving "Shared Reality" in the Communication Game: A Social Action That Creates Meaning

E. Tory Higgins • Columbia University

Editors' Notes

This selection further elucidates the social nature of interpersonal communication. Not only do communicators take into account the differences between themselves and potential recipients of their messages, but they also tailor their messages to what they believe their audiences know and feel. They try to produce clear and concise messages that fit their audiences' attitudes and beliefs. What is particularly striking is that the way messages are communicated to others affects the way the communicators themselves later remember and feel about the message topic. Thus, for example, the motivation to communicate good news to one's audience can fashion not only what one says and how one says it, but this message tuning will also affect one's own later beliefs and feelings about the original information. Thus, in a twist on a popular adage, "Saying is believing." However, even though tuning a message to suit the audience introduces a bias in one's own thoughts and feelings about a topic, it is highly functional by creating broad areas of interpersonal agreement. It affords a basis for common ground and a "shared reality."

Discussion Questions

1. According to the authors, what is the difference between "putting oneself in someone else's shoes" and "seeing the world through another person's eyes?"
2. On what evidence do the authors conclude that the way messages are tuned to suit an audience affects the communicators' own thoughts and feelings about the subject matter?
3. In what way does the research reviewed in this selection go beyond Grice's (1975) notion of adequate communication?
4. What does the author mean when he refers to communication as social action?

Suggested Readings

Fleming, J. H. (1994). Multiple-audience problems, tactical communication, and social inter-action: A relational-regulation perspective. In M. P. Zanna (Ed.), Advances in experimental social psychology (Vol. 26, pp. 215–292). New York: Academic Press.

Sedikides, C. (1990). Effects of fortuitously activated constructs versus activated communication goals on person impressions. *Journal of Personality and Social Psychology, 58,* 397–408.

Zajonc, R. B. (1960). The process of cognitive tuning and communication. *Journal of Abnormal and Social Psychology, 61,* 159–167.

Authors' Abstract

This paper reviews research on the 'communication game' (Higgins, 1981a) that supports two sets of conclusions. The first set of conclusions concerns communication as social action: (a) Communicators tailor their summary of target information to suit their audience's knowledge of or attitudes toward the target; that is, they achieve 'shared reality' with their audience and thereby perform a social action; (b) Communicators' different motivations to achieve 'shared reality' with their audience influences the extent to which they tailor their message to suit the audience, as evident in 'super-tuning', 'anti-tuning', and 'non-tuning'; (c) When there is a delay between successive messages about a target, communicators' use their first message to construct their second message even though the two audiences have different characteristics. The second set of conclusions concerns how communication as social action creates meaning: (a) Communicators use their message summaries about a target as a direct source of information about the target even when the message distorted the original target information to suit the audience, and these message summaries in turn influence the communicators' own memory and impressions of the target; (b) As the delay since communicating about the target increases, communicators' use of their message as a source of target information persists or even increases; (c) Communicators' messages about a target to suit their audience can have either beneficial or detrimental effects on the accuracy of their memory and impressions of the target.

Role Enactment and Role-Taking

Interpersonal communication is social action in at least two major ways. First, it involves role enactment. Second, it involves role-taking (or per-spective-taking). Although there are other ways in which interpersonal communication is social action, our research on the communication game has been concerned mainly with these two, especially the second. Thus, the present paper will focus on the implications of these two variables.

Role Enactment

Role enactment is a quintessential example of 'so-cial' action. In the traditional view, role enactment relates to conduct that adheres to a certain position in the social structure rather than to individuals *per se*. Role expectations is the conceptual link between social structure and role enactment. As defined by Sarbin & Allen (1968), role expectations 'are comprised of the rights and privileges, the duties and obligations, of any occupant of a social position in relation to persons occupying other positions in the social structure' (p. 497). Role enactment, in terms of role expectations, then, is social action. Sarbin & Allen (1968) also point out that role expectations operate as imperatives concerning a person's cognitions as well as his or her conduct during role enactment. Thus, role en-actment is social action that can influence meaning.

In a classic communication study, Zajonc (1960) found that subjects assigned the role of 'transmit-ter' of information represent the information in a more unified and organised way than subjects as-signed the role of 'recipient' even prior to the com-munication taking place. Several subsequent stud-ies replicated and extended this basic finding (for a review, see Higgins, 1981a). The results of these studies suggest that even preparation for role enactment can influence how information is processed. Many of these earlier studies, however, confounded role assignment with expectations of receiving additional information about the target. To control for this problem, role assignment and target information expectations were manipulated separately in a study by Higgins, McCann, & Fondacaro (1982). Consistent with previous conclusions about the 'transmitter' or 'speaker' role, the 'transmitter' role was found to influence cognition independent of target information expectations. Together, the results of this literature suggest that speakers tend to polarise and distort stimulus information in preparation for message production in order to meet their role-related obligation to produce clear, concise messages. The 'cognitive tuning' literature, then, provides an excellent example of how taking into account others, in this case others' expectations about one's role obligations, influences the representation of social information.

Role-taking

Successful role enactment requires taking into account the expectations and standards of others. Role-taking or perspective-taking involves inferences about how others would respond to a particular stimulus or situation. Successful role enactment, therefore, requires role-taking. There are two basic kinds of role-taking: (a) 'putting oneself in someone else's shoes', or situational role-taking, which involves inferring how you would respond if you were in the situation of another person; and (b) 'seeing the world through another person's eyes', or individual role-taking, which involves inferring how another person would respond if he or she were in your situation (see Higgins, 1981b). Role-taking is a fundamental process underlying all social interaction, including interpersonal communication. A basic rule of interpersonal communication is that each participant should take their partner's characteristics into account (Grice, 1971; Mead, 1934; Piaget, 1926).

ROLE-TAKING 1: TAILORING MESSAGES TO SUIT THE AUDIENCE'S KNOWLEDGE

In considering the nature and consequences of people following this rule, the communication literature has focused mostly on communicators taking into account their audience's knowledge of a topic (see, for example, Clark & Haviland, 1977; Fussell & Krauss, 1989; Glucksberg *et al.*, 1975; Grice, 1975; Higgins, 1977). We also considered this case in our research on the communication game. Our particular concern, however, was to examine how taking into account another's knowledge influenced the representation of social information; that is, how this type of social action creates meaning (see Higgins *et al.*, 1982).

Half of the communicators believed that their audience had received basically the same information about the target person, and the other half of the communicators believed that their audience had received different information about the target person. In fact, all subjects received exactly the same target person information. All communicators were asked to *describe* and *interpret* the target person information for their audience. To follow the rule of saying something worthwhile (Grice, 1975), the communicators with the same target information as the audience should emphasise interpretation over description (i.e. give their personal opinion) whereas the communicators with different target information than the audience should emphasise description over interpretation. Indeed, the communicators who believed they had different target information than the audience were more likely to emphasise description over interpretation (i.e. produce messages in which the target information was neither deleted nor evaluatively polarised).

What was the effect of this social action on meaning? All subjects recalled the original target person information both before and after producing their message. As shown in Table 1, the recall of the communicators who emphasised interpretation over description was less accurate after they produced the message than before (i.e. more deletions, distortions, or evaluative polarisations). Some decrease in accuracy over time would be expected simply because of the increased delay between input and recall. Thus, it is all the more remarkable that the recall of the communicators who emphasised description over interpretation was, if anything, *more* accurate after they produced the message than before (see Table 1). Social action in this case supported accurate recall.

These results indicate that not only do communicators take their audience's knowledge into account in producing their message, but that this social action impacts on their own later knowledge of the subject of the message (i.e. changes in

TABLE 31.1. Mean pre- to post-message change in reproductions on 'unchanged' measure [1] and 'polarisation' measure as a function of an audience with the 'same' or 'different' target person information

	Pre- to Post-Message Change in Reproductions	
	'Unchanged' measure	'Polarisation' measure
Audience knowledge		
Same	−9%	+22%
Different	+3%	−29%

[1]The 'unchanged' measure was the number of original target descriptions that were reproduced without deletion or distortion of the basic information.

memory). It should be noted that these effects on the communicators' own knowledge were not simply a direct effect of the audience's supposed knowledge because the information about the audience's knowledge was available at the time of both their post-message *and* pre-message recall. Thus, differences in message production that took into account differences in audience knowledge, (i.e., social action), were critical in creating differences in meaning.

Although clearly important, the knowledge of one's audience about the subject of the message is not the only audience characteristic that communicators need to take into account. Indeed, from a 'social' perspective other audience characteristics might be even more important. One such characteristic is the audience's *attitude* toward the subject of the message. Everyone has had the experience of talking about someone to another person who one believes likes or dislikes the person being talked about. Most people feel some pressure to describe the target person in a way that does not conflict with the audience's attitude. But beyond this social pressure, taking into account the audience's attitude in producing one's message simply follows the rule that communicators should take their audience's characteristics into account. And there is considerable evidence that communicators do, in fact, tailor their message to suit their audience's attitude or opinion about the subject of the message (e.g., Higgins & Rholes, 1978; Manis, Cornell, & Moore, 1974; Newtson & Czerlinsky, 1974). How does this common social action influence social cognition? Much of the research programme on the communication game has explored the intricacies of this seemingly simple question. In so doing, some major issues about the

relation between communication and social cognition have been considered. Let us turn now to these issues.

ROLE-TAKING 2: TAILORING MESSAGES TO SUIT THE AUDIENCE'S ATTITUDE

Our first study on audience attitude effects involved undergraduates at Princeton who believed they were assisting in an experiment on communication as a source of information transmission by describing a target person to another student (the audience) who would use their message to try to identify the target person. Both the target person and the audience were supposedly in the same 'eating club' at Princeton. Prior to giving the communicator some written information about the target person, the experimenter casually mentioned that other information indicated that the audience either liked or disliked the target person.

This audience-attitude manipulation had a major effect on how the communicators summarised the target person information. The target person information contained evaluatively ambiguous behaviours of the target (e.g., behaviours that could be equally labelled 'confident' or 'conceited'), unambiguously positive behaviours of the target (e.g., clearly 'athletic' behaviours), and unambiguously negative behaviours of the target (e.g., clearly 'short-tempered' behaviours). As shown in Table 2, communicators labelled the target information more positively when they believed that the audience liked the target person than when they believed that the audience disliked the target person.

Did this social action of taking another's attitude into account in one's message production influence the communicators' own memory of the original target information? As predicted, it did. Table 3 shows that the communicators' reproductions of the target person information were significantly distorted in the evaluative direction represented by their audience's attitude. Additional correlational analyses comparing subjects' messages and recall also indicated that communicators tended to use their message more as a source of information two weeks later than immediately— after two weeks the message, as a summary of the target information, becomes a necessary additional source of information for reconstructive memory.

It was clear in this study as well that the effect of audience tuning on memory was not due simply to a direct influence of the audience's attitude

TABLE 31.2. Mean number of positive and negative message labels for ambiguous and unambiguous target descriptions as a function of audience attitude

	Message Labelling of Target Person Information			
	Ambiguous Target information		Unambiguous Target information	
	Positive label	Negative label	Positive label	Negative label
Audience attitude				
Like	1.3	0.6	1.8	0.4
Dislike	0.8	1.5	1.3	1.8

on memory (e.g., some kind of informational conformity effect). First, any direct effect of audience attitude on recall should be greater after 20 minutes than after two weeks because both salience of the attitude and the need to be consistent with it would be greater after a brief delay. But the recall distortion for unambiguous information was found only after the two week delay. Second, because of a supposed 'experimenter error', half of the subjects in the study were given the information about their audience's attitude and *expected to communicate* but did not actually communicate. These subjects did *not* distort their recall in the direction of the audience's attitude.

The strength of communicators' motivation to tailor their message about a target person to suit the attitude of their audience toward the target person is well illustrated in a study by Sedikides (1990; Study 2). This study used the same basic paradigm as the Higgins & Rholes (1978) study. But in this study the subjects read the target person information *before* they even received the communication instructions or learned about the audience's attitude. In addition, subjects' representation of the target person information had already been experimentally influenced by priming or activating particular trait constructs. Despite all this, the subjects still tailored their summaries of the target person information to suit the attitude of the audience. Moreover, consistent with the results of

our studies, the communicators' own personal impressions of the target person were more consistent with their audience-tailored message than with the primed constructs.

These memory and impression effects from tailoring messages to suit the audience's attitude are another example of how social action can create meaning. What is especially interesting about such cases is that the communicators take their audience into account in producing their message, but do *not* take this audience-tuning sufficiently into account when they later use their messages in reconstructive memory. This is precisely why social action can create meaning. It is very difficult, if not impossible, for communicators to calibrate the extent to which their message reflects just the target information itself (i.e., the data) versus their tailoring of the messages to suit the audience (i.e., the communicative context). Communicators are likely to overestimate the extent to which their message was determined by the data, and, therefore, the social action of audience-tailoring is likely to create meaning (e.g., produce memory distortions).

ROLE-TAKING 3: TAILORING MESSAGES TO SUIT SUCCESSIVE AUDIENCES

In the Higgins & Rholes (1978) study, the communicators produced a single message to a single audience. Most interpersonal communication stud-

TABLE 31.3. Mean percentage of positive and negative reproduction distortions for ambiguous and unambiguous target descriptions as a function of audience attitude

	Reproduction Distortions of Target Person Information			
	Ambiguous Target information		Unambiguous Target information	
	Positive distortions	Negative distortions	Positive distortions	Negative distortions
Audience attitude				
Like	25%	19%	6%	2%
Dislike	3%	28%	1%	12%

ies have used this basic paradigm. But interpersonal communication in everyday life often involves communicating about some subject to more than one person over time. Imagine that you had some knowledge about a person and summarised this knowledge for two different audiences, first for an audience you believed liked the person and then for an audience you believe disliked the person. We know from previous studies that you would probably summarise your knowledge of the target person in a somewhat positive manner for the first audience. But what would you do for the second audience? And would your impressions of the target person be influenced more by your message to the first audience or by your message to the second audience?

For a variety of reasons one might expect that the first audience would determine both subsequent messages and meaning construction. Traditional models of communication audience effects have stated that it is the first audience that is critical (e.g., Zimmerman & Bauer, 1956). And 'consistency' models generally suggest that people would be motivated to respond later to a target person in a manner that was consistent with their initial response to the target (see Abelson *et al.*, 1968). Recent social-cognitive models, however, raise the possibility that the time interval between the first and second messages might be critical in determining the impact of the second audience on message production and subsequent personal impressions.

If the stored details of the original target information become increasingly inaccessible over time, then communicators would increasingly rely on their first message as a source of target information—both for their subsequent message and for their own impressions of the target (see Higgins & Rholes, 1978). There may also be an increasing consolidation or integration of the representation of the target details and the message representation of the target (see Wyer & Srull, 1986). Thus, when there is a long delay between the first and second messages, the impact of the first audience on communicators' first message should produce a primacy effect on both the second message and subsequent personal impressions. But when there is only a brief delay between the first and second messages, the second message should be tuned to the second audience and have the greater impact on personal impressions by virtue of being both most accessible and the 'final word' on the target.

In a study by McCann, Higgins, & Fondacaro (1991) addressing these issues, the communicators interacted face-to-face with two audiences who were both confederates of the experimenter. All participants were male. The communicators believed that their summaries would help their audience make a decision about whether to select the target person as a roommate. Before the communicators gave their summary to the audience, the audience mentioned that he had met the target person briefly and that his initial impression of the target person was either positive or negative ('kinda liked' or 'kinda disliked' the target). The communicators received an essay describing various characteristics of the target. They summarised this information to two different audiences, either only 15 minutes apart (the Brief Intermessage Delay) or one week apart (the Long Intermessage Delay). In an orthogonal design, the first audience either liked or disliked the target person and the second audience either liked or disliked the target person. The communicators' own impressions of the target person were obtained one week after their second message.

Consistent with the results of previous studies, the communicators tailored their message to suit the expressed attitude of their first audience. The communicators' labelling of the target person information was more positive when they communicated to an audience who supposedly liked the target person than when they communicated to an audience who supposedly disliked the target person. It is notable that this audience-tuning effect occurred despite the audiences stating that their expressed attitude toward the target person represented only an initial impression based on a brief encounter with the target person *and* despite the fact that the audiences stated that an accurate description of the target person would be most useful in helping them decide whether to select him as a roommate. These results thus demonstrate the powerful effect of audience attitude on communicators' social action.

As predicted, the labelling in communicators' message to the second audience was tailored to suit the second audience's attitude when there was only a brief delay between the first and second messages. But when there was a long delay (one week) between the first and second messages, the evaluative tone of the second message labelling was determined by the evaluative tone of the first message labelling (see Figure 1). The results indicate that after the long delay communicators used the first message to represent the target person information and they used *this* first message representation as the basis for their second message. Thus for information-processing reasons, the communicators' second social action, after a long delay, was determined by their first social action.

When audience tuning did occur, this social action influenced communicators' own impressions of the target person one week later. And once again, the impact of social action on construction of meaning was most evident when there was the longest post-message delay—for the first audience attitude/long intermessage delay condition. Given that successive messages on some topic typically occur relatively far apart, the results of this study also suggest that it may, indeed, be the first message on a topic (i.e., the first social action), that has the greatest impact on creating meaning over time (see Zimmerman & Bauer, 1956).

This initial series of studies investigating the communication game clearly demonstrated that communicators take into account the characteristics of their audience when producing their message, both their audience's knowledge and their audience's attitudes. This research also demonstrates that this type of social action influences the communicators' own knowledge of the subject of the message—the 'saying is believing' effect. The next series of studies on the communication game focused on the motivational underpinnings of communicators' social action. Does the extent to which

communicators tailor their message to suit the audience (i.e., the extent of their audience-tuning) depend on their motivational orientation toward others? And how does this influence the construction of meaning? To answer these questions, it is necessary to consider the motivational underpinnings of interpersonal communication.

Achieving 'Shared Reality' as a Goal of Interpersonal Communication

As just mentioned, our initial studies demonstrated that communicators will tailor their message to suit their audience's knowledge of or attitude toward the subject of the message—a case of 'basic tuning'. Why does such basic tuning occur? The phenomenon of communicators tailoring their message to suit the knowledge of their audience can be understood, and has been understood (e.g., Higgins *et al.*, 1982), in terms of Grice's (1975) maxim of 'relevance'—while sticking to the topic at hand, say something worthwhile or 'new' for the audience (see also Clark & Haviland, 1977). But the 'relevance' maxim or 'given-new' contract does not seem applicable to the case of communicators tailoring their message to suit the attitude of their audience. Indeed, if communicators wanted to provide the audience with 'new' information they would express an attitude *contrary* to the audience's attitude. But, in fact, they tailor their message to match the audience's attitude. In addition, the communicators are not trying to be as

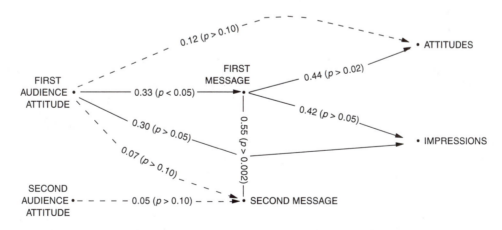

FIGURE 32.1 ■ Path analysis for the 'long inter-message delay' condition of the relations among the attitude of the first audience, the communicators' first and second messages about the target person, and the communicators' impressions of and attitudes toward the target person, plus the relation between the attitude of the second audience and the communicators' second message about the target person.

'truthful' as possible. Their messages are tailored to suit their audience's attitude rather than just being summaries of the target person information.

Applying Grice's (1975) 'cooperative' principle also fails to solve the problem because communicators could cooperate by providing the audience with as accurate and objective summaries as possible rather than tuning the message to suit the audience. It could be argued that subjects in the Higgins & Rholes (1978) study were cooperative because tailoring the message to suit their audience's attitude increased the likelihood that the audience would correctly identify the target person—a form of 'grounding' in the service of definite reference (see Clark & Brennan, 1991; Clark & Marshall, 1981). But in the McCann, Higgins, & Fondacaro (1991) study both the communicator and the audience knew that the communication was about the previously identified potential roommate. Moreover, the audience asked the communicator for his own personal impression. Nevertheless, the communicators in this study also tailored their message to suit the attitude of their audience. Why, then, did the communicators not cooperate by providing either objective summaries or their own impressions of the target person?

The 'communication game' approach suggests that there are many ways to be 'cooperative' depending on the goal or purpose of the interpersonal communication (see Higgins, 1981a). 'Cooperation' and 'grounding' are basic procedural principles or 'means' of communication. But what are the interpersonal goals or 'ends' that they serve? The now classic work by Brown & Levinson (1978) on politeness phenomena demonstrates that communicators will sacrifice the maxim of quality, as well as the maxims of 'quantity' and 'manner', for the sake of politeness. That is, some forms of cooperation are sacrificed for the other forms of cooperation. Interpersonal communication is rampant with such 'trade-offs' between forms of cooperation, and it is the specific goals of a communication that determine which forms (i.e., procedural rules) are given priority (see Higgins, Fondacara, & McCann, 1981).

The 'communication game' approach proposes that different 'means' or strategies would be selected or emphasised depending on the communicators' social-interaction goals (see Higgins, 1981a). These goals include 'entertainment' goals, 'task' goals, 'face' goals (i.e., impression management), and other social relationship goals, such as avoiding social conflict. For example, 'speech accommodation' is a strategy in which communicators shift their speech style to be similar to (convergence) or different from (divergence) the speech style of their audience in order to associate themselves with or disassociate themselves from their audience, respectively. Convergence is likely to occur when communicators are attracted to or seek approval from the audience (see, for example, Giles & Smith, 1979; Giles, Muiac, Bradac, & Johnson, 1987).

As we have seen, communicators also tailor their message to suit their audience's knowledge on a subject. Communicators need not be attracted to or seek approval from their audience for such social tuning to occur. And the social tuning itself can involve modifying the denotative and connotative content of a message as well as shifting the speech style. Thus, there are a variety of different forms and goals of social tuning.

For interpersonal communication to work at all, regardless of its goal, the communicator and the audience must share some mutual knowledge, such as who or what is being referred to in the message, who or what is the message subject or topic (see Clark & Marshall, 1981). To begin with, then, the communicator and audience must establish some common ground as a basic 'means' of communication. This does not imply, however, that the goal of the communicator is to achieve common ground with the audience in the sense of a 'shared reality' about the characteristics of the message subject. The communicator and audience need to agree that the communication is about 'X', such as a particular target person 'X', but they need not be motivated to have similar knowledge or opinions of the characteristics of 'X'. We propose, however, that the communicators in our studies *did* attempt to achieve 'shared reality' with their audience concerning the target person's characteristics. The 'communication game' approach emphasises the fact that participants in a communicative interaction often attempt to construct a common or shared reality (see Rommetveit, 1974; Ruesch & Bateson, 1968).

Communicators who believed that their audience had different information than them about the target person shared their knowledge of the target person by describing his characteristics to the audience. Communicators who believed that their audience had a particular attitude toward the target person produced messages whose evaluative tone matched the audience's attitude. Thus, the goal of the communicators' social action was to achieve 'shared reality'. The results of our studies show that this type of social action influences and creates meaning.

A dominant objective of social interaction in general is to establish a common 'social reality' (see Asch, 1952; Festinger, 1950; Sherif, 1936). Indeed, the concept of 'social reality' may capture the essence of the social psychology of cognition better than any other single concept. As described by Festinger (1950), beliefs, attitudes, and opinions vary in the extent to which there is physical evidence for them. It is extremely rare for a belief or opinion to be supported by hard facts of incontrovertible physical reality. The basis for holding most beliefs and opinions is social reality, the fact that others share the belief or opinion:

> . . . where the dependence upon physical reality is low, the dependence upon social reality is correspondingly high. An opinion, a belief, an attitude is 'correct', 'valid', and 'proper' to the extent that it is anchored in a group of people with similar beliefs, opinions, and attitudes. (1950: 272)

Thus, the very nature of most of our reality is social. The reality of our subjective meanings is anchored in the fact that others share the reality. This is especially true of opinion, beliefs, and attitudes about social objects, such as a target person. Therefore, when communicators achieve 'shared reality' with their audience about a target person, this 'shared reality' is likely to be treated *as reality* especially when the representation of the stimulus input (i.e., the physical reality) has decayed or become inaccessible.

By this reasoning, the impact on meaning from the social action of audience tuning largely derives from the fact that it involves achieving a shared reality. It would follow, then, that messages that do not achieve, or even prevent, a shared reality about a target person would not subsequently impact on communicators' memory and impressions of the target person, or at least would impact to a lesser degree. In order to consider this possibility in more detail, it is necessary to distinguish among different types of message modification as social action.

What Have We Learned, and What's Next?

The studies investigating the communication game have yielded consistent findings that permit some clear conclusions to be drawn. The first set of conclusions concern communication as social action. First, communicators generally take their audience into account and tailor their summary of target information to suit their audience's knowledge of or attitudes toward the target. That is, *communicators achieve 'shared reality' with their audience and thereby perform a social action.* Second, communicators have different motivations to achieve 'shared reality' with their audience that influence the extent to which they tailor their message to suit the audience. In addition to the basic level of audience tuning, there is 'super-tuning', 'anti-tuning', and 'non-tuning'. That is, *communicators perform different types of social action depending on their motivation to achieve 'shared reality'.* Third, when there is a delay between successive messages about a target, a later message will resemble the initial messages even if there is a change in the characteristics of the audience to whom the message is addressed. That is, *communicators' initial social action can determine their later social action.*

The second set of conclusions concern how communication as a form of social action creates meaning. First, communicators generally will use their message summaries about a target as a direct source of information about the target even when the message distorted the original target information in the direction of the audience. As a result, communicators' own memory and personal impressions of a target can become distorted. That is, *communication as social action can create meaning.* Second, as the delay since exposure to and communication about the original target information increases, communicators' use of their message summaries as a source of target information persists or even increases. That is, *the impact of communication on creating meaning persists or even increases over time.* Third, when communicators produce detailed descriptions of a target to suit their audience's need for such knowledge, the message production can improve the accuracy of their memory of the target information. That is, *communication can have both beneficial and detrimental effects on meaning construction.*

It is evident that communication as social action impacts on the construction of meaning—communicators come to believe what they previously said in their message. What underlies this 'saying is believing' effect? One possibility is that the supposed knowledge or attitude of the audience whom the communicator addresses, which in some studies includes the experimenter, directly influences the communicator's own memory and impressions of the subject of the message. This 'normative' or 'informational' conformity effect (see, for example, Deutsch & Gerard, 1955) is a classic alternative explanation for the 'saying is believing' effect. It has been addressed both in the role-playing literature (e.g., Hovland, Janis, & Kelley, 1953) and in the counter-attitudinal advocacy literature (e.g., Bem, 1967; Festinger, 1957; Wicklund & Brehm, 1976). Whether the explanation for the 'saying is believing' effect is 'active participation' (or personal 'improvisation'; see Hovland *et al*. 1953), 'dissonance reduction' (see Festinger, 1957; Wicklund & Brehm, 1976), or 'self-perception' (see Bem, 1967), normative or informational conformity is dismissed as a sufficient explanation. The role-playing and counter-attitudinal literatures report that the 'saying is believing' effect occurs only if the communicators are induced to believe that they themselves chose what to say in their message. This condition is 'active participation' in role-playing (involving personal 'improvisation'), 'high choice' in dissonance, and 'non-manded' in self-perception, each of which is necessary for the 'saying is believing' effect to occur. In these literatures, the alternative condition in which the 'saying is believing' effect does not occur is forced compliance or non-action (e.g., passive exposure to another's message).

Our studies testing the implications of the communication game were also concerned with ruling out simple normative or informational conformity as a sufficient explanation for our version of the 'saying is believing' effect. In the earlier discussions of these studies, various reasons were given for ruling out this alternative explanation. These include: (a) the communicators' knowledge of the audience's characteristics did not impact on meaning (i.e., communicators' own memory or impressions of the target) unless the communicators actually produced a message; (b) the communicators' knowledge of the audience's characteristics had a greater impact on meaning after than before message production; (c) path analyses revealed no direct effect from audience attitude to meaning, only a mediated path through message production; and (d) the impact of message production on meaning often increases over time.

The results of our studies, then, support the previous literature on the 'saying is believing' effect in dismissing simple normative or informational conformity as a sufficient explanation for the findings. But there is a fundamental difference between our version and explanation of the 'saying is believing' effect and those of the previous literature. The previous literature demonstrated self-persuasion effects of 'freely' advocating a position on some topic for some future general audience whose characteristics were basically unknown. Audience tuning was not an issue in these studies. In fact, the 'saying is believing' effect was thought to occur only to the extent that communicators considered the message to contain their own spontaneous, improvised arguments. The communicators were not expected to modify their messages by taking others into account. They were expected to produce their own personal messages. Thus, the 'saying is believing' effect was conceived as deriving from 'personal' action rather than from 'social' action. Indeed, 'social' action that involved taking others into account would have been associated more with the 'no choice' or 'manded' conditions involving forced compliance that diminishes the 'saying is believing' effect.

In contrast, the communication game studies *do* involve social action—communicators tailoring their message to suit the characteristics of the audience. And it is precisely this 'social' tuning action that produces the 'saying is believing' effect. When communicators did not tailor their message to suit their audience there was no clear 'saying is believing' effect—the 'anti-tuning' of the low authoritarians and the 'non-tuning' of the low self-monitors. These latter two responses are, if anything, more 'personal' than the usual audience-tuning response. Thus, the 'saying is believing' effect was *less* clear when the message were *more* 'personal'. In addition, the 'saying is believing' effect found in our 'social' action studies tended to persist or even increase over time whereas the 'saying is believing' effect found in previous studies of 'personal' action tended to decrease over time.

This comparison of the 'saying is believing' literatures raises an important issue for future study. In some cases social action, such as direct compliance to the demands of an audience (including the experimenter), diminishes the 'saying is believing' effect. But in other cases social action produces a strong 'saying is believing' effect, such as tailoring a message to suit the audience's characteristics (i.e., to achieve 'shared reality'). Thus *social tuning* must be distinguished from *social compliance* as forms of social action. The results of these literatures suggest the following intriguing possibility:

> In comparison to 'personal' action, social action in the form of social compliance reduces the 'saying is believing' effect whereas social action in the form of social tuning increases the effect.

Why might social action in the form of social tuning be an especially powerful force in creating meaning? Social tuning not only involves taking others into account but it also involves achieving a common understanding of the world that facilitates interaction with the audience. Establishing shared realities is basic to social regulatory systems. Socialisation involves people learning how others respond to the world, including how others respond to them, and using this knowledge in self-regulation (see, for example, Higgins, 1989). As a basic feature of the self-regulatory system, social tuning is charged with motivational significance. This motivational significance may be the reason that social tuning is such a powerful force in creating meaning.

The proposed distinctions between personal and social action and among forms of social action could be tested in future studies. For example, an experiment might have people produce basically the same message on some subject but under different phenomenological conditions, including 'personal' (e.g., freely choosing to write an essay that reflects a particular attitude toward the subject of the message (as in standard dissonance studies)), 'social compliance' (e.g., experimenter instructions to tailor a written message to suit an audience with a particular attitude toward the subject of the message), and 'social tuning' (e.g., freely writing a message to an audience with a particular attitude toward the subject of the message (as in standard communication-game studies)). The written message should have the greatest impact over time in the 'social tuning' condition because only in this condition are they produced for the purpose of achieving 'shared reality.' Different social tuning conditions could also be manipulated. For example, the in-group versus out-group status (in relation to the communicator) of both the audience and the message subject (i.e., the target person) could be varied. This would vary both the extent of the motivation to achieve 'shared reality' and the object of this motivation (i.e., to share reality with the immediate audience versus an alternative 'inner' audience). In this way, the issue of how communication as social action creates meaning could be examined within the more general framework of social- and self-regulatory systems —a framework that considers the 'ends' as well as the 'means' of interpersonal communication.

The implications of communicators' motivation to achieve 'shared reality' for other areas of social psychology could also be examined in future studies. In recent years there has been an increasing interest in the effect of communication processed on social-cognitive phenomena. Much of the interest has focused on the implications of Grice's (1975) maxim of relevance (see, for example, Hilton, 1990; Schwarz, *et al.*, 1991; Strack, Schwarz, & Wanke, 1991). But communicators' motivation to achieve 'shared reality' could also influence social-psychological phenomena. For example, what inference would observers make about a communicator's attitude on a subject when the communicator produces a negative message about the subject to an audience that the communicator knows has a negative attitude toward the subject? If observers understand that communicators are motivated to achieve 'shared reality' with their audience, then they should infer that the communicator's real attitude is probably less negative than indicated by the message. Indeed, there is evidence that observers do make this inferential adjustment (see Newtson & Czerlinsky, 1974).

Why, then, do observers not make a similar adjustment in other cases, such as those reflecting the 'fundamental attribution error' (Ross, 1977) or 'correspondence bias' (Jones, 1979). In the classic example of this phenomenon (Jones & Harris, 1967), observers inferred a direct correspondence between communicators' pro-Castro speech or anti-Castro speech and the communicators' true personal attitude toward Castro even though they knew that the experimenter had assigned the communicators to the position they advocated as part of a debate. What is notable about this case is that the communicators were not comunicating to an audience that they believed held a particular attitude toward Castro. And the observers knew this. Thus, the observers would not infer that the message content derived from a motivation to achieve 'shared reality' with an immediate audience. Indeed, the observers might infer that the messages content, apart from just the position advocated (i.e., 'pro' or 'con'), was tuned toward some 'internal' or 'personal' standard of the communicator. This would produce the 'correspondence bias'. But this explanation differs from the usual explanation of 'correspondence bias' in that it does not postulate that observers are insensitive to situational influences on the actor's behaviour (in this case, situational influences on the communicator's message). It is just that observers' major focus regarding situational influences is on audience-tuning. This perspective would predict that the 'correspondence bias' would disappear if the observers believed that the debaters were trained to use a strategy of imagining that they were communicating to an audience who held the position to be advocated.

A final comment. It has been over ten years since the 'communication game' approach to communication and social cognition was introduced. In the following years, my colleagues and I have been especially intrigued with how the social action of audience tuning can create meaning over time. The next stage is to consider how the impact of social action on creating meaning varies for different forms of social action (e.g., super-tuning versus anti-tuning versus non-tuning; social tuning versus social compliance). Of special interest are the implications of communicators being motivated to achieve 'shared reality' with their audience. By taking an increasing 'social' perspective on interpersonal communication, perhaps its role in 'social' psychology will be better understood.

ACKNOWLEDGMENTS

This paper was a plenary Keynote Address delivered at the 4th International Conference on Language and Social Psychology, Santa Barbara, August 18–23, 1991. The research described in this paper was supported by Grant MH-39429 from the National Institute of Mental Health.

REFERENCES

Abelson, R. P. *et al.* (1968) Psychological implication. In R. P. Abelson, E. Aronson, W. J. McGuire, T. M. Newcomb, M. J. Rosenberg and P. H. Tannenbaum (eds) *Theories of Cognitive Consistency: A Source Book*. Chicago: Rand McNally.

Adorno, T. W., Frenkel-Brunswick, E., Levinson, D. J., & Sanford, R. N. (1950) *The Authoritarian Personality*. New York: Harper.

Asch, S. E. (1952) *Social Psychology*. Englewood Cliffs, New Jersey: Prentice-Hall.

Austin, J. L. (1962) *How To Do Things With Words*. Oxford: Oxford University Press.

Bem, D. J. (1967) Self perception: An alternative interpretation of cognitive dissonance phenomenon. *Psychological Behaviour, 74,* 183–200.

Berg, K. S., & Vidmar, N. (1975) Authoritarianism and recall of evidence about criminal behavior. *Journal of Research in Personality, 9,* 147–57.

Brown, P. and Levinson, S. (1978) Universal in language use: Politeness phenomena. In E. Goody (ed.) *Questions and Politeness: Strategies in Social Interaction* (pp. 56–289). New York: Cambridge University Press.

Clark, H. H., & Brennan, S. E. (1991) Grounding in communication. In L. B. Resnick, J. M. Levine, & S. D. Teasley. (eds) *Perspectives on Socially Shared Cognition* (pp. 127–49). Washington, DC: American Psychological Association.

Clark, H. H., & Haviland, S. E. (1977) Comprehension and the given-new contract. In R. O. Freedle (ed.) *Discourse Production and Comprehension*. Norwood, New Jersey: Ablex.

Clark, H. H., & Marshall, C. R. (1981) Definite reference and mutual knowledge. In A. K. Joshi, B. L. Webber, & I. A. Sag (eds) *Elements of Discourse Understanding* (pp. 10–63). Cambridge: Cambridge University Press.

Deutsch, M., & Gerard, H. B. (1955) A study of normative and informational social influences upon individual judgment. *Journal of Abnormal and Social Psychology, 51,* 629–36.

Epstein, R. (1965) Authoritarianism, displaced aggression, and social status of the target. *Journal of Personality and Social Psychology, 2,* 585–9.

Festinger, L. (1950) Informal social communication. *Psychological Review, 57,* 271–82.

———— (1957) *A Theory of Cognitive Dissonance*. Evanston, Illinois: Row, Peterson.

Fiske, S. T., & Taylor, S. E. (1984) *Social Cognition*. Reading, MA: Addison-Wesley.

French, J. R., & Raven, B. (1959) The bases of social power. In D. Cartwright (ed.) *Studies in Social Power*. Ann Arbor, Michigan: Institute of Social Relations.

Fussell, S. R., & Krauss, R. M. (1989) The effects of intended audience on message production and comprehension: Reference in a common ground framework. *Journal of Experimental Social Psychology, 25,* 203–19.

Garfinkel, H. (1967) *Studies in Ethnomethodology*. Englewood Cliffs, New Jersey: Prentice-Hall.

Giles, H., & Smith, P. M. (1979) Accommodation-theory: Optimal levels of convergence. In H. Giles & R. St. Clair (Eds.), *Language and Social Psychology*. Oxford: Blackwell.

Giles, H., Mulac, A., Bradac, J. J., & Johnson, P. (1987) Speech accommodation theory: The first decade and beyond. In M. McLaughlin (Ed.), *Communication Yearbook* 10 (pp. 13–48). Newbury Park, CA: Sage.

Glucksberg, S., Krauss, R. M., & Higgins, E. T. (1975) The development of referential communication skills. In F. Horowitz, E. Hetherington, S. Scarr-Salapatek, & G. Seigel (eds) *Review of Child Development Research* (Vol. 4). Chicago: University of Chicago Press.

Goffman, E. (1959) *The Presentation of Self in Everyday Life*. Garden City, NY: Double-day.

Grice, H. P. (1971) Logic and conversation. The William James Lectures. Harvard University, 1967–8. In P. Cole & J. L. Morgan (eds) *Syntax and Semantics (Vol. 3): Speech Acts*. New York: Academic Press.

Grice, H. P. (1975) Logic and conversation. The William James Lectures, Harvard University, 1967–68. In P. Cole & J. L. Morgan (eds) *Syntax and Semantics (Vol. 3): Speech Acts*. New York: Academic Press.

Gumperz, J. J., & Hymes, D. (eds) (1972) *Directions in Sociolinguistics: The Ethnography of Communication*. New York: Holt, Rinehart & Winston.

Harvey, O. J., & Beverly, G. D. (1961) Some personality correlates of concept change through role playing. *Journal of Abnormal and Social Psychology, 63,* 125–30.

Higgins, E. T. (1977) Communication development as related to channel, incentive, and social class. *Genetic Psychology Monographs, 96,* 75–141.

——— (1981a) The 'communication game': Implications for social cognition and persuasion. In E. T. Higgins, C. P. Herman, & M. P. Zanna (Eds.), *Social Cognition: The Ontario Symposium*. Hillsdale, NJ: Erlbaum.

——— (1981b) Role taking and social judgment: Alternative developmental perspectives and processes. In J. H. Flavell & L. Ross (Eds.), *Social Cognitive Development: Frontiers and Possible Futures* (pp. 119–53). New York: Cambridge University Press.

——— (1989) Knowledge accessibility and activation: Subjectivity and suffering from unconscious sources. In J. S. Uleman & J. A. Bargh (Eds.), *Unintended Thought* (pp. 75–123). New York: Guilford Press.

——— (1990) Personality, social psychology, and person-situated relations: Standards and knowledge activation as a common language. In L. A. Pervin (Ed.), *Handbook of Personality*. New York: Guilford Press.

Higgins, E. T., Fondacaro, R., & McCann, C. D. (1981) Rules and roles: The 'communication game' and speaker-listener processes. In W. P. Dickson (Ed.), *Children's Oral Communication Skills*. New York: Academic Press.

Higgins, E. T., King, G. A., & Mavin, G. H. (1982) Individual construct accessibility and subjective impressions and recall. *Journal of Personality and Social Psychology, 43,* 35–47.

Higgins, E. T., & McCann, C. D. (1984) Social encoding and subsequent attitudes, impressions, and memory: 'Context-driven' and motivational aspects of processing. *Journal of Personality and Social Psychology, 47,* 27–39.

Higgins, E. T., McCann, C. D., & Fondacaro, R. (1982) The 'communication-game': Goal-directed encoding and cognitive consequences. *Social Cognition, 1,* 21–37.

Higgins, E. T., & Rholes, W. S. (1978) 'Saying is believing': Effects of message modification on memory and liking for the person described. *Journal of Experimental Social Psychology, 14,* 363–78.

Hilton, D. J. (1990) Conversational processes and causal explanation. *Psychological Bulletin, 107,* 65–81.

Hovland, C. I., Janis, I. L., & Kelley, H. H. (1953) *Communication and Persuasion: Psychological Studies of Opinion Change*. New Haven, Conn.: Yale University Press.

Jones, E. E. (1979) The rocky road from acts to dispositions. *American Psychologist, 34,* 107–17.

Jones, E. E., & deCharms, R. (1958) The organizing function of interaction roles in person perception. *Journal of Abnormal and Social Psychology, 57,* 155–64.

Jones, E. E., & Goethals, G. R. (1972) Order effects in impression formation. Attribution context and the nature of the entity. In E. E. Jones, D. E. K. Danouse, H. H. Kelley, R. E. Nisbett, S. Valins, & B. Weiner (Eds.), *Attribution: Perceiving the Causes of Behavior*. Morristown, NJ: General Learning Press.

Jones, E. E., & Harris, V. A. (1967) The attribution of attitudes. *Journal of Experimental Social Psychology, 3,* 1–24.

Kelley, H. H. (1979) *Personal Relationships: Their Structures and Processes*. Hillsdale, NJ: Erlbaum.

Manis M., Cornell, S. D., & Moore, J. C. (1974) Transmission of attitude-relevant information through a communication chain. *Journal of Personality and Social Psychology, 30,* 81–94.

McCann, C. D., & Hancock, R. D. (1983) Self-monitoring in communicative interactions: Social-cognitive consequences of goal-directed message modification. *Journal of Experimental Social Psychology, 19,* 109–21.

McCann, C. D., & Higgins, E. T. (1992) Personal and contextual factors in communication: A review of 'the communication game'. In G. R. Semin & V. Fiedler (Eds.), *Language, Interaction and Social Cognition* (pp. 144–72). London: Sage.

McCann, C. D., Higgins, E. T., & Fondacaro, R. A. (1991) Primacy and recency in communication and self-persuasion: How successive audiences and multiple encodings influence subsequent evaluative judgments. *Social Cognition, 9,* 47–66.

McGuire, W. J. (1969) The nature of attitudes and attitude change. In G. Lindzey and E. Aronson (eds) *The Handbook of Social Psychology*. Reading, Mass.: Addison-Wesley.

Mead, G. H. (1934) *Mind, Self, and Society*. Chicago: University of Chicago Press.

Mehrabian, A., & Reed, H. (1968) Some determinants of communication accuracy. *Psychological Bulletin, 70,* 365–81.

Miller, N., & Campbell, D. T. (1959) Recency and primacy in persuasion as a function of the timing of speeches and measurements. *Journal of Abnormal and Social Psychology, 59,* 1–9.

Morris, C. (1938) Foundations of the Theory of Signs. *International Encyclopedia of Unified Science* Vol. 1, No. 2. Chicago: University of Chicago Press.

Newtson, D., & Czerlinsky, T. (1974) Adjustment of attitude communications for contrasts by extreme audiences. *Journal of Personality and Social Psychology*, 30, 829–37.

Piaget, J. (1926) *The Language and Thoughts of the Child*. New York: Harcourt Brace.

Rommetveit, R. (1974) *On Message Structure: A Framework for the Study of Language and Communication*. New York: John Wiley & Sons.

Ross, L. (1977) The intuitive psychologist and his shortcomings: Distortions in the attribution process. In L. Berkowitz (Ed.), *Advances in Experimental Social Psychology* Vol. 10 (pp. 173–220). New York: Academic Press.

Ross, L., Amabile, T. M., & Steinmetz, J. L. (1977) Social roles, social control, and biases in social-perception processes. *Journal of Personality and Social Psychology, 35,* 485–94.

Ruesch, J., & Bateson. (1968) Communication: The social matrix of psychiatry. New York: W. W. Norton & Company.

Sarbin, T. R., & Allen, V. L. (1968) Role theory. In G. Lindzey and E. Aronson (eds) *Handbook of Social Psychology, Second edition, Vol. 1* (pp. 488–567). Reading, Mass.: Addison-Wesley.

Schwarz, N., Strack, F., Hilton, D., & Naderer, G. (1991) Base rates, representativeness, and the logic of conversation: The contextual relevance of 'irrelevant' information. *Social Cognition, 9,* 67–84.

Sedikides, C. (1990) Effects of fortuitously activated constructs versus activated communication goals on person impressions. *Journal of Personality and Social Psychology, 58,* 397–408.

Shannon, C. E., & Weaver, W. (1949) *The Mathematical Theory of Communication.* Urbana, Ilinois: University of Illinois Press.

Sherif, M. (1979) *The Psychology of Social Norms.* New York: Harper & Brothers.

Snyder, M. (1979) Self-monitoring processes. In L. Berkowitz (Ed.), *Advances in Experimental Social Psychology* Vol. 12 (pp. 85–128). New York: Academic Press.

Strack, F., Schwarz, N., & Wanke (1991) Semantic and pragmatic aspects of context effects in social and psychological research. *Social Cognition, 9,* 111–25.

Thibault, J. W., & Riecken, H. W. (1955) Authoritarianism, status and the communication of aggression. *Human Relations, 8,* 95–120.

Thomas, W. I., & Znaniecki, F. (1918) *The Polish Peasant in Europe and America,* Vol. 1. Boston: Badger.

Watzlawick, P., Beavin, J. H., & Jackson, D. D. (1967) *Pragmatics of Human Communication.* New York: W. W. Norton.

Weber, M. (1967) Subjective meaning in the social situation. In G. B. Levitas (Ed.), *Culture and Consciousness: Perspectives in the Social Sciences* (pp. 156–69). New York: Braziller.

Wicklund, R. A., & Brehm, J. W. (1976) *Perspectives on Cognitive Dissonance.* Hillsdale, NJ: Erlbaum.

Wyer, R. S., & Srull, T. K. (1986) Human cognition in its social context. *Psychological Review, 93,* 322–59.

Zajonc, R. B. (1960) The process of cognitive tuning and communication. *Journal of Abnormal and Social Psychology, 61,* 159–67.

Zimmerman, C., & Bauer, R. A. (1956) The effect of an audience on what is remembered. *Public Opinion Quarterly, 20,* 238–48.

The Cognitive Functions of Linguistic Categories in Describing Persons: Social Cognition and Language

Gün R. Semin • The University of Sussex
Klaus Fiedler • The University of Giessen

Editors' Notes

Whereas the previous two selections focused on the way the audience of the message affects the shaping of the message, the present selection focuses on how subtle properties of language are used in order to convey a specific intended meaning. As the authors demonstrate, the same action can be described at different levels of abstraction. The specific level chosen is indicative of the causal locus of the action (whether located in the subject or the object of the sentence), the extent to which the action reflects enduringness, and the degree to which it is likely to be verifiable and disputed. The authors distinguish between four categories of lexical descriptors, namely Descriptive Action Verbs (DAVs), Interpretive Action Verbs (IAVs), State Verbs (SVs), and Adjectives (Adjs). These four categories are assumed to define a continuum of abstractness. This hypothesis is corroborated through the finding of monotonic trends on the dependent variables, running from DAVs to Adjs. The results suggest that different linguistic categories are functional in directing message recipients to different characteristics of the actor or the situation. Thus, communicators can use abstractness to draw recipients' attention to those aspects of an event that they deem important. In this way, lexical properties of language can be used to fashion the conclusions that recipients reach, thereby increasing the effectiveness of the communication.

Discussion Questions

1. What are the differences between the four linguistic categories?
2. In what way do the linguistic categories direct attention to the subject versus the object of a sentence?
3. In what way, does study 2 go beyond and supplement the findings of study 1?
4. Why are decontextualized linguistic forms used despite their lack of disconfirmability and their likelihood of being disputed?

Suggested Readings

Brown, R., & Fish, D. (1983). The psychological causality implicit in language. *Cognition, 14*, 237–273.

Hilton, D. J. (1995). The social context of reasoning: Conversational inference and rational judgment. *Psychological Bulletin, 118*, 248–271.

Schwarz, N., Strack, F., Hilton, D. J., & Naderer, G. (1991). Judgmental biases and the logic of conversation: The contextual relevance of irrelevant information. *Social Cognition, 9*, 67–84.

Authors' Abstract

Three studies examined the cognitive implications of linguistic categories in the interpersonal domain. On the basis of conceptual and linguistic criteria, we advance a four-level classification that distinguishes between verbs and adjectives in the interpersonal domain. These four levels (in terms of increasing abstractness) are descriptive action verbs, interpretive action verbs, state verbs, and adjectives. Results from the first two studies reveal a systematic relation between the respective linguistic category and the temporal stability of the quality expressed in the sentence, the sentence's informativeness about the subject, the sentence's verifiability and disputability, and the sentence's informativeness about a specific situation. Results from the last study support the four-level linguistic classification and its differential cognitive functions. Implications for social cognition and personality research are discussed.

In the three studies reported in this article, we examine the cognitive functions of different linguistic categories used to describe persons and their behaviors. The aim is to elucidate how language mediates between social cognition and social reality. The interface between language and social cognition remains a relatively neglected issue in the burgeoning field of social cognition (cf. Fiske & Taylor, 1984; Markus & Zajonc, 1985; Wyer & Srull, 1984). Aside from work on aspects of communication processes such as speech acts (cf. Clark, 1985; Kraut & Higgins, 1984), there are a few studies that have examined the social cognitive implications of different linguistic categories in the interpersonal domain (e.g., Au, 1986; Brown & Fish, 1983; Fiedler, 1978; Kanouse,

1972; McGuire, McGuire, & Cheever, 1986; Semin & Greenslade, 1985).

This article's aim is to advance a general framework for the cognitive implications of linguistic categories in the interpersonal domain rather than focusing on specific properties of interpersonal verbs (e.g., presupposed responsibility, causality, etc.) and adjectives separately.

In the literature on the psychological implications of verbs and adjectives there exist different distinctions (e.g., action verbs vs. state verbs, Brown & Fish, 1983; immediate terms [verbs] vs. mediate terms [adjectives], Semin & Greenslade, 1985). These distinctions are informative and have yielded interesting theoretical and empirical results; however, as we shall see, there has been no cross-referencing between these frameworks and an absence of an overall framework. Here we would like to introduce a general taxonomy for the terms used in the interpersonal domain with the following examples: (a) A is *talking* to B; (b) A is *helping* B; (c) A *likes* B; and (d) B is an *extraverted* person.[1]

In the first example we have a neutral description of an action. A is talking to B and no interpretation of the action is involved, merely a description of it (cf. immediate terms, Semin & Greenslade, 1985). There is concrete reference to a behavior that allows the behavior's classification and its discrimination from other behaviors such as drinking, smoking, and so forth. The statement is uncontentious in that it is easily verifiable. A number of verbs fall into this category, for example, *hold, visit, call*, and the like. However, in the second example (A is helping B), the verb does not involve the mere description and classification of a specific behavior but also its interpretation. There exist an abundance of verbs that fulfill not only the function of behavior classification and discrimination but also interpretation (e.g., *encourage, mislead, cheat, flatter*, etc.). Although these verbs fulfill a similar function in describing a concrete behavior (i.e., their external reference can easily be established and the truth value of the statement can be examined), they nevertheless also involve something more than mere description. These verbs are *interpretive action verbs* (IAVs) (e.g., action verbs, Brown & Fish, 1983) in contrast to those in the first example, which are *descriptive action verbs* (DAVs). The third example (A likes B) is the description of a person in a situation. However, the verb's status is qualitatively different from the first two examples. In this case, the statement refers to the psychological state of Person A in relation to Person B. The statement does not maintain a concrete reference to a specific behavior episode or event. It is in fact an abstract statement that usually cannot be verified objectively by an observer, has a hypothetical interpretive status, and refers primarily to the psychological state of Person A in the situation in question. These types of verbs (e.g., *love, respect, abhor, trust*) are referred to as *state verbs* (SVs; cf. Brown & Fish, 1983; Miller & Johnson-Laird, 1976). The fourth example is identical to the *mediate terms* category introduced by Semin and Greenslade (1985) and in this article is referred to as *adjectives* (Adjs). It serves to discriminate Person A from other persons who are introverted, anxious, reserved, and so forth, and allows a classification of Person A in relation to others. These terms are abstract and maintain only a mediate reference to empirical events and actions.[2]

When the corpus of all interpersonal terms in the lexicon is considered, the classification of most terms as DAVs, IAVs, SVs, or Adjs is in a sense obvious. Even in the absence of objectively defined criteria, the meaning of the categories as outlined is often sufficient to discriminate between terms on an intuitive level. There are, however, problematic instances or borderline cases that require more than these general specifications for their classification. Because the classification of the terms is treated here as an independent variable, it is essential to provide explicit linguistic criteria above and beyond the previous specifications. The following are the criteria that were explicitly used to classify interpersonal terms in Study 1.

1. The distinction Adj versus DAV, IAV, and SV is given unambiguously and formally and in terms of qualities/properties of persons (Adj) versus actions or psychological states.

2. The distinction SV versus IAV and DAV consists of the fact that SVs are detached from observable behavioral events (cf. Table 1). SVs refer to mental and emotional states or changes therein as opposed to overt behavior. IAVs and DAVs, but not SVs, normally have a clearly defined beginning and end for an action. In-

[1]Nouns referring to properties and propensities of persons were not included in the studies reported here. The present research is deliberately confined to the psychological and semantic functions of linguistic terms in the emphasized, explicit predicates of sentences. Terms in the role of presuppositions are excluded from the analysis because they involve fundamentally different processes of inference and reference. Such terms may be regarded as characteristic of the impact of presuppositional information (cf. Fillmore, 1971; Loftus, 1975). The social roles and condensed actions expressed by nouns such as *father or thief* typically occur as presuppositions in sentences (e.g., *The father did not care for his children* or *The thief felt remorse*). In cases where the same noun appears in the position of the focused predicate (*The young man is the thief*) the noun use may be regarded as an adjectival case.

[2]Although this may be seen as one of the main functions of adjectives in the interpersonal domain, most adjectives may also be used to classify behaviors (e.g., an extraverted behavior, a polite behavior, etc.) that are taken to be behavioral instances of a particular trait. The main referent of adjectives, however, remains persons rather than specific instances of behaviors in everyday life, and the general usage is person rather than behavior centered.

TABLE 32.1. The Classification Criteria for the Three Verb Classes

Category	Criteria	Examples
State verbs	Refer to mental or emotional states; no clear definition of beginning and end; do not readily take the progressive form; not freely used in imperatives	like hate notice envy
Interpretive action verbs	Refer to general class of behaviors; have a defined action with a beginning and end; have positive or negative semantic connotations	help cheat inhibit imitate
Descriptive action verbs	Refer to one particular activity and to at least one physically invariant feature of the action; action has clear beginning and end; usually do not have positive or negative connotations	call kiss talk stare

deed, the distinction between state and overt action verbs is one commonly made in the linguistic literature (cf. Miller & Johnson-Laird, 1976). In those exceptional cases in which the distinction is ambiguous (most notably with verbs of judging, cf. Au, 1986) the instances can be disambiguated in the context of language use.[3]

3. From a conceptual point of view, the most difficult distinction concerns the delineation of DAVs versus IAVs. The interpretive versus descriptive contrast alone is insufficient because interpretiveness is a matter of degree rather than an absolute feature. Many DAVs have an interpretive component, although IAVs involve a greater depth of interpretation. However, it is difficult to specify such a criterion explicitly. Another possibility is presented by the argument that many IAVs have a pronounced evaluative component (e.g., positive IAVs such as *help, amuse, encourage* vs. negative IAVs such as *cheat, attack, harm*), whereas DAVs do not (e.g., *phone, talk, hold*). This may also be regarded as problematic because there are several DAVs that imply positive social relations (*kiss, hug*) or negative social relations (*kick, shoot*) and some IAVs that appear to be neutral in valence (e.g., *influence, interact with, select*). One might argue that the evaluative aspect of DAVs such as *kiss* or *kick* is mainly a matter of pragmatics, whereas in the case of IAVs it is the semantics of the terms themselves that are positive or negative, but this in itself would only complicate the distinction.

Therefore, we used the following criterion, which can be applied with reasonable objectivity

in the classification of these terms: DAVs are descriptive in the sense that there is at least one physically invariant feature shared by all actions to which the term is applied (e.g., *kiss* always involves the mouth, *phone* always involves the phone, *kick* always involves the foot, etc.). In contrast, there is no physically invariant feature in the case of IAVs, which refer to a multitude of different actions that may have nothing in common (e.g., there is no single common feature shared by the different instances of *helping, hurting, challenging*, etc.).

Some important cognitive implications of the categories we term IAVs and SVs have been investigated by Abelson and Kanouse (1966), Caramazza, Grober, Garvey, and Yates (1977), Fiedler (1978), McArthur (1972), and more recently by Brown and Fish (1983). These studies address the issue of the causality implicit in verbs. The consistent finding across these studies is the following: When a sentence in the form of subject–verb–object is presented and the subject's task consists of judging the locus of causality of the behavior expressed in the verb, then sentences including IAVs are regularly attributed to the subject, whereas sentences including SVs are attributed to the object. For example, the sentence *Bob helps Mike* implies that the cause of the behavior in question is Bob's helpfulness rather than Mike's helpworthiness. However, the sentence *Ted likes*

---

[3]Depending on the context, verbs of judging (such as *accuse, blame, praise*) may denote an overt (speech) action or a mental state or attitude. We do not consider these instances as examples for the classification. However, it should be pointed out that the disambiguation of these instances in fact provides evidence for the classification advanced here.

Paul points to Paul's likability rather than Ted's likingness as the implicit cause of behavior. The issue of causality implicit in language provides additional ideas about the psychological variables related to the four-level classification.

First, it has repeatedly been shown that sentences containing SVs are more person-specific, whereas sentences containing IAVs are more situation-specific (cf. Abelson & Kanouse, 1966). Thus, given the IAV sentence *Bob helps Mike*, the frequent inference made is that Bob helps other people as well and that Mike is helped by other people. However, the likelihood to generalize the SV sentence *Ted likes Paul* to other persons is less (Abelson & Kanouse, 1966). On the other hand, this sentence, although more person-specific, allows for more generalization over time—*to like* refers to a more enduring state than *to help*. Extrapolating from this difference to the other two categories, Adjs and DAVs, an important feature of the proposed four-level classification emerges: Adjectives should be even more person-specific (i.e., refer to traits or dispositions) than SVs, and DAVs should be even more context-specific in their reference than IAVs.

Second, IAVs may induce an observer perspective because they refer to observable, manifest behaviors (help, hurt, inhibit, etc.). On the other hand, SVs often refer to nonobservable, subjective states of the sentence subject (like, admire, abhor, etc.) and might therefore induce an actor perspective, which usually gives rise to more situation attributions (cf. Jones & Nisbett, 1972). Although this difference is not readily extrapolated to the extreme categories (DAVs and Adjs) for which subject attribution is almost always trivial, the social psychological processes underlying the actor–observer discrepancy may be related to different levels of language use. Thus, it is tempting to consider the possibility that language may be regarded as reflecting or mediating the different attributional tendencies of actors and observers (or listeners and speakers, cf. Farr & Anderson, 1983).

Third, the causal information implicit in IAVs and SVs might be attributed to the fact that IAVs often refer to controllable, voluntary behaviors, whereas SVs typically describe uncontrollable affects or cognitive states. The usual linguistic test for a state verb (cf. Miller & Johnson-Laird, 1976) is that they do not freely take the progressive form (e.g., *He believes in Santa Claus* and not *He is believing in Santa Claus*; cf. Kenny, 1963; Ota,

1963). Furthermore, as Brown and Fish (1983) and Miller and Johnson-Laird (1976) noted, these verbs are not freely used in imperatives. The examples Miller and Johnson-Laird (1976, p. 474) quoted are *Know the answer! Need money!* etc. The analogous extension of this observation to Adjs appears to be ambiguous where some imperative forms appear to be inadequate when trait terms are used (e.g., *be extraverted*), whereas others are quite acceptable (*be friendly, be polite*), although the reference of such sensible imperative forms is highly situated. Broadly speaking, however, another psychological function that the different linguistic forms can serve may lie in the communication of which behaviors are externally controllable. This aspect appears to be related to the criterion of enduringness or temporal stability mentioned earlier. What is malleable or changeable lends itself to external control. What is stable or endurable is not open to control.

Fourth, Brown and Fish (1983) have considered the possibility that the morphology of language as a system may underlie the causal impact of IAVs and SVs. Thus, it is worth noting that most adjectives derived from IAVs (e.g., helpful) are attributive to the natural sentence subject, whereas the majority of adjectives derived from SVs (e.g., likable) are attributive to the object of the behavior in question. Brown and Fish refute this possibility by arguing that English derivational morphology provides enough suffixes to derive from IAVs and SVs adjectives that are applicable to both subject and object attributes.

Pilot Study and Study 1

The aforementioned criteria constitute converging linguistic guidelines to discriminate among the four categories in the interpersonal domain. One could argue that these four linguistic categories are organized on a concreteness–abstractness dimension. At the one end are DAVs that maintain an immediate reference to concrete behavioral events, whereas Adjs, at the other end, maintain an abstract reference to a person's psychological properties (traits, dispositions). The issue addressed here is the general psychological implications of the concreteness–abstractness dimension along which the four linguistic categories are ordered. With more abstract reference of the linguistic category one would expect the terms to imply more temporal stability and to be more informative about a person. However, the more abstract linguistic categories also would by implication be less informative about specific situations and less verifiable and more disputable than concrete terms. Thus, our aim was to examine psychological properties that vary systematically over the four categories rather than focusing on particular features that are distinctive of some of the four categories (e.g., the susceptibility of traits to behavioral evidence, Rothbart & Park, 1986; causality implicit in IAVs and SVs, Brown & Fish, 1983; Fiedler & Semin, in press; types of presupposition in specific interpersonal verbs, Fillmore, 1971). The first two studies constitute an examination of those psychological features that differentiate among the four categories on this dimension.

One such feature is the *enduringness* of the quality ascribed to the person in question. Sentences with DAVs do not permit the inference of any stable characteristics or qualities about a person. In the case of Adjs, however, there is an assumption of a temporal stability of the quality in question, namely a disposition or trait. The two intermediate categories refer to different durabilities of characteristics in time; that is, *lying* refers to a characteristic that is manifested in an action, whereas *loving* refers to a psychological state of longer duration, but not a permanent state (exceptions in both cases are regarded as pathological). It would therefore appear that there is a dimension of enduringness, a psychological propensity that varies between the four categories.

Another interrelated implication is this: How much information do sentences with these linguistic categories yield about the subject? In the case of DAVs, this information is minimal and increases as a function of the category from IAVs to SVs to Adjs. To say that someone is talking (DAV) contains less information about the subject than to say someone is threatening somebody (IAV), in contrast to saying someone abhors somebody (SV), in contrast to saying someone is brutal (Adj). This criterion is referred to as *subject informativeness*.

Symmetrical to the subject informativeness criterion, one can also consider how much information such sentences contain about specific situations in which the subject of the sentence might be, namely the *situative informativeness*. To say that someone is extraverted (Adj) does not reveal much about a specific and concrete situation. However, examples such as someone is talking to, phon-

ing, or holding somebody else (DAVs) are directly associated with concrete events and therefore reveal something about a particular situation. In this case, we would assume a descending situative informativeness from DAVs to Adjs, Adjs being least informative about specific situational characteristics.

The concreteness–abstractness dimension also implies that the degree to which sentences containing either of these categories can be objectively verified by a potential observer will vary. In the case of DAVs the observer/listener should have no problems verifying the content of the sentence. This is similarly the case with IAVs, although there may be some debate about interpretation in this instance. In the case of SVs the problem becomes considerable because the only person who can attest to the truth value or falsity of the statement is the actor to whom the sentence refers. Finally, the ascription contained in Adj sentences is in principle completely open to debate. We refer to this property of the classification as the issue of *verifiability*.

The last criterion concerns a social property highly related to verifiability, namely, *disputability*. This issue concerns the contentiousness of the propositions contained in statements with any of these four categories. The assumption is that the likelihood of disagreement about the propositions contained in statements will increase from sentences containing DAVs to sentences containing Adjs as a function of their concreteness–abstractness.

In the following studies we attempted to establish whether the four categories differentiate along this dimension of abstractness–concreteness. This was done by providing subjects with minimal sentences (e.g., S is *successful* [Adj], S *visits* someone [DAV], S *harrasses* someone [IAV], S *likes* someone [SV]). All the terms were sampled from the interpersonal domain. By using the aforementioned five criteria as dependent variables (subject informativeness, situative informativeness, enduringness, verifiability, and disputability), we designed the pilot study and Study 1. The aim was to examine whether the analytically derived four-level classification would yield a corresponding unidimensional empirical classification on the basis of the psychological implications of these linguistic categories.

Method

Participants. Eighty undergraduate students at the University of Sussex, Brighton, England, participated in this study on a paid voluntary basis. They participated in small groups of 4 to 8 persons.

Procedure. Each participant received a booklet. The cover page contained the following general instruction:

This is a psycholinguistic study in which we are investigating how informative different verbs and adjectives are in describing persons. In order to examine this, verbs and adjectives will be presented to you in what one may call minimal sentences. Your task consists in answering several questions concerning the information conveyed in each sentence about the subject of the sentence. Obviously, the informativeness of such minimal sentences is limited. However, they do vary in their degree of informativeness about persons. These differences in information conveyed about persons is precisely what we are interested in finding out.

Subsequently, they were provided with eight such minimal sentences (of which two were constructed with DAVs, two with IAVs, two with SVs, and two with Adjs, presented in a random order) to form an idea of the type of sentences to expect in the questionnaire. They were then provided with the five questions that constituted the dependent measures as an overview of the types of questions that they would answer after each sentence. Finally, the instruction sheet ended with the following qualification:

You may find some of these questions difficult to answer for particular sentences. Do not hesitate to draw any possible inferences from the sentence that you are provided with in order to be able to answer all five questions. Please work through this questionnaire carefully and do not omit any of the sentences or the questions associated with each sentence.

TABLE 32.2. Randomly Selected and Typical Stimulus Terms

Linguistic category			
DAV	IAV	SV	Adj
Randomly selected stimulus terms			
call†	attack†	abhor	altruistic†
catch	blackmail†	admire†	brutal
find†	correct†	accept†	fair†
hold†	command	commiserate	foolish
lift†	denigrate†	envy†	ignorant†
phone†	deride	fear	friendly
photograph†	denounce†	desire†	jealous
prepare†	encourage	hate	offensive
pull aside†	excite	hold in contempt	patient†
stare	harrass†	like†	peaceful†
stop	hurry	love†	quiet†
summon	intervene	mourn for	shrewd
take something			strange
from	hurt†	prefer†	stubborn
tickle†	manipulate†	respect†	successful†
touch	mislead	recognize	sympathetic
visit	restrict†	suspect	youthful†
wake up†	thank	understand†	vain†
watch	threaten†	worry	virtuous†
Typical stimulus terms			
dance	amuse	detest	aggressive
dial	betray	dread	anxious
drive	cheat	envy	charismatic
hug	deceive	esteem	impulsive
kiss	disobey	like	intelligent
push	flatter	loath	moody
shout after	harm	notice	outgoing
touch	help	pity	pessimistic
wash	save	remember	reliable
wave	warn	trust	reserved

Note. DAV = descriptive action verb, IAV = interpretive action verb, SV = state verb, and Adj = adjective. Terms with a dagger were used in the experimental study.

Each of the 80 subjects received in their booklet only 36 of the 72 randomly selected stimulus terms (cf. Table 2). The presentation of the stimulus items was randomized for each subject.

Selection of stimulus materials. A representative sample of terms for the four linguistic categories was drawn by (a) defining the population of all English interpersonal terms and (b) drawing from this population a random sample that fulfilled several restrictive criteria. The aim of this exhaustive procedure was to ensure the generalizability of any empirical differences that we would obtain to the population of all terms. The selection of these terms was obtained on the basis of the broad criteria mentioned in the introduction and not the more explicit criteria (cf. Table 1).[4]

The basic population of terms was selected from a small English dictionary (Langenscheidt, 1967) that contains only the most common English words. Using a more exhaustive English dictionary would have made this extraction task insurmountable. A basic catalogue of 50 DAVs, 322 IAVs, 33 SVs, and 846 Adjs was extracted and assigned by the authors' consensus according to the criteria that all terms (a) referred to interpersonal behaviors; (b) were not of a metaphoric or ambiguous meaning; (c) were not derived from the same word stem or from another term; (d) did not represent participles, negations, or comparatives; and (e) appeared more frequently than 10 per million according to the Thorndike-Large count.

The 72 terms were drawn randomly from this population for each of the four linguistic categories (see the first half of Table 2). There were 18 terms per category.

A small pilot study was conducted to test the efficacy of independent criteria for the four-level classification. Four naive subjects were provided with the 54 verbs used in Study 1. Adjectives were not included because they are unequivocal. The subjects were asked to classify these verbs (each presented on a separate index card) into three groups (i.e., DAVs, IAVs, and SVs) along with the following instructions: (a) descriptive action verbs—objective identification of an elementary behavior (e.g., to address someone), in general no evaluation involved; (b) interpretative action verbs—interpretation of a behavior as belonging to a general action class (e.g., to help), which could be manifested through a variety of different behaviors and the interpretation typically involves an evaluation; and (c) state verbs—internal (i.e.,

emotional or mental) states or changes of state and no overt actions (e.g., to grieve).

The 4 subjects used in this pilot study correctly classified 100% of DAVs, 88.89% of IAVs, and 87.5% of SVs, providing evidence for the appropriateness of the broad criteria used to classify interpersonal verbs into these three categories.

Dependent variables. Each minimal sentence was accompanied by five questions, one for each of the criteria of subject informativeness, enduringness, verifiability, disputability, and situative informativeness. The respective questions were (a) How revealing is the attribute (action) about the subject of the sentence? (subject informativeness), (b) How enduring a quality does the attribute (action) in this sentence express about the subject? (endurability), (c) To what extent can the content of the above statement be objectively verified? (verifiability), (d) If the above statement were mentioned by someone, how likely is it that it could potentially lead to disagreement? (disputability), and (e) How much does the above sentence reveal about a specific and concrete situation in which the subject is? (situative informativeness).

Results

First of all, the mean ratings (across all participants) of the 72 linguistic terms (cf. the first half of Table 2) were obtained for the first study. The covariances among the mean ratings on all five dependent variables provided the input for a multiple discriminant analysis with the intention of (a) confirming the classification and (b) understanding its relation to the five criteria. The solution successfully separated the four linguistic categories. Of the 72 terms, 61 (i.e., 84.72%) were classified correctly, and of the remaining 11 displaced cases, only 1 was not placed in the neighboring category. In fact, each of the five dependent criteria alone is sufficient to reproduce the order of at least three of the four stages in the classification. This can be seen from the graphic rep-

---

[4]The selection of the items for this study was conducted with a broad set of criteria (mainly with reference to the distinction between the interpretive action verb [IAV] and descriptive action verb [DAV]), and not the more explicit distinction between IAV and DAV. Therefore, some items in this study were included under DAV, such as *prepare* and *stop*, which on closer inspection did not fall into the DAV category. Indeed, in the analysis of the data these two items are empirically classified under DAV (cf. Results section).

resentation of the categorywise means and variances for the five individual criteria in Figure 1A. As can be seen from Figure 1A, Adjs are the category with the highest subject informativeness, refer to the most enduring quality, are the least verifiable (except for SVs), give rise to the highest amount of disputability, and are the least informative about a situation. DAVs follow precisely the opposite pattern. SVs and IAVs occupy the predicted intermediary positions, with the exception of subject informativeness and verifiability. Aside from these descriptive statistics, the F statistics for the differences among the four groups were highly significant for each criterion. The within-groups correlations among the five criteria range from .07 to .70 (accounting for .005% and .49% variance) and suggest that the contribution of each individual rating was not merely a result of their redundancy.

Of the three canonical discriminant functions that can be extracted in the case of the four groups, the first accounts for 82% of the systematic variance, leaving no more than 9.97% and 7.93% to be explained by the second and third dimensions, respectively. This means that the psychological differences of the linguistic classes can appropriately be described as a monotonic order along a single dimension of concreteness–abstractness. Considering the (standardized) coefficients of the five variables on the dominant first discriminant function, the strongest contribution ($b = .61$) is

because of the rating of situative informativeness (i.e., how much a sentence reveals about a specific and concrete situation). Enduringness ($b = .53$) also contributed substantially, whereas the criteria of disputability ($b = .30$), person informativeness ($b = .29$), and verifiability ($b = .37$) maintained moderate relations to the first discriminant function.

The random selection of stimulus terms actually suppresses the strength of the relations that could be obtained with a more typical sample of terms. Typical, in this context, refers to choosing exemplars for the four categories within the strict definitional criteria advanced in the introduction (cf. Table 1). To this end a replication of the pilot study was conducted with 40 new terms (second half of Table 2) that were chosen carefully to comply with the explicit criteria advanced earlier. Twenty subjects from the University of Sussex participated in this study. The methodology used was identical to that in the previous study, except that 7-point rating scales were used instead of 9-point rating scales. We performed exactly the same analysis. The results were identical (cf. Figure 1B). However, in this case the solution successfully separated 97.5% of the cases, with only one adjective (aggressive) being misclassified as an SV. Essentially, the same detail for the discriminant analysis was obtained (of the three discriminant functions, the first explained 86.5% of the variance, etc.).

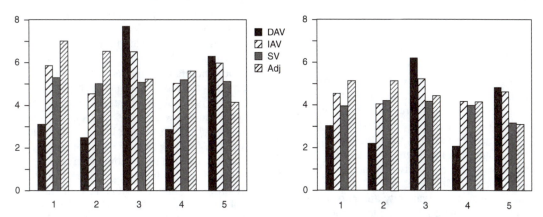

FIGURE 32.1 ■ Mean ratings and variances of the four classes of linguistic terms in terms of subject informativeness (1), enduringness (2), verifiability (3), disputability (4), and situation informativeness (5). (DAV = descriptive action verb; IAV = interpretive action verb; SV = state verb; and Adj = adjective. 1 = high values under SU indicate high subject informativeness; 2 = high values under EN indicate high enduringness; 3 = high values under VE indicate high verifiability; 4 = high values under DI indicate high disputability; and 5 = high values under SI indicate high situation informativeness.)

Discussion

The results of these studies support the assumption that the four linguistic categories are organized along a dimension of concreteness–abstractness and that their systematic ordering along this dimension is related to the cognitive implications of the linguistic terms as measured by the five dependent variables. These cognitive implications include the informativeness of sentences regarding the subject or the situation, and the enduringness, verifiability, and disputability of the proposition expressed in the sentence. In general, as one moves from DAVs to IAVs to SVs, and, finally, to Adjs, subject informativeness increases, situative informativeness decreases, and the sentence appears more endurable, less verifiable, and more likely to be the object of disagreement or dispute. The regularity by which the linguistic classes are monotonically related to these cognitive implications is consistent with the assumption of a common psychological dimension underlying all four word classes. Moreover, the proportion of 84.72% correct classifications in the first study and of 97.5% correct classifications for the replication from the discriminant analyses seems impressive, particularly if one considers the systematic sampling procedure for the first study that allows the results to be generalized over the whole lexicon.

Nevertheless, the conclusions that can be drawn from this study are limited. The main reason is that this study is confined to the cognitive implications of the semantic descriptions of the terms themselves and does not examine the interactions of these terms with given person types and situations. How are these terms used to describe specific persons in specific contexts? In other words, what is the impact of these linguistic classes in sentences including more than just *subject–verb–object*? If it can be demonstrated that the contextualized use of these categories is affected by the nature of the linguistic category on the dimension of concreteness–abstractness, then this would have substantial implications for a range of studies in social psychology and personality that rely on verbal material in the interpersonal domain. Essentially, this would mean that one would have to control for the regularities produced by the linguistic features of the categories used in such studies.

Study 2

To address the aforementioned issues, we conducted another experiment that examined the cognitive functions of the four linguistic categories. This study's aim was to test the differential semantic and psychological implications of these linguistic categories in their contextualized usage.

A study was designed (derived from Semin & Greenslade, 1985) in which the subjects' task consisted of judging the likelihood that a target person would manifest a series of behaviors (DAVs, IAVs, and SVs) and attributes (Adjs) in a particular situation. The characteristics of the target person were manipulated by providing subjects with brief pen pictures of an extravert, an introvert, and a Machiavellian. Orthogonally, the situation factor was manipulated by providing different behavioral settings, that is, a seminar, a party, and a business deal.

If DAVs constitute the most concrete categorical reference in the interpersonal domain, then their use should be affected by variations not only in information about both situations and persons, but also in their interaction. Different persons have different concrete behavioral styles, different situations have different behavioral requirements, and a person who is of a specific dispositional nature generally behaves differently in different situations. Concrete behavioral variations of this nature should be picked up by DAVs. On the other hand, if Adjs are the most abstract category, then it is unlikely that they will be influenced by variations in situations. Indeed, adjectives were judged in the first study to be least informative about concrete situational features. Furthermore, the Adj end of the concreteness–abstractness continuum is regarded as the most informative about persons (cf. the criteria of subject informativeness and enduringness in Study 1). Thus, the relative impact of the target person manipulation should increase from DAV to Adj and the relative impact of the situation manipulation should decrease.

In addition, an increasing reliance on interpretive processes should be observed with an increase in abstractness of category (from DAVs to Adjs). The more abstract categories are expected to be mediated by semantic interrelations (i.e., conceptual similarity). Therefore, one would expect semantic similarity to account for an increasing amount of the covariance in the inferences from more abstract sentences; namely, covariations of likelihood judgments should be predictable from independent conceptual similarity judgments.

The resulting study consisted of a 3 × 3 (Target Persons × Situations) between-subjects factorial design for each of the linguistic categories. The items consisted of a series of behaviors (DAVs, IAVs, and SVs) and adjectives that subjects had to judge with respect to their relative likelihood of occurrence for a specific target person in a specific situation. Independently, conceptual similarity judgments between all the items of a given category were obtained.

Method

Participants. One hundred and five undergraduate students at the University of Sussex, Brighton, England, participated in this study on a paid voluntary basis. Fifteen were assigned to the conceptual similarity task and the remaining 90 were assigned randomly to the experimental conditions. They participated in small groups of 3 to 5 persons.

Overview. Each participant received one of nine booklets. Their task consisted of judging the characteristics and behaviors that a target person would manifest in a particular situation. The first independent variable was varied such that each booklet contained a specific reference to one of three situations (i.e., a seminar, a party, or a business deal). The description of the target person was varied orthogonally to the situation variable. The target person was described as either a prototypic extravert, a prototypic introvert, or a Machiavellian. The design was therefore a 3 × 3 between-subjects factorial involving three target person conditions and three situation conditions for each of the four linguistic categories. The items for the four linguistic categories were presented in a randomized order as 40 stimulus terms (10 for each of the four categories of DAVs, IAVs, SVs, and Adjs). There were 10 subjects per cell. The subjects' task consisted of judging the likeliness that the target person would manifest each of 30 behaviors and 10 adjectives in a given situation.

Procedure. All participants received a booklet. The cover page contained the general instructions for the experiment and described it as "an examination of the behaviors that people manifest in a situation and the characteristics they display." They were then provided with a description of the target person and a situation and were asked to judge the likelihood that the target person would manifest a particular set of behaviors and adjectives.

Manipulation of the target person. Participants were given one of three target person descriptions. A third of the subjects were presented with a description of a typical extravert, a third with that of a typical introvert, and the final third with that of a typical Machiavellian. The extravert and introvert descriptions of the target persons were taken from the Eysenck Personality Inventory (Eysenck & Eysenck, 1976) and the Machiavellian description from Christie and Geis (1970).

Manipulation of the situation. After receiving the general instructions and the description of the target person, subjects were provided with one of three situation conditions. Depending on their situation condition, subjects were asked to imagine the target person in either a seminar, party, or business deal situation.

Dependent measures. After receiving these instructions and descriptions, participants were asked to judge the likelihood that a target person would manifest each of a series of 30 behaviors and 10 adjectives in a specific situation. They used a 7-point scale with ends labeled *not at all frequently* (1) and *very frequently* (7).

The 30 behaviors consisted of 10 DAVs, 10 IAVs, and 10 SVs that were selected from the first study and were the 10 most discriminating members of their respective linguistic categories. The 10 Adjs were also extracted from the first study using the same criteria. (These items are marked with a dagger in Table 2.)

Conceptual similarity. Fifteen participants were presented with 180 pairwise combinations (45 for each linguistic category) in a random order over a monitor, with the following instructions:

> Your task in the following study consists in judging the similarity in meaning between pairs of words. For each pair you have to indicate how similar or dissimilar they are in meaning. For this task you have a 9-point scale at your disposal, where scale position 1 indicates *not at all similar* and the scale position 9 indicates *highly similar*.
>
> Please give your judgment for each pair by pressing the corresponding key on the keyboard.

Participants were then given instructions about how to use the keyboard.

TABLE 32.3. Correlations Between Co-Occurrences and Abstracted Semantic Relations

Situation	DAVs P1	DAVs P2	DAVs P3	IAVs P1	IAVs P2	IAVs P3	SVs P1	SVs P2	SVs P3	Adjs P1	Adjs P2	Adjs P3
S1	−.19	−.20	−.00	.50	.08	−.07	.14	.12	.22	.32	.50	.11
S2	.06	.20	.09	.05	.04	−.04	.54	.24	−.10	.72	.48	.11
S3	.34	.05	.10	.56	.10	−.05	.11	.22	.15	.36	.36	.43
r^a		.050			.142			.205			.392	

^{a}Z-transformed average rs for each 3 × 3 matrix.
Note, P1 = extravert target; P2 = Machiavellian target; and P3 = introvert target; S1 = seminar; S2 = party; and S3 = business deal. DAVs = descriptive action verbs; IAVs = interpretive action verbs; SVs = state verbs; and Adjs = adjectives.

Results

Conceptual similarity. The first hypothesis examined concerned the degree to which the usage of the linguistic categories was influenced by the conceptual interdependence between the items within each linguistic category. To examine this hypothesis, an independent Pearson product-moment correlation matrix (the interitem correlations of the likelihood ratings for the 10 stimulus items across the participants in each cell) was computed for each of the nine cells of the design separately for each linguistic category. The nine interitem correlation matrixes under each linguistic category were then correlated with the independently obtained conceptual similarity judgment matrixes for the respective linguistic categories (mean similarity between item pairs obtained on the basis of conceptual similarity judgments independently for each of the linguistic categories: DAVs, IAVs, SVs, and Adjs). This involves correlating interitem likelihood judgment rs, obtained separately for each cell of the 3 × 3 design, under each linguistic category, with interitem conceptual similarity. As can be seen in Table 3, the average correlation between the conceptual similarity matrix and the respective behavior (DAVs, IAVs, and SVs) and adjective (Adjs) increases as a linear function of linguistic category from .05 (DAVs) to .14 (IAVs) to .21 (SVs) to .39 (Adjs). This distinctive pattern supports the proposed relation; namely, that there is an increased reliance on mediation by abstract, semantic, or logical relations implied between the terms from DAVs to Adjs.[5]

The differential impact of the situation and person manipulations. To examine the differential sensitivity of the different linguistic categories to the orthogonally manipulated contextual variables in the design (namely, situation and target person), four multivariate analyses of variance

(MANOVAS) were conducted. The first analysis was carried out with the verbs under the DAV category. Our hypothesis suggests that DAVs should be affected by both context manipulations and their interaction. As expected, the multivariate main effect for the target person was significant, $F(20, 144) = 5.08, p < .001$, as well as the multivariate main effect for situations, $F(20, 144) = 1.91, p < .015$, and the Target Person × Situations interaction, $F(40, 274.87) = 1.98, p < .001$. The univariate effects suggest that for the target person factor, 7 of the 10 DAVs gave rise to significant main effects; for the situations factor, 3 of the 10 DAVs produced significant main effects; and, finally, 5 of the 10 interaction terms were significant.

In the case of IAVs our hypothesis suggests only a main effect for the target person manipulation. The MANOVA for IAVs revealed a significant multivariate main effect only for the target person factor, $F(20, 144) = 9.62, p < .001$, with a nonsignificant situations main effects, $F(20, 144) = F < 1$, and a nonsignificant interaction term, $F(40, 274.87) = 1.14$. An examination of the univariate main effects for the target person main effect revealed that all IAVs but one were significant (cf. Table 3).

In the MANOVA for SVs, a pattern similar to that for IAVs is obtained. There is only a significant multivariate main effect for the target person factor, $F(20, 144) = 9.94, p < .001$.

Finally, the MANOVA for Adjs revealed a sig-

---

[5]One might argue that the results in Table 3 are an artifact resulting from the fact that there is little variance in the pairwise similarity ratings for descriptive action verbs (DAVs) and that this variance increases from DAVs to adjectives (Adjs). The evidence does not support this. The respective variances of semantic similarity ratings for DAVs, interpretive action verbs, state verbs, and adjectives are the following: .71, 1.32, 1.35, and 1.01. None of the $F(9.9)$ values reach significance.

nificant multivariate main effect for target person, $F(20, 144) = 14.11$, $p < .001$, and the Target Person × Situations interaction was also significant, $F(40, 274.87) = 1.66$, $p < .01$. The situation main effect was nonsignificant ($F < 1$). All the univariate target person main effects were significant; in the case of the interaction, only two univariate effects reached significance.

The patterns obtained through these four multivariate and univariate analyses are in line with the predictions advanced, namely that DAVs are differentially sensitive to both properties of the target person and situation manipulations as well as to the interaction. The monotonic decline of this sensitivity for situations from IAVs to SVs to Adjs is not directly apparent from the multivariate and univariate analyses. To examine these particular relations, we used an additional statistic that allowed us to make specific comparisons and thus examine the hypotheses concerning the differential sensitivity of the four linguistic categories for the contextual parameters as manipulated by the target person and situation factors. This additional index is obtained by calculating the respective η^2 for the multivariate terms. Eta squared is a measure approximating the amount of variance explained (cf. Moosbrugger, 1978; Tatsuoka, 1971). A comparison of η^2 for the different terms of the multivariate analyses of each of the four linguistic categories allows us to examine the hypothesis more precisely. According to the hypotheses and the results from the pilot study and Study 1 we would expect the amount of variance explained through the target person multivariate main effect to increase from DAVs to Adjs. As can be seen in Table 4, this is the case. Furthermore, we would expect the amount of variance explained for the situations factor to decrease from DAVs to Adjs. This predicted relation is found for DAVs, IAVs, and SVs. In the case of Adjs we find that the amount of variance explained for the multivariate situation main effect is smaller than for DAVs but greater than in the case of IAVs and SVs. Thus, adjectives do not follow the predicted trend for the situation manipulation. Nevertheless, the overall pattern of η^2 differences is in general agreement with the predictions and with the findings of Study 1: With increasing abstractness from DAVs to Adjs, the inferences are increasingly dependent on characteristics of the target person, in line with their higher subject informativeness. Conversely, information about the situational context becomes

TABLE 32.4. Amount of Variance Explained by the Contextual Factors and Their Interaction

Factors	Amount of variance (%)			
	DAVs	IAVs	SVs	Adjs
Main Effects				
Target Person	65.7	81.7	82.4	88.6
Situations	37.6	21.2	14.2	22.1
Interaction				
Target Person × Situations	68.1	44.1	40.7	56.2

Note. DAVs = descriptive action verbs; IAVs = interpretive action verbs; SVs = state verbs; and Adjs = adjectives.

increasingly important as one moves from SV to IAV to DAV, in line with the higher situation informativeness of specific terms shown in Study 1. The perfect monotonicity of these trends is violated only by the unexpectedly high impact of situational factors on Adj sentences (22.12%). Although we lack a cogent explanation for this datum, there are three possible explanations for this finding. One possibility is that the 3:1 ratio of verbs to adjectives may have created a set (in some of the judges some of the time) to interpret sentences as actions rather than traits (e.g., interpreting *an extravert in a seminar being fair as an extravert acting fairly in a seminar*), thereby producing an η^2 for Adjs that is similar to IAVs. Alternatively, the single datum may simply be a result of chance fluctuations. One final and serious possibility emerges if one considers Rothbart and Park's (1986) study. This study shows quite clearly that there is a broad range of variation among adjectives with respect to the ease in imagining behaviors that confirm or disconfirm an adjective. That is, some adjectives appear to be more directly associated with concrete behaviors than others, and it is possible that this factor may have contributed to this unexpected finding.

Finally, it should be noted that the overall pattern obtained through the comparisons of the h^2 across these main effects runs in the opposite direction to the correlations obtained between the conceptual similarity matrixes and the co-occurrence matrixes for the situations factor, and in the same direction for the target person factor (cf. Table 3). This produces a pattern that is in general agreement with the predicted inverse relation between the increasingly decontextualized or abstracted reference from DAVs to Adjs and the decreasingly situated and contextual sensitivity in the reverse direction.

General Discussion

What are the implications of the semantic and psychological functions of the four most commonly used linguistic categories in the description of persons and their behaviors? One of the more immediate and obvious implications for social psychological and personality research concerns the relation between the type of research question addressed and the types of verbal instruments used as dependent variables. The differential sensitivity of these linguistic categories as qualitative and interpretive comments on behavior at one end of the continuum (the prototypical case being Adjs) or as concrete comments on the situational and personal parameters of ongoing action (the typical example being DAVs) has serious consequences for questionnaire construction. Our studies suggest that these different linguistic categories, in fulfilling different functions, direct observers' attention to different aspects of an ongoing episode. Whereas DAVs allow an observer to differentiate situational and personal parameters of ongoing action, this sensitivity decreases gradually from IAVs to Adjs. Although there is an increased sensitivity to person parameters, there is a qualitative difference in that the use of these terms gradually becomes governed more by abstract, logical, or semantic relations than by the specific contingencies of the situations. This is demonstrated in Study 2 by the increase in the amount of variance accounted for by semantic similarity from DAVs to Adjs. The concrete implication of this theoretical framework has been drawn out by Semin and Greenslade (1985) in relation to the systematic distortion hypothesis (e.g., Shweder, 1982). According to the systematic distortion hypothesis, in its most concisely stated form, "*inferences* about personality contain a systematic bias in that propositions about 'what is like what' are substituted for propositions about what is likely, and *memory* for personality relevant events contains a systematic bias in that attitudes, affects, and behaviors that are conceptually associated are recalled as if they covaried" (Shweder, 1982, p. 66). In this case, Semin and Greenslade were able to argue and show that the choice of linguistic category for ratings is the major factor contributing to systematic distortion. Thus, if subjects are asked to describe targets in terms of adjectives, then the patterns of co-occurrence between adjectives are largely accounted for by abstract relations existing in language, giving rise to results predicted by the systematic distortion hypothesis. However, the use of a mixture of DAVs and IAVs to describe persons' behaviors in situations from memory does not yield the hypothesized bias. Disregarding the role of such linguistic factors inevitably leads to a confusion between cognitive processes and the different functions that language fulfills in the description of persons and their behaviors.

In conclusion, it appears that although decontextualized linguistic forms are often immunized against disconfirmation and do not easily lend themselves to critical examinations, they nevertheless fulfill the functions of cognitive economy. If we were to avoid abstract linguistic forms in our communications and rely exclusively on concrete descriptive forms, then the obvious result would be a communication breakdown. This would also mean having to store all concrete references, which would lead to an insurmountable information overload for human memory. Additionally, the rules governing conversation require, as Grice (1975) pointed out, the cooperative principle. This involves (among other things) the requirement that in conversation the contribution be as informative as possible (maxim of quality) while not making it more informative than required (maxim of quantity). It should also be brief and orderly. This means that statements should not contain more information than necessary for comprehension. Thus, to the extent that senders and receivers share some background information, descriptive terms will be replaced by interpretive and decontextualized terms. One final conclusion that emerges in the light of these three studies is that in the examination of social cognitive processes, language as a mediator between social reality and social cognition needs to be more carefully considered than it has been to date.

ACKNOWLEDGMENTS

The writing of this article was facilitated through an ESRC (UK) Personal Grant, G 00 24 2033, to the first author.

Thanks are due to the anonymous reviewers whose detailed comments helped to improve the manuscript substantially.

REFERENCES

Abelson, R. P., & Kanouse, D. E. (1966). Subjective acceptance of verbal generalizations. In S. Feldman (Ed.), *Cognitive consistency: Motivational antecedents and behav-*

ioral consequents (pp. 171–197). New York: Academic Press.

Allport, G. W., & Odbert, H. S. (1936). Trait names: A psycho-lexical study. *Psychological Monographs, 47* (1, Whole No. 211).

Au, T. K. (1986). A verb is worth a thousand words: The causes and consequences of interpersonal events implicit in language. *Journal of Memory and Language, 25,* 104–122.

Brown, R., & Fish, D. (1983). The psychological causality implicit in language. *Cognition, 14,* 233–274.

Caramazza, A., Grober, E., Garvey, C., & Yates, J. (1977). Comprehension of anaphoric pronouns. *Journal of Verbal Learning and Verbal Behavior, 16,* 601–609.

Christie, R., & Geis, F. (1970). *Studies in Machiavellianism.* New York: Academic Press.

Clark, H. H. (1985). Language use and language users. In G. Lindzey & E. Aronson (Eds.), *Handbook of social psychology: Vol. 2* (3rd ed., pp. 179–232). New York: Random House.

Cunningham, J. D., & Kelley, H. H. (1975). Causal attributions for interpersonal events of varying magnitude. *Journal of Personality, 43,* 74–93.

Cunningham, J. D., Starr, P. A., & Kanouse, D. E. (1979). Self as actor, active observer, and passive observer: Implications for causal attributions. *Journal of Personality and Social Psychology, 37,* 1146–1152.

DiVitto, B., & McArthur, L. Z. (1978). Developmental differences in the use of distinctiveness, consensus, and consistency information for making causal attributions. *Developmental Psychology, 14,* 474–482.

Eysenck, H. J., & Eysenck, S. (1976). *Manual of the Eysenck Personality Inventory.* Sevenoaks, England: Hodder and Stoughton.

Farr, R. M., & Anderson, T. (1983). Beyond actor-observer differences in perspective: Extensions and applications. In M. Hewstone (Ed.), *Attribution theory* (pp. 45–64). Oxford, England: Blackwell.

Fiedler, K. (1978). Kausale und generalisierende Schlüsse aufgrund einfacher Sätze [Causal and generalizing inferences from simple sentences]. *Zeitschrift für Sozialpsychologie, 9,* 37–49.

Fiedler, K., & Semin, G. R. (in press). On the causal information conveyed by different interpersonal verbs: The role of implicit sentence context. *Social Cognition.*

Fillenbaum, S., & Rapaport, A. (1971). *Structures in subjective lexicon.* New York: Academic Press.

Fillmore, C. J. (1971). Verbs of judging: An exercise in semantic description. In C. J. Fillmore & D. T. Langendoen (Eds.), *Studies in linguistic semantics* (pp. 273–296). New York: Holt, Rinehart & Winston.

Fiske, S. T., & Taylor, S. E. (1984). *Social cognition.* Reading MA: Addison-Wesley.

Goldberg, L. R. (1977). *Language and personality: Developing a taxonomy of trait-descriptive terms.* Invited address at the Division of Evaluation and Measurement, 85th Annual Convention of the American Psychological Association, San Francisco.

Grice, H. P. (1975). Published in part as "Logic and conversation." In P. Cole & J. L. Morgan (Eds.), *Syntax and semantics: Vol. 3. Speech acts* (pp. 365–372). New York: Seminar Press.

Heider, F. (1958). *Psychology of interpersonal relations.* New York: Wiley.

Jones, E. E., & Nisbett, R. E. (1972). The actor and observer: Divergent perceptions of the causes of behavior. In E. E. Jones et al. (Eds.), *Attribution: Perceiving the causes of behavior.* Morristown, NJ: General Learning Press.

Kanouse, D. E. (1972). Language, labelling and attribution. In E. E. Jones et al. (Eds.), *Attribution: Perceiving the causes of behavior* (pp. 121–136). Morristown, NJ: General Learning Press.

Kelley, H. H. (1967). Attribution theory in social psychology. In Devine (Ed.), *Nebraska symposium on motivation* (Vol. 15). Lincoln: University of Nebraska Press.

Kelley, H. H. (1973). The processes of causal attribution. *American Psychologist, 28,* 107–128.

Kenny, A. (1963). *Action, emotion, and will.* New York: Humanities Press.

Kraut, R. E., & Higgins, E. T. (1984). Communication and social cognition. In R. S. Wyer, Jr., & T. K. Srull (Eds.), *Handbook of social cognition: Vol 3* (pp. 87–127). Hillsdale, NJ: Erlbaum.

Langenscheidt's Pocket Dictionary (1967). (45th ed.) Berlin: Langenscheidt.

Loftus, E. F. (1975). Leading questions and the eyewitness report. *Cognitive Psychology, 7,* 560–572.

Markus, H., & Zajonc, R. B. (1985). The cognitive perspective in social psychology. In G. Lindzey & E. Aronson (Eds.), *Handbook of social psychology: Vol. 2* (3rd ed., pp. 179–232). New York: Random House.

McArthur, L. (1972). The how and what of why: Some determinants and consequences of causal attribution. *Journal of Personality and Social Psychology, 22,* 171–193.

McGuire, W. J., McGuire, C. V., & Cheever, J. (1986). The self in society: Effects of social context on the sense of self [Special issue on the individual-society interface]. *British Journal of Social Psychology, 25,* 259–270.

Miller, G., & Johnson-Laird, P. (1976). *Language and perception.* Cambridge, England: Cambridge University Press.

Moosbrugger, H. (1978). *Multivariate statistische Analyseverfahren* [Methods of multivariate statistical analysis]. Stuttgart: Kohlhammer.

Norman, W. T. (1963). Toward an adequate taxonomy of personality attributes: Replicated factor structure in peer nomination personality ratings. *Journal of Abnormal and Social Psychology, 66,* 574–583.

Orvis, B. R., Cunningham, J. D., & Kelley, H. H. (1975). A closer examination of causal inference: The rules of consensus, distinctiveness, and consistency information. *Journal of Personality and Social Psychology, 32,* 605–616.

Ota, A. (1963). *Tense and aspect of present-day American English.* Tokyo: Kenkyushua.

Rosenberg, S., & Sedlak, A. (1972). Structural representations of implicit personality theory. In L. Berkowitz (Ed.), *Advances in experimental social psychology* (Vol. 6, pp. 235–297). New York: Academic Press.

Rothbart, M., & Park, B. (1986). On the confirmability and disconfirmability of trait concepts. *Journal of Personality and Social Psychology, 50,* 131–142.

Ruble, T. L. (1973). Effects of actor and observer roles on attribution of causality in situations of success and failure. *Journal of Social Psychology, 90,* 41–44.

Semin, G. R., & Greenslade, L. (1985). Differential contributions of linguistic factors to memory-based ratings: Systematizing the systematic distortion hypothesis. *Journal of Personality and Social Psychology, 49,* 1713–1723.

Shweder, R. A. (1982). Fact and artifact in trait perception: The systematic distortion hypothesis. In B. A. Maher & W. B. Maher (Eds.), *Progress in personality research* (Vol. 2, pp. 65–101). New York: Academic Press.

Tatsuoka, M. M. (1971). *Multivariate analysis*. New York: Wiley.

Wiggins, T. S. (1985). The interpersonal circle: A structural model for the integration of personality research. In R. Hogan (Ed.), *Perspectives in personality* (Vol. 1, pp. 1–47). New York: JAI Press.

Wyer, R. S., Jr., & Srull, T. K. (Eds.). (1984). *Handbook of social cognition. Vols. 1, 2, 3*. Hillsdale, NJ: Erlbaum.

Heuristic versus Systematic Information Processing and the Use of Source versus Message Cues in Persuasion

Shelly Chaiken • University of Toronto

Editors' Comments

The communication research discussed by Higgins (Reading 31) focused on how the attitudes of an audience can shape, albeit indirectly, the communicators' own attitudes. In such self-persuasion, it is as if the audience ended up "persuading" the source of the communication through the communicator's message being tailored to suit the audience's attitude. Typically, the situation is the reverse; it is the sources of messages who intend to persuade their audiences. The next two selections present models of how sources of messages persuade their audience. The present selection introduces the Heuristic Systematic Model (or HSM) of persuasion. The model assumes that there exist two distinct modes whereby persuasion may be accomplished—the heuristic mode and the systematic mode. In the heuristic mode, persuasion is accomplished by simple rules of thumb external to the message, such as the expertise of the source (the "experts are right" heuristic). In the systematic mode, persuasion is accomplished by a thorough processing of the contents of the message arguments themselves. The systematic mode is more likely to be used when the recipients' cognitive resources and motivation (e.g., involvement in the issue) are high, and the heuristic mode is more likely to take effect when the recipients' resources and motivation are low. The HSM is one of two dual-process models of persuasion that greatly influenced persuasion research over the last two decades. The other model, known as the ELM model (Petty & Cacioppo, 1986) is represented in the next selection.

Discussion Questions

1. What are the differences between a heuristic and a systematic strategy of processing information in a persuasive message?

2. What were the differences between the two experiments in Chaiken's study set? What were the reasons for these differences (i.e., what functions did each serve in testing the theory articulated by Chaiken)?

3. What checks did Chaiken include to ensure that her independent variables were manipulated as intended? What did these checks indicate?

4. In what ways do the two experiments reported by Chaiken (1980) provide convergent evidence for the author's main hypotheses?

Suggested Readings

Kelman, H. C. (1958). Compliance, identification, and internalization: Three processes of attitude change. *Journal of Conflict Resolution, 2,* 51–60.

McGuire, W. J. (1985). Attitudes and attitude change. In G. Lindzey & E. Aronson (Eds.), *Handbook of social psychology* (3rd ed., Vol. 2, pp. 233–346).

Chaiken, S., & Maheswaran, D. (1994). Heuristic processing can bias systematic processing: Effects of source credibility, argument ambiguity, and task importance on attitude judgment. *Journal of Personality and Social Psychology, 66,* 460–473.

Authors' Abstract

In Experiment 1, subjects read a persuasive message from a likable or unlikable communicator who presented six or two arguments concerning one of two topics. High response involvement subjects anticipated discussing the message topic at a future experimental session, whereas low involvement subjects anticipated discussing a different topic. For high involvement subjects, opinion change was significantly greater given six arguments but was unaffected by communicator likability. For low involvement subjects, opinion change was significantly greater given a likable communicator but was unaffected by the arguments manipulation. In Experiment 2, high issue involvement subjects showed slightly greater opinion change when exposed to five arguments from an unlikable (vs. one argument from a likable) communicator, whereas low involvement subjects exhibited significantly greater persuasion in response to one argument from a likable (vs. five arguments from an unlikable) communicator. These findings support the idea that high involvement leads message recipients to employ a systematic information processing strategy in which message-based cognitions mediate persuasion, whereas low involvement leads recipients to use a heuristic processing strategy in which simple decision rules mediate persuasion. Support was also obtained for the hypothesis that content-mediated (vs. source-mediated) opinion change would show greater persistence.

This research distinguishes between a systematic and a heuristic view of persuasion. Both conceptualizations regard message recipients as concerned with assessing the validity of the message's overall conclusion. According to a systematic view, recipients exert considerable cognitive effort in performing this task: They actively attempt to comprehend and evaluate the message's arguments as well as to assess their validity in relation to the message's conclusion. In contrast, according to a heuristic view of persuasion, recipients exert comparatively little effort in judging message validity: Rather than processing argumentation, recipients may rely on (typically) more accessible information such as the source's identity or other noncontent cues in deciding to accept a message's conclusion. In essence, a systematic view of persuasion emphasizes detailed processing of message content and the role of message-based cognitions in mediating opinion change, whereas a heuristic view de-emphasizes detailed information processing and focuses on the role of simple rules or cognitive heuristics in mediating persuasion.

When will recipients employ a systematic rather than heuristic processing strategy? A heuristic strategy has the economic advantage of requiring a minimum of cognitive effort. Certainly, judging message acceptability on the basis of noncontent cues is less effortful than receiving and analyzing persuasive argumentation. Countering this advantage, a heuristic strategy may be a less reliable means of judging message validity. In the long run, overreliance on simple decision rules may inflate Type 1 and Type 2 errors: Recipients may sometimes accept (reject) message conclusions they might otherwise have (correctly) rejected (accepted) had they invested the time and effort to receive and scrutinize argumentation. A functional perspective suggests that recipients will employ a systematic strategy when reliability concerns outweigh economic concerns, and a heuristic strategy when economic concerns predominate.

Reliability concerns should be paramount and a systematic strategy therefore employed when recipients perceive that it is important to formulate a highly accurate or veridical opinion judgment. Recipients are likely to hold such a perception under conditions of high "issue involvement" (Kiesler, Collins, & Miller, 1969) or high "response involvement" (Zimbardo, 1960). That is, when recipients receive messages on personally important topics or when recipients feel that their opinion judgements have important consequences for themselves (e.g., recipients may expect to discuss or defend their opinions, or to engage in behavior congruent with their expressed opinions) or for others (e.g., jurors' verdicts). When asked for an opinion on an unimportant topic or when one's opinion judgment is perceived as inconsequential, recipients may give economic concerns greater weight and employ a heuristic processing strategy.

This analysis has implications regarding the relative impact of source and message variables on persuasion. In the systematic view, recipients focus primarily on message content. Although source or other noncontent cues may sometimes be used as aids in assessing the validity of persuasive argumentation, such cues may be used in only a secondary manner. Thus, when recipients employ a systematic processing strategy, message characteristics (e.g., amount, comprehensibility, validity of persuasive argumentation) may exert a stronger impact on persuasion than source characteristics (e.g., credibility, likability). Conversely, in the heuristic view of persuasion, recipients avoid detailed processing of message content and instead rely on information such as the source's identity in judging message acceptability. Thus, when recipients employ a heuristic strategy, source characteristics may exert a greater impact on persuasion than message characteristics.

Consistent with the above reasoning, previous researchers have shown that source credibility significantly affects persuasion under conditions of low, but not high, issue involvement (Rhine & Severence, 1970) and response involvement (Johnson & Scileppi, 1969). Also, Petty and Capioppo (1979) recently found that a manipulation of argument strength had a greater persuasive impact when issue involvement was high. The present research systematically explored the utility of the systematic versus heuristic analysis of persuasion and its implications regarding the persuasive impact of source and message cues.

Experiment 1

Subjects read a persuasive message containing six or two arguments from a likable or unlikable communicator under conditions of high or low response involvement ("consequences"). It was expected that high involvement subjects would employ a systematic processing strategy and would therefore show greater opinion change in response to messages containing six arguments but would be unaffected by the likability manipulation. In contrast, it was expected that low involvement subjects would employ a heuristic strategy and would therefore express greater agreement with the likable communicator but would be unaffected by the arguments manipulation.

The experiment also explored opinion persistence. It was assumed that opinion change would persist to the extent that it was bolstered by topic-relevant cognitions. It was also assumed that recipients who adopted a belief on the basis of who the communicator was would possess fewer supportive cognitions than recipients who adopted a belief on the basis of what the communicator said. These assumptions led to the hypothesis that the presumably content-mediated (initial) opinion change manifested by high involvement subjects would show greater persistence than the presumably source-mediated opinion change manifested by low involvement subjects. To test this hypothesis, subjects' opinions were reassessed approximately 10 days after their laboratory participation.

Method

SUBJECTS

Subjects were 207 male and female University of Massachusetts undergraduates who participated for extra course credit in sessions containing up to six subjects. Nine subjects were eliminated because they suspected an influence attempt (three) or questioned the cover story (six). Data from 15 others were discarded because they were not administered the delayed opinion posttest (13), or because they associated the posttest with their laboratory participation (two). [1]

PROCEDURE

At the first (in actuality, the only) session of a "two-session experiment on opinions and group discussions," the experimenter explained that subjects would receive "discussion topics," give their opinions on these topics, and respond to another questionnaire. Subjects learned that at "the second session" they would be individually interviewed about their opinions on their assigned topics and then discuss their opinions in groups. After this introduction, each subject received a list of five topics and, via a sham random drawing, was assigned one of two topics (sleep habits or the trimester system) from this list.

Justifying the persuasive message, the experimenter stated that subjects would read an opinion interview conducted in a related study to "get an idea of what their own interview would be like." The experimenter noted that the related study had used the same topics but had employed university administrators and faculty, rather than undergradu-

ates, as subjects. Subjects then received an interview transcript (persuasive message, see below) to read. Afterwards, subjects completed a questionnaire that solicited their opinions on all five topics.

"As a second experimental focus" subjects next completed a questionnaire assessing their "reactions to the interview transcripts." This questionnaire contained the remaining dependent measures (see below). Finally, subjects were excused after being told that they would be scheduled for "Session 2" later in the semester.

Approximately 10 days later (mean delay = 10.39 days; range = 8–15 days), subjects were telephoned by an experimenter who was blind to experimental condition. Under the guise of conducting a campus opinion survey, the experimenter solicited subjects' agreement with various opinion statements, two of which corresponded to the positions advocated in the messages presented at the laboratory session. After probing for suspicion regarding the relationship between the posttest and the laboratory session, the experimenter thanked subjects for cooperating in the telephone survey. Subsequently, debriefing letters were mailed to all participants.

INTERVIEW TRANSCRIPTS

The transcripts began with an interview asking an interviewee (communicator) for background information. The communicator was portrayed as a male university administrator who worked with various student organizations. After praising or insulting undergraduates in response to a question from the interviewer, the communicator was asked for his opinion on his "assigned" topic (sleep habits or trimester system). The remainder of the transcript consisted of the communicator's statement of his overall position (see below) and his presentation of various supportive arguments.

INDEPENDENT VARIABLES

Perceived consequences. Response involvement, or perceived consequences, was manipulated by presenting subjects with a message on a topic iden-

---

[1]Including these 15 subjects in analyses performed on initial opinion change and other measures assessed at the laboratory session yielded findings virtually identical to those reported in the text.

tical to or different from the topic they were assigned to be interviewed on and discuss at the "second experimental session." Some subjects assigned to the sleep/trimester topic received a sleep/trimester message (high consequences), whereas others received a trimester/sleep message (low consequences).

Communicator likability. Likability was manipulated via the communicator's response to the interviewer's question, "How do you like working with undergraduates?" (cf. Eagly & Chaiken, 1975; Jones & Brehm, 1967). This response appears below. Phrases specific to the likable or the unlikable version are enclosed in parentheses or brackets, respectively.

> Well, as a matter of fact, I (really enjoy it a lot) [don't really enjoy it very much]. When I first started my job here at the university I was a little apprehensive about the idea of working so much with undergraduates. Over the years, (however, I've realized that my apprehension was unjustified) [I'm sorry to say, I think that my apprehension has been justified]. The undergraduates who I've met both in my work with various student organizations and in other settings as well, strike me as being pretty (responsible and mature) [irresponsible and immature]. They're really (concerned) [unconcerned], I think, with their role in society. I don't know, of course, but sometimes I think that the public too often (underestimates) [overestimates] the ability and maturity of today's college student. They (just don't give undergraduates enough credit) [give undergraduates more credit than they deserve]. Anyway, (it's no wonder that) [sometimes I wonder why] I continue to do the work I do. . . . For me, working with undergraduates (has been pretty) [really hasn't been very] rewarding.

Topic and position advocated. Two topics, sleep habits and the trimester system, were used. The positions advocated in the persuasive messages were "People should sleep much less than 8 hours per night," and "The university should switch from its two-semester system to a trimester system." Topics and positions were selected after pretesting with an additional 50 subjects who indicated their agreement with various opinion statements. The major selection criterion was that the two statements be counterattitudinal and have similar mean ratings on the 15-point agreement scale (Ms = 10.72 and 10.54 for sleep and trimester topics, respectively, where 1 signified strong agreement). Because of the study's focus on response involve-

ment (consequences) rather than issue involvement, an additional criterion required the topics to be rated similarly and not extremely on personal importance. The sleep and trimester topics were considered "neither important nor unimportant" (Ms = 8.07 and 7.34, respectively, on a 15-point scale) by pilot subjects (N = 22).

Number of arguments. Amount of persuasive argumentation was varied by preparing messages containing six or two supportive arguments. Two renditions of each message type were written. Each rendition of the longer message presented the same six arguments in a different (randomly selected) order. Each rendition of the shorter message contained two different arguments drawn randomly from the pool of six.

MEASURING INSTRUMENTS

Opinions. Immediately after message exposure, subjects indicated their agreement with the overall positions stated in the persuasive messages (see above) by marking 15-point scales anchored by *agree strongly* and *disagree strongly*. During the delayed telephone posttest, subjects indicated their agreement with similarly worded opinion statements by responding orally to 5-point scales anchored by *definitely agree* and *definitely disagree*.

Thoughts. On the questionnaire assessing their "reactions to the interview transcript," subjects were first given 3 minutes to list their "thoughts" about the communicator's statements. Thoughts were scored by two independent raters as message-oriented or communicator-oriented (M, C) and as positively, negatively, or neutrally valenced (+, −, 0). Examples of statements placed in each category along with interrater reliability coefficients (Pearson rs) are: M + (r = .86): "The economic advantages of the trimester agree with me"; M − (r = .88): "Reason for trimester not sound logically"; M 0 (r = .86): "He said REM (sleep) can be controlled"; C + (r = .82): "He was very polite"; C − (r = .82): "He was a little close-minded"; C 0 (r = .75): "Hesitant about talking about self." [2]

---

[2]Statements that could not be placed into any of the six categories were coded as "other thoughts" and were not analyzed. It should be noted that the present thought-scoring procedure parallels to a certain extent scoring procedures typically used by persuasion researchers (e.g., Osterhouse & Brock, 1970). Statements traditionally referred to as counterarguments and source derogations are, in the present scheme, termed negative message-oriented thoughts and negative

Source perception. Subjects next rated the communicator on 15-point bipolar adjective scales. Positive poles of the 12 scales used were warm, knowledgeable, modest, intelligent, approachable, competent, likable, trustworthy, pleasing, sincere, friendly, and unbiased.

Message comprehension. Next, subjects were asked to write down the message topic, its overall position, and each supportive argument that the communicator had presented. An argument was scored correct if in the opinion of two independent raters ($r = .86$) it accurately summarized an argument appearing in the message. All subjects recalled the message's topic and all but four (retained in the analyses) accurately specified its overall position.

Other measures. To measure the effort subjects expended processing message content, the experimenter covertly recorded the time each subject spent reading the interview transcript. On the last page of the reactions questionnaire, subjects rated the message topic's importance, their desire to be well informed on the topic, the effort they had spent reading the message, the relative amount of time they had spent thinking about the communicator's arguments (vs. his personal characteristics), and their interest in the communicator's arguments (all on 15-point scales). Subjects also indicated their age, sex, and assigned topics. In the laboratory, subjects wrote down their interpretations of the study; over the telephone, they were asked if they'd been in any similar opinion surveys. These responses were coded for suspicion.

Results

The design included two levels each of perceived consequences, communicator likability, number of arguments, message topic, subject sex, and message rendition (nested within levels of topic and number of arguments). Since preliminary analyses yielded few effects due to message rendition, all reported analyses ignored this variable. Of the

few sex and topic effects yielded by the reported analyses, only those relevant to the major hypotheses are presented here.

CHECK ON EXPERIMENTAL CONDITIONS

The communicator who praised (vs. insulted) undergraduates was judged more likable, $Ms = 4.22$ versus 8.83, $F(1, 151) = 125.14$, $p < .001$. Subjects recalled more persuasive arguments when the message contained six (vs. two) arguments, $Ms = 2.81$ versus 1.56, $F(1, 151) = 76.18$, $p < .001$. Finally, the consequences manipulation successfully induced the conditions thought necessary to foster systematic versus heuristic information processing: High (vs. low) consequences subjects expressed a greater desire to be well-informed on the message topic, $Ms = 6.24$ versus 7.05, $F(1, 151) = 3.69$, $p < .06$.

It is important to note that assignment to topics did not lead subjects to "strategically" shift their opinions (cf. Cialdini, Levy, Herman, Kozlowski, & Petty, 1976): Topic Assigned × Topic Received analyses of variance on subjects' initial and delayed opinions on the two topics yielded no significant effects due to topic assignment ($Fs < 1.0$). The topic-received main effect was significant on all four opinion measures ($ps < .05$), indicating that the persuasive messages successfully shifted subjects' opinions.

OPINIONS

Mean opinion change scores for the primary experimental conditions appear in Table 1.[3] Analysis on subjects' initial opinion change scores revealed main effects due to communicator likability,

---

communicator-oriented thoughts, respectively. Statements commonly referred to as supportive thoughts are, in the present scheme, termed positive message-oriented or communicator-oriented thoughts depending on whether they refer more to the message or more to the communicator. For each type of thought, each independent rater judged the number of such thoughts listed by each subject. Interrater reliability was calculated separately for each thought category by determining the correlation between the two raters' judgments.

---

[3] Initial opinions were measured on 15-point scales and delayed opinions on 5-point scales. For comparability, subjects' delayed opinion scores were transformed to 15-point scales (see Minium, 1970, p. 115). Opinion change scores were formed by subtracting the mean opinion expressed by an internal control group from each subject's (initial or delayed) opinion. All subjects receiving a sleep message formed an internal control group on the trimester topic for subjects reading a trimester message, and all subjects who received a trimester message served as internal controls on the sleep topic for subjects reading a sleep message. The opinions expressed by internal control subjects did not differ significantly from those expressed by an external control group of opinion-only pilot subjects: For the sleep topic, $M = 10.23$ versus $M = 10.72$ for internal and external controls, respectively, $t(137) = .80$; for the trimester topic, $M = 10.32$ versus $M = 10.54$ for internal and external controls, respectively, $t(142) = .34$.

TABLE 33.1. Initial and Delayed Opinion Change as a Function of Perceived Future Consequences. Communicator Likability, and Number of Arguments Presented: Experiment 1

	Likable communicator		Unlikable communicator	
Opinion change	Six arguments	Two arguments	Six arguments	Two arguments
High perceived consequences				
Initial	2.79	2.20	3.28	.48
Delayed	3.02	2.48	2.15	.94
Low perceived consequences				
Initial	3.16	1.98	1.41	.95
Delayed	2.53	.70	1.54	.47

Note. Cell ns range from 20 to 26.

$F(1, 151) = 4.16$, $p < .05$; number of arguments received, $F(1, 151) = 6.14$, $p < .05$; and message topic, $F(1, 151) = 4.56$, $p < .05$. Overall, greater initial change occurred given the likable (vs. unlikable) communicator ($Ms = 2.54$ vs. 1.51), six (vs. two) persuasive arguments ($Ms = 2.67$ vs. 1.47), and trimester (vs. sleep) messages ($Ms = 2.60$ vs. 1.59).

Planned comparisons on initial opinion change yielded findings supportive of the study's major hypothesis. As Figure 1 illustrates, high conse-

quences subjects showed greater initial opinion change in response to six (vs. two) arguments, $F(1, 151) = 4.62$, $p < .05$, but were unaffected by communicator likability, $F(1, 151) < 1.0$. In contrast, low consequences subjects showed greater initial opinion change given the likable (vs. unlikable) communicator, $F(1, 151) = 3.92$, $p < .05$, but were unaffected by the amount of argumentation provided, $F(1, 151) = 1.48$, ns. Although these results conformed to predictions, the differences between consequences conditions proved statistically weak on an overall basis. Of the interactions implied by the major hypothesis, neither the Consequences × Arguments nor Consequences × Likability interactions reached significance in the full analysis of variance ($ps = .24$ and .25, respectively), and the Consequences × Arguments × Likability interaction attained only marginal significance ($p < .10$).

To explore opinion persistence, a repeated measures analysis of variance employing time of posttest (initial vs. delayed) as an additional design factor was performed. A time of posttest main effect, $F(1, 151) = 3.96$, $p < .05$, revealed an overall trend for opinion change to dissipate over the 10-day posttest interval ($Ms = 2.07$ vs. 1.76).[4] The Time × Consequences × Likability interaction, $F(1,$

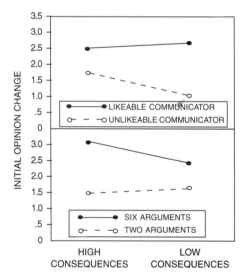

FIGURE 33.1 ■ Panel A depicts initial opinion change as a function of communicator likability and perceived consequences; Panel B depicts initial opinion change as a function of number of arguments presented and perceived consequences.

[4]Subjects' opinions were reassessed between 8 and 15 days after the initial posttest (mean delay = 10.39 days). Analysis of variance on days between posttest yielded no significant effects. Thus all experimental groups were subjected to approximately the same delay interval. Also, unless they were playing the role of "cooperative" subjects to the hilt, the low rate of suspicion or innocent mention of their earlier laboratory experience expressed by subjects during the "telephone opinion survey" suggested that the experiment had been successful in divorcing the context of the delayed posttest from the context of the initial opinion posttest.

151) = 4.00, $p < .05$, showed a data pattern roughly in accord with the hypothesis that greater persistence would be shown by high consequences subjects. Regardless of communicator likability, the opinion change manifested by high consequences subjects remained relatively stable between posttests: Ms = 2.48 versus 2.78, $F < 1.0$, for likable communicator; Ms = 1.88 versus 1.54, $F < 1.0$, for unlikable communicator. In contrast, opinion change declined significantly for low consequences subjects exposed to the likable communicator, Ms = 2.59 versus 1.65, $F(1, 151) = 7.24$, $p < .01$, although not for those exposed to the unlikable communicator, Ms = 1.18 versus 1.00, $F < 1.0$. The nonsignificant decrement in the latter condition probably reflects the fact that initial change in this cell was low and only marginally greater than zero, $t(43) = 1.99$, $p < .10$.

Paralleling the initial opinion change findings, the repeated measures analysis also yielded between-subjects effects due to likability ($p < .05$), arguments ($p < .05$), and a marginal effect due to message topic ($p < .10$). In addition, a Consequences × Likability × Arguments × Topic interaction ($p < .05$) was obtained. This interaction indicated that the primary experimental variables exerted a stronger impact on opinions within trimester (vs. sleep) message conditions even though the patterning of opinion change means was generally consistent within both topics.

COMPREHENSION AND THOUGHTS

In addition to the manipulation check noted earlier, the analysis on argument recall yielded a consequences effect ($p < .005$) and a Consequences × Arguments interaction ($p < .05$). Overall, high (vs. low) consequences subjects recalled more arguments (Ms = 2.40 vs. 1.98), and this difference was most pronounced given six persuasive arguments. Subjects reading trimester (vs. sleep) messages also recalled more arguments ($p < .001$).

Analyses were performed on each type of thought emitted by subjects (M +, M –, M 0, C +, C –, C 0) and also on three derived indices: Message-oriented minus communicator-oriented thoughts (regardless of valence), positive minus negative thoughts (regardless of orientation), and total thoughts expressed. For brevity, only the analyses on the derived indices are reported. Relatively more message-oriented than communicator-oriented thoughts were expressed by high (vs. low)

consequences subjects ($p = .06$), and also by subjects exposed to six (vs. two) arguments ($p < .005$) and the likable (vs. unlikable) communicator ($p < .005$). A likability effect on positive minus negative thoughts ($p < .001$) indicated that the likable communicator elicited more positive than negative thoughts, whereas the unlikable communicator elicited more negative thoughts. No effects obtained on total thoughts expressed.

SOURCE PERCEPTION

A factor analysis (varimax rotation) of the source ratings yielded two rotated factors, labeled *attractiveness* (e.g., warm, likable, friendly) and *expertise* (e.g., knowledgeable, intelligent, competent). These factors accounted for 55.8% and 10.2% of the variance, respectively. Factor scores were computed for each subject and treated by analysis of variance. The trustworthy, sincere, and unbiased scales, which loaded highly on neither factor, were analyzed separately. These analyses revealed that the likable (vs. unlikable) communicator was viewed as more attractive, expert, trustworthy, sincere, and unbiased ($ps < .005$).

Other Dependent Variables

High (vs. low) consequences subjects spent more time reading the persuasive message ($p < .005$) and reported spending more time thinking about the communicator's arguments than his personal characteristics ($p < .01$). Subjects exposed to six (vs. two) persuasive arguments also took longer to read the message ($p < .001$), spent more time thinking about the communicator's arguments ($p < .001$), expressed a greater desire to be well informed on the topic ($p < .005$), reported exerting greater effort reading the message ($p < .05$), and rated the topic as being more important ($p < .001$).

Correlational Analyses

Correlational analyses provided further information regarding the cognitive mediation of initial opinion change. Correlations between opinion change and perceptions of the communicator (source ratings, positive and negative communicator-oriented thoughts) were generally low and nonsignificant, with the exception of perceived expertise, which correlated positively with opinion change within both low and high consequences conditions ($r = .29$, $p < .005$, and $r = .25$, $p < .05$, respectively). As anticipated by the systematic versus heuristic analysis of persuasion, argument recall and both positive and negative message-oriented thoughts were significantly correlated with initial opinion change within high consequences conditions (recall: $r = .26$, $p < .05$; M +: $r = .41$, $p < .001$; M –: $r = -.32$, $p < .001$), but only negligibly related within low consequences conditions (recall: $r = .06$; M +: $r = .20$, $p < .10$; M–: $r = -.16$, $p < .15$).

Multiple regression analyses using initial opinion change as the criterion variable were also performed.[5] Within high consequences conditions, greater initial opinion change was predicted primarily by a greater number of both positive message-oriented thoughts ($p < .05$) and positive communicator-oriented thoughts ($p = .07$), fewer negative message-oriented thoughts ($p = .10$), and greater argument recall ($p = .11$). Within low consequences conditions, variables that significantly or marginally predicted greater initial opinion change included heightened perceptions of communicator expertise ($p < .05$) and a greater number of positive communicator-oriented thoughts ($p = .06$).

Experiment 2

A conceptual replication of the first experiment was conducted in order to extend the generality of the systematic versus heuristic analysis. This study included only the most theoretically interesting combinations of the arguments and likability variables and manipulated issue involvement ("personal relevance") rather than response involvement. In the 2×2 design of Experiment 2, subjects read a message consisting of either five persuasive arguments from an unlikable communicator or one persuasive argument from a likable communicator under conditions of either high or low personal relevance. It was predicted that subjects in high personal relevance conditions would be more persuaded by five arguments from an unlikable communicator than by one argument from a likable communicator. Conversely, low personal relevance subjects were expected to show greater opinion change in the one-argument/likable-communicator condition than in the five-arguments/unlikable-communicator condition. Experiment 2 did not examine opinion persistence and did not

include the full set of dependent measures employed in Experiment 1.

Method

SUBJECTS

Subjects were 80 University of Toronto undergraduates enrolled in the author's introductory psychology course who volunteered to remain after class one evening to participate in an "impression formation" experiment.

PROCEDURE

Each subject received one of four versions (representing the four experimental conditions) of an experimental booklet. The instructions printed on the cover page informed subjects that they would record their impressions of a "target speaker" after first reading a "partial transcript of an interview with the target" and a "transcript of a speech made by the target."

Communicator likability. The first page of the booklet presented the "interview transcript." The target speaker (communicator) was portrayed as a University of Toronto (U of T) administrator who had previously held a similar position at the University of British Columbia (UBC). Similar to the device employed in Experiment 1, the communicator's likability or unlikability was conveyed via his response to the interviewer's question, "By the way, how do you like U of T compared to UBC?" In essence, the likable communicator responded by praising U of T students and faculty and extolling the virtues of living in Toronto (at the expense of UBC and Vancouver), whereas the unlikable communicator responded by derogating U of T students and faculty and the city of Toronto (to the benefit of UBC and Vancouver).

Personal relevance of message topic. The next page of the booklet informed subjects that they would read a transcript of the "target's speech on

---

[5]Two (regular) multiple regression analyses were performed, one employing data from high consequence subjects ($n = 89$) and one using data from low consequences subjects ($n = 94$). Both analyses employed the following predictor variables: age, time spent reading the message, self-reported time spent thinking about the communicator's argumentation (vs. personal characteristics), attractiveness factor scores, expertise factor scores, arguments recalled, positive and negative communicator-oriented thoughts, and positive and negative message-oriented thoughts.

the issue of switching from a two-semester to a trimester system at the university." It was stated that the speech had been presented to a university committee charged with studying the issue. High (vs. low) personal relevance was manipulated by stating that, if the Committee approved a switch, the university would adopt the trimester system in the 1981 (vs. 1985) academic year.

Persuasive message. The last page of the booklet contained the persuasive message, whose overall position stated that "the University of Toronto should switch from its current two-term system to a trimester system." Opinion data from an independent group of control subjects ($N = 125$) indicated that U of T undergraduates disagreed moderately with this position ($M = 10.33$ on a 15-point scale on which 15 signified extreme disagreement). In the message, the communicator first stated his overall position and, if portrayed earlier as unlikable, provided five arguments supporting this position. If the communicator had been portrayed as likable, he presented only one supportive argument (drawn randomly from the pool of five arguments). Both messages ended with the communicator restating his overall position on the message topic.

Dependent measures. After examining their experimental booklets, subjects were given a one-page questionnaire. Subjects first wrote down the communicator's overall position (all subjects satisfactorily recalled the position) and then indicated their agreement with this position by marking a 15-point scale anchored by *strongly disagree* and *strongly agree*. Next, subjects rated the communicator on the following 15-point bipolar adjective scales: warm–cold, likable–unlikable, friendly–unfriendly, and sincere–insincere. On 15-point scales, subjects next indicated how personally relevant they considered the message topic to be, the relative amount of time they had spent thinking about the communicator's arguments (vs. personal characteristics), and the extent to which they typically agreed (disagreed) with people they liked (disliked). Subjects also indicated their sex and wrote down their interpretations of the experiment. Three subjects (retained in the analyses) were assessed as being suspicious of an influence attempt (two) or the cover story (one).

Results

The design included two levels each of subject sex, personal relevance of message topic, and source–

argument pairing (unlikable communicator–five arguments vs. likable communicator–one argument). Since preliminary analyses revealed no sex differences, subject sex was ignored in the reported analyses.

CHECK ON EXPERIMENTAL CONDITIONS

Subjects informed that the university planned to adopt the trimester (if approved) in 1981 (vs. 1985) judged the trimester issue to be significantly more personally relevant: $Ms = 5.58$ versus 7.42, $F(1, 76) = 5.62, p < .025$. No other effects were significant on this measure. The only significant effect on subjects' likableness ratings was due to the source–argument pairing variable, $F(1, 76) = 10.11, p < .005$: The communicator who praised (vs. insulted) U of T students and faculty and complimented (vs. derogated) Toronto was regarded as more likable ($Ms = 5.82$ vs. 7.75).

OPINION CHANGE

Opinion change scores (see Table 2) were formed by subtracting the mean opinion of the control group from each subject's opinion. As expected, the Relevance × Source–Argument Pairing interaction proved significant on these scores, $F(1, 76) = 4.30, p < .05$. Within low personal relevance conditions, significantly greater opinion change occurred among subjects in the likable-communicator/one-argument condition than in the unlikable-communicator/five-arguments condition, $F(1, 76) = 4.52, p < .05$. Within high relevance conditions, nonsignificantly greater opinion change oc-

TABLE 33.2. Mean Opinion Change and Use of the Liking Agreement Rule as a Function of Personal Relevance and Source Argument Pairing: Experiment 2

Dependent variable	Unlikable/ five arguments	Likable/ one argument
High relevance		
Opinion change	3.73	2.78
Use of liking/ agreement rule	7.25	10.30
Low relevance		
Opinion change	2.18	4.68
Use of liking/ agreement rule	8.75	8.95

Note. Higher numbers indicate greater opinion change and greater use of the liking/agreement rule. Cell $ns = 20$.

curred among subjects in the unlikable-communicator/five-arguments (vs. likable/one-argument) condition, $F < 1.0$. No other effects were significant on opinion change.

Other measures. The likable communicator (who presented one argument), compared to the unlikable communicator (who presented five arguments), was viewed as more likable ($p < .005$), warmer ($p < .005$), and friendlier ($p < .001$), but as less sincere ($p < .05$). No other effects were significant on these ratings.

It had been expected that low relevance subjects would report greater use of the liking/agreement rule. Although the means were in the expected direction, the relevance effect proved nonsignificant ($F < 1.0$) on subjects' reports of the extent to which they typically agreed (disagreed) with people they liked (disliked).[6] Analysis of this measure (see Table 2 for means) did yield a source–argument pairing effect ($p < .025$), and more interestingly, a Relevance × Source–Argument Pairing interaction ($p < .05$). The first effect indicates greater reported use of the liking/agreement rule among subjects in likable-communicator/one-argument (vs. unlikable/five-arguments) conditions. The interaction indicates that among subjects exposed to five arguments from an unlikable communicator, greater use of the liking/agreement rule was, as expected, reported by subjects within low relevance conditions. However, among subjects receiving only one argument from a likable communicator, those within high personal relevance conditions reported greater use of this heuristic.

No significant effects were obtained on subjects' ratings of the amount of time they had spent thinking about the communicator's arguments versus his personal characteristics.

Discussion

The systematic versus heuristic analysis of persuasion suggests that high levels of response or issue involvement lead message recipients to employ a systematic information processing strategy in forming their opinion judgments, whereas low levels of involvement lead recipients to employ a more economic heuristic strategy. Based on the assumption that systematic processing maximizes the persuasive impact of message cues and minimizes the impact of noncontent cues and that heuristic processing minimizes the persuasive impact

of message cues and maximizes the impact of noncontent cues, it was hypothesized that the initial opinion judgments of high involvement subjects would be more strongly influenced by the amount of argumentation provided in the message than by the communicator's likability, whereas the reverse would be true for low involvement subjects.

The two experiments provided converging evidence for this hypothesis. In the first study, high consequences subjects exhibited significantly greater initial opinion change in response to messages containing six arguments but were unaffected by the communicator's likability. Conversely, low consequences subjects exhibited significantly greater opinion change in response to the likable communicator but were unaffected by the amount of argumentation provided. In Experiment 2, subjects for whom the message topic was high in personal relevance showed slightly greater opinion change when receiving five arguments from an unlikable communicator than when receiving one argument from a likable source. In contrast, subjects for whom the topic was low in personal relevance exhibited significantly greater opinion change when they received one argument from a likable (vs. five arguments from an unlikable) communicator.

Analyses on the supplementary measures included in Experiment 1 yielded additional support for the assumptions underlying the major hypothesis. The fact that high consequences subjects expressed a greater desire to be well informed on the message topic corroborated the assumption that the consequences manipulation would engender differing levels of motivation for in depth information processing. The data were also generally

---

[6]Because this item appears to ask for self-reported use of the liking/agreement heuristic over an extended period of time, it is quite reasonable to argue that subjects' responses would not necessarily be affected by their present level of involvement (indeed, the results on this item conformed only partially to predictions). The rationale for including this item and thinking that it might reflect high and low involvement subjects' differential use of the liking/agreement rule is similar to the logic underlying Bem's (1972) self-perception hypothesis. Just as we might expect a person's presumably stable self-description of how honest he or she is typically to be influenced by a recent and salient honest (or dishonest) behavior on his or her part, it was expected that subjects' self-reports of their typical use of the liking/agreement heuristic would be influenced by whether or not they had just employed this rule in making their opinion judgments.

consistent with the assumption that these differ-ing motivational sets would lead high conse-quences subjects to employ a systematic process-ing strategy in which message-based cognitions would primarily mediate opinion change and would lead low consequences subjects to employ a heuristic strategy in which their perceptions of the communicator would primarily mediate per-suasion. High, compared to low, consequences subjects spent more time reading the persuasive message, reported spending more time thinking about the communicator's argumentation (vs. his personal characteristics), recalled more arguments, and generated relatively more message-oriented (vs. communicator-oriented) thoughts. Further, correlational analyses revealed that argument re-call, positive message-oriented thoughts, and nega-tive message-oriented thoughts were significantly correlated with and relatively good predictors of initial opinion change ($ps < .11$) for high conse-quences subjects. In contrast, these variables were negligibly correlated with and poor predictors of initial opinion change ($ps > .28$) for low conse-quences subjects. Finally, although perceptions of communicator expertise were significantly corre-lated with opinion change within both conse-quences conditions, perceived expertise proved to be a significant predictor of initial opinion change for low consequences ($p < .05$), but not high con-sequences ($p > .31$), subjects.

PERSISTENCE OF OPINION CHANGE

As noted previously, Experiment 1 provided ad-equate support for the assumption that message-based cognitions would primarily mediate initial opinion change within high consequences condi-tions, whereas source-oriented cognitions would primarily mediate opinion change within low con-sequences conditions. This assumption led to the hypothesis that greater opinion persistence would be manifested by high consequences subjects. In accord with this hypothesis, opinion change re-mained relatively stable over time within high con-sequences conditions but dissipated within low consequences conditions, although the decrease was significant only for low consequences sub-jects exposed to the likable communicator. The failure to detect a significant decrement within the low consequences/unlikable communicator con-dition is understandable, since initial change in this cell was not reliably different from zero, presum-ably because subjects used the communicator's unlikability as a discounting cue.

INVOLVEMENT AND PERSUASION

Finally, the current research has implications for understanding the impact of involvement on opin-ion change and opinion persistence. The fact that involvement exerted no main effect on initial opin-ion change in either experiment, as well as some recent demonstrations that greater involvement sometimes facilitates persuasion (e.g., Pallak, Mueller, Dollar, & Pallak, 1972; Petty & Cacioppo, 1979), contradicts earlier theorizing (e.g., Sherif, Sherif, & Nebergall, 1965; Triandis, 1971) and research (Miller, 1965; Sherif & Hovland, 1961) suggesting that greater involvement typically low-ers message persuasiveness. The systematic ver-sus heuristic analysis, which argues that greater involvement heightens recipients' tendencies to scrutinize message content, suggests that high in-volvement can both facilitate and inhibit persua-sion depending on the quality of persuasive argu-mentation. Indeed, Petty and Cacioppo (1979) recently found that involvement heightened per-suasion when a message contained strong argu-ments but inhibited persuasion when the message presented weak arguments. On the other hand, the finding in Experiment 1 that high consequences subjects showed relatively greater opinion stabil-ity suggests, in accord with previous correlational evidence (Watts, 1967), that opinion change in-duced under high involvement conditions results in greater persistence. This greater persistence pre-sumably occurs because high involvement fosters in depth processing of message content, which leads recipients to possess more topic-relevant cognitive supports for their adopted opinions.

ACKNOWLEDGMENTS

This article is based on a dissertation submitted in partial fulfillment of the doctoral requirements at the University of Massachusetts–Amherst. The author is grateful to Alice H. Eagly and Icek Ajzen for their counsel and to John W. Fee III and John Keenan, who served as experimenters in Experiment 1. John Bassili, Alice H. Eagly, Johnathan L. Freedman, Melvin Manis, and Wendy Wood provided helpful comments on earlier drafts of this manuscript. A report on Experiment 1 was presented at the meeting of the American Psychological Association, Toronto, Canada, August 1978. Experiment 2 was partially funded by a grant from the Humanities and Social Sciences Committee of the Research Board of the University of Toronto.

REFERENCE NOTE

1. Cook, T. D., & Gruder, C. L. *The sleeper effect predicted from the discounting cue hypothesis: A living phenomenon.* Unpublished manuscript, Northwestern University, 1979.

REFERENCES

Abelson, R. P. Script processing in attitude formation and decision making. In J. S. Carroll & J. W. Payne, *Cognition and social behavior.* Hillsdale, N. J.: Erlbaum, 1976.

Bem, D. J. Self-perception theory. In L. Berkowitz (Ed.), *Advances in experimental social psychology* (Vol. 6). New York: Academic Press, 1972.

Chaiken, S. *The use of source versus message cues in persuasion: An information processing analysis.* Unpublished doctoral dissertation. University of Massachusetts–Amherst, 1978.

Chaiken, S., & Eagly, A. H. Communication modality as a determinant of message persuasiveness and message comprehension. *Journal of Personality and Social Psychology,* 1976, 34, 605–614.

Cialdini, R. B., Levy, A., Herman, P., Kozlowski, L. T., & Petty, R. E. Elastic shifts of opinion: Determinants of direction and durability. *Journal of Personality and Social Psychology,* 1976, 34, 663–672.

Eagly, A. H. Comprehensibility of persuasive arguments as a determinant of opinion change. *Journal of Personality and Social Psychology,* 1974, 29, 758–773.

Eagly, A. H., & Chaiken, S. An attribution analysis of the effects of communicator characteristics on opinion change: The case of communicator attractiveness. *Journal of Personality and Social Psychology,* 1975, 32, 136–144.

Eagly, A. H., & Warren, R. Intelligence, comprehension, and opinion change. *Journal of Personality,* 1976, 44, 226–242.

Giesen, M., & Hendrick, C. Effects of false positive and negative arousal feedback on persuasion. *Journal of Personality and Social Psychology,* 1974, 30, 449–457.

Hendrick, C., & Giesen, M. Self-attribution of attitude as a function of belief feedback. *Memory and Cognition,* 1976, 4, 150–155.

Hovland, C. I., Janis, I. L., & Kelley, H. H. *Communication and persuasion.* New Haven, Conn.: Yale University Press, 1953.

Hovland, C. I., Lumsdaine, A. A., & Sheffield, F. D. *Experiments on mass communication.* Princeton, N. J.: Princeton University Press, 1949.

Johnson, H. H., & Scileppi, J. A. Effects of ego-involvement conditions on attitude change to high and low credibility communicators. *Journal of Personality and Social Psychology,* 1969, 13, 31–36.

Jones, R. A., & Brehm, J. W. Attitudinal effects of communicator attractiveness when one chooses to listen. *Journal of Personality and Social Psychology,* 1967, 6, 64–70.

Kiesler, C., Collins, B., & Miller, N. *Attitude change.* New York: Wiley, 1969.

Landy, D. The effects of an overheard audience's reaction and attractiveness on opinion change. *Journal of Experimental Social Psychology,* 1972, 8, 276–288.

McCroskey, J. C. A summary of experimental research on the effects of evidence in persuasive communication. *Quarterly Journal of Speech,* 1969, 55, 169–176.

McGuire, W. J. Personality and susceptibility to social influence. In E. F. Borgatta & W. W. Lambert (Eds.), *Handbook of personality theory and research.* Chicago: Rand McNally, 1968.

McGuire, W. J. The nature of attitudes and attitude change. In G. Lindzey & E. Aronson (Eds.), *The handbook of social psychology* (2nd ed., Vol. 3). Reading, Mass.: Addison-Wesley, 1969.

Miller, N. Involvement and dogmatism as inhibitors of attitude change. *Journal of Experimental Social Psychology,* 1965, 1, 121–132.

Miller, N., Maruyama, G., Beaber, R. J., & Valone, K. Speed of speech and persuasion. *Journal of Personality and Social Psychology,* 1976, 34, 615–624.

Minium, E. W. *Statistical reasoning in psychology and education.* New York: Wiley, 1970.

Mintz, P. M., & Mills, J. Effects of arousal and information about its source upon attitude change. *Journal of Experimental Social Psychology,* 1971, 7, 561–570.

Norman, R. When what is said is important: A comparison of expert and attractive sources. *Journal of Experimental Social Psychology,* 1976, 12, 294–300.

Osterhouse, R. A., & Brock, T. C. Distraction increases yielding to propaganda by inhibiting counterarguing. *Journal of Personality and Social Psychology,* 1970, 15, 344–358.

Pallak, M. S., Mueller, M., Dollar, K., & Pallak, J. Effect of commitment on responsiveness to an extreme consonant communication. *Journal of Personality and Social Psychology,* 1972, 23, 429–436.

Petty, R. E., & Cacioppo, J. T. Issue involvement can increase or decrease persuasion by enhancing message-relevant cognitive responses. *Journal of Personality and Social Psychology,* 1979, 37, 1915–1926.

Petty, R. E., Wells, G. L., & Brock, T. C. Distraction can enhance or reduce yielding to propaganda: Thought disruption versus justification. *Journal of Personality and Social Psychology,* 1976, 34, 874–884.

Rhine, R. J., & Severence, L. J. Ego-involvement, discrepancy, source credibility, and attitude change. *Journal of Personality and Social Psychology,* 1970, 16, 175–190.

Sherif, M., & Hovland, C. I. *Social judgment.* New Haven, Conn.: Yale University Press, 1961.

Sherif, C. W., Sherif, M., & Nebergall, R. E. *Attitude and attitude change.* Philadelphia, Pa.: Saunders, 1965.

Silverthorne, C. P., & Mazmanian, L. The effects of heckling and media of presentation on the impact of a persuasive communication. *Journal of Social Psychology,* 1975, 96, 229–236.

Snyder, M., & Rothbart, M. Communicator attractiveness and opinion change. *Canadian Journal of Behavioral Science,* 1971, 3, 377–387.

Stotland, E., & Canon, L. K. *Social psychology: A cognitive approach.* Philadelphia, Pa.: Saunders, 1972.

Triandis, H. *Attitude and attitude change.* New York: Wiley, 1971.

Watts, W. A. Relative persistence of opinion change induced by active compared to passive participation. *Journal of Personality and Social Psychology,* 1967, 5, 4–15.

Zimbardo, P. G. Involvement and communication discrepancy as determinants of opinion conformity. *Journal of Abnormal and Social Psychology,* 1960, 60, 86–94.

READING 34

Personal Involvement as a Determinant of Argument-Based Persuasion

Richard E. Petty • University of Missouri—Columbia
John T. Cacioppo • University of Iowa
Rachel Goldman • University of Missouri—Columbia

Editors' Notes

This selection presents a study conducted from the perspective of Richard Petty's and John Cacioppo's Elaboration Likelihood Model (ELM). Note the similarities between this selection and the preceding one. Both represent dual-process models whereby persuasion is accomplished via two qualitatively separate routes. (Compare them to Reading 13's presentation of a dual-process model of dispositional attributions.) Note also that one of the routes is likely to be taken under conditions where the recipient has limited motivation or cognitive capacity to process information (i.e., under low elaboration likelihood conditions), whereas the other route is more likely to mediate persuasion under high motivation and capacity (i.e., under high elaboration likelihood conditions). Note also the similarity in the experimental manipulations featured in this selection and the previous selection. In both cases, one of the independent variables involves a source characteristic (likeability in the previous selection; expertise in this selection) and a second independent variable involves a manipulation of a message characteristic (number of arguments in the preceding selection; quality of arguments in this selection). Nonetheless, the models differ in the concepts they employ to characterize the two modes whereby persuasion is accomplished. Chaiken's HSM distinguishes between heuristic and systematic processing modes, whereas Petty and Cacioppo's ELM distinguishes between peripheral and central routes to persuasion.

Discussion Questions

1. How do the authors conceptualize the difference between the central and the peripheral routes to persuasion?

2. According to the authors, why doesn't research by Chaiken (1980) provide definitive evidence for the existence of two routes to persuasion? What is the contribution of their study in this regard?

3. What were the main findings of the study? How do they fit with the ELM formulation?

4. According to the authors, what are two reasons why an increase in recipients' involvement might be associated with an increase in the importance of message arguments in persuasion?

Suggested Readings

Petty, R. E., & Cacioppo, J. T. (1986). The elaboration likelihood model of persuasion. In L. Berkowitz (Ed.), *Advances in experimental social psychology* (Vol. 19, pp. 123–205). San Diego. CA: Academic Press.

Cacioppo, J. T., & Petty, R. E. (1982). The need for cognition. *Journal of Personality and Social Psychology, 42,* 116–131.

Hovland, C. I., Harvey, O. J., & Sherif, M. (1957). Assimilation and contrast effects in reactions to communication and attitude change. *Journal of Abnormal and Social Psychology, 55,* 244–252.

Authors' Abstract

It was suggested that there are two basic routes to persuasion. One route is based on the thoughtful consideration of arguments central to the issue, whereas the other is based on peripheral cues in the persuasion situation. To test this view undergraduates expressed their attitudes on an issue after exposure to a counterattitudinal advocacy containing either strong or weak arguments that emanated from a source of either high or low expertise. For some subjects, the communication was high in personal relevance, whereas for others it was low. Interactions of the personal relevance manipulation with the argument quality and expertise manipulations revealed that under high relevance, attitudes were influenced primarily by the quality of the arguments in the message, whereas under low relevance, attitudes were influenced primarily by the expertise of the source. This suggests that the personal relevance of an issue is one determinant of the route to persuasion that will be followed.

In a recent review of the numerous approaches to attitude change that have developed over the past 35 years, Petty and Cacioppo (1981) suggested that these many approaches could be seen as proposing two distinct routes to persuasion. One, called the *central route*, views attitude change as resulting from a diligent consideration of issue-relevant arguments. The approaches that fall under this route have emphasized such factors as the comprehension, learning, and retention of message arguments (e.g., Eagly, 1974; McGuire, 1968; Miller & Campbell, 1959); the self-generation of arguments (e.g., Cacioppo & Petty, 1979a; Greenwald, 1968; Tesser, 1978; Vinokur & Burnstein, 1974); and the combination and integration of issue-relevant arguments into an overall evaluative reaction (e.g., Anderson, 1971; Fishbein & Ajzen, 1975; Wyer, 1974).

In contrast to this focus on the arguments central to the issue under consideration, a second group of approaches to persuasion has developed that emphasizes a more *peripheral route* to attitude change (Petty & Cacioppo, 1981). Under this second view, attitudes change because the attitude object has been associated with either positive or negative "cues." The approaches that fall under this second route have emphasized associating the advocated position with such basic cues as food (e.g., Janis. Kaye, & Kirschner, 1965) and pain (e.g., Zanna, Kiesler, & Pilkonis, 1970) or more secondary cues such as credible (e.g., Kelman & Hovland, 1953), attractive (e.g., Mills & Harvey, 1972), and powerful (e.g., Kelman, 1961) sources. These cues may shape attitudes or allow a person to decide what attitudinal position to adopt without the need for engaging in any extensive issue-relevant thinking. Furthermore, these cues can presumably influence attitudes whether or not any issue-relevant arguments are presented or considered (e.g., Maddux & Rogers, 1980; Norman, 1976; Staats & Staats, 1958).

Enough research has now accumulated in support of both routes to persuasion to clearly indicate that both processes operate (Eagly & Himmelfarb, 1978). Attitude change is not determined exclusively by either issue-relevant argumentation or simple cue association. A profitable direction for current research, then, is to document the differing consequences of each route to persuasion (if any) and to indicate the variables that determine which route will be followed. For example, in a recent review of attitude-change research, Cialdini, Petty, and Cacioppo (1981) concluded that one consequence of the different routes to persuasion was that changes induced via the central route tended to be enduring and predictive of subsequent behavior, whereas changes induced via the peripheral route tended to be more ephemeral and less predictive of subsequent behavior (see also Chaiken, 1980; Cook & Flay, 1978). Our goal in the present study was to explore the conditions under which each route to persuasion would be taken.

Specifically, we hypothesized that when a persuasive communication was on a topic of high personal relevance, attitude change would be governed mostly by a thoughtful consideration of the issue-relevant arguments presented (central route). On the other hand, when a message was on a topic of low personal relevance, we hypothesized that peripheral features of the persuasion situation would be more potent. As Miller, Maruyama,

Beaber, and Yalone (1976) noted, "It may be irrational to scrutinize the plethora of counter-attitudinal messages received daily. To the extent that one possesses only a limited amount of information processing time and capacity, such scrutiny would disengage the thought processes from the exigencies of daily life" (p. 623). Thus, persons must choose which stimuli should be scrutinized carefully and which are not worthy of extensive thought.[1]

Recent research has indicated that the level of personal involvement with an issue is one variable that influences the extent to which issue-relevant arguments will be considered. For example, Cialdini et al. (1976) found that subjects who expected to engage in a discussion with an opponent generated more supportive arguments in anticipation of the discussion when the attitude issue had high rather than low personal relevance. Also, Petty and Cacioppo (1979a, 1979b) have reported that subjects' message-relevant thoughts showed higher correlations with message acceptance when the issue was of high rather than low personal importance. Thus, the hypothesis that issue-relevant argumentation becomes a more important determinant of persuasion as the personal relevance of an issue increases has received some support (see review by Burnkrant & Sawyer, in press).

The complementing hypothesis—that peripheral cues in the persuasion situation become more important as the personal involvement with an issue decreases—has received less attention, although

---

[1]The notion that people sometimes devote considerable cognitive effort to processing a stimulus and at other times cognitive effort is minimal can also be seen in the recent psychological distinctions between mindfulness versus mindlessness (Langer & Imber, 1980), deep versus shallow processing (Craik & Lockhart, 1972), controlled versus automatic processing (Schneider & Shiffrin, 1977), and systematic versus heuristic processing (Chaiken, 1980). The notion that there are different *kinds* of persuasion was apparent in Aristotle's *Rhetoric*, but achieved the most contemporary recognition in Kelman's three process view of persuasion. In Kelman's (1961) system, the type of persuasion is determined primarily by the source of the message (expert sources produce internalization, attractive sources produce identification, and powerful sources produce compliance). According to the central/peripheral distinction, the central route is followed when issue-relevant argumentation is responsible for inducing change regardless of the message source. A person who changes simply because an expert, attractive, or powerful source endorses a particular position (without engaging in issue-relevant thought) would be following the peripheral route.

the available data are consistent with this view. For example, Johnson and Scileppi (1969) and Rhine and Severance (1970) found that a manipulation of source credibility was more impactful under low than under high-involvement conditions. In the most directly relevant study on involvement and type of persuasion to date, Chaiken (1980) exposed subjects to a message containing either two or six arguments, from a likable or dislikable source, under either high- or low-involvement conditions. She found that the message manipulation had a greater impact on persuasion under high involvement but that the source manipulation had a greater impact on attitude under low involvement. Although these data are highly suggestive, they do not provide definitive support for the two routes to persuasion because the particular message manipulation employed by Chaiken (number of arguments) has the ability to serve as a simple cue much in the same way that a source manipulation (likable or dislikable source) can serve as a cue. In other words, even if subjects did no thinking about the message arguments at all, it is likely that they would have realized that the message they heard had either relatively few or relatively many arguments. A simple desire to identify with a side that has many rather than few arguments may have been sufficient to produce the differential persuasion for the two- and six-argument messages under the high-involvement conditions. Thus, both the source manipulation and the message manipulation may have provided simple cues for message acceptance, making a cognitive evaluation of the message content unnecessary. It is sufficient to propose that under low-involvement conditions, the source cue was more potent but that under high-involvement conditions, the message cue was more potent.

The study reported here was designed to provide a more direct test of the hypothesis that under high-involvement conditions, a thoughtful evaluation of message content is the most important determinant of persuasion but that under low-involvement conditions, peripheral cues in the situation are more impactful. In the present study, all subjects heard a counterattitudinal communication. In addition to manipulating the personal importance of the message, the quality of the arguments that subjects heard in support of the advocated position was varied, as was the expertise of the source of the communication. By manipulating the quality of cogency of the arguments used in the messages, but keeping the number of arguments in the communications constant, the ability of subjects to evaluate the advocacy on the basis of a simple message cue (length) was eliminated. For the manipulation of message cogency to have an impact on persuasion, communication recipients must actually think about the merits of the arguments presented. Of course the expertise of the source of the communication could still provide a simple cue for message acceptance. Our hypothesis was that under conditions of high personal involvement, persuasion would be affected more by the quality of the message arguments employed but that under low-involvement conditions, persuasion would be tied more strongly to the expertise of the source.

Method

Procedure

One hundred forty-five male and female undergraduates at the University of Missouri participated in order to earn extra credit in an introductory psychology course. The design was a 2 (issue involvement: high or low) × 2 (argument quality: strong or weak) × 2 (source expertise: high or low) factorial. Subjects were tested in groups of 3 to 16 in cubicles designed so that no subject could have visual or verbal contact with any other subject. During any one session, it was possible to conduct all eight experimental conditions (if enough subjects were present).

The subjects were told that the University of Missouri was currently undergoing an academic reevaluation and that the new chancellor was seeking recommendations about policy changes to be instituted. To obtain a variety of opinions about the university and its future, the subjects were told that the chancellor had asked several individuals and groups to prepare policy statements. The subjects were further told that each of the policy statements had been recorded for possible broadcast on a campus radio station. The subjects were told that the psychology department was cooperating with the university administration in having the taped statements rated for broadcast quality.

After reading these background comments, the subjects heard one of the tape recordings over headphones. All of the tapes were made by the same male speaker and advocated that seniors be required to take a comprehensive exam in their major area as a prerequisite to graduation. After listening to the appropriate communication, subjects completed a dependent variable booklet and were then debriefed, thanked, and dismissed.

Independent Variables

Personal involvement. In the background material that subjects read prior to message exposure, half were told that the chancellor was seeking recommendations about policy changes to be instituted the following year (high personal involvement), whereas the other half were told that the chancellor was seeking recommendations about changes that would take effect in 10 years (low personal involvement). Clearly then, in the high-involvement conditions, the subjects would be affected personally by the advocated change, whereas in the low-involvement conditions they would not.

Source expertise. Half of the subjects learned that the tape they would hear was based on a report prepared by a class at a local high school (low expertise), whereas the remaining subjects learned that the tape was based on a report prepared by the Carnegie Commission on Higher Education, which was chaired by a professor of education at Princeton University (high expertise). Of course all subjects actually heard the same speaker.

Argument quality. Even though all subjects heard a message advocating the institution of senior comprehensive exams, the arguments used in support of the message conclusion were varied. In brief, the strong version of the message provided persuasive evidence (statistics, data, etc.) in support of the exam (e.g., institution of the exams had led to a reversal in the declining scores on standardized achievement tests at other universities). In contrast, the weak version of the message relied more on quotations, personal opinion, and examples to support its position (e.g., a friend of the author's had to take a comprehensive exam and now had a prestigious academic position). The messages were equivalent in length, and each contained elaborations of eight arguments. The strong arguments were selected from a pool that elicited primarily favorable thoughts in a pretest, and the weak arguments were selected from a pool that elicited primarily counterarguments in a pretest. The specific arguments employed in this study were adapted from the "strong" and "very weak"

communications described by Petty, Harkins, and Williams (1980). Pretest ratings of the two messages indicated that they did not differ in the extent to which they were "difficult to understand," were "hard to follow," or possessed "complex structure."

Dependent Variables

Subjects were told that because their personal views on the desirability of instituting a comprehensive exam might influence the way they rated the broadcast quality of the tapes, a measure of their own opinion was desired. Two measures of attitude were included. The first asked subjects to rate the concept "Comprehensive Exams:" on four 9-point semantic differential scales (good/bad, beneficial/harmful, foolish/wise, and unfavorable/favorable). Next, on an 11-point scale anchored by 1-"do not agree at all," and 11-"agree completely," subjects rated the extent to which they agreed with the proposal requiring seniors to take a comprehensive exam before graduating. The subjects' responses to the two attitude measures were converted to standard scores and averaged for an index of attitude toward comprehensive exams. The within-cell correlation between the two measures was 75.

Subjects then responded to a number of additional items including measures designed to maintain the cover story (e.g., ratings of speaker voice quality, delivery, enthusiasm, etc.). With one exception, the ancillary measures produced no significant effects and will not be discussed further. [2]

Next, subjects responded to three questions designed to assess the effectiveness of the three experimental manipulations. Finally, subjects were given 4 min. to list as many of the arguments from the message as they could recall. Two judges, blind to the involvement and expertise manipulations, rated each argument listed for accuracy ($r = .92$). Similar statements of the same argument were

---

[2] On the measure of speaker voice quality, a significant main effect for issue importance (better voice quality with low than high importance), and argument quality (better voice quality with weak than strong arguments), and a three-way interaction (uninterpretable) appeared. Since this pattern of data did not follow the pattern found on the crucial attitude measure, and since the within-cell correlation between voice quality and agreement was small and not significant ($r = .04$), this measure will not be given further consideration.

counted only once. Disagreements between judges were resolved by consulting a third judge.

No-Message Control

Although the primary aim of the experiment was to assess how personal involvement would affect the relative importance of argument quality and source expertise in influencing subjects' post-communication attitudes toward the topic, a no-message control condition was also conducted to assess absolute attitude change from a premessage baseline. An additional 18 undergraduates from the same subject pool were asked to participate in a "Survey of Campus Issues" study. [3] These control subjects gave their opinions on a number of different contemporary issues facing universities across the country. The fifth issue in each survey booklet concerned requiring seniors at the University of Missouri to pass a comprehensive exam in their major area as a prerequisite to graduation. The crucial issue was embedded in the context of many others to reduce the likelihood that subjects would spend an undue amount of time thinking about the issue, which could result in attitude polarization (see Tesser, 1978). Half of the surveys indicated that the exam requirement was being proposed for next year, and half of the surveys indicated that the exam requirement was being proposed to take effect in 10 years. Subjects recorded their attitudes on the issue on the same scales as those employed in the experimental conditions described previously. Since the manipulation of involvement in the control cells did not significantly affect the attitudes reported (p > .20), the data for these two conditions were combined.

Results

Experimental Groups

Preliminary 2 (personal involvement) × 2 (source expertise) × 2 (argument quality) × 2 (sex of subject) analyses of variance on each dependent measure produced no significant main effects nor interactions involving sex. Thus, this factor was ignored in all subsequent analyses.

Manipulation checks. To assess the effectiveness of the message quality manipulation, subjects were asked: "How would you rate the quality of the arguments used by the speaker to support the position advocated?" On a scale where 1 indicated

"not very good arguments," and 11 indicated "very good arguments," subjects hearing the strong arguments ($M = 8.9$) rated their quality as significantly higher than subjects hearing the weak arguments ($M = 4.5$), F(1, 137) = 51.02, p <.001. To assess the expertise manipulation, subjects were asked: "Regardless of how you felt about what the author had to say, how qualified did you think he was to speak on the topic?" On a scale where 1 indicated "not very qualified" and 11 indicated "very qualified," subjects hearing the high-expert speaker rated his qualifications as significantly higher ($M = 6.8$) than subjects hearing the low-expert speaker ($M = 5.7$) F (1,137) = 4.86, p < 03. In addition, subjects hearing the strong arguments rated the speaker as more qualified ($M = 7.6$) than subjects hearing the weak arguments ($M = 4.9$), $F(1, 137) = 39.2, p < .001$. Finally, to assess the personal relevance manipulation, subjects were asked to rate "How likely is it that the University of Missouri will institute comprehensive exams while you are a student here?" On a scale where 1 indicated "not very likely" and 11 indicated "very likely," subjects in the high-involvement conditions rated the likelihood as higher ($M = 5.5$) than subjects in the low-involvement conditions ($M = 2.7$), $F(1, 137) = 5.12, p < 0.2$. In sum, all three independent variables were manipulated successfully.

Attitude and recall measures. A three-way analysis of variance (ANOVA) on the index of attitude toward comprehensive exams produced two main effects and two interactions. A main effect for the expertise manipulation revealed that subjects agreed with the communication more when the source had high expertise ($M = .21$) than when the source had low expertise ($M = - .21$), $F(1, 137) = 16.24, p < .001$. Also, a main effect for argument

---

[3]The no-message control attitude data were collected at the suggestion of the *JPSP* reviewers approximately 2 years after the data from the main experiment. As a check on the stability of students' attitudes toward comprehensive exams over this period, control subjects' responses on the 11-point Likert-scale were compared with no-message control data on the same issue and scale collected in a pilot study that was conducted at about the same time as the main experiment reported here (the semantic differential measure was not collected in the earlier pilot study). A comparison of the two sets of control data collected about 2 years apart revealed no statistically significant difference (p > .20), suggesting that opinions on the issue over the intervening period were relatively stable. In any case, the statistical tests of the major hypotheses of interest in the present investigation could be and were conducted *excluding* the control data.

quality revealed that subjects agreed with the message more when it contained strong ($M = .36$) rather than weak arguments ($M = -.36$), $F(1, 137) = 20.35, p < .001$.

Of greater interest, however, were two interactions that qualified these two main effects. First, an Involvement × Expertise interaction, $F(1, 137) = 3.92, p < .05$, revealed that the expertise manipulation had a stronger effect under low personal-involvement conditions than under high (see top panel of Figure 1). In fact, a Newman-Keuls analysis of this interaction revealed that a source of high expertise produced significantly more agreement than a source of low expertise only under the low-involvement conditions. A complementing Involvement × Argument Quality interaction, $F(1, 137) = 6.05, p < .02$, demonstrated that the argument quality manipulation had a stronger effect under high personal-involvement conditions than under low (see bottom panel of Figure 1). A Newman-Keuls analysis of this interaction revealed that the strong arguments produced significantly more agreement than the weak only under the high-involvement conditions.

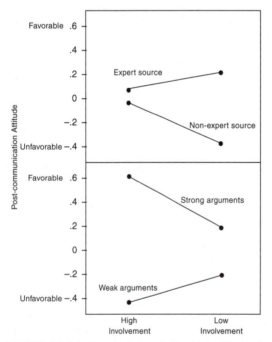

FIGURE 34.1 ■ Top panel: Interactive effect of involvement and source expertise on postcommunication attitudes. Bottom panel: Interactive effect of involvement and argument quality on postcommunication attitudes.

An analysis of the argument recall score revealed that subjects recalled more of the strong ($M = 4.2$) than of the weak arguments ($M = 3.2$), $F(1,137) = 14.93, p < .001$, but the personal involvement and expertise manipulations did not affect argument recall, and no interactions were obtained on this measure. Consistent with previous research, within-cell correlation failed to substantiate a relationship between argument learning and agreement for either the strong ($r = .05$) or weak ($r = -.09$) argument messages. When manipulations of argument quality are successful, it apparently has more to do with argument evaluation or elaboration than argument memorization (cf., Cacioppo & Petty, 1979b; Insko, Lind, & LaTour, 1976).

No-Message Control

In Table 1, the attitude scores have been restandardized to include the no-message control data. This table also provides pairwise comparisons of all eight experimental cells employing the Newman-Keuls test and a test of each experimental group with the control employing Dunnett's procedure (see Kirk, 1968).

Consistent with the two-way interactions reported previously, the Newman-Keuls analysis revealed that under high involvement, argument quality affected attitudes but source expertise did not. Under low involvement, however, the reverse pattern tended to occur. Attitudes of subjects in the no-message control condition fell in between the attitudes of subjects in the experimental cells, suggesting that the significant differences among the various experimental conditions may have resulted from a combination of both persuasion and boomerang processes. The largest (though nonsignificant) boomerang effects occurred in the two cells where nonexpert sources presented weak arguments. It is interesting to speculate that under low involvement, the tendency toward boomerang was produced primarily by a rejection of the message source, whereas under high involvement, the tendency toward boomerang was produced primarily by a rejection of the message arguments. Two experimental groups showed significant persuasion in relation to the nomessage control. This occurred when strong arguments, regardless of the source, were presented under high involvement. According to the present analysis, these are the two cells that should have resulted in the most favorable issue-relevant thinking.

TABLE 34.1. Standardized Attitude Scores for Experimental and Control Subjects

Arguments	High involvement		Low involvement		No-message control
	Expert source	Nonexpert source	Expert source	Nonexpert source	
Strong	.64$_a$*	.61$_a$*	.40$_{a,b}$	−.12$_{a,b,c}$	−.18
Weak	−.38$_{b,c}$	−.58$_c$	.25$_{a,b}$	−.64$_c$	

Note. Within the experimental cells, means without a common subscript are significantly different at the .05 level by the Newman-Keuls procedure.
* Experimental mean is significantly different from the control mean at the .05 level by Dunnett's test.

Discussion

Previous research on persuasion has tended to characterize attitude change as resulting from either a thoughtful consideration of issue-relevant arguments or from associating various positive or negative cues with the attitude object. Furthermore, researchers favoring one process have tended to downplay the importance of the other. For example, in a recent paper, Fishbein and Ajzen (1981) have argued that:

The general neglect of the information contained in a message . . . is probably the most serious problem in communication and persuasion research. We are convinced that the persuasiveness of a communication can be increased much more easily and dramatically by paying careful attention to its content . . . than by manipulation of credibility, attractiveness, . . . or any of the other myriad factors that have caught the fancy of investigators in the area of communication and persuasion. (p. 359)

The present study suggests that although the message content may be the most important determinant of persuasion under some circumstances, in other circumstances such noncontent manipulations as source credibility, attractiveness, and so forth, may be even *more* important. Specifically, in the present article, we have shown that when a persuasive message concerned an issue of high personal relevance, the effectiveness of the appeal was more a function of the cogency of the arguments presented in the message than of such peripheral cues as the expertise of the message source. On the other hand, when the message concerned an issue of relatively low personal relevance, effectiveness was more a function of peripheral cues than of the arguments presented. Interestingly, the long-standing tradition of persuasion researchers to employ messages that are

low in personal relevance (cf. Hovland, 1959) may be responsible for the voluminous number of studies emphasizing the influence of noncontent factors in persuasion and relatively ignoring issue-relevant arguments. Importantly, the present data suggest that it would be equally inappropriate to overemphasize the influence of issue-relevant argumentation and ignore the role of peripheral cues. Each type of persuasion occurs in some instances, and the level of personal involvement with an issue appears to be one moderator of which type of persuasion occurs.

There are at least two reasons why an increase in involvement might be associated with an increase in the importance of message arguments in producing persuasion. First, as an issue increases in its personal implications for the message recipient, it becomes more important to form a reasoned and veridical opinion. An attitude based on a careful examination of issue-relevant arguments will likely prove to be more adaptive and will certainly be easier to defend if challenged in the future. If people are motivated to hold "correct" opinions on personally important issues, and a consideration of the arguments relevant to an issue enhances the likelihood of veridicality, then it follows that people will be more motivated to scrutinize the arguments presented when an issue has many personal consequences than when personal consequences are few. When an issue has few personal consequences, it is unlikely that people will be motivated to do the cognitive work necessary to evaluate an advocacy on the basis of its arguments. The cognitive consideration of arguments is difficult work and is presumably best undertaken when the personal consequences of an issue are high. When the personal importance of the issue is low, people may be motivated less by a desire to be correct than by a desire to minimize cognitive work (cf. McGuire's "lazy organism," 1969, p. 198) or to manage the impressions of others (cf. Cialdini, Levy, Herman, Kozlowski, & Petty, 1976).

In addition to this motivational factor, it might also be that people have a better developed schema or framework for thinking about things that are relevant to the self than things that are irrelevant (cf. Markus, 1977). Thus, a second reason why the processing of issue-relevant argumentation may be greater under high involvement than under low is that people have a greater *ability* to do so. If an issue has high personal consequences, it is likely that the person has done considerable thinking about the issue in the past and has a large structure of preexisting information that can be useful in evaluating new information. Thus, a person might find it easier to evaluate the cogency of an argument on a topic of high rather than low involvement. Of course in the present study prior knowledge about the issue was identical for both high- and low-involvement groups, and thus the effect of involvement in the current study presumably hinged more on motivational than on ability factors. Nevertheless, it is still possible that when a person learns that a communication has high personal relevance, a self-schema is invoked, and this framework of self-relevant cognitions increases one's ability to evaluate the implications of the message arguments.

Our reasoning that a person's motives and abilities are typically different under high and low-involvement conditions suggests that some manipulations should be effective under high but not low involvement, but other variables should show the reverse pattern. The present study provides an example of one variable of each type. In addition, some variables might have effects under both high and low involvement, but the effects might be quite different in each case. For example, in a study on the effects of using rhetorical questions on persuasion, Petty, Cacioppo, and Heesacker (1981) found that using rhetorical questions enhanced message-relevant processing under low-involvement conditions (when thinking about the message would ordinarily have been low) but disrupted message-relevant processing under high-involvement conditions (when thinking about the message would ordinarily have been high).

The realization that an independent variable may have different (and even opposite) effects, depending on the level of personal relevance of a message, may provide some insight into the conflicting pattern of results that is said to characterize much attitude research (Fishbein & Ajzen, 1972). It may well be that there are two distinct routes to persuasion and that these routes are characterized by different antecedents and consequents (Chaiken, 1980; Petty & Cacioppo, 1979b, 1981). If so, future work could profitably be aimed at uncovering moderators other than personal involvement of the route to persuasion. These moderators could be variables within the persuasion situation or within the message recipient. In general, we suspect that any variable that increases the likelihood that people will be motivated and able to engage in the difficult task of evaluating the message arguments increases the likelihood of the central route to persuasion. On the other hand, any variable that reduces a person's motivation and/or ability to think about the message content would make the peripheral route more likely. These moderator variables would, therefore, include such things as message repetition and distraction, the number of people responsible for message evaluation, an individual's "need for cognition," and others (cf. Cacioppo & Petty, 1979b, in press; Petty et al., 1976, 1980).

ACKNOWLEDGMENTS

The data reported here are based in part on a master's thesis conducted by the third author under the supervision of the first two authors. The advice of thesis committee members Russell Geen, Donald Granberg, and Larry Siegel is acknowledged with thanks. We also thank Stan Wilensky and Don Fry for providing access to the University of Missouri learning lab facilities. This research was supported by National Science Foundation Grant BNS 7913753, and portions of this article were presented at the annual meeting of the American Psychological Association, September 1979, in New York.

REFERENCES

Anderson, N. H. Integration theory and attitude change. *Psychological Review*, 1971, 78, 171–206.

Burnkrant, R. E., & Sawyer, A. G. Effects of involvement and message content on information processing intensity. In R. Harries (Ed.), *Information processing research in advertising*. Hillsdale, NJ: Erlbaum, in press.

Cacioppo, J. T., & Petty, R. E. Attitudes and cognitive response: An electrophysiological approach. *Journal of Personality and Social Psychology*, 1979, 37, 2181–2199. (a)

Cacioppo, J. T., & Petty, R. E. Effects of message repetition and position on cognitive responses, recall, and persuasion. *Journal of Personality and Social Psychology*, 1979, 37, 97–109, (b)

Cacioppo, J. T., & Petty, R. E. The need for cognition. *Journal of Personality and Social Psychology*, in press.

Chaiken, S. Heuristic versus systematic information processing and the use of source versus message cues is persuasion. *Journal of Personality and Social Psychology*, 1980, 39, 752–766.

Cialdini, R. B., Levy, A., Herman, P., Kozlowski, L., & Petty, R. E. Elastic shifts of opinion. Determinants of direction and durability. *Journal of Personality and Social Psychology*, 1976, 34, 663–672.

Cialdini, R. B., Petty, R. E., & Cacioppo, J. T. Attitude and attitude change. In M. Rosenzweig & L. Porter (Eds.) *Annual Review of Psychology*, (Vol. 32). Palo Alto, Calif.: Annual Reviews, 1981.

Cook, T. D., & Flay, B. R. The temporal persistence of experimentally induced attitude change: An evaluative review. In L. Berkowitz (Ed.), *Advances in experimental social psychology* (Vol. 11). New York: Academic Press, 1978.

Craik, F. M., & Lockhart, R. S. Levels of processing: A framework for memory research. *Journal of Verbal Learning and Verbal Behavior*, 1972, 11, 671–684.

Eagly, A. H. Comprehensibility of persuasive arguments as a determinant of opinion change. *Journal of Personality and Social Psychology*, 1974, 29, 758–773.

Eagly, A. H., & Himmelfarb, S. Attitudes and opinions. In M. Rosenzweig & L. Porter (Eds.), *Annual Review of Psychology* (Vol. 29). Palo Alto, Calif. Annual Reviews, 1978.

Fishbein, M., & Ajzen, I. Attitudes and opinions. In M. Rosenzweig & L. Perter (Eds.), *Annual Review of Psychology* (Vol. 23). Palo Alto, Calif.: Annual Reviews, 1972.

Fishbein, M., & Ajzen, I. *Belief, attitude, intention, and behavior: An introduction to theory and research.* Reading, Mass.: Addison-Wesley, 1975.

Fishbein, M., & Ajzen, I. Acceptance, yielding, and impact: Cognitive processes in persuasion. In R. Petty, T. Ostrom, & T. Brock (Eds.), *Cognitive responses in persuasion.* Hillsdale, N. J.: Erlbaum, 1981.

Greenwald, A. G. Cognitive learning, cognitive response to persuasion, and attitude change. In A. Greenwald, T. Brock, & T. Ostrom (Eds.), *Psychological foundations of attitudes.* New York: Academic Press, 1968.

Hovland, C. I. Reconciling conflicting results derived from experimental and survey studies of attitude change. *American Psychologist*, 1959, 14, 8–17.

Insko, C. A., Lind, E. A., & LaTour, S. Persuasion, recall and thoughts, *Representative Research in Social Psychology*, 1976, 7, 66–78.

Janis, I. L., Kaye, D., & Kirschner, P. Facilitating effects of "eating while reading" on responsiveness to persuasive communications. *Journal of Personality and Social Psychology*, 1965, 1, 181–186.

Johnson, H. H., & Scileppi, J. A. Effects of ego-involvement conditions on attitude change to high- and low-credibility communicators. *Journal of Personality and Social Psychology*, 1969, 13, 31–36.

Kelman, H. C. Processes of opinion change. *Public Opinion Quarterly*, 1961, 25, 57–78.

Kelman, H. C., & Hovland, C. I. Reinstatement of the communicator in delayed measurement of opinion change. *Journal of Abnormal and Social Psychology*,1953, 48, 327–335.

Kirk, R. E. *Experimental design: Procedures for the behavioral sciences.* Beimont, Calif.: Brooks/Cole, 1968.

Langer, E. J., & Imber, L. Role of mindlessness in the perception of deviance. *Journal of Personality and Social Psychology*, 1980, 39, 360–367.

Maddux, J. E., & Rogers, R. W. Effects of source expertness,

physical attractiveness, and supporting arguments on persuasion: A case of brains over beauty. *Journal of Personality and Social Psychology*, 1980, 38, 235–244.

Markus, H. Self-schemata and processing information about the self. *Journal of Personality and Social Psychology,* 1977, 35, 63–78.

McGuire, W. J. Personality and attitude change: An information processing theory. In A. Greenwald, T. Brock, & T. Ostrom (Eds.), *Psychological foundations of attitudes.* New York: Academic Press, 1968.

McGuire, W. J. The nature of attitudes and attitudes change. In G. Lindzey & E. Aronson (Eds.),*The handbook of social psychology* (2nd ed.). Vol. 3. Reading, Mass.: Addison-Wesley, 1969.

Miller, N., & Campbell, D. T. Recency and primacy in persuasion as a function of the timing of speeches and measurements. *Journal of Abnormal and Social Psychology,*1959, 59, 1–9.

Miller, N., Maruyama, G., Beaber, R., & Valone, K. Speed of speech and persuasion. *Journal of Personality and Social Psychology*, 1976, 34, 615–625.

Mills, J., & Harvey, J. Opinion change as a function of when information about the communicator is received and whether he is attractive or expert. *Journal of Personality and Social Psychology,* 1972, 21, 52–55.

Norman, R. When what is said is important: A comparison of expert and attractive sources. *Journal of Experimental Social Psychology,* 1976, 12, 294–300.

Petty, R. E., & Cacioppo, J. T. Effects of forewarning of persuasive intent and involvement on cognitive responses and persuasion. *Personality and Social Psychology Bulletin*, 1979, 5, 173–176. (a)

Petty, R. E., & Cacioppo, J. T. Issue-involvement can increase or decrease persuasion by enhancing message-relevant cognitive responses. *Journal of Personality and Social Psychology,* 1979, 37, 1915–1926 .(b)

Petty, R. E., & Cacioppo, J. T. *Attitudes and persuasion. Classic and contemporary approaches.* Dubuque, Iowa: Win. C. Brown, 1981.

Petty, R. E., Cacioppo, J. T., & Heesacker, M. The use of rhetorical questions in persuasion: A cognitive response analysis. *Journal of Personality and Social Psychology,* 1981, 40, 432–440.

Petty, R. E., Harkins, S. G., & Williams. K. D. The effects of group diffusion of cognitive effort on attitudes: An information processing view. *Journal of Personality and Social Psychology*, 1980, 38, 81–92.

Petty, R. E., Wells, G. L., & Brock, T. L. Distraction can enhance or reduce yielding to propaganda: Thought disruption versus effort justification. *Journal of Personality and Social Psychology,* 1976, 34, 874–884.

Rhine, R. J., & Severance, L. J. Ego-involvement, discrepancy, source credibility, and attitude change. *Journal of Personality and Social Psychology*, 1970, 16, 175–190.

Schneider, W., & Shiffrin, R. M. Controlled and automatic human information processing: I. Detection, search, and attention. *Psychological Review,* 1977, 84, 1–66.

Staats, A. W., & Staats, C. K. Attitudes established by classical conditioning. *Journal of Abnormal and Social Psychology,* 1958, 57, 37–40.

Tesser, A. Self-generated attitude change. *Advances in Experimental Social Psychology*, 1978, 11, 289–338.

Vinokur, A., & Burnstein, E. The effects of partially shared

Persuasion by a Single Route: A View from the Unimodel

Arie W. Kruglanski • University of Maryland, College Park
Erik P. Thompson • Washington University

Editors' Notes

According to major twentieth-century philosophers of science such as Karl Popper and Imre Lakatos, scientific criticism and the pitting of competing theories against each other constitute a major vehicle for the advancement of science. Productive criticism should be based on true appreciation and respect of the work being reassessed. This selection represents such a respectful critique of the dual-process models featured in the two preceding selections. The unimodel outlined by Kruglanski and Thompson proposes an integration by collapsing the two modes of persuasion (whether heuristic/systematic or peripheral/central) into one. This integration is accomplished by identifying the major commonalities of the two processing modes. One issue concerns the presentation of evidence (e.g., about the source or about the message) that participants may view as relevant to the persuasive conclusion. In previous research one type of evidence was typically presented in a brief and simple format that rendered it easy to process (heuristic or peripheral), whereas the other type of evidence was presented in a lengthy and complex format that rendered it relatively difficult to process (central or systematic). According to Kruglanski and Thompson, this is why the heuristic or peripheral information exerted its impact under low motivation (where the motivation was sufficient to process easy information but insufficient to process difficult information), whereas the central or systematic information exerted its impact under high motivation. According to Kruglanski and Thompson, both dual-process models are "collapsable" into the same unimodel whereby subjectively relevant information impacts persuasion as a function of its difficulty and the recipients' motivation and ability to cope with the difficulty.

Discussion Questions

1. According to the authors, what is the common function fulfilled by heuristics and peripheral cues?
2. How might future research establish that there is process uniformity or process duality?
3. What are the "software" and "hardware" aspects of cognitive ability?
4. What do the authors mean by "inferred interactions" and "manifest interactions"?

Suggested Readings

Kruglanski, A. W. (1990). Lay epistemic theory in social cognitive psychology. *Psychological Inquiry, 1,* 181–197.

Kruglanski, A. W., & Mackie, D. M. (1990). Majority and minority influence: A judgmental process analysis. In W. Stroebe & M. Hewstone (Eds.), *European review of social psychology* (Vol. 1, pp. 229–261). New York: Wiley.

Authors' Abstract

Major current notions of persuasion depict it as attainable via 2 qualitatively distinct routes: (a) a central or a systematic route in which opinions and attitudes are based on carefully processed arguments in the persuasive message and (b) a peripheral or heuristic route in which they are based on briefly considered heuristics or cues, exogenous to the message. This article offers a single-route reconceptualization that treats these dual routes to persuasion as involving functionally equivalent types of evidence from which persuasive conclusions may be drawn. Previous findings in the dual-process literature are reconsidered in light of this "unimodel," and novel data are presented consistent with its assumptions. Beyond its parsimony and integrative potential, the unimodel offers conceptual, empirical, and practical advantages in the persuasion domain.

From a social psychological perspective, the 20th century may well be dubbed the Age of Persuasion. Unprecedented technological developments within less than 100 years have multiplied a thousandfold communicators' reach of their audiences. The advent of air travel (as well as increased efficiency of the railroad systems) has swelled the volumes of mail delivered to addresses. Its preponderance is often dismissed as *junk*—a term connoting deliberate persuasive intent: Someone is trying to sell us something or get us to do something we did not originally intend. The telephone, radio, television, computers, and fax machines lend hand to the conspiracy and inundate us with a barrage of persuasive messages fired at an exponential pace. Like intensely flowing tributaries to the rising flood of information menacing to engulf us, they seem bent on sweeping away our old attitudes, opinions, habits, or intentions and implanting new ones in their place. Of course, persuasion has a major positive aspect, beside its darker side and the potential for abuse. It constitutes the mainstay of effective education, psychotherapy, or counseling as well as of successful negotiation without which good interpersonal, intergroup, and international relations are unthinkable.

Given the ubiquity and importance of persuasion in today's world it is hardly surprising that its explanation has had high priority on the research agenda of many social psychologists. Over the last several decades, persuasion and attitude change have counted among the most thoroughly investigated topics of social psychological research, yielding exciting conceptual developments and a rich crop of intriguing findings (for a comprehensive review, see Eagly & Chaiken, 1993).

This hasn't always been so. *Persuasion* as a term did not even figure in the indexes of major early volumes introducing social psychology as a systematic field of study (e.g., Allport, 1924; McDougall, 1908; Ross, 1908), and influential midcentury texts (Asch, 1952; Newcomb, 1950) barely mention it in passing while discussing "propaganda." It was not until Hovland and his coworkers at Yale University (Hovland, 1957; Hovland & Janis, 1959; Hovland, Janis, & Kelley, 1953) launched their seminal Communication and Persuasion program that these issues began to receive their just desserts as major topics of social psychological inquiry.

The Yale research revolved about a classification system of persuasion variables growing out of Laswell's (1948) comprehensive question "Who says what in what channel to whom with what effect?" (p. 37). Initially, this led to a rather descriptive approach to persuasion research; for example, listing the variables within the *communicator* (i.e., the "who"), the *message* (i.e., the "what"), and the *audience* (the "to whom") categories. Over the years, research has moved from the mere itemization and interrelation of variables in Laswell's scheme to exploring the basic cognitive and motivational processes underlying persuasion.

Significant milestones on this road have been McGuire's (1968, 1969, 1972) reception-yielding model and the cognitive response model of persuasion (Greenwald, 1968; Petty, Ostrom, & Brock, 1981; for discussion see Eagly & Chaiken, 1993). Yet, the lion's share of current persuasion work was inspired by two major theoretical frameworks: Petty and Cacioppo's Elaboration Likelihood Model (ELM; e.g., Petty & Cacioppo, 1986) and Chaiken and Eagly's Heuristic Systematic Model (HSM). Although they may significantly differ in some respects (for recent comparisons, see Eagly & Chaiken, 1993; Petty, 1994), the ELM and HSM share a fundamental commonality: They both posit that persuasion may be accomplished via two qualitatively dissimilar "routes" or "modes." In ELM these are the *central* and the *peripheral* routes, in HSM they are the *systematic* and *heuristic* modes. Both models also stress that conditions that promote the extensive elaboration of message arguments will produce opinion change via one of the modes (the central one in ELM, and the systematic one in HSM), whereas conditions

that restrict the effortful elaboration of message arguments will bring opinion change via the remaining mode (the peripheral one in ELM, and the heuristic one in HSM).

It is difficult to overstate the dual-process models' contribution to understanding persuasion. Not only did they clarify why classical persuasion variables (e.g., source expertise) may yield different effects in different circumstances (Petty, 1994) but they also furnished invaluable insights into the complex ways whereby such variables may interact with factors in the persuasive context (e.g., recipients' involvement in the issue), and they fruitfully linked persuasion research to recent advances in social cognition, (Chaiken, Liberman, & Eagly, 1989; Eagly & Chaiken, 1993). This analysis is much indebted to those insights; indeed, we deeply venerate this work and the progress it has made possible. Nonetheless, our conceptualization substantially differs from the dual-process paradigm: We suggest a way of integrating its two component processes into one, and in this sense feature a unimodel of persuasion. The unimodel (a) adopts a more abstract level of analysis in which the two persuasive modes (of either ELM or HSM) are viewed as special cases of the same underlying process and (b) deconstructs the "Laswellian" partition between persuasively relevant categories.

It is not that the Laswellian categories are not real. The issue is that they do not represent meaningful distinctions that matter to persuasion. Take the distinction between the categories who and what; that is, the distinction between *source* and *message*. Even though these two may appear to be patently different, there is a sense in which their differences, although real, are irrelevant to persuasion. They turn out to constitute surface differences that share the same deep structure. In other words, what you see is not necessarily what you get.

Moreover, even though contemporary dual-process models have gone far beyond the variable listing approach inspired by Laswell's classification, they remain at least somewhat constrained by his scheme in retaining, as a basic premise, the Laswellian partition between persuasion based on source factors (that function, at least much of the time, as peripheral cues in the ELM and as heuristic cues within the HSM) and persuasion based on the message as such (referred to the central route in the ELM, and to systematic processing in the HSM). The unimodel, by contrast, unequivocally parts ways with the Laswellian scheme.

As a preview of what is to come, we first briefly review the two dual-process models (ELM and HSM) and highlight their commonalities. Second, we describe our logical method, or "rules of the game" for assessing process uniformity versus separateness. We then describe the unimodel and compare it with the dual-process frameworks. Next, we review empirical evidence, both old and new, relevant to this comparison. Finally, we draw the implications of our reconceptualization for theoretical, empirical, and practical issues in the persuasion domain.

Two Dual-Process Models

ELM

The ELM assumes that "there are two routes to persuasion that operate in different circumstances, and there are different consequences of each route to persuasion . . . (hence, the ELM) focuses on different persuasion processes that can operate in different situations" (Petty, 1994, p. 3). In fact, the model proposes a continuum of elaboration likelihood bounded at one end by the total absence of thought about issue-relevant information available in a persuasion situation and at the other end by complete elaboration of all the relevant information (Petty, 1994, p. 1). Extensive elaboration of the message information refers to persuasion via the central route, and reliance on message irrelevant cues refers to persuasion via the peripheral route. The ELM holds that "any variable that increases the likelihood of thinking increases the likelihood of engaging the central route" (Petty, 1994, p. 2). Prominent such variables are (a) personal relevance of the message, (b) whether the source is expert, (c) whether it is attractive, (d) whether it consists of multiple communicators versus a single one, or (e) whether the message recipient is high (or low) on the need for cognition (Cacioppo & Petty, 1982).

Processing information via the central route can be objective or biased. According to Petty and Cacioppo (1986):

> Relatively objective elaboration has much in common with "bottom up" processing since the elaboration is relatively impartial and data driven. Relatively biased elaboration has more in common with "top down" processing since the elaboration, for example, may be governed by a relevant attitude schema which guides processing in a manner lead-

ing to the maintenance or strengthening of the schema. (p. 136)

Although no explicit discussion of this point is offered, presumably peripheral processing is often "top down" as well, to the extent that it relies on "various persuasion rules or inferences" (p. 130) derived from prior beliefs and schemata stored in memory (e.g., "experts are right," or "poorly dressed people aren't smart").

Although the notion of peripheral processing usually calls to mind brief and simple cues, this need not be necessarily the case. As Petty and Cacioppo (1986) put it,

> In addition to the relatively simple acceptance/rejection rules . . . attitude change may be affected by more complex reasoning processes, such as those based on balance theory . . . or certain attributional principles. Importantly, even reliance on more complex inferences obviates the need for careful scrutiny of the issue-relevant arguments in a message. In other words, each of those processes (e.g., self-perception, assimilation, balance) is postulated to be sufficient to account for attitude change without requiring a personal evaluation of issue-relevant arguments. (p. 130)

An important aspect of ELM is its attention to motivational factors. According to Petty (1994),

> The ELM assumes that the default mode in persuasion settings is to understand the world and develop accurate views. Bias can be produced, however, when other motives are made salient . . . For example, if people came to feel that their autonomy to hold a particular view was threatened, the reactance motive could lead to defensive processing of a persuasive message. (pp. 1–2)

Also, when personal interests are very intense "as when an issue is intimately associated with central values. . . . Processing will either terminate in the interest of self-protection or will become biased in service of one's own ego" (Petty & Cacioppo, 1986, p. 148).

Although the central and peripheral "routes to persuasion" are assumed to qualitatively differ (cf. Eagly & Chaiken, 1993, p. 307) and be capable of operating in different circumstances, ELM affirms that they may occasionally co-occur. This would happen where a peripheral cue (like source expertise, or its minority–majority status) may help one decide whether the extent of processing issue-relevant information should be much or little (cf. Mackie, 1987). Furthermore, "at most points along the elaboration continuum there is likely to be some co-occurrence of processes and some joint impact. . . . That is the nature of a continuum" (Mackie, 1987, p. 4). Generally, the ELM proposes a "tradeoff between the impact of central and peripheral processes along the elaboration continuum . . . as the elaboration likelihood is increased central route processes have a greater impact on attitudes and peripheral route processes— a reduced impact on attitudes" (p. 4).

Petty (1994) advanced several hypotheses to explain why the impact of cues is reduced in conditions of high elaboration likelihood (Petty & Cacioppo, 1984; Petty, Cacioppo, & Goldman, 1981). The *cue-salience* hypothesis suggests that less attention may be paid to cues when participants are thinking about message content, although both high- and low-elaboration participants may have attended to the source (or another cue) when it was initially presented, it is "less *salient* (or spontaneously accessible) at time of attitude expression for the high elaboration participants presumably because of the extensive argument processing in which they engaged" (Petty, 1994, p. 5). A somewhat related notion, the *cue-loss* hypothesis, explains that

> Peripheral cues (have) an initial impact on attitudes but under high argument processing conditions . . . consideration of the issue-relevant arguments reduces the impact of the cues. This could occur, for example, if the cue is drowned out by the arguments or is undermined by the implications of the argument. (Petty, 1994, p. 5)

The *cue-extremity* hypothesis derives from Tesser's notion that increased thought about an issue may polarize one's attitudes toward it (e.g., Tesser & Conlee, 1975; Tesser & Cowan, 1977; Tesser & Leone, 1977). Specifically, "if high elaboration conditions lead to less thought about a peripheral cue and less thought about the cue leads it to be evaluated less extremely the cue would be expected to have a reduced impact on attitudes" (Petty, 1994, p. 5). Finally, the *cue-weighting* hypothesis

> assumes that the peripheral cues have relatively little impact on attitudes under high EL conditions *because* when people are highly motivated to process all the relevant information although aware of the cue do not consider it particularly relevant in making evaluative judgments . . . the cues are in essence discounted as irrelevant at the time of attitude judgment. This hypothesis isolates the reduced impact of the cues in the integration stage

of information processing. (p. 6)

Petty (1994) furthermore suggested that cues may be weighted less and arguments more because people come to have more "confidence" in their assessments of the arguments "if it turns out that confidence is the key to weighting, researchers can next turn to why differential confidence is produced"(p. 6).

Another important emphasis in ELM is the proposition that the same variable can serve different functions in the persuasion process. Specifically, "a variable serving as a peripheral cue can have some persuasion *impact* or outcome under both high and low elaboration conditions but the underlying processes producing these outcomes are postulated to differ" (Petty, 1994, p. 6). When the elaboration likelihood is low, a variable (e.g., source attractiveness) could serve as a cue; when it is high, the same variable could serve as an issue argument (e.g., an advertisement by a physically attractive source of a beauty product may imply that use of the product may have contributed to her attractiveness). Finally, when the elaboration likelihood is intermediate, the very same variable could determine the elaboration likelihood (e.g., an attractive source may prompt a more extensive processing of her message). For instance, when the personal consequences of, or prior knowledge about, an issue are moderate or unclear, people may not be sure if the message is worth thinking about or if they are able to do so. Under these circumstances characteristics of the message source can help a person decide if the message warrants close scrutiny. In a relevant study by Puckett, Petty, Cacioppo, and Fisher (1983), arguments were more carefully processed when they were associated with a socially attractive rather than a socially unattractive source. More specifically, the significant Message Quality × Source Attractiveness interaction was due to the joint tendencies for attractiveness to enhance agreement with the proposal when the arguments presented were strong, but to reduce agreement when they were weak (p. 188).

Research by Petty, Schumann, Richman, and Strathman (1993) on mood effects additionally demonstrated that a variable (positive mood in this case) can impact attitudes differently under varying levels of elaboration likelihood. Specifically, under low elaboration likelihood, positive mood can function as a heuristic and affect attitudes directly; under moderate elaboration likelihood, positive mood can reduce the overall level of elaborative processing; and under high elaboration likelihood, it can impact attitudes via the generation of positive message-relevant thoughts (see also Wegener & Petty, 1996).

Finally, and yet of considerable importance, the ELM holds that attitudes acquired via the central route differ in their consequences from those acquired via the peripheral route. The former are expected to manifest greater temporal persistence, be more predictive of behavior, and exhibit greater resistance to counterpersuasion than attitudes acquired via the peripheral route. The rationale for this hypothesis asserts that under the central route, the issue-relevant attitude schema may be accessed, rehearsed, and manipulated more often, strengthening the interconnections among the components and thus rendering the schema more internally consistent, accessible, enduring, and resistant than under the peripheral route (Petty & Cacioppo, 1986, p. 176). Evidence for differential consequences of attitudes formed via central versus peripheral routes is reviewed by Petty and Cacioppo (1986, pp. 175–182; as well as Petty, Haugtvedt, & Smith, 1995).

HSM

Chaiken et al. (1989) defined *systematic processing* as a "comprehensive, analytic orientation in which perceivers access all informational input for its relevance and importance to their judgement task, and integrate all useful information in forming their judgments" (p. 212). By contrast, heuristic processing is viewed as a more limited processing mode that demands much less cognitive effort and capacity than systematic processing. When processing heuristically, people focus on that subset of available information that enables them to use "simple inferential rules, schemata, or cognitive heuristics to formulate their judgments and decisions" (p. 213). Heuristic processing is furthermore regarded as "more exclusively theory driven than systematic processing," and the mode of processing distinction is assumed to be "*not merely quantitative*" (p. 213, italics added), but *qualitative*. Specifically, heuristic processing is "more exclusively theory driven because recipients utilize minimal informational input in conjunction with simple (declarative or procedural) knowledge structures to determine message valid-

ity quickly and efficiently" (p. 216).

Much like the ELM, the HSM assumes that the dominant motivational concern of persons in persuasion settings is the desire to form or hold valid or accurate attitudes, and that "both heuristic and systematic processing can occur in the service of this goal" (Chaiken et al., 1989, p. 214). Moreover, the HSM holds that motivational variables may have similar effects on systematic and heuristic processing. According to this position, personal relevance does not

> influence only the magnitude of systematic processing . . . (but) also enhances the likelihood of heuristic processing, because (it increases) the cognitive accessibility of relevant persuasion heuristics and/or increases the vigilance with which people search (the setting or their memories) for relevant heuristic cues. (p. 226)

Consistent with this contention, Sorrentino, Bobocel, Gitta, Olson, and Hewitt (1988) found that participants high on certainty orientation were more influenced by source expertise when personal relevance was high (vs. low).

In its recent versions (Chaiken et al., 1989; Eagly & Chaiken, 1993), the HSM is featured as a multiple-motive model, encompassing defensive and impression management motivations in addition to the motivation for accuracy. The defense motivation is "the desire to form or to defend particular attitudinal positions. . . . The processing goal of defense-motivated recipients, then, is to confirm the validity of particular attitudinal positions and disconfirm the validity of others" (Chaiken et al., 1989, p. 234). In addition, the HSM posits an impression management motive, that, "When paramount, [causes the] desire to express attitudes that will be socially acceptable to potential evaluators, both real and imagined" (p. 234).

Just as with accuracy motivation, the "defense-motivated goal of confirming the validity of particular attitudinal positions, and the impression motivated-goal of assessing the social acceptability of . . . attitudinal positions" (Chaiken et al., 1989, p. 235) can prompt systematic or heuristic processing, according to their model. "In other words, the multiple-motive HSM views processing mode and processing goals as orthogonal; heuristic and systematic processing occur in the service of the individual's processing goal, whatever that goal may be" (p. 235).

An important premise of HSM is that systematic and heuristic processing can co-occur. Three possible effects of such co-occurrence are referred to as (a) the attenuation, (b) the bias, and (c) the additivity hypotheses. The *attenuation* hypothesis assumes that systematic processing may provide recipients with additional evidence regarding message validity, which may contradict the implications of the persuasion heuristics being utilized. Consequently, the impact of the heuristic cues may be attenuated. The bias hypothesis assumes that heuristic cues

> influence recipients' perceptions of the probable validity of persuasive messages, and they may also bias recipients' perceptions of message content. Thus, if a message is delivered by an expert, its arguments may be viewed more positively than if the message is delivered by a nonexpert. (p. 228)

The *additivity* hypothesis assumes that both message factors and heuristics should exert significant effects on recipients' attitudes. Yet

> most existing research indicates that when recipients are willing and able to process systematically, message content manipulations exert strong main effects on postmessage attitudes, whereas heuristic-cue manipulations exert no significant persuasive impact. . . . In other words, this research overwhelmingly demonstrates the attenuation effect, in which systematic processing overrides the judgmental impact of heuristic processing. (p. 233)

To account for these findings, Chaiken et al. (1989) proposed that a 2 × 2 design in which variations in argument quality are orthogonally crossed with heuristic cues (mostly source expertise) provides a weak test of the additivity hypothesis because "two of the study's four cells represent clear cut cases in which message content blatantly *contradicts* the expertise heuristic (i.e., expert/weak arguments, inexpert/strong arguments)" (Chaiken et al., 1989, p. 223). If so, "inclusion of no-heuristic-cue control conditions, . . . should make additive effects in the two noncontradictory cells more detectable" (Chaiken et al., 1989, p. 223).

A major emphasis in the HSM concerns the relation of persuasion phenomena to broader social cognition principles. This emphasis is particularly apparent in the treatment of persuasion heuristics. It is reflected in "the assumption that the judgmental impact of heuristic cues should be moderated by the availability, accessibility, and perceived reliability of their associated heuristics" (Eagly & Chaiken, 1993, p. 342; see Baker, 1993, for fur-

ther discussion of the role of information accessibility and relevance in persuasion). This social cognitive emphasis is assumed to be distinctive to their approach because "aside from the heuristic-systematic model, the relevance of accessibility logic to persuasion processes has not generally been recognized" (Eagly & Chaiken, 1993, p. 342). It is of interest, however, that according to the HSM, accessibility considerations may also enter into the systematic processing of persuasive messages. Thus, Chaiken et al. (1989) acknowledged that "systematic processing (depends) upon . . . cognitive factors (e.g., the accessibility of knowledge structures that influence perceivers' interpretation and evaluation of information)" (p. 213). Similarly, Chaiken et al. recognized the relevance of availability considerations to systematic processing in their discussion of prior knowledge effects on such processing (Wood, 1982; Wood & Kallgren, 1988; Wood, Kallgren, & Preisler, 1985). As they put it, "Possessing an evaluatively biased store of knowledge may enhance recipients' abilities to rebut counterattitudinal arguments and to generate proattitudinal arguments . . . (so that) more knowledgeable recipients may be less persuaded by counterattitudinal messages but more persuaded by proattitudinal messages" (Chaiken et al., 1989, p. 230).

Commonalities Between the ELM and the HSM

Undoubtedly, the ELM and the HSM differ in some respects. Those are explicitly treated in Eagly and Chaiken (1993, chap. 7) and Petty (1994, p. 4) and will not be revisited here. More relevant to our purpose are features that the two frameworks share. First, both posit the existence of two qualitatively different modes of persuasion, one is more thorough and extensive than the other. Second, both assume that engagement of the more extensive mode (i.e., the central or the systematic mode) depends on sufficient motivation and ability to process information. Third, both agree that persuasion accomplished via one of the modes (i.e., the central or systematic mode) is more persistent, more closely linked to subsequent behavior, and more resistant to persuasion than persuasion accomplished via the remaining (peripheral–heuristic) mode. Fourth, both assert that the two persuasive modes can co-occur, albeit the exact manner of their co-occurrence is depicted somewhat differently in the ELM and the HSM: Although it permits co-occurrence, the ELM adheres, nonetheless, to the notion of a continuum whereby a trade-off (hence, a negative correlation) governs the use of the two modes. The HSM, on the other hand, allows orthogonality in use of the modes so that they can augment each other, or clash in their influence.

Finally, both the ELM and the HSM imply that the desire to hold accurate attitudes and opinions is often the "default" motivation in persuasion contexts. Similarly, both models assume that beyond accuracy strivings, extensive processing (i.e., central or systematic) can be affected by alternate motivations. In brief then, even though they may differ in specific emphasis, the ELM and the HSM share considerable features in common, the most important of which is the presumption of two qualitatively different persuasion modes. But are these two modes truly different? And how can such difference (or its absence) be decided anyway? We turn to these matters next.

Persuasion by a Single Route

How Should Process Uniformity Be Established? The "Rules of the Game"

Our basic argument is simple: The crucial distinction between cues and/or heuristics on the one hand and message arguments on the other refers to informational contents relevant to a conclusion, rather than to a principled difference in the persuasion process as such. Accordingly, cues and message arguments should be subsumed as special cases of the more abstract category of persuasive evidence. We argue, in other words, that the different informational contents corresponding to the cue versus message argument partition do not, in and of themselves, have a general effect on persuasion, nor are they impacted differently by persuasively relevant variables. Instead, the same overall process may transpire irrespective of whether the informational grist for the persuasive mill is of the cue or message type.

Let us illustrate the special case argument with the following analogy. Consider the distinction between Tylenol caplets versus tablets. Both may be considered special cases of the same medication, and the distinction between them is irrelevant, for all intents and purposes, to the phenomena that

Tylenol is assumed to affect. Of course, a given caplet may differ from a given tablet in ways that are absolutely critical; for example, it may contain a different dosage, a different concentration, or a different purity of the drug. But caplets versus tablets, as a whole, need not differ on these dimensions. Once these differences are controlled for, it should not really matter what form of the drug is administered, because the process whereby Tylenol exerts its effects should be the same in both cases. In analysis of variance (ANOVA) terms, the form of the drug should yield no main effects, nor should it interact (cf. Kruglanski & Mackie, 1990) with other parameters relevant to Tylenol-relevant phenomena (e.g., pain symptomatology, gastric sensitivity, etc.).

Just as specific caplets may differ from specific tablets, specific cues and specific message arguments may also differ from each other in parametrically relevant ways. For instance, a specific cue may appear less (or more) relevant to a conclusion than a specific message argument, and this degree of relevance may in fact constitute a significant characteristic of persuasion. A specific cue may be less (or more) complex, salient, or accessible than a specific message argument, and complexity, saliency, or accessibility may qualify as an important element of persuasion. Finally, a specific cue may appear either before or after a specific message argument, and the order of appearance or presentation may constitute an important dimension of persuasion. The foregoing does not imply that cues as a category systematically differ from message arguments as a category in those particular ways. For on the same parametric dimension that a given cue may differ from a given message argument (e.g., relevance, complexity, or order of presentation), a particular cue may differ from another cue, and a particular message argument may differ from another message argument. Of course, within-category variability as such does not deny the additional possibility of between-category variability. However, as we now proceed to demonstrate, there is little reason to believe that arguments as a category differ from cues and heuristics as a category on parameters relevant to persuasion.

Thus, once differences on persuasively relevant informational parameters are controlled for, cue-based and message argument-based persuasion should be impacted similarly by various persuasively relevant processing variables (e.g., motivation and cognitive capacity). In other words, we try to show that, all things considered, the two modes of persuasion lack discriminant validity, or functional independence—a known criterion for arguing the dissociation of psychological systems (used by Tulving, 1983, pp. 59–60, among others, to argue the distinction between semantic and episodic memory, or by Sloman, 1996, p. 10, to discuss the distinction between associative and rule-based reasoning).

To apply the functional independence criterion to this case, however, it is incumbent on us first to outline what variables are, in fact, relevant to persuasion, as well as what the underlying process of persuasion may be. These issues are addressed in our unimodel of persuasion, described next.

The Unimodel

Our persuasion unimodel is based on the Lay Epistemic Theory (LET) of the processes governing the formation of subjective knowledge (Kruglanski, 1989). Such knowledge may consist of judgments, opinions, or attitudes individuals may acquire or alter in various circumstances. Thus, in agreement with Chaiken et al. (1989), we view persuasion as integrally related to the general epistemic process of judgment formation. We believe it to be a motivated process of hypothesis testing and inference dependent on individuals' cognitive capacity and affected by cognitive availability and accessibility (Higgins, 1996) of pertinent information. More generally speaking, it is a process during which beliefs are formed on the basis of appropriate evidence.

THE CONCEPT OF EVIDENCE

But how may the concept of evidence be understood? According to LET, *evidence* refers to information relevant to a conclusion. *Relevance*, in turn, implies a prior linkage between general categories such that affirmation of one in a specific case (observation of the evidence) affects one's belief in the other (e.g., warrants the conclusion). Such a linkage is assumed to be mentally represented in the knower's mind, and it constitutes a premise to which he or she subscribes. For example, an individual may be convinced that "if a candidate totally lacked political experience, he would make a poor president," or alternatively, maintain a belief in a conditional probability

whereby "given that a candidate lacked experience, the chances of her making a good president are low (say 15%)." In both cases, granting our knower's beliefs, the candidate's lack of political experience becomes relevant evidence for his or her expected presidential performance. More formally speaking, the conditional belief linking (hence rendering relevant) the evidence to the conclusion is the *major premise* of a syllogism. Affirmation of the evidence in a particular instance—for example, compelling information that a specific Candidate X (say, Forbes) indeed lacked all political experience—constitutes the *minor premise*. Jointly, the two premises yield the (logical or probabilistic) conclusion concerning Candidate X's future presidential attainments.

The LET notion of evidence is compatible with major analyses of this concept within the philosophy of inference (e.g., Achinstein, 1983; Carnap, 1962, sec. 86; Glymour, 1980; Hempel, 1965). More to the point, it is highly congruent with treatment of this topic in major social psychological models of persuasion. Most explicit recognition of those evidential properties is accorded by the probabilogical models of belief inference put forth by McGuire (1960) and Wyer (1970, 1974) and in the Bayesian analysis offered by Fishbein and Ajzen (1975, pp. 181–188). Kindred notions of evidence appear in dissonance and balance theories (for reviews see Kruglanski, 1989, chap. 5; Kruglanski & Klar, 1987), or in the theories of reasoned action (Fishbein & Ajzen, 1975) and planned behavior (Ajzen, 1991).

For instance, according to the theory of *planned behavior*, attitudes or evaluations of objects "follow reasonably from the beliefs we hold about that object" (Ajzen, 1988, p. 120). Thus,

> we learn to like objects we believe have largely desirable characteristics, and we form unfavorable attitudes toward objects we associate with mostly undesirable characteristics. Specifically, the subjective value of each attribute contributes to the attitude in direct proportion to the strength of the belief, i.e., the subjective probability that the object has the attribute in question. (Ajzen, 1988, p. 32)

In terms of this discussion, the object's (positively or negatively) valenced attributes, as well as the outcomes the object may mediate (e.g., the health-promoting consequences of a given drug), constitute relevant evidence for its overall "goodness" or "badness," thus determining one's attitude toward the object. Presumably, this is based on a major premise, whereby the overall positivity of an object is conditional on the positivity of its attributes or mediated outcomes. In other words, if the object's attributes or mediated outcomes are believed to be positive (the minor premise), the object merits a positive evaluation (i.e., a positive attitude toward it); if these attributes or mediated outcomes are negative, it merits a negative evaluation (attitude). In the same way, then, that an enumeration of Bill Gates's assets may be relevant evidence for his wealth, a listing of Mother Teresa's good works is relevant evidence for her human kindness (meriting a positive attitude toward her), and a listing of aspirin's positive health implications is evidence for its medical benefits (also warranting a positive attitude). In summary then, a listing of positive (and/or negative) attributes associated with an object or positive and/or negative outcomes the object mediates affects one's belief or subjective likelihood that it is good (or bad) in accordance with a major premise conditionalizing an object's overall "goodness" on the positivity of its attributes, outcomes, or both.

The dual modes of persuasion as specific contents of evidence. The foregoing notion of evidence is the integrative glue that binds together the dual modes of persuasion. Specifically, the distinction between heuristic (or peripheral) cues and message arguments is now assumed to represent a difference in contents of evidence relevant to a conclusion, rather than a qualitative difference in the persuasive process as such. Consider a statement ascribed to Dr. Smith, a noted environmental specialist, whereby "the use of freon in household appliances destroys the ozone layer, and therefore ought to be prohibited." This argument may seem to be persuasive evidence to a recipient whose background knowledge included the (major) premise that "if something contributes to the thinning of the ozone layer (then) it should be prohibited." Dr. Smith's specific argument supplies the minor premise that "the use of freon in everyday appliances does destroy the ozone layer." In other words, Dr. Smith's pronouncement constitutes the "evidence" that, granting the major premise, warrants the conclusion that "the use of freon ought to be prohibited." Such orderly and logical processing of a message argument from evidence to conclusion has been typically considered the hallmark of persuasion by the systematic or central route.

But consider now a recipient who did not subscribe to the notion that "anything that causes the thinning of the ozone layer ought to be prohibited." Alternatively, this same recipient might be strongly committed to the assumption: "If an opinion is offered by an expert, (then) it is valid." This assumption may serve as a major premise of a syllogism, and the realization "Dr. Smith is an expert" may serve as a minor premise, hence furnishing evidence that (granting the major premise) points to the conclusion "Dr. Smith's opinion (that the use of freon ought to be prohibited) is valid." Such reliance on source attributes (such as expertise) has been typically regarded as characteristic of persuasion via the peripheral or the heuristic route. Yet from our unimodel's perspective, the two persuasion types share a fundamental similarity in that both are mediated by if–then, or syllogistic, reasoning leading from evidence to a conclusion.

MOTIVATION AND COGNITIVE CAPACITY

The foregoing, highly schematic (i.e., syllogistic or probabilogical) depiction of the evidence concept conceals the considerable amount of cognitive work often involved in constructing the evidence from the various bits and pieces available to the recipient in a given persuasion setting. The evidence may have to be gleaned from a thicket of informational detail in which it is embedded. Furthermore, the major premises that lend evidence its perceived relevance may need to be retrieved from memory, or may need to be made accessible beyond some functional threshold of activation. The memory search and activation processes occur partially in reaction to information presented to recipients in a given persuasive setting, including the heuristic/cue-related information, as well as the message as such. Thus, in a proper sense, they constitute a "cognitive response to persuasion" (Petty, Ostrom, & Brock, 1981). Moreover, such activities often entail considerable "cognitive work" that is quite painstaking and laborious. It is here that motivation and cognitive capacity enter into the equation; if the information is lengthy, complex, or unclear, the distillation of intelligible evidence may require a considerable amount of processing motivation and capacity. Similarly, if processing motivation and capacity are relatively low, only relatively simple and straightforward evidence will register, and thus exert a significant persuasive impact. In what follows, we address first motivational and cognitive ability concerns in general. Then, we relate them to the specific issue of persuasion via single versus dual modes.

MOTIVATION

In agreement with the ELM and the HSM, the LET also assumes that persuasion, and the formation of subjective knowledge more generally, is substantially affected by motivation (e.g., see Kruglanski, 1989). The variety of possible motivations that may impact knowledge formation is quite considerable. An individual trying to crystallize a judgment on some issue may desire accuracy and confidence on the topic. However, the relative weight given these two epistemic properties may vary, often outside the individual's awareness (Austin & Vancouver, 1996). The greater the proportional weight assigned to confidence or assurance as such, the stronger the individual's motivation for nonspecific cognitive closure (Kruglanski & Webster, 1996). In contrast, the greater the proportional weight assigned to accuracy per se, the stronger will be the individual's tendency to avoid closure and remain open-minded. The needs for nonspecific closure or the avoidance of closure are nondirectional in that they do not bias the judgmental process toward any particular conclusions. Another epistemically relevant, nondirectional motivation is the need for cognition (Cacioppo, Petty, Feinstein, & Jarvis, 1996); that is, the proclivity for, and intrinsic enjoyment of, complex thinking and information processing (see also Thompson, Chaiken, & Hazlewood, 1993).

Additionally, the judgmental process is affected by various directional motivations, or needs for specific closure (Kruglanski, 1989, 1990). Such specific closures refer to contents that appeal to the knower for some reason, representing preferred conclusions he or she may wish to reach. These may encompass a broad range of possible conclusions including self-esteem concerns (including ego-defensive or enhancing motivations implicating conclusions favorable to one's self as the preferential closures), impression management concerns (implicating as preferential closure conclusions that one is favorably evaluated by significant others), concern with one's economic and physical well-being, with one's good fortunes in various domains, and so on. Each such category

of preferred conclusions may be treated as a specific goal, considerably expanding the set of persuasively relevant motivations discussed in the persuasion literature so far. In short, according to LET, persuasion may be affected by a broad range of motivations including the three motivations specified in HSM (i.e., accuracy, defensive, and impression-management motivations) but also by additional motivations (e.g., need for nonspecific closure, need for cognition, and assorted needs for various specific closures).

The LET assumes that, generally speaking, all epistemic motivations impact the same broad parameters of judgment formation. These include initiation of a judgmental activity by a discrepancy between an actual and a desired epistemic state (whose specific nature depends on the momentarily operative motivation) and its termination when the discrepancy has been removed. Beyond initiating and terminating the epistemic activity, motivation may importantly affect the course of the persuasive encounter including its extent and direction. These may depend on both the quality and the magnitude of the underlying motivation for the activity. For example, the higher the need for (nonspecific closure; i.e., the greater its magnitude), the less extensive the information processing. By contrast, the higher the motivation for accuracy, or more specifically for the avoidance of closure, the more extensive the information processing (for discussion see Kruglanski, 1996b; Thompson & Kruglanski, 1998).

As implied earlier, motivation may also affect the direction of cognitive activity accompanying persuasion or judgment. Because a goal constitutes a cognitive structure (Austin & Vancouver, 1996; Bargh & Gollwitzer, 1994; Kruglanski, 1996a, 1996b; Srull & Wyer, 1986), its activation may spread to associated cognitions, increasing their accessibility (Higgins, 1996). This, in turn, may impact the construal of subsequent events (Higgins, Rholes, & Jones, 1977; Thompson, Roman, Moskowitz, Chaiken, & Bargh, 1994). Motivation may also affect selective attention to relevant stimuli. The attention-grabbing properties of goal-relevant objects have been demonstrated in several studies (Berscheid, Graziano, Monson, & Dermer, 1976; Erber & Fiske, 1984; Ruscher & Fiske, 1990; Taylor, 1975).

In sum, the LET assumes that all instances of knowledge formation, including persuasion, are potentially impacted by a broad variety of motivations that affect the course of the judgmental process; that is, its extent (or depth) and direction. Later, we argue that these motivational effects are the same irrespective of whether the evidence for the judgments is contained in heuristics or cues, versus message arguments. Now, however, let us consider some cognitive ability concerns of pertinence to persuasion.

COGNITIVE ABILITY: ITS "SOFTWARE" AND "HARDWARE" ASPECTS

Both the ELM and the HSM stress that persuasion importantly depends on the recipient's cognitive ability. It seems important to further distinguish between a "software" aspect of ability, which we refer to as *capability*, and a "hardware" aspect, referred to as *capacity*.

Capability. The capability notion refers to the knower's possession of active cognitive structures that enable the reasoning process involved in the production of knowledge and judgment. In this sense, cognitive capability refers to the epistemic "software" that is stored in the individual's memory and selected or rendered operative in particular circumstances. As noted earlier, beliefs representing the major and minor premises from which judgmental conclusions are derived need to be both mentally represented or available (Higgins, 1996) in the individual's mental repertoire, as well as sufficiently accessible, to be used in a specific instance. Take, for example, a physician who, after consulting an MRI scan, concludes that the patient has a slipped disk. This physician must have available and accessible (a) the mental representation linking a specific MRI pattern with disk slippage and (b) the representation asserting that the specific imaging pattern did indeed turn up.

Availability and accessibility of mental representations in a given content domain may both determine the extent of information processing and bias its direction. Extent of processing might be affected, for example, if a knower possessed many (vs. few) beliefs of the major premise type linking different types of evidence to conclusions about a given object. The application of multiple conditional beliefs may require the processing of different types of evidence, thus enhancing the amount (and duration) of processing. Occasionally, such evidence may give rise to conflicting inferences, requiring even further processing.

The biasing effect of mental representations

(prior knowledge) refers to the fact that the presence of specific premises may direct the knower's attention selectively to categories those premises specify (see Spiegel, Kruglanski, & Thompson, 1998). For example, a premise specifying that "Only *unlit* streets in New York are dangerous" (i.e., "only if a street is unlit is it *then* dangerous") may bias the individual's attention toward the degree of lighting, whereas a premise specifying that "only streets between the 70th and the 90th are dangerous" may direct one's attention to the street number.

Recent empirical evidence has confirmed the importance of belief accessibility in the processing of both message and cue information in persuasion situations. With respect to message processing, Fabrigar, Priester, Petty, and Wegener (1998) found that experimentally increasing the cognitive accessibility of participants' attitudes toward an issue increased processing of subsequent persuasive communications, as evidenced by an enhanced persuasive impact of strong (vs. weak) message arguments. According to one explanation proposed by Fabrigar et al., this was due to spreading activation from the primed attitude to related knowledge and beliefs, which were subsequently utilized in participants' elaboration of the message arguments. Also, Howard (1997) reported that highly familiar (and hence, accessible) arguments (e.g., don't put all your eggs in one basket) had greater persuasive impact than less familiar arguments of comparable length and semantic meaning (e.g., don't risk everything on a single venture) for participants low (vs. high) in issue involvement, high (vs. low) in distraction, or low (vs. high) in need for cognition. With respect to the impact of heuristic and peripheral cues, Maio and Olson (1998) found that misrepresenting one's attitude toward a likable communicator increased subsequent agreement with the communicator's position toward an issue, presumably because dissimulation heightened the accessibility of participants' genuine attitude toward the source, and thus enhanced the operation of a "likability heuristic." Thus, recent research, as well as theoretical statements within the dual-process models, confirms our unimodel's position that availability and accessibility of relevant knowledge structures can enhance the judgmental impact of both heuristics and cues and persuasive arguments.

Capacity. The "hardware" aspect of cognitive ability refers to the "state of the machine," given the individual's degree of alertness, energy level, or cognitive load. It refers, in other words, to attentional capacity limitations on the amount of processing the knower is capable of carrying out at any given moment (Kahneman, 1973). Thus, under conditions that tax the knower's cognitive capacity, he or she should be less able to process extensive bodies of information than under conditions where his or her capacity is relatively unencumbered. Again, we assume that cognitive capability or capacity considerations are unrelated to whether persuasion is accomplished via cues and heuristics or message arguments. We revisit this point later.

THE UNIMODEL AND THE DUAL-MODE FRAMEWORKS: COMPARE AND CONTRAST

As the foregoing discussion attests, the unimodel shares important points in common with the two dual-mode frameworks. All three formulations assume that the elaboration of persuasively relevant information can vary in extent. Similarly, all three assume that such elaboration can be affected by motivational and cognitive ability considerations. The unimodel differs from the dual-process frameworks, in that it (a) recognizes as relevant to persuasion a broader range of motivations than do the dichotomous models; (b) distinguishes between the software and hardware aspects of cognitive ability; and (c) is more explicit about the evidence concept, which it shares with prior, classic models of persuasion (McGuire, 1960; Wyer, 1970, 1974). It is this concept that warrants our essential claim for the unimodel, namely that heuristics or cues and message arguments all constitute forms (or content categories) of persuasive evidence.

It is instructive to consider this claim in reference to the motivation and cognitive ability factors outlined earlier. Specifically, we propose that these factors exert an identical impact on the processing of heuristics or cues and message arguments. To see why this is so, it is necessary to clarify at the outset what we take the terms *cues* and *heuristics* to signify. Essentially, we define them as information types extraneous to the message arguments as such. This definition is hardly esoteric. On the contrary, it is thoroughly consistent with discussions of these terms in the dual-mode literature. Both theoretically and empirically, cues and heuristics were invariably juxtaposed to message arguments. Even though in the ELM a

specific bit of information (e.g., about the source's expertise) can act as a cue in some cases, and in other circumstances function as a message argument, it cannot serve as both at the same time (Petty, 1994). This suggests that the cue and argument *functions* are fundamentally different. In other words, within the ELM, the same bit of information can fulfill different functions in different circumstances. Cues have been contrasted with message arguments in the HSM research program as well. For example, although Chaiken and Maheswaran (1994) measured participants' cognitive responses both to the source (*Consumer Reports* article vs. K-Mart brochure) and also to the message (promoting the XT–100 answering machine), they calculated their "valenced index of *systematic processing* . . . [as] . . . the net positivity of subjects' positive and negative cognitive responses to *specific product attributes* [i.e., those mentioned directly in the communication]" (p. 465, italics added).

By contrast, in our unimodel, the function fulfilled by cues and heuristics and message arguments is essentially the same. Both serve as forms of evidence, hence they are functionally equivalent. As we see it, there is no inherent difference between a cue and heuristic function, and a message argument function, in the persuasion process.

We can now turn to the issue of whether heuristics and cues and message arguments are impacted differently by motivation and cognitive ability. Note that in this connection cues or heuristics, as information types extraneous to message arguments, need not systematically differ from arguments in their difficulty of processing. Thus, message arguments may be presented in a clear, succinct form requiring little decoding effort; in an oblique form; or replete with irrelevant detail that may render them extremely laborious to digest. Similarly, persuasively relevant information extraneous to the message (i.e., cues or heuristics) can be presented briefly and succinctly, or in a form that is particularly long and unwieldy. In fact, the notion that peripheral cues need not be very simple and straightforward, but rather could be elaborate and complex, was explicitly noted by Petty and Cacioppo (1986, p. 130).

If heuristic cues and message arguments do not systematically differ in their length or complexity, it follows then that their processing should not require systematically different amounts of either cognitive capacity (the hardware aspect of cognitive ability) or processing motivation. More generally, the effects of capacity or motivation should be the same irrespective of whether the evidence is comprised of cues and heuristics or message arguments. Again, precedent for this notion exists in statements from the dual-process literature. For instance, Chaiken et al. (1989) noted that "motivational variables such as personal relevance do not influence only the magnitude of systematic processing. These variables . . . also enhance heuristic processing" (p. 226).

The directional biasing effects that various motivations or cognitive capabilities (the software aspect of cognitive ability) may induce also should have a similar impact on information irrespective of its evidential type. In reference to cognitive capability, Chaiken et al. (1989) noted that "heuristic processing depends on whether cognitively available heuristics are activated or accessed from memory" (p. 217). Similarly "systematic processing (depends) upon . . . cognitive factors (e.g., the accessibility of knowledge structures that influence perceiver's interpretation and evaluation of information" (p. 217). With regard to motivation, Chaiken et al. explicitly stated that "the multiple-mode HSM views processing mode and processing goals as orthogonal; heuristic and systematic processing occur in the service of the individual's processing goal whatever that goal may be" (p. 235).

By now we have seen that heuristics and cues or message arguments share the same evidential structure, that they do not differ systematically in their length or complexity, and that they should be impacted similarly by cognitive ability or motivational factors. However, one still might ask whether these two forms of evidence differ systematically in any other way germane to persuasion. For instance, are message arguments as a category more or less relevant to persuasive conclusions than are heuristic cues? A moment's reflection suggests that this could not be the case. Both message arguments and heuristics or cues may vary widely among themselves in their relevance to the conclusion. In fact, the "strong" or high-quality arguments in ELM research are such precisely because they are more relevant to the conclusion than are "weak" or low-quality arguments. Similarly, Chaiken's work on the reliability of heuristics (Chaiken, 1987; see also Chaiken et al., 1989; Eagly & Chaiken, 1993) indicates that heuristics may differ in their perceived relevance to a conclusion. For instance, some people may

subscribe to the premise "friends give good advice," whereas other people may not. For the former person, the friendship status of the communicator is relevant to the validity of his or her advocacy, whereas for the latter, it is not. Although it is clear that both cues and heuristics and message arguments may exhibit within-category variability in relevance, can one assume that one of these categories is systematically more relevant than the other? The answer appears to be no. For a devoutly religious person, a "heuristic" involving the authority of God or of a central ecclesiastical text may seem more relevant to the veracity of a particular opinion than does a logically impeccable message argument of lowly, secular origin. In contrast, to an individual who is deeply suspicious and distrusting of institutional authority in all its forms, a message argument (even a technically flawed one) may nearly always appear more relevant to a conclusion than does information portraying a communicator as a renowned expert in the area. In short, the relevance of evidence to a conclusion is subjective, and fundamentally orthogonal to whether the evidence is a cue or heuristic or a message argument.

Is message-related evidence systematically more accessible in memory than heuristic evidence? The answer, again, seems to be no. As Chaiken et al. (1989) pointed out, different heuristics may differ in their accessibility, as may the premises relevant to different message arguments. Nor should one expect that message arguments as a category will be more or less accessible than cues and heuristics as a category. Does message-related evidence differ from heuristic or peripheral evidence in ordinal position—another variable known to affect persuasion (Hovland, 1957)? In other words, is it inevitable that recipients encounter cues and heuristics before they encounter message arguments? Once more, no. Ordinal position, after all, is under the control of the presenter and has little to do with the content or type of information per se. For instance, the authors' credentials in "op-ed" pieces are often conveyed at the end of the article, that is, after the reader has been exposed to the "message" as such.

AN INTERIM SUMMARY

It is time now to take stock, and revisit the "routes to persuasion" question: How many of them exist? According to our LET-inspired unimodel, most knowledge formation—persuasion being a specific case—is affected by a process wherein conclusions are inferred from subjectively appropriate evidence. This process, in turn, requires the construction of evidence both from the information presented and also from background notions stored in memory. Also, it is affected by the availability and accessibility of relevant knowledge structures influencing the recipient's cognitive capability to construct the evidence, by the type and amount of information presented, by the recipient's motivation to process this information deeply (vs. superficially), and by the recipient's cognitive capacity (or available attentional resources) for doing so. Applying our "rules of the game" for deciding process uniformity, the material reviewed thus far seems strongly consistent with our unimodel. This analysis, incorporating numerous statements in the dual-process literature, implies that heuristics, cues, and message arguments do not systematically differ on such persuasively critical variables as the accessibility or availability of premises related to conclusions, their degree of relevance to the conclusion, the length and complexity of information in which the persuasive information is embedded, or the order in which it is processed by the recipient. Moreover, heuristics and cues and message arguments do not appear to be impacted differentially by motivation or cognitive ability. In short, persuasion outcomes based on the processing of heuristics and cues, and of message arguments, do not appear to be functionally independent. Therefore, the case for the unimodel would seem to be solid. However, one minor obstacle mitigates against unequivocal acceptance of this conclusion: veritable mountains of published empirical evidence apparently suggesting the very opposite. We now proceed to examine this evidence in greater detail.

EMPIRICAL EVIDENCE FOR THE DUAL MODES

A major empirical point for the functional independence of psychological processes can be made through demonstrations that they are impacted differently by, and hence that they "interact with," other variables (Tulving, 1983). In the case of the dual-process models, the large body of empirical findings (for reviews see Eagly & Chaiken, 1993; Petty & Cacioppo, 1986) is commonly taken to suggest the presence of interactions between evidential content type (i.e., cue vs. argument) and

determinants of "depth of processing" (e.g., motivation and cognitive capacity) on such significant persuasion outcomes as attitude change, its persistence over time, its resistance to counterpersuasion, and its relation to relevant, overt behaviors. Two categories of such interaction effects may be discerned. One we call *inferred* interactions, because these are cases where a variable's effect (e.g., that of distraction) is empirically observed in research incorporating one evidence type only (e.g., message arguments). The implicit, albeit untested, assumption in such a case is that the effect in question would fail to be manifest with the alternative evidence type (e.g., with cues or heuristics). The other type we call *manifest* interactions. These are cases where one evidence type (e.g., heuristic cues) is actually observed to interact with a determinant of processing extent (e.g., issue relevance or need for cognition) in a way patently different from that of the other evidence type (e.g., message arguments). We first consider findings in these two categories, reconsider them in terms of our unimodel, and then describe the empirical evidence supporting our reformulation.

Inferred interactions. The inferred interaction category is exemplified by research on distraction (for a review see Petty & Cacioppo, 1986, pp. 139–141). In the classical work by Petty, Wells, and Brock (1976), distraction was found to enhance persuasion by low-quality arguments and to decrease persuasion by high-quality arguments. Petty and Cacioppo (1986) concluded that "distraction is one variable that affects a person's ability to process a message in a relatively objective manner" (p. 141). Although in agreement with this conclusion, our perspective raises the question (addressed subsequently) of whether distraction may not interfere similarly with the processing of cue-related or heuristic information. We present evidence relevant to this issue later.

In a study by Schumann, Petty, and Clemens (1990), the repetition of message arguments extolling the desirable properties of a new pen increased the correlation between the positivity of recipients' attitudes toward this object and their expressed intention to purchase it. Yet, it is unclear whether repetition of cue-based or heuristically based evidence (and the opportunity to thoroughly process it) might not affect the attitude–behavior correlation in much the same way. Here, the interaction between evidence form and repetition (as far as the attitude–intention relation is concerned) may be only inferred, rather than manifestly observed.

Cacioppo, Petty, Kao, and Rodriguez (1986) found that "attitudes toward the candidates in the 1984 presidential election predicted voting intentions and reported behavior better for people who were high rather than low in their 'need for cognition' " (Petty & Cacioppo, 1986, p. 180). They concluded that when dispositional factors enhance people's motivation or ability to elaborate message-relevant information, attitude–behavior correlations become higher. Yet, the need for cognition might also enhance people's motivation to process heuristic or cue-related information, thus increasing the correspondence between behavior and attitudes formed on the basis of information extraneous to the communication.

In research by Petty, Cacioppo, and Heesacker (1985), source credibility and message quality were deliberately confounded. Participants received either a high-quality message (in support of a senior comprehensive exam) delivered by a prestigious source or a low-quality message from a low-prestige source. They manipulated issue involvement to be high for half the participants (the advocacy was said to involve a change in policy at participants' own university), and low for the other half (the change was said to occur at a remote university). They found that under high personal relevance, the relatively positive attitude formed in the strong message/source (vs. weak message/source) condition persisted over a period of 10 to 14 days following exposure to the advocacy, whereas in the low-involvement condition the same difference did not emerge. Petty and Cacioppo (1986) concluded accordingly that "subjects who formed their initial attitudes based on a careful consideration of issue relevant arguments (high relevance) showed greater persistence of attitude change than those subjects whose initial attitudes were based primarily on the source cue (low relevance)" (p. 178). Yet, because of the confounding in this study of source prestige and message quality, one may not know for certain that an interaction occurred between evidential type and personal relevance with respect to the persistence of initial attitude change. Such an interaction is inferred, rather than being explicitly manifest, resting on the assumption that under high relevance recipients process primarily message arguments. If, however, high-relevance participants may be generally attentive to information, they might under some conditions (specified later) carefully process cue-related information as well (e.g., information about source expertise or prestige). Moreover, it is possible that it is the care and thoroughness of processing, rather than the type of information processed (i.e., cues and heuristics vs. message arguments), which is the critical factor in determining the persistence of attitude change.

Finally, Petty and Cacioppo (1986) cited previous work (e.g., Burgoon, Cohen, Miller, & Montgomery, 1978; McGuire, 1964) that "attitudes can be made more resistant by motivating or enabling people to engage in additional thought about the reasons or arguments supporting their attitudes" (p. 182). We agree, but add the injunction that this should be so irrespective of the content type of the evidence on which the attitude, or the change in attitude, was based. As Petty and Cacioppo acknowledged, thus far these issues have not been adequately addressed in empirical research.

Manifest interactions. If the foregoing inferred interactions studies allow ambiguity as to whether cue or heuristic versus message argument-based persuasion is impacted differently by various factors, the manifest interaction studies answer the question directly and affirmatively. Prototypical of this research is the classic study by Petty, Cacioppo, and Goldman (1981) in which the following variables were manipulated orthogonally: (a) personal relevance of the issue to message recipients, (b) the quality of the arguments in the communication, and (c) the apparent expertise of the source. The data indicated clearly that personal relevance had the opposite persuasive effects in regard to source expertise than it did in regard to argument quality. Whereas argument quality was a more important determinant of persuasion for high- (vs. low-) relevance participants, source expertise was the more important determinant for low- (vs. high-) relevance participants. Taken at a face value, these interactive results and many similar ones reported in the literature (for reviews see Eagly & Chaiken, 1993; Petty & Cacioppo, 1986) appear to constitute powerful support for the dual-process models. They imply that the content type of evidence does in fact matter, and that cues and heuristics (vs. message arguments) are impacted in diametrically opposite ways by the very same moderator variables. Confirmation of the dual-process approach would appear virtually inescapable unless an alternative account of these results were possible.

REINTERPRETING MANIFEST INTERACTION EFFECTS

Consider the research by Petty, Cacioppo, and Goldman (1981) cited earlier. In that experiment, cue information regarding source expertise (a) was presented to participants prior to the message arguments and (b) was considerably briefer (in terms of the sheer number of words it contained) than message argument information. As a consequence, it seems plausible that the cue and heuristic information in this case was much easier to process than the message argument information. But earlier we noted that cue and heuristic information need not be briefer, less complex, or easier to process than message information. If one takes this notion seriously, and also assumes that the amount, complexity, and ordinal position of information in the communicative sequence do matter to persuasion, then one may account for previous findings without according a necessary role to the content type of the evidence.

It is entirely possible, in other words, that the reason why message arguments have had a greater impact under high (vs. low) issue involvement is that they were both more extensive and also appeared later in the informational sequence, either of which would have made them less likely to be thoroughly processed. As such, message arguments were particularly likely to benefit from the enhanced processing motivation engendered in the high- (vs. the low-) involvement condition. Similarly, because the more extensive, and secondarily presented, message arguments failed to be processed carefully under the low-involvement condition; the brief, easily processed, and initially presented cue and heuristic information may have enjoyed a persuasive advantage in this situation.

The unintended covariation in the Petty, Cacioppo, and Goldman (1981) research between information length and ordinal position on the one hand, and the evidential type of the information on the other hand, is hardly unique. Quite the contrary, it is endemic in much of the work conducted with the ELM and HSM research programs. Thus, Petty's (1994) "State of the Art" review described six major (most frequently cited) ELM studies, and chapter 7 in Eagly's and Chaiken's (1993) volume discussed seven influential HSM studies. In all of this research, listed in Table 1, the message argument information was considerably more exten-

sive, elaborate, and easy to process than the cue or heuristic information. Furthermore, in 9 out of the 13 studies the cue or heuristic information appeared before the message arguments, and in the remaining 4 studies, concomitantly with the message arguments. (For instance, in the research by Wells & Petty [1980] the cue consisted of the communicator's head movements that occurred as he was delivering the message arguments.) If our analysis is correct, controlling for informational extent and ordinal position should eliminate the apparent differences in the way cues and heuristics versus message arguments have interacted with various factors known to affect persuasion (e.g., involvement) in past research. These notions were examined empirically by Thompson, Kruglanski, and Spiegel (1998). We summarize their results later.

Testing the Unimodel

Study 1

A major finding in the dual-mode literature has been that only message arguments but not cue-related or heuristic information drive attitude change when the issue is personally involving for the recipient (e.g., Petty, Cacioppo, & Goldman 1981). In contrast, when personal involvement is low, attitude change has been influenced primarily by cues or heuristics. As noted earlier, one reason for this may be that in the typical dual-mode study cue information is brief, whereas message argument information is relatively lengthy. When the issue is involving to the recipient, his or her motivation may be sufficiently high to prompt the relatively laborious processing that lengthy informational passages may require to yield a persuasive impact. According to the unimodel, however, the critical feature here is not whether the information is of the heuristic or cue versus message argument variety, but rather its length and complexity. Consistent with this logic, our first experiment utilized relatively long heuristic information manipulating apparent source expertise, followed by an equally lengthy paragraph containing message arguments about an issue. Cross-cutting the source expertise manipulation we varied the personal relevance of the issue. We predicted that the heuristic information in this case would have the greater

TABLE 35.1. Characteristics of Message Arguments and Peripheral/Heuristic Cues From Studies Featured in Petty (1994) and Eagly and Chaiken (1993)

Study	Type of Cue or Heuristic	Order of Presentation	Length of Arguments (A) and Cues, Heuristics (C)	Cues Seem Easier to Process?
ELM studies				
Heesacker, Petty, & Cacioppo (1983)	Source expertise	Cue first	A: *Several argument* C: 30-word statement	Yes
Petty & Cacioppo (1984)	Number of arguments	Simultaneous	A: 3 to 9 arguments C: —	Yes
Petty, Cacioppo, & Goldman (1981)	Source expertise	Cue first	A: 8 *elaborated arguments* C: Short statement	Yes
Petty, Cacioppo, & Schumann (1983)	Celebrity status	Cue first	A: 5 *one-sentence arguments* C: —	Yes
Petty, Harkins, & Williams (1980)	Group size	Cue first	A: 5-min videotape C: Short statement	Yes
Wells & Petty (1980)	Head movements	Simultaneous	A: Short spoken editorial C: —	Yes
HSM studies				
Axsom, Yates, & Chaiken (1987)	Audience response	Simultaneous	A: 5-min audiotape C: —	Yes
Chaiken (1979)	Source attractiveness	Cue first	A: 2 brief oral arguments C: —	Yes
Chaiken (1980)	Source likeability	Cue first	A: 2 or 6 short arguments C: Paragraph	Yes
Chaiken & Eagly (1983)	Source likeability	Cue first	A: *5-min message* C: Paragraph	Yes
Chaiken & Maheswaran (1994)	Source credibility	Cue first	A: *450-word description* C: Short statement	Yes
Maheswaran & Chaiken (1991)	Consensus	Cue first	A: *450-word description* C: Short statement	Yes
Ratneshwar & Chaiken (1991)	Source expertise	Cue first	A: 9-sentence paragraph C: 2 short paragraphs	Yes

Note. In column 4, the longer set of information is italicized; in some cases, cues had no "length" per se; also, in Chaiken (1980) and Ratneshwar and Chaiken (1991), cue and argument information were roughly equal in length. ELM = elaboration likelihood model; HSM = heuristic systematic model.

persuasive impact in the high (vs. low) personal relevance condition. Specifically, the tendency of recipients to be more persuaded by the expert source than by the inexpert source should be greater when personal involvement was high than when it was low.

PARTICIPANTS AND PROCEDURE

Participants in our study, all introductory psychology students at the University of Maryland, College Park (UMCP), read an introductory paragraph about a proposal to institute a policy requiring graduating seniors to pass a comprehensive exam in their major area of study. If implemented, par-

ticipants were informed, the proposal would take effect the following year either at several schools in the Midwest (the low-involvement condition), or at several Mid-Atlantic schools, including UMCP (the high-involvement condition). Following that, participants received information about a potential speaker at a conference where implementation of the proposal would be decided. This information included a one-page résumé listing the educator's academic credentials and activities, followed by a letter he allegedly wrote in support of the comprehensive exam proposal.

All participants read a sample résumé of "Mr. David Whittaker," initially described as a "BA in Communications from Lincoln State University."

Subsequently, however, the information diverged for the expert and inexpert conditions. In the expert condition, the résumé emphasized Whittaker's work on curriculum studies in higher education, including relevant publications and presentations at various professional meetings. In the inexpert condition, by contrast, the résumé listed instead Whittaker's work on physical education with an emphasis on special needs of elementary school students. All participants then read the same letter allegedly written by Whittaker to "Dr. Julian Bradshaw" of the "Interim Board on Improving Higher Education." After initially expressing strong support for implementing the exams, the letter listed six arguments in favor of the policy, adopted from Petty, Harkins, and Williams (1980). According to a pretesting, four of the arguments for the exams were moderately weak. They stated that the exams would "put the university at the forefront of a national trend," that "many parents were in their favor," that "the students' job prospects might be improved," and that the exams "would allow students to compare their achievements with students at other schools." Two of the arguments were strong, namely, that the exams "have been associated with a reversal in declining achievement test scores" and "with an increase in the quality of undergraduate teaching." After they finished reading the letter, participants responded to a variety of measures including manipulation checks on the expertise and issue involvement manipulations and the critical dependent variable; that is, their personal attitude toward the proposed exam policy.

RESULTS

Manipulation checks. Appropriate manipulation checks verified that participants exposed to the expert source perceived his expertise as significantly greater than those exposed to the inexpert source ($p < .02$), and that participants in the high- (vs. low-) involvement condition indeed appeared to be more personally involved in the issue ($p < .001$).

Attitude toward comprehensive exams. On the first page of participants' response booklet, they reported their personal attitude toward the proposed policy. First, they indicated "the extent to which you personally agree or disagree with the policy of requiring seniors to pass a mandatory comprehensive exam before they can graduate" by circling a number on a Likert-type, 9-point scale

ranging from –4 (*strongly disagree*) to 4 (*strongly agree*). Then they responded to three identically scaled semantic differentials to indicate the extent to which they thought that comprehensive exams for seniors ranged from –4 (*bad, harmful, foolish*) to 4 (*good, beneficial, wise*). The four scores were highly intercorrelated ($\alpha = .91$) and were combined to form an overall index of participant attitude. When the scores from this index were submitted to an Involvement × Source Expertise ANOVA, a significant interaction emerged, $F(1, 98) = 4.78$, p $< .05$. As shown in Table 2, issue involvement decreased participants' favorability toward the policy when it was advocated by the inexpert and increased their acceptance of the policy when it was advocated by the expert. Most important, although communicator expertise made no difference in participants' attitude when they did not expect the policy to affect them personally ($t < 1$), participants in the high-involvement condition evaluated the policy more favorably when it was advocated by the expert than when it was advocated by the inexpert, $t(48) = 2.18$, $p < .05$.

These results suggest that when the heuristic or cue information (in this case, information about the source expertise) is relatively lengthy and complex, participants under high involvement are more successful in realizing its implications than participants under low involvement. It begins to appear, then, that it is not the content or type of the evidence that matters but rather its length or complexity. Consistent with the unimodel, the motivational variable of issue relevance seems to have had the same effect on the processing of heuristic and cue (i.e., nonmessage) information as it has had on message argument information in prior research.

Study 2

Adequate processing of relatively lengthy and complex information requires not only the proper

TABLE 35.2. Attitude Toward Mandatory Comprehensive Exam Proposal as a Function of Outcome-Relevant Involvement and Source Expertise (Study 1)

Source	Involvement	
	Low	High
Inexpert	-0.01_{ab}	-0.95_{a}
Expert	-0.54_{ab}	0.22_{b}

Note. Logical comparisons not sharing a common subscript differ at $p < .05$.

degree of motivation, but also sufficient cognitive capacity. Capacity-depleting events such as distraction or cognitive load should, therefore, attenuate the persuasive impact of such information. Indeed, prior research (e.g., the classic experiment by Petty et al., 1976) has demonstrated that distraction does interfere with the processing of message information, thus increasing the persuasive impact of low-quality arguments, and reducing the persuasive impact of high-quality arguments. As Petty and Cacioppo (1986) put it,

> distraction is one variable that affects a person's ability to process a message in a relatively objective manner. Specifically, distraction disrupts the thoughts that would normally be elicited by a message. Distraction should be especially important as a thought disrupter when people are highly motivated and able to process the message. (p. 141)

The unimodel suggests, however, that capacity depletion would impact not only the processing of message arguments, but also of appropriately lengthy and complex heuristic information. Our second study explored this particular possibility.

The design of this study was the same as that of Study 1 except for two changes. For one, half the participants were run in a cognitive load (or distraction) condition. Also, to ensure that cognitive load would have an effect, all participants were run in a high-involvement condition to establish a sufficient baseline level of effortful processing. Second, and most important, a cognitive load manipulation was carried out. Half the participants were presented at the outset with a nine-digit number and were asked to rehearse it to themselves as they went through the materials, so as to be able to reproduce it later. Our interest was in seeing whether distraction would interfere with participants' ability to carefully process the information about the communicator's background, hence diminishing the persuasive advantage of the expert (vs. inexpert) source.

PARTICIPANTS AND PROCEDURE

Participants in the study were introductory psychology students at UMCP. They all received instructions identical to those in the high-involvement condition of Study 1. As in that experiment, participants all read a one-page (fictitious) résumé of Mr. Whittaker indicating that he was either relatively expert (or inexpert) in the domain of cur-

riculum studies in higher education. Half the participants, those in the distraction condition, were shown a nine-digit number prior to reading the educator's résumé and were asked to silently rehearse the number until they were asked to write it down later during the session. No similar request was made to the remaining half of the participants, who were run in the no distraction condition.

RESULTS

Manipulation checks. As in Study 1, participants exposed to the expert source viewed his expertise as significantly higher than those exposed to the inexpert source ($p < .001$). Furthermore, appropriate manipulation checks indicated that participants who rehearsed the nine-digit number while reading the source and message materials felt more distracted than those who did not rehearse a number ($p < .05$).

Attitude toward comprehensive exams. The measure of participants' attitudes was identical to that of Study 1 ($\alpha = .93$). When scores on this index were submitted to a Source Expertise × Distraction ANOVA, a significant interaction emerged, $F(1, 107) = 6.88$, $p < .01$. As shown in Table 3, distraction tended to increase participants' favorability toward the policy when it was advocated by the inexpert, but to decrease their agreement when it was advocated by the expert. Specifically, communicator expertise did not reliably affect participants' attitude in the distraction condition, $t(53)=1.22$, $p = .224$; however, participants in the no distraction condition evaluated the policy more favorably when it was advocated by the expert communicator than when it was advocated by the inexpert, $t(54) = 2.51$, $p < .02$. It would seem then that relatively lengthy and complex heuristic information requires both sufficient cognitive capacity, as well as processing motivation, to yield a persuasive impact, just as with comparably elaborate message information in prior research. When

TABLE 35.3. Attitude Toward Mandatory Comprehensive Exam Proposal Under High Involvement as a Function of Source Expertise and Distraction (Study 2)

Source	No Distraction	Distraction
Inexpert	-0.74_a	0.87_b
Expert	0.71_b	0.13_{ab}

Note. Logical comparisons not sharing a common subscript differ at p < .05.

such capacity is depleted, participants are less able to realize the implications of "heuristic" information about the source than they are when their attentional resources are fully at their disposal.

Study 3

In Studies 1 and 2, by using relatively lengthy and complex source background information, we demonstrated that differences in apparent source expertise could have a greater, rather than lesser, impact under conditions of either high motivational involvement or processing capacity, compared to conditions where those variables were constrained to be low. However, in those studies we did not attempt to replicate past finding using the more traditional, briefer presentation of source information. In Study 3, we employed the design and procedure of Study 2, but extended it by adding a short source background condition to create a $2 \times 2 \times 2$ (Source Background [inexpert, expert] × Distraction [no, yes] × Source Background Length [short, long] experimental design. We expected to replicate the Source Expertise × Distraction effect from Study 2 when the source information was relatively long, as before. However, when the source information was shorter, and therefore less difficult to process when one is distracted, we expected to find only a main effect of expertise.

PARTICIPANTS AND PROCEDURE

Participants were undergraduates at UMCP who took part either to partially fulfill a course requirement or in exchange for $7. The procedure was identical to that of Study 2, with the exception of the additional short source background condition. Here, source information was condensed from the one-page résumé to a brief, two-sentence summary (approximately 50 words). In addition, we included self-report checks on the amount of effort participants felt was required to read both the information about the source, as well as that contained in his communication. These scales ranged from 0 (*no effort at all*) to 8 (*a great deal of effort*).

RESULTS

Manipulation checks. As expected, participants rated the source as more expert in the expert (vs. inexpert) condition ($p < .001$) and they reported feeling more distracted when they had to rehearse

the nine-digit string than when they did not ($p < .001$). Finally, participants described reading the long versions of the source background as requiring more effort than the shorter versions ($p < .02$).

Attitude toward comprehensive exams. We submitted the same composite measure of attitude used in Studies 1, 2, and 3 ($\alpha = .92$) to an Expertise × Distraction × Background Length ANOVA. The pertinent means are displayed in Table 4. A significant main effect of source expertise, $F(1, 118) = 6.27, p < .02$, indicated that attitudes were more favorable when the source was an expert ($M = 0.43$) than when he was not ($M = -0.49$). This was moderated by a marginally reliable Expertise × Distraction interaction, $F(1, 118) = 2.77, p = 0.99$. Just as we saw in Study 2, the impact of the expertise manipulation was greater when we did not distract participants, $F(1, 61) = 8.99, p < .005$, than when we did, $F < 1$. Finally, the predicted Expertise × Distraction × Length interaction, $F(1, 118) = 6.10, p < .02$, reveled that the by now familiar two-way interaction between expertise and distraction was reliable only when background information about the source was relatively long, $F(1, 65) = 10.43, p < .005$, and not when it was shorter, $F < 1$. Thus, it appears that distraction does not interfere with the processing of short cue or heuristic information of the type traditionally used in prior research, but it does significantly interfere with the processing of cue of heuristic information when the latter is sufficiently lengthy and complex.

Study 4

As we have seen, in a typical persuasion experiment brief heuristic information (e.g., about source expertise) is followed by much lengthier and more complex message argument information. Accord-

TABLE 35.4. Attitude Toward Mandatory Comprehensive Exam Proposal as a Function of Source Background Information Length, Cognitive Load, and Source Expertise (Study 3)

| | Source Background Information Length | | | |
| | Short | | Long | |
Cognitive Load	No Load	Load	No Load	Load
Source expertise				
Inexpert	-0.52_a	-0.78_a	-1.05_a	0.65_{bc}
Expert	0.57_{ab}	1.08_b	0.81_{bc}	-0.43_{ac}

Note. Logical comparisons not sharing a common subscript differ at $p < .06$.

ing to our analysis, it is the length and complexity of the information or its position in the sequence, rather than its content (i.e., being comprised of message arguments or cues and heuristics), that determine its persuasive impact. If so, the same pattern of interactions (e.g., with issue involvement) previously found to distinguish cue and heuristics from message arguments should obtain with any two informational sets, the first of which is relatively brief and simple and the subsequent one relatively lengthy and complex. Consider, for example, two separate sets of arguments exhibiting these characteristics. If the unimodel analysis is valid, the early appearing, brief arguments ought to exert greater persuasive impact under low as compared with high involvement, whereas the later appearing, lengthier arguments ought to exert greater persuasive impact under high as compared with low involvement.

Our Study 4 put these ideas to an empirical test. To that end, we independently manipulated the persuasive strength of brief, initial arguments supporting the comprehensive exam issue, as well as the strength of subsequent, extensive arguments that comprised a traditional persuasive communication. These were cross-cut with a manipulation of the recipients' personal involvement in the issue. In line with our single-process approach, we predicted that exposure to strong (vs. weak) initial, brief arguments would result in greater agreement with the communicator's position when issue involvement was low. Conversely, we expected that exposure to strong (vs. weak) subsequent, lengthy arguments would result in a more favorable attitude toward the communicator's position when issue involvement was high.

PARTICIPANTS AND PROCEDURE

A total of 174 introductory psychology students (98 women and 76 men) at UMCP participated in a study allegedly about "how people form impressions of those who represent the interests of others." They read about a proposal to implement mandatory comprehensive exams at their university. In the high-involvement condition, they learned that if approved the policy would be implemented the following year, whereas in the low-involvement condition, they learned that it could not be implemented before 10 years hence. Participants were told that a number of educators had responded to a newsletter advertisement solicit-

ing opinions about several new educational programs, in preparation for a national educational conference where the acceptance or rejection of those policies would be decided.

Participants then read two initial, one-sentence arguments allegedly submitted by a particular educator on a form from the newsletter ad, followed by six arguments (several sentences each) that comprised a formal letter to the National Board of Education expressing the educator's support for the mandatory exam policy. Argument quality (weak vs. strong) was manipulated independently both for initial, brief arguments and for subsequent, lengthy arguments. After reading the educator's letter, participants completed the four-item measure of attitude, as well as a number of checks on the manipulations. Finally, participants were fully debriefed by the experimenter.

RESULTS

Manipulation checks. Participants who read the strong initial arguments rated this first set as higher in quality than did participants who read the weak, initial arguments ($p < .001$). Also, participants who read the strong, subsequent arguments rated this second set as higher in quality than those who read the weak, subsequent arguments ($p < .001$). Furthermore, participants rated the initial, brief arguments as requiring less processing effort than the subsequent, lengthy arguments ($p < .05$). Finally, participants rated the policy as more personally relevant when issue involvement was high versus low ($p < .001$).

Attitude toward comprehensive exams. The four-item index of participant attitude used in Studies 1, 2, and 3 ($\alpha = .93$) was used here as well. An Initial Argument Strength × Subsequent Argument Strength × Issue Involvement ANOVA conducted on these scores revealed main effects for initial argument strength, $F(1, 162) = 5.92$, $p < .02$, and for subsequent argument strength. $F(1, 162) = 9.68$, $p < .002$. These means are displayed in Table 5. As expected, strong (vs. weak) initial arguments produced greater agreement with the communicator's position ($Ms = 1.73$ and 1.03), as did strong (vs. weak), subsequent arguments ($Ms = 1.79$ and 0.91). Also consistent with our predictions, the main effects of argument strength for both the initial and subsequent arguments were qualified by the issue involvement factor; $Fs(1, 162) = 3.99$ and 6.59, respectively, both $ps < .05$.

As depicted in the left panel of Table 5, strong (vs. weak) initial arguments elicited greater agreement in the low-involvement condition, $t(77) = 3.15$, $p < .005$, than in the high-involvement condition, $t(89)$. $p < 1$. However, as shown in the right panel of Table 5, strong (vs. weak) subsequent arguments induced more favorable attitudes when issue involvement was high, $t(89) = 4.03$, $p < .001$, than when it was low, $t(7)$ $p < 1$.

These results lend greater generality to the evidence supporting our persuasion unimodel. In particular, they speak to its proposition that the important characteristics of persuasive evidence (such as length/complexity, order, perceived relevance) are independent of whether such evidence constitutes cues or arguments. Previously, we demonstrated that nonargument cue information (e.g., pertaining to the expertise of the source) can have a greater, rather than lesser, impact on participants' attitudes when that information is made similar in length and complexity to that of message argument information typically used in prior research. In this study we showed further that variations in participants' processing motivation had precisely the same moderating effect on the impact of brief, initially encountered persuasive evidence when that information was of the argument type as it has in past research when that information was of the cue or heuristic type. Variations in the strength of brief, initially encountered message arguments had greater impact on attitudes when issue involvement was low (vs. high), presumably because here participants' lesser elaboration of the subsequent, lengthier message arguments did not overwhelm the judgmental implications of the arguments they encountered earlier.[1]

TABLE 35.5. Mean Favorability Toward Mandatory Senior Comprehensive Exams in Study 4, as a Function of Issue Involvement and Strength of Initial, Brief Arguments (Left Panel), and as of Subsequent, Lengthy Arguments (Right Panel)

Issue Involvement	Initial, Brief Arguments		Subsequent, Lengthy Arguments	
	Weak	Strong	Weak	Strong
Low	0.93a	2.20b	1.51b	1.59b
High	1.12a	1.32a	0.33a	1.94b

Note. Scores could range from −4 (very unfavorable) to +4 (very favorable). Entries not sharing a common subscript in each panel differ at the $p < .05$ level.

Discussion

The results of Studies 1 through 4 support, by and large, the basic premise of the unimodel whereby the same persuasion process takes place irrespective of whether the persuasive evidence is contained in the message arguments or in the heuristic/cue-related information (e.g., about the source). Controlling for information length and complexity, the same persuasively relevant variables (processing motivation and cognitive capacity) seem to interact with heuristic/message argument information in the same ways that they were found to interact with message argument and heuristic information in prior research.

In these studies, when made appropriately lengthy, the heuristic or cue-related source information yielded no systematic effects under low issue involvement, unlike previous findings where it was found to exert its effects under such conditions. Moreover, whereas in prior research (e.g., Petty, Cacioppo, & Goldman, 1981) source information typically yielded no significant effects under high issue involvement, it did yield consistent effects across these studies.

An interesting question in regard to this last finding is whether the expertise effects in the high-involvement condition (in Studies 1, 2, and 3)

[1]In a recent consumer advertising study, Haugtvedt and Wegener (1994) found that when they presented successive messages of comparable argument strength that varied in their advocacy (i.e., pro–con, con–pro), the attitudes of participants in the low- (vs. high-) involvement condition were more heavily impacted by the implications of the second message, whereas those of high- (vs. low-) involvement participants were more affected by the implications of the first message. Although these results may seem to contradict the results in our Study 4, it also is possible that the Haugtvedt and Wegener findings had more to do with high personal relevance, prompting a stronger online issue evaluation goal, which would attenuate the "recency effect" of the second message, despite the fact that in the high- (vs. low-) relevance condition the latter message may have received more extensive processing (Hastie & Park, 1986; Mackie, Worth, & Asuncion, 1990). Thus, the stronger recency effect of the second message under low relevance may have counteracted the greater processing of the second message under high involvement, with respect to the statistical comparisons on participants' final attitude. Alternatively, conclusions reached through extensive processing of the initial message in the high-involvement condition may have biased the processing of the counteradvocacy in the second message, thus reducing acceptance of its position. Our experimental procedures differ in a number of other ways (e.g., length of argument sets, cover story, manipulation of argument strength) that make direct comparisons between the two studies difficult.

might have been mediated via biased elaboration of the specific arguments presented in the message. Although this would hardly explain why, contrary to the dual-process models, expertise information exerted no persuasive impact in the low-involvement condition, it would be consistent with the dual-process notion that heuristic and cue information may occasionally bias the (central route or systematic) processing of message argument information, particularly when message quality is moderate, mixed, or ambiguous (e.g., Chaiken & Maheswaran, 1994; Petty et al., 1993). According to this view, the reliable source effects obtained under conditions of high involvement (or of low distraction) could be due to the extent to which the respective manipulations biased or guided effortful elaboration of the presented message arguments, in Studies 1, 2, and 3, where we combined strong and weak arguments to create mixed-strength messages of moderate overall quality. An alternative possibility suggested by the unimodel is that when the cue and heuristic (e.g., source) information is relatively substantial in amount, elaboration of that material itself could lead to greater confidence in the veracity of the advocated position, as well as to the generation of novel arguments that buttress that stance.

Note first that biased elaboration of message arguments seems unlikely in reference to Study 4. First, Chaiken and Maheswaran (1994) found biased systematic processing of message arguments only when message quality was mixed or ambiguous. In our Study 4, message quality (both for the initial, brief arguments and for the subsequent strong arguments) was clearly weak or clearly strong. More to the point, no cue or heuristic information was varied in that particular study. Hence, the observed effects could not possibly be explained by the biasing effects of cues or heuristics on central or systematic processing.

Finally, in regard to Studies 1, 2, and 3, there is another, more direct way to address the biased elaboration issue, namely by looking at our participants' cognitive responses to the persuasive materials with which they were presented. Specifically, we conducted regression analyses in each study to test whether the Source Expertise × Involvement (or Distraction) effects we found on attitudes were mediated by the valence of participants' cognitive responses about the specific message arguments, or else (or additionally) whether these effects were mediated by the valence of

thoughts about the source, the issue, or new arguments not mentioned in the message. Note in this connection that in the dual-mode literature, biased central or systematic processing seems to refer exclusively to the elaboration of the specific message arguments as such. For instance, Petty and Cacioppo (1986) stated that "variables can affect persuasion by affecting motivation and/or ability to process message arguments in a . . . biased fashion" (p. 162); and methodologically, they instruct judges to examine all thoughts listed by participants and "to delete those that were clearly irrelevant to *the topic of the message*" (Petty et al., 1993, p. 11, italics added; see also Petty et al., 1995, pp. 119–122). Similarly, Chaiken et al. (1989) asserted that "heuristic cues may . . . function to bias recipients' perception of *message content* . . . In essence heuristic cues can be used to disambiguate *message content*" (p. 228, italics added).

In each of our experiments, participants were given 3 min after completing the main measures of attitude to list any thoughts they recalled having had while reading the materials earlier. These protocols were coded by independent judges (average agreement = 74%) as involving either the source (e.g., "He's well qualified to speak to this issue"), the presented message arguments (e.g., "It's dumb to think that having the exams will lead to higher salaries for graduates"), the issue globally (e.g., "Having the exams is a good idea"), novel arguments for or against the policy (e.g., "Having the exams will put pressure on professors to 'teach to the test'"), and unrelated statements (e.g., "It's hot in this room"). Coders also made the additional discrimination as to whether each thought was positive, negative, or neutral in valence. For each participant we created valenced indexes for the first four content categories by subtracting the number of negative thoughts from the number of positive thoughts.

Mediational analyses were conducted following the guidelines discussed by Baron and Kenny (1986). The results of these analyses (for detailed descriptions, see Thompson et al., 1998) indicated that although valenced thoughts about presented message arguments did predict attitudes, this particular cognitive response index was not in turn predicted reliably either by the Source Expertise × Involvement interaction (in Studies 1 and 3), or by the Source Expertise × Distraction interaction (in Study 2). Finally, the direct effect of the experimental manipulations on attitude remained largely unchanged in each study, even after controlling for the effect of thoughts about the presented message arguments. Thus, in these studies, there was little evidence that the critical experimental interactions were mediated by thoughts about presented message arguments.[2]

Were the experimental effects then not mediated by participants' elaborations in these conditions? The answer is that they were, albeit not by the specific elaborations on the presented message arguments as such. In Studies 1, 2, and 3, a combined valenced index of global issue- and novel argument-related thoughts did predict attitude reliably, was itself predicted by the relevant interactions, and did reduce the impact of those same interactions on the index of participant attitude. In other words, this valenced cognitive response index did mediate the effect on attitude of the Expertise × Involvement and Expertise × Distraction interactions. The moral of the story? It is that extensive processing of source information can instigate considerable thinking about the issue that, in turn, may impact the individuals' pertinent attitudes. However, such thinking is not tantamount to central or systematic processing in as far as the latter have been operationally defined by the dual-process models in terms of elaboration on the specific message arguments presented.

Further Dual-Process Issues

The foregoing studies hardly exhaust the plethora of issues dealt with in the voluminous dual-mode literature. Space constraints render this a nearly impossible mission for any article, this one included. Nevertheless, it would be appropriate to briefly touch on the implications of the unimodel for a few major such concerns.

Reduced impact of cues under high elaboration likelihood. As noted earlier, Petty (1994) explained the reduced impact of cues under high elaboration likelihood (e.g., with high issue involvement) by invoking the hypotheses of (a) attention decrement (less attention being paid to cues when participants are thinking about message content); (b) salience loss of the cues "because of the extensive argument processing in which they are engaged" (Petty, 1994, p. 5); (c) cue-loss, "if the cue is drowned out by the arguments or is undermined by the implications of the arguments" (Petty, 1994, p. 5); (d) reduced cue extremity, because of lesser

amount of thought about the cue when occupied with processing the message arguments (Tesser & Conlee, 1975); and (e) reduced cue weighting because by comparison with the message argument the cue may appear less relevant to the requisite judgments.

From the unimodel perspective, the *cue* and *message arguments* terms in Petty's (1994) analysis merely represent two types of information presented in sequence. The reduced attention, weight, saliency, or perceived relevance accorded to the brief, early appearing information could occur irrespective of whether it constituted either a cue or another message argument, as in our Study 4. Similarly, the more extensive, later appearing information could be a cue (e.g., extensive source information) rather than a message argument. In short, the patently reasonable hypotheses advanced by Petty to explain the reduced impact of cues under high elaboration likelihood may apply to all cases where either brief (or less apparently relevant) information of whatever type is followed by extensive (or more apparently relevant) information.

The co-occurrence of systematic and heuristic processing. The HSM stresses that heuristic and systematic processing can exert joint effects of three possible kinds: (a) the impact of heuristic cues may be attenuated by systematic processing whose implications contradict those of the cues; (b) heuristic cues may bias recipients' perceptions of message content; and (c) both message arguments and heuristics can exert independent, hence additive, effects on recipients' attitudes. But from the unimodel perspective all three types of joint effects (i.e., attenuation, bias, and additivity) should be possible under the appropriate circumstances irrespective of whether one type of information was heuristic and the other constituted a

---

[2]In Thompson et al. (1998, Study 3), regression analyses indicated that the main effect of source expertise on attitude was in fact mediated by our valenced index of participants' cognitive responses about the presented message arguments, but only in the short source background condition. Recall than in Study 3 issue involvement was fixed to be high for all participants. Thus, the overall set of conditions for these participants was much the same as for those in the high task importance condition of Chaiken and Maheswaran (1994), who also found that valenced thoughts about the presented communication mediated the source credibility effects on participants' final attitude. When the length of the source information in our study was constrained to be comparable to Chaiken and Maheswaran's, we replicated their biased systematic processing effect.

message argument, versus both representing heuristics, or both representing message arguments. Thus, we might see that the impact of argument A is attenuated by, biases the processing of, or exerts an independent effect with respect to argument B. Similarly, the impact of one type of nonargument, heuristic information (e.g., about the source's expertise), might be attenuated by, bias the processing of, or exert an independent effect with respect to another piece of heuristic information (e.g., about the source's trustworthiness), and so on.

Multiple roles for variables in persuasion. An important feature of ELM theorizing (e.g., see Petty, 1994) concerns the multiple possible roles a variable could play in persuasion. Specifically, in different circumstances any one variable could serve as a cue, a message argument, or a motivating factor affecting the extent of processing (Petty, 1994, p. 3).

It is noteworthy that the multiple roles concept is thoroughly compatible with our unimodel. From the present perspective, the notion that a variable (e.g., source expertise) could serve under some conditions as a cue (e.g., "She is an expert," "experts can be trusted") and under other conditions as a message argument (e.g., "She is an expert," "she was trained at Ohio State," "therefore, Ohio State training is good") could simply mean that the same information could be relevant to different inference rules, or probabilogical schemata, some related to the content of the message, other exogenous to its content. This does not mean to say that a variable plays a qualitatively different role when it fits one type of inference rule versus another. As noted earlier, the unimodel makes no distinction between the persuasive functions of cues and heuristics and message arguments. Both constitute types of evidence whereby conclusions can be reached. By contrast, the ELM assumption that the same information could occasionally serve as cue and at other times as a message argument implies that the cue and message argument functions differ. Finally, the unimodel is compatible with the notion that a given bit of information (either contained in the message arguments or exogenous thereto) could activate a processing goal, and hence be motivating. This follows from the increasingly recognized notion that motivation has a definite cognitive aspect, or that goals constitute a special type of knowledge structures (cf. Austin & Vancouver, 1996; Bargh & Gollwitzer, 1994; Kruglanski, 1996a, 1996b).

Concluding Comments

The arguments and data presented in this article suggest that, on the whole, heuristics and cues and message arguments do not systematically differ on epistemic variables pertinent to persuasion (e.g., their degree of relevance to various conclusions, their availability or accessibility, their length or complexity, or their ordinal position), nor do they systematically interact with variables pertinent to persuasion (like issue involvement or cognitive capacity). It seems fair to conclude then that these two information types do not really signify two qualitatively separate, or functionally independent, processes whereby persuasion occurs. Rather, they are functionally equivalent in the persuasive process, both serving as evidence for the evaluative inferences perceivers draw. In other words, this analysis seems compatible with our LET-based unimodel that explicates the essential components of persuasion (evidential premises, motivation, cognitive ability) implicated in all of its instances.

But can the unimodel notion be sustained? Is it compatible with what is generally known about the way our minds function? In what follows we briefly consider the single versus dual-process question in light of a major, pertinent distinction in cognitive psychology between two systems of reasoning—the associative and the rule-based (Sloman, 1996).

Associative and Rule-Based Models of Reasoning and the "Routes to Persuasion" Issue

The partition between associative and rule-based reasoning goes back to James (1890/1950). It currently relates to a recent debate in cognitive psychology between those who

> prefer models of mental phenomena to be built out of networks of associative devices that pass activation in parallel and distributed form . . . (and) those who prefer models built out of formal languages in which symbols are composed into sentences that are processed sequentially (the way computers function). (Sloman, 1996, p. 3)

In the context here, the dichotomy between associative and rule-based reasoning raises two fundamental questions: (a) To what extent does it map onto, and in that sense support, the current distinctions between the two persuasion modes in either the ELM or the HSM? and (b) What does it imply for the feasibility of our unimodel? We consider both questions in turn.

TWO REASONING SYSTEMS AND THE DUAL-PROCESS MODELS

Although the distinction between two modes of reasoning has had a distinguished history, it does not command as yet a general consensus in cognitive psychology (cf. Margolis, 1987; Sloman, 1996). For the sake of argument though, let us assume it is valid. The issue then becomes to what extent it relates to the two persuasion modes depicted in the ELM and the HSM. Our answer is that it does not; hence, this particular distinction seems rather irrelevant to the "routes to persuasion" issue.

First, rule-based reasoning is common to both persuasion modes, rather than constituting the defining characteristic of only one of the modes, according to both the ELM and the HSM. Systematic and central processing are quintessentially rule based, depending as they do on the quality (i.e., logical plausibility) of the arguments contained in the message. So too, however, are the heuristic and peripheral modes. Thus, in the HSM heuristics are virtually defined as "simple inferential rules" and heuristic processing is regarded as largely "theory driven" (Chaiken et al., 1989, p. 213). Similarly, in the ELM, peripheral processing is based on "various persuasion rules or inferences" (Petty & Cacioppo, 1986, p. 130). Furthermore, "In addition to the relatively simple acceptance and/or rejection rules, . . . (peripheral processing) may be affected by more complex reasoning processes, such as those based on balance theory . . . or certain attributional principles" (p. 130). It is true that peripheral processing is also said to include "rather primitive affective and associational process" (p. 129) such as classical conditioning (Staats & Staats, 1958; Zanna, Kiesler, & Pilkonis, 1970) or mere exposure (Zajonc, 1968) and in that sense it may encompass both associative and rule-based reasoning. However, there seems no good reason to believe that such affective and associative processes are restricted to any particular type of information, in this case information exogenous to the message arguments (i.e., to cues and heuristics), that may not be equally instigated by message arguments (e.g., emotion-laden ones) as well. In short, the associative–rule-based distinction between types of reasoning does not adequately map onto the currently proposed divisions between the two, qualitatively distinct persuasion modes. Hence, it does not really bear on the routes to persuasion question one way or the other.

THE MODES OF REASONING ISSUE AND THE UNIMODEL

Our unimodel of persuasion assigns a central role to (syllogistic or probabilogical) reasoning from evidence to conclusion; hence, it clearly belongs within the rule-based category. The possibility that persuasion may be occasionally accomplished alternatively (i.e., associatively) might thus restrict the generality of our formulation. It seems appropriate to repeat in this regard that the question of whether associative and rule-based reasoning qualitatively differ is far from being settled within cognitive psychology proper. In a recent review, Sloman (1996) noted that, as compared with the case for rule-based reasoning, "the case for associative processes in reasoning . . . is less compelling" and "any apparently associative process can be described as rule-based" (p. 11). Sloman (1996) went on to argue, nonetheless, that the hypothesis of two reasoning systems is supported by evidence that occasionally people may "simultaneously believe two contradictory responses" whereby belief is meant "a propensity, a feeling or conviction that a response is appropriate" (p. 11). He gives as a striking example the case of the Muller–Lyer illusion in which measurement and eye-balling yield disparate, yet highly credible, conclusions.

We admit to finding such data less than completely compelling evidence for qualitatively different systems in so far as credible, yet contradictory, conclusions seem equally attainable via different applications of the very same (e.g., a rule-based) system. Note that the rules being applied need not be objectively, but only subjectively, correct. For instance, applying simultaneously the rules "all professors are disorganized" and "all Japanese are organized" one may reach two incompatible conclusions about a Japanese professor. Similarly, two objectively "correct" rules may yield incompatible conclusions because one is applied incorrectly. For example, because in cases of erroneous application the counting rule may occasionally yield a different outcome than the multiplication rule, the person performing the calculations may feel subjectively assured (inappropriately, of course) that he or she has both counted and multiplied correctly, giving rise to two incompatible conclusions and a maddening impasse. In short, the "two incompatible conclusions" criterion does not seem a particularly compelling marker of a two systems framework. All things considered then, it seems fair to conclude that as of now our unimodel and various alternative rule-based models (McGuire, 1960; Wyer, 1974), remain viable as general depictions of the persuasion process.

Implications of The Unimodel

The unimodel represents a fundamental critique of the dual-process frameworks in one sense only. It disputes the central assumption of these frameworks that a qualitative difference in the persuasion process hinges on whether persuasion is accomplished by the processing of message arguments versus the processing of information exogenous to the message; that is, by cues or heuristics. Our conclusion as to the uniformity of process in these two instances is supported not only by our own analysis and empirical results, but also, strikingly, by statements of the dual-mode theorists themselves. As noted throughout, many of the arguments here (e.g., for the similar way in which various factors affect heuristic- or cue-based and message-based persuasion) were either explicitly articulated or at least strongly implied in the dual-mode literature. In this sense, this conceptualization merely spells out the logical consequences of considerations recognized at some level, but not fully followed through, within the dual-mode frameworks. Also, we essentially agree with the dual-mode theorists on the role that motivational and cognitive factors play in determining the extent to which available evidence gets processed. Third, as ample evidence attests (see Eagly & Chaiken, 1993, for a review), the dual-mode frameworks work very well in situations where brief cue, or heuristic, information is followed by more extensive message arguments. Where such situations are encountered the dual-mode frameworks may

work well indeed. How often they occur outside the lab, however, is more difficult to ascertain.

Occasionally, information about the source's reputation may need to be processed extensively and laboriously, and subsequent message arguments may be relatively brief, and require much less processing effort. For example, when an "expert witness" testifies in a legal case, there often may be extensive, torturous debate between the prosecution and the defense, as the respective sides attempt to establish (or undermine) before the jury the expert credentials of the witness (i.e., heuristic information). This may, in some cases, be followed by the expert making a couple of focused points about a fairly specific point of evidence (i.e., message arguments). In other cases, we may first read an elaborate essay in a magazine (i.e., be exposed to an extensive message) and only at its conclusion be presented with a byline specifying the writer's credentials. In all such fairly common situations, the current dual-mode analyses may not apply. In short, because of the infinite heterogeneity of real-world situations, the frequentist argument—that in the real world the cue or heuristic versus message argument distinction is confounded actuarially with the length and complexity of information, its relevance, or its ordinal position—is rather difficult to verify.

More important, the unimodel offers a number of serious advantages for persuasion researchers. Not the least of these is its considerable generative potential as a source of novel, testable predictions. In that regard, our studies merely scratch the surface. Although they call attention to the need to control for different types of persuasive information (i.e., heuristics and cues vs. message arguments) for length, complexity, and ordinal position, additional research is needed to demonstrate the need to control also for its perceived relevance to the conclusion and for the availability and accessibility of its premises (see Spiegel et al., 1998).

Furthermore, whereas prior dual-process research has stressed the biasing potential of heuristics or peripheral cues on systematic or central processing of presented message arguments, the unimodel predicts that the flow of bias can be bidirectional; that is, processing of initial arguments can bias the subsequent processing of nonmessage, cue information, just as initial cues can affect the interpretation of subsequently encountered communications. For instance, if the message argument impressed one as particularly compelling, one might process source information in a biased way by accentuating positive (and downplaying negative) information pertaining to source features such as expertise, trustworthiness, and likability.

Finally, the unimodel implies that major persuasive advantages, such as increased persistence of attitude change, resistance to counterarguments, and a link to behavior derive from the depth or extent of processing, rather than the type of information processed (i.e., heuristics and cues vs. message arguments). By contrast, in the dual-mode literature such properties typically are linked to the processing of message arguments. For instance, Petty and Cacioppo (1986) stated that

> the ELM predicts that people who come to accept an issue position because of a peripheral cue (e.g., source expertise) should be more susceptible to an attacking message than people who adopt the same issue position based on a careful scrutiny and elaboration of message arguments. (p. 182)

In addition, they asserted more generally that "Attitude changes that result mostly from processing issue-relevant arguments (central route) will show greater emporal persistence, greater prediction of behavior, and greater resistance to counterpersuasion than attitude changes that result mostly from peripheral cues" (p. 175).

In general, the unimodel forms a bridge between prior persuasion work that stressed the syllogistic (or probabilogical) processes whereby people's attitudes and opinions are formed or altered (McGuire, 1960; Wyer, 1970, 1974) and contemporary work highlighting both the extent and depth of information processing involved in persuasion, as well as the motivational and capacity factors that affect it. Whereas previous work affirmed that people's conclusions are largely consistent with their premises (cf. McGuire, 1960; Wyer, 1976), we assume that when persuasively relevant information is extensive or complex, this degree of consistency will be maximized when sufficient processing motivation and attentional resources allow recipients to fully apply their premises to the information at hand. These issues could be fruitfully investigated in future research.

The unimodel also abounds with implications for real-world persuasion contexts that expand the range of tools in the communicator's kit and lend increased flexibility to their endeavors. To mention just a few examples, it opens the possibility of effectively using contextual information exogenous to the message arguments (i.e., cuelike, heu-

ristic information) vis-à-vis issues of high personal relevance to the recipients. Similarly, it affords the possibility of effective persuasion via message arguments when the recipient's processing motivation is low, providing that such messages are appropriately terse and easily understood (e.g., Howard, 1997). It suggests that distraction and repetition techniques, to name a few, may work as well with persuasion driven by contextual information as with that based on message arguments.

Of special significance, the unimodel offers the fundamental conceptual advantages of parsimony and integration. Such integration consists not only in synthesizing the ubiquitous dual modes into one, but also in forging linkages to previous models of persuasion and attitude change, such as McGuire's (1960, 1968) and Wyer's (1970, 1974) probabilogical notions, the theories of reasoned action or planned behavior (Ajzen, 1988; Fishbein & Ajzen, 1975), or the various cognitive consistency models of attitude change like Festinger's (1957) or Heider's (1958). In all these approaches, as in the unimodel, the concept of persuasive evidence that supports (i.e., is consistent with) or undermines (i.e., is inconsistent with) a conclusion plays a major role (see Kruglanski, 1989, chap. 6; Kruglanski & Klar, 1987). These explicit ties to past theorizing and research both highlight the cumulative nature of our progress in understanding persuasion and take advantage of important prior insights and discoveries.

Finally, but by no means least important, the unimodel integrates the Laswellian dictum to which much social psychological research on persuasion heretofore was indebted. Specifically, Laswell's (1948) slogan of "who says what in what channel to whom and with what effect" (p. 37) traditionally has been taken to indicate the separateness of its various terms. Here, the unimodel implies a fundamental shift in perspective. Within our new paradigm neither the source, the channel, nor the message any longer represents a distinct entity in the world external to the perceiver. Nor are they treated as separate from the recipient as such. Rather, they all are part and parcel of the recipient's cognitive repertoire, represented (as premises and assumptions) in the belief systems that populate his or her mind. Although their distinctness may be what meets the eye, their profound commonalities and functional equivalence may be what ultimately matters for understanding the processes underlying the phenomena of persuasion.

ACKNOWLEDGMENT

Work on this article was supported by NSF Grant SBR–9417422, NIMH Grant RO1–MH52578, and a Research Scientist Award to Arie W. Kruglanski.

REFERENCES

Achinstein, P. (1983). Concepts of evidence. In P. Achinstein (Ed.), *The concept of evidence* (pp. 2–32). New York: Oxford University Press.

Ajzen, I. (1988). *Attitudes, personality, and behavior*. Chicago: Dorsey.

Ajzen, I. (1991). The theory of planned behavior. *Organizational Behavior and Human Decision Processes, 50*, 179–211.

Allport, F. H. (1924). *Social psychology*. Cambridge, MA: Riverside.

Asch, S. E. (1952). *Social psychology*. Englewood Cliffs, NJ: Prentice Hall.

Austin, J. T., & Vancouver, J. B. (1996). Goal constructs in psychology: Structure, process and content. *Psychological Bulletin, 120*, 338–375.

Baker, W. (1993). The relevance accessibility model of advertising effectiveness. In A. A. Mitchell (Ed.), *Advertising exposure, memory and choice* (pp. 49–87). Hillsdale, NJ: Lawrence Erlbaum Associates, Inc.

Bargh, J. A., & Gollwitzer, P. M. (1994). Environmental control of goal-directed action: Automatic and strategic contingencies between situations and behavior. In W. D. Spaulding (Ed.), *Nebraska symposium on motivation: Vol. 41, Integrative views of motivation, cognition, and emotion* (pp. 71–124). Lincoln: University of Nebraska Press.

Baron, R. M., & Kenny, D. A. (1986). The moderator–mediator variable distinction in social psychological research: Conceptual, strategic, and statistical considerations. *Journal of Personality and Social Psychology, 51*, 1173–1182.

Berscheid, E., Graziano, W., Monson, T., & Dermer, M. (1976). Outcome dependency: Attention, attribution, and attraction. *Journal of Personality and Social Psychology, 34*, 978–989.

Burgoon, M., Cohen, M., Miller, M., & Montgomery, C. (1978). An empirical test of a model of resistance to persuasion. *Health Communication Research, 5*, 27–39.

Cacioppo, J. T., & Petty, R. E. (1982). The need for cognition. *Journal of Personality and Social Psychology, 42*, 116–131.

Cacioppo, J. T., Petty, R. E., Feinstein, J., & Jarvis, B. (1996). Dispositional differences in cognitive motivation: The life and times of individuals varying in need for cognition. *Psychological Bulletin, 119*, 197–253.

Cacioppo, J. T., Petty, R. E., Kao, C. F., & Rodriguez, R. (1986). Central and peripheral routes to persuasion: An individual difference perspective. *Journal of Personality and Social Psychology, 51*, 1032–1043.

Carnap, R. (1962). *Logical foundations of probability*. Chicago: Chicago University Press.

Chaiken, S. (1987). The heuristic model of persuasion. In M. P. Zanna, J. M. Olson, & C. P. Herman (Eds.), *Social influence: The Ontario symposium* (Vol. 5, pp. 3–39). Hillsdale, NJ: Lawrence Erlbaum Associates, Inc.

Chaiken, S., Liberman, A., & Eagly, A. H. (1989). Heuristic and systematic processing within and beyond the persuasion context. In J. S. Uleman & J. A. Bargh (Eds.), *Unintended thought* (pp. 212–252). New York: Guilford.

Chaiken, S., & Maheswaran, D. (1994). Heuristic processing can bias systematic processing: Effects of source credibility, argument ambiguity, and task importance on attitude judgment. *Journal of Personality and Social Psychology, 66*, 460–473.

Eagly, A. H., & Chaiken, S. (1993). *The psychology of attitudes*. Fort Worth, TX: Harcourt Brace Jovanovich.

Erber, R., & Fiske, S. T. (1984). Outcome dependency and attention to inconsistent information. *Journal of Personality and Social Psychology, 47*, 709–726.

Fabrigar, L. R., Priester, J. R., Petty, R. E., & Wegener, D. T. (1998). The impact of attitude accessibility on elaboration of persuasive messages. *Personality and Social Psychology Bulletin, 24*, 339–352.

Festinger, L. (1957). *A theory of cognitive dissonance*. Stanford, CA: Stanford University Press.

Fishbein, M., & Ajzen, I. (1975). *Belief, attitude, intention, and behavior: An introduction to theory and research*. Reading, MA: Addison-Wesley.

Glymour, C. N. (1980). *Theory and evidence*. Princeton, NJ: Princeton University Press.

Greenwald, A. G. (1968). Cognitive learning, cognitive response to persuasion, and attitude change. In A. G. Greenwald, T. C. Brock, & T. M. Ostrom (Eds.), *Psychological foundations of attitudes* (pp. 147–170). San Diego, CA: Academic.

Hastie, R., & Park, B. (1986). The relationship between memory and judgment depends on whether the judgment task is memory-based or on-line. *Psychological Review, 93*, 258–268.

Haugtvedt, C. P., & Wegener, D. T. (1994). Message order effects in persuasion: An attitude strength perspective. *Journal of Consumer Research, 21*, 205–218.

Heider, F. (1958). *The psychology of interpersonal relations*. New York: Wiley.

Hempel, C. G. (1965). *Aspects of scientific explanation*. San Francisco: Free Press.

Higgins, E. T. (1996). Knowledge activation, application, and salience. In E. T. Higgins & A. W. Kruglanski (Eds.), *Social psychology: Handbook of basic principles* (pp. 237–275). New York: Guilford.

Higgins, E. T., Rholes, W. S., & Jones, C. R. (1977). Category accessibility and impression formation. *Journal of Experimental Social Psychology, 13*, 141–154.

Hovland, C. I. (Ed.). (1957). *The order of presentation in persuasion*. New Haven, CT: Yale University Press.

Hovland, C. I., & Janis, I. L. (Eds.). (1959). *Personality and persuasibility*. New Haven, CT: Yale University Press.

Hovland, C. I., Janis, I. L., & Kelley, H. H. (1953). *Communication and persuasion: Psychological studies of opinion change*. New Haven, CT: Yale University Press.

Howard, D. J. (1997). Familiar phrases as peripheral persuasion cues. *Journal of Experimental Social Psychology, 33*, 231–243.

James, W. (1950). *The principles of psychology*. New York: Dover. (Original work published 1890)

Kahneman, D. (1973). *Attention and effort*. Englewood Cliffs, NJ: Prentice Hall.

Kruglanski, A. W. (1989). *Lay epistemics and human knowledge: Cognitive and motivational bases*. New York: Plenum.

Kruglanski, A. W. (1990). Motivations for judging and knowing: Implications for causal attribution. In E. T. Higgins & R. M. Sorrentino (Eds.), *The handbook of motivation and cognition: Foundations of social behavior* (Vol. 2, pp. 333–368). New York: Guilford.

Kruglanski, A. W. (1996a). Goals as knowledge structures. In P. M. Gollwitzer & J. A. Bargh (Eds.), *The psychology of action: Linking cognition and motivation to behavior* (pp. 599–618). New York: Guilford.

Kruglanski, A. W. (1996b). Motivated social-cognition: Principles of the interface. In E. T. Higgins & A. Kruglanski (Eds.), *Social psychology: Handbook of basic principles* (pp. 493–520). New York: Guilford.

Kruglanski, A. W., & Klar, Y. (1987). A view from a bridge: Synthesizing the consistency and attribution paradigms from a lay epistemic perspective. *European Journal of Social Psychology, 17,* 211–241.

Kruglanski, A. W., & Mackie, D. M. (1990). Majority and minority influenced: A Judgmental process analysis. In W. Stroebe & M. Hewstone (Eds.), *European review of social psychology* (Vol. 1, pp. 229–261). New York: Wiley.

Kruglanski, A. W., & Webster, D. M. (1996), Motivated closing of the mind: "Seizing" and "freezing." *Psychological Review, 103,* 263–283.

Laswell, H. D. (1948). The structure and function of communication in society. In L. Bryson (Ed.), *The communication of ideas: Religion and civilization series* (pp. 37–51). New York: Harper & Row.

Mackie, D. M. (1987). Systematic and nonsystematic processing of majority and minority persuasive communications. *Journal of Personality and Social Psychology, 53,* 42–52.

Mackie, D. M., Worth, L. T., & Asuncion, A. G. (1990). Online versus memory-based modification of attitudes: Determinants of message recall-attitude change correspondence. *Journal of Personality and Social Psychology, 59,* 5–16.

Maio, G. R., & Olson, J. M. (1998). Attitude dissimulation and persuasion. *Journal of Experimental Social Psychology, 34,* 182–201.

Margolis, H. (1987). *Patterns, thinking, and cognition.* Chicago: University of Chicago Press.

McDougall, W. (1908). *Social psychology.* New York: Luce.

McGuire, W. J. (1960). A syllogistic analysis of cognitive relationships. In C. I. Hovland & M. J. Rosenberg (Eds.), *Attitude organization and change: An analysis of consistency among attitude components* (pp. 65–111). New Haven, CT: Yale University Press.

McGuire, W. J. (1964). Including resistance to persuasion: Some contemporary approaches. In L. Berkowitz (Ed.), *Advances in experimental social psychology* (Vol. 1, pp. 191–229). New York: Academic.

McGuire, W. J. (1968). Personality and attitude change: An information-processing theory. In A. G. Greenwald, T. C. Brock, & T. M. Ostrom (Eds.), *Psychological foundations of attitudes* (pp. 171–196). San Diego, CA: Academic.

McGuire, W. J. (1969). The nature of attitudes and attitude change. In G. Lindzey & E. Aronson (Eds.), *Handbook of social psychology* (2nd ed., Vol. 3, pp. 136–314). Reading, MA: Addison-Wesley.

McGuire, W. J. (1972). Attitude change: The information processing paradigm. In C. G. McClintock (Ed.), *Experimental social psychology* (pp. 108–141), New York: Holt, Rinehart & Winston.

Newcomb, T. M. (1950). *Social psychology.* New York: Drained.

Petty, R. E. (1994). Two routes to persuasion: State of the art. In G. d'Ydewalle, P. Eelen, & P. Berteleson (Eds.), *International perspectives on psychological science* (Vol. 2, pp. 229–247). Hillsdale, NJ: Lawrence Erlbaum Associates, Inc.

Petty, R. E., & Cacioppo, J. T. (1984). The effects of involvement on responses to argument quantity and quality: Central and peripheral routes to persuasion. *Journal of Personality and Social Psychology, 46,* 69–81.

Petty, R. E., & Cacioppo, J. T. (1986). The elaboration likelihood model of persuasion. In L. Berkowitz. (Ed.), *Advances in experimental social psychology* (Vol. 19, pp. 123–205). San Diego, CA: Academic.

Petty, R. E., Cacioppo, J. T., & Goldman, R. (1981). Personal involvement as a predictor of argument-based persuasion. *Journal of Personality and Social Psychology, 41,* 847–855.

Petty, R. E., Cacioppo, J. T., & Heesacker, M. (1985). *Persistence of persuasion: A test of the Elaboration Likelihood Model.* Unpublished manuscript, University of Missouri, Columbia.

Petty, R. E., Harkins, S. G., & Williams, K. D. (1980). The effects of group diffusion of cognitive effort on attitudes: An information processing view. *Journal of Personality and Social Psychology, 38,* 81–92.

Petty, R. E., Haugtvedt, C. P., & Smith, S. M. (1995). Elaboration as a determinant of attitude strength: Creating attitudes that are persistent, resistant and predictive of behavior. In R. E. Petty & J. A. Krosnick (Eds.), *Attitude strength: Antecedents and consequences* (pp. 93–130). Mahwah, NJ: Lawrence Erlbaum Associates, Inc.

Petty, R. E., Ostrom, T. M., & Brock, T. C. (Eds.). (1981). *Cognitive responses in persuasion.* Hillsdale, NJ: Lawrence Erlbaum Associates, Inc.

Petty, R. E., Schumann, D. W., Richman, S. A., & Strathman, A. J. (1993). Positive mood and persuasion: Different roles for affect under high- and low-elaboration conditions. *Journal of Personality and Social Psychology, 64,* 5–20.

Petty, R. E., Wells, G. L., & Brock, T. C. (1976). Distraction can enhance or reduce yielding to propaganda: Thought disruption versus effort justification. *Journal of Personality and Social Psychology, 34,* 874–884.

Puckett, J. M., Petty, R. E., Cacioppo, J. T., & Fisher, D. L. (1983). The relative impact of age and attractiveness stereotypes on persuasion. *Journal of Gerontology, 38,* 340–343.

Ross, E. A. (1908). *Social control: A survey of the foundations of order.* New York: Macmillan.

Ruscher, J. B., & Fiske, S. T. (1990). Interpersonal competition can cause individuating processes. *Journal of Personality and Social Psychology, 58,* 832–843.

Schumann, D. W., Petty, R., & Clemons, D. S. (1990). Predicting the effectiveness of different strategies of advertising variation. A test of the repetition-variation hypothesis. *Journal of Consumer Research, 17,* 192–201.

Sloman, S. A. (1996). The empirical case for two systems of reasoning. *Psychological Bulletin, 119,* 3–22.

Sorrentino, R. M., Bobocel, D. R., Gitta, M. Z., Olson, J. M., & Hewitt, E. C. (1988). Uncertainty orientation and persuasion: Individual differences in the effects of personal relevance on social judgments. *Journal of Personality and Social Psychology, 55,* 357–371.

Spiegel, S., Kruglanski, A. W., & Thompson, E. P. (1998, May). *Accessibility effects in a unimodel theory of persua-*

sion. Paper presented at the 10th meeting of the American Psychological Society, Washington, DC.

Srull, T. K., & Wyer, R. S., Jr. (1986). The role of chronic and temporary goals in social information processing. In R. M. Sorrentino & E. T. Higgins (Eds.), *Handbook of motivation and cognition: Foundations of social behavior* (pp. 503–549). New York: Guilford.

Staats, A. W., & Staats, C. K. (1958). Attitudes established by classical conditioning. *Journal of Abnormal and Social Psychology, 57,* 37–40.

Taylor, S. E. (1975). On inferring one's attitudes from one's behavior: Some delimiting conditions. *Journal of Personality and Social Psychology, 31,* 126–131.

Tesser, A., & Conlee, M. C. (1975). Some effects of time and thought on attitude polarization. *Journal of Personality and Social Psychology, 31,* 262–270.

Tesser, A., & Cowan, C. (1977). Some effects of thought and number of cognition on attitude change. *Social Behavior and Personality, 3,* 165–173.

Tesser, A., & Leone, C. (1977). Cognitive schemas and thought as determinants of attitude change. *Journal of Experimental Social Psychology, 13,* 340–356.

Thompson, E. P., Chaiken, S., & Hazlewood, J. D. (1993). Need for cognition and desire for control as moderators of extrinsic reward effects: A person × situation approach to the study of intrinsic motivation. *Journal of Personality and Social Psychology, 64,* 987–999.

Thompson, E. P., & Kruglanski, A. W. (1998). *"Freezing" on high (but not low) source expertise prevents "seizing" on the content of a communication: The role of time pressure in message-based persuasion.* Manuscript in preparation.

Thompson, E. P., Kruglanski, A. W., & Spiegel, S. (1998). *Evidence for a single-mode "Unimodel" of motivated reasoning in persuasion: The role of "cue" length and complexity.* Manuscript in preparation.

Thompson, E. P., Roman, R. J., Moskowitz, G. B., Chaiken, S., & Bargh, J. A. (1994). Accuracy motivation attenuates covert priming: The systematic reprocessing of social information. *Journal of Personality and Social Psychology, 66,* 474–489.

Tulving, E. (1983). *Elements of episodic memory.* Oxford, England: Oxford University Press.

Wegener, D. T., & Petty, R. E. (1996). Effects of mood on persuasion processes: Enhancing, reducing, and biasing scrutiny of attitude-relevant information. In L. Martin & A. Tesser (Eds.), *Striving and feeling: Interactions between goals and affect* (pp. 329–362). Mahwah, NJ: Lawrence Erlbaum Associates, Inc.

Wells, G. L., & Petty, R. E. (1980). The effects of overt head movements on persuasion: Compatibility and incompatibility of responses. *Basic and Applied Social Psychology, 1,* 219–230.

Wood, W. (1982). Retrieval of attitude-relevant information from memory: Effects on susceptibility to persuasion and on intrinsic motivation. *Journal of Personality and Social Psychology, 42,* 798–810.

Wood, W., & Kallgren, C. A. (1988). Communicator attributes and persuasion: Recipients' access to attitude-relevant information in memory. *Personality and Social Psychology Bulletin, 14,* 172–182.

Wood, W., Kallgren, C. A., & Preisler, R. M. (1985). Access to attitude-relevant information in memory as a determinant of persuasion: The role of message attributes. *Journal of Experimental Social Psychology, 21,* 73–85.

Wyer, R. S., Jr. (1970). Quantitative prediction of belief and opinion change: A further test of a subjective probability model. *Personality and Social Psychology, 16,* 559–570.

Wyer, R. S., Jr. (1974). *Cognitive organization and change: An information processing approach.* Hillsdale, NJ: Lawrence Erlbaum Associates, Inc.

Wyer, R. S., Jr. (1976). Effects of previously formed beliefs on syllogistic inference processes. *Journal of Personality and Social Psychology, 33,* 307–316.

Zajonc, R. B. (1968). Attitudinal effects of mere exposure. [Monograph]. *Journal of Personality and Social Psychology, 2*(Suppl. 9), 1–27.

Zanna, M. P., Kiesler, C. A., & Pilkonis, P. A. (1970). Positive and negative attitudinal affect established by classical conditioning. *Journal of Personality and Social Psychology, 14,* 321–328.

Group and Cultural System

The fundamental tendency of humans to coalesce in groups has been touted as a major evolutionary achievement that contributed greatly to the ascent of our species within the animal kingdom and the construction of civilization. Whereas alone we are in many ways inferior to other creatures (e.g., we are considerably slower than the cheetah, less alert than the antelope, less auditorily sensitive than the owl, and less well camouflaged than the ground-nesting bird), together we amply compensate for our individual frailties. According to this argument, it was by acting collectively that humans managed to secure food and to avoid becoming food themselves, as well as to launch the conquest of the universe for which not even the sky sets the limit. Indeed, group formation fulfills a variety of essential functions for individual members of our species—strength in numbers, specialization and differentiation of labor, intellectual cross-stimulation, and emotional succor. Belonging to groups increased our capacity to cope with adverse circumstances and set us on the extraordinary pathway from stone tools to space rockets.

Among the many functions groups serve for their members, one of the most central is the affordance of world-knowledge; that is, provision of a system of agreed-upon categories and beliefs whereby reality is apprehended, as well as a system of norms whereby acceptable patterns of conduct in goal pursuit are indicated. The notion that groups provide a sense of reality for their members has been stressed by classical social-psychological theories of group processes and continues to be central to contemporary analyses of social behavior. An essential pre-condition for the fulfillment of world-knowledge is that the reality conveyed by the group to its members be *shared*; that is, grounded in opinion uniformity or consensus within the group. Social-psychological analyses of group processes have, accordingly, emphasized the tendency of groups to exert pressures toward conformity. But what are the contents of the social reality that group members are pressured to accept? And how stable or static is a given group's "reality"? The changing of social reality by minority influence is addressed in the selection by Nemeth (1986). The article by Levine and Moreland (1994) discusses the passage of individuals through groups and the mutual influence that groups and individuals exert upon each other. The article by Abrams and Hogg (1988) explores two general motives for intergroup discrimination; a desire for cognitive coherence, and a need for positive self-esteem. Reid and Deaux (1997) analyzes the social and personal identities that make up our self-representations. The evolution of group norms is discussed in the articles by Jacobs and Campbell (1961) and Prentice and Miller (1993). Finally, the differences in social realities subscribed to by different cultures are depicted in the paper by Markus and Kitayama (1994).

Differential Contributions of Majority and Minority Influence

Charlan Jeanne Nemeth • University of California, Berkeley

Editors' Notes

A major social-psychological process occurring in groups is social influence. In order to forge the consensus that is required to establish stable social realities, opinion differences among group members need to be eliminated. This is typically accomplished by group members attempting to influence one another. Historically, such influence was conceptualized in terms of "pressures to uniformity" (Festinger, 1950) or tendencies toward "conformity" (Asch, 1956); that is, in terms of the influence that a majority exerts upon dissenting individuals or a minority faction. If that were the case, however, how would social change ever occur? This issue, raised by Serge Moscovici (1976) and his colleagues, focused investigators' attention on the issue of minority influence. After all, most types of social change commence with ideas in some individuals' heads that differ from the received views within the group. In the present selection, the author suggests that the process whereby minorities exert their influence is rather different from the process of majority influence. It also raises the provocative possibility that, however difficult to accomplish and fraught with conflict and strife, minority influence can have major beneficial effects on our thinking and problem solving. As "consumers" of majority influence we are mostly passive. But minority influence forces us to be active, stimulating our "creative" and critical juices, which makes us better judges and decision makers.

Discussion Questions

1. In what way does the author propose to broaden the conception of "influence"?
2. According to the author, what are the differences between majority and a minority influence?

3. How do the three studies reported in the article test the author's proposed theory of differences between majority and minority influence?

4. What are the differences between divergent and convergent thinking, and how does the present theory relate to these differences?

Suggested Readings

Kruglanski, A. W., & Mackie, D. M. (1990). Majority and minority influence: A judgmental process analysis. In W. Stroebe & M. Hewstone (Eds.), *European review of social psychology.* London: Wiley.

Moscovici, S. (1980). Toward a theory of conversion behavior. In L. Berkowitz (Ed.), *Advances in experimental social psychology* (Vol. 13, pp. 209–239). New York: Academic Press.

Wood, W., Lundgren, S., Quellette, J. A., Busceme, S., & Blackstone, T. (1994). Processes of minority influence: Influence effectiveness and source perceptions. *Psychological Bulletin, 115,* 323–345.

Author's Abstract

In most studies comparing majority and minority influence, there is an emphasis on influence in the sense of "prevailing." Within this context, evidence exists that majorities exert more public influence and that minority influence, when it occurs, tends to operate primarily at the latent level. In the present formulation, it is proposed that the differences between majority and minority influence are in fact more extensive once influence is considered in a broader context. In particular, it is proposed that exposure to persistent minority views fosters greater thought about the issue. Furthermore, this thought tends to be divergent rather than convergent, and as a result, people tend to be better decision makers because they attend to more aspects of the situation and reexamine premises. By contrast, it is proposed that exposure to persistent majority views fosters convergent thinking and leads to an unreflective acceptance of the majority position. Three experimental studies are reported that directly test some of the propositions, and the formulation is linked to available knowledge in the areas of social cognition, creativity, and problem solving both at the individual and group levels. Finally, some practical implications of this formulation for small group decision making and for society at large are offered.

During the 1950s and 1960s, the study of influence processes was primarily focused on the phenomenon of conformity. Literally hundreds of studies demonstrated and sought to explain the reasons why individuals would change their judgment, opinion, or belief in the direction of the position proposed by the majority (see Allen, 1965; and Kiesler & Kiesler, 1969, for reviews). As of the late 1960s, a number of researchers began to focus on the reciprocal process, that is, influence exerted by the individual or the minority of individuals on the majority's views (see Maass & Clark, 1984, for a review). A natural consequence of two such lines of research has been to understand if, why, and how the two forms of influence processes differ.

In general, those who have focused primarily on public movement to the proposed position have argued for similarities between the two processes and have assumed that the two forms of influence differ only in degree (see Latane & Wolf, 1981; Tanford & Penrod, 1984). Those who have focused on private influence have noticed an asymmetry between public and private movement to the proposed position as a result of the majority versus minority status of the source. Thus, these researchers have noted and theorized about the differential nature of these two forms of influence (Maass & Clark, 1984; Moscovici, 1976; Mugny, 1980; Nemeth, 1976).

The contention of the present article is that the differences between influence processes exerted by majorities and those exerted by minorities are in fact more extensive once the conception of influence is broadened from "prevailing" (whether this be public or private) to issues of attention, thought, and "novel" judgments or decisions. The formulation presented here argues that majorities foster convergence of attention, thought, and the number of alternatives considered. Minority viewpoints are important, not because they tend to prevail but because they stimulate divergent attention and thought. As a result, even when they are wrong they contribute to the detection of novel solutions and decisions that, on balance, are qualitatively better. The implications of this are considerable for creativity, problem solving, and decision making, both at the individual and group levels. First, the available literature on the issues involved in opposing views emanating from a majority versus a minority is reviewed.

Majority Versus Minority Influence

If one takes the perspective of direct public movement to the position proposed, numerous studies have documented the fact that majorities exert more influence than do minorities (see Tanford & Penrod, 1984, for a review). To illustrate the power of majorities relative to minorities for prevailing, a study of 225 juries showed that the majority position on the first ballot (i.e., held by 7–11 persons) was the final verdict in over 85% of the cases (Kalven & Zeisel, 1966). The process by which majorities and minorities exercise their influence, however, appears to be somewhat different.

From a theoretical point of view, movement to the majority position is due to two assumptions. One is that the judgments give information about reality; majority judgments are therefore likely to be correct. This has generally been termed *informational* influence. The other is that individuals want to be accepted and therefore wish to avoid the disapproval that emanates from maintaining a minority viewpoint. This is often termed *normative* influence (Deutsch & Gerard, 1955). Movement to the minority position is assumed to depend on the behavioral style of the minority, that is, the orchestration and patterning of the minority's verbal and nonverbal cues used in presenting its arguments. In particular, emphasis has been placed on the consistency of position over time and the confidence with which it is held (Moscovici & Faucheux, 1972; Moscovici & Nemeth, 1974).

Such behavioral styles clearly would not be irrelevant to the process of majority influence as well. However, the issue has been one of emphasis because majorities start with positive judgments and expectations (e.g., they are correct; their approval is important). Minorities are viewed negatively, sometimes with downright derision (Nemeth & Wachtler, 1983). As a result, the experimental evidence shows movement to the majority position on early trials of judgments or in early minutes of a discussion. Movement to the minority position occurs on later trials or later in the discussion (Nemeth, Swedlund, & Kanki, 1974). The assumption is that majority judgments are seriously considered from the beginning. Minority viewpoints need time because it is the consistency and confidence with which the minority positions are argued that leads one to seriously consider the position.

A second and potentially very important distinction between influence processes exerted by a majority and a minority is that majorities exercise influence primarily at the manifest level whereas minorities show their impact at a latent level. Numerous studies show compliance without private or latent change to majority views (Allen, 1965; Moscovici & Lage, 1976). Movement to the minority view is often detected at the latent level even when manifest movement is not found. For example, Moscovici, Lage, and Naffrechoux (1969) had a minority of confederates judge blue slides to be green. Although little public movement to green was observed (9%), over 35% of the subjects showed a modification of their judgments of blue and green in a subsequent task. Nemeth and Wachtler (1974) found no public movement to a minority view of low compensation on a personal injury case but found significant private movement on the deliberated case as well as on other personal injury cases. Mugny (1980) found that minorities had more impact on items indirectly related to the stated judgments than on those directly addressed by the minority. Using the blue slide procedure, Moscovici and Lage (1976) found manifest influence for the majority and latent influence for the minority. Thus, the evidence points to a differential relation between manifest and latent influence when the source constitutes a numerical majority rather than a minority.

Theorists have differed in their understanding of majority versus minority influence in part because of the definitions that they use and the specific findings that they emphasize. Latane and Wolf (1981), for example, posit that the processes by which majorities and minorities exert their influence are similar. Majorities, however, have more impact; they exert more influence by virtue of their greater numbers. Available research comparing the influence of majorities and minorities in terms of movement toward, or adoption of, the proposed position at a direct public level corroborates this hypothesis. Using this definition and set of findings, majorities tend to exert considerably more influence than do minorities (see Tanford & Penrod, 1984, for a review).

Other researchers have focused on the asymmetry between public and private influence and, as such, have argued that the processes of influence exerted by the majority in comparison with the minority are quite different. Moscovici (1980), for example, argues that majorities induce compliance behavior whereas minorities induce conversion behavior. The former tends to be at the public level; the latter tends to be at the private level. Moscovici basically argues that both majorities and minorities exert influence, that both forms of influence pose a conflict, however, the conflict is resolved in different ways. First, he assumes that majorities induce a "comparison process" whereby individuals focus on what the majority is saying. Minorities induce a "validation process" whereby individuals focus on the relation between the position and the object itself. Thus, there should be more private change with the latter. Second, he assumes that there are motivational considerations. In particular, people want to publicly comply with the majority (e.g., for their approval) and are reluctant to publicly agree with a minority (e.g., for fear of appearing deviant). Thus, the conflict induced by the opposition is resolved along the path of least resistance, which means that individuals resolve the conflict publicly in the majority situation and privately in the minority situation.

Mugny (1980) offers another refinement on the motivational aspect involved in avoiding public agreement with the minority by a consideration of "psychosocial identity." This refers to the fact that people attribute to themselves stereotypical attributes of the group who influences them. Thus, insofar as minority membership has negative connotations, movement to the minority viewpoint has negative implications for oneself. Thus, there is resistance to resolving the conflict by direct public movement.

What becomes important as a consequence of such formulations is that there is a recognition that public and private forms of influence exist and that majorities tend to exert their influence on the public domain whereas minorities tend to have their effect at the private level. As such, the impact of minorities tends to be underestimated by comparisons that rely on the public dimension of influence. Furthermore, the influence exerted by minorities may be deeper and more lasting, even though it may not be as immediately apparent.

Such theory and findings emphasize the differences between majority and minority influence, but they tend to view the differences in terms of conflict resolution. Furthermore, all of the formulations tend to define influence in terms of prevailing. Whereas Latane and Wolf (1981) and Tanford and Penrod (1984) have focused on direct prevailing, or adoption of the position as a function of the majority or minority, Moscovici (1980), Mugny (1980), Maass and Clark (1984), and others have focused on direct versus indirect prevailing, that is, public versus private acceptance of the proposed position. Thus, research on both majority and minority influence has tended to define influence in terms of prevailing. The operational definition is movement to the position proposed. In this context, even the distinctions between public and private, manifest and latent, tend to be linear in their conceptualization.

A Proposed Reconceptualization

The present proposition is that majority and minority attempts at influence stimulate differential thought processes and with them differential problem solving and decision making. Thus, the question is not simply whether or not individuals move toward (or away from) the position proposed or whether they do this publicly or privately but rather how they think about the issue and the consequences of such thought processes for the quality of the solutions they find and the decisions they make.

Though the present reformulation profits from the previously described theory and research, the origins of the present set of propositions precede most of this theory and research and stem from a study reported in 1976 (Nemeth, 1976). These results will be detailed later in this article. Briefly, however, it was recognized that influence processes emanating from a majority and a minority differ not only in degree or in the public versus private nature of the person's movement but also in the ways these processes affect attention and problem solving. Majorities induce a concentration on the position they propose; minorities stimulate a greater consideration of other alternatives, ones that were not proposed but would not have been considered without the influence of the minority. As such, it became clear that the differences between majority and minority influence were more extensive once influence was considered in a broader context.

Specifically, it is proposed that persons exposed to opposing minority views exert more cognitive effort. More importantly, it is hypothesized that the nature of that thought is quite different from that of persons exposed to opposing majority views. Those exposed to minority views are stimulated to attend to more aspects of the situation, they think in more divergent ways, and they are more likely to detect novel solutions or come to new decisions. Importantly, it is assumed that, on balance, these solutions and decisions will be "better" or more "correct." Persons exposed to opposing majority views, by contrast, focus on the aspects of the stimuli pertinent to the position of the majority, they think in convergent ways, and they tend toward adoption of the proposed solution to the neglect of novel solutions or decisions. The efficacy of their solutions and decisions will thus be tied to the correctness or usefulness of the position proposed.

The present reconceptualization thus argues that exposure to opposing views has very different consequences for attention, for thought, and for decision making and problem solving as functions of whether the source of that opposition is a majority or a minority. It further argues that there are creative contributions made by a dissenting minority, even when it is wrong. Its value lies not so much in the correctness of its position but rather in the attention and thought processes it induces. The implications for creativity and decision making, both at the individual and group levels, become considerable. First, the rationale behind such propositions will be examined and then the empirical support to date for the assumptions will be demonstrated.

In attempts to provide a rationale for the hypotheses that are being proposed, the elements that persistently differentiate between majority and minority influence will be considered. A number of these, considered in the light of available knowledge, undoubtedly contribute to the overall tendencies for differential attention, thought processes, and decision making. However, no single element appears to fully account for the differences proposed and found. Multiple psychological processes appear to be responsible.

One persistent difference between exposure to majority opposing views and exposure to minority opposing views is that subjects report being under much more stress in the former situation than in the latter one. The early studies of Asch (1956) documented the considerable stress evidenced by subjects exposed to a majority who differed from them in judgments of length of lines. Presumably, subjects assumed that they themselves might be wrong; moreover, they feared the disapproval of the majority if they persisted with their minority, or deviant, judgments. Studies of minority influence tend not to find evidence of much stress on the part of subjects; in fact, subjects tend to report derision of the minority and their opposing views (see Maass & Clark, 1984, for a review). Furthermore, a study comparing majority and minority influence in the same experimental setting found that subjects exposed to a differing majority view reported significantly more stress than those exposed to the differing minority view (Nemeth, 1976; Nemeth & Wachtler, 1983).

Evidence is considerable that arousal leads to a focus of attention (Easterbrook, 1959). More attention is allocated to the central task and less to the peripheral ones (Bahrick, Fitts, & Rankin, 1952). Thus, the arousal (stress) induced by the majority would be expected to narrow the focus of attention and increase the probability of the strongest or most dominant response and decrease the probability of competing responses. Zajonc (1965) has used such a formulation to explain the effects of presence of others, a drive state that presumably fosters the dominant response. This aids performance in simple tasks and hinders performance in complex tasks. Such a formulation is consistent with the well-known Yerkes-Dodson law (Yerkes & Dodson, 1908) that shows that the quality of performance is an inverted U-shaped function of arousal.

Pertinent to the present formulation, the high degree of stress reported by persons exposed to the opposing majority view may well cause a narrowing of attention and poorer performance on complex tasks whereas the moderate stress of those exposed to the opposing minority view may well be optimal for problem solving. This is quite likely a component of the differential processes hypothesized. However, it is further assumed that in the case of the opposing majority view, the attention is narrowed to the position proposed by the majority. Subjects, it is believed, are motivated to consider the truth or falsity of that position and attention is allocated to that position rather than to other possibilities. By contrast, it is believed that those exposed to the minority viewpoint are not only less focused but also that they are actually stimulated to consider more aspects of the situation and more possible conclusions. Part of the reason for these more specific hypotheses regarding focus of attention and thought comes from the differences in assumptions and motivations that separately characterize majority and minority influence.

A second aspect concerns these cognitive and motivational factors. When the influencing agent is a majority, individuals start with the assumption that the majority is correct (even when it is not) and that they themselves are in error (Asch, 1956). By contrast, they assume that the differing minority is incorrect and, in fact, manifest outright derision toward them (Maass & Clark, 1984; Nemeth & Wachtler, 1983). Furthermore, individuals are motivated to accept the majority position and to not accept the minority position. They fear the disapproval that results from maintaining or joining a minority view (Asch, 1956; Deutsch & Gerard, 1955). Thus, when individuals accept the minority view, they tend to do so at the private or latent level (Maass & Clark, 1984).

Because individuals assume and are motivated to assume that the majority is correct, they tend to publicly adopt the majority position. Here, it is assumed that the person is primarily concerned about the truth or falseness of the majority position. The world of alternatives is reduced to two: that proposed and that originally held by the subject. Thus, attention and thought processes should be centered around the majority position.

When the influence source is a minority, the assumption that the minority is incorrect and the disinclination to publicly adopt its position lead to an initial dismissal of the minority viewpoint. However, with consistency and confidence on the minority's part over time, people are stimulated to understand such alternative views (e.g., "How can they be so wrong and yet so sure of themselves?"). As a result, they are stimulated to reappraise the entire situation, which involves a consideration of numerous alternatives, one of which is the position proposed by the minority. As such, the thought processes are marked by divergence and, hence, the potential for detecting novel solutions or decisions.

A third important aspect is the role of conflict. In both the majority and minority situations, people are exposed to an opposing or alternative viewpoint that persists over time. This, in and of itself, demands effort to resolve the conflict, and in Kahneman's (1973) terms, such effort extends the capacity for attention. In addition to greater attention, it is assumed that exposure to persistent opposing views will also be a catalyst to greater cognitive effort. People will think more. Although this consideration might, at first glance, seem to argue that those exposed to the majority position might expend more effort because they report greater conflict, the reverse is hypothesized: namely, that those exposed to the opposing minority position will exert more effort at both the attentional and cognitive levels. The reason is that the conflict is generally resolved earlier for those in the majority condition. Thus, although they may expend a great deal of effort in judging the proposed position to be true or false, subjects exposed to the majority viewpoint decide relatively quickly to adopt that viewpoint or to resist it.

The available evidence shows that individuals often adopt the majority position on early trials or in early minutes of discussion (Asch, 1956). By contrast, individuals exposed to opposing minority views rarely adopt the proposed position quickly. Adoption, when it occurs, tends to be manifested on later trials or later in the discussion (Nemeth et al., 1974; Nemeth & Wachtler, 1974, 1983). The assumption is that those exposed to the majority view exert a good deal of effort prior to the decision to adopt the majority view, but after this decision they engage in relatively effortless and superficial information processing. Whether they have moved for informational reasons (an assumption that the majority is correct) or for normative reasons (to incur approval and avoid disapproval), the decision, once made, tends not to be strongly reconsidered. Separate from the issue of amount of cognitive work, it is clearly presumed that the effort is differentially focused as a result of the majority or minority status of the source. When the source is a majority, attention and cognitions are focused on the position proposed. When the source is a minority, attention and thought processes are widened to include additional information and alternative positions.

The assumptions about the amount of cognitive work bear some similarity to Moscovici's (1980) contention that majorities produce compliance whereas minorities produce conversion in that there is more active or "central" (Petty & Cacioppo, 1981) thought processing when the influencing agent is a minority. However, the Moscovici formulation concentrates on thought relevant to the object under discussion and to message-relevant thought. This is used to account for private adoption of the minority position. Moscovici hypothesizes that people think more about the minority's position and, thus, adopt it privately. The present formulation actually predicts the reverse, namely, that message-relevant thought appropriate to the proposed position is more characteristic of reactions to majorities. The action thought processing stimulated by opposing minority viewpoints is more *issue* relevant. People think divergently; they consider more viewpoints than simply the one proposed. The consequence of this is that the quality of the decision (whichever is selected) tends to be better because more alternatives are considered. Furthermore, novel correct solutions are capable of being detected. From this perspective, dissenting minority views take on importance both in terms of individual and small group decision making as well as in terms of the functioning of society at large. These issues will be explored after a review of the studies directly testing some of the proposed distinctions.

Research: Direct Tests of the Theory

To date, three studies that directly test the assumptions of the theory have been conducted.

Study 1

In the first study (Nemeth, 1976; Nemeth & Wachtler, 1983) subjects in groups of 6 were shown a series of eight slides with a standard on the left and a series of six comparison figures on the right (see Figure 1 for an example). They were asked to name all of the comparison figures that contained the standard. One comparison figure was very easy; nearly every subject could detect the standard embedded in the comparison figure (U in Figure 1). The other five were very difficult. Depending on the experimental condition, 2 of the 6 people (the minority) or 4 of the 6 people (the majority) were paid confederates who said the figure was embedded in both the easy figure (e.g., U) and in one other figure (e.g., E). Again, depending on the condition, this judgment was either correct or incorrect; that is, the difficult figure named by the confederates either did or did not contain the standard. In the example given (Figure 1), E is correct. Results underscored the importance of the source of influence as a highly significant variable; whether or not they were correct proved to be of less importance. Most importantly, the form of the influence exerted by a majority in comparison with a minority was quite different.

With respect to direct following (i.e., adoption of the proposed position), majorities exerted more influence than did minorities. If the confederates said the standard was embedded in comparison figures E and U, subjects were more likely to also state E and U in the majority condition than in the minority condition. However, subjects in the minority condition were more likely to find novel correct solutions than those in the majority condition. Subjects exposed to the minority view detected the standard in comparison figures not pro-

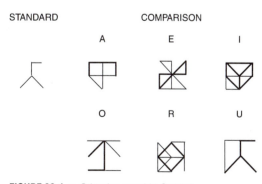

STANDARD   COMPARISON

FIGURE 36.1 ■ Stimulus used in Study 1.

posed by the minority. Furthermore, they were correct. Thus, they might find the figure embedded in the comparison figures I or R in the example, both of which are correct. Moreover, this was not due to guessing. There were no condition differences for novel incorrect solutions (A or O).

A secondary finding of some theoretical importance is the marginally significant interaction between source of influence and correctness, $F(1, 32) = 3.99$, $p < .06$. Subjects exposed to the minority viewpoint found more correct novel solutions whether the minority was correct or incorrect. Those exposed to the majority viewpoint found fewer correct novel solutions in general, but they were more likely to find them when the majority was incorrect rather than correct. Finally, subjects in the minority condition reported being under less stress than those in the majority condition. The minority source was also seen as less correct than the majority source.

The results corroborate other research showing that majorities exercise more influence in the sense of prevailing (Maass & Clark, 1984; Tanford & Penrod, 1984). Subjects are more likely to follow or adopt the exact position proposed by a majority than a minority of individuals. What the minority appears to stimulate, however, is a more active reexamination of the stimulus array. Individuals are finding solutions not proposed by the minority and solutions that they would not find by themselves, and their solutions are correct. Thus, it appears that the nature of the influence process is different when the source is a majority from when it is a minority. Majorities generate adoption of the proposed position but do not induce novel problem solving. Minorities are less able to get their specific position accepted but, in the process, appear to force a reexamination of the stimulus array so that correct and novel solutions are detected. This suggests that the minority may provide a creative contribution to problem solving whether or not their view is correct.

The interaction between influence source and correctness of the position provides some additional confirmation for differential processes induced by majority versus minority influence. The minority stimulates novel problem solving regardless of the correctness of its own position. The majority does not in general enhance such novel problem solving, but it is more likely to do so when its own position is incorrect. Thus, the possibility exists that breaking the assumption that the majority is correct may be a stimulant for more novel problem solving. People then search and find more correct solutions.

Study 2

Further evidence for the proposition that majority views confine problem solving to the position proposed whereas minority views stimulate both novel and better problem solving comes from a recent study of Nemeth and Kwan (1985b). In that study, subjects in groups of 4 viewed a series of slides, each consisting of a string of five letters with the middle three letters in capitals. An example would be *tDOGe*. They were asked to name the first three-letter word they saw. With exposure times of 1 s, all subjects saw *dog*. After five such slides, subjects were given feedback on the responses of the 4 subjects. In the majority condition, they were repeatedly told that 3 of the 4 saw the word formed by the backward sequencing of the capital letters (*god*) and 1 saw the word formed by the forward sequencing of the capital letters (*dog*). In the minority condition, they were told the reverse, that is, 1 saw *god* and 3 saw *dog*. They were then shown a series of 10 such letter strings and asked to form all the words they could from these letters. They were given 15 s for each letter string.

Subjects in the minority condition found more correct words. They achieved this overall performance by using all possible strategies—forward sequencing, backward sequencing, and mixed sequencing of letters. Subjects in the majority condition used the proposed strategy; that is, they found more words using a backward sequencing of letters. However, this was at the expense of finding words in the usual fashion, that is, forward sequencing. Thus, their overall performance was comparable to the control. In summary, those in the majority condition followed the strategy adopted by the majority but to the detriment of other possible strategies. Those in the minority condition adopted all possible strategies and used them to their advantage in finding more overall solutions.

Study 3

A third study (Nemeth & Kwan, 1985a) provides still more evidence for the hypothesized differences between majority and minority influence processes. The results also demonstrate the impact on thought processes even after the interaction with the majority or minority has ceased. In this study, a subject was placed in a cubicle with another person who was a confederate of the experiment. They were asked to judge 20 slides for color and perceived brightness. In fact, all of the slides were blue in color, Subjects, however, were told prior to their judgments that previous research found that approximately 80% of people judge these colors to be blue and 20% judge them to be green, or they were told the reverse. Thus, a judgment of *green* would be seen as either a minority or a majority judgment.

The confederate judged the color to be green on all 20 trials. Following this judgment session, subjects were asked for word associations to the words *green* and *blue*. Each word was repeated seven times. Using established norms for associations to these words, it was found that subjects exposed to the opposing minority judgment of *green* gave more original associations to both *green* and *blue*. They gave associations that were statistically less frequent. In contrast, those exposed to the opposing majority judgment of *green* gave more conventional responses, even more conventional than the control. Thus, those in the majority condition might give the statistically frequent responses of *sky* or *green* to the word *blue* whereas those in the minority condition might give the more original associations of *jazz* or *jeans*.

Results from these three studies provide evidence that majority and minority influence processes differ primarily in the form that the influence takes. In particular, majorities exert more influence in the sense of prevailing. People are much more likely to adopt the position they propose. However, in the process, subjects narrow the range of considerations primarily to that proposed and do not detect other solutions or "truths." Those exposed to minority viewpoints, although they are less likely to adopt the proposed viewpoints, are in fact stimulated to think in more divergent ways. They are more original, they use a greater variety of strategies, they detect novel solutions, and importantly, they detect correct solutions. Furthermore, this beneficial impact occurs even when the minority viewpoints are wrong.

Relevance to Other Literatures

In the present formulation, differences in attention, thought processing, originality, and quality

of decisions are hypothesized as a result of majority versus minority influence. A review of the existing literatures on these topics should extend the range of the formulation as well as add specificity and refinement to the present considerations.

One of the basic premises here is that individuals exposed to persistent minority views are actually better decision makers in that they attend to more aspects of the situation and they examine and reexamine premises. They manifest divergent rather than convergent thinking. By contrast, those exposed to persistent majority views tend toward convergence of thinking and to an unreflective acceptance of the majority position. As such, distinctions are made between relatively deep and superficial information processing and between relatively more complex and more biased search of the information. Such distinctions find their counterparts in a good deal of the social psychological literature.

Research on Attribution Processes and Social Cognition

One example of a distinction between complete and biased information processing can be found in attribution theories. Early work in that area emphasized the human being as a rational information processor. Keley's (1967) analysis of variance model, for example, portrays the individual as an "intuitive scientist" attempting to attain "cognitive mastery of the casual structure of the environment" (p. 193). The individual's limits in these endeavors, however, soon became apparent. He or she is often unable or unwilling to use basic logic or statistics and may rely on heuristics such as availability and representativeness (Nisbett & Ross, 1980; Tversky & Kahneman, 1974) or may be affected by motivational considerations such as self-esteem or self-presentation (see generally Bradley, 1978; Zuckerman, 1979). Thus, attributions can depend on careful search motivated by cognitive mastering or they can be biased either by inability or by social and psychological consequences of particular attributions (see generally Tetlock & Levi, 1982).

Such a distinction is also apparent in recent theorizing distinguishing between central and peripheral information processing (Petty & Cacioppo, 1981). Central processing refers to active issue-relevant thinking, a type of thinking that leads to relatively enduring change; peripheral processing is a reaction to persuasion cues in the situation and tends to be characterized by a more temporary attitude shift. Conceptually similar to this is the distinction between systematic and heuristic information processing (Chaiken, 1980). Systematic processing is characterized by more effort and by active attempts to comprehend the arguments of a message. Heuristic thinking is characterized by a usage of simple schemas (e.g., experts are usually correct; the longer a message the more valid its arguments). People use the script instead of actively processing the information. Such distinctions can also be found in Langer, Blank, and Chanowitz's (1978) work on "mindlessness" or Taylor's (1980) work on cognitive misery. In some situations, people are lazy cognitive processors in that they do not actively process the information that is available or, it could be added, fully consider the alternative ways of understanding such information.

The suggestions for counteracting this inadequate processing of information have taken various forms. Petty, Cacioppo, and their colleagues, for example, have pointed to the usefulness of making the issue more personally relevant, or of increasing personal responsibility (Petty & Cacioppo, 1981). Nisbett and Ross (1980) have provided evidence for the utility of statistical training. Moro's (1984) findings emphasize the importance of instructions to reflect. In most of these studies, the focus is on the individual, and attempts to make him or her a more active and thorough information processor tend to take the forms of experimenter-induced training, manipulations of role, or manipulations of the issue itself. All recognize the importance of motivation in information processing.

The present formulation can be viewed as relevant to the distinctions in that alternative minority views appear to stimulate more central or systematic processing whereas majority influence might be construed more in terms of peripheral or heuristic processing. Some consequences of this should be that individuals exposed to opposing minority views should be more likely to consider the quality of the message and be less bound by heuristics (e.g., length of the message). Those exposed to opposing majority views should be more affected by persuasion cues or by schemas such as "the majority is most likely to be correct" and manifest temporary attitude shifts. This would coincide with the persistent findings that those in

the majority condition show public compliance without private change whereas those in the minority condition show more private or latent than public or manifest influence. The present formulation differs from those research traditions in that there is an emphasis on influence and interaction. In particular it is exposure to differing views emanating from a minority that can stimulate more central processing.

Convergent/Divergent Thinking and Problem Solving

Perhaps the most relevant literature for the present purposes is that literature studying divergent versus convergent thinking and their relation to creativity and problem solving. Guilford (1956) defined divergent thinking as both more ideas (fluency) and more classes of ideas (flexibility). To illustrate, people can be asked to generate "uses for a brick." Within the classification of *building*, one could suggest building a home, a patio, or a monument. These are separate ideas but not separate classes of ideas. One could also use a brick as a *missile*. One could throw it through a window to make a point. This would constitute a different class of use. In his theory on cognitive structures, Zajonc (1955, 1960) makes a conceptually similar point with his terms *differentiation* (i.e., the number of attributes used to describe a social object) and *complexity* (i.e., the usage of different classifications of an object).

One of the important consequences of divergent thinking is that it appears to aid both problem solving and creativity. Many researchers recognize that the dominant response is often not the correct or best one (Moro, 1984). Thus, it is only with a careful search of alternatives that one can select the best solution or decision. In considering the notion of dominant versus subordinate solutions, many theorists have been influenced by Berlyne (1965), who argued that responses are hierarchically arranged. A given stimulus can evoke a number of responses, and the behavior chains between stimulus and response are not equally likely. Berlyne argues that the probability of elicitation is a function of reinforcement. Maier (1970) uses a similar notion in pointing to a hierarchy of possible solutions in many problem-solving settings. Maier argues that "tricky" problems are misleading in that they cause people to place low probabilities on the correct answer.

Another way of viewing the creation of inappropriate dominant responses comes from research on "set." Solutions that have been previously useful become dominant; they are used when they are no longer useful or best. The classic work by Luchins (1942) is illustrative of this phenomenon. People were given a series of water jar problems. For example, they were asked to find 100 gallons by using containers holding 21, 127, and 3 gallons, respectively. The formula $B - A - 2C$ (i.e., $127 - 21 - 6$) proved to be the solution over a series of problems. When then confronted with the problem of finding 20 gallons from 23-, 49-, and 3-gallon containers, individuals tended to use the dominant but no longer best formula of $B - A - 2C$ (e.g., $49 - 23 - 6$). The best formula is $A - C$ (i.e., $23 - 3$), a solution that is relatively easy if one has not been exposed to the previous problems. Within this context, it is beneficial for individuals to diverge their thinking, to consider more alternatives, to refrain from adopting the dominant solution or the first solution that comes to mind.

Creativity

The previously described research is also directly related to creativity because the notions of both divergent thinking and originality (statistical infrequency) are presumed to be essential elements of creativity. Watson (1928) refers to "shifting about until a new pattern is hit upon" (p. 198) in his description of creativity. Newell, Shaw, and Simon (1962) point to novelty, unconventionality, persistence, and difficulty in problem formulation. Ghiselin (1963) emphasizes the "quality of uniqueness, recognizable and definable" (p. 37), which involves seeing new relations among old ideas and thinking of alternative solutions. Most emphasize the importance of flexibility of search among ideas and associations (Guilford, 1956; Mednick, 1962).

The research on this issue has tended to concentrate on individual differences. Who is creative, how are these people detected, and what form does their creativity take? As such, creativity has often been construed as a skill. More recently, Amabile (1983) has emphasized the motivational aspects in her demonstrations. In particular, variables that undermine intrinsic motivation appear to reduce creativity. Thus, evaluation, time pressures, and reward can, under some circumstances, undermine creativity, presumably because some of the individual attention is diverted from the task itself and

from the nonobvious aspects that might be used in achieving a creative solution (Amabile, 1983). Thus, greater attention and cognitive work, particularly aimed at the novel as well as the obvious elements of the stimulus or problem situation, should enhance creativity.

The proposed framework and research findings support such contentions and point to the importance of influence processes on creativity. In particular, minority views can stimulate considerations of the nonobvious. Subjects detected novel solutions (Nemeth & Wachtler, 1983), used more varied strategies (Nemeth & Kwan, 1985b), and thought in more original ways (Nemeth & Kwan, 1985a). Thus, like Amabile (1983), the importance of motivation for creativity is recognized, but the consideration of the more social aspects of the process would be expanded from situational constraints and properties of the task to interaction. It is the contention here that interaction with persistent minority views is a mechanism for stimulating the kinds of thought processes that can be characterized as creative.

Group Creativity and Decision Making

Creativity at the group level has been studied in quite a different way because it, by definition, involves interaction. On this point, the bulk of the literature finds that the group is less than the sum of its individuals. McGrath (1984) summarizes this research: "Individuals working separately generate many more and more creative (as rated by judges) ideas than do groups . . . the difference is large, robust and general" (p. 131). The culprit appears to be a tendency for uniformity. People are reluctant to voice novel or deviant views for fear they will be ridiculed. Thus, the diversity of viewpoints is unexpressed in most groups, and therefore there is a reduced likelihood of finding creative solutions. Most attempts at enhancing group creativity have attempted to remove this culprit by instructions. People are encouraged to give as many judgments as come to mind and to refrain from evaluating those judgments. Brainstorming instructions, for example, operate on these principles (Osborn, 1953). The success of such instructions, however, has been limited, presumably because people still fear that such evaluation is, in fact, taking place (Taylor, Berry, & Block, 1959).

Research under the rubric of group decision

making has been frustrated by similar concerns. Research often shows that "the pooled output of noninteracting individuals is better than that of an interacting group" (Hackman & Morris, 1975, p. 46). Again, the mechanism by which resources can be harnessed to better productivity is assumed to be in the interaction process. Hackman and Morris (1975) have pointed to the importance of effort brought to bear on the task by the members, the performance strategies, and the knowledge and skills of the members. Hoffman (1959, 1965), Hoffman and Maier (1961), and others have recognized that pressures for uniformity are an impediment to good problem solving. They have stressed the value of heterogeneity, assuming that persons differing in category (e.g., age, skill, personality) will provide diverse approaches to problems and therefore performance will be improved. By and large, the research supports such assumptions though the question remains, "On what dimensions should group members be heterogeneous?"(Hoffman, 1959, p. 113).

The recognition that majority views and strains to uniformity can be impediments to good group decision making is also apparent in Janis's (1972) work on political "fiascoes." There, the problem is that cabinet-level decisions are often made by groups that are highly cohesive and insulated. This fact promotes "groupthink," evidenced by a tendency to inadequately survey alternatives and objectives. As a result, poor decisions can result. To counter this tendency, Janis makes several suggestions, such as having a person play devil's advocate, calling in outside experts, having the leader refrain from taking a position, and so forth, all of which should promote diversity of expressed views.

It is undoubtedly apparent that there is a compatibility of thought between the present formulation and these research literatures in that diversity of views is seen as an aid to creativity and group decision making. The emphasis, however, is somewhat different. The present formulation emphasizes the role of conflict, of exposure to differing views over time. Whether the fact of differing views (i.e., a plurality of opinion) is sufficient to invoke a reappraisal of the situation and a consideration of alternative viewpoints is questioned. Furthermore, it is assumed that instructions or role playing creates good intentions but that an active consideration of alternatives is more likely to come from confrontation with persons honestly differing in viewpoint and persisting in that difference.

Complications, Reflections, and Practical Consequences

In a good deal of the referenced research, there is a concern about the fact that people often take the path of least effort. They do not carefully scrutinize the issues or the arguments given. They do not fully reflect on alternatives. They are reluctant to voice novel ideas. As a result, both individuals and groups can be poor at problem solving and decision making. Correctives for this state of affairs can be considered on many levels, but the present formulation argues that dissenting minority views, even when wrong, stimulate reappraisal and a consideration of more alternatives. As a result, minority views provide a creative contribution to problem solving and decision making.

In this context, it is important to underscore the fact that it is not being argued that opposition or conflict between opinions per se is what stimulates such productive thought processes. Opposing views emanating from a majority have the reverse effect, leading to a convergence of thought, a tendency to focus on the position proposed to the neglect of other considerations. Thus, it becomes important to recognize that opposing views have different effects depending on whether their source is a numerical majority or minority.

When they are an initial minority, they stimulate the divergent thought processes; when they are an initial majority, they foster convergent thinking.

The functional consequences of these two forms of influence are complex. Under some circumstances, the influence exerted by the majority can be beneficial. It is almost always efficient if the majority is correct, because individuals and the group are more likely to accept that correct position. However, even under these circumstances, one would register caution because the agreement appears to be a consequence of unreflective submission rather than independent thought. Furthermore, it is assumed that the finding of truth or correct solutions is a more likely consequence of the divergent thinking characterized by persons exposed to dissenting minority views.

The creative contributions of minority views are

argued to both the individual and the group levels in the present article. The presence of minority views, much like the literature on hererogeneity, aids the consideration of more alternatives because different alternatives are represented by different individuals. In this sense, groups can be divergent even if the individuals are not. The presence of dissenting minority views and the expression of those views thus aid the consideration of alternatives at a group level. In addition, the process of confrontation of viewpoint makes each individual a better problem solver or decision maker by stimulating him or her to examine and reexamine premises.

Some Applications

If one takes seriously the importance of minority views for the stimulation of productive thought processes that aid problem solving and decision making, several practical consequences follow. For example, efforts to underrepresent minority views can suppress their active expression and are seen as undermining the quality of decision making. An illustration can be taken from the area of law: There has long been a tension between wanting community representation on juries and feeling that not all persons are capable of the onerous duties of jury service. Originally this took the form of qualifications for service by which certain categories of people were excluded from service by statute. More recently, it has taken a subtler form because there are few restrictions by category, yet juries in the United States, Great Britain, and France consistently underrepresent certain categories of persons (Nemeth, 1980, 1984). By and large, juries are "male middle aged, middle minded and middle class" (Lord Devlin quoted in Pope, 1961, footnote 10). Added to this underrepresentation of certain categories (and we assume certain view points), there have been efforts to suppress the effective expression of dissent. One example is the Supreme Court rulings allowing for nonunanimity of verdict (*Apodaca, Cooper, & Madden v. Oregon*, 1972; *Johnson v. Louisiana*, 1972). If unanimity is not required, the conflict in the deliberation appears to be less robust, the number of comments giving information and opinions is fewer, the functional deliberation time is shortened, and jurors believe that justice has been less

well administered (Nemeth, 1977). In perhaps an exaggerated version of such effective suppression of dissent, France has three judges deliberate with nine jurors on both culpability and punishment, eight votes of which are needed for a decision (Nemeth, 1984). From the perspective of this framework, such practices and rulings actually undermine the aims of justice by rendering the jurors less likely to consider all the facts, examine premises, consider multiple interpretations, and so on, and perhaps less likely to render a just decision.

At the level of society, the principle becomes even more important. As John Stuart Mill (1859/1979) argued, the protection of minority views from the potential tyranny of the majority is important as a democratic principle. However, he also argued that there are functional consequences to the allowance of, and confrontation with, dissenting viewpoints. Diversity and confrontation provide the impetus for detecting truths primarily because they stimulate thought (Nemeth, 1985). From this perspective, robust dissent is not only a manifestation of a democratic principle, but it is the mechanism by which better solutions are found and better decisions are made.

ACKNOWLEDGMENTS

I am very grateful for the help provided by the three reviewers of this manuscript. Many of their suggestions have been incorporated, and I am happy to acknowledge their contributions. I also wish to thank Ofra Mayseless, Eleanor Rosch, and Philip Tetlock for their reading of the manuscript and/or helpful comments.

REFERENCES

Allen, V. L. (1965). Situational factors in conformity. In L. Berkowitz (Ed.), *Advances in experimental social psychology* (Vol. 2, pp. 133–175). New York: Academic Press.

Amabile, T. (1983). *The social psychology of creativity*. New York: Springer-Verlag.

Apodaca, Cooper, & Madden v. Oregon, 92 U.S. 1928 (1972).

Asch, S. (1956). Studies of independence and conformity. *Psychological Monographs, 70* (9, Whole No. 416).

Bahrick, H. P., Fitts, P. M., & Rankin, R. E. (1952). Effect of incentives upon reactions to peripheral stimuli. *Journal of Experimental Psychology, 44,* 400–406.

Berlyne, D. E. (1965). *Structure and direction in thinking*. New York: Wiley.

Bradley, G. W. (1978). Self-serving biases in the attribution process: A reexamination of the fact or fiction question. *Journal of Personality and Social Psychology, 36,* 56–71.

Chaiken, S. (1980). Heuristic versus systematic information processing and the use of source versus message cues in persuasion. *Journal of Personality Psychology, 39,* 752–766.

Deutsch, M., & Gerard, H. G. (1955). A study of normative and informational social influence upon individual judgment. *Journal of Abnormal and Social Psychology, 51,* 629–636.

Easterbrook, J. A. (1959). The effect of emotion on the utilization and the organization of behavior. *Psychological Review, 66,* 183–201.

Ghiselin, B. (1963). Ultimate criteria for two levels of creativity. In C. Taylor & F. Barron (Eds.), *Scientific creativity: Its recognition and development* (pp. 30–43). New York: Wiley.

Guilford, J. P. (1956). The structure of intellect. *Psychological Bulletin, 33,* 267–293.

Hackman, J. R., & Morris, C. G. (1975). Group tasks, group interaction process and group performance effectiveness: A review and proposed integration. In L. Berkowitz (Ed.), *Advances in experimental social psychology* (Vol. 8, pp. 45–99). New York: Academic Press.

Hoffman, L. R. (1959). Homogeneity of member personality and its effect on group problem solving. *Journal of Abnormal and Social Psychology, 58,* 27–32.

Hoffman, L. R. (1965). Group problem solving. In L. Berkowitz (Ed.), *Advances in experimental psychology* (Vol. 2, pp. 99–132). New York: Academic Press.

Hoffman, L. R., & Maier, N. R. F. (1961). Quality and acceptance of problem solutions by members of homogeneous and heterogeneous groups. *Journal of Abnormal and Social Psychology, 62,* 401–407.

Janis, I. L. (1972). *Victims of groupthink.* Boston: Houghton Mifflin.

Johnson v. Louisiana, 92, U.S. 1935 (1972).

Kahneman, D. (1973). *Attention and effort.* Englewood Cliffs, NJ: Prentice-Hall.

Kalven, H., Jr., & Zeisel, H. (1966). *The American jury.* Boston: Little, Brown.

Kelley, H. H. (1967). Attribution theory in social psychology. In D. Levine (Ed.), *Nebraska symposium on motivation* (pp. 192–241). Lincoln: University of Nebraska Press.

Kiesler, C. A., & Kiesler, S. B. (1969). *Conformity.* Reading, MA: Addison-Wesley.

Langer, E., Blank, A., & Chanowitz, B. (1978). The mindlessness of ostensibly thoughtful action: The role of "placebic" information in interpersonal interaction. *Journal of Personality and Social Psychology, 36,* 635–642.

Latane, B., & Wolf, S. (1981). The social impact of majorities and minorities. *Psychological Review, 88,* 438–453.

Luchins, A. S. (1942). Mechanization in problem solving—The effect of Einstellung. *Psychological Monographs, 54* (6, Whole No. 248).

Maass, A., & Clark, R. D. III. (1984). Hidden impact of minorities: Fifteen years of minority influence research. *Psychological Bulletin, 95,* 428–450.

Maier, N. (1970). *Problem solving and creativity: In individuals and groups.* Belmont, CA: Brooks-Cole.

McGrath, J. (1984). *Groups: Interaction and performance.* Englewood Cliffs, NJ: Prentice-Hall.

Mednick, S. (1962). The associative basis of the creative process. *Psychological Review, 69,* 220–232.

Mill, J. S. (1979). *On liberty.* New York: Penguin. (Original work published 1859)

Moro, C. E. (1984). *Modification of response hierarchy and its effects on influence and cognitive structures.* Unpublished doctoral dissertation, University of Michigan.

Moscovici, S. (1976). *Social influence and social change.* London: Academic Press.

Moscovici, S. (1980). Toward a theory of conversion behavior. In L. Berkowitz (Ed.), *Advances in experimental social psychology* (Vol. 13, pp. 209–239). New York: Academic Press.

Moscovici, S., & Faucheux, C. (1972). Social influence, conformity bias and the study of active minorities. In L. Berkowitz (Ed.), *Advances in experimental social psychology* (Vol. 6, pp. 149–202). New York: Academic Press.

Moscovici, S., & Lage, E. (1976). Studies in social influence III: Majority versus minority influence in a group. *European Journal of Social Psychology, 6,* 149–174.

Moscovici, S., Lage, E., & Naffrechoux, M. (1969). Influence of a consistent minority on the responses of a majority in a color perception task. *Sociometry, 32,* 365–380.

Moscovici, S., & Nemeth, C. (1974). Social influence II: Minority influence. In C. Nemeth (Ed.), *Social psychology: Classic and contemporary integrations* (pp. 217–249). Chicago: Rand-McNally.

Mugny, G. (1980). *The power of minorities.* London: Academic Press.

Nemeth, C. (1976, August). *A comparison between conformity and minority influence.* Paper presented at the International Congress of Psychology (joint meeting of the Society of Experimental Social Psychology and the European Association of Social Psychology), Paris.

Nemeth, C. (1977). Interactions between jurors as a function of majority *vs* unanimity decision rules. *Journal of Applied Social Psychology, 7,* 38–56.

Nemeth, C. (1980). Jury trials: Psychology and the law. In L. Berkowitz (Ed.), *Advances in experimental social psychology* (Vol. 14, pp. 309–367). New York: Academic Press.

Nemeth, C. (1984). Processus de groupe et de jurys: Les Etats-Unis et la France. In S. Moscovici (Ed.), *Psychologie sociale* (pp. 229–251). Paris: Presses Universitaires de France.

Nemeth, C. (1985). Dissent, group process and creativity: The contribution of minority influence. In E. Lawler (Ed.), *Advances in group processes* (Vol. 2, pp. 57–75). Greenwich, CT: JAI Press.

Nemeth, C., & Kwan, J. (1985a). Originality of word associations as a function of majority vs. minority influence. *Social Psychology Quarterly, 48,* 277–282.

Nemeth, C., & Kwan, J. (1985b). *Minority influence, divergent thinking, and detection of correct solutions.* Manuscript submitted for publication.

Nemeth, C., Swedlund, M., & Kanki, G. (1974). Patterning of the minority's responses and their influence on the majority. *European Journal of Social Psychology, 4,* 53–64.

Nemeth, C., & Wachtler, J. (1974). Creating the perceptions of consistency and confidence: A necessary condition for minority influence. *Sociometry, 37,* 529–540.

Nemeth, C., & Wachtler, J. (1983). Creative problem solving as a result of majority *vs* minority influence. *European Journal of Social Psychology, 13,* 45–55.

Newell, A., Shaw, J., & Simon, H. (1962). The processes of creative thinking. In H. Gruber, G. Terrell, & M. Wertheimer (Eds.), *Contemporary approaches to creative thinking* (pp. 63–119). New York: Atherton Press.

Nisbett, R., & Ross, L. (1980). *Human inference: Strategies and shortcomings of social judgment*. Englewood Cliffs, NJ: Prentice-Hall.

Osborn, A. F. (1953). *Applied imagination*. New York: Scribner's.

Petty, R., & Cacioppo, J. (1981). *Attitudes and persuasion: Classic and contemporary approaches*. Dubuque, IA: William C. Brown.

Pope, J. (1961). The jury. *Texas Law Review, 39,* 426–448.

Tanford, S., & Penrod, S. (1984). Social influence model: A formal integration of research on majority and minority influence processes. *Psychological Bulletin, 95,* 189–225.

Taylor, S. E. (1980). The interface of cognitive and social psychology. In J. H. Harvey (Ed.), *Cognition, social behavior, and the environment* (pp. 189–211). Hillsdale, NJ: Erlbaum.

Taylor, D. W., Berry, P. C., & Block, C. H. (1959). Does group participation when using brainstorming facilitate or inhibit creative thinking? *Administrative Science Quarterly*, 23–47.

Tetlock, P. E., & Levi, A. (1982). Attribution bias: On the inconclusivity of the cognition–motivation debate. *Journal of Experimental Soc. Psychology, 18,* 68–88.

Tversky, A., & Kahneman, D. (1974). Judgment under uncertain heuristics and biases. *Science, 185,* 1124–1131.

Watson, J. (1928). *Behaviorism*. London: Kegan Paul.

Yerkes, R. M., & Dodson, J. D. (1908). The relation of strength of stimulus to rapidity of habit formation. *Journal of Comparative Neurology Psychology, 18,* 459–482.

Zajonc, R. B. (1955). *Cognitive structure and cognitive tuning*. Unpublished doctoral dissertation, University of Michigan.

Zajonc, R. B. (1960). The process of cognitive tuning in communication. *Journal of Abnormal and Social Psychology, 61,* 159–167.

Zajonc, R. B. (1965). Social facilitation. *Science, 149,* 269–274.

Zuckerman, M. (1979). *Sensation seeking: Beyond the optimal level of arousal*. Hillsdale, NJ: Erlbaum.

READING 37

Group Socialization: Theory and Research

John M. Levine and Richard L. Moreland • University of Pittsburgh

Editors' Comments

One of the most important characteristics of humans as a species is our sociability, and an important expression of human sociability is our membership in groups. Most persons belong to various groups, be it their high school class, a business organization, their professional community, or a religious association. Often we aren't born into groups but instead join them. When we do, we are newcomers and are treated accordingly. Over time, our involvement with the group's activities and its objectives may deepen and our status in the group may grow. Thus, there is an important developmental dimension to group membership. As the authors describe it, we move from the periphery of the group to its center, and our commitment to the group as well as the group's commitment to us increases proportionately. However, nothing is forever, and our centrality in the group may also wane in the course of time. Our involvement in the group may decline as other, more youthful and energetic members with fresh ideas vie to occupy positions of leadership in the group. Ultimately we may leave the group (e.g., retire), and our past membership in the group becomes part of the group's history, conserved in the group's collective memory.

Discussion Questions

1. What are the three psychological processes assumed to underlie group socialization?
2. What do the authors mean by the term *decision criteria*? What is being decided, when is it being decided, and by whom?
3. What are the major findings of the Pavelchak, Moreland, & Levine (1986) studies on reconnaissance processes?

4. What is meant by the notion of staffing level? What are the consequences of overstaffing and understaffing? What empirical evidence is there to support the authors' suggestions in regard to staffing?

Suggested Readings

Levine, J. M., Bogart, L. M., & Zdaniuk, B. (1996). Impact of anticipated group membership on cognition. In R. M. Sorrentino & E. T. Higgins (Eds.), *Handbook of motivation and cognition: Vol. 3. The interpersonal context*. New York: Guilford.

Moreland, R. L., Hogg, M. A., & Haines, S. C. (1994). Back to the future: Social psychological research on groups. *Journal of Experimental Social Psychology, 30*, 527–555.

Stasser, G. (1992). Pooling of unshared information during group discussion. In S. Worchel, W. Wood, & J. A. Simpson (Eds.), *Group process and productivity* (pp. 48–67). Newbury Park, CA: Sage.

Authors' Abstract

In an effort to conceptualize the temporal change and reciprocal influence that characterize relationships between groups and their members, we have developed a model of 'group socialization' that describes and explains the passage of individuals through groups (Moreland & Levine, 1982). The goal of the model is to clarify the changes (affective, cognitive, and behavioral) that groups and individuals produce in one another from the beginning to the end of their relationship. The model assumes that the relationship between the group and the individual changes in systematic ways over time and views both parties as potential influence agents. It is meant to apply primarily (but not exclusively) to small, autonomous, voluntary groups, whose members interact on a regular basis, have affective ties with one another, share a common frame of reference, and are behaviorally interdependent. Thus, the model is relevant to many different kinds of groups, including sports teams, work units, social clubs, and religious sects.

In this chapter we first summarize our model of group socialization. We then present theoretical elaborations of two key components of the model (commitment and role transition) and use the model to clarify several other aspects of group dynamics. Finally, we review some empirical studies stimulated by the model.

The Group Socialization Model

Three psychological processes are assumed to underlie group socialization–*evaluation, commitment,* and *role transition*. Evaluation involves efforts by the group and the individual to assess and *maximize* one another's *rewardingness*. Commitment, which depends on the outcome of the evaluation process, is based on the group's and the individual's *beliefs about* the *rewardingness of* their *own and alternative relationships*. Finally, role transitions, which occur when *commitment reaches a critical level* (decision criterion), involve *relabelling* the individual's relationship to the

group and thereby changing how the two parties evaluate one another. The relationships among these three processes are shown in Figure 1.

Before discussing these processes in more detail, it is important to clarify our use of the term *group*. When we state that a group evaluates a particular person, feels commitment as a result, or has a decision criterion regarding a role transition, we do not mean to reify the group as an entity apart from its members. Rather, we view a 'group' response to an individual as a consensual response based on the shared views of the people who make up the group. When a faculty committee evaluating an assistant professor decides that her research

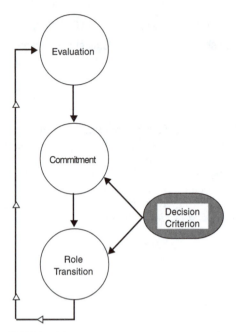

FIGURE 37.1 ■ Psychological processes in group socialization.

accomplishments have been excellent and feels highly committed to her as a result, but believes that she should publish several more papers in order to be promoted, it makes sense to talk about group responses. This is not to say, of course, that groups always reach consensus easily or that all members have an equal impact on the group's responses. Nonetheless, most groups develop informal or formal mechanisms for reaching consensus about individual members.

Evaluation involves assessments of the rewardingness of relationships. Because every group has goals that it wants to accomplish, it evaluates individuals in terms of how much they contribute to goal attainment. This evaluation involves deciding which goals the person is expected to contribute to, determining the behavioral dimensions on which these contributions will be assessed, developing normative expectations for each dimension, and finally comparing this expected behavior against the person's actual behavior. If the individual fails to meet the group's expectations, the group may take some form of corrective action to reduce the discrepancy between expected and actual behavior. The individual engages in a similar evaluation process to determine how well the group satisfies his or her personal needs.

While evaluating the present rewardingness of their relationship, the group and the individual also may think back to how rewarding their relationship was in the past and think ahead to how rewarding it will be in the future. Both parties may also evaluate the past, present, and future rewardingness of their alternative relationships. These six evaluations combine to produce feelings of commitment on the part of the group and the individual. Commitment will be higher to the extent that both parties (1) remember their past relationship as more rewarding than previous alternative relationships, (2) view their present relationship as more rewarding than current alternative relationships, and (3) expect their future relationship to be more rewarding than future alternative relationships. A discussion of the complexities associated with combining evaluations of past, present, and future relationships can be found in Moreland and Levine (1982).

Commitment can have important consequences for the behavior of both the individual and the group. When an individual feels strong commitment toward a group, the person is likely to accept the group's goals and values, feel positive affect toward group members, work hard to fulfil group expectations and attain group goals, and seek to gain or maintain membership in the group. Similarly, a group that feels strong commitment toward an individual is likely to accept the individual's needs and values, feel positive affect toward the individual, work hard to fulfil the individual's expectations and satisfy his or her needs, and seek to gain or retain the individual as a group member. Because relationships between groups and their members are smoother if the two parties feel equally committed to one another, they may 'test' one another's commitment from time to time (e.g. by mentioning attractive alternative relationships that they might enter).

Because the group's and the individual's commitment levels change over time, the nature of their relationship changes as well. These changes are governed by decision criteria, or specific levels of commitment indicating that a qualitative change in the relationship between the two parties is warranted. When a group's commitment to an individual reaches its decision criterion, the group will try to initiate a role transition. An individual whose commitment to a group reaches a personal decision criterion will make a similar effort. When a role transition occurs, the individual's relationship with the group is jointly relabeled, and the parties alter their expectations for one another's behavior. Role transitions often involve special ceremonies (i.e. rites of passage) designed to clarify that an important change has taken place. Following a role transition, evaluation continues, producing further changes in commitment and subsequent role transitions. In this way, the individual can pass through five phases of group socialization (investigation, socialization, maintenance, resocialization, and remembrance), separated by four role transitions (entry, acceptance, divergence, and exit). Figure 2 illustrates how the relationship between a group and an individual might change over time.

Initially, the group and the individual go through an *investigation* phase. During investigation, when the individual is a prospective member, the group engages in recruitment, looking for people who might contribute to the attainment of group goals. Similarly, the individual engages in reconnaissance, looking for groups that might contribute to the satisfaction of personal needs. If the commitment levels of both parties rise to their respective entrance criteria (EC), then the role transition of *entry* occurs and the individual becomes a new member.

The second phase of group membership is *socialization*. During socialization, the group attempts to change the individual so that he or she can contribute more to the attainment of group goals. Insofar as the group is successful, the individual undergoes assimilation. At the same time, the individual attempts to change the group so that it can contribute more to the satisfaction of personal needs. Insofar as the individual is successful, the group undergoes accommodation. If the commitment levels of both parties rise to their respective acceptance criteria (AC), then the role transition of *acceptance* occurs and the individual becomes a full member.

During the *maintenance* phase, both the group and the individual engage in role negotiation. The group attempts to find a specialized role for the individual that maximizes his or her contributions to the attainment of group goals, while the individual attempts to find a specialized role that maximizes the satisfaction of his or her personal needs.

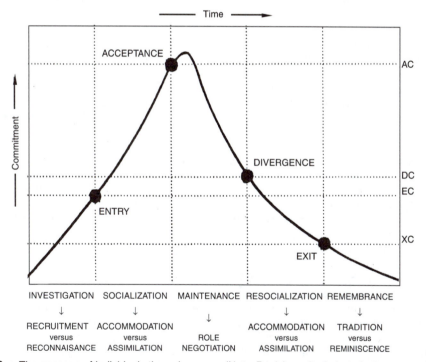

FIGURE 37.2 ■ The passage of individuals through groups. (Note: Decision criteria include the entry criterion (EC), acceptance criterion (AC), divergence criterion (DC), and exit criterion (XC). Reproduced from Moreland & Levine (1982) by permission of Academic Press.

If this role negotiation succeeds, then the commitment levels of both parties remain high. But if role negotiation fails and the commitment levels of both parties fall to their respective divergence criteria (DC), then the role transition of *divergence* occurs and the individual becomes a marginal member.

The fourth phase of group membership is *resocialization*. During resocialization, the group tries to restore the individual's contributions to the attainment of group goals, and the individual tries to restore the group's contributions to the satisfaction of personal needs. To the extent that both parties are successful, assimilation and accommodation again occur. If the group's and the individual's commitment levels rise to their respective divergence criteria, then the individual is returned to full membership. This special (and unusual) role transition might be called *convergence*. But if the commitment levels of both parties fall to their respective exit criteria (XC), then the role transition of *exit* occurs and the individual becomes an ex-member. This second and more common outcome of resocialization is shown in Figure 2.

Finally, the relationship between the group and the individual ends with a period of *remembrance*. During remembrance, the group recalls the individual's previous contributions to the attainment of group goals, and these memories become part of the group's tradition. Similarly, the individual engages in reminiscence about the group's contributions to the satisfaction of his or her personal needs. Both parties may also engage in an ongoing evaluation of their relationship, if they continue to influence one another's outcomes. Feelings of commitment between the group and the individual eventually stabilize at some level.

Figure 2 is an idealized representation of how the relationship between a group and an individual might change over time, and so it masks several complexities (see Moreland & Levine, 1982). For example, group and individual commitment levels may undergo sudden dramatic shifts, rather than changing gradually as the figure suggests. Group and individual decision criteria may not be stable over time, and changes in decision criteria can influence how long individuals spend in particular membership phases. If two adjacent decision criteria are quite similar, for example, the membership phase they demarcate will be very short. In contrast, if adjacent decision criteria are quite different, the membership phase they demarcate will be very long. Some decision criteria may vary in their positions relative to one another, which can produce variability in the number and order of role transitions that different individuals experience. For example, exit can occur during the investigation and socialization phases under certain circumstances. Finally, the figure assumes that the group and the individual share the same set of decision criteria and are equally committed to one another throughout their relationship. To the extent that this is not the case, conflict is likely to occur in the relationship.

Research on the Initial Phases of Group Socialization

Our group socialization model suggests many hypotheses about a range of small group phenomena, including group development, innovation in groups, and group culture. Our own program of research, however, has focused on the investigation and socialization phases of group membership. Below we describe three studies that clarify how individuals and groups behave during investigation. Investigation is the initial phase of group membership and involves reconnaissance of groups by individuals and recruitment of individuals by groups. These studies were not generally designed as formal tests of the group socialization model, but rather as efforts to obtain basic information about one of the membership phases identified in that model. This strategy was dictated by the paucity of research on investigation and the importance of this phase for the subsequent relationship between a group and its members.

Why has so little attention been paid to investigation? One reason is methodological. Most researchers investigate laboratory groups, in which several strangers are brought together for a brief period of real or simulated interaction. Under these conditions, issues of joining simply do not arise. A second reason for the failure to study investigation is theoretical. Most group theories are static rather than dynamic, ignoring temporal changes in the relations among group members. As a result, researchers tend to neglect issues of joining, even in natural groups where they are relevant.

This lack of attention to investigation is unfortunate, because the initial phase of group socialization is critical to the long-term success of both groups and individuals. Groups that do not engage in effective recruitment of new members have difficulty accomplishing their goals, and individuals who do not engage in effective reconnaissance of new groups have difficulty satisfying their needs. Unsuccessful investigation, particularly if prolonged, can have serious consequences for both parties.

Individual Reconnaissance

In order for reconnaissance to proceed successfully, the individual must do three things. First, the person must identify potentially desirable groups. This involves *deciding what kinds of groups he or she wants to join* and then determining the availability of these groups in the environment. Second, the person must evaluate the degree to which membership in available groups will satisfy his or her personal *needs*. This involves acquiring information about the probable *rewardingness* of memberships in these groups. Finally, assuming that commitment to a particular group exceeds the individual's entry criterion, he or she must take steps to enter that group. For this role transition to occur, the person must often convince the group to accept him or her as a member.

Many factors can influence the reconnaissance process, including a prospective member's acquaintance with group members, attraction to group activities, and prior experience in other groups. This last factor is particularly interesting, because although prior experience has been found to predict later group participation (Hanks, 1981; Hanks & Eckland, 1978), the psychological mechanisms underlying this relationship have not been investigated. Specifically, no attention has been given to how prior group memberships affect the subsequent reconnaissance activities of former members.

In one study (Pavelchak, Moreland, & Levine, 1986), we explored the impact of high school group experiences on the reconnaissance activities of freshmen at a large university. Prior to the fall semester, 1550 freshmen completed an orientation questionnaire assessing their experiences in high school groups and expectations about college groups. On the evening before the first day of class, many new students attended a university-sponsored Activities Fair, which was designed to introduce them to campus groups. On the two evenings following the Fair, a representative sample of 220 students who had completed the orientation questionnaire were interviewed by telephone about their behavior at the Fair.

Reconnaissance begins when the individual attempts to identify potentially desirable groups. We predicted that students whose experiences in high school groups were more positive would try harder to identify potentially desirable college groups and that this activity would be mediated by the belief that memberships in such groups were useful for achieving personal goals. Several questions in the orientation questionnaire were used to test these hypotheses. First, we measured students' perceptions of the enjoyableness and importance of their high school group memberships. Next, we assessed students' beliefs about the value of college group memberships for achieving important personal goals. Finally, we asked students to list campus groups that they had already considered joining and to name which group (if any) they were most likely to join. Students who named such a group were labeled 'joiners'; those who did not were labeled 'loners'. We estimated each student's efforts to identify potentially desirable groups by counting the number of prospective groups mentioned and noting whether the person was a loner or a joiner.

Complete data were provided by 1134 students. We used structural equations analyses to test our hypotheses about the determinants of reconnaissance activity. Figure 3 shows the standardized solution for a model based on our hypotheses. Underlying constructs are drawn as circles; measures of those constructs are drawn as boxes. Parameter values linking circles to boxes represent the estimated validities of construct measures; parameter values linking constructs to one another represent the estimated strengths of particular causal relationships. Some parameters (in parentheses) were set to 1.00 either for scaling purposes or to ensure that the variance in all the constructs could be identified. All parameter estimates were statistically significant. As the causal model in the figure indicates, the paths that we expected emerged quite clearly, although there was also an unexpected direct path linking high school group experiences to college reconnaissance activity. The overall chisquare for the model was nonsignificant, which is remarkable for so large a sample, and the ratio of the chi-square to its degrees of freedom was small. In addition, all of the model's residuals were small and showed no clear pattern. Consistent with predictions, students whose ex-

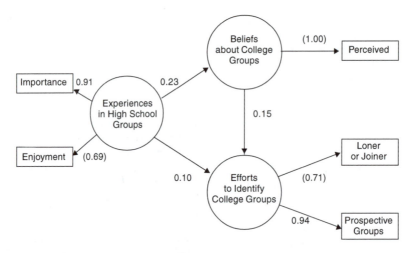

FIGURE 37.3 ■ Causal model relating students' experiences in high school groups, beliefs about the usefulness of college groups for achieving personal goals, and efforts to identify potentially desirable college groups. Reproduced from Pavelchak, Moreland & Levine (1986) by permission. © 1986 American Psychological Association.

periences in high school groups were more positive (i.e. important and enjoyable) tried harder to identify potentially desirable college groups, primarily because of their belief that memberships in such groups would be useful for achieving personal goals.

Once new students have identified potentially desirable campus groups, they must next evaluate the probable rewardingness of belonging to those groups. These evaluations require information about the rewards and costs associated with membership in each group. Because such information is often difficult to obtain, prospective members may not have an accurate picture of what lies in store for them after they join the group. In fact, research on reconnaissance in business settings suggests that people are frequently inaccurate in evaluating prospective groups (Louis, 1980; Van Maanen, 1977; Wanous, 1980). They tend to be overly optimistic, focusing on the rewards rather than the costs of group membership. This optimism has negative consequences for new members after they join the group, producing anger and resentment when the group is not as rewarding as they expected it to be.

Although students should make relatively positive evaluations of campus groups they are considering joining, we expected this optimism to be tempered by previous experience in relevant high school groups. Compared to inexperienced students (i.e. those who be-

longed to high school groups that were similar to the college groups they considered joining) should be familiar with both the rewards *and* the costs of membership and hence should make more balanced evaluations of the college groups. We also expected that experienced students' evaluations of college groups would be influenced by the kinds of experiences they had in relevant high school groups. Specifically, we predicted that the more positive a student's experiences in a high school group, the more optimistic he or she would be about belonging to a similar group in college.

These hypotheses were tested using data from 499 joiners. These students had listed the rewards and costs they expected to experience in their chosen college group, rated the strength and probability of each reward and cost (on 10-point scales), and indicated their overall commitment to their chosen group on a special 'feeling thermometer'. We determined if the joiners had prior experience in a relevant group by comparing the campus group they expected to join with the groups they had belonged to in high school. To qualify as relevant, a high school group had to have the same name as its college analogue (e.g. the marching band). Using this criterion, we found 229 students with and 270 students without prior experience in a relevant high school group.

Looking at the data for all the joiners, we found that the students were indeed optimistic about the group they had chosen. They believed they would experience significantly more rewards than costs in their chosen group (Ms = 2.53 and 1.22). They also expected the rewards of group membership to be significantly stronger than the costs (Ms = 9.14 and 3.55) and believed that the rewards were significantly more likely to occur than were the costs (Ms = 8.85 and 5.05). As predicted, however, this optimism was tempered by prior group experiences. Compared to the inexperienced joiners, the experienced joiners listed significantly more rewards (Ms = 2.68 and 2.41) *and* significantly more costs (Ms = 1.39 and 1.09) associated with college group membership. In addition, they assigned significantly higher likelihoods to the costs they listed (Ms = 5.46 and 4.71).

Next, we examined the responses of joiners who belonged to a relevant high school group to see if their evaluations of college groups reflected their prior experiences. We correlated the enjoyment and importance ratings that these students made of their relevant high school group with the evaluations that they made of the college group they had chosen. Consistent with our hypothesis, students whose experiences in a relevant high school group were more positive were indeed more optimistic about belonging to a similar college group. Specifically, students whose high school group membership was more enjoyable and important expected the rewards of membership in their prospective college group to be significantly more positive and felt significantly more committed to that group on the feeling thermometer.

Our group socialization model suggests that when a prospective member's commitment to a group rises to his or her entry criterion, that person will attempt to join the group. One factor that may stimulate prospective members to join desirable college groups is previous experience in relevant high school groups. Our hypothesis about the role of previous experience was based on Fazio and Zanna's (1981) discovery that attitudes formed on the basis of direct experience are more predictive of subsequent behavior than are attitudes formed by indirect means. Membership in a relevant high school group can be viewed as a form of direct experience with its college analogue. This experience should strengthen the linkage between students' feelings of commitment toward that college group and their attempts to join it. We therefore predicted that subjects who wanted to join a campus group would be more likely to approach that group if they belonged to a relevant high

school group than if they did not.

Our sample for testing this hypothesis was restricted to members of the telephone interview sample who were joiners, who attended the Activities Fair, and whose chosen group was represented at the Fair. Thirty students (14 with and 16 without prior experience in a relevant high school group) met these criteria. During their interview, these students were asked questions about their behavior toward groups at the Activities Fair, including which groups they wanted to visit, which groups they actually visited, and which groups they registered with. In spite of our small sample size and the difficulty some students had contacting groups at the Fair (because the Fair was crowded and group representatives came and left at different times), we obtained evidence for our hypothesis. Students who belonged to a relevant high school group were more likely than those who did not belong to (1) want to visit their chosen group (64% versus 31%), (2) actually visit that group (50% versus 25%), and (3) leave their name with the group (43% versus 19%). As we predicted, then, subjects who wanted to join a campus group were more likely to approach that group if they belonged to a relevant high school group than if they did not. Additional analyses indicated that this effect did *not* extend to campus groups that were similar to the student's chosen group. In fact, students were *less* likely to approach such groups if they belonged to a relevant high school group than if they did not. Apparently, previous experience caused students to be very selective in their choice of new groups.

The findings of this study suggest that prior membership in a group can indeed affect the behavior of ex-members of that group. People who had positive experiences in one group setting were more optimistic about their probable group experiences in a second setting and more likely to seek membership in groups they found desirable. These results raise several interesting questions. For example, how does prior experience in a high school group affect a person's later adjustment to a similar college group? Given that 'realistic job previews' can avert new employees' disappointment about negative aspects of their jobs (Caldwell & O'Reilly, 1985), perhaps experience in a high school group facilitates adjustment to a similar college group. In addition, *why* were students who belonged to a relevant high school group more likely than others to approach their chosen college group? Attitudes acquired through direct experience may have stronger effects on behavior for several reasons, such as a larger informational base, greater accessibility, and so on (Fazio & Zanna, 1981).

In a second reconnaissance study (Brinthaupt, Moreland, & Levine, 1991), we investigated three possible sources of optimism about future experiences in groups. First, prospective members' optimism may reflect the recruitment efforts of the groups that they plan to join. Because most groups attempt to foster a positive public image, particularly when recruiting new members, the information that prospective members receive may be positively biased. Prospective members may thus be optimistic because they have been given more information during their recruitment about the rewards than about the costs of group membership. Second, prospective members' optimism may reflect their efforts to cope with feelings of dissonance about the group that they plan to join. Although prospective members do not yet belong to the group, they may express their commitment to it in several ways, such as attending the group's meetings or praising the group to friends and relatives. These behavioral manifestations of commitment may produce dissonance when costs associated with group membership are discovered. The desire to reduce such dissonance may cause prospective members to seek and remember positive information about the group, while avoiding, discounting, or forgetting negative information. Finally, the optimism of prospective members may arise from a general need for self-enhancement. There is substantial evidence that people (at least nondepressed people) want to view themselves in a positive light. One way to achieve this goal is to harbor self-serving illusions (Taylor & Brown, 1988). These illusions include overly positive self-evaluations, an exaggerated sense of personal control, and unrealistic optimism about the future. The last illusion is especially intriguing. There is evidence that the average person believes he or she is more likely than others to experience positive events and less likely to experience negative events in such domains as health, marriage, and career (Alloy & Ahrens, 1987; Hoorens, 1993; Weinstein, 1980, 1987). Perhaps this illusion affects expectations about group membership as well.

We conducted a study to investigate these three sources of optimism among prospective group members. Two hundred college freshmen were asked to list, for both themselves and the average student, the rewards and costs of membership in a campus group that they were interested in joining. They were also asked to rate the strength and probability of each reward and cost (on 10-point scales). Students then answered five questions about the recruitment activities of the group (e.g. 'Has the information that you received from these group members been primarily positive or negative?', 'How much time and energy have group members spent trying to convince you to join this group?') and five questions about possible reasons for feeling dissonant about their chosen groups (e.g. 'How much time and effort have you put into finding out information about the group?', 'To what extent are people outside of the group, such as your friends or relatives, aware of your interest in joining this group?').

As we found previously (Pavelchak, Moreland, & Levine, 1986), subjects were optimistic about membership in their chosen groups (see Figure 4). Subjects expected to experience significantly more rewards than costs in their chosen group. They also viewed these rewards as significantly stronger than the costs and as significantly more likely to occur.

To simplify subsequent analyses we constructed a composite index of optimism that reflected the difference between the expected overall rewardingness and costliness of group membership for each subject. We also constructed separate recruitment and dissonance scales by combining subjects' responses on the relevant questions. In both cases, subjects' responses on the various questions were highly correlated, and coefficient alphas were high (0.78 and 0.80). To assess the effects of recruitment and dissonance on optimism, we performed two kinds of analyses. First, we regressed the optimism index on the recruitment and dissonance scale scores. Second, we carried out extreme groups analyses comparing the optimism scores of subjects in the top and bottom quartiles of the recruitment and dissonance scale distributions. These analyses indicated that neither group recruitment effort nor dissonance was an important determinant of prospective members' optimism.

Next, we examined the impact of self-enhancement on optimism (see Figure 5). We have already seen that subjects were optimstic about how they

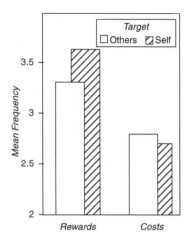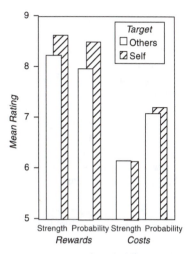

FIGURE 37.4 ▪ Expectations about the rewards and costs of group membership for self and other. (Note: Strength and probability ratings could range from 1 to 10).

would fare in their chosen groups. As the figure shows, subjects were also optimistic about how others would fare in these groups. Of course, the critical test of self-enhancement as a source of optimism rests on the *difference* between subjects' expectations for themselves versus others. Comparisons of the reward measures indicated that subjects expected significantly more rewards for themselves than for others, regarded their own rewards as significantly more positive than the rewards of others, and believed that their own rewards were significantly more likely to occur than those of others. Comparisons regarding costs indicated that subjects expected significantly more costs for others than for themselves. Finally, the mean optimism index score based on subjects' expectations for themselves (140.40) was significantly greater than a similar score based on subjects' expectations for others (91.14). Taken as a whole, these data suggest that self-enhancement is indeed an important source of optimism among prospective group members.

Were subjects especially optimistic for themselves because they expected to experience *different* rewards and costs than others would experience, even within the same groups? To explore this issue, we compared the various rewards and costs that each subject listed for himself or herself and for others. Each reward and cost was classified as either 'shared' (experienced by both oneself and others) or 'unique' (experienced by either oneself

or others, but not both). When we compared the shared and unique outcomes of group membership, we found similar patterns in the two cases. Subjects were more optimistic for themselves than for others on *both* shared outcomes and unique outcomes. For example, someone who expected everyone in a group to make new friends still believed that he or she would make more and better friends than others would. This optimism about shared outcomes is especially strong evidence for self-enhancement.

Finally, we investigated whether the type of campus group that subjects wished to join influenced their sources of optimism. We focused on the four types of groups that were most popular in our sample: fine arts and media groups, sports and recreation groups, student governance groups, and fraternities and sororities. Fraternities and sororities were perceived as making stronger recruitment efforts than the other types of groups, and they also elicited stronger feelings of dissonance. Separate regression analyses were conducted for each type of group using recruitment scale scores or dissonance scale scores to predict scores on the self-optimism index. Only one regression equation was significant: dissonance predicted optimism for students planning to join fraternities and sororities. These data suggest that dissonance, if aroused, can indeed influence optimism. Finally, self-enhancement was consistently associated with optimism. For all four kinds of groups, subjects' scores on the self-optimism index were significantly higher than their scores on the other-optimism index, and the size of this effect did not vary as a function of group type.

These results led us to attribute students' optimism about campus groups to a general need for self-enhancement, but cognitive as well as motivational forces could lead people to assume that the future will be better for themselves than for others. Perhaps it is easier for people to imagine how *they themselves* would cope with the rewards and costs of group membership than to imagine how *others* would do so. It would be useful, therefore, to know *why* prospective members expect campus groups to be more enjoyable for themselves than for others. Another unresolved issue is whether our students were really *overly* optimistic about their chosen groups. To what extent do the expectations of students who plan to join a campus group match the actual rewards and costs experienced by those same students after they become group members? Finally, little is known about the kinds of expectations that groups have for their prospective members. Are groups, like individuals, optimistic about their future relationships?

Group Recruitment

The two studies reviewed thus far dealt with a neglected aspect of group process, namely the reconnaissance activities of prospective members during the investigation phase of group membership. More research attention also needs to be devoted to the other side of investigation, namely the recruitment activities of groups.

One potentially important determinant of a group's recruitment activities is its staffing level. The staffing level of a group is defined as the difference between how many people actually belong to the group and how many people are needed for optimal performance. Research suggests that, compared to members of adequately and overstaffed groups, members of understaffed groups work harder, engage in a wider variety of tasks, assume more responsibility for the group's performance, and feel more involved in the group and important to it (e.g., Arnold & Greenberg, 1980; Perkins, 1982; Petty & Wicker, 1974; Wicker *et al.*, 1976; Wicker & Mehler, 1971).

Apart from altering their effort and involvement in the group, members of under- and overstaffed groups could also respond to staffing problems by trying to alter group composition. That is, understaffed groups could decide to become more 'open' to new members, whereas overstaffed groups could decide to become more 'closed' (see Ziller, 1965). Both strategies would affect the number of full members who belonged to the group and thereby alter its staffing level. Efforts by understaffed groups to obtain more full members seem quite consistent with our group socialization model— understaffed groups are probably more committed to their members than are overstaffed groups, because members of understaffed groups work harder to achieve group goals and are more difficult to replace. As a group becomes more understaffed, it thus becomes more likely to (1) seek many recruits during the investigation phase of membership, (2) adopt a relatively low entry criterion for the role transition from prospective member to new member, (3) emphasize accommodation rather than assimilation during the socialization phase of membership, and (4) adopt a relatively low acceptance criterion for the role transition from new member to full member.

We recently conducted a study designed to identify the problems associated with under- and overstaffing and to test the above hypotheses regarding the impact of staffing levels on group recruitment and socialization practices (Cini, Moreland, & Levine, 1993). Our data came from interviews with the leaders of 93 campus groups, ranging from social clubs to honoraries. Leaders were asked about the actual and ideal staffing levels of their group, how small or large the group would have to become before staffing problems arose and what kinds of problems would develop, and the group's recruitment activities toward prospective members and socialization activities toward new members.

Some interesting differences between leaders' perceptions of under- and overstaffing were observed. When asked whether their groups could ever become too small or too large, 87% of the leaders agreed that understaffing was possible, whereas only 62% agreed that overstaffing was possible, a statistically significant difference. To determine how small or large a group must become to seem understaffed or overstaffed, we divided the number of members that each leader regarded as too few or too many by the actual size of his or her group. The results are summarized in Figure 5.

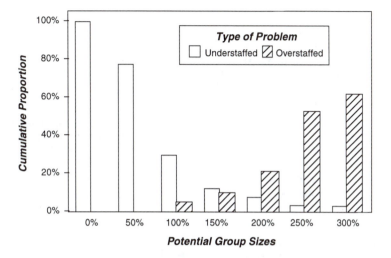

FIGURE 37.5 ■ Sensitivity to under- and over-staffing. Reproduced from Cini, Moreland & Levine (1993) by permission. © 1993 American Psychological Association.

The figure contains two cumulative frequency distributions, one for understaffing and the other for overstaffing. The horizontal axis shows a range of potential group sizes, expressed as percentages of actual group sizes. The vertical axis shows the cumulative proportion of leaders who would regard their groups as under- or overstaffed at each potential size. As indicated by the steeper slope for under- than for overstaffing, groups were much more sensitive to having 'too few' members than 'too many'.

Leaders mentioned about the same number of problems for under- and overstaffing, but they described different problems and different solutions in the two cases. The most common problems arising from understaffing were poor group performance, fatigue and burnout, loss of resources, and member homogeneity. The most common solutions for these problems were to recruit more members or reorganize the group. The most common problems arising from overstaffing were apathy and boredom, alienation, disorganization, strained resources, and clique formation. The most common solutions for these problems were to encourage current members to work hard, restrict membership in the group, punish deviates more harshly, or divide the group into subgroups. We were surprised to find that, even though under- and overstaffing produced about the same number of problems, more solutions were proposed for under- than for overstaffing. Perhaps the problems produced by understaffing are more difficult to solve, or the solutions applied to those problems are less effective. We did find that the solutions proposed for understaffing were more 'generic', in the sense that they could be applied to a broader range of problems. Because they were less closely linked to specific problems, these solutions may have been less effective.

Analyses of the relationships between group staffing level (defined as ideal group size divided by actual size) and investigation and socialization practices indicated, as predicted, that understaffed groups were relatively open to prospective and new members. Regarding prospective members, groups that were more understaffed wanted significantly more recruits, had significantly lower entry criteria, sought significantly fewer special qualities in recruits, and were significantly more likely to allow members to enter the group at any time. Regarding new members, groups that were more understaffed gave new members significantly fewer special duties, evaluated the behavior of new members significantly less often and used significantly fewer evaluation methods, were significantly more lenient with new members who caused problems, and had significantly lower acceptance criteria. These results were quite robust—effects of staffing level on the recruitment of prospective members and socialization of new members were similar across different types of campus groups and different levels of leader experience.

Many intriguing questions remain about the impact of group staffing levels on recruitment and socialization practices. For example, when staffing problems arise in a group, do all members respond in similar ways or are there individual differences in responses to under- and overstaffing? And what role do people outside the group, such as authorities, play in detecting a group's staffing problems and shaping its responses to them? Finally, can the same group be understaffed for some tasks and overstaffed for others, and how could its recruitment and socialization practices be altered to cope with such diverse problems?

REFERENCES

Alloy, L. B., & Ahrens, A. H. (1987). Depression and pessimism for the future: Biased use of statistically-relevant information in predictions for self and others. *Journal of Personality and Social Psychology*, 52, 366–78.

Arnold, D., & Greenberg, C. (1980). Deviate rejection within differentially manned groups. *Social Psychology Quarterly*, 43, 419–24.

Aronson, E., & Mills, J. (1959). The effect of severity of initiation on liking for a group. *Journal of Abnormal and Social Psychology*, 59, 177–81.

Brinthaupt, T. M., Moreland, R. L., & Levine, J. M. (1991). Sources of optimism among prospective group members. *Personality and Social Psychology Bulletin*, 17, 36–43.

Caldwell, D. F., & O'Reilly, C. A. (1985). The impact of information on job choices and turnover. *Academy of Management Journal*, 28, 934–43.

Cini, M., Moreland, R. L., & Levine, J. M. (1993). Group staffing levels and responses to prospective and new members. *Journal of Personality and Social Psychology*, 65, 723–34.

Fazio, R. H., & Zanna, M. P. (1981). Direct experience and attitude-behavior consistency. In L. Berkowitz (Ed.), *Advances in experimental social psychology* (Vol. 14, pp. 161–202). New York: Academic Press.

Feldman, D. C. (1989). Socialization, resocialization, and training: Reframing the research agenda. In I. L. Goldstein and Associates (Eds.), *Training and development in organizations* (Vol. 3, pp. 376–416). San Francisco: Jossey-Bass.

Fine, G. A. (1976, September). The effect of a salient newcomer on a small group: A force field analysis. Paper presented at the meeting of the American Psychological Association, Washington, DC.

Fromkin, H. L., Klimoski, R. J., & Flanagan, M. F. (1972). Race and competence as determinants of acceptance of newcomers in success and failure work groups. *Organizational Behavior and Human Performance*, 7, 25–42.

Gerard, H. B., & Mathewson, G. C. (1966). The effects of severity of initiation on liking for a group: A replication. *Journal of Experimental Social Psychology*, 2, 278–87.

Hanks, M. (1981). Youth, voluntary associations, and political socialization. *Social Forces*, 60, 211–23.

Hanks, M., & Eckland, B. (1978). Adult voluntary associations and adolescent socialization. *Sociological Quarterly*, 19, 481–90.

Hogg, M. A. (1987). Social identity and group cohesiveness. In J. C. Turner, M. A. Hogg, P. J. Oakes, S. D. Reicher, & M. S. Wetherell (Eds.), *Rediscovering the social group: A self-categorization theory* (pp. 89–116). Oxford: Basil Blackwell.

Hogg, M. A., & McGarty, C. (1990). Self-categorization and social identity. In D. Abrams & M. Hogg (Eds.), *Social identity theory: Constructive and critical advances* (pp. 10–27). New York: Springer-Verlag.

Hoorens, V. (1993). Self-enhancement and superiority biases in social comparison. In W. Stroebe & M. Hewstone (Eds.), *European review of social psychology*, Volume 4 (pp. 113–40). Chichester: Wiley.

Kaplan, S. R., & Roman, M. (1961). Characteristic responses in adult therapy groups to the introduction of new members: A reflection on group process. *International Journal of Group Psychotherapy*, 11, 372–81.

Kram, K. E., & Isabella, L. A. (1985). Mentoring alternatives: The role of peer relationships in career development. *Academy of Management Journal*, 28, 110–32.

Kruglanski, A., & Mackie, D. M. (1990). Majority and minority influence: A judgmental process analysis. In W. Stroebe & M. Hewstone (Eds.), *European review of social psychology* (Vol. 1, pp. 229–61). Chichester: John Wiley.

Levine, J. M. (1989). Reaction to opinion deviance in small groups. In P. Paulus (Ed.), *Psychology of group influence* (2nd ed., pp. 187–231). Hillsdale, NJ: Erlbaum.

Levine, J. M., & Moreland, R. L. (1985). Innovation and socialization in small groups. In S. Moscovici, G. Mugny, & E. Van Avermaet (Eds.), *Perspectives on minority influence* (pp. 143–69). Cambridge: Cambridge University Press.

Levine, J. M., & Moreland, R. L. (1990). Progress in small group research. *Annual Review of Psychology*, 41, 585–634.

Levine, J. M., & Moreland, R. L. (1991). Culture and socialization in work groups. In L. Resnick, J. Levine, & S. Teasley (Eds.), *Perspectives on socially shared cognition* (pp. 257–79). Washington, DC: American Psychological Association.

Louis, M. R. (1980). Surprise and sense making: What newcomers experience in entering unfamiliar organizational settings. *Administrative Science Quarterly*, 25, 226–51.

Merei, F. (1949). Group leadership and institutionalization. *Human Relations*, 2, 23–39.

Miller, C. E., & Komorita, S. S. (1986). Coalition formation in organizations: What laboratory studies do and do not tell us. In R. J. Lewicki, B. H. Sheppard, & M. H. Bazerman (Eds.), *Research on negotiation in organizations* (Vol. 1, pp. 117–37). Greenwich, CT: JAI Press.

Moreland, R. L., & Levine, J. M. (1982). Socialization in small groups: Temporal changes in individual–group relations. In L. Berkowitz (Ed.), *Advances in experimental social psychology* (Vol. 15, pp. 137–92). New York: Academic Press.

Moreland, R. L., & Levine, J. M. (1984). Role transitions in small groups. In V. L. Allen & E. van de Vliert (Eds.), *Role transitions: Explorations and explanations* (pp. 181–95). New York: Plenum.

Moreland, R. L., & Levine, J. M. (1988). Group dynamics over time: Development and socialization in small groups. In J. E. McGrath (Ed.), *The social psychology of time: New perspectives* (pp. 151–81). Newbury Park, CA: Sage.

Moreland, R. L., & Levine, J. M. (1989). Newcomers and oldtimers in small groups. In P. Paulus (Ed.), *Psychology of group influence* (2nd ed., pp. 143–86). Hillsdale, NJ: Erlbaum.

Moreland, R. L., & Levine, J. M. (1992). The composition of small groups. In E. J. Lawler, B. Markovsky, C. Ridgeway, & H. A. Walker (Eds.), *Advances in group processes* (Vol. 9, pp. 237–80). Greenwich, CT: JAI Press.

Moreland, R. L., Levine, J. M., & Cini, M. A. (1993). Group socialization: The role of commitment. In M. Hogg & D. Abrams (Eds.), *Group motivation: Social psychological perspectives* (pp. 105–29). Hemel Hempstead: Harvester Wheatsheaf.

Moscovici, S. (1985). Social influence and conformity. In G. Lindzey & E. Aronson (Eds.), *The handbook of social psychology* (Vol. 2, pp. 347–412). New York: Random House.

Mugny, G., & Perez, J. A. (1991). *The social psychology of minority influence.* Cambridge: Cambridge University Press.

Nash, D., & Heiss, J. (1967). Sources of anxiety in laboratory strangers. *Sociological Quarterly, 8,* 215–21.

Nash, D., & Wolfe, A. W. (1957). The stranger in laboratory culture. *American Sociological Review, 22,* 400–5.

Nemeth, C. (1986). Differential contributions of majority and minority influence. *Psychological Review, 93,* 23–32.

Pavelchak, M. A., Moreland, R. L., & Levine, J. M. (1986). Effects of prior group memberships on subsequent reconnaissance activities. *Journal of Personality and Social Psychology, 50,* 56–66.

Perkins, D. V. (1982). Individual differences and task structure in the performance of a behavior setting: An experimental evaluation of Barker's manning theory. *American Journal of Community Psychology, 10,* 617–34.

Petty, R. M., & Wicker, A. W. (1974). Degree of manning and degree of success of a group as determinants of members' subjective experiences and their acceptance of a new group member. *Catalog of Selected Documents in Psychology, 4,* 1–22.

Putallaz, M., & Gottman, J. M. (1981). An interactional model of children's entry into peer groups. *Child Development, 52,* 986–94.

Sagi, P. C., Olmsted, D. W., & Atelsek, F. (1955). Predicting maintenance of membership in small groups. *Journal of Abnormal and Social Psychology, 51,* 308–11.

Staw, B. M. (1980). The consequences of turnover. *Journal of Occupational Behaviour, 1,* 253–73.

Steiner, I. D. (1986). Paradigms and groups. In L. Berkowitz (Ed.), *Advances in experimental social psychology* (Vol. 19, pp. 251–89). Orlando, FL: Academic Press.

Stryker, S. (1968). Identity salience and role performance: The relevance of symbolic interaction theory for family research. *Journal of Marriage and the Family, 30,* 558–64.

Stryker, S. (1987). Identity theory: Developments and extensions. In K. Yardley & T. Honess (Eds.), *Self and identity: Psychosocial perspectives* (pp. 89–103). New York: John Wiley.

Stryker, S., & Serpe, R. T. (1982). Commitment, identity, salience, and role behavior: Theory and research example. In W. Ickes & E. S. Knowles (Eds.), *Personality, roles, and social behavior* (pp. 199–218). New York: Springer-Verlag.

Sutton, R. I., & Louis, M. R. (1987). How selecting and socializing newcomers influences insiders. *Human Resource Management, 26,* 347–61.

Taylor, S. E., & Brown, J. D. (1988). Illusion and well-being: A social psychological perspective on mental health. *Psychological Bulletin, 103,* 193–210.

Tuckman, B. W. (1965). Developmental sequence in small groups. *Psychological Bulletin, 63,* 384–99.

Tuckman, B. W., & Jensen, M. A. C. (1977). Stages of small-group development revisited. *Group and Organization Studies, 2,* 419–27.

Turner, J. C. (1985). Social categorization and the self-concept: A social cognitive theory of group behavior. In E. J. Lawler (Ed.), *Advances in group processes* (Vol. 2, pp. 77–122). Greenwich, CT: JAI Press.

Turner, J. C., Hogg, M. A., Oakes, P. J., Reicher, S. D., & Wetherell, M. S. (Eds.). (1987). *Rediscovering the social group: A self-categorization theory.* Oxford: Basil Blackwell.

Van Maanen, J. (1977). Experiencing organization: Notes on the meanings of careers and socialization. In J. Van Maanen (Ed.), *Organizational careers: Some new perspectives* (pp. 15–45). New York: John Wiley.

Vaught, C., & Smith, D. L. (1980). Incorporation and mechanical solidarity in an underground coal mine. *Sociology of Work and Occupations, 7,* 159–87.

Wanous, J. P. (1980). *Organizational entry: Recruitment, selection, and socialization of newcomers.* Reading, MA: Addison-Wesley.

Weinstein, N. D. (1980). Unrealistic optimism about future life events. *Journal of Personality and Social Psychology, 39,* 806–20.

Weinstein, N. D. (1987). Unrealistic optimism about susceptibility to health problems: Conclusions from a community-wide sample. *Journal of Behavioral Medicine, 10,* 481–500.

Wells, L. E., & Stryker, S. (1988). Stability and change in self over the life course. In P. B. Baites, D. L. Featherman, & R. L. Lerner (Eds.), *Life-span development* (pp. 191–229). Hillsdale, NJ: Erlbaum.

Wicker, A. W., Kirmeyer, S. L., Hanson, L., & Alexander, D. (1976). Effects of manning levels on subjective experiences, performance, and verbal interaction in groups. *Organizational Behavior and Human Performance, 17,* 251–74.

Wicker, A. W., & Mehler, A. (1971). Assimilation of new members in a large and a small church. *Journal of Applied Psychology, 55,* 151–6.

Zander, A. (1976). The psychology of removing group members and recruiting new ones. *Human Relations, 29,* 969–87.

Zander, A. (1977). *Groups at work.* San Francisco, CA: Jossey-Bass.

Zander, A., & Cohen, A. R. (1955). Attributed social power and group acceptance: A classroom experimental demonstration. *Journal of Abnormal and Social Psychology, 51,* 490–92.

Ziller, R. C. (1965). Toward a theory of open and closed groups. *Psychological Bulletin, 64,* 164–82.

Ziller, R. C., & Behringer, R. D. (1960). Assimilation of the knowledgeable newcomer under conditions of group success and failure. *Journal of Abnormal and Social Psychology, 60,* 288–91.

Zurcher, L. A. (1970). The 'friendly' poker game: A study of an ephemeral role. *Social Forces, 49,* 173–86.

Comments on the Motivational Status of Self-Esteem in Social Identity and Intergroup Discrimination

Dominic Abrams • The University, Dundee, England
Michael A. Hogg • University of Melbourne, Australia

Editors' Notes

The distinction between in-groups, groups to which an individual belongs, and out-groups, groups to which an individual does not belong, has been of primary importance in the social-psychological analyses of intergroup relations. A significant phenomenon concerning this distinction is that of in-group bias—the tendency of group members to overvalue characteristics, objects, or outcomes associated with the in-group and undervalue those associated with the out-group. The reasons for the in-group bias have been the topic of much theorizing and research. The most widely known proposal is the Self-Esteem Hypothesis (SEH) whereby individuals' group membership confers upon them self-esteem in proportion to the group's prestige. In the present selection, the authors critically examine the Self-Esteem explanation of in-group bias or inter-group discrimination. They point out that the in-group's value to the individual derives not merely from its prestige but also from its ability to gratify the individuals' other motives, and primarily the motive for coherence or a firm "self-evaluation." This selection exemplifies the incisive examination of empirical research in light of a guiding conceptual analysis. The authors derive the implications of the SEH, examine them in light of general knowledge about the self-esteem construct, compare them with the empirical findings, and offer a summary assessment of the state of the art in this domain of study.

Discussion Questions

1. What are the two motivational hypotheses contained in social-identity theory? What do the hypotheses state? What phenomenon do they explain?

2. What are the alternative interpretations the authors offer of the Oakes and Turner (1980) experiment?

3. Is self-esteem a dependent or an independent variable in relation to intergroup behavior?

4. According to the authors, under which conditions will self-evaluation or self-esteem motives predominate? In your opinion, is self-evaluation the only (or most important) type of knowledge a group membership may afford?

Suggested Readings

Leary, M. R., Tambor, E. S., Terdal, S. K., & Downs, D. L. (1995). Self-esteem as an interpersonal monitor: The sociometer hypothesis. *Journal of Personality and Social Psychology*, *68*, 518–530.

Tajfel, H., & Turner, J. C. (1986). The social identity theory of intergroup behavior. In S. Worchel & W. G. Austin (Eds.), *Psychology of intergroup relations* (2nd ed., pp. 7–24). Chicago: Nelson Hall.

Turner, J. C., & Oakes, P. J. (1989). Self-categorization theory and social influence. In P. B. Paulus (Ed.), *Psychology of group influence* (2nd ed., pp. 233–275). Hillsdale, NJ: Erlbaum.

Authors' Abstract

The background and development of motivational hypotheses in social identity theory are examined, revealing two general motives for intergroup discrimination: a desire for cognitive coherence, or good structure; and a need for positive self-esteem. The latter (self-esteem hypothesis: SEH) has received most attention. Both the theoretical and empirical bases of the SEH are largely rooted in research using the minimal group paradigm. However, it remains unclear whether self-esteem is to be considered primarily as a cause or an effect of discrimination. When real social groups are considered the SEH appears to provide only a partial explanation, and a variety of more or less powerful alternative social motives may underlie discriminatory behaviour. We explore some social-structural, individual and interpersonal limits to the SEH, and we call for an awareness of these motives and a re-examination of the good-structure thesis. The SEH, as it stands, provides only a partial contribution to our understanding of the relationship between social identity and discriminatory intergroup behaviour.

Introduction

The social identity approach to intergroup relations and group processes (Tajfel, 1978, 1982; Tajfel and Turner, 1979; Turner, 1981, 1982; see Hogg and Abrams, 1988) embodies an important and far reaching proposition that intergroup discrimination is motivated by individuals' desire to achieve and maintain positive self-esteem. In making an ingroup psychologically positively distinctive from an outgroup, one's self-image as a group member is thereby enhanced. Our purpose in writing this paper is to explore the ramifications of what we shall term the 'self-esteem hypothesis'

(SEH), for theory and research on social identity. Although the hypothesis has been specifically applied to the desire for positive distinctiveness, that desire is itself predicated upon a need for positive self-esteem. We intend to concentrate only on the following points: (i) self-esteem is not the only motivation specified by Tajfel and Turner's (1979) theory; (ii) the SEH is unclearly stated, and is hence difficult to test; (iii) the operationalization of 'self-esteem' may be of key import when conducting such tests; (iv) it may be useful to draw a distinction between minimal and real group contexts when applying the SEH; (v) that social-structural relations between groups, and group members' beliefs about these relations will determine the nature of the association between discriminatory behaviour and self-esteem; and (vi) while the SEH is possibly of use as a general explanatory concept, other social motivations can be more influential in the determination of specific intergroup behaviours.

From Tajfel's early work on social perceptions and categorization the first mention of motivation is his reference to 'the emotional, or if one prefers the term, value relevance of the classification to subjects' (Tajfel, 1959, p. 20). He went on to develop this idea in his (Tajfel, 1969) conceptualization of stereotyping and prejudice as a search for coherence: The 'need to preserve the integrity of the self-image is the only motivational assumption we need to make in order to understand the direction that the search for coherence will take' (Tajfel, 1969, p. 92). This line of reasoning closely resembles those of balance theorists (see Abelson, Aronson, McGuire, Newcomb, Rosenberg and Tannenbaum, 1968) in positing a need for an integrated and coherent set of cognitions (in this case, including cognitions about self), and is clearly related to the general assumption underlying contemporary social cognition that people have a need for cognitive parsimony (see Markus and Zajonc, 1985).

When the concept of social identity was introduced (Tajfel, 1972) the 'coherence' view became displaced in favour of a social self-enhancement view, derived from Festiger's (1954) theory of social comparison processes. Social comparisons in intergroup settings are designed to attain a 'positively valued distinctiveness from other groups' (Tajfel 1972, p. 3); the motive is to 'achieve a satisfactory concept or image of the self' (Tajfel, 1974, p. 4) through positive social identity.[1] In a

formal theoretical statement by Tajfel and Turner (1979) self-esteem was explicitly referred to as a motivation behind intergroup behaviour. In their analysis of relations between large scale social groups they suggest that where low status groups acquiesce to majority rule, 'the price of this has been the subordinate group's self-esteem' (p. 37). This 'price' rests on the further assumption (borrowed directly from social comparison theory) that 'individuals strive to maintain or enhance their self-esteem: they strive for a positive self-concept' (p. 40). It follows that groups compete, not just for material resources, but for anything which can enhance their self-definition; i.e. for positive social identity (Oakes and Turner, 1980; Turner, 1978a, 1980, 1981, 1982 (see p. 33); Turner, Brown and Tajfel, 1979; Turner and Giles, 1981, Chap. I).

We have identified two themes in the account of motivation in the literature on social identity; one for cognitive coherence (which is affectively positive), and the other for an evaluatively positive self-concept. We shall investigate the latter, since it has predominated in the literature, before widening our discussion to embrace the former.

The Oakes and Turner (1980) Experiment

The SEH was initially tested by Oakes and Turner (1980), and it is worth considering their experiment again. They adopted Tajfel, Billig, Bundy and Flament's (1971) minimal group paradigm in which subjects are divided into two groups (merely labelled X-group and Y-group) on the basis of an *ad-hoc* and trivial criterion. Within this paradigm it is commonly found that subjects allocate money or points in a way that favours the ingroup over the outgroup, even if such a strategy fails to optimize absolute ingroup rewards. It is also usually the case that these rewards are allocated to anonymous ingroup and outgroup members, and not directly to self (see Tajfel, 1982). The SEH was partly invoked in order to explain this apparently irrational and antinormative behaviour (Billig and Tajfel, 1973; Turner, 1980; but *cf.* Bornstein, Crum,

---

[1]Billig (1985, p. 89) believes that the introduction of a self-*evaluative* aspect was primarily to be able to explain social change: a task originally rendered problematic by reliance on the categorization process alone.

Wittenbraker, Harring, Insko and Thibaut, 1983; Branthwaite, Doyle and Lightbrown, 1979). In Oakes and Turner's (1980) study, half of the subjects were so categorized, and were allowed to allocate rewards, while the other half merely sat, and read a newspaper. The categorized subjects displayed discriminatory behaviour, but were also found, subsequently, to have higher self-esteem than did their newspaper-reading counterparts.

We shall consider two problems with the Oakes and Turner (1980) study, both of which have theoretical and empirical ramifications. First, the results, as reported, can be interpreted as reflecting the self-esteem *lowering* effects of reading a newspaper article, or differential self-esteem levels contingent on inequality of psychological significance of having participated in an experiment as against having merely waited and read a newspaper to while away the time. Certainly, the self-esteem factor scores of newspaper subjects were more strongly negative than those of the categorization subjects were positive. Any replication of this experiment should probably incorporate a categorization–non-discrimination condition in order to investigate this possibility. The problem here is that self-esteem is a *relative* state rather than an absolute one, and the question is, if discriminatory intergroup behaviour does elevate self-esteem, it elevates it relative to *what*?

A second problem concerns the indices of self-esteem and their use in the Oakes and Turner study. Three valid self-esteem scales are combined by mixing the items together (mingling the scales, rather than asking subjects to respond separately to each). The consequences of this are difficult to predict, but it is unlikely that the validity of any of the scales remained intact. Furthermore, the Rosenberg Self-Esteem Scale is designed as a measure of global self-esteem, but subjects were asked to respond in terms of 'how you feel at this moment'. If it is possible that subjects experienced some confusion when completing these mixed format measures, there may be legitimate doubts about the interpretation of their responses as measuring self-esteem. We shall return to the issue of measurement below.

Two Self-Esteem Hypotheses

Perhaps the key problem in Oakes and Turner's test of the SEH is that the hypothesis is cast in a way which does not entirely reflect Turner's (e.g. 1982) theoretical statements. This is because the SEH can in fact be seen to embody *two* unstated corollories: (i) successful intergroup discrimination will enhance social identity, and hence self-esteem (as tested by Oakes and Turner); (ii) low or threatened self-esteem will promote intergroup discrimination because of the 'need' for positive self-esteem.

In other words, self-esteem is both a dependent and an independent variable in relation to intergroup behaviour: it is a product of specific forms of intergroup behaviour, as well as a motivating force for those very behaviours.

A third possibility is that, as Oakes and Turner (1980) acknowledge, self-esteem may be elevated by intergroup behaviour independently of the positive distinctiveness of social identity. Hogg, Turner, Nascimento-Schulze, and Spriggs (1986) ruled out an explanation of Oakes and Turner's results in terms of mere salience (or positive self-stereotyping as an ingroup member; also see Lemyre and Smith, 1985). When category salience and discrimination were orthogonally manipulated only the latter led to higher self-esteem (supporting corollory 1). On the other hand, Abrams (1985) found that by changing the amount of attention paid to the categorization it was possible to increase or reduce discrimination. It therefore seems likely that salience, discrimination and self-esteem are more usually bound up together.

Corollary 1

Lemyre and Smith (1985) have recently reported findings from a relatively complex minimal groups experiment designed to investigate the relationship among these variables. Briefly, it was found that 'ingroup favouritism . . . restored self-esteem for categorized subjects' (p. 668), leading Lemyre and Smith to conclude that their results are 'consistent with social identity theory; given categorization, discrimination in favour of one's own group results in a relative increase in self-esteem. Categorization in itself was not sufficient, nor was cognitive differentiation of the ingroup and the outgroup' (1985, p. 668). It should be noted that, while supporting corollory 1, this study does not allow a test of the motivating aspect of self-esteem (corollory 2). Lemyre and Smith themselves allude to this; 'it is difficult to avoid the conclusion that we engaged in ingroup formation in order to promote . . . well being . . . although the issue of intention has not been explicitly addressed here . . . '(p. 669).

Vickers, Abrams and Hogg (1988) conducted a minimal group study to investigate the relationship between social categorization, intergroup discrimination, self-esteem, and local norms of cooperation. Relevant to present discussion is the finding that subjects for whom the local norm of cooperation was salient subsequently expressed strong intergroup discrimination but experienced *lowered* self-esteem (measured on Julian, Bishop and Fiedler's (1966) semantic differential). Vickers *et al.*, argue that this lowering of self-esteem is due to violation of the norm of cooperation. Here intergroup discrimination may serve to delineate groups and social identity but does not serve to enhance (or indeed to satisfy a *need* for) positive self-esteem.

Corollary 2

Corollary2, that low self-esteem motivates intergroup discrimination is also relatively unsupported. Abrams (1982,1983) reported two experiments in which pretested self-esteem (on Rosenberg's scale) was positively associated (*r*'s in the mid-twenties) with ingroup bias across a variety of dependent measures, thus disconfirming the hypothesis.

In an intriguing study, designed to simulate the social relations between Turks, Italians and Germans in West Germany (see Schonbach, Gollwitzer, Stiepel and Wagner, 1981), Wagner, Lampen and Syllwasschy (1986) constructed a three-group minimal group experiment in which one of the groups was of higher status than the others. Subjects (in a low status group) were most discriminatory against the other low status outgroup, as Tajfel and Turner would predict (see also Brown and Abrams, 1986). However, discrimination was not associated with heightened general self esteem relative to pretest scores using Coopersmith's (1967) semantic differential measure.

Sachdev and Bourhis provide some indirect evidence from a programme of minimal group studies charting the limits of minimal group discrimination. In one experiment (1984) they varied the relative numbers of ingroup and outgroup members and predicted directly from social identity theory that 'since minority group membership confers a relatively insecure and negative social identity, minorities should show more discrimination and less fairness than majorities. Discrimination . . . serves to achieve (or maintain) a positive social identity' (p. 47). The hypothesis was, by and large, unsupported: both minorities and majorities expressed comparable degrees of discrimination. In two experiments, Sachdev and Bourhis (1985,1987) studied the effects of power inequality and status inequality, respectively and found that the greater the stable power or status the greater the discrimination. This seems to work *against* the SEH, which would predict that the *less* the power/status, the lower the group-identity contingent self-esteem, and thus the greater the subsequent discrimination.

In their power study Sachdev and Bourhis (1985), found that 'high and equal power group members reported that they felt more comfortable, satisfied and happy than lower and no power group members about their group membership' (1985, p. 430). Of course, here we cannot know whether these measures monitor self-esteem, though presumably they are related to it, nor whether they reflect power *per se* or the discrimination that Sachdev and Bourhis discover to be positively correlated with it. In their status study Sachdev and Bourhis (1987) explicitly acknowledge that their (almost identical) results suggest that 'status *per se* can contribute to group members' social identities over and above the contribution made by discrimination'(p. 289), a view supported by Wagner *et al.*'s (1986) finding that low status groups experienced lowered self-esteem. It appears that in these modified minimal group studies the lower power/status groups resort to different behavioral and perceptual strategies to attenuate their inferiority. Discrimination may only be the strategy of groups with already relatively positive self-esteem (but see below, and van knippenberg, 1984) and of groups which confront each other as equals.

Another study with data on subjects' pretest self-esteem levels is by Crocker and Schwartz (1985). Subjects were divided into high and low self-esteem, on the basis of a tertile split of pretest Rosenberg scores, and then were divided into minimal groups and rated the personality of ingroup and outgroup members. Crocker and Schwartz report that although 'there was a strong tendency for low self-esteem subjects to be more prejudiced in the sense of rating outgroups negatively, there was no evidence of their greater ethnocentrism or ingroup favouritism, which requires rating the outgroup negatively relative to the ingroup' (p. 383), and go on to conclude that their results 'are not consistent with a self-enhancement through social comparison interpretation of ingroup favouritism effects' (p. 384).[2] Crocker and Schwarts's findings have recently been replicated by Crocker, Thompson, McGraw and Ingerman (1987).

Crocker and McGraw (1985) report an interesting field study of the relative influence of global self-esteem and group status on prejudice and ingroup favouritism. Their results reveal that lower self-esteem appears to motivate ingroup favouritism only for subjects in higher status groups. In lower status groups it is the higher self-esteem individuals who display greater ingroup favouritism. Thus the relationship between self-esteem and intergroup behaviour is clearly not a mechanical or direct one.

Crocker et al., (1987) report a minimal group study and a field study which, taken together, show that low self-esteem engenders ingroup and outgroup derogation rather than ingroup enhancing intergroup discrimination. It is people with high self-esteem, particularly those whose status is under threat or at risk, who indulge in discrimination. One test of both corollories of the SEH was conducted by Hogg et al. (1986), Experiment 2). They pre-tested self-esteem (using Oakes and Turner's composite measure) and then retested after subject had allocated points to ingroup and outgroup. The SEH predicts that low self-esteem at pre-test should promote discrimination, and should rise to a higher level by post-test. High pre-test self-esteem should attenuate or maintain discrimination (thereby maintaining a positive self-image) but need not rise or fall, by post-test. In fact, while levels of discrimination did not differ between high and low (pre-test) self-esteem subjects, lows did show a significant rise in self-esteem, whereas highs did not.

Limits to the SEH

Not surprisingly, these data provide only moderate support for the SEH. Tests of the SEH are unlikely to yield useful interpretable results until the SEH is more completely articulated and parameters placed around it. It suffers from at least two general shortcomings. First, it over-implicates self-

esteem in intergroup behaviour; self-esteem can, under some conditions, be incidental or even irrelevent. The posited 'need for positive self-esteem' has not more logical link with manifest intergroup behaviour, than does a 'need for nourishment' (people do not eat outgroup members, except in certain notable cases!). Second, the term 'self-esteem' is so general as to allow considerable variation in its operationalization. For example, many of the large scale studies adopt indices of global self-esteem, which may indeed be predictive of intergroup attitudes. However, Tajfel and Turner's (1979) and Turner's (1982) hypothesis refers quite clearly to the esteem in which specific self-images are held, that is social identity-dependent self-esteem. The salience of these self-images fluctuates across situations, and thus global self-esteem measures are largely insensitive to them (Fleming and Courtney,1984; Fleming and Watts, 1980; Wells and Marwell, 1977).

Although, as we described above, the introduction of a motive for positive self-evaluation may have helped explain social change (see Billig, 1985) and the variability of intergroup strategies at the macro-social level of analysis, the importance of the SEH in its more specific form has been its role in explaining discrimination in minimal group experiments (e.g. Turner 1975, 1978a,b). In these contexts it must necessarily be a transitory self-image which is made positive. Not only is there little reason to presume the effect will overflow to bathe the entire self-concept, but there is good reason to argue for its psychological containment. The debate as to whether minimal group experiments produce both normative discrimination and fairness (e.g Billig, 1973; Bornstein et al., 1983; Branthwaite et al., 1979; Turner, 1980,1983) attests to the fact that multiple pressures may operate. It is entirely reasonable that a personal self-image as being 'equitable' would be threatened if one engaged in discriminatory behaviour in order to enhance social identity (Vicker et al. (1988) provide data consistent with this argument). However, rather than propose continual conflict between the guilty personal, and the proud social, self-images in the arena of the self-

---

[2]Given this reasoning, it is rather surprising that Crocker and Schwartz made no reference to social identity, the SEH or positive distinctiveness. It should also be remarked that Crocker and Schwartz use a global rather than specific self-esteem measure. Perhaps different results may have emerged if the latter had been used.

concept (resulting in neutral self-esteem?) we propose that each self-image is a discrete entity, and is only rarely likely to be dragged into conflict with others. Global self-esteem may be a reflection of the total positivity of many self-images over time, but will provide at best an insensitive indicator of short-term variations in the positivity of specific self-images.

This view is entirely in keeping with Turner's social identification model, but has not really been reflected by the methodology employed by formal tests of the **SEH**. Wagner *et al.*'s (1986) experiment also supports this view. Although global self-esteem was unrelated to discrimination, specific self-esteem related to ingroup attributes was raised following discrimination. In addition, experiments which have reported ingroup bias in terms of trait adjective ratings, affective ratings and performance evaluation ratings (e.g. Brown and Abrams, 1986) are, in effect, directly tapping the relative esteem in which subjects hold their own group. To further access self-esteem using formal scales may be merely an additional, and ironically *indirect* approach.

Social Structural Limits on the Applicability ot the SEH

The discussion above has been concerned with issues which stem quite directly from research using the minimal group paradigm. In such highly controlled laboratory situations subjects may have little else to gain but self-esteem. In real group contexts the **SEH** may merely be *one* of a great many possibilities concerning the motives for intergroup discrimination.

Tajfel (1981, Chaps 14, 15) points out that large, stable and psychologically ligitimate status differences may exist between social groups. Under such conditions, low status (minority) group members may compete with ('social change' strategy), attempt to become assimilated into ('social mobility' strategy), or may find new dimensions on which they compare favourably with (an example of 'social creativity') the high status (majority) group. All of these strategies can be seen as satisfying self-esteem based motives. However, the postulation of such a motive as fundamental does not help a great deal in predicting what specific social groups do to achieve positive social identity in particular social contexts. For example, social categorization studies by Turner (1978b) and Mummendey and Schreiber (1984) were only able to predict with any accuracy the strategies used by subjects from consideration of the perceived legitimacy and stability of the status relations between the groups. In a more naturalistic laboratory study (related to Lemaine's, 1974, field work) Mummendey and Schreiber (1983) found that positive ingroup evaluation was preferentially achieved *without* indulging in relative outgroup derogation on the same comparison dimension, and that this latter strategy was only resorted to when no other alternatives were available. These findings have clear relevance for the work by Sachdev and Bourhis, and Crocker and colleagues, discussed earlier.

Where the differences between groups are highly institutionalized, and ideologically legitimized, it may be that both groups accept the status quo (*cf.* Hyman and Singer, 1968; Olson, Herman and Zanna, 1986; Suls and Miller, 1977), making no moves to transcend boundaries between groups. It is likely, under such conditions, that majority discrimination against the minority is also institutionalized (e.g. doctor–nurse roles, white–black status and power differentials in South Africa). If the intergroup context involves a normative and habitual pattern of discrimination, that discrimination will bear little or no relation to prior or subsequent self-esteem. Not only is self-esteem largely irrelevant in determining majority group members' behaviour, but there may be strong social sanctions against *failing* to discriminate. The obverse situation may also exist. Social norms prescribe who may not legitimately be the object of discrimination. For example, it is unlikely that abusing a physically handicapped person would be a socially viable way for non-handicapped adults to gain self-esteem, and even considering such action may provoke feelings of shame. The argument here is very much that used by Pettigrew in his classic 1958 cross-national study of the authoritarian personality. Pettigrew provided data to support his view that prejudice and discrimination is the expression of a culture of prejudice not individual psychological needs.

Beyond these formal social limits on the relationship between discrimination and self-esteem, it also seems likely that majority group members (e.g. white Britons) may not always be aware that they belong to a distinct social group (i.e. whiteness is not an informative self-categorization, *cf.*

McGuire and McGuire, 1982). So, as the security of a majority group increases, the self-esteem of its members becomes less susceptible to the favourability of intergroup comparisons. Other social groups largely become irrelevant. Here then, intragroup social comparisons, personal aspirations to adhere to cultural norms and the position of the individual within the society defined by the group (e.g. British) may be far more immediately relevant to the individual's self-esteem than are intergroup relations (Codol, 1975). While any social categorization *may* be rendered salient in certain contexts, and need for a positive self-image may motivate subsequent intergroup behaviour it is also plausible that certain broader socio-structural factors may effectively 'fix' the level of self-categorization at the interpersonal plane and thus restrict individuals' modes of self-esteem regulation. In this analysis self-esteem does not motivate intergroup discrimination, rather it is governed by real intergroup relations, either directly due to self-evaluative consequences of social identity, or indirectly due to restrictions on effective channels for achieving or maintaining self-esteem. The notion of levels of categorization comes from self-categorization theory (Turner, 1985; Turner, Hogg, Oakes, Reicher and Wetherell, 1987), and the emphasis on the socio-structural determination of self-esteem owes much to Tajfel's (1981) concern with the esteem of the group as a *whole*. An individual's self-esteem could be plausibly associated with the esteem in which his or her group holds itself, but that, in turn, is unlikely to be a cause of intergroup behaviour, so much as an aspect of it.

But even this is problematic. It is the thorny issue of the relationship between social status and evaluation, and self-esteem. Does low status group membership mediate low self-esteem, and if so under what circumstances? Presumably it does, otherwise self-esteem cannot be a force for social change. However, the relationship, where it has been studied, is not clear. For example, Stephan (1978), reviewing evidence concerning the effects of desegregation in the United States, concluded that desegregation had no impact on black self-esteem; a point which was confirmed by Stephan and Rosenfield's (1978a) pre–postdesegregation study, in which attitudes to both ingroup and outgroup were more hostile after desegregation, although self-esteem was unaffected.

According to Rosenberg (1977) inter-racial contact can lower self-esteem among blacks because whites are a dissonant comparison reference group. On the other hand, Krause (1983) found that contact had no such effect. There is also evidence that positive self-esteem is associated with more positive racial attitudes (Rosenfield, Sheehan, Marcus and Stephan, 1981), and that *increases* in self-esteem are associated with increasingly positive inter-racial attitudes (Stephan and Rosenfield, 1978b). While these correlational data do not disconfirm the **SEH**, it is possible that some third variable (e.g. social status, income) may determine both self-esteem and racial attitudes. Research on the association between self-esteem and delinquency (Kaplan, 1980; Rosenberg, 1979) meets with similar problems, and again conclusions are hard to draw (Bynner, O'Malley and Backhman, 1981; McCarthy and Hoge, 1984; Stager, Chassin and Young, 1983; Wells and Rankin 1983).

Furthermore the interpretation of findings can be difficult due to inherent problems in the accurate and appropriate measurement of self-esteem. Milner concludes, in the context of British race relations, that 'low self-esteem is not an automatic consequence of being black in a racist environment' (1984, p. 103), it depends upon the wider sociohistorical milieu, the more local racial context, the specific context of testing, and the age of the respondent. 'Overall self-esteem may be satisfactory, but tested in inter-racial contexts in which blacks are believed to be low achievers, for example in educational institutions, inter-racial comparisons of self-esteem may disfavour blacks. In this way, much of the disparity between different research findings can be reconciled, in particular, differences between earlier and later studies (reflecting social change in the interim), and between older and younger children (reflecting both social change and individual identity development)' (Milner, 1984, pp. 103–104). A similar analysis is provided by Louden (1978). There is empirical evidence for this contextual influence on self-esteem of members of large scale allegedly lower status (and higher status) groups in the context of sex group membership (Hogg, 1985; Hogg and Turner, 1987) and in the context of Asians and Anglo-Saxon British adolescents (Hogg, Abrams and Patel, 1987).

In summary, *real* intergroup behaviour seems most often to be based on factors such as the distribution of wealth and power (Ng, 1982); material resources (Caddick, 1981); the nature of goal relations between groups (Brown, 1978; Brown and Abrams, 1986; Sherif, 1967); and religious or political values. Despite this self-esteem is still an important variable to consider since it is primarily a *psychological* construct, whereas those mentioned above tend to be more sociological.

Individual and Interpersonal Limits on the SEH

Social identity theorists have largely ignored the voluminous literature on self-esteem. One major issue is what effects chronic levels of self-esteem might have on an individual's negotiation of intergroup contexts. A plausible hypothesis is that individuals with low self-esteem will be psychologically less well equipped to engage in competitive intergroup behaviour.

This hypothesis is consistent both with findings reported above and with research which indicates that lowered self-esteem, depression and learned helplessness can co-occur (Beck, 1967; Abramson, Seligman and Teasdale, 1978; Metalsky, Halbestadt and Abramson, 1987). It may be that without what Langer (1975) calls an 'illusion of control' low self-esteem people lack the initial confidence to discriminate in self-favouring ways (Alloy and Abramson, 1982). A downward spiral could then develop in which the person becomes decreasingly confident of his or her social identity, leading to a sort of discriminatory impotence. Self-esteem may therefore become increasingly depressed.[3]

Such individuals appear to lack the functional cognitive biases of those with normal self-esteem. Normal self-esteem is associated with unwarranted optimism, and viewing oneself with a rosy glow (Lewinson, Mischel, Chaplin and Barton, 1980; Nelson and Craighead, 1977; Rozensky, Rehm, Pry and Roth, 1977). If such self-congratulatory biases are actually indicative of a healthily operating cognitive system, it follows that, in an intergroup setting these biases might well appear as stereotyping and discrimination. Therefore, those with high self-esteem are more likely to discriminate than those with low self-esteem. The interesting prediction can also be made that low self-esteem may render individuals cognitively unable to perceive in a self-favouring way, and this cognitive deficiency will further impede elevation of self-esteem through discrimination.

Here we are referring to extremes of self-esteem.

However, consistent with the principle underlying the argument, there is recent evidence that it is high self-esteem and non-depressed individuals who are more likely to engage in self-enhancing social comparisons (e.g. Crocker and Gallo, 1985; Crocker, Kayne and Alloy, 1985; Crocker and McGraw, 1985; Crocker and Schwartz, 1985; Crocker *et al.*, 1987, Tabachnik, Crocker and Alloy, 1983).

Aside from the minimal intergroup context, discriminatory behaviour is usually visible to other individuals. Self-presentational concerns (Jones and Pittman, 1982; Schlenker, 1982) may well moderate the association between discrimination and self-esteem (Baumeister, 1982; Reid and Sumiga, 1984). It may be possible to elevate self-esteem not so much by discriminating, and by eliciting favourable evaluations from others. Thus, it is not only self-enhancing social comparisons with the outgroup, but also the social approval gained from ingroup members (*cf.* Arkin, 1981) which elevates self-esteem. A further intriguing possibility is that a person could be overtly friendly towards an outgroup member (for example at interdepartmental meetings) while psychologically and covertly positively differentiating. This scenario was also suggested by Stephenson (1981) who noted that negotiators may operate simultaneously on two levels. It is important for them to gain *interpersonal* approval in order to 'win the ear' of their counterpart, but it is also crucial to *win* at an interparty level. Success in both aims will inevitably raise the negotiator's self-image at both levels.

Meaning and Coherence as Sources of Motivation

The centrality of self-esteem in social psychological theorizing (Wylie, 1979) has given rise to an emphasis on self-enhancing processes (e.g. Tesser and Campbell, 1980, 1982; Tesser and Paulus, 1983). However, both Tajfel's early work (1969, 1972), and Festinger's (1954) social comparison

---

[3]Another related motivation concept which is of relevance is power, perhaps best captured by Nietzsche's 'will to power' but see also Ng (1980) and Codol (1984). Self-esteem might be a product of successful control or of simply achieving desired goals. As is the case for 'control' (Mikula, 1984) self-esteem is probably a product of what power can achieve, or of the possession of power itself.

theory embody another primary motive—to know oneself. That is we may have a drive for 'self-evaluation' *per se*, in addition to a need for 'self-enhancement', through social comparison.

At the most human extreme, it has been proposed that individuals aspire to a state of self-enlightenment, or self-actualization (Maslow, 1954; Rogers, 1951). Any obstacle to attaining such a goal may also threaten self-esteem and the integrity of the self (Rosenzweig, 1944; Hall, 1961). Therefore, in this conception, self-esteem is a reflection of the coherence of the self, as well as its evaluative valence.

Such formulations often suffer from being highly individualistic. Nevertheless, the possibility of a desire to make one's experiences and one's self meaningful, what Bartlett (1932) referred to as a search after meaning, does seem to be accepted by many (e.g. Berkowitz, 1968; Katz, 1960; Reykowski, 1982) and this notion, in different guises, is an important motivational foundation of current social psychology (e.g. research into attribution, social representations and social influence). In the same vein Tajfel (1981) highlights the broadly social explanatory functions of stereotypes attached to group membership: explanations which can be internalized by individual group members through the process of self-categorization which is now posited as being responsible for group, or social identity related activity and conduct (Turner, 1985; Turner *et al.*, 1987; also see Hogg and Abrams, 1988).[4]

Theories have also often emphasized the need for balance between different forces and components of the self (Festinger, 1957; Freud, 1922; Heider, 1958). With respect to intergroup behaviour, it is certainly possible that discrimination is produced by making consonant the characteristics ascribed to self and ingroup (Cooper and Mackie, 1983; Horwitz and Rabbie, 1982). This can be theoretically understood as part of a self-categorization process which in the context of a salient social identity renders self more similar to the ingroup norm than the outgroup (Turner, 1985).

The foregoing discussion of social comparison processes has been relatively uncritical of the assumption that self-knowledge *is* gained through social comparison. However, such approaches, along with symbolic interactionist views of the self (e.g. Cooley, 1902) have been criticized for viewing self-construction as a passive, cognitive process. In particular Gecas and Schwalbe (1983) ar-

gue that people are motivated to be efficacious (*cf.* Bandura, 1982; McClelland, 1975; Deci, 1975) and that only through action can we know ourselves (see also Marx, 1844/1963). Their view is that action may boost self-esteem if it occurs in valued contexts. As such, 'social structural conditions enable and constrain efficacious action, influence the meanings we give to it, and are in turn reproduced by it' (Gecas and Schwalbe, 1983, p. 87). This argument is particularly relevant to intergroup behaviour. Wars give meaning to nations (Simmel, 1955) just as industrial conflicts reinforce distinctions between management and unions. Increasing group cohesiveness and distinctiveness may lead to heightened self-esteem simply by clarifying the relevant social identification, though research reviewed earlier suggests that category salience alone may not be sufficient and that action in terms of the category is necessary. So, competing in the Olympic Games may be sufficient to elevate national pride and patriotism, without necessarily winning anything. If social comparisons are relevant here they may be comparisons with one's group in the past, or with some ideal state, just as easily as with other groups (*cf.* Jaspars and Warnaen, 1982).

Given that both self-evaluative and self-enhancing motives may exist, it is important to address the question of which conditions favour the predominance of each. It seems that, under conditions of fear, people are more concerned with self-evaluation, at least as regards emotions (*cf.* Cottrell and Epley, 1977). Generally, however, self-enhancement seems dominant since people avoid self-esteem threatening situations rather than seize the opportunity to find out more about themselves (Bramel, 1962; Pepitone, 1964). Indeed, people may often prefer to compare themselves with dissimilar (worse) others, thereby gaining self-esteem, than with similar others (Brickman and Bulman, 1977; Brown and Abrams, 1986; Tesser and

---

[4]Perhaps Billig's (1985) fears that, in social identity theory, categorization is associated with stability not change would be allayed by the greater emphasis in self-categorization theory on the cognitive process of categorization than on self-esteem. The motivation here is for maximally meaningful structure, and the cognitive process which produces it is categorization. The behavioural manifestation of this process may be intergroup discrimination, acquiescence, elevated self-esteem, depressed self-esteem, in fact virtually anything. However, a *predictable anything*: predictable from socio-cultural factors and contextual variables.

Campbell, 1980), contrary to Festinger's hypothesis. As mentioned above, it is also possible that self-enhancing social comparisons can be made with similar others (ingroup members) by competing in terms of displaying *normative* beliefs and behaviours (Codol, 1975). Reykowski (1982) argues that, in fact, both self-defining and self-enhancing motives are aspects of a personal meaning system, and hence, are highly related.

Summary and Conclusions

It has been the purpose of this paper to explore the theoretical and empirical derivation of the Self-Esteem Hypothesis in social identity theory, and the implications of the SEH for intergroup behaviour. The minimal group context does not reveal many of the social motives which may influence the behaviour of real groups, but rather, tends to encourage self-enhancing motives. Even so, the evidence for self-esteem as either a basis for or a consequence of minimal intergroup discrimination is mixed. This may be a result of methodological problems or may be because self-esteem is only indirectly associated with discrimination. A number of other mediating motives may exist, perhaps the most central of which is a need for a coherent self-conception—an idea which is consistent with Tajfel's early understanding of intergroup discrimination. Another motive which deserves attention is the search for meaning. Perhaps it is this above all else which motivates behaviour—a view consistent with assumptions underlying much of contemporary social psychology. In the intergroup context meaning may be achieved by intergroup discrimination which may enhance self-esteem, but there are many other avenues open to the seeker after meaningful structure, and there are many outcomes for the search. While categorization may be the cognitive process which maximizes meaning, the accompanying *activity* and the self-evaluative or self-conceptual outcome depends very heavily on social context.

ACKNOWLEDGEMENTS

We wish to thank Susan Condor and Nick Emler for comments on issues raised in this article. A more comprehensive and detailed version is available on request. An earlier version entitled 'Social identity, self-esteem and intergroup discrimination' was presented at the 1984 Annual Conference of the British Psychological Society Social Psychology Section, Cambridge. Correspondence concerning this article should be directed to Dominic Abrams, who will be taking up a post at the Institute of Social and Applied Psychology, The University, Canterbury, Kent CT2 7LZ from January 1989.

REFERENCES

Abelson, R. P., Aronson, E., McGuire, W. J., Newcomb, T. M., Rosenberg, M. J. and Tannenbaum, P. H. (Eds). (1968). *Theories of Cognitive Consistency: A Sourcebook*, Rand-McNally, Chicago.

Abrams, D. (1982). 'How does identity influence behaviour?' Paper presented at the Annual Conference of the Social Psychology Section of the British Psychological Society, Edinburgh.

Abrams, D. (1983). 'The impact of evaluative context on intergroup behaviour'. Paper presented at the Annual Conference of the Social Psychology Section of the British Psychological Society, Sheffield.

Abrams, D. (1985). 'Focus of attention in minimal intergroup discrimination'. *British Journal of Social Psychology*, 24, 65–74.

Abramson, L. Y., Seligman, M. E. P. and Teasdale, J. D. (1978). 'Learned helplessness in humans: critique and reformulation', *Abnormal Psychology*, 87, 49–74.

Alloy, L. B. and Abramson, L. Y. (1982). 'Learned helplessness, depression, and the illusion of control', *Journal of Personality and Social Psychology*, 42, 1114–1126.

Arkin, R. M. (1981). 'Self-presentation styles'. In: Tedesch. J. T. (Ed.) *Impression Management Theory and Social Psychological Theory*. Academic Press, New York.

Bandura, A. (1982). 'Self-efficacy mechanisms in human agency', *American Psychologist*, 37, 122–147.

Bartlett, F. C. (1932). *Remembering*, Cambridge University Press, Cambridge.

Baumeister, R. F. (1982). 'A self-presentational view of social phenomena', *Psychological Bulletin*, 91, 3–26.

Beck, A. T. (1967). *Depression: Clinical, Experimental, and Theoretical Aspects*, Harper and Row, New York.

Berkowitz, L. (1968). 'Social motivation'. In: Lindzey, G. and Aronson, E. (Eds) *The Handbook of Social Psychology*, Vol. 20, Addison-Wesley, Reading, Massachusetts, pp. 50–135.

Billig, M. (1973). 'Normative communication in a minimal intergroup situation', *European Journal of Social Psychology*, 3, 339–343.

Billig, M. and Tajfel, H. (1973). 'Social categorization and similarity in intergroup behaviour', *European Journal of Social Psychology*, 3, 27–52.

Billig, M. (1985). 'Prejudice, categorization and particularization: From a perceptual to a rhetorical approach', *European Journal of Social Psychology*, 15, 79–103.

Bornstein, A., Crum, L., Wittenbraker, J., Harring, K., Insko, C. A. and Thibaut, J. (1983). 'On the measurement of social orientations in the minimal group paradigm', *European Journal of Social Psychology*, 13, 321–350.

Branthwaite, A., Doyle, S. and Lightbown, N. (1979). 'The balance between fairness and discrimination', *European Journal of Social Psychology*, 9, 149–163.

Bramel, O. (1962). 'A dissonance theory approach to defensive projection', *Journal of Abnormal and Social Psychology*, 64, 121–129.

Brickman, P. and Bulman, R. J. (1977). 'Pleasure and plain in social comparison'. In: Suls, J. M. and Miller, R. L. (Eds)

Social Comparison Processes, Hemisphere, Washington, D. C.

Brown, N. J. (1978). 'Divided we fall: An analysis of relations between a factory workforce'. In: Tajfel, H. (Ed.) *Differentiation Between Social Groups*, Academic Press, London.

Brown, R. J. and Abrams, D. (1986). 'The effects of intergroup similarity and goal interdependence on intergroup attitudes and task performance', *Journal of Experimental Social Psychology*, 22, 78–92.

Bynner, J. M., O'Malley, P. M. and Bachman, J. G. (1981). 'Self-esteem and delinquency revisited'. *Journal of Youth and Adolescence*, 10, 407–441.

Caddick, B. (1981). 'Equity theory, social identity and intergroup relations'. In: Wheeler, L. (Ed.) *Review of Personality and Social Psychology*, Vol. 2, Sage, London.

Codol, J. P. (1975). 'On the so-called "Superior conformity of the self" behaviour. 20 experimental investigations', *European Journal of Social Psychology*, 5, 457–501.

Codol, J. P. (1984). 'Social differentiation and non-differentiation'. In: Tajfel , H. (Ed.) *The Social Dimension: European Developments in Social Psychology*, Vol. 1, Cambridge University Press, pp. 314–337 and Editions de la Maison des Sciences de I'Homme, Paris.

Cooley, C. H. (1902). *Human Nature and Social Order*, Schoken Books, New York.

Cooper, J. and Mackie, D. (1983). 'Cognitive dissonance in an intergroup context', *Journal of Personality and Social Psychology*, 3, 536–544.

Coopersmith, S. (1967). *The Antecedents of Self-Esteem*, Freeman, San Francisco.

Cottrell, N. B. and Epley, S. W. (1977). 'Affiliation, social comparison, and socially mediated stress reduction.' In: Suls, J. M. and Miller, R. L. (Eds) *Social Comparison Processes: Theoretical and Empirical Perspectives*, Hemisphere Publishing Corporation, Washington.

Crocker, J. and Gallo, L. (1985, August). 'Prejudice against outgroups: The self-enhancing effects of downward social comparisons'. Paper presented at the annual convention of the American Psychological Association, Los Angeles, CA.

Crocker, J., Kayne, N. T. and Alloy, L. B. (1985). 'Comparing oneself to others in depressed and nondepressed college students: A reply to McCauley', *Journal of Personality and Social Psychology*, 48, 1579–1583.

Crocker, J. and McGraw, K. M. (1985). 'Prejudice in campus sororities: The effect of self-esteem and ingroup status'. Unpublished manuscript, Northwestern University, Evanston, IL.

Crocker, J. and Schwartz, I. (1985). 'Prejudice and ingroup favouritism in a minimal intergroup situation: Effects of self-esteem', *Personality and Social Psychology Bulletin*, 11, 379–386.

Crocker, J., Thomson, L. J., McGraw, K. M. and Ingerman, C. (1987). 'Downward comparison, prejudice, and evaluations of others: Effects of self-esteem and threat', *Journal of Personality and Social Psychology*, 52, 907–916.

Deci, E. L. (1975). *Intrinsic Motivation*, Plenum Press, New York.

Festinger, L. (1954). 'A theory of social comparison processes', *Human Relations*, 7, 117–140.

Festinger, L. (1957). *A Theory of Cognitive Dissonance*, Stanford University Press, Stanford.

Fleming, J. S. and Courtney, B. E. (1984). 'The dimensional-

ity of self-esteem: II. Hierarchical facet model for revised measurement scales', *Journal of Personality and Social Psychology*, 46, 404–421.

Fleming, J. S. and Watts, W. A. (1980). 'The dimensionality of self-esteem: some results for a college sample', *Journal of Personality and Social Psychology*, 39, 921–929.

Freud, S. (1922). *Group Psychology and the Analysis of the Ego*, Hogarth Press, London.

Gecas, V. and Schwalbe, M. L. (1983). 'Beyond the looking-glass self: social structure and efficacy-based self-esteem', *Social Psychology Quarterly*, 46, 77–88.

Hall, J. F. (1961). *Psychology of Motivation*, J. B. Lippincott, Philadelphia.

Heider, F. (1958). *The Psychology of Interpersonal Relations*, Wiley, New York.

Hogg, M. A., (1985). 'Masculine and feminine speech in dyads and groups: A study of speech style and gender salience', *Journal of Language and Social Psychology*, 4, 99–112.

Hogg, M. A., Abrams, D. and Patel, Y. (1987). 'Ethnic identity, self-esteem and occupational aspirations of Indian and Anglo-Saxon British adolescents', *Genetic, Social, and General Psychology Monographs*, 113, 487–508.

Hogg, M. A. and Abrams, D. (1988). *Social Identifications: A Social Psychology of Intergroup Relations and Group Processes*, Routledge, London.

Hogg, M. A. and Turner, J. C. (1987). 'Intergroup behaviour, self-stereotyping and the salience of social categories', *British Journal of Social Psychology*, 26, 325–340.

Hogg, M. A., Turner, J. C., Nascimento-Schulze, C. and Spriggs, D. (1986). 'Social categorization, intergroup behaviour, and self-esteem: Two experiments', *Revista de Psicologia Social*, 1, 23–37.

Horwitz, M. and Rabbie, J. M. (1982). 'Individuality and membership in the intergroup system'. In: Tajfel, H. (Ed.) *Social Identity and Intergroup Relations*, Cambridge University Press, Cambridge.

Hyman, H. H. and Singer, E. (Eds) (1968). *Readings in Reference Group Theory and Research*, Macmillan, New York.

Jaspars, J. M. F. and Warnaen, S. (1982). 'Intergroup relations, ethnic identity and self-evaluation in Indonesia'. In: Tajfel, H. (Ed.) *Social Identity and Intergroup Relations*, Cambridge University Press, Cambridge.

Jones, E. E. and Pittman, T. S. (1982). 'Toward a general theory of strategic self-presentation'. In: Suls, J. (Ed.) *Psychological Perspectives on the Self*, Erlbaum, Hillsdale, New Jersey.

Julian, J. W., Bishop, D. W. and Fiedler, F. E. (1966). 'Quasi-therapeutic effects of intergroup competition', *Journal of Personality and Social Psychology*, 3, 321–327.

Kaplan, H. B. (1980). *Deviant Behaviour in Defence of Self*, Academic Press, New York.

Katz, D. (1960). 'The functional approach to the study of attitudes', *Public Opinion Quarterly*, 24, 163–204.

Krause, N. (1983). 'The racial context of black self-esteem', *Social Psychology Quarterly*, 46, 98–107.

Langer, E. J. (1975). 'The illusion of control', *Journal of Personality and Social Psychology*, 32, 311–328.

Lemaine, G. (1974). 'Social differentiation and social originality', *European Journal of Social Psychology*, 4, 17–52.

Lemyre, L. and Smith, P. M. (1985). 'Intergroup discrimination and self-esteem in the minimal group paradigm', *Journal of Personality and Social Psychology*, 29, 660–670.

Lewinson, P. M., Mischel, W., Chaplin, W. and Barton, R. (1980). 'Social competence and depression: The role of illusory self perception', *Journal of Abnormal Psychology*, 8–9, 203–212.

Louden, D. (1978). 'Self-esteem and locus of control: Some findings on immigrant adolescents in Britain', *New Community*, 6, 218–234.

McCarthy, J. D. and Hoge, D. R. (1984). 'The dynamics of self-esteem and delinquency', *American Journal of Sociology*, 90, 396–410.

McClelland, D. C. (1975). *Power: The Inner Experience*, Irvington, New York.

McGuire, W. J. and McGuire, C. V. (1982). 'Significant others in the self-space: sex differences and developmental trends in the social self'. In: Suls, J. (Ed.) *Psychological Perspectives on the Self*, Erlbaum, Hillsdale, New Jersey.

Markus, H. and Zajonc, R. B. (1985). 'The cognitive perspective in social psychology'. In: Lindzey, G. and Aronson, E. (Eds) *The Handbook of Social Psychology*, 3rd edn, Vol. 1, Addison-Wesley, Reading, MA, pp. 137–229.

Marx, K. (1963). [1844] *Early writings*, Bottomore, T. B. (Ed. and Trans.), McGraw-Hill, New York.

Maslow, A. H. (1954). *Motivation and Personality*, Harper, New York.

Metalsky, G., Halbestadt, L. J. and Abramson, L. Y. (1987). 'Vulnerability to depressive mood reaction: Toward a more powerful test of the diathesis-stress and causal mediation component of the reformulated theory of depression', *Journal of Personality and Social Psychology*, 52, 386–393.

Mikula, G. (1984). 'Justice and fairness in interpersonal relations: Thoughts and suggestions'. In: Tajfel, H. (Ed.) *The Social Dimension: European Developments in Social Psychology*, Vol. 1, Cambridge University Press, pp. 204–227 and Maison des Sciences de I'Homme, Paris.

Milner, D. (1984). 'The development of ethnic attitudes'. In: Tajfel, H. (Ed.) *The Social Dimension: European Developments in Social Psychology*, Vol. 1, Cambridge University Press, pp. 89–110 and Maison des Sciences de I'Homme, Paris.

Mummendey, A. and Schreiber, H. J. (1983). 'Better or just different? Positive social identity by discrimination against or by differentiation from outgroups', *European Journal of Social Psychology*, 13, 389–397.

Mummendey, A. and Schreiber, H. J. (1984). 'Social comparison, similarity and ingroup favouritism: A replication', *European Journal of Social Psychology*, 14, 231–233.

Nelson, R. E. and Craighead, W. E. (1977). 'Selective recall of positive and negative feedback, self-control behaviours, and depression', *Journal of Abnormal Psychology*, 86, 379–388.

Ng, S. H. (1980). *The Social Psychology of Power*, Academic Press, London.

Ng, S. H. (1982). 'Power and intergroup discrimination'. In: Tajfel, H. (Ed.) *Social Identity and Intergroup Relations*, Cambridge University Press, Cambridge.

Oakes, P. J. and Turner, J. (1980). 'Social categorization and intergroup behaviour: Does minimal intergroup discrimination make social identity more positive', *European Journal of Social Psychology*, 10, 295–301.

Olson, J. M., Herman, C. P. and Zanna, M. P. (Eds) (1986). *Relative Deprivation and Social Comparison: The Ontario Symposium*, Vol. 4, Erlbaum, Hillsdale, N. J.

Pepitone, A. (1964). *Attraction and Hostility*, Atherton, New York.

Pettigrew, T. F. (1958). 'Personality and socio-cultural factors in intergroup attitudes: A cross-national comparison', *Journal of Conflict Resolution*, 2, 29–42.

Reid, F. J. M. and Sumiga, L. (1984). 'Attitudinal politics in intergroup behaviour: Interpersonal vs. intergroup determinants of attitude change', *British Journal of Social Psychology*, 23, 335–340.

Reykowski, J. (1982). 'Social motivation', *Annual Review of Psychology*, 33, 123–154.

Rogers, C. R. (1951). *Client-Centered Therapy*, Houghton Mifflin, Boston.

Rosenberg, M. (1977). 'Contextual dissonance effects: nature and causes', *Psychiatry*, 40, 205–217.

Rosenberg, M. (1979). *Conceiving the Self*, Basic Books, New York.

Rosenfield, D., Sheehan, D. S., Marcus, M. M. and Stephan, W. G. (1981). 'Classroom structure and prejudice in desegregated school', *Journal of Educational Psychology*, 73, 17–26.

Rosenzweig, S. (1944). 'Frustration theory'. In: Hunt, J. M. (Ed.) *Personality and the Behaviour Disorders*, Vol. 1, Ronald Press, New York.

Rozensky, R. H., Rehm, L. P., Pry, G. and Roth, D. (1977) 'Depression and self-reinforcement in hospitalized patients? *Journal of Behaviour Therapy and Experimental Psychiatry*, 8, 35–52.

Sachdev, I. and Bourhis, R. Y. (1984). 'Minimal majorities and minorities', *European Journal of Social Psychology*, 14, 35–52.

Sachdev, I. and Bourhis, R. Y. (1985). 'Social categorization and power differentials in group relations', *European Journal of Social Psychology*, 15, 415–434.

Sachdev, I. and Bourhis, R. Y. (1987). 'Status differentials and intergroup behaviour', *European Journal of Social Psychology*, 17, 277–293.

Schonbach, P., Gollwitzer, P. M., Stiepel, G. and Wagner, U. (1981). *Education and Intergroup Attitudes*, Academic Press, New York.

Schlenker, B. R. (1982). 'Translating actions into attitudes: on identity-analytic approach to the explanation of social conduct'. In: Berkowitz, L. (Ed.) *Advances in Experimental Social Psychology*, Vol. 15, Academic Press, New York.

Sherif, M. (1967). *Group Conflict and Cooperation*, Routledge and Kegan Paul, London.

Simmel, G. (1955). *Conflict and the Web of Group Affiliations*, Collier-MacMillan, London.

Stager, S. F., Chassin, L. and Young, R. D. (1983). 'Determinants of self-esteem among labelled adolescents', *Social Psychology Quarterly*, 46, 3–10.

Stephan, W. G. (1978). 'School desegregation: an evaluation of predictions made in Brown versus Board of Education', *Psychological Bulletin*, 85, 217–238.

Stephan, W. G. and Rosenfield, D. (1978a). 'The effects of desegregation on race relations and self-esteem', *Journal of Educational Psychology*, 70, 670–679.

Stephan, W. G. and Rosenfield, D. (1978b). 'Effects of desegregation on racial attitudes', *Journal of Personality and Social Psychology*, 36, 795–804.

Stephenson, G. M. (1981). 'Intergroup bargaining and negotiation', In: Turner, J. C. and Giles, H. (Eds) *Intergroup Behaviour*, Blackwell, Oxford.

Suls, J. M. and Miller, R. L. (Eds) (1977). *Social Comparison*

Processes, Hemisphere, Washington D. C.

Tabachnik, N., Crocker, J. and Alloy, L. B. (1983). 'Depression, social comparison, and the false consensus effect', *Journal of Personality and Social Psychology, 45,* 688–699.

Tajfel, H. (1959). 'Quantitative judgement in social perception', *British Journal of Psychology, 50,* 16–29.

Tajfel, H. (1969). 'Cognitive aspects of prejudice', *Journal of Social Issues, 25,* 79–97.

Tajfel, H. (1972). 'Social categorization'. English Ms. of, 'La categorisation sociale'. In: Moscovici, S. (Ed.) *Introduction a la psychologie sociale,* Vol. 1, Larousse, Paris.

Tajfel, H. (1974). 'Intergroup behaviour, social comparison and social change'. Unpublished, Katz-Newcomb lectures at University of Michigan, Ann Arbor.

Tajfel, H. (1978). *Differentiation Between Social Groups: Studies in the Social Psychology of Intergroup Relations,* European Monographs in Social Psychology, No. 14, Academic Press, London.

Tajfel, H. (1981). *Human Groups and Social Categories: Studies in Social Psychology,* Cambridge University Press, Cambridge.

Tajfel, H. (1982). 'Social psychology of intergroup relations', *Annual Review of Psychology, 33,* 1–39.

Tajfel, H., Billig, M., Bundy, R. P. and Flament, C. (1971). 'Social categorization and intergroup behaviour', *European Journal of Social Psychology, 1,* 149–178.

Tajfel, H. and Turner, J. C. (1979). 'An integrative theory of intergroup conflict'. In: Austin, W. G. and Worchel, S. (Eds) *The Social Psychology of Intergroup Relations,* Brooks-Cole, Monterey, California.

Tesser, A. and Campbell, J. (1980). 'Self-definition: the impact of the relative performance and similarity of others', *Social Psychology Quarterly, 43,* 341–347.

Tesser, A. and Campbell, J. (1982). 'Self-evaluation maintenance and the perception of friends and strangers', *Journal of Personality, 50,* 261–279.

Tesser, A. and Paulus, D. (1983). 'The definition of self: private and public self-evaluation management strategies', *Journal of Personality and Social Psychology, 44,* 672–682.

Turner, J. C. (1975). 'Social comparison and social identity: some prospects for intergroup behaviour', *European Journal of Social Psychology, 5,* 5–34.

Turner, J. C. (1978a). 'Social categorization and social discrimination in the minimal group paradigm'. In: Tajfel, H. (Ed.) *Differentiation Between Social Groups: Studies in the Social Psychology of Intergroup Relations,* Academic Press, London.

Turner, J. C. (1978b). 'Social comparison, similarity and ingroup favouritism'. In: Tajfel, H. (Ed.) *Differentiation Between Social Groups: Studies in the Social Psychology of Intergroup Relations,* Academic Press, London.

Turner, J. C. (1980). 'Fairness or discrimination in intergroup behaviour?. A reply to Braithwaite, Doyle and Lightbown', *European Journal of Social Psychology, 10,* 131–147.

Turner, J. C. (1981). 'The experimental social psychology of intergroup behaviour'. In: Turner, J. C. and Giles, H. (Eds) *Intergroup Behaviour,* Blackwell, Oxford.

Turner, J. C. (1982). 'Towards a cognitive redefinition of the social group'. In: Tajfel, H. (Ed.) *Social Identity and Intergroup Relations,* Cambridge University Press, Cambridge and Maison des Sciences de L'Hommes, Paris.

Turner, J. C. (1983). 'Some comments on "The measurement of social orientations in the minimal group paradigm", *European Journal of Social Psychology, 13,* 351–368.

Turner, J. C. (1985). 'Social categorization and the self-concept: A social cognitive theory of group behaviour'. In: Lawler, E. J. (Ed.) *Advances in Group Processes: Theory and Research,* Vol. 2, JAI Press, Greenwich, CT, pp. 77–121.

Turner, J. C., Brown, R. J. and Tajfel, H. (1979). 'Social comparison and group interest in ingroup favouritism', *European Journal of Social Psychology, 9,* 187–204.

Turner, J. C. and Giles, H. (Eds) (1981). *Intergroup Behaviour,* Blackwell, Oxford.

Turner, J. C., Hogg, M. A., Oakes, P. J., Reicher, S. D. and Wetherell, M. S. (1987). *Rediscovering the Social Group: A Self-Categorization Theory,* Blackwell, Oxford and New York.

van Knippenberg, A. (1984). 'Intergroup differences in group perceptions'. In: Tajfel, H. (Ed.) *The Social Dimension: European Developments in Social Psychology,* Vol. 2, Cambridge University Press, Cambridge, pp. 560–578 and Maison des Sciences de I'Homme, Paris.

Vickers, E., Abrams, D. and Hogg, M. A. (1988). 'The influence of social norms on discrimination in the minimal group paradigm'. Unpublished manuscript, University of Dundee, Scotland.

Wagner, U., Lampen, L. and Syllwasschy, J. (1986). 'Ingroup inferiority, social identity and outgroup devaluation in a modified extended minimal group study', *British Journal of Social Psychology, 25,* 15–24.

Wells, L. E. and Marwell, G. (1977). *Self-Esteem: Its Conceptualization and Measurement* Sage, Beverley Hills.

Wells, L. E. and Rankin, J. H. (1983). 'self-concept as a mediating factor in delinquency', *Social Psychology Quarterly, 46,* 11–22.

Wylie, R. (1979). *The self-concept.* Revised Edition Vols. 1 and 2. Lincoln: University of Nebraska Press.

Relationship Between Social and Personal Identities: Segregation or Integration?

Anne Reid and Kay Deaux • City University of New York

Editors' Notes

The previous selection investigated the underlying motivation for highlighting a given group membership or social identity. The present selection inquires into the structure of our self-identity and about the relation between the *personal attributes* and *category membership* components of one's identity. After all, each of us has many components. We have individual attributes (e.g., we may be gifted, temperamental, or blond) and social category attributes (e.g., we may be Americans, students, or stamp collectors). The question raised by the authors is whether our social selves and our personal selves are sequestered or whether they are clustered together or intermixed. Note in particular the method adopted to study the research question. This method consists of first collecting questionnaire data that inquires about the participants' identities and attributes, then collecting recall data a week later at a second session, and finally collecting ratings of the relations between attributes and identities at a third session another week later. Together, these analyses afford a graphical representation of an individual's identity structure that provides an answer to the research question.

Discussion Questions

1. What are the different ways in which self-cognitions might be organized?
2. How do the present authors use their data to answer the question about the organization of social and personal attributes in memory?

3. What do the authors conclude from their data in regard to the segregation and the integration models? Which one of the two is apparently more valid?

Suggested Readings

Brewer, M. B. (1991). The social self: On being the same and different at the same time. *Personality and Social Psychology Bulletin, 17,* 475–482.

Deaux, K., Reid, A., Mizrachi, K., & Ethier, K. A. (1995). Parameters of social identity. *Journal of Personality and Social Psychology, 68,* 280–291.

Ellemers, N., Wilke, H., & Van Knippenberg, A. (1993). Effects of the legitimacy of low group or individual status on individual and collective status-enhancement strategies. *Journal of Personality and Social Psychology, 64,* 766–778.

Trafimow, D., Triandis, H. C., & Goto, S. (1991). Some tests of the distinction between private self and collective self. *Journal of Personality and Social Psychology, 60,* 649–655.

Authors' Abstract

Recognition that self-representation includes both social and personal identities raises questions about the cognitive organization of these elements. Two models of identity structure are compared: (a) a *segregation* model (D. Trafimow, H. C. Triandis, & S. G. Goto, 1991), which assumes that (social) identities and (personal) attributes are two distinct categories, and (b) an *integration* model (K. Deaux, 1992), which proposes that identities and attributes often coexist in a limited set of cognitive structures. Clustering of self-relevant information in free recall was used to assess cognitive organization in a sample of 57 students. Identities and attributes clustered separately at greater-than-chance rates, consistent with the segregation model. More detailed analysis of recall data, in which individual patterns of association between identities and attributes were considered, provides stronger support for an integration model of self-representation.

How is the self best characterized? This question has engaged theorists for nearly a century, dating from the early work of James (1890/1950) and Mead (1934/1962) to the more recent activity in social cognition (Greenwald & Pratkanis, 1984; Kihlstrom & Cantor, 1984; Linville & Carlston, 1994). In offering their analyses of the self, the majority of theorists assume some form of multiplicity, believing that the self is more accurately and usefully viewed as a composite rather than as a unitary entity. Although theorists agree on this general tenet, different models offer different concepts to parse out the total self package. Thus, researchers variously view the self as made up of separate self-schemas (Markus, 1977); actual, ought, and ideal selves (Higgins, 1987); possible selves (Markus & Nurius, 1986); self-prototypes (Kihlstrom & Cantor, 1984); or roles and identities (McCall & Simmons, 1978; Stryker, 1980).

One major basis of characterizing aspects of the self, which has gained increasing prominence in recent years, is the distinction between aspects of identity that are collective and related to social group membership versus features of identity that are personal and presumably more individuating. This general distinction has several related forms. Social identity and self-categorization theories (Hogg & Abrams, 1988; Tajfel, 1981; Turner, Hogg, Oakes, Reicher, & Wetherell, 1987) contrast personal identity, in which the stress is on personality characteristics and behaviors (e.g., intelligent, hardworking) that differentiate one from others, with social identities that derive from group memberships (e.g., African American) and provide the basis for common identification. Luhtanen and Crocker (1992) elaborated on this distinction in proposing two distinct forms of self-esteem, one personal and one collective, that are based on different aspects of the self-concept. A similar partition between collective and private or individualistic aspects of the self was made by Greenwald and Pratkanis (1984) and by Triandis (1989).

General agreement that a conceptual distinction can be made between group-based and individual-based aspects of the self is unfortunately not accompanied by a consensual position on vocabulary. Terms for group-based aspects of identification include *collective, allocentric,* and *social identity;* the contrasting type of self-cognition has been termed *individualistic, private, idiocentric* and *personal identity.* Our preference is to use the term *identity,* or *social identity,* to refer to social groups or collective categories of membership. We use the term *attribute* to designate the personality traits, characteristics, and behaviors that an individual uses in self-description. With this terminology we hope to avoid some of the confusion that results from the differing theoretical uses of *personal identity* (Deaux, 1992). Specifically, we want to differentiate our use of *identity* and *attribute* as elements of self-*structure* from the theoretical distinction between social and personal identity offered by social identity and self-categorization theories, in which the emphasis is on dynamic shifts in focus of attention (Turner et al., 1987; Turner, Oakes, Haslam, & McGarty, 1994).

The presumption of different aspects of the self, and in particular the distinction between identities and attributes, raises questions about the organization of self-structure. With the increased interest of investigators in cognitive organization and memory representation, these questions about self-structure take on new importance in research on the self.

One Basket or Two?

Trafimow, Triandis, and Goto (1991) recently addressed this question, suggesting two possible models of organization of self-cognitions. One possibility, which they ultimately discarded, was a "one-basket" model in which information about both identity and attribute is stored in a single cognitive structure. From this perspective, retrieval of self-related elements from memory should be predicted solely on the basis of frequency. Thus, if a person has more personal attributes than social identities, then attributes are more likely to be re-

called on request. Priming one aspect of the self—for example, social identities—should be no more likely to elicit social identities than attributes, according to a one-basket model.

The second model proposed by Trafimow et al. (1991) was termed a "two-basket" model. This model presumes that personal attributes are stored separately from social identities, that is, that there are two distinct and nonoverlapping self-representations. This model, which we term the *segregation model,* is illustrated in the top half of Figure 1.

Self-descriptions within the same basket are assumed to have some degree of association with one another, by virtue of their common category membership. Consequently, if an identity is made accessible, other identities stored in that same basket should be more accessible than any personal attributes in the other basket. Trafimow et al. (1991) tested this assumption in two ways, focusing on the kinds of items listed by respondents on Kuhn and McPartland's (1954) *Who Am I?* scale. First, they predicted that priming a social identity would result in more frequent listing of social identities and that priming a personal attribute would

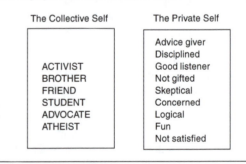

FIGURE 39.1 ■ The relationship between social and personal identities: two alternative models. Social identities appear in uppercase letters; personal identities or attributes appear in upper and lowercase letters.

result in more frequent listing of attributes. Second, they predicted that the retrieval of an item in one category—for example, a personal attribute—would increase the probability of retrieving another item in that same category.

In general, their results were consistent with a two-basket model. Different primes led to different rates of retrieving either attributes or social identities (although the trends were relative, rather than absolute, in that respondents always listed more personal attributes). Furthermore, and more relevant to the present study, patterns of identity listing showed greater-than-chance clustering by category; When a respondent listed a social identity, it was more likely to be preceded by another social identity than by an attribute (and similarly for the sequence of attributes). Although these patterns were in the predicted direction, the data had a considerably less-than-perfect fit to a two-basket model, in which all social identities would be retrieved in sequence and then all personal attributes (or vice versa). This lack of fit to an ideal model suggests that additional principles may be needed to account for the structure of self-representations.

Two Baskets or More?

Trafimow et al.'s (1991) results quite clearly suggest that self-representations are stored in something more complex than a single cognitive structure. At the same time, they leave open the question of just what the alternative organization might be. Although the bifurcation of social identity versus personal attribute has an appealing simplicity, some investigators have proposed that social and personal aspects of the self are not so easily separated (Breakwell, 1986: Deaux, 1992, 1993: Rosenberg & Gara, 1985). According to this position, social identities and personal attributes are often inextricably linked and thus would be represented within the same cognitive structures. Attributes, defined as personality traits or behaviors, are viewed as not necessarily constituting a separate form of identity; rather, they often provide the content and meanings of social categories. Thus, defining oneself as a professor can implicate traits such as intelligent, curious, and hardworking. Similarly, the meaning of being a Catholic might be inseparable from seeing oneself as spiritual, honest, and concerned for the welfare of others. This model, which we term the *integration* model, is represented in the bottom half of Figure 1.

From the perspective of the integration model, most individuals would have more than two organizing structures for self-related features, many of which would contain some combination of social identity and personal attribute. In the simple version of this model, a person would have as many structures as he or she has social identities; each of these social identities would, in turn, be associated with a set of personal attributes. In a somewhat more complex version of the integration model, such as that proposed by Rosenberg and Gara (1985), social identities that share common attributes might be combined in a single structure as represented in Figure 1.

The links between identities and attributes are thought to originate in at least two ways: (a) from culturally shared social representations that provide ways of interpreting common social categories (Breakwell, 1993; Moscovici, 1981) and (b) from specific individual experiences that give personal meaning to a categorical self-definition. Although the latter route produces more idiosyncratic links between identity and attribute, both routes are consistent with the assumption that attributes provide meaning to the more general categories of self-definition.

Comparison of the Segregation and Integration Models

Predictions of self-representation, organization, and recall derived from the segregation model are quite straightforward. As outlined by Trafimow et al. (1991), identities referring to social or group membership should always cluster together, distinct from the cluster of personal attributes. Making one versus the other category accessible should increase the probability that a person would draw from the primed category; a shift to the other category would be predicted only if category accessibility changed or if the first category were exhausted.

Predictions from the integration model are somewhat more complex and require a more detailed analysis of the social identities that an individual endorses and the specific attributes that are associated with each social identity. Thus, the integration model would predict that certain attributes are linked with certain identities and that those associated identities should be likely to cluster together in any test of report or recall. Put more concretely, the characteristic of intelligence, if associated with being a professor, should be more likely to be recalled with that category than with another personal attribute—such as physically fit—that might be primarily linked to the social identity of marathon runner. Attributes could be represented in the same cognitive structure if they had similar links to the social identity represented in that structure. Similarly, two or more social identities might be linked by common meaning: For example, being a psychologist and being a professor, although definably different identities, might have considerable shared meaning and hence occupy a common structure.

We designed this study with three goals in mind. First, we provide a conceptual replication of Trafimow et al.'s (1991) study in which we assessed identity-attribute sequences using a measure of recall rather than open-ended listing of identities. Second, we test the power of each model using a different dependent measure, specifically the overall clustering of items in free recall. According to the segregation model, recall should be organized in terms of two major clusters. According to the integration model, recall should be organized in terms of several clusters, each of which combines identities and attributes. Given the assumption of idiosyncratic identity-attribute links, the appropriate test of the integration model requires an examination of associations between identities on an individual basis. Third, we explore some unique implications of the integration model that predict differences within attribute-attribute and identity-identity pairings.

Method

OVERVIEW

Our goal in this study was to assess the organization of social identities and personal attributes in people's self-representations. In a first session, participants named each of their important social identities and provided a list of trait attributes associated with each. In a second session, 1 week later, each respondent was asked to recall the identities and attributes that he or she had named. Clustering patterns in order of recall served as an index of cognitive structure. In a third session,

several weeks later, participants rated the degree to which each attribute was associated with each identity, providing the data necessary for a hierarchical classes (HICLAS) analysis of identity structure (DeBoeck & Rosenberg, 1988).

PARTICIPANTS

Fifty-seven undergraduate students (36 women and 21 men) from a large New York City college participated in the study. The ages of the respondents ranged from 17 to 25 years with a mean of 19.5. Sixty-one percent of the sample was White, 9% was African American, 7% was Hispanic/Latino/Chicano, 11% was Asian American, and 7% was West Indian. The remaining 5% did not specify their ethnicity. Five people were eliminated from the analyses because they failed to provide usable data. Respondents participated in the study for both course credit (Sessions 1 and 2) and financial payment (Session 3).

PROCEDURES FOR DATA COLLECTION

Session 1. Participants were tested individually in the first session. Each student completed the first stage of the identity elicitation interview (Rosenberg & Gara, 1985), which provides a list of identities and attributes. To introduce the task, the interviewer explained that people can define or describe themselves in terms of social categories or groups to which they belong. Some examples of these categories, such as sex, ethnicity, occupation, and political and religious affiliations, were provided for purposes of illustration. After hearing this brief description, participants were asked to generate a list of self-relevant social identities. The interviewer then asked each respondent to list the attributes that he or she associated with each social identity. Finally, respondents completed a short demographics questionnaire in which they indicated their sex, age, ethnicity, and year in school.

Session 2. One week later, each participant was given a list of the identities and attributes that he or she had generated in the previous session, presented now in a single alphabetical order. Alphabetical order provided an essentially random ordering of attributes and identities, thus avoiding a bias toward either the integration or the segregation model. Participants were asked to rate each item on the list in terms of its importance to their self-concept, using a 5-point scale on which 1 = *not important* and 5 = *extremely important*. We included this step to remind participants of the identities and attributes they had reported a week earlier, thereby improving rates of recall.

After completing the importance ratings, but before doing the recall task, students worked for 5 min on a distractor task, which consisted of a word search puzzle on an innocuous topic. The purpose of this interpolation was to increase the likelihood that the sequencing of participants' free recall in the next stage of the procedure would be based on long-term memory (i.e., self-structure) rather than short-term memory (i.e., the immediately preceding alphabetical order).

When they had completed the distractor task, participants were asked to recall as many of the items from the importance rating task as possible. They were told to list the items in whatever order occurred to them. This recall task provided the data for assessment of identity-attribute organization.

Session 3. Several weeks later, participants were contacted and asked if they would participate in a third session, for which payment of $10 was offered. Twenty-nine members of the original sample agreed to return for this additional session.[1] Respondents in this sample did not differ in age, sex, or ethnicity from those students who did not participate in the third session. They also did not differ in identity-relevant measures, including the number of identities and attributes generated at the first session or the number of identities and attributes recalled at Session 2 (all comparisons were nonsignificant).

At this third session, each participant was provided with a set of individually constructed rating forms on which they were asked to indicate the extent to which each attribute they had named in the first session was associated with each of their named identities (Rosenberg & Gara, 1985). These ratings were made on a 3-point scale (0 = *never*, 1 = *sometimes*, 2 = *always*); in subsequent data analysis the 1 and 2 responses are combined to provide the binary data necessary for HICLAS analysis (DeBoeck & Rosenberg, 1988; Rosenberg & Gara, 1985). This analysis, explained in more detail in the Results section, produces a graphical representation of a person's identity structure that shows the association and overlap between both identities and attributes.

Results

DESCRIPTIVE SUMMARY

Participants in the study listed an average of 7.1 social identities (SD = 1.3), a figure closely approximating those reported in previous studies of identity (Deaux, 1991; Ethier & Deaux, 1994). The average number of attributes generated was 50.4 (SD = 23.2). On the recall task in Session 2, participants recalled on average 5.2 (73%) of their social identities (SD = 2.1) and 20.1 (40%) of their attributes (SD = 9.6). In addition, participants listed an average of 2.1 attributes that were not part of their original list. Virtually no identities were falsely recalled.

ANALYTIC STRATEGY

The basic data for analysis were the respondent's recalled identities and attributes. Each item in a respondent's list was coded as either an identity (I), if it referred to a social role or a social group, or an attribute (A), if it referred to a trait, behavior, or other personal characteristic.[2]

We used three approaches to data analysis, each of which relies on the order and sequence in which identities and attributes were recalled. The first approach is based on the strategy adopted by Trafimow et al. (1991), who used conditional probability scores to assess the likelihood that identities and/or attributes succeed each other. In the second approach we considered the overall pattern of clustering in recall lists. To test the segregation model, two clusters are defined (identities and attributes). For the integration model, which takes into account each individual's particular associations between identities and attributes, the number of clusters varies across individuals as a function of their initial identity listings. The third approach, which uses HICLAS analysis (DeBoeck & Rosenberg, 1988) to determine associations between identities and attributes, provides a more finely grained analysis of self-structure and allows

---

[1]Three participants who did not recall a sufficient number of identities at Session 2 were not contacted for this portion of the study, nor were the 5 people originally eliminated for unusable data in Session 1.

[2]The designation of an item as an identity or attribute was based on participants' initial listings of identities and attributes in Session 1.

the test of predictions unique to the integration model.

Conditional probabilities of identity–attribute pairings. In Trafimow et al.'s (1991) experiments, participants were given either private or collective primes and then asked to complete Kuhn and McPartland's (1954) 20-statement "Who am I?" listing, with the assumption that the sequence of self-descriptions would reflect self-structure. In the present study, participants were asked to recall material they had generated earlier, but the assumption that sequence would reflect the organization of self-representations was the same. In Trafimow et al.'s procedure each participant was required to produce 20 statements; in our procedure the length of the recall list could vary (the average list length was 25.3 items).

Following the procedure of Trafimow et al. (1991), we calculated four probability scores for each recall list in which one or more social identities were recalled ($N = 51$): the probability of an identity following an identity, $p(I|I)$; the probability of an identity following an attribute, $p(I|A)$; the probability of an attribute following an attribute, $p(A|A)$; and the probability of an attribute following an identity, $p(A|I)$. [3] We used within-subject analyses of variance to test the comparisons predicted by the segregation model.

Consistent with the results of Trafimow et al. (1991), the probability of retrieving an identity given that the previous response was an identity was greater than if the previous response was an attribute, $p(I|I) = .33 > p(I|A) = .16$, $F(1, 50) = 18.79$, $p < .001$. Similarly, the probability of retrieving an attribute given that the previous item was an attribute was greater than if the previous response was an identity, $p(A|A) = .84 > p(A|I) = .67$, $F(1, 50) = 18.79$, $p < .001$. These results are similar in magnitude and direction to those reported by Trafimow et al. (1991, Experiment 2), as shown in Table 1.

It is important to note that these similar patterns of findings are the result of two somewhat different methods of eliciting identities. Participants in Trafimow et al.'s (1991) study produced free-response lists after receiving either group or individual primes. In our procedure, participants at the initial session, 1 week prior to recall, generated a list of identities and then produced a set of attributes for each identity. Each of these procedures might be suspected of biasing the resultant output in a direction favoring the segregation or integra-

TABLE 39.1. Mean Conditional Probabilities of Identity and Attribute Sequences, With Comparison to Data From Trafimow, Triandis, and Goto (1991, Experiment 2)

Probability	Present study	Trafimow et al. (1991)
$p(I|I)$	.33	.46
$p(A|A)$	.84	.73
$p(I|A)$	.16	.17
$p(A|I)$	.67	.51

Note. I = identity; A = attribute.

tion models, respectively. The similarity of the patterns, however, argues against such a procedural bias.

At a conceptual level, the fact that two quite different methods of eliciting self-descriptive material led to similar outcomes suggests that a consistent form of mental representation is guiding the output. The precise form of this representation is not clearly specified, however. At a very general level, the assertion that identities and attributes cluster together separately is supported. Yet these patterns are far from perfect. In the pure case, one would expect that the I | I and A | A figures would both approach 1.0, and the I | A and A | I cases should approximate 0. The obtained data are quite discrepant from these norms, suggesting that other strategies of coding self-descriptive information may also be operating. In the second and third analytic approaches we explored this possibility, providing a basis for contrasting the segregation and integration models.

Overall patterns of clustering. The analysis of conditional probabilities tests the frequency of specific sequential pairs of identities and/or attributes. Another approach to analyzing lists of self-relevant material is to consider the overall pattern or clustering of items.

The segregation model would predict that recall would be organized in terms of two major clusters: one of identities and another of attributes. (In the absence of a prime, the order of these two clusters would be random.) The integration model,

---

[3] Trafimow et al. (1991) used a different notation system: they used G (referring to *group*) for what we term *identities* (I) and I (referring to *idiocentric*) for what we term *attributes* (A). In addition, they initially coded a category that they termed *allocentric*, used for characteristics that connoted interdependence and sensitivity to others, but the frequency of those items was quite low, and the category was not included in their reported analysis.

which assumes that social identities are linked to specific sets of attributes, would predict that clustering patterns would reflect these distinct cognitive structures. Accordingly, the number of clusters would vary by participant, with each cluster containing a combination of one or more identities and some number of attributes.

We analyzed the sequencing of items in recall in terms of an adjusted ratio of clustering (ARC), developed by Roenker, Thompson, and Brown (1971). ARC scores can range from +1 to –1; a score of 0 indicates chance clustering. Furthermore, because the value of an ARC score is relatively unaffected by the number of categories or the total number of categories recalled, it offers a reasonable basis for comparing the predictions made from the two models, which rely on different numbers of categories.

To test the prediction derived from the segregation model, we analyzed recall lists in terms of the clustering of items in one of two categories: identities or attributes. We calculated an ARC score for each respondent ($N = 52$) and then summarized scores across respondents. The average ARC score was .23 (individual scores ranged from –.30 to 1.00). This degree of clustering is significantly greater than what would be expected on the basis of chance ($z = 4.6$, $p < .001$).

To test the integration model, which is based on idiosyncratic combinations of identities and attributes, it is necessary to refer to the original lists of identities and attributes provided by participants in the first session. In the first session, respondents listed their identities and the attributes they associated with each identity. On the basis of this information, associated items (i.e., an identity plus its linked attributes) were assigned the same code number, whereas items that were not associated received different code numbers. Thus, if a person initially indicated that his or her identity as a student could be characterized by intelligence, studiousness, and future-orientation, those three attributes would be scored with the same code as *student*. Intrusions, that is, items appearing in the recall list that were not originally generated by respondents, were treated as nonoccurrences and ignored in the analysis.

We calculated an ARC score for each respondent ($N = 52$) on the basis of the number of identity clusters that he or she named; Summarized over participants, the average ARC score was .34 (individual scores ranged from –.50 to 1.00). This

degree of clustering is significantly greater than what would be expected on the basis of chance ($z = 11.33$, $p < .001$).

These results provide support for both the segregation model and the integration model, though the support for the latter is stronger. The fact that both models gained some support is not surprising, because both models predict that there will be some grouping on the basis of attributes. For the segregation model, all attributes should cluster together, distinct from the cluster of identities. For the integration model, subsets of attributes are predicted to cluster together, each associated with its own identity category. Thus, the predictions of the two models overlap to some extent. The stronger results for the pattern of clustering predicted by the integration model, however, argue in favor of the more complicated pattern of organization.

The analysis of clustering, using a single identity and its associated attributes as initially generated by respondents, serves as one test of the integration model. However, it does not fully take into account the premise of the integration model, namely that more than one identity as well as more than one attribute may be contained within a single cognitive organization. This assumption, which requires more detailed representation of identity–attribute associations, is tested by HICLAS analysis.

Hierarchical classes of identity structure. Disjunctive HICLAS analysis, as developed by DeBoeck and Rosenberg (1988), provides a means of determining, for each individual respondent, the degree to which identities and attributes are associated with one another. HICLAS is based on the binary matrix of association between identities and attributes and produces a hierarchical model of an individual's identity structure. Initially, the investigator chooses the number of ranks for the analysis, which can be considered the number of blocks at the base of the resulting pyramid. On the basis of both past research findings as well as the goodness of fit to the present data, we chose a Rank 3 solution. [4]

In the present analysis, we used individual HICLAS outputs such as the hypothetical one depicted in Figure 2 as the basis for determining

---

[4]The average goodness of fit was .83 and ranged from .52 to 1.0 in individual solutions: generally, a goodness-of-fit ratio greater than .70 is considered acceptable (S. Rosenberg, personal communication, May 1992).

which identities and attributes were associated with each other. Identities and attributes were considered to be associated if (a) they occurred in the same class or (b) they were in connected classes. As an example of the first case, the HICLAS output in Figure 2 shows that daughter and sister occupy the same class, by virtue of being described by the same set of attributes. The second case of association derives from the hierarchical assumptions of this particular model. One identity class may subsume one or more other classes, or it may be subsumed by a more general, superordinate class. In Figure 2, these circumstances are illustrated by the association of lawyer with the superordinate class (woman) as well as with two subordinate classes (partner and volunteer).

On the basis of these coded associations, we analyzed the order of recall of items in terms of probabilities, similar to our first analysis and that of Trafimow et al. (1991). Rather than considering only whether items were identities or attributes, however, we also considered whether they were associated (matched) or not associated (unmatched) with one another. Thus, a matched at-

TABLE 39.2. Mean Conditional Probabilities of Obtained and Expected Identity–Attribute Pairings

| | Type of item pairing | | | | | |
| | Obtained | | Expected | | | |
Probability	M	SD	M	SD	F(1.25)	p
p(MA|A)	.63	.28	.56	.29	6.58	.02
p(MI|I)	.54	.40	.44	.23	3.11	.09
p(MI|A) and p(MA|I)	.59	.26	.55	.25	1.18	.29

Note. M = matched: A = attribute: I = identity.

tribute–identity (MA | I) pairing is one in which an attribute follows an identity with which it is associated, that is, contained within the same class or related superordinate or subordinate class. An unmatched attribute–identity (UA | I) pairing is one in which an attribute follows an identity with which it is not associated. In all, we coded for three types of sequences: matched attribute-attribute pairings (MA | A), matched identity–identity pairings (MI | I), and matched attribute-identity or identity–attribute pairings (MA | I or MI | A). Obtained mean probabilities for each of these paired sequences are shown in the second column from the left in Table 2.

To determine whether these obtained probabilities were greater or less than what would be predicted by chance alone, we computed base rates of association from each participant's HICLAS solution. We accomplished this by calculating the proportion of all possible identity–identity, attribute–attribute, and attribute–identity (identity–attribute) pairings that would have been coded as matched had they been paired sequentially in recall. The mean probabilities for each of the paired sequences expected on the basis of chance alone are shown in the third column from the left in Table 2.

When one compares the probabilities obtained from respondents' recall lists with those expected on the basis of HICLAS alone it becomes apparent that association, in addition to type of self-cognition (identity or attribute), plays a role in the storage of self-relevant information. Respondents recalled matched attribute–attribute pairings at levels well above the base rate, $F(1,25) = 6.58$, $p = .02$. Similarly, when two identities were recalled together, they tended to be matched at a rate greater than that predicted by chance, $F(1,25) = 3.11$, $p = .09$. Finally, although matched attribute–identity

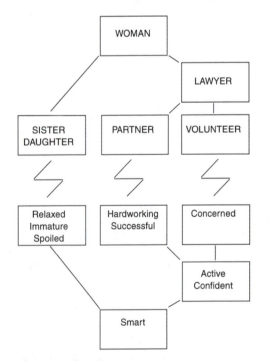

FIGURE 39.2 ■ A hypothetical hierarchical classes analysis output. Identities appear in uppercase letters; attributes appear in upper and lowercase letters.

and identity–attribute pairings were not significantly more likely than would be predicted by chance alone, the means were in a direction consistent with the integration model.

Discussion

A segregation model of self-representation, such as that offered by Trafimow et al. (1991), posits that social identities and personal attributes are represented separately in memory. According to this model, the social identities that an individual has are linked together, and attention to or recall of one of these collective representations will facilitate thought and recall of other social identities. Stored separately are personal attributes, which also are linked among themselves in thought and memory. Although Trafimow et al. (1991) speculated that further subdivisions could occur within each of these two self-structures—for example, there could be subsets of personal attributes such as musical-related traits—they were clear in their position that "the distinction between private and collective self-cognitions is both meaningful and important" (p. 653).

Although we do not deny the conceptual distinction between social identities and personal attributes, we suggest that an integration model, in which identities and attributes are inextricably linked to one another, offers a better way to conceptualize the organization of self-structure. From this perspective, attributes serve to give meaning to the social categories to which people belong. In claiming a social identity, people use attributes, traits, and behaviors to say what the category is and what it means to be a member of the category. Thus the integration model suggests that self-structure consists of a set of identity clusters, each of which may contain one or more identities and attributes. Although more elaborate in its analysis of cognitive structure than earlier models of multiplicity, the integration model certainly shares assumptions with early discussions by James (1890/1950) and Mead (1934/1962), as well as with more recent versions of role theory and identity theory (Stryker & Statham, 1985).

The two positions are not totally incompatible. Attribute–attribute linkages are expected in both models, for example, but the extent and specification of these linkages differ in the two models. Whereas the segregation model predicts that all attributes will be linked and distinguished from all identities, the integration model predicts with more specificity which attributes and which identities might be linked. In addition, the integration model is unique in predicting specifiable links between identities and attributes. Given some areas of overlap, it is perhaps not surprising that the data reported here provide some support for both positions. Although we replicated the results of Trafimow et al. (1991), the overall pattern of results provides stronger support for an integration model of self-representation.

In the first analysis of conditional probabilities, we found, as did Trafimow et al. (1991), that attributes are more likely to be linked to other attributes and identities to other identities. Yet these patterns, though statistically different from a chance distribution, are also at a considerable distance from a perfect fit to a two-basket model. Such a disparity suggests that an alternative representation is needed, in which the linkages predicted by the segregation model are only part of a more complicated story and in fact may be the by-product of different organizational strategies.

Additional analyses provided support for this alternative position. In the first test, we considered the overall pattern of clusters in recall and tested a two-basket model against our hypothesized multiple-basket model. Because the predictions of the two models partially overlap, as noted above, it is not surprising to find that the clustering analysis provides some support for both strategies. However, the results were stronger for the more differentiated integration model, in which clusters are idiosyncratic combinations of identities and attributes.

This supportive pattern of results occurs even though the analysis of clusters does not take into account all of the premises of the integration model. Specifically, the integration model assumes that identities can be conceptually linked to other identities as well as to attributes. In the clustering analysis, attributes could be linked only to a single identity, reflecting the initial statements of the respondent.

The second test of the model, in which HICLAS techniques are used, makes possible a more sensitive definition of the individual self-structures, permitting one to chart the overlap between some identities and attributes in a single cluster. In this case, the predictions are unique to the integration model. The support of these predictions, in contrast to a null hypothesis derived from the segregation model, further argues for the more complex representation suggested by the integration model.

An integration model does not deny the utility of distinguishing personal attributes from social identity in operational terms; rather, it stresses the need to consider the ways in which these two aspects of the self interrelate. The distinction between social and personal identity is common within the theoretical tradition of social identity and self-categorization (Hogg & Abrams, 1988; Turner et al., 1987). However, although this distinction is sometimes described in terms of a difference in the content of self-description, it more appropriately characterizes a difference in emphasis or focus: on the one hand consideration of the ways in which one is different from other people, and on the other hand an emphasis on the commonality of collective membership (Deaux, 1996). Turner et al. (1994) specifically made the point that it is not particular attributes that distinguish personal from social identity, but rather the kind of comparison that is being made with that dimension. Personal attributes can be used either to describe how one is similar to others in a social category or to highlight one's unique characteristics. Thus, it is important to distinguish between structure and process when using these common terms.

Although we argue that personal attributes provide meaning to social categories, we do not claim that clusters of attributes cannot exist apart from any social category. Indeed, the HICLAS analysis that we used allows for groups of attributes that have no one-to-one correspondence to a social category. Certain personality traits may also occupy a superordinate position, essentially characterizing all social identity categories and hence not serving to differentiate among them. A characteristic such as honesty, for example, might be the kind of trait that would inform all aspects of self-relevant behavior. (Even here, however, one can think of counterexamples, such as one in which honesty might be linked to a religious identity but not included in a work identity.)

It also is possible to consider social identities that are not given meaning by personal attributes. When one first claims a group membership, for example, a lack of experience may mean that for some period of time the social identity exists without much personal meaning. Available social representations might help define the category in some general terms, but these characteristics might not immediately be incorporated into the self-structure.

Just how attributes and social identities come to be linked together is an important issue for research. The relative weight that cultural representations have in defining a social identity, versus the impact of individual experience, is a question worth pursuing. So, too, are issues of change in self-representation: How fluid are the attribute–identity linkages over time? Questions of self-structure are often framed in static terms, but such structures are surely subject to modification as a function of choice or circumstance.

Many other issues related to self-structure remain to be pursued. In considering the overlap between various identities, for example, one might question whether certain types of social identity are more likely than others to share attributes. An analysis of identity clusters by Deaux, Reid, Mizrahi, and Ethier (1995) suggests several different types of social identity, characterized by different psychological dimensions and including distinct exemplars. Perhaps identities that are part of the same cluster are more likely to overlap in self-structure, depending on similar kinds of meanings and attributes to characterize them. If so, approaches to diagnosing self-structure that are more nomothetic than the ones presented here might be possible.

At the same time, the methods we used here focus on individual patterns of association and offer important tools for the analysis of self-structure which is, as most theorists assume, idiosyncratic in its development and form. Only with such an approach is it possible to reveal the kinds of associations that an integration model proposes and to explore the critical questions of meaning that a segregation model cannot address.

ACKNOWLEDGMENTS

This research was supported by Grant BNS-9110130 from the National Science Foundation.

We thank Michael Gara, Seymour Rosenberg, and members of the Identity Research Seminar at the City University of New York Graduate Center for their helpful comments on an earlier version of this article. Some of the findings reported here were presented at the 101st Annual Convention of the American Psychological Association in Toronto, Ontario, Canada, in August 1993.

REFERENCES

Breakwell, G. M. (1986). *Coping with threatened identities*. London: Methuen.

Breakwell, G. M. (1993). Integrating paradigms, methodological implications. In G. M. Breakwell & D. V. Canter (Eds.), *Empirical approaches to social representations* (pp. 180–201). Oxford, England: Clarendon Press.

Deaux, K. (1991). Social identities: Thoughts on structure and change. In R. C. Curtis (Ed.), *The relational self: Theoretical convergences in psychoanalysis and social psychology* (pp. 77–93). New York: Guilford Press.

Deaux, K. (1992). Personalizing identity and socializing self. In G. Breakwell (Ed.), *Social psychology of identity and the self-concept* (pp. 9–33). London: Academic Press.

Deaux, K. (1993). Reconstructing social identity. *Personality and Social Psychology Bulletin, 19,* 4–12.

Deaux, K. (1996). Social identification. In E. T. Higgins & A. Kruglanski (Eds.), *Social psychology: Handbook of basic mechanisms and processes* (pp. 777–798). New York: Guilford Press.

Deaux, K., Reid, A., Mizrahi, K., & Ethier, K. A. (1995). Parameters of social identity. *Journal of Personality and Social Psychology, 68,* 280–291.

DeBoeck. P., & Rosenberg, S. (1988). Hierarchical classes: Model and data analysis. *Psychometrika, 53,* 361–368.

Ethier, K. A., & Deaux, K. (1994). Negotiating social identity in a changing context: Maintaining identification and responding to threat. *Journal of Personality and Social Psychology, 67,* 243–251.

Greenwald, A. G., & Pratkanis, A. R. (1984). The self. In R. S. Wyer & T. K. Srull (Eds.), *Handbook of social cognition* (Vol. 3. pp. 129–178). Hillsdale, NJ: Erlbaum.

Higgins, E. T. (1987). Self-discrepancy theory: A theory relating self and affect. *Psychological Review, 94,* 319–340.

Hogg, M. A., & Abrams, D. (1988). *Social identifications*. New York: Routledge & Kegan Paul.

James W. (1950). *The principles of psychology*, New York: Dover. (Original work published 1890)

Kihlstrom, J. F., & Cantor, N. (1984). Mental representations of the self. In L. Berkowitz (Ed.), *Advances in experimental social psychology* (Vol. 17, pp. 1–47). New York: Academic Press.

Kuhn, M. H., & McPartland, T. S. (1954). An empirical investigation of self-attitudes. *American Sociological Review, 19,* 68–76.

Linville, P. W., & Carlston, D. E. (1994). Social cognition of the self. In P. G. Devine, D. L. Hamilton, & T. M. Ostrom (Eds.), *Social cognition: Its impact on social psychology* (pp. 143–193). New York: Academic Press.

Luhtanen, R., & Crocker, J. (1992). A collective self-esteem scale: Self-evaluation of one's social identity. *Personality and Social Psychology Bulletin, 18,* 302–318.

Markus, H. (1977). Self-schemata and processing information about the self. *Journal of Personality and Social Psychology, 35,* 63–78.

Markus, H., & Nurius, P. (1986). Possible selves. *American Psychologist, 41,* 954–969.

McCall, G. J., & Simmons, J. L. (1978). *Identities and interactions* (rev. ed.), New York: Free Press.

Mead, G. H. (1962). *Mind, self, and society*. Chicago: University of Chicago Press. (Original work published 1934)

Moscovici, S. (1981). On social representations. In J. P. Forgas (Ed.), *Social cognition* (pp. 181–209). New York: Academic Press.

Roenker, D. L., Thompson, C. P., & Brown, S. C. (1971). Comparison of measures for the estimation of clustering in free recall, *Psychological Bulletin, 76,* 45–48.

Rosenberg, S., & Gara, M. A. (1985). The multiplicity of personal identity. *Review of Personality and Social Psychology, 6,* 87–113.

Stryker, S. (1980). *Symbolic interactionism*. Menlo Park, CA: Benjamin/Cummings.

Stryker, S., & Statham, A. (1985): Symbolic interaction and role theory. In G. Lindzey & E. Aronson (Eds.), *Handbook of social psychology* (3rd ed., Vol. 1, pp. 311–378). New York: Random House.

Tajfel, H. (1981). *Human groups and social categories: Studies in social psychology*. Cambridge, England: Cambridge University Press.

Trafimow, D., Triandis, H. C., & Goto, S. G. (1991). Some tests of the distinction between private self and collective self. *Journal of Personality and Social Psychology, 60,* 649–655.

Triandis, H. C. (1989). The self and social behavior in differing cultural contexts. *Psychological Review, 96,* 506–520.

Turner, J. C., Hogg, M. A., Oakes, P. J., Reicher, S. D., & Wetherell, M. S. (1987). *Rediscovering the social group: A self-categorization theory*. Oxford, England: Basil Blackwell.

Turner, J. C., Oakes, P. J., Haslam, S. A., & McGarty, C. (1994). Self and collective: Cognition and social context. *Personality and Social Psychology Bulletin, 20,* 454–463.

The Perpetuation of an Arbitrary Tradition through Several Generations of a Laboratory Microculture

Robert C. Jacobs • University of Colorado Medical School
Donald T. Campbell • Northwestern University

Editors' Notes

The present selection is notable for both theoretical and methodological reasons. It compellingly demonstrates how a social phenomenon as complicated as the perpetuation of norms through several generations of group membership can be studied in the laboratory. The investigators use a clever procedure to study this generational phenomena. Specifically, the group interaction is divided into cycles such that after each interactional cycle a veteran member leaves the group and a new one enters it as a replacement. Thus, the group membership changes from a given interactional cycle to the next, and following a number of cycles the group membership is completely different from that which entered the experiment. Since the original publication of the Jacobs and Campbell paper the generational design has been used many times in research designed to investigate the determinants of norm stability in a group. Sophisticated statistical techniques for analyzing data (on individual and aggregate levels) obtained in such generational designs have been recently devised by the methodologist David Kenny. (See Kenny and Kashi's, 1999 article in the *Handbook of Social Psychology* Fiske and Gilbert [Eds.]).

Discussion Questions

1. How was an extreme cultural norm established in the present study?
2. How did the investigators use the autokinetic effect to study the perpetuation of group norms?

3. What was the major dimension of experimental variation in the present study? What did it represent theoretically?

4. How would you summarize the major findings of the study? What do they teach us about the permanence of group norms? Can you think of other experiments that would benefit from Jacobs and Campbell's generational design?

Suggested Readings

Asch, S. E. (1951). Effects of group pressure upon the modification and distortion of judgments. In H. Guetzkow (Ed.), *Groups, leadership, and men* (pp. 177–190). Pittsburgh: Carnegie Press.

Hardin, C., & Higgins, E. T. (1996). Shared reality: How social verification makes the subjective objective. In R. M. Sorrentino & E. T. Higgins (Eds.), *Handbook of motivation and cognition, Volume 3: The interpersonal context* (pp. 28–84). New York: Guilford Press.

Kahneman, D., & Miller, D. T. (1986). Norm theory: Comparing reality to its alternatives. *Psychological Review, 93,* 136–153.

Sherif, M. (1935). A study of some social factors in perception. *Archives of Psychology*, No. 187.

Since Sherif's (1936) classic studies on the formation of "social norms" in laboratory groups, there have been sporadic efforts to bring the process of cultural transmission into the laboratory. While much small group research might be so interpreted, the present study was in particular inspired by Sherif's studies, by Rose and Felton's (1955) "experimental histories of culture," and by the preliminary report of experiments on the evolution of "microcultures" by Gerard, Kluckhohn, and Rapoport (1956). In the latter two studies and in the present one, there is an effort to demonstrate a perpetuation of "cultural" characteristics that transcends the replacement of individual persons. In the present study confederates have been employed to establish an extreme cultural norm, the inculcation and survival of which is then studied as the confederates are one by one taken out of the group, naive new members gradually introduced, who then unwittingly become the further transmitters of the belief to still newer entrants.

The specific culture trait and the ecology of the group relative to such traits should obviously affect the success in the indoctrination of each new generation, and the rate of erosion of the tradition by innovation. In the Rose and Felton (1955) study, group interpretations of Rorschach cards were employed, a material offering considerable latitude for cultural arbitrariness and idiosyncrasy. In the Gerard, Kluckhohn, and Rapoport (1956) study, the groups were continually faced with new instances of a very difficult puzzle series, and were continually confronted with evidences of the lack of perfection of their traditional solutions, a situation encouraging the evolutions of more adaptive norms, and unfavorable to the perpetuation of pure superstition. For the present study, a task was sought which would allow as much latitude for cultural arbitrariness as the Rose and Felton situation, and which would, in addition, make possible the ready quantification of effects. The original Sherif (1936) autokinetic movement situation was judged to provide this; if a person views a pinpoint of light in an otherwise totally blacked-out room, the light soon appears to move. The illusion is a strong one for most persons, and is apparent even to those who know the light to be stationary. As Sherif has shown, naive respondents are very suggestible as to the degree of movement seen, and laboratory group norms on the amount of movement are rapidly established without the respondents being aware of the fictitiousness of their judgments.

So labile is the autokinetic experience or at least the translation of it into judgments of linear extent, that one reading the reports of studies employing it might expect that an arbitrary group norm once established would be passed on indefinitely without diminution; that once well indoctrinated, the naive group members would become as rigid and reliable spokesmen for the norm as were the confederates who preceded them; that each new generation would unwittingly become a part of a self-perpetuating cultural conspiracy propagating superstition and falsehood.

But the autokinetic experience is not completely labile. The very fact that sophisticated observers under strong "suggestion" to see the light remain fixed still perceive movement, shows this. Haggard and Rose (1944), in attempting to condition perceived movement on a right-left dimension, found for most respondents a strong rightward bias. In preliminaries to the present experiment, we learned that for our setting, respondents reporting alone produced mean individual judgments over 30 trials of from .64 to 6.67 inches, and with individual judgments rarely if ever approaching the arbitrary cultural norm of 15 to 16 inches which the confederates in our study provide. It is the presence of this potential natural norm that makes our inculcated cultural norm truly "arbitrary," and provides a counterpressure to the cultural tradition in its transmission across the experimental generations.

Method

Respondents

The 175 respondents who took part in this experiment were students, enrolled in introductory social sciences courses. They were unsophisticated concerning the autokinetic phenomenon and were unadvised as to the nature of the experiment previous to the time of serving in it. The respondents were assigned randomly to the six conditions involved. The number of respondents participating per group is shown in Table 1.

Materials, Apparatus, and Common Procedure

The experiment took place in a completely darkened, windowless, fan-ventilated room. The respondents were seated in a row 8 feet from a box designed to emit a small pinpoint of light. A 1 rpm induction motor was attached in series with the lamp, and a single switch controlled both. The motor was used solely as an auditory effect supporting the illusion of movement.

All respondents were blindfolded when brought into the experimental situation and were asked to put their blindfolds on whenever the door was opened to allow old respondents to leave and new ones to enter. This gave the respondents little if any knowledge of the size and arrangement of the experimental room. The individual respondents received the following instructions:

> This is a movement experiment. It is designed to test the students' visual perceptions with respect to space. In the next room is an apparatus that will project a small light. A few seconds after we begin, the light will move. It may move in a wavy motion or pattern or it may follow a recognizable course. However, your specific task will pertain merely to judging the distance that the light moves from the time that it appears until it is turned off. All judgments should be made in inches along a straight line connecting the starting point and the ending point on each trial.

Respondents going into group conditions received these additional instructions:

> You are going to join a student (or number of students) who are already serving in this experiment. . . . You will be seated in the seat on the far left. To simplify recording procedure I will ask you to report your judgments beginning with the person on the far right and ending with you on the far left. When I stop you the person on the far right will leave, each of you inside will move right one seat, and a new person will be brought in.

Each trial was 5 seconds in length and after each block of 30 trials a ventilation fan was turned on by the experimenter. During this time in the group conditions, the "oldest" member of the group was taken out, other members moved to the right one seat, and a new member introduced. In the solitary conditions, respondents were told that ventilation took place as a health requirement. The ventilation period was timed to take approximately the same amount of time that was necessary to give instructions to a new respondent and bring him in in the other conditions.

Experimental Conditions

Table 1 shows the main feature of the six treatment conditions. (These have been given designa-

TABLE 40.1. Experimental Paradigm

Condition	Size of Group	Number of Confederates	Trials per Generation	Number of Generations	Generations per Respondent	Number of Replications	Number of Naive Respondents
C-1-0	1	0	30	–	4	24	24
C-3-0	3	0	30	10	3	3	30
X-2-1	2	1	30	9	2	3	27
X-3-2	3	2	30	10	3	3	30
X-4-3	4	3	30	11	4	3	33
X-3-1	3	1	30	9	3	3	29

tions summarizing the group's construction. C and X stand for control and experimental. The first digit indicates the size of the group, while the second digit indicates the number of confederates present in the first generation.) There are two control conditions. In C-1-0 each respondent judged the movement of the light in solitude for four periods (called generations for the group conditions) of 30 judgments each. In C-3-0 respondents were run in groups of three, replacing one each generation (or 30 trials), for a total of nine generations.

A major dimension of experimental variation was the number of "culture-bearing" confederates with which the first naive respondent found himself placed. In experimental groups X-2-1, X-3-2, and X-4-3, the initial generation consisted of a solitary naive respondent sitting to the left of one, two, or three confederates who gave their judgments before he did, and who had been instructed to give judgments between 15 and 16 inches. The experimental variation in number of confederates was expected to produce cultural traditions of increasing strength. Confederates were recruited from the same subject pool as were the naive respondents. All were pledged to secrecy, with apparent success.

Another mode of manipulating cultural strength was explored by adding X-3-1, a group of two naive respondents led by one confederate. Thus C-3-0, X-3-1, and X-3-2 provide a set of three-person groups of 0, 1, and 2 confederates in the first generation.

The confederates who were present in the starting condition were removed one at a time, after each round of 30 judgments. Thus the groups with more confederates present in the first generation likewise had some stooging present for more generations. The shifting of members one chair to the

right each generation, plus the rule of responding in turn from right to left, insured that on each trial a confederate or the eldest member of the group spoke first.

Each of the groups was replicated three times, while 24 respondents were run in the solitary control condition. The conditions were given in a counterbalanced order insuring that the differences in respondent selection from one part of the term to the other were kept independent of treatments.

Results

Control Treatments

Figure 1 shows the results for the two control conditions. It will be noted that for C-1-0 the mean of the 24 respondents starts at 3.80 and decreases steadily generation by generation to a value of 2.90. This decrease is highly significant statistically, being found in the individual records of 21 of the 24 respondents, for which, by a two-tailed sign test, $p < .0002$.

The three-person group control, C-3-0, shows very comparable mean levels, and likewise a general decline. The effect is not so clearly significant and is beclouded by the mutual influence that the group situation introduces. In the three replications, two groups declined, while one started abnormally low and increased. Comparing Generation 1 with the last generation with three persons present, Number 8, average judgment changes were 3.93–2.90, 6.72–2.03, and 1.72–2.49. Notice that in spite of the idiosyncratic norms of Generation 1, the three replications became more similar as the process of successive replacement went on. Of the 27 respondents present in more than one

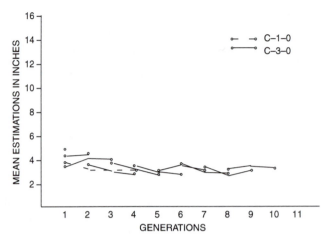

FIGURE 40.1 ■ Mean judgments of the control groups.

generation, 16 showed declines between their first and last generations.

In graphing C-3-0, the data have been averaged in a different fashion from the foregoing. To show the successive replacement and overlapping generational character, the careers of each successive replacement have been plotted separately. The plotted points represent the average of the three replications; that is, each plotted point represents the average judgment of three individual respondents, each taking the corresponding role in the three separate groups replicating this control treatment.

The two types of control established such similar reference standards that they cannot both be used conveniently as visual base lines in the graphing of the result of the experimental treatments.

For this reason, in Figures 2, 3, and 4, only C-1-0 has been plotted. This plotting has been done in such a manner as to provide a parallel for each new starting generation in the experimental group. Thus in Figure 2, where each respondent stays only two generations, the first two generations of data from C-1-0 have been repeatedly plotted. In Figure 4, all four generations of C-1-0 are needed as a comparison base.

Transmission of Arbitrary Norms over Total Replacement of Indoctrinator

Figures 2, 3, 4, and 5 present the transmission results from X-2-1, X-3-2, X-4-3, and X-3-1. The

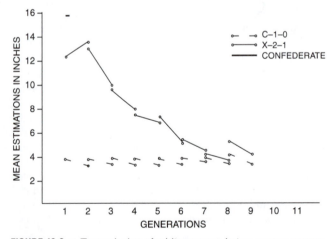

FIGURE 40.2 ■ Transmission of arbitrary norm in two-person groups.

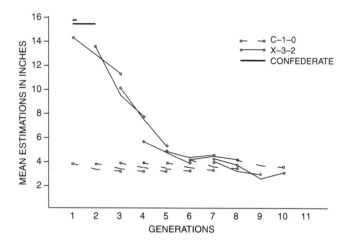

FIGURE 40.3 ■ Transmission of arbitrary norm in three-person groups.

first question that we ask of the data is whether or not the naive respondents, once indoctrinated by the confederates, have themselves transmitted any vestiges of the arbitrary cultural norm once the original indoctrinators have passed on. To test this, one can examine the judgments of the first generation of respondents to judge without any confederates present. For X-2-1, X-3-2, and X-4-3 these values are 12.07, 9.79, and 9.82. Each of these differs significantly ($p < .01$) from the C-1-0 control group by t test, when the mean of the 3 experimental respondents is compared with the mean of the 24 control respondents. For X-3-1, the mean is 5.34, not significantly different from the C-1-0 value of 3.80.

By pooling groups X-2-1, X-3-2, and X-4-3, we can compare to the 24 C-1-0 respondents 9 experimental respondents newly introduced at each of several generations beyond the final confederate. For the first such generation, $M = 10.57$, t = 7.25, $p < .0001$; for the second, $M = 7.80$, t = 3.74, $p < .0001$; for the third, $M = 6.06$, t = 4.02, $p < .0001$; for the fourth, $M = 5.08$, t = 2.04, $p < .03$; for the fifth, $M = 4.37$, t = 1.31, $p < .10$. Thus the arbitrary norm is transmitted in some degree up through the fourth and perhaps the fifth generation beyond the last confederate. By the sixth it has entirely disappeared, the mean of 3.60 being slightly below the control value of 3.80.

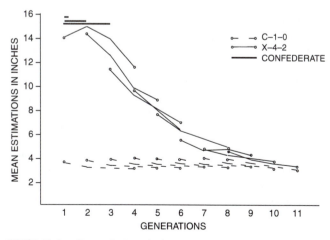

FIGURE 40.4 ■ Transmission of arbitrary norm in four-person groups.

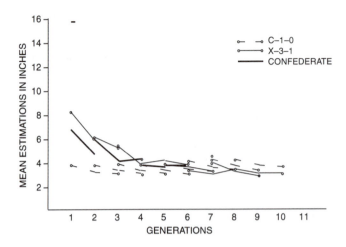

FIGURE 40.5 ■ Transmission of arbitrary norm in three-person group initiated by one confederate and two naive respondents.

Differences in Strength of Induced Traditions

The experimental comparisons were introduced in the expectation that induced cultures of differing strengths and persistence would be produced. In fact, there was some expectation that the strongest conditions might produce an arbitrary culture which would persist without apparent diminution. No condition produced a culture of any such strength, and among the three experimental groups starting with one naive respondent, the number of confederates in the groups had little if any clear-cut effect. In the first generation, with all confederates present, the means for the naive respondents were, for X-2-1, X-3-2, and X-4-3, respectively, 12.23, 14.37, and 14.13; X-2-1 was expected to be lower than the others. The difference between 12.23 and 14.37 is significant ($t = 2.16$, $df = 4$, $p < .05$, one-tailed test). The absence of a difference between X-3-2 and X-4-3 is against our expectation. The literature on this point is confusing. Asch (1951) finds almost no effect from a single confederate, whereas we, in X-2-1, and Goldberg (1954) and Kidd (1958) find strong effects from a single other. Asch finds the effect to increase strikingly when the confederates are increased to 2 and again to 3, whereas 4, 8, and 16 others have little or no greater influence than 3. Goldberg and Kidd find no significant gains between 1 and 3 (that is, between 2- and 4-person groups) in spite of large numbers of cases.

A comparison of the overall strength of the induced cultures is difficult because of the fact that in the larger groups not only are the culture-inducing confederates more numerous, but they are also retained for more generations. Thus it would seem unfair to compare all groups at the fourth generation from the beginning, since X-4-3 would have had a confederate in the immediately preceding generation, while X-2-1 would have been without a confederate for three generations. Perhaps more appropriate is a comparison of strength in the first generation subsequent to the removal of the last confederate. The values are, respectively, 12.09, 9.79, and 9.82. The smallest group, X-2-1, seems strongest at this stage although the differences do not approach significance. But this comparison is not exactly fair, either, because for X-2-1 the confederate, when present, dominated the culture, while for X-4-3 the final confederate had his influence diluted by the vocal presence of two not completely loyal naive respondents. By the fifth postconfederate generation, these three values are 4.69, 3.90, and 4.55. Lacking both striking differences and an optimal comparison, it seems fair to conclude that no differences in effective cultural strength have been achieved by thus manipulating group size.

One manipulation did indeed provide indoctrinations of varying magnitude. The naive respondents of X-3-1 were significantly different from C-1-0 only in the first generation, that is, with the confederate present ($t = 3.88$, $p < .01$). But even at this stage the naive respondents of X-3-1 were significantly less indoctrinated than those of X-3-2 at Generation 2, when it likewise consisted of but one confederate and two naive persons ($t = 4.69$, $p < .001$, 10 df). Thus manipulating the ratio of confederates to naive judges has little effect when achieved through adding more confederates, but has great effect when achieved through manipulating the number of naive respondents. As Asch (1951) has noted, this adding of a "true partner" seems to have an effect disproportionally greater than would be expected from the simple fact of diluting the majority. This dimension has not been systemically explored, however. In the present setting it would be interesting to compare groups of varying size in which the naive-to-confederate ratio was held constant, as through a group consisting of two confederates and two naive respondents, to be compared with X-2-1, etc.

Judgments as a Compromise between Own and Other's Observations

The deterioration of the cultural norm occurs, in part, because each naive respondent makes judgments somewhat lower, somewhat closer to the natural norm, than do the confederates or elder citizens serving as his mentors. Of 36 naive respondents serving for the first time in X-2-1, X-3-2, and X-4-3 during the first four generations (where some significant strength to the cultural norm was still present) 34 made mean judgments lower than the average of their mentors (for which, $p < .0000001$). This clear-cut fact we take as supporting the interpretation that each judgment represents a pooling of the person's own observations (the value for which we infer from the control group) with the reported observations of others. In the resulting compromise the person's own observations are not given much weight, but they are given some.

In the first generation of the experimental groups, the conditions are simple enough so that we can make some estimates of this relative weighting of own observations and other's reports. For the first naive respondent in X-2-1, the other's (confederate's) report averages 15.52. The own observation is inferred from C-1 to be 3.80. If the naive respondent weighted his own observation equally with the report of the confederate, his judgment would fall halfway between these values, at 9.66. Instead, the judgment is 12.23, much closer

to the confederate's. Rather than regarding the confederate as an equally good observer as himself, the respondent has weighted the confederate's opinion 2.6 times as heavily as his own. The formula for the weighting ratio is (12.23-3.80)/ (15.52-12.23). Assuming each confederate to be equally weighted, and solving for the weight given a single confederate's opinion, we get values of 4.6 for X-3-2 and 2.5 for X-4-3. Since these ratios are based upon the performances of but three naive respondents each, they are quite unstable, and are provided here primarily for illustrative purposes. Similar computations for the later generations have been omitted because of the difficulty of taking into account the reciprocal effect of new respondents upon the older naive respondents acting as indoctrinators. The first generation situation is computable just because the confederates were unresponsive to the judgments of their fellows.

Whatever the weighting ratio, as long as some weight is given own observations, and as long as own observations deviate in a consistent direction from the cultural norm, the arbitrary culture is doomed to deterioration eventually, at least in the limited sanction system of this laboratory. While the question has not been stated in this form, the relative respect for own observations over the reports of others is much higher in less ambiguous situations, as Asch (1951) has shown. It is easy to understand how the ambiguities of the autokinetic situation lead to lack of confidence in own opinion, but it is perhaps an indication of human trust that this same ambiguity does not lead to a proportional lack of confidence in the reports of others.

Forgetting and Reciprocal Influence

If the previous factor of compromise weighting were all that was involved, the deterioration in culture as graphed in Figures 2, 3, and 4 might have been of a stair-step fashion, with each new inductee starting lower than his indoctrinator, but once started, holding to his initial level through the several generations of his life in the group. As can be seen from the graphs, this is not the case. Instead, the respondent is less loyal to the old culture the longer he stays in the group. Of the 36 naive respondents introduced in the first four generations of X-2-1, X-3-2, and X-4-3, 31 made lower mean judgment on their last session than on their first (for which, p < .00001).

In the present design, three factors are confounded in generating this effect. While we have not extricated them, it seems well to mention them. The first factor is the autonomous decline noted previously in the control groups. In terms of absolute magnitude, this would seem to account for little of the total effect.

A second factor is forgetting. Were a respondent to judge with the leadership of a culture-bearing confederate, and then to judge in isolation for several sessions, he would in these later sessions be pooling his immediate visual impression of the stimulus with the remembered reports of the other in a previous session. As these memories dimmed, their weighting could be expected to diminish, and the relative weighting of own observation could be expected to increase. No doubt in the present situation forgetting of indoctrination provides some of the decline within the judgment series of a single respondent.

A third possible source of this within-respondents decline in loyalty to the arbitrary culture is the effect of the new group member upon his elders. Since judging was always from eldest to youngest on any given stimulus presentation, this would have to involve an influence carrying over from one turn to the next. We feel sure that some such influence was present, but its demonstration would require a separate experiment placing confederates in the final answering position.

Discussion

In presenting these materials to our colleagues, we have found them most fascinated by the fact of the cultural transmission surviving total replacement of specific individuals, and by the fact of naive respondents becoming unwitting conspirators in perpetuating a cultural fraud. This demonstration was of course our main intent, and this outcome was inevitable if the conformity research upon which we built had any transfer validity. But while these results are highly significant statistically, they fall short of our expectations. The inculcated arbitrary norms turn out to be eroded by innovation at a much more rapid rate than we had expected. We have hardly provided a laboratory paradigm for the examples of tenacious adherence to incredible superstition with which anthropologists and students of comparative religion provide us.

Of course, a relative weakness in strength is to be expected in a laboratory example. Mature individuals are undergoing transient indoctrination by unknown age-mates, as opposed to the natural setting of the teaching of the very young by tribal adults over a period of years. Fewer confederates are involved than in the tribal situation, although the effect of number upon degree of conformity is unclear in the laboratory. More important, there are no sanctions rewarding conformity nor punishing innovation. Furthermore, it is even possible that the subject of judgment in our experiment is less ambiguous than the subject material of religious belief, for example. There is, after all, a fairly clear consensus among our naive solitary observers. In our situation, the spontaneous deviations from orthodoxy were all in the same direction, whereas for many arbitrary items of culture the deviations may lack such concerted direction.

Nonetheless, the outcome may well warn us against the assumption that a purely arbitrary cultural norm could be perpetuated indefinitely without other sources of support. Even if people weigh the opinions of their elders many times that of their own direct observations, the collective effect of their own observations probably soon erodes a *functionless* arbitrary belief. Where we observed tenacious bizarre cultural belief we must look to more than mere tradition, suggestibility, or conformity, to explain its retention. Latent functions (e.g., Merton, 1949) at the personal or societal level must be present to counteract the pressures from continuous spontaneous innovation in a more natural direction. For example, Moore (1957) and Aubert (1959) have recently suggested such latent functions to superstitious magical lotteries used in the selection of hunting and fishing sites. As our understanding of the requisites of individual and social life further increases, we may expect to discover such latent functions for many if not all of those "meaningless" superstitions which stubbornly persist.

Summary

In an autokinetic judgment situation in which solitary judgments of movement averaged 3.8 inches, confederates were used to establish arbitrary "cultural norms" of 15.5 inches. The transmission of this norm was studied as one at a time confederates and old members were removed from the group while new members were added. Significant remnants of the culture persisted for four or five generations beyond the last confederate. Gradually in each of the 12 experimental groups the arbitrary norm decayed and the group judgments drifted away from it back to the natural norm found in the control groups. The size of group had no clear effect upon the endurance of the norm established, although a group beginning with one confederate and two naive respondents was markedly weaker than the others and transmitted no culture beyond one generation.

Major effects are interpreted in terms of a judgment process in which each respondent weighs the reports of others and his own observations, achieving a compromise between them. Even with the respondents giving the reports of others from 2.5 to 4 times the weight of their own observations, slight "innovations" result which rapidly cumulate to erode the original arbitrary cultural norm. Details of the process and analogues to the cultural transmission of bizarre beliefs are discussed.

REFERENCES

Asch, S. E. Effects of group pressure upon the modification and distortion of judgments. In H. Guetzkow (Ed.), *Groups, leadership, and men.* Pittsburgh: Carnegie Press, 1951. Pp. 177–190.

Asch, S. E. *Social psychology.* New York: Prentice-Hall 1952.

Aubert, V. Chance in social affairs. Inquiry, 1959, 2, 1–24.

Gerard, R. W., Kluckhohn, C., & Rapoport, A. Biological and cultural evolution: Some analogies and explorations. *Behav. Sci.,* 1956, 1, 6–34.

Goldberg, S. C. Three situational determinants of conformity to social norms. *J. abnorm. soc. Psychol.,* 1954, 49, 325–329.

Haggard, E. A., & Rose, E. Some effects of mental set and active participation in the conditioning of the autokinetic phenomenon. *J. exp. Psychol.,* 1944, 34, 45–59.

Kidd, J. S. Social influence phenomena in a task-oriented group. *J. abnorm. soc. Psychol.,* 1958, 56, 13–17.

Merton, R. K. *Social theory and social structure.* Glencoe, Ill.: Free Press, 1949.

Moore, O. K. Divination, a new perspective. *Amer. Anthropologist,* 1957, 69, 72.

Rose, E., & Felton, W. Experimental histories of culture. *Amer. social. Rev.,* 1955, 20, 383–392.

Sherie, M. *The psychology of social norms.* New York: Harper, 1936.

Sumner, W. G. *Folkways.* Boston: Ginn, 1906.

Tarde, G. *The laws of imitation.* (Paris ed., 1890) New York: Holt, 1903.

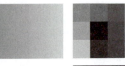

READING 41

Pluralistic Ignorance and Alcohol Use on Campus: Some Consequences of Misperceiving the Social Norm

Deborah A. Prentice and Dale T. Miller • Princeton University

Editors' Note

The present selection explores the phenomenon of "pluralistic ignorance." Individuals can perceive incorrectly a group norm, and consequently believe they deviate from the norm when in fact they do not. This intriguing phenomenon can arise when there is general conformity to a particular behavior (e.g., drinking alcohol) that is at variance with most individuals' attitudes (e.g., against drinking alcohol). Because there is a tendency for an individual to infer others' attitudes from their behaviors, an individual wrongly believes that his or her private attitude differs from those of most others in the group. Prentice and Miller investigate these issues in the context of a highly important social problem of norms and attitudes toward alcohol use at a university campus. The investigators find strong evidence of pluralistic ignorance and track its consequences for students' subsequent attitudes and behaviors, including the students' feelings of identification or disidentification with the campus community at large. Another interesting aspect of this selection is the investigators' systematic and insightful attempt to deal with other possible alternative interpretations of their findings. Overall, this selection is an excellent example of the application of social-psychological theory to an understanding of an important real-world issue.

Discussion Questions

1. What is the theoretical and methodological significance of the use of friends' presumed attitudes in study 2?
2. What is the explanation for the apparent inconsistency between the phenomena of "pluralistic ignorance" on the one hand and the "false consensus effect" on the other hand?
3. What is the authors' explanation for the gender differences in attitudinal shifts over time?
4. What are the alternative possible interpretations of the data identified by the authors in the general discussion section, and how do they rule out these interpretations?

Suggested Readings

Katz, E. (1981). Publicity and pluralistic ignorance: Notes on the "spiral of silence." In H. Baier, H. M. Kepplinger, & D. A. Reumann (Eds.), *Public opinion and social change* (pp. 28–38). Wiesbaden: Westdeutscher Verlag.

Miller, D. T., & Prentice, D. A. (1996). The construction of social norms and standards. In E. T. Higgins & A. W. Kruglanski (Eds.), *Social psychology: Handbook of basic principles* (pp. 799–829). New York: Guilford.

Ross, L., Greene, D., & House, P. (1977). The "false consensus effect": An egocentric bias in the social perception and attribution process. *Journal of Experimental Social Psychology*, *13*, 279–301.

Authors' Abstract

Four studies examined the relation between college students' own attitudes toward alcohol use and their estimates of the attitudes of their peers. All studies found widespread evidence of pluralistic ignorances: Students believed that they were more uncomfortable with campus alcohol practices than was the average student. Study 2 demonstrated this perceived self–other difference also with respect to one's friends. Study 3 tracked attitudes toward drinking over the course of a semester and found gender differences in response to perceived deviance: Male students shifted their attitudes over time in the direction of what they mistakenly believed to be the norm, whereas female students showed no such attitude change. Study 4 found that students' perceived deviance correlated with various measures of campus alienation, even though that deviance was illusory. The implications of these results for general issues of norm estimation and responses to perceived deviance are discussed.

Pluralistic Ignorance

Although the social psychological literature offers little evidence of how people identify social norms, it does provide some striking examples of systematic errors in norm estimation. Many of these examples come from research on pluralistic ignorance. *Pluralistic ignorance* is a psychological state characterized by the belief that one's private attitudes and judgments are differ-

ent from those of others, even though one's public behavior is identical (Miller & McFarland, 1991). It develops most commonly under circumstances in which there is widespread misrepresentation of private views. In these cases, people's tendency to rely on the public behavior of others to identify the norm leads them astray, for the social norm that is communicated misrepresents the prevailing sentiments of the group. If participants understood this state of affairs, the situation would be self-correcting. However, they typically make the mistake of assuming that even though others are acting similarly, they are feeling differently. Their own behavior may be driven by social pressure, but they assume that other people's identical behavior is an accurate reflection of their true feelings.

The research reported in this article was designed to explore these consequences of pluralistic ignorance. In all four studies, we examined pluralistic ignorance in the context of students' attitudes toward alcohol drinking on campus. We chose this particular issue because attitudes toward drinking are currently in a period of transition at Princeton, as the university becomes more sensitive to the negative effects of alcohol use on academic and social life. Many theorists have argued that pluralistic ignorance frequently accompanies such periods of social change, with private attitudes changing more quickly than social norms (see Breed & Ktsanes, 1961; Fields & Schuman, 1976; Miller & McFarland, 1991). Thus, we expected the issue of alcohol use to provide an excellent context for our empirical studies.

Alcohol Use on Campus

Alcohol use by college undergraduates has become a major concern of university administrators and public health officials across the country (Berkowitz & Perkins, 1986; Maddox, 1970; Straus & Bacon, 1953). A recent survey revealed that whereas the use of other recreational drugs has dropped significantly over the past 2 decades, alcohol use has declined more slowly (Barringer, 1991). According to the College Health Association, alcohol is the single greatest risk to the health of university students. One powerful predictor of adolescent alcohol use, and of other forms of substance use, is peer influence (e.g., Graham, Marks, & Hansen, 1991; Kandel, 1980; Perkins, 1985; Stein, Newcomb, & Bentler, 1987). Moreover, the impact of peers appears to increase, rather than decrease, as adolescents mature (Huba & Bentler, 1980; Zucker & Noll, 1982).

The alcohol situation at Princeton is exacerbated by the central role of alcohol in many of the university's institutions and traditions. For example, at the eating clubs, the center of social life on campus, alcohol is on tap 24 hours a day, 7 days a week. Princeton reunions boast the second highest level of alcohol consumption for any event

in the country after the Indianapolis 500 (Clitherow, 1991). The social norms for drinking at the university are clear: Students must be comfortable with alcohol use to partake of Princeton social life.

In the face of these strong norms promoting alcohol use, we suspected that students' private attitudes would reveal substantial misgivings about drinking. Within their first few months at college, students are exposed to vivid and irrefutable evidence of the negative consequences of excessive alcohol consumption: They nurse sick roommates, overlook inappropriate behavior and memory losses, and hear about serious injuries and even deaths that result from drinking. They may have negative experiences with alcohol themselves and may notice its effects on their academic performance. This accumulating evidence of the ill effects of alcohol is likely to affect their private attitudes but not the social norm: Indeed, believing that others are still comfortable with alcohol, students will perpetuate that norm by continuing to adopt a nonchalant demeanor that masks their growing concerns. If this analysis is, in fact, correct, we should find clear evidence of pluralistic ignorance regarding students' comfort with alcohol use on campus.

The present studies sought to document the existence of pluralistic ignorance regarding alcohol use and to investigate some of its consequences for individuals' attitudes and behavior. Study 1 was designed to demonstrate pluralistic ignorance by showing a divergence between private attitudes and the social norm as well as a belief in the universality of that norm. Study 2 extended this effect by showing a similar divergence between private attitudes and perceptions of the attitudes of one's friends. Study 3 explored the extent to which individuals respond to pluralistic ignorance by internalizing the social norm over time. Study 4 examined the behavioral manifestations of alienation produced by feeling deviant from the norm. The first three studies focused on comfort with alcohol use; the fourth study examined attitudes toward the university's policy banning beer kegs on campus.

Study 1

In our first study, we tested the assumption that students' attitudes toward alcohol drinking on campus are characterized by a divergence between private attitudes and perceptions of the social norm. We also examined the extent to which social norms are imbued with an illusion of universality by asking subjects to estimate the variability, as well as the central tendency, of other students' attitudes.

Method

Subjects. Subjects were 132 undergraduates, who voluntarily attended a mass testing session in which they participated in this and other short studies for pay. The sample included 69 women and 63 men, with approximately even distribution of women and men across the 1st- through 4th-year classes.[1]

Procedure. Subjects responded to a brief, one-page questionnaire that was included in a large booklet. The questionnaire was preceded by a page of instructions on how to use the response scales. The first question asked the following:

1. How comfortable do you feel with the alcohol drinking habits of students at Princeton?

Subjects indicated their own comfort by circling a number on the corresponding 11-point scale (1 = *not at all comfortable* and 11 = *very comfortable*). Then they were asked to estimate the comfort of other students:

2. How comfortable does the average Princeton undergraduate feel with the alcohol drinking habits of students at Princeton? (Please circle the average student's response and then bracket the two values between which the attitudes of 50% of students fall.)

Again, subjects indicated the average student's comfort by circling a number on the corresponding 11-point scale and then bracketed the two numbers on the same scale within which they believed the attitudes of 50% of students fall.

Results and Discussion

We expected that students would vary in their own comfort with alcohol drinking on campus but that they would believe other students to be uniformly more comfortable than they are. Means and standard deviations for the two comfort questions are presented in Table 1. Subjects' ratings indicated a sharp divergence between their own comfort and

TABLE 41.1. Ratings of Own and Average Student's Comfort With Alcohol Drinking in Study 1

Measure	Self	Average student
Women		
M	4.68	7.07
SD	2.69	1.68
Men		
M	6.03	7.00
SD	2.76	1.57
Total		
M	5.33	7.04
SD	2.73	1.63

Note. All ratings were made on 11-point scales (1 = *not at all comfortable* and 11 = *very comfortable*).

their subjective estimates of the comfort of others. A 2 (sex) × 2 (target) analysis of variance (ANOVA) revealed a highly significant main effect of target, $F(1, 130) = 55.52, p < .0001$: Respondents were much less comfortable with the alcohol drinking habits of Princeton undergraduates than they believed the average student to be. This main effect of target was qualified by a significant Sex × Target interaction, $F(1, 130) = 9.96, p < .005$, indicating that the gap between ratings of own and others' comfort was substantially larger for women than for men. Nevertheless, the self–other difference was significant for both male, $F(1, 62) = 10.35, p < .005$, and female subjects, $F(1, 68) = 51.95, p < .0001$.

A closer analysis of the distributions of comfort ratings indicated that students' perceptions of the attitudes of others converged on a highly consistent norm. Although their own comfort ratings spanned the entire 11-point scale in a relatively uniform distribution, their estimates of the average student's comfort assumed an almost perfectly normal distribution, with high agreement on an average of approximately 7. A statistical compari-

[1]The data for Studies 1, 2, and 4 were collected at Questionnaire Day sessions, which are organized by the psychology department each semester. These sessions are advertised in the student newspaper with notices posted around campus and are also announced in the large introductory-level psychology courses. Students come to a large lecture hall anytime during the afternoon or evening, fill out a questionnaire booklet anonymously, and receive $6 for their participation. To ensure that participants feel completely anonymous, we collect demographic information regarding only their sex and class. Although the samples are self-selected, they typically represent a cross-section of the undergraduate population in terms of these demographic characteristics.

son of the variances of the two distributions revealed a highly significant difference, $F(131, 131) = 2.99, p < .0001$.

In addition, subjects' estimates of the variability of others' attitudes provided strong evidence for the illusion of universality. The median estimate of the range within which the attitudes of 50% of students fell (i.e., the interquartile range) was 4, with a lower bound of 5 and an upper bound of 9. (We use medians here to facilitate comparison with the actual distribution. The means are very close to the medians in all cases.) Thus, students' subjective distributions of attitudes toward drinking on campus had a mean of approximately 7, with an interquartile range from 5 to 9. By contrast, the actual distribution of attitudes, as reflected by subjects' own comfort ratings, had a mean of 5.33, with an interquartile range from 3 to 8. These distributions demonstrate the two defining features of pluralistic ignorance: A divergence of subjective from actual norms and an illusion of universality.

Study 2

The results of Study 1 provided strong support for our expectation that students' attitudes toward campus alcohol practices would be characterized by pluralistic ignorance. However, two methodological features of the study allowed for alternative interpretations of the results. First, our question about the social norm asked students to rate the comfort of the average Princeton undergraduate with alcohol drinking on campus. Although we believed that ratings of the average student would provide a good indication of the perceived norm, it is also possible that the category "average student" lacked psychological reality for our subjects. Second, we asked the two comfort questions in a fixed order, with the question about the self always preceding the question about the average student. It is possible that subjects rated the average student as more comfortable simply because they made that rating second.

To preclude these alternative explanations for the findings of Study 1, we conducted a second study, in which we manipulated the order of the self and other questions and included an additional question that assessed the comfort of the respondent's friends with alcohol drinking on campus. Unlike ratings of the average student, ratings

of friends were certain to be made with a group of real people in mind.

Method

Subjects. Subjects were 242 undergraduates, who voluntarily attended a mass testing session in which they filled out this and other questionnaires for pay. The sample included 145 women and 97 men, with an approximately even distribution of women and men across the 1st- through 4th-year classes.

Procedure. Subjects answered the two questions asked in Study 1 (minus the variability estimates) and a third question that asked them to rate how comfortable their friends feel with the alcohol drinking habits of students at Princeton. Half of the subjects (77 women and 44 men) rated themselves first and the average student second; the other half (68 women and 53 men) rated the average student first and themselves second.

Results and Discussion

Means and standard deviations for the three comfort questions are shown in Table 2. A 2 (sex) × 3

TABLE 41.2. Ratings of Own and Others' Comfort With Alcohol Drinking in Study 2

Measure	Self	Friend	Average student
Self-question first			
Women			
M	5.84	6.49	6.96
SD	2.69	2.42	1.41
Men			
M	6.02	6.82	7.11
SD	2.66	2.12	1.20
Total			
M	5.91	6.61	7.01
SD	2.68	2.32	1.34
Other-question first			
Women			
M	5.06	6.13	7.16
SD	2.47	2.34	1.72
Men			
M	5.87	6.94	7.47
SD	2.54	2.12	1.37
Total			
M	5.41	6.49	7.30
SD	2.50	2.24	1.57

Note. All ratings were made on 11-point scales (1 = *not at all comfortable* and 11 = *very comfortable*).

(target) × 2 (question order) ANOVA revealed a highly significant effect of target, $F(2, 476) = 54.52, p < .0001$. Pairwise comparisons of the three means indicated that ratings of own comfort were significantly lower than ratings of friends' comfort or of the average student's comfort (using Tukey tests, with $p < .05$). The main effect of target was qualified by a significant Target × Order interaction, $F(2, 476) = 3.45, p < .05$, indicating that the differences between comfort ratings for the three targets were greater when the question about the average student came first. However, separate pairwise comparisons within each form of the questionnaire showed that ratings of own comfort were significantly lower than ratings of the other two targets for both question orders. Friends' comfort was rated as intermediate between own comfort and the average student's comfort in all cases, but the difference between ratings of friends and of the average student was significant only when the average student question came first (for all reported differences, $p < .05$).

Students' perceptions of the comfort of the average student again converged on a highly consistent norm. Ratings of the average student were significantly less variable than ratings of the self, $F(241, 241) = 3.14, p < .0001$, and of friends, $F(241, 241) = 2.46, p < .0001$. Not surprisingly, ratings of friends' comfort showed considerable variability across subjects, although still not quite as much variability as self-ratings.

These results, especially concerning perceptions of friends, raise some interesting questions about the relation between local (friend) and global (campus) norms and about the role of these norms in producing pluralistic ignorance. In the case of alcohol use on campus, both types of norms are on the side of greater comfort with alcohol than students privately feel, and thus it is difficult to disentangle them. In theory, however, local and global norms may be quite distinct and may contribute independently to producing the perceived self–other differences. Misestimation of the local norm may occur because, as in the bystander and classroom cases, students base their estimates on observations of their friends' public behavior and erroneously assume that that behavior is diagnostic of their private attitudes. Misestimation of the global norm may be driven, in part, by a similar process but may also be influenced by the collective representation of Princeton as a drinking campus and by the importance of a liberal position on alcohol to the college student identity. We return to a consideration of the mechanisms underlying pluralistic ignorance in the general discussion.

In summary, the results of Studies 1 and 2 confirmed our intuition that students' comfort with alcohol use on campus would manifest the classic characteristics of pluralistic ignorance. Although the subjects in these studies were volunteers and thus may not have been representative of the student body (a weakness we remedy in the next study), we believe that the phenomenon demonstrated here is quite general: Undergraduates believe that everybody is more comfortable with drinking than they are themselves (see also Perkins & Berkowitz, 1986). The situation of drinking on campus shares much in common with the classic examples of pluralistic ignorance cited in the introduction. In all cases, individuals assume that others' outward display of comfort and ease reflects their actual feelings, even though those individuals' own identical behavior is somewhat at odds with their internal states.

Study 3

Armed with evidence for the validity of our assumptions about the alcohol issue, we designed the next two studies to explore some of the consequences of pluralistic ignorance. Study 3 addressed the question of how individuals respond to pluralistic ignorance over time. One prediction is that when individuals perceive their attitudes to be different from the normative attitudes of their social group, they will gradually change their attitudes in the direction of the group norm, either because they are persuaded by the group's position or because they internalize the sentiments that they originally expressed inauthentically. This conformity prediction has considerable precedent in the social influence literature, which has always placed a heavy emphasis on conformity as a means of resolving self–group discrepancies (see Moscovici, 1985). However, in the case of alcohol use on campus, the presence of irrefutable evidence of the ill effects of excessive drinking might make it very difficult for students to decide that they are, in fact, comfortable with the drinking norms. If students are unable to internalize the (perceived) normative position, we should observe no reduction in pluralistic ignorance over time.

To examine the extent to which students would change their attitudes to reduce pluralistic ignorance, we surveyed a random sample of college sophomores at two time points: Initially, in September, when they had just returned from summer vacation and had had little recent exposure to college drinking norms, and then again in December, after they had spent several months as active members of the college community. We assumed that 8 to 9 weeks between interviews would be sufficient to observe internalization effects, if such effects existed. In addition, we asked two questions to assess their recent and typical levels of alcohol consumption. Although we expected no mass changes in drinking habits over the course of the semester we were interested in the relation of drinking behavior to both private attitudes and estimates of the norm. These behavioral questions were included in both interviews.

We tested for internalization effects in two ways. Our first expectation was that students would increasingly adopt the normative position toward alcohol use on campus over the course of the semester. Thus, we predicted that their private attitudes would show a change in the direction of greater comfort over time. Our second expectation was that internalization would result in greater consistency among private attitudes, estimates of the norm, and drinking behavior. Thus, we predicted that the correlations among these variables would increase over time.

Method

Subjects. Fifty 2nd-year undergraduates (25 women and 25 men) participated in this study. We chose 2nd-year students because we assumed that they would be familiar with student culture and, in particular, with norms for drinking but that they would still be new enough at the university to be concerned about fitting in. Subjects were selected at random from the student telephone directory and were each interviewed twice over the telephone.

Procedure. Subjects were contacted for the first interview during the 2nd or 3rd week of the fall term. They were asked to participate in a telephone survey of students' attitudes toward the university's alcohol policies. The interviewer explained that their telephone numbers had been chosen at random from the telephone directory and that their responses would be completely anonymous. Over 90% of the students contacted agreed to participate.

The interview began with several questions about the university's alcohol policies that are irrelevant to the present investigation. The critical questions regarding their own attitudes toward drinking and their estimates of the average student's attitude were as follows:

1. Now, I'd like to know how you feel about drinking at Princeton more generally. How comfortable do you feel with the alcohol drinking habits of students here? I'd like you to use a 0-to-10 scale, where 0 means you're not at all comfortable and 10 means you're very comfortable.
2. How comfortable would you say the average Princeton undergraduate feels with the alcohol drinking habits of students here at Princeton, where 0 means not at all comfortable and 10 means very comfortable?

Subjects responded to each question by giving the interviewer a number from 0 to 10. Finally, subjects were asked about their own drinking habits. After reassuring them of their anonymity, the interviewer asked two open-ended questions.

3. How many alcoholic drinks have you had in the last week?
4. How many alcoholic drinks do you have in a typical week during the semester?

Subjects estimated their weekly alcohol intake. At the conclusion of the interview, subjects were informed that we would be calling back later in the term to find out whether people's attitudes had changed over time. The interviewer explained that "When we do [call back], we would like to talk to you again, so if you could let your roommates know that you're the survey person, we'd really appreciate it."

Approximately 8 weeks after the first interview, subjects were recontacted for the second interview. All 50 students again agreed to participate. They were asked the same questions as in the first survey, including the questions about their own comfort with drinking, the average student's comfort with drinking, and their recent and typical alcohol intake.

Results

Attitudes and norms. The social psychological literature contains many compelling demonstrations

TABLE 41.3. Ratings of Own and Others' Comfort With Alcohol Drinking in Study 3

Group	September		December	
	Self	Average student	Self	Average student
Women				
M	6.08	7.16	5.94	7.74
SD	2.47	1.55	3.10	1.20
Men				
M	5.84	7.48	7.08	7.58
SD	3.01	1.45	2.70	1.27
Total				
M	5.96	7.32	6.51	7.66
SD	2.75	1.50	2.91	1.24

Note. All ratings were made on 11-point scales (0 = *not at all comfortable* and 10 = *very comfortable*). We added 1 point to each observation to make the scale comparable with the scale used in Studies 1 and 2.

of the power of social influence to move individual attitudes in the direction of the social norm. We tested the prediction that people will internalize what they perceive to be the social norm by examining changes in subjects' ratings of their own comfort and the average student's comfort with alcohol drinking over the course of the semester. Means and standard deviations for the two comfort questions are shown in Table 3. (We added 1 point to each observation to make the scales comparable with those used in Study 1). Inspection of the means suggests that in the face of relatively stable social norms, men, but not women, did indeed bring their own attitudes into line.

Inferential statistics confirmed this observation. A 2 (sex) × 2 (target) × 2 (time) ANOVA revealed a significant three-way interaction, $F(1, 48) = 3.92$, $p = .05$. Female subjects rated themselves as significantly less comfortable with alcohol drinking than the average Princeton undergraduate across both interviews; for target main effect, $F(1, 24) = 11.94$, $p < .005$; Target × Time interaction, $F < 1$.

Male subjects showed a similar self–other difference in the first interview, $F(1, 24) = 8.24$, $p < .01$; by the second interview, the difference was eliminated, $F(1, 24) = 1.69$, $p > .10$; Target × Time interaction, $F(1, 24) = 3.92$, $p = .06$. Thus, men behaved in the way social influence theorists would expect: They changed their own attitudes toward drinking in the direction of the social norm. Women, on the other hand, showed no change in attitudes over time.

Correlational analyses provided further evidence of internalization among male, but not among female, subjects. If individuals respond to perceived deviance by bringing their attitudes into line with their perceptions of the norm, we would expect the correlation between attitudes and norms to increase over time. Male subjects showed just such an increase. Correlations between attitudes and norms are presented in the top line of Table 4. For men, the correlation between attitudes and norms increased from .34 in the first interview to .76 after 8 weeks. For women, the attitude-norm correlation showed a substantial decrease from .60 in the first interview to −.08 in the second interview.

Again, as in Studies 1 and 2, estimates of the comfort of the average Princeton student with alcohol were much less variable than subjects' own comfort ratings. A statistical comparison of the variances of the two distributions yielded a highly significant difference at both time points, $Fs(49, 49) = 3.36$ and 5.51 for the first and second interviews, respectively, $ps < .0001$.

Drinking behavior. We examined the relation of private attitudes and social norms to drinking behavior as well. Subjects' estimates of the number of drinks they had had in the past week and the number of drinks they had in a typical week correlated highly ($r = .78$ for the first interview and .93 for the second interview) and so we averaged them to form a single index of drinking behavior at each interview. Means and standard de-

TABLE 41.4. Correlations Among Drinking Behavior, Own Attitudes, and Estimates of Others' Attitudes

Measure	Women		Men	
	September	December	September	December
Own and others' attitudes	.60**	−.08	.34†	.76***
Behavior and own attitudes	.56**	.45*	.28	.59**
Behavior and others' attitudes	.13	−.16	−.11	.34†

† $p < .05$, one-tailed. * $p < .05$, two-tailed. ** $p < .01$, two-tailed. *** $p < .001$, two-tailed.

TABLE 41.5. Self-Reported Drinking Behavior

Group	September	December
Women		
M	3.60	1.79
SD	5.28	2.92
Interquartile range	0–5	0–3
Men		
M	5.74	6.44
SD	8.74	7.26
Interquartile range	0–9	1–9

Note. Drinking behavior was measured by averaging subjects' estimates of the number of alcoholic drinks they had in the past week and the number they had in a typical week.

TABLE 41.6. Predicting Own Attitudes From Drinking Behavior and Estimates of Others' Attitudes

Group	Adjusted R	Adjusted R^2
Women		
September	.75**	.56
December	.36†	.13
Men		
September	.44*	.20
December	.85**	.73

† $p < .05$, one-tailed. * $p < .05$, two-tailed. ** $p < .001$, two-tailed.

viations for this index are shown in Table 5.[2] We expected drinking habits to be reasonably stable among our sophomore subjects, and indeed an initial ANOVA revealed a significant gender difference in drinking ($M = 2.69$ for women and 6.16 for men), $F(1, 46) = 5.17$, $p < .05$, but no change in drinking over time ($F < 1$) nor any Sex × Time interaction, $F(1, 46) = 1.61$, $p > .10$.[3] However, correlational analyses provided some indirect evidence of increased consistency of attitudes, norms, and behavior again among male, but not among female, subjects.

Correlations of behavior with attitudes and norms are shown in the last two lines of Table 4. For female subjects, both sets of correlations remained fairly stable over time. The attitude–behavior correlation was around .5 at both interviews, and the norm–behavior correlation was not significantly different from zero at either time point. For male subjects, both the attitude behavior and the norm–behavior correlations increased over the course of the semester: The attitude–behavior correlation went from .28 at the first interview to .59 at the second interview, and the norm–behavior correlation went from –.11 at the first interview to .34 at the second interview.[4] Of course, we can draw no causal inferences on the basis of these results. Still, the pattern of correlations for men is quite consistent with the operation of conformity pressures to bring attitudes, norms, and behavior into line.

On final set of analyses lent further support to this conclusion. We performed separate multiple regression analyses for men and women within interviews to test a model of individual attitudes as a joint function of drinking behavior and social norms. The results of these analyses are shown in Table 6. For women, their own comfort with drink-

ing was predicted quite well from their drinking habits and their estimates of others' comfort with drinking at the start of the term; that prediction grew substantially worse over time. For men, the opposite was true: Their alcohol drinking habits and their estimates of others' comfort with drinking provided a relatively poor prediction of their own comfort at the start of the term, but that prediction became much better over time.[5] Again,

---

[2]Initial exploration of the distribution of scores on the drinking measure (separately for men and women at each time point) revealed several outliers: Two men and one woman in September and one man and one woman in December reported levels of drinking that were extremely high compared with the rest of their distribution. To ensure that these points did not unduly affect the results, we analyzed the data three ways: (a) including these values, (b) replacing them with the closest values that were not outliers (i.e., with the value of the inner fence; see Tukey, 1977), and (c) excluding them. The patterns of results from these three sets of analyses were identical and led to the same substantive conclusions. Thus, in the text, we report the results of the analyses with all values included; the results of the two alternative analyses are provided in footnotes.

[3]With replacement of outliers: in September, women ($M = 3.22$, $SD = 4.06$), men ($M = 5.13$, $SD = 7.04$); in December, women ($M = 1.61$, $SD = 2.31$), men ($M = 6.46$, $SD = 7.16$). With exclusion of outliers: in September, women ($M = 2.72$, $SD = 3.64$), men ($M = 3.53$, $SD = 4.51$); in December, women ($M = 1.39$, $SD = 1.95$), men ($M = 4.70$, $SD = 5.76$). For all analyses, the sex difference was the only significant effect.

[4]With replacement of outliers: attitude–behavior correlations in September and December, respectively, for women were .57 and .44 and for men .26 and .59; norm–behavior correlations in September and December, respectively, for women were .11 and –.22 and for men –.17 and .33. With exclusion of outliers, attitude–behavior correlations in September and December, respectively, for women were .50 and .31 and for men were .00 and .53; norm–behavior correlations in September and December, respectively, for women were .06 and –.30 and for men were –.42 and .26.

[5]With replacement of outliers: women in September ($R = .77$), in December ($R = .33$); men in September ($R = .45$), in December ($R = .82$). With exclusion of outliers: women in September ($R = .73$), in December ($R = .10$); men in September ($R = .32$), in December ($R = .80$).

these results for men are consistent with theorizing about conformity pressures in social groups; the results for women, on the other hand, suggest increasing alienation over the course of the semester.

Discussion

The pattern of results in this study clearly indicates internalization on the part of men and alienation on the part of women. The obvious question raised by these results is why men and women responded to pluralistic ignorance so differently. Because these gender differences were not predicted, we have no ready-made explanation for them. However, one potential explanatory factor is suggested by the finding that male subjects reported an alcohol consumption rate over double that reported by female subjects. One interpretation of this difference is that alcohol consumption is a more central or integral aspect of male social life than of female social life. If so, men might be expected to feel greater pressures to learn to be comfortable with alcohol. By contrast, women, and particularly women at historically male institutions, may be accustomed to finding themselves at odds with the social norm concerning alcohol. As a result, they may have come to view that norm as less relevant to their behavior than to the behavior of men.

Another possibility is that men are simply more inclined to "react to feeling deviant from the norm with conformity," whereas women react to deviance with alienation. Although this suggestion that men conform more readily than women runs contrary to previous theorizing about gender differences in influenceability (see Eagly, 1978), there is some supporting evidence for it in the literature on gender differences in ego defenses. Considerable research suggests that in the face of ego threat, men react with externalizing defenses, such as projection and displacement, whereas women react with internalizing defenses, such as repression and reaction formation (Cramer, 1987; Levit, 1991). In the case of pluralistic ignorance, these differences in ego defenses may translate into a greater tendency of men to internalize the norm: Whereas women turn against themselves for being deviant, men take constructive steps to be less deviant.

One final point deserves consideration. Although men appear to have been able to resolve pluralistic ignorance through internalization, it is important to note that at the beginning of their 2nd year in college, both men and women were experiencing pluralistic ignorance in equal measure. Furthermore, Studies 1 and 2 provided evidence of pluralistic ignorance in a cross-section of the male population, including older as well as younger students. These findings suggest that internalization of the norm may provide only a temporary resolution of the perceived self–other discrepancy in comfort with alcohol; when social pressures are less immediate (e.g., during school breaks) or when those pressures change (e.g., as they do in students' 3rd and 4th years at Princeton), men may experience recurring concerns about students' excessive drinking habits.

Study 4

Study 3 provided evidence that, at least for women, pluralistic ignorance cannot easily be resolved through internalization. In Study 4, we explored the link between pluralistic ignorance and feelings of alienation from an institutional norm and from the institution itself. We were particularly interested in testing Noelle-Neumann's (1986) contention that people will be unwilling to express their opinions publicly when they feel that those opinions are deviant. This hypothesis, applied to a context of pluralistic ignorance, yields a provocative prediction; namely, even when people's private attitudes are in line with the norm of the group, they should be hesitant to express those attitudes if they mistakenly believe they are deviant.

To test this hypothesis, we needed a case of pluralistic ignorance in which the attitude in question had clearly available means of public expression. Such an issue arose in the fall of 1991 when the university instituted a campus-wide policy banning kegs of beer. The keg ban was imposed unilaterally by the president of Princeton, who saw it largely as a symbolic act designed to demonstrate the university's concern about drinking on campus. The policy was immediately unpopular: Editorials appeared in the student newspaper and other publications, and there was even protest from alumni groups (who would no longer have kegs at reunions).

Despite the apparent consensus around a negative attitude toward the keg ban, we suspected that private sentiments were not nearly so negative. It was a time of great concern about alcohol use on campus, and many students privately expressed approval that the president of the university was willing to take action on the issue. Also, because the ban affected only kegs, students would still be free to drink bottled beer and other forms of alcohol if they wished. In short, it was a symbolic act that was unlikely to have dire consequences for social life at Princeton.

Thus, the keg ban provided the perfect issue for our investigation of the behavioral manifestations of alienation. We expected that we would find evidence of pluralistic ignorance on the keg ban issue, with people's private attitudes being much less negative than the prevailing social norm. In addition, unlike general comfort with alcohol, attitudes toward the keg ban had a clear means of public expression: We could ask students how willing they were to participate in social actions designed to protest the ban. Our hypothesis was that regardless of their actual attitude toward the keg ban, feeling deviant from the norm would inhibit students from taking any action to protest the ban and might produce more general symptoms of alienation from the university as well.

Method

Subjects. Ninety-four undergraduates voluntarily attended a mass testing session, in which they participated in this and other short studies for pay. The sample included 52 women and 42 men, with approximately even distribution of women and men across the 1st- through 4th-year classes.

Procedure. Subjects responded to a brief, two-page questionnaire that was included in a large booklet. The questionnaire was presented as a study of attitudes about the keg ban, about alcohol use on campus, and about life at Princeton more generally. The first question assessed their attitudes toward the keg ban:

1. How do you feel about the university's new policy banning kegs on campus? Please indicate your feelings by circling a number from 0 to 10.

Subjects circled a number on the accompanying scale, with 0 labeled *totally opposed* and 10 labeled *totally in favor*. Next, they were asked to estimate the attitudes of other students, using a comparative scale:

2. Compared to you, how does the average

Princeton undergraduate feel about the university's policy banning kegs on campus?

Subjects circled a number from 1 to 5 on the accompanying scale, with the numbers labeled *much more negative, somewhat more negative, about the same, somewhat more positive*, and *much more positive*. The next two questions concerned their willingness to take social action to protest the keg ban:

3. How many signatures in protest of the ban would you be willing to go out and collect? Please circle a response from 0 signatures to 100 or more signatures.
4. How much of your time would you be willing to spend discussing ways to protest the ban? Please circle a response from no time to 10 or more hours.

Subjects circled a number from 0 to 100 (in increments of 10) to indicate how many signatures they would be willing to collect and a number from 0 to 10 (in increments of 2) to indicate how many hours they would be willing to discuss. Finally, they answered two questions that were designed to measure their connection to the university:

5. What percentage of reunions do you expect to attend after you graduate from Princeton?
6. How likely are you to donate money to Princeton after you graduate?

Subjects circled a number from 0 to 100 (in increments of 10) to indicate the percentage of reunions they expect to attend and a number from 1 (*not at all likely*) to 9 (*very likely*) to indicate how likely they are to donate money to Princeton after graduation.

Results

We divided subjects into two categories on the basis of their responses to the question of how the average student feels about the keg ban compared with themselves. Forty women and 29 men indicated that the average student was either much more negative or somewhat more negative about the keg ban than they were; these subjects constituted the *others-more-negative* group. Eleven women and 11 men indicated that the average student felt about the same as they did; these subjects constituted the *others-the-same* group. (Two men and 1 woman indicated that the average student

TABLE 41.7. Ratings of Attitude Toward the Keg Ban, Willingness to Take Action, and Connection to the University of Comparative Attitude of the Average Student

| | Average student's attitude | | | |
| | Woman | | Men | |
Measure	More negative	Same	More negative	Same
Keg ban attitude				
M	4.70	0.64	4.97	1.09
SD	2.55	0.92	2.61	1.30
Signatures				
M	6.05	49.09	3.14	30.00
SD	19.04	27.00	8.48	33.47
Hours				
M	0.40	2.55	0.34	1.45
SD	1.03	1.57	0.94	1.81
% reunions				
M	33.88	57.27	34.29	47.27
SD	22.37	25.73	24.10	29.70
Donations				
M	4.65	6.27	4.69	6.00
SD	2.28	2.32	2.54	2.49

was more positive than they were; because this group was too small to analyze, the responses of these subjects were discarded.) The distribution of subjects into these two categories confirmed our expectation that students' attitudes toward the keg ban, like their general comfort with alcohol, would be characterized by pluralistic ignorance: They showed a systematic tendency to believe that the average student felt more negatively about the keg ban than they did.

We predicted that subjects who believed themselves to be different from the average student would be less likely to take social action against the keg ban and would be less connected to the university compared with subjects who believed themselves to be the same as the average student, controlling for actual attitudes toward the ban. Means and standard deviations for the attitude and behavior questions are shown in Table 7. Not surprisingly, subjects' own attitudes toward the ban corresponded to their comparative ratings of others' attitudes: Subjects in the others-more-negative group expressed more favorable attitudes toward the ban than did subjects in the others-the-same group, $F(1, 90) = 48.26, p < .0001$. However, even controlling for this difference in private attitudes, subjects who felt that their attitude was different from the norm still were less willing to take action against the ban.[6] A 2 (sex) × 2 (com-

parison group) analysis of covariance, controlling for attitudes, yielded a significant effect of comparison group on willingness to collect signatures, $F(1, 90) = 18.94, p < .0001$, willingness to work hours, $F(1, 90) = 10.99, p < .005$, and percentage of reunions expected to attend, $F(1, 89) = 8.10, p < .01$. The effect of comparison group on likelihood of donating money was not significant, $F(1, 90) = 1.08, p > .10$, although the means were in the expected direction. There was also a significant gender difference in willingness to collect signatures, $F(1, 90) = 4.57, p < .05$, and a marginally significant gender difference in willingness to work hours, $F(1, 90) = 3.42, p < .07$. None of the Sex × Comparison Group interaction effects were significant.

Discussion

These results provide clear evidence that people who feel deviant from the norm of their social group are inhibited from acting. Regardless of their actual position on the keg ban, subjects who believed that others felt more negatively than they

---

[6]The use of analysis of covariance as a way of equating the two groups on attitudes is a reasonable but not perfect strategy; see Huitema (1980) for a full discussion of the assumptions and limitations of this statistical approach.

did were less likely to act on the ban and were also less connected to the university, as measured by their plans to attend reunions after graduation. These results demonstrate that mistakenly believing oneself to be deviant is associated with considerable alienation from the group. However, it is also important to note that the results of this study are correlational and do not enable us to make causal statements about the precise role of feeling deviant on the keg ban issue in producing the observed effects.

The results of this study, combined with those of Study 3, provide an interesting picture of the consequences of pluralistic ignorance regarding alcohol use for male and female students. For men, the pattern of results followed quite closely the predictions of the social influence literature: When they perceived their attitudes to be different from the normative attitudes of their group, men showed signs of alienation (Study 4) and responded to their perceived deviance by changing their attitudes in the direction of the norm (Study 3). For women, the pattern of results was more anomalous: They also showed signs of alienation when they perceived their attitudes to be deviant, but did not respond by moving toward the norm. Indeed, if anything, they appeared to grow more alienated over time (Study 3).

We believe that the most parsimonious account for these results focuses on the different relations of men and women to both the norm in question and to the group. As noted in connection with Study 3, norms related to alcohol use are likely to be much more central for men than for women. Likewise, fitting in at the university is likely to be more critical for men than for women. Even though Princeton had admitted female students for more than 2 decades, male students are still both the statistical and the psychological norm. (Many of the university's institutions and traditions were developed when it was an all-male school.) Thus, whereas Princeton men are likely to feel strong conformity pressures, Princeton women may have less ability and less motivation to conform to the norms of the group. They may see some degree of deviance and alienation as inherent in their position within a historically male institution. Of course, this explanation is speculative, but it is consistent both with previous theorizing about social groups (e.g., Festinger et al., 1950) and with the present results.

General Discussion

In pursuit of an answer to the question of how people respond to perceived differences between themselves and the group, social psychologists have largely ignored the more preliminary questions of how, and with what degree of accuracy, people identify social norms. In most laboratory investigations of social influence, the task of identifying group norms is eliminated by fiat of experimental design. (If the norm is measured at all, it is only done so as a manipulation check.) In real-world social groups, however, the task of identifying the group norm can be highly complex and demanding, so much so that members' estimates of the norm are often seriously in error. The present studies documented significant errors in college students' estimates of social norms relating to comfort with alcohol (Studies 1, 2, and 3) and attitudes toward a new university-mandated policy to reduce alcohol abuse (Study 4). Especially interesting was the systematic nature of the errors: Students erred by overestimating their fellow students' support for the status quo. Indeed, they assumed that the average other student was more in favor of the status quo than they themselves were. In short, students were victims of pluralistic ignorance: They believed that the private attitudes of other students were much more consistent with campus norms than were their own.

Norm Misperception: Possible Interpretations

The reported discrepancy between students' own attitudes and those they attribute to their friends and peers may have many sources. The least interesting interpretation, from a psychological standpoint, is that the reported discrepancy is merely that: a reported discrepancy that does not reflect true perceptions. By this impression management account, students may not actually think they are deviant but only portray themselves as such. Their descriptions of themselves as deviating from the status quo could simply constitute strategic attempts to present themselves as nonconformists, as people who are less supportive of their group's norm than the average group member. By presenting themselves in this way, the students might have hoped to convey the impression (if they assumed that the researcher disapproved of the group's norm) that they were more mature, more progressive, or more enlightened than their peers.

An impression management account could be applied to virtually all the studies that have reported erroneous perceptions of one's own attitudinal or behavioral deviance. The form that pluralistic ignorance takes in these studies is almost always the same: Subjects report that they are more sympathetic to the positions or concerns of some out-group than are their peers. For example, Whites portray themselves as more sympathetic to Blacks than their fellow Whites (Fields & Schuman, 1976), teachers portray themselves as more sympathetic to students than their fellow teachers (Packard & Willower, 1972), and prison guards portray themselves as more sympathetic to prisoners than their fellow guards (Kauffman, 1981).

Although it is possible that students in the present studies were motivated to portray themselves as more sympathetic to the position of the university administration than their fellow students, there are a number of reasons to doubt this self-presentational account. First, the anonymous nature of the data collection provided subjects with very little incentive to self-present. Second, the finding in Study 4 that subjects' estimates of their attitudinal deviance correlated positively with various measures of alienation, even when equating for their own attitudes, is hard to reconcile with a self-presentational interpretation. Subjects not only described themselves as being out of step with the social norm, but also they acted as though they were out of step with this norm. Even more problematic for the self-presentational account is the finding in Study 3 that male subjects moderated their perception of their deviance over time by shifting their attitudes toward their estimates of the social norm. If these subjects were attempting to present themselves as being more progressive or enlightened than their peers, it is unlikely that they would have reported their attitudes to be closer to the norm at one time than another. In short, the present findings are much more consistent with the view that the pluralistic ignorance observed in the present studies represented authentic perceptions of deviance and not just ones offered for public consumption.

Another possible interpretation of students' perceived deviance focuses on the representativeness of the public data from which they inferred others' attitudes. These data may have been skewed in the direction of the perceived norm. For example, campus publications may have tended to express more pronorm opinions than antinorm opinions. Similarly, students who strongly supported campus norms may have expressed their attitudes more vociferously than those who only weakly supported them or who disapproved of them. Korte (1972) offered the following general summary of this process:

> The side of an issue representing a cultural (or subcultural) value is more prominent, more frequently and loudly advocated by its adherents. From the point of view of the individual, this source of bias constitutes an unrepresentative sampling of the relevant population. (p. 586)

Through an accurate reading of a biased distribution of publicly expressed opinions, students may have been led to erroneous perceptions of their peers' attitudes. Interestingly, this account implies that pluralistic ignorance could arise without students misrepresenting their true opinions. It suggests that pluralistic ignorance may require a silent majority but not a dissembling one.

We cannot rule out the biased sample hypothesis, but it has difficulty accounting for the data on friends' attitudes in Study 2. There, We found that subjects revealed pluralistic ignorance not just when estimating the attitudes of the average princeton student but also when estimating the attitudes of their friends. It seems implausible that students would use the public expressions of their vocal friends to infer the private attitudes of their silent friends. Inferences concerning the population of a campus must be estimated from a sample of that population, but inferences concerning the population of one's friends need not depend on sample-to-population generalization.

Two other possible accounts of the pluralistic ignorance observed in these studies focus on student's interpretation and encoding of their own and others' behavior. The first of these accounts, which we call the *differential interpretation hypothesis*, suggests that students display pluralistic ignorance in their reactions to alcohol issues because they (a) present themselves as being more supportive of campus norms than they are and (b) fail to recognize that others are also misrepresenting their true feelings. The first of these points is well documented: Many authorities have noted that group members often display more public support for group norms than they privately feel (Goffman, 1961; Matza,1964; Schanck, 1932). As Goffman (1961) stated," When the individual presents himself before others, his performance will tend to incorporate and exemplify the officially accredited values of the society, more so, in fact, than does his behavior as a whole" (p. 35).

Comfort with alcohol and opposition to alcohol restrictions may not be officially accredited campus values, but they may serve a similar function. Alcohol on most college campuses, and certainly on the princeton campus, is not simply a critical feature of social life: It is also an important source of in-group–out-group polarization. Nothing is more central to the power struggle between students and the administration, faculty, and larger community than campus alcohol policy. Thus, even if students do not privately support the student position on alcohol, they may feel compelled to do so publicly out of a sense of group loyalty. Acknowledging that the other side has a point, or is not all bad, can carry a stiff social penalty.

There may be many reasons for students to exaggerate publicly their support for campus alcohol norms, but why not assume that their peers' public behavior is similarly inauthentic? One possibility, suggested by Miller and McFarland (1987, 1991), is that people hold a general belief that they are more fearful of appearing deviant than is the average person. Thus students may be disposed to accept as authentic the public pronorm behaviors of their peers, despite recognizing that their own public pronorm behaviors are inauthentic.

A final explanation for the observed pluralistic ignorance points to potential differences in the way students encode their own and others behavior. According to this differential encoding account, students may fail to recognize how pronorm their public behavior actually is, mistakenly believing that their private discomfort with alcohol practices is clear from their words and deeds. If students do suffer from an *illusion of transparency* (Miller & McFarland, 1991), they might reasonably assume that because the words and deeds of others signal more comfort than they themselves feel (and supposedly express), they must be alone in their discomfort.

Although both the differential interpretation and differential encoding hypotheses are plausible accounts of pluralistic ignorance in the present con-

text, we have no direct evidence to support or distinguish between them. It is quite possible that the two operate in parallel, along with other biases, to make pluralistic ignorance an overdetermined phenomenon. Future research could shed light on these accounts by determining whether students do (a) misrepresent their private attitudes in their public pronouncements or (b) generate different interpretations for what they saw as similar public behavior in themselves and others.

Before leaving our analysis of pluralistic ignorance effects, we should comment briefly on the apparent inconsistency be tween this phenomenon and the well-documented *false consensus effect*: people's tendency to overestimate their similarity to others (Marks & Miller, 1987; Ross, Greene, & House, 1977). The two phenomena are different but are not incompatible (see Suls, 1986). The norm misperception that arises in cases of pluralistic ignorance is most appropriately operationalized as a mean difference between that actual group norm and the perceived group norm; false consensus, on the other hand, is most appropriately operationalized as a positive correlation between ratings of the self and ratings of others. Theoretically, it is possible for there to be both a positive correlation between people's judgments of self and others and a mean difference in self–other rating. Indeed, we found precisely this pattern of results in Study 1 (for the self–other correlation, $r = .37$, $p < .001$) and in Study 2 ($r = .27$, $p < .01$). Thus, although students anchored their estimates of the average student level of comfort on their own (hence the positive correlation), they also perceived there to be a systematic difference between their comfort level and the comfort of others. Nisbett and kunda (1985) provided numerous other examples in which subjects displayed both false consensus effects and systematic biases in central tendency estimates.

Norm Misperception: Social and Psychological Consequences

What are the consequences of mistakenly assuming that the views of one's peers are different from one's own? Although illusory norms may not have the force of overt social pressure behind them, they still can have powerful social and psychological consequences.

Social consequences. Pluralistic ignorance has traditionally been linked to two consequences; The social construction of emergency situations as nonemergencies and the perpetuation of unsupported social norms. Defined broadly, the pluralistic ignorance found in the present studies may have had both of these consequences. Consider emergency nonintervention first. We obviously did not focus on emergency situations directly in these studies, but it is quite possible that most of our subjects had witnessed situations involving alcohol abuse that they viewed as potentially serious. If so, we can surmise that the pluralistic ignorance dynamic described by Latané and Darley (1970) may have been replicated frequently on the princeton campus, resulting in (a) the withholding of assistance to inebriated students about whom all members of groups were concerned and (b) increased confidence on the part of nonacting, but nonetheles concerned, bystanders that they were much less cool about the consequences of excessive drinking than were their friends and fellow bystanders.

The role of pluralistic ignorance in perpetuating unsupported or weakly supported social norms in the present context is also easy to sketch. Alcohol may have continued to play a central role in campus life not because students wanted it that way but because they thought that everyone else wanted it that way. For example, students themselves might often, or even generally, be indifferent to the availability of alcohol at a party, but they may assume that most other students have a strong preference for parties at which alcohol is present. This logic could have many consequences, the most obvious of which is that students, assuming that more people will come to parties that serve alcohol, will seek out parties with alcohol. It also suggests that students hosting parties will assume that they must provide alcohol to satisfy their guests. In short, attempts to institute alcohol-free social activities or institutions may fail to generate support because students mistakenly (and self-fulfillingly) assume they will not be widely supported.

One additional social consequence illustrated by the present findings is that individuals may actually conform to their mistaken estimates of the group norm. Previous research on substance use has shown that people's estimates of the prevalence of drug use among their peers influences their own use, whether these estimates are accurate or inaccurate (Kandel, 1980; Marks, Graham, & Hansen, 1992; Sherman, Presson, Chassin, Corty,

& Olshavsky, 1983). Similarly, in Study 3, male subjects modified their private attitudes over time in the direction of the position they mistakenly assumed was held by the average student. In effect, they achieved a level of comfort that few students initially felt simply because they thought that everyone felt that way. This analysis highlights the fact that the norms of a social group may be largely independent of the norms of the group members (Turner & Killian, 1972). The desire to be correct and to fit in may lead people to conform, even without social pressure, to what they (mis)perceive to be the norm of the group. In these cases, pluralistic ignorance will be highly ephemeral. If people come to believe what they mistakenly attribute to everyone else, then an originally erroneous perception of the situation will become accurate at the private, as well as the public, level. Misjudgments of others will drive out correct judgments of the self.

Psychological consequences. Our discussion suggests that the social consequences of pluralistic ignorance are significant. However, as the present research indicates, pluralistic ignorance has powerful psychological consequences as well. As documented in our studies, many of the consequences of mistakenly perceiving oneself as deviant are not much different from the consequences of accurately perceiving oneself as deviant. Discomfort, alienation, and an inclination to move in the direction of the majority appear to characterize the phenomenology of illusory deviants as well as real deviants. Indeed, because victims of pluralistic ignorance will typically be involuntary deviants, they may experience the pain of their deviance quite acutely. They may lack the comforting belief that they chose to march to the beat of a different drummer.

Whether victims of pluralistic ignorance do or do not experience their deviance more acutely than voluntary deviants, we have evidence that they manifest real symptoms. For the male subjects in Study 3, for example, the pain of perceiving themselves as deviant may have been a critical factor motivating them to conform to the (illusory) norm of their social group. Moreover, the present findings suggest that people may be much less inclined to conform to majority influence, real or imagined, than is generally assumed by social psychologists. Female subjects in Study 3 retained their (self-perceived) deviant attitudes, a response consistent with other signs of alienation found in both male and female subjects in Study 4. These results raise the possibility that conformity may not play as dominant a role in resolving self–group discrepancies as most psychological equilibrium models have posited.

Conclusions

The reported studies illustrate a number of important points about the relation between private attitudes and social norms. Taken together, they indicate that people can often err considerably in situating their attitudes in relation to those of their peers and that these errors have real consequences, both for the individual and for the group. Because little research attention has been given to questions of norm estimation, we know very little about the processes through which individuals identify and represent the norms of their social groups. The present results suggest that further attention to these questions may lead to a better understanding of the ways in which norms can perpetuate social problems, like alcohol use, and can inhibit social change.

The findings of these studies have practical implications as well. In particular, our analysis of the role of pluralistic ignorance in perpetuating dysfunctional social norms has clear implications for programs designed to effect social change. Programs aimed at the individual, such as informational campaigns or individual counseling sessions, may change private attitudes, but they are likely to leave social norms, and in many cases public behavior, untouched. Indeed, our research suggests that recent attempts by universities to raise consciousness about alcohol abuse on campus may have been effective at changing the attitudes of individual students (see also Trice & Beyer, 1977) but not at changing their perceptions of the attitudes of their peers. A more effective way to facilitate social change may be to expose pluralistic ignorance in a group setting and to encourage students to speak openly about their private attitudes within the group. Such an approach would promote social change by demonstrating that it has, in effect, already occurred at the individual level and simply needs to be acknowledged at the social level.

ACKNOWLEDGMENTS

The preparation of this article was facilitated by National Institute of Mental Health Grant MH44069 to Dale T. Miller. We thank Jenifer Lightdale and Carolyn Oates for their assistance with data collection and analysis.

REFERENCES

Allport, F. H. (1924). *Social psychology*. Boston: Houghton Mifflin.

Asch, S. E. (1951). Effects of group pressure upon the modification and distortion of judgments. In H. Guetzkow (Ed.), *Group leadership and men* (pp. 177–190). Pittsburg, PA: Carnegie Press.

Barringer, F. (1991, June 23). With teens and alcohol, it's just say when. *New York Times*, P.1.

Berkowitz, A. D., & Perkins, H. W. (1986). Problem drinking among college students: A review of recent research. *Journal of American College Health, 35,* 21–28.

Breed, W., & Ktsanes, T. (1961). Pluralistic ignorance in the process of opinion formation. *Public Opinion Quarterly, 25,* 382–392.

Cialdini, R. B., Kallgren, C. A., & Reno, R. R. (1991). The focus theory of normative conduct: A theoretical refinement and reevaluation of the role of norms in human behavior. In M. P. Zanna (Ed.), *Advances in experimental social psychology* (Vol. 24, pp. 201–234). San Diego, CA: Academic Press.

Clitherow, R. (1991). What is to be done? Alcohol abuse at Princeton. *The Princeton Tory, 7*(March), 8–13.

Cramer, P. (1987). The development of defenses. *Journal of Personality, 51,* 79–94.

Crandall, C. (1988) Social contagion and binge eating. *Journal of Personality and Social Psychology, 55,* 588–598.

Eagly, A. (1978). Sex differences in influenceability. *Psychological Bulletin, 85,* 86–116.

Festinger, L., Schachter, S., & Back, K. (1950). *Social pressure in informal groups.* New York: Harper & Row.

Fields, J. M., & Schuman, H. (1976). Public beliefs and the beliefs of the public. *Public Opinion Quarterly, 40,* 427–448.

Goffman, E. (1961). *Asylums: Essays on the social situation of mental patients and other inmates.* Garden City, NJ: Anchor Books.

Graham, J. W., Marks, G., & Hansen, W. B. (1991). Social influence processes affecting adolescent substance use. *Journal of Applied Psychology, 76,* 291–298.

Huba, G. J., & Bentler, P. M. (1980). The role of peer and adult models for drug taking at different stages in adolescence. *Journal of Youth and Adolescence, 9,* 449–465.

Huitema, B. E. (1980). *The analysis of covariance and alternatives.* New York: Wiley.

Kandel, D. B. (1980). Drug and drinking behavior among youth. In A. Inkeles, N. J. Smelser, & R. Turner (Eds.), *Annual review of sociology* (Vol. 6, pp. 235–285). Palo Alto, CA: Annual Reviews.

Kauffman, K. (1981). Prison officer attitudes and perceptions of attitudes. *Journal of Research in Crime Delinquency, 18,* 272–294.

Kelman, H. (1958). Compliance, identification, and internalization: Three processes of attitude change. *Journal of Conflict Resolution, 2,* 51–60.

Korte, C. (1972). Pluralistic ignorance about student radicalism. *Sociometry, 35,* 576–587.

Latané, B., & Darley, J. (1970). *The unresponsive bystander: Why doesn't he help?* New York: Appleton-Century-Crofts.

Levit, D. B. (1991). Gender differences in ego defenses in adolescence: Sex roles as one way to understand the differences. *Journal of Personality and Social Psychology, 61,* 992–999.

Maddox, G. L. (Ed.). (1970). *The domesticated drug: Drinking among collegians.* New Haven, CT: College and University Press.

Marks, G., Graham, J. W., & Hansen, W. B. (1992). Social projection and social conformity in adolescent alcohol use: A longitudinal analysis. *Personality and Social Psychology Bulletin, 18,* 96–101.

Marks, G., & Miller, N. (1987). Ten years of research on the false-consensus effect: An empirical and theoretical review. *Psychological Bulletin, 102,* 72–90.

Matza, D. (1964). *Delinquency and drift.* New York: Wiley.

Miller, D. T., & McFarland, C. (1987). Pluralistic ignorance: When similarity is interpreted as dissimilarity. *Journal of Personality and Social Psychology, 53,* 298–305.

Miller, D. T. & McFarland, C. (1991). When social comparison goes awry: The case of pluralistic ignorance. In J. Suls & T. Wills (Eds.), *Social comparison: Contemporary theory and research* (pp. 287–313). Hillsdale, NJ: Erlbaum.

Moscovici, S. (1985). Social influence and conformity. In G. Lindzey & E. Aronson (Eds.), *The handbook of social psychology* (3rd ed., Vol. 2, pp. 347–412). New York: Random House.

Newcomb, T. M. (1943). *Personality and social change.* New York: Holt, Rinehart & Winston.

Nisbett, R. E., & Kunda, Z. (1985). Perceptions of social distributions. *Journal of Personality and Social Psychology, 48,* 297–311.

Noelle-Neumann, E. (1986). *The spiral of silence.* Chicago: University of Chicago Press.

O'Gorman, H. J. (1975). Pluralistic ignorance and White estimates of White support for racial segregation. *Public Opinion Quarterly, 39,* 313–330.

Packard, J. S., & Willower, D. J. (1972). Pluralistic ignorance and pupil control ideology. *Journal of Education Administration, 10,* 78–87.

Perkins, H. W. (1985). Religious traditions, parents, and peers as determinants of alcohol and drug use among college students. *Review of Religious Research, 27,* 15–31.

Perkins, H. W., & Berkowitz, A. D. (1986). Perceiving the community norms of alcohol use among students: Some research implications for campus alcohol education programming. *International Journal of Addictions, 21,* 961–976.

Ross, L., Greene, D., & House, P. (1977). The "false consensus effect": An egocentric bias in social perception and attributional processes. *Journal of Experimental Social Psychology, 13,* 279–301.

Schanck, R. L. (1932). A study of community and its group institutions conceived of as behavior of individuals. *Psychological Monographs, 43*(2), 1–133.

Sherif, M. (1936). *The psychology of social norms.* New York: Harper.

Sherman, S. J., Presson, C. C., Chassin, L., Corty, E., & Olshavsky, R. (1983). The false consensus effect in estimates of smoking prevalence: Underlying mechanisms. *Personality and Social Psychology Bulletin, 9,* 197–207.

Stein, J. A., Newcomb, M. D., & Bentler, P. M. (1987). An 8-year study of multiple influences on drug use and drug use consequences. *Journal of Personality and Social Psychology, 53,* 1094–1105.

Straus, R., & Bacon, J. M. (1953). *Drinking in college.* New Haven, CT: Yale University Press.

Suls, J. (1986). Notes on the occasion of social comparison theory's thirtieth birthday. *Personality and Social Psychology Bulletin, 12,* 289–296.

Trice, H. M., & Beyer, J. M. (1977). A sociological property of drugs: Acceptance of users of alcohol and other drugs among university undergraduates. *Journal of Studies on Alcohol, 33,* 58–74.

Tukey, J. (1977). *Exploratory data analysis.* Reading, MA: Addison-Wesley.

Turner, J. (1991). *Social influence.* Pacific Grove, CA: Brooks/Cole.

Turner, R., & Killian, L. (1972). *Collective behavior* (2nd ed.). Englewood Cliffs, NJ: Prentice-Hall.

Zucker, R. A., & Noll, R. B. (1982). Precursors and developmental influences on drinking and alcoholism: Etiology from a longitudinal perspective. *Alcohol consumption and related problems* (Alcohol and Health Monograph No. 1, pp. 289–327). Rockville, MD: National Institute on Alcohol Abuse and Alcoholism.

A Collective Fear of the Collective: Implications for Selves and Theories of Selves

Hazel Rose Markus • Stanford University
Shinobu Kitayama • Kyoto University

Editors' Notes

Of long-standing interest to anthropologists, the concept of culture has recently become a major topic of interest for social psychologists as well. This is readily understandable in this day and age. International travel, the Internet, and economic globalization are increasingly shrinking geographic distances and bringing remote worldviews and exotic belief systems to our attention on a daily basis. In addition, as Samuel Huntington has recently argued in his work on "the clash of civilizations," the conflict lines in the post–cold war world seem to be increasingly drawn along the lines of culture. But what do these have to do with the science of social psychology? The present selection delineates several ways in which the concept of culture has relevance for the way social psychologists go about their business. Two major and interrelated ways are: (1) identifying culture and cultural differences as a major topic of inquiry for social psychologists; (2) fostering a new understanding of how our own scientific work, according to the authors, betrays a typically Western, individualistic orientation. Their discussion raises intriguing questions about the interrelation of culture and psychological processes. A major issue is how we, as human beings, are *similar* in our social psychological actions, perceptions, and feelings and how we are *different* as a function of our culture.

Discussion Questions

1. What are the main ways in which the individualist and the collectivist models of self differ?
2. What are the main normative tasks of the independent and the interdependent selves?

3. What are the implications of the different emphases in the American and the Japanese cultures for child rearing, media practices, and business practices?

4. According to the authors, what are the implications of the "collective fear of the collective" for psychological theorizing and research?

Suggested Readings

Fiske, A. P. (1992). The four elementary forms of sociality: Framework for a unified theory of social relations. *Psychological Review, 99*(4), 689–723.

Markus, H. R., & Kitayama, S. (1991). Culture and the self: Implications for cognition, emotion, and motivation. *Psychological Review, 98,* 224–253.

Miller, J. G. (1984). Culture and the development of everyday social explanation. *Journal of Personality and Social Psychology, 46,* 961–978.

Schweder, R. A. (1994). You're not sick, you are just in love. In P. Eckman & R. J. Davidson (Eds.), *The nature of emotion* (pp. 32–44). New York: Oxford University Press.

Authors' Abstract

Drawing on recent analyses of the self in many cultures, the authors suggest that the cultural ideal of independence of the self from the collective has dominated European-American social psychological theorizing. As a consequence, the existence of considerable interdependence between the self and the collective has been relatively neglected in current conceptual analysis. The authors (a) argue that a group's cultural ideal of the relation between the self and the collective is pervasive because it is rooted in institutions, practices, and scripts, not just in ideas and values; (b) show how a given cultural ideal, whether it is independence or interdependence, can shape the individual's experience and expression of the self; and (c) discuss how a comparative approach may enrich and expand current theory and research on the interdependence between the self and the collective.

Our cultural nightmare is that the individual throb of growth will be sucked dry in slavish social conformity. All life long, our central struggle is to defend the individual from the collective.

—Plath, 1980, p. 216

Selves, as well as theories of selves, that have been constructed within a European-American cultural frame show the influence of one powerful notion—the idea that people are independent, bounded, autonomous entities who must strive to remain unshackled by their ties to various groups and collectives (Bellah, Madsen, Sullivan, Swidler, & Tipton, 1985: Farr, 1991; Sampson, 1985; Shweder & Bourne, 1984). This culturally shared idea of the self is a pervasive, taken-for-granted assumption that is held in place by language, by the mundane rituals and social practices of daily life, by the law, the media, the foundational texts like the Declaration of Independence and the Bill of Rights, and by virtually all social institutions. The individualist ideal as sketched in its extreme form in the opening quotation might not be explicitly endorsed by many Americans and Europeans. Some version of this view is, however, the basis of social science's persistent belief in the person as a rational, self-interested actor, and it occasions a desire not to be defined by others and a deep-seated wariness, in some instances even a fear, of the influence of the generalized other, of the social, and of the collective.

Asocial Social Psychology

Although a diverse group of European and American theorists (e.g., Geertz, 1973; Gergen & Gergen, 1988; Gilligan, 1982; Icheiser, 1943; Moscovici,

1984; Shweder & Bourne, 1984; Tajfel & Turner, 1985) have found fault with the individualist model of self and its ability to reflect and account for social behavior, for the most part this critique has gone unheeded in the empirical analysis of behavior. A scrutiny of any current American textbook in social psychology reveals that social psychologists, the very group committed to understanding the social nature of the mind, approach the analysis of social behavior with a distinctly asocial model of the self.

In current social psychology, the healthy self is characterized as one that can maintain its integrity across diverse social environments and can successfully fend off challenge and attacks from others (Greenwald, 1980; Markus, 1977; Rosenberg, 1979; Tesser & Campbell, 1983). Although "social" identities are regarded as significant in some situations, they are typically viewed as separate from the more important and more defining "personal" identities. (Crocker & Luhtanen, 1990; Ovserman & Markus, 1993; Tajfel, 1981). Moreover, in many textbooks, there is an abiding concern that the social group will somehow overwhelm or disempower the autonomous, agentic self. It is the troublesome aspects of social behavior—conformity, obedience, groupthink, deindividuation, risky shift, diffusion of responsibility, and stereotyping—that are the main focus of conceptual analysis (see, e.g., Myers, 1993). Social behavior is very often presented as in opposition to individual behavior and construed as compromising individual behavior. This perspective, we contend, follows directly from a culturally held view of the self as distinctly separate from the exogenous collective.

Further, we suggest here that one major stumbling block to realizing the goal of this special issue—understanding how social aggregates influence individuals' thoughts and actions—and, in fact, to developing a comprehensive and fully "social" social psychology, is the unchallenged, heavily scripted, cultural view that the individual is, a priori, separate and self-contained and must resist the collective. This individualist view, what might be called America's civil religion (Gates, 1993), works to keep many of the social and interdependent aspects of the self relatively invisible.

Recent analyses of the self in cultures other than the European-American (e.g., Daniels, 1984; Derné, 1992; Markus & Kitayama, 1991; Triandis, 1990; White & Kirkpatrick, 1985) reveal some very different perspectives on the relation between the self and the collective. Japanese culture, for example, emphasizes the *inter*dependence of the individual with the collective rather than independence from it. The analysis of non-European. American view of self has two notable benefits. First, such an analysis can illuminate some central characteristics of these non-Western cultures themselves. Second, and more important for our purposes, it can help uncover some aspects of European-American social behavior that are not well captured in the current social psychological theories.

Culture and Self

Independence of Self from the Collective—A Cultural Frame

The model that underlies virtually all current social science views the self as an entity that (a) comprises a unique, bounded configuration of internal attributes (e.g., preferences, traits, abilities, motives, values, and rights) and (b) behaves primarily as a consequence of these internal attributes. It is the individual level of reality—the thoughts and feelings of the single individual—that is highlighted and privileged in the explanation and analysis of behavior; the collective level of reality recedes and remains secondary. The major normative task is to maintain the independence of the individual as a self-contained entity or, more specifically, to be true to one's own internal structures of preferences, rights, convictions, and goals and, further, to be confident and to be efficacious. According to this *independent* view of the self, there is an enduring concern with expressing one's internal attributes both in public and in private. Other people are crucial in maintaining this construal of the self, but they are primarily crucial for their role in evaluating and appraising the self or as standards of comparison (see Markus & Kitayama, 1991; Triandis, 1990, for a discussion of the independent or individualist self). Others do not, however, *participate* in the individual's own subjectivity.

The independent view of self does not, of course, argue for a permanent separation of self from the collective, but it strictly prescribes the terms of the relationship between the two. According to this model of the self and the collective, there are indeed positive outcomes of the social matrix of behavior—people cooperate, they love one another, they show concern and sympathy, they value friendship, they help each other, they care about those in need, they volunteer, they give to charity they are compassionate, and at times they perform heroic acts in behalf of others. In fact, according to many recent analyses, North Americans are among the most concerned and committed people in the world (Bellah et al., 1985; Withnow, 1992). For the most part. however, from the perspective of the individualist ideal, such prosocial behavior is *intentional* and *voluntary*, treated more as an exception to be admired and rewarded. It is not to be taken for granted, as it is in more collectively oriented cultures. Acts that are motivated primarily by the desire to improve another person's situation are seen as opposing self-interest and as costly to the individual. In many respects, interdependence is cast as a matter of personal discretion, not a moral imperative (Miller, Bersoff, & Harwood, 1990). Similarly, European-Americans also value groups and group activity (de Tocqueville, 1835/1969), especially when such activity involves pulling together to solve a difficult problem or overcome a barrier. Again, however, collectively oriented behavior is typically understood as voluntary and as purposely and temporarily engaging the separate self to participate in the collective for the purpose of realizing a shared goal.[1]

Interdependence of the Self and the Collective—An Alternative Frame

The pervasive influence of the individualist ideal in many aspects of European-American social behavior has appeared in high relief as we have carried out a set of studies on the self and its functioning in a variety of Asian countries, including Japan, Thailand, and Korea (Kitayama & Markus, 1993; Kitayama, Markus, & Kurokawa, 1991; Markus & Kitayama, 1991, 1992). What has become apparent is that the European-American view of the self and its relation to the collective is only *one* view. There are other, equally powerful but strikingly different, collective notions about the self and its relation to the collective.

From one such alternative view, the self is viewed not as an independent entity separate from the collective but instead as a priori fundamentally interdependent with others. Individuals do not stand in opposition to the confines and constraints of the external collective, nor do they voluntarily choose to become parts of this external collective. Instead, the self *is* inherently social—an integral part of the collective. This interdependent view grants primacy to the *relationship* between self and others. The self derives only from the individual's relationships with specific others in the collective. There is no self without the collective; the self is a part that becomes whole only in interaction with others (e.g., Kondo, 1990; Kumagai & Kumagai, 1985; Lebra, 1992). It is defined and experienced as inherently connected with others. In contrast to the European-American orientation, there is an abiding fear of being on one's own, of being separated or disconnected from the collective. A desire for independence is cast as unnatural and immature.

The major normative task of such a self is not to maintain the independence of the individual as a self-contained entity but instead to maintain *inter*dependence with others. Rather than as an independent decision maker, the self is cast as "a single thread in a richly textured fabric of relationships" (Kondo, 1990, p. 33). This view of the self and of the collective requires adjusting and fitting to important relationships, occupying one's proper place in the group, engaging in collectively appropriate actions, and promoting the goals of others. One's thoughts, feelings, and actions are made meaningful only in reference to the thoughts, feelings, and actions of others in the relationship, and consequently others are crucially important in the very definition of the self. (For more detailed descriptions of the interdependent self, see Hsu, 1953; Kondo, 1990; Markus & Kitayama, 1991.)

Interdependence in this sense is theoretically distinct from social identity (e.g., Tajfel & Turner, 1985; Turner & Oakes, 1989), which refers to social categorizations that define a person as a member of particular social categories (e.g., American, male, Protestant, engineer). Social identity, in the framework of Turner and colleagues, is always defined in counterpoint to personal identity, which

---

[1]For an analysis of the failure of teamwork in American corporations, see Hackman (1993), who argues that many American corporate teams are teams in name only. Typically, they are not stable or meaningfully interdependent. Moreover, they do not have control over their own affairs, and rewards and incentives are not at the team level but are given to individuals.

is all the ways a person is *different* from his or her in-groups. The key feature of interdependence is not distinctiveness or uniqueness but a heightened awareness of the other, and of the nature of one's relation to the other, and an expectation of some mutuality in this regard across all behavioral domains, even those that can be designated as private or personal.

Rooted in a Cartesian tradition, most European-American never question the natural and obvious separation of self and the collective. The notion of a self that in some respects transcends the limits of the individual's physical body and is inherently connected with others can be partly demystified by envisioning different ways of experiencing or knowing the self. Neisser (1988), for example, makes a useful distinction among five types of self-knowledge—ecological (i.e., the self as perceived with respect to the physical environment), interpersonal (i.e., a sense of self in human interchange), extended (i.e., a sense of self based on personal memories and anticipations), private (i.e., an awareness of self based on experiences not shared with others), and conceptual (i.e., one's theory of self). Building on the idea that self-representation is a plural phenomenon and can assume a diversity of forms, it is possible to hypothesize that although everyone has some store of private and ecological self-knowledge, from the interdependent perspective it is the self-in-human-interchange, or self-in-relation that is granted primacy in individual experience. In this view, a type of *intersubjectivity*, rather than a private subjectivity, would be the strongest, most elaborated aspect of self.

Differences in the Enculturation of the "Basic" Tasks

Although both European-American and Asian cultural groups recognize that independence from others and interdependence with others are essential human tendencies or tasks, these two tasks are weighted and organized quite differently in the two groups. The notion of the autonomous individual in continuous tension with the external collective is "natural" only from a particular cultural perspective. From an alternative perspective, such an arrangement appears somewhat unnatural and contrived. In Japan, for example, the culture in its dominant ideology, patterns of social customs, practices, and institutions emphasizes and fore-grounds not independence from others but interdependence with others. Interdependence is the first goal to be taken care of; it is crafted and nurtured in the social episodes and scripted actions of everyday social life, so that it becomes spontaneous, automatic, and taken for granted. Although independence is also essential for social functioning, it remains a tacit and less culturally elaborated pursuit. It is left to the intentions and initiatives of each individual member, and so its pursuit is relatively optional and is the focus of personal and unofficial discourse because it is not strongly constrained or widely supported by socially sanctioned cultural practices.[2]

The Cultural Shaping of Psychological Processes

In Figure 1, we have illustrated how the "reality" of independence is created and maintained in

---

[2]The reason that some cultural groups "do independence," highlighting in their practices and institutions the separation between the self and the collective, while others, "do interdependence," highlighting in their practices and institutions the interconnection between the self and the collective, is a mystery that is only now being analyzed (see e.g. Fiske, 1990; Taylor, 1989). These analyses begin with the notion that groups everywhere have a need to solve some questions about social existence. One of the most significant questions is, What is the self and what is not the self? In approaching this question, different groups make very different ideological commitments, drawing on diverse ontologies and philosophies.

According to one account, European-American culture naturally elaborates the individual level of reality—the person's seemingly separate and private store of thoughts, feelings, and proclivities—because it is rooted in an ontological tradition that favors, according to Lebra (1992), the "theistic/Cartesian split self." (Here *split* refers to the mind/body split and the self/other split as well as the cognitive/affective split.) Lebra argues that the goal of this ontological system is self-objectification. In this view, there is a highlighting of division between the experiencer and what is experienced, and becoming separate and independent from the surrounding context (both the natural and the interpersonal) is emphasized.

Lebra (1976) contends that Asian cultural groups, in contrast to those in the West, will more readily elaborate a social or interpersonal level of reality—the way in which the self is a connected and relational phenomenon—because they are tied to an ontological tradition that favors a notion of the submerged self, in which the goal is not self-objectification but instead freedom from self. Lebra argues that the perspective of the "Shinto-Buddhist submerged self downplays division between the experiencer and what is being experienced." It is connection with others and the surrounding context, rather than separation, that is emphasized.

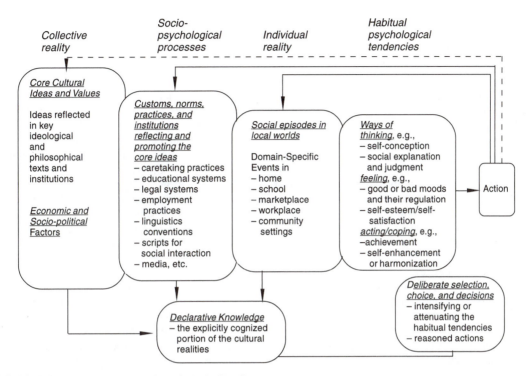

FIGURE 42.1 ■ Cultural shaping of psychological reality.

selves, as well as in theories of selves. According to this view, a cultural group's way of self-understanding is simultaneously related to a set of macrolevel phenomena, such as cultural views of personhood and their supporting collective practices, and to a set of microlevel phenomena, like individual lives and their constituent cognitive, emotional, and motivational processes.

Collective reality. Under the heading "collective reality" we have included cultural values and their related ecological, historical, economic, and sociopolitical factors. For example, the United States is a nation with a rich tradition of moral imperatives, but the most well elaborated is the need to protect the "natural rights" of each individual. This core cultural ideal is rooted most directly in the Declaration of Independence and the Bill of Rights, which protect certain inalienable rights, including life, liberty, and the pursuit of happiness. This highlighting of individuals and their rights is objectified and reified in a variety of democratic political institutions and free-market capitalism. In Japan, as throughout Asia, the prevalent ideological and moral discourses are not tied to individual rights but to the inevitability of a strict hierarchical order and to the achievement

of virtue through cultivation of the individual into a "social man" (Yu, 1992). This core cultural ideal is anchored in the works of Confucius and Mencius and finds expression in an array of economic, political, and social institutions.

Sociopsychological products and processes—transmitting the core ideas. The cultural ideals and moral imperatives of a given cultural group are given life by a diverse set of customs, norms, scripts, practices, and institutions that carry out the transformation of the collective reality into the largely personal or psychological reality. These sociopsychological products and processes objectify and make "real" the core ideas of the society (Bourdieu, 1972; D'Andrade, 1984; Durkheim, 1898/1953; Farr & Moscovici, 1984; Geertz, 1973; Oyserman & Markus, in press). For example, in the United States, the idea of human rights (including liberty from the thrall of the collective) as inherent and God-given gains its force from a large array of legal statutes protecting individual rights. In this way the individual gains superiority to the collective.

Child-rearing practices in the United States, rooted in Freudian theory and filtered through Dr. Spock and most recently the self-esteem movement, also work to develop the constituent elements of the self and to reinforce the importance of having a distinct self that the individual can feel good about. A recent study (Chao,1993), for example, found that 64% of European-American mothers, in comparison with 8% of Chinese mothers, stressed building children's "sense of themselves" as an important goal of child rearing. Many American mothers take every opportunity to praise children and to help them realize the ways in which they are positively unique or different from their peers. Training in autonomy and the development of the appreciation of being alone also comes early. Day-old children sleep alone in their cribs, often in separate rooms from their parents (Shweder, Jensen, & Goldstein, in press). On the playground, children are taught to stand up for themselves and fight back if necessary (Kashiwagi, 1989).

Another important quality of personhood, from the independent perspective, is the capacity to make one's own choice. In much of Western culture, but especially in North America, there are numerous examples of everyday scripts that presuppose the actor's right to make a choice. It is common for American hosts to instruct their guests, "Help yourself." With this suggestion, the host invites the guest to affirm the self by expressing some of those preferences that are thought to constitute the "real self." American children, then, are socialized to have distinct preferences. Long before the child is old enough to answer, caretakers pose questions like "Do you want the red cup or the blue cup?" With such questions, mothers signal to children that the capacity for independent choice is an important and desirable attribute. And the availability of choice gives rise to the need for preferences by which to make choices.

The practices of the media further create and foster the objectivity of the autonomous, independent self. Advertising in the United States makes appeals to nonconformity, originality, and uniqueness. A hard-sell approach is common in which the product is presented as the best or the leader of its kind, and purchasing it is claimed to reveal that the consumer has the "right" preferences or attitudes (Mueller, 1987; Zandpour, Chang, & Catalano, 1992). For example, Chanel recently marketed, in both the United States and Europe, a men's cologne with the strikingly unsubtle name of *Egoïste* and the slogan "For the man who walks on the right side of the fine line between arrogance and awareness of self-worth."

Perhaps the most powerful practice of all for the purpose of creating a shared concern with independence is that of advancing, promoting, and compensating people according to their "merit." This practice places a lifelong emphasis on inner attributes, capacities, and abilities as the "real" measures of the self and encourages people to define and develop these attributes.

In many Asian cultures, there is an equally diverse and powerful set of sociopsychological processes in each of these corresponding domains, but these practices are rooted in a view of the self as an interdependent entity. For example, in place of (or, to a certain extent, in addition to) the emphasis on human rights, there exist dense systems of rules and norms that highlight the duties of each individual to the pertinent collective, whether it is the company, school, or nation. Moreover, there are many fewer statutes protecting individual rights, and the Japanese resort to court suits to secure their rights far less readily than European-Americans (Hideo, 1988).

In the course of interpersonal interaction, the Japanese are encouraged to try to read the partner's mind and to satisfy what is taken as the partner's expectations or desires. A Japanese mother does not ask for a child's preference but instead tries to determine what is best for the child and to arrange it. Rather than asking a guest to make a choice, Japanese hosts do their best to prepare and offer what they infer to be the best possible meal for the guest, saying, for example, "Here's a turkey sandwich for you. I thought you said you like turkey better than beef last time we met."

Child rearing in many Asian cultures places a continual emphasis on understanding and relating to others, first to the mother and then to a wide range of others. The rules of interdependence are explicitly modeled, and the goal is to maintain harmonious relationships (Hsu, 1953). Interdependence can be found in all domains. In stark opposition to American practices and Freudian wisdom, cosleeping and cobathing are common in Japanese families. The emphasis is not on developing a good, private sense of self but on tuning in to and being sensitive to others. Punishing or reprimanding Japanese children often involves not the withholding of rights and privileges but a threat to the relationship. Mothers will say, "I don't like children like you" or "People will laugh at you" (Okimoto & Rohlen, 1988).

With respect to media practices, Japanese advertising often uses soft-sell appeals that focus on harmony or connection with nature or with others (Mueller, 1987). In classified ads, employers explicitly seek individuals with good interpersonal relations, as opposed to self-starters or innovators (Caproni, Rafaeli, & Carlile, 1993). A focus on relationships is also evident in all types of business practices. Japan stands out from all countries in the West because of its emphasis on durable and pervasive ties between government and industry, between banks and businesses, and among corporations. Okimoto and Rohlen (1988) contend that the emphasis on organizational networks and human relationships is so strong that Japanese capitalism can be labeled *relational capitalism*. In the pursuit of long-term relationships and mutual trust, Japanese corporations operate quite differently, often, for example, forgoing the maximization of short-term profits with the hope of gaining a long-term market share. And in contrast to the European-American emphasis on merit for promotion and compensation, wages and advancement in the majority of Japanese companies and institutions are tied to seniority in the system. In addition, employment in large corporations is typically permanent, and there is little lateral entry from the outside—all publicly scripted collective practices that foster and promote a view of the self as inherently relational and interdependent.

Beyond the caretaking, legal, business, and media practices we have alluded to are a host of others, including educational and linguistic practices, and all the scripts and institutions that structure everyday social interactions. An important element in understanding which practices will become socially established is how the practices reflect and carry the group's underlying cultural values. Americans, for example, will be particularly susceptible to ideas and practices that directly follow from individualism (Sperber, 1985). Other practices—welfare and universal health care programs are good examples—will have a more difficult time taking hold in the United States.

Local worlds—living the core ideas. The third segment of Figure 1 represents the specific settings, circumstances, and situations of everyday life that make up an individual's immediate social environment and in which particular customs, norms, and practices become lived experience. The local worlds—home, school, the work-place, the community center, the church, the restaurant, bar, or cafe, the marketplace—and the specific activi-

ties or episodes they support—helping a child with homework, shopping for a gift, drinking with friends, discussing politics, playing baseball, working with others to meet a deadline—demand specific, culturally appropriate responses if a person is to become a valued member of the family, school, workplace, or community.

It is within the demands and expectations of these domain-specific, recurrent social episodes that people, often quite unknowingly, live out the core cultural values. So Americans are likely to create and live within settings that elicit and promote the sense that one is a positively unique individual who is separate and independent from others. For example, in many American schools, each child in the class has the opportunity to be a "star" or a "Very Special Person" for a week during the school year. Likewise, Japanese will create and live with situations that promote the sense of self as interdependent with others. In Japanese schools, children routinely produce group pictures or story boards, and no child leaves to go to the playground or lunch until all members of the group are ready to leave.

Habitual psychological tendencies reflecting the core ideas. As a result of efforts to respond or adjust to the set of specific episodes that constitute the individual's life space, episodes that have themselves been shaped by norms, practices, and institutions supporting the cultural group's core ideas, a set of habitual psychological tendencies is likely to develop. The final segment of Figure 1 represents the individual's "authentic" subjective experience—particular, proceduralized ways of thinking, feeling, striving, knowing, understanding, deciding, managing, adjusting, adapting, which are, in some large part, structured, reinforced, and maintained by the constraints and affordances of the particular social episodes of the individual's local worlds. In this way, people who live within a society whose daily practices and formal institutions all promote independence will come not just to believe that they are, but to experience themselves as, autonomous, bounded selves who are distinct from other members of the collective. This will be evident in many ways of thinking, feeling, and acting, but it is particularly evident when people are asked to characterize themselves.

For example, by the time they are young adults, many Americans will seek an optimal distinctiveness from others (Brewer, 1990) and will "naturally" experience an ambivalence about their collective nature and a deep concern with being categorically perceived or socially determined. The journalist Barbara Ehrenreich (1992) describes an interchange with an acquaintance who has just rediscovered her own ethnic and religious heritage and now feels in contact with her 2000-year ancestral traditions. The acquaintance asks about Ehrenreich's ethnic background. The first word to come out of Ehrenreich's mouth in answer to the question is "None." She is surprised at how natural and right her answer seems, yet slightly embarrassed. She reflects and decides that her response when asked the nature of her ethnicity was quite correct. Her identity, she claims, comes from the realization that "we are the kind of people that whatever our distant ancestors' religions—we do not believe, we do not carry on traditions, we do not do things just because someone has done them before." Her ethnicity, she contends, is rooted not in a given group but in the ideas "Think for yourself" and "Try new things." In conclusion, Ehrenreich tells of asking her own children whether they ever had any stirring of "ethnic or religious identity." "None," they all conclude, and she reports, "My chest swelled with pride as would my mother's to know that the race of 'None' marches on."

A tendency to define one's "real" self as distinct from one's social groups and obligations is characteristic of both younger and older cohorts of Americans as well. In a series of studies with young children, Hart and his colleagues (Hart, 1988; Hart & Edelstein, 1992) asked American children to imagine a "person machine" that makes the original person disappear but at the same time manufactures other people, copies of the original, which receive some but not all of the original person's characteristics. The respondent's task is to judge which new manufactured person—the one with the same physical attributes (looks like you), the one with the same social attributes (has the same friends and family), or the one with the same psychological attributes (same thoughts and feelings)—will be most like the original person. By ninth grade, Hart et al. (Hart, Fegley, Hung Chan, Mulvey, & Fischer, 1993) finds that most respondents believe it is the copy with the original's psychological characteristics that is the most similar to the original.

These findings are consistent with those of several other studies of cultural variation in self-cat-

egorization (Cousins, 1989; Triandis, 1990) and suggest that, for American students, it is the internal features of the self—the traits, attributes, and attitudes—that are privileged and regarded as critical to self-definition. From this perspective, the significant aspects of the self are those that are the inside, the private property—one's characteristic ways of behaving, one's habitual thoughts, feelings, and beiiefs (e.g., think for yourself, try new things)—the elements that do not explicitly reference others or the social world. Such internal attributes are also mentioned by the Japanese, but they appear to be understood as relatively situation specific and therefore elusive and unreliable (Cousins, 1989) as defining features of self. For the Japanese, the critical features are those attributes—social roles, duties, obligations—that connect one to the larger world of social relationships. (For other detailed examples of the cultural shaping of judgment, self, and emotion, see Kitayama & Markus, 1993, in press; Markus & Kitayama, 1994.) In a study examining response time for self-description, Kitayama et al. (1991) find that Japanese respondents are decidedly slower to characterize themselves than American respondents and that this is particularly true for positive attributes.

The top level of Figure 1 indicates feedback loops from each individual's action. The most immediate and frequent feedback occurs at the micro level. Most obviously, what an individual does influences the very nature of the situation in which he or she has acted. There are, however, people who at times contribute, through their actions, not just to the micro level but also to the more macro level. The bottom level of Figure 1 represents a more cognitive influence. Some portion of the social realities—both macro and micro—can be represented cognitively. This cognized portion of culture is shaded in each segment of the figure. The articulated, declarative knowledge of cultural values, practices, and conventions may be recruited in modulating social action, either facilitating or inhibiting the automatized psychological tendencies. Importantly, however, psychological tendencies can develop independently of this second, articulated route of cultural influence. In this way, cultural values and beliefs can cause differences in psychological processes even when these beliefs (e.g., a fear of influence by the collective) are not cognitively encoded and overtly articulated. Of course, the values and beliefs often are encoded cognitively, but this current analysis implies that cognitive representations need not be central in the cultural shaping of psychological processes. Instead, we suggest that psychological processes and behavior can be best understood as an important, but only partial, element of the dynamic cultural and historical process that involves the systematic (though by no means error-free or "faxlike") transmission of cultural imperatives to shape and define the nature of the specific, immediate life space—the microlevel reality—for each individual.

Implications of a Collective Fear of the Collective for Psychological Theorizing

Using Asian cultures, particularly Japan, as a point of reference and standard, we have sketched how the European-American fear of the collective may arise and how it is naturalized, enacted, and embodied so that people rarely see or feel the collective nature or source of their behavior and instead experience themselves as separate and self-contained entities. A large set of mutually reinforcing everyday rituals, social practices, and institutions work together to elaborate and objectify the culture's view of what the self is and what it should be. Independence and autonomy are thus the "natural" mode of being—in Geertz's (1975) terms, they become "experience near" phenomena. The subjective authenticity or "naturalness" of this mode, however, is a function of the degree of fit between habitual psychological tendencies and the cultural and social systems that are grounded in these cultural imperatives.

Theorists of European-American behavior have also been extremely influenced by the prevailing ideology of individualism. They have often viewed the self as in tension, or even as in opposition, to the "ruck of society" (Plath, 1980) or the "thrall of society" (Hewitt, 1989). The source of all important behavior is typically "found" in the unique configuration of internal attributes—thoughts, feelings, motives, abilities—that form the bounded, autonomous whole. As a consequence, the ways in which the self is, in fact, quite interdependent with the collective have been underanalyzed and undertheorized. It is our view that there are a number of important reasons for theorists to go beyond theories that are directly shaped by the cultural ideal of individualism and

to consider a broader view of the self.

First, and most obviously, although current descriptions of the largely independent and autonomous self could be argued to be reasonably adequate for European-American selves, a growing body of evidence suggests that they are simply not valid for many other cultural groups (see extended discussions of this point in Markus & Kitayama, 1991; Triandis, 1990; Triandis, Bontempo, & Villareal, 1988). Second, although the cultural ideal of independence is very influential in the nature and functioning of the European-American self, it does not determine it completely. For example, with respect to the bounded or fixed nature of the self, there are a variety of studies that reveal the self as decidedly malleable and its content and functioning as dependent on the social context. Typically these studies are not integrated with the literature that suggests stability of the self (e.g., Fazio, Effrein, & Falender, 1981; James, 1993; Jones & Pittman, 1982; Markus & Kunda, 1986; McGuire & McGuire, 1982; Schlenker, 1980).

Third, at least in the United States, the analysis of the selves of those groups in society that are somewhat marginalized—women, members of nondominant ethnic groups, the poor, the unschooled, and the elderly—reveals a more obvious interdependence between the self and the collective. For example, women describe themselves in relational terms (Gilligan, 1982; Jordan, Kaplan, Miller, Stivey, & Surrey, 1991), and they do not reveal the "typical" preference for being positively unique or different from others (Josephs, Markus, & Tafarodi, 1992). Other studies reveal that those groups that are in the minority with respect to language, skin color, or religion are decidedly more likely to define themselves in collective terms (Allen, Dawson, & Brown, 1989; Bowman, 1987; Husain, 1992). Further, Americans with less schooling are more likely to describe themselves in terms of habitual actions and roles, and less likely to characterize themselves in terms of psychological attributes, than those with more schooling (Markus, Herzog, Holmberg, & Dielman, 1992). And those with low self-esteem show a marked tendency to describe themselves as similar to others (Josephs et al., 1992). These findings suggest that those with power and privilege are those most likely to internalize the prevailing European-American cultural frame to achieve Ehrenreich's "ethnicity of none" and to "naturally" experience themselves as autonomous individuals.

Fourth, a number of recent studies show many Americans to be extremely concerned about others and the public good (Bellah et al., 1985; Bellah, Madsen, Sullivan, Swidler, & Tipton, 1991; Hewitt, 1989; Withnow, 1992) and to characterize themselves in interdependent terms. For example, a recent representative sample of 1,500 adults, aged 30 or over, found that although Americans indeed characterized themselves in terms of trait attributes and not social roles or obligations, the most frequently used attributes were *caring, responsible, loved*— all terms that imply some concern with a connection to the collective (Markus et al., 1992). Even if, as we have suggested, this connection is clearly voluntary and done on one's own terms, the prevailing model of the self could be modified.

And finally, increasingly throughout social psychology, there are indications that the individualist model of the self is too narrow and fails to take account of some important aspects of psychological reality. For example, within social psychology specifically, there is a great deal of evidence that people are exquisitely sensitive to others and to social pressure. People conform, obey, diffuse responsibility in a group, allow themselves to be easily persuaded about all manner of things, and become powerfully committed to others on the basis of minimal action (Myers, 1993). Despite the powerful cultural sanctions against allowing the collective to influence one's thoughts and actions, most people are still much less self-reliant, self-contained, or self-sufficient than the ideology of individualism suggests they should be. It appears in these cases that the European-American model of self is somewhat at odds with observed individual behavior and that it might be reformulated to reflect the substantial interdependence that characterizes even Western individualists.

Alternative Views of the Self and the Collective

In trying to formulate the collective sources of the self among Europeans or Americans, models of the self and the collective "Asian style" may be particularly informative.[3] If we assume, as does Shweder (1991), that every group can be considered an expert on some features of human experience and that different cultural groups "light up" different aspects of this experience, then Asian

cultures may be an important source of conceptual resources in the form of concepts, frameworks, theories, or methods that can be employed to "see" interdependence. Even though interdependence American style will doubtlessly look quite different from interdependence Japanese style, an analysis of divergent cultural groups may further any theorist's understanding of the possibilities, potential and consequences, both positive and negative, for socialness, for engagement, for interdependence, and for the ties that bind.[4]

The first step in expanding theories of the self and the collective seems to require being deliberately self conscious about what is being taken for granted in the initial formulation of the problem and about the labels that are used. If a theorist accepts the notion that the self is constantly striving to defend itself from the collective, then influence by others is viewed as a weakness or as failure. Looking for possible consequences of such behavior will be seen as just so much rationalization. Yet, from the perspective of a model that acknowledge interdependence between the self and the collective, social influence, acknowledgment of others, attunement with others, imitation of others, the inhibition of private thoughts or feelings even yielding to others can be framed quite differently. Such actions can be construed as essential positive, and empowering (Azuma, 1986; Weisz, Rothbaum, & Blackburn,1984).

Consider the phenomenon of conformity. It typi-

---

[3]Some of the most important work suggesting the need for alternative models of the self comes from feminist theorists who have argued in the last 15 years that relations have a power and significance in women's lives that has gone unrecognized (Belenky, Clinchy, Goldberger, & Tarule, 1986; Gilligan, 1982; Jordan et al., 1991), The development of a psychology of women has shown that the "Lone Ranger" model of the self simply does not fit many women's experience because women's sense of self seems to involve connection and engagement with relationships and collective. In this work, being dependent does not invariably mean being helpless, powerless, or without control. It often means being interdependent—having a sense that one is able to have an effect on others and is willing to be responsive to others and become engaged with them (Jordan, 1991).

[4]Interdependence in Japan is a collective, multiply represented and reinforced goal. As interdependence is the prescribed way of being a self, there is relatively little ambivalence about it in public discourse. It is hard to be otherwise, and interdependence seldom seems a matter of conscious, active choice. Yet, in many European and American groups, interdependence is for the most part not culturally sanctioned and maintained, and it is left for people to deliberately negotiate on their own terms.

cally occurs when there is an ambiguous stimulus situation. Although conformity is obviously a necessary integrative mechanism, it is often cast as yielding to the collective, and investigators work to explain why it is that individuals feel the need to give in. This same behavior could be viewed as the mutual negotiation of social reality or as attunement with the other. Indeed, In Japan giving in to another is typically not a sign of weakness; rather, it can reflect tolerance, self-control, maturity. A recent study by Horike (1992) revealed that "conforming naturally to others" was the most important factor underlying humanness among Japanese respondents.

Or consider the phenomenon of groupthink. This occurs when members are deeply involved in a very cohesive group. It is said to occur when "members striving for unanimity override their motivation to realistically appraise alternative courses of action" (Jains, 1982, p. 9). Here, as with conformity, groupthink is viewed as a weakness, a failure of the autonomous self. Even given negative consequences like the Bay of Pigs invasion (said to be a result of groupthink), this same behavior could be analyzed as consensual decision making. By reconstituting "conformity" and "groupthink" as socially legitimate processes of mutual negotiation for consensual understanding and definition of the focal situation or issue, it may be possible to advance a somewhat different perspective on the link between the collective and individual thought and to more fully consider the nature and consequences of socially induced thought. Similarly, deindividuation could be seen from an alternative perspective on the self and the collective, not as a loss of self—the ultimate failure from the perspective of individualist ideology—but as the purposeful inhibition of one's thoughts and feelings, a clearing of the screen, to allow one to be receptive to others.

Another model of the self and the collective could also provide an alternative view of two of psychology's oldest problems—the inconsistency between attitudes and behavior and the inconsistency between personality and behavior. From an interdependent perspective, such behavior does not have to be framed negatively and does not have to give rise to great theoretical consternation. Interdependent selves do not prescribe or require consistency between one's internal attributes and one's actions. In fact, such consistency may reflect, not authenticity, but a lack of flexibility, rigidity, or even immaturity.

We have argued here that the cultural frame of individualism has put a very strong stamp on how social psychologists view the individual and his or her relation to the collective. Although this individualist view has provided a powerful framework for the analysis of social behavior, it has also, necessarily, constrained theories, methods, and dominant interpretations of social behavior. Because individualism is not just a matter of belief or value but also one of everyday practice, including scientific practice, it is not easy for theorists to view social behavior from another cultural frame, and it is probably harder still to reflect a different frame in empirical work. But the comparative approach that is characteristic of the developing cultural psychology (e.g., Cole, 1990; Stigler, Shweder, & Herdt, 1990) may eventually open new and productive possibilities for the understanding and analysis of behavior.

For example, just as social influence, from the perspective of an interdependent cultural frame, can be seen as the mutual negotiation of social reality, helping can be seen as a result of obligation, duty, or morality, rather than as voluntary or intentional (e.g., Miller et al., 1990). Similarly, emotion can be viewed as an enacted interpersonal process (Rosaldo, 1984) or as an interpersonal atmosphere, as it is characterized in some non-Western theories (White, 1990). Further cognition can be seen as an internalized aspect of communication (Zajonc, 1992), and the early idea of the social and interactive nature of the mind (e.g., Asch, 1952; Bruner, 1990; Vygotsky, 1978) can be taken much more seriously than it has been. In general, viewing the self and social behavior from alternative perspectives may enable theorists to see and elaborate at least one important and powerful universal that might otherwise be quite invisible—the ways in which psychological functioning (in this case, the nature of the self), as well as theories about psychological functioning (here, theories of the nature of the self), are in many ways culture specific and conditioned by particular, but tacit and taken-for-granted, meaning systems, values, and ideals.

ACKNOWLEDGMENTS

The authors would like to acknowledge the support of the National Science Foundation Grant #BNS9010754 during the time this article was written.

REFERENCES

Allen, R. L., Dawson, M. C., & Brown, R. E. (1989). A schema based approach to modeling an African American racial belief system *American Political Science Review, 83,* 421–442

Asch, S. E. (1952). *Social psychology.* Englewood Cliffs, NJ: Prentice-Hall.

Azuma, H. (1986). Why study child development in Japan? In H. Stevenson, H. Azuma, & K. Hakuta (Eds.), *Child development and education in Japan* (pp. 3–12). New York: Freeman.

Belenky, M. F., Clinchy, B. M., Goldberger, N. R., & Tarule, J. M. (1986). *Women's ways of knowing, The development of self, wise, and mind.* New York: Basic Books.

Bellah, R. N., Madsen, R., Sullivan, W. M., Swidler, A., & Tipton, S. M. (1985). *Habits of the heart: Individualism and commitment in American life.* Berkeley: University of California Press.

Bellah, R. N., Madsen, R., Sullivan, W. M., Swidler, A., & Tipton, S. M. (1991) *The good society.* New York: Knopf.

Bourdieu, P. (1972). *Outline of a theory of practice* Cambridge: Cambridge University Press.

Bowman, P. J. (1987). Post-industrial displacement and family role strains: Challenges to the Black family. In P. Voydanoff & L. C. Majka (Eds.), *Families and economic distress.* Newbury Park. CA: Sage.

Brewer, M. B. (1990, August). *The social self; On being the same and different at the same time.* Presidential address to the Society for Personality and Social Psychology presented at the annual meeting of the American Psychological Association, Boston.

Bruner, J. (1990). *Acts of meeting.* Cambridge, MA: Harvard University Press.

Caproni, P., Rafaeli, A., & Carlile P. (1993, July). *The social instruction of work. The role of newspaper employment advertising.* Paper presented at the European Group on Organization Studies conference, Paris, France.

Chao, R. K. (1993). *East and West. Concepts of the self reflected in mothers' reports of their child-rearing.* Unpublished manuscript, University of California, Los Angeles.

Cole, M. (1990). Cultural psychology: A once and future discipline? In J. J. Berman (Ed.), *Nebraska Symposium on Motivation,* 1989 (vol. 37, pp. 279–336). Lincoln: University of Nebraska Press.

Cousins, S. (1989). Culture and selfhood in Japan and the U. S. *Journal of Personality and Social Psychology, 56,* 24–131.

Crocker, J., & Luhtanen, R. (1990). Collective self-esteem and ingroup bias. *Journal of Personality and Social Psychology, 58,* 60–67.

D'Andrade, R. (1984). Cultural meaning systems. In R. A. Shweder & R. A. LeVine (Eds.), *Cultural theories: Essays on mind, self and emotion* (pp. 88–119). New York: Cambridge University Press.

Daniels, E. V. (1984). *Fluid signs: Being a person the Tamil way.* Berkeley: University of California Press.

Derne, S. (1992). Beyond institutional and impulsive conceptions of self: Family structure and the socially anchored real self. *Ethos, 20,* 259–288.

de Tocqueville, A. (1969). *Democracy in America* (J. P. Mayer, Ed., G. Lawrence, Trans.). Garden City, NY: Anchor. (Original work published 1835)

Durkheim, E. (1953). Individual representations and collective representations. In E Durkheim (Ed.), *Sociology and philosophy* (D. F. Pocok, Trans.) (pp. 1–38). New York: Free Press. (Original work published 1898)

Ehrenreich, B. (1992, March). The race of none. *Sunday New York Times Magazine,* pp. 5–6.

Farr, R. M. (1991). Individualism as a collective representation. In V. Aebischer, J. P. Deconchy, & M. Lipiansky (Eds.), *Idéologies el representations sociales* (pp. 129–143). Cousset (Fribourg), Switzerland: Delval.

Farr, R. M., & Moscovici, S. (Eds.). (1984). *Social representations.* Cambridge: Cambridge University Press.

Fazio, R. H., Effrein, E. A., & Falender, Y. J. (1981). Self-perceptions following social interactions. *Journal of Personality and Social Psychology, 41,* 232–242.

Fiske, A. P. (1990). *Making up society: The four elementary relational structures.* New York: Free Press.

Gates, H. L., Jr. (1993, September 20). Let them talk. *New Republic,* pp. 37–49.

Geertz, C. (1973). *The interpretation of cultures.* New York: Basic Books.

Geertz, C. (1975). On the nature of anthropological understanding. *American Scientist, 63,* 47–53.

Gergen, K. J., & Gergen, M. M. (1988). Narrative and the self as relationship. In L. Berkowitz (Ed.), *Advances in experimental social psychology* (Vol. 21, pp. 17–56). New York: Academic Press.

Gilligan, C. (1982). *In a different voice: Psychological theory and women's development.* Cambridge, MA: Harvard University Press.

Greenwald, A. G. (1980). The totalitarian ego; Fabrication and revision of personal history. *American Psychologist, 35,* 603–618.

Hackman. (1993, October). Why groups don't work. Paper presented at the ICOS. University of Michigan, Ann Arbor.

Hart, D. (1988). The adolescent self-concept in social context. In D. Lapsley & F. Power (Eds.), *Self, ego, and identity: Integrative approaches* (pp. 71–90). New York: Springer-Verlag.

Hart, D., & Edelstein, W. (1992). Self understanding development in cultural context. In T. M. Brinthaupt & R. P. Lipka (Eds.), *The self definitional and methodological issues.* Albany: State University of New York Press.

Hart, D., Fegley, S., Hung Chan, Y., Mulvey, D., & Fischer, L. (1993). *Judgement about personal identity in childhood and adolescence.* Unpublished manuscript.

Hewitt, J. P. (1989). *Dilemmas of the American self.* Philadelphia: Temple University Press.

Hideo, T. (1988). The role of law and lawyers in Japanese society. In D. I. Okimoto & T. P. Rohlen (Eds.), *Inside the Japanese system: Readings on contemporary society and political economy* (pp. 194–196). Stanford, CA: Stanford University Press.

Horike, K. (1992, July). *An investigation of the Japanese social skills. What is called "hito-atari-no-yosa" (affability).* Paper presented at the 25th International Congress of Psychology, Brussels, Belgium.

Hsu, F. L. K. (1953). *Americans and Chinese: Two ways of life.* New York: H. Schuman.

Husain, M. G. (1992, July). *Ethnic uprising and identity.* Paper presented at the 11th Congress of the International Association for Cross-cultural Psychology, Liege, Belgium.

Icheiser, C. (1943). Misunderstandings in human relations: A study in false social perception. *American Journal of Sociology, 55* (suppl.).

James, K. (1993). Conceptualizing self with in-group stereotypes: Context and esteem precursors. *Personality and Social Psychology Bulletin, 19,* 117–121.

Janis, I. L. (1982). *Groupthink: Psychological studies of policy decisions and fiascoes.* Boston: Houghton Mifflin.

Jones, E. E., & Pittman, T. S. (1982). Towards a general theory of strategic self-preservation. In J. Suls (Ed.), *Psychological perspectives on the self* (Vol. 1, pp. 231–262). Hillsdale, NJ: Lawrence Erlbaum.

Jordan, J. V. (1991). Empathy and self boundaries. In J. V. Jordan, A. G. Kaplan, J. B. Miller, I. P. Stivey, & J. L. Surrey (Eds.), *Women's growth in connection* (pp. 67–80). New York: Guilford.

Jordan, J. V., Kaplan, A. G., Miller, J. B., Stivey, I. P., & Surrey, J. L. (Eds.). (1991). *Women's growth in connection.* New York: Guilford.

Josephs, R. A., Markus, H., & Tafarodi, R. W. (1992). Gender differences in the source of self-esteem. *Journal of Personality and Social Psychology, 63,* 391–402.

Kashiwagi, K. (1989, July). *Development of self-regulation in Japanese children.* Paper presented at the tenth annual meeting of the International Society for the Study of Behavioral Development, Jyvaskyla, Finland.

Kitayama, S., & Markus, H. (1993). Construal of the self as a cultural frame: Implications for internationalizing psychology. In J. D'Arms, R. G. Hastie, S. E. Hoelscher, & H. K. Jacobson (Eds.), *Becoming more international and global: Challenges for American higher education.* Manuscript submitted for publication.

Kitayama, S., & Markus, H. (in press). A cultural perspective on self-conscious emotions. In J. P. Tangney & K. W. Fisher (Eds.), *Shame, guilt, embarrassment and pride: Empirical studies of self-conscious emotions.* New York: Guilford.

Kitayama, S., Markus, H., & Kurokawa, M. (1991, October). *Culture, self, and emotion: The structure and frequency of emotional experience.* Paper presented at the biannual meeting of the Society for Psychological Anthropology, Chicago.

Kondo, D. (1990). *Grafting selves: Power, gender, and discourses of identity in a Japanese work place.* Chicago: University of Chicago Press.

Kumagai, H. A., & Kumagai, A. K. (1985). The hidden "I" in *amae*: "Passive love" and Japanese social perception. *Ethos, 14,* 305–321.

Lebra, T. S. (1976). *Japanese patterns of behavior.* Honolulu: University of Hawaii Press.

Lebra, T. S. (1992, June). *Culture, self, and communication.* Paper presented at the University of Michigan, Ann Arbor.

Markus, H. (1977). Self-schemas and processing information about the self. *Jormal of Personality and Social Psychology, 35,* 63–78.

Markus, H., Herzog, A. R., Holmberg, D. E., & Dielman L. (1992). *Constructing the self across the life span.* Unpublished manuscript. University of Michigan, Ann Arbor.

Markus, H., & Kitayama, S. (1991). Culture and the self: Implications for cognition, emotion, and motivation. *Psychological Review, 98,* 224–253.

Markus, H., & Kitayama, S. (1992). The what, why and how of cultural psychology: A review of R. Shweder's *Thinking through cultures. Psychological Inquiry, 3,* 357–364.

Markus, H., & Kitayama, S. (1994). The cultural construction of self and emotion: Implications for social behavior. In S. Kitayama & H. R. Markus (Eds.), *Emotion and culture: Empirical studies of mutual influence* (pp. 39–130). Washington, DC: American Psychological Association.

Markus, H., & Kunda, Z. (1986). Stability and malleability in the self-concept in the perception of others. *Journal of Personality and Social Psychology, 51,* 1–9.

McGuire, W. J., & McGuire, C. V. (1982). Significant others in self space: Sex differences and developmental trends in social self. In J. Suls (Ed.), *Psychological perspectives in the self* (Vol. 1, pp. 71–96). Hillsdale, NJ: Lawrence Erlbaum.

Miller, J. G., Bersoff, D. M., & Harwood, R. L. (1990). Perceptions of social responsibilities in India and in the United States: Moral imperatives or personal decisions? *Journal of Personality and Social Psychology, 58,* 33–46.

Moscovici, S. (1984). The phenomena of social representations. In R. M. Farr & S. Moscovici (Eds.), *Social representations* (pp. 3–69). Cambridge: Cambridge University Press.

Mueller, B. (1987, June/July). Reflections of culture: An analysis of Japanese and American advertising appeals. *Journal of Advertising Research,* pp. 51–59.

Myers, D. (1993). *Social psychology* (4th ed.). New York: McGraw-Hill.

Neisser, U. (1988). Five kinds of self-knowledge. *Philosophical Psychology, 1,* 35–59.

Okimoto, D. I., & Rohlen, T. P. (Eds.). (1988). *Inside the Japanese system: Readings on contemporary society and political economy.* Stanford, CA: Stanford University Press.

Oyserman, D., & Markus, H. R. (in press). Self as social representation. In S. Moscovici & U. Flick (Eds.), *Psychology of the social.* Berlin: Rowohlt Taschenbuch Verlag Gmbh.

Oyserman, D., & Markus, H. R. (1993). The sociocultural self. In J. Suls (Ed.), *Psychological perspectives on the self, volume 4: The self in social perspective.* Hillsdale, NJ: Erlbaum.

Plath, D. W. (1980). *Long engagements: Maturity in modern Japan.* Stanford, CA: Stanford University Press.

Rosaldo, M. (1984). Toward an anthropology of self and feeling. In R. A. Shweder & R. A. LeVine (Eds.), *Culture theory: Essays on mind, self, and emotion* (pp. 137–157). Cambridge: Cambridge University Press.

Rosenberg, M. (1979). *Conceiving the self.* New York: Basic Books.

Sampson, E. E. (1985). The decentralization of identity. Toward a revised concept of personal and social order. *American Psychologist, 40,* 1203–1211.

Schlenker, B. R. (1980). *Impression management.* Pacific Grove, CA: Brooks/Cole.

Shweder, R. A. (1991). *Thinking through cultures: Expeditions in cultural psychology.* Cambridge, MA: Harvard University Press.

Shweder, R. A., & Bourne, E. (1984). Does the concept of the person vary cross-culturally? In R. A. Shweder & R. A. LeVine (Eds.), *Culture theory: Essays on mind, self, and emotion* (pp. 158–199). Cambridge: Cambridge University Press.

Shweder, R. A., Jensen, L. A., & Goldstein, W. M. (in press). Who sleeps by whom revisited: A method for extracting the moral goods implicit in practice. In J. Goodnow, P. Miller, & F. Kessel (Eds.), *Cultural practices as contexts for development.* San Francisco: Jossey-Bass.

Sperber, D. (1985). Anthropology and psychology: Towards an epidemiology of representations. *MAN, 20,* 73–89.

Stigler, J. W., Shweder, R. A., & Herdt, G. (Eds.). (1990). *Cultural psychology: Essays on comparative human development.* London: Cambridge University Press.

Tajfel, H. (1981). *Human groups and social categories: Studies in social psychology.* Cambridge: Cambridge University Press.

Tajfel, H., & Turner, J. C. (1985). The social identity theory of inter-group behavior. In S. Worchel & W. G. Austin (Eds.), *Psychology of intergroup relations* (pp. 7–24). Chicago: Nelson-Hall.

Taylor, C. (1989). *Sources of the self: The making of modern identities.* Cambridge, MA: Harvard University Press.

Tesser, A., & Campbell, J. (1983). Self-definition and self-evaluation maintenance. In J. Suls & A. Greenwald (Eds.), *Psychological perspectives on the self* (Vol. 2, pp. 1–31). Hillsdale, NJ: Lawrence Erlbaum.

Triandis, H. C. (1990). Cross-cultural studies of individualism and collectivism. In J. J. Berman (Ed.), *Nebraska Symposium on Motivation,* 1989 (Vol. 37, pp. 41–143).

Triandis, H. C., Bontempo, R., & Villareal, M. (1988). Individualism and collectivism: Cross-cultural perspectives on self-ingroup relationships. *Journal of Personality and Social Psychology, 54,* 323–338.

Turner, J. C., & Oakes, P. J. (1989). Self-categorization theory and social influence. In P. B. Paulus (Ed.), *The psychology of group influence* (2nd ed.). Hillsdale, NJ: Lawrence Erlbaum.

Vygotsky, L. S. (1978). *Mind in society: The development of higher psychological processes* (M. Cole, V. John-Steiner, S. Scribner, & E. Souberman, Eds.). Cambridge, MA: Harvard University Press.

Weisz, J. R., Rothbaum, F. M., & Blackburn, T. C. (1984). Standing out and standing in: The psychology of control in America and Japan. *American Psychologist, 39,* 955–969.

White, G. M. (1990). Moral discourse and the rhetoric of emotion. In C. Lutz & L. Abu-Lughod (Eds.), *Language and the politics of emotion* Cambridge: Cambridge University Press.

White, G. M., & Kirkpatrick, J. (Eds.). (1985). *Person, self, and experience: Exploring Pacific ethnopsychologies.* Berkeley and Los Angeles: University of California Press.

Withnow, R. (1992). *Acts of compassion.* Princeton, NJ: Princeton University Press.

Yu, A. B. (1992, July). *The self and life goals of traditional Chinese: A philosophical and cultural analysis.* Paper presented at the 11th Congress of the International Association for Cross-Cultural Psychology, Liege, Belgium.

Zajonc, R. B. (1992, April). *Cognition, communication, consciousness: A social psychological perspective.* Invited address at the 20th Katz-Newcomb Lecture at the University of Michigan, Ann Arbor.

Zandpour, F., Chang, C., & Catalano, J. (1992, January/February). Stories, symbols, and straight talk: A comparative analysis of French, Taiwanese, and U. S. TV commercials. *Journal of Advertising Research,* pp. 25–38.

Appendix: How to Read a Journal Article in Social Psychology

Christian H. Jordan and Mark P. Zanna • University of Waterloo

How to Read a Journal Article in Social Psychology

When approaching a journal article for the first time, and often on subsequent occasions, most people try to digest it as they would any piece of prose. They start at the beginning and read word for word, until eventually they arrive at the end, perhaps a little bewildered, but with a vague sense of relief. This is not an altogether terrible strategy; journal articles do have a logical structure that lends itself to this sort of reading. There are, however, more efficient approaches–approaches that enable you, a student of social psychology, to cut through peripheral details, avoid sophisticated statistics with which you may not be familiar, and focus on the central ideas in an article. Arming yourself with a little foreknowledge of what is contained in journal articles, as well some practical advice on how to read them, should help you read journal articles more effectively. If this sounds tempting, read on.

Journal articles offer a window into the inner workings of social psychology. They document how social psychologists formulate hypotheses, design empirical studies, analyze the observations they collect, and interpret their results. Journal articles also serve an invaluable archival function: They contain the full store of common and cumulative knowledge of social psychology. Having documentation of past research allows researchers to build on past findings and advance our understanding of social behavior, without pursuing avenues of investigation that have already been explored. Perhaps most importantly, a research study is never complete until its results have been shared with others, colleagues and students alike. Journal articles are a primary means of communicating research findings. As such, they can be genuinely exciting and interesting to read.

That last claim may have caught you off guard. For beginning readers, journal articles may seem anything but interesting and exciting. They may, on the contrary, appear daunting and esoteric, laden with jargon and obscured by menacing statistics. Recognizing this fact, we hope to arm you, through this paper, with the basic information you will need to read journal articles with a greater sense of comfort and perspective.

Social psychologists study many fascinating topics, ranging from prejudice and discrimination, to culture, persuasion, liking and love, conformity and obedience, aggres-

617

sion, and the self. In our daily lives, these are issues we often struggle to understand. Social psychologists present systematic observations of, as well as a wealth of ideas about, such issues in journal articles. It would be a shame if the fascination and intrigue these topics have were lost in their translation into journal publications. We don't think they are, and by the end of this paper, hopefully you won't either.

Journal articles come in a variety of forms, including research reports, review articles, and theoretical articles. Put briefly, a *research report* is a formal presentation of an original research study, or series of studies. A *review article* is an evaluative survey of previously published work, usually organized by a guiding theory or point of view. The author of a review article summarizes previous investigations of a circumscribed problem, comments on what progress has been made toward its resolution, and suggests areas of the problem that require further study. A *theoretical article* also evaluates past research, but focuses on the development of theories used to explain empirical findings. Here, the author may present a new theory to explain a set of findings, or may compare and contrast a set of competing theories, suggesting why one theory might be the superior one.

This paper focuses primarily on how to read research reports, for several reasons. First, the bulk of published literature in social psychology consists of research reports. Second, the summaries presented in review articles, and the ideas set forth in theoretical articles, are built on findings presented in research reports. To get a deep understanding of how research is done in social psychology, fluency in reading original research reports is essential. Moreover, theoretical articles frequently report new studies that pit one theory against another, or test a novel prediction derived from a new theory. In order to appraise the validity of such theoretical contentions, a grounded understanding of basic findings is invaluable. Finally, most research reports are written in a standard format that is likely unfamiliar to new readers. The format of review and theoretical articles is less standardized, and more like that of textbooks and other scholarly writings, with which most readers are familiar. This is not to suggest that such articles are easier to read and comprehend than research reports; they can be quite challenging indeed. It is simply the case that, because more rules apply to the writing of research reports, more guidelines can be offered on how to read them.

The Anatomy of Research Reports

Most research reports in social psychology, and in psychology in general, are written in a standard format prescribed by the American Psychological Association (1994). This is a great boon to both readers and writers. It allows writers to present their ideas and findings in a clear, systematic manner. Consequently, as a reader, once you understand this format, you will not be on completely foreign ground when you approach a new research report— regardless of its specific content. You will know where in the paper particular information is found, making it easier to locate. No matter what your reasons for reading a research report, a firm understanding of the format in which they are written will ease your task. We discuss the format of research reports next, with some practical suggestions on how to read them. Later, we discuss how this format reflects the process of scientific investigation, illustrating how research reports have a coherent narrative structure.

TITLE AND ABSTRACT

Though you can't judge a book by its cover, you can learn a lot about a research report simply by reading its title. The title presents a concise statement of the theoretical issues investigated, and/or the variables that were studied. For example, the following title was taken almost at random from a prestigious journal in social psychology: "Sad and guilty? Affective influences on the explanation of conflict in close relationships" (Forgas, 1994, p.

56). Just by reading the title, it can be inferred that the study investigated how emotional states change the way people explain conflict in close relationships. It also suggests that when feeling sad, people accept more personal blame for such conflicts (i.e., feel more guilty).

The abstract is also an invaluable source of information. It is a brief synopsis of the study, and packs a lot of information into 150 words or less. The abstract contains information about the problem that was investigated, how it was investigated, the major findings of the study, and hints at the theoretical and practical implications of the findings. Thus, the abstract is a useful summary of the research that provides the gist of the investigation. Reading this outline first can be very helpful, because it tells you where the report is going, and gives you a useful framework for organizing information contained in the article.

The title and abstract of a research report are like a movie preview. A movie preview highlights the important aspects of a movie's plot, and provides just enough information for one to decide whether to watch the whole movie. Just so with titles and abstracts; they highlight the key features of a research report to allow you to decide if you want to read the whole paper. And just as with movie previews, they do not give the whole story. Reading just the title and abstract is never enough to fully understand a research report.

INTRODUCTION

A research report has four main sections: introduction, method, results, and discussion. Though it is not explicitly labeled, the introduction begins the main body of a research report. Here, the researchers set the stage for the study. They present the problem under investigation, and state why it was important to study. By providing a brief review of past research and theory relevant to the central issue of investigation, the researchers place the study in an historical context and suggest how the study advances knowledge of the problem. Beginning with broad theoretical and practical considerations, the researchers delineate the rationale that led them to the specific set of hypotheses tested in the study. They also describe how they decided on their research strategy (e.g., why they chose an experiment or a correlational study).

The introduction generally begins with a broad consideration of the problem investigated. Here, the researchers want to illustrate that the problem they studied is a real problem about which people should care. If the researchers are studying prejudice, they may cite statistics that suggest discrimination is prevalent, or describe specific cases of discrimination. Such information helps illustrate why the research is both practically and theoretically meaningful, and why you should bother reading about it. Such discussions are often quite interesting and useful. They can help you decide for yourself if the research has merit. But they may not be essential for understanding the study at hand. Read the introduction carefully, but choose judiciously what to focus on and remember. To understand a study, what you really need to understand is what the researchers' hypotheses were, and how they were derived from theory, informal observation, or intuition. Other background information may be intriguing, but may not be critical to understand what the researchers did and why they did it.

While reading the introduction, try answering these questions: What problem was studied, and why? How does this study relate to, and go beyond, past investigations of the problem? How did the researchers derive their hypotheses? What questions do the researchers hope to answer with this study?

METHOD

In the method section, the researchers translate their hypotheses into a set of specific, testable questions. Here, the researchers introduce the main characters of the study—the subjects or participants—describing their characteristics (gender, age, etc.) and how many of them were involved. Then, they describe the materials (or apparatus), such as any questionnaires or special equipment, used in the study. Finally, they describe chronologically the procedures of the study; that is, how the study was conducted. Often, an overview of the research design will begin the method section. This overview provides a broad outline of the design, alerting you to what you should attend.

The method is presented in great detail so that other researchers can recreate the study to confirm (or question) its results. This degree of detail is normally not necessary to understand a study, so don't get bogged down trying to memorize the particulars of the procedures. Focus on how the independent variables were manipulated (or measured) and how the dependent variables were measured.

Measuring variables adequately is not always an easy matter. Many of the variables psychologists are interested in cannot be directly observed, so they must be inferred from participants' behavior. Happiness, for example, cannot be directly observed. Thus, researchers interested in how being happy influences people's judgments must infer happiness (or its absence) from their behavior—perhaps by asking people how happy they are, and judging their degree of happiness from their responses; perhaps by studying people's facial expressions for signs of happiness, such as smiling. Think about the measures researchers use while reading the method section. Do they adequately reflect or capture the concepts they are meant to measure? If a measure seems odd, consider carefully how the researchers justify its use.

Oftentimes in social psychology, getting there is half the fun. In other words, how a result is obtained can be just as interesting as the result itself. Social psychologists often strive to have participants behave in a natural, spontaneous manner, while controlling enough of their environment to pinpoint the causes of their behavior. Sometimes, the major contribution of a research report is its presentation of a novel method of investigation. When this is the case, the method will be discussed in some detail in the introduction.

Participants in social psychology studies are intelligent and inquisitive people who are responsive to what happens around them. Because of this, they are not always initially told the true purpose of a study. If they were told, they might not act naturally. Thus, researchers frequently need to be creative, presenting a credible rationale for complying with procedures, without revealing the study's purpose. This rationale is known as a *cover story,* and is often an elaborate scenario. While reading the method section, try putting yourself in the shoes of a participant in the study, and ask yourself if the instructions given to participants seem sensible, realistic, and engaging. Imagining what it was like to be in the study will also help you remember the study's procedure, and aid you in interpreting the study's results.

While reading the method section, try answering these questions: How were the hypotheses translated into testable questions? How were the variables of interest manipulated and/or measured? Did the measures used adequately reflect the variables of interest? For example, is self-reported income an adequate measure of social class? Why or why not?

RESULTS

The results section describes how the observations collected were analyzed to determine whether the original hypotheses were supported. Here, the data (observations of behavior) are described, and statistical tests are presented. Because of this, the results section is often intimidating to readers who have little or no training in statistics. Wading through complex and unfamiliar statistical analyses is understandably confusing and frustrating. As a result, many students are tempted to skip over reading this section. We advise you not to do so. Empirical findings are the foundation of any science and results sections are where such findings are presented.

Take heart. Even the most prestigious researchers were once in your shoes and sympathize with you. Though space in psychology journals is limited, researchers try to strike a balance between the need to be clear and the need to be brief in describing their results. In an influential paper on how to write good research reports, Bem (1987) offered this advice to researchers:

> No matter how technical or abstruse your article is in its particulars, intelligent nonpsychologists with no expertise in statistics or experimental design should be able to comprehend the broad outlines of what you did and why. They should understand in general terms what was learned. (p. 74)

Generally speaking, social psychologists try to practice this advice.

Most statistical analyses presented in research reports test specific hypotheses. Often, each analysis presented is preceded by a reminder of the hypothesis it is meant to test. After an analysis is presented, researchers usually provide a narrative description of the result in plain English. When the hypothesis tested by a statistical analysis is not explicitly stated, you can usually determine the hypothesis that was tested by reading this narrative description of the result, and referring back to the introduction to locate an hypothesis that corresponds to that result. After even the most complex statistical analysis, there will be a written description of what the result means conceptually. Turn your attention to these descriptions. Focus on the conceptual meaning of research findings, not on the mechanics of how they were obtained (unless you're comfortable with statistics).

Aside from statistical tests and narrative descriptions of results, results sections also frequently contain tables and graphs. These are efficient summaries of data. Even if you are not familiar with statistics, look closely at tables and graphs, and pay attention to the means or correlations presented in them. Researchers always include written descriptions of the pertinent aspects of tables and graphs. While reading these descriptions, check the tables and graphs to make sure what the researchers say accurately reflects their data. If they say there was a difference between two groups on a particular dependent measure, look at the means in the table that correspond to those two groups, and see if the means do differ as described. Occasionally, results seem to become stronger in their narrative description than an examination of the data would warrant.

Statistics *can* be misused. When they are, results are difficult to interpret. Having said this, a lack of statistical knowledge should not make you overly cautious while reading results sections. Though not a perfect antidote, journal articles undergo extensive review by professional researchers before publication. Thus, most misapplications of statistics are caught and corrected before an article is published. So, if you are unfamiliar with statistics, you can be reasonably confident that findings are accurately reported.

While reading the results section, try answering these questions: Did the researchers provide evidence that any independent variable manipulations were effective? For example, if testing for behavioral differences between happy and sad participants, did the researchers demonstrate that one group was in fact happier than the other? What were the major findings of the study? Were the researchers' original hypotheses supported by their observations? If not, look in the discussion section for how the researchers explain the findings that were obtained.

DISCUSSION

The discussion section frequently opens with a summary of what the study found, and an evaluation of whether the findings supported the original hypotheses. Here, the researchers evaluate the theoretical and practical implications of their results. This can be particularly interesting when the results did not work out exactly as the researchers anticipated. When such is the case, consider the researchers' explanations carefully, and see if they seem plausible to you. Often, researchers will also report any aspects of their study that limit their interpretation of its results, and suggest further research that could overcome these limitations to provide a better understanding of the problem under investigation.

Some readers find it useful to read the first few paragraphs of the discussion section before reading any other part of a research report. Like the abstract, these few paragraphs usually contain all of the main ideas of a research report: What the hypotheses were, the major findings and whether they supported the original hypotheses, and how the findings relate to past research and theory. Having this information before reading a research report can guide your reading, allowing you to focus on the specific details you need to complete your understanding of a study. The description of the results, for example, will alert you to the major variables that were studied. If they are unfamiliar to you, you can pay special attention to how they are defined in the introduction, and how they are operationalized in the method section.

After you have finished reading an article, it can also be helpful to reread the first few paragraphs of the discussion and the abstract. As noted, these two passages present highly distilled summaries of the major ideas in a research report. Just as they can help guide your reading of a report, they can also help you consolidate your understanding of a report once you have finished reading it. They provide a check on whether you have understood the main points of a report, and offer a succinct digest of the research in the authors' own words.

While reading the discussion section, try answering these questions: What conclusions can be drawn from the study? What new information does the study provide about the problem under investigation? Does the study help resolve the problem? What are the practical and theoretical implications of the study's findings? Did the results contradict past research findings? If so, how do the researchers explain this discrepancy?

Some Notes on Reports of Multiple Studies

Up to this point, we have implicitly assumed that a research report describes just one study. It is also quite common, however, for a research report to describe a series of studies of the same problem in a single article. When such is the case, each study reported will have the same basic structure (introduction, method, results, and discussion sections) that we have outlined, with the notable exception that sometimes the results and discussion section for each study are combined. Combined "results and discussion" sections contain the same information that separate results and discussion sections normally contain. Sometimes, the authors present all their results first, and only then discuss the implications of these results, just as they would in separate results and discussion sections. Other times, however, the authors alternate between describing results and discussing their implications, as each result is presented. In either case, you should be on the lookout for the same information, as outlined above in our consideration of separate results and discussion sections.

Reports including multiple studies also differ from single study reports in that they include more general introduction and discussion sections. The general introduction, which begins the main body of a research report, is similar in essence to the introduction of a single study report. In both cases, the researchers describe the problem investigated and its practical and theoretical significance. They also demonstrate how they derived their hypotheses, and explain how their research relates to past investigations of the problem. In contrast, the separate introductions to each individual study in reports of multiple studies are usually quite brief, and focus more specifically on the logic and rationale of each particular study presented. Such introductions generally describe the methods used in the particular study, outlining how they answer questions that have not been adequately addressed by past research, including studies reported earlier in the same article.

General discussion sections parallel discussions of single studies, except on a somewhat grander scale. They present all of the information contained in discussions of single studies, but consider the implications of all the studies presented together. A general discussion section brings the main ideas of a research program into bold relief. It typically begins with a concise summary of a research program's main findings, their relation to the original hypotheses, and their practical and theoretical implications. Thus, the summaries that begin general discussion sections are counterparts of the summaries that begin discussion sections of single study reports. Each presents a digest of the research presented in an article that can serve as both an organizing framework (when read first), and as a check on how well you have understood the main points of an article (when read last).

Research Reporting as Story Telling

A research report tells the story of how a researcher or group of researchers investigated a specific problem. Thus, a research report has a linear, narrative structure with a beginning, middle, and end. In his paper on writing research reports, Bem noted that a research report:

> . . . is shaped like an hourglass. It begins with broad general statements, progressively narrows down to the specifics of [the] study, and then broadens out again to more general considerations. (1987, p. 175)

This format roughly mirrors the process of scientific investigation, wherein researchers do the following: (1) start with a broad idea from which they formulate a narrower set of hypotheses, informed by past empirical findings (introduction); (2) design a specific set of concrete operations to test these hypotheses (method); (3) analyze the observations collected in this way, and decide if they support the original hypotheses (results); and (4) explore the broader theoretical and practical implications of the findings, and consider how they contribute to an understanding of the problem under investigation (discussion). Though these stages are somewhat arbitrary distinctions—research actually proceeds in a number of different ways—they help elucidate the inner logic of research reports.

While reading a research report, keep this linear structure in mind. Though it is difficult to remember a series of seemingly disjointed facts, when these facts are joined together in a logical, narrative structure, they become easier to comprehend and recall. Thus, always remember that a research report tells a story. It will help you to organize the information you read, and remember it later.

Describing research reports as stories is not just a convenient metaphor. Research reports *are* stories. Stories can be said to consist of two components: A telling of what happened, and an explanation of why it happened. It is tempting to view science as an endeavor that simply catalogues facts, but nothing is further from the truth. The goal of science, social psychology included, is to *explain* facts, to explain *why* what happened happened. Social psychology is built on the dynamic interplay of discovery and justification, the dialogue between systematic observation of relations and their theoretical explanation. Though research reports do present novel facts based on systematic observation, these facts are presented in the service of ideas. Facts in isolation are trivia. Facts tied together by an explanatory theory are science. Therein lies the story. To really understand what researchers have to say, you need to consider how their explanations relate to their findings.

The Rest of the Story

> There is really no such thing as research. There is only search, more search, keep on searching. (Bowering, 1988, p. 95)

Once you have read through a research report, and understand the researchers' findings and their explanations of them, the story does not end there. There is more than one interpretation for any set of findings. Different researchers often explain the same set of facts in different ways.

Let's take a moment to dispel a nasty rumor. The rumor is this: Researchers present their studies in a dispassionate manner, intending only to inform readers of their findings and their interpretation of those findings. In truth, researchers aim not only to inform readers, but also to *persuade* them (Sternberg, 1995). Researchers want to convince you their ideas are right. There is never only one explanation for a set of findings. Certainly, some explanations are better than others; some fit the available data better, are more parsimonious, or require fewer questionable assumptions. The point here is that researchers are very passionate about their ideas, and want you to believe them. It's up to you to decide if you want to buy their ideas or not.

Let's compare social psychologists to salesclerks. Both social psychologists and salesclerks want to sell you something; either their ideas, or their wares. You need to decide if you want to buy what they're selling or not—and there are potentially negative consequences for either decision. If you let a sales clerk dazzle you with a sales pitch, without thinking about it carefully, you might end up buying a substandard product that you don't really need. After having done this a few times, people tend to become cynical, steeling themselves against any and all sales pitches. This too is dangerous. If you are overly critical of sales pitches, you could end up foregoing genuinely useful products. Thus, by analogy, when you are too critical in your reading of research reports, you might dismiss, out of hand, some genuinely useful ideas—ideas that can help shed light on why people behave the way they do.

This discussion raises the important question of how critical one should be while reading a research report. In part, this will depend on why one is reading the report. If you are reading it simply to learn what the researchers have to say about a particular issue, for example, then there is usually no need to be overly critical. If you want to use the research as a basis for planning a new study, then you should be more critical. As you develop an understanding of psychological theory and research methods, you will also develop an ability to criticize research on many different levels. And *any* piece of research can be criticized at some level. As Jacob Cohen put it, "A successful piece of research doesn't conclusively settle an issue, it just makes some theoretical proposition to some degree more likely" (1990, p. 1311). Thus, as a consumer of research reports, you have to strike a delicate balance between being overly critical and overly accepting.

While reading a research report, at least initially, try to suspend your disbelief. Try to understand the researchers' story; that is, try to understand the facts—the findings and how they were obtained—and the suggested explanation of those facts—the researchers' interpretation of the findings and what they mean. Take the research to task only after you feel you understand what the authors are trying to say.

Research reports serve not only an important archival function, documenting research and its findings, but also an invaluable stimulus function. They can excite other researchers to join the investigation of a particular issue, or to apply new methods or theory to a different, perhaps novel, issue. It is this stimulus function that Elliot Aronson, an eminent social psychologist, referred to when he admitted that, in publishing a study, he hopes his colleagues will "look at it, be stimulated by it, be provoked by it, annoyed by it, and then go ahead and do it better. . . . That's the exciting thing about science; it progresses by people taking off on one another's work" (1995, p. 5). Science is indeed a cumulative enterprise, and each new study builds on what has (or, sometimes, has not) gone before it. In this way, research articles keep social psychology vibrant.

A study can inspire new research in a number of different ways, such as: (1) it can lead one to conduct a better test of the hypotheses, trying to rule out alternative explanations of the findings; (2) it can lead one to explore the limits of the findings, to see how widely applicable they are, perhaps exploring situations to which they do not apply; (3) it can lead one to test the implications of the findings, furthering scientific investigation of the phenomenon; (4) it can inspire one to apply the findings, or a novel methodology, to a different area of investigation; and (5) it can provoke one to test the findings in the context of a specific real world problem, to see if they can shed light on it. All of these are excellent extensions of the original research, and there are, undoubtedly, other ways that research findings can spur new investigations.

The problem with being too critical, too soon, while reading research reports is that the only further research one may be willing to attempt is research of the first type: Redoing a study better. Sometimes this is desirable, particularly in the early stages of investigating a particular issue, when the findings are novel and perhaps unexpected. But redoing a reasonably compelling study, without extending it in any way, does little to advance our understanding of human behavior. Although the new study might be "better," it will not be "perfect," so *it* would have to be run again, and again, likely never reaching a stage where it is beyond criticism. At some point, researchers have to decide that the evidence is compelling enough to warrant investigation of the last four types. It is these types of studies that most advance our knowledge of social behavior. As you read more research reports, you will become more comfortable deciding when a study is "good enough" to move beyond it. This is a somewhat subjective judgment, and should be made carefully.

When social psychologists write up a research report for publication, it is because they believe they have something new and exciting to communicate about social behavior. Most research reports that are submitted for publication are rejected. Thus, the reports that are eventually published are deemed pertinent not only by the researchers who wrote them, but also by the reviewers and editors of the journals in which they are published. These people, at least, believe the research reports they write and publish have something important and interesting to say. Sometimes, you'll disagree; not all journal articles are created equal, after all. But we recommend that you, at least initially, give these well-meaning social psychologists the benefit of the doubt. Look for what they're excited about. Try to understand the authors' story, and see where it leads you.

Author Notes

Preparation of this paper was facilitated by a Natural Sciences and Engineering Research Council of Canada doctoral fellowship to Christian H. Jordan. Thanks to Roy Baumeister, Arie Kruglanski, Ziva Kunda, John Levine, Geoff MacDonald, Richard Moreland, Ian Newby-Clark, Steve Spencer, and Adam Zanna for their insightful comments on, and appraisals of, various drafts of this paper. Thanks also to Arie Kruglanski and four anonymous editors of volumes in the series, *Key Readings in Social Psychology* for their helpful critiques of an initial outline of this paper. Correspondence concerning this article should be addressed to Christian H. Jordan, Department of Psychology, University of Waterloo, Waterloo, Ontario, Canada N2L 3G1. Electronic mail can be sent to chjordan@watarts.uwaterloo.ca.

REFERENCES

American Psychological Association. (1994). *Publication manual* (4th ed.). Washington, D.C.

Aronson, E. (1995). Research in social psychology as a leap of faith. In E. Aronson (Ed.), *Readings about the social animal* (7th ed., pp. 3–9). New York: W. H. Freeman and Company.

Bem, D. J. (1987). Writing the empirical journal article. In M. P. Zanna & J. M. Darley (Eds.), *The complete academic: A practical guide for the beginning social scientist* (pp. 171–201). New York: Random House.

Bowering, G. (1988). *Errata*. Red Deer, Alta.: Red Deer College Press.

Cohen, J. (1990). Things I have learned (so far). *American Psychologist, 45,* 1304–1312.

Forgas, J. P. (1994). Sad and guilty? Affective influences on the explanation of conflict in close relationships. *Journal of Personality and Social Psychology, 66,* 56–68.

Sternberg, R. J. (1995). *The psychologist's companion: A guide to scientific writing for students and researchers* (3rd ed.). Cambridge: Cambridge University Press.

Author Index

Subject Index